ALSO BY COLIN FLETCHER

River: One Man's Journey Down the Colorado, Source to Sea (1997)

The Secret Worlds of Colin Fletcher (1989)

The Complete Walker III (1984)

The Man from the Cave (1981)

The New Complete Walker (1974)

The Winds of Mara (1973)

The Man Who Walked Through Time (1968)

The Complete Walker (1968)

The Thousand-Mile Summer (1964)

ALSO BY CHIP (C. L.) RAWLINS

In Gravity National Park (1998)

Broken Country: Mountains & Memory (1996)

Sky's Witness: A Year in the Wind River Range (1993)

A Ceremony on Bare Ground (1985)

THE COMPLETE WALKER IV

THE *Complete*
WALKER IV

FULLY UPDATED AND REVISED

COLIN FLETCHER
& CHIP RAWLINS

*Illustrations by Vanna Prince &
Hannah Hinchman*

ALFRED A. KNOPF

New York   2002

TO MY MOTHER

who understood that walking for fun
is no crazier than most things in life,
and who passed the information along.

C.F.

Contents

Preface to the Fourth Edition

This fourth edition arrives seriously late: *Walker III* appeared in 1984, and most of its gear gospel, even much practice gospel, is now old testament. You can blame the updatage delay on my stalwart powers of procrastination, but at last, here we go again. With a difference.

This time, two of us are at it.

I'm now pushing 80, don't expect to live much beyond 120, and am already backpacking far less ambitiously. So I'm no longer in intimate touch with the most current gear. Obvious solution: co-opt a partner. The trick: find the right one. Perfection, it seemed to me, would be a longtime backpacker, a generation or two younger than me, conversant with gear but no mere gearhead; a proven writer, in tune with the book.

Chip Rawlins—who helped me with snowpack forecasts for my last book, *River,* and whom I'd met briefly in Wyoming—belongs, in his own words, to "the generation inspired by the first edition of this book. With frame-pack squeaking and agave staff in hand, I set out in the late 1960s to explore, and have made a life of it." Along with walking for pure pleasure, he worked as a backcountry ranger. In the late '80s and early '90s he shifted to wilderness hydrology and acid rain monitoring; in the course of this work he logged over 4000 miles afoot and another 1600 on skis—and received the U.S. Forest Service National Primitive Skills Award. Since leaving the Forest Service in 1992 to write, he has mapped glaciers, studied mountain streams, and thereby kept his soul in condition. His ongoing love affair with walking has so far off-sprung two poetry books and two of prose.

When we talked about coauthorship, Chip seemed eager. And here we are, in tandem.

Every part of the book has passed our twofold scrutiny. Much of the old nontechnical stuff stood up okay, but I've nipped-and-tucked it all and refurbished the writing to my new satisfaction. Chip has backpacked many miles researching equipment and has rewritten nearly all the material on gear and some on technique. So the book speaks with two voices.

In a sense, so did earlier editions. Vanna Prince's illustrations backed up the text beautifully. Vanna was keeping the faith for this edition, too, and had nearly all the drawings done when she went on a long-awaited European trip; but minutes after getting off the return flight she suffered a massive stroke. She died 10 days later. Chip and I feel a loss that is more than professional. Even in late life, Vanna sparked; illuminated; leavened. We miss her. But her work lives on in this edition—and will, in some form, in any future revisions.

Extending that thought: perhaps I should admit my fragrant hope that by handing the walking staff over to Chip—partially this time, totally later, if all goes well—I've given the book a chance to live on, post-Fletcher.

In this edition, for clarity, we'll preface all my material, old and new, with the label COLIN and all Chip's with the label

CHIP: Reading this edition might seem like listening in. But *The Complete Walker IV* is more than just a private talk between Colin and me. During the long and healthy life of this book, readers have written bales of letters ranging, as Colin observed, "from bloody silly to brilliant." And the result is a deepening of our collected experience.

Not all the experience that went into *Walker IV* took place out-of-doors. During the rewrite, Colin and I also worked closely with trusted advisors, editors, and our all-important illustrator. By the time of her death, Vanna Prince had finished more than a hundred new drawings for this book. To get the details right, she made a pilgrimage to Wyoming, sketching away cross-legged as I stuffed packs, set up tents, and demonstrated stoves—and learned to appreciate her as an artist and, no less, a friend. Looking through her unfinished sketches can still catch me up. But six months after she died, the momentum of writing and publishing carried us to the point where we had no choice but to find an illustrator for new drawings and alterations to some of Vanna's old ones. And Hannah Hinchman, who added drawings to my book *Sky's Witness*—along with publishing two fine books of her own—has stepped in to complete the work.

In the years since the third edition appeared, some good things have worn out. In their stead, designers and makers have proposed new means of getting us over the next hill and out of the rain. We've tried them out, adopting the most useful and graceful solutions: as we walk, so we learn.

New alloys, resins, fibers, and manufacturing techniques have thoroughly changed the look and feel of outdoor gear. Simple things like the water bottle have elaborated into "hydration systems" with filters, pumps, bladders, tubes, and valves. And, for good or ill, the cottage-industry fringe that once produced outdoor equipment has become a $5-billion global industry.

To keep track of what's what has become difficult in itself, let alone determining what works and what's just passing fancy. For gear and technique are not separate matters; rather, one nudges the other, and is in turn nudged back. Yet even as we differ spiritedly on the particulars, in the long run (or long walk) some changes simply prove more embraceable than others. For instance, these words were laid down not with a fountain pen, nor yet with a typewriter, but on a computer. Or computers: Colin uses an IBM-clone and I use a Macintosh laptop.

Other practica: Given the lengthening combination of mailing address, phone number, and Internet Web site, the contact information formerly in the text has mostly migrated to appendixes. Be aware too that although frequent mention is made of trade names, we elected to leave out the ®, saving gallons of ink.

The tension between our inexhaustible monkey-fascination with the new and strange, and the immemorial truth of nature is not limited to the terrain of this book. When we shift our gaze to the backcountry itself it is clear that while some things (like gravity) have not changed, others have. Human population in 30 years has leaped and bounded. Permits, user fees, and restrictions in general have predictably increased, while favorite and once remote campsites are overrun. And as we seek out ever remoter and quieter spots, the horde seems poised to follow.

This is not to say that either Colin or I have run out of places to walk. But it is to confess that as writers we must adopt practices that are increasingly subtle and furtive. So as we focus minutely on gear and techniques, we will talk about places themselves in fuzzily general terms.

COLIN: In a sense, nothing we write about has changed since the first edition. Equipment and techniques are mere means to an end, and the things we're writing toward are timeless. Cloud shadows still scud across sunlit peaks. Fleeing lizards still corner frantically around creosote bushes, flinging out little spurts of sand. Both Chip and I now have hilltops very near our present homes—different from and yet not different from the flat, grassy one mentioned on page 9—that we can climb for exercise and short-term mulling and sanity; hills on whose summits we can sit for days, when the need arises, in space and beauty and silence, so that we can sweep the daily clutter aside and penetrate surfaces and consider what to do with the rest of our lives—or perhaps just so that we can, severally and a thousand miles apart, wrestle with the preface to a new edition of an old book.

Then there are the wider, ephemeral-constant, wilderness moments that hang long and vivid in memory. Years ago, beside a remote Alaskan river, I met my first moose and then, minutes later, still high from that enlightenment, had a caribou stroll up to within eight paces of where I stood upright in the open. The caribou eyeballed me with a long and strangely glassy stare; then it began to angle slowly away—and I saw the huge, suppurating wound on its haunch, probably bear-inflicted, that had no doubt glazed the poor beast's mind. Snowshoeing for a week in the Sierra Nevada, I once sat at 10,000 feet, cradled in the silence and softness and harshness of a cupped basin, and watched its rocky slopes as the sun of yet another turning summer beat down from a cloudless sky and began to cleave and slough off into the past, in massive cake chunks, the rich white legacy of what we humans had regarded as an extraordinarily stormy winter. No, if you back off just a little ways, nothing much has changed since I wrote the first edition. Essentially, the old writ stands.

And here, once again, is the old and also, this time, new-new book.

Summer 2001

Authors' Notes

Several fibers woven into this book have been plucked from *The Thousand-Mile Summer,* originally published by Howell-North Books, and from *The Man Who Walked Through Time, The Winds of Mara,* and *The Secret Worlds of Colin Fletcher* (a title, though not a book, that I regret), all published by Alfred A. Knopf. To protect readers of these books from echo trouble, I've identified the rare passages in which I found it necessary to reuse any lengths of fabric.

A few strands also have come from articles of mine that have appeared in *Field & Stream, Sports Afield, Reader's Digest,* and the *San Francisco Chronicle,* and I wish to thank the publishers for their permission to rework the material.

C. F.

While passing on what I've learned outdoors, I've tried not to reprise tales from two previous books: *Sky's Witness: A Year in the Wind River Range* and *Broken Country: Mountains & Memory,* both published by Henry Holt & Co., and from pieces in *High Country News, Northern Lights, Sierra, Backpacker,* and various anthologies. Even so, a few things might sound familiar.

Perhaps, given the laws of physics and the intractability of human nature, they've also happened to you.

C. R.

For a list of the many individuals who helped us with this book, see pages 825–28.

WARNING! PRICES, ETC.

We've made a strenuous effort to get prices, weights, and other exactifications right. But in the time it has taken to get this book finished, some of these things have changed. And more of them will, by the time it's in your hands.

There's often a considerable gap between the manufacturer's suggested retail price (what we quote, mostly) and what the alert bargain hunter will pay. Corporate silliness (when we asked the weight of their flashlight, all they could quote was the shipping weight of a case of them) as well as packaging trends (heat-sealed blister packs) have at times made it difficult to get exact weights without actually buying all the gear mentioned—and we mention a hell of a lot in the following pages.

Still, for whatever lapses you might find in this fourth edition we must two-headedly bear the brunt of responsibility. And hope we can count, once again, on your forgiveness.

WHY WALK?

Now shall I walk
Or shall I ride?
"Ride," Pleasure said:
"Walk," Joy replied.

W. H. Davies

Why Walk?

Sanity is a madness put to good uses.

George Santayana

COLIN: I had better admit right away that walking can in the end become an addiction, and that it is then as deadly in its fashion as heroin or television or the stock exchange. But even in this final stage it remains a delectable madness, very good for sanity, and I recommend it with passion.

A redeeming feature of the condition is that no matter how heavily you've been hooked, you can still get your kicks from very small doses.

Ten minutes' drive from the apartment in which I used to live, there was a long, grassy ridge from which you could look out over parkland and sprawling metropolis, over bay and ocean and distant mountains. I often walked along this ridge in order to think uncluttered thoughts or to feel with accuracy or to sweat away a hangover or to achieve some other worthy end, recognized or submerged. And I usually succeeded—especially with the thinking. Up there, alone with the wind and the sky and the steep grassy slopes, I nearly always found after a while that I was beginning to think more clearly. Yet "think" doesn't seem to be quite the right word. Sometimes, when it was a matter of making a choice, I don't believe I decided what to do so much as discovered what I had decided. It was as if my mind, set free by space and solitude and oiled by the body's easy rhythm, swung open and released thoughts it had already formulated. Sometimes, when I'd been straining too hard to impose order on an urgent press of ideas, it seemed only as if my mind had slowly relaxed; and then, all at once, there was room for the ideas to fall into place in a meaningful pattern.

Occasionally you can achieve this kind of release inside a city. One day some years ago, when I had to leave my car at a garage for an hour's repair work, I spent the time strolling through an industrial area. I crossed a man-made wasteland, then walked up onto a little-used pedestrian bridge over a freeway. Leaning on its concrete parapet, I watched the lines of racing, pounding vehicles. From above they seemed self-propelled, automatic. And suddenly, standing there alone, I found myself

3

looking down on the scene like a visitor from another planet, curiously detached and newly instructed. More recently I've discovered a sandhill near the place I now take my car for repair. This desiccated oasis among encroaching industriana still supports on one flank a couple of windswept pines. Its center cradles dips and hummocks that are smooth and flower-decked. And there, while the 21st century ministers to my horseless carriage, I can lie and read and lunch and doze, cut off, in a quiet urban wilderness. Most cities offer such veiled delights. In walking, as in sex, there's always a good chance you'll find, almost anywhere, given enough time, something that wows you.

But no one who has begun to acquire the walking habit can restrict himself for long to cities, or even to their parks or less intentional enclaves. First he explores open spaces out beyond the asphalt. Then, perhaps, he moves on to car camping and makes long, exploratory, all-day treks. But in due course he's almost sure to find his dreams outreaching these limitations. "For the human spirit needs places where nature has not been rearranged by the hand of man." One of the joys of being alive today is the complexity of our human world. We have at our fingertips more riches than anyone has ever had: books by the zillion; CDs and movies and TV by the ton; the Internet; also the opportunity to move around almost as we please. But in time the sheer richness of this complexity can sand-bag you. You long for simplicity, for the yin to that yang. You yearn—though you may not openly know it—to take a respite from your eternal wrestling with the abstract and instead to grapple, tight and long and sweaty, with the tangible. So once you've started walking down the right road, you begin, sooner or later, to dream of truly wild places.

At this point you're in danger of meeting a mental block.

Even in these mercifully emancipated decades, many people still seem to become alarmed at the prospect of sleeping away from officially consecrated, car-accommodating campsites with no more equipment than they can carry on their backs. When pressed, they babble about snakes or bears or even, by God, bandits. But the real barrier, I'm sure, is the unknown.

I came to comprehend the reality of this barrier—or, rather, to recomprehend it—30-odd years ago, during a four-day walk through some coastal hills. (I was walking, as a matter of fact, in order to sort out ideas and directions for the first edition of this book.) One warm and cloudless afternoon I was resting at a bend in the trail—there was a little triangular patch of shade, I remember, under a rocky bluff—when some unexpected tilt of my mind reexposed a scene that I had completely forgotten. For all the vividness of the vital features, it remained a curiously indistinct scene. I wasn't at all clear when it had happened, except that it must have been more than 15 years earlier. I still do not even remember for sure whether it happened in Africa or North America. But the salient contours stand out boldly. I had come to some natural boundary. It may have been the end of a trail or road, or the fringes of a forest or the rim of a cliff, I no longer know which. But I do know that I felt I'd gone as far as a man could go. So I just stood there looking out beyond the edge of the world. Except for a wall of thick, dark undergrowth, I'm no longer sure what I saw, but I know it was wild, wild, impossible country. It still looms huge and black and mysterious in the vaults of my memory.

All at once, without warning, two men emerged from that impossible country. They carried packs on their backs, and they were weather-beaten and distilled to bone and muscle. But what I remember best of all is that they were happy and whole. Whole and secure and content.

I talked to them, briefly and in considerable awe. They had been back deep into the wilderness, they said, away from civilization for a week. "Pretty inaccessible, some of it," admitted one of them. "But there's a lot of beautiful country in there—some of the finest I've ever seen." Then they walked away and I was left, still awestruck, looking out once more into the huge, black, mysterious wilderness.

The awe that I felt that day still hangs in my memory. But my present self dismisses it. I know better. Many times in recent years I've emerged from wild country, happy and whole and secure and content, and found myself face-to-face with astonished people who had obviously felt that they were already at the edge of the world; and I know, now I have come to consider the matter, that what I have seen on their faces is exactly what those two men must have seen on mine, many years ago on the edge of that other wilderness. And I know now that the awe is unwarranted. There's nothing very difficult about going into such places. All you need is the right equipment, a reasonable competence in using it, a tolerable degree of physical fitness, and a clear understanding of your own limitations. Beyond that, all you have to do is overcome the fear of the unknown.*

---

*You'll see that I tend to write of walking as if it is something that must be done alone. Most people prefer company, and by all reasonable standards they're right. For efficiency and comfort and the rewards of sharing, and above all for safety, a walking party, like a political party, should consist of at least two or three members.

But I like to walk alone. And therefore, when I'm being honest, that is how I tend to write. It doesn't matter, though: if you choose, sensibly, to travel in twos or threes or twenties, just about everything I have to say still applies. You miss something, that's all. You never quite learn, for instance, that one of the riches a wilderness has to offer is a prolonged, deep silence.

There's one notable exception to my rule. When you and your companion are newly in love, the two of you walk with minds interwoven, and the bond enriches everything you see. And that is the best walking of all.

But be warned that solitude, for all its sweet sound, is not everybody's bag. I know one woman, very experienced at backpacking in groups, who discovered that when she at last ven-

Once you've overcome this fear of the unknown and thereby surmounted your sleeping-out-in-the-wilderness block, you are free. Free to
go out, when the world will let you slip away into the wildest places you
dare explore. Free to walk from dawn to dusk and then again from dawn
to dusk, with no harsh interruptions, among the quiet and soothing
cathedrals of a virgin forest. Or free to struggle for a week, if that's what
you want at that particular time, toward a peak that has captured your
imagination. Or free, if your needs or fancies of the moment run that way,
to follow a wild river to its source, fishing as you go, or not fishing. Free,
once you've grasped the significance of this other reality, to immerse yourself for two months in the timeless silence of a huge desert canyon—and
to learn in the end why the silence is not timeless after all.

But long before the madness has taught you this kind of sanity you
have learned many simple and valuable things.

You start to learn them from the very beginning. First, the comforting constants. The rhythm of boots and walking staff, and their different
inflections on sand and on soil and on rock. The creak of harness as small
knapsack or heavy pack settles back into place after a halt. And the satis-
factions of a taut, controlled body. Then there are the small, amplified
pleasures. In everyday life, taking off your socks is an unnoticed chore;
peeling them off after a long day's walk is sheer delight. At home a fly is
something that makes you wonder how it got into the house; when you're
lying sprawled out on a sandbar beside a remote river you can recognize a

---

tured out on her own, as she had long been dreaming of doing, she was too nervous to sleep
more than fitfully. And when she told other people about her fear she found that a surprising
number of them shared it. Several, faced with the reality, the first night out from roadhead,
got the shakes and hightailed for home. Some people seemed to feel the problem was almost
universal. One man commented that "even Colin Fletcher says he takes two or three nights to
get over it." This is a masterpiece of misinformation. I have my fears, but sleeping alone in
wilderness is not one of them. Very much the reverse.

Then there are those who only talk solitude. Not long ago, traveling cross-country at
10,000 feet in the Sierra Nevada, following a faint game trail and a train of thought that I'd
been trying to board for a long time, I met a young couple strolling near their rockbound
lakeside camp. They crowded around me—which takes some doing when you have only two
bodies at your command—and began talking. Wasn't it wonderful up here away from everybody? So peaceful. Why, only yesterday they'd been on the main trail, over the other side of
that crest, and they'd met 14 people inside of two hours. Fourteen! That was simply too
crowded, so they'd struck away from the trail. And now it was wonderful, being out here on
their own. Why, I was the first person they'd seen all day. . . . I began to ease on around the
lake. My companions eased with me, still talking. Hoping to catch up with the fast-vanishing
train of thought, I dropped a couple of hints. They fell on stony ground. When, in desperation, I was gently but firmly explicit, my companions looked surprised, almost shocked—and
sorely disappointed.

In other words, although "solitude" and "loneliness" describe identical physical conditions, the mental states stand poles apart. For more, see page 626, footnote.

fly as something to be studied and learned from—another filament in the intricate web of the world. Or it may be a matter of mere money: five days beyond the last stain of man, you open the precious little package of blister-cushioning felt pads that's marked "$3.65" and discover, tucked away inside, two forgotten and singularly useless $20 bills. Yet two days later you may find your appetite suddenly sharp for civilized comforts that a week earlier had grown flat and stale. Once, toward the end of a week's exploration of a remote headwater basin, I found my heart melting at the thought of hot buttered toast for breakfast. And in the final week of a summer-long walk I even found myself recalling with nostalgia the eternal city hunt for parking.

But well before such unexpected hankerings arise, your mind as well as your body has been honed. You have re-remembered that happiness can have something to do with simplicity. And so, by slow degrees, you regain a sense of harmony with everything you move through—rock and soil, plant and tree and cactus, spider and fly and rattlesnake and coyote, drop of rain and racing cloud shadow. (You have long ago outgrown the crass assumption that the world was made for man.) After a while you find that you're gathering together the whole untidy but glorious mishmash of sights and sounds and smells and touches and tastes and emotions that tumble through your recent memory. Then you begin to connect these ciphers, one with the other. And once you begin to connect, only to connect, nothing can stop you—not even those rare moments of blackness (when all, all is vanity) that can come even in the wilderness.

When you get back at last from the simple things to the complexities of the outside, walled-in man-world you find that you're once more eager to grapple with them. For a while you even detect a meaning behind all the complexity. We are creatures of our time; we cannot escape it. The simple life is not a substitute, only a corrective.

For a while, I said, you detect new meanings. For a while. That's where the hell comes in. In due course the hot buttered toast tastes like damp sawdust again and the parking hassle is once more driving you crazy and the concrete jabs at your eyes and the din and the dirt sicken you, and all at once you realize that there is no sense to be discovered, anywhere, in all the frantic scurryings of the city. And you know there's only one thing to do. You're helplessly trapped. Hooked. Because you know now that you have to go back to the simple things.

You struggle, briefly. But as soon as the straight-line world will let you slip away, or a little sooner, you go. You go in misery, with delight, full of confidence. For you know that you will immerse yourself in the harmonies—and will return to see the meanings.

This is why I recommend walking so passionately. It is an altogether positive and delectable addiction.

. . .

Naturally, not everyone understands.

A smooth and hypersatisfied young man once boasted to me that he had just completed a round-the-world sight-seeing tour in 79 days. In one jet-streamed breath he scuttled from St. Peter's, Rome, via the Pyramids, to a Cambodian jungle temple. "That's the way to travel," he said. "You see everything important."

When I suggested that the way to see important things was to walk, he almost dropped his martini.

Walking can even provoke an active opposition lobby. For many years now I've been told with some regularity that by walking out and away I'm "escaping from reality." I admit the statement puts me on the defensive. Why, I ask myself (and sometimes my accusers as well), are people so ready to assume that chilled champagne is more "real" than water drawn from an ice-cold mountain creek? Or a dusty sidewalk than a carpet of desert dandelions? Or a Boeing 747 than a flight of white pelicans soaring in delicious unison against the sunrise? Why, in other words, do people assume that the acts and emotions and values that stem from city life are more real than those that arise from the beauty and the silence and the solitude of wilderness?

For me, the thing touched bottom when I was gently accused of escapism during a TV interview about a book I'd written on a length-of-California walk. Frankly, I fail to see how going for a six-month, thousand-mile walk through deserts and mountains can be judged less real than spending six months working eight hours a day, five days a week, in order to earn enough money to be able to come back to a comfortable home in the evening and sit in front of a TV screen and watch the two-dimensional image of some guy talking about a book he has written on a six-month, thousand-mile walk through deserts and mountains.

As I said, I get put on the defensive. The last thing I want to do is knock champagne and sidewalks and Boeing 747s. Especially champagne. These things distinguish us from the other animals. But they can also limit our perspectives. And I suggest that they—and all the stimulating complexities of modern life—begin to make more sense, to take on surer meaning, when they're viewed in perspective against the more certain and more lasting reality from which they have evolved—from the underpinning reality, that is, of mountain water and desert flowers and soaring white birds at sunrise.

Here endeth the lesson.

But perhaps you're an unbeliever and need proof—a no-nonsense, show-me-some-practical-results kind of proof.

I can tell you now that I've had an unholy awful time with this introductory chapter.* I wrote it a dozen times, over a period of several months, and a dozen times it utterly refused to say what I wanted it to say. In the end I drove an hour out of town, parked the car on a dirt road, heaved the pack onto my back, walked for another hour, and then camped on the flat, grassy summit of a familiar hill. That was two evenings ago. I'm still there. In front of me the long grass is billowing like the sea. Far beyond it and far below sprawls the city. It is very gray. But here on my hilltop there is only the grass and the wind and the sky.

From time to time since I climbed up here I've strolled around my domain. Once I went down a few hundred feet with the pack on my back and filled all four canteens at a spring. But mostly I've sat up here in the shade of my poncho awning. I've looked at the billowing grass. I've looked beyond it at the sprawling gray city and have listened to the roar from a freeway that feeds it. I've consulted with a number of hawks, mice, beetles, and trees. And this morning—after two nights and one day of bitter, bitter struggle and many, many words—I suddenly relaxed and began to write. I don't say I'm yet satisfied with what I've written. But I think it will do.

I'm years down from that hilltop now, but before we move on to consider the ways and means of walking I must point out two pitfalls that you should bear in mind, always—or as always as you can manage.

First, make sure the ways and means remain just that. They'll always be threatening to take over. They'll tend, particularly at the start of a trip, to imprison your thoughts on a treadmill of trivial worries: "Is that a blister forming on my right heel?"; "If the storm breaks, will that little tarp really keep me dry all night?"; "My God, is the water going to last out?" And any sudden small problem is liable to inflate without warning and fill the horizons of your tight little world. It all sounds very silly, I know; but anyone who has traveled on foot, especially alone, will recognize the syndrome. I should like to report that experience cures such nonsense. Unfortunately, it doesn't. It helps; it helps a lot. But I still find, especially on long trips with a sharp physical challenge, that I need at least a few days of "shakedown cruise." On a two-month journey I once made through Grand Canyon it took me all of two weeks to break free.

Whether you like it or not, the trivia are always there. Never underrate them: either you subdue them or they subdue you. A single blister can blacken the most shining day. And if you're miles from anywhere,

*I've let this little story stand as it appeared in the first edition, because that's the way it happened, sort of inside the book.

soaked through and shivering and with no confidence in your ability to contrive a warm, dry shelter for the night, you'll be deaf to the music of raindrops drumming against your poncho and blind to the beauty of clouds swirling around sawtooth peaks.

The important thing, then, about running your tight little outdoor economy is that it must not run you. You must learn to deal with the practical details so efficiently that they become second nature. Then, after the unavoidable shakedown period, you leave yourself free to get on with the important things—watching cloud shadows race across a mountainside or passing the time of day with a hummingbird or discovering that a grasshopper eats grass like spaghetti or sitting on a peak and thinking of nothing at all except perhaps that it's a wonderful thing to sit on a peak and think of nothing at all.*

The second pitfall is more subtly camouflaged. Naturally, your opinions on equipment and technique must never fossilize into dogma: your mind must remain open to the possibilities of better gear and to new and easier ways of doing things. You try to strike a balance, of course—to operate efficiently and yet to remember, always, that the practical details are only a means to an end. But I'm not altogether convinced that after years and years of it—when you've at last succeeded in mastering most of the business and people have begun to call you an expert and someone may even ask you to write a book on the subject—I'm not at all sure that it's then possible to avoid the sobering discovery that you've become, ex officio, a very tolerably accomplished fuddy-duddy.

If you recognize these minor pitfalls and are careful and lucky, so that you don't tumble into them too often, you'll discover as the years pass that walking becomes a beautiful, warm, round pumpkin that sits up on a shelf, always ready to be taken down. There are moments, sure, when you worry if time hasn't tamed it, just a touch. Moments when you fret that perhaps it has turned into something safer, like a self-replenishing bank account. But most of the time, when you look up and see it sitting there on the shelf, waiting, it remains round and warm, a magical thing to have around the place. You wonder, sometimes, what in God's name you'd have done with your life if you'd failed to fall victim to the addiction.

It wouldn't be the same round and personal pumpkin, of course, if you hadn't grown it yourself.

In the beginning there was all the worrying that could smother the important things, the things that mattered. But as years rolled by you

---

*It would probably be a good thing if you reread this paragraph at least once—and tried to remember it. This is essentially a "know-how" book, but we must never lose sight of the fact that what matters in the end is the "feel-how" of walking.

fretted less and less about the damned equipment and about just where you'd go and how long it would take and where you'd camp. You still took care, mind. Still went carefully through your checklist beforehand—for long trips, went through twice, maybe three times. Still retained a habit of watchful but nonparanoid attention to detail. But you always knew, now, with more than thin logic, that these were only means. And you were able, easily and naturally, to go out longer, higher, remoter, farther into what was once jeopardy. So there were glaciers and deep desert canyons and mountaintops with views to the edge of the planet, of yourself.

And the things that mattered now gleamed and flashed sooner, more and more often, more and more momentously: sunrise behind Spanish moss; aching feet in a cool, caressing creek; a moose, chomping knee-deep in marsh, that in profile had been a harmless and rather comic creature but that suddenly swung its head up, alert, and looked directly at you and instantly became a very large and very serious and potentially menacing citizen; or that focused moment in which a perfectly ordinary scrub jay decamped from an oak limb, refolded its wings, like the scarabs, and as silently swooped away—blue and smooth-gray and white, at ease and elegant, provoking you to sudden envy.

Perhaps, if you found it suited you, you learned about solitude. Real solitude. Not the kind with 2 or 10 or 20 other tarps strung up beyond the next tree bole. Not the kind where for half the day you talk with other humans instead of with the rest of the world, with yourself. Instead, the kind where you feel cheated if you meet more than two people a week, a bit bruised if you have to exchange more than one-word greetings. The kind in which you learn about silence and peace and the wider circles.

You still don't do silly things, of course—whether you decide that solitude is for you or not. As the years go by, in fact, you play it closer and closer. You still checklist equipment, preview the mountain cold or desert heat, and finger the five-day forecast; and you take fewer and fewer risks, particularly when you're on your own. But you know a bit more about what you're doing now, so you are freer for the things that matter, for the meanings. They're still the same: the roughness of granite; good, clean, voluntary sweating, unprodded by money or other master; a bighorn materializing out of mist, momentarily close and understood, weathered gray and green, sagacious, magnificent; or just sunlight slanting through junipers. Still the same. But you know how to reach them now.

For in the end it's always there, sitting up on the shelf, round and warm and shining, waiting to be taken down. The flat, logical sector of you tends to think of it as therapy. So sometimes, as I say, you wonder if the years haven't tamed it a touch. But you know, if you stop to think, that at any moment, just when you least expect it, a lily or a thunderstorm or a moose, or just more sunlight slanting through different junipers, will tingle you into goose pimples. Or a rockface or river, a snake or sudden snowstorm will up and scare the arse off you—to the immense benefit of your little universe. So it's never really tamed, thank God. And it's always sitting up there on the shelf—that big, beautiful pumpkin—just waiting for you to wave the wand and turn it into something much more magical than a carriage.

HOUSE ON YOUR BACK

Meticulously organized, the flower of complex and collective thought, the loaded pack—like the space module—is fully a vehicle of our century's last quarter, and sits squarely on contemporary shoulders.

Bruce Berger

Ground Plan

COLIN: As long as you restrict your walking to one-day hikes you're unlikely to face any very ponderous problems of equipment or technique. Everything you need can be stuffed into pockets or if necessary into a convenient little pouch slung from waist or shoulders. And if something should get left behind, why, home is always waiting at the end of the day's road. But as soon as you start sleeping out you simply have to carry some kind of

A house on your back.

Obviously, there's a difference between the kind of house you need to carry for a soft, summer weekend in the woods and for a month or more in wild mountain country. But it's convenient and entirely possible to devise a standard structure that you can modify to suit a broad range of conditions. In the first two editions I tried to instruct mainly by describing in detail the fairly full-scale edifice, very simply modifiable, that I had evolved over a considerable number of years. If some of the architecture seemed too elaborate for your needs, all you had to do was simplify toward harmony with those needs. By the third edition, things had grown more complicated. An avalanche of new equipment meant that my house tended to get more markedly modified for different kinds of trips. And I was more likely to switch from one kind of pack to another—thereby altering not only what went inside but some details of how I operated. As in earlier editions, I discussed most techniques as they applied to trips of at least a weekend, and often in terms of more ambitious journeys. Again, if my suggestions were too intricate for what you had in mind, you simply simplified.

Basically, this method stands. But for the packful of reasons I've listed in the preface (pages ix–xiii), most current specifics will in this edition be written by Chip Rawlins, and will describe his gear.

In spite of these changes, the book remains highly subjective (well, bi-subjective)—and therefore should give many experienced walkers a whole slew of satisfying chances to snort with disagreement. I make no apologies. Backpacking is a highly subjective business. What matters to me or to Chip is what suits us, individually; but what matters to you is what suits you. So when we describe what we've found best, try to remember that we're really saying that there are no truly objective criteria, and the important thing in the end is not what we or other self-styled experts happen to use or do, but what *you* find best. Even prejudice has its place— a technique or piece of equipment that you've devised yourself is much more satisfying to use than an "import"—and in your hands it may well prove more efficient. In fact, the whole game lacks set rules. Different backpackers, equally experienced, may under the same conditions carry markedly different gear. And I'm always being amazed at the very wide variation in the ways people operate. Again, one of the most important things for a backpacker to be able to do is extemporize—mostly in the field but sometimes also in planning. And extemporizing is something that can't really be taught—though the right mind-bent can, I think, be encouraged. Given all this, then, the most a book can do is suggest guidelines.*

Guidelines are all we can offer for another reason too:

The current state of the mart.

In 1968 I wrote in the first edition that backpacking was "in a stimulating if mildly confusing state of evolution—or perhaps I mean revolution—in both design and materials" and also in distribution methods. In the second edition I noted that "the ev- or rev-olution continues." By the third edition the process had spun into high gear. Boot making had begun to throw off century-old traditions. Cold-weather clothes were slanting out in new directions. So was raingear. And almost all fabrics—for tents, sleeping bags, and packs as well as clothing—were stronger and lighter and came with more effective coatings. Drastic changes had swept through the peripheries too, from compasses to flashlights.

For this edition, change has shifted into overdrive. So our choices and practices are, like everybody's, in a state of flux—and some of our solemn, carefully updated advice will soon be outmoded again. But that matters less than it may seem to. Although we'll often be describing spe-

---

*Before writing the original version of this book, my advice to those genuinely interested in walking was to forget the books and get on with it, relying on the two finest teachers in the business—trial and error. I'm not at all sure a piece of me doesn't still stand by that advice.

cific items, the essence will once again lie not so much in the items themselves as in the principles that govern choice—those vital factors an intelligent backpacker should keep his or her eyes skinned for.*

After *Walker III* appeared, a Utah reader of earlier editions reported that he had already made several of the changes to new equipment that I'd now suggested. "See," he wrote, "you were successful in teaching not just specifics but the underlying function of equipment and the ideas behind choosing it."

Custom suggests that we avoid trade names. But only by discussing brands and models can we adequately indicate the details. And if we recommend one pack or jacket over another it's because we find it suits our needs better, not because, for crying out loud, we're mad at Mr. Madden or starry-eyed for Ms. Moonstone.

And now, gratefully and thankfully, over to

CHIP: When Colin and I first theorized about this update, we despaired somewhat. That is, the sheer range of outdoor gear available is stunning, though if you're trying to describe it comprehensively, "daunting" is a better word. In the last decade, not just the amount but also the rate of change has accelerated. Boot making leapt away from leather and tradition and has since made a partial leap back. Some raingear now *s-t-r-e-t-c-h-e-s*. New cold-weather clothes make lightweight winter trips (once oxymoronic) a brisk possibility. Whole classes of things such as water filters have flashed into existence and are diversifying into subclasses. And what one reader calls DMS (Digital Madness Syndrome) has added global positioning units, cellular phones, and electronic watches that also perform as alarms, timers, altimeters, barometers, compasses, and address books.

To get a feel for this, let's start at ground level. When the *Complete Walker* was first issued, I rushed out to get boots with soles made by Vibram, the original waffle-stompers. There were two sorts: the Montagna and the Roccia. I chose Montagnas. Now the Vibram flyer on my desk

---

*This is the last damned time I'll genuflect at the gender altar. But know ye that when I write "he" or "him" or "his," I always mean, terribly equally, "she"/"her"/"hers." Almost always, anyway.

Well, all right, maybe you're on to something if you think you detect a curmudgeonly, dinosauric impatience in my tone (though not, I hasten to add, in Chip's). But my problem is not with feminist aims, only overtouchiness among many tribulated pressure groups, including my own environmentalists. Things can easily get out of hand, you know. The odious but currently vogued "waitpersons," for example, won't pass close scrutiny: its last syllable is gender specific. So should we switch to "waitperchildren"—which is, even by true-believer standards, a rout of the language?

Anyway, I refuse to pockmark our text with repeated "he or she"s.

lists 32 different flavors. Besides the Montagna and Roccia (chocolate and vanilla), they range from the flattish #7510 Grip (for optimum traction) to the toothy #1450 Clusaz (a highly technical self-cleaning style for aggressive outdoor hiking). And these 32 soles are only a small part of what Vibram now offers.

In matters of gear, my practice was to swap with friends, dig deep in bargain bins or find part-time work in an outdoor shop to gear up at a discount. Thus, I tended to acquire things that were returned, scuffed, discontinued, or oddly colored, and to hang on to them until they were thoroughly tattered, bent, and delaminated. That's still my basic instinct.

But for purposes of this book, I had to augment my usual process of slow-destruction-in-the-field and explore the terra incognita of New Stuff. To be honest, I get a buzz in the presence of New Stuff. So at first the trade shows were like bushwhacking the American Dream. I fondled Eco-fleece and Powerstretch, hitched hipbelts and crawled into tents, and got a howling bellyache from bulk latte and free samples of energy bars. And each day I stuffed my faithful, faded Lowe pack with what salespersons are wont to call "literature."

I returned from that first show with 135 lbs. of catalogs, workbooks, and flyers. At the second show I pulled on seams, counted stitches, and cut the "literature" load to 60 lbs. By the third, a reaction had set in: I was tired of seeing New Stuff. After that, I found excuses not to go (and avoided a tornado that struck the trade show in Salt Lake City in August 1999). And I also returned to familiar ground: the fact is, even the most dedicated walker can break in only so many pairs of boots and still have feet left to walk on. So how can any one person hope to keep track?

Don't worry about it. To keep track is human—to make tracks, divine. As Colin observes, the essence lies not so much in a thing itself as in how it fits into your life afoot. So rather than trying, theoretically at least, to cover the universe of gear (for publications that attempt this, see page 24), instead we'll focus on how you can assemble (or refurbish) your portable house in a coherent way. There are decisions to be made at the outset. Just as even the most perfectly built igloo will never be much use in the Sonoran Desert, so some suites of gear are suited to a certain climate or landscape. And your own character and bent are crucial—some of us are minimalists by nature while others are maximalists or even hypermaximalists. Given your chosen landscape and yourself as benchmarks, the choices are not so difficult as they may seem.

When I was inspired by the first edition of this book to take up a staff and stride forth, most equipment was made and sold by backpackers with a knack for design who learned business as a necessity. Some owned shops, like the original Ski Hut in Berkeley, or were mountain guides. By the third edition that was not necessarily so. Success had forced many into roles as manufacturers and executives. Some, like Patrick Smith, "founder and grand pooh-bah designer" who has parted from Mountainsmith, still spend much of their lives outdoors. But the companies have passed into other hands. For instance, Mountainsmith now belongs to Western Growth, a venture-capital firm. Likewise, the present "outdoor industry" employs ranks of perfectly decent yet thoroughly un-outdoorsy folk. Thus, at trade shows one hears more of "high-touch shoppers," "specialty doors," and "big-box shifts" than of wild weather and narrow escapes.

COLIN: On a purely intellectual level, of course, results have often been beneficial. Fierce competition has generated more varied products of keener design at a larger number of sources. Technological and workmanship standards have, by and large, risen to new high levels. The pressure is so great that virtually every product niche has been filled and you're pretty sure to be able to find something appropriate to your particular needs. In fact, it's now easy to find good equipment, while to pick up really bad stuff you almost have to put your mind to it, at least in reputable "mountain shops"—that pleasant and useful misnomer for "backpacking stores." Of course, some models are better than others—and probably more expensive. In other words, we are better served—economically, anyway. This state of affairs is known, I understand, as capitalism. And the organizations that implement capitalism inevitably reflect, in their natures and structures, the sea changes of the past decade (though "reflect" may possibly be the wrong word). I don't mean only internal adjustments, such as a growing tendency to concentrate corporate energies on production and to rely for technical design, especially of such complicated items as tents, on outside consultants—who may also design for competitors. The most far-reaching change has been the rush to conglomeration (aka merging). The accelerating rush. Rumor has it that AOL Time Warner already plans takeovers of Microsoft, Madagascar, Wales, and Asia.

CHIP: The trend has spread as business in general has globalized (or perhaps "globularized" is a better word). It's not just the decisions made by profit-minded CEOs who wouldn't be caught dead with a backpack, but a deeper and more fundamental separation. Recently I set up a new tent and found what I first thought was excess dark thread sewn into the seams. But this turned out on closer inspection to be someone's long black hair. Did it belong to a woman supporting her children, or a young farm girl from the hills of southern China? What was her life like? Where did she sleep? I spent part of that long winter night thinking hard about the effects of globalization on human beings.

For the sake of fact, I visited a local shop to find out where gear comes from these days. Going From the Skin Out (FSO), much of the underwear and insulating fleece was made in the U.S. (or overseas possessions thereof), and likewise the socks, except for some excellent ones from Northern Ireland, with much of the wool coming from New Zealand. Shorts, shirts, and midlayers had a mix of U.S. and Far Eastern origins. The parkas and shell pants were made in China, Taiwan, and Bangladesh. Shoes and boots were by far the most polyglot: Italy, Czech Republic, Hungary, Romania, Morocco, Korea, Vietnam, and China. Packs were made in the U.S., Canada, Korea, and Indonesia. Without exception, down sleeping bags were made in China, with some synthetic-fill bags from the U.S. The tents were split between Taiwan and China. Thus, we backpackers are as globalized as anyone else, and should face up to it.

Another long-playing irony has been the effect of the outdoor industry on the outdoors. Over the years some companies have tried hard to reduce their environmental impact, and among them Patagonia deserves particular credit for tackling this in a straightforward way, with reports in their catalog. The effort has met with some genuine success. Fabric mills now use recycled soft-drink bottles to spin synthetic fleece and seek out dyes that aren't active poisons—in the U.S., Japan, and western Europe at least. But since the conversion of private costs into public liabilities is one of the cornerstones of capitalism, some firms have relocated their toxic habits to the "developing world." And those at companies that have spent millions to clean up their acts are disheartened by a general lack of recognition, let alone practical support in the form of sales.

But rather than speaking in general terms, let's look at two companies known for their excellent gear, and two different approaches to the capitalist game.

The North Face started out as a Berkeley, California, shop run by two backpackers who made some of the packs and sleeping bags that they sold. Their gear gained a devoted following, which over the next 20 years grew to national and international proportions. But as the present CEO, William Simon, told the *New York Times,* "They were dedicated to making good products, but they weren't profit-oriented." So the company passed through various hands and in the early 1990s was sold in a management-backed buyout. In 1996, The North Face raised $56 million with the sale of stock, which was used to pay debts and build a test lab with chambers capable of producing rain, hail, snow, winds, and temperatures of −40°F (as the outdoors is rumored to do). The firm also moved its base-camp from Berkeley to Carbondale, Colorado, announced a new footwear line, and bought up La Sportiva, the highly esteemed maker of mountain boots.

I used North Face packs during seven years of wilderness monitoring and found the quality superb. You could stake your life on their tents, and I did. So while I hoped to test some new gear of theirs for this book, my letters went unanswered and I never made it through the automated phone system. At the trade show they ran the door to their large display room like a border post. So—I gave up.

The *Times* quotes Bob Woodward, who started out in Berkeley with Sierra Designs and who now publishes an outdoor trade newsletter, as saying that The North Face "is going as fast as it can to become a street apparel company." Tents such as the VE-25 are still in the lineup, along with functional packs and other "real" gear. The company has a sterling record of honoring warranties, fixing, and replacing. But the bottom-liners who make decisions seem to be slouching toward fashions with the "outdoor look."

Under a photo of a squeaky-looking chap barking into a cell phone, the *New York Times* also quotes Ed Schmults, formerly at Patagonia, now president of Moonstone Mountaineering: "The industry is in a particularly aggressive process of change right now. It's an attractive market, and the big-money companies see an opportunity here." Unsurprisingly, outfits such as Polo Ralph Lauren and Tommy Hilfiger are busily cranking out parkas, fleece vests, hiking boots, and even backpacks. Is the stuff any good? According to Kristin Hostetter, equipment editor for *Backpacker* magazine, the answer is mostly no. Among outdoor hard-liners, fashion is known as the "F-word."

If commuters choose to look like Everest climbers, at considerable expense, neither Colin nor I dare say them nay. But here's the rub: the entry of the Fashion Monsters into the field might skim the cream from the market, the cream being those who dash out to buy high-end products at full retail price. And this skimming makes it harder for the companies that make real gear to survive.

Are we at the mercy (such as it may be) of a decreasing number of corporate leviathans? Generally speaking, yes. But perhaps not in every case. Here's a counterexample. In 1974, Mike Pfotenhauer and Laurie White started making custom packs under the Osprey label. I saw a few on the trails—plain old blue, but with a distinctive cut. By 1986, Osprey was wholesaling packs to shops, with competitors offering to buy the company. This is the route taken by many owner-designers: build it up, then cash it out. But instead, Pfotenhauer moved to Colorado, hired a small group, mostly Navajo, to sew packs and then settled in for the long haul.

In April 1998, I visited Osprey headquarters in Dolores. Up front, in a room with zero decor, I met the sales crew. They were getting ready for a meeting that would be held out of backpacks in a remote sandstone canyon. Despite the crunch, marketing manager Erik Hamerschlag took me back to the cutting room. Likewise zero-decor, it held huge tables flanked with bolts of bright fabric, sheets of foam, and hanging patterns. A computer program fit the patterns like puzzle pieces into the width of the fabric, to cut down on waste. The cut materials were trucked down the hill to the plant in nearby Cortez. Operating over short distances and on a monthly schedule, Osprey's staff could respond quickly to shifting demand. That was better, Erik said, than having to hustle huge advance orders, with the production work contracted overseas a year or two ahead. At Osprey, if someone came up with a bright idea, they could change an existing design at relatively short notice.

We returned to the front, where a striking young woman wobbled on platform sandals, clutching a sheaf of scrawled lists and getting things set for the campout. "Time to go," Erik said, and sent me down the hill to the plant. It was a nondescript sheet-metal building on the outskirts of town, where another Erik, Erik Wegener, walked me through. We began where the fabric was unloaded and traveled in handcarts to clusters of sewing machines and assembly tables. Most of the workers were women, Navajo and Ute, and they were friendly and talked in an unconstrained way. Others listened to portable radios. It seemed a decent place in which to work.

As I watched the pieces become packs, one woman showed me a trick she'd developed in order to sew a hipbelt more easily. Farther along, someone was cutting a piece of foam. "This is Mike," Erik said, introducing me to Mike Pfotenhauer, the founder and CEO.

Folding, peering, and trimming off minute slices, he was figuring out a way to cut the pads for a hipbelt so that when it was stitched it would take on a complex curve, like molded belts that cost a great deal more to produce. Besides the hands-on design process, he explained, they'd devised ways to use common pieces in several different packs and to streamline the physical work. So, despite their sophisticated design, the packs were simpler to make.

Finally, Wegener took me to his own area, where finished goods were lined up on ceiling-high racks. "We ship tomorrow," he said, "and this'll be a madhouse." Osprey, he explained, had gained momentum quickly, and they were operating at the limit. Later, on the phone, Erik Hamerschlag filled me in. Rather than going offshore to "sourcing" companies or assuming the debt for a large, new plant they'd decided to hold the line through other means: "Our dealers hang banners and our packs get reviewed. But at this point we aren't placing ads." That's hardly the sort of thing one expects to hear from a marketing manager.

In the Osprey catalog, everyone, from Mike Pfotenhauer to the cleanup crew, fits without crowding into a single photo. The differences between The North Face and Osprey are many, but the crucial distinction in my mind is that one has become a global enterprise while the other is still a maker of packs.

But—while I like dealing with small to midsize companies, I can't say that "small is beautiful" as far the gear itself goes. As Colin has observed over the years, size, success, and quality don't necessarily bear a consistent relation to one another.

Just as gear has changed, so have the paths by which it travels from maker to walker. And given the burst of computer commerce, these promise to shift even more quickly in the near future. My preference (perhaps sentimental) is to step into a local retail shop like Trailhead Sports in Logan, Utah, where I worked part-time. I like looking someone in the eye, asking questions, and arguing the fine points. The enduring virtue of the independent, local shop is that those who work there tend to be active hikers.

But times are increasingly tough for such local havens. One reason over the years has been mail-order catalogs, which have the advantages of buying in quantity and not having to maintain a retail store. More than once, I had people come into the Trailhead to try on a parka or pack and then breeze out, announcing that they could get it from a catalog for 10 percent less.

Recreational Equipment, Inc. (REI), one of the largest catalog sellers, began in 1938 as a co-op for Seattle climbers who had trouble getting quality mountain gear. When I joined, about 1970, the co-op had a catalog that offered packs, tents, and so forth from makers like Sierra Designs. There were also REI-brand products that tended to be sturdy yet Spartan: my first good sleeping bag was an REI Skier on which I gladly blew my food budget for two months, having nearly frozen to death in one of those flannel hunting-dog sacks. Good gear at a reasonable price continues as an REI staple, but under the leadership of a former Sears executive, the co-op embarked on the Way of Hugeness, extending its mail-order reach and opening retail stores (50 at last count). It has also engulfed a number of the companies that supply it with gear. And these days, the opening of a new REI outlet often signals the closing of independents.

A related trend among high-end makers is a shift from distributing only through backpacking (or specialty) shops to "big-box" sporting goods chains, which can command discounts in return for huge advance orders. While it boosts short-term profits, the practice is likely to hurt, if not kill, a great many specialty stores. One populist (and encouraging) trend is the appearance of stores selling "recycled" backpacking gear, though the amount of unscuffed gear for sale is perplexing.

Other long-running channels for backpacking gear include the colossus of the East, L. L. Bean, the Campmor catalog (still in endearingly trashy black-and-white), Canada's Mountain Equipment Co-op, and Japan's Snow Peak (for addresses, see Appendix III). Meanwhile, some local shops have expanded their reach with ads in national magazines and with mailings of flyers and catalogs. Some also produce their own gear. Others, such as Sierra Trading Post, focus on overstocks, seconds, or surplus. Along with its regular on-line catalog (which reported a "fivefold increase" in sales for 1998), REI has started its own Web site outlet, as have many other makers and suppliers of outdoor gear.

Sales via backpacking catalogs are still climbing, but the catalogs have changed noticeably. Besides daydream potential, a catalog should display tables of weights, volumes, boiling times, and such. But these comparative tools are now perishingly rare, having lost out to ever-glossier photos and fatuous sales pitches.

Another tack has been taken by Eastern Mountain Sports (EMS), which opened new retail stores across the U.S. and set up on the Web, but stopped printing a catalog. Instead, they offer separate brochures for each class of products and for techniques such as first aid. Given the rising costs of printing and mailing, and the frenzied lurch of computer commerce, the mail-order catalog might soon follow the way of the fiercely partisan, hole-in-the-wall backpacking shop.

Catalogs are the most fleeting form of

Helpful literature.

Again, a comprehensive list is neither possible, nor, given the volume of the flood, likely to do much except sweep you off your feet. So let's hop from one boulder to the next. One of the most provocative books is *Beyond Backpacking,* a guide to lightweight hiking by the protean Ray Jardine: engineer, climber, and through-hiker. Besides a wealth of practical lore and serious rethinking, it has plans for making ultralight gear. Karen Berger has written useful how-to books, most recently *Advanced Backpacking,* and Bruce Hampton's and David Coles's updated *Soft Paths: How to Enjoy the Wilderness Without Harming It* is a practical guide to new techniques. Other instant classics include *How to Shit in the Woods* by Kathleen Meyer and *How to Have Sex in the Woods* by Luann Colombo. *Backpacker* magazine and The Mountaineers Books launched a series that so far includes books on backcountry cooking, first aid and medical treatment, making camp, Leave No Trace techniques, and tips from experts (for a list of books, see Appendix IV).

Fortunately, dear old *Backpacker* survived engulfment by Ziff-Davis and is now under the sign of Rodale Press, which publishes *Organic Gardening* and *Men's Health.* But the days of strict advertising guidelines and a policy of not giving detailed directions are so long gone that they aren't even a memory. So in a recent issue, along with ads for packs, boots, and other staples, is a speeding Cadillac Catera (whatever the hell *that* is), with a command to "Think about more horsepower than a BMW 328i." I'd rather not. The content is more encouraging, with a contentious lead article on trailguides, a piece on camping with Mom, and a too-brief guide to repairing old gear, with a list of cobblers and tinkers, in itself worth the cover price. The ads in the Marketplace section in the back are a prime source for gear.

Backpacker gear reviews are consistently one of the best parts of the magazine. My own results agree with theirs about 75 percent of the time, with differences owing to stature, pain threshold, and boneheadedness. Editor's Choice Awards (not only for *Backpacker* but for other magazines) seem less reliable, since they tend to be given in advance for striking new concepts, some of which don't bear out. For instance, an award-winning boot felt great in the house, but after a week in the Big & Scratchy the revolutionary coating peeled off and one of the lace lugs tore out. Plus, it flexed in a way that chewed skin off the tops of my toes. (The maker claims that these troubles have been fixed, but after three strikes I remain wary.) In any event, *Backpacker* also publishes an annual Gear Guide in March, including the tables of weights, measures, and such gone missing from catalogs, along with useful introductions, brief comments, and the dates of review. They also maintain an extensive Web site with listings of gear, a women's page (including potential hiking partners), and other things not in the paper version. Above all, *Backpacker* is the only national magazine devoted entirely to backpacking.

Another survivor is *Outside.* While it has grown glossier and zoomier, with more attention to extreme and frenzied pursuits than to backpacking, there is still a core of excellent writing (Mark Jenkins, for instance) and concern for the outdoors. In the 1980s, *Outside* carried tests, a function now corralled in the annual Spring Buyer's Guide. This has comparative tables, but is more notable for flashy photos and breezy reviews that verge on sales-chat. It also includes kayaks, canoes, mountain bikes, cameras, watches, and sunglasses from other planets.

A genuinely new entrant (from the publishers of *Outside*) is *Women Outside,* which debuted in 1998. But despite ads for packs, boots, etc. (and the infamous Catera) the content is even less foot-to-earth than that of *Outside.* (Though I did enjoy the piece on cheerleaders.) A rough-and-tumble newsprint equivalent is *Wilds Woman* (subtitled "Women Getting Wild Outside") that also rounds up reviews of gear, rock groups, and "grrlz on film." Stray pieces on hiking and backpacking show up in *Men's Journal* (which also publishes an annual gear guide), and in *Women's Health and Fitness, Men's Health,* and *Walking* (a women's magazine on fitness and grooming rather than the outdoors).

A solid annual treatment of gear is published by *Climbing,* with coverage of tents, boots, crampons, packs, and stoves. While the range is limited (27 stoves versus 43 in the *Backpacker* guide) the accompanying text is full of hard-won details, for instance a sidebar on modifying a stove to hang. If you don't mind photos of people in tights with agonized looks on their faces, it's a valuable supplement.

From its former hook-and-bullet status, *Sports Afield* now courts backpackers with a focus on hiking and camping *sans* kill, and environmental coverage. The ads are a curious mix of packs, tents, parkas, sport utility vehicles, guided hunts, rifle scopes, and chewing tobacco.

Besides the perennials, any well-stocked newsstand will yield more specialized and considerably stranger magazines, focused not so much on backpacking as on the sort of person who might occasionally backpack. *Mountainfreak,* from Telluride, Colorado, is goofy and eclectic, with rock climbing, Forest Service misdeeds, the impact of trekking on Nepal, permaculture, alpine herbs, fly-fishing, Tibet, tattoos, music, and yoga (or what a friend calls "Pasta-farian culture"). *Orion* looks at our relationship to nature in a penetrating way, with fine writing and beautiful design. In that line, Colin likes *Resurgence,* a magazine published in England that hails itself as "an international forum for ecological and spiritual thinking." The refreshingly plainspoken *Wilderness Way* covers do-it-yourself gear, foraging, and primitive skills.

Regional tabloids, subtitled "sports guide" or the like, abound with articles on destinations, personalities, controversies, resource politics, and ephemera-in-general. Since most are ad-supported, they take few risks with gear reviews.

Adventure travel (or eco-tourism, a term with the same effect on my hackles as "wilderness management") is served by such as *Adventure Journal* and *Global Adventure* (from the U.K.). Along with gear reviews, these run ads from guide services and resorts.

A monthly newsletter, *Expedition News,* has sprung up to gauge the flow of sponsorship dollars and track the success or embarrassment of various industry-supported adventures. The publisher claims that such subsidized expeditions "are a way for people to learn about the world," which is in a certain way true.

Further publications (e.g., books on first aid or backpacking with children) are covered in the sections dealing with each subject or listed in Appendix IV.

The current state of the Ms.

During 16 years with a backpacking woman, Linda (Baker, then Rawlins, and now Baker once more), I've noticed significant changes. Between bouts with formal education, she worked outdoors as a surveyor, a forest researcher, a mapper of lost trails, and then as leader of a trail crew. Early on, she talked about the lack of essential gear—not cute sleeveless tops, but boots, packs, and long underwear—to fit her form. She discovered the Lowe Contour pack, a bisexual design that soon led to the womanly Sirocco. Accurately proportioned women's parkas, wind pants, and the like appeared from Patagonia and others. But boots lagged, as makers thriftily relabeled men's styles with equivalent women's sizes.

However, as the 1990s progressed, those who took the measure of contemporary women and redesigned their products accordingly have been rewarded. With a great many women not only active in backpacking but seeking outdoor careers, the bush telegraph quickly spreads the word on what fits.

Now, Lowe Alpine reports that 59 percent of its clothing is labeled for men (or unisex) and 41 percent for women, a shift from the prevailing ⅔ to ⅓ mix. Some rising stars like Mountain Hardwear emphasize that their clothes and sleeping bags are "designed by women for women." But men still run the show: a random sampling of sales and design personnel (based on the business cards I kept) yields 63 percent male to 37 percent female (with Gardner, Hadley, Drew, Paige, and Sam being, as I recall, women). There's no doubt that CEO-types are still predominantly male, and production stitchers mostly female.

But there are other concerns. One of these could be called a rise in *trail fear.* Violent crimes on popular trails, vandalism at trailheads, and thefts from unattended camps have made trail crime a subset of street crime, as one reader writes "in a manner most blasphemous." This breaks my heart. I do see more women on the trails, but few of them are hiking solo. A bronze-goddess friend even carries a .44 magnum pistol "for bears." (Though for both inter- and intraspecies self-defense, pepper spray might work better.) One male reader who came to a shelter on the Appalachian Trail in a storm found a party of women reluctant to let him in, and wrote "I do not yet know how to cope with *the look.*"

Still, despite media-borne waves of apprehension, the backcountry is safe. Compared to interstate highways, shopping malls, parking lots, kitchens, and bathrooms, the genuine hazards are few. But the sense of being alone and far from help—fear itself—can be hard to shake. Simply, one of the best ways to shake it is spend more time outdoors. Working for the Forest Service, Linda mapped so many trails by herself that she thinks nothing of tossing her gear in a pack and heading out alone for a few days of fishing in the high country. And I've met many other women who take challenging solo trips. The deeper the well of outdoor experience, it seems, the less fear.

One spring I hired a woman named Robyn Armstrong as field assistant and we spent the summer camped in remote places. The first thing we established was that she was safe with (and from) me. We had rough going at some points, but the result was a lasting friendship. So, despite the great divide between the sexes, if men err on the side of kindness and women in the direction of trust, our prospects out-of-doors are bright.

Schools and seminars

Colin got much of his early outdoor experience in the British marines and I had mine with the U.S. Forest Service. So our shared preference for solitude might owe in part to that. But some of our closest cousins—chimps, gorillas, and baboons—do nearly everything in company, and aboriginal people travel in bands. Thus, the group-bonding approach of Outward Bound and the National Outdoor Leadership School (NOLS) is a natural one. And, in a culture where vital outdoor skills have been lost, it's a necessity.

Still, my first sight of outdoor-school students was a neat line of 20 orange dots (their packs) up a snow-and-talus gully. I recall thinking that a loose rock or a slip up top could wipe out all below. And over the years I've seen organized groups do magically dumb things in that same imita-

"If nothing else, school has prepared me for a lifetime of backpacking."

tive way. On organized trips the greatest hazard seems to be not Unforgiving Nature but an unskilled or careless instructor. Still, for those who haven't the patience for trial and error, schools are a reasonable shortcut.

There are also a great many boot camps and survival schools for "at-risk" youth, collectively nicknamed "hoods in the woods." The worst of them have killed their charges in the name of reform and profit. But there are other quite different nonprofit groups, such as Wilderness Inquiry and Big City Mountaineers, that offer disabled people and disadvantaged youth a chance at the green world, and these deserve more popular support (see Appendix V).

But it's time to get our eyes back on the trail.

When planning a house on your back, the weightiest matter is

Weight.

COLIN: The rules used to read:
1. If you need something, take it.
2. Pare away relentlessly at the weight of every item.

Basically, these rules still stand. But a tide race has set in toward ultralightweight gear, and emphases have shifted:
1. Strive to reduce to a minimum the number of items you carry (often by sensible multiple usage).
2. Gossamerize every item toward vanishing point.

Result: loads that by old standards are featherweight.

CHIP: Of course there are strong crosscurrents. Countering the tug toward Unbearable Lightness is a tendency to seek Total Comfort. Devotees of the former vie for increasingly longer trips with spookily light loads, while the latter bake focaccia in trail ovens and take calls on their cellular phones.

Earl Shaffer, in 1948 the first to hike the entire Appalachian Trail, still hews to low-tech essentials. When he repeated his feat 50 years later and finished just before his 80th birthday, he carried a military-surplus rucksack with the sidepockets and hipbelt removed. Inside were a down sleeping bag; a down vest; a plastic poncho (which also served as ground-cloth and tarp); extra pants, shirt, undershorts, and socks in plastic bags; a recycled plastic jug for water; and widemouth plastic jars for oatmeal, crackers, and peanut butter. He was crowned with a pith helmet and headnet (with stocking cap for chill nights) and wore a long-sleeved plaid shirt and cotton workpants. On his feet were Red Wing 8-inch leather workboots with the heels pared down.

But Shaffer seems like a raving gearhead compared to Emma "Grandma" Gatewood (1888–1975). In *Beyond Backpacking,* Ray Jardine describes her as hiking in plain, black sneakers and wearing a plastic rain cape and an old shower curtain for weather protection, with her food and spare clothing in a cloth sack slung over her shoulder. In 18 years of hiking she traversed the Appalachian Trail twice, walked most of the long trails in the eastern U.S., and then hiked the 2000-mile Oregon Trail in less time than the original wagon trains took for the trip. "Most people are pantywaists," said Grandma G. "Exercise is good for you."

Foraging and scavenging can also lighten your load. In a *Backpacker* article, Andy Dappen tells of a trip he and brother Alan took on a 47-mile coastal trail in British Columbia. The coast being rich in both sea wrack and hiker discards, they scrounged cans to make cookpots and a stove, found a fry pan on a sea-stack, slept on foam padding from a deck-chair cushion, caught cod, netted crabs, and picked berries. They also scavenged T-shirts, shorts, socks, gloves, bandannas, rope, bottles, utensils, and plastic sheeting. Given a food- and trash-rich environment, this sort of trek can broaden your thinking and enrich your repertoire of skills. The big sacrifice, Dappen admits, is comfort. For three nights before finding the cushion they slept poorly. The other sacrifice is time. In spare environments, the desert or alpine tundra, one can spend much of the day foraging and still go hungry.

All of which our hunting-and-gathering ancestors proved for uncountable millennia, though there is value in proving such things for oneself, even in an elective way.

Technological tides have made lightness more bearable: warm 1.8-lb. sleeping bags, 10-oz. water-shedding breathable parkas, and 3-oz. stoves make it possible to float without suffering. While on the other hand, internal-frame packs with padding like that of Mercedes bucket seats have made it equally possible, in the short term at least, to hump foolish loads in return for luxury. Of course, in the long term gravity always wins.

A purist approach is self-reinforcing. For instance, the Ray Jardine–style pack is 2600 cu. in (with an 1100-cu. in. extension collar), lacks padding, frame, or hipbelt, and weighs about 14 oz. So it is beautifully adapted to very light loads, and performs less well as the weight increases. (*But,* says Ray, so do you.) For the ultralight through-hiker, intent on covering as many miles as possible with the least effort, it's revolutionary. Yet in my case, with occasional payloads of such unwieldy things as a 100-foot tape, bank stakes, and a current meter, it just won't do.

In the same way that you might launch yourself on the curve of Unbearable Lightness, you might also opt for a cushy 0° sleeping bag (no chance of the slightest chill), not three layers of clothing but six (likewise), and, gee, why not bring the espresso pot (and matching cups). Not sure which fly rod to take? How about both? Of course to contain these ample furnishings you'll need one of those Mercedes-upholstered packs, at 7 or 8 lbs. And given the accumulated poundage, your feet will cry for stout, supportive boots with springy insoles. So it goes. One of my self-indulgingest friends is fond of quoting Blake: *The road of excess leads to the palace of wisdom.*

Having enjoyed it both ways, I tend to choose the Light. Though not for abstract reasons. For seven years I did field hydrology in a wilderness, which meant that my pack might hold a 40-lb. payload of float tube, drysuit, fins, meters, cables, bottled lake samples, and other things that I could neither eat nor wear. Since a normal heft of food and camping gear would top me out at an unbearable 80 lbs., I sought out the lightest equipment and shaved ounces madly.

The Forest Service wouldn't buy light gear, so I did. And when I took my light gear on fun trips, I thought my feet had grown wings. But I didn't achieve Unbearable Lightness without tears, and frozen ones at that. A late-season solo into the Wind River Range of Wyoming dealt me a science-load of about 35 lbs. Since it was 10 miles in with a forecast of snow flurries and moderate (30°F) temperatures, and I knew of a sheltered camping spot just above 10,000 feet, I minimalized with a 1.8-lb. synthetic sleeping bag, a 1.2-lb. bivouac bag, and a dinner of curry ramen. I hiked in through intermittent snowfall, got my samples jugged, and set up the snow collector. Then I cooked my Spartan meal and kipped into my bivy sack, as spindrift hissed from the overhangs. But then it quit snowing. The sky cleared and the temperature plummeted to a thrilling 3°F.

At that point (2:00 a.m.) the curry ramen kicked in. I woke up cold, with a volcano in my guts. I erupted from the bivy sack, dug a quick pit, and hunched under a diamond-hard sky while my entire body turned inside out. Returning to the bivy, I shivered for a half hour and then repeated the process. Emptied out, I donned my entire inventory of clothing and dove back into my bag, but by then I was deeply, tooth-chatteringly chilled. So I rose again and built a small fire, with a flat reflector stone behind and converging rockfaces at my back. It took an hour to get warm (and sleepy). Then I crept into the bivy sack and blinked out until the sun woke me.

The lesson (beyond forevermore avoiding that brand of curry ramen) is this: never, never, ever place your entire trust in gear. If you aspire to lightness, whether high-tech or low-, you need an array of primitive backup skills. The point is not to live in a rabbity state of fear, but to stay somewhat flexible in your approach.

Given a preference for lightness, I don't always practice it. A recent late-October trip took me into a trailless part of the Wind Rivers, where I expected to see no one for five days. It had snowed and melted off, except in the shade, to about 10,000 feet. Besides testing gear, I was studying a stream and needed to wade. I wasn't sure whether I could follow the stream out or would have to climb back out of the gorge and retrace my route. The clouds promised a storm. So I took a 4-season tent, plenty of backup clothing, and extra food. Being large and bony, I also took a self-inflating foam pad. Because I expected foraging bears trying to put on a last coat of fat before denning, I also took a Garcia Cache (2.5 lbs.). And I indulged my spirit with a good, thick (1-lb.) book. Thus, my pack weighed 41 lbs. 7.5 oz., and From the Skin Out (FSO) my load was 46 lbs. 13.4 oz. The storm hit the first night, with strong winds and 4 inches of wet snow. It snowed on and off during the trip, and in the bottom of the gorge the leafy undergrowth held sodden clots of white. The wading was slick and the water icy. I misjudged one crossing and had to swim with the pack, which made me glad for the waterproof stuff sacks and extra clothes. My route was choked with brush and deadfall and at last narrowed to a pulse-pounding drop-off, so I had to reverse course, climb out, and camp on an exposed ridge with clouds roaring past. No hungry bear visited. But in other respects, I not only used what I brought, but was glad of it.

Not long before, in mid-September, I'd been seized by Unbearable Lightness. Despite freezing nights, I decided to see whether I could pull off a working trip, collecting stream data, with a fanny pack. In (and on) it, I managed to load a good ultralight sleeping bag, a titanium pot and spoon, an insulated mug shorn (Fletcher-fashion) of the handle, and a pellet stove. Underwear, socks, a knit cap, an anorak, and shell pants were tucked in the corners. Having to wade, I packed sandals and neoprene socks. On top went a pad and a bivouac bag in a single tight roll. One mesh sidepocket held a 1-quart water jug while the other held a canister (single-malt Scotch) with two days' food, both sprayed blaze orange so a hunter wouldn't blaze away at my trophy hindparts.

Ultralight fans tend to use the term *packweight,* which doesn't include water or food. So my *packweight* was 14 lbs. 14.1 oz. With the food and a full quart of water, I was actually carrying 18 lbs. 8.2 oz. What with clothing and boots, my FSO weight was 21 lbs. 1.6 oz. (the Mountainsmith fanny pack had auxiliary shoulder straps, which I used). The route, much of it off-trail, undulated for 15 miles between 9000 and 10,500 feet. Having a light load and low center of gravity eased the bushwhacking, so I sloped off into the tangles and saw some country I hadn't visited before. During the night it snowed lightly, but I slept warm and dry. The only lack was food—with 1.1 lbs. for two very long days I stayed hungrier than usual. For an overnight jaunt that's not a problem, but for longer trips and through-hikes it most certainly is. For load lists and weights for these and other trips, see Appendix II.

COLIN: Yes, Unbearable Lightness offers huge advantages, but it's easy to gloss over uncomfortable facts. Although the lighter load helps—helps a ton—that's not the whole truth, so help me God. Backpacking isn't all traveling. It's also sleeping and loitering and eating, for example. So backpacking pleasure is also comfortable sleep, cozy warmth at all times, and perhaps a few heavy luxuries—short of the complete works of Sir Arthur Conan Doyle (page 659)—not to mention a full belly. I note that many light-gear enthusiasts seem to skimp on the food. Yet there's general, though not total, agreement that to stay healthy and fully active the average person needs a daily ration of around 2 lbs. of dehydrated food, and some stories of ultra-Spartan rations frankly sound harder to swallow than the food.

CHIP: Of course, one of the benefits of lightening up your gear is that it allows you to carry good food: I regularly pack fresh fruits, vegetables, even potatoes, which were a major dietary item on Mark Jenkins's epic bike ride across the Soviet Union, which he describes in his book *Off the Map*. Even with dire loads on winter expeditions, and a largely freeze-dried regimen, I usually take fresh garlic, an onion, carrots, bell pepper, and similar whole foods to gnaw raw or add to the pot. I've long dried my garden produce, including such delights as plum tomatoes and scallions, for backpacking use. And the olive oil and vinegar I carry for mixing hummus dresses wild-green salads. In the course of hundreds of trips, I've noticed that an unrelieved diet of freeze-dried meals, energy bars, and the like results in a sense of deprivation. In my cowboying years, I saw that horses fed on bagged pellets and grain still had an ardent need to graze. Lacking grass, they would chew the tops off pine fence posts.

That is, beyond a mere slate of proteins, fats, and carbohydrates, we poor beasties need something to chew that resembles food. So—be pound-wise, but don't skimp.

Both approaches, the Road of Excess and the Gossamer Gallop, have been around for some time. Most backpackers choose neither exclusively but instead adopt some of the best elements from both. For instance, at the Total Preparedness end is a Coleman Pro-Lock pocket tool, with which I could probably rebuild a radial aircraft engine, that weighs 8.4 oz. My Victorinox Tinker (i.e., Swiss Army knife), with a 2½-inch blade and scissors but no pliers, is fine for most repairs at 3.2 oz. But I just got a Coast Micro-plier pocket tool with both pliers and scissors (small but usable), and a knife blade just long enough to clean a fish, at a snappy 1.8 oz. That gives me 6.6 oz. to play with: the weight of a medium-size potato. Or two paperback mysteries. Or, God help us, a mini espresso maker.

Having suffered exquisitely under expeditionary loads of 85 lbs. or more while traversing icy logs, swollen streams, and breakable snowcrust, I think that any residual toughness so gained was simply not worth the wear and tear. Really, the only good part is having lived to tell the story. Preferably from a good, deep chair, with stiff drink in hand.

The maximum for backpacking *as an enjoyment* is perhaps one-third of body weight. A well-conditioned body can handle more weight, if necessary, and training routines can help (page 41). A reasonable load would be one-fourth or one-fifth of body weight. Unbearable Lightness would kick in down around one-eighth.

Age is another ponderable. A good way to make children (or dogs, for that matter) hate backpacking is to load them too heavily. Young people are also somewhat awkward; that is, they have more resilience but less in the way of grace. As aging makes us less resilient, it can also make us— given any luck at all—far more efficient and graceful. As they say in the Hindu Kush: *An old goat has the surest step.*

For old goats as well as aspiring ones, the process of refining your game is part of the fun. Along with choosing one item of gear or another, you can follow the Fletcherist practice of lopping your toothbrush and tearing the labels off tea bags: set aside all your trimmings and then triumphantly weigh them all together. If you're serious, you'll soon acquire a good set of scales. I use a Hansen Commercial 860 for loads up to 60 lbs. and a Chatillons Improved Spring Balance for weights below 18 oz., with a Pesola Spring Balance for nitpickery under 100 grams (all available from Forestry Suppliers; see Appendix III). A further note on weight: while I'm bound by convention to pounds and ounces, given any good sense whatsoever you'll do your reckoning in grams and kilos.*

Again, the paring process is a profound sort of fun. At each pass of the blade, you can choose whether to drop your total weight or keep it neutral by adding some prized indulgence. The range of gear now available offers so many opportunities that it's hard, unless you throw caution

---

*The English have virtues, but their system of weights and measures is not one. (COLIN: Hear, hear!) In fact, as England edges into the European Union, grocers there can be fined for weighing out their goods in pounds and ounces. But the U.S. remains a stubborn holdout.

(and your savings) to the wind, to exhaust them all. For instance, clothes and sleeping bags should be in waterproof sacks. But cookpots are quite happy in mesh bags at half the weight. Should you wear mountain boots, at 3 lbs. 6 oz.? Or trail-running shoes, at half the weight? To go up on the glaciers, you'll need boots. But what about aluminum crampons, at half the weight of steel ones? There are also radical shifts, such as choosing a solar-powered campsite for long trips (for an explanation, see page 604). If you're replacing worn gear, you can refine your outfit, piece by piece. But don't be in too much of a hurry: let things wear out. Then see if you can get by without them. A good way to know the worth of a thing is to do without it for a while. If you find you can, then not only do you shed weight, but it costs nothing at all.

Cost

It's not just a fantasy but a verifiable fact that the cost of good backpacking gear has risen much less steeply than the price of—a car, for instance. In 1980 the MSR model G stove, not including fuel bottle, cost $60.75. You could get a reasonably equipped Saab sedan of that era for about $7500. The current XGK Expedition stove will nip you for $90, not bad as inflation goes, while the postmillennial Saab rolls out at $30,000-plus. And in the backpacking realm, some prices have remained nearly the same. The 1980 Bleuet (the company is now known as Campingaz) Globetrotter cartridge stove cost $21; the present Twister 270 fires up for $22, with a built-in piezoelectric lighter. Has the quality gone to hell? In a word, no. It's a great little stove.

But in 20 years, vast frontiers of expenditure have opened: computers and video systems to name just two. (Not to mention cosmetic surgery.) So while today's average backpacker probably spends less as a percentage of income, we tend to whine a great deal more. The pricing system that's evolved in response falls into three categories. The best off-the-shelf gear is called *high-end.* An example is the MSR Dragonfly stove, which roars, simmers, and burns everything but walrus blubber, at a cool $100. Then there is the solid, though not necessarily stolid, *midrange.* The Coleman Peak 1 Apex II is a good multi-fuel stove at roughly the same weight for $65. Still lower there lurks what is called *price-point* gear. While the term implies that low price is the only factor, there are surprises waiting for those unblinded by snob appeal. Such as the cute little Markill Devil stove, which claims a quicker boiling time than either of the above, at half the weight, for $20. If you don't need to melt cubic yards of snow, the Devil might suit you fine.

There is also the realm of the specialized and hair-raisingly expensive, like the Primus Titanium stove—a 3-oz. blowtorch for $200—that is generally called *trick.* Beyond *trick* is *custom,* the sweet stratosphere of McHale Packs and Limmer boots. True custom gear might set you back now, but also might last a lifetime.

In specialty shops, the high-end is high indeed but is generally worth the bite in terms of durability. The midrange is likewise good. While the price-point is usually decent. But if you venture into a "big-box" chain store, you might find that its high-end barely touches the specialty midriff. The midrange falls at knee-level. And the low end can be subterranean indeed. Having worked with outdoor programs that plumbed the depths of cheap gear, I tend to avoid it. It's harder to use, breaks down fast, and is often not worth fixing. Some conglomerates field one line for specialty shops and another for discounters, so brand name isn't necessarily the key. If you want to spend less, then bone up on the basic materials (e.g., Polarguard fiber for sleeping bags) and take the time to count stitches and slide zippers. If something looks useful, pounce. For many years, my 3-season bag was a screeching yellow beast I plucked off the trash pile at a firefighting camp. The zipper was blown, so I duct-taped the foot closed and used it that way for years. Then Linda (bless her) replaced the bad zipper. That scrounged bag (originally costing 20-some dollars) was home base for almost a decade. The moral? If the pudding tastes good, don't worry about the price.

Still, if you're working out your trajectory, or thinking about a one-shot winter camping trip, the answer might be

Renting.

Trailhead Sports, in Logan, Utah, where I worked for some years, had an active rental program. I learned a lot by fitting, maintaining, and fixing rental gear. Quite often, we sold it at the end of the season at a steep discount. Some shops give a credit based on rental fees if you buy as a result. Some chains, Eastern Mountain Sports (EMS) being perhaps the best example, maintain strong rental programs. As of this publication, the rates average:

	Per day	*3-day weekend*
Tent, 2-person	$15.00	$20.00
Pack	10.00	15.00
Sleeping Bag	10.00	15.00
Pad	5.00	10.00
Totals	$40.00	$60.00

Of course, at 60 bucks a pop, renting is not a way to go for very long. And there are risks attached. Deposits are usually the daily rate times 10.

If you return gear dirty or trashed, despite the fact that it wasn't really your fault, etc., etc., most shops will whack you for cleaning, repair, or replacement. So rent if you must, but keep your eyes pegged—for the same outlay you can score heavily at a garage sale or gear swap. There are also "recycled" outdoor shops where moderately good deals can be haggled. Another good bet is to find a thrift shop in a capitalist haunt like Jackson Hole. At season's end (when the colors of both leaves and fashions change), you can reap such shocking bargains as to feel positively guilty.

Of course, in an age of oversupply and hyperdemand, it's also possible to get burdened with bargains. So it always makes sense to think in terms of

EQUIPMENT FOR A SPECIFIC TRIP.

COLIN: Most decisions about what to take and what to leave behind will depend on the answers you get in the early stages of planning when you ask yourself "Where?" and "When?" and

"For how long?"

We have already looked (on pages 32–33) at the kinds of differences that can arise in equipment choice for a weekend as opposed to a week. Beyond a week the problems change. Food is the trouble. For 10 days, most people need around 20 pounds of it; for two weeks, almost 30. And such weights reach toward the prohibitive. I don't think I've ever traveled—as opposed to operating from a base camp—for more than 10 days without food replenishment. (For replenishment methods—by outposts of civilization, caches, airdrops, etc.—see pages 703–10.)

As far as equipment is concerned, then, even a very long journey boils down in essentials to a string of one- or possibly two-week trips. Besides replenishable items, all you have to decide is whether you'll be aching too badly before the end for a few extra comforts. A toothbrush, a paperback book, and even camp footwear may be luxuries on a weekend outing, but I imagine most people would think twice about going out for two weeks without them.

What makes a very real difference is that the longer the trip, the greater the uncertainties about both terrain and weather; but here we begin to ease over into

"Where and When?"

The two questions are essentially inseparable (see, again, pages 31–33 and 40; and for planning from maps, page 623). Terrain, considered apart from its weather, makes surprisingly little difference to what you need carry. The prospect of sleeping on rock or of crossing a big river may prompt you to take a self-inflating mattress, as opposed to a closed-cell foam pad for snow, or nothing at all for sand (page 443). In cliff country you may elect to take along a climbing rope, even when on your own (page 657). Glaciers or hard snow may suggest ice axe and crampons (pages 101–4). But that's about all. And snow and ice, in any case, come close to being "weather."

In the end it is weather that governs most of the decisions about clothing and shelter. Now, weather is not simply a matter of asking, "Where?" and answering, "Desert," "Rainforest," or "Alpine meadows." You must immediately ask, "When?" And from the answer you must be able to draw accurate conclusions.

In almost any kind of country the gulf between June and January is so obvious that your planning allows for it automatically. But the difference between, say, September and October is not always so clear—and it may matter a lot. (One of my advisers calls it "transition weather.")

A convenient source of accurate information is the U.S. National Climatic Center; above all the series of booklets *Climatography of the United States.* Each booklet (one per state) has a general climate summary and a map showing weather station locations. For each station it tabulates monthly averages of temperature and precipitation: means and extremes, highs and lows. Also, mean number of days with temperatures above 90°F and below 35°, 12°, and 0°. And snow and sleet data, including greatest depths. For some stations there are data on relative humidity, wind speed, barometric pressure, and hours of sunshine and heavy fog. The tables tend to be printed rather fuzzily, but they're peer-hard legible. Booklets run $2 each (plus a service and handling charge of $5, or $11 for orders over $50) from the National Climatic Data Center (NCDC), 151 Patton Ave., Room 120, Asheville, NC 28801-5001, 828-271-4800, fax 828-271-4876.

CHIP: Libraries might have a compilation (in huge format) called *Climatic Atlas of the United States.* Found in the Government Documents section, it reports daily maximum, minimum, average, and extreme temperatures, along with temperature ranges. It also includes frost-free dates, solar-heating indices, rainfall, snowfall, percentage of sunshine, and wind speed and direction. Some of this information is displayed on tables, and some on maps of the U.S. But look at the dates—the weather is changing significantly in some parts, and older data may be misleading.

COLIN: The NCDC also generates a blizzard of other information, including a climatic map of the U.S. and data on freeze/frost incidence, hourly precipitation, and storms. There's some worldwide information, too. A single-sheet list (free) summarizes what's available. A 132-page booklet, *Products and Services Guide* (also free) gives greater detail, including the many Web systems available through its home page, *www.ncdc. noaa.gov*—including such goodies as *Climatic Extremes and Weather Events, Temperature Extremes, El Niño/La Niña, Global Measured Extremes of Temperature and Precipitation, Summary of the Day* (8000 U.S. sites), *U.S. Monthly Precipitation,* and *Global Climate Model* (100-year run).

Many larger national parks, such as Yellowstone, Yosemite, and Death Valley, have weather data available on their Web sites, and those of other parks have links to weather information. Almost all national parks can provide some weather information through their listed phone numbers.

In Canada the prime equivalent to the U.S. Climatography Series is *1961–90 Canadian Climate Normals,* available on paper or diskette. The books cover six regions and give average and extreme monthly values of temperature and precipitation for all stations in Canada with 20 or more years of information, and monthly average wind, sunshine, and moisture for stations that record them (prices in Canadian dollars: *British Columbia,* $30.95; *North,* $19.95; *Prairies,* $37.95; *Ontario,* $26.95; *Quebec,* $32.95; *Atlantic,* $22.95; full set, $200. Diskettes for each region are $40; for all of Canada, $200). All of the information in the books/diskettes plus monthly data for the period of need from more than 6900 sites across Canada is compiled on a CD-ROM disk: *Canadian Monthly Climate Data and 1961–1990 Normals,* with enabling software for MS-DOS or compatible systems, $200. A list of the available information for Canada may be found at *www.msc-smc.ec.gc.ca/climate/index.*

The Canadian Climate Normals Atlas covers 1961 to 1990 and gives mean daily temperatures, mean daily maximum and minimum temperatures, total rainfall, total snowfall, and total precipitation. The set of two diskettes—temperature and precipitation—come in two versions: PXC graphics files that can be used with several off-the-shelf software packages, and CUT and MAP formats intended for Geographic Information Systems (GIS) such as SPANS. (Both versions are $50 Canadian.)

To order any of the above, or for more Canadian information, contact the Climate and Water Products Division, Environment Canada, 4905 Dufferin Avenue, Toronto, Ontario M3H 5T4 or e-mail *Climate.Services @ec.gc.ca.* (Make checks payable to the Receiver General for Canada.)

Monthly figures can never tell the whole story, but these booklets (certainly the U.S. ones, which I've used for years) can be a great help in planning a trip. In deciding what night shelter you need, it may be critical to know that the lowland valley you intend to wander through averages only 0.10 inch of rain in September (20-year high: 0.95 inch) but 1.40 inches in October (high: 6.04 inches). And decisions about what sleeping bag and clothing to take on a mountain trip will come more easily once you know that a weather station 8390 feet above sea level on the eastern escarpment of the 14,000-foot range you want to explore has over the past 30 years averaged a mean daily minimum of 39°F in September (record low, 19°F) but 31° in October (low, 9°); by applying the rough but fairly serviceable rule that "temperature falls 3° for every 1000-foot elevation increase," you can make an educated guess at how cold the nights will be up near the peaks. Remember, though, that weather is much more than just temperature. See especially the windchill chart, page 748.

A wise precaution before any trip that will last a weekend or longer is to check on the five-day forecast for the area. Such forecasts are given every few minutes on National Oceanic and Atmospheric Administration (NOAA) VHF radio stations that now form a network covering most of the country. You can buy small sets that receive them, starting at a few ounces and $29. Or, for taped, local reports check the telephone book under "U.S. Government, Department of Commerce, National Weather Service."

CHIP: For the computerized, a wide array of weather reports and data banks can be found on the Internet by activating a search for "weather." Some interesting Web sites I found (all prefixed by *http://www*) were Weather Satellite Views, which displays satellite images and forecasts for North America at *aerohost.com/weather-satellite.htm;* the Interactive Weather Information Network, with continuous updates from the National Weather Service, at *iwin.nws.noaa.gov/iwin/main.html;* and The NOAA Weather Page, which lists sources of weather information at *esdim.noaa.gov/weather_page.html.* Many server home pages have links for weather reports. To hone your personal forecasting skills, a good, portable book with over 300 photographs is *The Audubon Society Field Guide to North American Weather* ($19). Also good (though not packable) are a Global Climate Chart and an Atmosphere Chart (both $20) available from Forestry Suppliers (see Appendix V).

COLIN: But the finest insurance of all is to have the right friends. I have one who is not only a geographer with a passion for weather lore but also a walking computer programmed with weather statistics for all the western United States and half the rest of the world. I try to phone him before I go on even short trips to unfamiliar country. "The Palisades in early September?" he says. "Even close to the peaks you shouldn't get night temperatures much below twenty. And you could hardly choose a time of year with less danger of a storm. The first heavy ones don't usually hit until early November, though in 1959 they had a bad one in mid-September. Keep an eye on the wind, that's all. If you get a strong or moderate wind from the south, be on the lookout for trouble." By the time he has finished, I'm all primed and ready to go.

For keeping an eye on the weather during trips, see page 759.

Unless you have the only infallible memory on record, you ought to have a couple of copies of a

Checklist of gear.

It should be a full list, covering all kinds of trips, in all kinds of terrain, at all times of year. On any particular occasion you just ignore what you don't want to take along.

Eventually everyone will probably evolve his own list. But many local and national hiking organizations (see Appendix V) are happy to supply beginners with suggestions. So are some commercial firms. Appendix I is a full list that might be a useful starter. You can photocopy it and check from the loose pages, conveniently buttressed by a clipboard. But as soon as experience permits, draft your own list.

FURTHER PLANNING

Unless you are fit—fit for backpacking, that is—you should, at least as early as you start worrying about equipment for a trip, worry like hell about

Getting in shape.

The only real way to get used to heavy loads is to pack heavy loads— though what you mean by "heavy" will depend on your experience, ambition, frame, muscles, and temperament. I certainly try to fit in one or two practice hikes in the week or two before any long wilderness trip. Sometimes I even succeed. Whenever possible, I make this conditioning process seem less hideously Spartan by stowing lunch in the pack and eating it on a suitable peak, or by adding work papers and setting up temporary office under a tree. Or I may carry the pack on one of the walks I regularly take in order to think, feel, sweat, or whatever. As far as the exercise goes, I find that it makes no difference—well, not too much difference—whether I walk in daylight or darkness.

Even if your regimen doesn't permit such solutions, make every effort to carry the pack as often as you can in the week or two before you head for wilderness, if only to prepare your hips for their unaccustomed task. Details of distance and speed are your affair, but take it easy at first and increase the dose until at the end you're pushing sweaty hard. If possible, walk at least part of the time on rough surfaces and up hills. Up steep hills. Not everyone, of course, has the right kind of terrain handy, but at a pinch, anywhere will do. The less self-conscious you are, the freer, that's all. You may blench at the thought of pounding up Main Street with a 40-pound pack (all those damned traffic lights would wreck your rhythm anyway), but, pray, what are city parks for? And many big metropolitan areas now have nearby hiking trails.

If the pressures of time, location, family, and *amour propre* combine to rule out fully laden practice hikes, attack the problem piecemeal. Your prime targets are: feet, legs, lungs, and shoulders.*

Legs are best conditioned by walking, jogging, or running. Especially running. And especially up hills. For those with limited time at their disposal, running is currently the most popular and perhaps the most efficient answer. I suspect that a not inconsiderable number of those pent-up citizens who pant around Central Park Reservoir at their various rates and gaits may be preparing for a week or weekend along the Appalachian Trail. I know at least one who often is. Nowadays there are "par courses" in some cities: you run from one exercise station to the next, do your chosen stint there, and discipline and improve yourself by monitoring the overall torture time. Frankly, I find a much more pleasurable, though possibly less effective, regimen is tennis—singles, not doubles—played often and earnestly. An alternative, gentler on knees and backs, is running in place (and doing other fun exercises) on a small trampoline, indoors or out.

The finest conditioner for your lungs—probably even better than carrying loads—is, once again, running, especially up hills, up steep hills.

Because all the weight of a pack used to hang from the shoulders, people still connect backpacking with "sore shoulders." There's a certain residual truth in the idea: any but the very best modern packframes, properly adjusted, can leave unready shoulders a mite stiff. But with the hip-belt that is the crux of today's pack suspension, it is on your hips that the real load bears. And, brother, does it bear! I go for sumptuously padded

---

*CHIP: And don't forget your skin. Current medical wisdom suggests that sunburns are to be scrupulously avoided, particularly for the fair-skinned. (Dark-skinned people also get sunburns and should exercise due care.) A program of skin conditioning for a trip is to spend limited but regular time in the sun after applying sunscreen or sunblock (for details, see page 645).

belts and I'm fairly often in harness, but I still find, on the second morning of most trips with heavy loads, that I wince as I cinch the belt tight—the way it must be cinched—on hip muscles still complaining about yesterday. And on that second morning, if not earlier, any hips that have never undergone the waistbelt trauma under a heavy load, or have not done so for a long time, are just about guaranteed, I hereby warn, to complain fortissimo.

CHIP: Besides sore muscles, another lookout is pressure sores. These appear where your bones protrude, often at the points of your pelvis, and are slow to heal on the trail. Padding helps, but having a hipbelt and yoke of the right size and cut helps even more (see page 170). So does reducing your packweight.

When I was young I endured slings, arrows, and sores, and healed quickly, ready for more. But such wear and tear is cumulative. The present tendency (risking what threatens to become a minor jeremiad) is to think that you can simply buy your way out of this. Pressure sores? Get more padding. Aching feet? Buy stouter boots. But the practical limits of this strategy are clear, unless you also choose to hire a sedan chair, porters, and a cook.

The best course, which I discovered at length and Colin confirms, is to maintain a steady level of condition, whether through tennis, jogging, or climbing stairs, and then pile on a bit extra before a big trip. Not being much for running or tennis, my current favorite is pedaling a mountain bike on dirt roads at a heart-pounding clip.

When we last hiked, Colin would occasionally interrupt our rather brisk pace by excusing himself to dash up a hill, snorting like a bull, at an age when most men can only fart like one. So this is not a case of *ipse dixit,* but a well-proven pudding indeed.*

COLIN: I'm afraid all these strictures end up sounding ferociously austere. But Arcadian ends can justify Spartan means. Many a beautiful backpacking week or weekend has been ruined at the start by crippled, city-soft muscles—because their owners had failed to recognize the softness, or at any rate to remedy it.

Harbor no illusions about how much difference fitness makes to backpacking. A study conducted at the University of Texas, El Paso, in

---

*COLIN: Don't kid yourself, though: age matters. For one thing you become less resilient and must pay more attention. But there's one easy way, beyond sweat, to mitigate the tolls of time. Just before reaching 60 Fletcherheit, I underwent a cautionary conversion, and now, at 26 Celsius, I find I'm still going reasonably strong.

1974 indicated that physical fitness appears to be more closely related to pack-carrying performance than is either age or weight. I buy that.

There's a certain forest to which I retreat from time to time for a two- or three-day think-and-therapy walk. Normally I go when mentally exhausted from work and muscularly out of practice. I start, mostly, in the evening. I am glad to camp a little way up the first, long hill and then to plod on next morning until I reach a little clearing on the first ridge, where I often stop to brew tea. Sometimes it is by then time for lunch. But once, in order to think out the shape of a book, I went to my forest only 10 days after returning from a week spent pounding up a Sierra Nevada mountain. I was fit and alert. And that purgatorial first hill flattened out in front of me. I stayed in high gear all the way; although I had as usual started toward the end of the day, I reached the ridge clearing in time to choose a campsite by the last of the day's light.

So even if you can't manage practice hikes, try to do something. Start early. Start easy. Work up. You may find that you actually enjoy what you're doing, especially if you organize the right palliatives (hilltop lunches, subarboreal offices, daydreams, tennis). And when you stride away from the roadhead at last, out into Arcady, you will very likely discover that getting in shape has made the difference between agony and ecstasy.

Getting in shape for high altitude

Up high, your body works less efficiently, especially at first. There is wide variation: some people tolerate high altitude well, others poorly. And the more practiced you are, the better you tend to play the game. But current gospel maintains that physical condition has no effect—at least on the more serious forms of distress, known as "acute mountain sickness." In fact, fitness may make you drive too hard, and so overtax your body.

Symptoms of what could properly be labeled "acute mountain sickness" rarely occur below 8000 feet. (For much, much more on that subject, see page 750.) But if your body is tuned to operate at sea level you may well experience as low as 6000 feet enough mild initial distress, such as shortness of breath, to impair your efficiency and enjoyment. And a little higher you may begin to suffer headaches. You can dampen such distress almost to extinction if you acclimate correctly—that is, give your body time to make adjustments (mainly increasing the depth and rate of breathing) so that it can perform properly under the new conditions. If you're making your first energetic trip into high mountains and don't know what your threshold of tolerance will be, pay particular attention to this acclimation process.

The body does most of its adjusting in the first three days, with the first two the most important. So those are the days to watch. I seem to tolerate high altitude fairly well, at least up to 16,000 feet, but if I'm going over about 10,000 I take pains to arrange that I cannot get out of the car and immediately, with my body still tuned for sea level, start to walk toward those beckoning peaks. When checking gear at home I leave such details as rebagging food and waxing boots to be done at the roadhead. Other things being equal, I choose a roadhead as high as possible—at 6000 or 7000 feet or more. And I tend to drive until late at night to reach it. Sometimes I drive clear through the night. Then I more or less have to sleep up high for at least one night, or part of a night (or day); and by the time I've slept late and then gotten all my gear ready there's normally only an hour or two of daylight left—just enough for a leisurely walk and then another night's sleep up high before I can even begin serious walking.

Not everyone will want or even be able to apply my particular built-in brakes at the roadhead, but try to devise your own version. If time and terrain permit, it's naturally better to start low and let the body adjust slowly, as you gain elevation. But the slope must be reasonable or the pace slow, or both. I know one family that on its first Sierra backpack trip ignored warnings and tried too much, too high, and too early, so that everyone suffered headaches and the other malaises of "mountain sickness" and came down vowing never to set pack on back again.

Even when you ought to know better you can still do stupid things. A few years ago, after sleeping one night at a 9000-foot roadhead and a second night just above it, I pushed too hard on the third day, with a very heavy load, and was pretty tired, as well as somewhat dehydrated, by the time I camped at dusk on a 13,000-foot peak. That night, for the only time in my life so far, altitude ruined my sleep. All night I kept coming awake to find myself gasping for breath. It was not pleasant. And as soon as dawn broke I betook my shaken self down a talus slope that ended at 10,000 feet. There I camped. All day I sat. Next morning I felt fine. For the rest of that week—walking along a ridge, camping twice at 13,000 feet, only once below 12,000—I experienced no further distress. I had learned, vividly, what I had long known in a general way: for the first three days up high, you take things easy. I now know that this "periodic breathing" or "Cheyne-Stokes syndrome"—in which you repeatedly stop breathing for as long as 10 or 15 seconds—is common under such conditions and *in the absence of other symptoms* appears quite harmless. (See page 751.)

Even after the first few days of adjustment you must still take things much easier than at sea level. But that is a walking rather than an acclimating matter, so see page 121.

Be prepared, by the way, for your body to make readjustments when you return quickly, as you often will, to sea level or thereabouts. For two or three days you may feel somewhat sleepy.

CHIP: Or worse. For years I lived at 7000 feet and worked in the mountains between 10,000 and 11,000 feet. When a fellowship took me to Stanford University, at an elevation of tens rather than thousands, I felt awful. At the medical center they explained that while the percentage of oxygen was the same at my accustomed heights, the vapor pressure was less. Thus, up high my bloodstream needed more red cells to draw the necessary O_2 from the air, and my blood was too thick for sea level. For this reason, the ancient Incas placed strictures on travel between the coast and the high Andes. In my case, the rarifying effect of academe soon thinned my blood nicely. When I returned to the heights, I had to endure the obligatory puffing and blowing. But inseparable from the body is the mind.

Pretrip Sickness

COLIN: If you're what laymen call a hypochondriac but perceptive doctors classify as someone merely overaware of how the old organism is functioning, and if you're in the throes of planning a really challenging trip, funny things can happen.

In order to deal with them you must first get yourself a good doctor—the kind you've come to trust down the years, so that eventually you can call him and say, "Look, Glenn, I feel this and this and this. Am I ill or have I got Fletcheritis?"*

Almost 40 years ago, just before embarking on my two-month, length-of-Grand-Canyon walk, I was deep in the pit of logistics, economics, equipment, permissions, and all the other hassles when I was laid low by some new and inopportune affliction. For two days, or maybe three, I languished in bed, weak as a winter butterfly, sweating intermittently, deeply depressed at the prospect of the year's postponement that would

---

*Fletcheritis is a recurring and scurvy condition (typically, a horrendous slump with variegated symptoms, uniformly exhausting and dire, or semi-dire) that oozes into existence at such moments of crisis as the onset of a new book.

A different doctor, whom I had acquainted with the correct medical terminology, once told another patient, "Hm, in my opinion you've got Fletcheritis."

The patient stared, round-eyed. "My God, what's that?"

"Well, the way to cure it is to go away and get drunk. And if possible, laid. Then call me tomorrow and tell me how you feel."

The patient duly called. "You were dead right," he said. "I feel great."

result from a two- or three-week delay. At last I phoned my Doctor Glenn, described the symptoms, and put the Fletcheritis question.

"Are you afraid of this trip?" he asked.

"I don't think so. Not beyond a reasonable awareness that there's a physical challenge."

We talked a bit more, and eventually the doc rather tentatively suggested that perhaps I shouldn't go.

Within half an hour, still bedridden, I'd made the one phone call needed to bring preparations to a grinding halt.

Within another half hour I found myself out in the garden, standing in brilliant sunshine, throwing a golf ball in the air—and catching it and generally beaming at the world. The moment I realized what I was doing I rushed back indoors and rephoned the doctor.

"It was just the pressure of all the perishing hassles, wasn't it?" I said.

"Probably."

"And there isn't a damned thing wrong with me."

"No. But it might come on again, down in the Canyon, you know."

"It won't," I said.

And it didn't.

The moral of this story is, I guess, that every walk of life falls under the sway of the Testicular Imperative: "Either you have the world by them, or it has you."

CHIP: Just as troublesome is temporary insomnia. I tend to sleep poorly the first night on the trail. This condition is not uncommon—I once bought an army-surplus sleeping bag and found a bottle of sleeping pills tucked in the foot. Another remedy is to blur the transition between your house on a street and the house on your back. A week or so before, spend a night or two in your sleeping bag. Get out your stove, check the gaskets, and fire it up. Cook a meal out back and make tea. If you have a nearby spot, pitch your tarp or tent and sleep out. Beside shaking out any last-minute problems with your gear, this helps you adjust to such things as having to fiddle with a 60-inch zipper before relieving yourself at night. As conditioning goes, a pretrip stretching of habits can prove just as salutary as dashing up hills.*

---

*In a science journal (alas, I didn't note which one) I came across a paper suggesting that it's actually somewhat unnatural to sleep straight through a night. People who live without constant artificial light tend to wake up after four or five hours, to be awake for an hour or so, and then to sleep another two or three hours. After a week or so under the sky, my sleep cycle changes this way. I've worried about it, making the sleepless hour worse. But it seems that the worry is more of a problem than the sleeplessness.

COLIN: The planning question that seems to haunt almost all inexperienced hikers is

"How far can I expect to walk in a day?"

For most kinds of walking, the question is wrongly put. Except along flat, straight roads, miles are just about meaningless. Hours are what count.

Naturally, there's a connection—of sorts. I have only once checked my speed with any accuracy, and that was more or less by accident. It was during my summer-long walk up California. One afternoon I followed the Atchison, Topeka, and Santa Fe for 9 arrowlike miles into the desert town of Needles. It so happened that I began at a mileage post, and I checked the time and jotted it down on my map. I traveled at my normal speed, and I recall no difficulty about stepping on ties (as so often happens when you follow a railroad track), so it must have been straightforward walking on a well-banked grade. I took a 10-minute halt at the end of the first hour; and exactly 1 hour and 55 minutes after starting I passed the 6-mile mark. I would guess that this 3-miles-per-roughly-50-minutes-of-actual-walking is about my norm on a good level surface with a pack that weighs, as mine probably did that day, around 40 lbs. In other words, 7 hours of *actual walking* is roughly the equivalent of a 20-mile day on the flat, under easy walking conditions—provided you are fit, practiced, and motivated.

But on trails you'll rarely come close to 20 genuine miles in 7 hours. Mostly, 2 miles an hour is good going. Off trails, over really rough country, the average can fall below half a mile. The nonsense that hikers commonly talk about mountain miles walked in one day is only equaled, I think, by the drivel they deliver about loads.

But if you now ask the amended question, "How many hours can I expect to walk in a day?" it remains difficult to give a straightforward answer. The thing is seamed with variables. On any given day—provided you're well rested and not concerned with how you'll feel next morning—you can, if you're fit and very powerfully motivated, probably keep going most of the 24. But what really matters in most cases is what you're likely to keep up, fully laden, day after day. Even a rough estimate of this figure demands not so much a grasp of arithmetic as an understanding of human frailty. I've published elsewhere a table representing a typical day's walking on the desert half of my California trip—a day on which, beset with all the normal and fascinating temptations of walking, I pushed tolerably hard, though not even close to my limit. Mildly amended to fit more general conditions, that table may help explain the difficulties of computation:

	Hours	Minutes
Walking, including 10-minute halts every hour	7	
Extension of half the 10-minute halts to 20 minutes because of sights, sounds, smells, ruminations, and inertia		30
Compulsive dallying for photography and general admiration of the passing scene— 4⅔ minutes in every hour		30
Photography, once a day, of a difficult and utterly irresistible object (this will seem a gross overestimate to nonphotographers, an absurd underestimate to the initiated)	1	
Conversations with mountain men, desert rats, eager beavers, or even bighorn sheep	1	
Cooking and eating 4 meals, including tea	3	30
Camp chores		30
Orthodox business of wilderness traveler: rapt contemplation of nature and/or navel		30
Evaporated time, quite unaccountable for		30
Sleep, including catnaps	8	59
Reading, fishing, additional rest, elevated thinking, unmentionable items, and general sloth		1
Total	24	

Nonwalks, sort of

Please don't assume from all this talk of miles and hours that sheer walkery lies at the heart of every backpacking trip. Even when you set out with walking as your prime aim things don't always turn out that way. Sometimes you find that what you really want to do is loiter along or even just loaf around a camp that you thought was just an overnight stop. Or planned extraperambulatory activities (page 669) may hold the walking to a subservient, get-me-there niche. A special case, growing in popularity, is physical do-gooding. Mostly, that means making or maintaining trails, but there are other forms of helping the wilderness. Some years ago, I went up from time to time, often with one or two others, into what was once untouched wilderness, and slowly repaired a small section of the damage inflicted by bulldozers as they "fought" a forest fire. The practical impact of any such project on your equipment and planning may be small—a need for work gloves, stout boots if you're shoveling earth, maybe pack modification to carry tools, even including a chain saw (if you have permission to use one); but I very much want to inject a word about projects of this kind. I strongly recommend them as good for the soul: to my surprise, the work we undertook over a period of maybe five years has turned out to be one of the most rewarding things I've ever done with my life. Frankly, I like to operate in parties of one or maybe two, and find that things glow warmer when free of help from any organization. I'm aware, though, that most people prefer to work in groups and may have difficulty in matching their desires with suitable tasks.

CHIP: Wilderness Inquiry is a group that promotes and supports outdoor activity for disabled people and Big City Mountaineers organizes walking and camping trips for urban youth: both groups need qualified trip leaders. The American Hiking Society, Student Conservation Association, Sierra Club, and Appalachian Trail Conference, among others, sponsor a lengthy menu of service trips that combine hiking with trail building and maintenance. Conservation groups need volunteers to survey roadless areas and document conditions on the ground. Some parks and reserves have Adopt-A-Trail programs. Budget-pinched land and wildlife agencies offer a great many internships and volunteer positions that will get you out on two feet with a house on your back. (For addresses, see Appendix V.)

Permits and other controls

COLIN: A new and increasingly intrusive element in planning is the system that now meters backcountry visitors in many national parks and forests. You cannot legally go backpacking in them without a permit. To make sure of getting permits for the most popular places you may have to apply far ahead of time. If you arrive unheralded at the entry station you may be turned back. And the thing doesn't end there. Before you go in you'll likely have to specify not only your route but also the location of each night camp. For all its good intentions, the system is already a pesky affliction. It threatens to become a plague.

The reason for the system is clear and understandable: so many people now want to go into the backcountry that, in order to protect it and also the visitors' enjoyment, entry must be controlled.

The trouble lies in the nature of the controls. Most people, whether they recognize it or not, go into backcountry because they want to leave behind for a spell the human-dominated world, ruled by linear thinking: by immersing themselves in a world of curves that operates on quite different grids of meaning—or perhaps I mean webs of meaning—they hope to emerge with broader perspectives. Almost anyone who has spent a few days in wilderness, alone or in quiet company, understands the antithesis between the two worlds. And it's there, though not always so clearly recognizable, in any backcountry journey. But present control methods are the aggressively linear kind that will be the obvious and inevitable first choice of almost any human organization: to make absolutely sure of getting a permit you must delineate your plans weeks or even months ahead; and to satisfy the permit ranger you may have to set in concrete—or pretend to do so—even what you will do once inside and "free." In other words, this key does not fit this door. The system is, I suggest, self-defeating.

Its shortcomings reach out far beyond the philosophical: it generates traumas and hassles that range from minor to monumental. Many permit rangers perform their duties with perception and restraint, and the instructional sermons they deliver with the permits may even succeed in helping teach the uninitiated how to treat the backcountry; on the other hand, the system also guarantees employment for the kind of person who has revelled in rasping domination of his fellows since long before Shakespeare bewailed "the insolence of office"—the arrogant broad-brimmed Gauleiter who can, single-handed, tarnish anyone's entry into what was meant to be a beautiful experience. Most of us have brushed with such fauna. But many of the system's failures derive from its very nature, not from warts on its enforcers. With time as precious as pearls, you have ignored speed limits and generally busted your ass in order to reach roadhead by midafternoon—but still arrive half an hour after the permit ranger has shut up shop: if you're going to be legal you have to hang around until opening time the next day. (True, if you can phone ahead and if you hit a cooperative ranger you may be able to get a permit pinned to a bulletin board; but that's big "if" country.)

CHIP: As in dealing with any form of bureaucracy, the keys are a) start early, and b) double-check. Most agencies requiring permits have come up with a system for handing them out, but these are often perversely inconsistent, with the potential to become maddening. The most popular spots, national parks, suburban wilderness areas, and the like, are the most bureaucratized. Some have a lottery system for permits and this can be annual, seasonal, or monthly (often with cancellations opening up at short notice). Others hand out a limited number of permits per day, on a first-come basis. In all cases you should ask not only about fees but about deadlines: if permits are available only on alternate, odd-numbered Tuesdays when it's not raining, then so be it. You are being put over a hurdle (or many), and if you want to hit the popular spots you'll just have to hop on cue. Unless you have *in hand* a numbered receipt or some other incontrovertible evidence, it's also wise to double-check your status by calling back, checking the Web site, etc.

More common is an on-demand system, with a trailhead register. This log-in, log-out arrangement gives agencies some useful data and also makes it easier to track missing hikers. Having duly registered, some of us feel rather more secure, while others have that creepy sensation of being watched from on high. For years, I signed registers with assumed names (John Ruskin, Sid Vicious, Belle Starr) and accurate destinations. But quite often I didn't know quite where I intended to go, that being precisely the point. So I wrote things like "the Gateless Gate" or "101 Central Park West." What struck me at the time was that having a set itinerary for my wandering went hard against my instincts. And this leads to a trend more troubling than permits per se.

Besides permits, some jurisdictions now have "designated" campsites as well. The bureaucratic reason for this is "to prevent resource damage," but the spots designated are often such a mess that a sane person wouldn't camp there: trampled and shat upon to the point that they resemble a dirt-floored hovel with a broken toilet and the walls knocked down. Incessant use tends to attract animal scavengers ranging from horseflies through skunks to garbage-addicted bears. Unofficially, these are called "sacrifice areas." What they have been sacrificed to, of course, is us. In the five years from 1993 to 1998, visits to national forests in the U.S. increased from 729 million to over 900 million. Politics also factor in: during that same time, the appropriation for national forest recreation programs dropped from $261 million to $218 million. That is, legislators ever-eager to subsidize commercial logging, mining, and grazing are unwilling to put public money in the service of public recreation. Caught in the squeeze, the U.S. Forest and National Park Services have come up with a "fee demonstration program." In the past, most fees collected for recreation went back into a general pot rather than being used where they were collected. The new program allows parks and forests to take additional bites (for example, a $10 per head wilderness fee and a $5 parking permit billed as an "Adventure Pass") while keeping 80 percent for local repairs and maintenance. This, it is claimed, will prevent such disgraces as the recurring, massive sewage spills into the rivers of Yellowstone National Park. While the program seems reasonable on its face, in the long term it threatens to price a lot of good people out of the wilds, like closing the church doors to all but a select group of tithe payers.

A parallel incursion has been a series of attempts by legislators and their cronies to "privatize" the outdoors, which in effect means handing over public campgrounds, trailheads, and the like to profit-oriented business. There has also been a huge jump in the commercial use of wilderness areas by outdoor schools, guide services, adventure-travel bureaus, video producers, and so forth.

The grand solution, of course, is to scorch some pale legislative butt and demand that the personal, muscle-powered, *recreational* use of public lands be supported (as a great many less worthy things are) with the taxes we pay. As far as the impact of crowding on the land itself, Colin set forth a ringing proposal in the previous edition of this book.

COLIN: It has long seemed to me that a valid alternative permit system would radically reduce or eliminate all piecemeal, man-contrived controls and replace them with a natural, more or less self-regulating arrangement that still protects both the land and human experience. Now, devising such a system is not easy. Nor is embracing it. Out in the civilized, linear world where the relevant decisions must be made, it is difficult to retain a grasp of the curved, weblike modes of thinking at stake—even though you vividly remember the feel of the values they generate. In addition, our political and legislative machinery remains unpracticed in such solutions. And any plan that fits is almost sure to run head-on into the often unintentional but still undeniable tendency of bureaucracies, including the National Park and U.S. Forest Services, to extend their fiefdoms.

Still, somebody has got to try.

The filter-by-natural-obstacles system I propose is not new, at least in essence. But until *Complete Walker III,* it had not, I think, been seriously put forward in print. Its salient measures:

- Move roadheads back as far as possible, or at least as far back as is necessary to reduce usage and protect the land.
- Reduce and if necessary eliminate trail maintenance of the kind that encourages easy access (broadening, making easy grades, removing all encroaching brush, and, especially, fallen trees and rocks). Continue minimal maintenance to prevent erosion at specific points.
- Force the Park and Forest Services to quit advertising. That is, to eliminate or at least radically reduce their well-intentioned efforts to tell people "what's out there." They do so not only with maps and brochures but also with strategically placed rangers trained to dispense information—and graded on how well they do it. Such a policy was once valid. For "social," human-dominated areas served by roads, such as the floor of Yosemite Valley or Cade's Cove in the Smokies, it still is. But for today's pressured backcountry it makes no sense. After all, what goes on, essentially, is that one public hand encourages an influx of backpackers while the other hand tries to impose a curb because the numbers have grown too big.*

---

*Lumping the National Park Service and the U.S. Forest Service together, as I've done for simplicity, isn't really fair. Managing visitors forms only a small part of the USFS's jobs, and that fact often shows. But the NPS is deeply and basically concerned. It mostly does a superb job of running the roadbound, straight-line parts of its domain. Unfortunately the same principles and mind-sets tend to guide its backcountry management. And that goes so gratingly against the grain that I sometimes feel the whole permit system, if not unconstitutional, damned well ought to be. If the Founding Fathers were around now, with roadless country so shrunken and precious, perhaps it would be.

Please note that I am *not* advocating a simple dropping of the permit system and throwing open of the backcountry. That would be crazy. I suggest replacing the present controls with others, of an entirely different, nearly self-regulating nature, that would remove the current and growing barriers to human enjoyment *while still protecting the land.*

I also do not suggest that the permit system be abandoned everywhere, overnight. That would cause chaos. But I do believe that it should be replaced as soon as possible in suitable trial areas—which probably means large, rugged tracts where cessation of trail work would quickly make access a lot more difficult. Then, when the new system had been tried and its worst bugs swatted, we should consider extending it, perhaps in modified form, to many or even most backcountries. It may well turn out that no filter-by-natural-obstacles system will work in certain easily accessible areas, such as those used or overused by weekenders who demand easy access and may be perfectly happy to pay for it with the permit hassle. I'm sure there will be teething difficulties anyway. And I do not pretend to have fine-focused all ramifications and implications. Frankly, I lack the technical expertise. I suggest, though, that once the plan's essence and the changed mode of thought behind it have been genuinely accepted, then details of application and such related matters as fire-protection policy, rescue stance, and backcountry ranger stations could be hammered out. Others would solve themselves.

The plan isn't perfect, of course. Like our form of democracy, it may be the worst system you could imagine—except for all the others that have been tried. But at least its key fits the backcountry door.

CHIP: The erosion of soil from a trail can be stopped with a well-placed log and a few rocks. But the cultural erosion of wilderness, and the very idea of *wildness,* into a sort of on-demand commodity is less simple to fix. Nor is it my task to do so.

Despite sheaves of blistering comments and impassioned letters, I've noted my limited ability to steer the great ship of Public Policy through these reefs and shoals. So I tend to grip my own tiller (so to speak) and chart my own modest course. To wit: I hold my "permit" trips to a few each year, to lessen my role in overcrowding. Avoiding the famous trails, I do a great deal of aimless wandering, wondering, and vagabondage-in-general, at times even lacking a map. And increasingly, I simply depart on foot (or bike) from home, in search of obscure and scruffy borderlands where I can get my required dose in small, sweet sips. I regularly practice "stealth" hiking and camping, which quantizes the Leave No Trace ethic in the direction of sheer invisibility. And I continually look for places that haven't been written about and then do not write about them. None of this pays very well, but—

In April 1988 an article by Jon Krakauer in *Outside* extolled a certain lake as "maybe the prettiest place in all the Rockies" and displayed the obligatory "Access and Resources" box. Since I happened to be monitoring that very lake for acid rain and snow impact (I'll skip the irony), I was fiercely curious about the effect of a single page in a national magazine. For my unsanctioned study I interviewed Forest Service front-deskers, campground hosts, and local lodgekeepers and outfitters, all of whom noted the influx to that particular area. People called asking about "you know, that place in *Outside.*" On my science trips that summer I saw not only a human stampede, but also the aftermath—trampled campsites, candy wrappers, toilet-paper blossoms. Wilderness rangers reported loud arguments over campsites and even fisticuffs. As the season passed, several delicate stretches of trail were pounded so heavily that they washed out and slid into lakes and streams.

I also looked at trailhead registers for 1984 to 1988. As near as I could tell, Krakauer's piece contributed to a jump in use at that trailhead of 10,410 visitor/days, or 21 percent above the previous year (and of 12,359 visitor/days, or 24 percent higher than the five-year average). That is, a single article by a single writer can have immense effect. In such cases, the oft-repeated argument that by publicizing wild places one is attracting more defenders is eminently self-serving.

However, a greater threat to wildlands, wildlife, and wildness in general is the savage encroachment of motorized use. While hiking this past year I saw dozens of former foot-and-horse trails that have been beaten out by four-wheel-drive and all-terrain vehicles into roads, many of them quickly deepening into gullys. From these routes of invasion, wheel tracks set off at random across hillslopes and meadows. I've seen hill-climbing gouges and ATVs driven along shallow streams while the fat, beer-guzzling chaps on them wielded spinning rods. On ski trips, I've also seen hundreds of snowmobile tracks crossing wilderness boundaries. So while agencies tighten their regulations on essentially law-abiding back-packers and collect higher fees from those willing to help, the motorized Huns and Vandals largely have their way. Virtually the only time they suffer consequences is when they drive off a cliff or set off an avalanche, costing the public a whacking great sum for rescue.

Speaking of rescue . . .

Letting some responsible person know where you're going and when you'll be back (with electronic variations)

COLIN: I still think it should be automatic to file some kind of registration (with ranger, friend, or soberish aunt) before you walk out into any kind of country—whether for a few hours or several weeks. It's not merely a question of your own safety. If you don't, people will eventually come out to look for you; and if they have nothing to go on except the place your car was parked and perhaps the vague recollections of someone you happened to chat with, they'll waste a great deal of time searching in useless places. And they may expose themselves to unnecessary dangers—on the ground and in the air.

In busy national or state parks and forests your permit is hardly enough. Its aim is control. And rangers can't keep tabs on everyone who comes out. So, everywhere, cast about until you can find someone who strikes you as thoroughly reliable. Your life may depend on his reliability. If you travel solo, it would certainly be wise to make some such registration. A little to my surprise, I find I almost always do.

It's probably sensible, at least in some cases, to leave a map marked with your proposed route—if you have a route. And even if you're simply going to wander and have no idea where you'll end up, *state a date and hour by which you'll return*—or will emerge elsewhere and immediately check back by phone. Let it be clearly understood that if you haven't reported back by the time specified, then you're in trouble. In fixing the deadline, allow yourself a little leeway. And once you've fixed it, make hell-or-high-water sure you meet it. I repeat: make hell-or-high-water sure you meet it.

CHIP: The proliferation of cellular phones has added some odd variations. When I was mapping glaciers in a remote part of the Rockies (we saved weeks by using a fancy GPS rig-up) from our camp on a ridge at 11,000 feet, my colleagues would call home nightly on their cell phones. Why the GPS mapping didn't bother me while the phone calls did, I'm not sure. Organized groups have taken to using cell phones, and so have individuals for their own varying reasons, from trepidation to logistics. But this seems to me a subtle yet profound form of cultural erosion, the further wearing-away of wilderness.

A reasonable compromise would be to take the damned thing, but to seal it in a plastic bag with duct tape and stow it in the medical kit, for use only in dire need. Having acquired a tiny and madly expensive cell phone at a charity raffle, I gazed on it for some weeks and then gave it to Linda, having decided that I don't want it in my pack. What I love most about long walks outdoors is precisely the peaceful, self-reliant lonesomeness. Should I break a leg, I might feel differently. But so far, so good.

Two veiled elements of planning that are often overlooked

COLIN: When you leave civilization and enter wilderness you need time to convert from the linear coordinates of the human world to the softer web of wilderness. The interval required for fairly full recovery from this jolt—which is really an extreme case of "culture shock"—commonly runs to about three days. That's what I find, anyway. And until you complete your readjustment to the new "culture"—or, rather, to the lack of culture—you don't operate well. You tend to stumble on loose stones, select inefficient routes, hesitate or even balk at mildly challenging scrambles, and spend twice as long as normal choosing campsites. But after three days, give or take some, this nonsense passes and you are back in stride.

When you leave wilderness and reenter civilization you must, of course, reconvert. And you weather a corresponding withdrawal period. If you reenter by car, for example, you're likely to find that for 20 minutes after leaving trailhead you drive poorly, even a little unsafely. And although your eyes are newly and widely opened, what you see—or at least what you do with what you see—may remain strangely unfocused. I find that once I'm back home I can soon go about routine business halfway adequately but that it will be three days before I have readjusted well enough to do serious, delicate work.

I'm almost sure I have never read anything explicit about these dual phenomena, but I don't think there can be any doubt about their existence. Any experienced backpacker to whom I mention them immediately recognizes the reality. "Yes," said one friend who moves frequently between the two worlds, "I guess you could say I live in a perpetual state of maladjustment."

It seems to me that the two-way condition could usefully, if a little cutely, be called "trail lag." It should certainly enter—by any name you like—into your planning calculations.

There's another phenomenon you might do well to consider, too. An expectancy barrier is a well-known and superbly efficient human device— either self- or other-induced—for ensuring that an experience falls thuddingly short of its billing. The condition runs rampant in such fields as mutual friends ("Oh, you *must* meet John—you two will get on like a house on fire") and movies ("The funniest show since Genghis Khan— promise me you won't miss it"). Don't forget that an expectancy barrier lurks on the preboundaries of almost every backpacking trip—ready to cast its shadow over the round and beautiful pumpkin that sits waiting up there on the shelf. I can suggest no antidote beyond an alert and ongoing skepticism.

Foundations

COLIN: The foundations of the house on your back are your feet and their footwear, and the cornerstone is a good pair of

BOOTS.

Before surveying the boots now available we ought to consider some non-technical fundamentals:*

What a boot is meant to accomplish. The *upper* must be pliant enough to let your foot bulge slightly under load but must give it the necessary support. It must conform to the foot's minor idiosyncrasies, preferably without being broken in. It must protect the foot. It must repel water. It should, to some degree, breathe. The *sole* must be joinable to the upper in a waterproof, nonseparating way. It must provide safe traction on all expected surfaces—but, ideally, do so in a way that won't damage fragile land. It must cushion your foot against the worst sole bashing it's likely to sustain. It must support that foot when it's bearing an unusually heavy load. Yet it can't be too rigid because it must encourage, or at least not unduly impede, the foot's complex natural walking movements.

We'll consider most of these criteria later, piece by piece, but we must take a look right now at an important word used twice in the last paragraph.

Support, as applied to boots, is difficult to define. In a general sense it probably means something like the holding-together-against-abnormal-strain that professional athletes achieve when they tape their ankles, or that we mortals achieve with Ace bandages. More specifically, it seems to

---

*The uncomfortable fact is—as I've rediscovered every time I approach this chapter for a new edition—that boots, though basic, are boring. So I'm delighted to leave current details to Chip. But some of my old general stuff stands. Try to stay awake. Boot camp's important.

mean three discrete things: First, sufficient lateral rigidity to prevent feet from twisting severely under loads on uneven surfaces. Second, arch support of a kind that will prevent flattening under overload yet leave boots longitudinally flexible enough "to let your feet work"; that is, will mimic, at least to some degree, the spring action of your arches—an action vital to the feet's cushioning effect on the rest of the body. Such flexible reinforcement of the natural arch is normally achieved by inserting between midsole and insole a contoured shank.

CHIP: Traditionally the shank was a thin piece of steel, but in many boots it's now either enclosed in or replaced by a plastic shank or frame. Besides stiffening, the other function of a shank or frame is to protect against bruises from stones or abrupt edges. One clear advantage of plastic is that it can be curved closer to the shape of your foot. Another is that midsole frames can be formed with openings at the ball and heel for shock-absorbing inserts. The use of plastic also extends to the heel, with molded cups and supports standing in for layers of glued and stitched leather, fiberboard, or other material.

COLIN: *Weight* is even more important on the feet than on the back. In his classic 1906 book, *Camping and Woodcraft,* Horace Kephart calculated the results of wearing boots just 1 pound too heavy: "In ten miles there are 21,120 average paces. At one extra pound to the pace, the boots make you lift, in a ten-mile tramp, over ten tons more foot gear." In 1953 the successful Mount Everest expedition came to the conclusion that in terms of physical effort 1 pound on the feet is equivalent to 5 pounds on the back. A consensus of informed opinion now seems to support that assessment. Anyway, today's trend is certainly toward lightness.

CHIP: Outdoor footwear—which now includes not only backpacking boots but highly adapted species for trail running and canyoneering, and even sandals—has complexified to say the least. So some general categories will help us to sort the catch-of-the-day. (For reference, the weights given here are for *pairs,* men's size 9 and women's 7, with some comparisons to my own size 12s. But some makers list the weight per boot. And still others seem to weigh their boots without laces or footbeds. So you might want to take your own scale to the store.) In any event, let's start with the big ones and work our way down the foot chain:
  • *Mountaineering boots* are the stiffish types chosen by walkers whose taste runs to glaciers or alpine snowfields. Traditionally made of leather with stitched welts (the layer that joins the boot top to the sole) and full-length steel shanks, these boots reach above the ankle and have thick, lugged soles that mate with crampons. Koflach, Asolo, and others intro-

duced plastic shells with a mechanical pivot at the ankle and removable liners. While these work wonders on steep ice and snow, I was never able to walk in them with any degree of comfort. Recently, with superb boots from European firms such as La Sportiva, leather is once again in favor. But new materials and fibers such as Keprotec (Kevlar fibers wrapped around stainless-steel cores) are swimming up into the light. Weights (per pair) go from about 3 lbs. up to 5 or so. Prices hover at elevations around $200, and up, up, up.

• *Off-trail boots* were once called heavy hikers, but "heavy" is an unpopular word these days. For uneven terrain and the loads that go with long treks, these are the ticket, and some work with crampons for mountaineering. The most traditional boots, such as the custom Limmer, the Alico Sport Guide, the Danner Mountainlight, and the Merrell Wilderness, have features like stitched welts and leather linings that once signaled quality, along with devoted followings. Newer models combine leather uppers with cemented (though potentially replaceable) outsoles, some sort of shank or frame, molded midsoles, and synthetic linings of wicking fabrics such as Cambrelle. Inner membranes of Gore-Tex or Sympatex are common, though they won't save your feet if the boot leaks. Middle-ground boots have protective rubber toe caps or *rands* (pieces of rubber inserted between the sole and upper, folded upward and glued). Good examples like the La Sportiva Makalu, Montrail Moraine, Salomon Authentic 7, and Vasque Super Hiker are both sturdy and increasingly light. The radical end ("rads") of the spectrum runs to synthetics, though dabs of leather are found, often coated or dyed in supernatural hues. An advantage of the rads is that each component can be made from a material suited, whether in terms of stiffness, shock absorption, or breathability, to its intended function. Weights for off-trail boots average 3 lbs. and change. Some makers claim shocking lightness, which makes me wonder if they forgot to weigh the other boot. Prices range from $150 to over (perhaps well over) $200.

• *Regular old backpacking boots* might be tagged "rough trail," "midweight," "light backpacking," "long-distance hiking," "mountain trekking," or "cross-hiker," which suggests a certain grouchiness—maybe it's the price. These over-the-ankle boots span the trad-to-rad continuum noted above. While full-grain leather has a strong following (e.g., the ubiquitous Vasque Sundowner), the tip now twitches toward combinations of synthetics with various leathers: Nubuk (top-grain with a sanded surface and a great many spellings), and split-grain (i.e., suede). Soles are almost universally glued (with a few well-stitched exceptions) and may incorporate molded midsole/frame components. Rather than gluing, a few makers, like Asolo, injection-mold plastic directly onto the upper for a seamless bond. The outsole (the black part) now comes in a boggling diversity of patterns and depths. This simplifies one thing at least: it's easier to track someone on a crowded trail than it used to be. Weights range from 2.5 lbs. to just under 4, and prices from $100 to $200 plus.

• *Trail boots* are meant for maintained paths, day hikes, weekend trips with light packs, and general scuffery. They've also become standard for postal carriers, students, and the little old ladies who once sported tennis shoes. Topping out around the ankle bone or thereabouts, they tend to be either suede or fabric reinforced with leather. Most common is nylon, though synthetic leather and hemp have surfaced. Midsole/frame architecture is found in about half of this class, and outsoles tend to be softer with shallower patterns (a nonmarking sole—gray or tan—helps avoid domestic wrath). Weights span the range from 2 to 3 lbs. and prices from $50 to $150. One thing to beware: the very popularity of this class has spawned fashion look-alikes that lack the substance needed for actual trail use.

• *Running-shoe cousins* are increasingly used not just for easy walks but for serious endeavors. Inspired by the early success of the Nike Lava Dome, makers now attach tags like "trail running," "cross training," "multi-sport," or "adventure racing." Trailworthy breeds differ from street shoes in having a slightly higher cut, less open-weave mesh, an extra protective layer for the toe, and a denser outsole. Weights descend from 2 lbs. to mere ounces. List prices start around $35 and peak well over $100 for the techi-est breeds, with models changing fast.

• *Sandals* were used for serious hiking in biblical times and have made a millennial comeback. My love affair began when a disgruntled chap returned a Grand-Canyonized pair of size 12s to the store where I worked. Loath to pack heavy waders for alpine hydrology work, I cut off the straps that blistered his heels and wore them with neoprene divers' socks. Soon, I was donning them to wade creeks and simply stopped taking them off. Some of the present horde are simple footbeds with straps while others look more like half-finished shoes, but some basic choices present themselves. The first is between an open- or a strap-toe (one that encircles your major digit with webbing). The second is along a range from simple (continuous webbing, one buckle, plain footbed) to complex (padded straps, connective hardware, plastic superstructure, and shaped footbed). The soles need to absorb shock, and some styles have molded arch supports and curved stabilizers at the insteps. The front of the sandal should curve upward enough that, as you raise your foot, there's not much air between your toes and the footbed. Straps should have enough play that you can wear socks on chill nights. Leather footbeds (made popular by Birkenstock) are comfortable at first, but wetness and grime tend to glaze them quickly. Weights for sturdy footpads are 20-some ounces. Prices (for those that hold together) start around $35 and swoop up to $90.

Certain features are naturally common to all breeds of boot.

Lacing and laces

While laces have not changed much, the ways of conducting them have. *Eyelets* (punched holes with or without grommets) are still around, especially in the lighter breeds. *D-rings,* mounted with metal clasps and rivets, are likewise still in favor, along with lugs or hooks from the ankle up.

Before looking at new means, let's review the deficiencies. Eyelets and grommets tear out, notably at the instep and other stress points. D-rings, given more mechanical efficiency, tear out very seldom, but the rivets needed to attach them create pressure points. Metal hooks or lugs likewise create pressure points and also (when poorly attached) pull out. While nylon laces resist breakage along their length, they're vulnerable to a sharp edge. So examine all grommets, D-rings, and lugs for sharp edges and burrs. Metal grommets can wear through to a razor edge. Some makers use flat D-rings rather than round ones, and if they aren't smooth they're hell on laces. If your laces get fuzzy, look for the cause. A needle file, a scrap of fine sandpaper, or a cut-down emery board (for fingernails) can save you an eventual wail on the trail. That said, let's look at some new ways of doing the same old boring job.

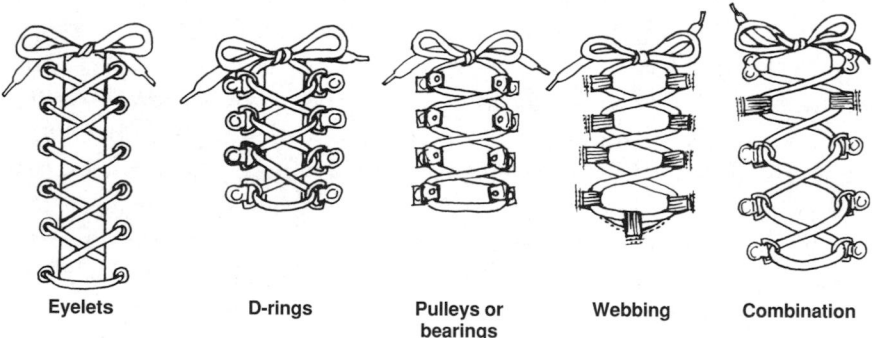

| Eyelets | D-rings | Pulleys or bearings | Webbing | Combination |

Velcro came and went, having a tendency to cut loose when dirty or wet. Plastic D-rings also disappeared, being subject to wear—a braided lace impregnated with grit acts like a mini–chain saw. But plastics are reappearing in place of metal in various forms. Variations include speed lacing (sort of a stamped or molded D-ring sans ring) and tiny pulleys with swiveling steel bodies and bronze wheels. A similar riff is a speed-lace lug with a ball bearing, called an "easy-roller." These allow friction-free adjustment with a slight penalty in terms of heft.

Locking hooks reign at the ankle or just below, with tapered throats that catch the lace and allow snuggery round the ankle with less tension at the toe and instep. Many lighter boots have flat loops of webbing in the forefoot: the width provides enough friction to resist seesawing by laces as you walk, the sewn attachment avoids the pressure point created by rivets and lugs, and the soft loops don't catch on things.

Most boots have a combination of the above. My off-trail boots mount flat Ds from toe to instep, then a locking D-ring set in a nylon base, then a loop of flat webbing at the ankle (where hooks tend to catch), topped by two open hooks. This works nicely.

Whether the laces run through eyelets, D-rings, or webbing, one significant change is from a layout that's symmetrical with respect to the boot to one that angles. Look at your bare foot. A line drawn across the base of the toe joints slants back toward the outside, and so does the contour of your forefoot. So some makers, Garmont for instance, now mount the outer lace points farther back.

Laces, given occasional washing and replacement, seem not to break. Flat laces are rare and braided nylon cord the standard. Rather than carry spares, I dig into my general repair kit for a hank of 2- to 3-millimeter nylon cord long enough to add a tie-out to a tarp, serve as a clothesline, or provide spare laces (on the theory that I'm unlikely to need all three at once). I also carry a foot or two of ⅛-inch shock cord that can also save a trip when new boots act up. On a pair that spread out in front and developed a nasty, toe-chomping flex, I knotted a loop of shock cord at the flex point to pull the Ds together. On my backcountry ski boots I use shock cord, permanently tied, on the forefoot. This promotes a snug but toe-wiggling warmth, and I can lace the ankles very tight indeed. Another repair-kit boon is a scrap of the heat-shrink tubing sold for electrical projects, which works wonders when lace-ends unravel.

Tongues

tend not to flap as freely as they once did. *Gussets* (or folds) attaching them to the uppers now extend over the instep and beyond. This keeps water and trash out, and heat in. Makers claim that wicking liners solve the sweat problem, which is *somewhat* true. Most tongues are faced with leather to resist abrasion and backed with fabrics, foams, and liners. The elegant trads employ leather throughout, with buttery gussets—sheer pleasure. In all cases, check the folds for internal lumps or ridges. On some boots, the tongue/gusset part may be a single piece that extends without seams into the upper, with sewn-on leather strips for D-rings or eyelets. While this design resists water, it may also bunch up and rub. Also be wary of separate, internal tongues, which scrooch off to the side unless tabbed with Velcro. The upper tongue should fold to conform to your shin as it grades into your ankle.

Liners and linings

The uppers may be lined with a breathable membrane of Gore-Tex, Sympatex, etc. For a while debate raged, but the consensus is that this doesn't hurt and often helps. In sodden conditions—hiking through willow bogs after a foot of wet snow—I notice that my feet do stay drier. That is, while my socks get damp, my boots no longer slosh internally. Most boots also have one or more layers of foam inside. This adds comfort and warmth (or hotness), and can conceal various boot-making sins. So put your forepaw in and feel around. Tongues are necessarily padded, but you don't want foam in the toe where it can cramp your wiggle. Likewise, there should be little or no foam in the heel. The place for a distinct cushiness is along the sides and about the ankle. Here's a simple test: with your thumb outside the boot, slip your fingers in and rub hard. If the foam shifts, don't buy the boot. It will bunch, raise blisters, and wear out, in that order. The innermost layer is called the *liner.* Cambrelle, nylon, and various three-bar knits, all synthetic, have supplanted leather. They don't get soggy and are generally durable. Traditional boots may be lined at the ankle with leather, which doesn't catch grit, burrs, and grass awns like knit fabric.

Scree collars

On above-the-ankle boots, the outers are cut lower at the back with a distinct roll or two made of leather or knit and filled with foam. These don't so much keep out scree as cushion the Achilles tendon and ankle— the bigger and stiffer the boot, the more help they are. By contrast, mid- and low-cut shoes curve up in the rear to protect this same area.

Soles

A closet poll reveals that about half of my outdoor shoes have Vibram soles, no two with the same pattern. Skywalk is another widely used brand, while some makers use self-labeled soles. So here, too, the range is wide. But some general principles hold true. Off-trail boots should have deep-lugged soles of a tough, carbon-black rubber. Given ice, snow, wet rock, slick mud, ball-bearing gravel, and similar delights, there is no substitute. Another aspect is pattern, which governs the *contact area.*

Simply, each sole has parts that touch and parts that don't, and the ratio between the two is crucial. The less the contact area, the greater the pressure (in pounds per square inch). On wet, glacier-polished granite, for instance, a pattern of deep, narrow lugs contacts less rock and increases the pressure. In turn, this decreases the chance of slippage. On a soft surface the lugs sink in, increasing both the contact area and the number of angles at which the sole resists slipping. Summed up, the reason lugged soles work so well is that their contact area, pressure, and array of angles all change as the surface does.

New rubber compounds have bettered both grip and wear resistance. Some outsoles employ two or three compounds. Others, like the Vibram Bifida, have inner layers or inserts of a lesser density (measured in durometers) in a grid or honeycomb pattern to make them lighter and to absorb shock.

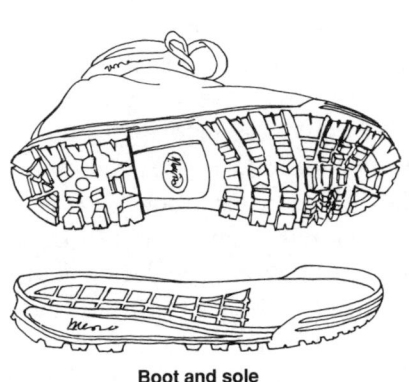
Boot and sole

Responding to complaints about trail damage and to studies of biomechanics, designers now use computer programs to divide the foot into thrust, grip, and brake zones, and design new soles on which no two lugs are alike in size and shape. There are grooved friction surfaces, angular wedges for traction and *kickoff,* and rounded center bobs that don't pick up mud. Toes and heels are canted to provide a more natural take-off and landing for the foot, along with a slight lengthwise curve for a forward-rolling effect known as *rocker.* Instead of 90-degree edges, new one-piece outsoles have tread patterns that curve up along the sides. Some running-shoe cousins also have curious lobes on the outer instep (the out-step?) to prevent ankle rollovers.

In general, the heavier the boot, the more lugged and angular the sole. Midweight trail boots tend toward circular, round-shouldered patterns. Running-shoe cousins have soles that are shallower and squigglier yet. Sandals have flattish soles arrayed with grooves. Another principle is that the lighter the shoe, the more contact area it should have on a hard surface. A final one is that as the shoes become lighter, the soles get softer.

Choosing your boots

COLIN: First, hold the objectives tightly in mind: you want to walk in comfort; you do not want to get unnecessarily tired; you want to keep your feet as dry as possible. To achieve these ends you must balance weight against support and protection. In the past, boots probably tended to be too heavy, but today the trend is toward lightness (and longitudinal flexibility, so that your foot can "work"). And you should certainly not buy a tank when a VW will do. But don't forget that the nature of your feet, your load, the terrain, or the weather may sometimes demand a tank.

Second—because there is now a boot for almost every backpacking niche—you must know just what you'll be demanding of the pair you choose.

If you intend to walk only in cities or suburban parks, unladen, then—provided you have strong feet and ankles—you can probably get by with tennis or running shoes. Some people even use them for much rougher walking. (I once wore running shoes for a day hike on Mongolian grasslands, but the place had been grazed lawnlike and I had no more suitable footwear within 10,000 miles.) Sneakers or running-shoe cousins, low-cut or ankle-length, are certainly fine for such jaunts—and for fair-weather work with light loads on trails or across friendly terrain. If you have suspect ankles or rain seems likely or the terrain gets rough, you may want to forget the sneakers and go with only ankle-length, top-of-the-line running-shoe cousins or lightweight boots. And if the weather promises to be really foul or if the load gets over, say, 35 pounds (though that figure will vary prodigiously person to person), then you may prefer heavier backpacking boots. Here, ability and experience count. An athletic and experienced walker may be able to carry heavy loads over rough terrain wearing lightweight boots that on a tyro would mean courting injury. For the latest on off-trail boots, see page 74. As a general principle, titrate the heaviness of your boots against the heaviness of your hiking.

These are only guidelines, of course. No two people have the same feet—or mind-set. A few happily pack 40-pound loads across talus while wearing low-cut cheapies. Others get out their backcountry heavies for a stroll around the park. And it's important to recognize that, even beyond such personal preferences, every choice is a compromise: no single boot will work best in all situations. Finally, if you find our guidelines fudgy to the brink of uselessness, remember that, as I said at the start, we are really looking at a continuum of boot styles, not a series of sealed-off categories.

Once you've decided what you'll be demanding of your boots and go to a store to buy them, try to have your decisions ready to put into words. A good salesman told me, "We try to tailor sales to customers' needs, but we have to work with the information they give us and it's often pretty vague." No matter how experienced you are, you'll probably find that in the store you still, like me, feel the need for guidance through the thickets of current brands and models. Even if you hike like crazy, all year round, you buy new boots only once every few years, and you tend to forget the rules. But the salesman is at it all day and every day. So if you feel confident that the one you get is an experienced backpacker and knows what he's talking about, lean heavily on his advice. In the end, though, you have to rely on your own judgment, feelings, and even hunches. So the more you know, the better shod you'll be.

In making your choice, the first criterion should be quality.

If, like most of us, you lack technical competence, judging a boot's quality is largely a matter of common sense; of impression rather than specifics. But remember that a maker who cuts corners is likely to cut all corners. So, in both new-tech and traditional boots, examine the stitching on uppers. If it's weak-looking, beware.

For more on the rather specialized subject of judging the quality of uppers and also sole attachment in traditional boots, see page 70.

In new-tech boots the nub question is the sole attachment's reliability. But the answer seems to be that, beyond gross and obvious deformity, looking won't tell you much. Other than rely on the maker's reputation, all you can do is wear the damned things and see if they hold up.

The second criterion in choosing your boots is fit.

The third criterion is fit.

And the fourth criterion is fit.

In fitting the boots, think of yourself as trying to put a glove on your foot. But don't picture a skintight glove. What you need is a boot that fits snugly at the broadest part of the foot (the trick is deciding exactly what "snugly" means, and in the end you always have to make your own decision, based on experience).

For details on judging fit, see below. But don't pay rapt attention to sizes. Base your decision on the feel of the boot. If the size is not the same as last time, it doesn't matter a damn. Different boots marked as the same size may vary appreciably.

CHIP: When companies maintained their own factories, sizes were fairly consistent within brands. But as they turn to "outsourcing," one model might be made in Morocco and the next in Korea, and fit quite differently. Further, some brands are marked in European or U.K. sizes, and conversion tables vary enough to increase the confusion (for a trustworthy size conversion chart, adapted from *Backpacker,* see the next page).

But the rule-of-toe remains simple: try 'em on. Numbered size refers to length. Width goes from AAA narrow to EEE wide. An average women's width is a B. Average men's is a D. Elegant trad leather boots may come in narrow, medium, or wide, as do the best fabric-and-leather ones. But since many outdoor boots come in only a single width, this leads to considerable focus on the *last,* or foot form, used by different makers. Merrells are kind to my widespread Balti-porter toes, while Asolos, for instance, are not. But a smarter way to think of this is in terms of volume. What I need is a high-volume toe. The rest of my foot is average in volume. You can jigger this somewhat according to your choice of socks and insoles (see page 84). But the true test is how the boot feels at the end of a long day.

SIZING CHART

European	U.K.	U.S. Men	U.S. Women
32	13*	1	2
33	1	2	3
33.5	1.5	2.5	3.5
34	2	3	4
34.5	2	3	4
35	2.5	3.5	4.5
35.5	3	4	5
36	3.5	4.5	5.5
36.5	3.5	4.5	5.5
37	4	5	6
37.5	4.5	5.5	6.5
38	5	6	7
38.5	5.5	6.5	7.5
39	6	7	8
39.5	6	7	8
40	6.5	7.5	8.5
40.5	7	8	9
41	7.5	8.5	9.5
41.5	7.5	8.5	9.5
42	8	9	10
42.5	8.5	9.5	10.5
43	9	10	11
43.5	9.5	10.5	11.5
44	9.5	10.5	11.5
44.5	10	11	12
45	10.5	11.5	12.5
45.5	11	12	13
46	11.5	12.5	13.5
46.5	11.5	12.5	13.5
47	12	13	
47.5	12.5	13.5	
48	13	14	

*This 13 is a children's size.

When shopping, take the socks you intend to hike in and any orthotics you use. It's best to try on boots after being on your feet, so take a few brisk turns around the park before hitting the store or go late in the day. With the boot unlaced, stand up and push your foot forward—you should be able to slip your index finger down at the back of your heel. When you sit and lace the boots, your heel should move back to fill this space. Stand and weight each foot, then walk around. Most important is how the boot fits across the top of your arch: laced tight, it should feel snug in a comforting way and keep your foot stable.

Second, your toes shouldn't touch at the front or top. If they do, the length is too short and/or the volume too low. This leads to ingrown nails, blisters, and metatarsal mayhem. Most people's feet swell with sustained walking, and while you can loosen the laces at the arch and ankle, that won't increase the length or the volume of the toe.

Third, your heel and the boot should move as one. If they don't, you'll acquire serious blisters or even festering wounds. Heel lift means a) the boot is too long and/or b) the geometry of the arch and lacing don't match your foot. A *very* slight heel lift can be scotched with the proper insole, but it's smarter to try another boot.

As a general matter, turn the boot upside down and place your stocking foot against it. The closer the outlines match (except at the toe) the better. If your feet lap over, that's where the boot will rub. But soles, especially stiff ones, much larger than your feet can exert surprising torque and not only cause chafing but also stress injuries to feet, ankles, and knees and even the lower back.

The flex point can also cause trouble, especially for those with toes that are either short or long in proportion to their foot size. The bottom of your foot flexes just behind the ball and the top somewhat forward of that, along the bases of your toes. Good boots do the same. Bad boots develop accordion folds over your toes and gnaw at them savagely. (While you may be tempted to beat them with a stick and shriek *BAD BOOTS,* this won't help.) The distance from heel to ball (of your foot, that is) and the height of your arch are further ponderables. The average woman's foot tends to have more delicate toes, a slim and less steeply angled instep, and a high and narrow heel bone. Some shops have an inclined surface to test how a boot feels on slopes, a great help in the fitting process. Another help is to find someone who has gone through the FitSystem workshops given by Phil Oren (see Appendix III).

Runners speak freely of *pronating,* but to others it's a mystery. Simply stated, it's the way your foot rolls inward, toward its unsupported edge. If you are at all prone to pronate (three out of four people are) the weight of a backpack will increase this tendency. You can discover this by gazing at the soles of your favorite shoes. If the tread is worn along the inner edge, you pronate. Another check is to set a well-worn shoe on a flat surface and look from the rear. If it has a perceptible inward slant, you've been pronating in it—might as well confess. Pronation puts more stress on the bones of your feet and ankles, and increases your chance of sprains and strains. So one way or another, you should try to correct or at least lessen it as you walk. Some boots have a built-in support for the inside of the arch. Special over-the-counter or prescription footbeds can help, too. You can also reduce pronation somewhat by strengthening your feet (see page 108).

Judging quality

is largely a matter of seeing how a boot fits and wears over time. But since the idea is to avoid unnecessary suffering, you need to learn something of the shoemaker's trade. So the last shall be first—the *last* being the foot-shaped form around which shoes are built. Traditionally, lasts were carved of wood and jealously guarded. Recently, makers began to use computer scans of the human foot to assemble large databases. For instance, those at Montrail claim to have digitized measurements of around 1 million pairs. Sorting this data according to size, gender, etc. they feed it into computer programs and come up with molded plastic lasts that provide a better fit in about 80 percent of all cases. This has also been a great leap toward better boots for women.

Vasque Sundowner and cutaway view

Given the basic form, there are two construction methods.

Board lasting crafts a shoe starting with the permanent insole, or *board.* This is fixed to the last, and the upper is shaped, sewn, and glued around it. (A point of confusion is that what most of us call the insole—the removable, squishy part directly beneath the foot—is properly the *footbed.*) If you pull out the removable footbed you will see the "board," with distinct edges and perhaps spots of glue. Once hard-tanned leather, boards are now made of pressed fibers (the commonly used salpa is a pressed leatherboard) or plastic. Board lasting gives a boot stiffness and lends a stable platform to the foot.

Slip lasting begins by sewing the upper together. It is then slid like a sock onto the last. If beneath the removable footbed you find fabric or leather stitched around the outer edge or even down the center, the boot is slip-lasted. Lacking the board, the upper can be shaped more closely to the curves of the foot, so this method yields a glovelike fit (desirable for rock-climbing or running shoes). But it depends for stiffness and support on the midsole and outsole.

Once the boot is lasted, the methods converge, as the midsole and outsole are attached. Traditionally, a leather *welt,* a separate piece stitched at the joining of the uppers with the board, provided a way to sew on the midsole. The midsole was a flat layer of stiff leather, to which the rubber outsole was finally glued. This method was labor-intensive and leak-prone, but made it possible to resole boots several times.

More common these days is a rubber or plastic midsole. On board-lasted boots, a sheet-rubber midsole (often gray or tan micropore) absorbs shock. A plastic midsole/frame can be used with either type of last to provide support via a stiffish molding that curves up at the toe, at the sides, and around the ankles and heel. This can be combined with a springy-steel shank and also incorporate glass or carbon fiber. Under the ball and heel may be inserts of shock-absorbing material like neoprene or Evazote (EVA) plastic, and these can extend to the sides as well. Tecnica laminates a fabric grid on the outside of the shock-absorbing layer that not only protects it from sharp rocks but also looks zippy. All these sole components are molded, glued, and squashed together, then cemented to the upper. They can be seen as different-colored strata at the side and instep of the boot, and tested with a thumbnail. Rough-terrain boots might also have rubber toe caps or rands to fend off abrasion and lend grip in cracks.

Whatever the lasting method, the outsole is cemented to the midsole. The flat tops of traditional outsoles were roughened with a wire brush for gluing, but most now curve in the shape of the foot and have internal patterns or inserts to absorb shock. While village repair shops could replace old stitch-down Vibrams, resoling the newest types is a difficult and specialized endeavor (see Appendix III, page 789).

Here's a lowdown on leather:

Top-grain or *full-grain* (2–3 mm) is the outermost skin of the critter. The term "full-grain" is misleading because mature hides are too thick for boots, so something has to go. On a top-grain hide, the soft, fibrous inner part is shaved off. While logic might lead you to believe that the outer skin of the hide is also the best surface for a boot, consider this: a cow's skin is covered with a great, greasy pelt of hair. And it's the hair, not the skin, that sheds rain and wards off cold. Still, top-grain leather looks good, waterproofs well, and is usually a mark of quality. *Anfibio* is a tanning process that lends water repellency to top-grain leather.

Nubuk, nubuck, nubuc, nabuk, or for all I know, *gnubuk* (2.5–3 mm), is a top-grain piece that's lightly sanded (or *micro-abraded,* as the wizards of marketing say) to remove surface imperfections in color and grain. This allows makers to use strong but less costly hides. Whatever it's called, it's pretty stuff that soaks up waterproofing nicely (at the cost of some prettiness).

Rough-out (2.5–3 mm), as distinct from suede, is often used in mountaineering and rough-terrain boots. The idea is that it won't show cuts and scrapes like top-grain. Both the top grain and the fuzzy inner surface are removed, leaving the *corium,* or fibrous matrix, which is the strongest part of the hide. If the piece is used inside out, it may be called *reverse-grain.* Perwanger of Italy, a well-known tanner, treats rough-out leathers with silicone, wax, and the like to repel water.

Suede (1–2 mm) is the inner layer shaved off a top-grain piece and then buffed to a nap that varies from fine to dreadlocked. Quality suede is solid enough, though porous. It soaks up waterproofing like mad, with most compounds changing the color and texture (for treatment see page 87). Bad, furry-looking suede soaks up water despite being treated and can be torn apart with ease.

While a few traditional boot makers such as Alico Sport stick with an all-leather lineup, most now use fabrics combined with leather for stiffness and reinforcement. Du Pont Cordura is a staple, in new colors and weaves, with nylon mesh in the lighter ranges, but new fabrics appear almost daily. Keprotec, from the Swiss firm Schoeller, is made by wrapping an aramid yarn around stainless-steel fibers, then interweaving it with nylon. While fabric can be ideal for quarters (the side panels), tongues, and padded ankles, it should be avoided where abrasion is likely. Synthetic leather is found on trail-running shoes where lightness, strength, and water repellency are important. And so far it seems to hold up as well as nylon fabric or mesh.

In traditional boots quality could be judged by the grain of the leather, a one-piece upper, even stitching, a tight welt, the easy folds of tongue and gusset, and smooth lacing components. Bad stitching is easy to spot, but the new cemented construction hides other vital details. Poor quality lurks in mismatches, gaps, color bleeds or blotches, raw edges, excess material, or misalignment. Pulling out the removable footbed can give you further insight: tatty stitches, blobs of glue, or ragged margins on the insole board should warn you off—be wary of any sign of haste and indifference.

So—you've tramped to a dozen stores, tried on a hundred different boots, and after serious toe flexing and head scratching settled on the ideal pair. Still, resist the temptation to slather on the dubbing and tramp off to the nearest trail. Instead, wear them indoors for a week, with clean socks, and walk only on carpet or well-mopped linoleum (no concrete, *por favor*). If they don't fulfill your dreams, you can return them. But any visible wear or slathering will earn you the hairy eyeball back at the store. You can't blame the dealers: persons who think nothing of purchasing a used car find it unthinkable to buy used shoes.

My (our) choices

In the '80s I had a three-boot stable: plastic Koflachs for alpinism, top-grain Vasque Sundowners for mileage, and low-cut fabric-and-suede Nike Lava Domes for scuffing around. I put by far the most miles on the Sundowners. Despite having to reglue the sole at the toe after every other trip, I walked thousands of miles and and utterly demolished two pairs with great satisfaction (for illustration, see page 70).

Linda wore blocky Kastingers, switched to lightweight nylon-and-suede Nikes, and then converted to Sundowners after finding that Vasque used a genuine women's last. We liked our Sundowners for several features: one-piece top-grain uppers; outsoles that worked in mud, snow, and slop but were still flexible and relatively light; midsoles with a shock-absorbing pattern; and Gore-Tex liners that seemed to work.

Taking on the research for this book gave me a chance to discover some new favorites while not entirely breaking faith with old ones. So what follows are the boots, shoes, and sandals that I (we) now wear regularly. I will hasten to say that this by no means indicates that we tried and rejected all else. Rather, it reflects a slightly expanded version of the way most people choose boots. That is, by a mix of instinct, hearsay, prejudice, and blind chance, with the unerring hindsight of experience.

If at some points my classification differs from those in catalogs or gear guides, that's because I'm a wearer and wearer-out. (A current marketing practice is to retag a boot in a hotter sales category with no change in design.) So here are various boots I have known. As I write about each pair I'll be wearing them, to summon up memories.

• *Mountaineering boots.* For rough hiking with talus scrambling, step kicking, snowshoeing, cramponing, and other full-contact pursuits, I like La Sportiva's Makalu. It has the one-piece upper, steel shank, and sturdy feel of a traditional mountain boot but is somewhat lighter (and you can walk in it). The outsoles are Vibram Clusaz, cemented, with aggro lugs that pick up less snow and guck than Montagnas and grooves for step-in crampons. The forepart of the sole is curved for a natural stride and the toe flexes smoothly. The break-in time was zero, and I've never had a blister, unique in my experience with this class of boots. Since my feet are different sizes, I

La Sportiva Makalu

usually end up snug left and slack right. But the Makalus fit both feet with neither pinch nor slack, owing to a new last called the P-Fit (P for Perfect) that works like a charm. The toe box is roomy. The one-piece uppers of rough-out leather have no seams to leak or chafe, and a single piece of black, top-grain leather forms a bellows over the tongue: a neat bit of work. I shook down the boots snowshoeing at timberline for several days with step-kicking detours that would reduce most leather boots to costly sponges. But the 3-millimeter silicone-treated Perwanger leather showed only one wet patch at the toe. Snowshoeing tends to gnaw the ankles, while step kicking bruises toes, but I suffered neither. They're great boots and they come in women's sizes as well. Weight per pair is 4 lbs. 6 oz. and the cost around $250, the same range as similarly good boots from Garmont, Lowa, Raichle, et al.

• *Off-trail boots.* Since science trips took me up mucky approaches onto a hinge-season snowpack, I wanted a nice, chunky walking boot with enough edge-ability to traverse frozen slopes. The solution: Vasque Super Hikers. The one-piece uppers are crafted in Italy from cappuccino-colored nubuk with the most elegant set of curves ever seen in a hiking boot. The Skywalk soles have opposing patterns at toe and heel for kickoff and braking, and a smooth, upcurved arch. The midsole is a shock-absorbing polyurethane in a discreet

Vasque Super Hiker

mocha. The insoles (boards) consist of a ribbed steel shank wrapped in Dacron and imbedded in Hytrel, an "advanced chemical" from Du Pont that doesn't stiffen with cold. The liners are three-bar knit, and the tongue and ankle are leather-lined. These boots and my feet have identical flexes. They look as if they'll resist demolition for years to come, so I can't give a final report, let alone an autopsy. Vasque says 3 lbs. for men's size 9, which raised my eyebrows. With laces, footbeds, and waterproofing my size 12s weigh 4 lbs. 3 oz. The bite was $215.

By staying much the same over the years, the Danner Mountainlight II has gone from a Gore-Tex-lined upstart to a stitched-down stalwart. The Vibram Kletterlift soles have lugs at the instep (good for mossy logs), and the midsoles are layered rubber and EVA. The top-grain uppers have leather-lined ankles a bit lower than average, since they lack a bulgy scree collar. They could use a locking hook midway. The

Danner Mountainlight II

footbeds are Danner Airthotic, a springy plastic that cups the heel and extends just forward of the instep. "Airthotic" sounds like a respiratory ailment, but these footbeds do have advantages: they don't absorb sweat, they don't wear out the heels of your socks, and they brush clean. The Mountainlights do take breaking in and should be treated with nonsoftening compounds, but they'll repay your patience with a neat, precise feel and endless resolings. They cost about $200. Weight is 3 lbs. 10 oz.

• *Regular old backpacking boots.* This is a crowded niche, so I'll touch briefly on several boots (all available in both men's and women's sizes). The Vasque Sundowner (page 70) need not be rehashed except to say that besides the classic burgundy it now comes in brown, black, and nubuk. And, too, that the redesigned outsoles no longer cut loose at the toe.

Alico's Italian-made leather boots are sleekly traditional, and a great many issue incognito from retailers such as Eastern Mountain Sports, so you may have worn a pair without knowing it. I got the Ultrex (sounds like an exotic, horned beast) with a top-grain top and a glued Vibram Bifida sole. The Sympatex liners and insulated footbeds make these good cold-weather boots, and I tested them with a November snowshoe trip over a high plateau: warm feet and no blisters. On the descent (with the webs strapped to my pack) of steep, brushy slopes and rocky canyons

Alico Sport Ultrex

leading down to a windswept valley, the Ultrexes snugged my arches and ankles without jamming my toes. Wide or high-volume feet will find prime habitat in this boot, and the uppers promise to outlast more than one set of soles ($210, 3 lbs. 6 oz.).

Linda was taken by the good looks of the Montrail Skyline GTX, but also came to appreciate the friendly fit, which coddled her bone spurs and bunions. The break-in was mercifully brief, and the Skyline not only holds up but holds out against water better than most fabric-and-leather boots. At 2 lbs. 2 oz. for women, 2 lbs. 10 oz. for men, and $135, they're also a damn good value.

One of the lightest 4-season boots on the market is the La Sportiva Storm GTX. Along with the mystery letters ("GTX" apparently means Gore-Tex) the Storms were suede, in contrasty colors. The fabric quarters and ankles looked soft, perhaps leaky, and the glittery labels pissed me off. So I put 'em through hell. But after a week of wet October snow, rocky slopes, rotting deadfalls, sodden brush, and willow bogs, I began to look on them with something like reverence. The suede (treated once) never got spongy. The Vibram Kamen soles, medium-aggro with deep-lugged heels, held well on a variety of nassssty surfaces. Though my feet got moist, I couldn't wring droplets out of my socks. And each snowy morning the boots were actually sort of dry inside. Built on the same last

La Sportiva Storm GTX

as the Makalus, they have a glovey fit with good arch and ankle support. For fans of advanced chemicals, there's more of that Hytrel stuff, glopped around a steel shank. The Gore-Tex liners have tightly sewn seams. I *still* think the label chews llama butt. But otherwise, the Storm GTX (Gratefully Termed Exceptional) is one sweet little bootie. I pray that La Sportiva survives the gaping jaws of The North Face. The catalog says men's are 2 lbs. 12 oz., women's 2 lbs. 7 oz., both $190. Here on earth, my size 12s, with footbeds, laces, and Nikwax, weigh 3 lbs. 4 oz.

The Tecnica Voyageur got a *Backpacker* Editors' Choice Award. And it feels both substantial and light on the foot. The uppers are Schoeller Keprotec and crinkle-coated Crosta leather, the lining plentifully padded. The Tecni-Lite composite sole is EVA inside nylon mesh with a

Tecnica Voyageur TCY

polyurethane skin. The overall effect is sort of an interstellar tweed. For some reason these boots made me nervous. Linda, on the other hand, laced hers up and set off immediately. Here's her take: "As I walked, the locking hooks at the base of the ankle caught each other and bent, causing them to protrude further. When a narrow passage forced my feet close together, I did a face-plant." During her trek, the coating on the Crosta leather peeled. Otherwise, she found them comfortable but leaky, and wished she'd gotten the waterproof TCY model. So I shook down my TCY Voyageurs with a series of long day hikes. The coating stayed put, but the toes developed a carnivorous flex that was partly cured by bridging the D-rings with shock cord. Then one of the lace-hooks pulled out, earning a cougar scream.* I spoke of these discontents to a Tecni-Person, who informed me that they had all been Fixed. In the interest of fairness I polled several friends who use these boots and heard rave reviews. At 3 lbs. and $150 ($180 for the waterproof TCY) you can find out for yourself. La Sportiva, Garmont, and others now make boots with roughly the same suite of materials.

*For more on cougar screams, see page 105, footnote.

• *Trail boots.* The Vasque Exodus 2 Mid is a genuine hybrid, slip-lasted in front and board-lasted in the rear with a molded heel counter and a high, padded tongue. Linda found them rather stiff at first, but patience improved the relationship to "something like love." In earth-toned leather, nylon, and Gore-Tex, they combine the support of a boot with the agility of a scrambler. They lace with D-rings and hooks, and hold up nicely, at 2 lbs. for women, 2 lbs. 4 oz. for men, and $140 for all.

My test case for lace-loops of webbing was the Asolo Pantera Mid, with 11. The ankle bears two hooks, but otherwise it's Loop City. Gone are the pressure points. After two years the top-most loops, which get reefed each time the boots go on, show only a mild fuzz. The Panteras are stout, with leather overlays sewn to the slip-lasted nylon uppers. The midsoles curve high to frame the heel, instep, and toe. The out-

Asolo Pantera Mid

soles have a medium bite with a grippy gray sector. (If you pronate like crazy, you should be wary of high-friction rubber on the inside of the sole, where it's likely to trip you up.) At 2 lbs. 8 oz. (2 lbs. 11 oz, size 12) and $100, these will also get walked around town a lot. There's no women's Pantera, but Asolo's Ripcord is similar, at 2 lbs. 4 oz. and $80.

• *Running-shoe cousins.* Having worn out several pairs of Nike Lava Domes in the 1980s, I did the same in the '90s with Merrell Solos, and have now adopted a trail-running shoe, the Montrail Vitesse (men's 1 lb. 8 oz., women's 1 lb. 4 oz.; $80). I first looked askance at the synthetic leather, lobed midsole, and the wraparound inner that replaces the tongue. But they've held up and delivered such comfort that I find

Montrail Vitesse

myself lacing them up for all manner of trips. The purely mechanical advantage of lightness is clear. So—why not just use plain running shoes?

But here are a few points against. Compared to trail shoes, running shoes break down faster, especially with the added weight of a pack. Open mesh admits not only water but also, and more important, abrasive dirt. Light colors and gloss finishes deteriorate fast with dirt and abrasion. And loud colors and reflective panels can make you conspicuous on the trail and scary in flash photographs.

Renowned through-hiker Ray Jardine treats running shoes as disposable, buying several brands so his feet won't be subject to a recurrent misfit, and plans on between 300 and 1000 miles per pair. For a long-distance hike, the equation is this: if you leave your job and rearrange your life to do the Pacific Crest Trail, you don't want to be hobbled by your boots. But through-hiking is a highly specialized pursuit. For most of us day hikes predominate, with semiregular weekend overnighters and, with luck, a few longer outings each year. And since I love good boots, something in me rebels at the notion of disposability. It reminds me of Amundsen on his South Pole trek, killing some sled dogs to feed the others—expedient, but not to be done without thought.

In any event, you won't lack for choice. Running-shoe cousins are a dense population these days, with weights ranging from 2 lbs. 8 oz. down to a shocking 12 oz. and with prices inversely proportional, from $20 in discount bins up to $100.

• *Sandals.* I'd used sandals for wading creeks and as camp shoes, but generally hiked in boots until a new pair gave me blisters at the start of a

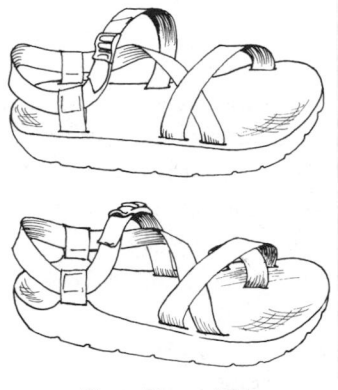

Chaco Elan and Z-2

trip. So I pressed on in my new sandals, Chaco Elans. For a week along the Continental Divide, I wandered—alpine tundra, streams, talus, and bedrock—savoring the delicious lightness while my blisters healed (for more on sandals and foot care, see page 111). With a 45-lb. pack, I worried about the lack of ankle support but experienced no soreness whatsoever. There was one grip-up crossing a snowfield when, being too lazy to put on my boots, I almost slid off into a lake. The other contretemps occurred back at the trailhead when a structurally perfect young woman in pink spandex shorts bent over in front of me to tighten her laces. Distracted, I tripped and almost butted her goat-fashion from behind. Which also could happen wearing boots.

The following spring my friend José, who runs a bookstore in Moab, Utah, challenged me to a series of slickrock, sandal-hiking loops. Not only did Chacos make exposed friction climbs less scary than in lugged boots, but they carried me over (and through) dunes, oakbrush, cactus patches, streams, and quicksand. My subliminal guidance system registered stubs, spines, loose rock, etc. and steered my naked toes accordingly. I was careful in a highly conscious way when descending rubble fans, crossing patches of cactus, or crawling along ledge overhangs. Otherwise, I just walked, feeling the air between my toes. Despite my suffering a bad case of adrenaline fatigue, the week's damage amounted to a few inconsequential scratches.

Since then I've done many bootless trips, with neoprene socks for snowdrifts and creeks, regular socks for nighttime warmth, and liner socks for daytime sun protection. While I don't think sandal hiking will save the world, the generic ills are few. The straps can chafe where they cross or double up, especially in sand, but you can affix moleskin and then keep your eye on it. The flattish soles tend to skate on loose or sloppy surfaces. Your insteps get poked by twigs and tufts. Pebbles creep in between foot and sandal, requiring a quick dance step. But in sum I prefer these mild irritations to confining my feet in sweaty, sticky socks. I now wear Chacos about 90 percent of the time when there isn't snow on the ground.

What should you look for in a hiking sandal? Anatomically designed, continuous straps that adjust by pulling through the footbed, with a one-buckle closure; polyester webbing, which is softer and faster-drying than nylon; as few plastic fittings, foam pads, etc. as possible; molded polyurethane (rather than sheet-rubber) footbeds with a distinct upcurve (1 to 1½ inches from ground to sole at the toe), not just a raised edge (which makes it harder to shed pebbles); and replaceable straps and soles. I like nonmarking Vibrams, but sticky 5.10 Aqua Stealth rubber adds grip.

Linda, a longtime fan of Teva's cushy footbeds, just adopted Chaco Z-2s, with toe straps for more lateral cling and contoured footbeds for more arch support. Besides Chacos, my former-favorite Alp Sports are now available as a style from Teva, the General Motors of the sandal world. I also tried Lizard Y-Hike Sandals, from La Sportiva. The Lizards had leather-covered footbeds that were likable around town, but dried slowly and glazed rather fast on the trail. But my first pair of Chaco Elans, with new soles, is still in the running after three years despite the fact that I wear little else from April through October. In basic black, they also work for formal occasions.

Footwear for special conditions

Special conditions might call for special boots.

But the ultimate and self-defeating outcome of specialization is to have dozens of pairs of boots and then fret over which ones to wear. Since—at the other end of the spectrum—lacking money is also a special condition, a few words are in order on cost. Hiking boots may be had for $20 to $30 at discount stores and in catalogs: Cabela's has nylon and suede hikers for $30, and Brigade Quartermasters lists an army-type jungle boot for $20 as "a reasonable value for normal wear. Not intended for hard, military use." Makers such as Hi-Tec sell reasonably good boots at comfortable prices. An inexpensive boot can see you through a season or two of moderate trips, if it fits. A good footbed will help. But a cannier approach is to look for a top-quality boot on sale. It may be a discontinued color or model, but if it fits, it fits.

If you're flush enough to specialize somewhat and you regularly combine walking with other pursuits, here are some notable subspecies:

Scrambling or *tech shoes* are intended for steep hikes and mild clambering. They have rubber toe caps and rands like climbing shoes, high-

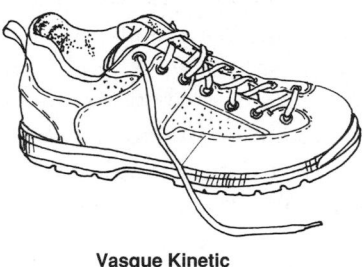

Vasque Kinetic

friction soles, and a close fit. I've used lightweight Vasque Kinetics for bike/hikes, and I also notice Garmont's "Sticky" series on rocky trails hereabouts. In general, tech shoes do nicely for scrambling, biking, and short walks but not for long ones. Some come only in men's sizes, but women's models can be had from Asolo, Columbia, Lowa, Merrell, Salomon, Tecnica, The North Face, Timberland, Vasque, and Yukon.

Canyoneering or *amphibious shoes* are curious hybrids. As kayakers sought lace-ups for rocky portages, canyon hikes involving wades and swims became a distinct specialty. Like the selkie of folklore fame, the off-spring favor one parent or other: the blue Patagonia CFS is a distinctly watery beast while the Hi-Tec Hydro Trail is more of a quick-dry running shoe. Besides nonabsorbent materials, what sets these low- to midcut shoes apart is quick drainage, meaning that water enters just as quickly. Weights are 20-some ounces per pair, and prices go from $50 to $135. A few points: Beach slip-ons fall apart when you hike in them, and your feet get bruised by rocks. Hiking barefoot in wet, grit-filled shoes is punishing, so use liner socks or thicker ones of neoprene or lined membrane (page 92). A caution for canyoneers is to avoid the shiny, round-edged soles found on sailboard shoes, which can dump you quicker than you can say "compound fracture."

Boots for the wet and cold come in both traditional and madly innovative forms. As Colin observes, our feet are in worse shape than any other part of the body to cope with long spells of abysmally wet weather. And because of the constant flexing and scuffing, nearly all boots seem in time to get wet and all feet to get cold. The challenge is to slow this process down.

COLIN: Forty-odd years ago, two summers of slogging through trailless tracts of western Vancouver Island convinced me that for cross-country travel in rain forests, where your route often lies over or along slippery fallen tree trunks and where undergrowth is always snatching at your legs, the only satisfactory footwear is a pair of calked knee boots. A logging source from up there confirms that nothing has changed. "From a safety and practicality standpoint," he writes, "calks are the only way to go. If you are not walking around downed timber or fallen logs, certainly a heavy Vibram-soled boot will suffice, but calks will always provide much-needed extra traction."

Another summer in the muskeg-and-lake country of Canada's Northwest Territories taught me that in such places you need a stout and roomy pair of leather-topped rubber boots. At that time the Maine Hunting Boot by L. L. Bean was standard for such conditions, and for wet snow. Such boots are reportedly admirable for much eastern wilderness—the sort of flat, soggy terrain in which old tote roads skirt or even transect spruce and cedar swamps. They're especially good when hiking is largely a means to camping or hunting or fishing, and a day's backpacking may amount to no more than 5 miles and is unlikely to exceed 12. The Maine Hunting Boot has now evolved, and in many places the current standards for soggy conditions—for ski operators in the West, for example—are calf-length boots by Sorel of Canada with leather uppers, injection-molded lug soles, and thick, removable felt liners that can be hand-washed. Many boots now have liners of Thinsulate and other synthetics that have less tendency to get soaked and can survive a washing machine. You can dry any liners off overnight, in your sleeping bag if necessary, or carry a spare pair.

CHIP: Schnee's (pronounced *Schnay's*) in Bozeman, Montana, makes a superb line of *pac boots* (the generic term for a rubber-footed model with a removable liner). Columbia also makes updated pacs, while Asolo's new plastic-framed Globaline series lets you walk through snow and slop with more in the way of ankle support. Recently, Salomon and other makers of ski-touring boots have applied their knowledge to lightweight "winter hikers" that promise waterproofing and insulation with better support and fit than the rubber-footed types provide.

COLIN: In certain parts of the country—because of local conditions or innate human conservatism or both—a specific style of boot may remain as traditional as the dialect. You can always ask a reputable dealer about parochial preferences. Of course, there's no law that says you have to take his advice.

For deep snow or cold, an alternative to packing an extra pair of specialized boots is to use

Overboots.

CHIP: Mountaineers have worn them for years with crampons or snow-shoes. But full-coverage overboots haven't been much good for the sort of trek that takes you up a hot, dusty trail into subalpine mud and then over a snowy pass. Recently, a company called Neos brought out a full-coverage overshoe with a front-zipped Cordura top that acts as a gaiter and a lug sole. Neos urges you to wear them over anything from hiking boots to moccasins, but I found that the wide, flexible sole torqued a running shoe around in a potentially blistering way. With over-the-ankle hiking boots and a squeak-tight fit, it was a different story. On a blizzardy midwinter campout with a lot of exploratory snowshoeing and postholing, my boots and socks stayed dry and my feet warmer than they'd have been with regular gaiters. Given the width, they don't edge terribly well on steep, hard snow, but they do pack small and weigh 2 lbs. 5 oz. (XL, 21-inch tops) with prices according to height from $55 to $80. Yet even as I write this, it appears that they have dropped the lean and serviceable model I tried for a heavier, insulated version.

Neos Overboot

Which brings us quite naturally to

Gaiters.

Once known as spats (short for "spatterdash"), these keep water, snow, mud, dirt, seeds, burrs, yak dung, pygmy shrews, etc. from infiltrating your boots. The biggest gaiters in the swamp are the supergaiters, which have a tight-fitting rubber rand or a cord that cinches them just above the exposed sole of the boot. Wild Country makes an insulated supergaiter with a stretchy rand at around $95 that works best on snow and under crampons. La Sportiva has plain ($85) and insulated ($99) supergaiters cut for their boots. In rocky terrain, rubber rands seem to tear and the cords and cables to snap. So most hikers choose mortal-gaiters that hook on a lace and cover the upper part of the boot. All have coated nylon around the boot and some have waterproof-breathable fabric above. It's best to find a pair that hug your boots, but if you intend to use them with several different pairs you might want elasticized bottoms instead. Some gaiters will work with midcut boots, and a few will also lend cover to running shoes. You need a cord or strap under the instep (it shouldn't absorb water and should either firmly resist abrasion or be replaceable). Heights vary, ankle to knee, with the midelevations tending to droop, so I go either high or low. Side zips with flaps have largely given way either to rear zips or the front-opening Velcro closures introduced by Outdoor Research in the early 1980s that allow you to adjust your laces and to ven-

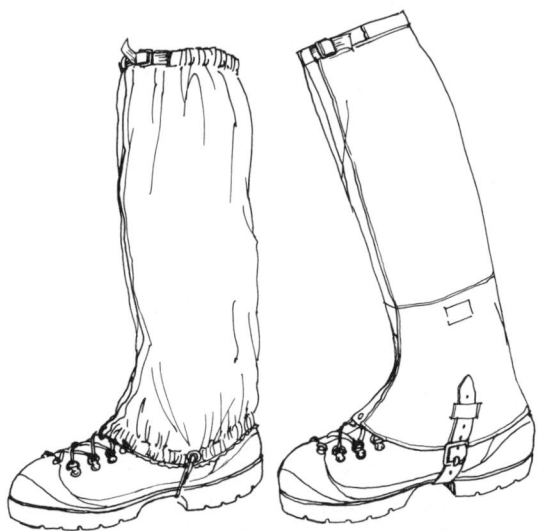

tilate with a simple tug. (NOTE: Since gaiters trap the moisture rising from your boots, it's vital to let it out, either by periodically undoing the gaiter, or leaving an opening near the top of the zipper or Velcro. Mountain Hardwear just brought out gaiters with mesh ventilating panels, which I've yet to try.) Mostly I've worn—but not worn out—the same pair of Outdoor Research Crocodiles (18 inches high, 10.2 oz., now about $50) since 1985.

The simplest gaiters have elasticized cuffs and no closures: they slip on before your boots, and consequently are lighter and cost less. There are now stretch models that shed enough grief for moderate conditions. I've used La Sportiva Gaskets (7 inches high, 2.3 oz., $25) with shell pants on snowshoe trips and also on late-summer hikes to ward off dust and grass awns. They fit tight around your boot tops or can be secured under the instep with cord. Similar, but with a convenient front-opening Velcro closure, are Outdoor Research Flex-Tex low gaiters, which in the last year have replaced my regular gaiters on nearly all my trips, summer and winter (7.5 inches high, 3 oz. per pair, $32).

Since gaiters take a lot of punishment and are a frequent source of complaints, in the last decade many former makers have quietly dropped their gaiters (if not their pants). These days, gaiters can be had from Camp, Lowe, Powderline, Savage, Sequel, and Sova, from a low bite of $15 to a toothy high of $100. The real Lizard King, however, is Seattle's Outdoor Research, with 11 distinct species.

Also in the animal kingdom are dog boots—see the Department of Canine Affairs, page 183.

Insoles,

or *footbeds,* as shoemakers prefer to call them, are enormously improved as a result of research into biomechanics and new materials. The footbeds that come with new boots vary a lot. Some are quite good, with a liner, pierced foam, shock inserts, and such. Others are a mere sheet of foam with fabric on top. In general, factory footbeds are thinner and tend to flatten out faster than accessory types. But since the array is staggering, let's look at what footbeds are meant to do.

First, they absorb shock. Traditional shoemakers used cork for this. Next came foam-rubber footbeds that worked for a short time, then fell apart. A breakthrough was Spenco Medical's infusion of tiny nitrogen bubbles in neoprene for a shock-absorbing, water-resisting footbed. The nitro-bubbly is underlain by a molded heel stabilizer and arch support, and lined with decay-resistant knit. Both Colin and I have used them with satisfaction, and Spenco offers a variety of shapes and sizes. Viscoelastic materials such as Sorbothane are even better at damping shock, but are heavy and prone to delaminate, so they tend to appear as inserts at the heel. Newer still is the use of air chambers (like heavy-duty bubble wrap) by makers such as Ortho-Air. And, harking back to tradition, the Footfix Ultra ($24) by Spirakut blends cork and EVA plastic to lend firmness and . . .

Second, to insulate. The first insoles I used were wool felt, in winter boots. They were springy and worked like a charm. But by evening they'd tripled in weight from moisture. They dried slowly. Left out, they froze hard. So the insulating properties of modern footbeds come from non-absorbent closed-cell foams. Since these resist moisture and your feet give off lots, most insoles are lined with wicking fabric. The idea is to conduct the moisture toward the lining of the boot, and using the action of your stride, pump it out the ankle. There are footbeds (called Dryz) for hot weather, and there are cold-weather varieties with synthetic fibers betwixt liner and foam, and still others with hidden recesses for chemical heat packs (from Heat Factory, $25) or even battery-powered elements. If you have perennially frigid digits, these last may tempt you, but they seem more suited for sitting than walking.

Third, footbeds resist wear. As your socks scrub away at the inside of the boot, the first thing to go is the knit liner on the footbed. New knits peel less easily, but some high-quality footbeds like the Footfix Ultra and the Saluber from Alico Sport are topped with leather. The ultimate wear resister is slick plastic, as in Danner's partial Airthotics (see page 75). This leads us to—

Fourth, they stabilize and support. Besides padding and insulation, footbeds are meant to compensate for weakness and eccentricity among feet, and to correct bad walking habits (see pages 69 and 108), which takes a certain firmness. So, from the bottom up, full-length orthotic footbeds combine a heel cup and arch of springy, stiff plastic with a layer of closed-cell foam and a fabric (or leather) liner. There may be viscoelastic inserts at the heel and perhaps the ball of the foot. While performing different tasks, all these layers must hang together. So it comes as no surprise that the bugaboo is delamination. Another concern is that the footbed should neither shift in the boot (too small) nor wrinkle around the edge (too big). There are standard sizes (that can usually be trimmed slightly at the front) while others are trim-to-fit.

Footbeds can correct minor problems with fit, which often have to do with volume. Superfeet offers firm stabilizers in two volumes (about $30), and Vasque offers foam footbeds in three—high-volume red, medium blue, and low-volume green (all $8). As far as the *fit,* a high-volume footbed will be thin and a low-volume one thick. But the fit of a boot shouldn't depend on the footbed, any more than the fit of a suit depends on your underwear.

Some are designed for specific problems: Montrail's Integrafit ($18) and SofSoles Motion Control ($28) reduce overpronation. Inflammation of the plantar fascia, the connective spring that runs from the ball to the heel, can be helped by the Bauerfeind ViscoSpot (about $50). But if walking gives you persistent pain, you should stop throwing $20 bills at it and seek out a podiatrist or orthopedist who can prescribe custom footbeds such as those from Arch Crafters, who use a scanning platform linked to a computer to create a precise contour map of your feet. Custom boot makers are sometimes able to build orthotic (or *pedorthic,* which sounds just as strange) inserts. My friend Mitchell Black, an accomplished outdoorsman, does this sort of work in Buffalo, Wyoming (for a list, see Appendix III). Colin tells me that for several years he's worn custom-made plastic orthotics for backpacking and tennis: "Once you get used to these, they're fine. But make sure you put them under some good cushioning, such as a Spenco accessory footbed."

Even the best footbeds break down. I usually go through two to three sets before resoling or replacing a boot.

It makes excellent sense to get new footbeds when you start

Breaking in new boots.

Though there's less breaking than bending these days. And seldom do we resort to folkloric methods, like standing in a ditch until the boots are soaked and then walking until they're dry; or less drastic, pouring in hot water then dumping it out, followed by a sustained walk-in. The best thing is not to get leather (nor the pressed leatherboard used for insoles and heel counters) completely soaked. The heat and moisture from your feet, with whatever treatment you use, will soften what needs softening.

COLIN: Frankly, all I've ever done to break in new boots is to take short, easy walks, with little or no load at first, and gradually increase load and distance. At the very beginning, even wearing the boots around the house helps.

For a major backpacking expedition—the kind that threatens to wear out a pair of boots—you obviously have to start with new ones. After all, you wouldn't set out on a transcontinental road rally with worn tires. For such expeditions, breaking in the new boots can present a problem. The theory is simple: the boots will take care of themselves during those practice hikes you plan to take for several weeks beforehand in slowly increasing doses that will painlessly harden your feet and muscles. But I've found that in practice the press of administrative arrangements just before the start rises to such a frantic peak that there's no time for any practice hikes worthy of the name. So you start with flabby muscles, soft feet—and stiff boots. And this is no laughing matter. It's not simply that sore feet soon take the joy out of walking. They can make walking impossible. Just before my Grand Canyon trip, while putting out a food cache and at the same time trying rather belatedly to harden my feet and soften a new pair of boots, I attempted too much in a single day, generated a blister, developed an infected heel, and had to postpone the start for a week. Fortunately I'd planned an easy first week's shakedown cruise. But even with an old pair of insoles in the boots my feet barely carried me through the second critical and much harder week of the trip. I offer no solution to this kind of problem (which can also crop up on shorter journeys), but I suggest that you at least make every effort to allow time for a gentle shakedown cruise at the beginning.

Caring for boots

CHIP: Wear your new boots indoors for a week and be sure the affection is mutual. Then venture out. The sidewalk is an unforgiving place to start out a pair of boots. So disobey the signs and walk on the grass. Or find a path through the park (with a view of the zoo). And treat your new boots like a new love: don't rush it.

Once you've settled in, the first big issue is treatment. And, like in-laws, the boot makers will usually put in a word or two. Most boots have a tag or a packing slip in the box that suggests one treatment over others. Some, like Vasque, recommend their own (Natur-Seal paste, liquid, cleaner, and spray), but this isn't mere commercial back-scratching. Leather should be treated in accord with its tanning process: vegetable or chrome-tanned uppers need wax or liquid-silicone-based compounds. Oil-tanned leathers need to be topped up with petroleum distillates. The finish is important, too: Nubuk and suede look like merry hell after a dose of anything remotely oily. (Neat's-foot oil was the mainstay for years, though wild rodents seem to regard it as a delicacy and it's reputed to attack certain plastics.)

Breathability is another aspect. In general, the more porous the leather, the thinner the treatment: silicone sprays and clear liquids with daubers prevail (but be warned—they are known to loosen glues).

To keep boots in good shape, you need to be concerned about a) water repellency, b) maintaining the finish, and c) maintaining the structure.

Water can be repelled by physical barriers, like greases or waxes, or more subtly by chemistry, like silicones and polymers. Sno-Seal, Bee Seal Plus, and Granger's G-Wax are based on beeswax with oils to condition leather. Biwell, which I've used for centuries, comes in two flavors: Classic for all-leather boots, and Trekking (with silicone) for fabric and leather. Aquaseal has a line of paste and liquid waterproofing. Sealer for leather welts on stitch-down boots comes in tubular form from Granger's and Sno-Seal. Lexol makes good conditioners for leather, often found in saddle shops.

Sprays like Kiwi Camp-Dry and Sno-Seal Waterguard, with about 10 percent silicone, have been around for years but are said to loosen glues and to muck up waterproof-breathable membranes. Tectron makes oft-recommended sprays and daubs for fabrics (the acronym is DWR, for Durable Water Repellent), and sells kits with cleaner, protector, conditioner, a brush, and a cloth.

The finish of top-grain leather can be restored by cleaning with saddle soap or gel, and then conditioning with oil, wax, or silicone-based treatments. The finish of nubuk and suede, once they're treated and dried, is resurrected by light sanding or buffing with a brass-bristled brush. Fabrics can be vacuumed and/or brushed, either dry or with a cleaner. (I have a friend who sprays off his boots when he washes his car after a trip.)

Since (according to the *New York Review of Boots*) postmodern boot crafters characteristically blend *au naturel* with synthesized elements in an intricate and multilayered composition, when it comes to waterproofing you may be faced with a maddening paint-by-numbers approach. That is, sprays or daubs for the fabric, and waxes for the leather.

But the English, notorious for their cooking, have nevertheless turned the boot world upside down with a *water-based* proofing known as Nikwax. The theory is that to transport a waterproofing compound to its proper site, water is the best medium. That sounds good, philosophically. But it takes a leap of faith to *moisten* your new boots and apply something that resembles skim milk. Having a lineup of test boots gave me a chance to try it in an objective way. Or semiobjective. I began with a pair of two-tone Euro-suede boots that I found suspect. Anglophobia rampant, I damped them down and Nikwaxed them, then repeated the process. When they dried, I buffed the suede lightly. And then I stomped through snow and primordial muck for a week.

The stuff works! It's the closest I've come to a religious conversion in years.

The magic of Nikwax is a polymer based on the same EVA plastic used for footbeds and midsoles, combined with a wax transformed at the molecular level to make it elastic. Using a water base allows these ingredients to be concentrated: 35 percent active versus less than 13 percent with a solvent base. And they end up in the very spots water does, coating fibers and flexing with them, while leaving open space between for breathability. Once the water is blocked, the treatment beads up on the surface, so you know when to quit. An added boon is the company's claim that water-basing avoids "evaporating over 500 tons of organic solvents and propellant gases per year into the atmosphere."

So while there might not be anything new under the sun, there are some new things under the rain. The gnomes of Nikwax purvey their nostrums not only for suede but for top-grain, nubuk, fabric-and-leather boots, waterproof-breathable clothing, down, cotton, and maps. They also have buttery dubbing for oil-tanned leather, and a gel that cleans both leather and fabric and works better (though more slowly) than the car wash. Though a mud-coated boot may suffer less from a quick (i.e., microsecond) pass with the car-wash wand than from a vigorous brushing that scratches the grain. (But avoid soap or wax.)

For my Chaco sandals, the car-wash wand sluices abrasive grit out of the strap channels in the sole, that being the main culprit in wearing out straps.

While synthetics take less in the way of care than leather, each and every boot deserves a decrudding after a dirty walk. If they're wet, dry them out on your feet or in the sun. The same goes for waterproofing.

Never put your boots in the oven unless you're preparing to eat them.

No leather boot should get much warmer than body temperature, and many of the plastics and cements now used are *thermosetting*: they cut loose when heated.

Porous fabrics and suede benefit from a light brush and a vacuum before using a cleaner. You should also pull out the footbeds for a brush or light scrub (but no machine wash, *por favor*) and vacuum or brush out the insides of the boots. Leather liners can stand a light treatment with Boot Guard or the current equivalent. Antifungal powders are better applied to feet than boot linings, where they screw up the wicking properties. Antifungal sprays can be found in drug- and discount stores, but some have solvents that damage Gore-Tex and other membranes, so read the fine print. Aquaseal has a new odor eliminator called MiraZyme that mixes with water and is claimed to be "hypo-allergenic, 100 percent natural, and biodegradable."

Minor fixery can be done at home or at local shops. Vulnerable stitches can be armored with plastic compounds like Aquaseal or Freesole, or a light coat of epoxy (but don't do this to a stitch-down welt). If you're competent, you can restitch gaping seams, but I've found that fishing line and dental floss can cut wet leather. So I use waxed linen thread for leather, and polyester for fabrics.

Look to your soles—the black rubber tread might wear nearly flat and still be replaceable, but any damage to the midsole can condemn an otherwise good boot. If you visit a local repair shop, check for outdoor boots on the shelf. The original dealer might recommend a place, or see Appendix III for a list (compiled by asking boot makers, retail shops, et al.) of reputable repair centers that specialize in outdoor footwear.

How long should a pair of boots last? As Colin observes, that depends on the boot, the terrain, and how you walk—"As with cars, spouses, and daydreams, so with boots: some people are gentle on them, some are downright murderous."

My only answer is the one I gave years ago when I was guiding, and a client in all innocence asked me, "How long does it take for a deer to become an elk?"

It varies.

SOCKS

Since by now you're tired of hearing that new materials and techniques have vastly improved, let's cut to the chase. There are *tons* of great socks out there, and the choices for the most part are between better and best.

Good socks make more difference in comfort for less difference in price than any other item of backpacking gear. But too often they are an afterthought. To counter that haphazardness, let's look at what socks do.

They protect your feet from your boots and vice versa. The sock should hug your foot while slipping smoothly across the lining of the boot, reducing friction. Liner socks reduce it still more by providing yet another interface. The resilient knit of a sock cushions your foot and may fill in excess space in the boot. And since your feet constantly shed skin cells, give off moisture and oils, and offer habitat for bacteria and fungi, your boots need protection, too. Socks should trap this organic foot crud, along with any dirt that gets into the boot, before it can permeate the liner. So, like any filter, they need to be changed frequently.

Socks regulate temperature and moisture. Since these interact, the insulating and wicking properties can be fine-tuned by the blend of materials. Most outdoor socks use at least two fibers, so let's consider the common ones (for more on fabrics and fibers, see page 505). First, the naturals: Wool, particularly fine merino, is a perennial favorite for warmth, springiness (called *crimp*), and absorbency. Cotton socks have blistered more feet than the gratings of Hell, but cotton's absorbency makes it useful in hot-weather blends. Silk is thin and resilient, for liners or blends.

Among the synthetics, acrylic has long been used for loft and cushioning, with new forms such as Lumiza that also absorb some moisture via tiny pores. Nylon is used for stretch, strength, and durability. Polyester (variously known as Capilene, ThermaStat, etc.) is spun and treated in a number of ways to provide insulation and wicking. CoolMax fibers have channels to increase surface area and transport moisture quickly. Duraspun is, likewise, a wicking fiber. Polypropylene (Meraklon, Thermax) is another plastic fiber treated to pass moisture without absorbing it, and is usually layered or blended. Other synthetics have crept in: Teflon is used to reduce friction. Lycra, spandex, etc. are used to provide stretch and recovery. Outlast is sort of a mystery, despite lots of colorful diagrams and graphs that claim it can absorb heat and release it later. (Outlast consists of tiny beads of paraffin encapsulated in plastic. Since wax melts around body temperature, and in changing state from solid to liquid absorbs a disproportionate amount of heat, the beads can literally store it. As the beads cool, and the wax changes back to solid form, this heat is released, tending to even out skin temperature. With water, the change in state can absorb or release 80 times the amount of energy — 1 calorie—it takes to raise or lower it $1\,°C$ in liquid form. So the potential is there. The problem is whether the amount of wax incorporated in a fabric is enough to make a difference in practical terms—see page 507.)

As far as how these miracle fibers actually work, you have two ways of finding out: one is to read what the manufacturer says, consult tests in *Backpacker* and other magazines, and ask store employees. The other is to trust your own sensory apparatus and indulge in some trial and error.

Sock architecture is now so intricate that it can be hard to judge a certain fiber per se. For instance, the natty Wigwam Ultimax Outdoorsman combines 38 percent acrylic, 32 percent olefin, 15 percent stretch nylon, 9 percent wool, 4 percent stretch polyester, and 2 percent spandex. And proportions vary in different parts of the sock. Another favorite, from Northern Ireland, the Bridgedale GTX has wool, nylon, polypropylene, and Lycra in blends for specific zones. So does the Dahlgren Dri-Stride Hiker, with 90 percent merino wool and 10 percent nylon in the toe and heel, where high moisture and high wear are the rule; the instep and arch are 75 percent Duraspun and 25 percent stretch nylon; and the leg is 90 percent Duraspun and 10 percent elastic. The wool absorbs moisture and the Duraspun transports it up and out. The Wick-Dry sock layers a water-repellent yarn like CoolMax next to the skin with absorbent merino wool on the outside. And some yarns themselves are a blend of two or more fibers, such as hydrophilic (water-loving) wool with hydrophobic (water-hating) polypropylene. These variations may be seen from the outside as different colors and textures, and more clearly from the inside where the various knits and joins are visible.

Since dealers get nervous when you start taking apart packages to turn the socks inside out, examine your sense-tested favorites at home. Do your nerve endings favor a uniform thickness or extra padding? The SmartWool and Wigwam Ultimax socks I like are basically uniform. Others with lots of extra cushioning in the toe, heel, and underfoot—the luxurious, densely looped Rohner Trekking sock—go well with roomy boots when I expect some battering from talus, a heavy pack, etc. While large terry loops can be cooler, small, dense terry loops are better for backpacking since they don't pack down with heavy use or snag toenails. Cushioning tends to add volume, and that leads to another aspect.

Cramming a thick sock into a boot can actually make your feet colder by constricting your circulation. If you wear the same boots year-round, Ridgeview makes a constant-volume set of socks, the Hemisphere system, with CoolMax for hot times, Duraspun for moderate ones, and ThermaStat for the cold, combined with about 10 percent nylon. They're uniformly midcalf height and black, with different-colored toe seams so you can tell them apart at 0500 hours.

The opposite, a variable-volume sock (High, Medium, Low) from Wick-Dry, can fine-tune the fit of your boots. These come in sets, marked L and R (Liberal and Reactionary?), and have Teflon yarn at the heels and toes to ease friction. Those who are cursed, as I am, with feet of slightly different sizes, and who don't give a rat's prat about matched colors, can combine a pair of low-volume socks with a pair of high, for two Hi-Lo sets. Of course, having left and right socks derails this approach.

In the sock circus, Ballston, Wigwam, Fox River/Wick-Dry, Thorlo, Patagonia, Ridgeview, and Rohner have been star performers for years. A newer entrant is SmartWool, with long-lasting, nonitchy merino socks that have a civilized demeanor and lovely little loops inside. Colin has used them for a lot of tennis and a little backpacking and says they're "truly great." (SmartWool also makes itchless wool underwear; see page 508.) On a different slant, Wyoming Wear has come up with Fleece Feet, stitching Malden Mills's Polartec into a sock that excels in wet and cold. These were first sold for use with sandals, but flatter seams let them work in boots, too. By far the lightest thing around, they're the only thickish sock that can be rinsed and wrung out before lunch, hung in the sun, and then worn: they dry that fast. The caveat is that they don't hug the foot like a stretchy knit. The king of stretchy knit is Bridgedale; their socks have zones of such pronounced huggery that one feels encircled by a loving hand.

Weight? Wyoming Wear Fleece Feet (per pair, for size-12 cloven hooves) are 2.4 oz., SmartWool Hiking 3.3 oz., Ultimax Outdoorsman 3.6 oz., Rohner Trekking 3.6 oz., and my old gray mammoth woolies are 4.2 oz. Prices in specialty shops commence at about $6 for light summer socks and proceed to $20-plus for deluxe trekking and wintery types.

Liner socks have a single layer of one of the materials discussed above. While advances in socks proper have somewhat diminished their use, I still employ them in several ways. They can reduce friction when breaking in boots or on sustained trips, add a wicking layer next to your skin, and boost the warmth of normal-weight socks. They also provide a nice prefilter for organic crud—it's easy to wash and dry liners on the trail, allowing you to change more frequently. Trail runners and the unbearably light may wear liners alone. I use them with sandals against sun and chafing. A clean pair at night can boost the warmth (and hygiene) of insulated booties and sleeping bags. Weights run from 1 oz. to 2 oz. or so, prices $5 to $12.

Socks for special conditions

In dire straits, plastic bread bags still work, slipped betwixt a liner and a regular sock. But coated-nylon vapor-barrier-liner (VBL) socks have practically vanished, for good reasons: they bunched and blistered feet and were portable growth chambers for microorganisms. One of my winter expedition partners wore VBL socks, and when he took them off at night I had to exit the tent, no matter *how* cold it was. (For more on VBLs, see page 517.)

For unrelenting wetness and chill—stumping around on the melting ice of glaciers—I've worn neoprene Gator Sox ($21 and 5 oz. dry). These work like a diver's wetsuit, holding moisture in place so your body can warm it. For anything short of actual wading, they're more comfortable over a thin liner sock, or in a fleece-lined version ($28, 5 oz.). I've also used them when snow swept thrillingly in on my sandal adventures. As with VBL socks, they tend to get grippingly funky inside, so they need frequent rinsing and drying, if possible inside out in the sun. You can (and probably will) dump antibacterial and antifungal powders into them. (With sprays, check a tiny patch for melting first.) Without these precautions, sustained use can lead to the skin on your feet wrinkling up and peeling off, along with various nasty infections. Neoprene is somewhat fragile, but I've stitched tears with polyester thread and patched holes with Aquaseal.

Also promising for hikers are Danalco SealSkinz. These pedic entities comprise a knit outersock (with toe and heel seams) laminated to a seamless stretch membrane of MVT (signifying "moisture vapor transpiration") and lined with either CoolMax or ThermaStat. A sweater-style Lycra cuff completes the ensemble. SealSkinz may be worn alone or over liner socks and they feel reasonably good in sandals, shoes, and boots (in basic black, $30). If you plan to crawl (or fish) there are matching gloves ($28.50). On a sodden trip in May with temperatures in the 40°F range (a wretched day for boots, not to mention feet) it rained and hailed all one morning as I hiked. So I stowed my wet boots and pressed on in sandals and SealSkinz. Hard rain turned the trail into a streamlet. Between downpours it hailed, so the puddles were topped with a half inch of floating ice balls. After a half hour of sanely picking my way around, I decided to make a go of it. So I slushed through every puddle, waded each milky runnel, and kicked through ankle-deep drifts of hailstones, feeling the little hard spheres crunch and melt under my feet as I strode on. My feet did get cold when actually immersed, as they would even in rubber boots, but otherwise I stayed shockingly comfortable. In fact, my feet were better off than they'd have been in soaked leather boots. When I stopped for lunch under a mossy, overhanging boulder, the SealSkinz were dry inside.

A truly waterproof-breathable sock amounts to a striking breakthrough. Still, despite ad photos of fools like me lolloping through creeks, having waterproof socks doesn't mean you can walk unscathedly in (let alone on) water.

The care and feeding of socks

Here's the care label on nearly every pair of socks in about 20 outdoor shops: *Separate colors. Turn inside out. Machine wash warm, no bleach. Tumble dry low. Do not iron.*

Actually, *Do not iron* appears on only about half the labels, but it insulted me every time. (A friend advises me that ironing cotton socks is indeed a custom, since heat kills germs and bugs. It also kills synthetic fibers.) The necessity of using Woolite and avoiding detergent and tumble dryers seems to be diminished with modern wool blends, which are processed to remove the parts of the fibers that shrink and cause itching, though synthetic blends benefit from fabric softener. Some liners (silk, polypropylene) should be washed in cold water and air dried.

Besides being social anathema, dirty socks can cause overheating, chilling, or blistering. In hot weather, you might change literally on the hour, rotating sweat-drenched socks to the mesh pockets or loops of your pack to dry. On extended trips, socks should be rinsed or washed often enough to keep a clean, dry pair handy. Doing this in a clear stream or the tea billy is subadvisable. Instead, a heavy-duty plastic bag makes a good wash-a-teria. Leave it in the sun to warm the water with the socks inside, then agitate (or let it slosh as you walk). I seldom add soap, but on a long, dusty trip you may need biodegradable cleaner (see page 564). The outside mesh pockets now found on packs are handy for bag washing, air drying, and also for transporting nasty, reechy socks you'd rather not have inside.

Colin reports patching a holed sock with a disc of moleskin. I tried this and it works best if you cut a disc of moleskin to overlap the hole on the inside and then apply one of duct tape for the outside, so they stick to one another through the opening. In the past I darned my ragg wool socks, although when practiced by flashlight at low temperatures, darning soon becomes damning. Colin further reports: "In the six months and thousand-plus map miles of my California trip (many more on the ground) I wore out nine pairs of mediumweight (4-oz.) wool socks, worn without liners." My recent experience is that rather than developing holes, socks à la mode tend to lose their stretch, a phenomenon a friend calls "bag-out." Another omen is fuzzing (the cutting loose of fiber ends) or pilling (as the ends ball up). In that event, it's best to retire the socks from trail use and wear them to meetings, etc.

As for longevity, my SmartWool socks have kept their shape and cushioning longest, with slight fuzzing and no pilling. The Bridgedale GTX Trekker is another durable standout.

Socks should extend at least 2 inches above your boots. In hot or dusty conditions, it helps to turn your socks down over your boot tops.

This keeps dust out of the boot and evaporates moisture more quickly. A common rubber band or a light stretch gaiter (see page 83) helps keep things in place.

CAMP FOOTWEAR

One of the indescribable pleasures of being in camp is to take off your boots. Rugged types go stark barefoot, and I have done so, too. But the hazards of stumbling around barefoot in the dark are significant. Soon after the start of Colin's Grand Canyon trip, his feet were so sore that he spent a day and a half resting near a spring, wearing moccasins for the many small chores that need doing around camp. His then-favorites were moosehide, by Minnetonka Moccasin, but they wore out fast in rocky terrain. Running shoes of all stripes have long been favorite campwear, and they are fast being overtaken by sandals.

For winter camping, the proper camp footwear is insulated booties or mukluks (page 563).

AIDS AND ATTACHMENTS

Walking staff

COLIN: Although the vast majority of walkers never even think of using a walking staff, I unhesitatingly include it among the foundations of the house that travels on my back. I've been solemnly advised that doing so is "even further out of the mainstream" than when I wrote the earlier editions of this book. Okay, call me Eddy. But I still take my staff along almost as automatically as I take my pack. It's a third leg to me—and much more besides.

On smooth surfaces the staff helps maintain an easy rhythm to my walking and gives me something to lean on when I stop to stand and stare. Over rough going of any kind, from tussocky grass to pockety rock, and also in a high wind, it converts me when I'm heavily laden from an insecure biped into a confident triped. It does the same, only more so, when I have to scramble across a chasm or a big boulder or a mildly obstructive stretch of rock and keep reaching out sideways for a balancing aid or backward for that little extra push up and over. And it does the same thing, even more critically and consistently, when I cross a steep, loose slope of talus or gravel or dirt, or wade a fast-flowing creek or cross it on a log. In marshland or on precarious rock or snow, and in failing light or darkness anywhere, it tests doubtful footing ahead. It reconnoiters bushes or crevices that I suspect might harbor a rattlesnake. It pushes or slashes aside poison oak or ivy. It's useful for pushing up and pulling down balanced bundles of food hoisted into trees to foil bears (page 732). After rain it knocks water off leaves that hang wetly across the trail. It often acts as the indispensable upright needed to rig a shelter from rain or sun with fly sheet, groundsheet, or poncho (pages 425, 434, 435). Occasionally, held down by a couple of heavy stones, it serves as ground anchor for the windward side of such a shelter (illustration, page 435—in lieu of canteen). When I've camped in some casual and unconsecrated place I often use the staff, just before leaving, to rough up the ground where I've slept so that no one, but no one, could see the signs. It has also performed successfully as a fishing rod. It has acted as a marked measuring stick, to be checked later when a rule is available, for the exact length of fish, rattlesnakes, and other dead animals. It forms a rough but very ready monopod for steadying binoculars if my hands are shaking from exertion, or for a camera if I need to shoot with a shutter speed slower than $\frac{1}{60}$ second. It is, of course, invaluable whenever I meet a unicorn: deftly placed, it helps disguise me as a conspecific, and therefore as acceptable company. And day in and day out, at almost every halt, it props up my pack and gives me a soft and stable backrest (pages 186–87). (As I'm lazy enough to believe that being able to relax against a soft backrest for even a 10-minute halt is no minor matter, I'm almost inclined to regard this function of my staff as one of its most vital.) It may well be, too, that the staff also gives me a false but subconsciously comforting feeling that I am not after all completely defenseless against attack by such enemies as snakes, bears, and men.

Down the years, my various staffs have surprised and pleased me from time to time by accomplishing new and unexpected chores. Once I decided halfway up a short rockface that it was unclimbable with the heavy pack on my back. I slipped the pack off and held it with knee pressure in a sloping crevice and took a short length of nylon cord from an outside pocket and tied it to the head of the staff and then to the pack-frame. Then I jammed the foot of the staff on a convenient ledge and angled its head up against the bottom of the pack so that it held there without my knee and thereby freed the knee and the rest of me for the short and relatively simple climb (unencumbered) to the top of the rockface—where I had a safe stance from which to reach down without difficulty and pull up the pack and attached staff. One cool and windy afternoon when I was booted and fully clothed, the staff rescued, with about an inch to spare, an empty plastic water canteen that the wind had blown into a river no less wet than any other river and a good deal bigger and stronger than most. One night when I was camped in a cave I tied the staff onto the nylon cord from which my candle lantern (page 599) was suspended—and thereby furnished myself with a convenient handle by which I could, without moving my lazy butt an inch, adjust the candle lantern into the various specific positions I wanted it for cooking, writing notes, or contemplating cave or universe. And one super-soggy morning it enabled me to stay fully inside my tent while I reached out and with its tip dug a shallow diversionary ditch in spruce needles so that the tent alcove, in which I was about to cook breakfast, gradually changed from a lake into a mere morass.

Of course, other writers have extolled the virtues of staffs, directly or indirectly. J. R. R. Tolkien, in *The Two Towers,* wrote: "I have no fitting gifts to give you at our parting . . . But take these staves. They may be of service to those who walk or climb in the wild." And Carlos Castaneda's Don Juan hints at an additional transcendental use: "By forcing the hands into a specific position," he says, "I was capable of greater stamina and awareness."

Down the decades, one corner of my gear closet has grown a small leaning coppice of staffs. (Well, a semi-coppice. Perhaps I shouldn't admit it, but long-handled housecleaning implements, ingloriously interplanted, account for half the growth.) Mostly, the staffs are in honorable virtual retirement. But every time I look at the stout bamboo I used on my 1958 walk up California—now worn down by a dozen years of grinding toil to a bare 3-feet-10-inch length, wounds bandaged with rings of red ripstop tape—its weather-beaten surface and especially the brown patina at the second knot, where my hand usually gripped, still generates echoes of warm affection (or soggy sentimentality). Other old friends trigger mixed memories: The bamboo that briefly succeeded the original. A thin ash model that snared my favor for a few years (equivalents still appear erratically in stores and catalogs). A hefty fiberglass affair (no longer commercially available) that manifests an endearing use-induced bow. Also some lightweight metal jobs. One of them, the beautifully balanced Nomad—aluminum alloy, with four interchangeable neoprene handles, weighing only 12 ounces with the shortest—is the survivor of a pair that, somewhat to my surprise, have for years, between them, under most conditions, been my almost automatic choice. (The preferred, anodized version succumbed during a six-month raft trip down the Colorado, source to sea, when I had to backpack 60 dry-river miles in Mexico: I stumbled and sat down on the staff as it lay angled up against my just-removed pack. No lightweight metal staff, and precious few others, can weather such abuse, and mine didn't.) Nomads, by LL Engineering, long ago fell victim to Herblock's Law: "If it's good, they've stopped making it." But until very recently the unanodized, scruffily spray-painted survivor remained my default staff. Then, after trying several telescoping models and finding none fully satisfactory, I discovered (via Chip) Stoney Point's Explorer. It balances perfectly in the hand. Its three hard-tempered aluminum alloy sections telescope from 25 to 63 inches. The quarter-turn locking system actually seems, by God, to lock: so far, I've experienced none of the unexpected, infuriating, and potentially danger-ous collapses endemic to most telescoping staffs. And I find the black anodized finish damn near beautiful. My basic E-XC Explorer (10.5 oz., $40) has a foam grip, a hardwood knob that unscrews to disclose a camera mount (standard ¼-20 "with take-up wheel for monopod use"), wrist strap ("adjustable, with breakaway safety feature"), and a rubber foot cap that pulls off to expose a hardened steel tip. Optional: snow boot, shoul-der strap (also breakaway protected), and a V yoke that replaces the hard-wood knob "for long-lens camera support or shooting rest." It's early days yet, but the Explorer threatens to become my new default staff. For Chip's parallel preferences, read on.

CHIP: For pure organic elegance, the agave staff, with a pithy center and fibrous sheath, is hard to improve on. Finding a prime specimen, I var-nished it, wrapped the bottom 16 inches in duct tape (to protect against sharp rocks), and added a crutch tip. Agave staves weigh next to nothing and no one sells them, thank heaven, nor should. I also like a nice, stand-ing dead lodgepole pine about 1¼ inches thick. I can choose one and adapt it (two minutes with a pocketknife), then leave it on my way out. But I keep a special lodgepole staff with feet and tenths notched into it for measuring the depth of streams.

A handsome traditional line of staves is made by Gastrock Stöcke (sold in the U.S. by Mountain Properties) in various woods and finishes, including natural bark, each with a steel spike under a rubber tip, topped with a camera mount or an inset compass. They vary in length from 32 to 60 inches and in price from about $14 for a youth size to $54 for one with a brass camera mount. In a different tradition is the Lathi (*Lah-Tee*), a rat-tan staff used by the Indian Police for "crowd control" but also good for gentler pursuits. According to Brigade Quartermasters (a catalog of mili-tary and survivalist items, not for the faint of heart) it is strong, flexible, and "tough enough to deflect edged weapons." About 1¼ inches thick, the Lathi comes in 48-inch length for $18 and 72-inch for $20. A more curi-ous variation is the Walking Stick Flute, a 4-foot bamboo staff that's topped with a compass and drilled with an octave-and-a-half major scale so you can woo the muse during rest stops—it comes with an instruction booklet (Real Goods, $70).

Having given up the excellent Stoney Point Explorer to Colin, I've been using a Tracks Superlite 3 (9.5 oz., $60) from Cascade Designs.

Given experience (some bad) with twist-lock devices, I like its simple, locking button, especially since a line machined into the aluminum lets you know where the button is. The Tracks staff is crowned with a walnut knob that gets polished with use and unscrews to reveal a camera mount. To support a tarp, I poke the mounting screw up through a grommet, screw the knob down, then crawl under the tarp and adjust the height—comfortably out of the storm. It has a removable rubber foot and small basket, and it telescopes to 25.5 inches to stow on the pack when I need both paws free. Cascade Designs makes several telescoping, folding, two-piece screw-mount, and traditional one-piece staffs, from $25 to $60.

Trekking poles have a partisan following, but an equally vocal group of detractors. Friends who found themselves unable to backpack because of knee or lower-back problems have been able to take it up again by using a pair—no argument about that. Reinhold Messner, a peerless mountaineer lacking most of his toes, says "poles make it possible to walk on four legs like animals do." Partisans also claim they relieve literally tons of stress on the knees and also turn a hike into an upper-body workout.

But, say the detractors, that upper-body workout occurs because not only are you carrying an extra pound or so in each hand, you are lifting each one about a thousand times per mile. I tried the adjustable Trek'R 3 system (21 oz., $90) from Cascade Designs, which gets the same good review as the Superlite Staff. I also tried Leki Makalu trekking poles. I won't pretend disinterest, being a longtime user of Leki's ski poles. (I tested one with an impromptu ski vault over a granite boulder, thus saving my life while bisecting the poor pole, which they replaced.)

The Leki Makalus (1 lb. 4 oz., $130) have a 15-degree angled grip that keeps your wrist straight, with the grip itself shaped out of a blend of plastic and cork. The shock-absorbing internal spring feels strange at first and then nice; it can be set for full bounce, half bounce, or no bounce. Unanticipated was the Turbo Disc, a thumbwheel that dials in a release tension for the breakaway wrist straps (nice for those unexpected boulder vaults). Small trekking baskets for hard snow are included. Rubber tips, a regular ski basket, and a deep-powder basket are available. So the Makalus are a year-round proposition.

But after that techno-rhapsody, I hasten to say that I don't even use a simple hiking staff all the time. A staff *feels* good, but the extra movement does slow you down (imagine an Olympic sprinter with a walking stick). So on trips where sheer distance-per-day is the object, I might go without. But for rocky, stream-wading, balance-intensive routes, I invariably use one. Sans knee problems, I'd rely on a pair of trekking poles only for humping heavy loads in rough, slippery, or steep terrain.

But couples might employ a pair of trekking poles as two singles, to double-up-on-demand (helpful in the event of sprains). Besides Stoney

Point, Cascade Designs, and Leki, pole and staff suppliers include Alico, Alpina, Komperdell, Life-Link, and Simond. Attachments range from useful to bizarre.

COLIN: My staff fixation has apparently generated bemused merriment among many readers of earlier editions. But by no means among all. Several have sent messages of support, both pragmatic and sentimental. Others supplied new stavic suggestions. One who recommends a yucca (i.e., agave) staff, cut about September, adds that he has used it in groups as a makeshift, largely psychological "railing" (held between two stalwarts) to help nervous people past exposed sections of trail, and also as a "yucca belay" by lowering it to where a scrambler in difficulties can grasp it. Another reader sent photographs of a remarkable survival kit that fits inside his self-built wooden staff. Yet another reader writes that "a broomstick makes a very serviceable and cheap staff, and if you leave the end on and happen to be hiking around October 31st, can speed your travel considerably." A third reader, who totes a 134 cm piece of hickory ("bound with nylon thread to stop a split"), finds "the big rubber tip a remarkably prehensile organ for picking up bits of plastic, foil or paper which litter the trail"; he had always wondered, he says, about

> carrying 20 ounces for a little stability and a few gimmicky uses, but it gradually dawned on me on [one] trip that the staff takes a tremendous load off my feet. And when I got home I pressed the staff down on a scale in the manner I would engage while vigorously climbing a steep slope, and discovered I was intermittently taking 30 pounds off my feet. While modern suspension systems take the load off my shoulders and back, nothing else takes any weight off my feet, which are, after all, the part of me that feels by nightfall as though a hippopotamus had been jumping up and down on them all day.

Now, why didn't I think of that really beautiful justification for my staffophilia?

One small but constantly recurring matter: you cannot conveniently lift a pack onto your back while holding a staff. Where possible, lean the staff against something before you lift the pack so that once you're loaded up you can easily take hold of it. But even in open places there's no need to waste the not inconsiderable energy expended in bending down with a heavy load on your back; just hook one foot under the staff, lift it with your instep, and take hold of it when the top angles up within reach of your hand. With practice you'll probably find yourself flipping the head of the staff up with your foot and catching it at apogee. You'll soon get used to laying the staff ready for this maneuver on a low bush or stone or across a depression in the ground before you hoist up the pack, so that afterward you can slide a toe under it. If you forget the precaution and can't get a toe under, simply roll the staff onto your instep with the heel of the other foot. It sounds gymnastic but is really very simple.

There are, I admit, times when a long staff, unless it telescopes or breaks down into sections, becomes a nuisance.

If you have to swim across a fast river, for example, it can tangle dangerously with your legs. In calm water it's easy enough to pull the staff safely along behind on a length of nylon cord (illustration, page 692). But when a fast-water situation was plainly going to arise on one trip beside the Colorado River I left my regular staff behind and on the first day cut a 4-foot section from the stem of a dead agave, or century plant. With the thicker end carefully rounded it made a very serviceable third leg. During river crossings it tucked conveniently out of the way in the bindings of my packframe, protruding only very slightly at the top (page 694). The odd thing was that by the end of two weeks I was feeling for this little staff the same kind of affection that I lavished on my regular bamboo one—so much so that when it broke on the next-to-last day and I had to cut a fresh length of agave, I stuffed the scarred, foot-long stub into my pack and carried it all the way home. More soggy sentimentality.

A staff is also a nuisance, even a hazard, if you have to do any climbing that demands the use of two unencumbered hands. Occasionally, on short and unexpected pitches, I've pulled the staff up after me on a nylon cord, or lowered it ahead. If you know you're likely to face some rock climbing it may be worth leaving your regular staff behind and cutting a temporary one that can be discarded and replaced (climbing was a contributory reason for my doing so on that Colorado trip). If you expect to do very much climbing, there are three solutions: do without a staff, use one that telescopes or breaks down, or take along an

Ice axe.

COLIN: You may carry an axe on certain trips because you know you may need to cut steps in ice or hard snow or, more likely, to self-arrest in case of a fall on steep snow or ice (I was very glad of one on an April ascent of Fuji); and even if you use the axe little if at all for ice or snow work it will serve as a reasonably efficient staff, even in the pack-prop role. It is also, incidentally, a splendid instrument for extracting stubborn tent pegs from packed snow—and in its old age, I'm told, for gardening. When not in use it straps conveniently onto your pack.

CHIP: For walking across hard snow or low-angled glaciers, an all-around pick on a longish shaft works best. But how long? Some people choose a too-long axe by trying it out on a flat surface. The flaw here is that on a flat surface, you don't need an ice axe. Since it stays in your uphill hand, the spike needs to touch down upslope with your arm comfortably bent at the elbow. So, extend your arm and measure the distance between your fingertips and the ground: this is the *longest* it should be. If you're trying one out at the store, wrap your fingers around the pick and relax your arm—the spike should dangle at least 2 or 3 inches above the ground. Or stand on the stairs and rest the spike on the next step up; your arm should be bent at a comfortable angle. Being 6 feet 4 inches (193 cm) tall, I take a longish 80 cm ice axe for casual rambles. Steeper ground requires a shorter axe.

There's no harm in a few notes on technique. The ice axe is held pick-forward in your uphill hand. When you change direction, stop and switch hands. Besides maintaining your balance and probing suspect patches of snow or ice, the ice axe serves as a brake if you fall, a technique called self-arrest. This should be learned from an experienced friend or instructor, and then practiced obsessively. Some, though not all, axes come with a wrist loop on a gliding ring and I recommend one, since an abrupt slip is likely to cause you to drop the axe, or in falling to plant the pick deeply and have it torn from your grasp by your momentum. This happened to me while traversing steep snow above a cliff band—I slipped on hidden ice, lost my ice axe, and nearly went over the edge. A soft patch of snow allowed me to self-arrest with toes and fingertips. Then I had to climb back up and retrieve my firmly lodged ice axe. So if your axe lacks a loop, get some ½-inch webbing and make one. At first, it's irritating to switch it from hand to hand, but soon becomes automatic. Also helpful are rubber guards for the tip and and spike, to protect packs, etc. in transport. You can buy a ready-made guard, but a scrap of plastic fuel hose works just dandy.

Traditionally, axes had forged steel heads and weighed 2 lbs. or more, but for moderate snow and glacier trips I now use a Camp HL 50 aluminum ice axe with a glide ring and wrist loop ($80) that weighs, at 80 centimeters length, a mere pound. (Camp is an Italian company distributed in the U.S. by Adventure 16.) While the aluminum pick and spike are in no way meant for clawing up steep, rocky, technical routes, I love the lightness. For ice walkers, the all-around axe with aluminum shaft and a chrome-moly steel head and spike starts at around $50. Thick, molded grips are undesirable for all-around use because they interfere with the penetration of the shaft in hard snow, though a close-fitting rubberized grip is okay. For smooth shafts, a neat wrap of friction tape adds grip without bulk. If you intend actual climbs, a precision tool such as the Black Diamond Alpamayo axe (1 lb. 13 oz., $80) will give you the necessary peace of mind.

Crampons

COLIN: Although crampons are essentially ironmongery for climbers they are sometimes worth carrying if you expect to cross ice or hard snow. And not only steep snow. A flat snowfield that has weathered hard may develop basins and ridges and even savage pinnacles that in naked boots create considerable and potentially dangerous obstacles. I once discovered by accident, when I climbed out onto the lip of an ice-covered gully on Mount Shasta, that when you're carrying a heavy load crampons can transform a sloping slab of very soft rock from a nasty barrier into a cakewalk.

CHIP: Technical crampons with stiff frames and raptorial front points aren't much good for walking, so look for a pair that will flex with your boot sole. This is accomplished with a hinged, springy steel strip with holes to adjust the length. To keep the crampon on, the traditional means are crisscrossed straps, but many boot soles now have molded grooves to accept a step-in toe bail and a heel binding that levers up into position and secures with an ankle strap. These made me nervous at first, but they don't pop off and are blissfully simple. The "new-matic" style binding (with a toe cup for climbing boots with narrow, weltless toes) might work on hiking boots, but I haven't had the chance to try.

Certain crampons won't fit certain boots—not just a matter of length but of sole design, width, and geometry—so take your boots to the store. (By the same token, when buying new alpine boots, take your crampons along.) Always fit them up before leaving home. A special wrench might be included. If adjustment takes both a wrench and screwdriver *at the same time,* prepare accordingly. The bails should match up with the grooves in your sole, and the crampon frame shouldn't stick out more than ¼ inch beyond the edge of the sole or heel. If it does, look for an adjustment. Some crampons come in Left and Right while others are symmetrical, but strap buckles should *always* be front or outboard, not on the inside where they might catch.

The business end(s) of a crampon are the points: 12 is the usual number, but there are 8-point models like the Camp Pioneer (22 oz., $65) and 4- or 6-point forefoot or instep crampons for use with hiking boots on moderate snow (these are spooky on steep downslopes). New nonslip thingies appear regularly and most fade away in short order. The latest is the Yaktrax Traction Device, a plastic webwork coiled with nonrusting steel springs that works best on boots with welts or grooves at the toe and heel (6 oz. a pair, $18). Another way to lighten up is an aluminum crampon like the 12-point Camp LC 480 (18 oz., $90), which I now use for glacier walks. These confer the same benefit as lighter boots, given careful placement—the aluminum points are vulnerable to the rocks that are frozen into alpine ice. On crampons of all sorts the points must be kept sharp: file lightly across the narrow edge (you want a chisel point, not a shark's tooth). The built-in file on a pocket tool is good for touch-ups.

Since crampons turn your feet into Tyrannosaurean talons, watch your step, especially in narrow slots. I've poked a few holes in my gaiters, but never drawn blood. Crampons weighted with rocks can also be used to anchor tent pegs, in hard snow. But when camping in steep terrain it's better to keep them on your boots in case you have to make a quick exit (park the boots in the vestibule of your tent). Weird rubber tip guards are available for transit, but crampon pouches with protective plastic sheets are less trouble.

As Colin points out, the most joyous and efficient way to travel over snow is on skis. But that lies outside our orbit: on skis you are no longer walking. So if you want to travel the snowpack as a walker, you should get acquainted with

Snowshoes.

Quoth Colin: "Snowshoes will allow you to travel (sweating hard, but sinking in less than a foot at every step) across snow into which you would otherwise go on sinking forever if God had not arranged that human legs eventually converge."

Traditional bent-ash and lacquered-rawhide snowshoes are among the noblest artifacts of humankind, but the lacquer cracks and the rawhide saturates and snaps, and there you are. On monster-packed science trips when the snow was thawing with rocks and stumps poking out, I found my then-newfangled Sherpa aluminum-framed snowshoes so marvelously indestructible that I elevated my old wood and rawhide webs to the status of art: I hung 'em on the wall.

But when I started testing snowshoes for this book, the mercurial nature of liking itself worried me somewhat. That is, I knew that external variables like weather and internal ones like what I had for breakfast would influence how well I liked a given pair of webs. So, to level the playing field, I took four pairs of snowshoes on each trip and switched off hourly. While this strained my pack, and at times my patience, the comparative insights it gave me were worth the grunt.

Besides frames of aluminum tubing, the revolutionary shifts in snowshoes are waterproof lacing and decking, a rod or hinge to improve the action and tracking, metal cleats, and technologized bindings. Let's take them in order.

The choice in decking (among other things) is between soft and hard. Semi-rigid plastic decks are rugged but prove cacophonous on crusty snow. So my preference is a soft, flexible deck of Hypalon (the coated nylon fabric used for rafts) or the lightweight Diamondkote used by Sherpa on their Tech Lightfoot (4 lbs. 3 oz., $209). This may be attached to the frame by lacing (which Sherpa favors to provide more traction on slopes, though it also adds drag) or by lapping the decking over the frame and riveting it to itself (a method used by Atlas, Redfeather, Tubbs, and most others). In years of hard use, I've broken neither lace nor rivet.

Since plastic decks are slicker than rawhide webbing, modern snowshoes have cleats, shark's teeth of steel or aluminum that run crosswise under the toe, for grip on slopes. Recently, lengthwise cleats have appeared near the toe, for traverses, and also at the heel for descents. My present love, the fire-engine red Atlas 1033 (4 lbs. 8 oz, $250), sports all three. Aluminum cleats are lighter, but steel ones are tougher for crossing rock or gritty mud. Like crampons, they should be filed sharp at the tips. The beautiful Canadian Ursus snowshoes, which I haven't tried but would like to, have conical, machined cleats of stainless steel that are replaceable, like huge track-shoe spikes.

The hinge, to which the binding attaches, can be a metal rod or a coated strap. Rods allow free rotation, so when you lift your foot the tail drops to the snow. Some designs let you adjust the degree of rotation for varying depths of snow. Fixed straps have a bit of spring, according to the width and stiffness, that flicks the tail up out of the snow and reduces the drag. But given too much spring, the tails will catapult wet snow up into your backside: don't underestimate the psychological effect of a constant barrage from the rear. While testing a particularly springy pair I progressed from mild annoyance through active piss-off to cougar screams.* Most stores frown upon your flummoxing over their carpets in snowshoes with sharp cleats, but you can test the rotation by holding the binding in one hand and moving the tail of the shoe up and down.

Metal parts do ice up, so some makers coat or anodize the cleats, which helps. The Redfeather Blackhawk shoes (3 lbs. 6 oz., $237) I tried were springy as hell but also had the least exposed metal and the best

---

*THE COUGAR SCREAM: Magazines seldom walk on the dark side of product design. But over the years my partners and I have come up with a scale of badness, ranging from the *?* (pronounced "huh?"), through the *grunt* and the *curse,* to the *cougar scream.* The first three are self-evident. The *cougar scream* memorializes truly ugly situations. Say, the main-panel zipper on your pack fails on a steep ridge and your stove and cookset go clanking a thousand feet down and into a crevasse. Cougar screams may also acknowledge grand stupidities of design and cheap betrayals in execution. The saving grace is that it's far, far better to let out a maddened screech than to heave the offending item at a rock, thus doing further damage to one's survival prospects.

For the dedicated record keeper, ?'s, grunts, curses, and cougar screams are customarily calculated on a per-trip basis.

resistance to icing. They also had plastic cleat guards to protect against shredding packs or upholstery. To the same end, full-length carrying bags are available from several makers.

Bindings vary a lot. The simplest have a flexible piece of coated fabric with holes that lace up with a narrow strap, and a second strap around the heel. These take some fiddling to achieve a good fit. More elaborate ones have a semi-rigid frame with straps and ratcheting buckles. These are simpler to adjust, but the Tubbs Expedition shoes (MTN 36, $287) I tried had stiff plastic straps that clacked down on the decking with every step, driving me bats. The Atlas Switchback binding had molded plastic wings and webbing straps that cinched down easily with my gloves on and never needed readjusting. Both Atlas and Ursus have special snowshoes that attach to a boot with a crampon on it, and Ursus has an optional step-in binding.

Flotation (i.e., how far you sink in the snow) depends on your weight versus the surface area of the snowshoe, so in places with a fluffy snowpack like the northern Rockies you need more area. Likewise, the added weight of a pack demands a bigger snowshoe. But the bigger they are, the more awkward walking becomes. Narrow shoes, like the Sherpa, traverse better, and some have an offset frame to prevent stepping on toes with tails. My Atlas 1033 webs are 8½ inches wide, and that's about the maximum without adopting a spraddle-legged gait. The toes should curve up: 4 inches is nice for deep, soft snow. On a hard snowpack you can get by with less. The elegant tails on wood-framed shoes kept them tracking straight, but new hinges and bindings make this unnecessary, so most snowshoes are what's called a modified bearpaw shape.

A completely new approach is the Denali from Mountain Safety Research, with a molded, one-piece plastic deck/frame combination. They're noisy on a hard snowpack but are simple, rugged, and cheap ($109). Full-length cleats to each side make them traverse beautifully, while the low curve of the tip makes them best for dense or crusted snow. The Denali Ascent ($150) has toothier cleats under the foot and a heel lift for steep climbs. Two flotation tails (9.5 inches, $25; 13.5 inches, $30) attach in seconds for deep snow and heavy packs, and there's a children's model, the Little Llama, for $60.

The Little Bear Saguache snowshoe (sold by L. L. Bean as the Winter Walker, at 2 lbs., $99) has a one-piece deck/frame of Lexan, in translucent hard-candy colors. The cleated frame is rugged and impervious to freeze-up. The lace-up binding, with a rubber heel strap, has a wide base that works best with oversize, insulated boots. Little Bear's new buckle-up Lobo binding fit my hiking boots better, though it still slopped around on slopes. Summed up, these are good, low-maintenance recreational webs rather than mountain tools. Little Bear also makes jazzy Lexan models for kids.

Jogging on snowshoes is *en vogue,* but the short, asymmetrical jogging types aren't much good for backpacking. In penniless times, I've used the one-piece, molded snowshoes sold by snowmobile dealers and sometimes found in junk shops ($3 or so). The bindings were worthless, so I made my own with scraps of raft fabric, rivets, and grommets, and romped on my bargain beauties for several winters. Since after all you may *hate* snowshoeing, normal caution dictates renting different makes and sizes before taking the plunge.

To snowshoe the flats, a pac like the Sorel or even a mukluk will do. But mountain trips with packs require a stiffer boot. I've used both plastic mountaineering boots and hiking boots with gaiters or overshoes (see page 81), and now gaze with longing on the new insulated winter hikers. For balance, a ski pole helps. I use a single one and swap hands, but some websters prefer two. An adjustable pole is likewise nice, but if you aren't picky, ski-town thrift shops have barrels of old ski poles from which to choose.

A few notes on technique are in order. Since your feet have, in effect, quadrupled in size you'll have to shorten your stride and adopt a rolling, bearish gait. The deeper the snow, the shorter your step, and in deep fluff you may need a two-stage stride, with a tentative step to pack the snow before shifting your weight. If you sink, stop and take a few breaths before trying to thrash out. You might need to pack several steps or grab a tree. Avoid bridging a gap, since this can bend or break the frame. When crossing logs, either turn sideways and step entirely over, or face front, center the ball of your foot (and the cleats) on the log, then step up just enough to clear it with your trailing shoe. Don't jump logs or brush—catching the tail of a shoe means a full face-plant. Snowshoe ads show people running and jumping, but they don't show the spectacular crashes that result. If you want to jog on webs, do it on groomed trails, open meadows, or solidly frozen lakes. In rocky or wooded areas, don't run on unpacked snow, and avoid jumping. If you do have to jump a creek, land with both shoes as flat as possible. (Or find a bridging log and take the snowshoes off to cross.)

Slopes require thinking rather than instinct. Short, gentle slopes can be herringboned, with toes out and the tails of the shoes overlapping as you step up. If the snow is crusty, you can climb straight up by lifting your heels to engage the cleats. Heel elevators, an option on mountaineering models, allow straight-line (and strenuous) ascents. But on most steep slopes you'll choose to traverse, i.e., cut across the angle of the slope. Cleats help, but edging the shoe into the snow with a slight kick and then angling the heel of your boot to the uphill side packs a stable platform. The pole should be in your uphill hand. On very steep slopes you can hold your pole (or poles) across your body in both hands, points uphill, to balance and self-arrest. If the snow is hard and the surface is melting, it can be safer to tie the snowshoes on your pack and kick steps. Going downhill, keep your weight forward to engage the cleats, or if you have heel cleats you can boink them in decisively. If you do slide, crouch and stay as low as possible to avoid a face-first dive. Glissading on snowshoes is fun, sort of. The secret (especially if you're wearing a pack) is to bend your knees and stay low. Or take the webs off, set one on the other (cleats down), and sit on them, using the pole to brake and steer while emitting the necessary whoops. It doesn't hurt to find a steep slope with no rocks or trees (let alone creeks or cliffs) below, to practice your glissades.

For more on snow camping in general, see pages 438 and 496.

CARE OF FEET

COLIN: Some people seem to have naturally tough feet. But even those not so blessed can improve their situation. Some years ago a reader advised me: "If you go barefoot whenever you can, you'll most likely develop lovely leathery feet." She was right. Whenever possible I now go around with nothing on my feet (and et cetera, which also feels nice), and because of that—or maybe because of improvements in boots or a lowering of ambitions or something entirely different—it's years since I had real foot trouble. The fact remains, though, that human feet are delicate instruments: they embody 52 separate bones (about one-quarter of the body's total), along with related muscles and tendons; they sweat through some 250,000 glands. And for all but the most blessed toughfoot, it pays to take stringent precautions before and during any walk much longer than you're currently used to, or with a load much heavier than you've very recently carried. If you don't yet understand the value of such precautions, then you've never generated a big, joy-killing blister with many miles still to go.

Getting your feet ready

This vital task is best achieved by practice—by taking time out beforehand to work up slowly from a few gentle miles, unladen (if you're in really bad shape), to a long day's slog with a load as big as you mean to carry (page 41). But somehow (page 86) you rarely seem to have the time to take out, and even more rarely the determination to take it. It helps, though, to wear your boots—especially new ones—as much as you can for a week or so before you go, even if only around the house. For years the only substitute I've known—and a poor one at that—has been to toughen up the skin (soles, toes, and heels particularly) by regular applications of rubbing alcohol for a week or so beforehand. If you put the alcohol bottle beside your toothbrush, it's not too difficult to remember this simple half-minute chore, morning and night. But alcohol tends to dry the skin, and I'm told that tincture of benzoin works better. My limited experience suggests that it does—though it's a little messier to use. Unfortunately, it has become a special-order item at most drugstores.

Some people who habitually get blisters in certain places on their feet say they ward them off by covering the sites in advance with tape, moleskin, or Adhesive Knit (page 113).

CHIP: If you're subject to athlete's foot (a fungus that devours dead skin cells) you already know that the hot, moist environment of a boot creates extremes of fungal hunger. Since dead skin, or callus, is what protects your feet from chafing, you don't want your resident fungi to eat it all up. So start treating for athlete's foot before you hit the trail with over-the-counter sprays or liquids (more effective than powders). Or better yet, go barefoot before the trip and wiggle your toes in the sun: the fungi don't like ultraviolet rays.

If you suffer from excess callus or corns, then there are various abrasive or chemical strategies. Wearing sandals gives me thick callus around my heels, which can crack and hurt like mad. My sandal-crazed friend José squeezes Superglue into these cracks and pinches them shut, but somehow I can't bear gluing myself. Instead, I've tried abrasive devices from Dr. Scholl's, which work fine but wear out fast on my dinosaur-grade calluses, and have recently figured out that a power sander works like magic. (VITAL NOTE: *My electric sander has a flat, rubber-padded, vibrating placket. Disc or belt sanders are hazardous for pedicures—don't even think of using one on your feet.*) Anyhow, during sandal season, twice a week I rev up the sander (with coarse paper) for a callus reduction and vibrating foot massage. Laugh if you like, but I just finished a summer of sandal hiking without a single painful heel crack. (Colin raises an eyebrow and tells me that he uses a nonmotorized pumice stone.) While on trips I've also used coarse sandstone, finding a hand-friendly piece, or simply rubbed my heels across bedrock. Post-abrasion, I apply Neutrogena Foot Cream (2 oz., $4.75), a pleasant-smelling gel that makes the skin more elastic without diminishing the protective effect of a good layer of callus.

Trim your toenails meticulously, looking for ingrown edges and sharp corners that dig into adjacent toes on the downhill grind—it's alarming to de-boot and see the toe of your sock soaked in blood. If jammed toes are a problem, there are between-toe pads available.

Stress-related aches and pains can also be warded off to some extent. The problem is that civilization has tended to flatten the surfaces on which we walk to the extent that it seriously weakens our feet, not to mention ankles, knees, etc. Much can be accomplished with conditioning jaunts over cobbles, clods, roots, tussocks, and so forth. Or toss knotted towels, sofa pillows, stuffed animals, and such on the floor of your urban cell and tramp determinedly over them while listening to the financial report.

If the boots that fit you perfectly at home tend to destroy your toes on the trail, you might have a weak arch and a problem called *elongation.* To test, recruit a friend, spouse, or dependent. Lay a piece of paper down and stand on it barefoot, and have them trace the outline of each foot. Then load your pack and heft it, line up your heel, and repeat the tracing in a different color ink. If, on the second try, your insteps and toes extend more than ¼ inch beyond the original outline, you should take action. First, try some barefoot conditioning—if it hurts too much, stop. Second, when you get measured for boots, stand up. And third, get a corrective footbed (page 84).

If you turn your ankles a lot, get a fat piece of surgical tubing or a bungee cord (4 feet long) and center it on your instep. Stretch the cord and then pull with the outside hand and resist with your ankle while counting to 10. When that palls, reverse the pull. Repeat. Jumping rope also helps.

If you've had sharp, burning pain under your heel on getting out of bed, then your plantar fascia, the bundle of tissue that forms a spring between the ball and heel of your foot, is likely to get inflamed with the added stress of backpacking. Conditioning on uneven ground helps, and so do orthotics (page 85).

Pronation is excessive rotation of the foot inward (a common condition), and supination is excessive rotation outward. For a diagnostic, see page 69. A corrective footbed with the proper firmness helps. But if you have the same complaint on every trip, regardless of socks or boots, see a doctor or call the American Podiatric Medical Association for a referral (1-800-366-8227) or access their Web site at *www.apma.org.* For makers of custom boots and footbeds (also called orthotics or pedorthics), see Appendix III.

If you don't have serious problems with your feet, by far the most organic, cheap, and simple approach to conditioning is to go barefoot or wear sandals. Regular airing scotches athlete's foot and builds up healthy callus. Barefooting also trains you to walk with grace and foresight.

On the march

COLIN: The important thing is to begin easily. People who backpack into the bush for once-a-year vacations all too often find the whole week or fortnight ruined at the very beginning by too much ambition and too little discretion. Their feet never recover from the pounding of the first day or two. A gentle shakedown cruise (pages 41 and 86)— a day or a week, depending on the total length of the trip— can make all the difference. On my thousand-mile California walk, although I began with stiff new boots and soft city feet, I suffered only one blister—a minor affair generated by an ill-advised insole experiment. During the first week, though, I averaged fewer than 7 miles a day, over very easy going. In the Grand Canyon my feet fared less well. But I began with a barely cured infected heel and because of it had worn nothing but moccasins for almost two weeks. If it hadn't been for two days of easy ambling at the start and a further four days of taking it fairly easy, I'd probably have been crippled before I got fully started.

It's essential that you continue to take precautions until your feet are comfortably lasting out the longest day and the heaviest load—even with steady downhill work, which gives them a much more brutal hammering than they get on the level or uphill. On long, hard treks I rarely seem to reach this point for at least a week or two.

CHIP: When my fieldwork included walking 50 or more miles per week, I had very few foot problems. At the start of the season new boots could give me a blister or two, and a long day under a heavy pack made me feel as if all those little foot bones were grinding together. But I seldom used anything other than water and soap. Though benzoin is reputed to toughen skin, an athletic trainer tells me that it's intended simply to hold tape in place. I occasionally dust my tootsies with footpowder—a sample-size container lasts the season and can be refilled. On a trip to Mexico I got a large sifter of O-Dolex Talco Desodorante (150 grams, 5 pesos), which should hold me for years. While the improved wicking properties of socks and boot liners mean much less messing around with your feet, some bits of wisdom still hold.

COLIN: Taking your boots off and airing your feet whenever you can certainly makes good theoretical sense. Heat is the cause of all blisters— though softening of the skin by unwicked-away sweat may also con- tribute. Locally, the heat comes from the friction of a rucked sock or an ill-fitting boot. But it seems reasonable to suppose that the overall temperature of your feet makes a big difference. I certainly find deserts the hardest places on feet. And that's not really surprising: few people realize how hot the ground underfoot can be. In the Grand Canyon I repeatedly checked air and ground temperatures. With air temperature about 85°F I would get a ground reading on unshaded rock (and that meant just about any rock) of around 115° or 120°. On unshaded sand the mercury would go well past the last gradation of 120°. When air temperature climbed over 90° I had to be careful where I left the thermometer, for fear the mercury would blow off the top.*

A reader recommends as "freaking marvelous" this simple exercise for tired feet: After you've removed your boots, slowly flex them forward, wiggle at extreme extension, flex fully backward, rewiggle, repeat as often as needed. My evaluation: "freaking marvelous." A sort of miniservice version that I find useful on the march for any forefoot discomfort, especially when going downhill, is to simply wiggle your toes occasionally inside your boots.

CHIP: When my feet get hot, I have a mental picture of the Red Queen bellowing "OFF WITH HIS *BOOTS!*" And off they come. If it's sunny and I'm near a lake, my barefoot lunch might become a naked one. But always, I beat the dust and seeds out of my socks, turn them inside out, and drape them in the sun (on the end of a staff or weighted with rocks). In hot weather I retire the sweaty pair to the mesh pocket on my pack and change, rotating the two pairs as required.

Soaking your feet in cold water reduces swelling but also softens your skin, so give them ample time to dry before socking up. A strip cut from the end of a viscose pack towel is a handy foot dryer that can be run between your toes and then hung on your pack (where it might also keep bears away). Another therapeutic move is to prop your feet up so they're higher than your torso, on a rock, log, or dependent child. Ten minutes of this reduces swelling.

Sandals provide an easy out for tortured feet. I switch them on and off with boots, and find that it not only helps my feet but soothes my inner aborigine.

---

*An article by A. Court in the *Geographical Review* (1949, no. 2, pages 214–20) gives these figures for extreme conditions in American deserts: air at 5 feet (which is where official readings are taken), 125°F; at 11 feet, 150°F; at 1 inch, 165°; at ground, 180°. This kind of heat layering is by no means confined to deserts. See, for example, page 439. Interesting temperatures recorded during World War II at a naval research center in Imperial Valley, California, on a day when the official air temperature touched 120°F, include 145° in the gasoline in a 50-gallon drum left in the sun, 155° in the vapor above the gasoline, and 190° on the seat of a jeep.

Remedial treatment

COLIN: If, in spite of all your care, your feet need doctoring, start it early. The moment you feel what may be the beginnings of a blister, do something about it.

First remove any obvious and rectifiable local irritant, such as a fragment of stone or a rucked sock. Then cover the tender place. Cover it even if you can see nothing more than a faint redness. Cover it, in fact, if you can see nothing at all. Being a "hero" is being a bloody fool. The covering may only be needed for a few hours; if you take it off at night and let the air get at the skin you may not need to replace it next morning. But if you do nothing at the first warning you may find yourself inside the hour with a blister that will last a week.

For covering, a piece of surgical tape or a Band-Aid will do in a pinch, provided its adhesive surface is efficient enough to prevent rucking—a requirement not always met when the trouble is on your toes. But for years now I have, like most backpackers, patched with the oddly miraculous devices known as "moleskins." The original Dr. Scholl's Moleskins—sheets of white felt, adhesive on one side, that you can cut to suit your blister or sore spot—are sold in most drugstores. Now, it used to be that a moleskin was a moleskin was a moleskin. No more . . .

CHIP: Most backpacking shops stock a heavy-duty variant called Moleskin Plus (three 4-by-3½-inch sheets, $4). Dr. Scholl's Molefoam is moleskin bonded to latex, for extra padding (two 4-by-3½-inch sheets, $3.50, applicable, they say, to boot liners as well as feet). Spenco Adhesive Knit is thinner but no less tenaciously adhesive, although it seems to come off more easily when you want it to. It also comes packaged with the marvelous 2nd Skin, a sterile gel in sheet form. Spenco developed 2nd Skin to treat burns and wounds where exposure to air was painful. Sharp scissors are needed to cut a patch of the gel. Once it's in place (as the pain sweetly disappears) you apply a somewhat larger patch of Adhesive Knit. If the edges are not round, then round them, since pointy patches peel. The trick is to let your skin dry before applying the knit covering and to have plenty of overlap all the way around. The combination is surprisingly rugged and you don't have adhesive gummed directly to the raw spot. For fastest healing, it should be changed two to three times a day.

Spyroflex is a new laminate of open-cell dressing material with a breathable, stretchy outer knit. It's available in precut Skin Savers ($5) for preventing blisters, while 2-by-2-inch Blister Dressings ($5) and 4-by-4-inch Abrasion Dressings ($7) come in sterile packets.

Other molesome species turn up in prestocked first-aid kits (page 648). Band-Aid (Johnson & Johnson) recently debuted Blister Block, a precut stick-on cushion. I just bought both Spyroflex and Band-Aid varieties for eventual testing, but as Colin says, "I'm damned if I'll go get blisters deliberately, just for your edification, buster (or, of course, bustress)."

Some of my friends (self-designated hardguys) take great delight in duct-taping their blisters. Since duct tape sticks like a limpet but has no other therapeutic advantage—it traps moisture and tends to tear out chunks of flesh when pulled off—you're probably better off saving it for true emergencies (a spot of footpowder keeps it from sticking to the wound). On a long trek, an hour or two spent resting, airing, and sunning your feet (though not sun-burning for heaven's sake) can save considerable anguish later on.

COLIN: If you generate a blister in spite of all your care—or because you weren't careful enough—and if it's either very deep or isn't yet very bulbous, the best treatment is probably just to cover it. If the blister is close to the surface and has already inflated you will need to burst it before you can walk with comfort. Pierce it with a needle, from the side, down near the base of the balloon, so that all the liquid can drain away. I carry several needles, primarily for repair work, in my waterproof matchsafe. Sterilize the needle first, in a sterilizing agent if you carry one (rubbing alcohol won't do) but, failing that, in a flame—far better than nothing, in spite of the carbon deposits. If you've got to keep walking and if the loose skin of the balloon doesn't ruck up when deflated, it's probably best to leave the skin in place and cover it, and to cut it away only when the skin beneath has had time to harden. If you can rest long enough for the skin to harden—which it does more quickly when exposed to air—or if the deflated outer skin puckers so badly that it seems likely to cause further damage as you walk, then you should remove it by scissoring carefully around the edges of the blister. Take care to keep the exposed area clean. And leave no dead skin likely to cause new chafing. Once the newly exposed skin has dried, hasten hardening with tincture of benzoin or even rubbing alcohol. If you must keep walking, and apply a moleskin or other adhesive cover, use a thin fragment of gauze—or, better, 2nd Skin—to prevent the cover from sticking directly to the still tender skin. A sprinkling of footpowder can also help reduce friction, and so can an antiseptic of a kind that will lubricate as well as reduce the danger of infection.

But never forget that a blister is a sign of failure. The efficient way to deal with foot trouble is to avoid it. Preharden. On the march, and especially in the early days of a trip, attend assiduously to preventive measures. And nip tribulations in the bud.

THE FOUNDATIONS IN ACTION

A book on walking should no doubt have something to say about the simple, basic, physical act of walking.

On the most fundamental level, advice is probably useless. Anyone old enough to read has almost certainly grown too set in the way he puts one foot in front of the other to alter it materially without devoting a great deal of time and determination to the task.*

On the other hand, it's very easy to improve by a little conscious thought what I regard as the most important single element in the physical act of walking: rhythm. An easy, unbroken rhythm can carry you along hour after hour almost without your being aware that you're putting one foot in front of the other. At the end of a really long day you'll be aware of the act all right, but as long as you maintain a steady rhythm very little of your mind need be concerned with it. And your muscles will complain far less than if you've walked all day in a series of jerky and semicoordinated movements, sometimes pushing close to your limit, sometimes meandering.

With experience you automatically fall into your own rhythmic pace. (At least, mostly you do. There'll still be days when you have to fight for it, and not always with total success.) But when you first take up real walking you may have to think deliberately about establishing a stride and a speed that feel comfortable. And both stride and speed may be rather different with and without a load.

You'll almost certainly have to concentrate at first on the important matter of not disrupting the rhythm unless absolutely necessary. This means stepping short for a stride when you come to some minor obstacle such as a narrow ditch, or even marking time with one foot. I can't emphasize this unbroken-rhythm business too strongly.

---

*I'm no longer convinced that this is so. At least, the necessary time and even determination may be a lot less than I imagined. A course of Rolfing showed me that it can alter your gait as well as stance—while also giving you a new and effective tool to deal with certain nagging back and other anatomical problems.

CHIP: I remain un-Rolfed, but have changed my step from duckfooted to straight, largely through several thousand miles of ski touring—with my feet aligned by ski bindings and stiff boots—along with a bit of subliminal effort. I notice now that my right foot swings out and then self-corrects before touching down.

A Massachusetts reader writes: "You are right to stress rhythm, but it can be improved with coordination of breathing, arm movement and a [simple] mantra . . . [that] quickly becomes unconscious, bringing the whole self to a deeper unity."

Of course, rhythm is not always a simple matter of constant stride and speed. In fact it remains so only as long as you walk on a smooth and level surface. The moment you meet rough going underfoot or start up or down a gradient, you have to modify stride or speed or both.

Climbing a gentle slope means nothing more than a mild shortening of stride, though leaning forward slightly may help too. But long before a mountainside gets so steep that you start reaching out for handholds, stride becomes a meaningless word. Now you put your feet down almost side by side at one step, a foot or more apart at the next, depending on the immediate local gradients and footholds. Even the rate at which you move one leg past the other—slowly and deliberately and almost laboriously, though not quite—may vary in response to changes in the general gradient. Yet the old rhythm persists. I'm not sure where the relationships lie. It is not—though I have sometimes thought so—that you continue to expend the same amount of energy. Steep climbing takes more out of you, always (page 196). But the fact remains that although you must change gear in an almost literal sense at the bottom and top of a steep hill, you can maintain the deeper continuity of the old rhythm. The pulse is still there, somewhere, if you know where to feel for it.

Downhill walking, though less sweaty than climbing, is less easy than it ought to be. In broad theory you merely relinquish the potential energy you gained with such labor as you climbed; but in practice you do no such thing. At every step you expend a great deal of effort in holding yourself back—and this effort too demands a deliberate change of gear. If the gradient is at all severe you reduce both stride and speed as much as you think necessary to prevent yourself from hammering hell out of knees and ankles and feet (especially feet). Again, though, you find with practice that it's possible to maintain the essence of the old rhythm.

You may also have to apply a conscious effort to maintaining your rhythmic pace when you come to certain kinds of rough going—soft sand or gravel that drags at your feet like molasses; talus that slides away from under your feet like a treadmill; rough rock or tussocky grassland that soon disrupts an even stride; or prolonged sidehill work that puts an abnormal strain on foot and leg muscles and may also present something of a problem in balance.

Walking after dark, especially on pitch-black, moonless nights, can also destroy your customary rhythm. If you've been walking in daylight and simply keep going, little trouble seems to arise. But if you get up in the middle of the night and hike out into darkness you may have a surprise in store. I wrote in *The Thousand-Mile Summer* about the only time I traveled at night on my California walk. It was in Death Valley. The first night inside the Valley I had no sleeping bag, and I failed, dismally, to stay asleep (see page 479, this book). At 3:30 I got up from the gully in which I'd camped and headed north into the darkness. There was no moon. From the start I found myself walking in a curious and disturbing state of detachment. The paleness that was the dirt road refused to stay in positive contact with my feet, and I struggled along with laborious, unrhythmic steps. All around hovered hints of immense open spaces and distant, unconvincing slopes. Time had lost real meaning back in the gully; now it lacked even boundaries. When dawn gave the landscape a tenuous reality at last I was still two hours away from my next cache. In those endless two hours I completely failed to reestablish my usual rhythmic pace.

Next night I was on the move by 9:30. This time, bright moonlight made the physical world something real and conquerable. I could plant my feet firmly and confidently on the solid white road. But soon after eleven o'clock the moon set. The world narrowed to hints of colossal open space, to a blur that achieved reality only through jabbing at my feet. Distance degenerated into marks on the map. Time was the creeping progress of watch hands. All through the long and cold and dismal night that followed I had to struggle to hold some semblance of my usual daytime rhythm. I succeeded only marginally. But I succeeded far better than on the previous night. In recent years I seem to have had no such problem at night. I guess it's just practice.

A delicate sense of balance is vital to good walking, day or night. And it's not just a matter of being able to cross steep slopes without tightening up. Your body should always be poised and relaxed so that you put down your feet, whatever their size and whatever your load, with something close to daintiness. Before I walked through the Grand Canyon I met the one man who seemed to know much about hiking away from trails in its remote corners. Trying to get some idea of whether I'd be able to cope with the rough, steep country that he crossed with such apparent ease, I asked him to tell me, honestly, if he was a good climber. "No," he said, "definitely not. I'd say I was a very mediocre climber indeed. But in the Canyon it's mostly walking, you know, even though it can be pretty tricky walking at times." He smiled. "I guess you could say, come to think of it, that maybe I don't dislodge quite as many stones as the next guy." I knew then that he was a good walker.

One of the surest ways to tell an experienced walker from a beginner is the speed at which he starts walking. The beginner tends to tear away in the morning as if he meant to break every record in sight. By contrast, the experienced walker seems to amble. But before long, and certainly by evening, their positions have reversed. The beginner is dragging. The expert, still swinging along at the same easy pace, is now the one who looks as though he has records in mind. One friend of mine, a real expert, says, "If you can't carry on a conversation, you're going too fast."

The trap to avoid at all costs, if you want to enjoy yourself, is spurious heroism—the delusion that your prowess as a walker rests on how dauntlessly you "pick 'em up and lay 'em down." It's a sadly common syndrome.

The actual speed at which you walk is a personal and idiosyncratic matter. Settle for whatever seems to suit you best. It's really a question of finding out what you can keep up hour after hour in various kinds of terrain carrying various loads. Until you know your own limits, aim for a slow, rhythmic, almost effortless pace. You'll be surprised, I think, at the ground you cover. The miles will come to meet you. In time you'll learn that, generally speaking, the way to hurry is not to hurry but to keep going. To this end I have two walking speeds: slow and slower. See also page 121. Note (page 194) that the energy expended in walking doubles, roughly speaking, with each mile-per-hour increase in speed; and that the best way to prevent a buildup of lactic acid in the muscles is to walk more slowly.

For a different look at the basic facts of walking, see an excellent article by James Tabor in *Backpacker* magazine, April/May 1981. It propounds, in more scientific terms, more or less what I've said here, but it also adds new insights into the extraordinarily complicated act of walking.

The halts you choose to take are a matter of personal preference, but frequent and irregular halts are a sure sign of an inexperienced hiker.

Unladen, it may be a good thing to keep going hour after hour without disturbing your rhythm. But if you're carrying a sizable pack you'll almost certainly find that, no matter how fit you are, you need to get the weight off your back for a short spell about once an hour. I halt every hour with fairly mechanical regularity, modifying slightly to suit terrain. I like to get to the top of a hill before I stop, for example; and I often halt a few minutes early or late to take advantage of convenient shade or water or a pleasing view. In theory I rest for 10 minutes. (In the first 5 to 7 minutes of rest the body flushes out about 30 percent of the lactic acid buildup in muscles, only 5 percent in the next 15 minutes.) But it is horribly easy to let a halt drift on for 20 or even 30 minutes, and when I slip the pack off I often, as protection, activate my wrist-Casio's stopwatch mode. In the past I would often, when I had a map, mark on it the halting place and also pencil in the exact time I stopped: I'm no longer sure why I began doing so, but I went on doing it because the penciled figures on the map acted as a reminder and spur. They also helped me judge how I was progressing across a given kind of country and made it easier to estimate how far I should be able to travel in the next hour or afternoon or day or week. In fact I still sometimes pencil in halt sites and times for that purpose.

At each halt I take off my pack and prop it against a rock or a tree or the staff and lean against it. I try to relax completely. Sometimes, warding off the attractions of scenery, animals, and the map, I quickly succeed. If I fail I may use Selective Awareness (page 124); I may even doze off for a few minutes. Getting started again may demand considerable willpower, especially toward the end of a long day; but within a few paces I slip back into the old, regular rhythm. And mostly I will hold it, unbroken, for another 50 minutes.*

Desert walking

In deserts, think "water" incessantly. At times you may need to carry 2 gallons of the stuff, or even more. You must certainly plan every move with known sources in mind; and remember that a spring marked on a map is not a sure and certain source unless confirmed by recent firsthand evidence from a person you feel sure you can trust (for hints on calibrating trustworthiness, see page 639). For more on water—dehydration, conservation, how much to carry, how often to drink, sources, purification, desert stills, caches, and canteens—see pages 230 to 265. In low desert, except in midwinter, consider walking early and perhaps

---

*Any other man stops and talks.
But the walking man walks.
—song, "The Walking Man"

late in the day, or even at night—but don't ignore possible rhythm difficulties (page 115) and rattlesnakes (pages 711–22). Desert walking in winter or early spring can be delectable; but you must still think "water" all the time.

A Southern California reader offers some interesting thoughts: "Most of my walking is done in the desert and much of that when it's hot. Why? The challenge (if snow, ice and subfreezing temperatures are allowable obstacles for the climber, then why not obstacles of the other extreme?), the virtual assurance that one will escape from ORVs and (I confess it) other hikers, and—I like hot weather. Yet there are times when one wants and needs shade. I have tried a space blanket (silver side up) and six aluminum tent poles—three for each prop—for protection on lava fields and the like. A bit unsteady in a wind but even a droopy awning gives shade."

CHIP: Ray Jardine describes using his own reengineered umbrella with a reflective Mylar cover for desert hiking. To carry your own traveling patch of shade might be a brilliant tactic, if you can stop giggling. But I hasten to add that few umbrellas are seen in Wyoming, owing to gusty and insistent winds. (GoLite sells a Jardine-style hiking umbrella, 9.5 oz., $23). Jardine's book *Beyond Backpacking* has plans for the Mylar cover and pointers on wilderness umbrella technique.

Winter walking

Where summers are grindingly hot, winter can be the time for extended walks. Water holes fill up and some desert plants flower and bear fruit in winter. The main difference is that you should be prepared for a cold snap, blustery winds, or a cold drenching rain as a matter of course. Walking tends to keep you warm, so calculate your thickest layer for sitting still at nighttime temperatures.

Moist coastal belts present their own winter conundrums. Most residents avoid walking, stay indoors, and drink heavily. But the unrelenting wet and cold also spark innovation. The overall shift to synthetics began on the Norwegian coast with Helly Hansen. It is under such inhospitable conditions that new materials like Polarguard and neoprene, and new ideas like the SealSkinz waterproof socks and gloves, develop and are tested. That this takes place not to advance the human prospect, but to escape the constant misery of wet feet, cold hands, a wet butt, etc. should not diminish our thanks.

Where it snows (YES!) walkers can adopt the necessary ambulatory means like snowshoes and overboots (page 104), and press on. Snow camping takes some getting used to, both for hazards and for joys, but it's a keen and bracing variation. In steep country, you should know something about avalanches, which, if scary, are generally predictable (for books, see page 753). In ski regions, avalanche forecasts are broadcast daily, and land-management agencies have toll-free lines with recorded reports. Heavy snowfall and strong winds are the most dangerous combination. The smart thing to do is to stay out of the backcountry until a spell of clearing—and the natural settling of the snowpack—eases the danger. Or, if you're caught out, stay put (or find the nearest safe place to camp) for at least a day or two after the storm clears, to let the critical slabs crack loose. It's actually sort of enjoyable to lounge in a safe spot and watch big slides peel off and thunder down. Having worked and played all my life in the avalanche-prone central Rockies, I've managed not to get caught, but some of my friends have not been so lucky, and some have died. So, while I don't fear avalanches, exactly, I do take them very seriously.

Overall, though, my experience has been that you have more to fear from what's under the snow than from the slopes above. Big rocks, deadfall logs, brush, and creeks all create voids in the temporary support structure known as the snowpack. If you stumble into one you can take quite a fall, ending on a sharp stub or in freezing water up to your hocks. Then, you have to scramble out of your self-made pit. If the place is familiar, you might have some idea what's under the snow, but otherwise you should try to picture it. Rockfaces, slanting deadfalls, and the sound of running water should prick your nerve endings. If in doubt, stop and probe with a pole or staff. In fact, the abiding discipline of winter travel is a deliberate, nerve-twitching observance of what lies ahead. It might be a stove repair at 35°F below or an April creek roaring under fragile snow bridges. But the common element is to first imagine the consequence of each and every action. Which distracts you, quite pleasantly I think, from those abstract terrors that throng the dark and the cold.

Walking at high altitudes

COLIN: Even if you acclimate properly (see page 44), you must, once you get up high, walk differently. "How high" is not really answerable with a figure: your body, on any given day, will respond more accurately. But as a guideline it's probably safe to say that most people will have to adjust over 10,000 feet, and that many will have to do so a lot lower.

First, you must learn to modulate your rhythm—to dead slow. Even at sea level there's nothing so becomes a walker as modest slowness and languidity;

But when the mountain air blows in your ears,
Then imitate the action of a tortoise;
Slacken the sinews, throttle down the blood,
Deflect ambition with delib'rate pace,
And lend the legs a loitering aspect;
Let them creep through the hours of the day
Like a brass clock; let the body dawdle
As languidly as doth a smoker
Drag slow-foot through the grass, like a tippler
O'erfilled with mild but tasteful potion.
Now ope the teeth, and stretch the nostril wide;
Draw slow the breath, and suck down every intake
To his full depth!—On, on, you noble Walker,

whose blood is thin from scaling this full height, and remember that not only during the first three days of your body's readjustment but on, on into the fourth and fifth, Henry, and beyond that for as long as you stay up high, you must strive to keep moving in this consciously imposed, almost ludicrous slow motion.*

If you do it properly you won't get breathless unless you go very high indeed. And your heart won't pound. (I maintain that if your muscles feel the strain of walking when you're up high then you're asking too much of your heart.) If you forget to hold your legs in check, and revert to something like your normal pace, you'll probably begin to gasp and to feel your heart triphammering. You will therefore rest—and lose time and momentum. But if you tortoise along you can often keep going for the full regulation hour with no more distress than at sea level. (For a discussion of "acute mountain sickness," see page 750.)

Remember, always, about those deep, slow breaths—preferably taken in rhythm with your steps. (Up really high, try taking more breaths to the step.) By dragging each breath down into the full depths of your lungs you will at least in part make up for the reduced oxygen in the air. If you find your brain isn't functioning very well—and up high there will assuredly be times when it does not—stop and drag down several extradeep breaths that expel every lurking unoxygenated residue from your lung cellars. You may begin to think better at once. And this treatment will as often as not remove or at least moderate the headaches that are apt to afflict you for a spell. I keep battling headaches with such deep breathing, and it is many years since I needed to resort to aspirin.

---

*It distresses me to discover that for two editions and 25 years just about everyone seems to have read this passage, in spite of the Henry-hint, as a mere Fletcher efflation; so here I come, following the Bard again, once more unto the breach, dear friends, once more.

Once you've mastered these simple lessons you'll be ready to sample the simple joys of walking around on top of the world.

There remains the matter of what you do with your mind while your body walks. Mostly, I find that everything takes care of itself. My mind soars or grubs along or meanders halfway in between, according to the sun or cloud, the wind or rain, the state of my metabolism, the demands of the hour or other elements beyond my control. But there are times when, in the interests of efficient walking, you need to discipline your thoughts. If the way ahead looks long and tiresome, and above all if it slopes steeply and inexorably upward, on and on, then you're liable to find that the prospect presses heavy on your mind and that the depression acts as a brake on your body and that its lethargy further depresses your mind—and so on. The syndrome is pandemic to mountains, and especially to those high enough for the thin air to brake directly on mind and body. Some years ago, in early November, I went up Mount Whitney. I wandered up, acclimating slowly, savoring the emptiness and silence of the country (I had chosen November for horde avoidance); but I was carrying a considerable load—my plan, eventually scuttled by weather, was to camp on the summit—and on the long, final pull each step became a wearisome, mind-demanding effort. Ahead, the trail curved on and up, on and up. As I climbed, the air grew thinner, even less sustaining. My mind sagged under the burden of step-by-step effort. And then I remembered something. My paperback for the trip was *Zen in the Art of Archery,* and while reading it in my tent the night before I'd decided to try applying one of its lessons. I immediately began to do so. "I am the summit," I told myself. "I am the summit. I am the summit." I focused my mind on the statement, close. And very soon, very easily, I believed it: my insignificant self and the apex of that huge blade of rock were the same thing—or at least they occupied the same point in space and time. Yet the space was in another sense still above me. The time, I think, was a nudge ahead in the future. Or perhaps it was the present. Anyway, I held the concept tight and firm, so that there was no room for anything else. (Excluding other ideas wasn't difficult: at 14,000 feet you can rarely cope with more than one at a time.)

It seemed to work. The effort of climbing—of pulling self and load on and up, on and up, step by laborious step—faded away. To say that I floated upward would, I guess, be hyperbole; but when I reached the summit in a physical sense I was, I think, less tired than I have ever been at such a high and crowning moment.

That experience on Whitney turned out to be only a start. In the years since I have employed for all manner of purposes—from nonanesthetic dentistry through giving up smoking to controlling pre-tennis-tournament nerves—a technique devised by Dr. Emmett Miller that he calls "Selective Awareness." It's not altogether unlike transcendental meditation: you put yourself into a kind of hypnotic trance that's really no more than a controlled focusing of the mind and relaxing of all muscles. Selective Awareness has often proved invaluable to me on walks. Not long ago, as I was coming down from a weeklong trip into some familiar mountains, darkness fell when I was still a couple of hours from roadhead. In itself, that didn't matter: moonlight illuminated a trail I knew well, and I had a good flashlight. But it had been a hard week, and when I stopped for my final rest, barely an hour from the car, I felt suddenly exhausted. Directly ahead, beyond a creek, the land rose precipitously for what I knew was the last, 10-minute climb before a long, steep descent. For a few moments I wondered how the hell I was going to make it up and down that final ridge. Then it occurred to me to rest with Selective Awareness, the way other people apparently do with yoga. After 5 minutes, or maybe 10 (time seems suspended when you're in that state), I emerged feeling totally refreshed. I went up the hill as if it were a plain and I a lightly loaded gazelle. And then I glided happily down to the car.

Walls

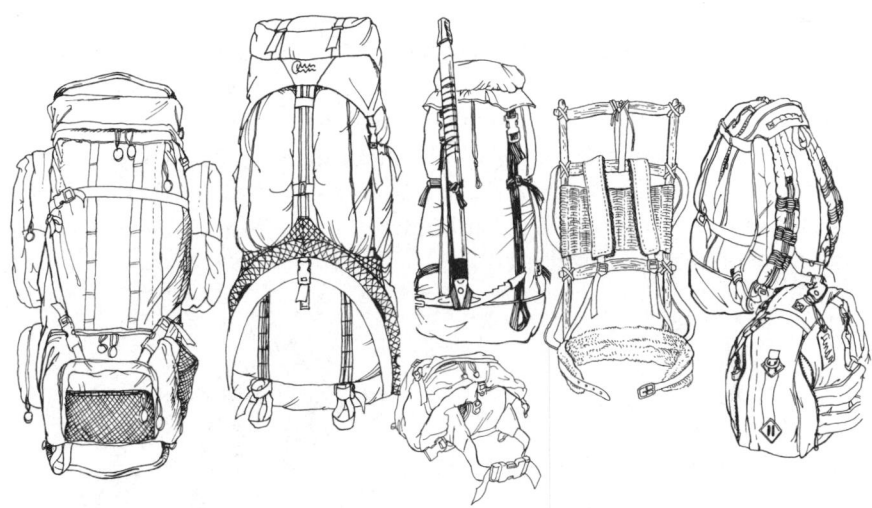

COLIN: Next to your boots, no item of equipment is more likely to make or mar your walking than the pack that forms the walls of your house. For the pack is more than a shell that contains and protects everything else. It also embodies the crucial interface between you and your load: that artful combination of hipbelt and shoulder harness known as the suspension system. And there grief can lie—unless you get everything just right.

If a trip will last only a few hours, of course, you may not need a pack. You can stuff everything you want into pockets. Or you may take one of those small pouches—not really houses at all, just pottering sheds—that are known as

FANNY PACKS.

CHIP: These are also known as waist or lumbar packs, which seems sort of neo-Victorian. The simplest of these arse-kits still consist of a pouch sewn to a piece of flat webbing, at $12–$20, while the most elaborate ones hold over 1000 cu. in., have padded belts and suspensions, and cost more than $100.

The nicest thing about them is where the load rests: tucked into the curve of the spine and close to your center of balance. My first fanny pack was the zip-off top pocket of a blue Lowe Liberty pack (circa 1980). Stuffed drum-tight, with an anorak lashed to the top, it tailed me up uncounted peaks. But the simple bun-bag has its drawbacks. With more than 10 pounds it sags woefully unless the hipbelt is tight enough to bisect you. That's also about the load limit of the detachable top pockets now found on full-size packs.

Technically speaking, fanny packs are going in two interesting directions.

First, with increasing volume they take on padding, external pockets, compression and stabilizer straps, and flexible stays for support. The largest now bump the volume of a day pack and hold about 20 pounds, with the hipbelt supplemented by light shoulder yokes, or "strapettes," as they're called by Mountainsmith, the Colorado company that took the first leap in this direction. To put it bluntly, bun-bags have reached a state of refinement that invites abuse.

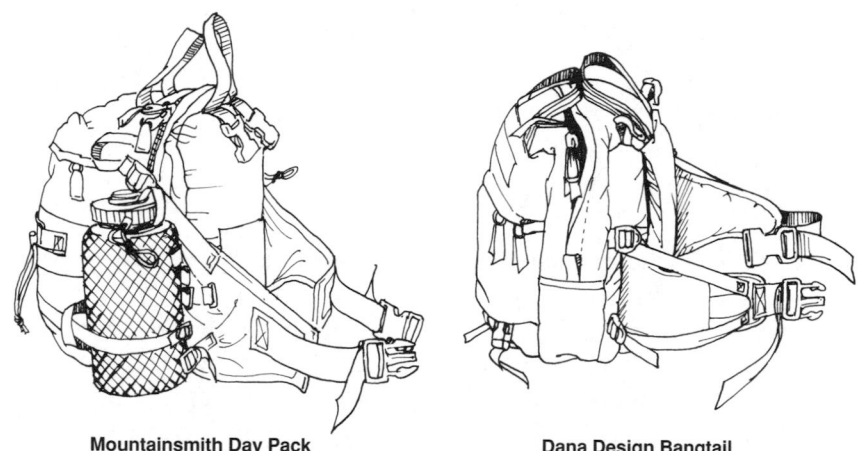

Mountainsmith Day Pack　　　　　**Dana Design Bangtail**

I took the Mountainsmith Day Pack (despite the name, a fanny pack at 1254 cu. in., 1 lb. 9 oz., $80) for an off-trail, overnight trip in freezing weather. I carried a bivy sac, pad, sleeping bag, pellet stove, cookpot, water bottle, and a two-day supply of food. Not only did I survive, but the lightness and maneuverability let me indulge my penchant for bush-whacking (for details, see page 32 and Appendix II).

Second, some makers are fielding multipurpose bun-bags. More rectilinear than classic models, they have a tuck-in hipbelt, briefcase-style handle, and clip-on shoulder strap. On workdays they bulge with file folders and laptop computers. On weekends, stuffed with shell jackets and energy bars, they go hiking and biking. A good one I've used that way (while getting a chuckle out of the name) is Dana Design's Bangtail (1 lb. 13 oz., $80).

DAY PACKS

Now part of everyday life, day packs abound in every conceivable combination of strappery, zippery, and pocketry, not to mention an explosion of colors. As demand has ballooned, the once-simple sack-with-straps has picked up features (not all of them desirable) and high-end models have gotten madly sophisticated. The classics like Gregory's Day-and-a-Half pack (far right, page 125) have been refined, with tougher fabrics, smoother zips, and contoured straps. But too much choice can be perplexing: JanSport, for instance, recently introduced 28 new day packs, some for hiking and climbing and others for laptop computers or wet swimming suits. Model names offer clues (Bitterroot and Chasm versus Megabyte and Gridlock). But a great many of the day packs found in discount stores are neither designed nor built to handle serious outdoor use.

In any size, the cause of most discomfort is poor strap geometry. Small day packs don't need much structure, but at higher volumes (above 2000 cu. in.) look for stays, a foam back or a framesheet, and perhaps a hipbelt. Other things to look at include the layout of internal or external pockets (some of mesh), and whether there are means to lash gear outboard. Some models have bungee cords, handy for light, bulky things like sweaters.

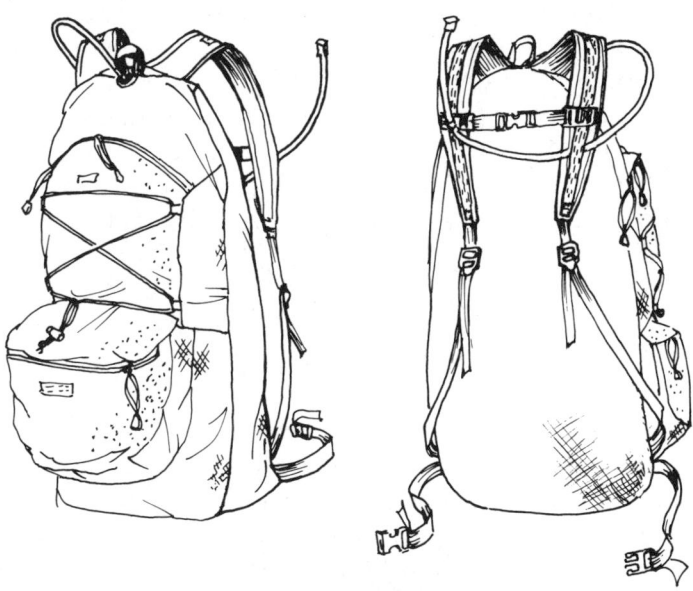

Platypus Thunderhead

An increasingly popular variation on the classic day pack is the *hydration pack,* which is built around a good-size plastic bladder with a drinking tube (above). I tried a Platypus Thunderhead (from Cascade

Designs, 3 liters of water, 550 cu. in. for sundries, 1 lb., $38) and found it useful for hot-weather hikes. A slim hipbelt keeps it from bouncing, the 10-inch width makes it somewhat cooler than average, and two zippered pockets plus a bungee give scope for a windbreaker and lunch.

As gear has slimmed down it has become feasible to use day packs for overnight trips. To accommodate the extra gear, look for side compression straps, a webbing daisy chain or lashpoints to attach a sleeping pad, and similar options. Increasingly, for day-tripping duties I use either specialized ultralight models (page 160) or the detachable versions found on travel packs (page 163).

Between day packs and full-size models is a growing middle ground that will do for long days or lightweight weekend trips.

MIDSIZE PACKS

The jump in the numbers of midsize (2500–4500 cu. in.) packs reflects a couple of trends. The first is that mountaineers, skiers, photographers, and other gearheads tend to overload their day packs, which has led manufacturers to puff up the volume. The second is the shrinking weight and bulk of outdoor gear in general: it's no longer necessary to pack a huge, reeking wad of clothes. Tents and sleeping bags can be found at half their former weight, while tricky little 3-ounce stoves and titanium pots have streamlined cookery; and so on. Thus, going light no longer demands quite the masochistic fervor that it once did.

Still, most people choose midsize packs for gear-intensive day trips, snowshoeing, etc. My first was the Pingora (third from left, page 125), painstakingly sewn by my climbing partner Jay Goodwin. In 20 years it hasn't popped a single stitch, and despite the many midsize packs now available, I still favor it.

FULL-SIZE PACKS

Whatever pack you choose, once you decide to stay out for several days at a time you'll find you must carry a genuine house on your back. Early in the game, from the 1950s to mid-'70s, that was a pack with a large, visible, often creaky external frame of aluminum tubing: the *E-frame.* In the '70s, packs appeared with internal frames of aluminum stays hidden in fabric sheaths, and these *I-frame* packs were quickly adopted by mountaineers. As I-frame packs improved, they claimed more of the market, and today dominate it.

I-frame packs begat *travel packs,* wildly popular these days, and also *ultralight packs.* All of the above come in varying sizes and configurations, so before we elaborate further, let's define our terms.

External-frame packs evolved from the old wooden-frame packboards used by hunters and foragers, some of which (and whom) have been found frozen in glacial ice. The first American patent for a frame backpack went to a Mr. Merriam in 1886, but the expression—"backpack"—wasn't much used until the 1900s. In the 1916 classic *Camping and Woodcraft,* Horace Kephart observed that "Backpacking is the cheapest possible way to spend one's vacation in the wilderness." While armies on several continents used frames (iron!) to support clumpy rucksacks, the first commercially successful frame pack was the Trapper Nelson, which employed the still-basic form: a rectangular frame with a bag on the back and a harness on the front. Variations on this theme have included pads, backbands, hipbelts, foam, and the use of plastic for all or part of the frame. Designs have matured (some to the brink of senility), but the basic architecture endures.

Internal-frame packs began as frameless sacks for mountaineering, basically duffels with shoulder straps. The cut was narrow and cylindrical, as free of hoops, loops, or bumps as possible. Riding close to the body, they were hot, uncomfortable, inconvenient to pack, and also rather dashing. Then someone came up with the notion of putting thin, flat, flexible bars of aluminum inside the bag where they wouldn't catch, either parallel or in an X. These stood the pack up for easier access and kept it clear of the wearer's back.

From a simple beginning, I-frames are evolving an intricate structure in the same way that soft-bodied creatures grew complex skeletons to bear their (our) weight on land. Stays are still mostly aluminum, but polycarbonate, carbon-fiber, and other advanced chemicals provide light, boingy alternatives. Other forms of support are wands and hoops of fiberglass or Delrin. Large packs now tend to have a framesheet of resilient plastic, in concert with stays, hoops, and other concealed wonders.

Travel packs are I-frames modified to bear the rigors of mechanized travel. Ideally, they withstand being crammed into luggage racks or baggage compartments and can pass through the guts of strap-devouring airport luggage systems, but also ride well on the back. The boom in "adventure travel," which caters to a demand for the predictably exotic, has mushroomed the number of travel packs. Convergent evolution has given us travel packs with both good suspensions and ingenious ways to conceal them, and some of these are good all-purpose choices.

Ultralight packs originated with two different but equally fanatical groups: mountaineers who adopted the fast-and-light ethic of Yvon

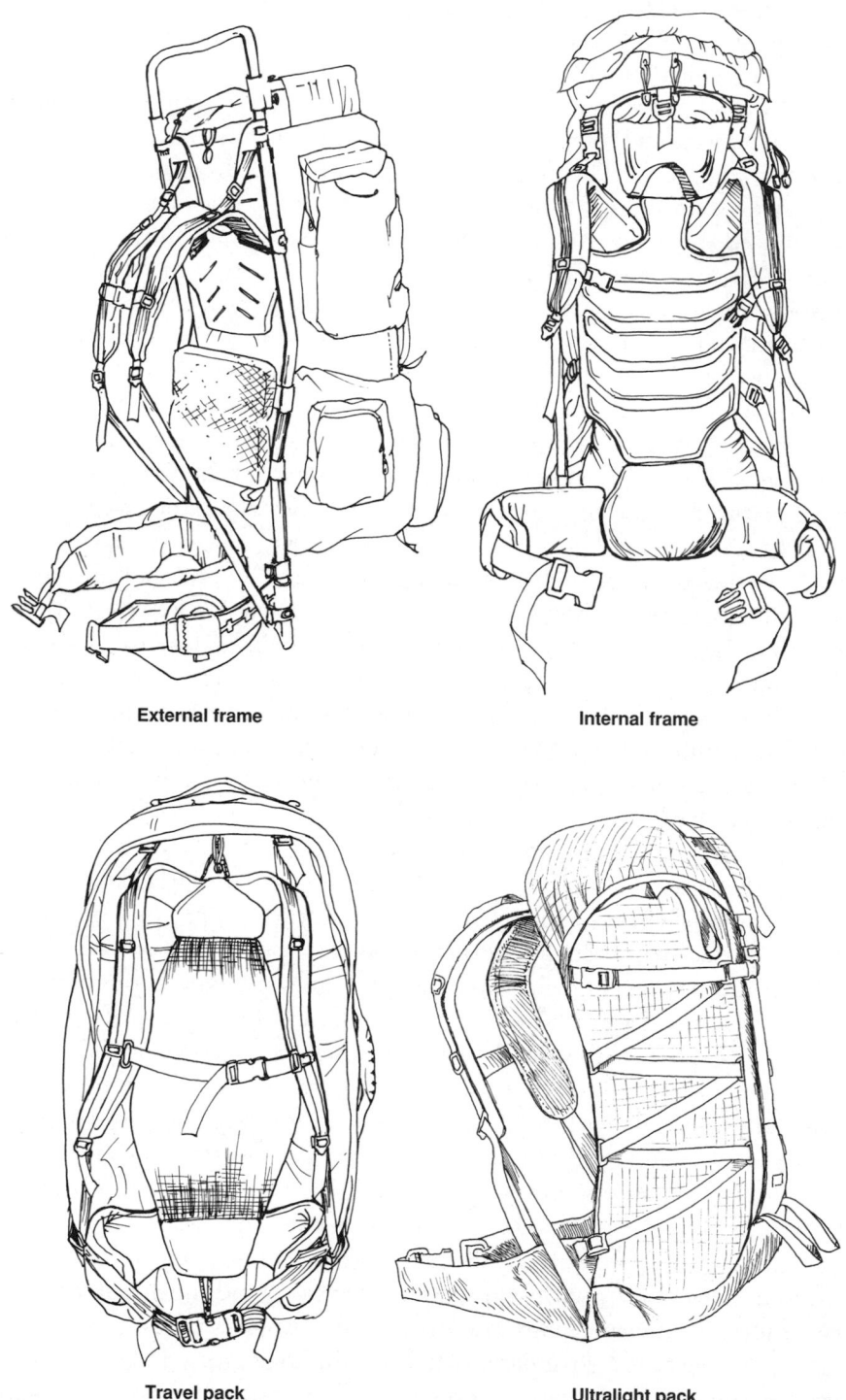

External frame

Internal frame

Travel pack

Ultralight pack

Pack types

Chouinard, and long-haul hikers obsessed with shaving every ounce. Some early ultralight packs had so little structure that they were miserable to carry and were sewn of such thin fabric that they verged on disposability. The newest generation pares weight in sensible ways: light but durable fabrics, carefully rationed padding, fewer compartments and zippers, and thinner straps and smaller buckles. I have a cherished Mont-Bell expedition pack designed by Doug Robinson (5500 cu. in., 3 lbs. 13 oz., no longer available). It needs careful loading but has stood up time and again under vicious burdens like battery boxes and bundles of ice screws without hurting my back. And a saving of 3 pounds out of the box is not to be sneezed at.

DECIDING WHAT KIND OF PACK OR PACKS YOU NEED (OR WANT)

COLIN: The question used to be simply, "What kind of pack will suit me best?" One set of walls, it was assumed, would serve for any version of the house on your back. That was how most people operated. I certainly did. But, as with boots, complexity has opened things up or—if you prefer to see it that way—taken its toll.

You can, of course, still stick to one pack. Most people probably will. But if you do much backpacking of varied kinds you may now decide that you need more than one—because today, much more clearly than yesterday, no one pack is "best." Under different conditions each type offers specific advantages. "The industry," of course, rejoices. Its profound sociological aim: "three or four packs in every American closet." And I, for one, have succumbed. Mind you, my downfall—or uplifting—has been helped along. Some makers regard Chip and me as pros and occasionally send us new products to test. So when you make your own decisions you should probably, in weighing our personal examples, bear that dollar-relevant factor crisply in mind.

CHIP: Scanning the racks in outdoor shops reveals that the decision between E-frames and I-frames is now overwhelmingly resolved in favor of the I-. Some shops no longer stock E-frames, and I spoke with young employees who regard them (and me, for asking) as quaint.

Discounting herd instinct, this reflects two trends. One is the increasing grace of I-frame design, which has given us packs that are comfortable and can carry the sort of loads that most of us wisely avoid. The other is the increasing athleticism of the outdoor population. Whereas a simple walkabout on cleared trails was once the rule, we now bushwhack, rappel, scramble, and canyoneer. If, in nautical terms, the E-frame descends from the Spanish galleon, the I-frame is more closely akin to the kayak. That is, it not only hugs the human body, but, having its bones beneath the skin, resembles one.

An early stab at this intimacy was the Jensen Rivendell Pack, which lacked a frame. Rather, it hugged the hips with a sleeping-bag compartment, surmounted by two vertical tubes. Stuffed tight, it gained structure from the contents. I carried a knockoff made by Wilderness Experience and liked it well enough, though my back sweated up and pimpled.

Introduced in the 1970s, the Lowe Expedition pack balanced huggery with standoffishness, and gave our backs a bit of breathing room. Others like Wayne Gregory and Dana Gleason soon seized the initiative and launched a new tradition of bloody-great-I-frame-sacks. Then E-frame makers like JanSport and Kelty caught the wave, and now sell far more I- than E-frames.

In the 1980s, Lowe also led the way with I-frame packs for women, first the Contour IV and then the Sirocco. Most makers now offer either women's models, or a women's suspension having more taper to the hipbelt, a friendlier strap contour, and so on. But getting the I-frame pack that fits both your body and your purposes can still be a dicey process (for more on fit, see page 169).

Though fewer E-frame packs are sold these days, I still see a great many out on the trail. The E-frame is a proven design and has come down significantly in price, and there are other good reasons for picking one. If you hike in a dignified way, on trails or in open country, the E-frame may please you. If you're somewhat disorganized, it provides a traveling bin into which you can dump gear in no certain order. It allows the breeze to cool your back. Professional beasts of burden, like outdoor-program leaders, choose E-frames for sheer capacity. If you hunt or shuttle awkward loads, most E-frames allow you to shed the packbag and tie a load directly to the bars. If you have small children, the E-frame accommodates more than one sleeping bag and also lets you lash a tired child's pack to the top bar. And they also make perfect backrests.

Another advantage is precisely that of the classic Model T Ford: interchangeable parts. A worn-out hipbelt or a sun-rotted sack can be taken off and replaced, and there's tremendous scope for tinkering.

Yet the longtime disadvantages are still there. E-frames are damnably awkward to load in a car seat or trunk. Airlines and cabdrivers hate them. Their center of mass tends to be high and your load may shift unpredictably. The top bar snags—*oof*—on low limbs. They get creaky with age. Metal parts—clevis pins and split rings—poke holes in tents and catch sweaters or long hair. Some of these disgruntlements have been soothed by new materials and designs, but not all.

If, on the other hand (or foot), you love bushwhacking, scrambling, and slithering, then the I-frame is your bet. I-frames are the only choice for winter pursuits like snowshoeing and skiing. Some previous objections, such as having to stuff one's sleeping bag into a cramped bottom compartment or a lack of organizer pockets, can be finessed by choosing a sack with a zip-out divider and adding accessory pockets.

If it sounds like I favor I-frame packs, well—I do. For a seven-year project collecting water and snow samples in the Wind River Range I used a North Face I-frame of frightening capacity to carry loads of 90 or so lbs. It wasn't always comfortable—no pack is at that weight—but for the off-trail scrambling, snowshoeing, and ski mountaineering my work demanded it was the right tool.

But are internal frame packs really better? Not necessarily. And I'm not just dodging the wrath of devotees whose love for their scuffed Kelty Tioga or REI Cruiser defies both time and fashion. Besides all the scuffed and faded E-frame packs one sees in constant use, there are new designs to bring converts into the fold.

Still, the majority will be happiest with an I-frame. They do cost more, and tend to run about 1 pound heavier than an E-frame of the same volume. But they load easily into compact vehicles, which in turn tend to be cheaper than large ones. So I, for one, would urge you to spend rather more on your pack and less on a car.

Meanwhile, the refinement of travel packs makes them increasingly viable as either a first or all-around pack. Given a range from suitcases-with-straps to full-dress expedition packs with travel covers, in theory all you have to do is find the right point on the spectrum, and pounce.

COLIN: In practice, though, an iceberg looms. One immutable law of the universe has it that the more functions a device is designed to perform, the less perfectly it can perform each of those functions. No adjustable wrench works as well as a closed-end wrench on its designated nut. And no near-suitcase will fit and ride as efficiently as a sophisticated I-frame. So any travel bag involves compromise. Sometimes that may be fine. If you're making a Tuesday-so-it-must-be-Belgium tour of Europe, say, but hope to squeeze in one weekend of light-load backpacking afterward, then something down toward the Samsonite end of the spectrum might suit you admirably. If, on the other hand, you're planning some serious backpacking in the mountains of southern China but can't determine just how you and your equipment will be transported to base camp, you'll probably be well served by a near-expedition I-frame with certain travelwise modifications.

But the problem is rarely as simple as that. For one thing, your needs probably fluctuate from year to year, trip to trip. And in the end your decision will no doubt ride on the range of your activities and the depth of your pocket. If you spend half your life backpacking and mountaineering and ski touring and canoeing and adventure traveling, in roughly equal doses, and if money is no object, then you could—if you bow to consumerism and ignore the needless resource consumption—buy a dozen different packs, each perfect for its own niche, including two or three along the travel-bag spectrum. If, on the other hand, you're appreciably poorer than Croesus, do a fair amount of backpacking in varied terrain, and are now dreaming of a cut-rate trip to Nepal, you might look very seriously at a travel bag that's a mildly modified I-frame expedition bag.

In between—and in between is where most choices will no doubt lie—you just have to make your own assessments about where you'll come down among the many makes and models that are strung out along the travel-bag spectrum (see page 163).

Pack volume

CHIP: Besides the type, another major concern is volume. Sizewise, your *numero uno* all-around packbag should be a comfortable home. It should accept your worldly chattels without bits hanging out like passengers on a third-world bus. Such festooning not only makes for poor load distribution and screwy weight shifts, but also courts disaster in rain or snow. The idea that sheer capacity invites overloading is true to *some* extent, but I think it's better to cultivate a sense of discipline than to have your pack impose it on you. For lesser loads, options like bellows pockets, compression straps, and removable components can scrunch the outside dimensions down to that of the payload.

Most of us have a rough idea of how big a pack we need. But to refine that rough idea, here's a formula (one that my mathematical adviser describes with a grin as "empirically based," i.e., the result of trial and error) to calculate the volume (*V*) in cubic inches of your ideal pack:

$$V = b\,n\,R\,s\,g\,\text{p}$$

b = body weight in pounds + 30
n = square root of the number of days out (For example: $\sqrt{1} = 1$,
    $\sqrt{2} = 1.4$, $\sqrt{3} = 1.7$, $\sqrt{4} = 2$, $\sqrt{5} = 2.2$, $\sqrt{7} = 2.65$,
    $\sqrt{8} = 2.83$, $\sqrt{9} = 3$, $\sqrt{10} = 3.16$, etc.)
R = Resilience (and Complexities)
    0.75: sleeps naked on bedrock, hikes barefoot, eats small animals raw
    1.00: sound sleeper, feet always warm, laughs in the teeth of the wind

1.50: pleasantly normal

2.00: cold sleeper, comfort hound, serious photographer or gourmet chef

2.50: feet of ice/special diet/multiple phobias/needs background music

s = season:

4: summer

5: spring or fall

8: winter

g = gear type

0.9: ultralight

1.0: light

1.2: average

2.0: cast-iron and canvas

p = party size (with packs)

1.5: solo

1.0: two

0.7: three

0.6: four (or more)

Feel free to use values between the buttons; for instance, you might be a slightly cold sleeper—try an R-factor of 1.6.*

Here are some sample calculations. I weigh 215 lbs., average four days out per trip, sleep warm, prefer my food cooked, am most active in spring and fall, use light gear, and usually hike solo. Hence, for V = bnRsg$p$:

$$V = 245 \times 2 \times 1.00 \times 5 \times 1.00 \times 1.5 = 3675 \text{ cu. in.}$$

For ultralight gear, the pack size comes out as 3308 cu. in. Extend the trip to 10 days and the result is 5806 cu. in. for light gear and 5226 cu. in. for ultralight.

For four days in winter with light gear and a partner, it works out this way:

$$V = 245 \times 2 \times 1.00 \times 8 \times 1.0 \times 1 = 3920 \text{ cu. in.}$$

Make that a full week and it comes out 5194 cu. in. These results correspond to the packs I actually use.

Linda weighs 115 lbs., averages three days out per trip, sleeps cold,

---

*My mathematical friend Harvey also suggested using a constant (the 30 lbs. added to body weight) and making the number of days a square root. He helped me rein in other factors while striving to keep the whole thing somewhat simple. Further suggestions are welcome.

enjoys backpacking in high summer, has average-weight gear, and often goes solo. Hence:

$$V = 145 \times 1.7 \times 2.0 \times 4 \times 1.2 \times 1.5 = 3550 \text{ cu. in.}$$

But for a four-day fall solo trip, her volume would be 5220 cu. in. compared to my 3675 cu. in. Besides average versus light gear, the difference is R, resilience. She's a cold sleeper and needs roughly twice the insulation that I do, so for freezing temperatures she'd want a fluffy sleeping bag and more clothing, items that take up considerable space.

An odd result can suggest a change—getting lighter gear, for instance. But at the extremes, the equation either breaks down or conveys a rarefied form of truth; e.g., on a four-day winter trip, a 175-lb. camper with feet of ice, multiple phobias, and average-weight gear (with a partner) would require a 9840-cu.-in. pack. Of course, no one could be comfortable carrying a 9840-cu.-in. pack (if such a thing exists).

The problem can be dealt with in more than one way: a) suffer, b) get a sled for the extra gear, c) talk your partner into pulling it, d) stay home and watch the Adventure Channel, e) come up with a better formula.

Before we closely examine the various breeds of packs, we need to consider what they have in common. First:

SUSPENSION SYSTEMS.

COLIN: The suspension system forms the core of every pack. And the marrow of almost every suspension system is now

The hipbelt.

Things were not always so. When Dick Kelty pioneered aluminum-frame packs in the early 1950s he inherited from the wooden Yukon packboard, essentially unchanged, the ancient and obvious method of hanging a load on the human body: a pair of simple shoulder straps. For years almost the sole advance was a little padding on the straps. Then, in the early 1960s, Trailwise introduced a belt that did more than attempt—as had a few earlier, flimsy affairs—to reduce a pack's sway. At first the new hipbelts were unpadded and rather narrow. But they revolutionized backpacking. A nonhiking friend once slipped my E-frame pack on when it held about 55 pounds and was appalled at the deadweight on his shoulders. I told him to fasten the belt—one of the early, narrow, unpadded kind. "Why," he said when he'd done so, "it practically takes the sting out of the load!" It does too. The belt removes almost all the weight from the shoulders and puts it on your hips.

That's where it belongs. The human backbone has evolved from a system designed primarily for horizontal use, with the weight taken at anchored endpoints. Our newfangled upright stance has therefore assured us a rich legacy of back trouble. Packs with suspension systems consisting only of a shoulder harness imposed fierce vertical pressure on the easily damaged spine. They also put a heavy strain on the muscles of shoulders, neck, and back, hastening fatigue. A hipbelt removes this pressure and strain and transfers the weight to the simple, strong, and well-muscled structure of hips and legs. It also lowers your center of gravity.

The hipbelt has evolved slowly toward bigger and mostly better things: from a simple 2-inch-wide belt of cotton or nylon webbing, through broader Ensolite-padded affairs covered with nylon fabric, to sumptuous foam creations, 4 inches deep or more at the back. If you carried heavy loads you welcomed each advance: the broader and better-padded the belt, the less sting to the load, and the less second-morning hipbelt trauma (page 43).

We seem to be reaching a limit, though. It's not only a limit imposed by added weight and increased heat in the small of the back. For some time the trend in the best packs has been toward broad, contoured (*curvilinear*) belts designed to fit snugly on the hips. But practical difficulties emerged. The new belts look magnificent. They feel fine too—in the store. Yet I've found, along with many people, that under a heavy load most of them tend, after a while, to slide downward in a way that their contouring is specifically designed to prevent. The result is crampingly uncomfortable. At first I thought the trouble might lie in my shape. Everybody's hips and arse are idiosyncratic. (Women, with their broader hip design, have the belt advantage, statistically, over us straighter-up-and-down men.) It seems, though, that I'm far from alone. And some kind of consensus on the reason has now built.

After years of doubt, two fundamental facts of belt design seem to be generally, though still not universally, accepted. First, a fully encircling belt works better than sidestraps from the base of frame or bag. Second, the essential element in a fully effective encircling belt is a continuous, unbroken base of some semistiff material such as webbing. The explanation may be obscure but the pragmatic evidence has grown overwhelming. Unfortunately it seems to be difficult, going on impossible, to sew broad webbing around a curve so that it lies naturally. There are ways around the problem, but they involve such labor-consuming measures as padding layered with foams of differing consistency—and the finished products, though dulcet, are therefore expensive.

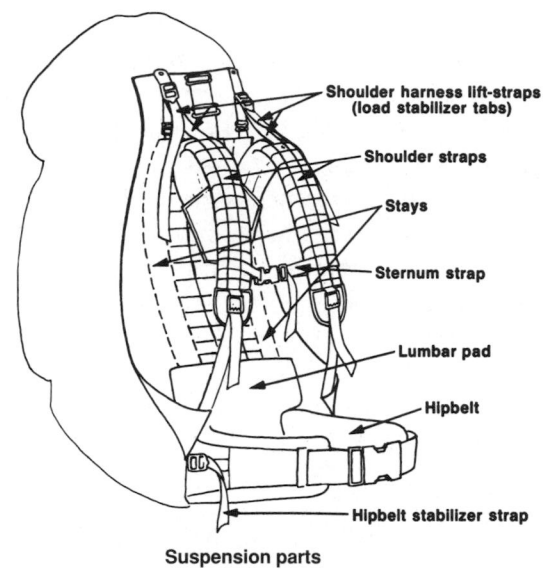

Suspension parts

CHIP: The drive to make the hippest possible belt has led on one hand to complex molding and lamination. Stiff foam or plastic distributes the weight while soft foam padding reduces pressure points. Molded belts are covered in an abrasion-resistant fabric like Cordura with a softer lining, which may be mesh or have wicking characteristics. Some layers are pierced, to circulate air. The best molded-foam hipbelts are almost magically comfortable and, yes, they cost like screeching hell.

On the other hand lies improved fabrication—basic cutting and sewing. I visited the plant of a company whose designers lean this way and watched them slice a foam laminate and then stitch through the nylon covering to form a tapered curve like that of a molded belt. Not requiring a mold, however, this method costs less and allows them to change their design without a huge investment.

But gravity can't be bought off: under really heavy loads, all hipbelts tend to slip. Hitching and tightening have limits, as far as proper digestion and circulation go, plus you can get pressure sores. Most vital is a good fit (see page 169). A patch of high-friction fabric also helps keep the belt from edging down. Some makers line the hipbelt with a faintly sticky mesh, a boon on slick synthetics though not entirely happy on bare skin.

With E-frames, in order to make the suspension bend where the waist does, some makers tried canting their frames forward at the bottom while others, such as JanSport, added flexible plastic hipbelt wings that pivot on the frame. The hipbelt on the Gregory Evolution (yes, Gregory makes an E-frame pack) mounts on a molded "floating bridge." The belt on Dana Design's LoadMaster attaches to a fiberglass "cross-link" rather than to the frame. Different though they are, all these systems seem to work.

Back to I-frames. Another vital aspect is how the hipbelt attaches to the pack. The simplest are sewn on. If they fit, peaches. If not, purgatory. One step up is a removable belt that slides under the lumbar pad and catches with Velcro. Such belts come in sizes and also in different tapers. Next up are wings that attach separately. On my Mont-Bell ultralight, the wings stick down with Velcro to the body of the pack, with the lumbar pad Velcro-ed (if that's an acceptable verb) over the top—simple, and it works.

Farther along are hipbelts like Gregory's, with stiff plastic wings that bolt to a framesheet, adjusting to 16, 18, or 20 degrees of taper. Over these go molded, segmented pads of firm foam with a soft, wicking liner. Does this feel as good as it sounds? It does! Like expensive wines, expensive hipbelts are not invariably better than low-priced ones, but your odds improve.

The hipbelt buckle

of toothy metal is now a relic, at least as original equipment. Even Kelty has replaced their metal quick-release camlock with a plastic side-release buckle.*

Velcro closures tried in the 1980s proved to gather lint, dirt, snow, and to be less than dependable, drawing grunts and curses. Fortunately, in the last decade and a half, the plastic side-release buckle has shed some of its fragility. I used to break them often enough, by stepping on them or slamming them in a car door, that I began carrying a spare. The new ones are tougher plastic with a more positive engagement and a simpler release, and lighter in the main. Some, like Kelty's Scherer Cinch, now allow easy adjustment on both sides.

(*Fastex, Duraflex, Airloc, Nexus*—O brave new world, that has such buckles in it!)

But they still break. Last winter I broke one and had to ski out with an expedition-size pack slithering like a boa constrictor down around my

---

*COLIN: I still prefer the metal camlock, and substitute it for the plastic job on any heavy-load pack that'll accept it. I've never had one break or jam or even whimper. It lets me cinch tighter, more easily. And it quick-releases with a fumble-proof finger flip—though admittedly you then have to unthread the belt end. The metal Kelty camlock is still available from local stores or from American Wilderness at 1-800-284-0365, for about $10.

hips. The problem, besides intense cold, was a thin little guide fence on the receiving end. Latching up with gloves on, I jammed the male part in at an angle and snapped the crummy little fence clean off. When I reported this, with some heat, to the makers of the pack, they let slip that the same buckle had just failed on an Everest climb. So carrying spares on long trips isn't a foolish precaution.

The yoke, or shoulder harness

was slower to change than the hipbelt, even though its function had altered: instead of taking the full load the yoke was called upon to keep the upper part of the pack near the body. Near enough, that is, to harmonize in terms of movement but not so close as to be hot and confining. Single-pin shoulder harnesses, adjustable only for length, did this poorly. Trailwise and other frame-pack makers soon increased the number of attachment points so the width could be varied, added a mesh back panel, and crossed the straps. This added variations for load, slope, slippage, expansion, sore muscles, and all the other elusive factors that add up to either comfort or torture.

Most E-frame makers have moved from the original drilled tubes and clevis pins to plastic frame parts with molded slots to adjust for torso length and width. Once under way, the change in yokes tracked that of hipbelts: rather than the boxy neck gnawers I suffered for years, straps now tend to have a gentle curve, with rounded edges and tapered ends. The best are made of laminated foams that tend to be somewhat stiffer than in the past, but are lined with softer fabrics. On women's models, yokes taper around the trapezius muscles to fit a smaller neck and are shorter overall with more outward curve to the chest. Among full-breasted women a frequent complaint about close-fitting I-frame suspensions is that the shoulder-strap buckles dig in at the sides. In this case, look for a shoulder strap that adjusts at both ends (or a different pack).

The suspension of a full-size pack includes four other major components: a sternum strap, stabilizer straps on the yoke and hipbelt, a backband or back panel, and a lumbar pad. We'll take them in order.

The sternum strap

attaches to the shoulder straps at either end. It adjusts to bodily dimensions such as neck and breast size, and also to changes of clothing, from silk T-shirts to antarctic layers of pile. All have a clip buckle dead center, and most now slide vertically on a piece of flat webbing and can be adjusted without taking off the pack. (Colin: "Also, dammit, without your meaning it to happen!") Another nicety is an elastic tension loop that allows you to breathe. Since you breathe rather often, the elastic eventually gives up the ghost. So a key feature of sternum straps is that they can be replaced.

The sternum strap should spread the load, not the brute gravitation of the pack itself but the fore-and-aft burden, with respect to the spine. Most women choose a higher and narrower configuration, while men prefer low and wide. When crossing a creek or traversing an avalanche track, always disconnect your sternum strap, so that in the event of panic you have only to deal with the hipbelt buckle.

As I-frames took off, the critical relation of load-to-back made other adjustments desirable, and this gave birth to

Stabilizer straps.

The tall, cylindrical top of the I-frame pack tended to lean away from the body and to reef annoyingly at the shoulder straps. So a pair of straps running from the upper face of the pack to the yoke (originally a feature of the Trailwise E-frame pack) was added to I-frame suspensions to limit this motion and to adjust the angle between the load and your back.

Upper stabilizer (or load-lifter) straps are meant to be adjusted with the pack on, and some can be repositioned at both ends (i.e., where they attach to the shoulder strap and also at the packbag, a feature that's desirable if you're tall). But a single height adjustment is okay if it yields the desired 45-degree angle—reckoning from the load down to a line across the top of your shoulder. If the strap describes a lesser angle, the pack's too short for your torso.

The same logic soon led to the use of flexible struts on either side of the hipbelt. Called by a variety of names—snuggers, trim straps, delta straps, or load-transfer straps—these do several things. They limit the side-to-side travel and the pivot of the hipbelt, and they regulate the weight transfer from pack to hipbelt, adjusting how the load carries, from high-and-tight to low-and-loose. On suspensions with flexible rods, straps may run between the rod ends and the hipbelt.

Patrick Smith, at Mountainsmith, doubled the number of straps between the hipbelt and load, to form a pair of triangles. These delta straps, as he calls them, are strikingly effective on fanny packs and also help on full-size I-frames by tucking the weight more neatly into the curve of the spine. But six (four on the hipbelt and two on the yoke) seems to be the practical limit.

The backband or back panel

All E-frames suspend the frame and keep it off your back with either a mesh panel or a foam pad. Older frames had double bands, but a broad single band is now the norm. The backband is held in tension by various means: the simplest have grommets and laces, while others consist of a foam pad covered in mesh, stretched by nylon straps. The tension should be, as Colin puts it, near-tympanic. A refined form is found on the Dana Design LoadMaster, which sports a triangular panel of grippy mesh that tapers down to a single strap to stretch the panel vertically. Gregory's Evolution frame has a molded foam panel, with grooves for air circulation, that mounts on the plastic centerpiece.

I-frames have back panels that range from Spartan (a flat sheet of foam clad in mesh) to elaborate (thermomolded foam laminates bonded to wicking knit fabrics). Don't be seduced by luscious contours. A back panel that works aesthetically might not fit your particular back, and this is the one part of an I-frame pack that's not adjustable. Some people like body-hugging ribs that distribute pressure while others prefer simple foam blocks with plenty of airspace between, drawing us inexorably down to

The lumbar pad,

that island of support that nestles over the crucial lumbar spine. These don't exist on E-frames with encircling hipbelts, but on the majority of other packs they act not only as padding but also as a structural element. The lumbar pad covers the crucial juncture of hipbelt and sack, and in some instances is backed with Velcro to hold the hipbelt in place. Because there tends to be more downward force at the base of the lumbar pad than anywhere on the hipbelt, high-friction fabric, either in a patch or on the whole, prevents slippage.

Now that we're through with the suspension system, we can look to the storage space.

PACKBAGS

Regardless of what sort of frame it's on, a packbag should be strongly stitched of a tough and waterproof fabric. Packs of canvas and leather are now fashion items, with nylon most common. But polyester, aramid, Kevlar, and other materials are creeping in, with fancy combination weaves that owe to developments in fields like auto air-bag technology.

But first, some definitions. The weight of a fabric is measured in *denier,* which is the weight (in grams) of a 1000-meter length of the thread used to weave it. Thus, 600-denier Cordura (the ubiquitous packcloth) is woven of thread that weighs 600 grams per 1000 meters. High-denier fabric tends to be more abrasion-resistant and is used for the bottoms of packs. But it's also, owing to thicker threads with more space between, less waterproof. So most packcloth is *coated* on the inside, where the gunk won't scrape off as quickly. For more on coatings, see below. Meanwhile, let's look at structure.

The basic weave seen in nylon oxford has been augmented by new combination weaves. For instance, Gregory uses a 500-denier ripstop of nylon Cordura with a grid of high-strength Spectra fiber in a contrasting color, giving the cloth a windowpane pattern. JanSport's Hex-Stop packcloth looks like a honeycomb, but thankfully lacks the contrasting hues.

Another new weave is the D^2 (or Dual Denier) developed by Dana Design—after which a slight p-p-pause is in order. Anyhow, a 420-denier high-strength filament nylon is woven in a grid three "picks" (i.e., threads) wide. Within this grid, under less tension, goes a thicker 500-denier Cordura. Visible as little checks, the Cordura stands out from the filament grid to resist abrasion. Overall, the dual-denier fabric has a suppler hand and is lighter overall than standard packcloth.

Another approach is lamination. While rubber-impregated nylon, like the DuPont Hypalon that was developed for rafts, has been around for some time, the new laminated fabrics are curiouser still. A distinctive diamond pattern is showing up in new packs from Cirqueworks and European biggies like VauDe. It's a three-ply weave, faced with 420-denier waterproof nylon, on a diagonal grid of 1000-denier aramid for strength, and lined with a light 40-denier nylon ripstop for internal sleekness.

Kevlar, a fiber used in whitewater canoes, shows up not only in weaves but in seams. Vortex, a small Utah firm, uses bright yellow Kevlar thread to bar-tack the straps on its packs.

Beyond durability, another concern is keeping water out. Coated fabrics have been around for decades, and the earliest coatings tended to peel. My Lowe Liberty pack (circa 1980) now sheds little brown globs inside. New coatings are better, or at least newer, so they don't peel as much. Fully impregnated fabrics like Hypalon are not only waterproof but also airproof. They're also heavy, so they show up mostly in crampon patches or "beavertails" (those rear flaps that compress the load and corral your snowboard, snowshovel, etc.). In general, coatings should be thin and they belong *inside* the pack. Wherever a coated fabric is pierced by stitching, water can get in, so high-grade packs have their seams taped inside. But not all needle holes can be taped—around stays and waistbelt attachments, for instance. So a careful application of seam sealer or water repellent helps keep your load dry.

The colors used in packs have changed, or perhaps circled uneasily. The original cotton canvas, in buff or brown or olive drab, would soil and fade to a gentle tone. Then came early frame packs of nylon in "international" orange, a screaming shade meant to facilitate search-and-rescue. A few years along, when blending into the landscape was again an ideal, packs were made in synthetic-but-earnest greens or browns, and Lowe's baby blue was considered flashy. Black is perennially a sign of Serious Intent, and thus much favored by hardpersons. Yet in the last decade, packs in fashionable shades like copper and rust and indigo crept onto our backs. And more recently has come a revival of fluorescent hues: shrill scarlet, livid lime, and odious orange, all patchworked with black in a way that signals both raw aggression and brooding intent.

Besides the applied-physics aspect (black packs are dark inside and absorb more heat from the sun) and presentability (light colors soon get stained), the main concern is whether you choose to stand out or to blend in. And that should be left up to you.

Once you've decided on the type of frame and the volume (and the color), there are four further decisions that overlap somewhat:

1. Compartments or full-length cavernous sack
2. Top-loader, panel-loader, or a hybrid
3. Pockets (fixed, interchangeable, none)
4. Overall proportion (tall, short, tubular, broad)

So let's take them in order:

1. *Compartments or full-length cavernous sack?* Just as a house is divided into rooms, so are most packs. Even so, for sheer efficiency (capacity divided by the weight of material) the cavernous bloody-great-sack has no equal. To test this proposition, I loaded an undivided 5500-cu.-in. sack to tympanic tension (with real gear, not foam pillows) and carried it a few miles to let the contents settle. I then transferred the load to a multi-compartmented sack of the same rated volume, and *the load wouldn't fit.* I've tried this more than once and the principle holds. That is, compartments and pockets are convenient but they waste space. And, of course, while empty space doesn't weigh much, the fabric needed to enclose it does. I don't mind having to take everything out to get to my sleeping bag, since that's my usual unpacking process. (The trick is to find a stuff sack for your sleeping bag that fits the basement of your pack; see page 178.) Some panel-loading sacks have internal straps for the sleeping bag rather than a divider, an arrangement that suits me fine.

But the usual floor plan is a large upper room with a basement apartment for the sleeping bag. Lowe packs are notable for having the divider steeply angled, which improves weight distribution and makes it easier to get your sleeping bag in. But most dividers are dead level. Removable (or at least fold-back) versions are increasingly common, and often a nuisance. There are center-puckering ones with drawstrings, zippered ones that are supposed to lie flat when not in use (and don't), and strap-and-buckle versions. With the divider removed or disengaged, the hangy-downs that attach it can get caught up in the loading process. So it goes. Some packs will balloon rearward unless the divider is engaged. Another thinkpoint is that even when you fold the divider back, you are still carrying the weight of it. (Since most dividers don't come out they're hard to weigh, but my best guess is 7–10 oz.) The only times I've folded a divider back was to haul bulky snow samples out of the mountains or to carry unwieldy items like a full-size surveyor's tripod in. So while both Colin and I favor undivided sacks (in the way that artists like lofts), most backpackers seem to want their dorsal domiciles divided into rooms.

2. *Top-loader, panel-loader, or a hybrid? Top-loaders* were the starting point in packbag design and are still without a doubt simpler, lighter, and more durable than panel-loaders. To load them properly you must stand them upright, and to reach what lies on the bottom, all else must come out (panel-loading packs are not simply a frivolous fillip of the technological baroque).

But if top-loaders appeal to you, scrutinize the way in which the top battens down. The main entry of a top-loading pack is a pucker, with a drawstring in a fabric casing, cinched through a cord lock. Simple or ultralight packs have a single pucker, but most have two. The outer drawstring keeps the load from mushrooming. The inner drawstring closes the *spindrift collar,* a ring of lighter fabric that keeps out airborne grief and may also lend auxiliary load space. A frequent malady is the sudden ripping of the

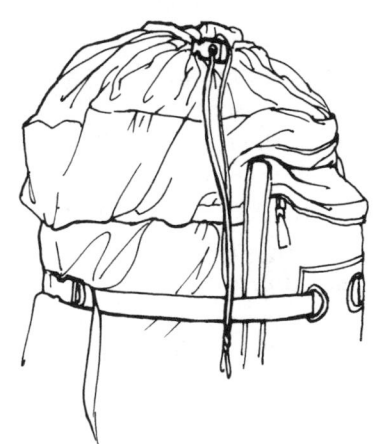

Drawstring top

outer drawcord from its casing (two cougar screams), so the spot where it surfaces should be reinforced with a grommet, doubled fabric, extra stitching, or all three. (Hint: It helps if you don't jerk on it like a madman.) Many sacks now back up the main drawstring with a top-compression strap. Some of these anchor on the outside of the pack and cinch over the top of the spindrift collar while others fasten inside (in which case light-colored webbing adds visibility).

Over the double pucker rides a top pocket. Some top pockets are sewn on, opening with one or two clip buckles while others "float" on adjustable straps to let you overload the pack, or to remove the pocket entirely. Of lasting interest is how well the top pocket's flap (or skirt) hugs the pack's contours. The outer edge of the skirt should overlap the bag's rim by 2 to 3 inches, with a tailored cut or elastic sides to snug it down. Imagine yourself on a high ridge with rain blowing not merely sideways but upward, and judge accordingly.

Less obvious but no less important is the color of a top-loading pack. Black is the color of my true-loved midsize Jay Goodwin (for philosophical reasons). Consequently the pack is Stygian within. A dial thermometer in a black leather case was lost for six months. So if you carry a black top-loader, use a headlamp to unpack and be sure to up-end it after every trip.

The *panel-loader* was (according to JanSport) invented by JanSport in 1971. Nearly all makers offer them, and some makers now sell nothing but. My first really good pack, a Lowe Liberty (circa 1980), was a panel loader, and I've had others over the years. The panel opens the pack up in the way a suitcase does, to allow precision loading and a leisurely gathering-in. The encircling zippers give rapid access to any part of the load. But this very convenient openness also means that things can fall—inconveniently—out. If you've ever unzipped a panel and had your stove in its cookpot drop out and roll down a steep snow slope, then we share this particular insight. Another minus: when a panel-loading pack is laid flat for loading, the suspension suffers in snowy or muddy or thorny spots. But above all, the rub, the Achilles' heel, the fatal flaw is that around that zippily convenient panel lurks 3 or 4 feet of *zipper.* Zippers are more tractable these days than the dragon-toothed, beard-eating nightmares of the past, but are still the weak link. So if you buy a panel-loader make sure that crucial zippers are backed up by compression straps or some other means of keeping your treasures corraled. Or, if you're one of those lucky people who actually thinks ahead, when the zipper starts to get cranky, have it replaced. Lowe Alpine has graciously performed two zipper renewals on my old Liberty pack.

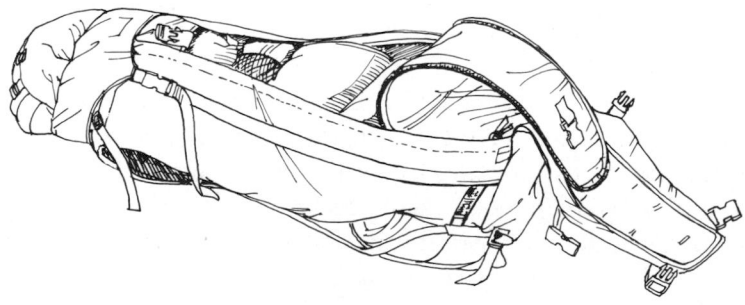

Pack with panel, unzipped

A new company, Lodestone, introduced a line of packs-without-zippers, but they (the company, that is) folded before I could get my trembling mitts on one.

In these days when purity is perishingly rare, so is the pure top- or panel-loading pack. Most often, one finds a top-loading upper compartment and a lower one with a zippered panel, known as a *hybrid loader*. (Grammarians had better not dwell on that.) Having covered the virtues and vices of both parents, we needn't belabor the offspring. But if you have to jam and cram, then do your worst in the top-loading sector and treat the zippered parts with care. Another more recent hybrid mates the drawstring top compartment with a zipper access. The Arc'Teryx Bora 95 has a zipper down the left side, while the entire rear panel of the Osprey Advent unzips and flops out like a great big tongue. The Mountainsmith Alpenfire pack that Linda's been using lately has a single zipper in a J shape to access both the sleeping-bag compartment and the right side of the pack (which gives it a lopsided grin). Another means of entry, found on smaller packs, is a zipper that arcs like a rainbow over the top. Again, if you tend to cram your pack to bursting, this type is likely to blow, so check for backup straps or tabs. Or get a "pure" top-loader instead. A unique hybrid is the "X-access" system on the Camp 7 P.O.D. pack, with four overlapping panels that open outward, like a budding gentian. But the concept, while interesting, hasn't really caught on.

3. *Pockets (fixed, interchangeable, none)?* Besides the major partition, there may be attics, closets, cabinets, and dustbins. Some top pockets double as arse-kits, a useful option, although high-end makers go overboard with padded waistbelts, etc., adding unnecessary weight. A greater concern is whether the load you actually carry matches up with the available space. Most full-size packs also have storage in the rear: a big zippered stash (miscalled a kangaroo pocket, since marsupials are strictly front-loaders) or a mesh sleeve. Each side might sport one or two pockets, or means to attach them.

External pockets promise convenience, and to some extent deliver it: one for the fuel bottle, one for the water bottle, one for the binoculars, and so forth. But in practice (and practice is all) one finds that these appliances are all either somewhat larger or smaller than the available pocket. A friend who's run a backpacking shop for years claims that the savvy of a backpacker is inversely proportional to the number of fixed pockets on his pack. "Geeks love pockets," says he. (Ahh—I hear the howls of the mob already.)*

So let me hasten to say that some *very* good packs have fixed pockets:

---

*COLIN: I love them, too—for specific things (pages 685–87).

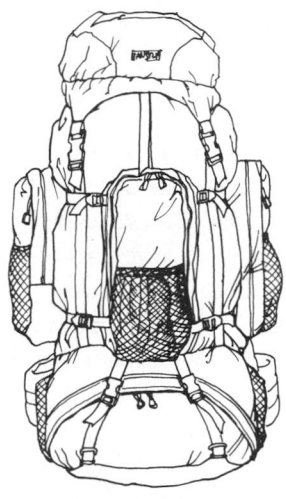

JanSport Rockies   **Vortex STX**

the JanSport Rockies (above left) has one rear and one per side, with three additional mesh sleeves, for six altogether. While the Vortex STX (above right), sort of a Porsche Speedster as packs go, hath none.

My reflection (as opposed to my friend's provocation) is that the desire for fixed pockets tends to decrease as a function of steepness. That is, mountaineering packs have fewer fixed pockets because *pockets catch on things.* Whereas packs meant for level-footed travel may be enhanced by auxiliary compartments (one for the Bible, one for the sextant, and so forth).

But in this instance, you most certainly can have it both ways. One fixed pocket astern won't lessen the expeditionary swank of a good sack. And—depend on it—even the most starkly unpocketed model will have patches, tabs, sliders, buckles, and compression straps to attach whatever you choose.

Nearly every maker of packs sells a nice, sober sidepocket with the proportions of a brick. I've long used a vintage Gregory brick pocket as my main ditty bag, and have a pair of Lowe Kit Pouches that, by virtue of trickily sewn tabs, can barnacle onto a pack upright or sideways, or hang via tabs at the ends. Several makers supply mesh pockets (for water and fuel bottles, pestilent socks, etc.), organizers with built-in filing systems, and culinary pockets for spoons, spices, etc. Pouches and sheaths abound for cameras, crampons, fly rods, snowboards, water bladders: you name it. VauDe even makes a detachable and self-sealing pouch for packing out human waste (page 702). JanSport has an elaborate modular pocket system that gives you the option of carrying virtually the entire contents of your pack outside it. So the key here is to focus on your real needs/obsessions. Scout leaders will want a large first-aid pocket, with moleskin, dressings, and tranquilizers easy to hand. Fishmeisters will want rod, reel, and all those glinting, feathery bits for that moment when Leviathan rises. Meditative types might want to check out Osprey's Vector Easy Chair (a buttock pocket). And although it might only seem this way to me, JanSport's #49705 insulated "tool scabbard quart" seems made for a bottle of Pouilly-Fuissé and a corkscrew.

Once you've picked out your pockets, the question arises: what should go in each one? And then how do you find it? Some packers prefer to code pockets by color: fuel red, water blue. When I use pockets, they're monochromatic; the most-used item, say a water bottle, goes in the pocket where my right hand naturally lights. From there, I assort things in the manner of a clock face: water at two o'clock, raincoat at four, and so on. The fuel bottle, which comes out late and goes in early, is at ten o'clock. Lefties should reverse the order.*

4. *Overall proportion (tall, short, tubular, broad)?* Opposites attract, sometimes wildly so. Nevertheless, the overall shape of your packbag should closely resemble your own. When you try on packs, look at yourself calmly and without vanity in the mirror. If you're by God built on the horizontal plan, it's damned silly to get one of those tall, tubular sacks that will rear up above your head and throw you off balance with every sneeze. Instead get something like a Kelty White Rim, Slickrock, or Zuni—wider I-frame bags. Kelty's E-frames are also built lower and wider than, for instance, JanSport's. Gregory's I-frames are tall and slim, while I-frames by Cirqueworks and Mountain Tools are tailored to the compact mesomorph. If you use a staff or trekking poles or intend to ski with the pack, a wide packbag or fixed sidepockets will scuff your elbows in a maddening way.

Another issue lurks just out of sight: the back of your head. If it bumps on your pack 35,000 or so times in the course of a trip, it might just put you in an unreceptive mood. Some makers build in a recess (my Arc'Teryx pack has one that would fit a pteranodon), but if the pack's too tall or short for your frame, your head will miss it.

And, in deeply mysterious fashion, that brings us to

Z-z-z-zippers!

They make grand schemes possible, as far as pack design, not to mention tents, clothes, and so on. But when they fail they fail absolutely, at the worst possible moment—on the summit, as lightning flicks its bright tongue from the wall of cloud to the west.

*COLIN: Different-colored pull tabs on the zippers let you have it both ways.

Like plastic clip buckles, zippers are now far, far better than they were. But they're still the most vulnerable part of a pack or any outdoor gear. Metal zippers have given way to nylon coil designs, which are smoother and somewhat self-repairing. But they do melt (don't ask). Likewise, keep 'em out of sand or grit—it doesn't hurt to blow or spritz zippers clean after a trip. A vacuum-cleaner brush attachment does a nice job, and so do handheld plant sprayers. Oily sprays like WD-40 have a way of staining fabrics, but I've run the butt of a candle over a cranky zipper as a temporary fix. There are wax-based zipper lubes on the market, though most attract dust and grit, in which case you might occasionally daub them clean with alcohol. At least one combination zipper lube/lip balm has been cooked up but doesn't yet have FDA approval. But that does suggest the fragrant possibility that lip balm can get a balky zipper through a trip. Those with pliers on their pocket tools can try parting the edges of the slider, returning it to the end of the track, and then squeezing it back on with slightly less clearance, which might get you home at least.

Arc'Teryx, a Canadian firm not given to fantasy, just introduced waterproof zippers on their parka pockets and bravely left off the obligatory storm flaps. But the main zipper is a tried-and-true nylon coil type. Stay tuned.

Another aspect of zippery and pocketry is that pack makers now decorate each zipper pull with a handy little loop. Handy, that is, unless you bushwhack. On catching a branch tip or stub, these little loops will, at best, simply stop you dead in your tracks. At worst, the resulting inertial gradient will have Consequence. This happened to me when I was skiing with a full pack down a narrow, tree-spiked ridge, admittedly at unsafe speed. As I slalomed the trees, the handy little zipper loop handily hooked a stub on a whitebark pine, around which I subsequently orbited, skis outermost, and then French-kissed with my head.

While this rated *at least* three cougar screams, I could manage only one.

So I now snip off each and every little standard-equipment snare and replace it with a swallowtail, thus: take a 4- to 5-inch piece of light, bright cord or nylon ribbon, double it, and slip the loop through the zipper pull. Then thread the two ends through the loop and, gripping the pull with your other hand, jerk smartly.

Another means is to loop cord through the zipper pull and then clamp it close to the pull with one of those aluminum collars used to cinch light cable. Artistic types can run it snugly through a fancy bead (or beads, to color-code your load). Meanwhile, designers who actually *use* packs have come up with alternatives; for instance, Vortex molds a grippy rubber tab over each pull. But most continue to festoon their products with little death loops, so beware.

. . .

So far, we've been looking at features common to both I- and E-frame packs. But now it's time (the Walrus said) to talk of E *or* I. And the question of precedence naturally arises. If *The Complete Walker* were stringently alphabetical, E-frames would come first, and likewise, if this were a history of backpacking. But since both Colin and I, not to mention most of you gentle readers, now sling our frames with I-frame packs—the I's have it.

INTERNAL-FRAME PACKS

An endearing quirk of the human beast is the regular turning of tables. I'm just old enough to recall when faith in I-frames, except in climbing circles, fell somewhere between bad taste and rank heresy (a close friend once called them "infernal frames"). Yet now, anything short of a snorting disdain for E-frames is met with a similarly long-nosed squint.

Our abiding interest, though, should be in what works. And that seems like a stepping-off point for a discussion of that most crucial element—

The frame.

First came aluminum stays, in pairs, either parallel or crossed in an X. Besides lightness, an advantage of aluminum is that flat stays can be bent to follow the back's curve, though for years I was too superstitious to do this.

On one trip, when I-frames were new, my coconspirator in the ascent of a peak kept stopping to remove and rebend his stays. But (since his load included a canned ham and a half-gallon jug of wine) he couldn't get the balance *quite* right. At last, mere yards below the gleaming summit, where we planned to bivouac and attain perfect enlightenment, he dug in his heels again. Rebending his previous bends and swearing a blue streak, he lost his balance, slipped on the snow, and *made* a blue streak. He did manage to self-arrest with the stay, twisting it into something like a giant, dull fishhook. Which object he gazed at solemnly, and then, with a cougar scream, flung into the void. We never did find the damn thing. Thence and therefore, I decided to keep my stays safely out of sight.

Dumb, I admit. Stays are meant to be bent. And a great many makers now prebend them, so you might get a good fit right out of the box. But if not, it makes sense to do your bending at the store, with help, or in a considered way at home (see Fitting, page 167). Along with flat bars there are extruded beams, meant to be flexible lengthwise and torsionally rigid. Above all, a stay must have *zing*. So besides bendable aluminum, these supporting members of I-frames are now made of zingier things: fiberglass, carbon-fiber composites, Delrin, and polycarbonate.

Diverging from two simple flat stays, I-frame designs now incorporate wands, arches, hoops, bows, framesheets, tension panels, and so on, under a mad array of proprietary names. Hence, a few examples (of full-size packs) are in order.

Lowe relies on two aluminum stays, prebent to an average contour, and on some packs adds a flexible Delrin hoop called a "crossbow." This arches in a sheath around the load, at an angle controlled by several straps (pack second from left, page 125). The "bow" is intended to do two things: to transfer weight to the waistbelt, in the way a flying buttress does for cathedrals, and to compress the upper part of the pack, preventing weight shifts.

Dana Design's new ArcLight I-frames have a single aluminum stay in the center with a crosspiece at shoulder height. Two full-length fiberglass rods transfer weight to the hipbelt and are topped by a nylon crosspiece that shapes a recess for the head. Backing all this is a plastic framesheet. The setup is easy to adjust and comfortable—except for the diagrams in the catalog, you wouldn't know all that stuff was in there.

Framesheets of thin plastic have caught on like a sparkler in rabbitbrush, since they lend something like the support of an E-frame while being, technically, internal. Gregory now uses a curved framesheet of high-density polyethylene (HDPE) backed with two alloy stays. The limiting factor is that HDPE framesheets can be curved in only one direction. At least this is the claim of the youngsters at Granite Gear, who base their packs on 3-D molded framesheets. These are more rigid than flat sheets of HDPE, but their complex curvature reduces their *need* to flex (see next page).

Is anything getting simpler? The answer is yes, the reason is *cost*. While colossal firms have shifted their manufacturing to low-wage plants overseas, smaller domestic outfits must now rack their brains for ways to simplify production in order to keep labor costs under control.

One striking success is Osprey's Flexion Series I-frame, with one center stay, an oval framesheet, and a Delrin hoop. This Spartan but comfortable rig is mated to a taco-style packbag sided with panels of thin, stiff foam: instead of compression straps at the sides, it has two straps across the back that draw the "taco" in. I tried one, and it works. It also rolls up tight (like an enchilada) for compact storage.

As pack volumes decrease, internal structure gets simpler: A 2500-cu.-in. pack might be framed with stays, or a framesheet, or a flexible hoop—needing, at most, two out of three. A common layout in the mid-

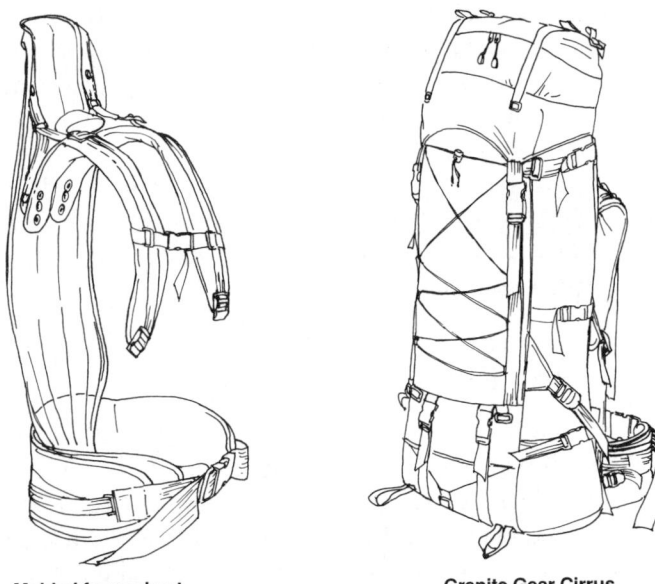

Molded framesheet   **Granite Gear Cirrus**

size and daypack range is a framesheet and single center stay. Ultralights are another story (page 160).

One perplexing aspect of the frames themselves is that, being internal, they're hard to see. Most catalogs have diagrams of how the frame is made and how it works. But before dropping $400 plus on a new I-frame pack, it makes good peasant sense to get down on the floor with it and poke around. For one thing, look at the degree to which the frame components are permanently sewn or glued in place or, on the other hand, removable and replaceable.

Having the back panel and lumbar pad sewn to the bag is a frequent arrangement. This is good for coupling the load to the suspension, but since the lumbar pad and back panel are both foam, and are covered in either mesh or stretch fabric, they are relatively delicate. (Come to think of it, they are somewhat like our own lower parts.) So, when setting down your pack, be gentle.

Makes and models of I-frames

Colin and I undertook this update knowing that we couldn't possibly cover everything. So we looked instead for representative items. In part this was a studied process, with hours spent poring over stacks of catalogs, magazines, and such. We kept our eyes open, on the trail and at trade shows. But there's also a random element, trusting that what catches one's fancy is somehow significant.

Partisanship enters in. Colin's *affaire de cœur* with Gregory packs is well known. At a crucial point in my life I met a blue Lowe Liberty, and like a lovestruck duckling, imprinted. Because they made genuine women's models early on, Linda also has a great *afición* for Lowe packs. Such loyalties are human.

But a restaurant critic who refused to dine at any but a few old favorites (or rehashed the glories of haunts long since closed) would not only do his readers a deep disservice but would also be boring. So in that spirit, we sampled the newest

Full-size packs.

Arc'Teryx packs are gorgeous, and my favorite in the over 6000-cu.-in. class is their cobalt blue Bora 95 (6040 cu. in., 7 lbs. 12 oz., $395; top right, page 130). It's flawlessly constructed, each piece cleanly cut with scrupulously taped seams and tight, even stitching. It's also a thoughtful piece of design. My gear goes in smoothly, and the stated volume is conservative in terms of what the pack actually holds. Even under winter-solo loads, the suspension is profoundly adjustable and has no pressure points whatever. You can pop the top pocket off in seconds for arse-baggery, and its cunning buckle/D-ring setup gives considerable scope for strapping on extra clothes, etc.

One nonpareil feature is the ¾-length rear pocket that will not only accept an iced-up tent and fly, but by virtue of heat-absorbing blackness, also melt out the ice and drain it through a strategically punched grommet. You have to try this truly thoughtful design to fully appreciate it. Like most Arc'Teryx packs, the Bora comes in various sizes, with a women's-fit package available.

There are bigger packs out there, like the Astralplane from Dana Design (7540 cu. in.), the 7000 (7300 cu. in.) from Vortex, and the Cirrus (7000 cu. in.) from Granite Gear. But for years, in the name of science, I carried a huge pack and am, frankly, over it. Besides, the bounty of light and compact gear now on hand makes huge packs unnecessary, except for all-out expeditions.

Here's a quick rationale. My relentlessly pared-down 3-season kit (including either a tarp and groundcloth or an ultralight tent) weighs 25 lbs. and occupies about 2500 cu. in. For a good, long trip, with no caches or drops, 65 lbs. isn't an unreasonable starting load. So a 6000-cu.-in. pack gives me a potential payload (food, water, etc.) of about 3500 cu. in./40 lbs. This amounts to a week of luxurious decadence or two or three times that, with Spartan virtue. For winter trips, more fuel, a stouter tent, and fatter clothes take up space, but instead of carrying water I can melt snow. Plus, I don't usually stay out as long, so a 6000-cu.-in. pack is about right. (For calculations on volume, return to page 134.)

In the well-accoutered backpacking class (5700–4250 cubic inches, that is, high-fives to low-fours) are a great many packs, in a range of volumes and harness sizes. Sticking to what Linda and I actually carried on trips, there are several standouts.

Dana Design's Swiftcurrent (5000 cu. in., 6 lbs. 4 oz., $340; see page 146) defines the hybrid-loader concept. An undivided sack with a drawstring top and internal straps for a sleeping bag, it has a full-length rear panel that gets around the stress problems of curved zippers by using two straight ones on a trapezoidal panel. Another problem with hybrid loaders is leakiness, but on the Swiftcurrent both zippers are covered by flaps, and the top pocket is tailored for a tight fit. I tested this inadvertently by fording a stream that turned out to be roughly twice as deep as I thought, and the Swiftcurrent kept the swift current out. It has the ArcLight frame described on page 152, with a suspension (in men's and women's versions) that's easy to adjust. Dana Design hipbelts are particularly yummy, and tinkering reveals that they work on packs by other makers with similarly Velcro-ed slots.

The Gregory Petit Dru Pro (4750 cu. in., 7 lbs. 4 oz., $430) is aimed at the hard-core female alpinist, but Linda ranked it high for backpacking

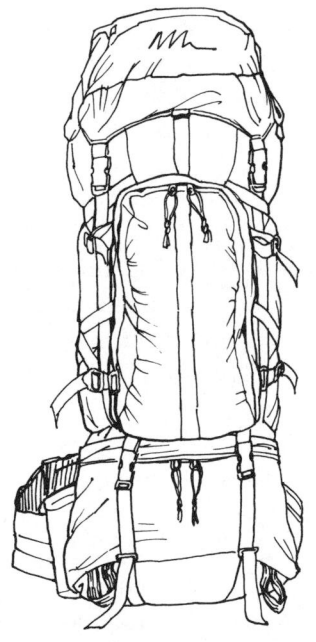

Gregory Petit Dru Pro

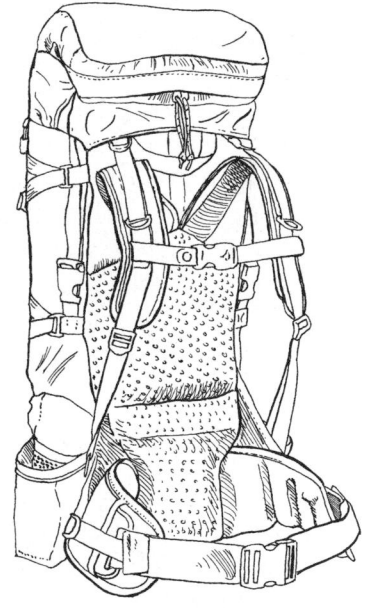

Gregory Palisade

as well: "The top pocket, main compartment, and rear pockets are sized so that my gear fits without juggling and the sleeper accepts a 0°F winter bag, with a divider that comes out. Color-coded straps make it easy to differentiate their functions, and the quick-release buckles on the V-compression straps let me add sidepockets, carry a fly rod, etc." A hydration system comes with the pack. The Gregory Pro series offers a range of packs, sizes, and adjustments.

For the all-around backpacker, the Gregory Palisade (5400 cu. in., 7 lbs. 4 oz., $285) sports the same logical arrangement of pockets and straps and a similar frame, yoke, and waistbelt. The sleeping-bag hutch was a bit tight for my winter-weight long. But Gregory's Contour stuff sacks end the frustration of trying to cram a tubular sleeping bag into a rectangular space. Meanwhile, the Palisade carried so well that at times it seemed more like an antigravity pod, lifting me up rather than weighing me down. But the tall, narrow profile makes the pack rather tipsy—to discourage you from tying anything on top, Gregory leaves off the usual rigging points.

The elegantly simple Gregory Thru Hiker (5350 cu. in., 5 lbs. 2 oz., $230) is a lightweight, undivided top-loading bag on the same Adventure Series frame and suspension as the Palisade. In a lighter-weight fabric, it has two pairs of side compression straps with big mesh scoops low down, intended for water bottles, etc. (One unintended consequence being that when you set the pack down in snow, little chunks are forced through the mesh, building into a good-size snowball.) Rear accessory loops and a bungee give scope for parkas, raingear, and ice tools. I developed a soft spot for the Thru Hiker because it was one of the very, very few packs that actually weighed *less* than the catalog claimed. Also, it made me feel noble, which is harder to explain.

For pocket lovers, the JanSport Rockies is another good carry (regular: 5400 cu. in and 5 lbs.; tall: 6200 cu. in. and 5 lbs. 5 oz.; both $170; page 148, left). Besides the two main compartments and hundreds of pockets, there's a wide range of adjustment, and the wishbone-shaped back padding disperses heat nicely (but spreads out under really heavy loads). As packs go, the Rockies is both good-natured and modestly priced.

Other good values in this range are the REI Traverse series packs—for some years I used a Valhalla Traverse (4500 cu. in., 5 lbs. 9 oz., $160) for slickrock trips because the clean side profile was good for slot-canyon shrugs. The Lowe Australis 80 (4880 cu. in., 4 lbs. 11 oz., $155) is another well-designed basic pack. But it has a reflective crisscross bungee cord that really wakes you up the first time you flash a light on it—it looks like a ghost in a corset. An increasing number of packs and tents have reflective parts, to help you find them if you're lost in the dark.

Stealth campers might steer clear of glow-in-the-dark parts for the same reason.

Linda swore by the Lowe Alpine Contour IV for years until the fully feminized Sirocco came out, and she now swears by that, having carried one for thousands of miles on trail-mapping and building projects (the Sirocco II is 4200 cu. in., 6 lbs. 2 oz., $240). The unpocketed exterior is medium-tall and slim. The waterproof sleeping-bag stash has trapezoidal zips that make it easy to stuff in a big sleeping bag.

Lowe Sirocco II   **Mountainsmith Alpenfire 48**

But lately she's been test-firing a Mountainsmith Alpenfire 48 (4800 cu. in., 5 lbs. 15 oz., $280). The pack has a lopsided grin, owing to a big J-shaped zipper that accesses both the right side of the top compartment and the sleeping bag. Says she: "I was skeptical of the zipper arrangement, but wound up liking how accessible it made spare clothes and such. My winter bag fit fine and the storage space was thoughtfully designed." She found the foam-block suspension to be comfortable and well ventilated, except for a bit of strap chafing low down on the yoke, which extended padding would solve.

Vortex Packs are made in Salt Lake City, Utah, next door to a favorite Mexican restaurant. So after touring the plant I came away full of green chile with a flame-red STX pack (see page 148, right; about 4500 cu. in., 5 lbs. 13 oz., $330). I say it's about 4500 cu. in. because it has a broad spindrift collar and a floating top pocket that let you extend the volume smoothly without messing up the balance. What sets Vortex off is, *numero uno,* a molded-foam back panel that's actually shaped like your back; i.e., the pads curve up in the center to fill the valley of your spine.

I didn't expect to like this, but did. *Numero dos,* the stays, rather than being aluminum, are polycarbonate, extruded in a shape that my western background leads me to call a Flying U. Polycarbonate is "unbreakable, half the weight, and 12 times as strong as aluminum." *Numero tres,* all the straps and daisy chains go into at least two seams and are bar-tacked with Kevlar thread. I used the STX for snowshoe tests, carrying winter bivouac gear *and* three extra pairs of webs. I also used it for stream-channel studies that involved 100-foot tapes, bank stakes, field guides, and other unwieldy junk, with constant in-and-out. This relentless abuse produced one small hole, poked by a bank stake that I jammed in sideways—it was snowing like hell—and some loose stitches in the nylon tape around the lumbar pad. But Vortex's warranty promises to repair any damage, even if it's your fault: a refreshing, no-guilt-trip approach.

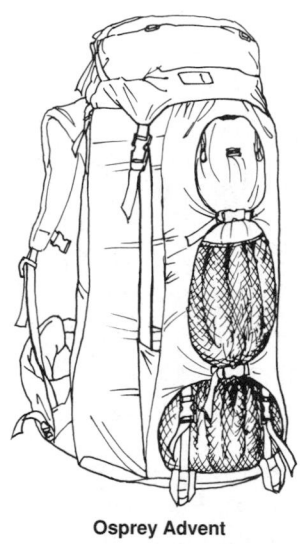
Osprey Advent

Osprey Isis

Along with hybrids we should look at the mutants. I picked the Osprey Advent (men's large: 4600 cu. in., 5 lbs. 15 oz., $290) from the Straightjacket Series. If you're used to straps and more straps, these packs are inscrutably smooth, with buckles in all the wrong spots. Some of the weirdness owes to the buckles centered in back that, pulling on taco panels of thin, stiff foam, provide whole-body compression. The pack also has hidden buckles on the side that let you roll the pack into itself for compact storage (see page 166). I set out with a 43-lb. load and a fine-edged skepticism. But after a week the Advent had become sort of a pet. The foam-panel compression worked like a dream. I was logging stream-channel data, so the combination of drawstring top and bomb-bay zipper panel was handy: the undivided sack opens wide like a duffel. The top pocket is roomy and converts to an arse-kit. The big mesh pocket on the back is good for stowing my dripping stream gear. The updated Advent has these features plus an improved bottom design and a mesh scoop on each side for water bottles, etc.

As much as I liked the Advent, the hipbelt managed to score two red zeros on my pelvic goalposts. (Back home, I discovered that a Dana Design molded belt would fit and, taking the hybrid idea one step further, stuck one on.)

But the foam-taco concept is brilliant, from the 5600-cu.-in. Osprey Mutant to the 1100-cu.-in. Skimmer. My artist friend Hannah, who finished up the illustrations for this book, uses the Scarab (2000 cu. in., 2 lbs. 7 oz., $125) for her sketchpads, journals, and paintboxes. Besides the Straightjacket Series, Osprey also makes the more conventional Vector Series packs (such as the Isis pictured on the previous page) with a focus on interchangeable components. There's also a subspecies of travel Ospreys (see page 165).

Midsize I-frame packs

For me (over 6 feet tall and 215 lbs.) midsize stretches from about 4250 cu. in. down to 3500 or so, while for Linda (5 feet 4 and 115 lbs.) the midrange tops off where mine bottoms out. But the following for these packs has developed so that they are now available in corresponding sizes. For example, the wildly popular Gregory Reality ($220) comes in four sizes, from a 4050-cu.-in. large (5 lbs.) to a 3420-cu.-in. X-small (4

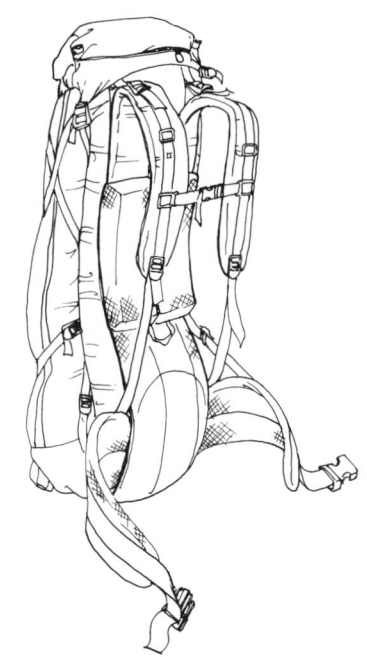

Mountainsmith MountainLight 3500

lbs. 7 oz.). An outstanding midsize value is the Kelty Tornado (men's: 3700–4000 cu. in., 4 lbs. 10 oz.; women's: 3600–3800 cu. in., 4 lbs. 8 oz.; both $130), which scored the highest rating in a recent *Backpacker* magazine test, at the lowest price.

I tried the midsize Mountainsmith MountainLight 3500 (3500 cu. in., 3 lbs. 10 oz., $240. Optional carbon-fiber stays shave 3.5 oz. and cost a sobering $60). Rather than leaving things off, Mountainsmith reduces the weight of all components, yielding a slim, undivided sack with a well-padded and highly adjustable suspension, in both men's and women's sizes. The 3500 has a top pocket with a zip ditty bag, side straps connected to a rear compression panel (with a Velcro shovel loop and rear bungee), and quick-release loops for ice tools. So, besides its suitability for weekend trips and through-hiking, the MountainLight works for climbing and ski tours. Last November I carried the midsize 3500 on a snowshoe trip across a high plateau and down narrow canyons. Low temperatures were around 15°F and it snowed at night, with gusts of wind. Despite the slender profile of the pack, my load of just over 30 lbs., including a solo tent, fit entirely inside with a Reflectix pad lashed on the back (for a gear list, see Appendix II). In distinctly wintry conditions I was not only comfortable but luxuriously so, and found once again that lightweight gear makes traveling the snowpack much easier. After only a short acquaintance, I've half-adopted the MountainLight 3500—it's good-looking, waterproof, and rugged for the weight. In summer I could easily get a full week out of it and am already plotting some off-trail scrambles.

In general, the virtues and flaws of each maker's midsize packs tend to echo those of full-size models. Features that are crucial on bigger sacks, like load-lifter straps, dividers, and hipbelts, are more clearly subject to the razor cut of performance versus weight. Another key point is that lighter loads—35 lbs. down to 20 or so—make happiness that much easier to find. If you're attracted to midsize packs and already have compact gear, then it's just a matter of arranging the furniture in your new traveling home. If you're starting out fresh, then you should choose gear that's especially suited to the snug little cottage on your back.

Ultralight I-frame packs

The first question is: just how light is ultralight? The logical way to decide is to divide the capacity by the weight of the pack. For a benchmark, about 50 cu. in. per ounce is the average for packs-in-general, while my old Mont-Bell Expedition 90 (5500 cu. in., 3 lbs. 13 oz.) weighs in at 90 cu. in. per ounce.

But the lightest of the light are spookily so: the Kelty Cloud 60 (5050 cu. in., 1 lb. 2 oz., $400) at 280 cu. in. per ounce and the Kelty Vapor 45 (4250 cu. in., 1 lb. 1 oz., $350) at 250 cu. in. per oz. These gossamer ghosts are made of white Spectra (transparent when wet). I've yet to get my hands on one for a tryout, but the concept is simple. The basic bag is very light and also lacking in structure. To increase the load-carrying capacity you can add frame elements, padding, and pockets, all of ultralight construction.

Minimalism is also carried to extremes on the GoLite Breeze (rated 2700 but actually about 3000 cu. in., at 12.4 oz. and $120). The Breeze is a Ray Jardine–style pack without stays, a sternum strap, or a hipbelt. Jardine's theory, expounded in *Beyond Backpacking,* is that your load should be kept so light that you don't need them. (GoLite, a new company, sells ounce-shaving clothes, a fly tarp, and a combination sleeping bag/pad similar to those used by Jardine.) The Breeze, at a thistledowny 244 cu. in. per oz., also lacks a top pocket (the top is a storm collar with a drawstring) but has big mesh pockets—not included in the volume figure above—on the rear and sides. Waterproofing's not a strong point, so GoLite recommends using their own silicone-impregnated nylon stow sacks (the 2000-cu.-in. stow, used as a pack liner, weighs a mere 2.5 oz.). I carried a Breeze with 21 lbs. of gear and food through canyons in

GoLite Breeze

the Medicine Bow Range and found it pleasant enough, though the slick nylon straps skated around on the shoulders of my microfiber parka. That could be solved neatly by lining the yoke with a knit fabric, or rudely with a few turns of athletic tape (or, says the maker, by keeping them tight). Despite its through-hiking origin, I found myself liking the Breeze as a day pack and also as a stuffable adjunct on suitcase trips when I might end up walking, on the spur of the moment, for a day or three.

While such diminishing weights are seductive, you should ask just what you're giving up. First comes structural support: stays are either attenuated or lacking, and framesheets unthinkable. Second comes padding: there may be a thin piece of foam that serves as a combination framesheet and backpad, while the yoke and waistbelt will be slender and minimally cushioned. Third is that most extremely light fabrics are neither wear-resistant nor durably waterproof. Fourth is sturdy hardware: you'll find fewer and smaller buckles and D-rings, mounted on thinner straps. And finally, while I didn't do a dollars-per-ounce ratio, cost does factor in.

Tricky in a different way is the Mountain Tools Jet VX-15 (tall: 1900 cu. in., 1 lb. 11 oz., $140). At 70 cu. in. per oz., the Jet is billed as an "adventure race pack," though the number among us who'll go dashing across the veldt with TV cameras aimed at their twitching posteriors is, thank heavens, small. What I found attractive was the potential for ultralight weekend trips. In contrast to undivided sacks, this one gives you some internal sorting options. On the outside are compression straps, a daisy chain, a removable set of ice-tool loops, and a crisscross bungee. The shoulder straps can mount two bicycle-type water bottles (via 15-

Mountain Tools Jet Pack

inch lengths of shock cord with locks—a slick idea adaptable to most packs). I thought the bottles might be off-pissing, but I scarcely noticed them unless I was thirsty. An even trickier option is the Race Module (6.4 oz., $45), a chest pouch that clips to the shoulder straps and the waistbelt (via elastic straps). The center pocket can hold binoculars or a small camera. The sides will take energy bars, sunscreen, a pocket tool, a flashlight, etc. The mesh sleeve on the back is good for maps (waterproofed—otherwise they get spongy with sweat). Again, I thought the full-width pouch might be annoying but it wasn't—you can munch, drink, and consult the map, all without breaking stride. Using the gear I did for fanny-pack trips (Appendix II), I was able to get two to three semicomfortable days out of this pack. But not being a racer, Adventure or any other kind, I used the Jet Pack most often (as I did the GoLite Breeze above) for gear-intensive day trips. Since my favorite day trips are those where you risk spending a night out, I like the potential of both these packs for tucking away a bivy sack, a down vest, booties, and a stove-cookpot combo—just in case.

Subultra, though very light indeed, is the Mountainsmith MountainLight series. The 5000 (5000 cu. in., 4 lbs., $290) clocks in at 78 cu. in. per oz. (or 83, with optional carbon-fiber stays). Also noteworthy is the Mountainsmith MountainLight 3500 (see Midsize Packs, page 159) at 60 cu. in. per oz. The carbon-fiber stays shave 3.5 oz. (for 65 cu. in. per oz.) and cost $60.

Also in the vicinity of the I-frame lurks a growing population of

Travel packs.

Good news: the suitcase-with-straps has evolved into something that actually rides like a pack. Not that the suitcase-with-straps is bad for what it is—a Patagonia MLC (Maximum Legal Carry-On) served me well on various aircraft, Mexican buses, and the beaches of Baja. But while I did pack things in it, it would be stretching the truth to call it a pack. And since carry-on rules have tightened, it's no longer legal.

Present specs at Denver International Airport are 22 inches long by 14 inches wide by 9 inches deep (for a volume of 2772 cu. in.). So if you don't want to check your bags, ultralight camping is the ticket. For some years, Linda has used an Eagle Creek travel pack (pictured, page 125, second from right) that I'd peg at about 2500 cu. in. It has a decent suspension system but lacks the scope for extended campouts. Of course your destination plays a part, too. In hot countries you can go part-naked and leave your sleeping bag at home (in favor of a silk sleep sack that weighs mere ounces). There are dozens of tidy little carry-ons, like the Lowe Alpine Voyageur 35 (2100 cu. in., 2 lbs. 4 oz., $90) that I now use. But in this range the technical demands are not huge, so there's no need to carry on further.

While there are zillions of so-called travel packs (some with retractable handles and roller-skate wheels), our focal point here is the full-size wheel-less sack. It should have enough volume for actual self-supported backpacking and a suspension that won't punish you for long days on the trail. And further, it must be at least potentially able to serve as your all-around backpack. Since most travel packs feature a detachable day pack (and some come with a duffel), for one price you can get luggage, a backpack, a day pack, and maybe a laundry bag.

The All-Is-One approach will appeal mightily to impoverished students and Thoreauvians. So I tested it by carrying travel packs on walks and scrambles with a full backcountry kit. The three categories that emerged are a) true backpacks with fully adjustable suspensions and travel covers or duffels, b) sleek hybrids with mildly adjustable suspensions that zip into hiding, and c) duffels with suspension systems that either zip away or detach, and perhaps some stays or stiff foam for structure.

At the packish end of the spectrum, the Madden Meridian (see page 164) gave one of my most comfortable carries, period, with a chunky 52-lb. load. It's also bombproof in the Madden tradition, of 11-oz. Cordura. But though the catalog spec was 5 lbs., the test pack I got was a striking 2½ pounds heavier. (A Mercedes is heavy, but you don't have to carry it on your back.) In any event, the Meridian (large: 5000 cu. in., 7 lbs. 8 oz., $270) has a fully adjustable suspension system that would support a tank. It also has suitcase handles, an excellent detachable day pack, and a clever

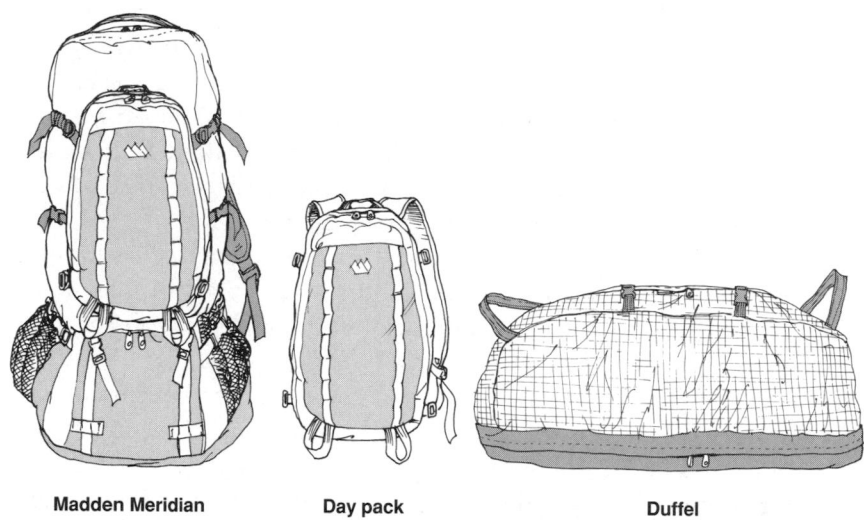

Madden Meridian   **Day pack**   **Duffel**

top stash to hold the voluminous Eclipse duffel (10,000 cu. in.) that guards the pack in transit and also acts as a rain cover. Made of Spectra fabric, the Eclipse duffel is listed in the catalog at 2 lbs. 7 oz. but actually weighed only 1 lb. 8 oz., which cancels out the difference in pack weight somewhat. It can be used to travel-ize any pack, as well as for laundry, personal concealment, and the like. Comfortably rugged, the Meridian might be the ideal pack for bush-flight backpacking in Alaska.

Lowe Alpine makes full-size Voyageurs (shown page 165) with a distinctly stylish turn and specialized features that Linda was mad for, e.g., two internal ditty bags that clip together to form an internal compression sleeve. Which, she points out, means you can pack clothing neatly, compress it, and not have to fight the main zipper. "This was obviously designed by a woman," she said, and in fact Lowe's chief pack designer is one Heidi Kessler. A related accessory is the Tux-Away, a garment portfolio that accepts a blazer and slacks, folds in thirds, and fits the narrow (12 inches wide) profile of the Voyageur pack. The Tux-Away can keep your dress clothes safe at the hotel, while you're off degenerating in the bush. My merely male senses did register a pair of sleeping-bag straps, and the fact that the perimeter zip allows you to treat the Voyageur as a top-loader or open it up duffel-fashion (a process that involves five clip buckles and two zippers—somewhat annoying for backpacking). Large Voyageurs come with a detachable day pack, with mesh yoke and room for 2 liters of wine, a baguette, cheese, fruit, a towel, and a scandalous novel. The zip-away suspension doesn't adjust for torso length but is otherwise quite good, and comes in men's and women's sizes. I took a Voyageur 65 (4000 cu. in., 6 lbs. 9 oz., $200) backpacking in the stony,

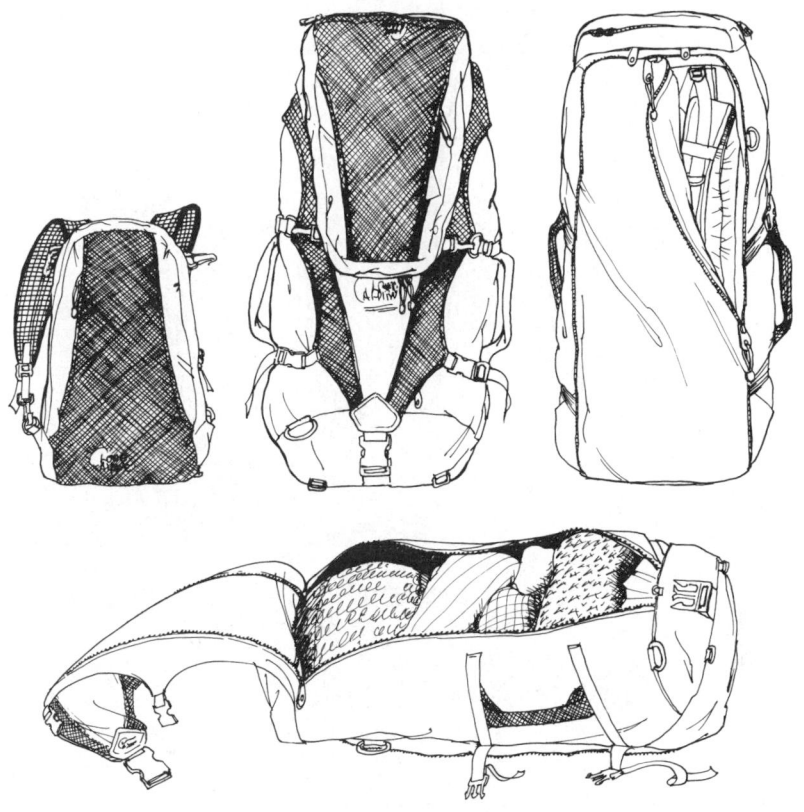

Lowe Voyageur, GS

wind-whacked Nevada desert with 43 lbs. and had (after rebending the stays) a happy time.

Osprey's foam-paneled taco construction is ideal for travel packs, providing full-body compression, load protection, and a sleek outer skin. I've not only backpacked with an early model, the Synergy, but used it for field schools that combined dirt-road transit in vans with canoeing, and lab sessions at a college. I've also used it for science trips, humping digital current meters, steel sounding rods, and the like. The current version is the Hejira (large: 4600 cu. in., 6 lbs. 13 oz., $269), with handy internal pockets and a detachable day pack. It also has a zip-away suspension (in sizes but not adjustable for length; see page 130, bottom left) with a foam back panel, a padded waistbelt, and cleverly hidden buckles that won't catch in a luggage system. The Hejira is a very good backpack, the only lack being a top pocket. The cute baby sister is the Departure (large: 3200 cu. in., 4 lbs. 3 oz., $230), which can sneak through the carry-on slot.

Osprey also has simple taco-style backpack/duffels called Transporters (large: 7800 cu. in., 4 lbs., $150; medium: 5400 cu. in., 3 lbs. 11

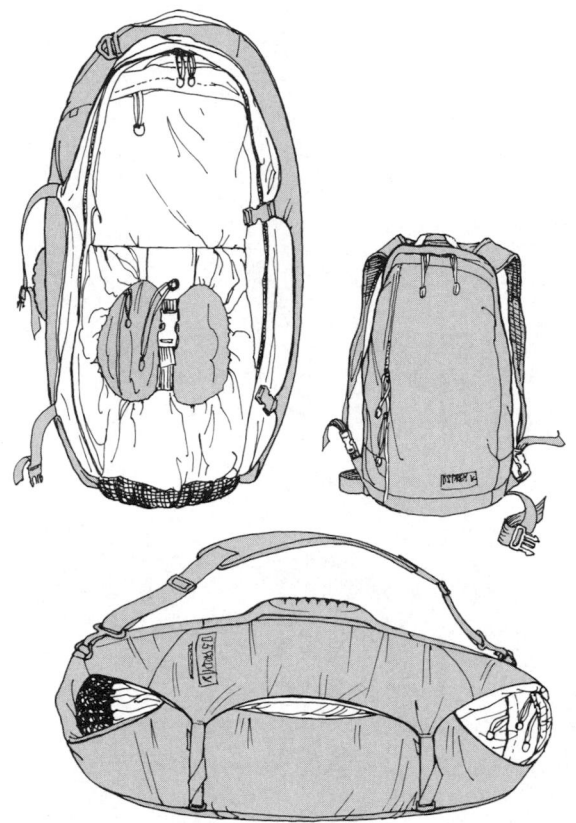

Osprey Synergy, day pack, rolled

oz., $130; small: 3700 cu. in., 3 lbs. 2 oz., $120). These have zip-cover suspensions with a contoured yoke, load-lifter straps, and a 2-inch web hipbelt, along with a suitcase grip and belay-strength shoulder strap. I wouldn't say they're great for backpacking, but they're definitely on the high side of okay—and the price is right.

Another new species is the really, truly

Waterproof pack.

Most packs are sewn of fabrics described as "waterproof," but if you dunk the packs, they fill up fast. So my generation swam rivers and slot pools with our packs wrapped in trash bags that inevitably ruptured. On his Grand Canyon trips, Colin refined the method (see page 690). But these days, for trips involving regular swims or wallows, or for the new sport of canyoneering, which involves butt kayaking, rappelling down waterfalls, and related lunacies, a truly immersion-proof pack may be in order.

The leader in this specialized field is VauDe, a German firm, with a line of eight waterproof packs. Their flagship Blue Canyon (5200 cu. in., 5 lbs. 11 oz., $400) is heavily impregnated and taped Cordura (slightly stiff) with roll closures like those on river drybags. VauDe's fabric and seam sealing seem near-perfect. With an advanced plastic I-frame, a highly adjustable suspension system, lush padding, and so on, it was suspiciously comfortable. But "immersion-proof"?

VauDe Blue Canyon roll closure

The demon in me wondered.

So I loaded up the Blue Canyon with real gear—sleeping bag, clothing, food bag, stove—and let the demon hose it down with a high-pressure nozzle. After 20 minutes or so, it showed no leaks whatsoever.

Then the demon and I repaired to a local creek—invigorating, since in my part of the world on April 23 the waters are not warm. I lay on my back in a pool and rolled back and forth, howling (or the demon did). Given as much maltreatment as I could stand, the Blue Canyon allowed about ¼ cup through each of the two closures. Not bad.

In a sulfurous mood, the demon clawed his way up to a waterfall and hung the Blue Canyon pack underneath, letting it spin for an hour. And yes, it did leak—about 3 cups. I tried the same test with a pro-quality drybag, made by Jack's Plastic Welding, that's proven stone-dry during several whitewater boat flips. It leaked, too, though the amount was teaspoons. But given the fact that neither I (nor the demon) could have survived an hour under that waterfall, I'd say the Blue Canyon's as waterproof as a backpack can be and still open easily. And it's comfortable.

If you're willing to sneeze at comfort, a thrifty alternative is a river drybag with a rudimentary suspension system. I tried the ProPack 115 from Cascade Designs (6940 cu. in., 5 lbs. 1 oz., $115), which has a removable hipbelt and yoke. It passed the wallow and waterfall tests with, respectively, teaspoons and cups. To fully assess the *ouch* factor I walked a 5-mile circuit. With 35 lbs. it was fine—a rubber rucksack. With 45 lbs. it was actively annoying. With 55 lbs. it was like bearing all the sins of your past life, mostly because the hipbelt is set rather high on the sack. I added a sternum strap—otherwise, the yoke gobbled my armpits. The Paragon Pack (Northwest River Supplies, about 6500 cu. in. and 6 lbs., $117) is a drybag with stays and a genuine suspension system. In either case, if you have only sporadic canyoneering in mind, the price sings out.

As a second line of defense, use waterproof roll-closure stuff sacks (page 179) for sleeping bags and clothes. For sunglasses, cameras, and other screw-upables, the watertight boxes from GSI, Pelican, and Otter are crushproof, and thus good for negotiating boulder piles, slot pools, and overhangs.

Weight distribution in I-frame packs

COLIN: Because the bag hugs your back and becomes almost an integral part of you, the way you arrange your gear in the bag is more important than in E-frames. In fact, it's critical. Maladjusted I-frames have the disturbing tendency to hang from the bearers' backs like ill-tempered baboons, and their natural complaints (the bearers', not the baboons') used to echo down backpacking's word-of-mouth corridors. Sometimes still do.

Makers differ mildly in their recommendations (for two, see below)—no doubt because of idiosyncrasies of their packs, gaits, or theories. But they agree on general principles. Above all, the foot of the pack must not carry a heavy load. Makers mostly agree that the way to achieve this end is to put your sleeping bag there. Some even provide separate zippered basement compartments with compression systems that coerce your sleeping bag into the most efficient conformation.

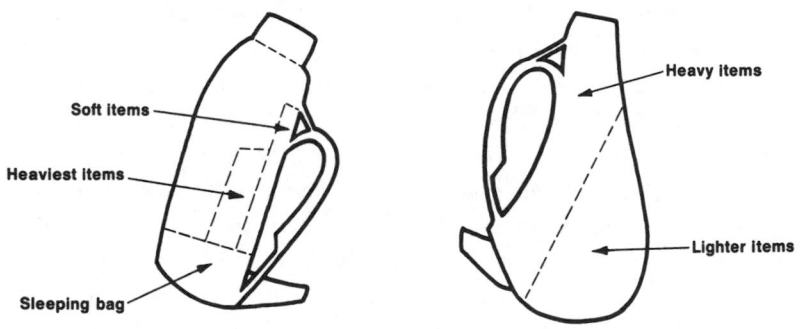

Weight distribution in I-frames

To keep the load close to your back you must, of course, pack heavy items well forward in the pack, or at least at the top, where the bag's natural lean and curvature will bring it closest to your balance line. Because the bag will, if properly adjusted, travel close to your back, you must take even greater care not to pack protruding articles along the forward surface where they might gouge your back. Instead, stuff in soft or flat and not-too-rigid items. The final touch to an efficient loading job is pulling tight on all compression straps.

Fitting a new internal-frame pack

Unless you adjust the suspension properly when you first try the pack on, it will hang there like one of those ill-tempered baboons. You're unlikely to give the wretched thing real consideration, let alone buy it. And if you're foolish enough to buy it you'll probably never get the slightly-mixed-metaphor monkey off your back.

If you're shopping in a store, seek help. Perhaps more than with any other backpacking item, you need the assistance of a salesman you can trust. Failing such trust—or if you shop by mail—read the instructions that come with the pack. Read them carefully. At first they may seem rather daunting. But the procedure is easy enough once you grasp the principles. We'll have to consider the more sophisticated kinds of suspension, so if you're eyeing a simpler pack, just cut some of the complicated cackle.

CHIP: Because frames, yokes, and hipbelts are often sized separately, you should have your measurements written down in advance of the actual decision, so you don't get swayed. Stores tend to display packs stuffed with foam blocks or plastic bags filled with foam peanuts, and they love to have you try them on that way, since even a maladjusted baboon will feel great. So for pack shopping I take two things along: my sleeping bag in a stuff sack, and a plastic bag of water-softener salt, with a handle. This lets me see how my sleeping bag fits and gives me 25 honest pounds to slip in.

Here's a preliminary process for finding the perfect fit.

1. Measure your torso length. Start from the seventh cervical vertebra. If you tip your head forward, you can feel it as a distinct knob at the base of your neck. From there, run the tape down your spine to the top of the iliac crest, the two bony protusions that flank it, slightly below your pelvic girdle (you can feel these easily). If you don't have a dressmaker's tape, you can use a steel carpenter's tape, which I just did and got 22½ inches. Torso length determines your pack/frame size. For example, Dana Design's ArcFlex frame is available in five sizes: 14 to 16 inches extra-small, 16–18 inches small, 18–20 inches medium, 20–22 inches large, and 22–24 inches extra-large. Their ArcLight frame comes in three sizes: 15–18 inches X-small/small, 18–21 inches medium/large, and 21–24 inches large/extra-large. Some I-frames come in two sizes: regular and large. There's usually an inch or two overlap in the sizes, so if you're tall with a short torso you should consider the larger size, and vice versa.

Once you decide on the frame size, you need to fine-tune the torso length. The yoke attachment should be centered between your shoulder blades, with the shoulder straps following the curve of your shoulders and the load-lifter straps angled down from pack to shoulder top at 45 degrees. Early I-frames had strap ladders (some still do—it's a good system), and you simply feed the yoke attachment through the proper step. Other length adjustments might initially be somewhat mysterious, involving hidden straps and obscure Velcro tabs. The instructions should at least hint at the location of such things, but if it's a used pack or is missing its little hanging reference library, then poke around. Often, the lumbar pad flops down, with a great unscritching of Velcro, and all is revealed. But on a few packs you need to grope under the back panel to find a hidden buckle.

Patience is all.

(I performed this ritual on an indecently large number of test packs and in only one case did my frustration rise to a full cougar scream. Since the pack in question had just gotten a *Backpacker* Editors' Choice Award, I suspect latent masochistic tendencies.)

Anyhow, with your torso length tentatively adjusted and the pack on, tilt your head back to see if there's clearance—if not, then you need either a different-size pack or perhaps some artful stay-bending (but hold off on that until step 4).

2. Measure for the hipbelt. Keep your pants (or whatever you wear for backpacking) on. The tape should be at the level of the iliac crest, not (for vanity's sake) up above your pelvis with your belly sucked spineward. If you use a steel tape, pull it tight. My girth is 38 inches B.C. (Before Christmas). Hipbelts come in three to five sizes (waif, Barbie, normal, comfy, and pro linebacker). The pads themselves should extend 2 inches beyond your hipbones, and there should be a 3- to 4-inch gap between them to allow for hipbelt adjustment.

The other hipbelt variable is angle or taper, which allows for the difference between waist and hips. Gregory puts a three-way taper adjustment where the hipbelt attaches to the frame, and Arc'Teryx has a Velcro adjustment on the belt itself. Dana and Osprey have differently cut belts. Most hipbelts are labeled "men's" or "women's" but cross-dressing is okay—a slim-hipped huntress can use a man's belt and vice versa.

3. Likewise, the harness, or yoke, may come in men's and women's cuts as well as sizes roughly corresponding to shirt size. The straps should give plenty of neck room. If they are curved, the curve should match the radius of your neck. The padding should extend 3 to 4 inches below your armpit, and the plastic adjuster buckles shouldn't dig in. The sternum strap should ride where you like it without being at one end or other of its travel. Lastly, extend your arms to the sides—if the straps ride up and bind, you need a different-size yoke.

4. Once all these ponderables have been duly pondered, then it's time to think about bending the stays (if they're aluminum, that is). Some stores have stay-bending experts, to save your trying to do it by yourself.

But here's the drill. With the pack on and weighted, feel where the bottom ends of the stays rest on your back. Then take them out, which might take some head scratching and a few grunts. If they slot into the hipbelt, you should take the hipbelt off the pack, slip the stays in, strap it on, and scrooch it down a bit at the sides to simulate the effect of a load. A properly bent stay follows the contour of your back, which is hard to see from in front, so get help or at least use a mirror. Bend the stay over a rounded surface—your thigh or the back of a sofa. Then bend the other stay to exactly the same curve and reinsert. Test by walking around with a load. In the pack, that is.

If all of the above trials work to your satisfaction, you'll have a pack that—potentially at least—fits.

COLIN: Next along the pathway to satisfaction there stands—second in importance only to that initial fitting—the daily, ongoing, hour-by-hour business of

Fine-tuning (or driving) an I-frame pack.

Coldly stated like that, the thing may sound like a hassle. But I have found—like most experienced people I've consulted—that with very little practice the process becomes almost automatic, demanding precious little time or thought.

There are, I guess, five somewhat separate ways in which you can fine-tune, or drive, your pack. Once you've fully grasped the underlying principles they are all matters of common sense, and really very simple. Please note that when I speak of adjusting some strap or fitting, the alteration is almost always very small. A ⅛-inch movement in a strap buckle may bring about a marked change in the way the pack rides.

The first fine-tuning procedure comes at the start of a trip or when you radically change the loading of your pack. At such times you must run quickly through key items of the fitting procedure. That is, you: Loosen all adjustments. Put pack on. Tighten shoulder straps to firm position. Cinch hipbelt tight. Tighten belt stabilizer straps. Possibly readjust shoulder straps. Adjust lift straps. And, finally, fasten and adjust sternum strap. The more sophisticated the pack, the longer all this will take; but even with the most sophisticated it need consume no more than about a minute.

You go through the second procedure, a sort of miniversion of the first, every time you put the pack on: Cinch hipbelt tight. Tighten belt stabilizer straps (if any). Possibly (but improbably) readjust lift straps. Fasten sternum strap. Walk. Elapsed time, maybe 30 seconds.

The third kind of tuning is another miniversion of the first. When you put the pack on after a camp or halt, as above, you find that because of some overlooked change in load or loading (lots of food eaten, or an item of a companion's gear taken aboard, or merely some rearrangement of your own gear) the pack doesn't sit quite correctly. The response is simple: Slacken off lift and sternum straps a touch, readjust shoulder straps until the load feels right, then readjust lift and sternum straps. A sub-version of this procedure may be needed on the move, particularly with a new pack: while you walked, hipbelt or harness has shifted a shade, and the fit is no longer exact. Your response will obviously vary with what feels wrong. Sometimes a simple readjustment of lift straps will be enough. But if the hipbelt has slunk lower you must hunch your shoulders to lift the pack higher and then recinch the belt. (We see this all too often, but it shouldn't happen with a really good pack, properly fitted and worn-in to your contours.) Once the hipbelt feels right, you'll probably have to readjust shoulder lift and sternum straps just a touch.

The fourth tuning procedure also occurs on the move. You've been walking for half an hour and, because you're out of practice or new to the game, the muscles taking most of the load have begun to rebel. Mostly, with a properly fitted pack, this means that the hipbelt is so tight it's crucifying your hips. But some people like to take part of the load on their shoulders, and it may be the shoulders that are aching. If so, all that's needed may be a very slight tightening of the sternum strap, to change minutely the places the shoulder straps bear. If more is needed, you adjust matters accordingly. That is, you manipulate the controls of your pack (which you can by now do with about as little conscious thought as you apply to manipulating the controls of your car) so that part of the load transfers from hip to shoulder, or vice versa. With a good pack you no more think of halting to make this readjustment (unless it involves tightening the hipbelt) than you think of stopping your car to change gear.

The fifth tuning procedure is the one that adds the final elegant touch to I-frame efficiency. It's a response to changing terrain. Mostly, that means hills. When you walk uphill with a load you tend to lean forward. So in order to keep the pack balanced on your hips, you slacken off the lift straps very slightly. And when you're going downhill and tending to lean farther back than when on the flat, you cinch up the lift straps just a touch. The difference this simple adjustment can make is astonishing. I now find I often make it—without even breaking stride, of course—even for an uphill stretch that's no more than 50 yards long. You can also adjust the lift straps—and perhaps the shoulder straps as well—in response to other changes in terrain. For rock scrambling or boulder hopping or crossing any rough country, tightening them will draw the pack more firmly against your back and reduce any tendency it may have to sway and so throw you off balance.

But perhaps I've already passed the point at which discrete quanta of logical responses are useful. In the end, fine-tuning boils down to something less obviously cerebral. If you use a sophisticated pack you'll probably find that with a little experience you repeatedly make minuscule readjustments almost without thought and often without quite knowing what you're responding to—and then, even when you stop to consider the matter, you're still not really sure whether you were responding to new terrain, wearying muscles, changes in the pack's conformation, or some combination of these. After all, that's mostly how you drive a car, isn't it? And when you reach that point with your pack, you're driving it. If you're not by that time halfway in love with it, then that pack is probably not for you.

Paying due attention to driving your I-frame pack may seem to mean some loss of simplicity and convenience. And maybe it does. But the loss is very slight. I find the gain overwhelmingly worth it.

EXTERNAL-FRAME PACKS

CHIP: These are showing renewed acceptance, owing to radical changes in the design of

The frames.

About the only thing unchanged since Dick Kelty built his first packframe in 1952 is the basic layout: straps front, load back. The aluminum tubing familiar to readers of the first three *Walkers* is still with us in some degree, though the old straight-backed configuration is gone for good. Even the lowliest E-frames now curve in a gentle S, to work with the muscles of the torso rather than against, and most have a rearward arc at the top and bottom to accommodate our heads and tails.

Another slant entirely is molded plastic, which has adherents at both the high and low ends of the scale. Newest out, though, are composite frames, with tubing for strength and plastic members to anchor the yoke and hipbelt.

Most frames have a bag that can be taken off (though some new designs won't allow this). With proper rigging, the bare frame can accommodate a haunch of moose, a case of mushroom soup, or an inflatable kayak (for more on that, page 674).

The three-quarter-length bag is so popular that most makers have dropped full-length sacks from their lines. (Although Colin still advocates them. And he's not alone.) While strapping a sleeping bag in a stuff sack to the frame is easy, you court some annoyances that may become dangers. In wet or snowy weather, each time you set your pack down you plunge your sleeping bag into sodden grass, dripping willows, greasy mud, or the like. While stuff sacks are widely claimed to be waterproof, most aren't. Dirt and gravel grind away at the fabric while sharp rocks and pointed stubs can puncture it. Further, the usual drawstring/flap arrangement can scoop water by the tablespoon each time you set the pack down or brush against wet foliage, let alone wade a creek and step into a hole. Only a truly heavy-duty coated stuff sack with a *waterproof roll closure* will keep your sleeping bag dependably dry. So, if you like the strap-on arrangement, get thee one (page 179). Or prepare to take your soggy lumps. A rain cover, sized to fit your pack, can also lend some peace of mind.

Makes and models of E-frames

The 1998 *Backpacker* Gear Guide lists 50 makers of packs, with 14 offering E-frames. As of 1999 the numbers were 52 and 15, i.e., stable. In various forms, E-frames can be had from Alps, Camp Trails, Dana Design/K2, Diamond Brand, EMS, Granite Gear, Gregory, JanSport, Kelty, Natalex, Peak 1, REI, Rokk, VauDe, and Wenzel (for addresses see Appendix III). The low price, for a child's pack, was $75, and the high was $485. But a good-quality, adult E-frame averages $150 to $250, roughly two-thirds of the price of an I-frame of the same quality and volume. Weights range from 3¼ lbs. for a youth pack to 7½ lbs. for a large frame with a full-length sack.

The two surviving "traditional" ("trad") giants are Kelty, born in 1952 in Dick Kelty's garage with sales of 29 packs the first year, and JanSport. JanSport was born in 1967, when Murray Pletz, a student, entered a contest sponsored by an aluminum company. Pletz's packframe won and he used the prize money to start a company named after his girlfriend. The long-running JanSport classic was the D2, which used small-diameter (16 mm) tubing with no color coating or welded joints. Now the D2 has become the Yosemite, with the same delicate-looking tubes and construction.

The JanSport frame is quite stiff, with subtle curves to fit the back (see facing page). Near the top is a pair of cast slip fittings, like those used on adjustable rowing frames, with sockets for a tube to shape the top of the sack. The overall length of the frame is fixed, but the plastic molding that holds the upper ends of the shoulder straps has 4½ inches of travel, for different-length torsos. A curved cross tube issues from two stationary fittings. This is where the backband rests. Below, two movable castings keep the plastic hipbelt wings in place when weighted yet when they are unweighted allow a 180-degree swivel, so the wings can fold flat for trans-

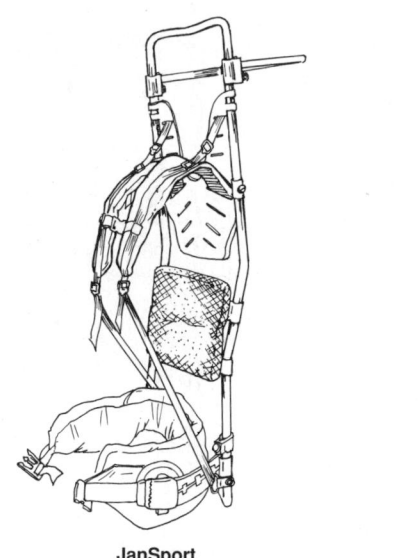

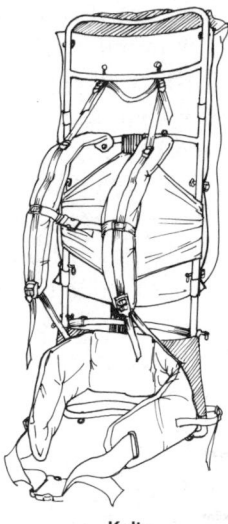

JanSport   Kelty

port. These lower cast joints have about 6 inches of up-and-down travel, so the suspension not only adjusts for torso length, but moves up or down with respect to the frame. Finally, the bottom of the frame comes off where clevis pins (the two and only) anchor the bottom ends of the shoulder straps.

Recently JanSport dropped its full-length Nepali, and now offers E-frames from the basic Scout (3 lbs. 4 oz., $90) to the three-quarter panel-loading Yosemite (5 lbs. 9 oz., $190).

Kelty uses a seamless, coated tubing of larger diameter, and its Tioga frame presents a conservative approach to parts metallic. That is, the upper yoke connects directly to the aluminum frame, avoiding plastic components, while the lower part of the frame telescopes, moving the hipbelt down to accommodate a longer torso. The practical difference is that while the JanSport frame has a fixed length, Kelty's can be adjusted for torso length without raising the height of the top bar—if you hike brushy country this makes a difference. Kelty has also focused on the hipbelt and yoke. With a broad, tapered hipbelt of laminated foam and tapered shoulder straps, Kelty delivers Cadillac comfort at a modest price. The trad classic Trekker Series starts at about 5 lbs. and $130, with the Tioga at 5 lbs. 15 oz. and $150, the Super Tioga at 6 lbs. 8 oz. and $185, and the jazzy purple-framed, Spectra-reinforced Ultra Tioga at 6 lbs. 5 oz. and $280.

Both the JanSport and Kelty frames are steadfastly comfortable and neither has that sloop-in-a-storm creak—after all, they've had 30-some years to get it right.

So let's look at further developments. Some years back, Coleman (aka Peak 1) introduced an innovative molded-plastic packframe. While it never made much of a dent in the high-end market (already lurching toward I-frames), it hit home with scout troops and outdoor programs for whom the combination of simplicity, comfort, and cheapness sounded a golden chord. Some Peak 1 frames incorporated Kevlar for strength, but the quality of the packbag lagged behind that of the frame, which the company tells me will soon be discontinued. Since the all-plastic frame is ideal for boatpacking (see page 674), I've kept one around over the years.

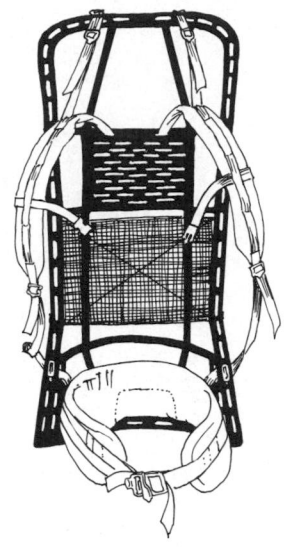

Peak 1 E-frame

Between the "trad" tube frames and full plasticity we encounter a new crop of hybrids. One of the best is Dana Design's LoadMaster, made of a 6066 T-6 aluminum alloy that's harder than the "furniture tube" used in cheap frames. Gregory uses that same 6066 T-6 alloy in the Evolution frame, while Kelty uses 6063-T6511. Read as addresses, these numbers indicate the same neighborhood, so let's leave it at that. Welded joints have been perfected to the extent that one no longer need worry about their breaking under normal use. (Having your pack fly off a roof rack at 70 mph is *abnormal* use.)

Let's look more closely at the Dana Design LoadMaster frame (which, owing to corporate ferment, may soon be known as the K2 LoadMaster). In any event, the perennial problem is how to bridge the gap between a rigid frame and a flexible (and somewhat tender) body. Dana uses a 25-millimeter loop of aluminum tube, in a handsome powder-coated finish, with a slightly smaller top bar that removes with two clevis pins (see the similar Terraframe, page 177). The frame also telescopes about 6 inches upward. The hybrid element lies in two flexible fiberglass "cross-links." The yoke is sewn to a panel, roughly diamond-shaped, that narrows to a strap at the bottom. This adjusts torso length while tympanizing the mesh back panel. Second comes a pair of fiberglass wands in a trapezoid, from the upper frame member to the hipbelt. These couple the load to the hipbelt and adjust the give between the frame and the suspension. The yoke and hipbelt are virtually identical to those on Dana's I-frames, i.e., excellent.

The Dana Design/K2 LoadMaster frame supports a range of packbags: the simple T-1 (4600 cu. in., 6 lbs. 7 oz., $270), the Shortbed (7 lbs. 3 oz., $280), the Longbed (6100 cu. in., 7 lbs. 5 oz., $300), and the intriguing Terraframe (7 lbs. 8 oz., $320, page 177). The Zen choice is the Flatbed (for which the cu.-in. measurement is arguably either zero or infinity, at 5½ lbs. and $200), a frame with fancy lashings and an under-slung "beavertail" for packing a haunch of moose, bass viol, etc.

Another cool hybrid is Gregory's Evolution E-frame. The load rests on two large-diameter alloy tubes with mild curves. The tubes are joined by a system of plastic components that resemble the fancy railway bridges of the last century. The upper curve and the yoke attachment are one fixed piece, intricately slotted and braced, with a wide range of adjustment. There's also potential for attaching objects from the mundane (sleeping pad) to the exotic (caged iguana). The lower member, called a "floating bridge," has a tail section that extends down 8 or so inches without touching the frame tubes, giving about 10 to 15 degrees of flex to the hipbelt attachment. This is different in concept from the Dana wands, but similar in effect. It's also called a "beavertail."

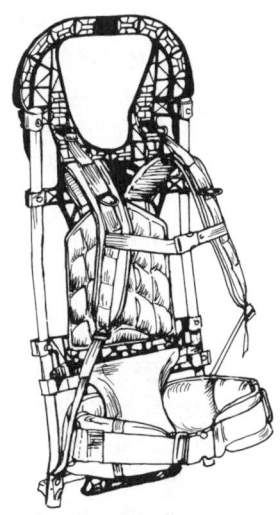

Gregory Evolution E-frame

One aspect of the vast proliferation of outdoor stuff is that far too many things end up being called "beavertails," and likewise dozens of unlikely objects are tagged as either "Revolution" or "Evolution." This leads to a state of mental overload I call *product blur.*

Back to the chase: the Gregory E-frame employs a yoke, hipbelt, lumbar pad, and molded back panel like those on Gregory I-frames. Other ergonomies include a bottom brace that allows the pack to sit upright and an upper one that holds the pack open for loading and gives it shape. Two forms are available, a panel-loader (4187 cu. in., 5 lbs. 10 oz., $230) and a top-loader (4568 cu. in., 7 lbs. 5 oz., $250). A color-coordinated, Evolution-frame-compatible, no-bungee-cord-required sleeping-bag stuff sack ($24) is recommended.

A recent development is the mating of an I-frame-type bag with an external frame. Which in a way brings us full circle to Colin's original preference for the full-length E-frame sack. The strongest entry is the Dana Design/K2 Terraframe (6100 cu. in., 7 lbs. 8 oz., $320) that mates the high-volume Terraplane sack to the LoadMaster

Dana Design/K2 Terraframe

frame. Dana Gleason, himself a high-volume person, says it's not just another E-frame, but a whole new thing.

I tried one, and it is lovely. If I took a lengthy, meandering trip across the steppes of Central Asia with a sample kit of anvils, I'd want none other. But it's not a step to be taken blindly. For one thing, the bag is permanently wed to the frame and suspension, so the option of ditching the bag and lashing on a raw leg of yak must be forsworn. This is also the case with the full-length Dana Design Longbed. The Shortbed and the T-1 bags can be detached.

E-frame fittings

Formerly, most bags were fitted with grommets and pinned to the frame. Clevis pins are still used, sparingly. JanSport has two per frame, to join the tubes and anchor the low ends of the yoke. Kelty has clevislike bosses fixed to the lower part of the frame that catch corresponding grommets on the bag. But these days the most common way of holding bag to frame is by Velcro tab. The JanSport Yosemite has six of these, reinforced by a removable tube that extends through a sleeve on the top of the bag. Removing the support tube subjects the Velcro tabs to a definite strain. But I slipped it out and loaded the bag with a vile burden (books of literary criticism) and the upper tabs held, though with faint squeaks of protest. This isn't an idle concern, since a recent *Backpacker* test reports that one unidentified pack fell off its frame and into a creek.

While tubular E-frames attach with Velcro, sewn sheaths, and metal bosses in combination, molded frames require other means, the most useful being a simple slot. Through the slot slips a flat steel slider on a sewn tab. You pull back and it jams. At first these seem chancy, but I've never had one fall out as I walked, though they do sometimes pop out in a car trunk. Other makers use threaded sockets with setscrews to anchor soft parts (bags, hipbelts, and yokes) to the molded frame. With fasteners of any sort, one thing to beware is a lack of weight-bearing surface. That is, a grommet or any other attachment with a small area and/or a cutting edge should be reinforced by layers of fabric, a nylon washer, or similar means.

And that's the E-frame news.

AUXILIARIES
Stuff Sacks

In the house on your back, these are the closets and cupboards. The generic stuff sack is a tube of nylon, sewn shut at one end with a drawstring and perhaps an internal flap at the other. It comes in various shapes and sizes, for sleeping bags, tents, poles, pads, cookpots, and sundry. It might be sort-of-ly waterproof. Since it takes a lot of stress from daily stuff-and-unstuffing, besides being used as a seat cushion, it tends to wear out fast. Seams give way and the drawcord tears out of its sheath. Being ubiquitous, it's often overlooked in terms of function. But there are think-points involved, to wit:

Waterproofness versus ventilation. In watery cases, whether monsoon or slot pool, it makes sense to double up on protection and keep your essentials like matches, sleeping bag, and extra clothes in truly waterproof sacks. I tried two types. The Cascade Designs Black Canyon Series (designed for boaters) is a coated Cordura, slightly stiff, with a drybag clip-buckle roll closure. One model has a rubber stopper that allows you to press out the air after the bag has been sealed. The heavy-duty fabric is a bit stiff to pack and the clip-buckled roll takes up space. The Outdoor Research Hydroseal stuff sacks (in a range of sizes) are a softer coated nylon with a roll closure secured with Velcro strips. The soft fabric packs nicely but seems less durable (though my two-year-old sack is still water-tight), and the Velcro has a way of latching on to the Velcro counterparts found on packs, etc. But these seem better for backpacking.

In any event, it makes sense to get a waterproof stuff sack for your sleeping bag, and one for your extra clothes. If I seem to belabor this point, that's because it can save not only a night's sleep but perhaps your life.

Mesh is good for things that need to drain and dry out, like water filters, and is generally about half the weight of a solid fabric. If you're undecided, some bags have one mesh side and one solid. Cookpots now come in mesh sacks that are light but don't corral soot. Even clean-burning cartridge stoves can deposit some, so beware.

Size and proportion. There are shapely developments, like the Gregory Contour Stuff Sack (S, M, L, all $20) that fits neatly in the sleeping-bag compartment, and the clever zip-open Cell Blocks from Outdoor Research, that are rectangular for a close fit both to gear and the inside of your pack. Long, skinny sacks protect sleeping pads and prevent the loss of tent poles and stakes (which are better left out of the tent bag—see pages 382, footnote, and 419).

Compression. These sacks have straps running length- or widthwise to reduce the volume of puffy things like sleeping bags and parkas (which shouldn't be stored in compressed form between trips). Waterproof, roll-closure sacks can also be compressed before closing—if they poof up in your pack that means there's a leak.

Weight. Further weight shaving can be done with ultralight sacks, such as the silicone-impregnated nylon Pouch Stow Sacks from GoLite (in six sizes, from 125 cu. in. and 0.5 oz. to 2000 cu. in. and 2.5 oz., $12–$33). Despite extreme lightness, the stitching is excellent, and the three largest sizes have internal collars that can be twisted before the drawstring is tightened for added water resistance.

Comfort. For cush-hounds, Liberty Mountain Sports has the Sova Convertible Stuff-sack Pillow that turns inside out to reveal a panel of fleece (8 by 18 inches, 4 oz., $12 in retail shops).

Convenience. Also worthy of mention are the small sacks or ditty bags that refine your sorting process and hold repair kits, herbal remedies, amulets, art supplies, and so forth. Stores have a mind-boggling array, and the purple cloth sacks that hold fancy jugs of whisky are popular: The possibilities are endless.

Office-on-the-yoke

Office-on-the-yoke

COLIN: Because I often walk without a shirt and therefore without a front pocket, I long ago—back in 1958—had a 5-by-6-inch pocket sewn onto the front of my yoke or shoulder strap, roughly where the shirt pocket comes. Into it go notebook and map, and sunglasses when not in use. Pen, pencil, and thermometer clip on to the rear, between pocket and strap, where they are very securely held—not, as they used to, in front, where removing map or notebook can flip them out unnoticed. I can't imagine how I ever got along without such a pocket—or one of the now-available commercial variants.

CHIP: These are so useful I thought there'd be dozens in catalogs. There are lots of belt pouches and travel wallets that hang around your neck, but rather few organizers that attach to a yoke strap. But I've got a medium-size Outdoor Research Possum Pocket (4 by 6 by 1½ inches, 2.5 oz., $18), likely inspired by Colin's original. It has a mildly padded back and an ingenious Velcro/snap combination that rotates from vertical to horizontal. That is, you can wear it on the yoke of a full-size pack, then swap it to the hipbelt of a fanny pack. The various flap pockets, slots, and sheaths are nicely thought out. At the moment, mine holds a Fox 40 whistle (hung on the loop), a signal mirror, a magnesium fire starter, a butane lighter, a Coast Micro-plier pocket tool, a 3-by-5-inch spiral notebook, mechanical pencil, sunglasses, lip balm, sunscreen, and an emergency packet of toilet paper. The Possum Pocket also comes in small ($16) and large ($20), in various colors.

For a better-equipped office, there are full-width chest pouches, like the Mountain Tools Race Module (page 162) that clips to the shoulder straps of the Jet Pack, adding useful capacity (and in hot weather, some sweat). Farther along this path is the gear vest, resembling those used by fly fishers, photographers, and field scientists. If you need quick access to an assortment of gear without having to shed your pack, this is a workable, if slightly bothersome, solution. The Peak 1 Gear Vest (7.5 oz., $28) has two layers of mesh with a zipper on either wing so the vest itself forms two large pockets (one with a grommet for a hydration tube). There are also four top-loading pockets and four D-rings. The vest attaches with plastic clips—some packs have D-rings in the proper spots and others can be easily adapted. I've used the Gear Vest with a Peak 1 plastic E-frame for boatpacking and portaging (see page 674) to hold rigging straps and other small items that might easily go astray.

Belt pouches

Belt pouches are almost as useful as hands. At the simple end, they consist of two or three pieces of fabric sewn together with a single zipper and two loops. Spiffier models sport internal organizers, mesh sleeves for water bottles, and concealed pockets for valuables.

On short kangaroo hops, a belt pouch may be all you need. On long treks, it holds your notebook, pencil, sunglasses, lip balm, and other talismans annoying to dig out of an overstuffed pack. Lay out the gear you want in constant reach and then look for a pouch that will accommodate it. Most pack makers have a pouch or two (which, despite how it might sound, is not a personal comment). A friend tells me that Dana Design makes one that attaches to the waistbelt of a pack, which he prefers to the office-on-the-yoke. Travel packsters like Eagle Creek have dozens, and so do accessory wholesalers like A-16 and Liberty Mountain Sports. Outdoor Research has a selection that's particularly well designed for backpacking. And last but not least, military-surplus stores have bins of curious pockets and tuckaways.

Enough. What do kangaroos have that you do not?

Child carriers

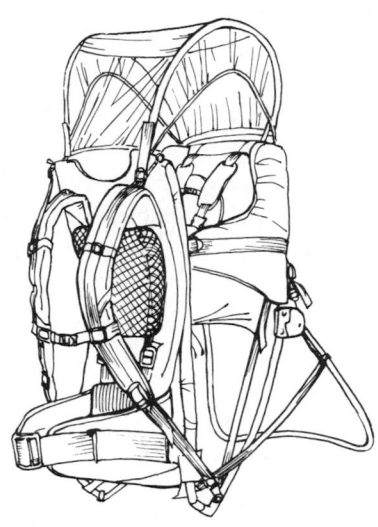

Kelty Elite kid carrier

In the grand tradition of W. C. Fields, neither Colin nor I have children and my friends seem reluctant to lend me theirs for testing purposes. So this is based on observation and random questioning of Mormon backpackers, who have a lot of experience in this regard.

Soft, front-loading infant carriers are good for casual walking. But for overnight backpacking, you're looking at an E-frame designed to contain a live, often wiggly load. So, first, there should be restraints to keep the child firmly ensconced, particularly if you fall. The little darling should face front (so as to pull your hair, vomit down the back of your neck, and kick you in the ribs when you lag—young children should not be trusted with whip or spurs). For babies there should be ample head and neck support, and overall dimensions that will expand to provide for growth. The carrier frame should have a tip-resistant bottom bar that swings out to let you set it down while cooking dinner, fending off maddened grizzlies, etc. Weather hoods, mosquito nets, and other refinements can help to ensure the succession of your little prince or princess.

The current standouts are Tough Traveler, with the Stallion (for large adults, $160) and the Filly (for smaller ones, $155), and a soft front-carrier called the Pony Ride ($75). A boggling assortment of snugglies for clothing, diapering, and sleepering youngsters are available, as are children's packs.

Along with a nice front-carrier, Kelty K.I.D.S. has an astounding array of both conveyances (not so much pack as palanquin) and gear for young children. The fully loaded Explorer ($230) comes with a hood, netting, zip-off kid pack, and diaper duffel. The Elite has a hood and a zip-off kid pack ($180), and so on down the line through the Trek ($150) and the Country ($120). Whether this is an oversight or a sign of the times, the stunning young model packing a baby in the Kelty catalog wears no wedding ring. Which brings up the fact that child carriers are particularly sanity saving for single parents—as the twig is bent, so the tree inclines.

As W. C. Fields said, "Anybody who hates children and dogs can't be all bad." I wouldn't go *quite* that far. But beyond the walls of your pack lies the

Department of Canine Affairs.

For backpacking bowwows there are presently dog packs, dog boots, collapsible dog dishes, and dog video games (in the form of a lightweight, fold-up, fang-resistant Frisbee). In a catalog not exactly devoted to backpacking, I saw a small carrier much like a kid pack, intended for a tiny dog (no doubt a potential shock to passersby). Dog sunglasses have not made an appearance. Or at least, not yet.

Pooch packs are made by some high-class companies like Mountainsmith (the cleverly named Dog I, for varmints under 35 lbs., is 760 cu. in., 1 lb. 6 oz., and $60; Dog II, for 35–65 lbs., is 1300 cu. in., 1 lb. 9 oz., and $70; and Dog III, 65 lbs. and over, is 2400 cu. in., 1 lb. 14 oz., and $80). Mountainsmith also makes dog harnesses for lightweight sleds. Ruff Wear's Approach Pack is a favorite with my dog-possessed friends (small $62, medium $66, large $70) with a suitcase-type handle for restraint or boost. Those with high-fashion mutts might prefer the Granite Gear Ruff Rider packs, which have a foam back panel, nonchafing tubular straps, and a Louis Vuitton–ish cut (small: 30–50 lbs., 900 cu. in., $45; medium: 50–80 lbs., 1100 cu. in., $48; and large: 80+ lbs., 1300 cu. in., $52).

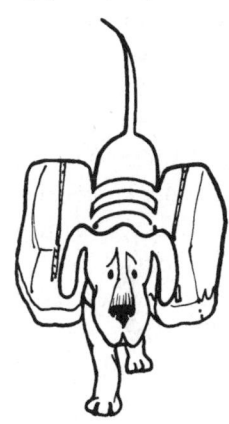

Dog with packs

These come in forest, royal, and red. There's also a folding Frisbee flyer for $13.50.

Wolfpack simplifies things with the clean-lined Banzai pack: three sizes for one price: $74. A-16 supplies the expedition-style Chief, with a mesh back panel, in Spaniel (1150 cu. in.), Shepherd (1310 cu. in.), and St. Bernard (1600 cu. in.) for $55. They also have the more Spartan Rover Series (500, 750, and 1000 cu. in., $40), along with Green Ban Herbal Dog Shampoo and Herbal Flea Powder (both 4 oz., $7.50). Not to mention the famous Reservoir folding dog bowl, in two sizes and colors ($13.50). They also sell the Pelican Pet-tracker Strobe ($15), a collar-mounted device that will annoy everyone within a half-mile radius by flashing for 8 to 10 hours.

Further pup stuff is available from Liberty Mountain Sports (likewise a wholesaler, so you need to visit a local shop). The basic black Sequoia dog pack comes in S/M ($24) and L/XL ($33). There are Paw Pals dog boots ($13), a fleece "cover-up" ($14–22), a collar-mounted collapsible dog bowl ($12), and an array of harnesses, leashes, chokers, and such. The Campmor catalog has a full page devoted to doggery, with folding bowls ($7–15), several models of dog packs ($24–48), a Stearns flotation vest ($15), Ruffwear Bark'n Boots, a new rubber-soled design with a D-ring and Velcro cinch ($33), and Zuke's Power Bones (canine energy bars) in beef, chicken, or peanut flavors. By far the largest selection of dog boots, though, is in the hunting-oriented Cabela's catalog. And there is likely an upscale retailer—L. L. Beast, perhaps—that will advance Fido to full consumer status. But I haven't seen it.

I did have friends with a tribe of backpacking cats. They made a teeny little pussy pack, but the test subjects consistently flopped down with a scornful glance: no go. My artist friend Hannah has a lordly black tom named Ratz, who hikes but would no more countenance wearing a pack than the Duke of Windsor would have worn a fake mustache. But a fleece patch attached to the shoulder strap or the top of your pack allows kitties, raccoons, and lemurs to ride when their wee legs tire out.

COLIN: Remember that in much backcountry, especially in national parks, dogs are forbidden. In others, such as U.S. Forest Service wilderness areas, they're permitted only if kept on a leash. In others they must be "under control."

I'm at best ambivalent. Cases clearly occur in which dogs harass wildlife. Barking dogs can be a pain, especially at night. Even someone repeatedly calling dogs to heel can disturb the peace and silence you've gone to find. But I recognize that some people's trips are enriched by being able to take their pets along, and there's something to be said for the practice—in the right places, and if extreme care is exercised to prevent the dogs from interfering with wildlife or with other backpackers.

A Vermont reader who took me to task for giving "short shrift to dogs" has put the case very well indeed—at least for eastern backcountry. "I have been backpacking with my dog for seven years," she writes. "Besides her own food she carries two 1½-quart canteens, maps, guidebook, and sundries. The point I wish to make is that dog owners should follow some basic rules, e.g.:

> "1. Keep the dog on leash always, day and night. It takes a little trouble first thing in the morning and just before bed, but it is worth it.
> "2. Never let the dog run up to—much less jump up on—other hikers.
> "3. At meal times, especially when with a group, tie the dog away where it won't get into food or knock the stove over.
> "4. Only bring a quiet dog. Several times after a night in a shelter with others, they have remarked, 'Your dog is so quiet. She never

barks.' Well, she does bark if other hikers approach after we have settled in, and growls if another animal approaches. (She scared off a large porcupine one night.)

"5. The dog owner must know how much weight his dog can carry (one-quarter to one-third of body weight) and get the dog in shape just as he does himself. He must also be as sensitive to the dog's need for water and shade as he is himself. And last, he must realize that a dog cannot travel consistently the long distances a human can."

CHIP: According to authors Tom Kirkendall and Vicky Spring, hikers tend to choose "even-tempered, steady dogs like golden retrievers—usually with a bandanna around the neck and a name like Fletcher"—immortality, of a kind.*

The idea that a dog will protect you from large predators is mostly illusion. I've talked with a number of people who've seen their dog dash into the brush, only to dash out again, pursued by a critter somewhat higher on the food chain. This happened to my former neighbor Sherm, who had to fend off a mountain lion with (appropriately enough) a mountain bike, while his Rottweiler cowered behind him. So, no matter how fearsome your dog may appear, it is simply no match for wild predators, and might well attract them.

Another potential source of agony is that commercial livestock grazing covers most of the western U.S., including some wilderness areas, and the sheepherders and cowboys can instantly (and legally) shoot any dog that chases sheep or cattle. I've heard this sad tale more than once, and think you should spare yourself and your pet that sort of abrupt ending.

Books on sharing your walks with a dog are listed in Appendix IV.

THE WALLS IN ACTION
Getting the pack onto your back

COLIN: You carry out this operation in the field many times each day, and the total energy consumed is considerable. At the end of an exhausting day it might even be crucial. So it pays to give the matter some thought.

The easiest way to load is to use a loading platform—a convenient rockledge or bank or fallen tree trunk—and just slip into the yoke.

Failing a loading platform—and rest assured that you'll mostly fail—you can sit down, enyoke, and then stand up with an easy if inele-

*Backpacker, April 2000, page 78.

gant sidle. With a back-breaking load this is about the only possible method. I believe it is the one the time-and-motion sages agree is the least expensive in energy.

Yet for all but the very heaviest loads I find that the simplest method is to hoist the pack up into position with an easy swinging motion, one hand gripping a shoulder strap and the other the small nylon hand strap that is now fitted to most good packs. Swing the pack up from whichever side comes naturally; but if you use an office-on-the-yoke (page 180) make sure you put it on the strap that slips onto your shoulders first. On the other side it will infallibly foul things up.

The question remains: "At what stage should I switch from the easy-swing-up to the sit-and-enyoke method?" My own answer is: "Not until somewhere around 60 pounds, and not even then for sure." I find that by swinging even a very heavy pack up onto a raised upper leg first, and then onto the shoulders without ever quite stopping, you use surprisingly little energy. Yet one experienced friend of mine sits-and-enyokes with a load as low as 40 pounds. To find out what suits you, experiment.

THE WALLS AS NONWALLS

Your more or less empty pack may from time to time act as windbreak on one side of a tent or bivouac, as ground insulation for your feet when they protrude out beyond a three-quarter-length air mattress or pad, or even as a pillow. If it's big enough, and uncompartmented, it could make a water- and windproof cover for the foot of your sleeping bag—though you'd have to check that it didn't soak the bag in the moisture escaping from your body. It could certainly make an emergency footsack in the horrendous event you burned or otherwise lost the use of your sleeping bag. On such occasions sleeve-with-drawstring tops are obviously best.

But for my money by far the most important auxiliary use is

The pack as backrest.

If you prop a full E-frame pack against something, it makes a very comfortable chair back. When the bag has been emptied or part-emptied it works better with the luxury padding of an air mattress or foam pad.

When you can, simply prop the pack against a tree or rock. But if, like me, you believe in resting on the smoothest and softest piece of ground in sight, there will 9 times out of 10 be no such convenience. So mostly you use your staff as the prop. It soon becomes almost automatic, the moment you halt—even for a 10-minute rest—to look for a rock or crevice or a tree or even just a clump of grass to wedge the butt of the staff

Colin with E-frame backrest

against. Failing all these—and here again you will fail regularly—just angle-prod the staff down into the soil until it holds firmly, with or without an assist from a stone, and then jam the top of the staff between the yoke and the top crossbar of the pack, hard up against the bag. (A hand strap holds it perfectly.) Fine-adjust the angle of the packframe, sit thankfully down, and lean back. But lean so that your back thrust is along the staff's axis. Otherwise the pack will assuredly skew. It will skew anyway, from time to time, no matter how careful you are. But care helps. This all sounds rather complicated, I know; but after a while the whole operation takes about four seconds—and virtually no conscious thought (unless your packframe has a rounded foot that skews and skids at a touch on almost any ground: no amount of conscious thought will teach such mavericks a lasting subservience).

An I-frame makes a scurvy backrest. Especially with a staff prop. Even when it's full you can rarely lean against it for more than about 30 seconds before it swivels and falls. And unpacked it's about as useful as a waterless waterbed. I find this a sad defect of character in such a noble item of equipment, and the first person to proffer a resolution gets an autographed copy of this book in glorious black-and-white. (Several readers of *Walker III* have proposed ideas, but none really solved the problem. For me, anyway.)

PACK, SWEET PACK

Whenever I'm out on my own, free from civilization, and my pack is in every way my home, containing everything on which my continued existence depends, I find that I develop a reluctance to move very far from it. Even a side trip of an hour or two involves a battle with this reluctance— an almost physical tearing away. For a long time I assumed that mine was an idiosyncratic caution, but I find—hardly to my surprise, come to think of it—that other lone backpackers quickly arrive at the same sensible state of mind.

Kitchen

FOOD

COLIN: Backpackers in embryo sometimes dream of just walking out and away and living off the land. There is a delightful simplicity about the idea, of course, and its allure is stiffened by obvious practical advantages: no heavy food in your pack; constant variety; fresh, vitamin-rich products at every plucking. It seems as if you could hardly ask for a more perfect fusion of romance and efficiency.

Forget it. Above all, forget the efficiency. There are no doubt a few places in which certain select souls could live off the land and still find time to do one or two other things as well, but my advice is to leave the happy dreams to those who have never tried it.

That doesn't mean ignoring what the land drops into your lap. See, especially, Euell Gibbons's *Stalking the Wild Asparagus;* other books listed in Appendix IV; and two little decks of cards—one for the western states, one for the eastern states—called *Edible and Poisonous Plants,* with color photographs and text (each deck weighs 3½ oz. and costs $7.95 postpaid; available from Plant Deck Inc., 15200 Twin Fir Rd., Lake Oswego, OR 97035, or phone 503-636-9018). I often supplement my regular rations with trout, and occasionally with watercress (though doubts are now raised about its safety) or a few wild strawberries. And I once came close to eating rattlesnake steak. But in most cases and places the time and energy you would have to expend in shooting, snaring, catching, or otherwise gathering in a day's food and then preparing it are simply better applied elsewhere. Anyway, such hunting and cropping have little place in today's pressured wilderness: even where not illegal, they're mostly unethical.

CHIP: As a ranger and hydrologist, I regularly included wild plants in my diet—but I lived for entire seasons in the same remote places. As Discorides wrote 2000 years ago: "Now it behooves anyone who desires to be a skillful herbalist to be present when the plants first shoot out of the earth, when they are fully grown, and when they begin to fade." But if long-term presence enhanced my knowledge of what plants I might use, it also made me more conscious of my effect. So I now limit my foraging to widely distributed and locally common plants and gather them well away from popular trails. Rather than stripping one plant or denuding a spot, I pick a few leaves or fruits and move on. I think that such gentle herbivory does little harm. But you need to know your plants very well indeed, since some (e.g., the common water hemlock, one of the carrot family, or the death camas, a lily with a bulb resembling a wild onion) can kill you in very short order while others can make you too sick to walk. The best and most wieldy guides focus on a certain region: my favorite is *Edible Native Plants of the Rocky Mountains* by H. D. Harrington, with precise drawings by Y. Matsumura (see Appendix IV). By photocopying a few pages for each trip, you can learn the local edibles at a leisurely pace.

COLIN: Emergencies are special cases (see, for example, page 713 for rattlesnakes as emergency rations). And a deliberate attempt to live off the land may be well worth it for the spiritual effect of sheer primitive simplicity. But for normal walking, when one of your objects is to get somewhere or to do something when you get there, like climbing or looking or lazing, I recommend unequivocally that you carry just about everything you expect to need.

In choosing what foods to take, consider:
- Nutritional values
- Weight
- Ease of preparation
- Palatability
- Packaging (with a special thought for litter)
- Cost

Some people carry fresh food for the first day or two out, and perhaps a package of sprouts for later germination (page 220). These are certainly sound nutritional practices. But the only practical answer for any trip of more than a couple of days—and the simplest answer for shorter ones too—is dehydrated food. Most mountain shops now carry a wide selection of freeze-dried items. They're tasty and said to retain most of their nutritional value, and they've largely replaced vacuum-dried foods. Both kinds are stable: provided water content remains below 5 percent, neither bacteria nor mold will grow on them, and insects won't even snack. Such foods aren't perfect, of course. They tend to be expensive and to make you fart like a bull, and they come in air-excluding foil or polyethylene envelopes that can't be completely burned and therefore must be packed out (see page 221). Other dehydrated foods, such as oatmeal, soup powders, spaghetti, rice, and couscous, line supermarket shelves. But read the cooking instructions before you buy them, resolutely reject those that must be cooked for an hour (unless you cook on an open fire and love it), and think twice about any that must be soaked overnight.

Less than 2¼ pounds of properly dehydrated food will satisfy your nutritional needs for a highly energetic day. Many people seem to function on far less. And you can adjust the cuisine to suit personal tastes and current conditions. You can concoct complicated, multiflavored dishes or keep the cooking childishly simple and still have a nourishing and palatable meal. Palatable, that is, for its time and place. A steaming mix of pemmican-like meat bar, rice, and gravy may hardly be the kind of dish you'd want to find on the table at home, but I assure you that at the end of a 20-mile hike it can taste better than a filet mignon in any restaurant.

In America, at least, we now have such a wealth of special backpacking foods, and of other foods eminently suitable for backpacking, that there's no longer any real problem about finding something that will do, only about making suitable decisions. But before we dip into our cornucopia we had better examine some general considerations.

There are two possible approaches to backpacking gastronomy:

Trial and Error, in which you follow personal preferences and are guided only by rules of thumb; and

The Scientific Nutritional Method, in which you calculate in calories and try to balance intake against energy output.

Trial and error

The advantage of this approach is that, although it involves a lot of built-in chance, your answers begin with a bias toward your individual requirements and evolve along the same axis. This is important, physiologically and psychologically. Each individual's alimentary system works in its own idiosyncratic way. And different people have very different philosophies of outdoor eating. Some like to make a meal out of making a meal. Some almost seem to make each trip one long making of meals. Then there are those who, like me, were born British and therefore are, as far as food goes, barbaric. (Hell has been described as a place in which the politicians are French, the police German, and the cooks British.) And at the extreme there sit—or stand or maybe even walk—those who never cook in the field or who even subsist entirely on pills.

I began, the way most people do, with the trial-and-error method. That is, I stood and looked at the packages in the stores and listened to a little advice and even took some of it. If I found I was at all hungry on a trip, I took a bit more next time. If—as was far more likely—I had a lot left over, I retrenched. If an item tasted good and/or seemed to keep my legs going like pistons, I tended to take it again. If not, not. Anything that turned out to be a nuisance to prepare, I promptly dropped. Continually, though never lavishly, I experimented. And in the course of time I developed a well-tested backpacking menu, entirely adequate for a barbarian.

But one day it occurred to me that the logical approach was the strictly rational, quantitative,

Scientific nutritional method.

It seemed to me that by tailoring a diet to my exact nutritional requirements under specified conditions and by paring vigorously away as usual at the half ounces, I could hardly fail to come up with the most economical menu—economical, that is, in terms of weight and energy. I might have to allow for a few personal fads and fancies, but that was all.

I chose, at that time, to ignore vitamins and minerals. But I examined fat and protein requirements closely. The gospel of the moment was that fats should constitute at least 20 percent of total caloric intake and could run to 35 percent or even more; and that you needed 45 grams of protein per day per 100 pounds of body weight (though your body could not assimilate the protein properly if you ate the full requirement at a single sitting).

Now, fats contain approximately 9 calories per unit of weight compared with 4 calories in the same weight of protein or carbohydrate, and they therefore form by far the most efficient food in terms of calories per unit of weight. Although no meaningful figures existed (the technical literature hedged, even cited "fast and slow stomachs"), it seemed to be accepted—and still is by most gospels—that the energy from fats and protein is released over longer periods than that from carbohydrates, and that they are therefore less efficient for booster snacks but eminently suitable for what might be called all-day or all-night background.

Fats can also raise palatability problems. At high altitude (and in extreme heat too) anyone's appetite is liable to falter, and you may find yourself revolting against the very thought of fats. A possible reason: fat needs more oxygen to "burn" than do other foods. But up high you may also abhor the thought of protein. The elevation at which such awkward things happen varies widely from person to person, even from trip to trip. It may start as low as 8000 or 9000 feet. It's apparently rather likely to happen above, say, 17,000 feet. Slow acclimation helps but doesn't necessarily cure. All you can really do is take along a fair variety of foods and hope there's always something in your pack that appeals to you. Sweet things are probably the best bet, but the range of sudden demands is unpredictable. Frank Smythe, struggling on and up, alone, toward the summit of Mount Everest, longed for frankfurters and sauerkraut; Ed Hillary, high on Cho Oyu the year before he climbed Everest, for pineapple cubes. I had always thought these reports a bit far-fetched. But on one trip I found myself feeling, at a mere 14,000 feet, the same craving for pineapple. Such vagaries of appetite are the results of a particular kind of stress. A soldier may face a similar situation, and the U.S. Army Food Service recognizes the palatability problem that can arise under combat stress. They have a saying: "It doesn't matter how many calories you give a man if he won't eat." In the mountains the trick is to guess right—short of pineapple cubes—and still keep your menu practical. It's as simple as that. And as difficult.

With these preparatory considerations out of the way I turned, in my search for a scientific nutritional method, to the first part of the basic problem: computing total energy supply.

First I set about learning how to calculate the nutritional content of various foods. Almost at once I discovered the U.S. Department of Agriculture's *Agricultural Handbook No. 8: Composition of Foods.* It proved invaluable—tables analyzed in detail the nutritional makeup of everything from abalone (raw and canned), through muffins, to zwieback. Today, life is simpler. Almost all prepared foods, including dehydrated and freeze-dried, must legally bear a list of contents and nutritional values, and this takes the sting out of calculations. Also, there's now the excellent paperback *Complete Book of Food Counts* by Corinne T. Netzer (see Appendix IV). It "contains over 12,000 listings" of the caloric, protein, carbohydrate, fat, cholesterol, sodium, and fiber content of a huge variety of very specific foods. Its introduction tells you that 3.57 ounces = 100 grams, 1 ounce = 28.35 grams; and even if you're not about to use these full and rather forbidding figures, you need rough conversion rates.

Agricultural Handbook No. 8 is no longer printed (though old copies may lurk in libraries). But anyone rabidly interested in the scientific approach to outdoor eating (or, for that matter, indoor eating) can now buy a CD-ROM that supersedes it—*Nutrient Database for Standard Reference (SR)*—from the U.S. Government Printing Office by phone (202-512-1800) or fax (202-512-2250), or on the Internet at *www.access.gpo.gov/su_docs/sale.html* (item # 001-000-04679-9, $17). *SR* is "the major source of food composition data in the United States and provides the foundation for most public and private sector databases."

You can download similar material—"food composition and nutrient information"—free, from *www.nal.usda.gov/fnic/foodcomp.* At this Web site you can also find "a wide variety of information and products. . . . including an online program which allows you to search for the nutrient content of individual food items expressed on a 100 gram or common measures." And you can get an abbreviated list by requesting a single free copy of *Nutritive Value of Foods, Home and Garden Bulletin No. 72,* from Nutrient Data Laboratory, Bldg. 005, Room 107, BARC-West, 103000 Baltimore Ave., Beltsville, MD 20705-2350; e-mail: *NDLinfo@rbhnrc. USDA.gov.*

At the time I did my "scientific nutritional" study, though, all I had was *Agricultural Handbook No. 8.*

By studying the *Handbook,* consulting various manufacturers, and reading much small print on many labels, I managed to calculate the caloric, protein, and fat content of each item on my standard food list for a seven-day period—the normal basis on which I plan. It's worth remembering, by the way, that figures for many foods can be only approximations. As a nutrition expert warned me: "No two wheat germs are quite alike."

Because the nutritional gospel, not to mention my tastes and the available foods, are now radically changed, I won't bother you with my item-by-item table from early *Walker* editions. The important thing is that the theoretical daily intake came out to 3830 calories, of which 900 were from fat. (For Chip's equivalent today, see pages 224–25.)

At first glance my caloric total struck me as a little low, but I postponed judgment. Naturally, I was relieved to find that, based on my body weight at that time (190 pounds), my diet provided more than the guideline minima then in vogue for both fats and protein: fats, 23.5 percent of total caloric intake as against a recommended minimum of 20 percent; protein, 152 grams as against the recommended minimum of 85 grams.

With these intake figures established I turned to the second part of the food-to-output tailoring process: calculating what my body needed for maintenance and exercise under various conditions. If I'd been starting from scratch, without a food list to evaluate, I'd probably have begun on this tack. I'm glad I didn't.

I soon learned that for maintenance alone (basal metabolism) the average person needs about 1100 calories per day per 100 pounds of body weight. In city-slob shape—which is the way I seem to start just about every backpacking trip—I then weighed, as I've said, around 190 pounds. So mere maintenance drained off 2090 calories from my daily total of 3830.

During the process of digestion the body consumes a certain amount of energy as heat. This factor is called, for some reason, *specific dynamic action.* It fluctuates between 6 percent and rather more than 10 percent of the total caloric intake. For simplicity, it's usually averaged at 10 percent. So in my case specific dynamic action accounted for another 380 calories: 2470 of the total gone, 1360 left. I began to wonder.

Next I got down to assessing energy output over and above these constants. I quickly ran to earth a table of fascinating figures. The moment I began to read the table I thought, "Ah, *this* is the answer. Now nothing can stop me."

THE ENERGY COST OF ACTIVITIES*
(exclusive of basal metabolism and influence of food)

	Calories per 100 lb. per hour
Walking: on hard, smooth, level surface, at 2 mph	45
at 3 mph	90
at 4 mph	160
(For walking on rough trails, multiply each figure by a very arbitrary factor of 2.)	
Standing, relaxed	30
Sitting, quietly	20
Eating	20
Dressing and undressing	30
Lying still, awake	5
Sleeping (basal metabolism only)	0
Shivering, very severe	up to 220
Sawing wood	260
Swimming, at 2 mph	360
Writing	20
Dishwashing	45
Doing laundry (light)	60
Singing in a loud voice	35

My source listed several other activities that made interesting reading, and all of them could, at a pinch and on a highly diversified walking trip, become ancillary pursuits:

Typewriting, rapidly	45
Driving an automobile	40
Bicycling (moderate speed)	110
Horseback riding, walk	65
trot	200
gallop	300
Running	320
Boxing	520
Rowing	730

*Most of these figures are derived from *Factors and Formulas for Computing Respiratory Exchange and Biological Transformations of Energy* by T. M. Carpenter (Carnegie Institute, 1948 ed.), page 136.

Come to think of it, campfire concerts often feature harmonica and recorder accompaniment, and I suppose there's no reason why it should stop there. So:

Violin playing	25
Cello playing	60
Piano playing, Mendelssohn's songs	35
Beethoven's *Appassionata*	65
Liszt's *Tarantella*	90

Almost all walking includes some uphill work. And it seems that, assuming a body efficiency of 30 percent, you use about 110 calories in raising every 100 pounds of body weight each 1000 feet of elevation. For practical purposes you can add the weight of your pack and clothing (FSO, or From the Skin Out) to body weight.

Armed with all these figures (but already suffering misgivings) I began to work out energy sums for an average fairly hard day's wilderness walking. I pictured myself, at 190 pounds, carrying a 50-pound pack, walking on a rough trail for 7 hours (with halts), gaining a total of 3000 feet in elevation, and otherwise doing all the things you do on an average day. Juggling with the figures I'd gathered, and trying to pin down the hours of a wilderness day along the lines of the table on page 49, I came up with:

	Calories
Basal metabolism (190 lb. @ 1100 cal. per 100 lb.)	2090
Climbing 3000 feet (240 lb. @ 110 cal. per 1000 ft.)	792
6 hours actual walking, at 2 mph (240 lb. @ 45 cal. per hour per 100 lb., times a factor of 2 for roughness of trail)	1296
3 hours dishwashing, laundering (light), making and striking camp, photography, compulsive dallying, and unmentionable activities (average: 50 cal. per 100 lb.-hours)	285
3 hours dressing and undressing, standing (relaxed), singing in a loud voice, cooking, and such items as evaporated time quite unaccountable for (average: 30 cal. per 100 lb.-hours)	171
3 hours eating, writing notes, and sitting quietly (halts, rapt contemplation, worrying, elevated thinking, general sloth) (average: 20 cal. per 100 lb.-hours)	114
1 minute lying still, awake (to nearest cal.)	0
8 hours 59 minutes sleeping (including catnaps)— i.e., basal metabolism, above	0
Total	4748
Plus specific dynamic action, 10 percent	475
Total day's energy output	5223

Even before I arrived at this figure and stopped to contemplate with dismay the gulf between it and my theoretical daily food consumption of 3830 calories, I knew something was going wrong with my neat little sums. Some of the figures in the energy-output table were obviously very rough approximations indeed. The efficiency with which you walk, saw wood, do laundry (light), or sing in a loud voice may vary drastically from day to day, even from hour to hour. And you perform most wilderness activities much more efficiently after you've been out for a week. Altitude tells too. And an arbitrary reclassification of the trail as "smooth" cuts the calorie total by 700 (including specific dynamic action)—which makes a huge difference.*

TOTAL	CALORIES PER HOUR	
Weight in pounds	*Level walking*	*10% incline*
110	200	380
120	215	380
130	228	433
140	240	456
150	252	479
160	264	502
170	272	517
180	280	532
190	300	570
200	318	604
210	334	634
220	350	664
230	366	694
240	382	724
250	398	754

But the biggest variable is the individual. All the figures are for average people, and although rough theoretical allowances can apparently be made for discernible differences due to age, build, sex, and even race, the critical question remains, "How do I, personally, function?" The spread, even between apparently similar individuals, can be wide. About 70 percent of people fall within a fairly narrow central efficiency range; but if you belong to the 30 percent in any one function—and the chances are that you do—then any computation may give highly misleading results.

*This table, adapted from the University of California, Berkeley, *Wellness Letter,* Vol. 2 No. 4, 1986, shows the number of calories per hour, according to body weight, that you use while walking at 3 mph on the level and up a 10 percent incline. For level backpacking, use total weight (body + pack + clothing), and for the 10 percent grade double the weight of the pack.

At this point in my investigations I began to suspect that the right approach to the food question was, after all, *trial and error* and not the strict, rational, quantitative, *scientific method*. With considerable misgivings I voiced this thought to several experienced research workers in the field of human nutrition. To my surprise, they tended to agree. Current knowledge, they said, left too many variables for any very meaningful quantitative balancing of energy input and output. The best way was to "get out in the field and establish bases for your own personal nutrition requirements." To do, in other words, just about what I had done in the first place.

Now, the last thing I want to suggest is that the scientific method turns out to be useless. If I thought so I'd hardly have inflicted several pages of it on you. Nowadays, with markedly changed nutritional gospels, and different foods available, I still routinely apply what I've learned to make rough calorie counts and even estimates of protein and fat content for almost any food list I assemble. And I'm convinced that even a little knowledge of the principles of human nutrition can be an invaluable aid to anyone striving to evolve a backpack diet that suits his needs. Had I known what I know now, my early trials would have been less tributary, my errors less gross.

So please don't write off my energy-input and -output tables as stillborn theorizing. Apart from anything else, what I learned about nutrition in the course of preparing them helped me build some solid-looking bridges across the gap they revealed between my actual intake and apparent needs. And down the years it has continued to color my thinking.

On long trips I usually take one day of almost total rest in every week of walking. Often I take two. On these days I normally eat less than on the others. So for the days that really demand energy I have rather more than the standard quota available—more than 4000 calories, almost certainly.

In addition, I tend to nibble away at small quantities of food throughout the day (used to, anyway), and this little-and-often kind of intake turned out to be the most efficient, especially for quick-burning carbohydrates.

But the really big factor, in more ways than one, may be my spare tire. I know from happy experience that my midriff begins to deflate after just a few days of walking with a load. On the California and Grand Canyon trips the tire vanished. The Grand Canyon trip was the only time I've ever done a before-and-after weighing, and in those two strenuous months I dropped from 194 to 174 pounds. I'm fairly sure that almost all the loss came in the very strenuous first half—a conclusion borne out by nutrition experts who say, "Weight loss is usually most marked at the start of any stepped-up exercise." I lost, then, something approaching 20 pounds in 30 days. Up to two-thirds of this loss, or about 14 pounds, is likely to have been fat. (Water would account for most of the balance.) Now, it seems that the body uses this fat just as efficiently as it does fat ingested by mouth. That is, it extracts 9 calories per gram, or about 4000 calories per pound. In other words, my 14 pounds of fat gave me an additional 56,000 calories in 30 days, or close to 2000 calories per day! Too many imponderables are involved in reaching this rather astonishing figure for us to accept it as at all accurate. But, to say the least, it makes the theoretical daily gap of 1300 calories between my apparent needs and actual intake yawn a great deal less capaciously.

In conclusion, then, it seems to me that the way to work out a good backpacking diet is to go on a shakedown cruise and find out by trial and error what suits you. If this sounds too unscientific for your temperament, call it "going out in the field and establishing personal nutritional bases." A useful starting point is the current U.S. Army formula for calculating optimum caloric intake (assuming no weight loss or gain): multiply your body weight in pounds by a factor that rises with activity level — 13 for sedentary, 14 for light, 15 for moderate, 16 for heavy. So if you weigh 170 pounds and are backpacking (heavy activity), you might aim initially at 2720 calories. To translate calories into ounces of food, consult nutritional labels, *The Complete Book of Food Counts,* or one of the other sources suggested on page 192. Remember that most backpackers, including me, tend to err on the side of taking too much food. From there, play it by ear. But keep one ear cocked in the direction of calories and their constituents. Ruminate on the notion of Konrad Lorenz, Nobel Prize–winning ethologist, that "Truth, in science, can be defined as the working hypothesis best fitted to open the way to the next better one." Think like a rough-and-ready computer. And don't forget to sing in a loud voice.

More than 30 years have passed since I made these sagacious calculations. Today, the energy-output data still hold. But nutrition is one of those fields of human ignorance that—like almost every damned aspect of backpacking (and just about everything else too)—is now in a state of near-manic, maybe explosive, flux. So we should reassess matters in the light of altered scientific "truth."

The dogma varies from month to month, expert to expert; but "ephemeral constants" include:

- *We need protein, carbohydrates and fat: for the right proportions, pick your month and favorite expert.* Note: some experts say we need only one, or maybe two, of these food groups.
- *Vitamins and minerals have moved, or at least are moving, from fringe lore into establishment gospel.* They're best absorbed from foods, but supplements are getting okayer.

- *Carbohydrates should mostly be complex, not simple and sugary.*
- *Eat as many different kinds of food as possible.* This studied complexity may be as important as any single facet of diet. It will help fill not only potholes we can see but those that surely lurk outside our present vision. It's possible that, provided a diet is varied and "healthy" (whatever you take that to mean), otherwise dangerous components may prove harmless.

For the low-sodium caper, see page 218.

Once you've selected your current nutritional gospel for eating at home, you may need to make a few modifications before you apply it to the house on your back. For example, a carbohydrate-rich diet, though it provides quick energy, doesn't stick well to most people's gut. So when backpacking you have to keep snacking. And while that's often just a matter of remembering to do so, it can under certain conditions prove inconvenient, going on impossible. Boosting your intake of protein and fat, which you metabolize slowly, takes care of that difficulty—and for many years I tended to eat rather more protein and fat when backpacking than I did at home. ("Me, too," said a doctor-adviser—to my surprise and pleasure.) Nowadays, I follow a different light.

In *Walker III* I wrote: "I have retained a healthy skepticism of extremists—the hyperhypoglycemites and -hyperlipidians, and the overholy 'holistics' who in reality have often been dazzled by a single beam and can no longer focus the whole. But I do my best to listen. Wisdom often underlies the chaff.

"Above all, I have studiously ignored all currently popular, widely touted diets, ranging from old-style high-protein hymnals to restrictive, soul-cramping, Pritikin-like regimens that proclaim, roughly speaking, 'Eat what you like, provided it isn't food.' "

So you'll be enchanted to hear that in 1996 I adopted Barry Sears's Zone Diet. Went on it but big. I'm still aboard—and delighted. Transformed, too.

Now, journalists and the medical establishment tend to mislabel The Zone as a "weight loss," "low-carbohydrate," or "high-fat" diet. It's none of these things. "Diet" nowadays suggests a regimen for losing weight; The Zone is a way of eating that permits your body to operate at full efficiency ("in the zone"). Its prime aim: controlling the insulin level of your blood so that it remains almost steady, without the peaks and valleys that normal eating generates. Among other huge benefits: marked reduction in heart disease. The Zone achieves these ends through a specific balance of carbohydrates, proteins and fats. This balance is 40-30-30 (calories from each group) and must be observed at every meal or carefully controlled snack. For convenience, balanced units (composed of whatever foods you choose—plain or fancy—with certain restrictions) are divided into "blocks." The number of blocks you eat each day depends on your size and level of exertion. There's more to it than that, but once you've grasped this essence, the regimen, though hardly simple, isn't too difficult to follow. If you need to lose weight, you will; if you don't, you won't.

I lost over 30 pounds in five months (from a semibloated 200-plus), and have maintained my around-170-pound level. Other benefits I've reaped: new mega-ergs of energy; lower blood pressure and cholesterol levels (six years earlier, I'd had a coronary bypass); to my surprise, and just as promised, a virtual absence of lactic acid formation—and therefore of weariness—in muscles during backpacking (and tennis). Also a cut of an hour in the sleep I need each night, and . . . But I must stop proselytizing, and just offer thanks to my unbigoted cardiologist who suggested The Zone.

Following the Zonic regimen when backpacking is less simple than following it at home, but it can be done. Even, I assure you, by the aged—who have less tolerance than the young for variance from its guidelines. For hints on specific food choices, see pages 205–16.

I hope you'll pay some attention to the many scientific pearls I've silk-pursed before you; but I also hope you nurture a healthy cynicism about all new knowledge, and can thereby, while slushing happily around in it, retain some semblance of wisdom. Bear in mind, constantly, that this whole field of nutrition is shot through with uncertainty. Figure-fouling idiosyncrasies do not end with wheat germs and humans. I once saw on a blackboard in the nutritional-sciences department of a famous university: "Lipids are inscrutable." But someone had struck out "lipids" and substituted "guinea pigs."

And now, with the scientific precepts safely under our hipbelts, we can at last consider

Dipping into the food cornucopia.

You must buy backpacking food differently from and much more carefully than the food you use at home.

The propaganda permeating our current crazy industrialized life tends to view calories as something to be avoided, or at least pared down. In backpacking, because you'll be exercising strenuously and carrying everything on your back, your object must be—within other constraints—to pack the maximum number of calories into the minimum number of ounces. So you compare all net weights (not the reconstituted weights of reputed servings, which depend on how much water you add). You check packaging for weight too—and for toughness and disposability (page 221). You read cooking instructions and choose the simplest (remembering, though, that meals with mixed ingredients and slightly complex cooking methods may taste better than those to which you just add water). You ignore cost to the limit of purse and temperament. You also ignore the "zesty richness" and "tangy flavor" and other alluring horseradish printed on the packages. What you want to know, in most cases, is how quick and easy this particular item will be to prepare when you're tired and hungry, how much better it will make you feel, and how long it will go on making you feel better. Advice on this score is useful only up to a point: what really matters, remember, is how the food suits *you*. And the only way to decide that is to experiment.

For our experimentation we now face a palate-boggling array of choices.

Freeze-dried foods have largely replaced vacuum-dried: they retain nutritional values better and are tastier and simpler to prepare. They also cost more. And, once opened, they must be used fast: exposed to air, their taste and nutritive values soon deteriorate.

CHIP: As far as backpackable foods go, three schools of cookery hold sway. Traditional, even aboriginal, is the idea of carrying bags of staples—couscous, bulgur wheat, parched corn, dried vegetables and fruits, dried meat, and spices—and combining them in varying ways. And for long or frequent walking trips, this is far and away the most efficient plan. Freeze-drying and precooking decreases the weight of these items without altering the strategy in any important way. One variation, employed by students and mendicants, is to economize radically by eating the same few items for long periods of time (the nutritional pitfalls being obvious, along with the distressingly real response I call the *gag factor*). Another variation is to select fresh or relatively unprocessed foods that offer higher nutritive value with only a slight increase in weight and/or cooking time. (A good source on the whole-foods approach is the relevant chapter in Ray Jardine's *Beyond Backpacking*—see Appendix IV.) Left to myself, I stock up on bulk staples and dry garden produce, then simply package these things before each trip while making a list of those others that are perishable or not on hand for a pretrip visit to the store. So I have at least one foot firmly placed in the middle ground.

The middle ground is occupied by the Supermarket Backpacker. As the hectic pace of American life spawns ever more quick-cooking food, this approach gains adherents. Some friends assure me that you can stock the larder-on-your-back with one judicious round of the local market prior to each trip. That's true, given that the market isn't a crossroads store in a one-horse town, where they respond to a request for "couscous" as an indecent proposal. Usually, I watch for sales on items I favor—Lipton's Cajun Rice and Sauce with Beans or the delicious Amore Tomato

Paste, Garlic Paste, and Pesto (all 4.5 oz. in a tube)—and lay in my seasonal stock.

But most visible is the school of cookery I call Pre-Fab Gourmet, with aluminized exotica such as Jamaican BBQ Chicken, Katmandu Curry, and Chili Pepper Pesto. While Mountain House (with which I became overly familiar as a Forest Service ranger, since they had the government contract) remains much as it was, with sturdy Italian and Asian touches, the other large suppliers—RichMoor, AlpineAire, and Backpacker's Pantry—now stud their menus with Thai this and Santa Fe that. Harvest Foodworks of Toronto offers a full range, from exotica (Tandoori Curry) to freeze-dried beef burgers, with cold-prep meats, crab, whitefish, and salads. They also have complete food kits for two (30-day, $449; 60-day, $869 Canadian).

Never loath to try something new in the way of eats, for this book I rehydrated and chomped my way through an array of Pre-Fab Gourmet cuisines. And even as a contrarian, I found the stuff—with few exceptions—delicious. Another strong drift is toward "natural" contents, low salt, and few or no preservatives or flavor enhancers such as monosodium glutamate (MSG). AlpineAire, RichMoor's "Natural High" label, and MSR Ecocuisine (organic foods in burnable packets) all tend this way, and companies list an increasing proportion of vegetarian meals.

COLIN: You can't help feeling a great deal of sympathy for the ideas, or at least emotions, that prompt the revolt against industrial buggering about what we eat. But it becomes a little wearying to be warned ad nauseam that consuming polluted "commercial" food is the reason you have warts, are impotent, and died last week. And organic food seems to generate not only energy but also haloes—the same appallingly human haloes that always lurk, ready for conspicuous wear, behind the knowledge that you have "seen the light," and it makes no difference whether your "truth," hidden from all lesser eyes, concerns "natural food," Islam, Jehovah Witnessing, the cooperative movement, or "ecology." Anyway, the point is that the "organic" movement generates a backlash. I confess that I sometimes find it difficult, faced by certain food purists, to stop their goddamn haloes from blinding me to real advantages that "natural" foods may offer. But if you are immune to such choler, or can survive it, and want to live on a preservative-free, unpesticided, health-and-halo-inducing diet, and also to backpack, then know ye that the world is full of little packaged jewels. I use them regularly.

CHIP: Being of two minds (if not mouths), I agree with Colin as to the halo factor. And yet as an enthusiastic and organic gardener, I try to support my tribe. One of my favorite suppliers, Paradise Farm Organics, began with Idaho farmer Mary Jane Butters's search for a way to market her crops. Her all-vegetarian Backcountry line includes Garlic Fry Bread with Basil, Organic Sweet Corn and Black Bean Chowder, Polenta, and Curried Lentil Bisque, in compact and burnable packets (she's also a source for MSR's Ecocuisine). Her mail-order catalog is a good stop for bulk cereals, dried fruits, and such. So far, everything I've tried is paradisacal.

Newer still is Trail Gourmet, an Ohio company that packages fast-cooking ingredients (e.g., couscous and angel-hair pasta) in small, clear packets, so you can see precisely what you're in for. And that's mostly good. Their Moroccan Vegetables with Couscous got the top overall score from both Linda (a former restaurant cook) and me, not only for savory, intriguing taste, but also for delivering realistic portions. David Hennel and Sue Boyce, both long-distance hikers, also supply lightweight, quick-cooking vegetables, fruit, rice, pasta, beans, and mixes in bulk (e.g., whole wheat couscous at $1.75 per lb. and refried black beans at $3.75 per lb.).

That brings up the issue, bluntly put, of *how much.* First, that means *how much* you need to stay healthy, happy, and alert for the term of your trip, and Colin covers that on pages 190 to 200.

Second, *how much* refers to the size of the servings each package contains. And my experience, alone and with partners over the years, confirms Colin's: most pre-fab portions are scant indeed. A 7-ounce freeze-dried packet labeled "for two" might satisfy one person of average appetite after a full day of exertion. Makers skirt the issue somewhat by labeling these "entrées," like the à la carte menu of a restaurant. But most backpackers consume them as one-burner meals. So be forewarned.

Third, *how much* refers to cost. In the Campmor catalog, which lists Backpacker's Pantry, RichMoor, Mountain House, and AlpineAire foods, the freeze-dried entrees (allegedly for two) range from $4.50 (Red Beans and Rice, Chili Mac) to a high of $8.50 (Santa Fe Chicken). While on the average this is less than it costs to eat at a fast-food joint, it does add up. A one-week menu from a freeze-dried food supplier, using only their products, totals 20,758 calories, or roughly 3000 calories per day, at a total cost of $146, or $20.86 per day. A combination of pre-fab and bulk foods can bring the cost down to less than $15.00 a day, and using all bulk staples can get you by for less than $10. Both Backpacker's Pantry and AlpineAire have good beef, chicken, and turkey packs. The only quibble is that some precooked, freeze-dried meats remain leathery after in-pouch rehydration, so brief simmering may be in order. The same two makers, plus RichMoor, have good vegetable packs: peas, corn, potatoes, refried beans, and green beans almondine. They also have useful mixtures, mainly peas, carrots, and corn, with trimmings available such as onions, celery, bell and/or chili peppers, and so forth, which tend to be labeled as a "Southwestern," "Santa Fe," or "Sicilian" vegetable mix.

For Bulk Staplers or groups, AlpineAire has bulk packages of grains (e.g., instant white rice, 16 oz.); beans (dehydrated black beans, 14 oz.); turkey (cooked, diced, freeze-dried, 8 oz.) and shrimp (cooked, whole, freeze-dried, 4 oz.); vegetables (the usual suspects, plus freeze-dried or dehydrated broccoli, cabbage, celery, mushrooms, and asparagus, in packs from 2 to 12 ounces); powdered cheese, milk, and sour cream (8–12 oz.); fruits (apples, blueberries, and strawberries); and maple syrup granules. Recently Mountain House began to offer freeze-dried and dehydrated foods in #10 cans, good news for those who repackage (page 221) and use up the contents over a fairly short period, say on a through-hike.

A logistical advantage of the bulk approach is that you can pack for a given trip, say 10 days, using food counts to make sure your nutritional needs are covered, while retaining the ability to vary your menu and portions as you go.

COLIN: Many people still tend to select backpacking foods purely for flavor and to assume that the nutritional values are there. They're wrong. Read all labels carefully—and remember that ingredients are listed in descending order of occurrence, by weight. Also that if the package bears a USDA symbol, which it certainly should, then the big-type title of a complete meal tells you a lot. "Beef Stroganoff," for example, must contain a minimum of 45 percent beef, while "Noodles and Stroganoff Sauce with Beef" may have only 21 percent and "Beef-Flavored Stroganoff Mixed with Freeze-Dried Beef" less than 1 percent. Similarly, "Chicken and Rice" contains more chicken than does "Rice and Chicken."

Note that unless your soul warps at the prospect, you can dehydrate some of your own foods. Dehydrating removes 90 percent of the moisture, as compared with 96 percent in vacuum- or freeze-dried items. Chip tells me that a dehydrator with 4 trays, expandable to 12, appears in the Campmor catalog for $80. Also listed: extra trays at $10 each; special plastic sheets for making fruit leather and drying sauces, etc., at $7 for two; and a book, *How to Dry Foods* by Deanna Delong, at $15. Other books on drying food for backpacking: *The Wilderness Cookbook* by McTaggart, Bryant, and McLeod; *High Trail Cookery* by Linda Yaffe; and *Trail Food: Drying and Cooking Food for Backpackers and Paddlers* by Alan Kesselheim. And drying tips appear in various books by Dorcas Miller, a regular contributor to *Backpacker* magazine. (For a list of books, see Appendix IV; for packaging, and storage desiccants, page 221; for making your own beef jerky, page 213).

Finally, remember that dehydrated foods are not the whole story.

Some people say, "Eat as fresh as you can for as long as you can"—and they carry fresh vegetables, meat, and other items for the first few meals (see page 220 for "grow-as-you-go" garden). While I certainly agree with the fresh-food principle, I never seem to follow it in practice. I have not experimented, as I've intended to do, with fresh bread. And in my parts of the following meal-by-meal review of present backpacking foods, I'm afraid I rather ignobly tend to ignore fresh-food alternatives.

The review, though it seems necessary, poses difficulties: I'm undoubtedly ignorant of many first-class items, particularly those sold only in the East; taste is perhaps the most wildly idiosyncratic corner of the idiosyncratic backpacking field; and attitudes toward meal making run it a close second. So while I shall follow my normal practice of stating personal preferences you'll find that I try to take a rather more objective view than usual. Remember too that personal tastes and attitudes toward meal making can change. I remain, at rock belly, a Britannic barbarian. But the years have taken their toll: America has corrupted me. I have to confess that at times, even far from civilization, I now yearn for parti-civilized food. And I often pander to this treasonable weakness. So my needs have evolved—but not necessarily progressed. A backpacker with a cuisine that's simple going on depraved can perhaps claim survival advantages.

Breakfast

I find this the most difficult meal. The basic requirements are at odds with each other. Nutritionally, you want something that will keep you going through a long morning's walking; but you often want to start walking immediately after eating, so the slow-digesting fats and proteins that fill the first requirement are the very items that, because of their demands on the body's energy output (page 191), should be avoided immediately before strenuous exercise. Even more to the point, the meal should, except on rest days, be very simple to prepare. I find that I eat most breakfasts in at least a mild hurry, sometimes in darkness, and nearly always in that pseudocatatonic post-eye-opening period when no one in his right mind would describe me as awake. And I have yet to discover the perfect meal to accompany the hot tea that is the only catalyst reasonably sure to jolt me toward interaction with a new day.

For years I ate 4 ounces of cold dehydrated fruit, soaked overnight. Later I alternated it with one of the Swiss-type cold-cereal-fruit-and-nut mixtures (Fini, Familia, Swissy, Alpen). But eventually I tired of the cloying sweetness, and—in those days before I converted to the Zone Diet (page 199)—if I wanted cold cereal, which is also useful as an odd-time filler, I used a sugar-free brand or mixture of brands (Grape-Nuts, small Shredded Wheat, for example; read supermarket labels for others). All-Bran can be helpful in the first days of a trip if, because of the suddenly changed way of life, your bowels need prompting. (An alternative, I'm told, is dried fruit, especially white figs.) Often I spiced up my cereal with Familia-or-similar. And I almost always added a protein booster.*

Immediately pre-Zone, my standard breakfast, especially in cool weather, was one or two 1-ounce envelopes of Quaker Instant Cereal (the regular flavor has no added sugar) with protein booster and, often, a sprinkling of Swiss cereal or gorp (page 212). Occasionally I substituted a 3-ounce package of ramen (Oriental noodles), boosted to taste. Both oats and ramen are cheap supermarket standards and very simple to prepare. As a variation and on hurry-up days, I often used Bear Valley Fruit'n Nut Pemmican or MealPacks (see page 214). These wads, though hardly a gourmet's delight, need no cooking: you just eat, right out of the wrapper. And they seemed to keep me going for hours.

Other alternatives included flavored nutritional drinks, but although I occasionally carried one I found I could rarely face it. On rest days, of course, when there's no need for speed, you can let yourself go: my favorite is small trout, caught either the evening before or, better still, that same morning. But don't kid yourself that trout are fuel fit for long-distance walking.

Note that freeze-dried menus offer not only "eggs with real bacon bits" but "omelettes" and also "hash browns," "blueberry flavor pancake mix," and other resistibles.

*A useful protein booster—for any meal—is Textured Vegetable Protein (TVP), made from cooked defatted soy flour. I use Bob's Red Mill TVP (10 oz., $2.19) from Natural Foods, Inc., Milwaukie, OR 97222, available in health-food stores and some supermarkets. In ¼ cup there are 12 g protein, 7 g carbohydrate, 0 g fat, and 594 mg potassium.

Another booster source: protein powder, based on milk or soy or some other delight. Sold in health food stores and good pharmacies. Brands come and go. Prices vary. The best contain 90 percent protein, and some boast a list of vitamins and minerals that stretches from here to Zanzibar.

It's a sound principle, likely to avert considerable suffering, that if some items of your diet are frequently repeated you should try for bland-tasting versions that will be swamped by other ingredients. Both these boosters meet that criterion.

IMPORTANT NOTE: Nutritionists, with considerable reason, quantify the protein, fat, and carbohydrate content of foods as percentages of total calories, not of total weight. I have followed their lead. So my figures will differ from those you find on packages. They normally show grams-per-serving of each commodity. To convert into nutritional terms, multiply protein and carbohydrate figures by 4, fats by 9 (that is, by the number of calories per gram); then reduce to percentages. We hope you have more fun doing so than we did.

CHIP: My breakfast strategy is to boil a pot of water, which provides for coffee, cocoa, or tea, the main meal, and a quick washup. So, although I never touch the stuff at home, both instant oatmeal and wheat-and-barley cereal (e.g., Grape-Nuts) stay on my trail menu. I usually add almonds and raisins or walnuts and currants, and then stir in dry milk before adding water. Sometimes I boost the content by adding a nutritional drink mix along with (or instead of) the dry milk, or by sprinkling in textured vegetable protein (TVP, facing page, footnote). On chill mornings, I stir in hot water and might also add margarine. Hot water turns flakes to unappetizing mush, but Grape-Nuts (or the generic equivalent) stands up to it well. Heritage O's, a multigrain cereal in 26.4-oz. bags (available from Paradise Farms Organics—see Appendix III—or natural-food stores, around $8.50), are equally crush- and mushproof, with a considerably lower gag factor.

But my favorite zero gag-factor breakfast is a toasted bagel with peanut butter and a dab of good jam. The bagel can be toasted on the point of a knife (plastic utensils are risky) over a stove on a low flame, or, even better, with the coals left in a Sierra Stove (page 336) after boiling up. Tricky little fold-up toasters also work, at the cost of ounces.

Since, of a morning, I like genuine coffee, I've tested a variety of brewing methods (page 280). I greet subzero winter dawns by loading the coffee with a few spoons of instant cocoa, a blend known in the low company I formerly kept as "smoking mocha."

COLIN: The important thing is to follow your own fresh or freeze-dried star, tailoring each breakage of a night's fast to suit your own mind and gut and the particular day that fans out ahead. A Texas reader speaks glowingly of grits.* And a New York couple recommend "at close of breakfast" (as well as at bedtime) a 1-ounce package of Swiss Miss, "a really dynamite cocoa" laced with nonfat dry milk and malt.

Lunch

Hot food seems to recharge me best. So for years I lunched on soup. Knorr products come in light, burnable, waxed-paper packages (discard the outer cardboard box), are easy to prepare, and seemed to satisfy me more than others I've tried ($1.50–$2.00—the packages vary somewhat in weight and markedly in calorie content, according to flavor, but average about 10 percent protein, 12 percent fat, and 78 percent carbohydrate).

---

*CHIP: In a firefighting camp, I heard this venerated southern breakfast food referred to as "buttered kitty litter," a comment that nearly precipitated an interregional riot.

But sometimes I replaced the soups with 3-ounce packages of ramen. Alternative cooked lunches: chili, sausage patties.

If, like many people, you make the lunch stop little more than an excuse to get the pack off your back for rather longer than usual, you can just sit down and devour part or even all of a Bear Valley Pemmican or MealPack Bar, or as I do now, a ZonePerfect Bar (page 215). Or you can carry bread, bagels, or tortillas and spread peanut butter or other goodies to your stomach's content. Or you can make lunch no more than another helping, perhaps bigger than normal, of your routine "trail snacks" (page 212). In practice you often have to operate this way, like it or not. I find myself doing so, for example, if it's too cold to stop for long without making camp or if I'm pushing for miles and the days are short.

CHIP: My being a raw-lunch beast probably owes to my living in a part of this earth that's either too maddeningly buggy or too bitingly cold for prolonged halts. Thus, I've made more midday repasts than I like on the contents of a pocket. Given some leisure, the first few days out I'll lunch on hard salami, an aged cheese like Asiago or dry Jack, grainy crackers, and an apple or orange. Later in the trip, my lunch staple is hummus, a fine-textured mix of precooked chickpeas and sesame paste, flavored with salt, pepper, garlic, herbs, lemon juice, or what have you, and generally eaten as a spread. Available in bulk sections of natural-food stores, it packs and keeps well. Besides water, I add a slosh of olive oil and a drizzle of balsamic vinegar, and mix it in a little pop-top container before leaving camp in the morning. Hummus can be eaten on crackers, bagels, tortillas, or in pita bread with whatever garnish suits you.

Britannic afternoon tea

COLIN: Most people can let four o'clock pass without stopping everything (as I am still unable to—despite American citizenship and almost half a century's U.S. residence); but few backpackers fail to drink tea or its nutritional cousin, coffee, at some point in the day. So I'll take this opportunity to air a few minor facts and one scurrilous innuendo.

First, the "facts." A little to my surprise, I find plain, straightforward Lipton tea best for sheer resuscitation power. Thirty bags see even me through the thirstiest week. I normally include a few fancier jobs, mint- or orange- or cinnamon-flavored, for rest-day kicks. Several readers have registered horror at my use of bags. One suggests instant tea, because "tea bags are simply unnecessary deadweight." But a sore-footed reader reports that used tea bags are excellent as a cleansing and soothing wipe for feet, and claims this toughens the skin (perhaps the same way tannic acid does for leather). A "lover of tea and hater of tea bags" counter-recommends a blend of genuine leaves (three parts Darjeeling, three parts Keemun, one part Ceylon, and a dash of Lapsang souchong) which, he avers, can actually be smoked and "will cure all ills, including future smoking of anything."

You carry such loose tea in a zip-top plastic bag and steep by means of a lightweight metal tea basket. A tea sock—cotton or silk on a stainless steel frame—can also be used for coffee. "Iced" tea, in crystal form, is more quickly and easily concocted than hot tea—add the coldest water around, then stir—but doesn't seem to pack the same wallop. Chip suggests brewing "sun tea" as you walk, in a clear Lexan bottle.

The resuscitative power of both tea and coffee stems, of course, from caffeine. And this is where innuendo lurks. I am indebted, or something (what *is* the antonym of "indebted"?), to a Texas reader for a 1974 report by Dr. R. M. Gilbert, published in *Addictions,* the quarterly publication of the Addiction Research Foundation of Ontario. (Note the tainted source.) This report turns up some mildly interesting facts: Tea leaves and coffee beans both contain about 1.5 percent caffeine, but because of preparation methods an average cup of coffee "is believed to contain" more than an average cup of tea (100–150 mg as against 50–75 mg). Tea, unlike coffee, also contains a related drug (another xanthine alkaloid) that neutralizes some of caffeine's rather complicated effects on blood vessels. Many soft drinks also contain caffeine (Coca-Cola: 43 mg per can), and so does chocolate ("about 25 mg per average bar"). The report goes on: "Five studies conducted at Stanford University in the 1960s indicated that caffeine in coffee both prevented and disturbed sleep, and elevated mood but not performance. It also caused characteristic dysphoric symptoms such as irritability, inability to work effectively, nervousness, restlessness, lethargy, and headache when taken by non-users, or not taken by regular users." This hodgepodge of alleged effects is labeled "caffeinism." "Illness otherwise unexplained may be caused by excessive ingestion of the xanthine alkaloids, including those in coffee, tea [and] cocoa. . . ."

Now, coffee and cocoa are mere foods. But such calumnies against the good name of tea are enough to depress the mood, if not the performance, of an Un-British Activities Committee. And worse follows. The report calls caffeine "a drug of concern." Perhaps the most insidious effect, it says, lies in the consequences of its withdrawal. "Many early morning blues are quite likely caffeine withdrawal symptoms. Inability to rise, the empty feeling behind the eyes, irritability, headache and fragility are all relieved by caffeine, but only at the cost of staying on the drug. . . . Studies with rats have shown that the after effects of caffeine on behavior (i.e., the withdrawal effects) are much more profound than the direct effects of the drug, even after one day's administration."

"Ain't this a bitch?" comments my reader-informant. It is indeed.

All I can personally hope for is that Hades has at least a caffeine-maintenance program. Otherwise it'll be just hell down there. Meanwhile, all this emotional stuff has gotten to me, and I must pause for my second fix of the day.

Dinner

Even more than at home, this is the main meal of the day, and probably your main protein intake: the day's walking or exploring or fishing or what-have-you is over, and you have both time to cook and also freedom from the inhibiting prospect of immediate strenuous exercise. The catalogs offer a wild array of dinners, and most now come with fairly simple cooking instructions—though they range from "add boiling water and take five" to shepherding several ingredients through the maze of stirrings and simmerings beloved of do-it-yourself gourmets. With all dinners—and other meals too—ignore such printed fiction as "serves four." If you need the kind of evening meal I do you should allow a total of around 7 ounces, dry weight, and include adequate protein and fat. If you travel solo and find a dinner pack too big, use only half and rubber-band the balance for another day.

Alternatively, you can concoct your own dinners. (For repackaging techniques, see page 221.) Your personal melding of 3 ounces of protein in some form with 4 ounces of vegetables (or whatever amounts seem to suit you) can form the foundation of dinner every night for a week, with very little pain. For the switcheroos are almost limitless. You can vary both protein and vegetable, and the mixtures thereof. The fat, too. You can ring sauce-and-gravy changes. You can shuffle and reshuffle your herbs, spices, and other trimmings. And you can modulate the amount of water so that you serve yourself anything from thickish soup to amorphous loaf. Mostly, though, you end up with what can only be called "stew." Some such variant—which one backpacking companion labeled Fletcher Stew (Boeuf Gallois Alfresco)—was for years my dinner, six days out of seven. Everyone evolves his own standbys.

For Zone eating, the best freeze-dried meals I've found so far come from more or less straight protein packages—turkey, chicken, beef, or fish (Backpacker's Pantry offers good ones)—plus separate vegetables or fruit. AlpineAire Foods' Larry North Gourmet Series (notably Beef Stroganoff, Chicken Rotelle, and Sierra Chicken) provide fairly well balanced three-block entrées (some need extra fat) but they're pasta-heavy: wheat is an "unfavorable" Zone carbohydrate. They're high in sodium, too. So are ZonePerfect four-block ready-to-serve meals—and they're semiliquid and therefore heavy. They also fail to fill me.

CHIP: For dinner, the Pre-Fab Gourmet will simply choose which aluminized package to open and then (removing the oxygen-absorber packet) douse the desiccated delights with boiling water: *voilà!* The Supermarketeer will perform slightly more of a ritual, bringing *x* cups of water to a rolling boil, adding the contents, reducing to a simmer, and stirring like a maniac until the stuff is (let us pray) tender. Meanwhile, the Bulk Stapler will attempt a single-burner *fougasse* of couscous, soy protein bits, garlic flakes, tomato crystals, and chili powder, ending up with Shocking Pink Gumbo. And, naturally, all three will sigh with satisfaction at that first laden spoonful.

I've tried it (dinner that is) just about every possible way, spooning Thai Satay from an aluminized envelope, stirring boxed materials vigorously (until semitender), and bulk-stapling odds and ends together. Particular meals—fresh-caught cutthroat trout with morel mushrooms and wild onions—stand out, as they should. But absent obvious mishaps, like dumping the pot onto your feet, dinner is tough to screw up.

But a few additional bits are needed to fully stock the larder on your back.

Sauce and gravy can brighten, thicken, or, as Colin says, "masculate" an otherwise lackluster potful into Fletchergullion. The choice is immense, from the sturdy Knorr Hunter Sauce mix to the exotics in the gourmet section. Or you can blend your own. I'm seldom without a vial of my diabolic hot sauce, home-concocted from a windowsill pepper garden, that adds considerable bang (with a mild laxative effect).

COLIN: *Herbs, spices, and other trimmings* can vivify any lunch or dinner. I carry three very small bags of herbs on each trip, ringing the changes on ground cumin seed, oregano, thyme, sage, and Italian herb mix. Other bags may hold garlic powder, dried onion flakes, and imitation bacon chips. Sometimes I add a ½-ounce package of dried mushrooms. ("Refresh in cold water 2 to 3 hours. Use the same as fresh mushrooms.") And I've learned that a sprinkling of roasted sunflower seeds imparts a subtle taste and texture to many meals.

But the vital element in dinner trimmings is variety: handle them properly and you'll dine off a different dish every night, even if the basics remain unchanged. Well, a vaguely different dish, anyway.

Desserts rarely grace my dinner menus, but you'll find fruits and other goodies in every food catalog. Try freeze-dried "ice cream" in solid form (not too much like ice cream, perhaps, but it sure as hell tastes good—though it lingers on fingers as well as palate). Another delectable: freeze-dried strawberries flavored with banana chips and a little sugar and lubricated with water and powdered milk. Failing a dessert, you can round off dinner very satisfyingly by a little judicious thieving from your stock of

Trail snacks,

which should be small, conveniently packaged items that don't melt, crumble, or make you unduly thirsty. They travel in an accessible pocket of the pack ("nibble pocket," page 358) or clothing. Pre-Zone, I nibbled at every halt, except perhaps the first of the day.

In harmony with current nutritional gospel, I also curbed my sugar intake. Curbed, but did not eliminate. I long ago banished the mint-cake candy that for years was my staple snack; but I always carried

Hard candies—individually wrapped. (Beware, though, of flimsy little wrappers that slip off more easily than a nightdress, creating sticky pockets and furry candies.) I also mixed in a few specials such as toffees and mints to pamper my postdinner palate. The candies' straight sugar was particularly useful toward the end of a morning or day, when I needed a sharp energy boost and knew I'd be eating a meal within an hour or two. But I might use the candies—sparingly, and buffered with more-balanced snacks—at other halts.

Gorp became my basic snack. The term embraces a wide spectrum of mingle-mangles, usually based on dried fruit and nuts, sometimes with chocolate or carob. In many supermarkets as well as natural-food stores you can now make your choice from a line of intriguing drums and ladle out as much as you need. I became enamored of a supermarket concoction called Tropical Trail Mix (date pieces, raisins, sunflower seeds, coconut chips, pineapple pieces, banana chips, papaya, almonds, and peanuts), but this is a field in which you can switch inamoratae (or inamorati) as often and unguiltily as you like. Make sure, though, that the loved one is somewhat nutty and not too sugary. Then life together should be satisfying and not a switchback of ups and downs.

Mixed nuts in small quantities also make good trail snacks, though I found they more often served to fill odd corners after a meal, especially at night, when their 82-percent fat content can be easily digested—and will help keep you warm. Now they're a Zone staple (page 199). Note that deer mice love nuts with deermonic passion and in order to gratify it will penetrate all manner of obstacles, including layers of thick plastic tucked under your knees at night.

Semisweet chocolate contains about 35 percent fat and in old-style theory is therefore unsuitable for use during or just before strenuous exercise. The balance is mostly sugar, laced with caffeine. I find that chocolate does not, in practice, produce any "heavy" effects—and always tastes good, under any conditions. As a result, I almost always carry it—and always finish it, down to the last morsel. So, I gather, do most walkers, theory or no theory. Supermarket semisweet chocolate, used mainly for cooking, is cheaper than "candy" chocolate, tastes just about as good, and melts less readily. Still, it melts. Try to keep out of direct sunlight. In deserts, avoid.

Banana chips are nutritious, easily digested, rich in potassium, middle-income in minerals, and delectable alone or conglomerated. Note that if prepared with coconut oil they can "go bad."

Beef jerky makes a protein- and fat-rich snack for any time of day, or for dropping into soup or stew—though it will not rehydrate because, unlike most dehydrated foods, it has been heated past the point at which tissue structure is irreversibly damaged, and no amount of soaking will soften its leathery soul. One lb. reputedly equals 3.5 lbs. of fresh steak, but quality seems to vary widely and I can offer no logical testing criteria. You can now buy turkey and even ostrich jerky—at a price in dollars and sodium.

A Pennsylvania reader who "fell in love with biltong in South Africa" gives this recipe for making your own jerky: "Take several pounds of good beef and soak it for 3 hours in salt water. A little fat left on adds to the flavor. Hang up in *dry* wind (cold is fine; just has to be dry), shielded from flies. Let dry for 2 days. Take down and pound peppercorns and any other spices you feel like adding into it. Hang up again to dry until the stuff is hard as a rock. It can be refrigerated and kept forever (or frozen) but will also keep *for weeks* without refrigeration. You will need very strong teeth to deal with the stuff, or preferably a strong knife (you can precut it before you hike) but it is delicious. The Boers thrived on it."

You can make low-fat jerky by using flank steak. And I'm told you can dry the stuff by laying it on cookie sheets in a gas oven, on pilot. If you slice thin, along the meat's grain, the job takes only 12 to 24 hours.

CHIP: The jerky-making gospel I learned is to start with an inch-thick chunk of meat, and with a very sharp knife cut around the edges, taking off a strip in a spiral until the center's reached. I'm told that cutting in a curve shortens the fibers of the meat, which lets it dry faster and makes it a damn sight easier to chew. My experience in drying deer, elk, and bison for staple use supports this. After cutting, I soak the strips in salt brine and afterward treat them the same as the biltong above, at times hanging them in the smoke of a low fire to keep the flies off and add savor. Further jerky counsel is to avoid too much pepper, soy sauce, brown sugar, liquid smoke, or other heavy flavoring, which on long trips can add to the gag factor.

Alternative snacks

Rice crackers aren't absolutely crushproof, but their small size makes them durable and easy to pack. In various interesting shapes and colors, with a light coating of soy sauce, they offer a fuss-free snack. Found in those intriguing bins near the gorp, the plain rice crackers also come mixed with sesame sticks, peanuts, dried peas, and spices—thus adding calories, flavor, and mess—under aliases such as Oriental Party Mix.

The Asian groceries now open in most cities are a source of arresting bits such as dried sour plums and dried seaweed, which are mostly low in calories and high in salt.

Energy bars. Some years ago, a reader gave Colin the recipe for what sounds like the prototype energy bar: "I throw raisins, dates, coconut, figs, prunes, pecans, walnuts and filberts in a heterogeneous mixture into the food chopper. I pack the dubious-looking mess which the chopper spews out into a 1-inch metal tube, ramming it down hard with a close-fitting rod. When the tube is nearly full, I lay it on waxed paper and push the cylindrical rod of 'gorp' out, wrap it in the paper, wrap that in foil, and stow it in the refrigerator. I suppose it would go rancid eventually at summer temperatures but I haven't noticed it after it has been out a week or so. On a hike one merely peels it like a banana."

This is in essence what most energy-bar makers do, with wide variations in philosophy and taste.

Bear Valley Fruit'n Nut Pemmican and MealPack Bars have been around for years and are still favorites for one sound reason: they're recognizably food. And that provides a simple, though not exactly scientific, way of sorting out the present tumble of bars (prefixed *Food, Energy, Performance,* etc). Bear Valley bars resemble the homebaked ration that Finis Mitchell lived on during his many Wind River Range rambles. They taste good, the only complaint being that they tend to be slightly dry. Also at the "food-ish" end of the spectrum are Peak Bars, round, tasty and cookie-like, which have caught on fast in the West. Odwalla Bars and Clif Bars are composed of identifiable bits with generally pleasant flavor. Some all-fruit bars, such as Grabbers, from Canada, rank high in both taste and carbo-kick. The difference, besides ingredients and flavor, is in the proportion of protein, fats, and carbohydrates.*

*Orthodox nutrition (the American Dietetic Association) presently recommends getting 10 to 12 percent of your daily intake of calories from protein, 25 to 30 percent from fat, and the remainder—58 to 75 percent—from carbohydrates. (The Zone system Colin adheres to, by contrast, supplies 30 percent protein, 30 percent fat, and 40 percent carbohydrates.) Of further interest is the proportion of saturated to unsaturated fats. Also important, in terms of how quickly energy is released, is the ratio of simple carbohydrates (most sugars) to complex ones from grains.

Other criteria include the type of grain (you might avoid wheat in favor of oats) and the sweetener (all-fruit, or those from rice or barley malt as opposed to generic corn syrup).

In the midspectrum lie various grainy extrusions, high in nutrition but hard on the eye. (Though doubtless good, cranberries lend a purplish brown hue with disturbing connotations, and the bars that featured them were met by repeated grimaces among fellow hikers as well as outright rejection by a dog.) As we devolve, bars made of finely ground ingredients and semiliquids (e.g., fruit, peanut butter, cocoa, honey, malt syrup) tend to have a slick-sticky texture that one reader reports as unpleasantly "vinyl-like." This textural unease is exacerbated by hot or cold weather—Power Bars in particular have a reputation for playing havoc with dental work. A further caveat with food bars is a fart potential that makes another reader call them "flammable fiestas." Thus, if you see bars as a significant part of your field ration, buy several brands for experimental chilling, heating, and devourment, to note the effects.

At the nonfood end of the spectrum (in appearance at least) are bars that look like candy: precise rectangles, often coated with chocolate or some simulacrum thereof. Balance Bars have 40 percent carbohydrates and 30 percent each of protein and fat. The ones I tried varied from nicely concentrated to chalky and *uck*-sweet, particularly when coated with chocolatey stuff. I tried ZonePerfect Bars too—somehow, regardless of their salutary effect, they just didn't seem like food.

The latest nutritive dribble is gel: GU, Power Gel, and other carbohydrate fixes come sealed in tubes or little plastic bladders ($1.00–$1.50 each), which you squeeze onto your eager tongue. Several of my fast-twitch climber friends recommend them highly and Linda, subject to low-blood-sugar crashes, also liked them a lot. Being a primitive in matters of sweets I can imagine *Star Trek* characters consuming such things, far from this Earth.

COLIN: Note Chip's opinion, above, on ZonePerfect Bars. I agree. But as a barbarian I'm overwhelmingly concerned with nutritional values—and by Zone criteria these bars (two blocks each) are nutritionally perfect. I always carry plenty for snacks, even occasional meals. Also as emergency rations. Don't try to live on them exclusively, that's all. Balance Bars come close and taste less like sawdust but lack certain ingredients. In hot weather, try to avoid all chocolate-coated bars.

For the carbohydrate in snacks, and also as fill-ins for meals, I carry dried fruit. For fat, nuts (especially almonds, peanuts, filberts, macadamias); also olive oil and Benecol Lite margarine (which, as promised, drove down my cholesterol and which, though best kept refrigerated at home, can be backpacked without loss of nutritional value, only of texture). For protein you can, if you're not sodium-sensitive, try turkey jerky, or ostrich ditto; and there are several palatable and effective "high protein" bars, including Met-Rx's Protein Plus and Worldwide Sport Nutrition's Pure Protein (labeled "low-glycemic"); also, less proteinly, Biochem's Ultimate Protein Bar. All these items are easy to measure into Zone blocks.

Overall, I find that my almost tireless leg pump alone is well worth the mild kitchen hassle of eating Zonic.

Finally, remember that trail snacks are not only for snacks: they may form your entire lunch; they can round off any meal; and for people who dine early they make the most convenient warming-effect-last-thing-at-night snacks (page 478). So whenever need strikes, delve into your personally evolved nibble bags of trail snacks, come up with whatever catches your fancy, serve to taste, and continue singing in that loud and cheerful voice.

A few words on some staple items:

Milk. Adding cream to nonfat milk (that is, milk from which the cream has been removed) sounds crazy; but with low-fat Milkman it seems to work. At least, that is what the makers say they do before drying their product; and the resulting powder dissolves at least as quickly as the Carnation Nonfat I used to favor, tastes distinctly better, contains about 25 percent more calories, and somehow seems to go appreciably further in normal use. A single foil envelope (3.44 oz./97 g; 360 calories; 36 g protein, 6 g fat, 44 g carbohydrate, battalions of vitamins; 12 envelopes for $9.69) makes 1 quart of reconstituted milk (butterfat: 0.5 percent), neatly fills (with a little shaking down before the final topping up) my plastic milk squirter (page 285), and unless used ultralavishly lasts me rather more than a single day.*

Granulated sugar. Use as a condiment, not a food. Even pre-Zone I used to take no more than 6 ounces, rather than the ½ pound or even 2 pounds I once did. Now, rarely any.

Margarine (rather than butter, because it keeps) improves almost any dish. (Liquid margarine, procured in squeeze bottles, is most convenient.) And because it is almost pure fat it has a higher energy/weight ratio than almost any food you can lay sticky hands on (204 calories per ounce, though "light" margarine might have between one-half down to one-

---

*CHIP: New on the market is a zero-cow mix called Instead of Yogurt (Sovex, P.O. Box 2178, Collegedale, TN 37315). Good for people with lactose intolerance, it comes in several flavors that go well with cold cereal. One problem: the packets balloon (and might pop) at higher elevations.

twentieth of this count, so read the label with care. These figures compare with 203 calories for butter, 159 for sunflower seeds, 144 for semisweet chocolate, 112 for Milkman dried milk, 109 for granulated sugar, 105 for spaghetti, 28 for raw brook trout [flesh only], 14 for raw brook trout [whole], 3 for watermelon [raw, whole], and 20 for zwieback. But note that salad or cooking oil packs 251). Pre-Zone, in spite of the then-current antifat strictures, I usually took 2 or 3 ounces of margarine for a week's trip. In trout country I often carried an extra 4 ounces, for frying.*

Fruit-drink mixes used to mean Wyler's or Kool-Aid or similar in some flavor that pleased you. (One reader wrote that he'd heard grape juice was the best thirst quencher, but I suspect his informant of being a straight-faced W. C. Fields.) Such sugary concoctions are pleasant quick-energy sources that disguise the taste of unappetizing water. But what you drink at halts can, much more importantly, also be a means of replenishing the electrolytes (potassium and sodium, and chloride radicals) that you lose in sweating. Gatorade, in crystal form, will do the job. But I found that Gookinaid ERG (Electrolyte Replacement with Glucose, developed by Bill Gookin, a marathon runner) does it even better and seemed to lie much more lightly on the stomach. ERG now comes in 1.8-oz. envelopes (makes 1 quart, $.95–$1.25), and 35-oz. plastic tubs (makes 5 gallons, $10–$12); but prices may be about to go up. The potassium-sodium ratio of ERG is reputedly calibrated with that of the average human sweat: according to the manufacturers, human sweat ranges from 31 to 47 percent potassium and 18 to 37 percent sodium; and ERG provides 42.1 percent potassium, 32.4 percent sodium—while Gatorade has 9.8 percent and 48.3 percent, respectively. The degree of dilution of the ERG is therefore important. If you need or are prepared to carry a full quart canteen, no problem. Otherwise, eye-stimate. This leads us into the whole question of

Electrolyte replacement. When you sweat you lose not only water but also the electrolytic salts, potassium, and sodium chloride (see above), and without them in the right proportions, electrical processes within the body become impaired. Unless you replace both water and salts you may suffer from heat exhaustion.

---

*This paragraph set me toying with the idea of a new appendix listing calories per ounce for a wide range of backpacking foods. In the end I decided "no." And not only because the job would be a pain in the butt. Such a list might dangerously mislead earnest people who ignored such vital factors as nutritional balance, minimum protein requirements, upper fat and sugar limits, vitamin and mineral requirements, and the need for some fiber and at least some variety—not to mention the vagaries of taste. Anyway, if you really want such figures, consult the new alternatives to *Agricultural Handbook No. 8* (page 192), which, as you've no doubt zwiebacked out, is what I did.

Electrolyte replacement was once seen as a matter of "salt" replacement. That is, replacement of sodium chloride. Hence the popularity of salt tablets (see below)—which actually often contain potassium chloride too. But it now seems generally accepted that, except possibly for people on very stringent low-sodium diets, no one is likely to suffer from sodium deficiency, no matter how much sweat pours out (note that most backpacking foods are riddled with salt), but that potassium deficiency after heavy sweating is entirely possible.

On a practical level, then, the response to heavy sweating should be replacement of *all* lost materials. First and most important, the water—if possible, in small, frequently consumed quantities so that no serious deficiency arises. Second, along with the water, potassium in the form of the chloride. And third—and possibly least important—the sodium. ERG accomplishes these aims perfectly, provided its concentration is right.

CHIP: Friends also recommend Cytomax, a sports drink that comes in orange, tropical, and peach flavors, with packets (that make 1 liter, $1.50) and 1.5-lb. cans ($20). I've tasted it—not bad—but haven't used it regularly enough to notice a difference from my usual water-plus-nibbles regimen. Label squinting does reveal that some sports drinks are high in maltodextrins—long-chain sugar molecules that are said to provide more kick with less digestive cost than common sucrose and glucose. If you intend to swill gallons of such stuff, there may also be things you don't want—stimulants such as caffeine, ephedrine, or norepinephrine (found in the Chinese herb *ma huang* and claimed to improve the digestion of fats, but which, according to mountaineer Mark Twight, "is a vasoconstrictor without peer, narrowing the blood vessels and making cold-weather injury more likely").*

A good principle is to first quench your thirst with water and then follow up with a few swigs of electrolyte replacer.

COLIN: Salt tablets, the old standbys, should probably be avoided, not only because the potassium/sodium ratio is wrong but also because consuming them without the right amounts of water can insult internal balances and cause serious illness. In cases of suspected heat prostration, Lite Salt (with half the sodium of regular salt and much more potassium) or No Salt (rich in potassium, almost sodium-free), taken in large quantities of water, are safer and more effective than tablets. As a preventive measure, use Lite Salt or No Salt in your shaker (as I've done for years) and sprinkle profusely over meals.

*Mark Twight and James Martin, *Extreme Alpinism,* page 77.

Some authorities now deny that any such precautions are necessary. Supply a little potassium, they say, and you can't get electrolyte deficiency. Along with a lot of people, I disagree. Twice—once backpacking in desert, once after a long summer day's tennis—I've suffered what I still can't see as anything but electrolyte deficiency. On the other hand, there seems little doubt that individual requirements vary widely. Years ago, when salt tablets were still standard, a Death Valley ranger told me, "When it reaches 110°F, I take one tablet a day. I need that one, but my stomach won't accept more. Yet there's a guy at Park HQ who has to take twenty a day. If he doesn't he ends up in the hospital."

Important footnote: It now seems generally accepted that too much sodium, at least in some people, raises blood pressure and can increase the likelihood of a heart attack. And don't assume that such strictures apply only to old crocks like me with marginally high blood pressure. There's some evidence that it pays to reduce sodium intake as early in life as possible.

Vitamins and minerals. See page 198. Some people backpack with the whole quinque-alphabet in tablet form. To improve performance on long high-altitude expeditions, others take vitamin E or stress-potency C and D complex. I used to rely on my fresh-food-at-home body reserve, plus additives in the dehydrated foods and maybe dried seaweed. But a flood of evidence—flowing not only from New Agers but also, increasingly, from the medical establishment—has converted me. At home and backpacking, I now swallow—spread out over each day—a rich and often-modified array of multicolored and -shaped pills and capsules. At home I rely on fresh greens and fruit to take care of my vitamin C needs. But when backpacking I take one 500-mg tablet every day I don't forget; and I carry a reserve so that if a cold strikes a couple of days out from the civilization that passed it along, I can suppress the effects with a first dose of 1000 mg. and then 500 every few hours. Of course, nobody but nobody in his right rutted mind believes Linus Pauling's assertions, in *Vitamin C and the Common Cold,* that vitamin C can also curb or even cure cancer. Well, almost nobody: Blue Cross of California has suggested that it may nullify the cancer-causing effects of sodium nitrite, a preservative often used in cured meats such as bologna, salami, and commercial jerky. So maybe even the ruts are being overrun.

Spirulina (*spear-oh-LEE-nuh*) is still sometimes touted as a vitamin source. It's a blue-green algal plankton, commercially harvested, mainly from a Mexican lake, and sold in pill, capsule, and powder form; when I wrote *Walker III* a growing band of enthusiasts were swearing blue-green murder that it did matchless things for their minds and bodies. Some even used it as their sole food on backpack trips. My skepticism at the time has hardened. And the mini-tumult has subsided—but not vanished. I guess the stuff could be a valid vitamin source.*

CHIP: In places where I know the plants well, I sometimes gather fresh greens (see page 188), but for long trips you can also equip the house on your back with a grow-as-you-go garden, by sprouting seeds and grains. The basic drill is to soak the seeds overnight, drain them, seal them in a zip-top bag or plastic bottle, and put them in a dark place in your pack. Rinse and drain them at least two to three times daily (using filtered water, so you don't inadvertently start a *giardia* farm). After they sprout, brief exposure to sun will green them up. Keep rinsing and devour promptly. For a steady supply, start a new batch every two to three days. For the best varieties and technical tips, consult any of the several hundred books available. Prepared sprout packs are sold in health-food stores and even supermarkets.

COLIN: It's probably wise to carry a small *emergency ration* of some sort, just in case of trouble. I now rely on an extra ZonePerfect Bar plus one Bear Valley Fruit'n Nut Pemmican Bar (page 214).

Morale-boosting: goodies. If you've been living on dehydrated food for days or weeks or months you won't hesitate, given half a chance, to call in at a café (as I could occasionally on the California walk) and order a red-blooded steak or whatever your fantasies have been featuring. Even under more Spartan conditions you may be able to engineer a change of pace, beyond such delicacies as small trout so fresh that it's a problem to keep them from curling double in the frying pan: consult your palate, and pack along one small, fully hedonistic meal.

On my Grand Canyon walk I included in each cache and airdrop one can of delectables—oysters, lobster, cocktail meatballs, fish appetizers, or frog's legs—and a small bottle of claret. The goodies were great. But the claret, oddly enough, didn't really fit in. And I decided that you simply didn't need alcohol in the wilderness. Not when you were on your own, anyway. Yet nowadays I find that I often, but not always, take along a snort of bourbon. This change no doubt indicates a heightening of common sense, mellowness, or depravity.

Purists still maintain that the only satisfactory container for booze is glass, but I find that the little hip flasks made of hard plastic leave bourbon unblurred. (Says Chip: Lexan is rugged, see-through, and lighter than

---

*CHIP: According to yet another reader who experimented with spirulina on an extended walk, "There is no such thing as a food substitute." He reports passing out on day 21 "from a lack of calories."

stainless steel, for a better net weight of Old Overcoat. Nalgene has nice loop-top pint bottles of Lexan, and GSI makes a 16-ounce Lexan flask in the traditional butt-hugging shape, for regular applications of Celtic medicine.) A reader writes that "Lemon Hart or Hudson's Bay Demerara rum, at 151 proof, gives you twice the mileage for half the weight." The math seems murky but the idea sound.

Even if you deplore solitary drinking there's no denying that a little Scotch or bourbon (or potent rum) can be very welcome in a group at the end of a day. Especially in a group of two. A bottle, or even half bottle, of champagne carried secretly in a male chauvinist's pack and then produced with a flourish from a cold creek at lunch or dinnertime may just possibly help melt a damsel's heart. And there is absolutely nothing, of course, to prevent a damsel chauvinist from trying her delicate hand at male heart melting.

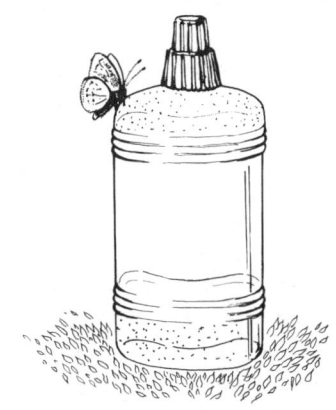

Packaging—and repackaging

The foil envelopes in which freeze-dried foods come (because air must be rigorously excluded until they're used) have a very long shelf life; but they will sometimes crack under bottom-of-the-pack buffeting—though the best are now becoming very tough indeed. The foil cannot be burned, cannot be burned, cannot be burned, and must be packed out, must be packed out, must be packed out. Note, for paranoid weight-saving moods, that the edges of many foil packages can be trimmed, especially up top, where holes for store display live.

The polyethylene that houses most vacuum-dried foods—and that also forms standard supermarket plastic bags—gives the illusion of being burnable. But in fact there's always a residue, and I now pack out such empties. Polyethylene is moistureproof for reasonable periods, but there's some degree of porosity (for an alternative, see Mylar, below). In damp climates the packages should if possible be stored or cached in airtight cans, preferably with some desiccant such as silica gel or Drierite (anhydrous calcium sulfate), which come with moisture indicators and can be regenerated by baking. (Silica gel from VWR Scientific Company, Box 7900, San Francisco, CA 94120, 1-800-841-0617; Drierite from them too, and from W. A. Hammond Drierite Company, Ltd., Box 460, Xenia, OH 45385, fax 937-376-1977.)

If you choose to buy in bulk (page 201) and repackage you must take certain precautions. Because of the very short storage life of freeze-dried foods after opening you can't satisfactorily repack them. But if you buy vacuum-dried products in bulk you can repackage into small amounts that suit your requirements by buying small heat-seal bags and sealing with a warm iron. Ditto if you dehydrate your own foods (page 204). Mylar affords a better air-and-moisture barrier than polyethylene, which is somewhat permeable. But Mylar is not readily heat-sealable. Laminated Mylar/polyethylene bags, eminently heat-sealable, can be bought in ½-pint, 1-pint, and 2-pint sizes. If you plan to do a great deal of repackaging, specialized heat-sealing equipment (available where cooking and food storage supplies are sold) will ease the task. For splitting out portions of bulk freeze-dried foods, Sears sells the Fresh Lock II vacuum sealer for about $40.

CHIP: Twist ties have gained ill-fame for turning up in unlikely spots— inside trout—and the alternatives work just as well. Plastic bags with durable zip closures come in an array of sizes, and with careful use and rewashing have sometimes lasted me for several trips. Not as reusable but madly useful are the snack-size (6.5 by 3.25 inches) bags, perfect for a daily portion of gorp or compact and oft-used things such as loose tea. National Outdoor Leadership School (NOLS) food guru Claudia Pearson, author of *NOLS Cookery,* recommends using plain plastic bags that are long enough to be loaded and then tied in a loose knot.

Crackers can be guarded with a stiffish container that fits their shape: Pringles potato-chip cans work (but wash out the greasy residue first). The canisters that hold fancy liquor are more durable and come in various shapes. Plastic freezer containers are also good. If you have a favorite cracker, memorize the dimensions—Stoned Wheat Thins are 65 millimeters square—or cut out a piece of stiff cardboard and tuck it in your wallet for rapid fit assessment.

Specimen food list

It hadn't occurred to me—before now—that a list of what I choose to eat for a week constitutes self-revelation. But so it does. I have a shameless passion for hot peppers, garlic, and strong coffee, and on the trip for which the food table was made, I indulged myself. At other times, veering toward self-denial (or shaving weight) I take not coffee but loose tea, and forgo delights such as salami and crisp apples.

This list differs from the one in the previous edition in some ways worth noting. While most of the gear on our various lists has grown lighter, my week's ration is 1 lb. 15 oz. heavier than Colin's in *Walker III.*

This is partly my self-indulgence (real coffee, salami) and partly a strong preference for fresh food (apples, onion, garlic). I'm also a bigger beast: 215 lbs. to Colin's 175 or so. Factoring his list by the difference in our weights, I'd be carrying 17 lbs. 4 oz. of food.

My specimen list (for a fall trip with freezing nights) lowers the calories—from 26,332 to 25,033 (that is, from 3762 calories to 3576 calories per day). The ratio from Colin's list in the third edition is 15 percent protein, 36 percent fat, and 52 percent carbohydrate. My list has 18 percent protein, 33 percent fat, and 49 percent carbohydrate. Backpacker's Pantry recommends 15 percent protein, 25 percent fat, and 60 percent carbohydrate. In contrast, the Zone goal is 30 percent protein, 30 percent fat, and 40 percent carbohydrate—dumping carbs in favor of protein. The upshot: whatever your preference, someone recommends it.

Rather than dousing and wolfing expensive prepacked entrees, I usually combine various bits with bulk staples. I happened to have a bulk pouch of freeze-dried chicken, so most nights I ate chicken-and-something. The something might be wild rice, mushrooms, garden veggies, and diced fresh garlic and onion. Or it was black beans, "Southwestern" corn, dried scallions, fresh garlic, and hot pepper sauce. The last night out was odds and ends.

I came home with a day-and-a-half's food: dry cereal, a couple of Bear Valley Bars, the leek soup mix, and ramen. But that's as it should be—if you come home having devoured every scrap and morsel, you aren't carrying enough.

To calculate the values for the accompanying food table, I used package labels and the *Complete Book of Food Counts* (see Appendix IV), which is handily portable and affordable but gives values based on widely differing units (e.g., cups, ounces, slices, teaspoons). Meanwhile, the required nutritional labels on packages tend to state counts by the "serving" (often canary-size) rather than for the package. By contrast, the USDA *Agricultural Handbook No. 8* and its many supplemental manuals give counts based on 100 grams, with helpful notes like "1 slice = 12 grams." To be truly scientific in your method, always double-check the units. (For more on this subject see Colin's discussion on pages 191–203.)

Given a list with calorie counts, it's not hard to shift food values around. Look especially for foods that are high in one column: freeze-dried chicken is almost pure protein, while margarine is fat, and dried fruit is nearly all carbs. Of further interest is the proportion of saturated to unsaturated fat, and also the balance of simple carbs (sugar) to complex ones (rice and pasta). By adjusting amounts you can change your intake markedly. Likewise, if money is a ruling variable, replace foods with a high cost-per-ounce (typically freeze-dried and/or prepackaged and/or self-indulging) with staple equivalents.

Net wt. (oz.)	Quantity	Item	Brand	Number of days	Energy value (calories)	CALORIES Protein	Fat	Carbo-hydrate	Protein (grams)	Cost ($)	Cost (per oz.)
		BREAKFASTS									
5.0	—	Wheat and barley cereal	(Supermarket)	2	541	67	5	469	14	2.49	0.08
5.0	1	Outrageous Outback Oatmeal	Paradise Farm	1+	570	48	90	432	12	3.63	0.21
3.5	—	Raisins	(Natural-food store)	3	333	12	4	317	3	0.67	0.19
14.0	4	Bagel, multigrain	(Bakery)	4	660	96	36	528	24	1.86	0.13
5.0	—	Peanut butter, chunky	Adams	4	937	131	675	131	33	0.50	0.10
2.5	4 tbsp.	All-fruit spread	(Supermarket)	4	160	0	0	160	0	0.85	0.34
3.8	1	Fruit 'n Nut Pemmican Bar	Bear Valley	1	420	68	104	248	17	1.49	1.49
6.0	—	Coffee, French roast	Coal Creek	6	n.a.	—	—	—	—	4.50	0.75
		LUNCHES									
8.0	—	Salami, hard	(Deli)	3	909	205	689	15	51	2.99	0.37
6.0	—	Cheese, Asiago	Stella	3	702	168	486	48	42	3.36	0.56
7.0	2	Bagel, onion	(Bakery)	2	330	48	18	264	12	0.93	0.13
14.0	2	Apple, Macintosh	(Supermarket)	2	177	4	4	169	1	1.13	0.08
6.0	—	Hummus	(Natural-food store)	4	726	120	270	336	30	2.02	0.34
8.8	18 pieces	Multigrain crispbread	Wasa	6	720	144	0	576	36	2.39	0.27
7.5	2	MealPack Bar, Coconut Almond	Bear Valley	2	792	128	216	448	34	2.98	1.49
		DINNERS									
8.0	1	Chicken, cooked, freeze-dried	AlpineAire Foods	5	1424	1280	144	0	320	27.81	3.48
6.0	—	Wild Rice, quick-cooking	Trail Gourmet	3	678	88	126	464	22	4.13	1.16
8.0	1	Garden Vegetable Mix	AlpineAire Foods	4	842	132	50	660	33	8.31	1.04
2.0	—	Mushrooms, sliced, dehydrated	Trail Gourmet	3	104	40	0	64	10	3.00	1.50
6.0	—	Black Beans, quick-cooking	Trail Gourmet	2	239	65	11	163	16	1.22	0.20
1.8	1	No-cook Southwestern Corn	Backpacker's Pantry	2	188	24	20	144	6	2.95	1.69
6.0	—	Couscous, bulk	(Natural-food store)	3	665	144	24	497	36	0.56	0.09
4.0	1	Corn & Black Bean Chowder	Paradise Farm	2	358	56	54	248	14	6.46	1.62
4.5	1	Classic Split Pea Soup	Paradise Farm	1	320	96	0	224	24	4.95	1.10
5.1	1	Cajun Rice & Sauce w/ Beans	Lipton	1	523	80	27	416	20	1.59	0.31
1.8	1	Leek Soup	Knorr	1	213	24	81	108	6	1.99	1.11
3.0	1	Ramen	(Supermarket)	1	396	40	144	212	10	0.16	0.05

Net wt. (oz.)	Quantity	Item	Brand	Number of days	Energy value (calories)	CALORIES Protein	Fat	Carbo-hydrate	Protein (grams)	Cost ($)	Cost (per oz.)
		TRAIL SNACKS									
12.0	—	Raw trail mix	(Supermarket)	7	1620	192	756	672	48	2.77	0.23
8.0	—	Mixed dried fruit	(Natural-food store)	7	534	22	0	512	5.5	2.50	0.31
8.0	—	Almonds, shelled	(Natural-food store)	7	1432	192	1080	160	48	2.50	0.31
8.0	—	Sunflower seeds, shelled raw	(Natural-food store)	7	1619	197	1274	148	49	0.54	0.07
6.4	4	Energy bar, mixed fruit	Grabber	4	604	10	18	576	2.4	3.98	0.62
4.8	2	Food bar, carrot-raisin	Odwalla	2	501	48	45	408	12	3.18	0.66
3.7	21	Hard candies	Werther's	7	427	0	63	364	0	2.99	0.23
2.0	2 bars	Bittersweet Baking Chocolate	Hershey's	2	290	0	162	128	1	0.60	0.30
		STAPLES									
2.0	1 head	Garlic, fresh	(Homegrown)	6	91	14	2	75	3.6	—	—
4.0	1	Onion, fresh	(Supermarket)	2	47	5	4	38	1.2	0.10	0.03
2.0	—	Diabolic pepper sauce	(Homemade)	6	16	0	0	16	0	—	—
1.0	2 tbsp.	Balsamic vinegar	(Supermarket)	7	24	0	0	24	0	0.29	0.29
1.0	—	Scallions, dried	(Homegrown)	7	6	2	0	4	0.4	—	—
8.0	—	Milk, dry nonfat	(Supermarket)	7	797	320	0	477	80	1.46	0.18
4.0	—	Margarine, liquid	(Supermarket)	7	834	8	826	0	2	0.52	0.13
2.0	—	Olive oil	(Natural-food store)	7	514	0	514	0	0	0.46	0.23
2.0	—	Brown sugar	(Supermarket)	7	221	0	0	221	0	0.08	0.04
2.0	—	Salt	(Supermarket)	7	n.a.	—	—	—	—	0.04	0.02
1.5	10 bags	Tea, assorted herb flavors	Celestial Seasonings	6	n.a.	—	—	—	—	1.75	1.17
9.0	5 packets	Electrolyte drink mix	Gookinaid ERG	5	959	0	0	959	0	5.75	0.64
4.5	—	Nutritional drink, chocolate	Balance	3	570	168	162	240	42	3.13	0.70
1.0	8	Multivitamin tablets	(Natural-food store)	7	n.a.	—	—	—	—	0.53	0.53
255oz. = 15lb. 15 oz.		**TOTAL FOR ONE WEEK**			25,033	4486	8184	12,363	1121	$128.09	
2 lb.	4.4 oz.	**DAILY AVERAGES**			3576	641	1168	1169	160	$18.39	

COLIN: No perfect food list for every trip exists, of course. It's not only that we have to meet the varying demands of weather, terrain, load, and trip length: our theories, tastes, and prejudices change; and most of us experiment.

I am not menu-minded. The meticulous culinary briefings that beguile so many people leave me emotionally inert, intellectually repelled. But there's no doubt about the general beguilement. Backpacking magazines and books steam with menus. One classified ad read: "FOOD PLANNING DONE! Prepackage for whole season. Nutrition tips. 3 week menu, shopping list, recipes for lightweight, inexpensive, spoilage-free eating. $3.25." And another: "DELICIOUS vegetarian backpacking menu and recipes. Detailed menu for 7 days. Send $3.00." Then there's a stack of books expressing attitudes quite different from mine: still in print after almost 20 years is *The Hungry Hiker's Book of Good Cooking* by Gretchen McHugh.

Menus, then, are not my bag. But there are valid reasons to come up with one. See pages 224 to 225. Offered primarily as an up-to-date starting point from which beginners can work out their own salvations, the selection is designed to suggest ideas and sources and at the same time to convey as much information as possible about quantities, nutritional values, and costs of items fairly readily available to western backpackers. Easterners, I'm afraid, and to a greater degree Canadians, may need to translate a few items.

My menus and cooking methods place me, I guess, somewhere around midway on the scale of current backpackers' eating systems.

At one extreme on the scale (upper or lower, take your pick) crouch the fancy cookers, simmering, steaming, sautéing, baking, and otherwise gourmeting; all terribly civilized. I'm afraid I have nothing of value to offer in this field—beyond drawing your attention to a couple of fancy utensils (page 265).

At the other extreme march the gustatory zealots.

CHIP: To lump a number of mutually exclusive eating disciplines—Anti-Cookers, Algae Eaters, Whole Grain Sprouters, Supplementarians, and Military Rationalists—into this single zealot category is to court the ire of all. But the common characteristic is that food zealots of all stripes tend to rank their current theory somewhat higher than food itself. Naturally, there's spirited contention and some outright nuttery. But in these specialized approaches there are also kernels of wisdom that should be rolled on the tongue, chewed meditatively, and, in some cases, swallowed.

COLIN: You can, of course, forgo cooking and ingest just as many calories as a gourmet. Of the items on Chip's sample menu the food bars, cold cereal, hummus, trail snacks, and staples demand no cooking; and with a little imagination you could increase and augment them into a 4000- or 5000-calorie diet. Starting from scratch it would be even easier.

Any noncooking regimen promises stunning advantages—and possible penalties.

The fundamental argument of noncookers is that an ounce of extra food provides far more calories for the body than does an ounce of fuel used to heat food. So far, so true. But if you don't cook you save much more than fuel weight. You need carry no stove or accessories, no pots, no utensils beyond a cup. Already we have eliminated over 4 pounds. But that's by no means the end of it: you can also get by with a far smaller tent, even in foul weather. (In snow, rabid noncookers say, you simply "eat" snow—letting body heat convert it to drink.) A tiny tent, or bivy sack, will save maybe 2 or 3 pounds, compared with a bigger model. And if you carry your noncooking to a spirulina extreme you eliminate in food alone, for a week's trip, 14 pounds or so.

Not cooking saves time too. "It makes life so simple," says my practitioner-informant. "On one recent trip I made a severe error: I forgot to take a book. And I repeatedly found that when I had done everything—taken all the pictures I wanted to take, washed myself, admired all the views—there was nothing to do. So I ended up walking all day." I suspect that most people find, like me, that on a normal backpacking day there is always enough, if not too much, to be done—and would revel in the richness of more spare time.

But it seems to me that noncooking may impose unacceptable burdens—even millstones. I mean more than the heavy load of deprivation laid on incurable fancy cookers or, even more onerously, on tea or coffee addicts. For I don't think we should write off the pure efficiency value—perhaps even survival value—of hot food. It could be dangerous to dismiss its effects as "psychological"—as if that were something utterly detached from "physiological." A thought, after all, "is" molecular movement—and as such can surely be affected by immediately available calories; furthermore, the nature of your thoughts in critical situations can radically influence your survival chances. And while it may be just possible to dismiss a hot breakfast drink as mere hedonism, I can only regard a hot dinner differently.*

---

*About that hot breakfast drink, though: A reader sent me a neat calculation, based on drinking one cup (¼ liter) of tea or other hot beverage to bring him back to early-morning life. If the drink is at 176°F/ °80°C (the upper limit of tolerability) it provides, in cooling down to body temperature of 86°F/ 30°C, 12.5 calories—enough for 7½ minutes of basal metabolism for the average person. And these calories are immediately available, surging through you, and

Just before dinner, at the end of a long, hard day's walking, there often comes a moment when you suffer from something suspiciously like incipient hypothermia (page 746). All day you've been sweating freely. As soon as you stop, you put on warm clothing. But for a few minutes, as the sweat dries, you feel not only on the verge of coldness but also mentally and physically sluggish. These symptoms are the classic early signs of hypothermia. I'm not suggesting that in most such cases they are at all dangerous, or even serious, but I notice that in my case they often persist until a hot meal sends warmth coursing through me. To overcome the sluggishness and prod me into preparing dinner, I often supply my body with quick energy in the form of a little sugar-rich food. And although that tends to help marginally, it's only after I get hot food inside me that I feel the internal radiators turn on. In other words, far below the danger level, your body may need hot food to get the furnace roaring. If hypothermia approaches the critical stage, of course, you may need hot food to keep the fires from falling below the point of no return—and flickering out (page 750). So a noncooking regimen, it seems to me, might possibly prove highly inefficient, even dangerous: in critical situations you would have no practical way of providing hot food when the need began to crystallize in your already sluggish brain.

Now, please do not read these thoughts as blanket condemnation of noncooking—any more than the preceding list of advantages as a blanket recommendation. I'm merely expressing cautious misgivings. Noncooking may turn out to be the Wave of the Future. I suggest, anyway, that it's possible, as so often happens in life, to benefit from the actions of extremists without stumbling into their snake pits. For alfresco eaters form a continuum, from the fanciest cookers to the spirulina Spartans. It has always been so. John Muir apparently used to subsist largely on bread. Teddy Roosevelt probably did not. And even down toward the austere end of the continuum you can ring almost infinite changes. Tibetans, I understand, favor a day-after-day menu that is soul sustaining in both hot and cold weather, easy to carry and prepare, and surprisingly palatable: hot tea with butter and salt, mixed to a gruel with parched barley. (Note that this traditional menu meets almost all our current complicated criteria—yea, unto a caffeine fix.) But if you want to travel with a light and simple kitchen, regard all such models as no more than signposts. Devise a menu that suits and satisfies your own tastes. Keep modifying it too. For years, whenever conditions demanded or indicated, I carried only a "rock-

---

therefore set you up to assimilate the main breakfast and get on with the day. As the reader wrote: "This system does not make me fast or efficient in the morning. Nothing can. But it does simplify getting up."

bottom, tin-can kitchen" (page 368) designed to boil water but do little more. Under that regimen I sometimes subsisted, ad nauseam—breakfast, lunch, and dinner—on meat bars, mitigated only by tea, trail snacks, and fruit drink. I once ad-nauseamed it like that for 10 days in some Arizona mountains and emerged fit and happy with lots of miles and no vomiting behind me—though I did cheat with one fancy rest-day lunch that tasted, I admit, transcendentally ambrosial. On other occasions I mitigated further with such thrilling variations as bacon bars, dry cereal, and dried fruit. Later, because I knew of no acceptable meat bar, I would substitute Bear Valley Pemmican—perhaps with soup for furnace-stoking dinner—and thereby cut the cooking even further. Or I might take Mountain House no-pot-needed packages (now fairly common) and, though losing some simplicity and a point or two on my ounce/calorie rating, achieve a more varied diet. I repeat, though, that the important thing is to suit your own taste and temperament. Experiment. And keep experimenting. You're limited by little but your imagination.

CHIP: Under certain conditions I give up cookery altogether. When it's hot out, my desire for hot food is lessened. And when mosquitoes, blackflies, no-see-ums, buffalo gnats (or whatever your local bane may be), reach their peak, making camp consists largely of getting under netting as fast as humanly possible. Whether it's the heat or the carbon dioxide that attracts bugs, any stove I've ever used has been a biomagnet. This makes cookery actively painful and also raises the question of whether you're getting enough extra calories to make up for the lost blood. Uncooked food itself need not be Spartan. Rich and tasty delights such as hummus or tabouli can be mixed sans flame. Some freeze-dried packets will rehydrate to edibility with unheated water (though meats, peas, and beans seldom reach tenderness). Ultralight through-hiking in warm climates is the milieu in which the no-cook theory flourishes and makes the most sense. For emergencies, astute pre-Prometheans carry a metal cup in which water can be heated and some fuel tablets (see page 335).

A similar bent is that of the Military Rationalists, who treat walks as do-or-die missions and subsist—chewing grimly—on packaged survival rations. These are typically high-calorie bars, and the ones I've tried so far have a monumental gag factor. The other problem is that such concentrated rations tend to clog up your pipes—no joke on the trail. In fact, Roald Amundsen and party tried to subsist on a concentrated ration during their first attempt on the South Pole and were turned back by constipation, which led to lethargy, hemorrhoids, and related miseries. The remedy is to eat dried fruit or other roughage and also to drink lots of

WATER.

COLIN: You can if necessary do without food for days or even weeks and still live, but if you go very long without water you assuredly die. In really hot deserts the limit of survival without water may be barely 48 hours. And well before that your brain is likely to become so addled that there's a serious risk of committing some irrational act that will kill you.

Dangers of dehydration

Too few people recognize the insidious nature of such thirst-induced irrationality. It can swamp you, suddenly and irretrievably, without your being in the least aware of it.*

WATER REQUIREMENTS

	Maximum daily temperature (°F) in shade	Available water per man, U.S. quarts					
		0 qt.	1 qt.	2 qt.	4 qt.	10 qt.	20 qt.
				Days of expected survival			
	120°	2	2	2	2.5	3	4.5
	110	3	3	3.5	4	5	7
NO	100	5	5.5	6	7	9.5	13.5
WALKING	90	7	8	9	10.5	15	23
AT ALL	80	9	10	11	13	19	29
	70	10	11	12	14	20.5	32
	60	10	11	12	14	21	32
	50	10	11	12	14.5	21	32

	Maximum daily temperature (°F) in shade	Available water per man, U.S. quarts				
		0 qt.	1 qt.	2 qt.	4 qt.	10 qt.
				Days of expected survival		
	120°	1	2	2	2.5	3
WALKING AT	110	2	2	2.5	3	3.5
NIGHT UNTIL	100	3	3.5	3.5	4.5	5.5
EXHAUSTED	90	5	5.5	5.5	6.5	8
AND RESTING	80	7	7.5	8	9.5	11.5
THEREAFTER	70	7.5	8	9	10.5	13.5
	60	8	8.5	9	11	14
	50	8	8.5	9	11	14

© Reprinted from *Physiology of Man in the Desert* by E. F. Adolph and Associates (Interscience Publishers, New York, 1947).

*The length of time a man can survive without water, or with very little, will clearly depend not only on his build, health, and state of mind but also on how much exercise he takes and on ambient temperature, humidity, wind, and available shade. Still, the above table makes interesting reading.

I described one such case in *The Man Who Walked Through Time*. In July 1959 a 32-year-old priest and two teenage boys tried to follow an old trail down one side of Grand Canyon to the Colorado. They carried little or no water. More than halfway down, hot and tired and already very thirsty, the priest made the barely rational decision to climb back to the rim. Before long the trio lost their way. Next morning, desperately dehydrated, they tried to follow a wash back to the river. Soon they came to a sheer 80-foot drop-off. The priest, apparently irrational by now, had all three take off their shoes and throw them to the bottom. Then he tried to climb down. A few feet, and he fell to his death. The boys soon found a passable route, but one of them died on the way down to the river. The other was rescued by helicopter a week later, 8 miles downstream.

I know only the bare outline of this story. But some years ago I interviewed many times, and eventually wrote a magazine article about, two boys who were trapped in the Mojave Desert. This is not a walking story, but it is the only case in which I know full details of the kind of irrationality that any dehydrated hiker could all too easily develop. The boys were Gary Beeman, 18, and Jim Twomey, 16. Their car bogged down near midnight in soft sand, 200 feet off a remote gravel side road. It was June. Daytime shade temperatures probably approached 120°F. Humidity was virtually zero. The only liquid foods in the car were two cans of soup and one of pineapple juice, plus 2 pints of water. By the end of the first day—during most of which the boys rested in the shade of some nearby rocks—they had finished all the liquid. That night, working feebly, they moved the car barely 15 feet back toward the firm gravel.

The second day, back among the rocks, both boys suffered delirium. At sunset Jim Twomey staggered toward the car. Suddenly he sank to his knees, pitched forward, and lay still. The older boy, Gary, saw him fall. In midafternoon he had staggered irrationally out from the shade of the rocks into blazing sunlight in order to "try to find some water," and had finally dug himself into the cool sand. Now he felt less lightheaded. He went over to his friend and bent over him. Jim's face was deathly pale. His mouth hung open. Dried mucus flecked his scaly white lips. Gary hurried to the car, searched feverishly through the inferno inside it, and at last found a bottle of after-shave lotion. He wrenched off the top and put the bottle to his lips. The shock of what tasted like hot rubbing alcohol brought him up short. He had a brief, horrible comprehension of his unhinged state of mind. Afterward all he could think was, "We need a drink. We both need a drink."

Desperately he ran his eyes over the car. For a moment he considered letting air out of the tires and somehow capturing its coolness. Then he was thinking, "My God, the radiator!" He had always known that in the desert your radiator water could save you; yet for two days he had ignored it! Again he had that terrible momentary comprehension of his state of mind. Then he grabbed a saucepan, squirmed under the front bumper, and unscrewed the drainage tap. A stream of rust-brown water poured down over the greasy, dust-encrusted sway bar and splashed into the saucepan. "That water," he told me later, "was the most wonderful sight I had ever seen."

After he had drunk a little, Gary found himself thinking more clearly. He went back and poured some water into Jim's open mouth. Quite quickly Jim revived. All at once Gary saw what should have been obvious all along: a way to run the car clear, using some old railroad ties they had found much earlier. He spent almost the whole night aligning the ties—five or six hours for a job that would normally have taken him 20 minutes. At sunrise he helped his half-conscious friend into the car and made what he knew—because they had now finished the radiator water—would have to be their last attempt, however it ended. Moments later, with wheels spinning madly and the bucking car threatening to stall at any second, they shot back onto the gravel road. Four hours later, after many sweltering halts for the now dry motor to cool, they hit a highway.

Since that day Gary has never driven into the desert without stocking up his car with at least 15 gallons of what he now calls "the most precious liquid in the world."*

Important: Note that I tell this story only to illustrate the quick onset and dangerous nature of thirst-induced irrationality. Today almost all cars come with coolant solutions containing ethylene glycol in their radiators, and ethylene glycol, even heavily diluted, is deadly poisonous to man. And the first symptoms resemble drunkenness or delirium, which in the desert could easily be misconstrued.

Conservation of body fluids

You can very easily, in your minute-by-minute behavior, take sensible steps to conserve your body's precious water. People brought up in hot climates often train themselves, early, to reduce losses on torrid days by keeping their mouths closed. Talking is reduced to the minimum. The

---

*When I asked Jim Twomey how he had felt when his friend came with the radiator water, he said, "Oh, I just wanted him to leave me alone. I was so tired. You know, I'm fairly sure I'd never have regained consciousness if Gary hadn't brought that water, and I guess it sounds a pretty horrible way to die. But it isn't. I wasn't suffering at all—just terribly tired. All I wanted to do was to lie down and go to sleep, quite peacefully, and never have to wake up again."

moist membranes of the mouth certainly lose a lot of water if exposed to free air, and such precautions are well worth taking.

Theory and folklore suggest you wear clothes that cover almost all your skin and so reduce perspiration loss. But other factors come into it, and in practice I tend to do exactly the opposite (page 502).

For recycling of body fluids in a solar still, see pages 253 to 257.

For replacement of essential electrolytes lost through sweating, see page 217.

How much water to carry

When you're backpacking you can't play it as safe as Gary Beeman learned to do and carry 15 gallons of water (1 U.S. gallon weighs 8⅓ pounds); but in any kind of dry country you'll have to carry more than you'd like to.

In the mountains you may not need to pack along any at all—though even in the mountains there are often long, hot stretches without a creek or lake or snowbank, and unless I'm sure of a regular supply I tend to carry at least a cupful in a canteen. In deserts, water becomes the most precious item in your pack—and often the heaviest. In the drier parts of Grand Canyon I left each widely spaced water source carrying at least 2 gallons. Together with the four canteens, that meant a 19¾-pound water load. At the start of several long dry stretches I carried a third gallon in a disposable plastic liquid-bleach bottle from a food cache. On such occasions I'd walk for a couple of hours in the cool of evening, drink copiously at dinner and breakfast, then leave in the morning, fresh and fully hydrated, on a long and waterless stretch that was now two critical hours shorter than it had been.

The amount of water you need under specific conditions is something you must work out for yourself. As with food, requirements vary a great deal (though see page 230 and its footnote).*

For me, half a gallon is under normal conditions a comfortable ration for a dry night stop, provided I'm sure of finding more by mid-morning. In temperatures around 90°F, and in near-zero desert humidity,

---

*Small, wiry people are generally regarded as better adapted to living in deserts than are big, muscular ones. In a sense this is true. As any solid increases in size, its volume is cubed every time its surface area is squared. So the bigger a person's body, the less surface area it has for each unit of volume; and the surface, or skin, is where we lose excess heat, mainly through perspiration. As usual, though, there are compensations—both ways. Although small men are able to keep their body temperature down more efficiently than are big men, this extra sweat efficiency means that they tend to drink more water for their size than big men do. And because a rough relationship exists in most cases between body weight and acceptable load (see page 34), big men can normally carry heavier weights—and therefore more water.

a gallon once lasted me 36 hours, during which I walked a flat but rather soft-surfaced 30 or so miles with no appreciable discomfort, though with no washing or tooth cleaning either. But I was steely fit at the time, and well acclimated; I wouldn't dream of attempting that stretch "cold" with so little water.

I always lean toward safety. I can recall only three occasions on which I've been at all uncomfortably thirsty, even in the desert; and lack of water has never even threatened to become a real danger. It pays to remember, though, that only a hair's breadth divides safety from potential tragedy. If you're alone, one moment of carelessness or ill luck could send you stumbling across the threshold: a twisted ankle miles from water would probably be enough; certainly a broken leg or a rattlesnake bite. I try to make some kind of allowance for such possibilities, but in the end you have to rely mostly on caution and luck. Perhaps the two are not altogether unconnected. An ancient Persian proverb has it that "Fortune is infatuated with the efficient."

How often to drink

The old Spartan routine of drinking water at infrequent intervals, and rarely if ever between meals, is perhaps necessary for military formations: only that way can you satisfactorily impose group discipline. But for individuals the method is inefficient. For one thing, you tend to drink unnecessarily large quantities when at last you get the canteen to your lips. And although thirst may not become an actual physical discomfort, you often walk for hours with your mind blinkered by a kind of dehydrated scum that seals off any vivid appreciation of the world around you.

In well-watered country I take a drink, if I feel like it, at any convenient creek or lake. (At least, I used to. See the section on *Giardia,* below.) Up high or in winter I sometimes suck snow or ice as I walk along. In deserts I drink a few sips of water at each hourly halt, swilling it around my mouth before swallowing. I'm almost sure I use less water this way. I certainly know that the little-and-often system keeps washing the first traces of that blinkering scum away from the surface of my mind, and so rehones the edges of my appreciation. And appreciation, after all, is the reason I'm walking.

Water sources

In assessing the purity of any water supply, the only safe rule is: "If in doubt, doubt." In the years since early editions of this book appeared, things have deteriorated so badly that in most places you should now maybe doubt any source except fresh rain pockets and springs (and, as we shall see, there are certain dangers even with springs). You can blame mankind, exploding toward disaster, or find some other scapegoat, but the sad fact remains that—as suggested in an excellent article in the May 1981 issue of *Audubon* magazine, by Bert Newman—"the days of drinking directly from streams may be over." It is difficult, standing beside a clear, cold, rushing mountain torrent in the Appalachians, Rockies, Cascades, or Sierra, to believe that such water is probably polluted. But the chances are, no matter how high you go, that it is. And the hazard now lurks there, too strong to ignore, almost everywhere in the U.S.—and, indeed, in the world.

The danger can stem from any one of many infectious organisms, but 9 or 10 of them (all except one transmitted by feces) account for most of the trouble. And in the U.S. the most common of these now seems to be a protozoan called *Giardia lamblia. Giardia* is most often passed from organism to organism in the form of a tiny oval cyst about 10 by 20 microns—though it may measure only 7 microns across. About 16,500 can fit on the head of a pin—to the exclusion of all angels in the vicinity. One stool from a moderately infected human can produce 300 million cysts—and the ingestion of as few as 10 or 20 of them can infect you. Once in the upper small intestine, the cysts hatch into active, wineskin-shaped trophozoites, then divide and multiply, and soon establish a ravenous colony.

Of the 16 million Americans who probably now have giardiasis (also known as "backpackers' disease"), many may be only carriers who remain perfectly healthy, showing no sign of the disease—yet can excrete cysts for months or even years. It remains unclear why some infected people get giardiasis symptoms while others do not. But the unlucky ones discover that the disease is no laughing matter. After an incubation period of from 7 to 14 days you suffer "a fulmination of diarrhea, cramps, visible bloating, weight loss, nasty burps, and anorexia (loss of appetite)." Get a bad case, and you may vomit too. As soon as possible, consult a doctor. In the backcountry, even more than "outside," the results can be serious. "Everything you eat promptly comes up or out," says one victim. In 7 days his weight plummeted from 165 lbs. to 115. And weakness and other symptoms may persist for months. All this stems, by the way, from an organism that, although long known to occur in humans, was until 40 years ago thought to be harmless to them.

Unfortunately, humans are only the start of it. Other animals that are sufferers and carriers include several of our hangers-on—cattle, horses, and dogs—that also travel the backcountry and are even less particular in their sanitation habits than the most undisciplined human. Also susceptible: rabbits, coyotes, deer—and, probably, beavers, who routinely defecate in creeks and therefore spread the disease like wildwater (hence the alternative name, "beaver fever"). The wildlife carriers make it seem overwhelmingly likely that once an area has become infested, *Giardia* will be there to stay.

Reasons for the recent spread of infestation remain obscure. Most likely culprit: man, in increasing numbers, with decreasing discipline. But livestock, especially horses, could be culpable. (Few dogs and no cattle visit such recently infested areas as Sequoia and Kings Canyon National Parks in the Sierra Nevada.) As with other imbalances in today's world, with its exploding human population, the root may be purely a matter of density. But, whatever the cause, the end result—and especially its probable permanence—is pretty damned sad.*

For treating water suspected of harboring *Giardia,* see next section.

Even today most springs are safe—from *Giardia* and other contaminants. But mineral springs, especially in deserts, can be poisonous. One culprit is arsenic.

What you do if you suspect an unposted bitter-tasting spring, I really don't know—though a lack of insect life would be good reason for doubting its safety. I would guess that if you're in danger of dying from thirst you drink deep; and that if you're not in danger you stand and ruminate for a few minutes, then walk on. Perhaps I should add that in out-of-the-way places I've come across some remarkably evil-looking springs, bubbling and steaming and reeking, and have discovered that the water was drunk regularly by some hardy local. But the only safe rule remains: "If in doubt, doubt."

CHIP: Another watch-out, common in the arid western U.S., is selenium (in trace amounts a necessary nutrient), and surface water can contain toxic amounts. The water itself may bear no visible sign, but experienced friends tell me that selenium smells "garlicky" and that plants such as princess plume indicate high levels. A distinctly visible sign of trouble is a whitish crust at the water's edge, indicating a high proportion of dissolved salts. If not actively poisonous such water may yet be highly laxative, with the same dangerous net dehydrating effect as giardiasis. So drink these waters only in direst need, and sample a small amount first.

In areas where mining took place, the acid drainage from tunnels or

---

*CHIP: Having suffered once from bacterial dysentery and once from a protozoan, I can attest that it's no joke. But for many years I drank untreated water from sources all over the map without a twinge. In fact, because I lived in remote spots, I scarcely drank *treated* water at all. And I wonder if one of the reasons for the rise in giardiasis as a problem might owe in part to our increasing intake of chlorinated municipal water, which likely attenuates the natural intestinal flora, leaving a wide-open niche for invaders such as *Giardia.* And come to think of it, both times I got the thermonuclear crud, I'd been living in town and drinking municipal water. But before publishing this in *Nature* I'll take it up with a microbiologist.

waste dumps can carry heavy metals (e.g., lead) into streams. Where there's farming or ranching upstream, nitrates, phosphates, herbicides, and pesticides might be found. Some filters can remove dissolved chemicals—see page 242.

COLIN: Don't rely on maps, by the way, for information about springs. Even the excellent U.S. Geological Survey (USGS) topographical series often show springs that dry out each summer or have vanished altogether due to some subterranean change. Other springs may fail in extra-dry years. Rely only on recent reports from people you feel sure you can trust. If any doubts linger, carry enough water to take you not only as far as the hoped-for spring but also back to the last water source.

Sometimes, of course, snow will be your surest, or only, source of water (page 370).

Water purification

CHIP: The following paragraphs might just as well be subtitled "Things You'd Rather Not Know." Even the clearest, coldest stream can yield an unheavenly, invisible host, all poised to ruin your internal neighborhood. Meanwhile, from the makers of potions and devices there issues a flood of test results and counterclaims that must also be filtered before being swallowed. In 1996, *Backpacker* ran a special report by Mark Jenkins that's still the most understandable treatment of the subject, paired with an exhaustive field test of water filters by Kristin Hostetter. A good book on the topic is *Purification of Wilderness Waters* by David O. Cooney. Cooney, a chemical engineer, provides detailed explanations of gazigglies and also charts the performance of chemical treatments and the most common filters circa 1998. I also consulted *Medicine for the Outdoors* by Paul S. Auerbach, M.D. (For a list of these and related titles, see Appendix IV.) To simplify a bit, I've compiled what I found as a table (see below).

Most belly vengeance involves three forms of gazigglies that spend part of their life cycle in your internal Shangri-la. *Protozoa* are free-living one-celled critters that form shelled *oocysts* (Oh, oh—cysts!) from 4 to 20 microns (a micron being one-millionth of a meter), so they're smaller than the eye can see. *Bacteria* are one-tenth that size, from 0.3 micron to 2 microns, and come in spheres (cocci), rods (bacilli), and spirals (spirillia). Some occur naturally in your gut, including strains of *E. coli,* where they're vital for digestion and general health. But in water they indicate contamination by other disease-causing types. *Viruses* are subcellular globs of nucleic acid coated with protein, from 0.02 to 0.1 micron (i.e., roughly one-tenth the size of bacteria). A whopping 97 percent of all waters harbored one of the three, Chuck Hibler, a Colorado parasitologist, told

WATERBORNE DISEASES

TYPE Species	Symptoms	Incubation/Lasts (in days)	Size range/ Absolute pore (in microns)	Treatment B-boil, I-iodine C-chlorine, F-filter
PROTOZOA				
Giardia lamblia	Diarrhea, cramps, bad gas, headache, fatigue	7–20/30–60	6–10/ 5	B, I, C, F
Cryptosporidium	Diarrhea, cramps, some gas, low fever, fatigue	2–10/7–10	4–5/ 2	B, F
Entamoeba histolytica*	Diarrhea, cramps, bloody stools, fatigue	7–30+/7–60+	5–20/ 4	B, I, C, F
BACTERIA				
E. coli	*"Turista:"* vomiting, diarrhea, fever	0.5–1.5/2–5	0.5/0.2	B, I, C, F
Shigella	Diarrhea, vomiting, fever	2–7/3–90	0.4/0.2	B, I, C, F
Campylobacter	Diarrhea, vomiting, fever	2–7/3–90	0.3/0.2	B, I, C, F
Salmonella	*Typhoid:* severe diarrhea, vomiting, fever	2–7/3–90	0.6/0.2	B, I, C, F
Vibrio cholera*	*Cholera:* severe diarrhea, vomiting, fever	2–7/3–90	0.5/0.2	B, I, C, F
VIRUSES				
Hepatitis A and E	Nausea, diarrhea, abdominal pain, jaundice	2–3/varies	0.02–0.1/>0.01	B, I, C
Norwalk virus	*Mild, flu-like:* vomiting, diarrhea, gas, headache	1–2/few	0.027	B, I, C
Rotavirus	*Flu-like:* vomiting, diarrhea, gas, headache	1–3/7–14	0.070	B, I, C
Echovirus	Fever, rash, vomiting—rarely meningitis	2–3/3–7	0.020	B, I, C
Poliovirus*	*Minor:* flu-like fever, headache, nausea	2–3/1–3	0.020	B, I, C
	Major: back and neck pain, stiffness, paralysis	5–7/4–7		

*Uncommon or unknown in the U.S.

Backpacker's Mark Jenkins, in a study involving 10,000 samples "from streams all across America, Alaska to Arizona, and we didn't find one without Giardia." So why is it that some of us, me included, have imbibed largely of wilderness waters without getting sick? One reason is that low concentrations of organisms in pristine, high-altitude waters are less likely to successfully colonize your internal habitat. Another is that resistance varies a lot: the young, the old, and those with weak immune systems can be vulnerable to a single gazigglum. Another is that some of us are hosts: post-illness, we carry the little monsters around without any symptoms.

This raises the probability issue. And the experts agree that the concentration, whether protozoans, bacteria, or viruses, is much greater in the host (and the waste products thereof) than when diluted in streams. So your chances of getting the Hollering Crud from direct contamination (food, hands, or shared utensils) are greater by far than those of getting it from the water—the freedom of the hills doesn't include freedom from dishwashing.

Another major concern is temperature. The dormant, shelled oocysts are very tough little customers. In water near freezing, *Giardia* cysts can survive more than 80 days. *Shigella* bacteria can camp for long periods in ice, and so can viruses. Boiling, on the other hand, wipes all of them unquestionably out.

BOILING TEMPERATURE OF WATER BY ELEVATION

Elevation (Feet / Meters)	Boiling Point (Degrees F)	Boiling Point (Degrees C)
0 / 0	212.0	100.0
2000 / 610	208.3	98.0
4000 / 1220	204.7	96.0
6000 / 1829	201.1	93.9
8000 / 2439	197.4	91.9
10,000 / 3049	193.7	89.8
12,000 / 3659	190.0	87.8
14,000 / 4268	186.3	85.7
16,000 / 4878	182.7	83.7

The boiling temperature decrease per 1000 feet is 1.83°F or 1.02°C.

The thermal death point (TDP) is the temperature at which no organism can survive for five minutes. In *Purification of Wilderness Waters,* author David Cooney gives a TDP for *Giardia* of 147°F (64°C). Other protozoans have TDPs from 147 to 169°F (64–76°C). Sustaining a temperature of 170°F (77°C) for a minute or two kills 'em all.

The drawbacks are several. Boiling takes significant time and fuel.

Cooling the water takes yet more time, and it tastes like hell unless it's poured between two containers to aerate. Teas or drink mixes can cover this to some extent. And also, boiling won't remove, and in fact may concentrate, nonvolatile poisons like arsenic.

The main types of chemical treatment are:

Chlorine. The amount of chlorine in city water supplies (less than 0.5 milligram per liter) won't kill *Giardia* or *Cryptosporidium* cysts, and even higher doses aren't very effective. Chlorine loses its punch in cold or alkaline water (with a pH above 7.5, found in lakes with limestone or dolomite bedrock and in desert "sinks" with no outlets). Neither does it work well in waters with high organic content (silt, algae, etc.). A contingent worry is that chlorine reacts strongly to organic matter in water, producing chloramines or trihalomethanes, both carcinogens. But for occasional use, liquid chlorine bleach (5 percent sodium hypochlorite) remains a cheap treatment, at 0.2 milliliter per quart with a 30-minute contact time—never use powdered laundry bleaches, nor any with additives. The former standby, Halazone, takes five tablets to treat a quart of water (30-minute contact) and is highly perishable, losing 75 percent of its chlorine after two days' exposure to air. Newer chlorine treatments include Aqua Mira (two bottles, 1 oz. each, about $12), that treats 115 liters using chlorine dioxide and phosphoric acid. These must be mixed, seven drops each, and allowed to stand five minutes before going into the water bottle, with a 20-minute contact time. Chlorine-treated water can also be used to wash fruits and vegetables. After sufficient contact time, adding ascorbic acid (vitamin C) will reduce the hypochlorite to a colorless, odorless chloride. This also works with iodine, which changes to iodide. The taste improves, but chloride and iodide don't kill gazigglies. So, since many drink mixes contain ascorbic acid, *never add anything to the water before the full contact time has elapsed.*

Iodine is cheap, lightweight, and thus much favored by mass-market outdoor programs, a circumstance that has brought a couple of problems to light. First, some people are rather allergic to it. (If you're allergic to shrimp, you might be sensitive to iodine.) And this is something you should determine before setting out, either with the help of a doctor or through home trials: get bottled water and treat it, drinking nothing else for a day to see what happens. But for the majority who aren't allergic, military testers claim that iodine is safe. Although other sources claim that it builds up to a toxic level in the body and shouldn't be used continuously for weeks or months. Second, iodine won't kill *Cryptosporidium,* perhaps the most common waterborne parasite of all. Third, it has a definite gag factor. And fourth, it is said to react with some foods and perhaps the aluminum in cookware: readers report purplish soups.

The most popular iodine tablets are Potable Aqua (tetraglycine hyperiodide, a bottle of 50 tablets; 1 ounce [0.2 ounce net]; $6). The tablets are only for treating water—they're poisonous if swallowed—and must be kept dry, since they lose one-third of their effectiveness if exposed to air for four days. So don't try to save weight by carrying them in a plastic bag; take the bottle along, always recap it tightly, and if it has been opened or is of indeterminate age, get a new supply. A yellow tinge is said to be a sign of deterioration. Potable Aqua Plus is a kit ($7) with the iodine pills as above and a neutralizer called PA (45 mg ascorbic acid per tablet) in a second bottle of 50. Similar, except for the green blister pack, are Coghlan's Drinking Water Tablets and Neutralizer. A less costly iodine treatment with unlimited shelf life is Polar Pur (99.5 percent iodine crystals, about $10), which treats 2000 quarts. Each bottle holds about 7.5 grams of iodine in little beads, with an insert to keep them in the jar. You fill the bottle with water (5 oz. or so) and wait for the iodine to form a saturated solution. The bottle says one hour. But the first time out, David Cooney found that after an hour at rest, less than one-third of the iodine had gone into solution and that full saturation took 5 to 6 hours. So you should fill a new bottle the day before you leave home. He recommends shaking the bottle at intervals. The gentle motion of walking helps, but tucking it into a gaiter is a more vigorous option. Just make sure the cap's tight. Once the bottle's in play, you use only part of the contents, adding fresh water each time, so it's easier to maintain the strength. On the side of the bottle are temperature-sensitive dots with a corresponding dosage scale, in capfuls. This works out nicely for clear water, but for cold, cloudy, or alkaline water you should double both the dose and the contact time.

Iodine *can* kill some protozoans, such as *Giardia*. But a published test using clear, cold (10°C/50°F) water showed that after 30 minutes virtually all commercial iodine treatments left more than enough *Giardia* cysts alive to make you sick, with some taking up to eight hours to kill all cysts. In the same tests, none of the chlorine treatments racked up a 100 percent kill.*

In water 20°C (68°F) and above, an hour or two of iodine treatment might kill nearly all the *Giardia* cysts. Yet another caution is that the tannins released by leaves and other organic matter react to form iodide ions, which (I repeat) do not kill gazigglies. And since iodine doesn't work on *Cryptosporidium,* many of these products bear labels urging the use of a filter.

If you're on a Thoreauvian budget, you can buy tincture of iodine (crystals dissolved in grain alcohol—a 1-oz. bottle costs less than $1). But

*Ongerth, J. E. "Backcountry Water Treatment to Prevent Giardiasis." *American Journal of Public Health,* 79: 1633, 1989.

it has to be measured out, and the good Dr. Cooney suggests the small plastic bottle intended for eyedrops—carefully washed out and labeled IODINE with indelible marker—with five drops per liter as the starting point. You can also get food-grade ascorbic acid (vitamin C crystals) and dash in ¹⁄₁₀ teaspoon per liter after the contact time, with a good shaking, to neutralize the *uck*.

Other universals: For best results, turbid water should be settled and/or filtered through a paper coffee cone before going into your drinking bottle. After you add water treatment, shaking speeds up the process. And since you've just put untreated water in your bottle, before you drink loosen the cap slightly and upend the bottle, letting enough water leak out to rinse the rim and threads.

Water filters and purifiers

have the the same object—to clean up your drinking water—but there are significant differences in how they work. After having standards for purifiers for some time, around 1998 the U.S. Evironmental Protection Agency (EPA) published standards for water filters. Devices that pass the test display a registration number, but it still pays to learn the basics.

A *filter* works by passing water but trapping microorganisms and particles. So the vital measurement is pore size, which can be stated in two ways: *nominal* pore size is an average, meaning that there are both smaller ones and larger ones. A nominal 5-micron filter may have some pores large enough to let a *Giardia* cyst through. A 5-micron *absolute* pore size means that no pore is larger than 5 microns, so the filter will trap *Giardia* cysts. Some filter makers claim to meet two of the three parts of the EPA standard for purifiers (see below). But no mechanical filter can remove viruses, which is the third part of the standard.

A *purifier,* as certified by the EPA, is able to "remove, kill, or inactivate all types of disease-causing microorganisms from the water, including bacteria, viruses, and protozoa cysts . . ." It must remove 99.9 percent of the protozoans and 99.9999 percent of the bacteria, and also inactivate 99.99 percent of the viruses, which are too small to filter out.*

To do this, the typical purifier combines a *physical* filter with *chemical* action: most have a resin matrix that releases iodine to inactivate bacteria and viruses. Others have a silver-impregnated element, or a bed of activated carbon. Silver inhibits bacterial growth in the filter itself, but

---

*U.S. EPA Guide Standard and Protocol for Testing Microbiological Water Purifiers, 1987. The test organisms are *Cryptosporidium* protozoans, klebsiella bacteria, and poliovirus and rotavirus. For more information, the U.S. Federal Emergency Management Agency (FEMA) has a Web site on water purification: *www.fema.gov/pte/foodwtr.htm.*

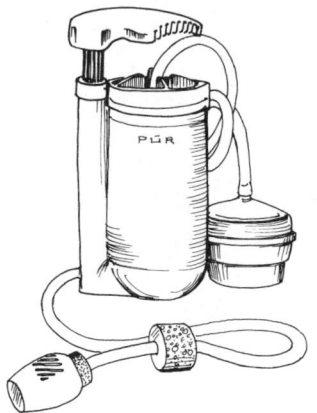

PUR Hiker

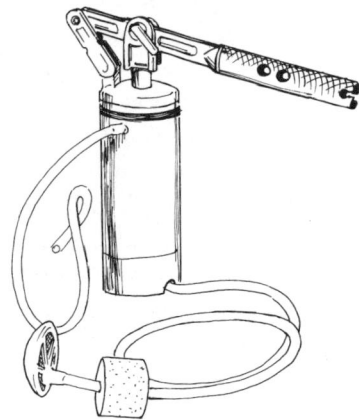

Sweetwater Guardian

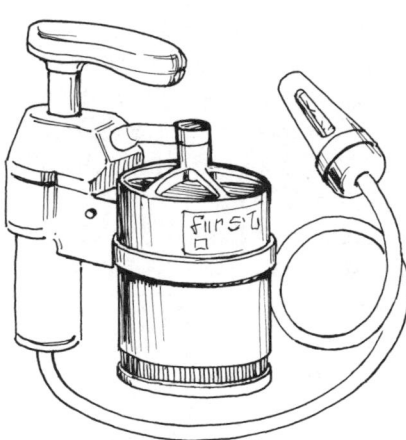

First Need Deluxe

MSR MiniWorks

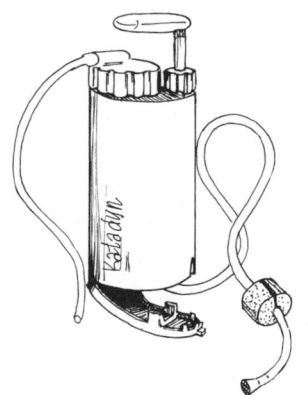

Katadyn Mini Ceramic

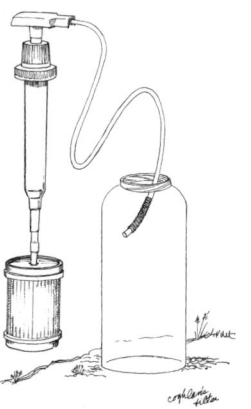

Coghlan's

doesn't have much effect on water passing through. Activated carbon (or charcoal) takes up dissolved chemicals by *adsorption* (meaning their molecules stick to the carbon particles) and can remove pesticides, herbicides, chlorine, and iodine, as well as funky odors and tastes in general. So carbon is commonly used either as part of the filter element or in add-on cartridges.

Filters for backpacking are made of ceramic, carbon, various fabrics or fibers, and plastic meshes or matrices. Because a filter with pores fine enough (2–3 microns) to trap small cysts will clog up very fast indeed when plastered with silt, algae, and other waterborne gunk, some filters deploy metal or fiber prefilters to catch the coarse material. The coarse screens can usually be brushed off when they clog. Then comes a midlayer of fibers or small-pored ceramic and backing that may be a core of carbon. Some fine-filter elements can be cleaned, by brushing, scouring, or backwashing, while others must be replaced. The carbon part retains chemicals and must be replaced. It's very important first that you be able to clean or replace the element in the field, and second that you be prepared to. That's the general poop. For specifics, we need to talk about makes and models. The following combines what the companies say, *Backpacker* tests, and my own subjective take after several seasons. (During which, as a matter of record, I experienced zero Belly Vengeance.)

The PUR Hiker (15 oz., $60, replacement filter $30) is sturdy, rounded, and easy to live with. *Backpacker*'s test crew rated it more than twice as high as the two runners-up. The body is a speckled plastic with a built-in pump and a thread-in filter cartridge that mates a pleated 0.3-micron absolute glass-fiber body (with a high 126-square-inch surface area) with an activated carbon core. Intake is via a plastic "acorn" with a removable (and easily cleaned) foam core. But you should be careful pulling the tube off to remove the foam—the little spurs that hold it break rather easily. A movable float lets you keep the intake off the bottom, which is smart. From the acorn, a flexible tube leads to the filter/pump unit. The pump has a well-shaped handle, a moderate (8-lb.) force, and a high output (1.24 liters per minute at 48 strokes). You can set it on a rock or your knee to pump, and the tubes are long enough to avoid a dunking. The filter resists clogging (it's rated for 757 liters) but it can't be cleaned, so carrying a spare might be in order for glacial melt, warm-water sloughs, or desert potholes. Replacement takes only seconds. The filter core seems resistant to freeze damage but can be fully drained and the innards dried out, just in case. The plunger comes out easily—for long trips a spare O-ring will cover you for maintenance. The outlet tube leads to a bottle adaptor that fits all but the popular 1-liter soda bottles. But you can pull it off and use the bare tube, saving ounces. Gripes are few: the main one is having to unscrew the filter and prime the pump, a matter of 10 seconds if you pull the outlet hose off first. Otherwise things get twisted. But if the filter is wet you might not need to prime it. The 0.3-micron pore catches protozoan cysts and almost all bacteria. PUR also makes a lighter, cheaper, lower-capacity filter, the Pioneer (8 oz., 0.75 liter per minute, $35) that threads onto a Nalgene widemouth bottle and comes with two replacement disks ($8, sold separately). But most back-packers will be happier with the Hiker or one of PUR's purifiers: the sim-ilar Voyageur ($75; $40 replacement), or the double action, T-handled Scout ($90; $45 replacement), which Linda has used with great satisfac-tion, or the self-cleaning Explorer ($130; $50 replacement).*

The Sweetwater Guardian (12 oz., $50; replacement cartridge $30) resembles those old iron homestead handpumps by virtue of its lever-action handle but is blessedly light in weight. Easy to hold and pump (only 2.0 lbs. of force), it nevertheless puts out a steady 1 liter per minute. The filter of glass fiber with a carbon layer has a 0.2-micron absolute pore size. It clogs more quickly than the PUR Hiker, but this is signaled by a squirt of water from the relief valve (see below) that prevents filter rupture or bacteria "push-through" when you pump too hard. Rated for 757 liters, the filter element can be cleaned in the field with a brush (included), taking only about 15 seconds. When it's worn out, a black grid pattern shows up. The replacement cartridge is roughly the same size and weight as the one for the PUR Hiker. The inlet is a plastic capsule with a 75-micron stainless screen that plugs into a flex tube and is good for shallow water. A 5-micron prefilter, called a SiltStopper, can be added betwixt inlet and cartridge (>1 oz., $10, with a three-pack of replacement elements costing $13). The outlet tube is plenty long, and the plastic adapter does fit smallmouth soda jugs. The outlet nipple and tubing are smaller than those on most flexible bladder systems (see page 262), though with some effort you can jam the stock outlet tube inside the tube from the bladder, and pump gently. Gripes: The handle needs to be deployed each time you pump, and some people report breaking the plunger, which can't be fixed. The pump itself doesn't come apart (as far as I could tell), so while the rubber washer is visible through holes, it can't be replaced. If you pump too hard or the filter starts to clog, the relief valve squirts—if you catch it in the face, it rates 0.5 cougar screams: find it before it finds you. (Hint: turn the pump shaft so the exit hole points away.) A Viral Guard cartridge, to upgrade the Guardian to a purifier, was sold until 2000 when Cascade Designs' own microbiologist found that "portable iodine resin bead technology, as used in the Viral Guard, does not meet the EPA standard *for purifiers* in a number of water conditions

*As this book went to press, PUR announced that its Stop Top Carbon Cartridge, meant to improve the taste of water, can interfere with antiviral action, and offered free replacements.

commonly found in the outdoors." Since EPA tests are performed in the lab, not the field, this might have gone unnoticed, but Cascade Designs—commendably—pulled the Viral Guard off the market. The Guardian, which I ended up liking rather well, and the Walkabout microfilters (0.2 micron, 9 oz., $40; replacement $19) are unaffected by the problem.

General Ecology's First Need Deluxe Purifier (15 oz., $80; replacement $36) is an amalgam of virtue and vice. It was the first filter (or purifier) I used. It was hard to hold and the cartridge clogged up quickly, but it was better than anything else around at that point. Further along, some friends invented a prefilter with stiff tubing and faucet strainers. I figured out how to backwash the cartridge before the company agreed that it could be done (now they give you directions). So this little beast has a history with me. The filter itself is a mysterious, blue plastic cartridge that can't be opened. Called a "structured matrix," it somehow removes 0.1-micron gazigglies with a 0.4 absolute pore size. It also captures dissolved chemicals with "molecular sieving" and "broad spectrum adsorption," and removes colloids and the smallest particles by "electrokinetic attraction." The rated life is 400 liters, which presumes relatively clear water and regular backwashing. This can be done in the field by pumping water slowly through the clogged filter into a liter or quart bottle, treating it with five drops of liquid bleach (or, according to the product engineer, with an iodine treatment). After the proper contact time (30 minutes) has gone by, disconnect the pump from the cartridge and clean it with a few squirts. Then connect the pump outlet to the outlet (i.e., the bottom) of the cartridge and pump the filtered water through *gently*. Little bits of stuff will come out of the cartridge inlet hole. Tapping the cartridge lightly against your hand between pumps will dislodge more bits. Pump all the treated water through and it's done. Though it's not a quick fix. A bottle of blue coloring is included to test the filter cartridge. Recent improvements are the ergonomic pump handle, a quick-release bracket that attaches the pump to the cartridge, and a self-cleaning mesh prefilter with a sliding float. The pump is double-action and fast (with a new cartridge) and can be taken apart for maintenance. The cartridge has gained a built-in set of adapters that thread onto a Nalgene widemouth bottle, and a small set for a Sigg (or equivalent) aluminum bottle. It won't match up with 1-liter smallmouth soda bottles, but you can slip on an outlet tube or the tube of a bladder system (also the case with the PUR Hiker and MSR MiniWorks). Since my gripes have been aired, they need not be repeated. The First Need Deluxe also includes an auxiliary nipple that converts the stuff sack (with a plastic bag as a liner) into a gravity system. You fill the bag, hang it, plug a hose to the pump inlet, give a few strokes to start the flow, and sit back as your bottle fills—Nice-a-roo. The rate depends on the drop between bag and bottle—with the stock 3-foot tube, it filled a 1-liter bottle in less than 10 minutes. A double-action pump is required, it seems, or you can use the cartridge alone and suck heroically on the outlet hose to start the flow. If the cartridge is too clogged to pump through, you can still filter water with gravity flow. General Ecology also sells the Microlite System purifier (1 micron, 8 oz., $44; replacement two-pack $8) and the Microlite filter unit alone (7 oz., $33).

MSR makes a chunky, solid filter called the MiniWorks (15 oz., $60; Marathon ceramic element $30) that justifies its weight with some distinct advantages. Like the Sweetwater, it has a pump handle, but the plunger is horizontal: easy to hold, with moderate force required to pump. The plunger and a rubber O-ring are housed in clear plastic, so you can spot problems. The element, housed in black plastic, is ceramic with an activated carbon core (0.3 micron absolute), and is cleaned with a scouring pad. This takes off the surface, exposing clean ceramic, for a relatively long life. A built-in gauge lets you know when it's worn out. The inlet has a spring weight over a plastic capsule with a dab of foam as a prefilter— easy to take out and clean, and also easy to lose. A float keeps it off the bottom. The outlet has a cap and threads that fit a widemouth Nalgene bottle or MSR's Dromedary waterbags. But it also has a nipple, so you can slip on a flex hose and use the adapter of your choice. The pricier Waterworks II filter ($130) has the Marathon filter element in a clear housing and an added PES membrane filter (0.2 micron absolute) that screens out the smallest pathogenic bacteria. Both models are easy to work on—for long trips a maintenance kit ($8.50) is in order. Gripes were few, though the flow rate (0.7 liter per minute) seemed a bit slow for the size and weight, and the ceramic element can be damaged by freezing.

Katadyn's Pocket Filter has been around for years and has the highest capacity (tens of thousands of liters), but I bypassed it for several reasons: a) at 1 lb. 10 oz., it's heavy; b) the handle is small and pump force is high; c) having to direct the outlet stream into the bottle is a cramp; and d) it costs $250. Colin used one on his solo Colorado River descent and had clogging troubles. The Katadyn Combi costs less ($160) but it's an ounce heavier. So I tried the Katadyn Mini Ceramic filter (8.5 oz., 0.2 micron, $90; replacement $60), which one of my friends called "a cute little booger." Compact and mechanically simple, it fits the hand nicely. The single-pump O-ring is easily examined and replaced. The ceramic element has a small surface area that clogs rather quickly but is easily scrubbed with an abrasive pad for a long life (7000 liters). The tiny stainless inlet strainer also clogs, so an equally tiny brush might be in order. The inlet hose stows neatly under a trapdoor, which popped open—I used a thick rubber band to hold it closed. The pump force was high and the flow rate was slow. And the outlet hose was too short and springy to stay in my bottle (though it did jam nicely inside the tube of a bladder system). So why did I like it? Hmmm. It's light and easy to pack. Has a long life. And it *is* cute.

The Coghlan's Water Filter or the similar Timberline Eagle (6 oz., $25; replacement $13) can be found in discount stores and even in supermarkets. It's neither durable nor easy to hold, but it gives me a certain Rube Goldberg–ish delight. The pump is the sort found in gallon jugs of shampoo, with the spout cut off to admit a skinny outlet tube. Into the inlet (the part that sticks down into the shampoo) fits a short tube with a sleeve inside that holds a 1-micron polyethylene and fiberglass element. This will catch *Giardia* and *Crypto* cysts (though not bacteria or viruses) and is rated for 400 liters, though it seems to clog quickly and can't be cleaned: carry a spare. The pump is a surprise in terms of sheer volume, but the teeny outlet hose couldn't accommodate the flow, and popped off in a magically off-pissing way (see below). Since this leads naturally to the gripes, the filter element itself is the inlet, so you have to immerse it in the creek. But the tubing tends to slip out of the pump, dropping the filter element. In fast water, that could be good-bye. Even in the event you don't lose it, "wild" water will have contaminated the inside of the filter element. If this happens, you should disinfect it, or at least pump a few cups onto the ground to wash it out. The best course is to duct-tape the join of the tubing to the pump. The tubing fits the filter nipple securely, and you do need to take the element off to pack it. But if you plop the element wet into a plastic bag, dribbles can also contaminate the outlet. So you should shake the water out of the filter before packing it, and a little cap might be in order (search in the parts boxes at a hardware store—if you want to take the parts-bin riff a little further, read on). Besides the duct tape, another slight modification does wonders for both the performance and your temper, to wit: I trimmed off the plastic around the pump outlet until I could slip a larger (1-cm) tube *over* it. This ends the pop-out problem and thence, the pump filled a 1-liter bottle with the same 36 strokes, in half the time. The stock outlet tube has a copper weight, and it still comes rocketing out of the bottle if you pump hard, so I added a thick rubber band to hold it in. Once I started to tinker, I couldn't quit—see the customizing section below.

Meanwhile, what with Mark Jenkins's article and Kristin Hostetter's field tests from *Backpacker,* supplemented by David Cooney's minibible, I was swamped with data. So, besides carrying all of the above filters on wilderness trips and risking La Vengeance by pumping water directly below sheep fords and hunting camps—with no evil results—I wanted to compare what matters to me: How many strokes to fill my bottle? How long will it take? And last but not by any means least—am I likely to smash this thing against a rock? So after a festive evening, I ratcheted myself up at 5:00 a.m. for a predawn (and precoffee) test.

5 A.M. WATER FILTER TEST: TO PUMP I LITER

Brand and Model	Number of strokes	Time	Grunts! *Cougar Screams*
PUR Hiker	62	0:55	1.0! (had to prime—hoses got twisted up—@ 0.5 grunt per hose)
Sweetwater Guardian	84	1:30	1.5! (lightweight intake zoomed around) *0.5* (if relief valve nails you) *1.0* (in the eye or crotch)
First Need Deluxe	40	0:46	1.5! (long intake—no *bueno* in shallow water)
MSR MiniWorks	111	2:00	0.7! (heavy, medium effort, slowish flow)
Katadyn Mini Ceramic	162	3:20	*0.25* (high effort, outlet hose too short)
Coghlan's Water Filter (*aka* Timberline Eagle)	36	1:02	*1.2* (Filter element fell off. Then, the hose popped off the pump, which squirted me in the crotch. But the price is right.)

Conclusions. To generalize, ceramic filters (Katadyn, MSR) are harder to pump, have lower flow rates, and clog more quickly. They're also likely to be damaged by freezing. But they're fairly simple to clean and maintain, with exceptionally long life. Fibrous filters (PUR, Sweetwater, Coghlan's), some backed up with carbon, have higher flow rates and higher maintenance costs, since the elements must be replaced at shorter intervals than those of ceramic.

A powerful pump and a thundering flow rate might seem like the Holy Grail, but some of the critters you're trying to catch can slim down to ooze through pores smaller than their normal size (and pressure may help them do this). So in the field, pump slow and steady. While micro-filters (absolute pore size smaller than 1 micron) seem to be sovereign against protozoans and bacteria in U.S. waters, EPA-certified purifiers (First Need, PUR, MSR) add protection against viruses. But since most depend on iodine resins or other time-sensitive means, once again it's best to pump at a slow, steady rate. This also prevents forcing unwanted crap through the filter. You can dependably purify water microbiologically by treating with chlorine or iodine, then filtering. Or, of course, letting it boil for one minute. Since none of these methods removes dissolved chemicals, a post-filter with activated carbon might be an asset.

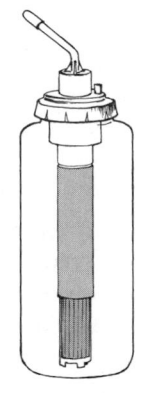

Exstream MacKenzie

Safewater Expedition

Bottle/filters. Bota of Boulder sells the Outback (2 microns, 5 oz., $18; replacement $9), a bike-type bottle with a filter cartridge that fits tightly inside the rim. You unscrew the top, take out the cartridge, then fill the bottle with "wild" water (leaving room for the cartridge, since otherwise, wild water spurts out around the edges and contaminates the tame side of the filter). You screw the top back on and tip it up, squeezing the bottle to force water into one of those push-pull nozzles. Unfortunately, the plastic of the bottle is stiffish and the filter offers enough resistance to make this an ordeal, especially with your arm cocked high. Those with a less-than-simian grip will be flummoxed.

Exstream Water Technologies outfits its MacKenzie bottle (9 oz., $45) with a 1-micron filter/EPA-registered penta-iodine purifier that will treat up to 26 gallons. This unit extends nearly the full length of the bottle, reducing the 1-liter volume somewhat. The bottle itself is a squeezable white plastic, demanding only moderate grip strength. The push-pull mouthpiece has a tiny outlet hole, probably to prevent overloading the filter, so it takes time to get a mouthful. Even so, the MacKenzie seems like a decent bet for overseas trekking and travel, where viruses are a concern.

Safewater Anywhere makes the Expedition bottle/filter of translucent plastic (1 liter, 6 oz., $40; and ½ liter, 5 oz., $35; replacement $25). The three-layered filter, of "medical-grade, micro-porous plastic," has 2-micron absolute pore (which is claimed to catch smaller beasties by offering a "tortuous path," in the manner of a Swiss cheese). It removes protozoans, bacteria, and a range of unsavory chemicals, but not viruses. Though small and lightweight, it's rated for 750 liters (over 185 gallons). The bottles have a widemouth screw cap on the bottom and a drinking nozzle on top, under a conical flip-cap. You take off the bottom cap to fill up, and find a prefilter "sock" of 25-micron fabric with a tail so you can pull it out and swish it clean—without removing it from the bottle. Once again, you have to immerse the bottle to fill it (in shallow water this means you pick up silt, algae, grit, etc., which the sock is intended to catch). Recapping the bottom, you let the drips drain off, flip open the double-gasketed top, squeeze, and drink from the mouthpiece. The flexible bottle and low-resistance element reduce the effort—it's grand to dip water from a cold, babbling brook and down it immediately. In places with plentiful streams and lakes you can save considerable packweight by dipping just enough to satisfy your thirst. But I had two quibbles, one specific and one general. Specifically, when I flipped up the cap to drink, I found droplets inside. Had the double gaskets leaked? (If you close it carelessly, they will.) But eventually I figured out that the mouthpiece was the guilty part. While this soothed my fears of contamination, it meant that the bottle had to be kept upright. The company promises a redesign and I wish them well.

So on to the general quibble: if you expose this, or any translucent container holding "wild" water to sunlight, things bloodywell grow in it. The company provides a mesh sleeve, encouraging you to sling it outside your pack. Naturally, this boosts the growth rate. All the zoo- and phytoplankters you're culturing not only add unwelcome color notes but if allowed to proliferate also clog the hell out of the filter element. Frequent changes of water help. Regular cleansings and dry-outs do, too. So does keeping it out of the light. (More on this when we get to hydration bladders, page 262.)

A slick little packet is Safewater's 3-oz. in-line filter cartridge (with a stainless 25-micron prefilter and the 2-micron filter element specced on the previous page, at $35), which plugs into the drinking tube of a hydration system. The same low-resistance element as in the Expedition bottles allows you to drink without inordinate hollowing of the cheeks. And given the general catch about putting "wild" water in your hydration bladder, it's not a bad system. Yet another application is gravity filtering. I rigged it to a bladder (a Platypus Big Zip, which opens for easy filling and cleaning). With a 5-foot drop, the Safewater cartridge filtered a liter in 58 seconds—no pump required. By the same token, since it has a built-in prefilter you could stick a tube on either end (upping the weight to perhaps 3.3 oz.) and simply suck up the blessed quench. This one goes into my ditty bag, for sure.

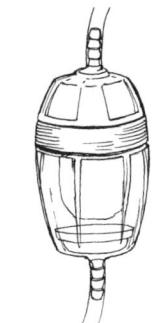

Safewater in-line cartridge

The newest development, and maybe a trend, is to minifilters that fit in the neck of a bottle or plug into the tube of a drinking bladder. This seems like a grand notion but in practice creates its own set of problems, some of which I stumbled upon. The Gatekeeper, from TFO, Inc. (0.6 oz, $12, two-pack $20), is a minuscule cartridge rated to filter 25 gallons. It snaps into the underside of a 28-millimeter cap/mouthpiece (included) that fits TFO and Platypus bladders (or the ubiquitous 1-liter soda bottle). A hearty squeeze—and patience—is required to get a mouthful. Nevertheless, the extraordinary lightness, low cost, and adaptability all make it attractive. I used a Gatekeeper–tonic bottle combo on a 70-mile trip during a prolonged drought, when I was forced to dip soupy water from beaver ponds and cow-flopped water pockets. Aside from the unsavory visuals, the only bad moment came when the teeny filter cartridge popped out of the cap as I unscrewed it and dropped into a creek—fortunately a mere trickle. Still, it bounced off downstream. I retrieved it, lashed the outside with rum, and then squeezed water through to flush out any stunned gazigglies—with no ill effects, except on the rum supply.

Customizing. Each of these models seems to have a particular advantage, which tempted me to try swapping things around. Needless to say, the makers do not condone this, and will curse me for even suggesting it. Understand—I'm not urging you to alter a single jot or tittle. But I can't resist. So here are various irresponsible substitutions and field-grade tips.

Truly mucky or tea-colored water should be settled, but if you're on the run you can rubber-band a coffee filter, etc., over the inlet boggle.

MSR uses a steel spring to weight their inlet hose, which, combined with a sliding float, gives you superior control of the depth. For squirrelly inlets, you can find a similar spring to slip over the hose. Or wrap some bare copper wire (10- to 14-gauge) tightly around a dowel, thence twisting it onto the errant tube.

The mighty bulk-shampoo pump (a mere 2 oz.), as modified above (page 248) with a fat outlet tube, can be used handily with different cartridges and inlet screens. For instance, I stuck the Sweetwater 75-micron inlet screen on as a prefilter and tubed the shampoo pump's outlet to the Safewater in-line cartridge, comprising a slick-and-thrifty system with two prefilters that weighs 6 ounces and will draw from the shallowest water pocket. A piece of foam pipe insulation (the kind with the slit) augments the grip—but don't cover up the vent holes. The detachable, durable, double-action First Need pump also lends itself to this unhallowed approach. (Just remember to stroke gently.)

Water in an emergency

COLIN: Cunning ideas are always being propounded about what to do if you run out of water. Typical examples are "Catch the rain in a tarp" and "Shake condensed fog off conifer trees" and "Dig in a damp, low-lying place." Then there are various crafty systems for distilling freshwater from the ocean. In an Armed Forces Research and Development publication I once ran across a description of what at first seemed a practical rig for sea-skirting backpackers: a series of foil sheets between which you heated salt water, either in the sun's rays or "by sitting on them." But right at the end came the killer: "With additional sheets, a survivor can obtain about one pint of water in 16 hours."

Unfortunately, the occasion on which you're really in desperate straits for water is pretty darned sure to come just when there is no rain, no fog, no damp place, and no ocean (not to mention no sheets of special foil). In other words, in the desert, in summer.

For years the only advice I'd heard that sounded even vaguely practical was "Cut open a barrel cactus." An experienced friend of mine says he rather imagines you'd "extract just about enough moisture to make up for the sweat expended in slashing the damned thing open." But the *Air Force Manual* (no longer available) exhorted you, when in a desert fix, to "cut off top [of a barrel cactus], mash pulp, suck water through grass straw or mash the pulp in a cloth and squeeze directly into the mouth."

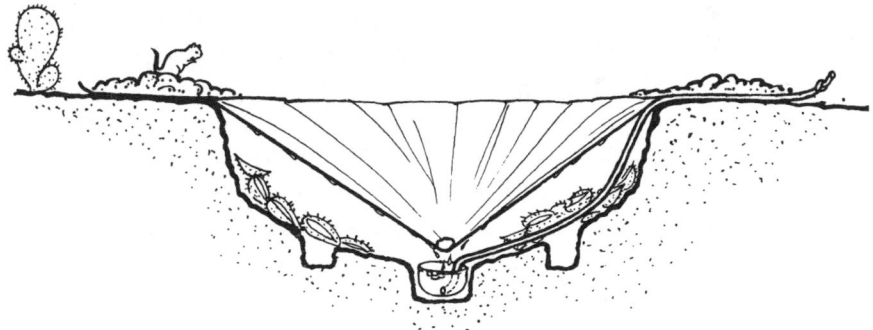

The *Manual* also gave details of the desert still described in earlier *Walkers*.*

*My sources:
1. "Solar Distillation of Water from Soil and Plant Materials: A Simple Desert Survival Technique," by Ray D. Jackson and C. H. M. van Bavel. *Science,* 149, No. 369 (September 17, 1965), pages 1377–79.
2. Private correspondence with Dr. Ray D. Jackson of the U.S. Water Conservation Laboratory, Phoenix, AZ.
3. "Water, Water, Everywhere," by Frank James Clifford. *FAA Aviation News,* 5, No. 1 (May 1966), page 10.
4. "Water, Water, Everywhere," by Joe Bailey. *The Airman,* 10, No. 8 (August 1966), pages 24–25. (Less technical detail than above, but one or two additional findings.)

Articles on the still have appeared in many other places, including: *The American Rifleman,* July 1970, page 35; *Outdoor Life,* August 1965, page 14; *U.S. Army Aviation Digest,* October 1965, page 18; *The Flying Physician,* July 1966, page 37.

The beauty of the device is that it works best in the time and place you're most likely to need it: summer desert. The hotter the sun, the more water you get. And the water is as pure and clear as if it had been distilled in a laboratory. An Air Force medical colonel called this still "the most significant breakthrough in survival technique since World War II"—and the colonel headed a team that experimented with the still for 25 days in the Arizona desert. The team essentially confirmed the findings of the original researchers, and there seems no reason why this still shouldn't save your life, or mine, if either of us ever gets into water trouble while backpacking in the desert—provided we have a clear understanding of what to do.

The still's only essential components are two items we might seem reasonably likely to carry: a container to catch the water and a 6-foot square of clear or almost clear plastic sheeting. Up to a point, the container is easy: a cooking pot or cup or a plastic bag or even a small piece of plastic sheet or aluminum foil shaped into a hole in the ground. But the container should be wide enough to catch *all* drops falling from the sheet—as a cup would not. And a metal container will get very hot and "boil off" some of its precious water. So a cooking pot will do but a plastic bowl or bucket will do better. The plastic sheet raises unexpected problems, but as we'll see there's a way out.

A desirable but not essential component for the still is a piece of flexible plastic tubing, 4 to 6 feet long (the kind sold for aquariums is fine). For other reasons, you might consider taking some (see footnote on page 353). Most water filters and drinking bladders (pages 242 and 262) have suitable lengths of tubing.

Constructing the still sounds a simple enough job for even a weak and scared man, provided he has kept a modicum of his cool: Dig a hole about 40 inches wide and 20 inches deep. Dig the sides straight down at first, then taper them in to a central cavity (see illustration, page 253). Failing a toilet trowel (page 698) or a staff or stout stick, your bare hands will do the job, provided the soil isn't too rocky. When the hole is finished, put your container in its central cavity. If you have plastic tubing you should tape it inside the container so that one end lies very near the bottom. Lead the other end up out of the hole and seal it by knotting, or doubling and tying with nylon. Next, stretch the plastic sheet over the hole and anchor it around the edges with soil. Alternatively, you can dig a circular trench, about 4 inches deep, a few inches beyond the perimeter of the still, in which to stuff the edges of the plastic—and so obviate any problem with dirt sliding down the sheet into the pit. Next, push the sheet down in its center until it forms an inverted cone with sides 25 to 40 degrees from the horizontal. The plastic should run 2 to 4 inches above the soil and touch it *only* at the hole's rim. Place a small, smooth stone or other weight dead center to hold the conical shape and reduce wind flutter. Pile extra soil around the edge to hold the sheet firmly in place and block off all passage of air. In high winds, reinforce with rocks or other heavy articles. Leave the free end of the plastic tubing uncovered—and clean. Estimated construction time: 15 to 30 minutes.

This simple structure works on the same principle as a conventional still: solar energy passes through the clear plastic and heats the soil (or added plant material—see below); water evaporates, condenses on the plastic (which is cooled by wind action), runs down to the point of the cone, and drops into the container. It takes one to two hours for the trapped air to become saturated so that water condenses on the plastic and begins to drip into the container. With a plastic tube you can suck up water at any time; without it you have to keep removing the container—and each time you do so you lose one half to one hour's water production.

The apparently simple business of the water running down to the point of the cone raises the first plastic sheeting difficulties. Clear plastic groundsheets are polyethylene, which is slick, especially when new; it sheds many drops before they reach the cone's apex—and can reduce yield by about half. Any used groundsheet will be scratched, and water will adhere rather better. And scouring the sheet's undersurface with sand might make a critical difference. (I don't suggest you do it ahead of time: just file the idea away in your mind for emergency use.) But there are other groundsheet difficulties. A sheet punctured in any way, even with small holes, will drastically reduce the still's yield. Possible remedy: patch with ripstop tape. Again, the thinner the sheet, the more efficient: 1 mil is ideal (dry-cleaner bags, for example—though they're polyethylene). But a 1-mil groundsheet is close to useless; mostly, they're at least 3 or 4 mil. Finally, any loss of transparency, such as accidental or deliberate scratching, will further reduce the still's yield. In other words, a transparent groundsheet, somewhat scratched and with all holes patched, will do at a pinch. But a thin special plastic, such as Du Pont's Tedlar, will do far, far better. Unfortunately, Tedlar is 20 times as expensive as polyethylene and is not readily available to the public. I don't at present know where you can buy any—either alone or as part of the complete desert-still kit that used to be sold by a California firm. I regret to report that Du Pont has steadfastly ignored my inquiries on both counts.

A sandy wash makes the best site for your still. Next best is a depression where rain would collect: months after a shower such places still retain more water than does nearby high ground. The finer the soil, the better. Make every effort to site the still where it will get day-long sunlight.

After long droughts you may be able to collect only small amounts of water from even favorable soil; but—and it's a gigantic "but"—you can probably save the day by lining the sides of the hole, under the plastic, with vegetation *cut open so that its moist interior is exposed.* Cactus is best. Prickly pear and barrel cactus yield most; saguaro comes next, cholla a poor fourth. Creosote bush helps very little.

The vegetation should not touch the plastic; it may flavor the water slightly. Small ledges made in the sides of the hole may make it easier to keep the vegetation in place.

Seawater or brackish water (as found in many desert lakes) can be purified by building the still where the soil is kept moist by the underlying water table. Or keep adding the polluted water—either into a trough (see below) or by pouring it well down in the hole, not up near the rim, where condensing water could touch the soil and carry impurities down into your container. If the soil is badly contaminated on the rim (by strong alkaline deposits, say) your precious harvest of water may be fouled, so raise the plastic slightly with small rocks placed underneath it, all around the hole. With these precautions you can even—cozy thought—operate in a region made radioactive by fallout.

Slightly modified, the still will purify water polluted by almost anything *except* antifreeze from a car radiator. So your body wastes become recyclable. To make full use of polluted material, dig a trough halfway down the hole (see illustration, page 253), line it if possible with a plastic sheet, and pour the material in.

Yield will depend on many factors, but it seems reasonable to expect at least a quart a day from a properly constructed still dug in desert sand containing some moisture or lined with cut cactus. And although there seems to be an upper production limit of about 3 quarts a day for such stills, that yield can in relatively moist soil or with a good vegetation lining be maintained for four or five days. After that, make a new still or replace the vegetation. These 40-by-20-inch stills are the optimum size: if you need more water—and have the necessary materials—make more stills rather than a bigger one. Given fleshy plants or polluted water, two stills should provide adequate drinking water for one person *for an indefinite period.*

If rain falls, your plastic cone will naturally capture it. It may capture other things, too. In the desert, water always attracts animals, and the air force colonel's team found that "many small rodents and snakes become trapped in the middle of the plastic"—unable to escape over its slick surface. If you're hungry these poor little bastards are obviously going to end up in your gut. (For thoughts on rattlesnake steak, see page 713.) And even if you don't feel hungry, remember that the animals contain precious fluids.

A word of warning: it occurs to me that the quoted yields of water were achieved by men practiced in the technique and operating with minds and bodies in good shape. Don't underestimate the possible effects of weakness and irrationality (page 230). But you can take care of the technique problem by personal experimentation. (If you experiment, make sure you fill the holes afterward.)

I'm ashamed to say that I've still not followed my own sage advice and given the rig a trial run. But the idea sounds to me like a practical proposition. A reader who had her Sunday School class of five-to-nine-year-olds build a still, guided only by my instructions in an earlier edition of this book, reports that the children constructed one, "completely on their own, in 1 hour 15 minutes. . . . And when the first drops of water began to collect and run down into the bucket, they jumped up and down yelling, 'It works! It works! WE DID IT!' "

For car and airplane users, it seems to me, the components should henceforth be standard emergency equipment, kept stowed aboard against a nonrainy day.*

Finding Water

CHIP: Having come of outdoor age in the deserts of Nevada and Utah, and on the Colorado Plateau, my instinct is to constantly search the landscape for sources of water. The discipline required is to always think about where water might be, whether you need it or not. Picture the way water drains, and follow the signs of surface runoff downhill. If water has left its mark—damp sand, ripple marks, dried mud—where has it gone? The two controlling variables are gravity and evaporation. I look for bedrock traps in washes and dry streambeds, or dig in shaded undercuts along banks. If there's damp sand or gravel, you're on the right track. The groundwater table is closest to the surface at the low points of the landscape and also along sharp changes in slope, like the base of a cliff or mesa or even a dune field. On exposed slopes, look for aquifers (water-bearing layers of porous rock or gravel), which show up as dark stripes or bands of vegetation. There may also be dark water stains or white evaporative

*CHIP: Annette McGivney, in *Backpacker,* September 1999, page 49, describes a "solar tree still" using a clear plastic bag that covers live vegetation and is tied tightly around the stem, making use of natural evapotranspiration. But an accompanying photo shows a small produce bag and the article claims a yield of "2–3 tablespoons"—scarcely worth the effort. With a large cooking bag (used for turkey, ham, etc.) and a plant like a cottonwood that has roots in the groundwater and a high transpiration rate, you might get enough water to make the effort worthwhile. But most desert plants have rather low rates of transpiration. A further problem with all of this distilling fiddle is that while you're devising and then waiting for the process to work, you're running out of survival time. And, too, you're stuck in one place. So I'd attempt distilling only when it's so hot that I had to shade up during the heat of day. For most backpackers (as opposed to pilots crashed in the Rub' al Khali), since you walked in, the sane thing to do is to walk out again—in the dark.

crusts below. Following such a layer to a shaded alcove may reveal a seep or pool. It also pays to learn what local plants are indicators of water on or near the surface. In my part of the Earth, cottonwoods, willows, sedges, bulrushes, cattails, reeds, and mosses all attest to a possible drink.

At sunrise and sunset, scan for the flash of water. It's not always where you'd expect. In Wyoming's Killpecker Dunes there are large ponds of meltwater from snowbanks covered up by drifting sand. Even in the deep desert, there are water pockets in the tops of some rock formations, while joints and crevices collect runoff and sluice it into hidden pools—Utah's Waterpocket Fold is the best-known instance, but most exposed formations have more "tanks" than you'd expect from a casual glance.

One tantalizing puzzle I encountered was a deep pocket with overhanging sides. It was 20 feet down to the water, and if I'd fallen in I'd never have gotten out. I had a 60-foot coil of parachute cord and a cookpot *without a bail.* I considered rigging a sling, but if my only pot fell out I'd have been in real trouble. I also pondered using a stuff sack with a rock in the bottom, but then my eyes lit on a sack of mesh. It fit nicely over the pot, a rig that even a dehydrated idiot could manage—and the fine mesh made a nice prefilter.

Water caches

COLIN: On both California and Grand Canyon walks I had to establish several water caches. Glass bottles, I discovered, kept the water clear and fresh. Whenever possible I buried them—as protection against the hoofs of inquisitive wild burros and the fingers of other thirsty, thieving, or merely thoughtless mammals.*

---

*On the California walk, at the southern end of Death Valley, an amateur rockhound operating from a pickup truck kindly gave me a gallon bottle of good drinking water that he had "found under a pile of stones, back up in the hills." The water tasted far sweeter than the alkaline spring I'd camped beside. But it brought on a bad case of worries: I became highly conscious that for three days ahead I'd be relying on water I'd cached out as I drove south through the valley two months earlier, and I hoped no thoughtless, light-fingered rockhound had stumbled on any of my caches. Fortunately, all the caches were buried and camouflaged. I found each one safe.

I also found them without difficulty. People often ask me how you can be sure of finding a cache again. The safest way is to draw in your notebook a sketch map showing important features such as gullies and bushes and rocks, and to pace out and record a few measurements from obvious landmarks. And then to mark the exact spot with a big stone. I did all these things. But I never actually used the maps. Each time, memory took me directly to the right place. City people sometimes express amazement at such a "feat." But once you've lived for a while in any wilderness its landmarks stand out quite clearly. Even a moderately practiced eye will detect at least as much difference between two neighboring desert gullies as between two neighboring downtown streets.

Unburied bottles are liable to crack from extreme heat (if you leave them in the sun) or from extreme cold (wherever you put them, if temperatures fall low enough for the water to freeze solid). I worried a good deal about the freezing danger in Grand Canyon, but found the unburied bottles at both caches intact, in spite of night temperatures several degrees below freezing. The bigger the bottles you use, the less danger that they'll freeze solid. One-gallon jugs, thoroughly washed, are good; 5-gallon bottles, though cumbersome, are better. Plastic bottles such as those used for liquid bleach or for distilled or spring water are lighter and perhaps stronger, but I've recently had some perforated by thirsty rodents. Big, strong plastic jerry cans (Igloo, Rubbermaid, etc.) used for river trips and car camping should be much safer.

Water left for even a few weeks in 5-gallon metal cans seems to take on a greenish tinge, apparently from algae, but can still be drunk with complete safety. And these 5-gallon cans are light and strong, and easily lashed to a packframe when caches have to be made on foot. Twice in the Grand Canyon I used 5-gallon cans in which my food had been stored (page 704) to pack water a half day ahead and so break a long waterless trek into two much safer segments.

Canteens, bottles, bags, and bladders

In buying canteens, take no chances. If you find one is leaking badly, miles from the nearest desert spring, it may well be about the last thing you ever find.

Metal canteens, which I used for years, are, for backpackers, essentially things of the past. But there is one feature of metal canteens that plastic cannot match. If metal canteens with felt jackets are wetted and put out in the sun, evaporation from the felt soon cools the water. You can rig a makeshift jacket for a plastic canteen with almost any article of wettable clothing, but because plastic is a poor conductor of heat the cooling system doesn't work very efficiently.

Today's bottles, of various plastics, are far lighter and cheaper—and in many ways tougher. On the score of toughness, metal naturally impresses you with greater immediate confidence. But on my Grand Canyon trip the felt covers of both my metal canteens developed gaping holes, and when the canteens came on side trips—slung from my belt by their convenient little spring clips—the bared aluminum banged against rocks and developed seep holes. I fixed the leaks with rubber air-mattress patches—but my confidence had been punctured too. The polyethylene canteens I also carried on that trip showed no sign of wear, and since that time I've used only plastic canteens. They've proved astonishingly tough. Once, at a "dry camp" on a steep hillside, a full 1-quart plastic canteen holding my entire overnight supply tumbled more than 100 vertical feet down a steep but nonrocky canyon. It went in big bounces, emitting a dull, heart-rending thud at each contact. But I found it, lying in a dry watercourse, safe and sound.

CHIP: For years I've used clear plastic soda bottles—the kind that contain anything from cola to mineral water. Having been sternly lectured in backpacking shops that the dire consequence of having one fail makes it mandatory to buy "real" water bottles at $6-plus a crack, I must respond with one well-chosen compound word. Soda bottles come in a range of convenient sizes, up to 2 liters, and various colors. Since high summer inspires in me a lust for gin and limes, my present standard is the 1-liter Schweppes Tonic. For testing, I randomly picked one out of my recycling bin, fitted it with a push-pull mouthpiece, filled it with water, and began to drop it from 90 inches—as high as my arm can reach. I dropped it 10 times on turf, 10 times on rocky soil, 10 times on boulders—not a single leak. So I started tossing it up in a spin and letting it come down on a concrete sidewalk, *thwap!* Twenty times. About every third *thwap,* the impact forced a small spurt from the mouthpiece, but it didn't leak. After that, I climbed a tree and pitched the bottle down onto the sidewalk a few times—the lobes on the bottom crunched up and the mouthpiece looked as if it had been chewed by a badger, but no leakee. So I filled the poor thing to the top and left it out overnight to freeze hard. Again, some water oozed out of the mouthpiece, but the bottle—battered, buffeted, and iced—proved steadfast.

By dint of relentless abuse, I found that the cap is the most vulnerable part: mouthpieces can be forced open by impact or freezing, and plain caps will crack if struck at just the wrong angle (a few turns of duct tape can shockproof them). But if I'm fool enough to drop my water bottle repeatedly on the cap, then I deserve to die. And in that sad event, the bottle can at least be recycled into a fleece pullover.

Meanwhile, I tried the same series of drop tests with a $6 Lexan bottle. Thicker and more rigid, it held up as far as not leaking, but rocks gouged the rigid Lexan deeply enough (in the same way that aluminum canteens can be gouged) to worry me.

The metal vessel is not dead, however. Sigg, Markill, and other European companies make elegant aircraft aluminum bottles with interior coatings that resist the acids in drink mixes, juice, wilderness lakes, etc. These weigh about an ounce less than widemouth Lexan bottles of the same size (the 1-liter Markill weighs 5 oz.) and cost roughly twice as much (the 1-liter Sigg is $13). Both companies offer insulating sacks, but for evaporative cooling, make your own cover from the sleeve of a cast-off cotton knit shirt.

Most made-for-backpacking bottles come in translucent polyethylene (high or low density) or transparent Lexan. The Nalgene catalog has a handy reference chart on which material does what, as well as cautionary notes (don't carry chlorine bleach, which makes plastic bottles leak). Polyethylene bottles get brittle with age and/or UV light: check them by flexing and look for hairline cracks. When buying a new bottle, look for refinements such as undroppable loop tops and measuring marks. If you have a water filter, then your bottle should fit the threads. Some makers pick a thread that matches only their products, forsaking all others. The closest thing to a standard is the 63-millimeter-wide mouth. I have a Nalgene widemouth of polyethylene—snatched from the water-quality lab I ran for years and converted (with Reflectix insulation and duct tape) for winter use—and a second one (repeatedly boinked in the torture test above) that came with a First Need purifier. Hunersdorf widemouth bottles (facing page, right), of lab-quality polyethylene with ribbed, easy-open caps, in sizes from 50 milliliters to 1.5 liters, are also favorites for their ruggedness and imperviousness to tastes and odors.

The faceted, polyethylene bottle with a loop top that Colin once favored (he's now gone Nalgene) can be had in four sizes (1 pint, 1.5 pints, 1 quart, 1.5 quarts, at $2–$6) from most backpacking shops. The loop has been strengthened so the bottle can be safely hung thereby. But, unless you're on a hanging bivouac, it shouldn't be.

COLIN: I long ago rejected the traditional idea that in thirsty country you carried a canteen clipped outside your pack, readily available: thirsty country almost always means sunny country, and direct sunlight soon turns even cold spring water into a hot and unquenching brew. In thirsty country I carry my canteen near the top of the pack but insulated under a down or pile jacket. In any case, a canteen clipped outside your pack, especially if swinging loose, is pretty sure to be a poorly placed load. Unless weight is a real problem I mostly carry four 1-quart canteens. Even when I don't expect to carry as much as a gallon for safety purposes, I feel it's worth the extra freedom they give me, at 3 or maybe 4 ounces a shot:

I can camp well away from water and, unless it's very hot, stay for 24 hours without a refill.

Water bottles make tolerably comfortable pillows, especially if padded with clothing. Bladders, too. In weather no worse than cool, the pillow routine also keeps the stopper from freezing (and for an infuriating minor frustration few things equal waking up thirsty in the middle of the night and finding yourself iced off from your drinking water). Simply putting the canteens on air mattress or foam pad may be enough to keep the stopper ice-free, but in really cold weather take one canteen to bed with you. If you think there's any danger at all of the others freezing solid, make sure they're no more than three-quarters full. That way, they can hardly burst.

No matter how many large canteens I take, I now nearly always add an Evenflo baby-feeder bottle (.5 pint capacity; 1 oz., $.73). It does more than boost my carrying capacity. In hot weather, particularly if walking along a riverbank or lakeshore where the water is suspect, I often fill it at every halt, add a Potable Aqua tablet, and slip it into a pack pocket. At the next halt I have, immediately available, just enough safe water to see me through another hot, dry hour. In the desert I've found such a bottle invaluable for collecting water from shallow rain pockets, and I've often been glad to have it for collecting water from other small sources. At a pinch, you can even use one for rescuing a little water from seeps that no ordinary canteen will even begin to tap; but for a better alternative see page 284. Baby bottles are also convenient for short side trips; one will slip into your pants pocket—though it can also slip out. These little bottles are tough too. Once, when mine held my last precious half pint of water and I dropped it on a boulder, it bounced quite beautifully. Warning: The two-piece lid (for fitting baby's rubber nipple) is a mild nuisance. To hold it in one piece and so prevent the inner disk from dropping off every time you remove the lid, just slap a piece of tape on top. Renew it occasionally. The tape will allow the disk to turn a fraction when you replace the lid, and so jam into a watertight joint—provided you keep the rubber nipple in place. Know ye that without the inner disk—or the nipple—the damned thing will leak.

True, the bottle/filter combinations (page 250) now let you do most of the baby bottle's jobs; but I'm still a fan. Second childhood, you say?

CHIP: My experience with bladders (except, of course, my own) is limited. But Linda adopted the drinking-bladder-and-tube setup at the first glance. And she remains a proponent of the Hydration Way: suck as you go. I have an odd resistance to it—the vision of overaged infants snoozling away with tubes in their mouths doesn't sit well. But there are sound physiological reasons for downing small amounts of water on a frequent basis, rather than taking huge, infrequent gulps, and equally sound ones for staying well hydrated. Sports physiologists claim that you're more subject to stress injuries when your body is short on H_2O. Another plus is sheer efficiency: you can hold a steady pace and sip without a stop. In bug-pestered areas, being able to drink without halting is a distinct advantage. Given all that, I might grow accustomed, sooner or later.

Platypus Thunderhead   Bladder

Meanwhile, I tried a Platypus Thunderhead that combines a slim day pack and a 3-liter bladder (1 lb., $75) while exploring an obscure range of mountains in the Mojave Desert. Days touched the 90°F range: hot but not killing. From a base camp with access to a spring, I chose a different canyon each day, approaching up sandy washes and climbing steep streambeds choked with boulders and prickly brush, past fantastic alcoves with signs of desert bighorn sheep (though I saw not one).*

Conclusions. the Thunderhead holds enough drink for a strenuous day in a comfortable, nonsloshing container (bladders flatten out as you empty them). The pack has zipper pockets for a lunch, guidebook, and survival ditty kit, with a rear bungee for what-have-you. Given a shove, a 4-liter bladder will fit. On a major trek, using two or three bladders, you can shuttle water from source to base camp, or cache ahead. (Although I've had no such trouble so far, left alone the bladders might be chew toys for thirsty critters.) Without the bladder and tube, the day pack weighs a mere 12 oz. and has a sternum strap and minimalist waistbelt, and a layer

---

*For the sake of both water quality and thirsty native wildlife, it's best to camp a moderate distance (and out of sight) of desert springs and water holes. You'll also—sans scritchings and thumps in the night—get considerably more sleep.

of foam that lends both padding and insulation. With the straps disengaged, it makes a reasonable pillow as well. The bladder and tube can be slipped into your full-size pack for the grand march.

My first try with a (nonevolutionary) bladder wasn't quite as happy, but it took place in winter. Filled up and loaded into a full-size pack that I'd then stuffed to tympanic pitch, it treated me, each time I even glanced at the bite valve, to a peevish squirt. Then (it was middling cold) the tube froze up—inspiring a cougar scream. You could insulate the tube with a sheath of foam or reflective bubble wrap, and so on, but unless you're a fast-twitch mountaineer the fumbling may be more trouble than it's worth.

Another point to ponder is that if you're melting snow, your bottle, bladder, or whatever had better have a mouth big enough to pour into from a pot without spilling. The MSR Dromedary and Dromlite bags have a 63-millimeter widemouth, as does the Nalgene Cantene. The new Camelbaks have a smaller but perhaps negotiable aperture. Platypus Big Zip models have a locking channel across the entire end opposite the screw cap. Ultimate Direction has a wide rolltop closure.

Other points, from my own trials and Jonathan Dorn's test in *Backpacker* (October 1999, page 83), may soon be rendered moot by onrushing changes in flexible water systems. But here is a gleaning.

The primary irk is the *bite valve:* it must allow a reasonable flow when chomped but shouldn't leak when bumped; it should have a good mouth-feel; and it should be simple to clean. Even the best valves wear out quickly, and a spare weighs next to nothing. If you unthinkingly stuff the tube end into your pack, the bladder can empty through a squished bite valve—but this can be prevented with a pinch fitting (such as hospitals use for IV tubes). Instant gratification has pitfalls: a hard-drinking friend dozed off, rolled on his bite valve, and flooded his sleeping bag: his cougar screams woke me up. Given the same size tube, you can use bite valves and lapel clips from different makers until you settle on a favorite.

Tubes rank second. Since a bladder might be pressurized by your load, the tube, cap, and all the connections need to be snug. So fill up and then give the bladder a good, hard squeeze before trusting it in your pack—or you might spend a thirsty night in a wet sleeping bag. The tube should reach from the bottom of whatever pocket the bladder is in to your mouth, without strain and also without loops to catch on brush. To keep it inboard, you can thread it under a load-lifter strap or under your arm (but in that case, be careful taking off your pack). A lapel clip (improvise with badge clip, binder clip, rubber band, or Velcro) dogs the tube onto your shoulder strap, and keeps the bite valve facing up—that, along with a puff of air after a drink, keeps the dribbles at bay. For shuttling or caching water, use a plain cap on the bladder. When greenish, tubes can be cleaned with a rifle patch or part of a cotton ball, propelled by a coat hanger.

Bladders themselves seem quite rugged unless they're stomped, run over, or punctured. There's a spectrum of materials: urethane (flexible, clear); polyurethane (flexible, translucent); polyethylene (easy to clean, slightly stiff); Mylar (reflective, opaque); and urethane-coated nylon (opaque and tough). Some early polyethylene bladders had stiff, laminated edges that were sharp enough to cut skin, cloth, etc. The shape of the bladder should accord with the chosen space in your pack. Some are long and sausagey while others are squarish, but in general the flatter the bladder, the better it packs (the Ultimate Direction Sport Tank has an internal baffle to thin the profile). Clear bladders with zip-top or rolltop closures are easy to fill, and you can add ice, snow, etc. Clear plastic also reveals the need for cleaning and lets you do a good job. To clean a bladder, add a mixture of hot water, baking soda, and white rice, agitate, and then thoroughly rinse. If you use drink mixes or employ an in-line filter (with "wild" water in the bag), then choose a clear bladder with a large opening, and add an overnight soak (with 1–2 tablespoons of liquid bleach) to your cleaning routine. TFO's Flexi-Flasks (and perhaps other translucent types) can be sterilized with boiling water and/or a microwave oven. Gregory recommends replacing its bladders regularly, at a cost of 2 for $10. Water bladders—and all the tubes, clips, shower nozzles, and hangy-downs appurtenant thereto—are made by Camelbak, Gregory, MSR, Nalgene, Platypus/Cascade Designs, Safewater, TFO (a neat double-capped version), and Ultimate Direction. Weights, prices, and specifications are changing quickly enough that it's pointless to quote them across the board.

KITCHEN UTENSILS

COLIN: Keep your utensils as few and as simple as you can, consistent with personal requirements of weight, comfort, convenience, and obscure inner satisfaction. Naturally, no two backpackers are likely to make identical choices. I know a man-and-wife team who never carry more than one cup and one spoon between them. At least, so they say. Other people like to pack everything, plus the kitchen sink.

When I wrote *Walker III,* my basic kitchen utensils weighed 1.3 lbs. Chip's standard utensil packet, using modern stuff, totals less than 1 lb. while accomplishing the same rock-belly tasks. But as we'll see in the following pages, any standard list should be far from immutable. As conditions demand, various items get added, subtracted, or replaced.

CHIP: Constant gear testing makes it hard to standardize, so this is the utensil kit I took on a lightweight trip last month:

	Weight in ounces
Cookpot with handles and lid (MSR Titan kettle, 0.85 liter)	4.1
Insulated mug (12-oz. Aladdin, with top, minus handle)	4.8
Spoon (Snow Peak titanium)	0.7
Tea ball (stainless steel with chain and hook)	0.5
Pocket tool with knife (Coast Micro-plier)	1.7
Salt and pepper (2 plastic film cans)	0.4
Mixing container (.5-cup pop-top for hummus, etc.)	0.9
Liquid margarine bottle (4-oz. Nalgene)	0.8
Olive oil bottle (2-oz. Nalgene)	0.4
Refillable butane lighter	0.5
Pot scrubber (green fuzzy type, 1.5 by 1.5 inches)	0.01
Fine-mesh sack	0.5
Total	15.31 ounces

While the cookery gear above is functionally equivalent to Colin's list in *Walker III,* there are differences owing to food habits (e.g., his milk squirter—page 285—versus my hummus mixer). But virtually every item is lighter—except the insulated mug, 1.8 ounces being a small price to pay for hot drinks staying hot (see cup tests, pages 274–75). Some of this drift toward lightness reflects my constant paring, but there's also a general trend toward lighter materials: the new titanium cookpots weigh about half as much as steel equivalents—at double the cost.

COLIN:

Pots. Spun aluminum-alloy pots were once standard. But in the slip-stream of allegations that the lead in many aluminum-alloy pots could taint food and cause poisoning, and that aluminum might trigger Alzheimer's disease, there came a swing to stainless steel—which distributes heat more evenly and is said not to pit or to taint food. Some versions were surprisingly light. Now, with improved nonstick coatings and a debunking of the Alzheimer's scare, aluminum has made a strong comeback.

The nesting pair of Sigg spun-aluminum pots that I used for close to half a century were highly practical units: corners rounded and easily cleaned; low profiles and broad bases to promote rapid heating; lids that doubled as plates or pans; bail handles that locked firmly—well, fairly firmly—into upright position. The smaller unit, alone, was big enough for simple solo cooking—and if in-pack space posed a problem, to house a stove. These pots were tough too. The smaller one, which for years traveled inside its mate, though sometimes alone and unprotected, still stands essentially unscathed. My original larger one withstood a dozen years of brutal use (it once bounced 150 feet down a talus slope in Death Valley) and then had to be retired only because it got so dented that cleaning became difficult. After a few decades its replacement began to mature—and even to usurp the niche in my affection once held by that old and honored friend. Naturally, I can't openly admit that I still use my trusted Siggs.

CHIP: Rather than resting on their laurels, Sigg recently introduced a delectable-looking cookset of Inoxal, which is aluminum bonded to an ultrathin liner of stainless steel, that includes three pots and fry pan, at $115 (I haven't yet gotten my hands on them for weighing in). But for more detailed permutations we should look at—

Nesting cooksets. For 20 years and several hundred trips my standby was a nesting stainless-steel set by Evernew (1 liter, 11 oz.; 1.5 liters, 13 oz.) NOTE: For pots that come with lids, the weights given are for pot plus lid. For sets that have a single lid to cover more than one pot, the lid's weight is given separately. If a pot lifter is required, its weight is included in the total for the set.

Peak 1 Trekker nesting cookset

The Evernew pots have locking, flat bails (handy and also hand scorching if left in the path of the flame), and lids with folding wire handles that double as fry pans or dishes. For sultry summer solos, I left the larger pot home. But on trips-for-two, and for winter snow melting, the 1.5-liter pot more than justified its weight. The bottoms were once copper-clad, but most of it has been scoured off. Yet the pots are rugged: the inside finish and the action of the bails are very nearly as good as the day I first lit a flame under them.

The Evernew brand is still around, and similar stainless-steel sets by MSR, Olicamp, Peak 1 (the Trekker set is shown above), and others all should give dependable service. Some have refinements like nonstick coatings or clips that fold over the lids and lock them down, all of which add weight. Early nonstick coatings tended to pit, peel, or flake. So I tested a GSI Glacier Extreme cookset, stainless steel with a three-layer Teflon coating, for over a year at home—equivalent to several years of backpacking use. At long last, the coating on the pot I used most often began to show pits and discoloration—the others are still perfect. The one bug in the soup was the GSI Diamondback lifter, which in time weakened enough to dump a pot of spaghetti (followed by a rousing cougar scream). It turned out that GSI had recalled the batch—bad alloy—and they sent me a new one with a stiffer constitution.

Rudimentary "mess kits" (pot with lid, fry pan, dish, and plastic cup) can be had for $6 in plain aluminum and in plain stainless steel for about $15. Quality varies a lot, so take your prospective set out of the box and check how the lids fit: some don't. Another common boo-boo is bad spot-welds on the brackets that mount the bails or folding handles—failure can not only dump boiling water on your feet but is also tough or impossible to fix in the field. So if there's any visible gap between the bracket and the pot, don't trust it.

Among the coated aluminum pots are some winners. Olicamp's Nova cookset is simple, with Silverstone-coated 1- and 2-quart pots, a 6.5-inch fry pan with lid, and a lifter ($36), all nested in a mesh sack. MSR's BlackLite set (17.1 oz., $33) consists of two pots (1.5 liters, 5 oz.; 2 liters, 7 oz.), one easily dented flat lid (3.5 oz.) that fits both pots, and a sturdy lifter (1.5 oz.). Another $10 buys the lidless fry pan (5.4 oz., the same as two extra-large eggs).

MSR BlackLite

The whole ensemble, mesh-bagged as the BlackLite Gourmet set, weighs just under 1.5 lbs. and costs $43. Stygian blackness makes these ideal for solar cookery (see page 609); they also feature nonstick coating and grooved bottoms to prevent skating. The MSR pot lifter left toothmarks in the nonstick coating along the rim, so I cut short bits of tubing (from a water filter) and slid them over the ravening aluminum jaws. (MSR's new LiteLifter weighs only 1 oz. and seems less Tefloniverous.)

Evolution cooksets are also quite good (I'm told). I first saw them in the backcountry and asked the cooks, who spoke highly of the handsome brick-red finish, nonstick coatings, and even heating. Along with the Outback Oven (page 270), they've migrated from Cascade Designs to Backpacker's Pantry.

Another keen aluminum cookset is the GSI Bugaboo, likewise nonstick. These well-shaped pots have rolled rims that pour smoothly and anti-skate grooves beneath. The lids double as fry pans. The four sizes (1 quart, 9.1 oz., $22; 1.5 quart, 12 oz., $25; 2.5 quart, 16 oz., $28; 4 quart with a locking bail, 24 oz., $44) are available separately or in sets.

The pretty blue Bugaboos aroused my rather jaded lust for New Stuff. And the few days I spent with them were blissful indeed—until Linda snaffled the 1- and 1.5-quart pots for her personal testing program. (Excellent, she tells me.)

GSI Bugaboo

There are also pot sets with lids that clamp tight for presoaking and storage. MSR makes StowAway Pots (four sizes from 0.5 liter to 1.6 liters, $12–$20), and Olicamp makes the Watertight Sealfood Containers (six sizes from 0.35 liter to 4 liters, $14–$35).

Fry pans tend to be acquired as part of a cookset, but lovers of crisp fish, over-easy eggs, and hand-rolled tortillas can get one separately, in 8-inch ($9–$13) up to 12-inch ($12–$17) sizes. Since the single-burner norm is food that's carbonized in the middle and raw on the edges, you need to move the fry pan constantly, especially if your stove has a small-diameter burner. A "wundergauze" (page 348) or metal diffuser can also avoid hot spots. Colin tells me he's stopped carrying a fry pan, preferring to bake fish over a small stick fire in a sheet of heavy-duty foil. But for ambitious cooks, a fry pan or dual-purpose pan is handy.

Fry-bake pans. Former National Outdoor Leadership School (NOLS) instructor Pam Banks designed an aluminum Fry-Bake Pan with a non-stick coating (8 inches, $65; 10 inches, $70) that's available from NOLS through mail order. Aficionados tell me they kindle a small twig fire on the lid for browning.

For fireless backpacking, great potential resides in the Outback Oven, from Backpacker's Pantry. This combines a steel diffuser disk and riser bar with a "convection dome" of reflective fabric to direct the heat evenly around the pan to an exit hole. The final refinement is a bi-metal thermometer set in the knob on top. This seemed at first to be sheer wankery. But having learned camp cooking over fires with cast-iron Dutch ovens, it didn't take me long to realize what could be done with the Outback Oven. That is, pizza, lasagna, rellenos, frittata, pita, cookies, scones, pies, and yes, *quiche,* on a single burner at a fraction of cast iron's weight. At first I used packaged mixes but also found it wondrously suited for the conversion of bulk staples (flour, cornmeal, etc.) to satisfying meals. It comes in 8-inch (18 oz., $45), 10-inch (24 oz., $50), and 12-inch Outfitter (43 oz., $90) sizes, with the pan and lid about half the stated weight. Accessories include a pot lifter, 1-oz. bamboo spatula/

Outback Oven

knife, and a 12-inch plastic cutting board with the Outfitter. For those with suitable 8-inch pots, the Ultralight kit (7 oz., $35, with a set-on-top thermometer that comes separately for $6.50) puts a bakery on your back. The diffuser plate (called a Scorch Buster, 2.8 oz., $13) helps to simmer thick soups and toast bagels. The fabric convection dome halves fuel consumption when melting snow (without the diffuser plate) and can be upended, with a black pot inside, as a solar melter. It also makes a decent (if silly looking) survival hat. And so on. But the Outback Oven can't be used on any stove with a built-in tank where heat from the burner pressurizes the fuel supply (e.g., Svea) at the risk of *kablooey*. And though a trim-to-fit reflector is included, you'd want to be cautious with stoves that mount the burner directly on a gas cartridge.

The BakePacker, sold by Adventure Foods, is an aluminum grid that holds bread dough, fish, etc. in a plastic cooking bag above 1 inch of boiling water (you supply the pot). The advantage is being able to mix things in the bag (no washup) and relative unscorchability. One disadvantage (perhaps only aesthetic) is that foods don't brown. A second one is having a food-coated plastic bag to dispose of. It comes in two sizes: Standard (7¼-inch diameter, 9 oz., $18) and Ultralight (5¾-inch diameter, 4 oz., $17).

Teakettles. For inveterate brewers-up, a stainless 1-quart teakettle with wee spout, folding handle, and mesh basket comes from Olicamp (at a guess, 13 oz., $25) as well as a titanium kettle holding just under a quart, with an adjustable handle (5.4 oz., $63). The Trangia Kettle is aluminum (6.6 oz., $14). MSR also makes a stainless teapot (9 oz., $23).

Fuel-saving devices. Mountain Safety Research's XPD Heat Exchanger, a ring of corrugated aluminum (6 oz., $30) that clamps on a 1.5- to 2-liter pot, has been around for some time. The catalog claims that it "ups heat efficiency by 25%"—certainly appealing. Yet a snow-seasoned friend calls that claim "extravagant, to say the least." He tried the XPD on an expedition and thought his trusty stove was malfunctioning because it took so much longer to melt snow. But once he took the heat exchanger off, boil times dropped. Intrigued, I borrowed an XPD and also got the Olicamp II Cooking System (see below). Granted a blustery finger-biter of a day, and applying real-world standards, with an MSR DragonFly stove I boiled 1 quart in a 1.5-liter pot. With the XPD it took 13:11 and without, 11:20. *Hmmm.* Thinking the stove's output might be fluctuating, I tried the test again on a gas kitchen stove. This timed out at 7:39 with the XPD and 7:22 without. Wondering if a wide 2-liter pot might be more efficient, I logged 8:04 with the heat exchanger and (double *hmmm*) 8:00 without. It seemed that a basic principle was emerging. For which, read on.

The Olicamp II Cooking System (20 oz., $35) is a stainless 2-liter pot with an integral windscreen that extends ¾ inch below the bottom of the pot, to which it's joined at the rim, above a ring of vent holes. The catalog claims that this double-walled wonder "increases cooking efficiency by 30–40%!" But again the boil times proved otherwise. Outside on the DragonFly stove it boiled a quart in 11:30, bettering the XPD, but still slower than a plain old stainless pot at 11:20. On the kitchen stove it boiled in 7:47, a bit slower than the XPD. Since the outer and inner walls of the Cooking System pot are joined at the top, I thought it might do better full, but indoors with 2 quarts it logged a dreary 15:09 while a plain-Jane stainless 2-liter pot boiled in 11:45.

Since I believe (local politics notwithstanding) that the laws of the universe are the same in Wyoming as elsewhere, what are we to make of these results—not only consistent, but consistently the opposite of the claims? Simply, my physics bump tells me that both devices increase the pot's surface area so that the net heat loss outruns the net gain. That is, instead of gathering heat they act like the cooling fins on a cylinder head.

By covering the pot completely with a reflective dome, the Outback

Oven (see page 270) does decrease the amount of fuel needed to melt snow. You cover the pot with the dome and run the stove at low throttle until the water steams. Then you remove the dome and crank the burner to attain boilage. If you try to reach a boil with the dome on, especially in cold weather, condensation drips can put out the stove.

Pressure cookers have long been used both to shorten cooking time (by about 70 percent) and to allow cooking with far less water. For high altitude areas, water-scant deserts, and fuel-short locales where the available foods such as rice, beans, yams, potatoes, and athletic goat all take considerable cooking, a pressure cooker can make the difference between eating quite well and damned badly. Some readers suggest the deluxe Duromatic, made by Kuhn-Rikon of Switzerland. The drawback is weight: my old 4-quart steel Presto ($10 at a garage sale, plus a new gasket and safety release) weighed 3 lbs. 12 oz. Trimming the plastic handles and replacing steel bolts with aluminum ones knocked off 4 oz. Somewhat lighter is the Chinese-made 3-liter aluminum GSI pressure cooker (3 lb. 6 oz., $62). Since the chunky handles weighed in at 4.4 oz., and the fat plastic knob-and-bar assembly at 9.2 oz, I took them off and replaced the top knob with a wooden dowel, getting it just under 3 lbs. without compromising safety. But GSI is dropping this model in favor of a hard-anodized 3.3-liter model at a thumping 4 lbs. 4 oz.

Having pressure-cooked for 20-some years without tie-dying my ceiling, I'd better underline the fact that it takes *constant attention*. In this case, an unwatched pot will not only boil but will also spew its contents, at a thrilling 250°F-plus, all over you and the surrounding landscape. Another caution is to allow pressure-cooked foods to cool before decanting into plastic bowls, cups, etc. (Lexan, for instance, melts at 265°.) For full tips, consult the directions supplied.

COLIN:

Cups and mugs. The Sierra Club stainless-steel cup (or Sierra cup, as it's now called — 10 fl. oz., weight 3 oz., about $5) is one of those simple but gloriously successful devices that man occasionally invents. It's tough. It cleans easily. Its rim rarely burns your lips, even with the hottest food or drink. The open-end steel-wire handle stays cool too, hooks over belt or bough or cord, and snaps easily and securely onto a belt clip. (A reader writes: "Have you ever found an efficient way, or even an inefficient way, to stop the occasional intolerable rattle of Sierra cup in belt clip?" Another responds: "Yes. Just slip the cup into a worn but clean sock. Or even a dirty sock.")

An Illinois reader made a simple but interesting modification to the Sierra cup handle. "The extra bend," he wrote, "affords a secure grip and

counterbalance that I have not found in any other cup. If you fill the cup with liquid you will get the full impact of its practicality." He sent me a modified cup and, by God, he was right! I've used the modified version for years, with advantage and pleasure.

Unfortunately, the Sierra cup has in certain wilderness circles become a badge of conformity: a dismal fate for a first-class article. The status symbol game hit a new high (or low) in the 1980s with Early Winters's brass-, silver-, or gold-plated Sierra Club cups. More in the outdoor spirit is the new Titanium Sierra Mug, from Olicamp, a slightly deeper version holding 11 fl. oz., with measuring marks, at a notable 1.55 oz. and $24.

Plastic cups, being less heat-conductive than the Sierra cup, should in theory keep food hotter. I once conducted a rather elegant experiment to clarify this point. Using a standard Sierra cup and a plastic one, I several times filled both cups with water of known temperature and then exposed them, side by side, to environments of known temperature.*

Unfortunately, the lightness and deepness of most plastic cups mean less stability (a real factor, this, and perhaps the main reason I continue, except when going ultralight, to carry a Sierra cup: I find that a plastic cup, when close to empty, tends to tip over if you rest a spoon in it). The smaller top area also means less convenience with the lumpy stews and even hamburgers that the Sierra cup handles with such surprising grace. And you cannot cook in a plastic cup—though a reader writes: "You can almost boil water in [one]. Heat stones in a fire. Drop them in the cup of

*Summary of results:

Water at start	Cool environment	Minutes exposed	Water temp. °F	
			Sierra	Plastic
Boiling	Garden, 58°F, windless	15	120	126
		18	112	118
		20	109	115
122°F	Freezer box, 15°F	5	96	100
Boiling	Freezer box, 15°F	10	120	126

I assume that any impartial observer would accept these figures, which were supported by lip-service tests, as clear demonstration (taking into account the time and temperature parameters probable in field use, and reducing all readings to two decimal places) that the plastic cup is, as a heat conserver, superior to the Sierra cup by a factor remarkably close, all expectations considered, to zero.

water. Use greenstick tongs or chopsticks." Finally, gung-hoers complain that no plastic cup is in the same class as the inverted Sierra cup when it comes to digging handholds in snow slopes.

CHIP: To those who camp at high elevations and latitudes, especially in winter, the insulated mug is right up there with Vibram soles. On subzero mornings, being able to set your mug right on the snow and guzzle hot brew while packing up is as near heaven as I expect to get. So is being able to retreat to the sleeping bag at night and slowly sip hot tea, as the world freezes up around you. So I take an insulated mug (with the handle trimmed off, of course) even on ultralight summer trips.

To follow up on Colin's experiment, in 1996 *Backpacker* tested an insulated travel mug (12-fl.-oz. Aladdin with lid) against lidless cups of double-wall stainless steel, single-wall Lexan, enameled steel, plain old plastic, and the venerable Sierra cup. After 10 minutes the insulated mug had cooled by 10°F. The rest, including the double-wall stainless, lost 30 to 35°, with the Sierra cup shedding nearly 40°. After 30 minutes the insulated mug was still 158° while the double-wall steel one was 119° and the rest had dropped well below that boundary (about 115°F) that signals "warm" to our senses.

Since *Backpacker* didn't mention outdoorsy variables, I tried the same test with some popular insulated mugs (and a stainless-steel cup for reference) in Cruel World conditions: just before dawn at 7200 feet, with a stiff 36°F mountain breeze. I measured the temperatures with a scientific thermometer that just fit into the drinking hole.

CRUEL WORLD INSULATED MUG TEST
(starting temperature in cup 189°F)

	Temperature °F		
Type and volume (fl. oz.)	10 *min.*	20 *min.*	30 *min.*
Whirley, sealed, 22 oz.	169	154	144
Whirley, regular, 13 oz.	162	149	138
Whirley with Reflectix, 13 oz.	169	156	146
Aladdin, regular, 12 oz.	164	152	142
Aladdin, cargo, 12 oz.	162	150	141
GSI stainless Bottle Cup, 18 oz.	124	100	86

Besides the fact that insulated mugs do an extraordinary job of holding heat, the results show other things. One is that volume helps, with the 13-fl.-oz. Whirley (5.7 oz., $3) outdone by a 22-ouncer of the same brand. Another is that even with a smaller diameter and slightly less volume, the 12-fl.-oz. Aladdin mug (5 oz., $3) with foam insulation held heat better than the Whirley, insulated with an air gap. But when I

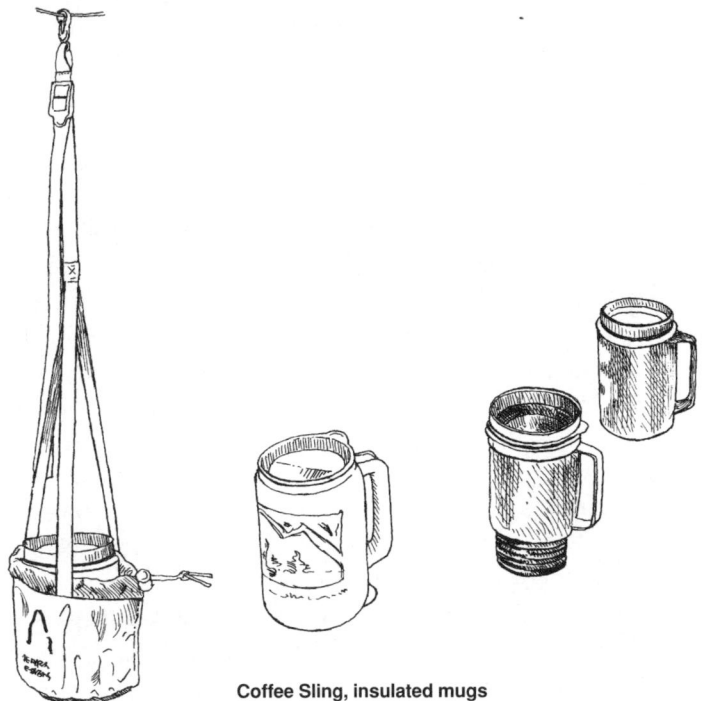

Coffee Sling, insulated mugs

popped the bottom off the Whirley mug and slipped a layer of Reflectix bubble insulation (page 451) into the air gap and glued a ¼-inch piece of Ensolite to the cap, its performance improved. (If space is an issue, you could leave out the insulation and easily stuff a week's worth of tea bags in.) While there wasn't much temperature difference betwixt the regular Aladdin mug and the "cargo" type (with a skinny corrugated bottom for car holders), it's worth noting that the cargo mug tipped over when I poured water into it. For stability, the broad-based Whirley design was best.

Since tipsiness is disastrous in a tent, a brilliant accessory is the 3-oz. Coffee Sling, devised by Fred Dieter and sold by Sierra Designs in packs of two ($20). This lets you suspend your insulated mug from a tent tab or branch and sip at your ease, while making it virtually impossible to spill. I batted a full mug (with lid) of coffee around and achieved significant spillage only by bouncing it off the side of the tent.

While the stainless GSI Bottle Cup (5.3 oz., $6.50) isn't a monster for heat retention, it has its uses. It snugs over the base of a 1-liter water bottle, holds 18 fl. oz., and has folding handles long enough to let you cook in the event of an unplanned night out. While spending a whole summer camped out, for bivouacs I used the classic kidney-bean-shaped 22-oz. U.S. Army canteen cup, of stainless steel with folding handles (9 oz., $5–$10). The shape makes it good for cooking with twig fires. An

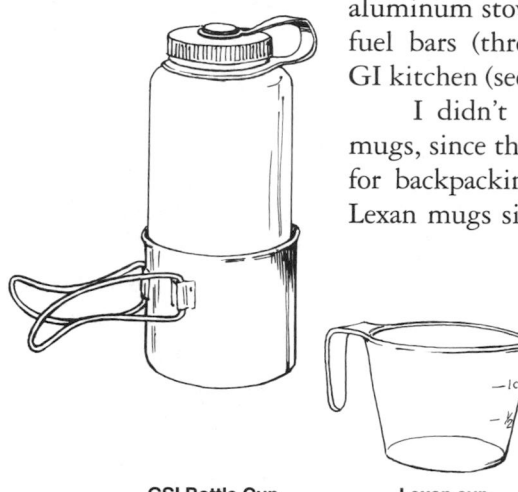

GSI Bottle Cup   **Lexan cup**

aluminum stove base (6 oz., $6) and trioxane fuel bars (three for a buck) turn it into a GI kitchen (see page 336).

I didn't try fancy stainless-steel travel mugs, since they're more for commuting than for backpacking. Nor did I try double-wall Lexan mugs since the ones I saw lacked lids. If insulation is optional, a plain 12-oz. Lexan cup with measuring marks is elegant, rugged, and cheap: GSI makes them in clear, cobalt, and emerald (2.8 oz., under $4).

Ultralight cookware. The unvarnished approach is to use a small pot from a light-gauge aluminum mess kit (Boy Scout vintage). But this also means thin walls and low volumes, with a corresponding loss of cooking qualities and durability. So it pays to seek out compromise of one sort or other.

Snow Peak, a Japanese firm begun in 1963, makes aluminum ware in compact sizes with dimensions unlike European- and U.S.-made sets. Their Solo Combo Cookset (1 lb. 1.5 oz., $100) is an oval pot, fry pan/lid, cup with folding handle, titanium utensils, and cutting board, with room inside to stow a compact stove and fuel cartridge. I've been using their Mini Solo cookset (8.2 oz., $56) that nests a ¾-liter pot inside a ⅓-liter cup (also stoveworthy), with a lid that fits both. The nonstick coating is fragile, so a paper towel or viscose wiper should go betwixt mug and pot.

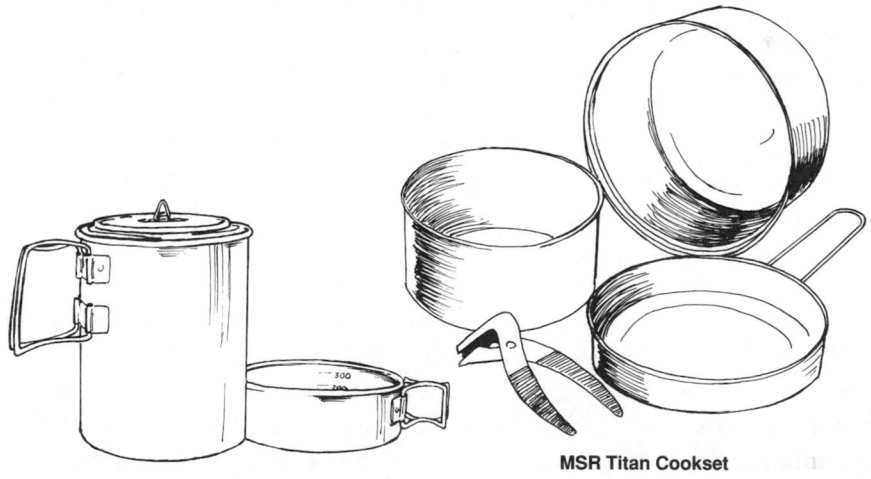

MSR Titan Cookset

Snow Peak Mini Solo Cookset

(In fact, abrasion from nesting and joggling ruins nonstick coatings more quickly than anything, except a major scorching.) The narrow (5-by-3.5-inch) shape is less than efficient at catching heat but does have its advantages: a 12-oz. insulated mug (minus handle) nests neatly inside. In turn, the mug holds Snow Peak's minuscule GigaPower stove (see page 331), a 2-oz. packet of loose tea, a tea ball, a scrubber, and a butane lighter. With a spoon slipped in and a 250 g gas cartridge in the bottom of the mesh sack, the whole thing fits into the left-hand water-bottle sleeve on my fanny pack. And an extra titanium pot will snug over the Snow Peak gas cartridge. I call this motley and ever-changing assortment:

THE FLYING KITCHEN

	Ounces
GigaPower stove	3.0
Mini Solo cookset	
300 ml. cup/pot	2.5
750 ml. pot	4.5
lid	1.0
mesh drawstring sack	0.5
insulated 12-oz. mug (no handle)	4.8
titanium spoon	0.6
tea ball	0.5
viscose pack towel, 3 by 12 inches	0.3
scrubber, 1.5 by 1.5 inches	0.1
refillable butane lighter	0.5
Total	1 lb. 3.0 oz.
plus a 7.7-oz. net gas cartridge	12.0
Total with fuel	1 lb. 15 oz.
(plus extra titanium pot)	
Olicamp Space Saver 0.8 liter, with lid	3.6
Grand total	2 lbs. 1.9 oz.

Titanium is not only light, as metals go, but is also stronger than aluminum and resists dents and scratches. The thin walls develop hot spots and need close watching, but these days the fast crowd will have nothing else. Light as a feather (but a real goose in terms of cash) is the MSR Titan cookset (see previous page): two nesting pots (0.7-liter, 2.8 oz.; 1-liter, 3.7 oz.), a lid/fry pan with folding handle (2.2 oz.), and a gripper (1.5 oz.) for a total 10.2 oz. and a cool $90. While this volume will do for two light eaters in warm weather, bush wolves will round out the set with the MSR Titan 2-liter pot with lid (7 oz. plus 1-oz. gripper, $80). To put it mildly, $170 is a lot to cough up for a cookset. More volume comes with Evernew's MountainLite T-set, with nesting 1.9-liter and 2.6-liter pots, each with lid and folding handle (1 lb. 2.6 oz., $85), with a titanium fry pan extra

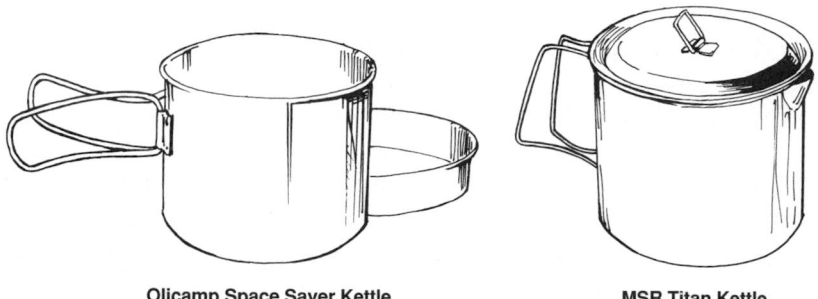

Olicamp Space Saver Kettle   MSR Titan Kettle

(4.2 oz., $30). On one-pot jaunts, I've carried the Olicamp titanium Space Saver Kettle (3.6 oz., $42), which will nest with the Flying Kitchen (above). The MSR Titan Kettle (0.85-liter, 4.1 oz., $50) with folding handles, a close-fitting lid, and subtle pour spout is another good solo cooker.

COLIN:

Fork. Redundant.

Spoon. Any tough, light spoon will do. One from a clip-together set will have two little protuberances that are not only ideal for hooking onto pot rims when you leave the spoon standing in one but also unbeatable for collecting dirt. Alternatively, you can bend over the top of a metal spoon so that it hooks over the pot rim rather than slipping down into the soup. Although you can't do this with Lexan plastic soup spoons (⅓ oz., <$1), they're so light and efficient that I find I nowadays almost always choose to take one, rather than my old metal friend.

CHIP: As if ⅓ oz. wasn't light enough, I just got a new Lexan spoon that's just big enough to be useful and weighs only ¼ oz. (in GSI's TEKK set, with a redundant fork and pointless knife, 0.7 oz., $2.50). Lexan, besides high strength and flexibility, also has the advantage of not marring non-stick coatings. But if you leave a Lexan utensil in a simmering pot, it will melt: I've got two spoons with Salvador Dalí lips. The bright side is that

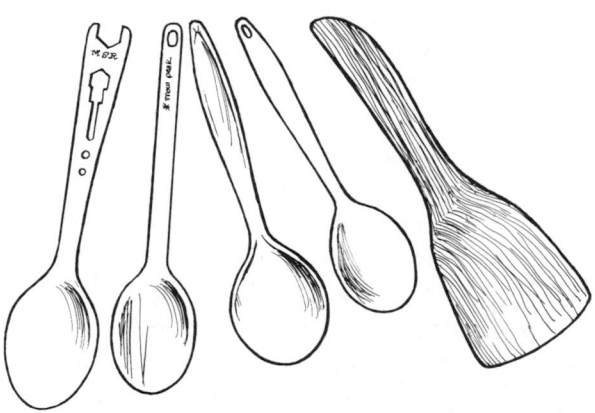

this allows you to *carefully* heat the handle and bend it into a gentle hook, to keep your spoon from pot diving. Although heating Lexan to the point of flexibility does seem to make it brittle. Titanium spoons, weighing twice what Lexan does but half as much as steel, won't melt outside a blast furnace. I've somehow acquired one from Snow Peak (0.6 oz., from a set with fork and sheath, 1.4 oz., $27) and a bigger one from MSR, the Titan Tool Spoon (0.8 oz., $15) with jet and cable wrenches for MSR stoves incorporated in the handle. (A stainless-steel Tool Spoon is 1.5 oz. and $6.)

Chopsticks expand your culinary horizons in inverse proportion to their weight and cost (0.3 oz., free at your neighborhood café)—perfect for ramen-slurping, trout-dismantling, and other spoon-defying tasks. Another choice bit of Eastern wisdom is the Utu (at right, facing page), a knife/spatula combo of bamboo that comes with the Outback Oven (or by itself; 0.6 oz, $4.50). The spatula is thin and stiff yet won't scratch coated pans. The handle is beveled into a knife of sorts, to divide freshly baked goods and spread jam—sharp, it ain't. But with pocketknife, spoon, chopsticks, and utu, I can cook and eat virtually anything on my personal menu, perhaps a notch or two above Colin's rock-belly Brittannic barbarism. If you aim ever higher, read on.

Miscellania. Makers of cookware tell me that a gourmet groundswell is boosting demand for all sorts of fancy armament—mostly for wilderness tête-à-têtes, or group trips on which intricate cookery can be appreciated. Kitchen kits, various implements, and sundry vessels in a compartmented pouch (from GSI, JanSport, Outdoor Research, and Sova, among others) aren't hard to find. But unless you get one as a present (it's the sort of thing that appeals to noncamping relatives), it makes sense to list what you actually carry and then look for a pouch that matches up. The failing of such kits is leaky containers. So look for pharmaceutical-grade bottles (e.g., Nalgene) and jars. MSR's Alpine Kitchen Cupboard is based on a plastic caddy that fits inside their cooksets and includes a sturdy folding ladle, spatula, and pasta drainer, and assorted plastic bot-

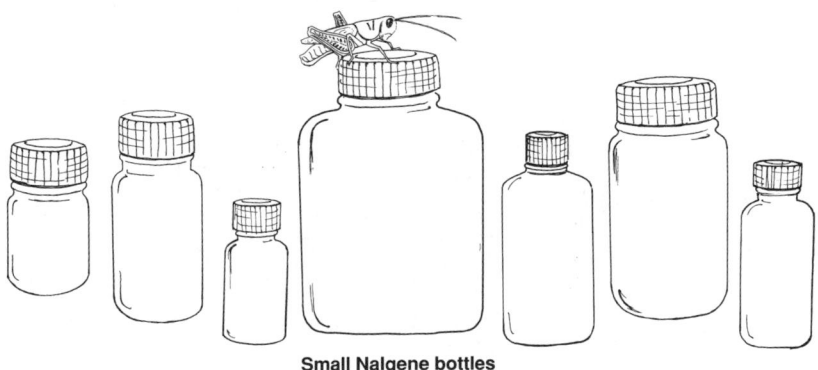

Small Nalgene bottles

tles (11 oz. and $20). Costlier iterations add a scrubber, a plastic cutting board, a mesh dish-draining bag, and suchlike. To lighten up, you might ditch the plastic cutting board from your kitchen kit and go with one of the thin, knife-resistant plastic sheets now showing up at cookery shops—an 8-inch circle weighs about ½ oz. Other firms offer graters, whisks, corkscrews, Lexan wine goblets, and cocktail shakers, and for all I know, solar-powered Cuisinarts.

Readers have suggested items such as an Ensolite "cozy" for keeping pots warm. I've dropped a balaclava or a folded-foil "hat" over them, and Colin has used sand or leaves—around the pot, not in it.

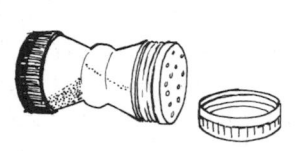

Salt and pepper shaker. Widely available are plastic, perforated lids with snap covers that fit recycled 35-millimeter plastic film cans (¾ oz. a pair, $2)— also useful for footpowder. Lexan combination shakers are clear, rugged, and unlikely to pop open, unlike those of softer plastic. GSI's weighs 1 oz. and costs $3 or so. The drawback is that salt and pepper shake out into the lids in transit, so uncap with care.

Caffeinic arts. Tea bibbers (and juicers) should skip this part. For those of us who are not, the array of infernal machines for the delivery of fresh-brewed coffee has proliferated. So I'll spiral downward from the most elaborate. If you pack fluorescent blue hair-coloring on backcountry trips, you'll feel naked without a mini espresso maker. I did an explosion test on a GSI stainless-steel 1-cup model (7.5 oz., $30) and rather than blowing up, it spewed out a jet of pure darkness—much more quickly than boiling water and brewing coffee. Aluminum models are lighter and cheaper. Teeny espresso makers work best on a small-burner cartridge

Mini espresso maker

stove; for broad-burners, MSR sells a three-prong Espresso Star adapter (0.8 oz., $11). The matching GSI demitasse cuplet is 4 oz. and $2.

Midway is GSI's JavaPress (10 fl. oz., $16; 33 fl. oz., $20) a Lexan press pot that makes excellent coffee. L. L. Bean purveys a Backpacking Java Press, a 20-oz. insulated mug with plunger built into the lid ($17.50). The truly mad will also require a hand coffee grinder (Olicamp's small: 5 oz., $18; large: 10 oz., $26). On the lighter side, the MSR Mugmate is a simple washable screen in a plastic frame (1 oz., $13) that works best with a medium-coarse grind (with fine-grind, you get sedimentary scum). Melitta-type filter cones (1 cup, 1.6 oz., $2) with paper filters yield good coffee if you wet the grounds and let them plump up before pouring away. Coffee socks (or silk aquarium dipnets) make decent coffee but get rank if put up wet.

For the minimalist, Coghlan's sells 1-cup paper cone filters with punched holes and a plastic wand to hold them up ($2), requiring only coffee and a good aim. Or you can get a box of No. 1 filters, punch the holes yourself, and use a chopstick. A Seattle reader suggests placing a small paper filter in an insulated mug, folding the edges down, adding coffee, and snapping down the cap. You trickle boiling water through the drinking hole until it backs up, signifying fullness. If it backs up right away, the filter is plugging the hole—rotate the cap. The nice part is that you can steep your brew without losing heat. But if you need to eyeball the process, leave the top off and use a fat rubber band to clamp the filter (10 No. 1 or No. 2 paper filters and a rubber band weigh a mere ⅓ oz.).

What to do with coffee grounds? I take them along (*en filtre*) when I seek the trees and then mix them with my own end products (page 699, footnote). However in places where self-composting is not a good idea, you should let coffee filters or tea bags drain and pack them out.

COLIN-THE-KNIFE: For some years I very happily used a Victorinox Tinker (3.2 oz., $25). In addition to a large and a small blade, it embodies an excellent pair of scissors, which I use a great deal, and slide-out tweezers and toothpick. It also grows a Phillips screwdriver, bottle-opener/screwdriver, can opener, and reamer, which I rarely if ever use. Some time ago I thought I'd lost my Tinker and, being on a lightweight kick, I bought a 2¼-inch Victorinox Classic (1 oz., $15) and it has largely (or, rather, small-ly) supplanted

Victorinox Tinker

the Tinker. It comes with one blade, scissors, tweezers, and toothpick—and also a "manicure blade" that I may just, in some paranoid gramparing moment, cut off.

The two reputable makers of Swiss Army knives, Victorinox and Wenger, both offer lifetime guarantees. Avoid imitators. The range of available models is now so rich that you can not only be sure of finding one that meets all your requirements and whims but also have a ball making the selection.

Knife sharpener. Sharpen at home. Standard for touching up in the field: a small Carborundum stone (3 inches, 1 oz., $5). Alternatives: a miniature steel (a good one comes with a sheath designed for Swiss Army knives but doesn't seem to be sold separately; another has diamonds set in the stainless steel and is said to be "great"); a substitute, which I've now adopted on ultralight trips: Carborundum sandpaper. But Fiskars now makes a sharpener (sold by Gerber and others) with ceramic rods, fine and coarse, set at the proper angles in a plastic body (0.5 oz., $3). The ceramic rods are somewhat fragile; sharpen with care.

CHIP: There are excellent folding knives made by Gerber, Kershaw, Spyderco, and others that lend themselves to sawing through frozen ropes, deboning moose, and other tasks that backpackers very seldom need to do. As pocketknives have sprouted files, hooks, awls, scissors, and so forth, they've diverged into

Pocket tools. Circa 1988, I got a Leatherman Pocket Survival Tool from the U.S. Forest Service as a "wilderness safety award" for staying alive—a state I seek to maintain, regardless. The pliers and robust file proved so useful that I added it to my ditty bag without leaving my ancient Victorinox Tinker pocketknife behind. I was dimly aware that the combination weighed over half a pound but felt prepared for anything short of neurosurgery. Most kitchens have a drawer with an ill-assorted jumble of tools, and the kitchen on my back was no different.

Backpacking shops now carry pocket tools by Coast, Coleman, Gerber, Kershaw, Leatherman, Schrade, Seber, SOG, Swiss-Tech, and dear old Victorinox (among others) at a range of prices. But before buying, check out your stoves and packframes (and don't forget seasonal specialties like ski bindings), noting the size and type of screws, nuts, and so forth. Then consider the exigencies of repairing zippers, eyeglass frames, fishing reels, blown grommets, and anything else you've had fail. And last, note your present assets, such as the wrench-worthy MSR toolspoon. If you have a faithful Swiss Army knife that you wish to supplement, unfold its blades one by one and think about what you actually use. Then make a list.

Some tools have pliers but no scissors, and some vice versa. Some even have lock-grip pliers (at 8-plus oz.), while pliers on the more knife-

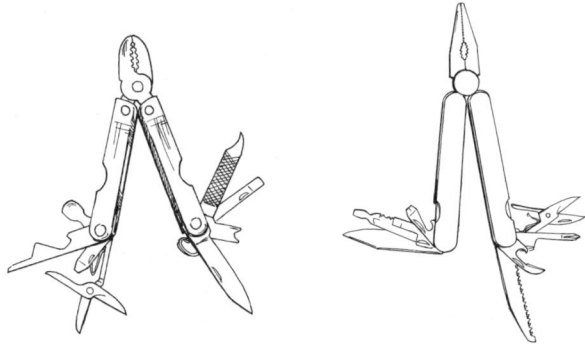

Pocket tools

like tools might be rather slim. The fine-jawed pliers on mini-tools make excellent tweezers as well. If you use a sparking tool to start fires or to clean fish regularly, a second knife blade is good. So consider your habits, blade by blade and bit by bit. With your list done, qualitative issues arise. For instance, locking blades are costly, but an unexpected fold-up can slice, pinch, or puncture you far from aid—and when pressure is exerted lengthwise, any nonlocking bit will fold up. So either pay up or take due care.

Sheer mass is also key. The Victorinox SwissTool is a gorgeous 23-featured artifact with individually sprung locking blades, though at nearly 10 oz. (and $90) it had better be. The new Leatherman Wave is likewise, amazing (at 8 oz., $80). Whence the cost factor again raises its ugly head. Since I lost my engraved Leatherman tool during a lean period, I replaced it with two relatively inexpensive tools from Coast Cutlery, of Portland, Oregon.

The Coast Micro-plier tool (above left) is 2.5 inches long when folded and has both serviceable pliers and Swiss-style scissors with enough bite to trim Grendelistic toenails. It also has a teeny slot screwdriver bit (eyeglasses, fly reel) as well as medium slot and Phillips drivers, a reasonable file, a wire stripper (also good for prying things open), a wire cutter, a scraper (for tanning mouse pelts?), and of course a wee knife blade, at 1.5 inches just long enough to clean a trout. And (as the replacement cost of my late-lamented Leatherman hovers around $50) the $15 price and 1.7-oz. weight looked good. So the Micro-plier tool now lives in my office-on-the-yoke (page 180). For winter, when a stainless-steel chill travels straight up my arm, I got the larger Coast Pocket Pliers (above right, 3¾ inches, 6 oz., $20) for their plastic-clad grip. (A trick that winterized my all-steel Leatherman was to nip a notch out of the leather flap on the sheath so that it could be slipped on and snapped with the blade out, giving an insulated grip.) The Coast Pocket Pliers sport both serrated and saw blades, as well as a can opener. To lessen the fold-up factor, I used a medium stone on the little shoulder that stops the knife blade, until the blade opened perfectly straight with respect to the grip. Locking blades are better.

A general principle is that the weight and complexity of your pocket tool should match the weight and complexity of your gear: the less you carry, the less you'll need in the way of techno-fixits.

COLIN:

Containers—for staples and goodies. Make sure all containers are easily distinguishable by sight and touch. Years ago I used to carry detergent powder and sugar in identical plastic boxes—and I can heartily unrecommend predawn cereal sleepily sweetened with detergent powder. I haven't carried detergent powder for years, and now, Zoning, I eschew sugar. But be warned!

Some people carry food items, and even water, in widemouth plastic bottles of various sizes. A whole family of cousins, in various shapes and sizes, sprinkles the catalogs. But Nalgene bottles seem by far the most reliable. They come in myriad shapes and sizes, rounded and squared, large- and smallmouth, 1 fl. oz. to gallons, in polyethylene, polypropylene, and Lexan. They're strong, the lids don't leak, and the plastic doesn't contaminate. Kitchen kits tend to have containers of lesser quality, a good argument for assembling your own.

For gourmets, multi-spice shakers (various weights, $4–$6) sort spices and flavorings in a container divided like a pie chart into six or so spaces with individual snap caps.

One solution for margarine and also for such potential pack wreckers as jam, honey, and peanut butter is a poly squeeze tube, refillable by disengaging the end clip (now markedly and mercifully improved) from Campmor, Coghlan's, and others (2 oz., 2 for $3; spare clips, 2 for $.50). You can carry exactly the amount you want in such a tube, up to 6 ounces, and so escape the limitations of prepackaged products. (Instead of margarine, I now carry much healthier olive oil—in one of the very small cylindrical Nalgene bottles. Size depends on trip.) I know one man who

Miscellaneous containers

carries a squeeze tube in his packet as a "cup" for quick drinks from trailside sources. It is the only thing, he says, that's any use for small rock seeps: you press the open tube against the rock and it conforms to the rock's contours and collects virtually all the seepage. The untethered caps are easy to lose, though.

I'm told you can break eggs into squeeze tubes, or even doubled zip-top bags, and halfway trust the yolks to be intact for morning fried eggs. Alternatively, buy yourself a hard plastic egg box, sextovular through duodecimovular (6 egger, $2.50; 12 egger, $3.50). In 1960 I used a biovular job with profit on a summer-long walk up England when I could often drop into a farmhouse in the evening and buy a couple of eggs for breakfast. But if shells break in such containers you get egg on much more than your face.

Milk squirter. I still use one of those pliable, squeezable polyethylene containers in which honey and mustard are sometimes sold. For refilling with milk powder, unscrew main top. For making milk, remove only the little dunce-cap top and squirt powder down onto water, tea, or coffee. Even in a raging gale you suffer virtually no loss. A simple but valuable device—and one that lasts. The Sue Bee honey container (12-oz. size) that I started with almost 35 years ago is still squirting strong. At least, I think it's still the same one. Supermarket shelves

Milk squirter

bear plastic containers in an array of shapes, sizes, and specializations, with food already inside. Wash and reuse.

Fire starters. Bookmatches, though useless in a high wind, are otherwise more convenient than wooden ones. I find a book a day more than enough.

A waterproof matchsafe holds about 20 large, wooden, strike-anywhere matches for use in wind or wet.

My first-line matchsafe is the screw-tight metal kind. I've carried it for years, but at one time grew unhappy with both the difficulty of opening it and also the way the metal attachment loop can pull loose. If it weren't for the usefulness of this loop, which permits you to tie the matchsafe to your belt, or to an inflatable vest on river crossings, I'd probably switch to a simpler plastic model (0.6 oz., $1.50 from Coghlan's), though the striking bar is only marginally effective. Chip has turned up alternatives: the Olicamp threaded matchsafe is milled from solid aluminum, with an O-ring seal and attachment point (1.5 oz., $10). For those who insist on heirloom quality, the Silva Matchcase Compass is machined of brass, with a spare lanyard, double silicon O-rings (with two spares), and of course a diminutive compass (4 oz., $18). At the opposite, frugal extreme, Chip's favorite matchsafe is a green plastic Mentholatum bottle (1.1 oz.) that holds 80-plus matches and has never leaked (given a smear of lip balm on the threads).

I'm always rather surprised at how rarely I use a matchsafe, but when I need one, I need it. And in practice I find I often carry two. (They're also convenient places to keep needles and a little thread.)

For extra safety you can coat match heads with candle wax, but you *must* remove the wax before striking—and I find that even then they're difficult to ignite. Now available: Greenlite water-resistant matches, 45 to a water-resistant box (four boxes, $2.40; 10 boxes, $3.60); and wind- and waterproof matches, 25 to a box (two-pack, $5.50). British Lifeboat Matches, chemically treated to burn in any wind, even when wet, with a 12-second burn time, come 25 to a sealed plastic container (¾ oz., $4.50).

CHIP: For snow camping in particular, a butane lighter saves you condensation-logged match striking (and launching little sulfuric rockets to burn holes in your tent and sleeping bag). I've got a refillable Ronson (0.5 oz., $1.50). Even when the gas doesn't light, the spark it generates will touch off a cartridge stove or priming cup. But beware: some supermarket lighters with piezoelectric ignitions (that convert the motion of a spring-loaded plunger to a spark) are awful, lighting an average of 3 out of 10 times—a real screamfest. There are also astonishingly high-tech refillable lighters with piezo ignitions, elaborate cases, and so forth for $10 to $50. Not sure why I haven't tried one. Meanwhile, the classic Zippo (2 oz. full, $20 and up, with replaceable flint), in essence a felt wick in a metal fuel tank, has the same virtue of sparkiness. Readers inform me that the Zippo works at high elevations in high winds, where pressurized gas lighters are known to flunk.

Lately, in place of a matchsafe—or for that matter, matches—I've been carrying a Magnesium Fire Starting Tool, by Doan Machine and Equipment (1.3 oz. without the little chain, $6). You can soak it in water, shake off the drops, and light a fire immediately. The drill is to shave magnesium bits off the bar, then ignite them by striking a knife or other steel edge on the sparking insert. For starting wood fires, the magnesium chips torch off with a brilliant white flame, undeterred by moisture. You can also nest the magnesium chips in a puff of fine (0000) steel wool and by blowing gently generate intense heat. Steel wool makes excellent tinder, and you can stuff quite a lot in a film can. My faith in this little whizbang was confirmed by an utterly matchless week, in October above

10,000 feet with blustery, spirit-dampening, hypothermic weather. I used the sparking insert to start my stove repeatedly without a miss.

COLIN: An ultralight *can opener* may be worth carrying if you don't have a Swiss Army knife with one. Ordinary canned foods make hopelessly inefficient backpacking fare, but you could need the opener for canned goodies that you include in cache or airdrop, or buy as a welcome change at a wayside store, or are given by some kind, heavy-toting, backcountry horseman. The old U.S. Army type P-38 crashed years ago, but Coghlan's now sells a slightly larger equivalent (0.4 oz., 2 for $1.19) that seems to be effective and tough. I'm told that some copies are not.

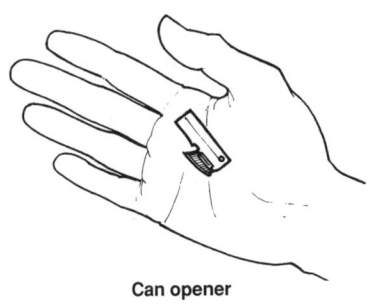

Can opener

Warning: These can openers are easily lost, especially in sand, so thread a small piece of red rag through the key-chain hole. On the rare occasions I now carry one, my opener goes into the office (page 180), wrapped in its own small plastic bag.

A prospector's magnifying glass, most often useful for examining rock samples and such sights as the horrifying head of a dragonfly, forms an emergency reserve for fire lighting. For years I carried a metal-cased 10-power glass that weighed 2 oz. (a current equivalent: the 16-power Naturalist's Loupe, Model 596, by Swift Instruments of Boston—also 2 oz., $20). Then I found a plastic-cased, 9-power substitute (¼ oz.) intermittently available from The Nature Company and from Audubon. An elephant treading on it might cause disruption, and the glass is no doubt of inferior quality. But I find it eminently practical as well as deliciously light. And its two swiveling lenses—4- and 5-power—give you added flexibility. Thread a thin nylon cord inside the end bar and you can hang it around your neck. This little gem seems to have succumbed to Herblock's Law ("If it's good, they've stopped making it"), but Bausch and Lomb offers a sturdier, fancier version with three lenses—5-, 10-, and 20-power (0.6 oz., $29).

A reader recommends a detachable camera lens as both magnifier and emergency fire starter. I rarely carry a full-size camera these days, but in an emergency I guess binoculars might do a fire job.

Keeping utensils clean

I generally carry a single "paper" washrag (actually rayon or similar, sold as Miracloth, Wash 'n Dri, or the like) for wiping pots clean (maybe

0.5 oz., around $.20). Several readers write that they take scouring pads of various kinds (Chore Boy, Scotch Brite, Brillo, or Dobie), which they swear will clean anything instantly, even in cold water. Others counsel presoaping the underside of pots and pans, so that "the black gunk washes right off (a trick any well-bred Girl Scout knows like the back of her hand)."

For notes on the actual practice of cleaning utensils, see A Sample Day in the Kitchen, page 359. For biodegradabilia, see page 358. For pots as washing machines, page 564.

HEAT SOURCES

Fires

The campfire is one of man's most ancient traditions (indeed, you could define man as "the fire-lighting animal"), and even today a fire is to many people half the fun of camping. Understandably so. For cheer and warmth as well as for cooking—not to mention for drying out you and yours—there is nothing quite like it.

The warmth is not very efficient—you tend to be toasted on one side, iceberged on the other (though see Chip's snazzy solution to this problem, page 351)—but there's no doubt about the cheer. Beside your fire you live in a private, glowing little world. All around you, fire shapes dance across rocks and bushes and tree trunks. A grasshopper that you've been watching as it basks on one verge, motionless, leaps without warning clear over the flames and out into the darkness. But most of the time you just sit and gaze into the caverns that form and crumble and then form again between the incandescent logs. You build fantastic worlds among those pulsating walls and arches and colonnades. No, not quite "build," for that is too active and definite a word. Rather, you let your mind slip away, free and unrestricted, roaming wide yet completely at rest, unconnected with your conscious self yet reporting back at some low, quiet, strangely decisive level. You sit, in other words, and dream. The East African has an almost limitless capacity for this masterly and delightful form of inactivity, and when his friends see him squatting there, lost, they understand and say in Swahili, poetically, *Anahota moto*— "He is dreaming the fire."

But there is another side to this shimmering coin. For many years now, in places it was both easy and reasonable to build campfires, I have almost always done without one. Perhaps laziness has a lot to do with it. But I'm very aware that a fire cuts you off from the night. I don't mean only that it makes most night animals give your camp a wide berth. Within the fire's domain you exist in a special, private, personal, isolated world. It's only when you walk away and stand for a while as part of the silence and immensity beyond that you understand the restriction. And then you find that the silent, infinite, mysterious world that exists beyond the campfire is truer than the restricted world that exists around it—and that in the end it is more rewarding. I walk out into wilderness primarily, I think, to reestablish a sense of unity with the rest of the world, with the rock and the trees and the animals and the sky and its stars—though perhaps I mean only that when I return to the city a renewed sense of this affinity is, above all, what I bring back with me. Anyway, a campfire, by its very charms, disrupts my sense of inclusion.

But if I do not build a fire I erect no lasting barriers. After I've cooked my evening meal on the little stove I use instead, and have switched off the stove and registered the unfailing astonishment I experience at the noisiness of its hissing, I am alone in and with the night. I can hear, now, the magnified sounds of its silence: a field mouse thinly complaining; a dry leaf rustling; a wedge of wind sliding down the far slope of the valley. And I can look deep into the shadowy blackness or the starlit dimness or the moonlit clarity. Or, best of all, I can watch the moon lever itself up and flood the starlit dimness into landscape. Always, over each of these separate mysteries, spreads the sky, total. And I, at the center—my center of it—am small and insignificant; but at the same time a part of it and therefore significant.

Then there are the ethical considerations.

A thousand charred forests bear black witness to the dangers of open fires. These dangers are as old as the dry summer hills; but in recent years new imperatives have crowded in on us. They depend, as do so many things, on numbers. Forty years ago popular wildernesses like the High Sierra were so lightly used that a backpacker could, within reason, light a safe, properly controlled cooking and campfire every night with a clear conscience. No longer. And it's not only that round black firesite pockmarks have in places become so common they rupture the sense of wilderness that people are presumably there to capture; or that too many fires—even small, safe fires—in such fragile places as meadows may seriously damage root systems. The fundamental and inescapable fact is that wood fires consume wood.

This slow consumption by humans does not at first seem to matter much. If you like tidy, parkland sort of country rather than genuine wilderness—which is rarely tidy, close up—then you may even like the result. I can do no more than differ with your aesthetic judgment. But dead and decaying wood is a component of the mechanism that has built what you find in the corner of the planet you have camped in. At moving margins—a meadow's edge, a forest's flank, the battlefront between soil and sand dune—it may be the most important component of all. It provides shade; holds soil and moisture; becomes home and food for plants and insects and even birds—and so sets off new chain reactions that soon employ more plants and insects and birds, then reptiles—and mammals too. And eventually—dust to dust—it re-becomes soil. A new, richer, more productive soil. Reduce the wood available for decay, and you slow down this process. Reduce it a bit more, and you halt all progress. Reduce a bit more, and you begin to impoverish the corner of the planet you've camped in. Natural accretion is slow; it moves by the decade, the century, the millennium. But our depletion is rapid: man consumes by the year, the day, the hour, the minute. And when he can find no more dead wood to consume, he begins to cut green wood. . . .

And now I have a confession to make. To make with reluctance. My draft of this section ecologized along to considerably beyond this point. When it was written I sent copies of it, for a check on facts and arguments, to two qualified outdoorsmen friends—one a geography professor and the other a doctor of ecology who drives airliners for a living. To my surprise, both came up fighting. Each suggested, independently, that I had employed a common current ploy: using tenuous and questionable "ecological" arguments to justify what was really a gut feeling. On reflection, I pleaded guilty. Each of them then proceeded to demolish my "ecological" arguments with an expertise beyond my grasp. In particular, they zeroed in on my use of the word "impoverish." In some areas it might be applicable; but fire-lighting man might equally be said to stimulate growth by releasing the nutrients bound up in dead wood. More had to be learned about the chemistry of such burning. Again, in much prime backpacking country, decades of successful fire prevention had created such an accumulation of fuel in the form of choked bush that when the inevitable fire came at last it was, instead of a cleanup operation, a holocaust. Hence my "charred forests."

Both my friends then said at some length that to them campfires were, anyway, "a part of it all." They extolled the warm skills and traditions of woodcraft. They listed all the campfire pleasures I had listed. They added more. For groups, they said, the pleasures multiplied: there is nothing like a campfire to promote community spirit within a heterogeneous party. My "sense of inclusion" idea had some merit in bright moonlight; but "what about a dark night?" Anyway, you only had to move away from a fire to see the stars. And too damned often there was a "hair shirt" element in doing without a fire. Maybe a campfire was even one of man's "deep evolutionary needs." And so it went on.

Now, both my friends are honest men, and both readily admitted that they were no doubt doing exactly what I had done: justifying gut feelings with any "logic" that came to hand. But both remained adamant.

They were very much attached to fires. They disagreed with me "one thousand percent." And they disagreed with terrible competence.

I am slightly intimidated but not, I find, convinced. I fail to detect the faintest tickle of a personal hair shirt. And I continue to feel that the building of campfires in much of today's wilderness is harming that wilderness. On further reflection, I think I may be talking less about genuine ecological damage than about fires' charring and jarring effect on the "natural," harmonious, nonhuman timbre of true wilderness—the quality I probably value above all. My opinion is no doubt based on gut feeling rather than logic. But I make no apologies for that. Rather the reverse. Few people accuse me of clear thinking, but I like to consider that on occasion I can *feel* with some accuracy.

Finally, I call for support on another friend who has spent long months backpacking around the High Sierra. He is a man who dotes on wilderness cooking and drools over smoke-tanged steak. He sees stoves as "revolting, noisy, heavy little bastards." But he has reluctantly concluded that in heavily used backcountry all wood fires should 'be banned. Since *Walker III* appeared, such a restriction has been imposed in many places at high-fire-risk times. And rightly so. But any broad, blanket ban would be a deplorable step in many complicated ways (see, for example, page 351), and I'm not sure I would really approve; yet I might well come to regard it as the lesser of two looming evils.

All this is very sad. As I've said, there is nothing like a fire for warmth and cheer. In real cold and wet, drying you and yours can be a crucial matter. And let us not forget such soft delights as "dreaming the fire" (or being choked by billows of smoke, or watching red-hot sparks spit onto hapless sleeping bags). Fortunately, there are still places in which even a protectionist more rabid than I would condone campfires: below high-tide mark, for example, on a beach littered with logging debris, as so many Pacific beaches are littered. And there are occasional times and places, even now, when I light my own small campfire (see, for example, page 368).

When it comes to cooking fires, I find myself in the same minority position—for the same reasons (a properly handled stove poses no fire hazard), plus others that are perhaps simpler to explain.

Cooking outdoor food on an open fire is the obvious as well as traditional way. (For operating with one, see page 350.) But a quarter of a century ago I bought a small gas-burning stove for use in a fuelless mountain area above timberline, and the stove turned out to be so efficient that very soon I virtually gave up open-fire cooking.

For me, a stove wins on every count except weight. When selecting a campsite you no longer have to worry about fuel supply or to hunt for wood as soon as you stop—an important advantage when you want to push ahead until dark, and always a comfort in rattlesnake country. Instead you light up the stove (an operation that takes only a minute or so, even with the less convenient kinds, once you're competent), then leave the meal to cook by itself while you set up camp—another sharp gain, especially when you're flop-down tired. And heat control is almost as easy and instant and exact as on the gas stove back home. On a stove, too, the outside of your pot stays bright and clean. You won't write this off as a minor benefaction if you've ever discovered that the plastic bag sheathing your fire-blackened pots in the pack has sprung a leak next door to the sleeping bag; or if you've woken up one morning to find that you unsuspectingly went to sleep the night before with one hand soot-black from handling a cooking pot in the dark. A stove allows you greater freedom in choosing campsites too; you need not worry about having firewood available, or about that appallingly combustible layer of pine needles. When it rains or snows, there's the huge advantage of being able to cook "indoors." Also, no matter what the weather—and this is vital to me—a stove makes it possible to cook and eat all meals comfortably cocooned in a sleeping bag (page 367). For groups, though, a fire yields one important practical advantage: you can heat more than one pot at a time—especially if you carry a grill or grate, as many experienced backpackers do.

It's true, of course, that even a small cooking fire offers, in miniature, any campfire's glowing, pulsing mysteries. It is at once a relaxing and yet stimulating change from modern home life—including its own emasculated shadow, the suburban barbecue. Then there are the smells. And food cooked on it can pick up a delightful tang. But to my mind these attractions hardly begin to offset the practical and ethical drawbacks. Nowadays, except when cooking trout, I almost always rely on a stove.

Stoves

suitable for backpacking come in two major species—liquid-fuelers and cartridge stoves—each subdivided into varieties according to design and the type of fuel, for the most part various fractions of crude oil. Also available: alcohol-burning stoves and a device (beloved by Chip) that burns deadwood, dung, and other natural fuel, fiercely, in a draft generated by a battery-operated fan.

CHIP: Among recent (and welcome) developments are stoves that not only burn several different liquid fuels but also provide genuine simmering (as opposed to pops, spurts, sputters, and clogs). On the cartridge side, there are now stoves that burn hot to the end of the canister, with cartridges that are themselves recyclable. But we should start out (as both Colin and I did) with liquid-fuelers.

Liquid-fuel stoves have refillable tanks either as integral parts of the stove or separated from the burner by a tube. In older stoves with built-in tanks (the Optimus Svea 123, Ranger 10, and Hiker 11), fuel is led from tank to burner jet by a wick that, abetted by a strainer, prevents dirt from reaching and clogging the nozzle. Fuel pressure comes initially from pre-heating, then is maintained by the stove's own warmth (though a detachable minipump can be used for initial pressurizing). These durable artifacts have inspired love in many a backpacker's heart but are now less popular for good reasons. Since heat from the burner is needed to pressurize the fuel, the tank must be close to the flame, which isn't the best place to store fuel. The tank must be sturdy and thick enough to distribute heat, i.e., heavy and generally small. The many cycles of heating and cooling are murder on rubber O-rings and gaskets. For every Svea devotee there's a former adherent who has blown one up (me). And many built-in tank stoves were enclosed in a nice, heavy steel box—marvelous for heaving onto a dogsled but not so for backpacking.

In any event, makers began to use a length of tubing to distance the fuel tank from the burner. Without heat to pressurize it, the tank needed a pump. So the next step was to design a pump with a pressure-tight fit to a standard fuel bottle. The first viable stove on this pattern, Mountain Safety Research's Model G (for gasoline), caught on in the 1970s with mountaineers and winter campers because of its amazing performance—like having a jet fighter buried nose down. It weighed about a pound, astonishingly light at the time, and with a 1-liter bottle the little beastie would roar for almost two hours. A separate folding windscreen, of heavy-gauge foil, added gobs of efficiency with a slight increase in awkwardness. By the '80s, the multi-fuel G/K had captured the affection of hard-core users, and soon thereafter it gained an X. Thus, a generation of Svea worshippers has been followed by a generation of XGK wallahs, who brandish their sooty, battered appliances with proud cries.

A good design being its own argument, the XGK soon spawned the FireFly (now extinct) and the WhisperLite, and has lately hatched the DragonFly, with, no doubt, more bugs to come. Meanwhile, other makers adopted the basic layout. The Optimus Explorer, Primus MFS, Sigg Fire-Jet, Peak 1 Apex, and other stoves using fuel bottles for tanks are to some degree XGK clones.

All liquid-fuel stoves with a separate tank and pressure pump route the fuel tube through the burner to vaporize the fuel, which otherwise squirts out of the jet in a stream, evident during the priming process.

Coleman, on the other hand, kept the steel tank underneath the burner to produce the first Peak 1 stove, a stocky, weighty, and wildly popular design with foldout moon-lander legs. Besides a resemblance to the old Army GS-1 gasoline stove (and the familiar Coleman lantern), the main selling point was that you didn't have to dribble raw fuel out and prime with an open flame. Despite balkiness in cold weather, and a tendency, if not warmed up properly, to emit pillars of fire, the original Peak 1 caught on fast and contributed steely genes to the current—and at 1.5 lbs. misnamed—Feather series.

Before going further, let's define what fuels these liquids be.

• *White gas* (or a brand-name equivalent such as Coleman Fuel, Blazo, etc.) is known for high heat output and relative cleanliness, except when priming—a sooty interlude.* It's also flammable as hell, so be constantly on the watch for leaks, to avoid potential blowups. In cities, bulk white gas has become less and less easy to find. Overseas, you can rarely buy white gas. In Europe a relatively common replacement is naphtha—a first distillate of gasoline that's very efficient but highly volatile.

• *Auto gas,* the lowest octane available, will burn in some stoves, with more soot, smoke, noxious fumes, and clogging than with white gas. High-octane gas has various additives (e.g., tetra-ethyl lead) to retard burning, so avoid it like the plague. Some stoves will also burn aviation gas (AV).

• *Kerosene* can yield reasonably high heat. Most multi-fuel stoves have a lower output, by 10 to 25 percent, with kerosene. But MSR claims that the new XGK Expedition stove logs an extraordinary 2.9-minute boil on kerosene (compared to 3.6 minutes with white gas). Being less refined, kerosene also yields smoke, soot, and clog-ups. While not explosive—an advantage—it demands long and careful priming. Starting up with solid or paste primer, alcohol, etc., has been standard practice, but new multi-fuel stoves have priming wicks or pads that let you use onboard kerosene. Still, besides floating scrims of soot, it leaves an oily scum and a smell on your fingers that's hard to wash off. (Hint: Get thin, latex or nitrile gloves for refueling and maintenance, and stow 'em in the stove sack. Otherwise, not only your hands but your mittens, sleeping bag, hair, and dreams will all reek of the stuff.) Semideodorized kerosene can be found in paint and hardware stores at $4 to $6 per gallon.

Availability is a strong point: in various forms, kerosene is used to fuel everything from antique lamps to trucks and aircraft. K-1 is the purest, but diesel works, as does Jet A, which I burned in lamps for many years with no problem, though reportedly both diesel and Jet A contain various additives.

---

*To avoid sooty priming, readers recommend various tactics. A Montana reader packs a few ounces of alcohol in a squirt bottle to stand in for fuel from the tank. There are safe-and-smokeless priming gels available in tubular form: just squeeze and light. A Maryland reader uses a tiny pencil torch (for delicate soldering) as both priming device and lighter. At this point, both MSR and Primus have added a priming wick to their multi-fuel stoves, not only cutting down on soot but also reducing both slosh and flare-ups.

• *Alcohol* is clean, safe, nonstaining, smokeless, and won't explode. But it doesn't generate much heat per gram. It also burns poorly in cold weather. Even so, I recently adopted a Trangia alcohol-burner and find that odorless and silent cooking is a distinct pleasure. To ward off the booze hound, grain alcohol (or ethanol—a compound of hydrogen, carbon, and oxygen) is "de-natured" by adding wood alcohol (methanol), which is poison. To help you remember, see below:

Methanol   **Ethanol**

$$\text{H—C—OH} \qquad \text{H—C—C—OH}$$

Pure grain alcohol burns just fine, but since it's regulated as a drink the cost is prohibitive (unless you're a bootlegger who also backpacks). The most predictable source of fuel alcohol (also called methylated spirit) is the hardware or paint store, where it costs anywhere from $5 to $9 per gallon.

Increasingly popular are multi-fuel or vari-fuel stoves, that burn more than one liquid, usually by changing a screw-in jet. (This should come with the stove in a plastic bag, with the needed wrench and perhaps some spare parts.) While mounting a different jet is not difficult in itself, getting to it can mean a laborious disassembly—followed by a quick screw—and an equally laborious reassembly: not something you want to do for the first time on a remote gravel bar, plagued by mosquitoes.

Cartridge stoves are fueled by interchangeable metal canisters containing pressurized, liquefied gas in amounts from about 3.5 oz. up to 1 lb. For backpacking stoves, the gases used are butane, isobutane, and propane.

Butane is safer than other cartridge gases because it doesn't vaporize as easily (see below). The penalty is lousy cold-weather performance. Beloved by summertime simmerers, for the benefit of the hasty majority it is commonly blended with isobutane and/or propane. Isobutane vaporizes (i.e., boils) at a lower temperature than does plain-Jane butane. So cartridges with isobutane perform somewhat better in cold weather. Methane, butane, and propane are all compounds of carbon and hydrogen called *alkanes*. Methane, CH_4 (natural gas), has a boiling point of $-161\,°C$. Propane, C_3H_8, boils at $-44\,°C$ ($-47\,°F$), so it's present in liquid form only in severe cold or under pressure. Butane, C_4H_{10}, boils at $-0.5\,°C$ ($31\,°F$), so it's safer for portable stove cartridges but doesn't vaporize worth a damn in freezing weather. Isobutane (C_4H_{10}, an isomer with the same formula as butane) has a different hookup and different properties, notably a lower boiling point: −10°C (14°F). So it vaporizes in colder weather. Here's what the molecules look like:

Methane

H
|
H—C—H
|
H

Propane

H H H
| | |
H—C—C—C—H
| | |
H H H

Butane

H H H H
| | | |
H—C—C—C—C—H
| | | |
H H H H

Isobutane

H H H
| | |
H—C—C—C—H
| | |
H   H
|
H—C—H

Blends predominate, mostly butane and propane. The ideal is to mix a cocktail of gases that burns hot and maintains pressure without being so volatile as to be unsafe in small, thin-walled vessels, which pure propane is. But most cartridge gas blends are still subject to the notorious pressure drop, which owes in turn to the way in which the gas is withdrawn.

Vapor withdrawal is just that: the puddle of liquefied gas emits a cloud of vapor, which pushes out, like a ghost escaping through a keyhole, into the stove burner. This system fights two laws of physics. First—as you use the stove the number of gas molecules crowded into the cartridge decreases and so does the pressure: the flame diminishes. Second—this drop in pressure is accompanied by a steady lapse in temperature. On the grand scale, the same phenomenon causes earth's air to cool, flowing over a mountain crest. It also makes spray cans chilly as the paint is exhausted. So cold weather delivers a double whammy. (Look up the *Ideal Gas Equation,* which is a blend of three historic gas laws: Boyle's, Charles's, and Avogadro's.)

Mountaineers, who use cartridge stoves in tent vestibules, even inside tents where a liquid-fuel stove would be madness (as opposed to mere foolishness), have a semisomnolent drill: Wake up just enough to stuff a cartridge in your armpit and Zen back as it warms. (For those who have trouble waking up, a cold gas cartridge in the groin does the trick, and how.) Attach warm cartridge to stove. Then, cook like a bunny.

I sometimes keep a second cartridge in my sleeping bag, to swap with the one on the stove. Part-arsed solutions, such as chemical heating pads, have been tried over the years. A chemical pad can slow cooling, lessening the pressure drop somewhat—in several tries, boil time decreased by about 15 percent, which doesn't seem like much; but with a half-empty cartridge this can reduce a 12-minute boil to 10. A reflective base under the cartridge and heat pad helps. The Primus heat pad produces about 1200 calories. But to regenerate the sodium acetate in the pad you have to immerse it in boiling water for "3–8 minutes or until all crystals are dissolved." Of course, idly boiling water for 3 to 8 minutes consumes quite a bit of fuel, which certainly outweighs the time (and *no* fuel) saved by the pad. So, to be honest, I'd rather stuff a cartridge in my crotch. Ending a trip with low cartridges, I've warmed two or three in my sleeping bag and swapped them between pots of water, letting the stove cool a bit. But resist the impulse to spur your lagging stove by wrapping your hands around the canister, which can frostbite you promptly.

Backpacker's Jonathan Dorn suggests setting the cartridge in water, using a shallow pan or pot lid. Even cold water works, since it has to give up 80 calories per gram in order to freeze (this is why fruit growers spray trees with water to protect them). But don't immerse the cartridge, so that when you lift off the pot the depleted canister breaches, like Moby Dick, and upends the stove. I've also seen heat exchangers of copper or brass (and recently decided to build my own—page 312).

But a more fundamental solution is available.

Liquid withdrawal ignores the ghostly vapor and instead drains the puddle of liquefied gas. Early liquid-feed cartridges resembled spray cans, with a wick or tube of some sort extending down close to the bottom. They had to be upright to work. The newest design (and a clever one at that) is the Coleman Powermax cartridge that rests on its side, separating the tank from the burner and providing the same stable profile as the ancestral MSR X-stove. I tested the Powermax cartridge (it mates only with Peak 1 X-series stoves) in severely cold weather against several liquid-fuelers (it won hands down). That made me curious enough to open up a cartridge in order to gaze upon its secret.

NOTE: **Do not** try this at home. I was prompted by, besides catlike curiosity, two vital circumstances. First, Peak 1 provides a "Green Key" to puncture empty Powermax cartridges, drain the residual gas, and allow recycling. Second, the Powermax cartridge is nonsparking aluminum, not steel. If you attempt to open up any cartridge—especially a steel one—with residual gas in it, you will likely blow yourself to hell-and-gone.

But let me tell the story: In order to see whether the Powermax cartridge would indeed provide a hot, steady flame to the end, I let one go full bore until the stove went out with a tiny *pop*. I then hefted the cartridge—*feels* empty—and shook it—*sounds* empty—but what's that weird rattle? I wielded the aforementioned Green Key, and a faint sigh of gas issued forth. Then, to be absolutely certain there wasn't any gas left inside, I let it sit for six months before excising the bottom with a hacksaw.

Then, with pounding heart, I peered inside. And what did I find? *For heaven's sake stop prodding me, Watson.*

Immediately, I perceived that the aluminum cartridge had an unusually slick internal coating of some resin. Resting upon the inner surface was a small tubular section of white plastic. Its posture owed to the weight of a lengthier tube, inserted therein, of a metallic substance, just over 3 inches in length. This was, in turn, conjoined to a transparent and flexible tube, apparently plastic, that traversed the remaining inches to the inside center of the cap. Upon removal (with needlenose pliers) the metal tube proved to be of steel, presumably for its weight. This, along with the flexibility of the transparent tubing, ensures that the inlet is ever drawn by gravity to rest, regardless of the vessel's orientation, beneath the surface of the liquid contents. Thus, said contents issue forth not as a ghost through a keyhole, but rather as a compressed liquid, unto the very end of their unoxidized existence.

Since the tip of the steel inlet tube, rotating in transit, could eventually cut through the thin-walled aluminum vessel, as a finishing touch the devisers have capped the steel tip with a plastic guard—*In all, a deucedly clever machination!*

Liquid-fuel stoves—mainly gasoline burners—have long been the standard for backpackers. But cartridge stoves offer advantages that are eye-catching to the inexperienced, and no less to some of the wise. So, my dear Watson, it becomes necessary to summarize the evidence in "The Case of

Gasoline versus Cartridge Stoves."

COLIN:

Heating efficiency. Gasoline used to outperform old-style vapor-feed cartridges roughly two to one. This apparent advantage was slightly reduced by the need to preheat most gasoline stoves, but was radically widened by the way vapor-feed cartridges lose efficiency as they empty, while gasoline stoves and liquid-feed cartridges burn at peak to the end. The best liquid-feed cartridges now rival or exceed the performance of small gasoline stoves.

Cold radically reduces the efficiency of vapor-feed cartridge stoves, but high altitude means lower external air pressure and therefore makes them work better, and as it is usually cold up high, performance becomes a seesaw balancing act. The effects of cold and high altitude on gasoline and liquid-feed cartridge stoves are less acute—though far from negligible.

Wind has a tremendous effect on the performance of almost all stoves (see table pages 309–10). So some stoves of both persuasions have built-in windscreens or broad pot supports to shield the flame. Others depend on external windscreens, with the fuel tank resting outside. Adding a windscreen is dangerous with some stoves, if the fuel tank is enclosed by it, so read the directions. Surprisingly, one stove, owing to burner design, actually performed better in a stiff breeze than in still air. For specifics and partial exceptions, see individual stoves, pages 310 and 329.

"But why all this fuss," I hear you mutter, "about what probably amounts to a couple of minutes' difference in boiling a quart of water?" The grisly fact is that when the wind is iceberging and you're tired and cramped as well as aching cold, and everything you do is difficult and so tends to get done inefficiently, then 2 or 3 minutes' difference registered under indoor test conditions may run to 10 minutes or 20 — or even to the difference between boiling and not boiling: as the water nears boiling point, loss of heat from stove and pot to a hostile environment increases and in the end may balance that generated by the stove, so that the outfit hunkers down into a docile but immovable state of equilibrium, maddeningly shy of boiling. (This condition follows Boyle's First Law: "The heating efficiency of a gas [or cartridge] stove varies in direct proportion to the goddamn ambient temperature." And it epitomizes, of course, Boyle's Second Law: "A watched pot never . . .") Even in cozy indoor tests such stalemates can occur when vapor-feed cartridges run low.

Heating efficiency forms by no means the only admissible evidence in this hotly contended case.

Reliability is even more critical. A stove that fails, miles and days from succor, can ruin a trip—and in winter could place you in real jeopardy. But this is a criterion not easily assessed. One stove expert writes: "Only many years of fooling with these little devils under many conditions will produce reliability information." The opinions given here and under specific model listings (pages 313–41) are based on my own and Chip's combined experience, heavily colored by the testimony of those who have spent years repairing stoves in busy mountain shops.

CHIP: Having fooled with more than my fair share of devils, I'd say that one reason for the popularity of the Svea 123 stove is its brass-bound toughness. You can drop one on a rock, and the rock will crack. Other than gaskets and such, there really isn't much to go wrong and if something does, it's simple to fix. Newer liquid-fuel designs are more complex, with considerable returns in safety and tractability. But this in turn means more parts, boosting the Murphy coefficient.

Cartridge stoves, too, are far and away more efficient and dependable than they were a decade ago. The coupling of cartridge to stove, once a rich source of torment, has been eased in nearly foolproof ways, with well-machined threads or twist-lock couplings replacing older puncture-fit or rubber-tip systems. Cartridges themselves are more consistent in weight and pressure, and seldom fail in use. *Piezoelectric ignitions*—little spring-loaded plungers that produce a spark without flint or steel—make lighting up easier. And recent leaps in design have brought cartridge stoves into the subzero realm, where once only liquid-fuelers might safely tread.

So, as of this edition, the reliability gap is becoming more a matter of design and quality than of liquid versus cartridge.

COLIN:

Weight. Two figures apply: what you start with, and what you pack out empty. So to assess the relative weight merits of liquid-fuel and cartridge stoves for any specific trip you must first estimate how much gasoline or how many cartridges you would need, given the maximum number of days you'll be out and the expected conditions. Then you calculate starting weights and finishing weights and compare the averages. For a specific example, see table below. In the past, some cartridges turned out to be as much as 20 percent short of fuel on delivery to the retailer, which complicates the process.

CHIP: To see whether this was still a problem, I weighed case lots of cartridges from Campingaz (formerly Bleuet), Coleman, MSR, and Primus. The weights were remarkably consistent, varying from the stated contents by 0.1 oz. at most. The cartridges were all at least a year old, so leaks are evidently not a problem. Some cartridges were dented in shipping, though none of the dents were bad enough to cause a leak or interfere with operation.

Below is a table based on my weights, in some cases different from those in the catalogs. This also seems like a good place to note gas mixtures. For the right-hand column I divided the net weight of gas by the total weight of the cartridge: the higher, the better.

HOW MUCH GAS CAN A GAS CARTRIDGE CART?

Brand, Type	Butane, Isobutane, Propane % gas blend	Net weight (g/oz.)	Total weight (oz.)	Ratio of net contents to total weight
Campingaz CV 470	B 80:P 20	450 g/15.88 oz.	22.7	0.70
Campingaz CV 270	B 80:P 20	220 g/7.76 oz.	13.2	0.59
MSR IsoPro*	B 5:I 72:P 22	227 g/8.00 oz.	12.7	0.63
Peak 1, 3250-712T*	B 70:P 30	227 g/8.00 oz.	14.0	0.57
Peak 1, 3100-712T*	B 70:P 30	100 g/3.53 oz.	6.5	0.54

Brand, Type	Butane, Isobutane, Propane % gas blend	Net weight (g/oz.)	Total weight (oz.)	Ratio of net contents to total weight
Powermax 730	B 60:P 40	300 g/10.58 oz.	13.7	0.77
Powermax 717	B 60:P 40	170 g/6.00 oz.	7.8	0.77
Primus 2202*	B 70:I 10:P 20	450 g/15.88 oz.	21.3	0.75
Primus 2207*	B 70:I 10:P 20	215 g/7.56 oz.	11.7	0.65
Olicamp Scorpion*	B 100	170 g/5.95 oz.	10.0	0.60

*With Primus-type thread. Campingaz and Powermax cartridges each have proprietary twist-lock tops.

The upshot is that for anything other than a very short trip or emergency arse-coverage, it doesn't make sense to carry small cartridges (except for the Powermax), because the weight of the container catches up with you. For example, 20 small steel cartridges give you 71 oz. of gas and 68 oz. of steel (bad). Ten medium cartridges give you 76 oz. of gas and 41 oz. of steel (better). While five large (15¾ g) cartridges give you 79 oz. of gas and 27 oz. of steel (best). Weightwise, the most efficient cartridge is the aluminum Coleman Powermax, in either size. The least efficient are the cute little 110 g steel numbers.

When I come home with gas left, I weigh the cartridge, subtract the weight of the container, and write on it with indelible marker the remaining amount of gas. When cartridges are too low to justify backpacking them, I use them with a lantern for picnics and car camping. Even a fairly powerful cartridge lantern, at 80 watts, consumes a small fraction of what a cartridge stove does, at 2800 watts. So a rundown cartridge will light a lamp for hours.*

That brings up the question of how much gas is enough. In clement weather, using the stove for breakfast and dinner, with conservation measures a longstanding habit, I average 3 oz. of cartridge gas per day. Most people seem to use about 5 oz. per day. Meanwhile an article in *Backpacker* estimated daily use for two, in mild weather, at 250 g (or 8.75 oz.) per day—an entire medium-size cartridge).

For long and/or cold trips the weight equation shifts strongly toward liquid fuel. It takes up less space per calorie and you can store liquid fuel in volume, while even the lightest cartridges saddle you with a fixed ratio of metal to gas. For liquid-fuelers, the MSR catalog suggests 4 oz. per person per day in temperate climes and double that when snow must be melted for drinking water. In the bluest cold of all—Antarctica

*A less than half-full cartridge (3.5 oz. of gas) kept a 100-watt Markill lantern alight for 3½ hours: 1 ounce of gas per hour.

or during midwinter ski tours in high latitudes—figure 12 to 15 oz. per soul per day.

Since burn time depends on the size of the cartridge or fuel bottle, a sounder measure of both efficiency and potential consumption is how much water can be boiled for a given amount of fuel. The 2000 catalog from MSR tabulates this vital statistic (albeit at the silly standard 70°F water temperature). Most efficient is the DragonFly, burning kerosene, with 28.4 quarts boiled per pint. Least efficient is the RapidFire, burning isobutane, with 12.0 quarts per pint. While Btu ratings give you a rough handle on both boil times and fuel consumption, the figures given by MSR come closer to a real-world assessment of how stoves perform.

COLIN:

Convenience. Cartridges win, nolo contendere. This is what catches the inexperienced eye: instant heat whenever you want it. Cartridge stoves are also cleaner and less noisy. And in cool weather you can relight them briefly to heat chilled food—an unreasonable operation with any tank stove.

Beginners boggle at the imagined difficulties of preheating gasoline stoves, but once you achieve competence (page 344), it is in fact a minor chore. Mostly, anyway.

Safety. Built-in tanks have pressure-release valves designed to prevent explosion. You hear and read lurid but apparently true stories of these valves sprouting jets of flaming vapor, but I know of no experienced user having such trouble. (Or didn't until Chip footnoted this paragraph.) This is not, by God, to say that it can't happen; only that I'm suspicious of half-screwed-down filler caps and grossly overheated bowls.*

For vital words on the danger of using automobile gasoline instead of white gas, see page 294.

CHIP: On the border of convenience and safety lies some dubious terrain. One reason a great many mountaineers and foul-weather campers choose cartridge stoves is that their relative predictability offers the potential (unanimously condemned by the makers) of cooking under tarps, in tent

---

*CHIP: After I'd cooked with it happily for 10 years, my Svea sprouted a jet of flaming vapor. The trouble was that I hadn't replaced the rubber gasket under the cap. That worthy item had cracked with age, and at last the operating pressure forced fuel out under the cap. Whence it ignited, a veritable pillar of fire. The moral is—for all stoves—examine rubber O-rings and gaskets before every trip, and replace them every 2 to 3 years without fail. Stoves that use fuel bottles as tanks have strainers or filters that need similar attention. Stoves with built-in tanks, like the Svea, also have internal wicks that need replacing at 5- to 10-year intervals.

vestibules, and even inside tents. This, as the makers rightly observe, can be dangerous: a flare-up can torch your tent, sleeping bag, and you (clad in melt-to-the-skin synthetics) as well. Carbon monoxide poisoning can lead to dementia and death. But, if to cook or not to cook is the question, under the lash of wind and freezing rime, it can seem more perilous not to.

So, to all corporate liability lawyers: *mea maxima culpa.*

Forgive me, strict sirs and madams, for I have simmered under my Heptawing as an incessant four-day rain hammered down. And have boiled, no less, in the vestibule of my Galaxy Ultralight as wind-driven snow hissed along the taut angles of the fly. And I committed these sins not just with cartridge stoves. I've gone so far as to prime and start an XGK outside, and then to place it brazenly on a snow ledge beneath the vestibule of a VE-25. And, yes, I performed this act not once but many times in two decades of ski mountaineering. *Yes,* counselors, I did pay great attention indeed to keeping all heat and flame away from the tent fabric and no less to venting dangerous fumes. Given a weather edge, I'll set up my stove outside under trees or overhangs, or even build tiny a half-igloo in arm's reach of the tent. But alas, some cold and wind-beaten times I simply had to get inside the effing tent and into my effing sleeping bag to cook my effing dinner in order to stay alive. I'm not saying it's a brilliant thing to do. Only that it's not inevitably fatal.*

Mishaps reported by readers include more than one blowup (i.e., rapid venting rather than outright explosion) of a gas cartridge. Damage to the rubber tip was cited, and in other instances overheating (one survivor admitted surrounding his piggyback cartridge stove with a foil windscreen and leaving camp to fish). Bad packing was also a problem. Stoves attached to cartridges had their fuel knobs turned on, filling the pack with combustible fumes (if you smell a persistent something, maybe it's not the refried beans). Stoves attached to cartridges got flexed and sprung leaks at the coupling. Metal fuel tubes got bent and cracked. Tubes of plastic and rubber were sliced or crimped. If you're a squeak-tight packer, then for your own self-preservation get a stove that fits inside your cookset or a good stiff plastic case. Liquid-fuel woes included in-pack leaks and clumsy spills (benzene pancakes, anyone?), megapoofs due to overpriming, and nozzilistic clogfests. Stupid modifications—drilling out jet holes—and imperfect field repairs were blamed for leaks, poofs, tosses, and other fiery effects.

In the Murphy Department, more features mean more moving parts. Which places you ever more at the mercy of the molders and fabri-

---

*COLIN: By no means inevitably. I too have under dire conditions committed the in-tent cooking crime—without even singeing my beard.

cators and inspectors. So, to balance my *mea culpa* above, I must say that you are a thumb-sucking idiot if you set out on a trip with an out-of-the-box stove you haven't fully tested yourself. By fully, I mean regularly for a week or longer. Fire it up *outside,* if possible, in roughly the conditions you predict for your trip (temperatures, winds, etc.). Be creative: to simulate freezing nights, you can place the stove and fuel bottle in a freezer, then take it outdoors to fire it up. The point is, first, to get thoroughly accustomed to all its works and pumps. And first again, if anything does go awry, to have the sad mishap occur well *before* the ski plane drops you off on the Greenland Ice Cap.

Over the years I've located sundry sneaky glitches—twisted gaskets, a munched O-ring, a piece of plastic film *inside* a fuel tank, a fuel line with a hairline crack—that might have trashed a trip—along with one scary production error. To wit: I noticed that an all-metal pump made a weird click with each stroke. But the stove worked perfectly. Still, I wanted to figure out what the hell was clicking before taking it on a real trip. So I tried it the next day, and it worked just as well. I wasn't quite nervous enough to take the pump apart, but after head scratching and peering could locate no visible sign of trouble. So, simulating actual conditions, I filled the fuel bottle, threaded the pump in, pumped it up, checked for leaks, let the pressure out, and placed it in a plastic bag, just as I would before leaving. The next morning, there was raw fuel in the bag.

Then I took it apart. The pump shaft was aluminum rod stock, and someone at the factory had sneezed and cut it 3 millimeters too long. So, with each full stroke, it bottomed out on the valve that holds pressure in the tank: that was the click. The steel valve was mounted in an aluminum plug, not threaded but pressed into the barrel of the pump with some sealant goop. My vigorous pumping had unseated the plug, allowing fuel to seep into the pump. From there, it drained out the airhole and into the bag.

So I *did* catch the problem.

The scary part is that if I'd taken it on the trip, it would have worked fine the first day or two. And if I'd left it out on the snow, the fuel leak might have gone unnoticed. That is, until my bravura pumping style had unseated the plug. Unaware, I'd have primed and lit and gotten the stove roaring, as pressurized fuel seeped invisibly into the pump. Then, as I gave a few final strokes to reach operating pressure, raw fuel would have spurted out the airhole, and instead of a Chip, I'd be a Cinder.

I speedily notified the maker. Besides the shaft-length glitch, I recommended they switch to a threaded plug. They never did acknowledge the message, but I presume they did the right thing (and the Swedish Army survives unburnt).

Meanwhile, *in partibus infidelium,* I removed the plastic knob, cut 3 millimeters off the outside end of the pump shaft, and replaced the knob: no click. I also cleaned, regooped, and re-pressed the aluminum plug. I tested my repairs on and off for a month, and have since used the stove on many trips. The moral is: give your new stove a full shakedown (and the chance to prove Murphy right) when the stakes are not high.

Fuel availability. White-gas stoves have the edge in the United States, Canada, and other overdeveloped nations. With the wholesale shift to unleaded auto gasoline, some multi-fuel stoves can burn the stuff without horrors. This has distinct advantages for finding fuel while through-hiking and on overseas treks. But you might want to filter it first: plastic funnels with screens catch the big chunks. Paper coffee filters can supplement the process. But in hamlets fringing on the Great Beyond, kerosene is a likelier find (see page 294).

Campingaz (formerly Bleuet) cartridges are sold worldwide. In the U.S. the old hole-punch type has been supplanted by a simple twist-lock coupling, but in Patagonia and other spots (as of 1999) only the old-style cartridges could be had. I've heard that an adapter is available overseas but couldn't find one on the 1999 parts list from the U.S. distributor.

Primus also sells a pierced cartridge. Available from the wholesaler A-16 are the rubber-tipped Optimus 702 wick-feed cartridges that fit the "Mousetrap" and Hank Roberts stoves (page 332). A more recent standard is the screw tip, which appears on cartridges from Husch, MSR, Optimus, Peak 1, Scorpion, Snow Peak, and others. But threaded cartridges carry different blends of gas (see table, page 300). As this goes to press, MSR has introduced the SuperFly, a cross-compatible stove with a "Multi-Mount feature that mates with canisters large and small." (Reminds me of a friend.) The spiffy Coleman Powermax cartridge mates only with the X series of Peak 1 stoves.*

It's not only wildly unsafe but downright illegal to transport stove cartridges on a passenger aircraft or train, since under certain conditions they become metal-clad bombs. If foolishly causing your own disfigurement or death (not to mention that of your fellow travelers) doesn't dissuade you, consider the present obsession with security—if you try to smuggle gas cartridges in a backpack, odds are you'll get popped at the airport check-in, where you face not just an unpleasant dialogue, but the loss of your ticket and more—a possible $25,000 fine.

Returning expeditions give away or sell leftover cartridges, which

---

*As this lurches into print, my muse at Coleman informs me that products now tagged "Peak 1" will be henceforth called "Exponent."

show up in street markets. I've heard rumors (perhaps unfounded) of clandestine refilling operations, which may not use the right mix (too much propane is perilous). So be wary of cartridges lacking plastic caps, or with visible signs of use.

With vapor-feed cartridges, the difference between full and half empty seems more crucial than that between different brands. While each firm recommends the use of their own, I've swapped threaded cartridges promiscuously and kept on cooking (in warm weather at least) with scarcely a grunt.

But, speaking in worldly terms, as far as availability, liquid fuel trumps.

Cost. Initial outlay: Simple vapor-feed cartridge stoves are markedly cheaper (at $20 or so). High-performing liquid-feed cartridge models cost the same as white-gas stoves with comparable Btu ratings. Multi-liquid-fuel models live at the top of the price range, but despite the temptation to style oneself an international expeditioneer, rather few backpackers ever use anything besides white gas. Special features, like integrated cooksets, hangup rigs, magnesium and titanium parts, or the increasingly common piezoelectric ignitions, bump the price.

Longevity/maintenance: Simple cartridge stoves are throwaways, with parts scarce or unobtainable, though most do have a removable jet. Cartridge stoves clog up infrequently, but on long trips take a wrench and cleaning needle. Fuel tubes are plagued by crimping, scuffing, cracking, or melting, and sticky control valves crop up on both types. A good cleaning works wonders. Liquid-fuel stoves usually come with a jet-cleaning tool and a multipurpose wrench, but overhaul kits (O-rings, gaskets, strainers, lubricants) are extra-cost items. A sweet exception: MSR stoves come with a spare set of rings-and-things.

Running costs: Liquid-fuel stoves win, wallets down. A gallon of white gas that costs $3 to $4 should last a season. Meanwhile, LP gas cartridges now cost $4 to $10 each, so if you got a $20 cartridge stove for thrift's sake, consider the cold-cash fact that you might easily shell out 5 or 10 times that per year for cartridge fuel. The pain can be dulled somewhat if you order cartridges by the case.

COLIN:

The litter problem. With gasoline stoves: nil. With cartridges: a growing menace. EMPTY CARTRIDGES MUST BE PACKED OUT. That seems no more than common sense, common decency. Yet many people either don't care or are too dim-witted to comprehend that they degrade the land, and themselves, when they toss empties away. Nickel refunds have been tried—but, sadly, didn't seem to catch on. Campingaz now offer retailers, for around $500, a device that sucks out all residual gas and makes cartridges safe for recycling. Check with your local stores.

A newly notable step up is the Coleman Powermax aluminum cartridge. The Coleman X-series stoves that run on this cartridge come with a "Green Key" to puncture the upper rim of the empty cartridge, allowing it to be safely recycled (see page 331).

Colin's verdict: If you feel you must be able to cook, yea unto boiling, any place, any time, under the most bloodcurdling or heavenward conditions, pronoz. judgment in favor of liquid-fuelers that burn gasoline. Or, in the hinterlands and the outback, consider kerosene.

If you can be sure of benign conditions, place high value on convenience and cleanliness, do not demand particularly quick cooking, and are not a litterlout, opt for a cartridge stove.

I find it highly relevant that many experienced backpackers, after affairs with the seductive cartridge stoves, seem to return to the gasoline fold—though they may, like me, continue to use cartridge stoves for short trips when all suns shine. Recently, with the improved cartridge stoves, I've found that the suns do a lot of communal shining.

Chip's verdict: My stove-for-all-seasons would be a multi-liquid-fuel wonder with a separate bottle/tank—probably one named after a bug. I've grown accustomed to the clankiness, setup time, priming, soot, *whoompfs,* and so forth, and over the years have acquired considerable low-light maintenance skills.

But recently, even in cold weather, I'll take a liquid-feed cartridge model for its near-zero fiddle factor. And yet . . .

This last summer I carried an alcohol burner on lightweight rambles and found myself bemused by its simplicity—no pump, no tubes, no nozzles; in fact, no moving parts at all. I quickly adjusted to waiting twice as long for water to boil. What won me over was the utter silence, like one hand clapping.

Choosing your model or models

COLIN: Getting someone to change his religion can be difficult, but the task is often simple compared with that of getting him to change his backpacking stove. So before you establish a stovial loyalty it's important to try to achieve what we often find difficult with early religious loyalties—bringing logic to bear. Note, by the way, that nothing in the Constitution says you must stick with one stove. Different conditions may call for different models. As we shall see, both Chip and I habitually ring the changes on a team of favorites and experiment with others.

Note that the only backpacking stoves worth considering used to come from Sweden, but in the 1980s they were challenged, and perhaps surpassed, by U.S.-made brands. Japan entered the field (and the U.S. market) soon thereafter; and since much of the world's metalwork is now done in China, backpacking stoves—being objects of commerce as well as religion—will no doubt follow the trend.

In deciding which stove or stoves best suit your temperament and your kinds of walking, the first criterion is obviously that the stove heats well. For the second edition of this book I therefore went to considerable pains to prepare and present comparative figures for heating efficiency of the leading models. The third time I managed to be briefer because performance figures for most stoves had appeared in trustworthy places, such as *Backpacker*'s Annual Gear Guide. Also, increased competition had not only eliminated stoves that didn't burn hot enough but also effected an ongoing refinement in other features, so that high heating efficiency, while necessary, is no longer sufficient. In fact, it's not always the prime criterion.

The table on pages 309 to 310 evolved from those in earlier editions of this book, from those in catalogs and in *Backpacker* magazine, plus the fruits of recent personal experiments (annotated as such). The stoves reviewed this time out are in the main a) widely available, b) proven in field use, or c) tested for a reasonable span by Chip or me, or both of us.

It's important that you don't treat the information in these (or any) tables as gospel. The fickleness of stoves remains one of the deeper mysteries of life. So every series of tests remains subject to the vagaries and variabilities of individual stoves (any stove may perform differently on successive burns), of fuels and cartridges, and of experimental conditions. But none of these things quite seems to explain why independent investigators, seeking only the truth, generate figures so disparate that you sometimes wonder if they all live on the same planet. Still, the disparities are a fact. I therefore rest confident that somebody somewhere will do similar tests and come up with wildly different answers (as, in fact, someone did, with gleeful savagery, after the second edition appeared). It's rewarding to know that your work can bring so much happiness into the world.

CHIP: This time out I decided not to test stoves that burn *only* kerosene (e.g., the sturdy and relatively quiet Optimus 10 Ranger) because I couldn't see any advantages for the backpacker over newer multi-fuel models. But a viable alcohol burner in various forms and a fan-assisted natural-fuel-burning stove mean that you can now, on occasion, say "no" to petroleum-based cookery.

Boil times are indeed a touchy subject—that's why most magazine gear guides simply repeat the figures supplied by companies (which I quote below). But existing as I do in the world of wind, snow, and mishap, I regard the boil times in magazine ads as errant fantasy. The convention is to time how long it takes 1 quart of 70°F water to reach a full boil at sea level in still air. This is convenient, and theoretically valuable for comparison. But the water in mountain streams runs cold: during the snowmelt, in the 40° range, warming as the season advances. For late summer, 50° to 60° is typical.

By definition, 1 calorie is the heat needed to raise 1 gram of water by 1°C: that's the brute equation. So cold water takes longer to boil—no mystery there. To melt snow or ice also involves a change in state, solid to liquid, that requires not 1 but 80 calories per gram. As the winter night falls, stove performance becomes a poignant issue—one might be moved to curse the milk of the mothers of the publishers of all those untouchable three-minute boiling times.

As we all know (or shall, by checking page 239), with increasing elevation water boils at lower temperatures. So boil time tends to shorten as the altitude increases (as opposed to "cooking time," which lengthens). But higher elevations have colder water (perhaps even snow) and chillier winds to suck heat out from under the pot. On a windy day, as your pot lingers just below the boiling point, you can see the rising bubbles chase around on the bottom with the gusts, mapping the loss of heat. Which, under the circumstances, might be a welcome distraction.

The stoves I tested had all been on one or more actual trips (that is, were field-proven) and were fueled with the maker's specified bottle or cartridge, full-to-the-line. Following the enclosed directions *to the letter,* I pumped, primed, lit, and let each stove warm up, then gave it one minute at full flame before setting on the pot and starting the clock. As any sensible person would, I stacked rocks into a rough enclosure to break the wind somewhat. Stoves (e.g., the MSR DragonFly) that come with external windscreens were tested both with and without—the difference is stark. I also bench-tested the stoves in still air. Summed up, these tests offer comparisons missing from the catalogs and also come closer to predicting what a stove will do under the quirky and subjective conditions encountered outdoors.

CRUEL WORLD STOVE TRIALS

These tests were performed at 7200 feet (the calculated boiling point being 198.9°F or 93°C) on several windy days, with temperatures in the high 30s to low 40s. I used 1 quart of 50°F (10°C) water in a 1.5-quart stainless-steel pot, lid on for the first five minutes. The second column was logged in still, 60°F air. The "manufacturer's specs" column lists boil times given by the makers. Stoves supplied with windscreens were also tested without (and in some cases, vice versa). Unless noted otherwise, cartridges were the same brand as the stove. All stoves were given the recommended start, warm-up, and one minute at full flame before timing.

FUEL: (*c*) *cartridge* (*w*) *white gas* (*k*) *kerosene* (*a*) *alcohol* (*s*) *solid*

	Boil time in minutes:seconds		
			Manufacturer's
Make and Model	*Windy*	*Still*	*Specs.**
MSR DragonFly (w)	7:25	7:06	3:30
no external windscreen (w)	9:35	6:54	
with windscreen (k)	8:59	7:41	3:54
MSR SuperFly (c); no external windscreen	5:48	4:59	3:00
with MSR Ascent reflector/heat exchanger	5:26		
Optimus Svea 123R (w)	7:38	6:44	7:00
Peak 1 Apex II (w)	7:39	6:12	4:00
Primus MFS (w)**	6:56	6:10	3:30
no external windscreen (w)	9:18		
external windscreen (k)	10:10	9:26	4:30
external windscreen (c)	6:10	5:56	3:00
no external windscreen (c)	8:25		
Campingaz Twister 270 HPZ (c)	7:34	4:15	3:30
Markill Dragon (c)***	6:20	4:26	2:50
Markill Spitfire (c)***	7:12	5:06	4:00
Olicamp Scorpion III (c)	8:35	6:02	4:00
Peak 1 Xtreme (c)	5:35	5:00	3:00
no external windscreen	5:53		
Peak 1 Micro (c)	5:15	5:49	3:30
Snow Peak GigaPower (c)	9:49	5:03	3:52
Sierra Basic 111A (fuel unknown)			4:00
(weathered pine)	7:36	—	
(hardwood twigs)	6:40	—	
(woodstove pellets)****	6:25	—	
(moose turds)	6:12	—	
Trangia Westwind (a)*****			
outside with external windscreen	18:11	14:26	15–18

*Source: Annual Gear Guide, *Backpacker,* March 1998, 1999, 2000.
**The Primus MFS can use liquid fuel or a gas cartridge.
***Markill cartridges were unavailable, so I used Primus.
****½ cup (3 oz.) of stove pellets will boil a quart of water and toast a bagel.
*****With a custom hanging rig made from a small saucepan (such as shown on page 340 and the pot 2 inches above the burner I got the boil time down to 9:14 (50°F water) and an amazing 6:20 with 70°F water.
COLIN: Wouldn't life be barren without footnotes?

What did I learn? First, what I already knew: that the boil times given by makers are unapproachable under field conditions. Second, and vital, that a good windscreen adds more bounce per ounce than any other single feature. Stoves without any wind-cheating capacity (e.g., the Snow Peak GigaPower) suffered badly in a breeze. And those supplied with windscreens (the MSR DragonFly) did poorly without one. The exception, a surprise, was the Peak 1 Micro, which actually burned hotter in a breeze than in still air.

For detailed write-ups on each stove, consult pages 313 to 341.

More on cartridge performance: In vapor-feed stove canisters, starting pressure ranges from around 55 pounds per square inch (psi) for blended fuel to around 30 psi for straight isobutane. As the butane/propane cartridge empties, pressure drops in a fairly smooth curve to around 18 psi, bottoming out when the cartridge is still a quarter full. Isobutane maintains a steady pressure of about 30 psi to the end.

What does this mean in arse-to-the-ground terms? Since the Peak 1 Micro stove burned hot and wasn't sensitive to wind, on a blustery sub-freezing morn I swapped different brands of medium (7–8 oz.) brand-new butane/propane cartridges, timing and weighing. I started with a warm (body-heated) cartridge. Then the stove/cartridge unit was allowed to sit a half hour and started cold, which increased boil times from 4 to 28 percent. Then I shut down for 5 minutes and started again, which lengthened boil times from 23 to 41 percent. This is like boiling a pot of water for hot drinks, another for the meal, and a final pot to wash up. A half-full cartridge warmed in a sleeping bag or with a chemical pad lost 35 percent, while a half-full cartridge, started cold, lacked 45 percent of its original punch. Below one-quarter full, most cartridges wouldn't boil a quart of water. Even the new MSR IsoPro cartridge, claimed to operate "down to −10°F/−23°C" proved disappointing. I tested it with MSR's new SuperFly stove: at 0°F, a 60 percent full cartridge that had been sitting outside burned lethargically and then died out after 14 minutes without boiling the water. I had to body-warm the IsoPro cartridge to get the stove started again, but it did boil water in 6:40. But when I tried a second pot, the cartridge had cooled enough to die out again, and by then my crotch was damn near glacial. Body-warmed, the IsoPro cartridge outperformed most competitors. But at −10°F, any vapor-feed cartridge is deadweight. Looking back at the table (How Much Gas Can a Gas Cartridge Cart, page 300) you can see that besides having 5 percent isobutane, the IsoPro cartridge has 22 percent highly volatile propane, a higher proportion than does Campingaz. But the Peak 1 vapor-feed cartridge has 30 percent propane and the liquid-feed Powermax, which triumphed in all my cold-weather tests, has 40 percent propane.

Between boils, I weighed cartridges: for vapor-feed cartridges, the amount of gas needed to boil 1 quart (50°F water, stiff breeze) averaged ¾ oz.

Since it was depressing to watch the stove go out time after time while the cartridges still held gas, I decided to build a gas-cartridge heater. The reason stove makers don't sell one is that they expect you, the idiot camper, to misuse it, blow yourselves up, and then sue. Figuring that I was immune to self-litigation, I made a trip to the hardware store and came home with brass sheet stock, ⅛-inch brass rod, and small springs. Given the object—to keep vapor-feed cartridges from dying in cold weather—the design constraints were clear: a) it couldn't interfere with heat transmission to the pot; b) it had to diffuse heat to the cartridge safely; and c) it had to collapse and pack inside a small pot.

After a happy burst of tinkering, I came up with the contraption pictured below. The bent brass rods (with springs slipped on to catch more flame) carry heat down to the brass collar without touching the cartridge. The collar diffuses the heat so the cartridge is warmed evenly. And the rods slip out of the drilled tabs on the collar for packing.

Cartridge heater

I tested it at temps from 0 to 10°F and found that while I still had to body-warm the cartridge to get the stove going well, after a few minutes the device transferred just enough heat to counteract the double whammy of chill air and the pressure drop. That is, the cartridge remained cool to the touch yet no frost formed. And I was able to melt snow and boil pot after pot of water until the cartridge was empty.

So far, so good. But if you build a similar device (which, understand, I don't urge you to do) you can blow yourself up in any of several ways. First, don't use any cartridge heater unless it's well below freezing. Second, don't place it inside a full windscreen or heat reflector. Third, the more propane in the gas blend (see table, page 300), the more careful you must be of overpressurizing. Fourth, don't boost the number and thickness of the heat-capturing rods: the cartridge should never, ever get hot. Summed up, you're trying to balance the combined effect of cold and the pressure drop, not to supercharge your stove.

The heat content of a given fuel—whether liquid or cartridge gas—is a matter of rock-bottom physics. For backpackers, the critical factors are a) how much fuel each stove can burn and b) how efficiently it applies the heat output to a pot, and the contents thereof. And for that, we need to delve into specifics of stove design.

Multi-fuel stoves

MSR XGK Expedition

This specialized classic—just as an F-15 is a specialized airplane—has been visibly updated from the Model GK of the 1970s. Gone are the creaky, swing-out pot supports, replaced with a silent stainless X. Along with the new pot support, it has a Shaker Jet weighted cleaning needle that lets you clear the orifice with a quick rattle between burns. The knurled adjuster screw is gone, and the vaporization tube has lost its spiral heat distributor. But the fat-foil windscreen (1.6 oz.) is the same, and peerless. And the new XGK Expedition is a sleeker version of the squat little salamander that melted and boiled well over a thousand quarts during my seven years of winter fieldwork. Sooty, heat-blued, and looking as if it had just been salvaged from a mine explosion—it was the familiar of my irascible ski partner Marty. Even in killing cold, his XGK never failed to light up. Once touched off, it roared, and the pile of snow blocks by the tent was magically transformed to steaming tea, rock-belly cuisine, and Swiss Miss with rum. Simmer? I never had much luck, but Marty could coax it into a slumbrous growl. It never clogged, not once. For all I know he's still using it.

XGK Expedition

The newest XGK, has gained the Expeditionary tag. And that's fitting. It burns white gas, unleaded, aviation gas, Stoddard solvent, naphtha, kerosene, and diesel. And it burns them with minimum fuss. (I haven't tried extra-virgin olive oil, but who knows?)

COLIN: Years ago, on one relatively easy 12-day trip, I soon became intensely grateful that I'd elected to take my MSR XGK. On the second day out I discovered that through a series of unlikely errors—which do little to soften my shame—my fuel bottle held not white gas but a mixture of regular, leaded automotive gas and SAE 30 oil, intended for a chain saw. By that second day the stove was repeatedly blocking. Yet when I switched to the K (for Kerosene) jet it once again functioned. I don't say it functioned at full roar. I had to keep cleaning the jet with the pricker provided, too. But I could cook, always. On the sixth day I reached my halfway food cache and found to my relief that the spare bottle of fuel indeed held white gas, and all I had to do was change back to the G (for Gasoline) jet and decoke the surge filter (which has been eliminated in later models). For the rest of the trip I had to clean out the jet occasionally, and the heat generated fell short of the stove's normal blowtorch level. I was back in something close to full business, though. And I doubt that any other stove would have seen me through so gastronomically unscathed.

CHIP: Despite ongoing refinements, the new XGK Expedition (15.8 oz., $90) is still a workhorse. A foil windscreen and reflector come with it. To tank it up, MSR fuel bottles come in three sizes: 11 fl. oz. (2.8 oz., $8); 22 fl. oz. (4.9 oz., $9); and the snowmelter's favorite, 33 fl. oz. (7.3 oz., $10). These weights include the cap (0.4 oz.), which you can leave off in favor of the stove's pump. (For more on fuel bottles, see page 342.)

Useful accessories include the Maintenance Kit ($13) and the Trillium Stove Base shown on page 313 (2.8 oz., $19), an aluminum trefoil that gives good footing on loose or frozen surfaces (and fits all MSR stoves).

MSR WhisperLite Internationale 600

The WhisperLite evolved in the mid-1980s from the now-extinct FireFly: a three-limbed critter with pot supports looped from the same steel rod as the legs. While the pump-in-tank setup is the same as the XGK's, the WhisperLite's fuel tube flexes so it can be packed inside a pot, and the stove itself is higher and wider—airy, compared to the XGK's Sterno-tin shape. It's also somewhat lighter and cheaper (14 oz., includes 1.6-oz. windscreen; $70).

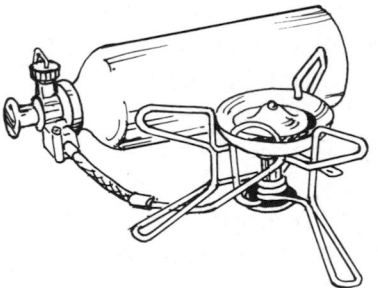

MSR WhisperLite Internationale

The post-Marxist multi-fuel version, the Internationale, has some of the same virtues as the XGK, and similar quirks. It doesn't roar, but it's not silent, either. It burns dependably hot on a wide range of fuels but lacks a minutely adjustable simmer. It has the self-cleaning Shaker Jet and a large-diameter fuel line to accommodate poor-quality hinterlands juice. And, even given the usual quota of thumbs, when it poops out you can *probably* fix it in the field.

Peak 1 Apex II

Light dawns in a north-facing cirque. The sun has yet to peer over the Divide. Amidst the boulders of a snow-covered moraine is a yellow tent. Zooming in we notice a squat red stove chugging away, like a lunar module trying to lift off, with a stainless-steel pot on top. The tent zipper opens and a shaggy head pokes out. "Not yet," it says.

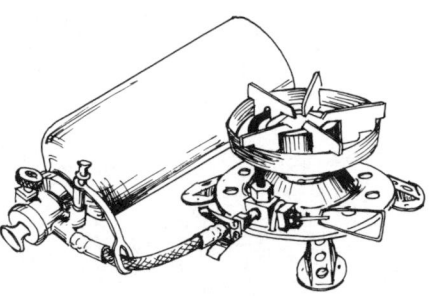

Peak 1 Apex II

That was my experience with this stove. Despite obsessive direction following, pumping variations, a thorough cleaning, and a barrage of evil language, I never could get much heat out of it. Rated at a lowly 7500 Btu for white gas (6500 for kerosene), it lacks the thrust of comparable multi-fuelers (10,000 Btu or so), and in a head-to-head boil-up with its cartridge cousin the Peak 1 Xtreme, it got smoked by a full two minutes. From a cold start, the flame is subject to flare-ups, and when it settles down it falls into a "slight pulsation" that I found more than slight—a *chug-chug-chug* that's annoying. On kerosene, it alternated between hopeless and infuriating. A knurled brass adjuster on the leveling leg stuck out, as did the inlet plug, and kept it from fitting into my 1-liter pot. The fuel-tube connector was attractive to dirt, and the wind baffles were pointed and edgy. And the thread on the pump will mate with no bottle other than a Peak 1 (a skimpy 22 fl. oz., included). The Peakèd Ones told me this was for safety reasons, since cheap knockoff fuel bottles had been known to rupture.

The current Peak 1 Apex II 445 weighs 1 lb. 3 oz. and costs $65.

A few savvy friends told me they truly esteemed their Apexes. So, to see if I'd gotten a lemon, I borrowed one that had gone on several expeditions. But it had been stored for some months, and when I pumped it up the fuel tube leaked.

I took that as an omen.

The same burner and multi-fuel capacity can be had with a built-in tank in the piggyback-style Peak 1 Multi-Fuel Stove 550, which burns white gas at 7500 Btu with a boil time of 4:15 and kerosene at 6500 Btu (1 lb. 5 oz., $60).

Primus MFS

If you hadn't guessed, the letters stand for "multi-fuel system." Subtitled "the ultimate expedition stove," this three-legger has the same bangproof appeal as the Svea, without the brass-bound cachet. And despite a problem with the pump, which I duly fixed, I ended up liking it enough to take it winter camping—in Wyoming, a serious commitment.

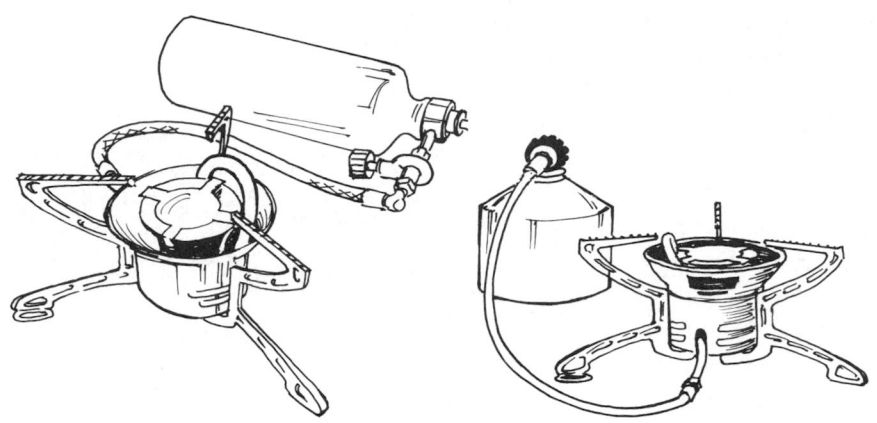

MFS with liquid and cartridge

As fuels go, the MFS is heterodox: one nipple handles kerosene or diesel, and the other white gas, unleaded auto gas, *or*—the big news—cartridge gas. In fact, this is the only multi-liquid-fueler that also mates with a cartridge. The trick is a brass valve that mounts directly to a screw-top gas cartridge, or to the outlet of an all-metal pump that fits into a standard fuel bottle. As ideas go, this one's snappy. How does it work?

On white gas, it primes and lights easily, with little or no flare-up, and then cranks out an honest 10,000 Btu. The shutdown drill is odd: one side of the pump has ON stamped into it, the other, OFF. Rather than shutting the valve, one is instructed to flip the bottle. In a minute or so, the flame dies and air is heard hissing from the jet. At which point you close the brass valve. The good part is that this clears fuel out of the supply tube. The bad part is that it's awkward.

On white gas, the MFS pops rather than simmers, but does so for quite a while without expiring. Kerosene is a different story. Changing the jet is semi-toilsome. A priming pad lets you heat the burner with kerosene from the tank (two minutes at least), but even with lengthy priming I couldn't get the stove to burn with the fuel valve open. Instead, it flared and spattered. By shutting the valve partway, I managed a steady flame, but within 5 to 10 minutes it would revert to flares and spatters. More than 10 to 15 strokes of the pump (i.e., overpressurizing) had the same effect. My thought was that maybe the vaporizer tube curves too far out of the direct flame (on the MSR XGK, which *cranks* on kerosene, it runs dead center). So, when priming again, I carefully tipped the MFS burner so the open flame licked the tube; this shortened the priming time but made no difference otherwise. At a medium flame, the MFS stove burned steadily, but with flutters of yellow flame, indicating poor combustion (i.e., carbon monoxide and soot). And with kerosene, the tank-flip shutdown produced a beard-frizzling flare-up.

The pleasant surprise is how well the MFS performs with a cartridge, putting out 10 percent more heat than on white gas—with no jet change—and with a benevolent simmer to boot. The brass valve unthreads in seconds from the pump/bottle unit: a unique multi-fuel scenario. That is, in base camp you can burn white gas for workhorse snow melting and switch to a cartridge for a bivouac. The vaporization tube serves as a preheater, extending the useful life of cartridges. But if there's any liquid fuel left in the line, lighting up with a cartridge produces a dragon's belch of flame. If there's any doubt, open the valve and let the cartridge hiss for 10 seconds, then shut down and check for liquid fuel. Burn it off with the valve shut, as during normal priming, then let the stove cool briefly before lighting.

Being able to switch from white gas to a cartridge on the spur of the moment sets the MFS apart. So despite the wavery learning curve, I came to like the thing, which has since transmogrified into the Himalaya Multi-Fuel 3288 (1 lb., $99 without fuel bottle or the pretty-damn-necessary windshield/reflector combo, 2.3 oz., $15). Lacking the cartridge option, it's sold as the Himalaya Vari-Fuel 3278 (14 oz., $63).

MSR DragonFly

Pulling this out of the bag, my first response was bewilderment. The parts—pump, burner—were familiar, but they were linked in a curious way. With the spring-steel legs unfolded and the burner rotated to an upright position, it began to look more like a stove. In fact, it looked as if an XGK had mated with a WhisperLite.

From papa, it has the green-chili-can burner cup, in newly finned aluminum. From mama it has the braided fuel line and springy tripod gear, in a whole new configuration. It has the Shaker jet but is missing the flame-licked preheater loop of the fuel tube. Instead, it has a second valve,

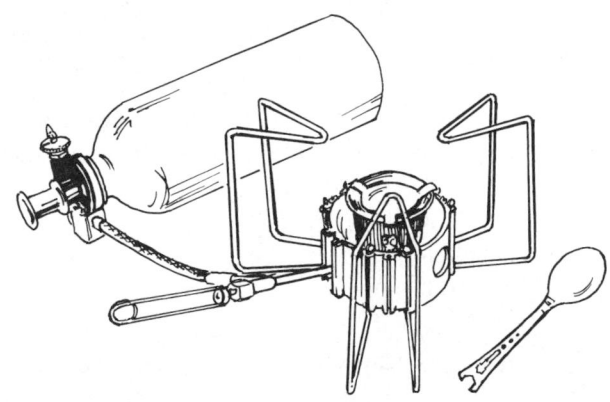

MSR DragonFly

in a brass Y on the stove. The valve stem mounts dual O-rings that are kept cool by incoming fuel from the tank. So the adjustment isn't subject to extreme heat, nor so far from the burner that there's a lag. In practice, this means both genuine simmering and an immediate flame response, heretofore the province of cartridge stoves. From the "cool-fuel" valve out, it's pretty much MSR-standard. The pump has a neat ceramic filter on the inlet tube and another in-line where the brass begins.

I took the DragonFly ski mountaineering and never had a harsh moment, whether torching snow or simmering soup. Not exactly compact, it does fit inside a 1.5-liter pot (if the pot's more than 4 inches deep) with pump, windscreen, and reflector. Take care, though—bagging and cramming can crimp the fuel line. Another thing to watch is getting crap in or on the brass tube that fits into the pump—a new in-line filter helps (with a spare in the parts kit), but a stray gob of pasta can have a disproportionate effect.

Given the DragonFly's civilized cooking qualities, the multi-fuel aspect is doubly attractive: one stove for both happy camping and overseas treks. To change to kerosene, you pop the flame spreader and use the MSR tool (or a broad screwdriver) to change the jet: not bad. The DragonFly digests kerosene happily, with no starting problems or flare-ups, but simmering yellows the flame, yielding carbon monoxide and soot. Once sooty, it's hard to clean, so priming with paste or alcohol is smart. Kerosene boil times are 10 to 20 percent longer than with white gas— also not bad. This is the most efficient of the MSR stoves, boiling 26.2 quarts per pint of white gas and 28.4 quarts per pint of kerosene. So I guess I'll get used to its looks. Stove and pump are 17.1 oz., with foil reflector (0.25 oz.) and windscreen (1.6 oz.), all for $100.

To make the bug fly, you also need a fuel bottle—MSR's 11-oz. bottle costs $8 and weighs 2.8 oz.; the 22-oz. is $9 and 4.9 oz.; and the 33-oz. is $10 and 7.3 oz.

Optimus Explorer 11

This multi-fuel design deploys the familiar brass-domed, low-decibel Optimus burner in the now-standard MSR setup, separated by a

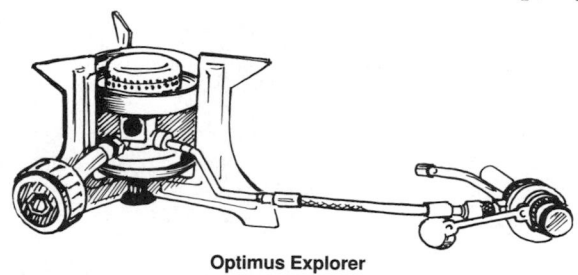

Optimus Explorer

fuel tube from the pump/tank. The Swedish Airborne Special Forces field-tested the Explorer in the Arctic, but the U.S. distributor was reluctant to send one to me. So all I can report are the specs in the brochure: 10,000 Btu, three-minute boil time on white gas, 1 lb. 3 oz., $118. According to *Backpacker,* October 1996, "testers liked the flame adjustability but not the temperamental performance and fussy setup."

Optimus Hiker 111C

The Hiker series is a long-running design, semi-indestructible and still clanking away with a good many outdoor schools. Since it weighs 3 lbs. 6 oz. and costs $160, the Hiker tends to be used by groups. As an artifact, it charms with its polished-brass domed burner and fuel cap against a black tank set in a black steel box. Perfect for 4-liter pots, it gives (quoth Optimus) three-minute boil times, it burns quiet and clean on white gas or alcohol, and the 12-oz. tank with built-in pressure pump yields about two hours at full flame. Kerosene wakes up minor demons—flaring and soot. Cruder fuels such as diesel don't agree with the Hiker, though they will burn—but use a funnel with a fine screen or a filter, and be prepared to give the stove your undivided attention.

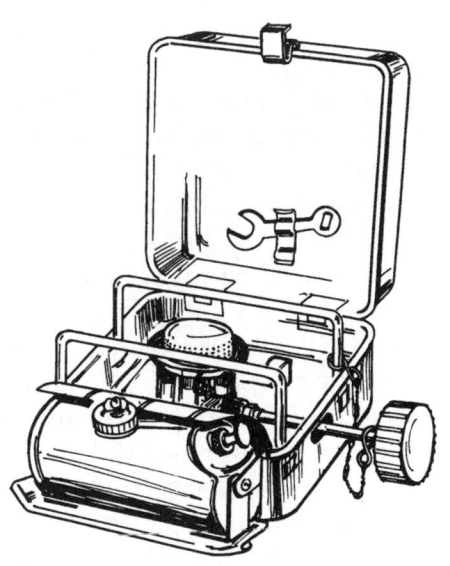

Optimus Hiker

Gasoline stoves

Optimus Svea 123R

COLIN: The Svea for years was probably the most reliable little stove ever made, and maybe still is—even though the newer models with a built-in cleaning needle seem to be rather less reliable and are decidedly more touchy for flame adjustment than the older ones. But even with the new-style models there are still very few things to go wrong. And the stove is reasonably stable. I've tipped a pot off a Svea only once during the 40-plus years I've used it (and most of that time it was virtually the sole stove I

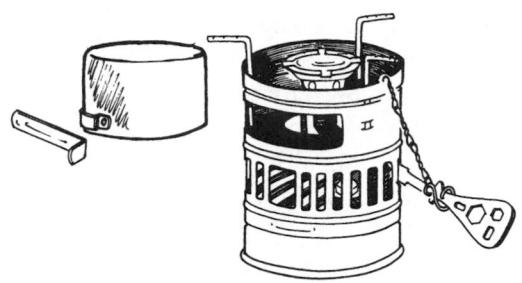

Optimus Svea 123R

used). The current model is still my trusted friend. Its predecessors have roared sturdily away for me at over 14,000 feet and in temperatures around 10°F. And none has ever let me down.*

Some people seem to find it difficult, going on impossible, to prime the Svea. But once you get used to a system that suits you (page 344) such complaints should fade away. And you can get an aluminum mini-pump to ease the priming process and boost the heat output (2 oz., $25).

A minor but very real bonus the Svea brings is its removable aluminum cover that doubles as pot or cup—hellishly hot on lips but a useful reserve in case of unexpected company or loss of your regular cup. I occasionally carry the cup on side trips away from my pack and brew tea in it over a small wood fire. But its main use to me is as a cup stand (illustration, page 366). By rotating the open end a couple of times on any rough surface except rock I can dig it in enough to form a raised, level, and stable platform. Even on rock you can experiment and soon find a firm base. Anyone who has watched precious tea or coffee spill from a tilted cup will understand the value of this instant table. In snow, where a hot cup quickly melts its own hole, I invert the cover and rest the cup in its hollow. The heat dissipates much more gradually, the food stays hot longer, and the cover, kept cool, sinks into the snow only very slowly. To correct even that minor fault I put the stove's Ensolite pad underneath once it's no longer needed for the stove. This cup stand may sound like the blatherings of a man blinded by personal loyalty to an old friend, but every time I use another stove I'm re-amazed at the way I chafe at not having the Svea cover to put my cup on. In fact, I sometimes take it along.

Note that in Chip's Cruel World stove trials (pages 309–10) the Svea 123R (1 lb. 3 oz., $78, tank capacity 4.5 oz.) was the only candidate to perform up to the manufacturer's specs. I'm not surprised.

---

*CHIP: One constant reader reports that a Svea stove unused for 11 years (with fuel of the same age) started up on the first try. "I am way beyond soggy sentimentality," he writes, and was so moved that he actually polished it. Rather than priming with liquid fuel or paste, he suggests using a pencil torch to heat the vaporizer tube.

MSR WhisperLite Shaker Jet

CHIP: This is the progenitor (and hissing cousin) of the WhisperLite Internationale 600, so go back to page 314 and reread. The differences are that this white-gas version lacks the fiberglass priming wick, the extra kerosene jet, and the large-diameter fuel tube (for that lumpy Third World diesel).

If the XGK is the expedition standard, the WhisperLite is the backpacker's friend. But my first date with one, at 10°F below zero, didn't work out: it clogged up and quit. Despite repeated (and increasingly frenzied) cleanings, for the rest of the trip it never put out more than a half-hearted flame—my partner dubbed it the Whimper-Lite. Home again, I tore it to bits, cleaned it, blew it out with compressed air, rinsed out the fuel tank twice, sun-dried it, added a sintered bronze inlet filter, and tried again. It worked perfectly and has ever since. If you have an old Whisper-Lite (or other MSR stove), the Shaker Jet is a worthy retro-fit. MSR lists a boil time of 3.9 minutes and an efficiency rating of 25.4 quarts per pint of fuel (weighs 14 oz., windscreen included, and costs $60).

Peak 1 Feather 400 and 442

COLIN: Over 20 years or so, successive versions of this stove have been bought by a great many people. But the buyers tend to be rather inexperienced backpackers, often those who mostly go on weekend trips. And the reasons seem fairly clear.

The Peak I Feather is in many ways a very good stove. It burns hot. Its quadrant-divided windshield means that one-fourth of the burner will often stay alight when the rest is blown out—and will then relight the whole circle. In tests the stove rates high in fuel efficiency. It also simmers nicely. It has a large 11.8-oz. tank capacity, and the convex base means that you use the last drop of fuel. It has a built-in pump, and in warm weather it's simple to light. It's at least reasonably reliable.

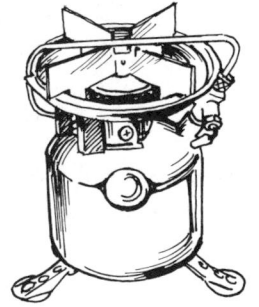

Peak 1 Feather

Starting the original Peak 1 in any kind of cold weather could be a pain. I had minor trouble in a windless 42°F. It is vital, I'm told, to follow starting instructions exactly, "with no jumping the gun on any step." But one experienced climber reported that on Mount Shasta, "we had to soak the damned thing in gas before it would start." Priming with paste (page 344) helps, and some users advocate letting the stove run in the LIGHT position for at least two minutes rather than the one minute prescribed in the directions. Otherwise the flame may turn yellow and the stove flood with liquid gasoline. And simmering, though easy in shielded situations, becomes problematical in even a 2- or 3-mile-an-hour wind. Simmering for an extended span can also lower the vaporizer tube's temperature so that the flame turns yellow and the stove eventually floods. (If the flame turns yellow, remove the pot and then switch back to HIGH until the tube reheats.) Because of such quirks the Peak 1 series tends to be less fuel-efficient than tests suggest. As one of my advisers said, "There are a lot of little things about this stove that people need to know." To promote easy starting, for example, it pays to set the fuel valve to START for 15 to 30 seconds before shutting it off, to clear the vaporizer.

Although reasonably reliable, the Peak 1 seems less so than other currently popular liquid-fuel stoves. And it's not easily repairable: to do anything, you need a Phillips screwdriver and small wrench; and the trouble usually lies in the valve system, which cannot be fixed in the field.

Finally, in both forms the Peak 1 Feather seems too heavy for solo backpackers—though this judgment is softened by the big tank, which means that you may need no extra fuel for a typical one- or two-night weekend trip. But I took it on a six-month raft trip down the Colorado in 1989—when weight wasn't a factor—and used it exclusively, with pleasure and zero problems.

To summarize, then, the Peak 1 Feather is a useful stove for 3-season use by parties of two or more when failure would not be devastating, especially in warm weather and when ease of use looms large and oz. paring does not.

The white-gas Feather 400 is rated at 7500 Btu, with a boil time of four minutes, weighs 1 lb. 7 oz., and costs $49. The Feather 442 Dual-Fuel can also burn unleaded auto gas; otherwise, it's identical except for a price of $55.

Cartridge stoves

CHIP: In 1980, *Outside* magazine's review of backpacking stoves covered 10 liquid-fuelers and only two cartridge models: the Bleuet Globetrotter S200S and the Hank Roberts Mark II Mini. Twenty years on, the *Backpacker* 2000 Annual Gear Guide listed 16 liquid-fuelers and 29 cartridge models (with one stove that takes both). Ergo, cartridges have definitely arrived. The basic layouts available include the commonplace *piggyback,* with the stove mounted on top of the cartridge; *freestanding,* with foldout legs on the burner and a tube connecting a separate fuel valve and cartridge; and *hanging,* with the stove mounted on a platform or in a circular windscreen with the cartridge underneath.

Bleuet/Campingaz 270 Series

I loved saying *"Bleuet,"* as these stoves and cartridges were called when I first encountered them. To cook even the plainest dish on a Bleuet gave it Gallic savor. While the stoves and cartridges are better now, the name isn't—"Camping Gaz" sounds like a digestive problem. And the recent compression, "Campingaz," is worse. How do you say it? *Campin' Gas?* Or *Camping Ass?*

In any event, the Bleuet (as I continue to think of it) was the first widely available butane cartridge stove, and is certainly still the most universally used.

COLIN: You can buy these stoves and cartridges all over the world: I've even found them in small African village stores. And the Bleuet is a workhorse that can surprise you, especially up high. During a 24-hour stay in a hut at about 16,000 feet on Kilimanjaro, with temperatures around freezing, mine brewed me many cups of tea and all regulation meals. Admittedly, I seem to remember that it was pretty slow work. And my cartridges may have been filled with the butane/propane mix commonly found overseas rather than with the less efficient straight butane then mandatory for safety reasons in the U.S. (The good reports from Everest many years ago that did much to build the Bleuet's reputation were of butane/propane cartridges under higher pressure.)

CHIP: Campingaz cartridges, with an 80 percent butane/20 percent propane blend and a valved connector in place of the older pierced type, are now standard in the U.S. For some years they were handled on these shores by Suunto, but are now distributed by Coleman, which might increase their availability. Stateside standards are the valved CV 270 (7.75 oz. net), the CV 470 (16 oz. net), and the pierced C-206 (6.75 oz. net). Note, for your own sake, that the Campingaz valve is not compatible with any other brand of stove (except the MSR SuperFly). In distantest parts, like Patagonia, you might find only the pierced type (for more on cartridges, see page 298). The adapter isn't listed for sale in the U.S., but given the modest weight and price of these stoves, true-Bleu fans could afford to own one of each type.*

Two models, both piggybackers, are available in the U.S.

The Turbo 270 updates the classic 206, with a broad flame pattern, an easy-to-reach jet, and a built-in reflector/windscreen. It comes with a

---

*Markill/VauDe Sports sells an adapter for pierced cartridges (page 328), but it mates with a Primus-type thread, not a Campingaz twist lock.

Campingaz Turbo 270

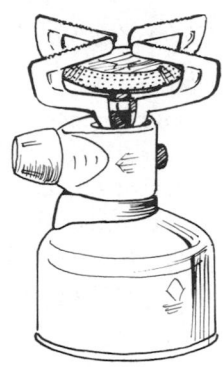

Campingaz Twister 270 HPZ

close-fitting pouch that tucks away; but getting it into the pouch requires complete disassembly, and putting the pieces together can provoke a surly grunt or two. Likable features are quietness and adjustability, down to a near-invisible simmer. Listed at 10,000 Btu with a four-minute boil time, it weighs 9.6 oz. and costs $33.

The Twister 270, so-called for the new locking valve connector, has a tighter flame pattern, four serrated foldout supports (best for small pots), and a streamlined blue plastic shroud (no, it doesn't melt). It packs in one piece and fits flat in a 1.5- liter pot. With a 10,000 Btu output and a 3:45 boil time, the Twister 270 weighs 8 oz. and costs a mere $22.

The one I packed around was the new Twister 270 HPZ. It has a broad flame pattern and four flat-folding serrated pot supports, lending stability to 2-liter and larger pots. The blue plastic fenders are Euro-cool, and a fat adjustment knob with click increments can tweak the flame down to a sub-sub-simmer. HPZ signifies piezoelectric ignition, activated by an ovoid red button and, to date, infallible. Rated at 11,000 Btu, the newest Bleuet offspring weighs 10 oz. and costs $33.

Given the height and inherent tipsiness of virtually all piggyback stoves, an accessory cartridge base is a necessary adjunct.

Primus Cartridge Stoves

Primus fields a broad and mostly excellent line of cartridge stoves (for fuel specs, see page 301) that change names more quickly than a race-track tout. The model numbers are more durable than the names, so if the Yellowstone Lite Trail (formerly PLS, for Primus Light Stove) soon reincarnates as the Cloudbiter Anti-Gravity, the number should still be 3266. And that's a good starting point.

The Yellowstone Lite Trail, #3266 (7 oz., $44), is a sweetly simple stove with a built-in windscreen and disassembles to fit in the palm of a hand. It burns hot, at 10,000 Btu and three-minute boil time, and has one

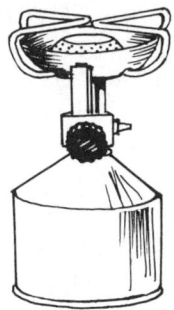

Primus Yellowstone Lite Trail

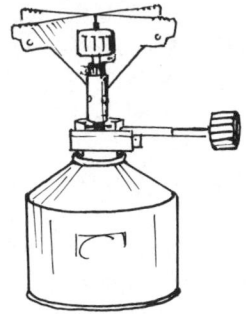

Primus Alpine Titanium

moving part—the valve that adjusts from subsimmer to scorch. When setting it up, the windscreen can be a puzzler at first (the 1998 *Backpacker* Annual Gear Guide, page 173, shows it in the wrong place) and some users report burning unwary fingers while adjusting the valve. A cartridge Footrest seems like a good idea. The stove also fits in a Windshield/Hanging Device (24 oz., $32), a rigid aluminum windscreen suspended by thin steel cables that not only does wonders for efficiency in cold, windy spots but also makes the stove virtually spillproof.

The #3243 Alpine Power Cook (not shown, but it resembles the Markill Vulcano, page 327) is pitched toward the hyperactive alpinist, with a howling 14,500 Btu output. Primus lists the boil time as "less than 3 minutes." It has a wide flame pattern and piezo ignition, weighs 7 oz., and costs $59. The foldout pot supports make it especially tipsy, so the Primus Footrest is included. A *Backpacker* (April 2000) test found this stove to be particularly weather worthy. It seems like the perfect match for the Windscreen/Hanging Device but might require fiddling to fit (for more on hanging stoves, see page 339).

Also summit-bound is the #3211 Alpine Micro (4 oz., $50), an ultralight with a minimal quadrant windscreen/pot support and piezo ignition. It sports a three-minute boil time and 11,000 Btu output with a tight flame pattern more suited to rapid snow melting and shovel-it-up cookery than gourmet tricks. The #3274 Alpine Titanium has the same specs with a 3-oz. weight and $129 price—that's $43 per oz. (Remember, too, that gas cartridges don't get any lighter just because you've got a supertwist stove.)

Last (deservedly so) on our Primus list is the Alpine Mini-Duo, a stove-lantern pairing that won a *Backpacker* Editor's Choice Award

Primus Alpine Mini-Duo Stove and Lantern

in 1997. As a notion, it's appealing—the two fit into a cute little box and weigh just under a pound. But the set costs a shocking $149. The stove is rated at 9000 Btu, with a boil time of four minutes, but I couldn't get anywhere near that (even in still air) and the swing-out pot supports are treacherous. The lantern has a chimney of unbreakable mesh instead of glass, but it puts out about 15 maddeningly flickering watts and can't be hung up.

Let's get it straight: with that same $149, I could get the snappy little Alpine Micro, a new headlamp, new batteries, a fifth of excellent rum, and still have $49 for the posttrip celebration.

Olicamp Scorpion I and III

The Scorpion first crawled out as the Evernew Pack-In Stove. But the one I bought, a parts-bin special, came in a bag labeled Olicamp, with a burner stamped "Grill," and a base with a cast-in glyph that reads "portm 2." It had, still has, a threaded gas valve and a skinny black-rubber fuel tube. My first freestanding tripod cartridge stove, it weighed

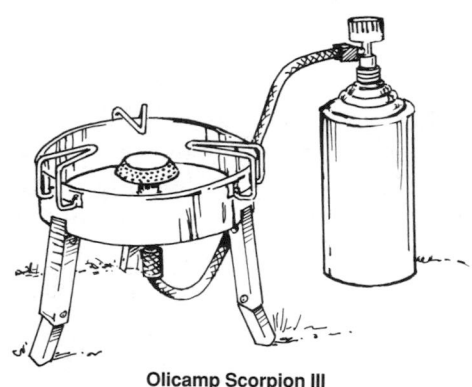

Olicamp Scorpion III

7.5 oz. and cost $12. I've used it happily for 20 years (an amortized cost of $.60 per annum so far, and declining). It was particularly great for science trips when on top of my backpacking stuff I carried 40-plus lbs. of sampling gear and ended the day in too vicious a temper for pumping and priming. The burner, tube, and valve weren't attached to the base, so I drilled

the appropriate holes in an aluminum dog dish and built my first hanging stove, with a fat rubber band to double the fuel tube so the cartridge didn't dangle.

It's not a raging blowtorch, but I've cooked hundreds of leisurely soups, fried up falafel and browned brook trout, and grown to appreciate its modest hiss. Maintenance so far is trimming the burner-ward end of the fuel line, which cracks, and poking it back on. (Recycler's note: the skinny, clear tubes used in home oxygen systems, and regularly tossed out, make decent replacements, with a teeny hose clamp.)

The present generation, Scorpions I and III, sport slightly different burners and a braided fiber sheath on the fuel line. The Scorpion I (shown with the Outback Oven, page 270) has a simple fold-up tripod base and costs $29. The Scorpion III has a stainless-steel windscreen with folding pot supports and double-jointed legs (shades of the flying saucers in 1950s films). For packing ease, the windscreen holds the burner, tube, and valve. One pot support detaches to serve as a wrench for the burner, and there's a cleaning needle included. In toto, 9.7 oz. and $38.

Scorpion sells spray-can-style butane cartridges, but these stoves do fine on other screw-top brands and blends. A neat accessory is the Double Valve (2.8 oz., $9.50) that lets you run two Scorpions, with individual controls, on a single cartridge.

Markill cartridge stoves

Sold in the U.S. by VauDe Sports, these German stoves somewhat resemble those from Primus. But with prices a full notch lower, Markill (Mar-*kill*) stoves are catching on fast in the States. Markill cartridges (also similar to Primus) weren't available in the U.S. when I tested, but the folks at VauDe Sports tell me that they're developing cartridges with different warm- and cold-weather gas blends.

Simple, cheap, and beloved of Scout troops (as well as backpacking satanists) is the Markill Devil. Listed with an eyebrow-raising 2:40 boil time, it weighs 8 oz., has a tight flame pattern, costs $20, and tucks into a wee stuff sack. It does lack a windscreen, so performance falls off steeply when the zephyr sings.

The Vulcano has nice foldout pot supports, a broad flame pattern, and a piezo lighter (built into the spring-loaded adjusting knob) but packs in a compact zip case. A bit slower to the boil, at 3:30, and lacking a windscreen, it allows more scope for cookery at 10 oz. and $27. A cartridge foot helps keep things on the up-and-up.

Blasting away atop a cartridge, the Dragon looks like a flying saucer trying to impregnate a grain silo. The listed boil time is 2:50 (see table, pages 309–10, for my take). It's a bit heavy, as piggyback stoves go (11 oz.), but the broad flame pattern, large windscreen/reflector, toothy fold-

Markill Devil   **Markill Vulcano**   **Markill Dragon**

out pot supports, piezo lighter (built into the adjusting knob), and hard case put it in the deluxe category, at a decent $30. Being tipsy, it needs a cartridge stabilizer. But the easy lighting, wide heat range, and tractability make it a good choice for ambitious camp chefs—I used it a lot with the Outback Oven (page 270).

A new Markill stove (not shown) is the Spitfire, rated at a four-minute boil (9 oz., $33), with a tight flame pattern, a built-in reflector/windscreen with four flip-out pot supports (that look vaguely like the pick of an ice axe), and a piezo ignition. The control stem has a clever sliding brass sleeve that lets it fold up as well, for stowage in a tidy plastic box. It's rugged, serviceable, compact, and an excellent value. A pared-down version that lacks the windscreen and reflector but comes with a folding three-footed cartridge base is the Hot Shot (4:30, 6 oz., $30).

The Markill Stormy Cookset gets high marks from alpinists. The Devil burner, with a fuel hose and valve, mounts in a windscreen with folding tripod feet and D-rings for hanging. A close-fitting pot and lid give the set a weight of 1 lb. 9 oz. and a tag of $109. The boil time (curiously, considering the spec for the Devil alone) is listed as 6:30. But the design aims at a steady output and high fuel efficiency rather than the fastest possible boil. In terms of capacity, it's somewhere between solitude and togetherness: two big eaters will end up scrapping.

Interesting Markill accessories are the *Stechkartuschenadapter* (aka Old-Style Gas Cartridge Adapter) #24960, which mates a screw-top stove with pierced cartridges and has integral stabilizing feet. Another is the *Kartuschenwärmer* (figure it out) that clings to a steel cartridge with magnets and transfers heat from the burner to counter the dread pressure drop.

MSR SuperFly

MSR fans who want a cartridge stove should check out the new SuperFly (4.6 oz., $40; with piezo lighter, 5.2 oz., $50). Hooked up to the also-new MSR IsoPro cartridge, it's rated at a three-minute boil. The big techno-leap is a "multi-mount" base that fits both threaded and non-threaded cartridges. An aluminum "grabber" slides sideways under the flange on top of the cartridge, and a large thread on the stove base guides its brass inlet into the hole and snugs it down. That is, it mounts on the cartridge without engaging either thread or click lock. It's a tight fit over the fat lip on a Primus cartridge but slips right onto the Campingaz, Peak 1 threaded (though not the Powermax), Olicamp Scorpion, and Snow Peak cartridges without any leaks. The quadrant pot supports keep the flame from blowing out but don't provide much shielding from the wind. The Ascent Hanging Kit (4.4 oz., $40), however, consists of a folding titanium stove support and a sheet-titanium windscreen and reflector.

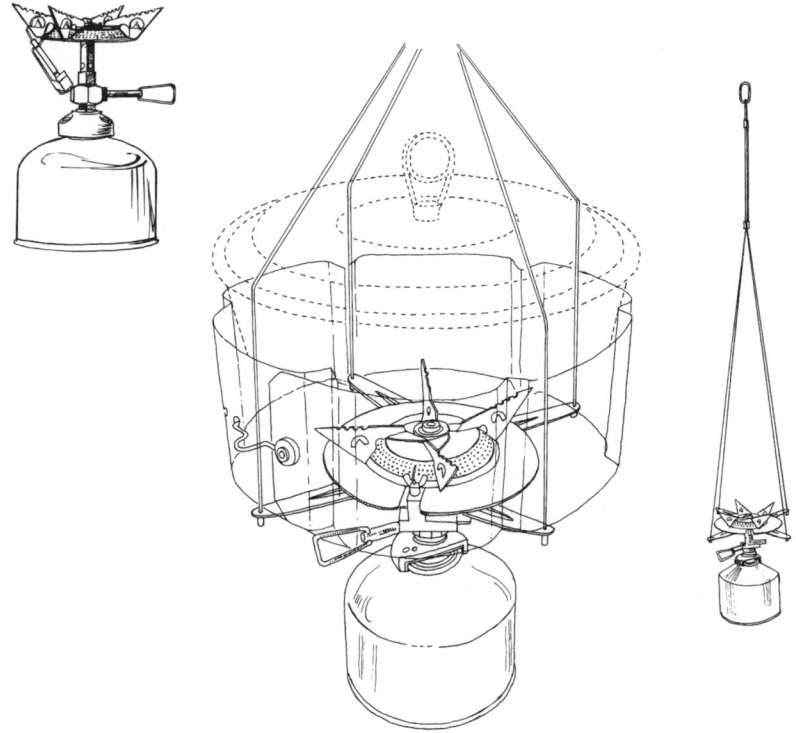

MSR SuperFly and Ascent Hanging Kit

Besides being extraordinarily light, the Ascent goodie practically disappears when folded: one sweet piece of design.

Peak 1 Micro

As we go to press, I find that this excellent little stove has been dumped, not for any fault of its own, but by Coleman's having taken on the Campingaz line. So this is a requiem. At 13,000 Btu, with sturdy folding pot supports, a heat exchanger, a boil time of 3:30, a 6-oz. weight, and a $25 tag, it was a sleeper. In cold, windy conditions and without a windscreen, it scorched the pants off everything else I tested (see table, pages 309–10). This owed, I thought, to a slight oversupply of fuel, so a stiff breeze simply adjusted the oxygen content. This bore out when I tried the Micro in perfectly still air and the boil time slowed by half a minute. There might be a few left in bargain bins: worth a look.

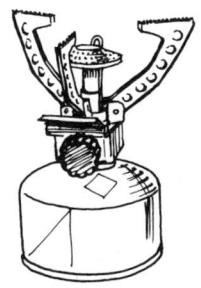

Peak 1 Micro

*Peak 1 X-Series**

When I first saw the brushed aluminum with its fancy graphics it looked to me like pure marketing. The claims—4-season performance, burns hot to the last drop—were too good to be true. But I was wrong. These stoves all run (as nothing else can) on the liquid-feed Coleman Powermax cartridge (see page 297). Which as far as cartridges go is quite simply the best thing going. Each stove includes a "Green Key" to prick holes in the empty cartridges, so they can be flattened and recycled.

The Powermax cartridge reclines, and the matching X stoves are freestanding, with magnesium-alloy frames. The burner has a medium-size pattern, with a brass heat exchanger extending, like a cocked finger, up into the fiery zone. This warms the liquefied gas so it vaporizes just before mixing with air, rather than in the cartridge. A brass tube extends out to the fuel line, in a braided metal sheath. This leads to a brass valve enclosed in a magnesium-alloy housing, with a springy support and a big adjuster knob on top. You can use these stoves with an external windscreen, but even in blustery conditions they log five- to six-minute boil times without one. And (I'm humbled, already) they do most assuredly burn hot and perfectly steady in subzero temperatures, until the cartridge is nearly dry.

The Xtreme 9720 is the lightweight of the X series at 11 oz., so that's the one Linda and I took as backup when we camped in March on a snow-covered glacial moraine. Our main stove for melting snow was supposed to be the liquid-fuel Peak 1 Apex (page 314). But in a boil-off, the Xtreme whipped it by a full two minutes. Plus it simmered like an Italian film star. So we ended up choosing the Xtreme for everything. I found I could deploy the legs, attach the cartridge, light up, and have a pot on in *17 seconds.* The magnesium tripod gear is stable, with grippy supports, but setting a pot on at an angle can fold it up abruptly. Forewarned, that's

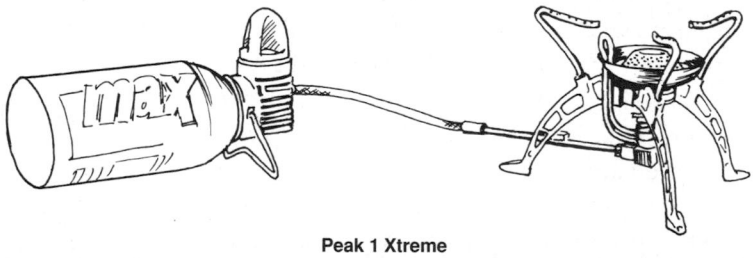

Peak 1 Xtreme

*As mentioned on page 305, many of Coleman's Peak 1 products are now known as Exponent products, and this stove will be the Exponent Xtreme. I didn't ask why. Nor, at this late stage, do I intend to go through the whole damn book and change it.

avoidable. But, subject to occasional fits of idiocy, I drilled three unsanctioned holes in the toes so I could anchor it with matchstick stakes. The Peakèd Ones rate the Xtreme at a zoomy 14,000 Btu, with a three-minute boil time, yet it consumes a mere 0.53 oz. of fuel for each liter boiled (in my tests, the average for all other cartridges was 0.75 oz.). So it's relatively fuel-efficient. For a summer week in the Utah canyons, cooking dinners and heating dishwater every night, with serious coffee swilling at dawn, Linda and I used up two 10.6-oz. cartridges. That's only 3 oz. of gas per day. Lord knows, $75 isn't cheap. But after brief tests, Colin and I agree: this one's worth the bite.

The other X-stoves merit some mention. The Xpert 9710 is a quadruped, with a 12,000 Btu rating, at 13.5 oz. and $60. Good points are its four-legged stability and lower price.

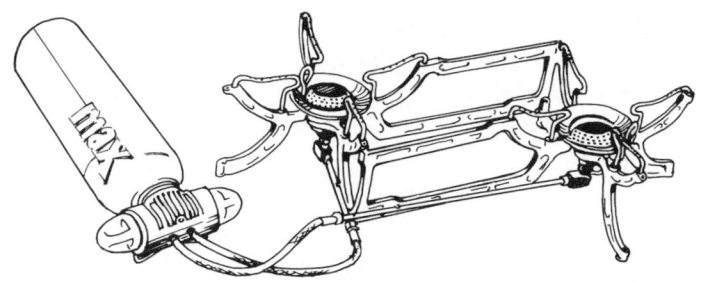

Peak 1 Xpedition

The Xpedition is unique: a collapsible two-burner (like two Xpert stoves engaged in an act of congress) with dual controls. The burners are 9 inches apart, so it can handle two 2-liter pots at once. Running off a single cartridge, it rates 10,000 Btu per burner, with a 3:45 boil time. With both jets at full howl, it gets 42 minutes out of a large Powermax cartridge, so for normal cooking, or anything other than continuous snow melting, you could probably get double that. It folds more or less flat—not a bad package. At 1 lb. 9 oz. and $90, the Xpedition bids fair to become the standard cooker for groups and families.

Snow Peak GigaPower

When the Japanese company Snow Peak brought its wares to the U.S., I snagged a stove for a test. It was called the *Chi,* which means energy. It looked like it was made by a jeweler and I was won over, even before I weighed it: 3¼ oz. Or 4, with the hard plastic case. Having garnered a 1999 Editors' Choice Award from *Backpacker,* it's now called the GigaPower, not as nice to my ears as *Chi:* three letters, three ounces, total wisdom.

In any event, this is the hot little number I've been using in my Flying Kitchen. It folds to fit—with rattling room—inside an insulated mug, adjusts from a microsimmer to a weasel's roar, and generally pleases merry hell out of me.

What's not to like? Well, it has a pinpoint flame pattern. With a 4-inch support span, it won't take a large pot. And lacking any wind protection whatsoever, it loses its *chi* in a stiff breeze. Nevertheless it's a great solo stove, at its best in tight bivouacs. I made a 1-oz. folding windscreen out of reflective fabric (from a discarded Forest Service fire shelter) that lowers the boil time

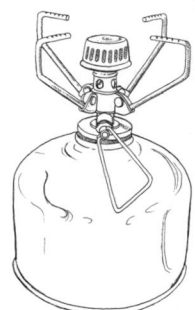

Snow Peak GigaPower

considerably, matching in fact the Peak 1 Xtreme (page 330).

The specs on the basic GigaPower GS-100 are 10,000 Btu, 3:52 boil time, 3.25 oz., $50. Variations include the GS-100A Giga Auto (ugh, who does these names?) with piezo ignition, 3.75 oz., $64; the GST-100 Titanium, 2.5 oz., $80; and the GST-100A Titanium Auto, with piezo ignition, 3 oz., $99.

New from Snow Peak is the GS-200D GigaPower Auto Detachable, a freestanding tripod that delicately resembles the MSR WhisperLite. The GS-200D is rated at 13,800 Btu, with a 3:52 boil time, and piezo ignition (10.4 oz., $100).

All Snow Peak stoves run on screw-top cartridges with blended fuel: their 110-g. net canister is $4, the 220-g. size is $5. Availability is spotty, but my stove works fine with Peak 1, Primus, and MSR IsoPro cartridges.

Hank Roberts Mini Mark III

COLIN: Many years ago, when I first saw this stove packed up like a large but tinny yo-yo, it struck me as just the sort of damn clever, impractical

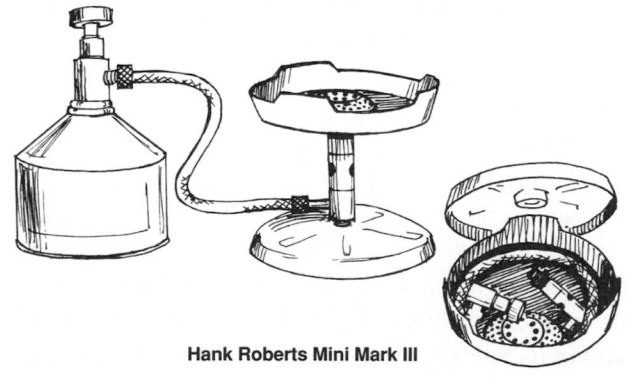

Hank Roberts Mini Mark III

little device I deplore. But it soon earned my respect. Assembling the stove and repacking the yo-yo turned out to be not the finicky business I'd feared but simplicity itself, and it heated very efficiently. True, it proved mildly temperamental—tending to flare or go out until it was warmed up (one minute or so); at the start, you had to watch the flame like an arsonist, adjusting the flow to keep it alive. And the close-to-the-burner cartridge, unless ventilated at all times, tended to overheat, with a considerable risk of explosion. Still, I soon began to carry the Mini stove on short, mild-conditions trips, and in spite of my general reservations about cartridge stoves, came to rate it high.

CHIP: High enough, in fact, that whenever I mentioned stoves to test for this edition, Colin kept asking, "What about the Hank Roberts?" I barely remembered seeing one in the Great Outdoor Shop in Pinedale, Wyoming, back when mammoths roamed the West, though I never got past the yo-yo stage. So I told him about Markill and Snow Peak. "That's all very well," quoth Colin, "but what about the Hank Roberts?" So I started to hunt. The local shop no longer stocked ol' Hank, and the *Backpacker* Annual Gear Guide didn't list him. But Pinedale's big general store surprised me by having a stock of Hank Roberts fuel cartridges. So I wrote down the phone number and reached a series of cryptic answering machines at a factory in Denver, from which I was referred to an 800 number in California. The California voice assured me that I really needed to talk to the people in Denver. And so on, Ping-Pong style. Finally, a sheet popped out of my fax. It bore patent numbers, a bar code, and a crude representation of a Roberts Mini Mark III stove.

It looks like they ran a box through their fax machine. According to that, the Roberts Mini Mark III stove is "Oderless [sic] and spot-free. No leakage on food or clothing. 7600 Btu's." The Mark III updates the aluminized yo-yo concept with dual filtration and a fuel line that moves the cartridge away from the burner. The valve now has threads (I think) rather than the old prong-and-ball system that gave Hank II such prime potential for rocketry. Roberts cartridges are apparently still wick-fed, though other screw-top canisters aren't, so performance might vary.

For Colin's sake, I'm still trying to get an actual stove to test. Roberts aficionados can try their own luck: 1-800-290-2267. The old-style rubber-tip Roberts cartridges (or the roughly equivalent Optimus 702) are available at Faler's General Store in Pinedale, Wyoming (and probably in other spots as well).

Before we lurch on to other types, a feature increasingly found on cartridge stoves is the

Piezoelectric ignition.

When you count the phosphoric pinholes in your sleeping bag, tent, parka, shell pants, etc., not to mention the aggravation of dampish crumbling matchheads and similar Promethean gripes, the piezoelectric stove lighter, now found on many cartridge models, is potent magic. Until it fails to work.

The lowest possible flow of gas is best for lighting up. If it's breezy, use a pan lid to shield the burner. If you fail otherwise, try turning the stove at an angle (but joggling a cartridge can produce flares). If it still doesn't work, look at the spark gap. If there's no visible spark, the unit is faulty. A 3- to 4-millimeter gap seems about right. If the tip gets bent and the gap is too short, or it's right above a hole in the burner, you can click like a madman with no result, despite a nice blue spark. I discovered this when testing two identical stoves—one lit and one didn't. The needlenose pliers on pocket tools are a means of adjustment, but some spark tips have a ceramic insulator—take care not to break it. A properly aligned piezoelectric ignition is about 97.3576 percent reliable.

Alcohol stoves

are said to be "explosion proof and absolutely safe." If you cock a jaundiced eye on the energy future, note too that neither form of fuel alcohol comes from fossil sources.

Various alcohol stoves such as the Optimus Trapper have appeared in the U.S., only to vanish from the market. The current best choice is the Swiss Trangia line, distributed in several configurations by Mountain Safety Research. The heart of the mild-mannered beast is an ingenious brass cup (3.7 oz.) about the size of a green chile can, with vent holes around the rim. One filling boils one liter, or thereabouts. While it's possible to knock this over and spill alcohol, the ghostly blue flames are easier to put out than a white-gas conflagration. The burner has a screw cap and a separate simmer ring that also puts it out when you're done.

The Trangia 25 is a burner, windscreen, and integrated cookset (1.5- and 1.75-liter nesting pots, 9-inch fry pan, lid, and lifter [2 lbs. 8 oz.]) in nonstick aluminum ($76) or Duossal, with a stainless-steel cooking surface and aluminum outer ($88). The Mini-Trangia 28-5 Cookset nests the same burner in a round pot support with some wind-baffling qualities, with 0.8- liter aluminum pot, nonstick fry pan/lid, and rudimentary lifter (11.5 oz., $26). The Trangia Westwind (6.6 oz., $20) is three flat pieces of aluminum that slot in a triangle around the burner, sort-of-ly blocking the wind while supporting a pot.

The first time I tried the Westwind, while testing cartridge stoves, it seemed agonizingly slow. But last summer I took it out several times and learned to love its quietness. Plus, burning alcohol actually smells good. A windscreen and base I made of reflective fabric (1.5 oz. total) shortened the boil time, and when I'm not in a rush or near-hypothermic, as I'm mostly not, I don't mind the waiting. While cooking, I could hear birds calling and even a squirrel's claws scratching on pinebark. *This,* I thought, and not the pressurized roar of a mini jet engine, is what I'm here for. If stoves were poems, this one would be a haiku.*

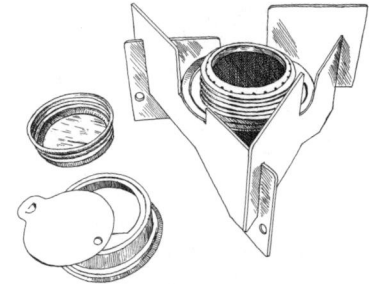

Trangia Westwind

Trangia Fuel Bottles are plastic, made for alcohol but okay with white gas and kerosene; but despite having the same thread as MSR, Sigg, etc., these plastic bottles *must not be used with a pressure pump.* The built-in pour spouts and locking tops are nice— the 0.5-liter is 4 oz. and $13, the 1-liter 5.5 oz. and $15. By volume, my alcohol consumption per trip (for the stove, that is) seems to be about 1½ times that of white gas.

Other stoves

COLIN: "Sterno" (solid alcohol in a can) is a word that used to reverberate around the woods. It now conjures up outdated pictures of cold, wet groups huddled hopefully around a small pot perched on a smaller can, waiting for water to boil. Waiting . . . and waiting . . . and waiting . . .

CHIP: Coghlan's sells a new Sterno-like product called Camp Heat in two-can packs. Chemically, it's diethylene glycol. Being gelled, it can't spill. Each can has a double set of caps to vary the output and a built-in wick that improves the efficiency. Each 270 g can burns four hours (for cooking) or six hours (for warming), depending on which cap is removed. Various pot-supporting devices for use with Sterno cans should perform just as well with Camp Heat. But still, the boil time is meditative at best.

The Esbit Stove (3 oz., $12 with 12 fuel tablets), distributed by MPI Outdoors, is made in Germany and issued to NATO troops (perhaps making them wish they were SATO troops). It burns "wax-based" fuel tablets that look like logger-size sugar cubes (watch your kids). I took the wee

---

*Lightning last-second update: With a custom hanging rig made from a Mirro 2 liter saucepan (sort-of-ly as shown on page 340) and supports that hold the pot 2 inches above the burner, I got the boil time down to a Cruel World 9:14 (50°F water) and an amazing 6:20 (with 70°F water). With no moving parts.

Esbit on a fanny-pack trip in nippy Wyoming weather (late September at 9500 feet) and we both escaped. That is, I escaped hypothermia and it escaped being thrown in the creek after an interminable wait for morning coffee.

Esbit Stove

The stove itself is a shallow steel box that unfolds to support a pot. The tablets light easily but blow out with equal facility, so you should erect a windscreen. In cool-with-slight-breeze conditions, it took two tablets to boil a pint of cold stream water. But it did boil. *Penitentes* and anchorites will consume 3 to 5 half-oz. tablets per day. A similar thingie is the "Tommy Cooker" from Brigade Quartermasters, for $8 with four 1-oz. trioxane bars (a toilet-cleaner blue that kids are unlikely to gnaw) that need to be snapped in two or three parts for use. The trioxane bars were army issue for the GI Canteen Cup Stove (6 oz., $6; also consult page 275) that works okay for heating—one fuel bar boosted 50°F water to 90°— but it isn't something you can cook with, really. And trioxane fumes make me sneeze like hell.

Sierra Stove

Made by ZZ Manufacturing, this was long known as the ZZ Zzip Ztove. In previous *Walker*s, Colin wrote that "although it looks like a Monty Python prop—great fun but of questionable use—it works."

Colin's account alerted me, but I didn't consider trying a Sierra Stove until Gary Holthaus, a fellow poet, told me he'd walked from the Canadian border to Colorado with one, and burned not a drop of gas or oil. Think of it: no fuel caches, cartridge-seeking frenzies, or petro-guilt.

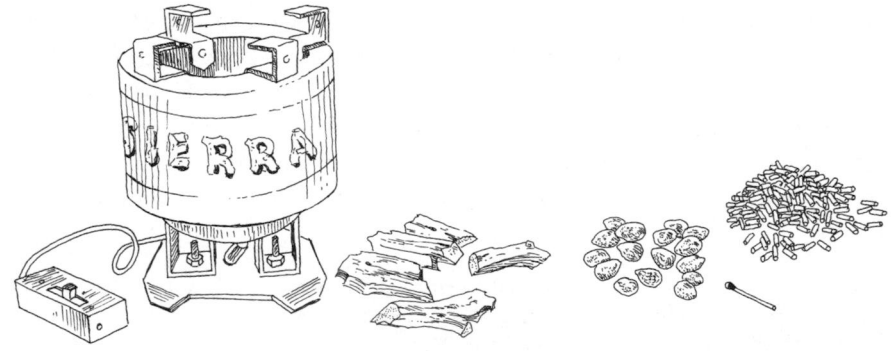

Sierra Stove and various fuels

Now that I've tried one—not only tried but fiddled and fondled and obsessed over—I'd say it's the key to truly unencumbered long-distance walking.

In effect, it's like a tiny blacksmith's forge. You kindle a fire in the double-walled combustion chamber, then switch on the blower fan. The airflow is preheated (and cools the fire chamber somewhat) before issuing from a double ring of holes, supercharging the little blaze. The fan is powered by a single 1.5-volt battery. AA size is standard, and a quality alkaline cell will give 4 to 6 hours of cook time. Once you have the hang of it, and given good fuel, the heat output matches white-gas and cartridge stoves (see table, pages 309–10).

Good fuel isn't hard to find. The instructions mention pinecones, which burn hot but exude so much resin that pots literally tar themselves to the stove. This happens with any resinous wood—desert shrubs (creosote) can be particularly awful, but pine, spruce, fir, and conifer-in-general make a sticky mess of your pot. So I look for nonresinous fuel: well-weathered deadfall pine, dry hardwood twigs, solid charcoal from old fires, and dung.

I'd read of the Bedouin delegating small kids to scoop up fresh camel flop and mold it into briquets. And above tree limit, at 11,000 feet in Wyoming, I cooked a meal with the neat, dried pellets of bighorn sheep. Suffice it to say that most large ungulates—bison, yak, elk, deer, pronghorn, caribou—produce burnable dung, but those on a woody diet excel: a moose wintering on twigs molds a marvelous fuel pellet, 1.4 inches long by $\frac{3}{8}$ diameter—about 1 gram dry. (Look in the willows along creeks.) Domestic cow-flop is by comparison a low-grade fuel. But it does work. Near Goblin Valley, Utah, courtesy of overgrazing, I cooked my breakfast with tumbleweeds and cowshit.

The drill I evolved is to stuff a plastic bag in an outside pocket after lunch. As I wander, my eye is peripherally peeled for silvery deadwood, seasoned twigs, solid charcoal, and of course, prime poop. With very little pausing, by dinnertime I have a nice bundle of all-natural fuel. Branches finger-size and up must be broken into segments: lay them across a crack in the rock and gently apply a fist-size stone. For kindling, the thin pages of Campmor catalogs are divine. But inner bark, rabbitbrush tops, and pine needles work, with fine twigs latticed above. On matchless trips, I've kindled my Sierra Stove with flint-and-steel or a Doan's magnesium fire starter, shaving chips into a little paper nest, or a tuft of extra-fine steel wool, then firing in sparks and blowing it into flame.

Commercial stove pellets can give you a concentrated reserve and extend your reach to shrubless expanses or alpine haute routes. A half cup (3 oz.) will boil a full quart of cold water and leave coals to toast a bagel or two. So the 6 to 9 oz. of pellets needed per day weighs about the same as the gas in a medium-size cartridge, without the steel canister. A 40-lb. sack of pellets costs $4. For starting pellets, gel or paste starters or a squirt bottle of alcohol or kerosene all work fine. Just don't squirt while the stove is burning. An aluminum tent peg of curved or angled stock makes a handy stoker—load it with pellets, slip it under the pot, and jiggle.

If you're used to gas, Zzip cooking requires a mental adjustment. Have your fuel stocked, in serviceable 1- to 2-inch chunks, before firing up, so you won't have to dash off to scrounge. Once the fire is hot, I replace twigs with charcoal and/or dung for a clean, hot flame. Some soot is a given, but regular stoking, a few twigs or turds at a time, keeps the heat even and the smoke under control. Letting it burn to coals and heaping on fuel gives you belches of smoke and hot flashes. With care—set the stove on sand, rock, or a reflective base—the fire hazard is low. But some woods produce propulsive sparks (for instance mesquite, both dry and charcoal).

More practica: On a trip where every bit of deadwood and dung was soaked by fog and rain, I set a Trangia alcohol burner in the combustion chamber and temporarily converted the Sierra Stove to liquid fuel (note that manufacturers disapprove of such tricks).

The newest Sierra Stove has a separate metal battery holder with a switch: OFF, LOW, and HIGH. I had problems maintaining good battery contact, and did some reengineering with a chunk of Ensolite. The fan was also loose on the motor shaft, needing a lick with a teeny Allen wrench. In regular use, the stove disassembles into two parts, with the base and battery-pack fitting inside the combustion chamber. This loads neatly and somewhat sootily inside a 1-liter stainless pot. The stuff sack is, appropriately, black. To power the fan, I experimented with various rechargeable batteries and a solar panel (results on page 605). For cold weather, a lithium cell is a nice backup. An optional D-cell setup will power the stove for up to 35 hours.

A common problem is installing the battery backward, whence it sucks flame back toward the motor. This seems unlikely, but a friend who has tested gear for several magazines borrowed my older-model Sierra Stove and pronounced it useless. It turned out that he'd put the battery in backward and it simply hadn't occurred to him to reverse it. The newest model has a battery box with + and − clearly indicated.

The potential not just for naturally fueled treks but, given advances in solar panels and rechargeable batteries, for completely sun-powered backpacking (see Solar Campsite, page 604) is exciting. Given my itch for second-guess engineering, this sooty little sucker makes me quiver like a stud-horse, imagining a 6-oz. titanium version.*

*Yow!!! Just announced: the Sierra Titanium Stove: 9.9 oz., $125.

Meanwhile, the un-re-engineered Sierra Basic 111A (14 oz., $52) is listed at an optimistic 18,000 Btu with a four-minute boil time. The Sierra Set (2 lbs. 3 oz., $72) includes a 1-liter stainless-steel pot with fry pan/lid, a windscreen, a crisscross grate for burning long sticks, fire tongs, and a packet of Zip Fire starter sticks. The windscreen, grate, and tongs are regrettably heavy sheet steel. I've not heard of motor failures, but for the ultraparanoid, a spare one is about $7. The specs and details seem to be continually in flux, which makes it more fun, I guess.

Hanging stoves

For years hanging stoves were part of the arcana of big-wall climbing, but recently they've come down from the vertical world to more general use. I've built several, using stoves from Bleuets to XGKs, and like them particularly in winter. It's nice to have a stove that isn't melting its way inexorably down into the snowpack, having to be chopped free the next morning. A hanging stove (and the pot thereon) is also tip-proof. And in any season, walkers with bad backs find stand-up cooking agreeable.

The Primus Windshield/Hanging Device (page 325) and Markill Stormy Cooker (page 328) have been around for years, and get high marks. The Bibler Hanging Stove (boil time 3:30, 1 lb. 13 oz., $85) looks like a Primus mounted in a cheap aluminum saucepan—I haven't tried one. All these are cartridge burners, subject to cold and pressure drop, though the Markill Stormy is designed to counter the problem somewhat by hanging the cartridge near enough to get burner heat (though not so near as to explode). Some homemade hanging stoves have brass or copper heat exchangers that conduct flame heat to the cartridge, and I've built an experimental one that works (page 312), though most stove and cartridge makers discourage their use. The only add-on commercial heat exchanger I've been able to locate is Markill's magnet-mounted version (page 328), adaptable to any steel cartridge, hanging or no.

MSR now makes the ultralight Ascent Hanging Kit (4.4 oz., $40), which consists of a folding titanium stove support with cables, a sheet-titanium windscreen, and a reflector. Besides being extraordinarily light, it folds very small for packing. The Ascent kit comes alone or with the SuperFly stove (page 328) that MSR recommends using with it. (I tried stoves from several other makers and they don't fit.)

But there are innumerable ways to adapt stoves to airy situations, using available bases like the MSR Trillium or by drilling vents and mounting-holes in thin-walled aluminum pots (see *Climbing*, 184, page 161). A pregnantly possible resource is an aluminum angel-food-cake pan ($8) with a removable bottom. For safety, cartridges should always mount under the windscreen/reflector rather than inside and should have some support other than the flexible fuel tube. Liquid-fuel bottles can be hung in the proper attitude underneath with a loop or two of fine cable. To reduce blowup risks, liquid-fuel stoves enclosed in hanging windscreens should be primed with paste. Another lookout is that your cookpot doesn't fit too tightly in the windscreen, or flames will come raging out the bottom. Tapered pots such as the GSI Bugaboos (page 268) work where straight-sided ones don't.

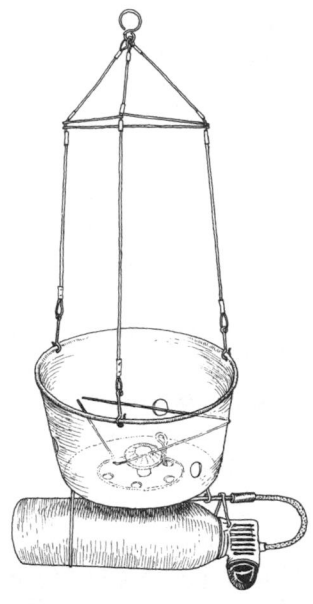

Homebuilt hanging stove

After many trials and errors, my latest homebuilt hang-up incorporates the Peak 1 Xtreme, stripped of the legs. The Xtreme (page 330) has a built-in preheater, and the liquid-feed Powermax cartridge really cranks in blue weather. I rigged the stove in a Mirro 2.8-liter aluminum saucepan ($6), with the valve and cartridge underneath, using ⅟₁₆-inch cable and swages, an extra spring, an S-hook, and a split ring (all together, about $10–$12). The Xtreme burner unthreads (gently, gently) so the stove can be packed inside the windscreen. After building several versions with permanently looped cable hangers, I co-opted the removable Primus Hanging Device (alone, about $12). The whole bang-up weighs 15 oz. For winter solos it's become my favorite stove, since it delivers uncanny five-minute boil times while swinging like a church bell in a 10°F wind.

Under the circumstances, a beautiful sight.

Current choices

COLIN: Because I've had to test most of the little devils (except the latest crop), I now own at least one each of most long-established and currently available stoves. But I find that in practice I mostly use only four.

For any kind of severe conditions I favor an MSR XGK because it burns like a blowtorch, even in the cold, up high and in winds, and because it's light and reliable and burns many fuels.

For general three-season backpacking I continue to use my Svea because it's so reliable and because, although 3 oz. heavier than the MSR, it is, for me, several minutes a day lighter in fiddle time. (I mean, I could probably operate the thing in my sleep.) A pinch of sentiment too? Possibly.

For one- or two-day trips when weather seems sure to cooperate, and especially if I want to keep my hands clean, I often save a few ounces by taking along a Hank Roberts or even a more ethereal alternative.

Other considerations can, of course, outweigh weight. In forested country, or when some other good fuel seems sure to be plentiful, I might well opt for a Sierra Stove.

CHIP: For deep-winter snow melting and also for unpredictable fuel scenarios, I've been carrying the MSR DragonFly. Despite the mildly awkward setup, it does all that a good stove ought to, including simmer, on a range of liquid fuels.

On the cartridge side I'm mightily taken with the winter-worthy, fuel-efficient Coleman Peak 1 Xtreme (by now the Exponent Xtreme) and the liquid-feed Powermax cartridge. Most often it hangs in my homebuilt rig. Drawbacks are the cost and limited availability of the aluminum cartridges.

For light/short/feral jaunts, the infinitesimal 3-oz. Snow Peak GigaPower cartridge stove fits in an insulated mug with room to spare. But the new MSR SuperFly, adaptable to many cartridge types and augmented with MSR's ultralight hanging kit, is a close rival.

The future? A growing distaste for Big Oil gives me a strong nudge toward the alcohol-burning Trangia Westwind. For simplicity, unbreakability, and quietness, it's hard to beat.

And, echoing Colin, I find the Sierra Stove a valuable adjunct. So much so that I'm developing a whole new long-distance strategy around it (page 604).

OPERATING YOUR STOVE

COLIN: Convenience is the cartridge stoves' strong point, and with them you don't really have to learn much except how to put a match to a burner or click a piezoelectric igniter. It's almost—though not quite—like lighting a nonpilot stove back home. But for such things as must or should be done, see under each model, page 313 and onward. For Keeping Cooked Food Warm and Protection from Wind, see pages 345 and 348.

Their convenience is undoubtedly the reason cartridge stoves consistently outsell small gasoline stoves. But the latter are really far better performers—or used to be—and, in the long run, less aching sources of grief. "At least 50 percent of the problems with gasoline stoves arise because people don't understand how to operate them," one experienced repair-

Safety

Don't be afraid of any stove. But each time you touch one, exercise meticulous care in every little act. Your first failure to screw a filler plug or cartridge fully home could be your last.

Examine and replace gaskets, O-rings, and other fast-wearing parts, and perform regular maintenance. Poorly maintained stoves are more likely to give you trouble, leading to haphazard attempts at repair. A vicious cycle.

Never have your face over a lit stove. The chances of a malfunction at such a time may be remote, but it would be devastating. Less obvious but more likely, and almost as dangerous, is the risk of the flame's igniting hair or beard or clothing.

Beware of big pots, especially with encircling windscreens. They can entrap so much heat that the cartridge or tank may explode. (In tank stoves the danger is especially great with leaded gasoline.) This can also arise with stoves having separate tanks and fuel lines, if the pot spreads the flame far enough out to heat the fuel bottle. Large pots and/or windscreens can also direct enough heat downward to melt rubber or plastic gas tubes. So can heat-retaining devices such as the Outback Oven.

Beware of sleeping bags near stoves. Nylon shells melt easily and are very difficult to extinguish. (I say only "Beware," not "Keep stoves away." As we shall see, I mostly cook with my stove close to my sleeping bag. But I take care.) Also vulnerable: the cuffs of down parkas and synthetic fleece gloves.

Stoves in tents. See pages 303 and 371.

man told me. "And today's instructions are often worthless." In other words, to make a gasoline stove realize its potential you must know what you're doing—from the start.

Fuel containers

All fuels deteriorate in storage. Before filling your fuel bottle or stove tank from a can that has stood for some time, always shake well and reduce the risks of trouble by pouring through a Coleman or similar filter.

When I filled my new Svea with Camplite fuel that had been standing in the garage for God knows how many months or even years, tested boiling time for a quart of water rose from 5 or 5½ minutes to between 7 and 8.

The most popular containers for backpacking, and the ones I use, are the cylindrical, spun-aluminum Sigg bottles, made in Switzerland (0.3 liter, 0.6 liter, 1 liter, 1.5 liters) ranging in price from about $8 to $14. Buy the bare aluminum, nonanodized kind, or the slightly more costly painted version: expensive anodized bottles are needed only for corrosive liquids, such as booze (page 220). All these aluminum bottles are extraordinarily tough. My original Sigg, though battered like a pug, was still sound after a dozen years; but dents finally reduced its capacity so severely that I retired it, with honor. Three decades later its replacement remains in good shape. You may have to replace a worn gasket every few years, but that's about all. If a stopper is hard to remove, apply overwhelming leverage by twisting a spoon or stick pushed through the stopper arch. The new Sigg bottles are designed for use with pressure pumps—old ones might not be. A full 1-pint bottle of white gas plus the starting tankful will just last me and my Svea or MSR a week, provided I exercise care. If snow or ice must be melted for water, I carry more bottles and/or larger ones.

CHIP: MSR bottles (having a deeper set of threads than the older Sigg bottles) are tested for the pressures involved with MSR stoves and come in three sizes: the 11-oz. costs $8 and weighs 2.8 oz.; the 22-oz. is $9 and weighs 4.9 oz.; and the 33-oz. is $10 and weighs 7.3 oz. These weights include the cap (0.4 oz.), which you can leave off in favor of the pump. New "for fast-and-light fanatics" are titanium fuel bottles that are somewhat lighter than the equivalent aluminum models, at enormously greater cost (0.4 liter, 3 oz., $60; 0.6 liter, 3.5 oz., $65; and 0.8 liter, 4.1 oz., $70).

Optimus makes pressure-resistant aluminum fuel bottles (0.6 liter, $10; 1 liter, $11), as does Primus (0.6 liter, $13; 1 liter, $14.50).

Peak 1 Apex aluminum fuel bottles (22 oz., 4.9 oz., $11) have a different thread than the cross-compatible ones on Sigg, Optimus, and MSR bottles. Coleman chose this as a way of making sure that substandard copycat bottles—said to rupture under pressure—couldn't be used with the Apex, but it can cause problems for groups and expeditions.

Because of different internal coatings, aluminum fuel bottles intended for white gas or kerosene shouldn't be used for alcohol. Nalgene makes red plastic bottles with a fluoropolymer inner coating that resists both gasoline and alcohol, and nice dripless spouts (16 oz., $10; 32 oz., $13). Trangia bottles are also plastic, with cleverly locking pour spouts in the caps (0.5 liter, 4 oz., $13; 1 liter, 5.5 oz., $15); they can be used to store white gas or kerosene. But *no* plastic fuel bottle should be used as a fuel tank for a stove or pressurized with a pump.

Filling the stove

Small funnels with brass mesh filters are found in every sporting goods store. Liberty Mountain Adventure has a lightweight squarish version (1 oz., $1.30) with the spout to one side, made for awkward stove and lantern tanks. Stoves with built-in tanks and small caps, like the Svea, need a delicate touch. The Ulti-Mate Pour Spout (1.5 oz., $4) is a two-piece cap for a standard (i.e., Sigg) bottle. The spout top opens with a half turn and delivers a narrow, steady, Svea-friendly stream. Trangia fuel bottles have a similar setup. The Nalgene fuel bottle has a reversible cone-shaped spout that works fine in tight quarters with a bit more jockeying.

When using a metal fuel bottle as a tank, note that stove makers recommend having about 20 percent of the volume empty for proper pressurizing. Some have a painted or embossed fill line. So if, for efficiency's sake, you carry your extra bottles completely full, you'll have to pour fuel out to make room for the pump and leave the necessary airspace. On long trips, my drill is to empty the first bottle, then pour off the extra from spare bottles to refill it, so all my spares are ready for use.

COLIN: You may sometimes have difficulty unscrewing your stove's knurled filler cap—especially on Sveas. Failing pliers, try nylon cord: loop it around the knurled portion and jam (not tie) it tight, then pull. It works, I promise. Or can.

Priming (preheating)

CHIP: Most liquid-fuel stoves are primed by burning something or other in the fuel cup under the jet and burner assembly. This can be fuel from the tank, alcohol from a squeeze bottle, priming paste from a tube, toilet paper, teabag wrappers, or any number of things. Some readers apply heat with a butane lighter or even a pencil torch. In-tank pressure pumps have made priming more predictable, but it can still be a pyrotechnic display, the main reason being too much fuel in the priming cup. This overflows, creating a lagoon of flame, or boils over, for a biblical pillar effect. Both Primus and MSR now add wicks or pads to regulate the priming flame. These also work nicely with white gas and can be retrofit on stoves that lack them. (The fiberglass cord used to seal woodstove doors makes good priming wick.)

Once the priming cup holds ¼ inch of fuel, or the pad is saturated, shut off the valve *completely.* Leaving it slightly open means further incendiary excitement, as fuel is pressurized by the heat and squirts out in a fiery jet.

Needless to say (or maybe not needless) you should never prime a liquid-fuel stove inside, under, upon, or adjacent to anything that can conceivably catch fire. On winter trips, I'd set up the XGK on the scoop of an aluminum snow shovel, prime it well away from the tent, and when it was burning steadily, move it closer. (For details on winter ops, see pages 370, 422, and 438).*

For vapor-feed cartridge stoves, stuffing a cartridge in your armpit is the equivalent of priming. They should be lit at the lowest-possible steady flow of gas—piezo igniters work best that way. Most cartridge stoves require a brief warm-up before wide-open operation. Most stoves using liquid-feed cartridges have preheaters that take a half minute or so to warm up.

Protection from wind

COLIN: Wind is a major difficulty in lighting a stove. A guttering warm-up flame does precious little warming up, and the stove will burn feebly, if at all. So make sure you shield it adequately. Cupped hands work reasonably well.

But wind remains a problem even when the stove is well alight. It drastically reduces the effective heat. And because this is something you can't see, the only way you know about it is that after a while you find the wretched water still hasn't come to a boil. Most of us, I fancy, tend to become careless about protecting our stoves from wind. Every now and then I get a reminder. I once spent a night on a mountain in winds that I later learned had gusted to 50 miles an hour, and was forced to sleep in a sheltered rock crevice. At the back of the crevice I found a beautiful little grotto of a kitchen that might have been made for my Svea. Although the elevation was over 12,000 feet, the stove burned in that perfectly protected place with the healthiest and boomingest roar I have ever heard it make, as if overjoyed at being given this chance to defy the rage outside. And my dinner stew that night seemed to start bubbling and steaming much more quickly than usual.

Sometimes a gust of wind will blow a stove clean out, particularly before the burner ring becomes red-hot, or when you lower the flame for

---

*COLIN: The trend is now toward "natural," recyclable everything. One reader reports that a neighbor, a contractor, "insists he warms the tank of his Svea by urinating on it." "Migawd!" says this correspondent. "Now we gotta study the science of Thermodynamic Urination."

As you see, priming your gasoline or kerosene stove is a creative and almost limitless field. For a ponderously well-rounded account of Svea priming lore, consult *Walker III*. No room here.

simmering. At such times, and especially when you're relighting it, a match left across the burner helps keep a reluctant flame alive.

To shield your stove you can build a makeshift structure with pack, boots, clothing, spare pots, or anything else you can lay hands on. (But take care not to overheat a cartridge stove.) Or you can, as I often do, carry a

Windscreen, reflector, and base.

CHIP: As if I hadn't known already, the Cruel World stove tests (pages 309–10) confirmed my notion that a windscreen should be thought of as a working part of the stove. Some stoves have built-in burner cups or quadrant-type pot supports that are somewhat effective, but the limiting factor is that the designer can't foresee the width of the pot you'll use. For safety, factory windscreens must leave plenty of room—sometimes too much for efficiency's sake.

The ideal solution, from the engineer's point of view, is to integrate the windscreen with a stove and cookset. The Markill Stormy Cookset (1 lb. 9 oz., $109) and Primus System Stove (2 lbs. 5 oz., $116) do this with the option of ground-based or hanging cookery (also see page 340). Mountain Safety Research has long supplied both a thick, crinkle-foil windscreen (1.6 oz., $5.25) and a reflector (0.25 oz., $3.25) with each stove—so far the lightest, most effective, and most adaptable solution. Primus sells a similar foil screen with a larger reflector for $10, and Sigg has a rigid, flat-folding windscreen at the same price.

The reflector fits around and under the burner, directing heat upward at the pot (and away from vulnerable fuel lines, cartridges, and whatever the stove is resting on). For cartridges, above 120°F/49°C is the danger zone, so I use a reflector on piggyback stoves in hot weather when ground temperatures can be surprisingly high (see footnote, page 112). A reflector should also be used under large-diameter pots, and one comes with the Outback Oven (page 269) to prevent cartridge overheating. I've made reflectors out of heavy foil or the fabric used in firefighting suits and shelters.

Back to windscreens: they should have an opening that lets you adjust the stove's fuel valve (without getting burnt fingers) and provides enough ventilation so the flame stays blue and the enclosed parts don't overheat. The Peak 1 windscreen (4.5 oz., $7) is a round aluminum one, included in some of their cooksets. Collapsible rigid windscreens, like the Primus folding model and the Olicamp hinged version (9.5 oz., $15), tend to blow over, so they need staking; some have stakes included—all of which adds weight. So over the years I've custom-cut MSR windscreens to fit various stoves, some with a ring of neat ½- to 1-inch holes around the bottom for cartridge cooling and and a deep U on top for adjustments. I've also made windscreens and reflectors from aluminized fabric (a discarded forest-fire shelter) that work nicely, with a stake or two, but won't stand direct flame as does thick foil.

For cooking on snow, heavily organic soils, or any meltable or burnable surface, a reflective stove base is good. There are commercial ones, like the MSR Trillium Stove Base (2.8 oz., $19), an aluminum trefoil that gives good footing on loose or frozen surfaces (and fits all MSR stoves). But I've tended to use things like aluminum snow-shovel blades or made

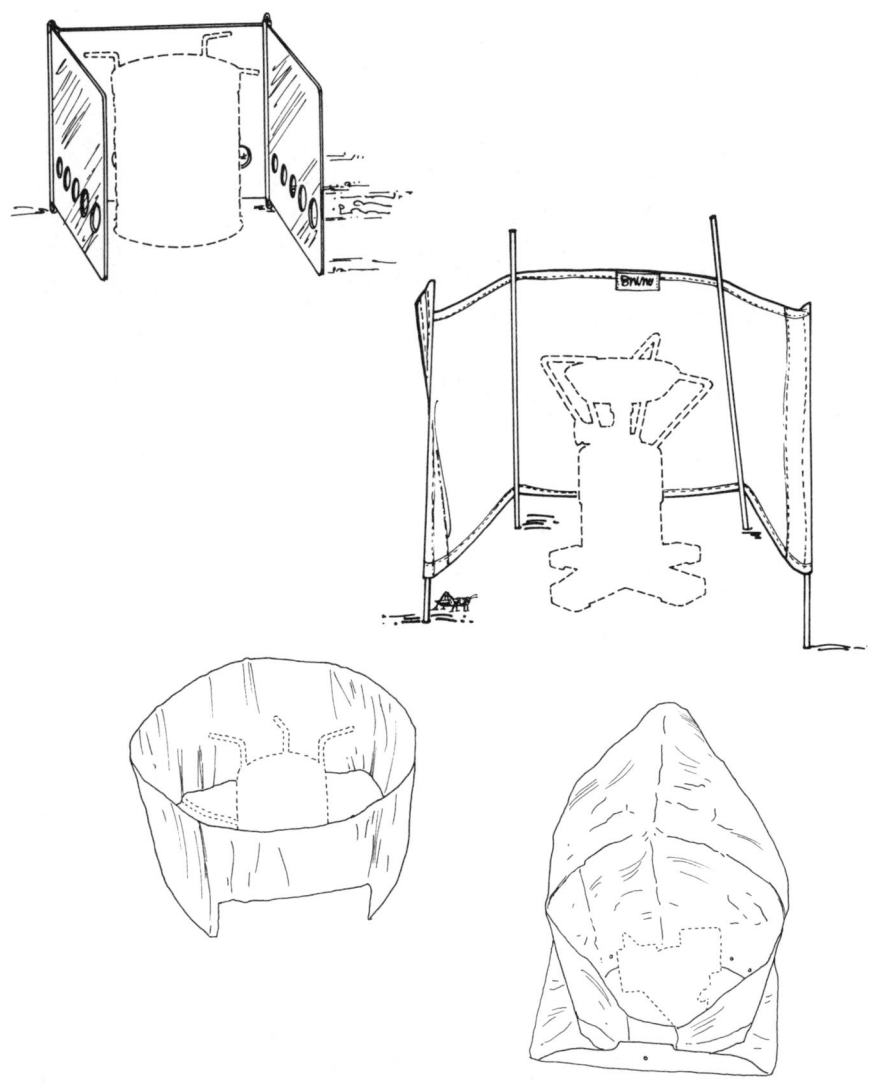

Four types of windscreen

my own. For several snow-blown years, I packed a 7-by-8-inch piece of thin Masonite with heavy foil glued on top and edges. The bare cross-hatched bottom froze to the snow, lending stability. But it weighed a hefty 5 oz. So I cut a piece of brown, corrugated cardboard (free) and covered it with foil tape: *perfecto* at 1.6 oz. For summer I cut a piece of the same shiny fabric I use for windscreens and punched a few holes, so the skinny stakes that hold the windscreen also anchor the base: 0.4 oz. See bottom right on page 347.

Wire-and-asbestos wundergauze

COLIN: Years ago a reader suggested that you could improve frying on almost any stove with one of those 6-inch-square wire gauzes with 4-inch-diameter asbestos centers (1 oz.) that are used in chemistry labs to attenuate Bunsen-burner heat. It works like a charm. I carry mine rubber-banded into a small, strong plastic envelope (to keep the inevitable soot closeted), bagged in with a metal windscreen to hold it flat. Reputedly, the wundergauze can double as a toaster—and also as a heat pad for cup or pot. But there are better ways of

Keeping cooked food warm.

With a gasoline stove the chore can pose problems. You can't leave the stove on low indefinitely: fuel is too valuable. And relighting any stove that needs priming is next door to unthinkable. In cold or windy weather you can wrap the cooking pot (if clean enough) in the sleeping bag or some other spare insulator, or can embosom it in dead leaves or some other natural insulant; or you can stand the pot on a small Ensolite stove pad like the one I've used for years to insulate the base of my Svea, or on a corner of your sleeping pad. One reader has suggested a foam pot cozy.*

When it's both desirable and reasonable to light a large campfire (not for cooking [page 350]), you can put the pot of cooked food beside it—close enough to keep warm, far enough away to keep clean. You have to keep reversing the pot so that half the food doesn't get cold, but you can do this very simply each time you pour or ladle out another cupful of food.

*CHIP: Combination pot lid/fry pans can be upended, to steam-heat the sauce while the pasta boils, to melt cheese, or to keep any number of things warm. But first make sure your cookset allows the upending. Cover the upper pan with a piece of foil.

Maintenance

As one of my stove advisers said, "Most trouble with backpacking stoves arises from stupidity or neglect." I guess stupidity ain't readily curable. But neglect is. Any gasoline stove that lacks a built-in cleaning needle comes with a little wire pricker for cleaning the jet. Carry it, always. You won't need it often, but when you do you'll need it badly. Likewise any included wrenches, cable tools, etc.

After a trip, don't leave your stove half full of fuel. It may separate out and gum up the works. But for stoves with built-in tanks, some experts advise leaving a little fuel in the tank to keep the wick damp, or maybe a dab of alcohol—which leaves no varnish. It pays to spray carburetor cleaner into the built-in-type tank occasionally to clean things out. And always use filtered gasoline. Fuel bottles should be rinsed with filtered stove fuel—small amounts of residual white gas can be poured into the tank of your auto without harm.

If you are—like Chip—the sort of person who repairs his own stove when it malfunctions, my advice is probably useless. But a reader reminds me that you can easily fix a leak around a fuel-adjusting shaft by packing with heavily waxed string of the kind used on water-pump seals.

Some of the big, quality mountain shops have stove repairers who know their business well. They can cure most woes. You can also buy replacement parts (MSR, Optimus, Primus, and Sigg all sell complete rebuild kits) and do your own work. But any of the little liquid-fuel stoves will eventually begin to show its age, and once it starts giving trouble no amount of replacing doubtful items such as generator or wick seems to work. The only remedy is to ditch it and buy a new one. Several people confirm this apparently illogical fact. I use my Sveas a fair amount, and five years seems to be about their life span. Specific troubles are not the only signs of aging. I've long suspected that heating efficiency eventually declines, and some years ago I checked my third Svea, already booked for retirement, against its new replacement: the new one boiled its quart in 5½ minutes; the old one took 7½.

Or was that my fourth Svea? I'm not sure. Rather surprisingly, I don't seem to generate a warm affection for individual stoves. But for Sveas as a tribe, yes. Very definitely. A reliable stove earns your gratitude times without number, at the most God-awful moments. Don't forget that. And if you're wondering whether our pages of print tell you a hell of a lot more about stoves than you wanted to know, ruminate afresh on the nature of that gratitude, and of its anguished opposite—and also on the pockmarking of wilderness by rampant woodcutters and by the scars of open fires.

OPERATING YOUR FIRE

Cooking fire

For years I have found that, except when stove fuel runs low or I brew tea on side trips away from my pack or I'm operating on a rock-bottom, tin-can menu (page 368), almost the only time I cook on an open fire is for frying fish or cooking them in aluminum foil. But I still light a fire occasionally, and so will other people, so we'd better take a look around.

For frying, I find that the best hearth is a two- or three-stone affair with a shallow trough for the fire. The stones must be flat enough to form a stable rest for the pan, and deep enough to leave space for a sizable fire. Wind direction and strength dictate the angle of the trough. A light breeze blowing down its length keeps flame and glow healthy; a high wind is best blocked off by the side stones, perhaps with an assist from others.

On the rare occasions I use an open fire with my cooking pots—and the last was long ago—I usually make a two- or three-stone hearth. A useful alternative that makes it easier to build and replenish a sizable fire and to control its heat is a double-Y-stick-with-crossbar rig (though very few places remain in which you can ethically cut sticks for the job):

The two forked (or, more often, branched) sticks must be planted firmly, and far enough apart to be safe from burning. As a precaution I may splash them from time to time with water. The crossbar must be tolerably straight and either green or wet enough not to burn too readily.

If there's even a hint of fire hazard I carefully seal off my fire, no matter which kind, with a circle of stones.

The hottest fire comes from small sticks; the best are those that burn fairly slowly and/or remain glowing for a long time. (See also Rock-Bottom, Tin-Can Kitchen, page 368.)

Another satisfactory cooking method that I occasionally use, especially for frying, is to build a small extension to the stone ring around a big campfire. It's simple, then, to transfer a few glowing embers from the main fire, and to keep replenishing them. If you build a fire in an untouched place, try to keep it small; then you can remove all, or almost all, traces when you leave. Pockmark scars, remember, are a major objection to open fires.

CHIP: Leave-No-Tracers advocate building fires on exposed bedrock or bare ground if possible. A fire cloth of the same reflective woven fabric I use for windscreens may be laid out and covered with a thin layer of sand or mineral dirt. Post-fire, scatter the hearthstones, scorched side down. The ashes and blackened dirt are allowed to cool, thoroughly stirred, and disposed of in some inconspicuous and nonflammable spot, with a drench if possible.

For fire precautions, see page 356.

Warming Fire

On page 31, I told how the unfortunate combination of an ultralight sleeping bag, a curry-based laxative, and a 3°F night forced me to build a quick fire for salvation. Left unsaid was that I had made similar fires for occasional coverless nights out, and have learned in my bones the difference between good warming fires and bad. In the mountains, I've also found the traces of fires built by the Shoshone for hunting and vision seeking: the coals, of course, are long gone, but the rocks remain in a distinctive arrangement, resembling the one I'd evolved by shivery experience.

So I'll pass along this ancient-meets-modern technique. First, get something at your back: a rockface, the back of a sheltering overhang, a big log, or a reflective survival blanket. This keeps the wind off and reflects the fire's heat. Second, find a reflector stone (or stones) and prop it upright 3 to 4 feet from your backdrop. This will direct the radiant heat toward you. Angled wings add reflecting power and shield the fire from wind. I noticed that the Shoshone also piled stones in two wings out from the backdrop, to break the wind and augment the reflector-oven effect. Let's see if I can do this with type:

```
        // === \\
        //   +   \\

    \\              //
    \\    YOU      //
  _____\\_____//_____
```

The fire's heat is directed into the larger enclosure where you sit or crouch, legs open to the warmth. For quick recovery, it's important to heat up not just your torso but also the big blood vessels on the insides of your thighs. It's surprising how much warmth you can get from a rather small fire using this technique. And if you're stranded, a modest heap of wood will keep you warm all night long.

Lighting a fire

COLIN: An outdoorsman's ability to start a fire—anywhere, anytime—is the traditional criterion for judging his competence, and for years I accepted it in an unthinking, uncritical sort of way. But now, if I try to assess my own competence, I find it surprisingly difficult to award a grade. Perhaps that's just because I'm not a prolific lighter of fires. But I suspect that the traditional criterion has outlived its validity.

Every modern outdoorsman should be able to light a fire, but the act is not, it seems to me, a particularly important or testing part of his life. There are exceptions, of course. In cold, wet country where you're always needing a fire for warmth or for drying out clothes, getting one alight quickly is both a testing and an important business. And doubly so in an emergency, without matches. But the generalization stands.

I certainly seem to have survived without undue discomfort on a meager and rather incoherent grab bag of fire-lighting rules that I've made up as I went along:

Carry plenty of matches, and *keep them dry.* (See waxed and also waterproof matches, page 286.) An old tip for helping keep a match alight in a stiff wind (it appears in the November 1915 issue of *Popular Mechanics*) is to cut and turn up the wood just above the striking material: the curled-up shavings will light easily and hold the flame.

What matters most in starting a fire is the kindling (once you've got a small but healthy fire going, almost anything will burn on it). Unless your kindling is very dry indeed and very small, use paper as a starter. If the whole place is dripping wet, look for big stuff that will be dry in the center and from which  you can cut out slivers that are easily split and shaved into serviceable kindling (the dry side of a dead cedar is a good bet, and so are the dead and sheltered twigs at the foot of many conifers), but don't overlook sheltered rock crevices and hollow trees (mice or other small animals will often store small sticks there, and you can rob them with remarkably little guilt). If you anticipate real trouble in starting a fire (if, for example, you had just one hell of a time doing so last night), carry along some kindling from

wood that you dried out on last night's hard-won fire; don't just stuff it
into your pack: wrap it in a plastic bag and keep out the damp air. If necessary, do the same with some fire-dried paper too; in really wet weather
even paper can be hard to light. Some people, when they expect bad conditions, take along some kind of starter: candles (which are dual-purpose
tools), heat tablets, or tubes of stove-priming paste.

If you need a fire to dry your gear out after a storm when every piece
of wood within miles is soaking wet, but you have a stove, the situation
demands precious little ingenuity—especially if your stove is an MSR (see
page 572).

The basic rules for the actual lighting of a fire are simple and fairly
obvious: Have plenty of wood ready in small, graduated sizes. Arrange the
sticks of kindling more or less upright, wigwamwise, so that the flame
will creep up them, preheating as it climbs. Keep the wigwam small.
Apply your match at the bottom. In the first critical moments, carefully
shield the flame from wind. If in doubt what to do with a just-started fire
that looks as though it may go out, leave it alone. If a fire with plenty of
hot coals under it happens to go out, put small sticks or tinder on the
coals, uprightish, and wait. Often the heat will recombust them spontaneously. A mild blowing applied after a decent interval will almost always
convert them into a sudden small inferno.*

With these simple rules I seem to have got by without serious trouble. Oddly enough, the only real difficulties I can recall have been in the
desert. Lighting a fire there is normally simple: you just break off a few
twigs of almost any growth, dead or alive, and it lights. But desert plant
life must, to survive, be adapted to absorb every drop of moisture. And it
does so alive or dead. One sharp shower of rain, and every plant or fragment of plant you break off will feel like damp blotting paper. I vividly
remember one cold and windy evening in Grand Canyon when a day of
intermittent rain had ended with a snowstorm. At dusk I found a shallow
rock overhang that offered shelter from both wind and snow but fell
appreciably short of coziness. Tired and damp and cold after a long day, I
wanted a fire more than anything else. But every piece of wood I could
find under the thin blanket of snow was soggy, clean through. I made a
few abortive attempts at starting a fire with the driest wood, but even the

---

*"In the old *Outing* magazine of about 1898 or 1899," writes a reader who was 15 or 16
at that time, "Stewart Edward White, one of the most experienced hunters and campers, gave
a lot of sound tips. I made one of his *Exhilarators* and used it to start balky fires successfully for
many years. It's a little blowtorch, made from a piece of small brass tubing, flattened out at
one end, and the other inserted in a rubber tube about 3 feet long. Blow through it to make
balky wood burn or to expedite a blaze."

For reasons you might be carrying a piece of tubing, see page 254.

scraps of paper from my pocket did little more than smolder. Because I was running desperately short of white gas I couldn't afford to use my stove as wood drier. But eventually I found the fairly thick stem of a cactuslike century plant or agave and managed to whittle some shreds of dry kindling from its center. It lit the first time, and I spent a cheerful and almost luxuriously warm evening.

It's only common sense to site a fire so that the smoke from it will blow away from your campsite—but it is also common sense to expect that the moment you light the fire the wind will reverse itself. Objective research would probably confirm the existence of something more statistically verifiable behind this expectation than the orneriness of inanimate objects: campfires tend to be lit around dusk, and winds tend to change direction at that time, particularly in mountain country.

Some people speak learnedly about the virtues of different firewoods. Frankly, I know almost none by name. But it doesn't seem to matter too much. It's no doubt more efficient to know at a glance the burning properties of each kind of wood you find; but you have only to heft a piece of dead wood to get a good idea of how it will burn. Generally speaking, light wood tends to catch easily and burn fast. Heavy wood will last well, though the heaviest may be the devil to get started, even in a roaring blaze.

I have never, thank God, had to produce a flame without matches. I haven't even given the matter the thought it deserves. The magnifying glass that I carry primarily for other purposes (page 287) is always there, but I have never, in spite of intermittent good resolves, actually tried it out. (For other emergency means, see page 352.) A reader suggests that a detachable camera lens might do a good job. Ditto binoculars. But the uncomfortable fact is that the day on which you need a fire most desperately is likely to be wet and cold, and even a camera lens would then be about as useful as a station wagon in outer space. So would the time-honored recipe of "rubbing two Boy Scouts together."

In an emergency it's theoretically possible to do the trick with a piece of string or bootlace that you wrap around a rotator of a stick whose end is held in a depression in a slab of wood. The idea is to twirl the stick fast enough and long enough to create by friction enough heat to ignite some scraps of tinder dropped into the depression. Simple, primitive men certainly started fires this way; but I have an idea that we clever bastards might find it extraordinarily difficult.

To be honest, I'm singularly unimpressed by the woodsy fanatic who's rich in this kind of caveman lore, especially if he'll pass it all on at the drop of a snowflake. I always suspect that he'll turn out to be the sort of man who under actual field conditions can stop almost anywhere, any time, and have a pot of water on the very brink of boiling within 2 hours and 35 minutes—provided it isn't actually raining and he has plenty of matches. But maybe you'd be right to chalk my cynicism up to plain jealousy.*

CHIP: In the 1970s, I learned to kindle fires using a "steel" (made from a round file, heated and hammered into a crescent) and a chip of flint or chert. It's not hard to strike a good spark—the trick is to catch it in good tinder. The best is carbonized cotton cloth (heated to blackness in a metal shoe-polish tin with a hole punched in the lid), but #0000 steel wool is also great. Natural tinder should be dry and fine-textured: the fibrous bark of sagebrush, juniper, or other resinous plants can be rubbed between your hands and then curled into a nest. Rabbitbrush tops are stunningly flammable. Around the fine tinder, you wrap a layer of coarser stuff. Have small sticks, etc. stockpiled. When the spark catches, blow it into flame, then jackstraw fine twigs and such until you have a nice little blaze. (Just remember not to brag up your skills.)

When I was hitchhiking through the Navajo Nation, a friendly old gentleman offered to show me the "traditional firestarting method." Whereupon he led me to a nearby trash pile, caught up the bottom of a shattered bottle, and focused it on a scrap of paper: bingo. For truly traditional methods, consult primitive survival guides.

Fire hazards

COLIN: These days the way you guard and leave your fire (on those occasions you judge it reasonable to light one) may well be a more valid criterion for judging your outdoor competence than the way you start one. A deliberately apprehensive common sense is your best guide. But here are some general rules, based on those laid down by the Forest Service:

- Never build a fire on deep litter, such as pine needles. It can smolder for days, then erupt into a catastrophic forest blaze.
- Clear all inflammable organic material from an area appreciably bigger than your fire, scraping right down to bare earth. (This destructive suggestion is unacceptable in much of today's tramped-over wilderness; but the need for it as a safety measure is another reason for forgoing fires.)

*At least one reader shares my cynicism. She writes:

"A terribly procedure-conscious walker from Stanford once told me: 'One evening in the Sierras, I lighted a fire in a snowstorm WITH ONLY ONE MATCH!'

"'Yes,' said his long-suffering wife. 'And it only took him an hour and twenty minutes to prepare it.'

"I call this sort of nonsense 'One-Match Machismo.' "

- Generally speaking, and where possible, build a ring of stones around your fire. It will contain the ash and considerably reduce the chances of spread.
- Never leave a fire unattended.
- Where a fire hazard exists, do not build a fire on a windy day.
- Avoid wood that generates a lot of sparks. The sparks can start fires in surrounding vegetation and your sleeping bag.
- Above all, *don't just put your fire out—kill it, dead.* Stir the ashes, deep and thoroughly, even if the fire seems to have been out for hours. Then douse it with dirt and water. You can safely stop when it's so doused you could take a swim in it.

Oddly enough, you can forgo such precautions in most kinds of desert—though not all (see Chip's footnote). The place is curiously immune to arson. I have only once seen an extensive "burn" in treeless desert. Individual bushes may catch fire rather easily, but vegetation is so widely spaced (a necessary adaptation to acute moisture shortage) that the fire rarely spreads. The heat and dryness of deserts would seem sure to cause fires in mass-inflammable vegetation, so perhaps susceptible species have been selected out by the natural process of destruction by fire.*

General fire precautions

Cultivate the habit of breaking all matches in two before you throw them away. The idea is not that half a match is much less dangerous than a whole one, but that the breaking makes you aware of the match and conscious of any lingering flame or heat. Bookmatches are rather difficult to break, but as I use mine only for fires or the stove I always put used matches into the former or under the latter.

The big match danger comes from smokers (I'm now two decades into my third Fifty-Year Trial Abstention Plan, and with this refurbished halo tilted rakishly over my bald crown, I feel comfortably smug). In some critical fire areas you're forbidden to carry cigarettes at certain times of year. In many forests you're not allowed to smoke while on the move, and can do so only on a site with at least a 3-foot clearance all around—such as a bare rock or a broad trail. Increasingly, smoking is restricted to posted locations that have been specially cleared. Even there, make absolutely sure you put your cigarette stub OUT. Soak it in water, or pull it

---

*CHIP: The invasion of cheatgrass and other highly flammable exotics, as a result of overgrazing, has radically altered this former fireproofness in much of the arid West. And each year, carelessly set fires contribute to the further spread of cheatgrass and other fire-dependent annuals. The fastidious practice of burning used toilet paper is a frequent cause—take care.

to shreds. If you doubt the necessity of following such irritating rules to the letter, make yourself go and see the corpse of a recently burned forest.

See also Garbage, next page.

THE KITCHEN IN ACTION
Packaging and packing

My kitchen travels, almost exclusively, in plastic bags. The most useful sizes are extra-small (snack size), small (sandwich size), medium (1-gallon capacity), and capacious (thick, pillow-size trash bags or the kind you can get from machines in some Laundromats—or, best of all, the heavy, translucent kind in which your butcher maybe gets his offal). Before knotting small and medium-size bags with food in them, expel most of the air. And secure them as high as possible, so that bag and contents can adjust to external pressures and occupy the minimum and most convenient space. To avoid frustration, knot bags loosely. If bags are too full for knotting, secure with a rubber band. Zip-top plastic bags have their uses too—especially the newer slide-lock type.

For heat-seal plastic bags, less permeable than the standard polyethylene kind, see page 222.*

Into the extra-small snack bags go my herbs and spices, spare salt, and bookmatches; also, if carried, can opener and stove-nozzle cleaner. Just about everything else goes into small or medium-size bags (plain open-ended or zip-top or slide-lock): dry cereal mixture (emptied from its heavy cardboard box); soup and gravy packages (they tend to split open); powdered milk packages (they split too, and you can picture, I'm sure, a faintly milk-coated kitchen on a rainy day); each day's dinner that is not a store-bought package but is instead my own make-up of grain or vegetables plus meat package or bar and perhaps sauce; the complete collection of very small bags containing herbs and spices; the various trail snacks that travel in my "nibble" pocket; trail snacks for the rest of the week; tea bags; fruit-drink mixes; and margarine container (always mildly greasy). Also, sometimes, the stove—though I now tend to use a stuff sack. The more rebellious items (cereal, soups, margarine, milk, chocolate) get double-bag protection. The blackened frying pan, if it comes along, slips inside two medium-large bags.

---

*CHIP: For perishables, I've adopted reusable Evert-Fresh bags, which allow gases that promote decomposition to escape and prevent moisture buildup. They make a surprising difference. Available in various handy-home catalogs, they're made by Evert-Fresh, P.O. Box 540974, Houston TX 77254-0974, 713-529-4593. The small size is most useful for backpacking.

All the food, bagged and unbagged, is then divided between two pillow-size bags. Into one bag goes everything needed for the current day—plus, perhaps, an extra dinner, so that I have a last-minute choice. I try to keep the top of the milk squirter pointed in toward the center of the bag, so that it doesn't keep poking holes in the plastic. Into the other bag goes the balance of the week's rations. (If you put the whole lot into one bag you'll never be able to find what you want.) Because it's difficult to find pillow-size bags that are strong enough you may have to use doubled bags—at least for the much-handled day's-ration bag. Once a day I choose the morrow's menu and transfer the rations (page 364).

Into one of the pack's upper outside pockets (my nibble pocket) go the between-meals trail snacks (page 212) and one mealworthy "pemmican" bar—so that if there's no time to stop for a regular lunch I need not unpack the main food.

Into one of the lower sidepockets go my baby-feeder water bottle (page 262), a package of fruit-drink mix, and water-purifying tablets.

Large canteens travel in the main compartment—loaded back or front, high or low, haphazardly or meticulously, according to whether full or empty, needed next halt or next day, requiring or not requiring insulation from hot sun (page 261).

The nesting cooking pots, or the single pot, travel in a large plastic bag, folded around so that no residual water can escape. Well, not much, anyway. My spoon and cup normally go inside the inner pot, though in well-watered country I often carried the cup ready for use on a belt clip. Pre-*Giardia,* that is. When space is tight the stove may, if it fits, travel inside the pot.

Garbage

The wilderness litter problem has reached grotesque proportions, and food wrappings are the most obvious—though not always most serious—source. No matter how carefully you select food that comes in burnable packages, you'll always find small items that can't be burned. And burying is no solution to litter: animals will soon smell the adhering food and dig it up. I stow all unburnable garbage (except tea bags, which I dismember and broadcast in bushes) in doubled, medium-size plastic bags that travel, easily get-at-able, in the cover pocket of the pack. Into these bags go empty foil wrappers from freeze-dried foods, soups, meat products, milk, and the like. Also used plastic bags, half-burned matches (usually), and, on the rare occasions I use them, cans. (Some people recommend burning cans before packing them out, to remove adhering food.) For those who smoke, add cigarette butts—especially if filter-tipped—to this list. I may fill several double-bagged garbage dumps, but the total weight rarely amounts to much. I've checked three times, with standard menus. Once, after 10 days in the mountains, my garbage totaled out at 12 oz.; another time, at the end of 7 desert days, at 9 oz.; and after another 7-day trip, at only 4 oz. A few ranger stations now provide ingoing backpackers with plastic garbage bags (which tend to be unnecessarily huge).*

For disposal of stove cartridges, see page 306.

I used to feel nothing but contempt for those who desecrate the countryside with litter. But I'm uncomfortably aware that once, in a mild alcoholic haze and pleasantly provocative company, I heaved an empty wine bottle out onto the virgin desert sand—and did it maliciously, with delight, with satisfaction. Like a good, rabid anti-litter man, I retrieved the bottle later. But the memory is still there, and although I continue to look on litterlouts with contempt and loathing I can in my more charitable moments feel a twinge of understanding. But only in the more charitable moments.

For further sermons, see pages 431 and 760.

A SAMPLE DAY IN THE KITCHEN**

(Not to mention the bedroom, and most other departments too. Meticulously applicable only to those who operate on the Fletcher in-sleeping-bag culinary system; but embodying, I hope, suggestions useful to those who for good—or merely conservative—reasons persist in getting out of bed to cook.)

Something stirs inside you, and you half-open one eye. Stars and blackness, nothing more. You close the eye. But the something keeps on stirring, and after a moment you slide another inch toward consciousness

---

*CHIP: For those areas where our food scraps and excretory wastes must be packed out, you can build a poop tube out of PVC pipe. Also, VauDe Sports makes a leakproof scat bag with a roll closure at both ends to allow a thorough cleanout. See page 702.

**COLIN: There are several similarities here to an account in *The Man Who Walked Through Time* (pages 19–24) of how I prepared an evening meal. Because the pith of this sample day is method, not details of diet, I've allowed the simple dishes I described in the original *Walker* to stand. And although I now tend to take one cooking pot rather than two, I've retained the older and rather easier bipottal system. Ditto, mostly, with clothing. The only serious amendment I might have made was to have you (traveling this sample day under the name Fletcher) respond to such a chilly morning by putting on hat or even balaclava very much earlier. You would probably, in fact, have been wearing the balaclava all night. These changes have been brought about by the passing of further years and residual hair.

Note that there are no bears in our chosen land.

There is one other thing. In the years since I wrote this section I've been increasingly impressed by the broad range of practices that exists among even highly experienced back-

and turn your head to the east and reopen the eye. It's there all right, a pale blue backing to the distant peaks. You sigh, pull up one arm inside the mummy bag, and check that the luminous hands of your watch say five o'clock.

After a decent interval you loosen the drawstrings of the mummy bag so that there's just enough room for you to slip on the shirt (which has been coiled around your shoulders all night, keeping the draft off) and the down jacket (which you've been lying on). Then, still half-cocooned in the mummy bag, you sit up, reach back into the pack (which is propped up against the staff, just behind your head), and take out your shorts (which are waiting on top of everything else) and the pillow-size bag containing the day's rations (which is just underneath the shorts). From the ticket pocket of the shorts you fumble out bookmatches and an empty Lipton teabag wrapper. You stuff the shorts down into the mummy bag to warm. Next you take the flashlight out of one of your boots (which are standing just off to the left of the sleeping pad). Then you put the teabag wrapper down in the little patch you cleared for the stove last night (on the right side of the bed, because the wind was blowing from the left last night; and very close to the groundsheet so that you don't have to stretch). You set the teabag wrapper alight and hold the stove (which is the Svea) by its handle with the base of the bowl just above the burning paper. Soon you see in the beam of the flashlight that gasoline is welling up from the nozzle. You put the stove down on the teabag wrapper, snuffing out the flame. Gasoline seeps down the generator of the stove and into the little depression in the bowl that encircles the base of the generator. When the depres-

---

packers. The differences embrace almost every sector, but quite a few emerge in the ground covered in the next few pages.

Instead of taking a long lunch, as I tend to, and then walking in the cool of evening, most people, most days, seem to make lunch a biggish snack and to camp early and take their rest or recreation then.

Most people probably still do not eat dinner and breakfast while semi-cocooned in their sleeping bags, as I do—though I've had some warm letters from converts.

One reader reports a first-thing-in-the-morning system that works well for him. At night he arranges everything for a quick getaway from camp. At first light he gets up without food, walks "for an hour or so until the sun comes up or I fully wake up," then has a leisurely breakfast. "This," he says, "breaks up the morning pretty good."

Then there was the very experienced backpacker who mentioned the other day that he never carried a bandanna. "But what do you use as a potholder, for example?" I asked. "A sock," he said. "Always have done."

And so it goes on. There's a huge range of viable variations. The important thing to remember is that none of them—well, almost none of them—is either "good" or "bad." If it suits you, it suits you.

So just bear in mind as you read the next few pages that all you're learning is what suits me.

sion is full you close the stove valve and ignite the gasoline. When it has almost burned away you reopen the valve. If you time it dead right the last guttering flame ignites the jet. Otherwise you light it with another match. The stove roars healthily, almost waking you up.

You check that the roaring stove is standing firm, then reach out for the larger of the cooking pots (which you half-filled with water after dinner last night—because you know what you're like in the morning—and which spent the night back near the pack, off to one side, where no restless movement of your body could possibly knock it over). You put the pot on the stove, with its lid inverted. Next you put on your hat (which was hanging by its chin band from the top of the packframe) because you are now conscious enough to feel chilly on the back of your head where there used to be plenty of hair. Then you reach out for the smaller cooking pot (which is also back in safety beside the pack, and in which you last night put two ounces of dehydrated fruit cocktail and a shade more water than was necessary to reconstitute it). You remove the cup from inside this pot (it stayed clean there overnight) and put it ready on the stove-cover platform (which is still beside the stove, where you used it for dinner last night). You leave the spoon in the pot (it too stayed clean and safe there overnight). You pour a little more water into the pot from a canteen, squirt in some milk powder (the squirter stood all night beside the pot), stir, and add about two ounces of cereal mix. Then you lean back against the pack, still warm and comfortable in the mummy bag (the hood tapes of which you retighten if necessary, just below your armpits) and begin to eat the fruit-and-cereal mixture. The pale blue band along the eastern horizon broadens.

Soon—without needing to use the flashlight now—you see steam jetting out from the pot on the stove. You remove the pot, lift the lid by its exposed rim (using a bandanna to insulate your hand), and swing-flip one tea bag inside. (You had put the tea bag ready on top of the pot at the same time as you took the cereal out of the day's-ration bag.) You leave the label hanging outside the pot so that later, when the tea is strong enough, you can lift the bag out. Then you turn off the stove. And suddenly the world is very quiet and very beautiful, and for the first time that morning you really look at the silhouetted peaks and at the shadows that are the valleys. You swirl the teapot a couple of times to suffuse the tea, take a few more mouthfuls of fruit-and-cereal, then pour a cupful of tea, squirt-add milk and perhaps spoon in a little sugar (the sugar container also spent the night beside the pots), and take the first luxurious sip. Warmth flows down your throat, spreads outward. Your brain responds. Still sluggishly, it takes another step toward full focus.

And so, sitting there at ease, leaning back against the pack, you eat breakfast. You eat it fairly fast today, because you have 20 miles to go and by eleven o'clock it will be hot. You pour a second cup of tea, and it helps too. Spoonful by spoonful, you eat the fruit-and-cereal. It tastes good. When it's finished you chew a stick of beef jerky. And all the time the world and the day are unfolding above and below and around you. The light eases from gray toward blue. The valleys begin to emerge from their shadow, the peaks to gain a third dimension. The night, you realize, has already slipped away.

Don't let the menu deceive you: there is no better kind of breakfast.

When the meal is over you wash up rather sketchily (there's plenty of water, but time presses). You rebag the food and utensils and stove and stow them away in the pack. The light moves on from blue toward pink. Still inside the mummy bag, you put on your shorts. And (because this is a day in a book) you time it just right. The sun moves majestically up from behind those distant peaks, exploding the blue and the pink into gold, at the very moment you need its warmth—at the very moment that the time arrives for you to pluck up your courage and forsake the mummy bag and put on socks and boots. Ten minutes later you're walking. Another half hour and you're wide awake.*

(This is only a sample morning, of course—a not-too-cold morning on which you know there is a hot and fairly long day ahead. If the night had been really cold, or the dew so heavy that it soaked the mummy bag and everything else, you would probably have waited for the sun to make the world bearable or to dry out all that extra and unnecessary load of water. If, on the other hand, the day promised to be horribly long, or its noonday heat burningly hot, you would have set the something to stir inside you even earlier—probably suffering a restless night thereby, unless you are a more efficient alarm clock than I am or carry a mechanical one of some sort—and would have finished breakfast in time to start walking as soon as it was light enough to do so safely. By contrast, this might have been a rest day. Then you would simply have dozed until you got tired of dozing, and afterward made breakfast—or have woken yourself up first by diving into lake or river. But whatever the variations— unless you decided to catch fish for breakfast and succeeded—the basic food theme would have remained very much the same.)

You walk all morning, following a trail that twists along beside a pure, rushing mountain creek. Every hour you halt for 10 minutes. At every halt you take the cup from the belt clip at your waist and dip it into the creek and drink as much of the sensuously cool water as you want. (Let

---

*Such perfect timing is not, I find, restricted to sample days in books. One reader, whose sole mentor for his first backpack trip was apparently an earlier edition of this book, reports that on his first morning, at precisely the moment he was ready to emerge from his sleeping bag, the sun rose.

us assume that this is one of those rare places in which you can still drink safely from creeks.) And at every halt—except perhaps the first, when breakfast is still adequately with you—you take one or more trail-snack bags out of the nibble pocket and munch a few delicacies. At each succeeding halt you tend to eat rather more; but without giving the matter much direct thought you ration against the hours ahead. In midmorning a stick of beef jerky helps replenish the protein supply. Later you boost the quickly available energy, and the fats too, with a piece of chocolate. At the last couple of halts you add candies to the menu.

Just after noon you stop for lunch. You choose the place carefully—almost more carefully than the site for a night camp, because you'll spend more waking hours there. You most often organize the day with a long midday halt, not only because it means that you avoid walking through the worst of the heat but also because you've found noon a more comfortable and rewarding time than late evening to swim and wash and launder and doze and read and write notes and dream and mosey around looking at rocks and stones and fish and lizards and sand flies and trees and panoramas and cloud shadows and all the other important things. A long lunch halt also means that you split the day's effort into two slabs, with a good long rest in between. Come to think of it, perhaps this after all is the really critical factor.

Anyway, you choose your lunch site carefully. You find a perfect place, in a shady hollow beside the creek, to prop up the pack and roll out the groundsheet and then the sleeping pad (and maybe, in cooler weather, even the mummy bag), and within three minutes of halting you have a setup virtually identical to the one you woke up in that morning.

The soup of the day is mushroom. The directions could hardly be simpler: "Empty the contents into 1 liter (4 measuring cups) of hot water and bring to the boil. Cover and simmer for 5–10 minutes." So you light the stove and boil as much water as you know from experience you need for soup (what *you* need, not necessarily 4 measuring cups). You stir in the soup powder, add a smidgen of thyme (after rubbing it lightly in the palm of your hand), lay the wundergauze over the stove's burner, replace the pot cover at a very slight tilt so that the simmering soup won't boil over, reduce the heat as far as it will go (a mildly delicate business), and then lie back and stretch out, tiredly but luxuriously. After five minutes you add a dollop of margarine to the soup, stir, and pour out the first cupful. You leave the rest simmering. When you pour the second cup you turn off the stove and put the pot in the warmest place around—a patch of dry, sandy soil that happens to lie in a shaft of sunlight. Within half an hour of halting you've finished the soup and dropped off into a catnap.

When you wake up you wash all pots and utensils—thoroughly now, because there's time as well as water. You do so well away from the creek, to avoid polluting it. You use sand as a scourer, grass or Miracloth as a cleaning cloth, biodegradable detergent as detergent, and the creek for rinsing. (If the pots had looked very dirty and you'd been "out" for a long time, or if an upset stomach had made you suspicious about cleanliness, you might—if there was fuel to spare—have put spoon and cup into the small pot, and the small pot and some water into the big pot, and boil-sterilized the whole caboosh. Or, more probably, you would combine this operation with making tea later.)

Next you do a couple of chores that you've made more or less automatic action after lunch so that you won't overlook them. You decide on the menu for the next 24 hours and make the necessary transfers from bulk-ration bag to current-day's bag—including the refilling from the bagged reserve of the containers of milk (an everyday chore) and salt (once, in midweek). You also replenish the nibble pocket with trail snacks. If necessary you put a new book of matches in a ticket pocket of your shorts or long pants or in a sidepocket of your jacket. (You carry a book in each.)

Finally, you refill the stove.

(Naturally, it doesn't matter much what time of day you choose to do these chores. In winter, for example, when the days are short, you'll probably just snatch a quick lunch or succession of snacks and will do the reapportionment and refilling during the early hours of the long, long darkness. But on each trip you try to get into the habit of doing the chores at about the same time each day, because you know that otherwise you may find yourself fumbling down into the pack for the bulk-food bag in the middle of a meal, and at the same moment hear the dying bleat of an almost empty stove.)

For the next two or three or four or even five hours you either do some of the many make-and-mend chores that always keep piling up (washing, laundering, writing notes, and so on), or you mosey around and attend to those important matters that you came for (rocks, lizards, cloud shadows), or you simply sit and contemplate. Or you devote the time to a combination of all these things. But eventually, when you know you ought to be walking again within half an hour, you brew up a sizable pot of tea (this particular day, remember, you too are walking on a British passport). And because there are still four hours to darkness and night camp and dinner, you chew a sampling of trail snacks or perhaps serve yourself some cold cereal. Then you pack everything away, hoist up the pack, and start walking—leaving behind as the only signs of occupation a rectangle of crushed grass that will recover within hours and, where the stove stood, a tiny circle that you manage to conceal anyway by pulling the grass stems together. These are the only signs you leave at any of your campsites, day or overnight.

You find yourself walking in desert now (a shade miraculously, it's true, but it suits our book purposes better to have it happen that way), and it is very hot. Because you expect to find no more water until you come to a spring about noon the following day, you've filled all six quart canteens you brought with you. Now you go easy on the water. You still drink as well as munch at every hourly halt. And you drink enough. But only just enough. Enough, that is, to take the edge off any emerging hint of thirst. At the first couple of halts this blunting process calls for only a very small sip or two. Later you need a little more. Always, before you swallow the precious liquid, you swirl it around your mouth to wash away the dryness and the scum. And sometimes you hold it in your mouth as long as possible so that it seeps bit by bit down your throat and gives long, delicious minutes of thirst-quenching sensation.

One canteen must always be nonfumble available at halts but, because direct sunlight would quickly turn its water tepid, you put it inside the pack—on top, but insulated by your jacket.

With an hour to go to darkness, and a promise already there of the coolness that will come when the sun drops behind the parched, encircling hills, you begin to feel tired—not so much muscle-weary as plain running out of energy. So at the hourly halt you pour some water into either your cup or the lid of one cooking pot, squirt-add milk, and pour in some cereal mixture. (Looked at objectively, this cereal snack has always seemed a highly inefficient business. It ought to be enough to take a booster bonus from the nibble pocket. But on the few long, hard days that such tiredness hits you, the cereal snack seems to work better.)

At this final precamp halt you empty into the inner cooking pot the dehydrated beans and mixed vegetables that are on the day's dinner menu (if they're the old, recalcitrant kind that need presoaking or prolonged cooking) and add salt and just enough water to reconstitute them. (Presoaked like this, they cook in 10 minutes rather than half an hour.) You know from experience how much water to add. It is surprisingly little: barely enough to cover the food. You add as little as possible, to reduce the danger of spillage, and from now on, when you take the pack off, you're careful to keep it upright.

You walk until it is too dark to go on (keeping a canny rattlesnake watch during the last hour, because this is their time of day—see page 711). You camp in any convenient place that's level enough, though it's a kitchen advantage, stovewise, to have adequate shelter from desert winds (usually down canyons at night).

Dinner is the main meal of the day but it's very simple to prepare. It has to be. You're tired now. And because the rising sun will be coercing you on your way again in less than eight hours you don't want to waste time. So as soon as you halt you roll out the groundsheet and pad and

sleeping bag and sit thankfully down and set up the kitchen just as you did last night and at lunchtime, except that because of a hump in the ground and a gentle but growing crosswind you find it expedient to put everything on the other side of the bed. Even before you take off your boots you empty the already soft vegetables out of the small pot into the big one, scraping the stickily reluctant scraps out with the spoon and swirling the small pot clean with the water you're going to need to cook the meal anyway. You add a little or a lot of water, according to whether you fancy tonight's stew in the form of a near-soup or an off-putty goo. (Only experience will teach you how much water achieves what consistency. For painless experience, start with near-soups that won't burn, and then work down toward goo. Your methods are rough-and-ready, so you will from time to time add the pleasures of surprise to those of variety.) You light the stove (using the flashlight to check when the gasoline wells up) and put the big pot on it, uncovered. Then you crumble one meat bar onto the vegetables and sprinkle in about one-fifth of a package of oxtail soup and a couple of shakes of pepper and a healthy dose of hand-rubbed oregano. You stir and cover. Next you take off your boots and put them within easy reach, on the opposite side of the bed from the kitchen, and put your socks in one of the boots with the sweaty lower portions hanging outside to dry. Then, if you feel they need it, you anoint your feet with rubbing alcohol, taking care to keep it well away from the stove. (If you're using an air mattress or inflatable pad, you inflate it at this stage: you never leave that breath-demanding chore until after dinner.)

At this point steam issues from the stew pot. You reduce the heat to dead-low or thereabouts (taking care not to turn the stove off in the process), lay the wundergauze across the burner, stir the compound a couple of times, inhale appreciatively, and replace the cover. While dinner simmers toward fruition you empty two ounces of dehydrated peaches and a little water into the small cooking pot and put it ready for breakfast, up alongside the pack, out of harm's way. Then you jot down a few thoughts in your notebook, stir the stew and sample it, find the beans are not quite soft yet. So you study the map and worry a bit about the morning's route, put map and pen and pencil and eyeglasses and thermometer into the second bedside boot, take off your shorts, and slide halfway down into the mummy bag out of the rapidly rising wind, and stir the stew again and find all ready. You pour-and-spoon out a cupful, leaving the balance on the stove because the wind is distinctly cool now. And then, leaning comfortably back against the pack and watching the sky and the black peaks meld, you eat, cupful by cupful, your dinner. You finish it—just. Then you spoon-scrape out every last possible fragment and polish-clean the pot and cup and spoon with your Miracloth or, failing that, a piece of toilet paper. If you use toilet paper you put it under the stove so that you can burn it in the morning. Then you put the cup and spoon into the breakfast-readied small pot, pour the morning tea water into the big pot, set the big pot alongside the small one and the sugar and milk containers alongside them both, put the current day's-ration bag into the pack (where it's mildly safe from mice and their night allies) and your shorts on top of it, lean one canteen against the boots so that you can reach out and grasp it during the night without doing more than loosen the mummy-bag drawstring, zipper and drawstring yourself into the bag, wind your watch, belch once, remind yourself what time you want the something inside you to stir in the morning, and go to sleep.*

---

*The elapsed time between halting and going to sleep will obviously vary with many factors, including how eager you are to get to sleep. It's difficult to give meaningful average times. You just don't measure such things very often. The only time I remember doing so was under conditions markedly similar to those of our sample evening. I was in no particular hurry, but I didn't dally. And I happened to notice as I wound my watch that it was exactly 40 minutes since I'd halted.

THE KITCHEN IN ACTION UNDER SPECIAL CONDITIONS

Rock-bottom, tin-can kitchen

Over the years I've several times met conditions that demanded and also permitted a radically simplified kitchen. The demands concerned weight: I wanted or needed to pare every eliminable ounce, down beyond my normal comfort requirements. The permission concerned fires: in the country I'd be walking through it had to be easy and ethical and preferably legal to build very small open fires any place I camped.

In one case I wanted to walk for 10 days along a desert mountain range that offered no possibility of replenishing food stocks but every chance that I'd at times need to carry 2 gallons of water. Faced with the prospect of a house that would put 25 lbs. of food and 16 lbs. of water on my back before I even began to install the standard furnishings, I cast around for ways to cut the load. Careful inquiries about the mountains revealed, as I'd expected, that the country I'd be walking through abounded with little sticks, presented no fire hazard at that time of year, and was so little traveled that small fire scars would probably heal before being seen by human eyes. I therefore opted for a rock-bottom, tin-can kitchen. I cast out my cooking pots and stove, and also the two gasoline containers (one of them half full) required for 10 days' stove cooking. That saved me 4.5 lbs. As sole cooking utensil I took an ordinary medium-size tin can with its top removed and a wire handle threaded through two holes punched with a nail near the carefully tamped-down rim. Total weight: 2 oz. The simplified menu (page 228) meant a saving of about 1.5 oz. a day, or a pound for the 10 days; and the simpler packaging meant a further saving of at least half a pound. Total saving: 6 lbs.—which feels like a hell of a lot, I assure you, when it means around 54 lbs. on your back

instead of 60. Anyway, it turned out to be a rewarding, unbackbreaking 10 days, and I didn't regret my decision.

Another time, conditions were different. I was planning one of my sudden, periodic, spur-of-the-moment, two- or three-day therapeutic disappearances into some local hills in which you are always, like it or not, going uphill or down. Mostly, I'm content to take it easy in there. But on that occasion I for some reason felt within me the urge to walk fast and, compared with the normal Fletcher-amble, furiously. So to keep my load down I again opted for my tin-can kitchen. And again it worked: I indeed walked fast and far and furious, reveling in the light load, and emerged amply restored. (Note: Both these trips took place before the days of ultra-light titanium cooking gear, but our wider current options don't undermine the general principle.)

The fire for a rock-bottom, tin-can kitchen should be small and concentrated, so that when you've covered your traces Sherlock Holmes would be hard put to discover you'd passed that way. You want fast, short-lived heat, so you use only very small sticks. And to make full use of their heat you build them up around the sides of the can.

A Wisconsin reader writes that he sometimes gives "a new twist" to the rock-bottom, tin-can kitchen by taking along a "stove" for firewood—made from a 1-pound tin can.

Clearly, any tin-can kitchen can be modified back toward "normalcy" in various ways to meet different conditions or wants.

High altitude

At sea level, water boils at 212°F / 100°C. But the boiling point falls for every rise in elevation (see table, page 239). When the water contains salt or other impurities the boiling point rises slightly. Marked weather changes, with shifts in barometric pressure, may raise or lower it.

As most outdoor cooking depends on the boiling point of water, food therefore takes longer to cook at high altitudes than at sea level. With my simple menus, and at the maximum elevations I normally reach (little over 14,000 feet), I pay almost no attention to the differences. I just sample and go by the taste and texture. But with more complicated dishes you should probably work out some kind of graduated compensation. The only time I ever noted any figures was at 14,246 feet. There, an egg boiled for 10 minutes turned out to be still slightly underdone. It would be difficult, I imagine, to find a more superbly useless item of information.

For pressure cookers, see page 272; for the vagaries of appetite at high altitude, page 191; of stoves, page 309.

In snow

CHIP: When I did fieldwork in Wyoming's Wind River Range, I camped quite often at high altitudes in white winter. The result is that I've come to regard snow not as an implacable enemy but rather a beautiful, if changeable, friend. For every commonly remarked disadvantage of snow there's a corresponding benefit. But it takes a certain degree of experience and attitude adjustment to discover the marvels of snow camping—and, like sex, the proof is in the performance.

You might have noticed that a lot of references to snow melting have crept into this book, which attests to its central importance in my life outdoors. For this, the salient characteristic is water content. Rocky Mountain powder snow is 10 percent or less water by volume, heavy maritime snow is about 50 percent or more, while glacial ice is 95 percent or more, depending on how many air bubbles remain. Obviously, the higher the water content, the less often you have to reload the pot. But the real hurdle is the state change (see page 309) since pushing solid water over that 1° hump to liquidity takes an astonishing 80 calories per gram. So even in the depth of winter, finding open water saves both time and fuel. Given that snow-covered stream banks offer undependable footing, it may also involve lowering pots on a string or ski-pole basket. In spring, when the snow is thawing, you can dig a pit and scoop liquid water from the bottom of the snowpack.

But otherwise, it helps to concentrate the water content. This can be gracefully combined with the labor of packing a tent site or digging a snow cave (only an idiot snow-camps without a shovel). After stomping out a tent platform, Zen back and let it *sinter* (a process whereby snow crystals that have been tumbled freeze together). Set up the tent and then excavate a skank pit (or foot well, among the civilized) at the entrance, so you can enter or exit standing. Stockpile the snow blocks you cut from the skank pit (or snow cave) in arm's reach, carving them neatly with the shovel into sub-fist-size blockettes. This is your water store, already concentrated by packing and sintering. Blocks of snow are also surprisingly good for mopping up spills in the tent. If the local snow looks dirty, shop around. But if you're boiling the water, small organic chunks won't hurt you, and might contain added nutrients. (Obviously, by mutual agreement, you should spot your pissing ground elsewhere.) Having a nice pyramid of snow blocks gives you the luxury of debooting and cocooning, with an uninterrupted melt.

Set up the stove near enough to be reached without exiting the tent—I sometimes carve out a little balcony in the skank pit, to get it out of the wind. You can also stack a protective half circle of snow blocks. Use a shovel blade or reflective base (page 347) under the stove. If you have a hanging stove, suspend it from a limb or a ski tip. (Since, even with the stove outside, fumes can fill up the tent, always unzip windows and roof vent partway.) Despite cooking in vestibules a lot, I seldom—more like never—cook inside a tent.

For parties, it's best to have one person act as undisputed stovemeister. Stovemeister duty involves refueling, priming, adjusting, and actively replenishing the pot with snow blocks to make full use of the heat. Once boilage is achieved, shift a new pot of packed and sintered snow immediately onto the flame (a splash of water speeds things up) or quickly replenish the first one. Keep the stove at full roar, since condensation drips can extinguish a low flame.

Before shutting down the stove, I always replenish the water bottles. You can tuck a warm bottle, temporarily, in the foot of your sleeping bag to promote optimum toe-temps. In deep cold, if you keep a tightly capped water bottle in your sleeping bag you can be assured of precious nighttime sips. I've insulated plain water bottles with Ensolite or Reflectix (page 451) and duct tape, and there are various insulated bottles and covers to be had. In moderate temperatures, a water bottle can be tucked under the edge of your bag, over the pad.

Once dinner, hot drinks, washup, and bottle filling are accomplished, shut off the stove and set on a last pot of snow to soak up residual heat. In the dim blue bitter morn, a pot of ice melts more quickly than fluffy, finger-biting snow.

On waking, drink several healthy swallows from your water bottle to start your body up, ignite the stove, and pour the rest into the icy pot.

Winter cooking is not qualitatively different than in other seasons. But you'll find yourself wanting more calories, either from fat or from the hot liquid in steam-fragrant stews and soups, rich cocoa, rum toddies, and other joys of the season. In deep cold, the muffled roar of a backpacking stove—that iconic and somehow lovable bit of high technology—is so comforting that I seldom mind the noise.

In a tent (especially, but not necessarily, in snow)

COLIN: Every time you convert your tent into a kitchen, two dangers lurk. Today the dangers are so well recognized that some experienced backpackers now try, when using a tent, to eat uncooked food as often as possible. But, as I've suggested (page 227), that may not always be desirable or even safe. And you must sometimes melt snow for water. When weather permits, you should certainly cook outside the tent. But weather doesn't always permit. At such times the only practical solution is to be achingly and constantly aware of the dangers and to exercise great care. But that exercising is easier said than done: the one time you really need a tent is in bad weather, up high, and under such conditions your brain is liable to be working at about 10 percent of normal capacity. That, I am sure, is how many of the worst kitchen-in-tent accidents occur.

The first danger is fire. In the cramped confines of a tent you're hardly likely to be absentminded enough, no matter what the altitude, to drop a still-glowing match. But any stove—gasoline, kerosene, or cartridge—being lit in low temperatures is apt to flare into a sudden oversize flame that can quickly engulf a tent. The instructions for MSR stoves go so far as to warn "Gasoline (appliance fuel) is hazardous: do not light any stove in a tent or indoors." But bitter cold and/or ferocious wind or even lashing rain (though see page 572) may make it impossible to do the job outside. If you absolutely must do it inside, be ready at any moment to hurl a flaming stove out into the quenching elements (see Chip's shovel-blade stove base, pages 347 and 370). As you may have to batten down tight while lighting the stove, in order to cut wind disturbance to the minimum, you can't always leave a zipper or drawstring undone. But at least you can be mentally ready, somewhere in the recesses of your mind, to pull them open at the first sign of trouble. I'm not sure that's enough; but under certain conditions you really don't have much choice.

An even more serious danger, and one more likely to occur, is carbon-monoxide poisoning.

Unless you ensure adequate ventilation, a burning stove can very quickly consume almost all the free oxygen in your battened-down little world. And a stove burning in a confined space that lacks a free oxygen supply will give off carbon monoxide.

It's important to understand the distinction between asphyxiation (lack of oxygen; presence of too much carbon dioxide) and carbon-monoxide poisoning. If you're starved of oxygen, your breathing will in time fill the space around you with carbon dioxide, and you will usually be warned of the danger of asphyxiation—even awakened from sleep by being made to gasp for breath (page 45—though also page 750). But carbon monoxide is a colorless, odorless, highly poisonous gas—the gas that occasionally kills people in enclosed garages. It does not warn you of danger by making you gasp for breath. And it does not extinguish or even dim a flame.

Carbon-monoxide poisoning is no mere theoretical hazard for campers—especially in snow, which can very effectively cut off all ventilation. Down the years there have been many tragedies and near-tragedies. Vilhjalmur Stefansson, in his book *Unsolved Mysteries of the Arctic* (1938), gives some graphic examples. The gas almost killed Willem Barents and his entire polar party when they holed up in a snow-encased cabin on Novaya Zemlya in the winter of 1596 and tried to keep themselves warm with "sea-coles which we had brought out of the ship." Stefansson himself was lucky to escape in 1911 when his four-man party found an old Eskimo snow-house, sealed the doorway too tight, and began cooking on a kerosene-burning stove. A kerosene-burning heater almost killed a man on the first Byrd Antarctic expedition of 1938, when a blizzard partially blocked the flue pipe. Stefansson maintains that the two men of the ill-fated Andrée arctic balloon party of 1897, whose bodies were not found until 1930, probably died from carbon-monoxide poisoning: a kerosene-burning Primus stove stood between their bodies, and there seems every reason to believe that their tent may have been partly covered by drifting snow.

Some years ago two young men apparently died from carbon-monoxide poisoning while camping in the Inyo National Forest of California. It seems almost certain that, in unexpectedly cold weather, they battened down their impermeable plastic-tube tent and for warmth left their Sterno stove (canned heat) burning when they went to sleep. They never woke up.

Now, I don't want to make you afraid of cooking in a confined space. But I do want to make you keenly aware of the dangers. It's vital to remember that, as becomes clear from the accounts of survivors from near-tragedies, you get no warning of carbon-monoxide poisoning beyond, perhaps, "a slight feeling of pressure on the temples, a little bit as if from an elastic band or cap." Unconsciousness may follow within seconds. Unless someone else recognizes the danger in time and lets in fresh air before he succumbs himself, you die.

The necessary precautions are simple. When you're cooking in a tent or other enclosed space, especially in snow, always make sure you have adequate airflow. In a high wind, that's hardly likely to be a problem. But if snow is falling, keep checking that the air vents don't become blocked, and keep clearing away drifted snow, so that the entrance is never in danger of being completely buried (see also page 437).

Bedroom

THE ROOF

COLIN: Under most conditions the best roof for your bedroom is the sky. This common-sensible arrangement saves weight, time, energy, and money. It also keeps you in intimate contact with the world you are presumably walking through in order to come into intimate contact with.

That world often mounts to its most sublime moments of beauty at the fringes of darkness; and the important thing, I find, is not just to see such beauty but to see it happen—to watch the slow and almost imperceptible transitions of shine and shadow, form and shapelessness. You cannot see such events by peering out occasionally from under a roof. Certainly you cannot lie under a roof and let yourself become a part of them, so that their meanings, or whatever it is that's important about them, move deep inside you. You must be out under the sky.

For me, the supreme place to watch beauty happen is a mountaintop.

I shall never forget a calm and cloudless autumn night when I camped roofless and free, yet warm and comfortable, on the very summit of Mount Shasta, in northern California. Shasta is an isolated volcanic pyramid that rises 10,000 feet from a broken plain. Its apex stands 14,162 feet above sea level. From this apex, as the sun eased downward, I watched the huge shadow of the pyramid begin to move out across the humps and bubukles of the darkening plain. At first the shadow was squat and blunt. And its color was the color of the blue-gray plain, only darker. As the sun sank lower, the shadow reached slowly out toward the horizon until it seemed to cover half the eastward plain. Its color deepened. The pyramid grew taller, narrower. At last its slender apex touched the gray and hazy horizon. There, for a long and perfect moment, the huge shape halted; lay passive on the plain. Its color deepened to a luminous, sumptuous, majestic royal blue. Then the light went out. The shadow faded. Night took over the gray but still humped and bubukled plain. And slowly, as the western sky darkened, the shapeless shadows moved deeper into everything and smoothed the plain into a blackboard. Soon a few small lights bloomed out of the dusk. But the real happenings were over, and after a while I went to sleep, high above the stage and yet a part of it.*

But you don't have to climb a 14,000-foot peak in order to sleep above and yet in the night. Years ago, when I felt the need for a new perspective on my tight little urban life, I'd go—often late at night—to the place in which I wrote the opening chapter of this book. I'd heave my pack into the car, drive for an hour, and park the car on a dirt road that wound steeply through a stretch of still-untrampled ranch country, recently set aside as a public park. An hour later, aided by a flashlight and the pleasurable excitements of change and darkness, I'd climb up onto the flat, grassy summit of an isolated and "unimproved" hill. This little tableland stood almost 1700 feet above sea level, and from it I could see the sprawling blaze of lights that ringed San Francisco Bay. I could watch tiny headlights creeping in and out of this web, like unsuspecting fireflies, along the freeways that linked it, eastward, with the black and mysterious continent. And when I had rolled out my mummy bag and cocooned myself inside it against the cold wind sweeping in from the Pacific, I could sometimes see as well, quite effortlessly, in the moments before I fell asleep, both a time when the shores of the Bay were as black as the rest of the continent and a time when the eastward view from this hill would blaze almost as brightly and beautifully and senselessly as the current thin ring around the blackness that was the Bay. I'd have found it almost pointless to camp on that hill in a tent.

But there is more to rooflessness than panoramas. Some worlds only come alive after dark, and my memory often cheers me with warm little cameos it wouldn't hold if I always roofed myself off from the night. Deep in Grand Canyon, inches from my eyes, floodlit by flashlight, a pair of quick, clean little deer mice scamper with thistledown delicacy along slender willow shoots. On a Cornish hillside, with the Atlantic pounding away at the cliffs below, the shadowy shape of a fox ambles unconcernedly

---

*Important safety note: mountain peaks, although superb, are treacherous. Some, like Shasta, are so big they make their own weather—and it can change within minutes. So if you're going to camp on a peak you must know what you're doing. Shasta, I understand, has killed a fair number of people; and before I decided to camp on its peak I made sure that (a) the weather pattern was stable in a way it rarely is in that part of the world; (b) I had a tent ready, should the weather change; and (c) a tentative evacuation-to-lower-elevations plan was always lurking ready at the back of my mind.

out of and then back into the darkness. On the flank of a California mountain, in sharp moonlight, a raccoon emerges from behind a bush, stops
short and peers through its mask at my cocooned figure, then performs a
long and comically exaggerated mime of indecision before turning away
and, still not altogether sure it has made the right choice, sea-rolling back
behind the bush.

Without a roof you wake directly into the new day. Sometimes I
open my eyes in the morning to see a rabbit bobbing and nibbling its way
through breakfast. Once I woke at dawn to find, 10 feet from my head, a
doe browsing among dew-covered ferns. Near the start of my California
walk, camped beside a levee that protected some rich farmland that had
been created from desert by irrigation with Colorado River water, I woke
in a pale early light to find myself looking into the rather surprised eye of
a desert road runner that stood on top of the levee, as still and striking as
a national emblem. There was a light frost in my little hollow, and I lay
warm and snug in my bag, only eyes and nose exposed, and watched the
bird. It watched me back. After a while I heard a noise off to the left. The
road runner came to life and retreated over the levee. The noise increased.
Suddenly, sunshine streamed over the dike. Soon a tractor pulled up, 20
feet from my bedroom, beyond some low bushes. A large and cheerful and
voluminously wrapped black man got down and swung his arms for
warmth and made an adjustment to the motor. Then, seeing me for the
first time, he grinned hugely and enviously and said, "Well, you look
warm enough. That's one of us, anyways."

Yet, in spite of the obvious advantages of rooflessness, most people
seem to assume that camping means sleeping in

TENTS.

In this connection I always recall the instinctive remark of a young lady
whose forte was indoor rather than outdoor sports, but who was for a time
the very close friend of an experienced outdoorsman. One close and
friendly evening she lifted the sheet above them both with the tips of her
pink toes so that it formed a neat little pup tent and exclaimed, "Look!
Camping out!"*

It amazes me, though, that most practicing backpackers also seem to
regard a tent as obligatory, even in fair and stable weather. An experienced
mountain-shop manager once told me, "People want to be in an enclo-

---

*No, come to think of it, it was a friendly afternoon.

sure. They seem to need the psychological 'safety' of four walls—even if part of the enclosure is only netting."

There are, of course, certain conditions under which a tent becomes desirable or even essential.

Very cold weather is one of them—the kind of weather in which you need to retain every possible calorie that your body generates. But in calm weather such conditions occur only when the temperature falls really low. That night I camped on the peak of Mount Shasta, the thermometer read 9°F at sunrise. Yet, with nothing for a bedroom except an Ensolite pad and a good sleeping bag, I slept warm and snug. But that night was dead calm. In almost any kind of wind, even when the temperature is up around freezing, you need walled shelter: all but the warmest sleeping bags, unprotected, lose too much heat (though a Gore-Tex shell helps). In a high wind you may also find it virtually impossible to cook food or do any other partway-out-of-the-bag chore. A cave may be the best hideout, but in most places good caves are rare. When you're on the move a tent is, unfortunately, the only dependable solution.

You also need a tent in any appreciable snowfall—if you want to be sure of reasonable comfort. And if it is also very cold a tent may be necessary for survival—though a snow cave (page 438) may be just as good.

It's my personal opinion—not very widely shared—that you rarely need a tent in rain. There are, as we shall see, lighter alternatives. When rain is heavy and prolonged and wind-driven, though, a tent may be the best answer (but see page 569 for a nontent that worked). And if mosquitoes or other insects routinely mount mass-formation attacks—as they often do during northern Canadian summers, for example—then a tent may be the only way to retain your sanity. To this end you can now choose among many tents with walls mostly of netting.

Unless you're an eager and habitually diurnal lover, privacy is no reason for taking a tent. You may need one overnight at a crowded road-head campsite; but, if once you start backpacking you persist in camping in crowded places, don't worry about a tent, consult a psychiatrist.

On the other hand, a tent may well be worth packing along if you're going to set up a semipermanent camp and move out from it each day—for fishing, hunting, climbing, or whatever. It's convenient then to be able to leave your gear unpacked and ready for use but still protected. Protected, that is, from any weather that may blow up, and also from most animals. Naturally, no tent will keep out every kind of animal. Ants can usually find a way in. So, less certainly, can mice. But a properly battened-down tent with a sewn-in floor will keep out most middle-size creatures that can be a daytime nuisance: birds (especially jays, which are sometimes called "camp robbers") and such inquisitive mammals as chipmunks and squirrels and, worst of all, pack rats. Fortunately, most of the big mammals—deer, coyote, bobcat, cougar—seem to steer well clear of anything that smells of man. There are two dire exceptions. One is light-fingered man—a breed that is, I sadly understand, becoming more wide-spread in backpacking habitats; the other is man-habituated bear—also becoming less rare. See page 733.

Outside North America the animal situation may be rather differ-ent. In parts of East Africa, for example, it is unwise, on account of lions and hyenas, to sleep in the open on your own. You don't need much pro-tection: almost anything that completely surrounds you seems to keep the predators off (a mosquito net is probably, though not quite certainly, enough). But it's important that you be completely surrounded. Lions, in particular, have been known to wander in through the open doors of tents. During a six-month East African safari, when I spent much of the time watching wild game and camping out alone, I soon gained confidence in the protection afforded by my 2-man A-frame tent. It had a zipper door at one end, a tunnel door at the other. By closing the lower halves of both entrances and fully closing their mosquito-net coverings, and by leaving a small mosquito-netted air vent above the tunnel door open, I maintained adequate ventilation. And the lions and hyenas that often circled around camp at night never bothered me.

Kinds of tents

In the last decade, catalogs and mountain shops have sprouted whole villages of new tents. But the initially confusing array can conveniently be categorized two ways: by function and by structure.

"4-season" models are all-weather units, designed to withstand the heaviest snow and rain and the fiercest winds. Now straddling the gap between 4- and 3-season models are "convertible" tents, that allow you to shed a pound or so by leaving at home one pole, or sections thereof, and perhaps a zip-out roof panel. "3-season" tents (a category that covers most modern backpacking tents) should see you through the worst that spring, summer, or fall can produce but will not assure protection from a deep-winter onslaught. The sturdiest of them might do so at a pinch; but some of the ultralightweights are really for late spring through early fall, or for mild climates. These are sometimes labeled "2-season."

But note that "season" categorizing depends a great deal on the driver. An experienced, resourceful mountaineer caught with his precau-tions down in an early blizzard would probably survive with the lightest 3-season tent or even a sketchy nontent shelter. Indeed, he might enjoy a passing comfortable rest. But an inexperienced, panicky, uninventive, fumble-fisted summer camper caught in a three-hour thunderstorm could, even if equipped with the latest 4-season wonder, soon get Godaw-ful wet and decline into misery and hypothermia. So learn your onions.

Another form of functional categorizing is body count. The labels "1-man," "2-man," "6-man" seem self-explanatory: and note that makers have now shifted to "1-person," "2-person," etc., or to other terms such as solo, duo, trio, quartet. But all such tags demand close and cynical scrutiny. Tent makers naturally rate their models according to the greatest number of human bodies that can be laid out, corpselike, on the floor. Smallish bodies too. But a tent that will accommodate x corpses will not accommodate x breathing individuals. Not through many rainy nights, anyway, let alone a weeklong blizzard.

It's my opinion, probably shared by most experienced solo back-packers, that for comfort, even for efficiency, someone on his own needs what the catalogs call a "2-person tent." A snowstorm once kept me more or less confined in a 2-man A-frame tent for four straight days; I was warm and tolerably comfortable and could cook and do all necessary chores without hazard. I would not have liked to spend those four days cooped up in a small, coffinlike 1-man tent I owned at the time.

With two or more people, lack of space takes an even greater toll. Pack any catalog-given number of normally stable personalities into a tent for a protracted spell and you can rest pretty damned sure that some emotional fur (or perhaps I mean fleece) will eventually fly. Extra roomi-ness for the same floor space will help. A tent in which you can actually stand up and move around helps even more. But in the end the only effec-tive response, almost always, is to lower the catalog quota. Remember, too, that backpackers carry packs. And they need to cook. So when you body-calibrate any tent for use in bad weather make allowance for accom-modating your pack and having it get-at-able, and also for cooking, either in the tent itself (for dangers, see page 371) or, better, in a vestibule. Tents that make allowance for such matters in their body counts are sometimes called "2-plus," "3-plus," etc.

The Bones—

CHIP: Taking our cue from nature herself, we can gain considerable insight from classifying tents in a quasibiological way. That is, according to their skeletal structure. With Darwin blurring thus gracefully into Bucky Fuller, our current bioarchitectural categories include:
1. *Macroinvertebrate* (no spine; i.e., a *bivouac bag*)
2. *Avian:* tarps and wings (zero to two straight poles)
3. *Pyramid* (one center pole)
4. *Traditional A-frame* (a straight pole or two-legged frame at each end);

Tent types

5. *Modified A-frame* (ridgepole and center hoop to add space);
6. *Hoop* (one, two, or three: think of a covered wagon without the wheels);
7. *Wedge* (two intersecting hoops)
8. *Dome* (three or more intersecting hoops)
9. *Hybrids* and *offbeats* (skeletal features from two or more of the above)

Each of these types has its own strengths, and corresponding liabilities. But taxonomic disputes can arise: for instance, is a bivouac sack with one hoop a true macroinvertebrate, or a merely an underdeveloped hoop tent? My take is that a *sack,* by definition, is in contact with its contents (you and your sleeping bag) while a *tent* isn't. So, until a second hoop lifts it off your feet, it's not a tent.

On the whole, hybridizing aims at reducing the liabilities of one type by introducing some feature of another. For instance, the tent I use most is a wedge that's been mildly hybridized with a true dome (page 407). The inner tent is a basic wedge, with poles curved in an X. But a short wand crosses over the X in a domish way, in a sleeve outside the fly sheet to form a tension eave. This adds two roomy vestibules to relieve the head-cramping wedge design.*

Another useful distinction is whether the tent is freestanding or must be staked out to hold its shape. Speaking in general, types 1 through 6 above are not freestanding while 7 through 9 mostly are. Tents relying on stakes-and-stretch to hold their shape can be lighter than freestanders, which need an extra pole or two and, usually, no fewer stakes (I counted). In practice, nearly all freestanding tents need to be staked or guyed for best performance, and may also have a stretch-and-stake fly sheet or vestibule.

Of course all tents, given their functional resemblance to sails, must be soundly staked or otherwise tethered while in use. Unless you're so utterly bored by it all as to savor the thrilling sight of your new $450 ultralight being wafted to the middle of an alpine tarn, where it—slowly and Poe-perfectly—sinks beyond all human ken.

Skeletal materials. In the late 1960s, when the first edition of this book was born, fiberglass was the favored skeletal material. But Stephenson had introduced precurved aluminum-alloy tubing to support its gossamer Warmlite hoop tents. Today, most quality backpacking tents and

---

*A curious but nevertheless real hazard of wedge tents is that, on being suddenly awakened (by the *thwump* of an avalanche or the scream of a real cougar) you'll rear up and bash heads with your partner. Knowledgeable doctors call this mutual skull trauma Bibler's Syndrome. Frequent sufferers are advised to sleep head-to-foot.

virtually all mountaineering tents have bones of aluminum-alloy tubing, in multiple sections joined with elastic shock cord.

Most aluminum tubing is *anodized,* an electrochemical process that adds a thin coat of color and protects the metal from corrosion (aluminum being fiendishly subject to pitting from seawater and even salty sea breezes). But even anodized poles have plain aluminum ferrules and inserts, so rinse them in freshwater if they've been exposed to corrosive influences. Curiously, tent-pole design has benefitted most from leaps in arrow making—that's the use for which the high-strength, small-diameter anodized tubing was intended. But arrows are straight. So another lurking gremlin of aluminization is that hoops and domes require you to flex a straight piece of tubing, thus weakening it. The pole-sleeve repair kits included with many such tents attest that abrupt bends-and-breaks are far from rare.*

These days, precured wands and connectors are increasingly com-mon—and desirable—particularly on small tents that demand tight pole arcs. Easton 7000-Series tube, in various diameters, is the standard, with 7075 and 7079 used in most quality tents. But the new DAC Featherlite tubing (from Korea) is a serious competitor. Sierra Designs is using it in the classic Flashlight tents, with much of the saving from a new connector that eliminates the insert (that piece of smaller, thicker tubing that forms the joint), making the pole set 15 percent lighter. But on a new solo tent, Sierra Designs now use Easton's UltraLite AC tube (which means not only Aluminum-Carbon but also Accelerated Cost). With overlapping connec-tors of Kevlar (not inserts, the Sierra Designers tell me, but *out*-serts) and Delrin pole tips, this new bone structure weighs a surprising one-third less than one of 7075 tube.

Fiberglass wands are still encountered, mostly on mid to low-price tents. But fiberglass tubing requires more thickness for adequate strength, so a tube with an inside diameter large enough for a reasonable shock cord is fat and correspondingly heavy. But carbon-fiber wands are

---

*Most broken poles result from rough transport (the disastrous car-trunk slam), inept or impatient setup, and clumsy falls (i.e., you on top of your tent). High winds rank a strong fourth. Large dogs are also significant malefactors. If you lack a pole-sleeve repair kit, a section of aluminum cut from a beer can, plus a hearty hi-ho silver wrap with duct tape will serve. But don't use so much that the wand won't fit through its sleeve.

COLIN: When carrying curved poles in your pack, pad them with soft gear or protect them with something strong and rigid—by packing them along one of the internal-frame stays or the framesheet. You can do the same with straight poles or can lash them, very securely, to the side frame of most external-frame packs or carry them, preferably in tent-pole bags, flush with the sides of internal-frame packs. Some such packs now come with pockets near the bottom to make things easier and safer. Wrapping poles in the tent often results in holes being poked through its fabric.

already showing up on tents, so the magic now applied to fishing rods might soon bring a further evolutionary flip-flop.

Shock-corded poles ensure, as Colin says, "that the sheer hell of pitching your tent in a gale or downpour or both becomes mitigated to a mere nightmare." Limp shock cord is a subsidiary evil. Decent-quality stuff has a double-braided sheath with a nylon outer, a cotton inner, and a natural rubber core. It tends to be glossy, while the nasty, cheap sort is a dull white and resembles candlewick. Don't be afraid to take out a wand and give it a stretch test in the store. But don't, no, *never* fling a wand out and let the sections snap together—this eventually cracks the tubing. Instead, starting at the center, straighten the sections out, easing them together with a discreet click, and working outward to the ends. When dismantling, reverse. (Thus, the Swami Tentananda hath sworn on the Millennial Catalog.)

The skin—

Besides a bony frame, a tent is a tent is a tent: by definition, cloth. Once rawhide gave way to woven fabric, in the many centuries before synthetics, cotton canvas was popular because the fibers swell when wet, creating a barrier against the rain. Nylon, developed for parachutes among other things, was lighter, thinner, and stronger. Being plastic, the fibers didn't absorb water, but neither did they swell up to exclude it. So the first nylon tents had two daunting problems. The smallest tear would zip clear across, becoming an unauthorized exit. And the necessary waterproof coating gave them the unrelenting humidity of a steam room. A weave known as ripstop solved the first problem. The second one—Demon Humidity—has proved somewhat tougher.

COLIN: Virtually all backpacking tents are still made with some form of nylon or polyester taffeta. (Ripstop is a taffeta with the weave reinforced every quarter-inch or less by thicker threads, clearly visible, that indeed stop most rips but can cause puckers across strained cloth.) Most inner tents are left uncoated and can therefore breathe. Fly sheets are urethane-coated and impermeable. Similar but heavier fabric is used—because the coatings suffer heavier abrasion—for the "bathtubs" that form most floors and lower sidewalls.

Single-needle stitching—a single line of stitches covered with bias tape—suffices for bathtubs, where the enemy is abrasion, not wind force. But some of the best makers regard it as a no-no for walls, where the fabric is lighter and under stress from wind. There, *double-needle stitching*—a double line of stitches—renders the seams stronger than the fabric itself. It also forms "shed seams"—constructed like shingles, so that gravity carries water down and away. Chip advises me that this is now called a *lap-fell seam,* which is preferable to an *overlock* or *bias-taped seam.* Laser or hot-cutting is best for nylon, since it fuses the threads and seals the edge against fraying, but these days most tent pieces are cut in thick stacks, so felling and treating with sealer are reasonable stopgaps. Floor seams should be factory-taped, rather than being sealed by the tenter. For maintenance of seams, see page 414.

CHIP: At present, regularly encountered tent fabrics are:
- Lightweight 40d (the *d* stands for denier; see page 142) 1.5-oz. nylon ripstop is used for backpacking tent canopies.
- High-tenacity 40d multi-ripstop 1.5-oz. polyester, for the canopies of mountaineering tents. Polyester doesn't stretch when wet, as nylon does, so it's better for severe-weather tents and fly sheets. It also holds up under ultraviolet (UV) light, which weakens nylon quickly.
- Coated 75d ripstop 1.9-oz. polyester, for fly sheets. Polyurethane is the most common coating, but new elastomeric polymers have more elasticity: they don't "bind" the fibers, allowing them to absorb more stress while still keeping water out. Coatings are ranked by the number of "passes," or applications. Good fly sheets have two-pass coatings. More would add unnecessary weight. Waterproofness is rated with a pressure test, and a good fly sheet tests at 80 pounds per square inch (psi).
- 2-oz., 70d nylon taffeta coated with three passes of polyurethane is used for bathtub floors. 100 psi is a good rating. Polyurethane coatings *hydrolize* (get gummy) when stored wet.
- 1.4- to 1.5-oz. 30d silicone-impregnated nylon ripstop (Soar Coat, etc.) is a parachute fabric used in ultralight tents, wings, and tarps. It's not as waterproof or abrasion-resistant as a conventional fly sheet and needs to be reinforced at stress points. But silicone impregnation doesn't hydrolize like urethane coatings, and a 2-person wing made from it weighs about 18 oz.
- No-see-um mesh (a nylon tricot) is finer than mosquito netting, at 20d. Dark colors allow more visibility.
- Power mesh is a heavy-duty netting used for pole sleeves and reinforcement.
- Waterproof/breathable laminates for tents consist of an outer layer (40d nylon or polyester) with a membrane layer, usually a stretched film (polytetrafluoroethane, PFTE, or similar). The inner surface is a nonwoven fabric (e.g., 1-oz. Du Pont Sonatra polyester) with a fibrous texture that increases the surface area in

order to promote wicking. While ultralight parkas are now made with two-layer laminates, tent fabrics need three. Besides Gore-Tex, there's ToddTex, Klimate, MemBrain, and a gaggle of new-comers, named and nameless.

- Clear film is used for windows and skylights in tents from Sierra Designs, Mountain Hardwear (theirs is called UVX), and others. Reportedly tearproof, it remains flexible to −66°F. (I've only tried it at a temperate −37°, and it was flexible as hell. And also completely iced over.)

COLIN: Gray, light green, or pale blue fabric—for main walls and fly sheet—means a soft light inside your tent in bright sunlight, and an inconspicuous camp (easier on everyone in heavily used backcountry), but can produce a cold and depressing ambiance in dim light. Orange or yellow fabric keeps the interior from getting too dark and oppressive in snowstorms and the like, stands out well in case of search-and-rescue (yellow is said to be best in dull weather, orange in sunlight), and catches the customer's eye in the store—but can generate near-psychedelic effects in glare. Currently popular: white, cream, and tan.

Tents derive their strength from a balancing act between *compression members* (poles) and *tension members* (fabric, guy lines). The straight, rigid poles of A-frames are extremely strong when compressed along their length, and in well-designed tents most of the tension is applied in that direction. The flexible wands of hoop tents and domes are, on their own, floppy and weak. But if tension is applied evenly around their curve they become laterally very strong. Such tension can come from fabric stretched in an unbroken surface across the semicircle of an end wall (though any door or window or other break radically reduces the effect); or it can come from fabric stretched tightly and evenly over the outside of the poles. Such tension comes most often and most purely from a fly sheet. These factors, and many more—such as the *bias* in all fabrics, which makes them stretchier one way than the other—are carefully balanced by today's tent designers, who often use computers to achieve optimum systems. Even for us users, understanding some of the implications offers practical advantages. It's certainly worth knowing, for example, that in most modern tents the fly provides much of the strength. In hoops and domes the fly can account for 85 to 90 percent. So in high winds, whether or not you need a fly for protection, rig it. Firmly.

CHIP: For some years, *double-wall* tents have predominated, with a separate waterproof outer fly sheet protecting a breathable inner tent from the lash of the elements. Between the two, air can circulate (at least in theory), lessening the problem of condensation. But there are also excellent single-wall tents around, either of coated (nonbreathable) fabrics with a crafty arrangement of mesh and vents, or of waterproof, breathable laminates (Gore-Tex, ToddTex, and sundry). Since condensation still ranks chief among tent gremlins, the fly sheets on double-wall tents are increasingly vented as well.

Together your body and the tent create a changing microclimate. The most important variables are sunlight and wind, while the heat and moisture you emit are relatively constant. Whatever the humidity and temperature of the outside air, your presence inside the tent adds both water vapor and heat. For comfort, the relative humidity in a tent should be 35 to 45 percent. What makes humidity relative is that it changes with temperature. At 32°F the air can hold 4.8 grams of water vapor per cubic meter. At 60° it can hold 13.5 grams. At 90° it can hold 33.5 grams. Water vapor remains invisible until the relative humidity reaches 100 percent—the *dewpoint*—and the air can no longer hold it. Then the water vapor becomes highly annoying, even life-threatening, as it beads up and drips onto clothing and sleeping bags, or sheets up on coated tent floors, sometimes pooling under pads and making the term "bathtub floor" a bit too exact for comfort.

To track the invisible vapor, I got an Oakton Digital Thermohygrometer (1.8 oz., $40, from Forestry Suppliers; see listing in Appendix III). This little wonder stick displays the temperature, from 32° to 122°F, and the relative humidity, from 2 to 98 percent. It also records high and low values for both, for as long as it's on. Battery life is 4000 hours. (Switching it on, I find that this paragraph is being written at 69.1° and 39 percent relative humidity.) Using it, I can literally map how moisture builds up or dissipates.

When I breathe on the wonder stick, the reading bounces from 39 percent to 76 percent relative humidity. Thus, on cool, still nights, one person's breathing can quickly saturate the air in a battened-down tent. Compared to the water content of breath, sweating is negligible. (Somewhat to my surprise, I found that it can be much drier inside a sleeping bag than outside: in a tent at 64°F and 64 percent humidity, the wonder stick registered 79° and only 33 percent inside my Polarguard bag.) The internal volume and surface area don't double from a 1-person to a 2-person tent, but the condensation problem does. At any rate, in cold weather, three or four breathers (people, dogs) can bedew (or befrost) the innards of a tent in very short order indeed. Tracked-in snow, wet clothes, and spills all boost the water content. If you add cooking vapors, you'll be enveloped in a garlic-scented fog.

The following table shows the temperature and humidity in various tents that were closed (fly zipped, tent door panel slightly open) or open (fly unzipped, tent door panel or vent fully open), compared to the surrounding air. I hung the instrument 2 feet from the floor, midway between bow and stern (so I wasn't breathing on it). To keep the body heat and breath moisture as constant as possible, all the tests were done with one person: me.

Looking at the results, we see that the humidity is higher inside the tent except when a) the sun is shining on it, or b) it has a peak vent. In both cases, heat is what drives the drying process.

HUMIDITY IN TENTS

Tent	Relative Humidity % at Temperature °F			
	Closed	Open	Outside air	Conditions
Moss Double Helix (d)	51% at 57°	42% at 56°	38% at 50°	Still, dark
Mountain Hardwear Nightview (d)	67% at 61°	—	50% at 47°	Still, first sun
Eureka Cobra (d)	56% at 53°	—	75% at 33°	Still, first sun
Sierra Designs	56% at 61°	53% at 57°	52% at 52°	Breezy, dark
Divine	77% at 58°	72% at 55°	62% at 49°	Still, predawn
Lightning (s)				
Eureka Zephyr XT with peak vent (d)	64% at 62°	55% at 65°	57° at 54°	Breezy drizzle
(after a night of rain)	50% at 62°	53% at 59°	55% at 40°	Slight breeze

Single-Wall (s), Double-Wall (d)

In a double-wall tent, water vapor is supposed to exit the breathable inner. If there's a breeze—*active ventilation*—enough air may circulate betwixt tent and fly sheet to carry the moisture off. If the air is still, moisture will condense on the fly sheet and, one hopes, roll off the ducky back of the inner tent to the ground. But if the inner tent has a flat roof panel of mesh with a pole crossing above it, you might wake to a fine, cold shower. Naturally, if the fly sheet touches the tent at any point, the condensation will soak through.

In still air, you depend on *passive ventilation*. Besides water vapor, bodies give off heat, and (this is called *thermodynamics*) the warm air rises. So you get a certain amount of ventilation with body heat alone—if there's someplace for the water vapor to go. But in most double-wall tents, especially classic domes, the warm, moist air is trapped in the inverted bowl of the fly (imagine a cloud forming and slowly descending over a mountain peak and you get the picture). Since the fly is cooled by outside air, you then get droplets.*

Humidity and temperature (°F) readings for a mesh-windowed double-wall tent (a Sierra Designs Flashlight CD) in still air are revealing.

Outside air	34% at 64°
Sidepocket	39% at 73°
Peak (inside tent)	46% at 74°

That is, as warmed air rises inside the tent, the humidity increases by 12 percent. If the outside air is cold and moist, the air under the fly can be quickly cooled to dewpoint. Adding a second person (and a bit of kissing) gives us more moisture still.

Outside air	34% at 64°
Sidepocket	50% at 76°
Peak (inside tent)	54% at 78°

So two people raise the relative humidity by 20 percent. If the outside air is already moist, you have a problem. First, the moisture beads on smooth, cool surfaces like a coated fly sheet, water bottles, etc.—a warning sign. Then, it condenses everywhere: eyeglasses fog, clothing grows dank, paperback books crinkle, and matchheads pulp.

Savvy makers of single-wall tents add peak vents, either as floppy tunnels, overhanging eaves, or down-slanting dormers with stiffening arches. Increasingly, peak vents or high/low venting options (i.e., a low intake and a high exit), show up on double-wall models as well. By giving moist air an exit, these make a difference, even on still nights when body heat alone drives the system. Here are figures for a peak-vented double-wall model (a Eureka Zephyr XT), with a barely perceptible breeze, just after a rain.

Outside air	55% at 40°
Sidepocket	51% at 59°
Peak (inside tent)	53% at 62°

The difference, compared to the first set of figures, is that the humidity at the peak is 2 percent *lower* than that of the outside air, even with the added moisture from my breath, rather than 12 percent higher, as it

*The only situation where body heat will warm an outer layer of fabric enough to keep condensation from occurring is in a bivouac bag of breathable laminate. I've stayed surprisingly dry on otherwise miserable slush-and-rime nights.

would be without a peak vent. So the thermodynamic engine is working to keep me dry. On still, cold nights a good venting system can be boosted with a candle lantern to keep frost off the walls.

In the absence of a built-in vent, look for door zippers with double sliders. Lacking such things, a tent can be made lighter. But shelf weight isn't the whole of it. Operationally, more condensation means you get less warmth from your bag and need rather longer to dry things out in the morning. If you pack up the least bit damp, you gain more weight (in water) than that 5 grams for a second slider.

But the most radical difference in internal weather is between sun and shade. In direct sunlight, a tent can become either a sweatbox or a quick-drying chamber, depending on ventilation. Given trees or rock outcrops to work with, you can locate a tent to catch early sun, for wake-up and dry-out. But, if you're staying in place, it's nice to have midday to late-afternoon shade, for a post-fishing nap. That is, you need to think of your tent as a microclimate within a microclimate.

Most quality tents on the market today will do a good job if you use them intelligently. For years, I've had good luck in all seasons with double-wall tents. I've also camped in single-wall tents on wet nights near the freezing point, when condensation is rampant, with reasonable comfort. The new breathable fabrics do work rather well, but they have their limits. The transport of moisture through the membrane depends strongly on surface area and to some degree on heat. If you're hoarding your heat inside a good sleeping bag, while wisely breathing outside it, you'll load the tent with moisture. So venting provides the margin between staying relatively dry and feeling like a bath sponge. Whether the walls are single, double, or for that matter limestone and stained glass, when the air is saturated, you'll get soggy in your tent.

SELECTING A TENT

COLIN: First, obviously, you must decide how many people you'll be housing. Then, if you're wise, and especially if you'll need the tent for cooking or holing up in during bad weather (and if you don't need that, I suggest maybe you don't need a tent), you look only at those catalog-calibrated for one more person than you expect. Next you decide whether you need a 4- or 3-season tent or even a lesser breed. And then you begin to weigh the pluses and minuses of each major kind of tent.

There is, of course, no single "best" kind: you must choose the one that seems most suitable for you and yours under each set or amalgam of expected conditions. Among the nubs you heft—in your own personal order of importance—are weight, degree of protection from rain and from snow, stability in wind, reliability (resistance to damage), difficulty of erection in fair weather and foulest, ease of access in ditto, roominess, cost, freedom from condensation problems, and whether guyed, guyless, or fully freestanding.

CHIP: As you ponder catalogs or prowl backpacking shops in your quest for El Campo Perfecto, it helps to repeat the mountaineer's longtime mantra: *weather is the crux.* That is, any tent you can carry is a temporary and fragile shelter. In order to shield you, it must not only resist the elements but also exist in some sort of harmonious relation to them. So your overarching consideration should be climate—where do you go, mostly? What season?

In the high mountains, you need sturdy protection. Strong winds, hard rain, or unexpected snow are best met with a substantial skeleton, an aerodynamic profile, multiple tie-downs, and a UV-resistant skin that sheds whatever the alpine gods throw at it. Haute mountaineering and winter touring in the snowy latitudes raise similar demands, along with stormy-day visibility, nondepressive decor (yellow, orange, white, tan), a roomy vestibule for storage and rank-weather cooking, and an arrangement of doors and vents that give you a) a second exit and b) airflow even when the tent is partly drifted in.

If you plan to use the tent mostly under the lash of white winter, look for snow flaps (to block the wind and anchor the fly), internal guy points, and adjustable vents. In extreme cold, sheer waterproofness is not quite as crucial (but direct sun can heat up a tent enough to melt accumulated snow, and surprise you). Ferrino, a venerable Italian firm, and Hilleberg, a Swedish one, both concentrate on severe-weather tents. Snow stakes (page 421) are seldom supplied with such tents but are absolutely required.

In cool maritime regions, rain is the crux. First off, you need a full fly sheet—with a flawless, two-pass coating—betwixt you and the firmament. Second, you should be able to set it up quickly enough that you don't get soaked from above in the process. And since rain splashing up from the ground will wet you just as nastily (with the addition of muck), look for sufficient overhang. A bathtub (or should we call it a lifeboat?) floor that rises high enough is a further need. Sloping entrances are at best inconvenient and at worst can render a tent uninhabitable. So look for a vertical or amply sheltered entry that doesn't let rain sluice down onto your sleeping bag or make the floor a literal bathtub. But you also need ventilation. So look for splashproof peak vents and strong airflow potential.

Where humid heat is the rule, rainproofness remains a concern while airflow becomes a full-blown obsession. Thus, options for raising or abbreviating the fly sheet, to woo vagrant breezes, must be eagerly sought. Likewise, flow-through ventilation (i.e., two opposing mesh doors) is precious. So is the presence of mind to pitch your tent with openings along, rather than across, the prevailing breeze. Under a wet-proof fly sheet, a generous expanse or even a full canopy of mesh can make sleep that much more possible. For sunny sites (and sleeping in) a light-hued fly appreciably lowers the sweat factor. In heavy, root-laced soils, skinny stakes work like a charm.

The dry heat of the desert can be pleasurable, but it takes its toll. Camping in open sites you need a light-colored fly of UV-resistant fabric and coating. Where you'll be welcomed by biting flies, gnats, and the uniquely vicious mosquitoes found in desert water holes, and it's too damned hot to drape your sleeping bag over your face, a full-mesh canopy is a sanity saver. A favorite dodge of mine is to pack a mesh canopy (leaving the full-coverage fly at home) with a lightweight tarp or wing for midday shade-ups and occasional thunderstorm coverage. Sand—rasping, grainy, infinitesimal—is a constant companion, so to forestall too great an intimacy (waking up with grit in your teeth and bumfurrow) a substantial threshold helps. This also averts the gritty destruction of the zipper. Likewise, a freestanding canopy lessens your dependence on sand-subverted stakeouts. Pin stakes are dead useless in sand, and angles are marginal, so your desert kit should include enough T-stakes (page 417) for a faith-promoting stretch-and-tether. (I've used snow stakes, but they bend if you hit a root or pebble.) In areas of windblown dunes (where rocks and wood are scant), flat panels of fabric with strategic loops—for burying—will keep your fly right and tight. For both extreme wetness and constant abrasion, an auxiliary groundsheet (now sold as a "footprint" with the same shape as each tent) can save your floor coating for another day.

Another tactical option is to pitch the fly without the inner tent, using the footprint or a lightweight groundsheet. And, given the right groundscape and beneficent weather (and few bugs), it can work out rather well.

Tent makers now publish not one but two or three weights for each model. *Packed* (or package) weight is what you lug home from the store: tent, fly, poles, stakes, bags, extra guy lines, etc. *Trail* (or minimum) weight is for the tent, fly, and poles. *Fastpack* weight is for the fly sheet, poles, and a fitted groundcloth (or footprint). Obviously, you can't pitch a tent without stakes. But since I toss all my tent stakes into one box and choose a set according to the ground I expect to traverse, I think of stakes as separate. I also find artful dodges that enable me to leave stuff sacks behind. So the weights we quote below are, unless otherwise noted, *trail* weights. That being the weight of what stands between you and the weather: tent, fly, poles.

TENTS—MODELS AND IMPRESSIONS

COLIN:

Bivouac bags,

for soloists only, evolved from old-style sleeping-bag covers—which never proved really acceptable because they either failed to breathe or let the rain in or both. Came Gore-Tex. And with it came, first, simple envelopes with entrance-and-breathe holes of various designs. Some people loved them—and still do. But, perhaps because the envelopes tended to induce claustrophobia (and also because they slumped unattractively on the salesroom floor, like body bags), they soon grew small hoops, top and often bottom, that held them clear of your sleeping bag.

I have yet to try a bivy, except on a salesroom floor—where, battened down in an envelope, I felt a most unusual moment of claustrophobia. But I'd guess that for certain Spartan soloists with low or medium metabolic rates they would, under certain conditions, fit like a glove.

CHIP: I have two bivouac bags, not a right and left, but rather a North Face and an Outdoor Research. My old North Face bivy is a simple envelope-style, with Gore-Tex top and coated bottom. I got it in case I managed to end up on top of something I couldn't get off. And soon I found myself carrying it on solo rambles, in case I busted a wing. Like a sleeping bag, it zips down one side, with a storm flap, and has a drawstring hood, but no other form of cover for the face. So in real storms, I slept (or tried to) with my head under a jutting rock or a low limb. But I also learned to rig a small tarp, which kept low-angle rain or blowing snow off my head and torso and allowed me to brew up in my sleeping bag. My North Face bivy weighs 1 lb. 3 oz. and I don't remember what it cost. The new North Face

Soloist Bivy (2 lbs. 2 oz., $269) has double-crossed wands for headroom, with a grief-gray skin and regrettable purple innards. (Those who don't mind the colors seem to like it well enough.) Meanwhile, Bibler, Integral Designs, Wild Country, Dana Design, and Outdoor Research all have vastly improved bivy sacks (with flaps and overlaps) that weigh about a pound and change.

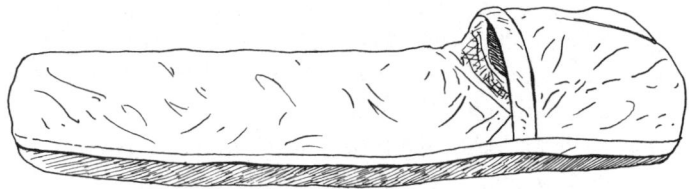

Envelope bivouac bag

Most bivy sacks have some sort of overlap at chest level, perhaps with mesh, that's more suited to sitting up on a ledge than to lying down. Since most nonclimbers would rather lie down, the next step up is to insert a wand or two for headroom. But wands or no, these overlap designs have one major weakness: getting in or out of them is pretty damned awkward, and exposes your sleeping bag to the elements. So for ultralight camping I've taken to using an end-opening bivy sack with a half circle of zipper around the top, near ground level. Outdoor Research has the widest selection of this type, with Gore-Tex laminate tops and coated underbellies.

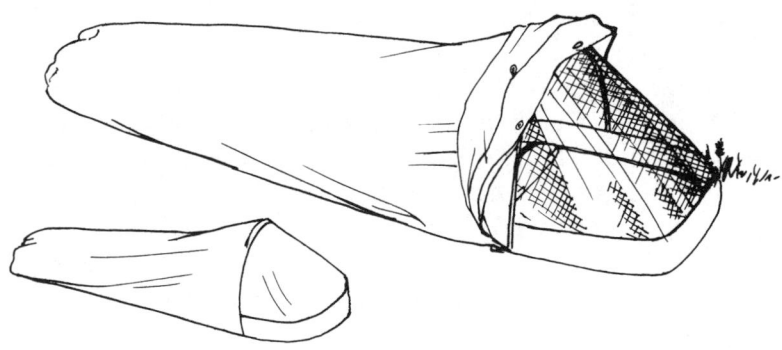

OR Deluxe Bivy

These include the mesh-protected Basic (1 lb., $180) and Standard (1 lb. 4 oz., $215), and several hooped styles. I've used the Outdoor Research Deluxe Bivy (1 lb. 10 oz., $250) for trips of a week or so in sullen weather, liking the anticlaustrophobic features. It's white inside with a shock-corded Delrin hoop for breathing room. The end-opening 5-foot zipper lets you ventilate while staying dry, and there's zip-up no-see-um mesh (both zips have double sliders). Other boons are sleeping-pad straps that reduce semiconscious thrashing and let you double your pad with Reflectix or a space blanket when sleeping on snow.

One night I slept out on a ridge above tree limit, at a low of 26°F, with 4 to 6 inches of horizontal snow. I could feel the wind buffeting me all along one side—a bivy sack can be raucous—and kept expecting to get cold, but I didn't. I left the hood unzipped slightly and about 3 cups of snow blew in while I slept. But I did sleep. In the morning, my lee side was solidly drifted in. There was slight condensation above my face, but my toes were toasty and my Polarguard bag was *dry*.

So I've gone from loathing all bivy sacks to liking this one. It's a tiny but livable space (I managed to read *The Name of the Rose* by headlamp on one weeklong trip). Outdoor Research also has an Advanced Bivy (1 lb. 15 oz., $280) and, for true intimacy, the Advanced Double Bivy (2 lbs. 15 oz., $410). A couple of all-mesh hooped sacks, the Bug (13 oz., $75) and the Double Bug (1 lb. 3 oz., $115), round things out.

Tarp and wing

Since Colin—El Maestro—has a detailed section on rigging tarps for various climatic entertainments (page 419), I'll confine this to new materials and some of the best single-sheet shelters to be had right now. Except, as noted, the weights don't include poles.

Several new mini-pavilions use 1.1-oz. parachute nylon. Silicone-impregnation boosts the waterproofness and ups the weight to 1.35 oz. per square yard. (Since seam tape won't stick to it, you need to seal the seams with silicone-based goop—see page 414.) The 5-by-8-foot SIL Tarp from Integral Designs (7 oz., $55) is intended either for two leprechauns or (more likely) as a head-and-torso shelter for a bivy sackster. This lets you flop on the bosom of Magna Mater and brew up, even in a drizzle. With a reinforced center loop and 16 loops around the edges, it configures easily. An 8-by-10-foot SIL Tarp with the same loop layout is also available (14 oz., $120). The light fabric turns wind and raindrops well enough, and is pleasantly translucent. It also stretches and sags when wet, needing alert adjustment. For more protection, the SIL Shelter (15 oz., $150) is a sophisticated tarp, 9 by 5 feet with a tricky overlap (no zipper) at one end that lets you pitch it tent-fashion with a trekking pole or stick. A reinforced cap at the peak keeps the pole from punching an impromptu grommet. But more often, wanting unimpeded floor space, I angled a line from the peak to a convenient rock or tree and then staked out the edges. With 15 loops around the edges, it pitches in a staggering number of configurations—a stretch-pentagon floor plan is most obvious: roomy for one, feasible for two.

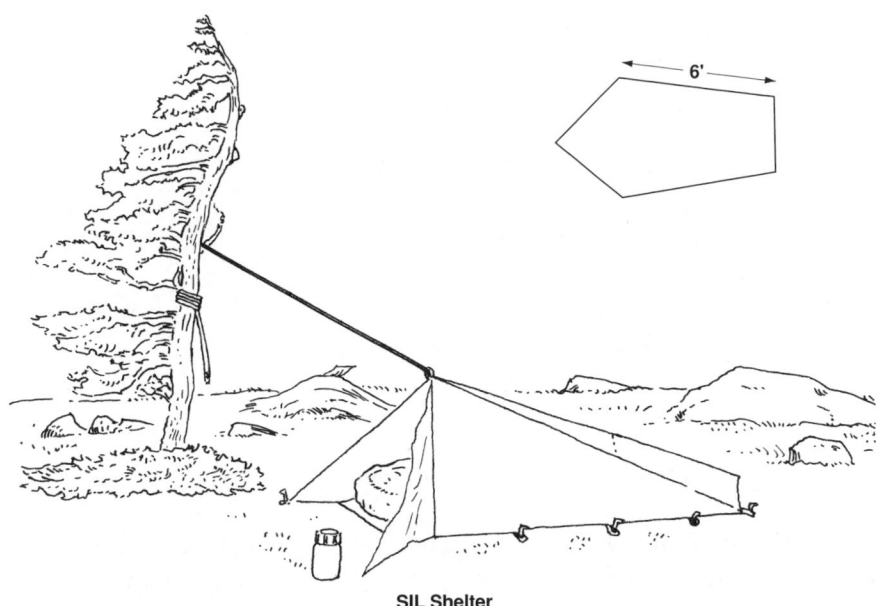

SIL Shelter

This same gossamer fabric is used in the GoLite Cave (1 lb. 2 oz., $185). Based on a Ray Jardine design, it pitches with trek poles or what-have-you and has lifter lines, to increase headroom, and down-slanting "beaks" to give more shelter at the ends. A fine-mesh bug shelter/floor combo, the Nest (1 lb. 3 oz., $75), feathers out underneath for those buzzing summer nights.

The Walrus Trekker (2 lbs. 10 oz., $89) is an A-frame, without the frame. Sewn from a rugged nylon-polyester blend and coated, it has Vel-cro-type cuffs to encircle trekking poles, aspen boles, or the leg of a sleeping giraffe. With a zip entry, it measures 9.5 by 10 feet, will shelter two big galoots (and a ballerina). Mountain Hardwear's Stingray, an 11+ by 12+ polyester tarp with extra-strong tie-downs, is a good choice for three-sies (tarp, 2 lbs.; poles, 1 lb.; $120).

I've used the Moss Heptawing (tarp, 2 lbs.; poles, 15 oz.; $165), for several years. In strong winds, its bat-curved 9.5 by 9.5 feet is unflap-pable—if occasionally wet at the edges—for two. Besides regular single-sheet camping, I've pitched the Heptawing as a rainy-day cardplayers' annex. The real discovery was that it fit perfectly over the all-mesh body of a Moss Double Helix, giving 360-degree views and gnat-free ventilation for two. On a heat-wavered trip through no-see-um plagued Utah canyons, this proved a good combo. One night Linda and I heard a throaty belch and a sound like someone slapping the sand: ka-*thwup.* A headlamp revealed one hell of a big desert toad, who (the *Chicago Manual of Style* be damned—I instinctively use "who" for animals rather than "which," and

Moss Heptawing

this toad was definitely a "who") paused in his gnat-lapping rounds to take us in. For wildlife encounters, a wing's the thing. The larger Moss Vistawing (tarp, 2 lbs. 14 oz.; poles, 1 lb. 7 oz.; $199) accommodates three human beings—or one skunk.

Pyramids

are, *in esse,* tarps with folded corners. Chouinard Equipment (long since bifurcated into Patagonia and Black Diamond) brought one out years ago, and under it—for three endless, rainy nights on a river in Idaho—I got eaten alive. While the tent itself did not hatch the bugs, it certainly seemed to concentrate them; and ever since, I itch at the mere sight of one. The fact that it also resembles (is a nylon copy of) an archaic canvas sheepherder tent called the "range tepee" blunts my acceptance of it as a revolutionary development. Unless you excavate a hole underneath, I find the space cramped, with the center pole in the way of practically everything. Some of my Egyptoid pals do like them, however.*

The original durable diamond is now sold as the Bibler Megamid: a cheap sleep for four (at 5 lbs. 8 oz., $178). Others include the netted and recontoured Moss Superfly 4 (5 lbs. 4 oz., $399) and the Mountain Hardwear Kiva (sleeps four, 4 lbs. 2 oz., $240).

My unreasonable dread is tempered by the Asage Stronghold Tipi, an 11-foot-diameter, eight-paneled version with steep, snow-shedding

---

*COLIN: I've used my old Chouinard pyramid occasionally for years—in low-bug-potential situations—largely because of its lightness (2.5 pounds complete). And although the center pole indeed mangles available space, the rig is still palatial for one, and on balance I've enjoyed being a live ringer for a dead pharaoh.

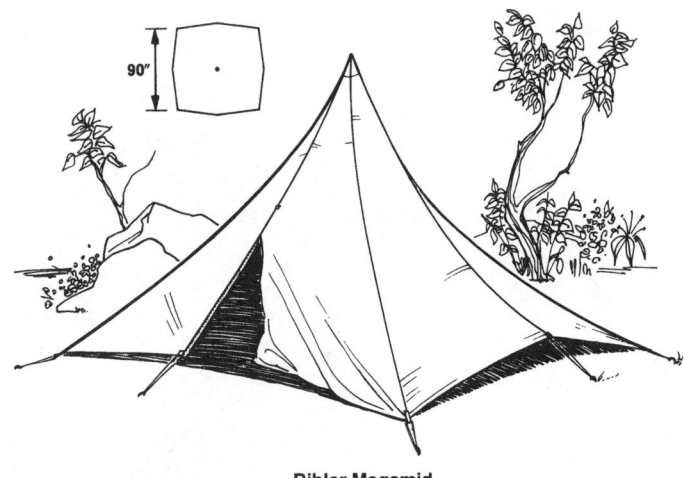

Bibler Megamid

walls, a standup center, and a hooded vent opposite a mesh window. Non-corporately made in Girdwood, Alaska, it weighs—pole included—5 lbs. 14 oz. and costs $347. Dreadlocks optional.

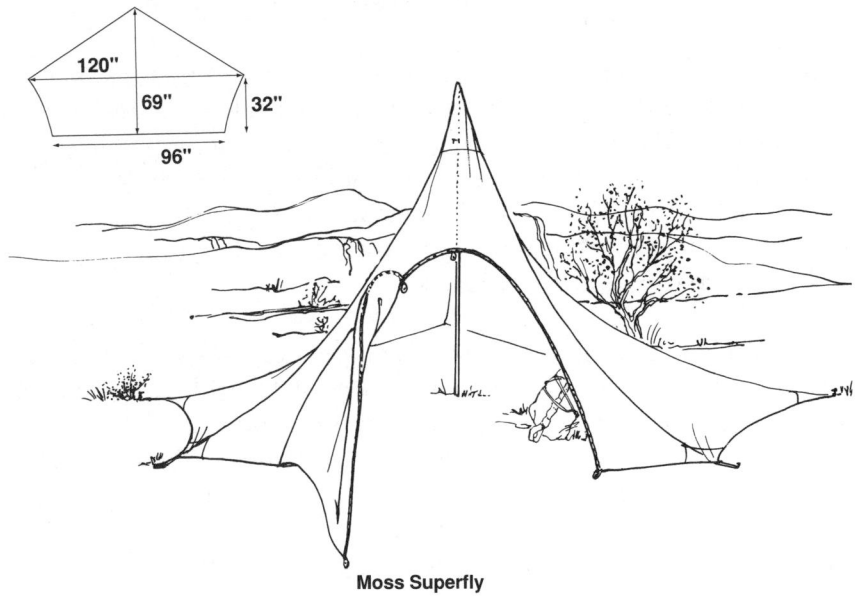

Moss Superfly

Traditional A-frame

COLIN: At one time most backpacking tents were A-frames. No more. A-frames tend to be rather heavier than equivalent hoop tents and domes, and their sloping sidewalls mean that they offer less roominess for the

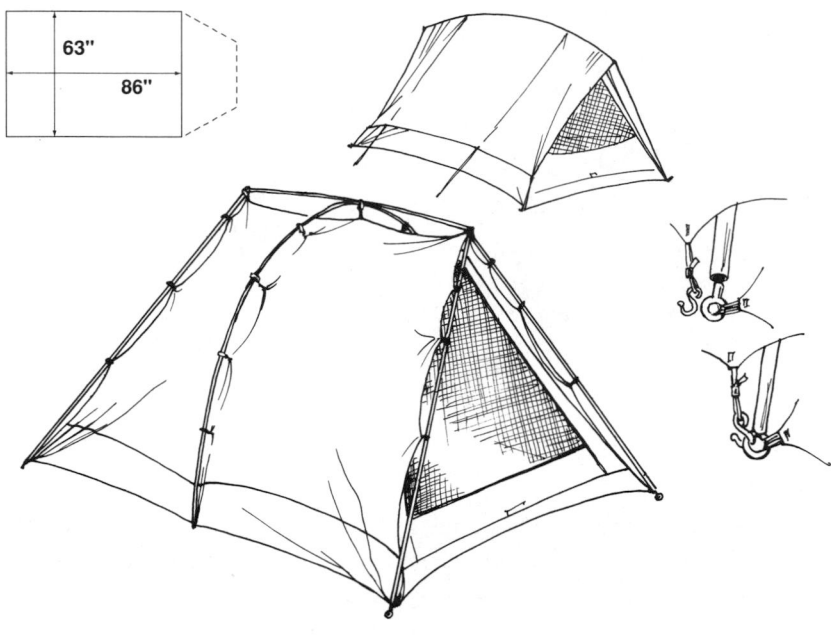

Eureka Timberline

same floor space. So they've become "old hat." But don't let that fool you. In a gale-whipped rainstorm the best of them are at least as easy to erect as most hoops or domes. They generate fewer condensation problems. And they tend to cost less than more fashionably shaped equivalents. Above all, they afford the surest protection against tempestuous snow, rain, and wind. And they remain perhaps the most reliable design. If I were planning a macho trip I'd still consider one.

CHIP: The longest-running A-frame design is the Eureka Timberline— over 2 million sold (I remember when the McDonald's sign said that). With a gently arched ridgepole that stretches a protective eave over the ends, it's a simple, sturdy, weatherworthy (and freestanding) tent. The 2-person model weighs 6 lbs. 10 oz. and costs $170, and larger versions are available. A lightweight variant with a stakeout vestibule is the Timberlite XT (4 lbs. 8 oz., $215). A lurking hazard is described in the footnote, page 381.

Modified A-frame

Once the most logical leap, in terms of design, this is now a dwindling category. But the tents in it tend to be very well proven indeed. A good example is the Walrus Rapeede, which is distinguished by a folding

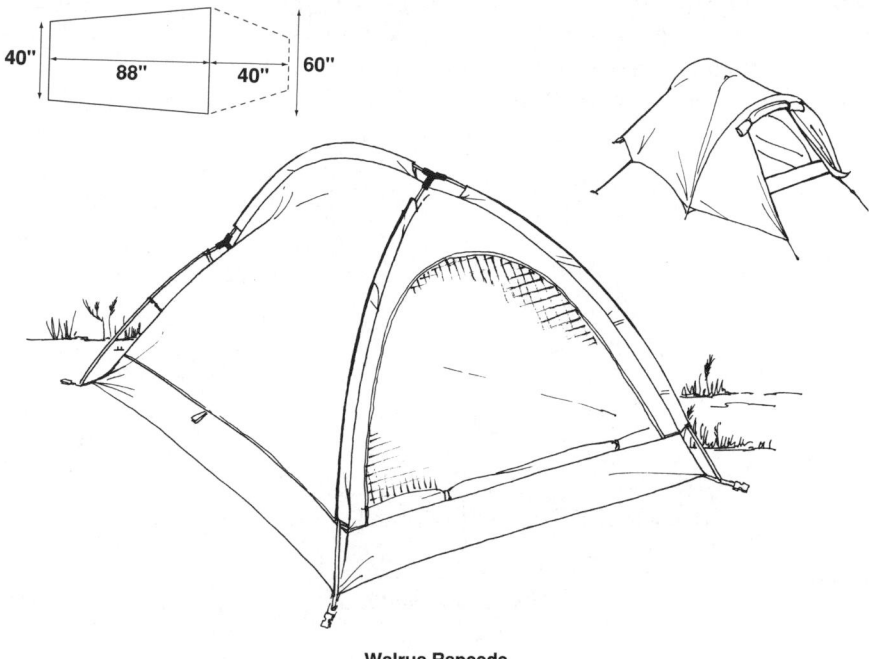

Walrus Rapeede

hub system—the poles stay in one piece—and a distinctively arched front and a smaller, low-arched rear A-frame (6 lbs., $229). An early sales pitch was that you could throw this tent up in the air and it would pitch itself, but better sense now prevails.

The Moss Outland is another proven 4-season mountain tent, for soloists (5 lbs. 12 oz., $409). It has a ridgepole that touches down at either end, with hoops rather than pointy frames at the ends. The tent itself is symmetrical, but the fly vestibule makes it look like a caterpillar abruptly changing its mind which way to go. Like most other Moss tents, this one is sweetly habitable under the vilest conditions, and should last for years.

Classicists, however, will prefer the Eureka Alpenlite 2XT, a lightweight 4-season variant of the Timberline A-frame, with white body and yellow full-coverage fly, front vestibule (with window), and good ventilation (for two, 6 lbs., $295).

By reason of shape—a flat-topped A—I'd almost judge the Sierra Designs Clip Flashlight a modified A-frame. But the experts call it a

Hoop tent.

COLIN: Because of their curved sidewalls, hoop tents offered more space for a given floor area and could be built lighter. Most models were easier to erect than all but the best A-frames. And although they at first looked fragile and most were in fact less sturdy than good A-frames, so that few were genuine 4-season units, they proved remarkably strong. One disadvantage: their curved wands remain more liable to damage, especially during erection or dismantling, than the thicker, rigid A-frame poles.

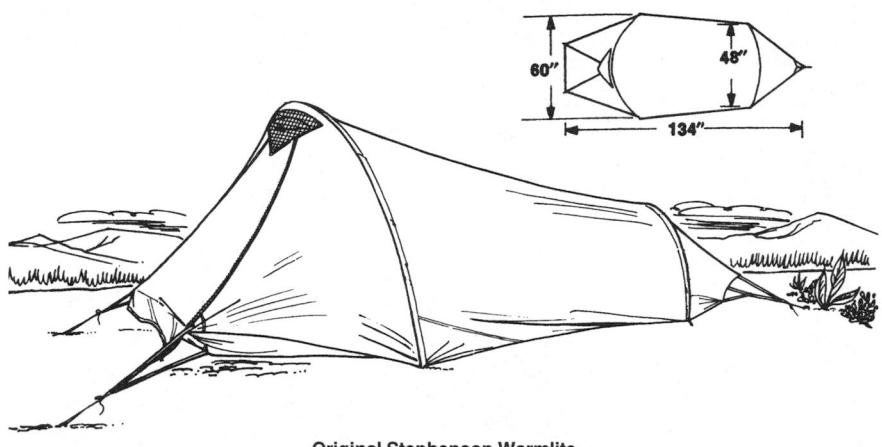

Original Stephenson Warmlite

Among the earliest and most innovative hoop tents were the Warmlite series by Stephenson, now of New Hampshire. The current line offers three sizes and many variations, with everything still designed for lightness, from anodized aluminum poles to impermeable, polymer-coated 1.4-ounce ripstop nylon walls (single or double; no traditional fly). As with all Warmlite products, the design is ingenious, if not always superbly practical, and the workmanship excellent. The tents seem to attract a small, enthusiastic group of true-believing users, but many people, including me, doubt their ability to stand up to severe weather, especially heavy rain, or to even reasonably careful everyday use. But you can't ignore a 2-person tent that weighs less than 3 pounds. And I still consider using my old 2-person, double-walled version occasionally when weight looms big and lousy weather small—that is, mostly, when I really don't need a tent. Warmlite tents are labeled by the number of sleepers, with an X for single-wall and an R for double-wall models. Current weights and prices for single-wall tents are: 2X—2 lbs. 5 oz., $460; 3X—3 lbs. 4 oz., $580; 5X—4 lbs. 11 oz., $780. For double-wall: 2R—2 lbs. 12 oz., $499; 3R—3 lbs. 12 oz., $625; 5R—5 lbs. 10 oz., $850.

CHIP: Post-Warmlite, less costly hoop tents were fielded by Moss, Early Winters, JanSport, and Sierra West. The advantages were a high ratio of usable space for the weight, and overall simplicity. The bad points were pronounced floppiness in wet or snowy weather, along with slope-slanting doors that didn't go well with bathtub floors. As Colin observes, "once you get rain into the bathtub you have . . . a bathtub." North Face updated the hoop design with the Westwind, a true 4-season mountain tent (and a personal favorite, now lost in the mists of time).

But the smash hit of the hoop genre is the Sierra Designs Clip Flashlight. The key to the design is the Swift Clip, a tough plastic hook on a loop of webbing, sewn into a seam of the inner tent. Rather than having to slip each wand through a full-width sleeve (a scream in a high wind), you simply stake the tent out, poke pole tips into grommets, and stretch the tent up to clip, cutting pitch time by at least four or five expletives. The fly drapes over the wands, with Velcro loops inboard, and you anchor it below with clip buckles. And dive in.

The Swift Clip is now used in all Sierra Designs tents, and clips-in-general are found on a great many other brands. A new-style Sierra Designs clip called the Cam-Loc adds wind resistance. Since the fly sheet is in contact with the full length of the pole, there seems not to be a great sacrifice in strength, compared to a sleeve.

Meanwhile the Flashlight CD now comes in the classic 2-body version (3 lbs. 10 oz., $189), and a 3-person Clip 3 CD (4 lbs. 10 oz., $249). Success has also spawned two solo offshoots. The affordable Light Year CD (2 lbs. 15 oz., $149) has a pointed, asymmetrical prow and angled entry, with a boot-width vestibule. Recently, I've been using the accelerated-cost version, the Ultra Light Year CD (2 lbs. 10 oz., $349) of the lightest possible fabric with the new Easton aluminum-carbon poles. The two-tone sage fly is great for stealth camping and casts a sylvan light inside. There's enough mesh for airy sleep and bug-free views. Despite the amaz-

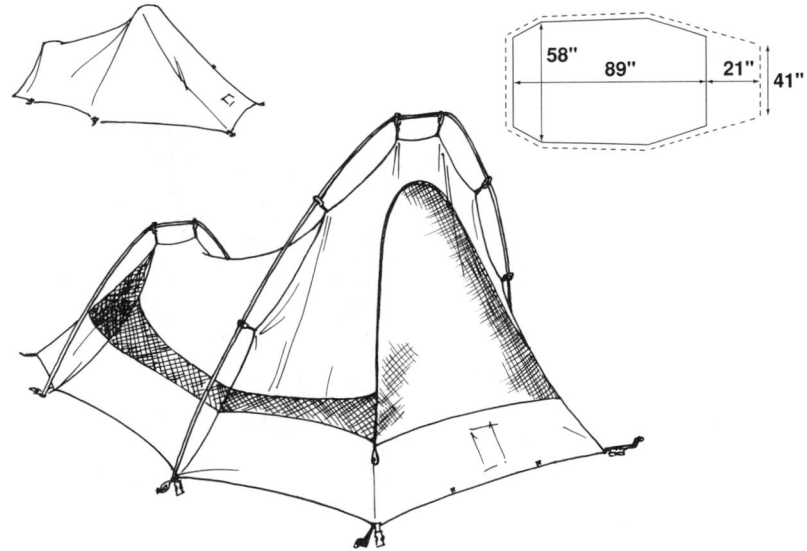

Sierra Designs Clip Flashlight

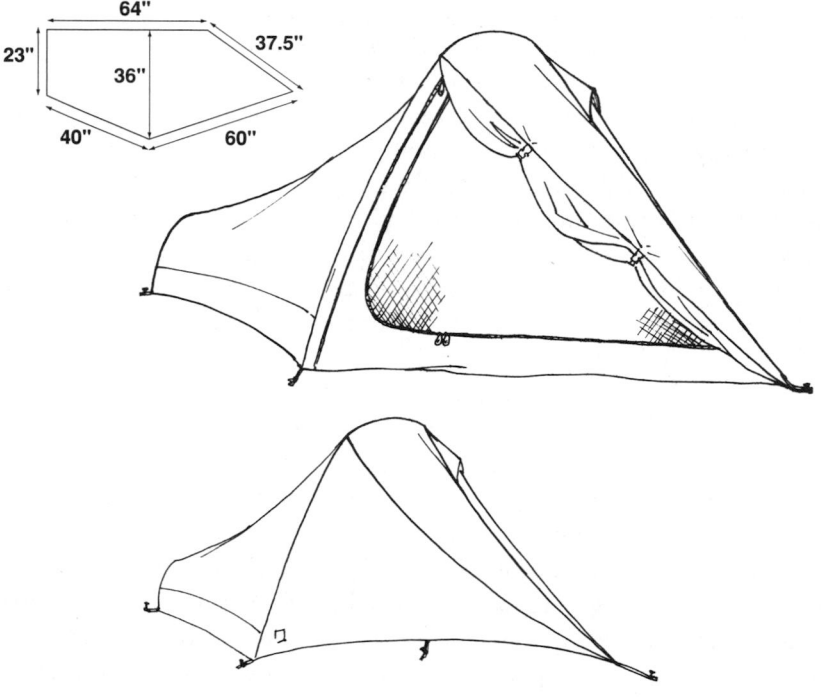

Sierra Designs Divine Lightning

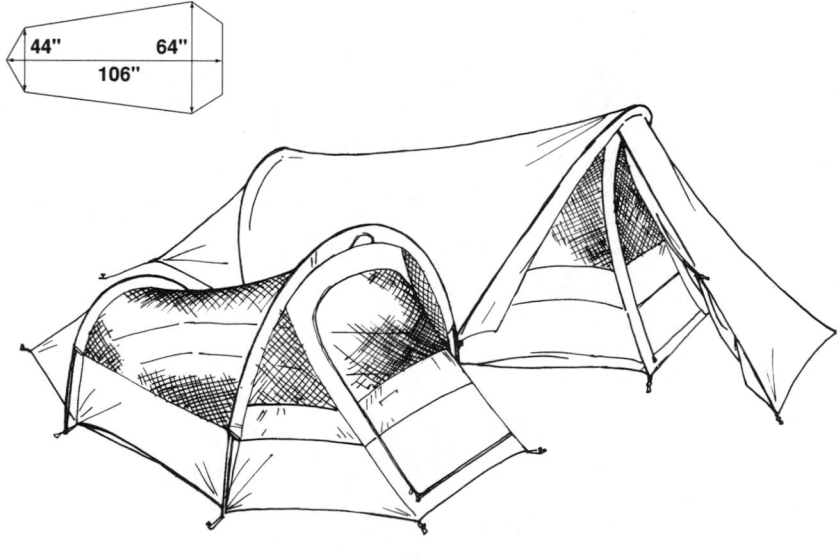

Walrus Arch Rival

ing lightness, it offers sufficient room for me (6 feet 4 inches) in a puffy sleeping bag to draw up my knees or (*Yes!*) sit up straight and pull on clean socks. For the sake of perspective, this tent weighs less (at 2 lbs. 9 oz.) *with* the poles than my Moss Heptawing (a sophisticated tarp, at 2 lbs. 12 oz.) does without them. The stitching and taping are perfect: I think it'll stand up to Wyoming weather. Or three seasons' worth, anyhow.

Earlier on, I used the similarly laid-out Sierra Designs Divine Lightning, a single-wall solo tent of a breathable laminate, for trips year-round. But with scant volume in the head and foot, I found it confining. Yet for Linda (at 5 feet 4 inches) it was indeed divine. While droplets and frost built up on the coated door fly (and dripped to the ground), the inside of the breathable portion stayed dry—the hooded peak vent helped.

Other noteworthy hoopsters (excuse the mind-numbing list) are made by Garuda, EMS, Eureka, Ferrino, Integral Designs, Kelty, L. L. Bean, Marmot, Mountain Hardwear, Noall, North Face, Peak 1, and VauDe. At the foot of the alphabet, Walrus has some of the nicest hoop tents around. The Walrus Micro-Swift is for petite solists (2 lbs. 13 oz., $119), while the Arch Rival is for two primates of average build (see previous page; 4 lbs. 4 oz., $169).

The Walrus Hurricane Hole (7 lbs. 5 oz., $318) is a unique three-hoop tent with a Euro-inspired exoskeletal design. That is, the three wands, with straps across the base, sleeve tightly inside the fly. This assembly can give you a truly striking demonstration of how a spinnaker works—until you learn to stake it down at one end and stay low while poling up. But once you get the fly-sheet protocol down, you can slip

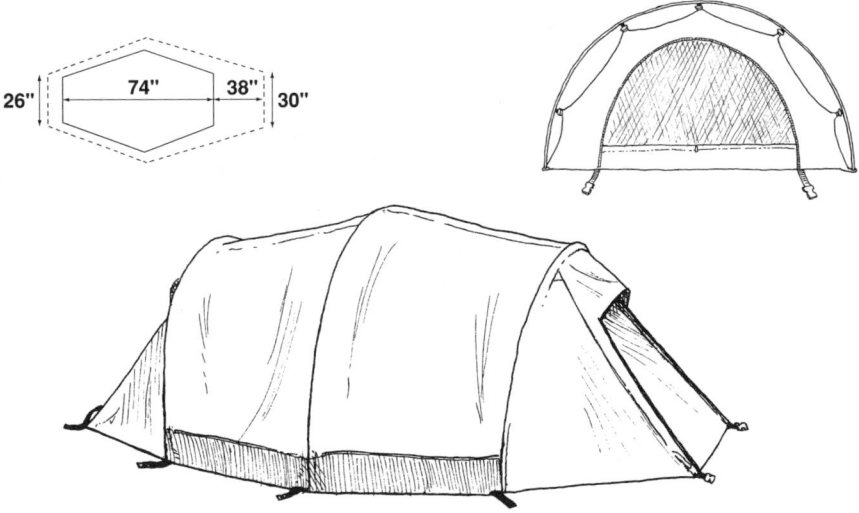

Walrus Hurricane Hole

inside—out of the storm—to suspend the floored inner tent in a sheltered and leisurely way, from elasticized clips. You can even pitch the fly, drag your pack inside, unload, lean out to start up the stove, and then finish deploying the inner tent while the first pot boils. With its ground-hugging pitch, internal flaps, double doors (each with vestibule), and large vent overhangs, this is a howlingly great winter or high-elevation tent. With an optional full-length floor (1 lb. 4 oz., $40) the coated fly can serve as a roomy single-wall shelter for three. I've been using the Hurricane Hole regularly as a reverse 3-season tent: fall, winter, and spring. Despite an optional mesh inner ($92), it's a steambath in summer. If you pitch it *exactly* in line with the breeze, it ventilates. Otherwise, not.

Hilleberg Akto

Similar virtues reside (as do a large number of Swedes) in hoop tents by Hilleberg. Now available in the U.S., Hilleberg's beautifully sewn and detailed line of tents includes a single-hoop soloist, the ultralight but commodious Akto (the Sami word for "alone" — 3 lbs., $340). By dint of a large center hoop sleeved into the full-coverage fly, with small carbon-fiber wands at the corners, the Akto offers nonslanting head- and foot-room. It easily accepts my 6-foot 4-inch frame in a lofty sleeping bag, but the one small bug-mesh window makes it best for cool nights, methinks. It comes (as do all Hilleberg models) with a spare pole section and extra fabric, for patches. In fact, Hilleberg specializes in hoop tents, some roomy enough for a string quartet—and their instruments.

While I enjoy the roominess of hoops, another highly useful breed is the

Wedge tent.

The gear guides call these domes, but they aren't, in the way that a mouse is not a ladybug. The first one I camped in, on a winter ski traverse, was a JanSport Half Dome. It was frosty and cramped, with (as I recall) a canopy of clinically depressed gray under a suicide-blue fly sheet. Or maybe it was the other way around. One night an avalanche cut loose below camp, and my partner—an unhygenic French Canadian hockey fan—reared up violently from his bag, just as I did the same. We bashed skulls so hard that I saw tiny flaming pinwheels for hours after. This also happens in A-frames (footnote, page 381).

Bibler I-tent

The upshot was that I absolutely refused to have anything to do with a wedge for many years. When friends raved about their Bibler I-tents (a renowned single-wall stalwart, ostensibly for two; 3 lbs. 12 oz., $575), I wrote them off as masochistic—my problem, not yours.

Most makers have a wedge or two in their line, for good reasons: it's the simplest possible layout, two flexible wands crossed in an X. It's free-standing. It gives maximum floor area for minimum material (and weight). The ughs include acutely angled head- and foot-space, limited storage area, and the slant-door bathtub syndrome. To get around this last, some makers have moved the door from the end to one side (or both), and added a third wand to stretch the fly out in an eave, which is mildly effective in calm weather. In turbulent storms, you get wet. Unless, that is, the fly sheet includes a real, zippered vestibule.

The king of the wedgies is Eureka, with 10 reasonably priced tents in various sizes. Of interest to backpackers are the Aurora (solo: 4 lbs. 12 oz., $195; duo: 6 lbs. 14 oz., $240); the solo Zephyr (3 lbs. 9 oz., $170); and the 3-verging-on-4-season Mountain Pass 2XT (for two, 6 lbs. 2 oz., $230). I've used a Eureka Zephyr XT (4 lbs. 12 oz., $180) for several trips and liked it. As fans of Moss tents have realized for some time, the white/tan/red color scheme is pleasant. With a full-coverage fly, peak vent, and two vestibules, it's winterworthy. And it's also one of the least-expensive solo tents that's actually comfortable for 4-season use—if you dig out a subvestibular skank pit (page 370). Otherwise you have to duck low to get in.

Kelty also has several wedges, with the convertible Jetstream neatly sleeping two (5 lbs. 12 oz., $330). In an age of haphazard instructions Kelty deserves credit for giving good tent-specific directions and also a general care-and-maintenance manual, with pitching and repair tricks, and a further section on the effects of wind and altitude—all in a funny, offhand style. Besides the famous I-tent mentioned above, Bibler has the palatial Ahwahnee (5 lbs. 4 oz., $750) with a big mesh windows, side entry, and an optional third-pole vestibule (1 lb. 8 oz., $150).

I've inserted a wedge into my solo/alto trips: the VauDe Galaxy Ultralight (5 lbs., $339). For two ballerinas (or a single galoot), it pitches extremely fast with a post-and-grommet setup on the two main wands and a clip system. At that point, you have the typical gossamer wedge, with two doors. What makes it stand out is a transverse pole on top that stretches the gleaming polyester fly, forming two deep-eaved vestibules,

VauDe Galaxy Ultralight

with full-arch zips. You can store a pack, even two, and still have room to cook. Lacking a peak vent, it ventilates with the double zips and a healthy overhang. Minor quibbles are some raw fabric edges inside and cheesy (but easily replaceable) shock cord in the poles. But this tent has pleased me mightily on trips with strong winds and snowfall, by allowing a sound, dry slumber. VauDe (a twist on the German word for "father") also makes the affordable standard Galaxy (6 lbs. 2 oz., $169) and Galaxy 3 (7 lbs. 2 oz., $199). Their catalog—of things both germane and Germanic—shows a number of intriguing tents.

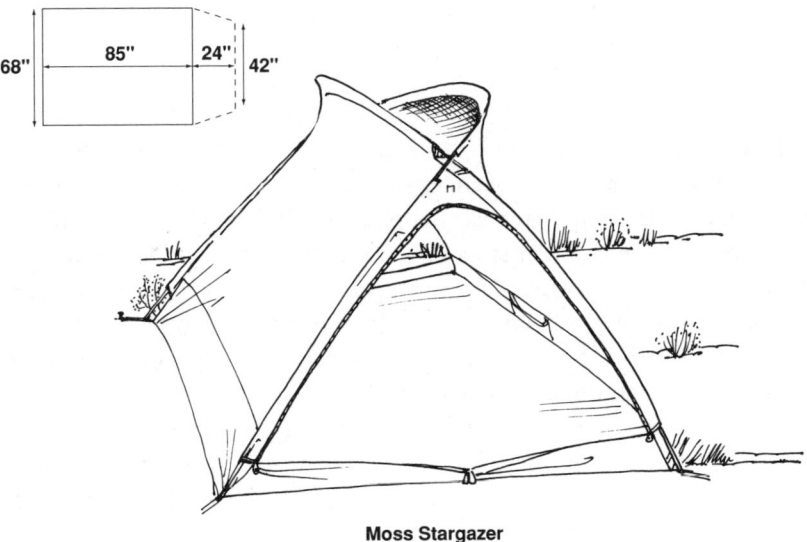

Moss Stargazer

A significant variation on the wedge (and the first tent Moss built) is the 3-season model now called the Stargazer (for two: 7 lbs. 8 oz., $389). The two wands cross twice, front and rear, increasing the headroom with a mesh skylight, which can also let condensation drip down: keep the fly snug. I think of it as a mushroom wedge. The Moss Starlet is a lightweight cousin (5 lbs. 4 oz., $379) with partial-mesh sidewalls. Both (and all Moss tents) are a clean combination of tan floor, white walls, and full-length red pole sleeves. The fly sheets are tan, for nice internal light in almost any weather.

If you add a third pole to a wedge, you enter the ever-more-complex world of

Domes.

COLIN: Domes are essentially hoop tents rendered remarkably rigid by single or multiple crossings of the hoops. This rigidity makes the best of them good 4-season tents. But the attractive and roomy structure complicates condensation-fighting ventilation (page 386). And domes tend to be difficult to erect under vile conditions ("Practically impossible after a little wine," says one practitioner). Most domes are entirely freestanding, and salesmen make a lot of this: "You can pick it up and move to another place without taking it down," they say. But that seems more a sales- than a tent-pitch. After all, how often do you really want to move house? Furthermore, a freestanding tent tends to be left unstaked, held down by only the gear inside, and a sudden wind may then pick it up and waft it away. Such unscheduled flights occasionally occur. It's true, though, that if the unmanned hang glider lands in a lake, its rigid structure proves a huge advantage: it may amphibianize the glider into a sailplane and deposit it, contents still dry, on the far shore. This, too, has happened. A more real if minor advantage of a freestanding tent is that you can erect it and set it to one side, ready for quick use in case of rain, and then sleep or rest nearby with an unobstructed view of scenery or stars. And a freestanding tent is certainly easy to dry: you just pick it up, shake the grossest moisture and crud out the open door, then stand it on end or hang it, floor facing the morning sun (if you can marshal a morning sun). In other words, such tents offer genuine field advantages; but I suspect that some of the bouncy sales talk may stem from advantages they offer in the mountain shop. There, as in the mountains (and as with all guyless models), they take up far less valuable ground space. What's more, they can be hung, leaned, and generally flung around in delightfully eye-catching poses. And I think we should all, when buying, maybe try, as a precautionary measure, to bear that morsel of information in mind.

JanSport pioneered large, practical dome tents. Later, North Face almost dominated the market with its VE series (VE = Vector Equilibrium, the Bucky Fuller geodesic design concept). Many domes tend toward high profiles—opting for headroom rather than wind-shedding strength. I have little experience with dome tents, and none in really bad weather, but they're certainly popular. The mountain shops—and the mountains too—teem with eye-pleasing, practical models.

CHIP: The North Face's first dome, the Oval Intention, was a landmark— absolutely the strongest mountain tent of its era. But the 17 poles in 13 different lengths (there might have been fewer while seeming like even more) did give me a bad moment or two in blizzards. For some years I lived in a series of VE tents—all government property—while practicing science at high elevations, and liked them except for the weight. The VE 23, 24, and 25 domes (respectively 3-season, 4-season, and expedition) were notable improvements. Today, the only VE tent left in the North

Face catalog is the VE-25 (10 lbs. 13 oz., $549), a four-pole (plus a hoop for the vestibule), 4-season shelter of exceptional toughness that will sleep three, in a pinch. While the VE designation has flown, North Face still makes a series of rugged VE-inspired domes that will accommodate from two to eight-plus.

Everybody (except Stephenson's) makes domes these days, so a full list is out of the question. Instead, it seems wise to reflect on Domes-I-Have-Known with reference to some overall qualities. Which makes me realize that I have owned only two: a Sierra Designs Omega CD and a Eureka Assault. Despite that, some of my personal milestones have come and gone under cover of one. Linda and I commenced our courtship with a game of strip poker in her sun-ravaged JanSport dome. And I can date my Forest Service years by the model of the North Face dome we camped in.*

But I've never really liked domes in the way I do hoops. Mostly, I suspect, because of the added weight.

Dome-tent design starts with two wands that cross (or double-cross). But where the third wand goes makes all the difference. On the old

Classic dome

---

*One season I slept out in my bivy sack to avoid run-ins with an overbearing coworker who resided in a VE-23 — I thought of her as the Dominatrix.

JanSport classic, three wands intersected on top, in the middle, making the floor an equal-sided hexagon. This made it shed rain beautifully, down the pie-slice walls, but also rendered it weak in high winds. A true geodesic structure gains strength from multiple pole-crossings, and this is why North Face domes work so well. Given the basic X, a third pole can cross at the front or the rear, for a stretched-hex floor plan. The Sierra Designs Omega CD (convertible, for two: 6 lbs. 2 oz., summer; 6 lbs. 8 oz., winter; $289 year-round) has a third pole arching up from the center to frame the front door (as do thousands of others). This lends more structure and height at the head, while the foot tapers off. The fly sheet stakes out to form an end vestibule with a plastic window: neat and effective.

Sierra Designs boosts the strength of the pole web in a couple of ways. One follows a longtime practice of mountaineers: wrapping shock cord around intersections to add wind resistance. Sierra Designs strings a short piece of shock cord (called a ShoK-Cert) to the large clips that hold the poles where they cross. Once wrapped around, it slots with a plastic bead back into the clip. The entirely new Cam-Loc clip slides freely until you turn a plastic twist key that grips the pole with a squeak. It weighs only 0.15 oz. more than a standard clip and is claimed to add 12 percent more strength.

Other makers, like Moss, claim that full-contact sleeves are by far the best for strength. The disadvantage is that the poles must be threaded through, one by one by one. Partial sleeves, that expose the crossings, are one variation that eases pole threading (as long as you remember to follow the seams). Another is the use of strong mesh for all or part, as in the Eureka Assault opposite. Some tents, like those from Marmot, combine mesh sleeves and clips. Quite a few now have color-coded tape or clips— including, as of 2000, that full-sleeve stalwart Moss, with a new wishbone-shaped clip.

The Eureka Assault (it seems they have a NATO contract) exemplifies another sort of three-pole dome. This also begins with an X, but the third pole arches, like a Neanderthal brow, across the wider dimension. The 2-person Assault (now updated as a four-poler called the Polar Storm XT: 10 lbs. 10 oz., $435) has two full doors and two vestibules. The layout is strong but also airy and convenient, letting you lounge as you cook and exit without having to crawl. (These double-door-and-vestibule tents are particularly beloved by dog owners because the pups can be bedded down in shelter without actually being in the tent proper.) The Marmot Swallow (for two: 6 lbs. 13 oz., $339) is a particularly good tent of this type, with mesh sleeves for the X and clips for the brow pole, and a dark high-visibility netting.

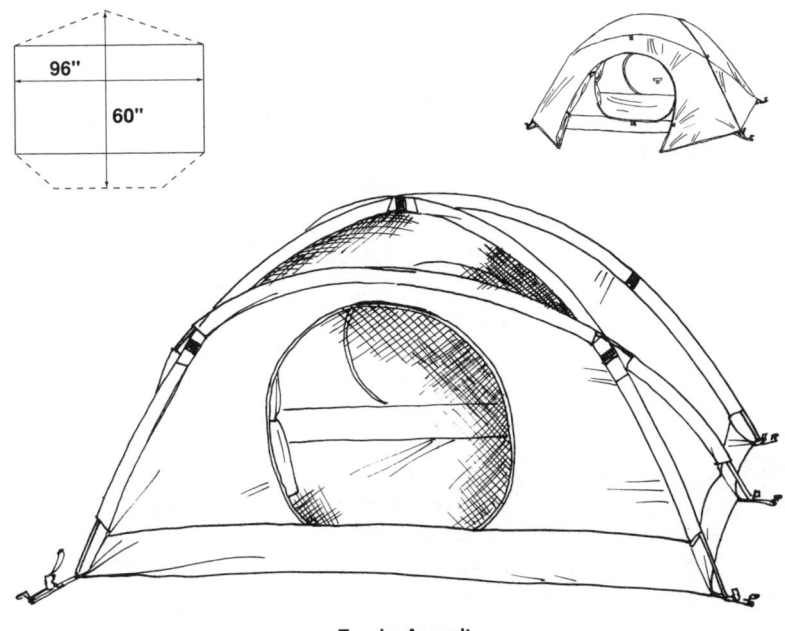

Eureka Assault

Adding a fourth pole is a move usually reserved for the stoutest 4-season tents. What you have at this stage is an X or a double-cross overlapped with a (). But let's talk about desirable or undesirable features.

Since most domes have sloping walls, there should be some weather protection for the door, either by steepening that part with a brow pole or by using an eave or a full vestibule. Another problem, particularly on "stretch" domes, is a flattish roof panel, especially one bordered by pole sleeves. While the fly might shed rain when tight, it will droop in the wet and become a rooftop mini-pond. Or, given freezing temperatures, you might wake up with a block of ice overhead. If the panel has a clear plastic skylight, then you can at least watch the process. Clear plastic windows are likewise appealing, once you get used to their being fogged most of the time you're actually inside your tent.

Being able to adjust the tension of the fly from inside is a definite plus. So is being able to reef up one end or the other on a warm night. Tie-downs should be no lower than one-third of the height of the fly, nor much higher than half. A too-high guy line turns your tent into a spinnaker. In a truly hellish gust, it's better for the tent to be blown flat (at least serving as a bivy sack) than to lift off.

One of the nicest stretch domes I've tried is the Nightview by Mountain Hardwear (7 lbs. 8 oz., $370). The proportion and angle, and a

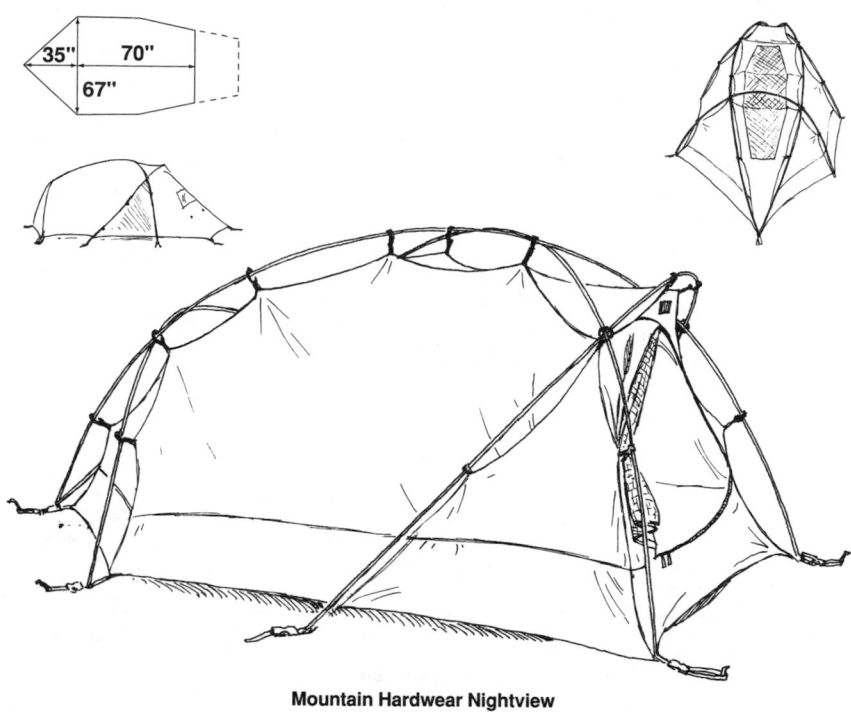

Mountain Hardwear Nightview

long mesh top panel (with a matching skylight in the fly), give the tent a unique architectural grandeur. Crawling inside, you can almost feel a monumental hush.

Hybrids and offbeats

One of my favorites, despite scant headroom, is the odd-but-engaging single-pole Moss Helix (in a solo and duo version). The one lengthwise wand swaps sides in the middle, like a rainbow with one foot in Belgium and the other in France.

The Walrus Warp 2 (duo: 7 lbs. 8 oz., $249) sort of blurs your vision at first. It's basically a wedge, but one side of the X is forked at both ends, framing two low mesh vents/windows. Two asymmetrical doors complicate the look, but not the livability—it's a superb 4-season tent that seems to be spawning variants.

Another offbeat that's lasted is an asymmetrical, three-pole design from Marmot—introduced in the Peapod, Nutshell, and Hardshell. Picture a narrow rectangle. The longest pole (like the one on the Moss Helix) starts in the southwest corner and rainbows all the way to the northeast. The middle-size pole begins in the southeast corner (framing the door)

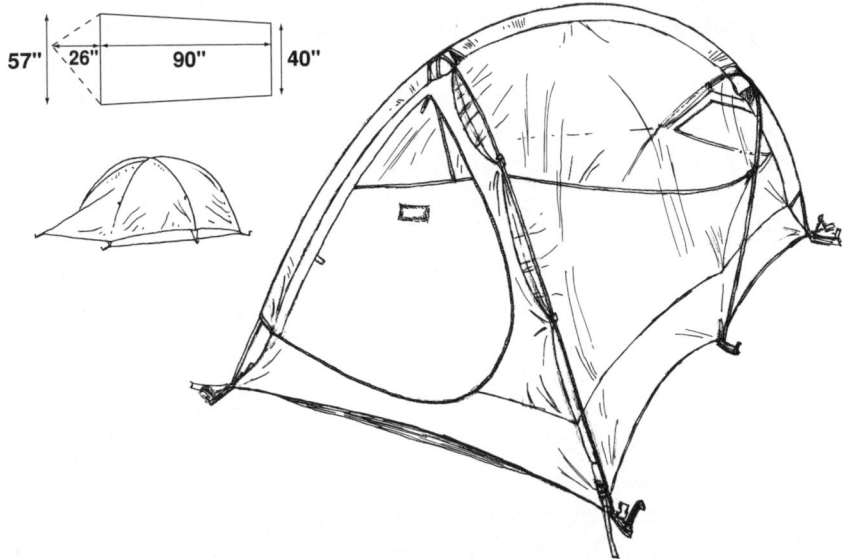

and touches back down halfway up the west side. The short pole starts halfway up the east side and grounds in the northwest corner (see the drawing above, and see also tent types, page 380, bottom right).

Marmot deserves thanks not only for exceptional gear but also for maintaining a "demo-locker" for testing purposes: they sent me a well-used Nutshell to test, and I loved it. It was light, set up fast, kept me dry under 4 inches of rainfall—and looking at it put me in a good mood. Marmot genes, yielding doors that zip (and fall) to one side now show up in many other tents. And the 3-season Nutshell is happily and anti-entropically still around (for two: 4 lbs., 10 oz., $259). It rides in an envelope-style sack that's probably easier on the tent than the usual tubular crammer.

But offbeats are hard to sell. So some of the best new designs wither and vanish, while the same old hoops, domes, and A-frames continue to dominate. It seems that tent buying, like housebuilding, is inherently conservative.

QUALITY AND OTHER CONCERNS

Tents, having large areas of several different fabrics and being terribly labor-intensive, vary enormously in quality. So here, by virtue of several decades of tenting, a few significant failures—and a great many attentive crawls on the floors of shops and trade shows—are some qualitative tips.

The tent should pitch evenly, with the seams along the margin of the floor, well above ground-level. All the stake loops should touch ground—on some poorly cut domes some loops can be far enough off the ground that you have to struggle (or add cheater loops) to stake the tent down. Seams should be straight and lie flat—no crinkles. If they're taped, make sure the tape lies clear and flat, with no wrinkles, bubbles, loose threads, or hairs to cause leaks. Coated fabrics should display an even finish—check with a glancing light.

On uncoated parts, since the optimal hot-cutting method is seldom used, for reasons of cost and laboriousness, look carefully for fray-prone edges where unraveling can reach a seam. The worst examples are usually inside the door arches, where the tent body is turned in along the zipper. One of my otherwise favorite tents had this problem, and I daubed seam sealer along the raw margin to stop the unraveling, which had almost reached a crucial zipper seam.

Tension points, at the base of clips or stake loops, should have fabric layered and sewn flat, not bunched up. Even tents with factory-taped seams can generally use extra seam sealing where loops join—pitch the tent and stretch it taut to open the needle holes before applying sealer. Avoid petroleum-based seam sealer in bottles with foam daubers (I've had the foam actually melt and adhere to the tent in nasty little glops). Instead, use sealer in a tube, with a narrow brush. The drill is to squeeze out a bead with one hand and follow along with the brush in the other to spread it and work it into the seam. Or, failing that, you can work as a team, with Squeezer closely followed by the Spreader. (Never, at the risk of your good nature, try sealing a tent on a windy day.) On flat-felled or overlapped seams, seal the smooth side. For urethane-coated fabrics (most) McNett Seam Grip earns the most kudos, with their Aquaseal running a close second. These are packaged with the proper brush, and a liquid accelerator adds strength and speeds drying. Let the tent dry fully, 24 to 48 hours, and then dust the sealed areas lightly with talc (Seam Grip is a glue) before stuffing it. (Incidentally, most makers now recommend stuffing rather than folding tents. A repetitively neat crease will weaken fabrics and damage coatings.) For those who'd rather avoid noxious fumes and stickiness, Seam Sealer 3 by Kenyon (2 oz., $4.50) is a water-based urethane compound. I recently sealed a tent fly with it, and besides being nearly odorless, it goes on smoothly and controllably with the built-in dauber. I double-coated all the fly seams and treated some of the spots where seams join and those where the stake loops join the tub floor three times, all with a mere ounce of sealer. It seems to do the trick, though I've yet to see it through a long downpour. Also just out and perhaps similar is Aquaseal Seam Sealer ("odorless, tough, elastic") in a 2-oz. bottle for $4. Silicone-impregnated nylon, in ultralight tarps and tents, should be sealed with McNett SILNet (also gluelike, 1.5 oz., $6) or the equivalent. Liquid daub-on silicone compounds have some seam-sealing effect but need to be reapplied frequently. Breathable laminates are generally factory-sealed with heat-bonded tape, but check the tag for a recommended sealer, usually the same brand as the cloth.

Cool-running zippers (see page 149) are another abiding concern. Double sliders are a help, for letting partners enter and exit single-door tents without footsicuffs, and for venting fly sheets with eaves.

One heartening evidence of care (over and above corporate cost cutting) is to open up a tent package and find quality stakes, stout cordage, and perhaps a pole-sleeve repair kit. Moss has long been exceptional in this respect. All Hail!

Pegs and guy lines

COLIN: If a campsite is too soft to hold your pegs firm (sand) or too hard for you to drive them in (yes, rock), and if the wind is not too strong (if it is, try to go someplace else), tie the guy lines to the middle of the pegs, lay them flat, and block them from sliding toward the tent with heavy rocks. For this job, strong sticks are even better than pegs: their greater friction reduces the chances of slippage. Either method works better than trying to tie guy lines directly onto all but ideally shaped stones. But it is often easier and safer to loop your guy lines around the lowest branches of a bush. Or you can tie a loop of nylon cord to the bush and thread the guy line through it so that you can more easily adjust the guy. See also the guy-line shock absorber, page 421. Various makers now have shock-absorbing kits of elastic cord with hooks or rings.

CHIP: One keen trick for windy conditions, via Kelty, is to plant the guy-line stakes halfway between the fly-sheet tie-outs. The guy line runs at an angle from one stake, through the tie-out loop, to the next. This provides built-in shock absorption because it avoids a straight-line jerk. I've used this tactic on the prevailing-wind side of a tent with success. Presumably, you could run a continuous, self-equalizing web of guy line around the entire fly. The problem is keeping the line on the stakes. I threw a loop around each stake while letting the line run free through the tie-outs on the tent. Which made me nervous, in the insistent, shifting winds we get here, about having the guy line saw its way through the fabric tie-out loops. Adding split rings to the tie-out loops could be a solution.

On climbing trips, camping on bedrock, I used to slot a wired stopper or two into cracks to anchor tent guy lines. This trick can be adapted by the intelligent nonclimber: tie your guy line around a sub-fist-size rock or section of tree limb. This can be slipped into a crack where it narrows.

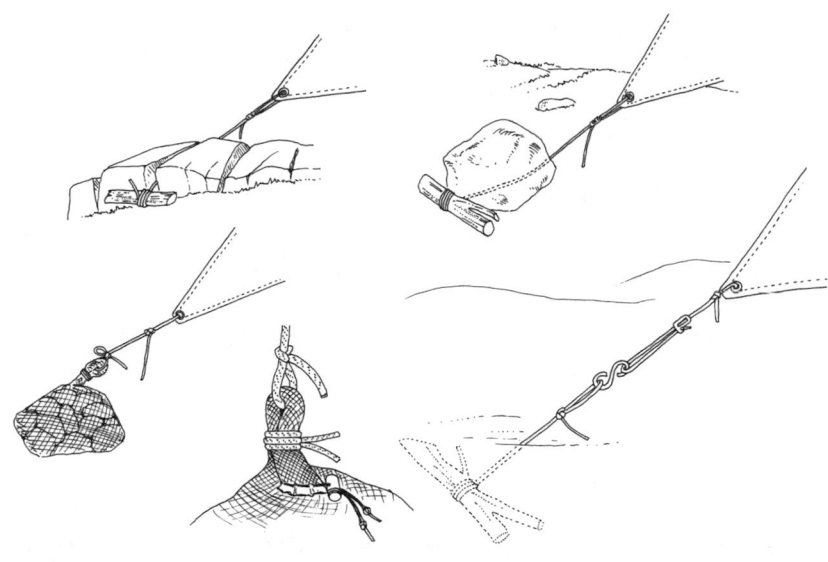

Staking variations

It can also be jammed against the far side of a large rock, with the line underneath, the advantages being that the pull is kept low and will at worst cause the large rock to slide rather than roll. Slings and shock cord give more scope for such tricks.

Where large rocks can't be had, you can fill a coarse mesh sack with smaller ones, or a stuff sack with sand for an anchor. But don't trust the drawstring. Instead, double the top of the bag and wrap it before tying off. An old scruff of a friend suggests using dirty socks for this, tied off in the center. They can (he claims) be filled with sand and buried or, in winter, if they're sufficiently damp, tied off and left out to freeze while the tent platform sets up, and then buried as deadfeet. He hit on this when his skiing partner insisted on the eviction of his socks from the tent, and they lacked a stake. Whether deadman or deadfoot (see page 421), loop it so that your knot isn't buried, using the figure-of-eight knot shown, or a bowline (see drawing). I tie a bowline by forming the initial loop, then doubling the end of the cord. This gives you a bowline you can untie with a jerk. Hilleberg sells "line-runners" that tie to the snow peg and hook to the guy line. Other stratagems involve fabric pieces with loops sewn on, sold by various companies— Bibler Soft Stakes for one. But you can set grommets in scrap

Figure-of-eight

Bowline

fabric and loop your own. Do not affix guy lines to wildlife, large dogs, or collapsed friends.

Adjustment can be done with tautline hitches (shown below), but most tent kits include guy-line adjusters, little infinity symbols of aluminum. Also good are nylon squibs with three holes, if they're set up right (both available from wholesalers and findable in most backpacking shops). They occasionally slip on glossy cordage. I usually ditch fray-prone factory guy lines and replace them with 2- to 3-millimeter cord from the bulk roll in a shop.

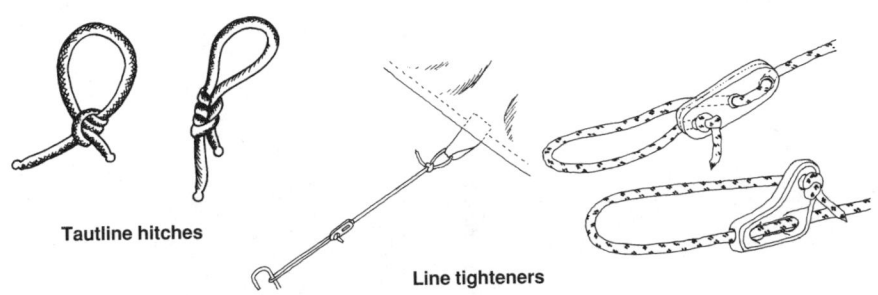

Tautline hitches

Line tighteners

Pegs are legion, with new configurations appearing as the millennium has come and gone. Basically, the shapes are pins, angles, Ts or Ys, I-beams, and curves. Most tents come with pin stakes. Cheapest are thin steel pins (a) (0.5–0.8 oz.) with a simple bend. These can rotate and lose guy lines, so push them down so the short end of the curve goes into the ground. Steel pins with loops (b) (0.6 oz.) tend to be square rod stock, and some are twisted, screw-fashion. Poking them in without turning negates the benefits of the thread, while screwing them in is tedious. But in rocky and rooty terrain, these sorts can work, via twist-and-tap, where fatter aluminum pegs fold up and fail. Thin aluminum pins (c) (4 millimeters, 0.3 oz.) bend so easily as to be semi-useless. Fatter ones (d) (6-plus millimeters, 0.4-plus oz.) with hook or loop ends are standard issue with better tents. Aluminum pegs, some with plastic hooks, that resemble 50d nails are rugged, if a bit heavy. The deluxe pin (e) is a 9-millimeter-by-9-inch-long (how's that for schizoid measurement?) 0.5-

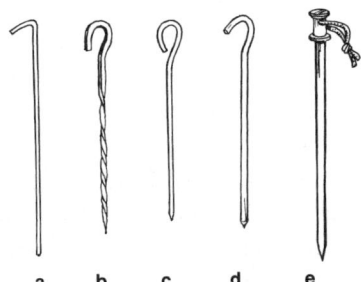

a   b   c   d   e

plus oz. Easton tube—the pointed end of an arrow shaft with a drilled spool top for driving.

Angles are an old design, but for backpacking, steel has given way to aluminum. Inexpensive ones curl over at the top (f) and will curl further if struck with any force. A better angle (g) is Easton 7075-T6, reinforced with a center bead and anodized—these come in 7.5-inch lengths with Moss tents, and perhaps others. They penetrate well, resist bending, and weigh 0.5 oz. The tops can injure bare feet, so watch it.

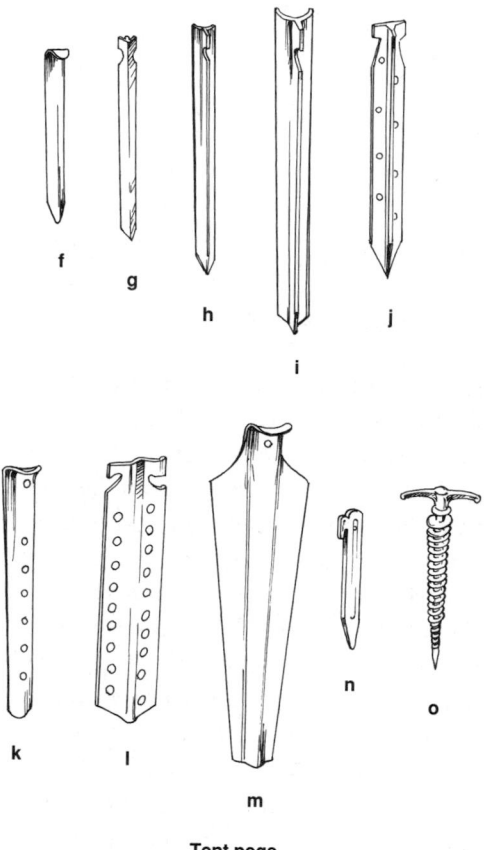

Tent pegs

Both T- and Y-pegs come in various gauges and lengths. At ¾ inch wide (h) they make good heavy-duty pegs for all-around use. The 1¼-inchers (i) are intended for sand and snow. They come in 7- (1.2 oz.), 9- (1.5 oz.), and 12- (2 oz.) inch lengths. The toughest pegs of all are Black Diamond T-stakes (j), also of 7075 T-6 alloy, which are 8 inches (1.8 oz.) and 9½ inches (2.1 oz.) long and cost $4 to $5 each: ouch! Even if you can get by for the most part with light pin stakes and tied-off bushes, it's smart to pack a few good T-stakes, especially with a hoop tent that needs to be stretched. They also work well for loose ground and snow.

The best snow pegs I've used are the curved ones (k) long made by the Seattle Manufacturing Company (SMC), 9 inches long (1 oz.), with holes. These allow disturbed snow to sinter and lock them in place. They also pack beautifully, spoonwise, with a rubber band. I've made my own snow pegs (l) of aluminum doorsill by cutting and drilling and smoothing.

Looking like one-eyed liver flukes are the extra-wide 14-inch sand-and-snow pegs (m) (3.4 oz.), made in Germany and wholesaled by Liberty Mountain Sports. For big tents, dry snow, and high winds, they can be worth the extra weight if you have to leave the tent and can't rely on ski tails. It's smart to drill a few more holes (and smooth the rims) so you get more anchor effect and can tie them off halfway.

Plastic pegs (n) are molded in an I-beam shape, in several sizes. Those supplied with backpacking tents are 6 to 7 inches long and weigh 0.6 oz. A new plastic twist peg called the Psyclone (o) takes aim at loose soil and sand and is popular enough that Liberty Mountain, the wholesaler, was out of stock when I tried to get one—more out of a sense of duty to you, dear reader, than any desire to insert such a thing into the bosom of our dear planet.

Since pegs pick up dirt and organic muck, and few campers choose to rinse and dry them, it's sheer folly to roll them up inside your tent, even in the measly little sacks supplied. Dirt aside, sharp peg points probably poke more holes in tents than do rocks and other natural features combined. So decide on an external pocket or other safe place, and keep your peg sack there.

TENTS IN ACTION

Pitching a tent in a high wind

COLIN: Every tent has its own stratagems for driving you to the brink of lunacy when you try to erect it in a high wind. But there are standard defensive measures with which you can counter. Before you unroll the tent itself and allow the wind to breathe berserk life into its billowing folds, have all the support weapons ready and waiting—poles, pegs, and an assortment of articles from pack or nature that are heavy enough to help hold down the wind-filled tent and yet smooth enough not to tear it. Then drive in the first peg partway. For obvious reasons, wind- and door-wise, this peg should be the one for the center guy line of the foot end of the tent—or, in guyless tents, for one of the corners at the foot end. In guyed tents, if possible, hook the line over the peg before you unfold the tent. Drive the peg fully home, so that the line cannot by any devilish means flap free. Then take a deep breath and unfold the tent. Unfold it slowly, close to the ground, and onto each foot or so of unfolding fabric put one or more of the heavy, smooth articles. Their size and nature will depend on wind strength and campsite: sometimes all you can use is the full pack; big stones, when available, are godsends, but they must be smooth. Failing adequate heavy support weapons, sprawl yourself over the whistling, flapping bedlam. Slowly, painfully, drive in the pegs that hold down the edges of the stretched-out floor. If no stones are handy, drive in the pegs with your heels. Unless you've attempted this maneuver from the prone position in a 30-mile-an-hour wind, brother, you haven't lived.

The sequence in which you tackle pole erection and the securing of the other guy lines will depend on the structure of your tent and the vagaries of your temperament, but in general you fix the windward end first and you try to keep everything flat on the ground until you're ready to lift the fabric quickly into a taut, unflappable position. You can't possibly accomplish such an act, but you might as well aim for it. Once you've come anywhere close your troubles are almost over. But if you get the tent up within double the time you figured on, count yourself a candidate for the Tent of Fame.

Once the tent is up you should check several times that no pegs are threatening to pull out. And because even the tautest tent will flap in a very high wind, or at least shudder, you may have to tighten the lines occasionally. End-to-end stability is the most vital factor, and it pays to place the head-end peg so that the adjustment knot or line tightener comes close to the apex of the tent and you can adjust it by simply reaching out from inside. If necessary, shorten the line by tying in a sheepshank.

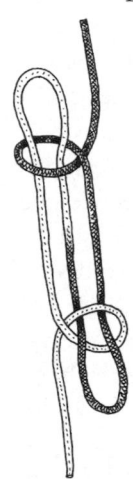

Sheepshank

Drainage moats

It was long the practice—and a wise one too—to dig a small ditch or moat around your tent even when there was little danger of heavy rain: if the rain came you diverted all invading surface water. Tents without floors almost demanded such precautions. And in a real deluge even the best floored tents can, unless moated, begin to ship water through a cookhole, the foot of a zippered entrance, or a worn sector of the waterproof floor and lower wall; and once the flood begins there is Noahscape.

But times have changed. A single large party of well-meaning but unaware people who assume they're being good woodsmen by meticulously moating each tent in their little village can turn a beautiful campsite, almost overnight, into a scarred eyesore. In today's heavily used backcountry such a place rarely gets, as it used to, a year or so's rest. And the disruption to the delicate drainage and soil-binding relationships of a fragile place may turn it within a few years into a rutted, eroded mess. "Ah," you say, "but I always travel alone." Maybe. But one moat-minded person camping in a place every day of the month (which is the kind of usage many backcountry campsites now suffer) is little different from 30 such people camping there for one night: although the damage will at first be confined to a smaller area, it will be locally more severe—and will soon force campers farther and farther afield. The result's the same.

So we must desist. What a man does in one of those fortunately rare cases when no amount of good site choosing and tent pitching can save him from the flood must be left to his own terribly human conscience. My guess is that, like me, he would reluctantly dig as small a moat as possible and fill it carefully when he strikes camp. But the routine digging of tent moats, though a perfectly reasonable practice when backpackers were few and far-flung, is in today's congested wilderness no more acceptable than digging a septic tank for your downtown office.

Pitching a tent in snow

In hard snow the only vital difference from pitching a tent elsewhere (unless you have to level a site) lies in the pegs. Ordinary round tent pegs are useless in snow. Special snow pegs are surprisingly efficient. Once you've driven them in, in fact, the only difficulty tends to be getting them out when you strike camp. The best extractor is the point of an ice axe. It's also a highly efficient tool for making holes in tent fabric.

Alternatives to snow pegs include "deadman" snow anchors—light alloy or fiberglass disks or slabs, usually about 6 or 8 inches across, with holes for tying in the guy line (or, better still, for tying in a loop of heavier cord through which you thread your guy line). You bury the anchor and stamp the snow firm on top of it, or maybe slide it in sideways. You dig it out with shovel, ice axe, ski, snowshoe, or whatever your ingenuity devises. Even more efficient are snow-filled stuff sacks carried specially for the job—perhaps with a small bungee cord as shock absorber on the guy line attached to it. An alternative: a *one-piece* rubber shock loop—not the untrustworthy kind crimped together with a metal clamp. Rigged like this

the line gains elasticity in a wind, and if the bungee cord or shock loop should break it will do so when the line is almost fully extended and can take the load without sudden strain. Either of these devices can, of course, be used on any guy line, in or out of snow.

A stick makes a serviceable snow anchor. It need be no more than a foot long and as thick as your little finger—with a loop tied to its center. Bury it in a small trench, dug at right angles to the tension. A real advantage: you needn't retrieve it.

In case of lost pegs or deadmen or substitutes, snowshoes or skis or ski poles or ice axes make good emergency replacements. Some people even use them regularly and so reduce their load—though that means, of course, that they probably can't move far from the tent without collapsing it.

In soft snow it's essential that before you attempt to pitch a tent you stamp or dig out the site. Do the job before you take anything out of your pack, and make sure you know beforehand how many paces or boot lengths you need for length and for width, allowing room for you to move around outside the tent during the pitching operation. Stamp out narrow extensions for any guy lines, and a broad one around the entrance. In bad weather this stamped-down or dug-out entrance area (see also page 370) will reduce the risk of drifting snow blocking all ventilation (pages 372 and 423). In good weather you'll find it invaluable as a place you can probably stand up in without snowshoes or skis. A little alleyway extension as a john is a worthwhile refinement.

The tent in action in snow

In snow camping, your tent is your castle. Outside, the world howls, white and hostile. Inside, you create a little domain of your own—cramped, imperfectly dry, and frigid by town-indoor standards; but livable and surprisingly snug. Of course, you have to work to keep it that way. Above all, you have to work at keeping things reasonably dry. Primarily, that means keeping the snow out. Brush all the snow you can off clothing and person before you crawl inside. Stamp as much as you can off your boots too. And don't wear them all the way in: swivel around before they come more than an inch or two over the threshold, take them off (less easily done than written), and immediately slip your feet down into the sleeping bag. Legs and body probably go into the bag too. (If you're covered with snowflakes or melted snow you must obviously brush off or dry or remove your outer layer before getting into the bag.) Then bang the boots together and get most of the remaining snow off them. In good weather hold the boots outside for this operation. In vile weather bang the snow onto something waterproof laid out just inside the entrance and empty it outside when you get a chance. You have to be careful not to get sleeping bag or clothing wet.

Boot-desnowing is not the only reason for having a waterproof mat of some kind just inside the entrance (I use the large tough plastic bag that wraps my cooking pots). This doormat collects most of the snow that inevitably comes with you when you crawl in, and also the smaller but by no means negligible amounts that dribble in whenever you have a small opening for ventilation. It also serves as an interim garbage can for all the foreign matter you'd just as soon didn't lie around inside: gas spilled when you're refilling the stove; water spilled when you're filling canteens after melting snow; food fragments; even, if you're feeling house-proud, the inevitable stray feathers from sleeping bag and down clothing. At convenient intervals you empty all this debris outside. Some people carry a small sponge for regular snow- and debris-cleaning. ("Otherwise," one of them says, "your friends use your socks.")

A waterproof mat also acts as a doormat when the weather is good enough for you to put on your boots outside: you tread on it in stockinged feet while you put on the boots. You can also stand on it in stockinged feet, just outside, when you have to answer the liquid calls of nature. The right kind of gloves make good short-service slippers, but the ideal is a pair of down or maybe pile booties (page 553). For more on sanitation, see page 700.

For techniques and precautions when cooking in and around a tent, see page 371 and maybe 303.

CHIP: Camping on snow or frozen ground, you'll get bad condensation on coated tub walls and floor. In snow or rainfall, there's also runoff from wet clothes and tent walls. So if you're spending a lot of time in your tent, you need to lift up your sleeping pad regularly and check for puddles. You can also get condensation between sleeping bag and pad, so don't abandon your tent with the pad and sleeping bag flat. Drape the bag through loops, off the floor, and tip your pad up on one edge. A reflective floor liner—a space blanket (page 758) or a Reflectix pad (page 451)—helps reduce floor condensation, and keeps you warmer in the bargain. If you're leaving the tent set up on snow during the day, open up the vents and leave the reflective barrier in place to keep your tent platform from melting down into a literal bathtub. Otherwise the tent will turn into a solar greenhouse by day, but with darkness and a hard freeze assume an ice-floored immovability. I've seen tents so frozen in that they had to be chopped loose.

COLIN: The most vital precaution of all when camping during a snowfall is to keep the tent from getting buried. You can buy lightweight aluminum shovels (page 438) to carry along for the job—and, of course, for clearing tent sites, digging snow caves (also page 438), or even clearing a route. But a snowshoe is a very efficient tool for keeping your tent unburied. In extremely heavy snow it may become necessary, if the snow keeps falling for a day or two, to take down your tent, raise the platform by shoveling in snow and stamping it flat, and then repitch the tent. Failure to guard against burial could prove fatal.

In mid-July 1958 a party of four climbers camped in stormy weather on an exposed Alaskan ridge at about 11,500 feet. They had two 2-man tents: a Gerry model made of permeable material and with two entrances, and an impermeable army mountain tent with only a sleeve entrance. On the second stormbound night a very heavy fall of snow formed a 10-inch-thick wind slab over the tents so quickly that none of the climbers appreciated the danger before morning. Around 6:00 a.m. one of the men in the army tent woke, breathing rapidly, and realized that the air was foul. Unable to find knife, boots, or gloves in the semicollapsed tent, he just managed to dig his way out through the clinging folds of the sleeve entrance, barehanded, then had to slide back inside to rest and warm up. (The outside temperature was around $-10°$F.) Suddenly he and his companion found themselves gasping for breath. The first man immediately started out the entrance again but was unable to free himself from the door, then stopped digging to rest—and lost consciousness. Around 8:30 a.m. one of the men in the Gerry tent dug free and saw him lying halfway out of the entrance, with evidence of frostbite. Carried into the Gerry tent, he soon recovered consciousness. His companion was found, still inside the army tent, motionless and not breathing. Four to five hours' artificial respiration failed to revive him. He had died, of course, from asphyxiation (lack of oxygen, presence of carbon dioxide) due to the tent's being buried.

Extremely bad snow conditions caused this accident, but contributory factors included the impermeable tent fabric, the clinging nature of the only exit, and a guying system that failed to preserve adequate internal airspace. (For a full report and analysis, see "Accidents in American Mountaineering," Twelfth Annual Report of the Safety Committee of the American Alpine Club, 1959, pages 22–4.) The story is a vivid object lesson in how alert you must remain—under conditions horribly conducive to weariness and boredom—when there is any danger of your tent's being buried by snow.

For more on blocked ventilation, see page 372.

Care of tents

Damp doesn't harm nylon tents the way it did old-style canvas-and-rope models (though nylon fly sheets actually stretch a little when wet, while cotton canvas tightens up). And once the weather swings around on your side the nylon tent dries out very quickly. But mildew can still form, and if you arrive home with a wet nylon tent you should dry it out. The simplest way is to erect it on the lawn, wash it if necessary with the garden hose, sponging off dirt, and just leave it to dry. If you have to do the job indoors, hang the tent by its normal suspension points. Some makers used to recommend washing nylon tents after use in a tumbler-type—not agitator-type—washing machine, cold, with mild detergent, then drying them in a spin drier. (To avoid grisly tangles, remove all guy lines.) But virtually all makers now cry, "Never!", and forbid the use of detergents. Nikwax, Granger, and others sell special tent-wash. Coated—and perhaps all—tent fabrics should be kept out of dryers.

For waterproofing seams, see pages 414 to 415.

NONTENTS

Your roof need not be a tent, of course. The several alternatives are all lighter than tents and easier to erect. All perform more efficiently as cool retreats in hot weather. And all are much cheaper. On the other hand, all are useless for protection against insects. None can approach the efficiency of a tent in blocking out a really high wind or in conserving warmth (though it's often overlooked that all of them, except in a very high wind, reduce the rate at which warm air from your body can escape, and so increase your warmth at night to a surprising degree). Although some of them repel the average rainstorm as well as most tents do, or even better, nothing rivals a good tent with fly sheet for protection from prolonged rain, whether a heavy downpour or a swirling, penetrating mountain drizzle.

You choose your roof, then, to suit expected conditions.

A fly sheet alone

You can use a standard fly sheet or have a special one made. Forty years ago, during a four-month walk up England through the soggy maw of what the British sportingly call summer, I relied entirely on a simple unit that I had made up from untreated nylon fabric. It worked fine.

Note that pyramid tents (page 396) are essentially fancied-up fly sheets.

CHIP: Colin's love for the freshest possible air has caught on big: many outdoor schools now teach their students to camp under tarps and some sell their proprietary designs—the NOLS Thelma Fly has 12 grommets, eight tie-outs, and a slight eave at each end (2-person: 2.8 lbs., $100; 3-person: 4 lbs., $125). Of course tarps and flies are also much lighter than they used to be (see page 394). Given light but water-shedding impregnated nylons and polyesters (and no less, sleeping bags and bivy sacks of Dryloft and Gore-Tex), single-sheet camping is a fertile field for personal innovation: a tarp is rather simple to make, and to modify as you go along. Ultralight swami Ray Jardine has an excellent chapter on sewing your own gear in *Beyond Backpacking* (see Appendix IV) with details on lap-felling seams, finishing edges, adding tie-outs, and other mortifications. He recommends Outdoor Wilderness Fabrics in Nampa, Idaho (800-693-7467); The Rain Shed in Corvallis, Oregon (541-753-8900); Seattle Fabrics in Washington (206-632-6022); and Quest Outfitters in Sarasota, Florida (800-359-6931). Lightweight fabrics can also be had from Stephenson's-Warmlite, and other suppliers show up in the classified section of *Backpacker.* If you're excited by gear making, then sewing your own made-to-measure tarp is probably the most rewarding way to start.

Plastic sheet (with attachments)

COLIN: This cunning and convenient though unlikely looking rig is strong, light, and very cheap. The plastic sheet is smooth, white, translucent .004-inch polyethylene, known as Visqueen, that is absolutely watertight and a great deal tougher than it looks. (Make sure, though, that you buy good-quality sheeting. One sample that I tried soon began to tear. And check that the material is translucent, not semitransparent, or it will make a scurvy sun awning.)

For normal solo use I favor the 8-by-9 size, but if really wet weather looms I may take the 9-by-12, which is entirely adequate for two (complete with eight tarp clamps and six strong pegs, about 2¾ lbs.).

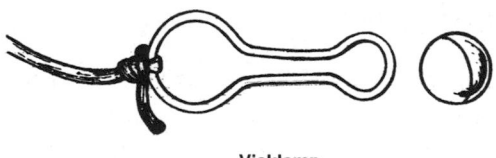

Visklamp

The sheets are plain, without grommets or attachments of any kind. You secure them with the improbable little two-part devices called Visklamps (¾ oz., $.40 each).

CHIP: For the life of me, I could not find a Visklamp anywhere on earth. In shops I got shrugs and at outdoor trade shows, superlatively blank

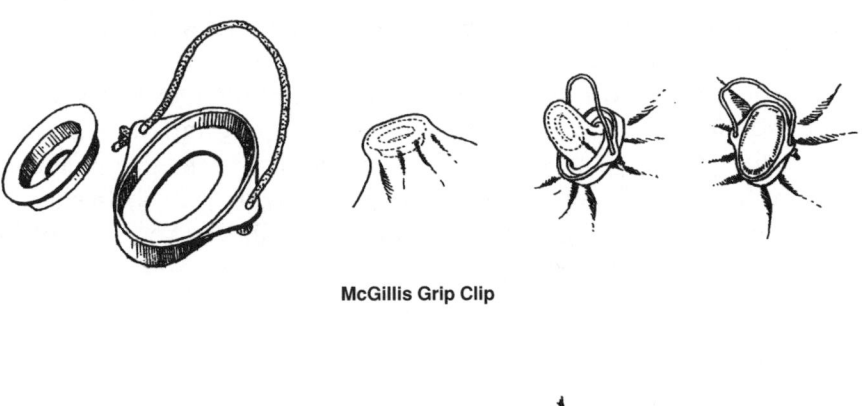

McGillis Grip Clip

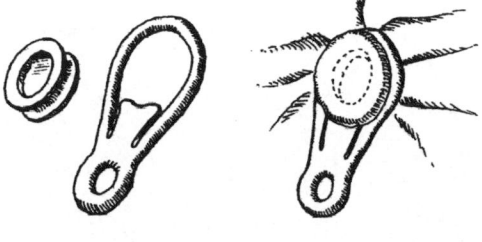

Coghlan's Tarp Holder

looks. One current successor is the Grip Clip, by McGillis Products, a two-piece plastic fastener with a loop of nylon cord. It works on the same principle while being lighter and less likely to tear out under stress. It's available from Sierra Designs and wholesalers in three sizes: small (0.25 oz.), medium (0.4 oz.), and large (0.5 oz.). Another contender is the Tarp Holder by Coghlan's, of flexible blue plastic with a built-in loop. It works, too (what else can you say about such things?), and weighs 0.7 oz. The advantage of the Grip Clip is lightness, while the built-in loop of the Tarp Holder gives you a straight pull. Coghlan's also has plastic grommets that mount in plastic sheeting without a special tool: use a smooth rock. (In fabric you have to punch or melt a hole.)

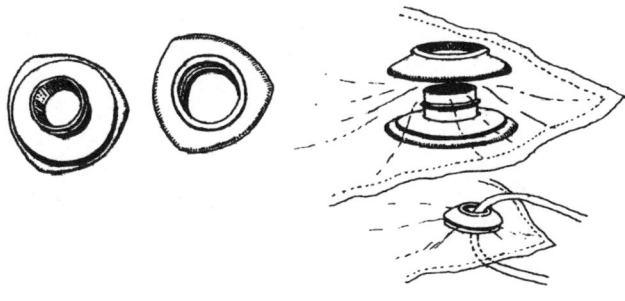

Coghlan's plastic grommet

COLIN: No matter what clamps you select, just use your imagination when our illustrations show a Visklamp.

For easy adjustment, run the guy line back from tent peg or substitute and thread through the clamp. Pull downward, using the clamp loop as a pulley. When the guy is tight, knot the free end at the clamp. You can then readjust the tension on any line without leaving your shelter.

The great advantage of this system is its flexibility. You can build an orthodox, tentlike bedroom:

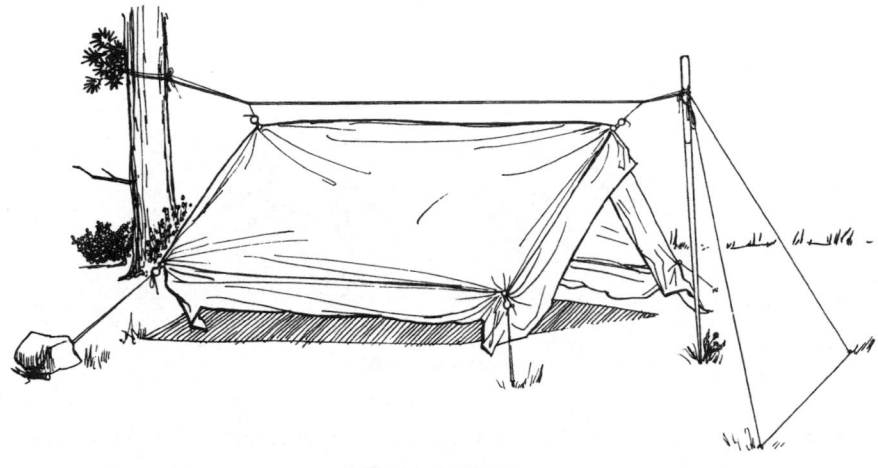

Tentlike bedroom

or a sort of eccentric rotunda (though you have to be careful about the angles, or you end up with almost no roof—only folds):

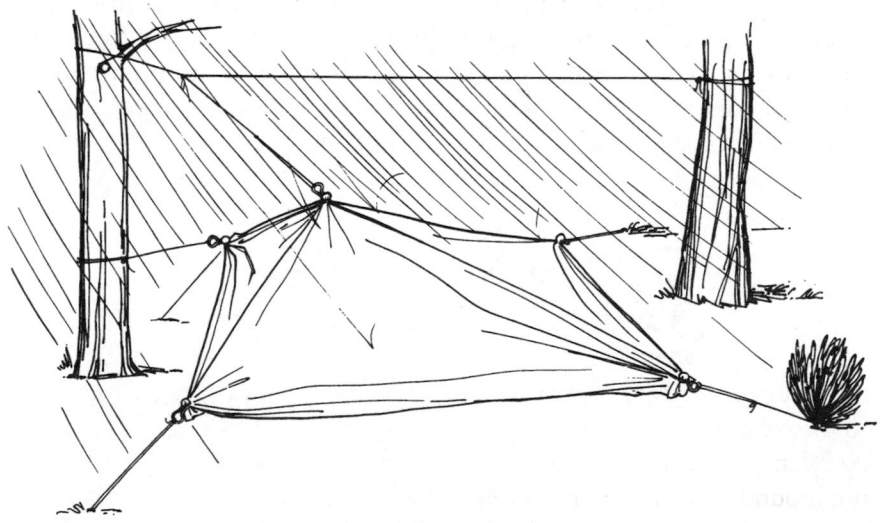

Eccentric rotunda

or a useful lunchtime shelter in wind-driven drizzle:

Lunchtime shelter

For further ideas, see variations on the poncho theme, pages 333 to 335.

CHIP: I've set up space blankets (the mildly reinforced laminated sort— see page 758) as tarps, but the small metal grommets rip out at the slightest breath of wind. Aluminized, nonstretch polyester with a reflective coating (called an emergency or survival blanket, in the same 5-by-7-foot size; 1.66 oz., $3) is mostly used as an ultralight groundsheet but can also be pitched as a tarp with clamps. I staked a piece out with Grip Clips on a moderately windy day, and did it ever *flap*—loud and appallingly bright, scaring birds and startling pilots for miles—but it didn't tear. At 0.06 oz. per square foot, you can't beat it for weightlessness. For those who disdain silver, glamorous gold costs about $5. For full-body shelter, you'd have to find a piece bigger than 5 by 7, or tape two together.

COLIN: An advantage of any such rig is that you can, by moving one or two clamps, very simply make a major readjustment to meet new conditions of wind or rain. And in most setups you can, while still in bed, slip one clamp loose and lift the roof aside for cooking or working or for looking around, and can immediately replace it if rain threatens or you want more warmth. Carrying this idea further, you can put up your shelter because you think it may rain or get cold enough to make you grateful for the roof's assistance, and can then remove one or more of the clamps (filing the stray piece in a pocket or some other instantly reachable place) and so enjoy all the freedoms of rooflessness and yet know that if it rains, even in the middle of the night, you can get the roof over your head in about 10 drops flat. I often rig such a ready-roof. In fact, it may be the prime reason I continue, despite raucous laughter from serious, haughty backpackers, to use my improvised shelter more than any other.

If you haven't used this prophylactic system and rain catches you unawares you can as an emergency measure simply spread the sheet over yourself. One recent summer, caught in a fierce and prolonged mountain thunderstorm that struck with about three minutes' warning just as I camped at dusk, I was even able to cook dinner under the quickly spread sheet. That night the storm cleared within a couple of hours, but even for sleeping you can wrap the sheet loosely around everything in a makeshift cocoon—taking care to leave an opening at your head for ventilation. (For details, drawing, and dangers, see pages 437 to 438.) This wraparound system, by the way, will help you keep warm, rain or no rain. Don't wrap yourself too tightly or your sweat may condense on the impermeable sheet and soak the sleeping bag.

I normally carry eight clamps and six aluminum tent pegs for this setup, but in really cramped and awkward corners a couple extra of each can make all the difference. Once or twice, when I needed more attachment points than I had clamps, I have just twisted up a tumor of plastic and tied the nylon directly to its neck. A reader recommends using a rounded pebble or even a ball of dirt.

One summer, when a desert afternoon wind was blustering across the plateau on which I'd camped, it repeatedly tore the sheeting at a Visklamp. So, although that has been my polyethylene's only failure, I would certainly not trust this rig in a full-scale mountain gale. But I almost always take it on summer trips of a week or so when there seems a chance of heavy rain. For its remarkable success in a wild November storm, see page 569. On short trips the wear factor can hardly become serious, but I'm not sure I'd rely on the plastic for a really long trip when I couldn't replace it.

Because the sheeting is white it doesn't make your den dark and dismal, even in oppressive weather. And because it's translucent-going-on-opaque it makes an excellent sun awning.

Visqueen is versatile stuff. It's exactly what you need for waterproofing your pack contents on major river crossings (page 688). And if you have to swim across a river on a packless side trip you can wrap all your clothes and gear in the sheet, tie it with cord, and have yourself a buoyant, watertight bundle that you can push or pull along (page 690). In any kind of terrain not covered by snow, the sheeting also makes a first-class marker for airdrops (page 705).

The use of plastic sheeting involves an important matter of principle that applies even more stringently to other items but which we had better examine before we go any further:

The ethics of using disposable plastic equipment.

Twenty years ago, in some of the more heavily used backcountry, certain popular campsites—whole meadows, even entire above-timber rock basins—were transformed into garbage dumps by discarded plastic groundsheets, tarps, and tube tents. Things are now less horrendous. But defilements continue.

The causes seem clear: an exponential increase in the number of human visitors; the inability of uneducated newcomers to grasp the gulf that yawns between behavior acceptable in a human society still sick with the no-deposit-no-return syndrome and behavior acceptable in an essentially nonhuman society with its fragile economics totally dependent on recycling; and the cheapness, lightness, efficiency, and wide availability of plastic sheeting molded to many backpacking uses. The remedies are less clear. One possibility is to limit, forcibly, the number of human visitors. This highly undesirable step has already been taken in many places. Another alternative is enlightenment of the uneducated (such as I am attempting now, I guess) or a more general attempt—which has had some success—to eradicate the no-deposit-no-return mentality. Another approach is to remove the plastic offenders from the marketplace. Several firms have, to their eternal credit, made the attempt. Horrified by the results of their legitimate business, they at first tried charging refundable deposits for disposable plastic items; and when that scheme proved ineffective they ignored profits and stopped selling plastic groundsheets, tarps, and tube tents. But it seems unlikely that all outdoor-equipment suppliers could be persuaded to follow this public-spirited lead—and even if they did so, the raw sheeting would still be available, and bought. (Retailers who continue to sell plastic items such as tube tents [page 432] point out, accurately, that much of the backcountry litter consists of empty stove cartridges and shredded packs—and that no one stops offering these items.)

In the end, only backpackers can stop the plastic defecation. So for all of us the question arises, "What should I, personally, do about it?"

Should we stop using such vastly useful articles—you and I, who would never by God dream of ditching a plastic groundsheet or anything else in a wild place? (I mean, after all, would we?) The sacrifice would without doubt generate a cozy holier-than-thou feeling—which is always rewarding, and the reason self-denial remains so improbably but perenni-ally popular.*

For me, the question also arises, "Should I remove all reference to the offending items from this book?" Such a course would certainly ensure that cozy glow of holiness; but I doubt its effectiveness. So for the time being I shall, a shade unhappily, continue to use certain plastic items—and let my plastic paragraphs stand. But I remain in a state of some confusion.

The trouble is, I think, that the situation in those sad campsites is simply another manifestation of the current general human malaise: imbalance with the rest of the world. And the only way to correct that imbalance lies through a broad change of heart and actions. See, for exam-ple, *Earth at a Crossroads* by Hartmut Bossel.

One of the worst sources of plastic litter has been the

Tube tent.

The standard form of this once-popular device is a tube of inexpen-sive polyethylene, usually 3.5 mil or lighter, about 9 feet long and 8 to 10 feet in circumference. The tube can be quickly strung up on any ridgeline. The weight of your gear and body—perhaps with an assist from smooth

---

*For years I have sporadically packed out some of the trash other people left behind. Although finding the act rewarding (that is, it made me feel good), I've always suffered from the bitter and inhibiting knowledge that it was an insignificant drop in a gigantic bucket. Then, for the last edition, a Texas reader offered an excellent idea: "No one person can clean up all that plastic and other gunk that has been left in the mountains. But there are a lot of civi-lized backpackers. If—in the later stages of every trip, when we aren't carrying so much and won't have to carry it so far—we all picked up at least one piece of abandoned plastic and schlepped it out with our own trash it would make one hell of a damn dent in the wilderness trash accumulation. Doing so gives a tremendous 'holier-than-thou' rush. In other words, schlepping somebody else's garbage on one's back for twenty miles, just to help save the wilderness, would appeal to all 'holier-than-thou' junkies. And it might soon become as trendy and aware to have a recovered abandoned groundsheet in one's pack as to have a Sierra Club cup on one's belt—and to casually mention it when you stop to chat with other walk-ers. . . . Can't you imagine a whole new leitmotif in casual conversation? Trash machismo!: 'Yeah, I carried thirty pounds of abandoned groundcloths down Mount Whitney in a January blizzard. Roughest descent I ever had. Published a note in *Mountaineering Gazette!*' . . . *Seri-ously,* though, and exaggeration aside, perhaps it should become a sign of conservation aware-ness to pack out more trash than you generated yourself. And while very few people would do this as isolated individuals (feeling that it would not make enough difference) they might do so if they knew they were part of a large group, all doing it. If, for example, it began to be urged in print by one or more of the authors they consider to have earned some attention, Mr. Fletcher, sir."

And here it is. Again.

stones—anchors the floor. Some models have grommets at each end for drawing the openings more or less closed. The lightest—and flimsiest— may weigh only 10 oz., cost $6.

Tube tent

Tyros tend to see tube tents as a wonderful idea; experienced back-packers, to steer clear. In rain the open ends are almost sure to let in some water—which will collect in puddles on the impermeable floor. If you batten down the ends to keep rain out, fierce condensation on the imper-meable walls may in time produce as many puddles. And if the ridgeline sags beware of the suffocation hazard, and of carbon-monoxide poisoning (page 372). Also, hail or even high winds can shred the thin plastic. That is why so many get left behind, particularly up high.

When certain states passed fire-retardant laws for tents, tube tents for a time faded away. But now they have eluded the law's embrace by assuming the names *tube shelters* or even *tube groundsheets.* The fact remains, of course, that a tube by any other name will burn as bright.

When the rain threat is minor I often rely for an emergency roof on my

Poncho or groundsheet.

Ponchos are now rare, but most of what I have to say about them as roofs also applies to groundsheets. Heavy ponchos mostly have grommets along their edges and it's a simple matter to string them up with nylon cord. Lightweight ponchos often lack grommets, but I used to have up to six or eight specially inserted. To build your roof you can string a ridge rope between trees and make an orthodox tentlike bedroom or you can attach the poncho by its corners to surrounding bushes and branches or to sticks held in position by stones. In heavy or driving rain you can stay surprisingly dry if you keep the roof so low that there's only just room for you underneath. I have on occasion carried one tarp clamp as a roof lifter for the poncho: with the low-level, battened-down roof, it makes life much more comfortable.

Poncho with trees

If you suspend the roof by the poncho's hood cord you don't risk damaging the fabric with the Visklamp (or a substitute) but you put the roof's high point in the wrong place and probably get some rain in through the hood opening.

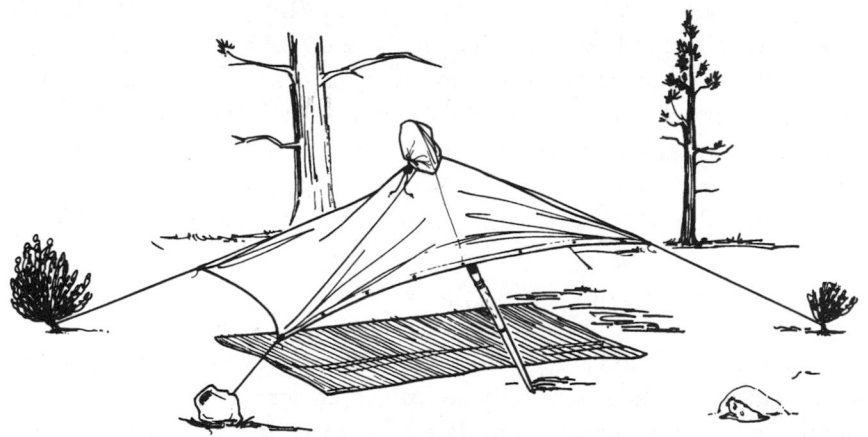

Poncho with staff

Under milder conditions you can use your staff either as an external upright or as an inside prop to force the roof pleasantly high above your head and also to keep it taut, so that rain doesn't collect in sagging hollows. When you use the staff this way, pad it at the top with something soft so that it won't cut the poncho.

A makeshift rig with a poncho, groundsheet, or tarp is especially useful in open desert, when you may find yourself in desperate need of protection from the sun at midday halts. The difference between the sun-scorched ground and your little coffin-shaped patch of shade will seem like the difference between hell and . . . well, something a comfortable half-hitch short of hell. (See figures for desert ground temperatures, page 112, footnote.) The awning will certainly make a critical difference to your sense of well-being and therefore to what you're capable of doing in the cool of evening. Under certain conditions it could even spell the difference between life and death.

On desert afternoons a strong wind often blows for hour after hour. When it does, the continuous flapping of the awning makes a hideous din, always threatens to tear grommets loose, and sometimes does. One way of reducing both noise and strain is to secure only three corners of the awning to fixed points and to tie a large rock on the downwind corner with a cord of such length that the stone will just rest on the ground under normal conditions, but will lift, and so ease the strain, when the roof billows under an especially strong gust.

A grommeted groundsheet can also make as effective a rain roof as a poncho. As it is usually bigger it will when new make an even better one—but groundsheets rarely stay unpunctured for very long.*

---

*CHIP: The coated nylon floor protectors (called "footprints") for tents make excellent groundsheets with bound edges and stake loops. Depending on the tent's size and floor plan, they can also be strung up as partial shelters.

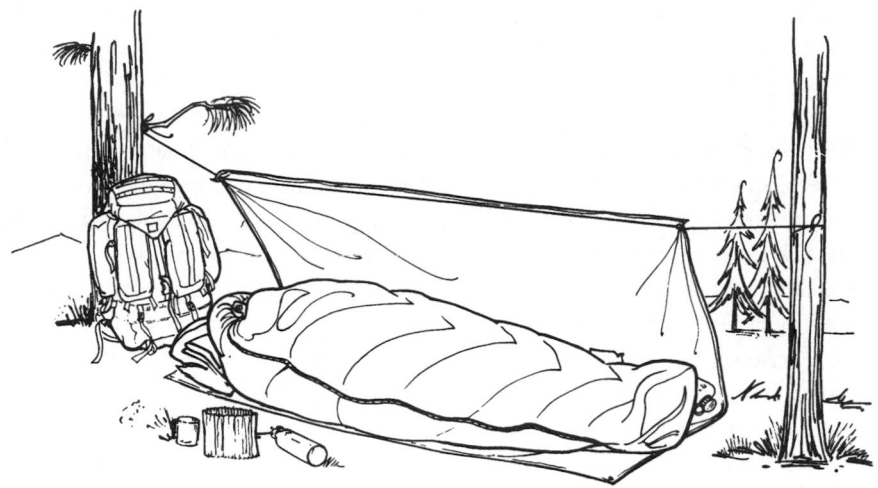

Economy-size groundsheets (which in our peculiar modern tongue are distinctly large ones) can be folded so that they act both in their normal role and at the same time as an angled wall that will protect you from driven rain (and from a cold wind, dry or rain-bearing). You can hold the angled edge down with full canteens or other heavy equipment, with your staff (anchored by large stones), or with smooth stones alone.

As sun awnings, clear plastic groundsheets are, of course, comprehensively useless—and translucent colored ones only a shade better. Black is beautiful.

Whether you choose to use your groundsheet or poncho as emergency rain roof depends on conditions. If you can race an approaching storm you'll probably be wise to consider rigging your capacious groundsheet over a dry piece of ground and doing without anything under your mattress. Then you'll be able to wear the poncho when necessary. Try to resist the temptation to use it as a groundsheet; it will certainly develop holes. If the ground is already wet you'll need the groundsheet as a floor, and the poncho goes up as roof.

Finally there's the problem of what to do about a roof when you go to sleep in the open, confident that no rain will fall, and wake up later to the pitter-patter of tiny raindrops or the clammy drift of drizzle. One solution is to unwrap your groundsheet (which, if it's big enough, is doubled under you) and cover yourself with the open side to leeward. If the weather gets worse you can quickly improve this makeshift cocoon by lacing the open side with nylon cord threaded through the grommets, if any (you get only mildly wet in the process). Another solution is to use the poncho in the same way, laced or unlaced. (If I harbor any doubts at all about the weather I go to sleep with the poncho ready, close at hand.) Better still is a combination of groundsheet and poncho: the groundsheet as main cocoon, the poncho wrapped like an elephant's foot around the bottom of your sleeping bag, which otherwise persists, steadfastly, in pushing out into the open. Provided the rain isn't too heavy, such a makeshift shelter can keep your sleeping bag surprisingly dry, and your-self totally so. (One good friend of mine, an experienced backpacker, holds with ferocity to the childiotic notion that if he erects any rain shelter more complicated than a poncho-groundsheet cocoon he is pandering to his weaker instincts.) But DryLoft-covered sleeping bags or bivy covers may mean that, except for your head, you need take no precautions against mist or very light rain (page 468).

The extent of the action you take when surprised by rain during the night depends on your sleepy estimate of the probable heaviness of the rain. If you think it's going to come down but good it pays to make the hard decision early and get up and rig poncho or groundsheet into an ade-quate roof. Of course, any man with an ounce of sense will rig a roof whenever there's a hint of doubt about the weather. I have at last learned to rig a ready-roof (page 435) at such times—with poncho or groundsheet if necessary. Well, have more or less learned.

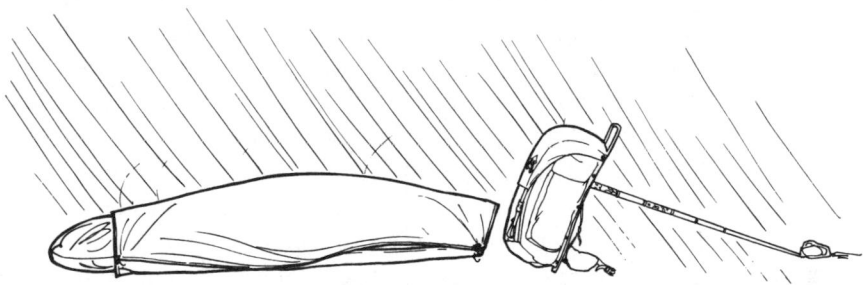

The cocoon bedroom in all its variants is also a useful makeshift measure in unexpected light snow. Even in dry weather it gives you a sur-prising degree of extra warmth, particularly in high winds. Remember, though, that unless there's adequate ventilation your sweat will condense and soak the sleeping bag. An unventilated cocoon—or a tarp or ground-sheet just spread over your sleeping bag—can be dangerous. In early April 1961 a young woman from the University of New Hampshire camped beside the parking lot of a New England ski resort. She had con-siderable winter camping experience. The weather had been warm and there was meltwater on the packed snow. It rained during the night. Then the weather cleared and the temperature fell. Presumably to keep the rain off, the girl had covered her sleeping bag with an impermeable plastic tarp. In the morning she was found dead. It was presumed that she had suffocated, for the edges of the tarp were frozen to the ground ice and she had been sealed in. The carbon dioxide that would normally have awakened her by making her struggle for breath may have been absorbed by the moisture collected under the tarp. Lesson: always leave plenty of ventilation at your head, especially if there's any danger of the tarp's being frozen to the ground.

Snow caves (and trenches)

A few experienced winter backpackers say they habitually travel without tents; for shelter, they dig snow caves. The trade-off is weight for time: you save several pounds; but you must camp early enough, and with enough energy left in you, to allow for from one to three hours of hard digging to make your cave—although, as we shall see, it's sometimes possible to get by with far less work. On balance, then, digging a cave may not make sense if you expect to move every day but may be eminently worthwhile if you expect to use it for several successive nights. Knowing how to go about the job, at least in principle, is certainly a useful hedge against an emergency.

CHIP: Snow camping without a shovel is like eating ice cream without a spoon. Companies like Life-Link that make ski poles and avalanche rescue equipment produce good ones—shovels, that is. A plastic-bladed "survival" shovel with a small-diameter handle (about $30–$35) is okay for casual camping. But for carving through avalanche debris or high-elevation wind slab a plastic blade will flex and bounce off—to the accompaniment of cougar screams—so a nice, stiff aluminum blade is preferable. Good aluminum shovels start at about $50 and "pro" models, with larger scoops and telescoping handles, might be $80 or more. Mine, which I thought I'd lost (I just went tearing all over the house in a frenzy and found it), is a Voile, made in Salt Lake City, Utah. The powder-coated blade is 9 inches wide and doubles magnificently as a stove platform. The lightweight handle (12 inches long, 6.5 oz.) is aluminum tube with a T made of PVC pipe. Total weight 23 oz. The deluxe handle (18 inches, telescoping out to 25, 11.5 oz.) has a plastic D-grip. Total weight 28 oz. For tight work in snow caves, you can shorten the handle and gouge away. Extended, it's good for excavating skank pits (page 370) and contouring snow shelters in general. In the mountains of the interior, with their airy, soft snowpacks, a shovel is all you need. For dense, maritime snowpacks from which blocks can be cut, you may also need a snow saw (12–18 oz., $25–$85). Life-Link makes a high-quality one. Emergency substitutes for digging include snowshoe, ski tip, spare ski tip, cookpot, a stick, or, as a last and unrecommended resort, hands (preferably protected by waterproof gloves). A friend who was buried thigh-deep in a slide on Teton Pass claimed to have dug himself loose with a pair of blade-type polycarbonate sunglasses: "Not," says he, "in any way recommended."

Shovel in hand, the question arises: where to dig? Avoid locating snow shelters (or tents for that matter) at the low point of a valley where cold air collects. Neither are ridge tops good, since the snow can be scoured thin on the upwind face and hide rock outcrops downwind. The best spot is on the flank of a slope. But not under a steep, high cornice, especially if wind can be expected. The reason the cornice is there in the first place is that snow has blown over a rise and been deposited, so if the process resumes you'll be up half the night digging out (and redigging and redigging) the entrance of your snow cave.

COLIN: Frankly, I have never dug a snow cave. But once, in a Sierra Nevada winter storm that brought 4 feet of snow yet left temperatures up around 25°F, I found a U.S. Air Force survival-training group dug in, apparently without sleeping bags, on a steep ridge. As far as I could make out (when I stumbled on them, visibility was down to about 10 yards), they seemed reasonably comfortable. They certainly sounded cheerful.

"If you know how to use it," an experienced cave digger once told me, "snow can be your friend." Apart from know-how, all you need to build a snow cave is plenty of time, good waterproof clothing—preferably including rain chaps, because most of the digging will be done on your knees—and lots of snow. The snow should be somewhat consolidated; otherwise there's a danger of the roof's falling in. The best site is a wind-packed drift or gentle slope, but at a pinch you can build almost anywhere there's enough depth, even on the flat. You dig a small entrance, level or sloping up (easier to dig), then hollow out a chamber just big enough for however many people are in your party. The excavated snow can be banked up into a windbreaking wall, just outside the entrance.

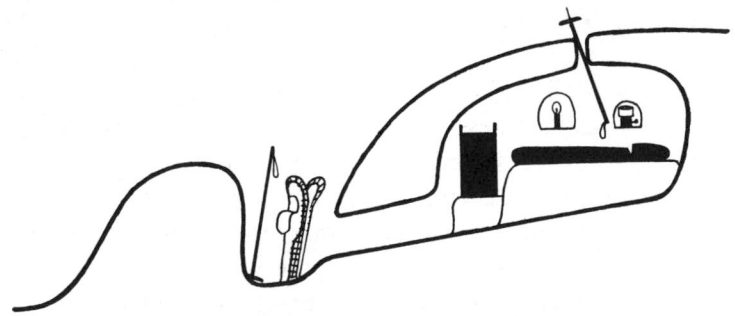

Inside the cave a raised platform for sleeping on puts you up where the temperature is highest, makes a convenient seating place, and keeps you and yours out of the watery runoff that tends to collect on the floor.

Because snow is an excellent insulator (it holds small air pockets, just as down does) the temperature in the cave, fueled by your body and cooking stove and maybe a candle or two, will often be above freezing. So roof and even walls may develop a coating of ice that appreciably strengthens the structure—and also drips. A domed interior not only makes the strongest roof but also encourages moisture to run down the walls instead of dripping maliciously onto you or your sleeping bag. But any cave tends to be a humid place, and a Gore-Tex-covered or synthetic-filled bag will assuredly perform better than a traditional taffeta-covered down model. You must, of course, have a groundsheet (or, better still, a reflective groundsheet—see pages 442 and 451) and also a self-inflating pad or some other good insulation under the bag. Into the walls of the cave, at convenient places, you cut little alcoves for cooking stove, candles, and anything else you fancy. Properly positioned, they can make the cave not just a convenient refuge but an attractive, even beguiling, little temporary home.

Roof thickness can vary from as little as 3 to 4 inches in well-consolidated snow to as much as 3 feet in new snow or the wetter kind commonly found in the East. The smaller the cave, the stronger the roof. The danger of collapse is apparently not great—though you're at first likely to feel nervous on that score as you lie looking up at the blank snow just above your head, especially if you're the body farthest from the entrance. A sensible precaution: always sleep with your shovel or other digging instrument at your side. Real danger of roof collapse can come from passing moose or people, particularly those on snowmobiles (mark the site carefully, especially in flat terrain) or from rain. Ventilation can be controlled, at least to some extent, by leaving the entrance open or partway open (a block of cut snow acts as door) and by cutting or poking a hole in the roof (though not directly above your sleeping place). Some people recommend leaving a ski pole or stick in the hole so that in case of heavy snowfall it can be kept open by jiggling from the inside. Others (who mis-holed) maintain that snow then falls into the cave, usually all over your bag.

The time needed to dig a good cave will vary with site, snow conditions, and, above all, the expertise of the digger or diggers. With luck and experience, two men (changing places: inside and shoveling to the entrance; outside and removing the shoveled snow) may get the job done inside two hours. But a solo digger, making his smaller residence, may finish in an hour. And shortcuts sometimes present themselves. A hummock in the snow may indicate a sapling curved and weighed down by the snow, and beneath it may lurk an almost ready-made cave; if you're on your own you may with care and imagination be able to complete a cozy little nest within 20 minutes.

CHIP: Igloo building is a craft verging on a fine art, on which I refuse to trespass. Igloos are wrought in dense, maritime snowpacks usually with a snow saw rather than a shovel. Slightly less fine, in aesthetic terms, but no less comfortable is the *quinzhee.* Used by the Athabascan tribes of the interior, where snowpacks are too soft and loose for cutting blocks, it depends on the natural freeze-bonding of disturbed snow grains. There's a good description of quinzhee building in *Winter: An Ecological Handbook* by James Halfpenny and Roy Ozanne. Briefly, you pick the spot and then build a heap of snow, layering it into an igloo shape. From the center, compass your task with a ski pole: 8 feet is a minimum diameter. Then it's heave-ho for as long as it takes to reach a smooth height of 4 feet or so. At that stage, a helpful trick is to lay a few pine tufts at several spots on the top and flanks of the mound before adding the last foot of snow. (These act as thickness markers, telling you—if light through the snow doesn't— when to stop gouging and start sculpting.) If the snow is very loose and dry, you might need to compact the layers with shovel or boughs as you build them. Once you have a sufficient heap—5 to 6 feet high—leave it alone. Dry snow takes longer to sinter (a crystal-bonding process involving water vapor), so in cold temps you might have to wait an hour or even two. Find a patch of late sun, or start melting snow for hot drinks and dinner.

Then the mound must be hollowed out, the same as a snow cave. The door should be at 90 degrees to the prevailing wind. As with a snow cave, start by cutting out a small dome shape, and then enlarge it a layer at a time. Watch for the pine-tuft markers. Another gauge is to break sticks to the proper length and push them into the walls and roof from outside, for the digger to spot. The roof should be about 8 inches thick and the walls 12 or more inches. Cave-ins usually occur during the hollowing process, so watching the digger (one at a time) is a smart move. Sleeping benches can simply be left in place, or built up with snow carved from the roof and the cold air trap (or skank pit). The finishing touches are to poke a high vent (small, then widen it out) while the spotter builds a snow wall on the windward side of the door, turning it into an L that overlaps the entrance by 2 to 3 feet.

An evenly domed quinzhee is structurally very strong. But over several days, the roof might sag: You might be able to add more snow on the outside, re-sinter, and then carve some out—I've never tried it. But the main cause of sag is overheating the interior. Snow is a superb insulator, and the common impulse is to pile inside, start the stove, light candles, and get it as warm as possible. It's also foolish. The condensation from breath and cooking vapor, along with snowmelt—drip-drip-drip— rapidly soaks your clothes and sleeping bags. And, just as on a wet day one notch above freezing, you end up with an unshakable chill. Second, and more basic, the structural integrity of a snow shelter owes all to the fact that snow is a crystalline solid. Above freezing, however, snow becomes water. After a few miserable stays, my reformed snow-shelter discipline has been to keep the inside air just under freezing—out of the wind it feels warm—while hoarding my personal heat inside sleeping bag, clothing, cap, booties, etc. Unless a blizzard shrieks, I cook in an alcove just outside the entrance. The upshot has been the ability to live comfortably in a snow cave or quinzhee for days on end.

One more thought: although it's nice to know that you can create nightly shelter with little more than a shovel and a strong back, the time and effort you put into a snow cave, igloo, or quinzhee is in practice only justified by a stay of 2 or more nights. Some groups build one going in and then catch a night on the way out. And a shelter in a popular spot might also be occupied by successive groups—a snow motel.

COLIN: If you lack the time, energy, know-how, or inclination to construct a cave or quinzhee you can maybe get by with a trench. You simply dig a "foxhole" 2 or 3 feet deep and just big enough for your sleeping bag not to touch the walls (but also as small as possible, to conserve body heat). Pile the excavated snow into an encircling wall. Then lay skis or snowshoes or tree branches across the open trench and cover them with a tarp or space blanket or whatever you have available. Secure it with snow. The result, says my informant, can be an astonishingly effective shelter, especially as protection against wind—though it's not really viable in stormy weather.

GROUNDSHEETS

Under benign conditions it's entirely possible to operate without a groundsheet. But I find I never do. You need one in most places to keep out the damp, in even more places to reduce wear and tear on such fragile items as pad or mattress and sleeping bag, and just about everywhere as a general keep-clean-and-keep-from-losing-things area for the gear you take out of your pack. A slippery groundsheet also forms a natural defense zone against ants and ticks and scorpions and their brethren. In addition, remember the groundsheet-as-roof-and-walls-or-even-cocoon (pages 433–38).

When your load problem is acute and the chances of rain slight (a combination that applied on my Grand Canyon trip) you can carry a light poncho that doubles as groundsheet. A groundsheet does highly abrasive duty, so don't expect the dual-purpose article to last very long as a waterproof poncho. In Grand Canyon mine, sure enough, didn't. But all the rain and snow fell near the start, just as I'd expected, and the arrangement worked out fine.

For a long trip on which you can't get equipment replaced you need a strong, though still lightweight, groundsheet. Coated nylon remains the best bet. But it's expensive. Typical urethane-coated groundsheets (reinforced with eight brass-plated grommets, so that they can double as tarps) run $30 to $40 in the 6-by-8-foot size, $50 to $60 for a 10 by 10, and $60 to $70 for a 10-by-12-footer. Weights run from just over 1 lb. to 3-plus lbs. Laminated, woven polyethylene (the ubiquitous blue plastic tarp) comes in myriad dimensions, with a groundcloth-size piece, 5 by 7 feet and about 14 oz., starting at $4. Space blankets (a mildly reinforced laminate with a reflective side, about 5 by 7 feet, about 9 oz., $15) are often used as groundsheets. Similar but several times lighter are sheets of aluminized, nonstretch polyester film with a reflective coating, called emergency or survival blankets (usually 5 by 7 feet, 1.7 oz., $3). And see Chip's elegant suggestion (page 435) about old tent floors. On all but the longest trips I have for years used ordinary 4-mil painters'-cloth plastic sheeting, often under the name Visqueen (10-by-25-foot roll, $12), available in rolls at builders' supply stores. You can cut it to the exact size you want for any given trip. Mostly, you use it single and small (say, 3 by 7½ feet). But if you're going light on overhead protection and therefore may need something to pull over your bag, you cut your cloth accordingly. Color matters little, unless you may want the sheet to double as an awning. Then, choose black. I almost always do.

Plastic groundsheets are waterproof—when unpunctured. But because they often get punctured and torn they form a considerable part of the plastic desecration of wilderness by uneducated oafs (see, please, page 431). Each of us must make up his own mind about his personal response to this messy problem.

MATTRESSES

When you're young and eager and tough, and the weather isn't too perishingly cold, you do without a mattress. I did so all through the six months of my California walk (except for the first few days when, to cushion the shock of changing from soft city life, I carried a cheap plastic air mattress that I didn't expect to last long, and which didn't). I soon got used to sleeping with my mummy bag directly on all kinds of hard ground, but I often padded the bag inside with a sweater or other clothes. On that trip temperatures rarely fell more than a degree or two below freezing, though on one occasion I slept on stones at 25°F. (That night I had a floored tent and a few sheets of newspaper, which make a very useful emergency insulator.)

But failing to use some kind of insulation under your sleeping bag (unless it's a foam bag) is, in all but consistently hot weather, grossly inefficient: your weight so compresses the down or synthetic directly beneath you that its air-holding and warmth-conserving property is cut almost to zero. And even when cold is no problem you're liable to find that if you've grown used to an ordinary bed, the change to unpadded bag-on-the-ground ruins your sleep for at least a few nights. This reduces both your efficiency and enjoyment, and the saving in weight just isn't worth it—unless you can be sure of finding soft, dry sand for a bed. Then all you need is a couple of wriggles to dig shallow depressions for shoulders and rump, and you've got yourself a comfortable sleep.

The traditional woodsman and Boy Scout routine was to build a mattress from natural materials: soft and pliable bough tips, or moss or thick grass. On the California walk I did for a while use branches from desert creosote bushes. But in today's heavily traveled backcountry camping areas the cutting of plant life is not merely illegal but downright immoral—an atrocity committed only by the sort of feebleminded citizen who scatters empty beer cans along our roadsides. Besides, the method is inefficient. Even when you can find suitable materials, you waste time in preparing a bed. And the bed is rarely as warm or comfortable as any of the modern lightweight pads or mattresses.

For perhaps 20 years the standard equipment under almost all conditions was an air mattress. These traditional devices have now almost, but not quite, disappeared from mountain shops. I still use one occasionally, though, when I judge the night won't be cold enough to make sub-sleeping-bag insulation a major problem but weight, or even just comfort, might be; when I think I might need it for a river crossing; when bulk poses a load problem; or if I want to spend a lot of time sitting and reading or writing, and like hell fancy the idea of an easy chair (though for a more comfortable chair, see page 451).

If you decide you want an air mattress for some reason, avoid at all costs—unless you want it only for a night or two—one of the cheap, thin, plastic jobs. They puncture and tear almost without provocation, and often don't get the chance to do either before a seam pulls open. Coated nylon does much better.

An air mattress amplifies the efficiency of your sleeping bag by keeping a cushion of air between it and the ground. The air can circulate within the tubes, though, and therefore passes heat by convection from warm body to cold ground—and especially to snow. But an air mattress also neutralizes the sharpest stones, supports your body luxuriously at all the right places, converts into an easy chair, and will if necessary float you and your pack across a river (pages 688–97). It also gets punctures.

An offshoot is the *down-filled air mat* (DAM). This unlikely device by Stephenson-Warmlite is an attempt to combine the sink-in comfort of an air mattress with the much greater insulation of small, trapped air pockets. A box-baffled, urethane-coated nylon shell, fitted with an air valve, is filled with goose down, as in a sleeping bag or jacket. The great gain compared with a self-inflating pad (see below) is reduced bulk for packing. But in case of a puncture you lose the backup of a conventional foam pad. And because your breath would soon soak the down you must inflate the DAM with a short plastic tube attached to a special sleeping-bag stuff sack that acts as pump. In addition, because DAMs are made in special conformations to fit specific Stephenson sleeping bags, they're damned expensive: $140. All are 3 inches thick. Weights: from 1 lb. 4 oz. to 1 lb. 9 oz.

Foam pads succeeded air mattresses as king of the backcountry underbed, and they ruled for perhaps a decade.*

Still air trapped in small enough chambers—less than ¼-inch diameter—forms an excellent barrier to heat transfer, and foam pads hold the air in just such small chambers and therefore insulate far better than air mattresses. They also tend to be lighter and cheaper—and puncture-immune. But they're bulkier, and most of them are far less comfortable—except on snow or sand or a deep pile of leaves or other soft underlayer. In addition, they make inferior chairs and will help you precious little on river crossings. On balance, though, they proved better than air mattresses and superseded them for general backpacking, especially in cold places. For years no one in his right mind has carried an air mattress for snow work.

For 20 years now, you've been able, under almost all conditions, to have the best of both worlds.

Self-inflating pads

It's very rare for a new piece of backpacking equipment to sweep aside, almost overnight, all the oldies. But Cascade Designs's Therm-a-Rest mattress virtually pulled it off. A Therm-a-Rest—or one of the later

---

*Note that, in spite of fire-retardants, all foams—and also many nylon fabrics as used in sleeping bags and other equipment—present serious fire hazards. I don't say they'll burst into flames at the drop of a match. But they'll burn. And foams may give off toxic gases. I'm not sure what you can do about it, beyond exercising reasonable care. But I feel I must sound this warning.

competitors—is at least as comfortable as an air mattress and insulates better than most pads. The idea is simple: an open-cell foam pad that is covered with a tough, waterproof, airtight nylon twill cover bonded to the foam. A valve at one corner enables you to control the air pressure in the foam's spaces. To deflate for packing you roll the mattress on a flat surface or your thighs, then close the valve. The mattress remains rolled and is reasonably compact. To inflate you simply open the valve: the mattress will slowly unroll, and within a few minutes—the time needed to erect a tent, say—it's ready for use. You can simply close the valve or you can—as I almost always do—blow more air in and then close the valve. Inflated that way, the mattress is more comfortable as well as a more efficient insulator. Rather to my surprise, I find that the harder it's inflated, the more comfortable it is. But you can experiment and then minister to your personal druthers.

Punctures occur only rarely (full instructions for repair come with each mattress, and there's now a repair kit—Hot Bond, $5—said to be good); even a punctured Therm-a-Rest is still a serviceable open-cell foam pad (for open- and closed-cell pads, see pages 449–51). Faulty valves can be replaced fairly simply (spares, $5). It's my experience, widely shared, that if you treat your Therm-a-Rest with anything less than brutality it will give good service. It is very well made and the makers stand sturdily behind their product—even, sometimes, beyond the two-year warranty.

I suspect that a Therm-a-Rest might even fill the special role of air mattress as flotation device for you or your pack (page 690)—though if you ever got water in that open-cell foam . . .

Naturally, all this joy does not come cheap—in ounces or dollars.

CHIP: But, like a good sleeping bag, the cost is reasonable if you reckon the years of good service. I bought my first Therm-a-Rest mattress, an orange ¾-length, in 1980. It cost me $39—a vicious bite at the time. But divide that by the 21 years since and you get $1.86 per year for a decent night's sleep. That's quite a bit less than if I bought a new, cheap air mattress every year. My original Therm-a-Rest does have drawbacks. The nylon shell is slippery. I sprayed and resprayed it with Slip Fix, making it look as if I'd blown my nose on it 10,000 times, and even the anti-slip coating has grown polished with use. In 1987, I punctured it once, mysteriously, dead center, and applied a neat patch from the kit. So, in hard and constant use, that's 0.05 punctures per year. About 1989, the original brass valve crapped out so I replaced it with a mitten-operable plastic one. All my pad lacks is a name.

The new Therm-a-Rest pads are topped with nonslip polyester and undergirded with a coated nylon oxford. The valve is long-lasting plastic.

The repair kit is likewise improved, with a heat-bonded patch (you use a pan of boiling water) rather than the old glue-on type.*

There are four Therm-a-Rest series: Luxury, Performance, Classic, and Discovery. The first three come in full- or ¾-length. But some full-length pads, at 77 inches, are fuller than others, at 72. The ¾-length pads are 56 inches or 47. Any pad with "Camp" in the title is both longer and wider (25 inches versus 20). Except for the CampLite I'm not listing the Camp-width pads, because they're on the heavy side for backpacking.

The Luxury Edition pads (full: 2 lbs. 5 oz., $110; ¾-length: 1 lb. 9 oz., $82) have round, widthwise channels in the foam, for lightness and also cushy butt-hugging thickness (2 inches). Topped with Softknit fabric, these verge on the indecent—if you have hidebound notions of roughing it, that is. But if you're heavy and bony, tending to bottom-out on regular pads, this one's the ticket. Just don't crow too loud, or your significant other will snag it (mine did).

The Performance Series is filled with LiteFoam, which is cut vertically with overlapping slots and then stretched across the width. The 1.6-inch-thick CampLite is both longer (77 inches) and wider (25 inches) than the standard 72-by-20-inch pad, while only weighing 4 oz. more (full: 2 lbs. 12 oz., $80; ¾-length: 1 lb. 15 oz., $70). After Linda selected my new Luxury pad for her personal suite, I adopted the 1-inch-thick UltraLite (full: 1 lb. 8 oz., $70; ¾-length: 1 lb., $54). Blown up taut, it gives me just enough flotation for comfort and packs beautifully—the ¾-length size rolls to a 4-inch diameter and is 10.5 inches long. In summer, I stick with ¾-length pads. In winter, I formerly used a ¾ pad and wadded up extra clothes under my feet. But, with the advent of ultralight models, I've switched to a full-length pad for snow camping, with a reflective layer beneath (page 451).

The Therma-a-Rest Classic Series is the old reliable Standard, 1.5 inches thick with improved foam and a nonslip woodsy green top (full: 2 lbs. 8 oz., $65; ¾-length, 1 lb. 9 oz., $50). The Discovery Series Explorer weighs the same, has the same warranty, and costs less (full: $50; ¾-length,

---

*To patch this type of pad: 1) Find the hole, using a bathtub, alpine lake, or large amounts of spit; 2) wipe the area around the hole clean and let it air dry; 3) put water in a pot with a relatively clean bottom and bring it to a boil; 4) always open the valve fully when making repairs; 5) work McNett Seam Grip or other recommended cement into any exposed foam and the inside of the fabric; 6) apply a thin slather of cement evenly around the hole; 7) unlimber the patch, trimming it if necessary, and peel the backing off without touching the inner surface; 8) gently smooth the patch on; 9) if the pot is funky, or perhaps in any case, spread a clean hanky or scrap of other thin cotton cloth over the patch; 10) take the pot off the stove and set it on the patch. Then go away. Leave it absolutely alone till the water has cooled.

$40). A combination cover with straps and pillow sleeve called the Therm-a-Wrap has just risen from the waves.

I visited Cascade Designs in Seattle and watched the birth of a Therm-a-Rest UltraLite pad—or a whole herd of them, actually—laminated, pressed, and bonded. Kitty Graham, my guide, had two dogs curled up by her desk—it seemed like a pleasant place to work.

Other makers are trying hard to get into the bedroom-on-your-back. Artiach, a Spanish company, makes a pad covered in a glossy, nonslip polyester called the Skin Mat. The covering does feel disconcertingly like skin, though not human skin. It's dark gray and crinkled, like those 1960s B-movie Martians that scared my smaller self. The Skin Mat's not scary, though. Instead, it rolls up compactly and has a light protective cover. As pads go, it's not bad, though it doesn't fully inflate without some puffing and I did pinhole it first time out. But I repaired it by rubbing cement over the hole—didn't need a patch. I have a regular 63-inch midlength pad (1.5 inches thick, 1 lb. 14 oz., $64). I've been using this as my winter pad, for several reasons. The length works out nicely, with a fat makeshift pillow of fleece. It's rather thin-skinned, but snow covers the world's horny hide. And there's nonslip "skin" on both sides of the pad, so it doesn't skate around on the Reflectix sheet I use underneath (which coated nylon does most annoyingly). Artiach also has a more conventional Confort Mat Series and a Compact Mat Series, all in long, ¾-length, and the distinctive 63-inch midlength size. Weights are from 1 lb. 5 oz. to 5 lbs. 5 oz. and prices range from $49 to $98.

Stearns takes a different tack with the Ergo Mat Series. The open-cell foam isn't bonded to the casing. This means you can puff it up a bit extra and get the full floating-air effect, with enough foam to keep you from bottoming, shouldering, hipping, or heeling out. (My friend Paco, aka Jack's Plastic Welding, has made river runner's pads this way for years, and they're the catfish's pajamas, though a bit hefty for backpacking.) Anyhow, the full-length Ergo Mat's tapered, mummy shape has three segments so you can vary the softness and thickness from back to bum to legs. There's also an inflatable, foamless pillow. Once you get it right, it's comfortable for the weight and bulk—combining the virtues of a self-inflater and a well-designed air mattress. The drawbacks are three plastic flap valves, but they're located so that rolling up the pad exhausts the air and then more or less automatically closes each valve in turn. Two snap-on straps are included. The pad I tried a few years ago, the Ergo Mat Long (77 by 22 by 1.5 inches, 1 lb. 10 oz., $54) had a somewhat slithery top cover, though the current catalog lists all variations as having nonslip fabric.

Other semi-aerated pad purveyors are Backcountry Designs, Coleman, Mountain Equipment Co-op, Paramount Outfitters, Slumberjack, Sunny Rec, and Wenzel.

Before the trip, open the valve, let the pad uncrimp, and then blow it up tight and leave it overnight, to let the foam expand. (If it's limp the next morning, take it back to the store.) To keep your pad in good shape, store it with the valve open so the foam doesn't lose its bounce. To pack it, roll it once to get the air out, then unroll, fold double along the length, and re-roll for storage *inside* your pack. Or roll it up once and cover it with some sort of bag or sheath for transport *outside* your pack. Lashing a pad unprotected to the top or rear of your pack exposes it to sharp stubs, thorns, rock crystals, etc. Keep mosquito repellents with DEET (diethyl-whatever) way away: it melts the urethane used to coat (i.e., hold air inside) synthetic fabrics. That is, power lounging after applying bug dope can ruin your day (and night). All the generic finger wags about UV apply. The trick is not to sacrifice your enjoyment to preservation: your pad need not outlive you.

Pads that (intentionally) don't inflate

COLIN: Naturally, not everyone will want a Therm-a-Rest. Some people are, for good, bad, or indifferent reasons, wedded to foam pads. These can be lighter and less bulky, not to mention cheaper. And cost may be a crucial factor, especially if you backpack only rarely.

Closed-cell foam pads have impermeable surfaces and trap tiny air pockets almost permanently. They therefore insulate extremely well and are mostly waterproof. But they compress very little and, although thin (⅜ through ½ inch), are bulky to pack. When a pad is new, indentations quickly disappear; but with age it becomes, like people, less resilient. And severe cold makes some foam stiff and brittle. The thinness and incompressibility mean that closed-cell pads do not cushion you well; but comfort can be increased—at considerable cost in weight and bulk—by laminating sheets together. Pads come in various hip- or full-length sizes, or in sheets you can cut to suit.

Most early closed-cell pads were Ensolite. It has been improved and joined by others, and we now have a spectrum of pads in a wide range of sizes, weights, costs, and resistance to cold and abrasion. For a few current spectrum points, see below. Others exist. More will assuredly follow—and wax and wane with the passing moons.

CHIP: Among the determined users of closed-cell pads are those who bivouac on puncture-rich ground: in talus caves, on desert pavement, or under snaggly scrub. (The more sybaritic members of the tribe also slip a ¾-length self-inflater inside the bivouac sack.) Generic single-layer slabs can be scooped up in discount stores for $5 to $10. Those in backpacking shops range from $10 to $20. Black Ensolite, which resists cracking in cold weather, comes in ½- and ¾-inch thicknesses and 6-foot lengths, for $30 to $45.

Wildly popular are two closed-cell pads from Cascade Designs. The Ridge Rest goes through a special press that leaves crosswise corrugations in the foam. This renders the pad slightly more compressible under body weight, for comfort. There's probably no one in the developed world who hasn't seen one of these, if only by the side of a highway, blown off the roof rack of some hapless soul. They're superb, as 3-season pads, and I use one regularly. But winter's a different story. If you don't get every bit of snow off them before going to sleep, or if there's frost falling from the inside of the tent, your body heat melts it and the neat little channels channelize it to the lowest point: right under your sleeping bag. The Ridge Rest Deluxe (two-tone purple and metallic green) is 72 by 20 by ¾ inches and 1 lb. 2 oz. for $29. The Ridge Rest Regular is ⅜ inch thick, 14 oz., and $20, with a ¾-length version a mere 9 oz. and $15.

The Cascade Designs Z-Rest goes into a different press, and comes out in a pattern you could call egg-crate (for hummingbird eggs). Rather than rolling, it folds up accordion-fashion, with the little eggules nesting into one another. This makes for compact, if rectilinear, packing. Even though it appears lighter, it weighs a bit more than the regular Ridge Rest: the 72-inch Z-Rest weighs 1 lb. and runs $30, while the ¾ size is 11 oz. and $24. Lighter people rave about how comfortable the Z-pads are, while bony heavyweights (me) tend to flatten the eggules at key points, and thus prefer the Ridge Rest. When I visited Cascade Designs, they were working on a new, ultraresilient, top-secret formula for Z-Rest foam. The enemies of these pads are solvents and heat: don't leave them under the rear window of a parked hatchback. A tangential use is to stiffen up the mattresses in Third World hotels or student rentals.

COLIN: *Open-cell foam pads* compress easily and are therefore more comfortable than Ensolite and its cousins. But to achieve the same insulation they must be about three times as thick (normal range, 1½ to 2½ inches). So they're bulkier, heavier, and more expensive. The bulkiness is more apparent than real: stuffed hard into a packbag, they compress halfway well. Open foam is often corrugated, in "egg-crate" or zigzag form, to increase comfort with minimum additional weight.

Because the open-cell structure soaks up water, the pads mostly come with covers—coated waterproof nylon underneath, with a nonslip blend on top to reduce slipperiness and permit perspiration to dissipate. A pleated pocket at the head of the cover may offer holding space for whatever pillow you choose to inject (page 486). Before the advent of the Therm-a-Rest, I used a Sierra Designs version of such a pad for years under most conditions except snow and found it as warm and trouble-free as Ensolite and almost as comfortable as an air mattress. A Georgia reader suggests a cheap, do-it-yourself covered pad: open-cell foam, 25½ inches wide, 1 or 1½ inches thick, with two industrial-strength plastic garbage bags slipped over opposite ends, joined amidships with duct tape, and punctured at one end (for air escape and easier packing) with slits placed at ½-inch intervals.

Meanwhile, evolution pads on.

CHIP: Mountain Hardwear has a new series of tapered pads, 1.6 to 2.4 inches thick, in 50-, 60-, 72-, and 77-inch lengths. Weights range from 1 lb. 12 oz. to 4 lbs. 6 oz., and prices from $42 to $89. Not inflatable—by any normal means at least—they have wiggly open-cell foam laminated to a sheet of closed-cell foam and nonslip covers with nice pillow sleeves. Everything I've seen from the Mountain Hardwear folks has been top-notch, and early reviews on these pads are good, except for the rolled-up size, which is bulkier than that of a self-inflater.

Reflectix insulation is grand stuff: thin aluminum foil on both sides, bonded to a 3/16-inch sheet of bubble wrap. I got a roll to insulate my work-shop, and liked the looks of it. So I cut off a 74-inch piece to take snow camping. The insulated part is 22 inches wide, with a 1-inch stapling strip on either edge. My pad liner weighs 10.5 oz. (or 1.7 oz. per foot). Camping in February, I noticed that I hadn't melted out my usual body trough in the snow under the tent floor. That's a first, since I radiate heat like a fresh-caught meteorite. The bubble wrap gives it minor effective-ness as padding: on snow, hardpersons can punch out hip and shoulder recesses and use Reflectix alone. It's slickery under sleeping bags, though, and knees and elbows tend to pop a few bubbles each time you roll, so the life span is limited. But mine has survived its third winter. Reflectix and similar products can be found in eco-solar-type catalogs, or at the local home center. A 25-foot roll (four full-length pads) costs $25.

Last and most curious is a hybrid sleeping pad/chaise, the subinfla-tionary PowerLounger, at 54 by 17.5 by ½ inches. The core is foam, while the nonslip cover has wing straps that elevate the upper third into a near-instantaneous backrest. The PowerLounger (1 lb. 14 oz., $51) is built by Crazy Creek Products, who also originated the backpacker's chair.

Chairs and nonchairs,

as *Variety* might put it, now do boffo biz with hike-happy hordes. Since Crazy Creek ranks first in time, let's take them as somewhat repre-sentative. There are two main types. The fabric and foam chair (no infla-tion) buckets around your buttocks in a way that's at first disconcerting. But once you get the way of it, you can be comfortable indeed. The Crazy

Creek original weighs 22 oz. and costs $37. Variants exist for canoes, stadiums, and other presently unimaginable spots. I saw a young couple using one in a futile attempt to ensconce their unhappy child on the back of an unhappier llama. The second sort is a fabric shell, with wands or stays, that warps a self-inflating pad into chairlike form. Crazy Creek makes the ThermaLounger in various widths and lengths from Mini to Camp, and weights from 15 oz. to 1 lb. 14 oz. Not only must the width be compatible with your pad, but length figures in too.

In a moment of weakness I got a Therm-a-Rest Lite 20 Easy Chair, in a color called Grape. (Hail to thee, blithe nylon—grape thou never wert!) Despite every intention of testing it rigorously, I haven't unwrapped it yet. It slumbers, vivid, beneath its plastic shroud. My fear is, I guess, that I'll head off on a walking trip only to spend more time lounging than walking. In any event, Cascade Designs has Easy Chairs to fit all of their pads (except the Z-Rest). As do most other pad-forming entities.*

I do rely, especially after lugging a heavy winter pack and being storm-cooped in a tent, on a self-supporting device. But it's not a chair. It's a construct of webbing, buckles, and modest pads called, in fact, the Nada-Chair (9.5 oz., $49). The back support, 6 by 20 inches, is crossed by 2-inch webbing loops that slip down over your knees and then buckle together, midthigh. It works the same way as a Crazy Creek Chair, but discreetly. You can't plunk down in it. You have to sit in a conscious way. But you can get out of it more easily. I find it pleasanter, on the whole, than a butt-enveloping slab of nylon. And it's certainly a lot lighter. Since you wear it rather than sit in it, it also works as a back brace for pounding a keyboard, as I'm doing now.

I'm not sure whether doubling up my sleeping pad in winter accords—philosophically at least—with my stringency in the matter of chairs. An eminent book reviewer once observed: "There is something of the anchorite in Rawlins."

I leave it up to you.

Hammocks and hanging shelters

COLIN: A reader once wrote from Liberia that he often used his army hammock from Vietnam for backpacking, "with no regrets . . . only a few reservations." Now, most people shy away from the idea of sleeping in a hammock, especially after a long day with a heavy load. I certainly do. But you may not. And I guess a light hammock can be useful as a bed if you want to keep cool (air all around you) in a place as hot as Liberia; if the

*COLIN: After initial skepticism, I've succumbed, blissfully, to the Easy Chair.

ground, every place, is soaking wet; if you're petrified beyond sleep by the thought of rattlesnakes or scorpions or other things that might go chomp in the night; if the local ground insects are a ravenously hungry host; or if you're an old-style sailor, landlubbering but pining. Other suggested uses: for slinging food and gear from trees, high above the ground, as protection against flood, bears, and other invaders; for rest, not sleep, at a base camp; and, with poles, as an emergency stretcher.

My Liberian correspondent's hammock seemed to be of some solid fabric: he didn't like or trust "the net-type sold for packers." But sold they are—or at least offered: knotless synthetic-mesh jobs described as rolling into "a pocket sized ball" and damn nearly doing so (main body 32 by 72 inches, 12 oz., $15). Also sometimes seen: a Mayan Indian design, "made of miles of 100% pure cotton lace, hand woven and hand tied . . . so big and strong it'll sleep three adults. . . . Easy to care for, will last and last" (10 by 11 feet, 3¼ lbs., $60). A selection of Mayan handwoven net hammocks and Brazilian cloth ones can be bought from a Boulder, Colorado, outfit called Hangouts.

CHIP: My uncle Sid, who spent an adventurous decade in South America, returned with a tribal hammock-for-two in which he'd slept regularly. According to him, the Indians, who practically live in their hammocks, bed down more or less crosswise. This greatly lessens the fundamental droop.

Two nylon models that I have actually seen and briefly occupied are the Blue Ridge Camping Hammock (4 lbs. 4 oz., $172, from Lawson Hammocks), which has two aluminum hoops to support the netting and fly sheet; and the Jungle Hammock (4 lbs. 3 oz., $169, from Clark Outdoor Products), which eschews hoops and uses separate rigging points for hammock and fly (four altogether). The Treeboat Hammock (3 lbs. 12 oz., $115), which I've heard about but haven't seen, is made by New Tribe of Grants Pass, Oregon. It has four-point web rigging with raindrip-stopping rings at each corner and slip-in fiberglass battens. For cool nights, a Quallofil underside is 2 lbs. and $55, while mosquito net runs 15 oz. and $40. The Treeboat two-hoop rainfly is 12 oz. and $70, while a three-hoop tent top with zip doors is 2 lbs. 7 oz. and $100. The New Tribe catalog has a vast assortment of tree-scaling gear, including hardware, cordage, shot pouches, special arrows (for reaching extra-high branches), and books like *The Tree Climber's Companion* by Jeff Jepson ($10.50) and *Recreational Tree Climbing* by Dick Flowers ($7.50).

Unfortunately, any bed that forms a catenary curve plays absolute hell with my back: I can't sleep, and the next morning can barely walk. Which rules out the army/navy/marine-surplus models (and private variations) for me.

But hanging one's bed from a tree does have a certain appeal. One April in southeast Alaska, I was looking for deer and brown bears with a biologically inclined friend. After boating to a snowcapped island, we walked for hours through a dank forest, clambering over roots and down trunks, all humped and festooned with soggy moss. The fact that I could scarcely walk, let alone run, on such stuff, along with the idea of horse-size bears emerging ravenous from their dens, made me mildly uneasy. There were occasional openings, called muskegs, nicely cushioned by organic muck, but our feet pressed down into groundwater at every step (imagine a floating sponge). There wasn't a nice dry flat patch of mineral dirt for miles. The only half-decent place I could see to sleep was on bedrock points, lashed by waves, or on pebbly beaches above the tidemark. As I was pondering this aloud, my friend pointed out the bear trail that paralleled the beach, so well traveled that each pawprint was deeply indented. "Lots of edible goodies wash up, so the bears patrol," he said. "Or at least the hungry ones do."

"So, uhhh, Nels—where do *you* sleep out here?"

"On my skiff, anchored out in that little cove."

For the skiffless, whether afoot or a-kayak, a ripe possibility is the Dryad DT 100 Suspended Shelter by the Canadian firm Terrelogic (7 lbs. 5 oz., $350). The photos in their brochure intrigued me, showing the Dryad hung between mangroves on an islet with no sand whatsoever, just interlaced roots. Another showed it 20 feet up (well out of claw range), hung from a single point. On a hike last spring down a narrow canyon, with the trail shelved on a timbered slope above a thundering creek, I'd thought: What a gorgeous place to camp, if you could just roost in a fir.

So I tested a Dryad (they render it drYad, which could conceivably be read as Dr. Yad. I do grow weary of strangely capitalized words). Picture

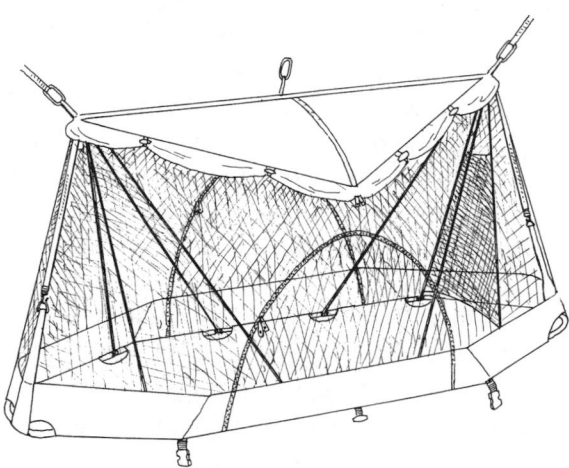

drYad hanging shelter

a double-wall tent with a floor you can trust. The suspension is quite good—the floor, with tapered ends, is framed by fat aluminum tubing that plinks together with shock cord.

When you get it plugged together, a lengthwise nonstretch Dacron strap reefs it tight. Suspended from eight lengths of nylon cord connected to thick webbing loops, the floor is level, tight, and distinctly more habitable than a droopy-ass hammock. In cool weather you'd want an insulating pad, or better, Reflectix insulation (page 451) trimmed to fit the floor.

My first night out was chill: 20°F. Even with the fly partly unzipped on both sides, there was condensation and frost. By morning the floor and the bottom of my sleeping bag were wet. Forests, the natural habitat of dryads, are both more humid and more still than open sites, so venting is crucial.* Double sliders on the door zips would help, and so would an overlap vent at the head. The rainfly could be made of a breathable laminate, tacking on further cost. Of course, in smiling weather, you can roll the rainfly up on one side or both, and lounge like a peeled banana on your airy, screened-in cot.

The built-in backrest was a surprise, adding great comfort for little weight. From a compact tuck it slips down two of the suspending cords. I also discovered that you can pluck bass-viol notes on the cords (the tone is quite good, for a tent). On my second—and considerably warmer—night out I rolled up the rainfly, plucked the cords, and sang "Bye-bye Blackbird" while rocking gently.

The Dryad is a camper's rig. Hard-core climbers are best served by a single-point porta-ledge and matching fly (Terrelogic makes one, the DT 200). But most climbers' ledges, while technologically awesome, are two or three times the weight of a tent and when folded are over 40 inches long. The Dryad, on the other hand, is *sort* of packable—once you get the hang of it. The frame disarticulates while remaining in its sheath, and the whole assemblage stuffs loosely into a sack that's 26 by 9 inches. Fearing punctures, I used some emery cloth on the edgier parts of the frame, and am looking at further unauthorized (or maybe "author-ized" is the perfect word here) changes, so that I can pack the frame separately.

I'd rate the whole concept as promising. In steep, forested country, it could be a godsend. For casual use, I'd rig the thing close to the ground.

To rig from one point, on high, you need slings and an extra-cost spreader bar. Most trekking poles are too short—a 5-foot span is needed.

---

*Having suggested venting options to the maker (brusquely rejected), I took the laws of physics into my own hands. Using a torch-heated tuna can, I hot-cut two openings and stitched two coated-nylon hoods over them, with stiffeners of electrical cable. The sewing was torture, but my supermodified Dryad is much less subject to condensation.

(You also need a tether or two, to keep it from swinging or spinning—unless you enjoy that.) I had to build a 7075-aluminum eave-stretcher pole, having snapped the original fiberglass one during a complex maneuver I'd rather not describe.*

If you need (or want) to suspend your bed more than a few feet off the deck, consult a book on big-wall climbing for relevant details and precautions. Get real carabiners (not those little keyholders) or steel rapid-links and use high-strength slings or cord. A safety harness and a pair of ascenders with *etriers* (stepladders of nylon webbing) and/or empirical knowledge of Prusik-loop technique is essential. Suspended camping needs to be practiced, since the inexorable effect of gravity can nudge the usual mishaps toward disaster.

Besides eco-activist tree sitters, the other prong of development for hanging shelters has been biologists who work in forest canopies. Dr. Nalini Nadkarni, of Evergreen State College in Olympia, Washington, the president of the International Canopy Network (*www.evergreen.edu/ican*), kindly gave me several leads. An article on safe rigging, with a diagram of a line-tossing apparatus that grafts a Wrist Rocket slingshot onto a spinning reel, is "An Improved Canopy Access Technique," by Gabriel F. Tucker and John R. Powell, *Northern Journal of Applied Forestry*, 8 (1), March 1991. Tree-climbing gear is available from Forestry Suppliers and from New Tribe.

Once you attain a major branch, you can rig separate slings for the shelter, keeping the main rope for ascent and descent. (In brown bear country, all anchors should be out of reach—the bear's that is.) My third time out, I rigged the shelter high, then hauled my pack up and hung it from a branch like a swinging cupboard. After which I cooked soup on my hanging stove. Other happy adjuncts were a mesh gear loft and a Sierra Designs coffee sling.

Obviously, I'm fascinated by the whole arboreal riff, and wonder whether human evolution took a wrong swerve.

SLEEPING BAGS

COLIN: For good reasons, we'll consider the fundamentals of warmth retention in the Clothes Closet, not here. See The Prime Purpose of Clothes, page 504, and The Fundamentals of Insulation, page 515. If you

---

*Okay—might as well come clean. While Dryad camping on high, I was trying to come up with an eco-sensitive method of taking a crap without actually rappelling. Nor did I wish to risk a rimshot inside the thing. So there I was, hanging outboard, paper bag in hand. There were unpredictable winds.

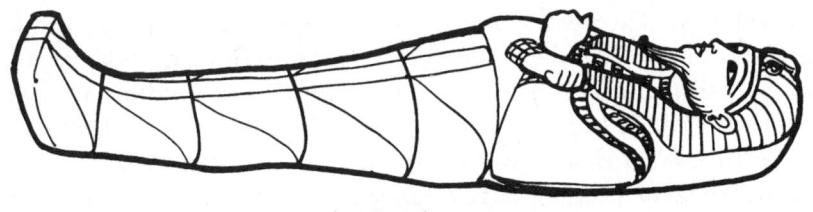

Ancient Egyptian mummy

Modern American mummy

can't be bothered to check those pages, at least remember that sleeping bags, like clothes, are not to "keep the cold out," as the old saying goes, but to conserve heat from the only available source—you; also that (although the distinction is less important than with clothes) the bag is not meant to make you as warm as possible, but to maintain *thermal equilibrium*—a state in which your heat production roughly balances your heat loss.

Because the first sleeping bags clearly evolved from the idea of stitching two blankets together, they took the rectangular form of a bed. But most backpacking bags are now mummy bags—designed for human forms rather than for small upright pianos.

A few people say they feel uncomfortably confined in mummy bags. Claustrophobics may certainly face difficulties; but if you've given mummies a fair trial and just cannot get used to any real or imagined constriction, you don't necessarily have to put up with the inefficiencies of the old rectangular piano-envelope. Although most backpacking bags are now distinctly form-fitting (in spite of a trend away from extreme sheathing), the catalogs still offer a continuum ranging from slim through mesomorphic to downright obese—some of these are tapered but unshaped—as well as old-style rectangular. Take your well-pondered pick. But remember that each size up means marginally greater weight and bulk. And, worse, that your body has to warm, all night long, a marginally greater volume of contained air.

CHIP: Between the strictly rectilinear and the infidel mummy lies a zone of compromise, known (depending on where you start) as either *semi-rectangular* or *modified-mummy*. Sensible persons once called these "barrel-shaped" bags, a term that now refers only to those without a permanently attached hood. The modified-mummy bags are tapered at head and foot, but not so closely as to be in any wise confining. But the enduring problem with all mummy bags is that real mummies, being dead, lie still on their backs. While backpackers, after a day of strenuous travel, don't.

A significant change over the last decade is in the number of makers offering a line of sleeping bags designed for women; at present: Eastern Mountain Sports, Kelty, Lafuma, L. L. Bean, Recreational Equipment, Rokk, Sierra Designs, Slumberjack, The North Face, and Woods Canada Ltd. In general, women's models have more insulation in the foot and/or torso. The cut is smaller in the shoulder and roomier at the hip. Linda gives high marks to the Sierra Designs Ella, a o°-down bag with a womanly cut, and most of the women I ask who own these bags prefer them to unisex types, but there are also complaints. One athletic female friend bought (and returned) a bag that she claims was "overwomanized," cut not for a kayaking, trail-running woman but for a steatopygous, Willendorfian Venus.*

Rather than offering "womanized" bags, quite a few of the best companies urge you to look carefully not just at length but also at the girth measurements at the shoulder, hip, and foot. Once you've measured your own girth, the rule of thumb is to add 2 inches for a close fit, 4 inches for an average fit, and 6 inches for a loose one. For instance, my ultralight Western Mountaineering Iroquois Long has a close-fitting 60-inch shoulder, a 52-inch hip, and a 38-inch foot. While the cold-weather Puma Long measures 63-54-39: ample room for a layer of fleece inside.

COLIN: Some outdoor lovers complain that mummy bags don't leave enough room for maneuver. Opportunists may face a problem here (though a local Don Juan advises: "You'd be surprised what has been achieved. As in all games, desire is very important"). Those who plan their amatory operations in advance should note that it's now possible to order most mummy-bag models with zippers on opposite sides so that they'll join convivially together. And any two bags with zippers of the same kind and length will conjoin—though the hoods will face opposite ways. See also doublers, page 476.

A battened-down mummy bag is a very efficient heat conserver. Old-style rectangular envelopes gave your head no protection at all, tended to leave your shoulders exposed too, and let a great deal of precious body heat escape through the bag's wide mouth. A mummy eliminates all

---

*Since Colin asked: the *Venus of Willendorf* (an Austrian town on the Danube River) is a well-known Paleolithic sculpture of a woman with exaggerated breasts, hips, and buttocks—an image said to represent fertility, or a personification of nature as female.

these faults. When you pull on the drawstrings of the hood, the fabric curls around your crown and not only protects head and shoulders but also bottles the body heat. On a really cold night you pull on the drawstrings until the opening contracts to a small hole around nose and mouth. If, like me, you prefer to sleep naked because you wake feeling fresher you may sometimes find cold air seeping down through the hole and moving uncomfortably around bare shoulders. All you need do is wrap a shirt loosely around your neck (though see Hoods, Collars, Zippers, etc., page 469). But this arrangement often holds the warm air in so well that you soon find you are too hot. To reduce the inside temperature (whether you're using a neck wrap or not) simply slacken the hood tapes a little. That will make a lot of difference: your head dissipates heat more quickly than any other part of the body (also page 469). (You won't question this statement if you're balding fast into coot country: you'll probably, like me, have taken to wearing a balaclava at night.) In warm weather you can leave the tapes undrawn so that the mouth of the bag remains as open as in old-style envelopes. In hot weather you can go two steps further—if you have the right kind of bag. A mummy bag designed for use only in cold weather (that is, for polar exploration, high-altitude mountaineering, and winter hunting) may have no zipper openings. So do some ultra-light bags. But although an uninterrupted shell is the lightest possible design and also conserves heat the most efficiently, such a bag is now very rare. It may do its special job well but it lacks versatility. In anything but chilly weather you're liable to find yourself sweating even though the mouth of the bag is open—with no alternative except getting partly or wholly out. A zipper opening solves the problem, and nearly all bags now come with side zippers reaching the ankles or thereabouts. The modification is not pure gain. To prevent air passage through the closed zipper it has to be faced inside with a down-filled draft flap, or the zipper zone has to be blocked with a broad extension of the main wall that snugs in tight when you close the zipper. Or there may be two full-length zippers. But even a single zipper and its flap add several ounces to the weight of a bag, and, no matter how good the blocking device, there is bound to be a slight loss in heat-conserving efficiency, but if you expect to operate at times in temperatures much above freezing, then the very great gain in versatility is well worth such minor drawbacks. Some mummy bags have zippers that open all the way around the foot so that you can ventilate your feet as well as the rest of you—and can also convert the fully opened bag into a flat though markedly tapered down cover, very useful for warm nights in the bush and cold ones back home in bed. Almost all bags now have two-way zippers: you can operate the zipper from both top and bottom, and by opening it partway at shins as well as shoulders you gain a valuable aid in the almost nightly game of adjusting your bed to suit different and changing air temperatures (page 478).

Of the major sleeping-bag components—fill, shells, and liners—

The fill

is what matters most. It must hold within itself as many pockets of air as possible, to act as an insulant between the warmed inner and cold outer air, and for backpacking purposes the best material is that which does this job most efficiently for the least weight. But there are subsidiary considerations: compactibility (the packed bag should not be too bulky); fluffability (the fill must quickly expand to its open, air-trapping state after being tightly packed); efficiency when wet; even, for a few people, possible allergic effects.

Traditional down-filled bags still dominate the high-quality field. But synthetic-filled bags, which have for years been nipping at their drawstrings, continue to make technical advances, and have just about caught up. Among high-quality bag makers, a few still stick exclusively with down. But most of the big producers have added synthetic lines or even gone all-synthetic.

Down is still the most efficient fill, warmth for weight. Compressed for packing, it's markedly less bulky than any known synthetic fill. It also fluffs back to its open, air-trapping state more quickly and totally. When not compressed it free-flows, almost like a liquid, so that it continuously and evenly fills, in a way no current synthetic will, a space that's always changing shape—as is a compartment in a sleeping bag. In addition, a good down-filled bag should, with real care, last 10 to 15 years, against 3 to 6 years for most current synthetics. On the other hand, down is useless when wet (synthetics retain at least some insulating property, and often most of it); once wet, it is difficult-going-on-impossible to dry in the field (synthetics dry much more readily); and over a long period of continual use, as in an expedition, dirt and repeated dampness tend to reduce its loft and therefore its efficiency (though see Gore-Tex shells, page 468). Down, unlike synthetics, can also generate allergies in rare individuals. It demands rather more care in maintenance. And high-quality down is now murderously expensive: on the Asian wholesale market, 600-fill is $16 per lb., 700-fill is $27, and 775 is $30, versus $6 per pound for the best current synthetics.

It's generally accepted that the best down comes from geese (mostly from China). Much learned discourse used to occur in catalogs and mountain shops—and to some extent still does—about the virtues of white versus gray goose down (probable ultimate verdict: the difference is either nil or very little), the adulteration of down with fluff (by law, "down" must be at least 80 percent *down*—that is, cluster and fiber rather than quills, beaks, etc.), and even the occasional perfidious sale of mere duck down under the name of "goose" (to be labeled "goose down," 90 percent of the clusters must actually come from geese). All new bags bear a sewn-in label showing government specifications of the fill—the American Society for Testing and Materials (ASTM) has ordained standards for down content and fill power. For some years, though, a generally accepted qualitative measure has been dampening this ongoing discourse. *Fill power* is not, thank God, yet another political rallying bleat: it shows the number of cubic inches an ounce of down will occupy. (The scale is not used for synthetics.) The best bag and garment makers use down with a fill power of 600, 700, or even 800, and somewhere in the blurb about their gear they will give the figure. Or should.

CHIP: Simply speaking, fill power comes from longer-tendriled, fluffier down clusters: 550-fill down has 56,000 clusters per ounce, while an ounce of 750-fill has 24,000. So good down takes up more space with the same weight of material. While there is no legal standard for fill power, the International Down and Feather Bureau recommends a test using a clear cylinder, marked with fill-power grades, with a 68.4-gram disk to gently compress the down. To reduce the variation owing to moisture content and packing methods, certified testing labs go through a five-day process of lofting and drying down samples, which means that the test batches are in optimal shape. Meanwhile, back at the plant, the down that goes into your sleeping bag is usually unconditioned. Thus, even down certified as 800-plus will give somewhat less than its rated performance after being crammed into a stuff sack and then lofted for a mere 10 minutes before you start butt-mashing it and sweating through it.

Even so, good down, in a well-made bag, has a distinctive resilience: poke it with your finger and it nudges back. Down also has amazing longevity. I have a bag made circa 1976 by Holubar of Boulder, Colorado, with 3 lbs. of down fill. I used it hard during 15 years of Forest Circusing, including six winters of snow sampling in the bitterly cold Wind River Range. I've washed it three times, always in special down soap, and except for a slight clumping in the hood, it's still lofty and winter-fit after 25 years.

COLIN: *Synthetic fills* with fancy names and low prices have been around for years. For backpacking, I wouldn't touch them with a walking staff. But the latest versions are a different kettle of fuzz.

Current trade names don't matter too much: they'll likely be gone tomorrow. But it's worth knowing that there are three main kinds of fill presently in use and that at least one novel form lurks in the wings:

1. Long, continuous-filament fibers that cling together and are used in thick, cohesive sheets known as *batts* (usually rated by weight per square yard). A 5-oz. layer, uncompressed, is about 1 inch thick. Currently dominant: Polarguard (a solid-core fiber that depends on bounce for insulating capacity), Polarguard HV (with a triangular cross section that gives more insulating capacity and makes it more compressible), and Polarguard 3D (also triangular and hollow-core, but finer and softer). Other continuous-filament contenders include proprietary fibers such as Lamilite.

2. Much shorter, noncontinuous-filament fibers that can be used either in cohesive batts, much like the long-fibered layers, or in a more amorphous (i.e., chopped) form. Current trade names: Hollofil (a simple hollow-core), Hollofil II (with four channels), and Quallofil (seven channels and a silicone finish).

3. Even-shorter-fibered forms somewhat resemble down, though they may be partially bonded or come in batts. Names still being juggled include Lite Loft, Micro-loft, Primaloft, and Thermolite Extreme. Some get good reviews: Primaloft 2 is said to be "like down, but amazingly water-repellent."*

All three forms can be "lubricated" by spraying with silicone or other liquids to reduce the "boardlike" quality and make them feel more silky, more downlike.

It looks as if we are now not far away from a synthetic that warms and wears as efficiently as down, perhaps in a form that can also be blown into compartments. If so, it will revolutionize the sleeping-bag and down-garment field. As the R&D man for a leading maker told me years ago: "If and when we get the right synthetic it will destroy down—because of its price, because it stays warmer when wet, and because it will be easier to take care of."

Thinsulate, a thin-fibered polyolefin/polyester synthetic insulation very popular in certain kinds of clothing (page 515), did not prove suitable for sleeping bags. Ditto pile and fleece (page 509), except for light, warm-weather bags. And foam bags seem to have faded into the night.

---

*CHIP: Reports from outdoor programs, which launder rental bags after every use, peg the effective life of most synthetic insulations at 6 to 8 machine washings. So, as with down, you're better off keeping your bag as clean as possible and washing it infrequently. Most sleeping-bag makers are mum on the subject. But Jerry Wigutow of Wiggy's, who is anything but mum, claims that his Lamilite synthetic insulation will withstand regular washing.

Two variations on the normal method of using fill now enjoy considerable vogue. Both appear mainly if not solely in down-filled bags.

One is simply to put 60 percent of the fill on top, 40 percent below—instead of the normal 50/50 division. Assuming a good insulating pad underneath, that makes theoretical sense: most of the heat you lose presumably escapes upward. But it seems to me that unless you tend not to move at all during the night, or always move the bag around with you when you do so (and some people apparently train themselves to do just that, even in mummy bags), then the "top" of the bag is by no means always on top. Most people lie at least part of the time on one side, and curled, so the underfilled portion tends to pull tight along your back—the most vulnerable area. That kicks a colander in the theory; but the fact is that many, perhaps most, down bags are now filled 60/40. Some, for mountaineering, even go 70/30 near the foot.

The second variation is to sew a shell with continuous baffles so that fill can be moved around, top to bottom. This is achieved by omitting the line of of blocking baffles that runs down the side of the bag opposite the zipper and keeps down from traveling, top to bottom, along transverse tubes (see next page). The idea is that in cold weather you shift down from bottom to top; in warm weather, vice versa. Satisfied users tell me it works, even when done in the dark. Frankly, I remain apprehensive of cold spots. But many bag makers now produce at least one model, usually a lightweight, built this way. Some, like Feathered Friends and Western Mountaineering, now use the down-shifting design for most of their bags, with block baffles reserved for the coldest-weather models.

The shell

Down demands one kind of internal construction; synthetics, quite another.

Down tends to move away from the points of greatest wear, notably from under your butt and shoulders (where it will be compressed and not very effective anyway) and also from the high point above your body (where, because heat rises, good insulation is vital). To minimize fill's movement the shell is therefore divided into a series of self-contained tubes that keep the down from moving very far (see above). Because of a general tendency for down to migrate from the head toward the foot of a bag, transverse tubes work far better than longitudinal.

If tubes are made by simply stitching through the inner and outer walls of the shell you are left unprotected at the stitch-through points. If some form of batting is inserted at these points (a simple and cheap system) there's some improvement. But not much. And except for a few ultralight models, all down sleeping bags now embody tube systems in which the tube walls—known as *baffles*—are constructed on one of four systems:

straight,

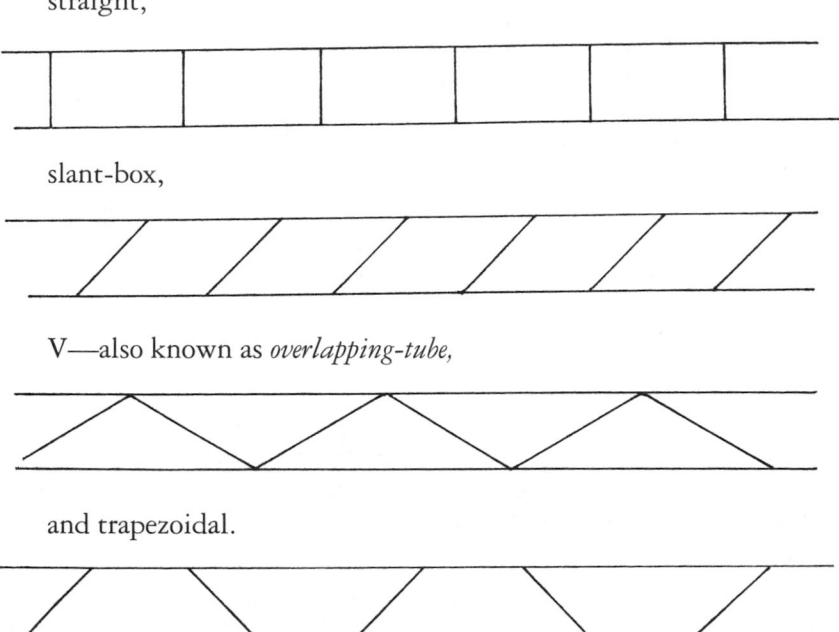

slant-box,

V—also known as *overlapping-tube,*

and trapezoidal.

CHIP: These days, most top-notch bags have a differential cut (i.e., an inner layer with a smaller girth than the outer shell) with minor variations. The problem of maintaining the proper distance between the liner and shell around a tight curve—along the sides and at the head and foot—has made trapezoidal, or wedge, baffling popular. Yet another trick is for inner liners to be larger than outer shells, in what's known as a *reverse*

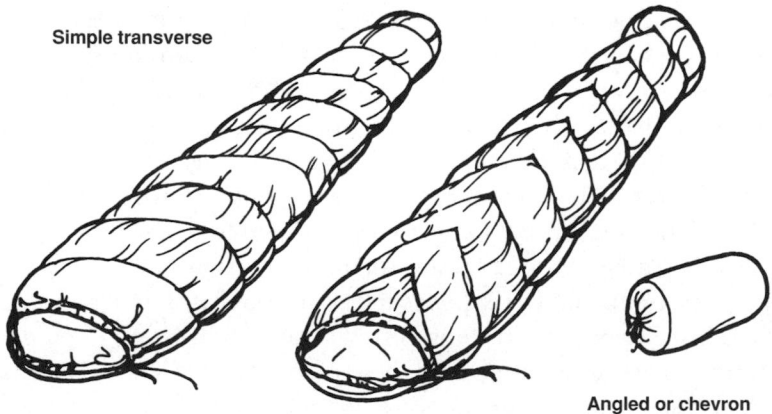

Simple transverse

Angled or chevron

differential cut, for instance in a hood. The loose down-filled fabric liner is meant to expand around your face and forehead and seal out drafts. But one of my favorite bags is a box-quilted (that is, *sewn-through*) down ultralight, so when arguments rage over cut-and-bafflement, it pays to keep an open mind.

As far as the visible geometry, transverse or chevron, the debate seems to have been resolved in favor of simple transverse tubes. The virtue of chevron-shaped baffles lies in preventing down shift while you sleep. But a chevron means more baffle material and longer seams, jacking up the cost. Canada's Integral Designs makes high-quality chevron-style bags filled with Primaloft—a downy synthetic.

In good-quality down bags, the width (or spacing) of the baffles seems to have settled between 5 and 6 inches. Cold-weather bags with side-block baffles tend to use wider spacing. Several makers, Marmot for instance, vary the width, using narrower tubes through the heat-producing torso and wider ones in the heat-shedding head and foot.

The baffles themselves—invisible in a finished bag—are made of a light and usually unspecified synthetic. No-see-um mesh is often used, being tough, lightweight, and flexible. Recently, mildly elastic tricot baffles have been used by Marmot and others to add more give at the weak point—where the baffle connects to the inner shell. A high-stretch baffle first showed up on bags from Mont-Bell, a Japanese firm with elegantly functional designs that didn't take hold in the U.S. But the idea was adopted under license by Sierra Designs. I've been testing one of these new bags and find that the flexy-stretchy system makes it more comfortable—for me at least.

COLIN: Long-fibered, continuous-filament synthetics, such as Polarguard, need no tubes. A single layer or combination of layers encircles the bag, with extra fill at the foot. Most such bags have quilt lines that look like baffle-tube seams, but in at least some cases they seem to be largely cosmetic: people are used to transversely sewn bags, say the makers, and demand "the down look." Actually, the quilting of continuous-fiber synthetic to the shell increases costs and may slightly reduce insulation efficiency—though it can be argued that a floppy, unsecured shell would be a nuisance, especially on the inside. The important thing with such bags is *edge stabilization,* which simply means that the layers (or at least the outer layers) are sewn securely to the shell along their edges. Otherwise they tend to pull away and leave an insulation-ruining gap, and the insulation ends up twisting on itself.

Edge stabilization is equally important with shorter-fibered synthetics, such as Quallofil, when they're used in batted layers. With such fills, quilting over the main surface is usually necessary—even when, as often happens, the batts have a lightweight scrim attached to one side to hold the material together structurally.

CHIP: Synthetic insulation is now arrayed in three main ways.

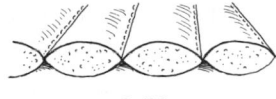

Quilting

1. *Quilting* encloses the insulation liner and shell, then stitches through all three layers. This is okay on your bed in the house but productive of cold spots outdoors. A variation on the quilt method, used mostly in ultralight bags, is to stitch the insulating batt to the liner at regular intervals while sewing it to the outer shell only around the edges. An ultralight Austrian Gold-Eck bag I've used for some time is made this way, and it is far warmer than I expected it to be by the weight alone.

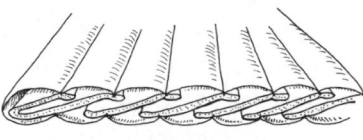

Shingling

2. *Shingling* laps one insulating batt over the next, like playing cards fanned out. This works on the same principle as slant baffles in down bags to eliminate cold spots. The drawback is that shingles can rip loose along the edges.

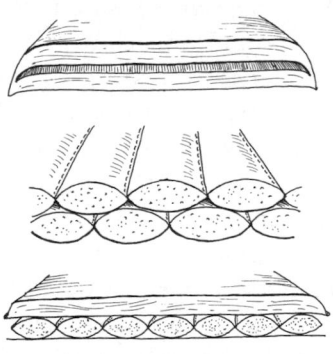

Layering

3. *Layering* follows the same principle as piling up blankets and quilts on your bed for a cold winter night. Potential combinations include two continuous batts, sewn at the edges; two

quilted layers with the seams offset to prevent cold spots; or various hybrids: a shingled layer combined with a quilted one, or a quilted one with a continuous batt. Layered bags offer great warmth and durability—at a price. One of my favorite synthetic bags, the Cascade Designs Quantum O° (now sadly discontinued), had layers of Polarguard 3D under a seamless top.

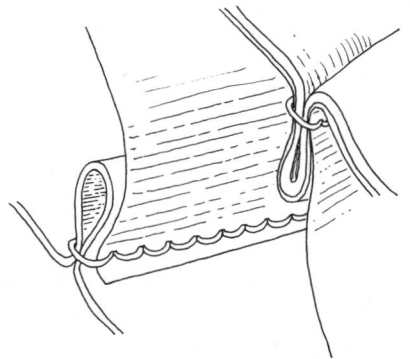

Tuck-stitiching

Some makers *tuck-stitch* the seams: the fabric is tucked inside and stitched on the inside, so the thread is hidden—safe from abrasion, snagging zippers, cracked toenails, frayed clotheslines, and other destroyers. Tuck stitching, a mark of quality, also increases costs. But Sierra Designs reports that a change to tuck stitching reduced sleeping-bag seam repairs at the factory from one per week to about one a year.

I first heard about ground-level side seams from the original owner of Moonstone Mountaineering, who, like a circuit-riding preacher, visited retail stores himself. Early nylon-shelled bags had tops and bottoms the same width, with lengthwise seams halfway up the sides. But, for the same reason the top sheet and blankets on your bed need to be wider than your mattress, the upper insulating layers in a sleeping bag should reach ground level. This is critical in a down bag with side-block baffles, and no less in a synthetic bag with more insulation above than below. But, as Colin observes, the whole scheme depends on keeping the upside up. If you corkscrew all night, so do the rules of thermal engagement.

The materials used in sleeping-bag shells have changed more slowly than the insulation. Nylon taffeta still predominates, in the 1.6-to-1.9-oz.-per-square-yard range. Lightweight forms, with a fine denier thread (30) are indeed soft and sexy, and by virtue of a high thread count (300+ per inch) quite downproof and somewhat windproof as well. Found on deluxe bags, a light 1.4-oz. nylon taffeta called 30 Max (30d, 350 threads per inch) is treated with Teflon to increase water repellency. This is used for both shell and liner, or as the liner for bags with shells of Gore DryLoft or the new microfiber polyesters. Ultralite Ripstop, a 30-denier parachute nylon with 280 threads per inch that weighs a mere 1.1 oz. is showing up in sleeping bags from high-end makers like Western Mountaineering. It's highly breathable and allows insulation to loft well but might tend to wear out more quickly.

A variety of polyester taffetas with trade names like Softech are available in shells and liners. Kelty's warm Pepper Series Polarguard bags have all-polyester shells and liners. One advantage of polyester over nylon is that it feels warmer at first touch, easing those first shivery moments in a sleeping bag.

Gore DryLoft is a lamination of a PTFE (poly-tyranno-fluoridated egg whites?—see page 539) membrane to a shell fabric. The original three-layer Gore-Tex was somewhat stiff and noisy for sleeping-bag shells, especially when cold. One dissenting reader compared it to "sleeping in a bag of popcorn." Such complaints prompted the use of increasingly light and supple fabrics for the two-layer DryLoft. For instance, DryLoft 830 is faced with a 30-denier nylon fabric with 280 threads per inch, weighing 1.1 oz. per square yard, and complaints about noise now range from rare to nil. People who camp in drippy spots—the Maritime Provinces, the Pacific Northwest, snow caves—or who use partial shelters like tarps tend to revere DryLoft and equivalents. But it shouldn't be thought of as a primary shield against the elements. One sticky problem with regular nylon taffeta is that it "wets out," forming a vapor barrier that traps moisture in the insulating layer and at times freezes hard. Polar expeditions report progressive ice-ups that turned their sleeping bags into hard-shelled coffins weighing 30 lbs. or more. Since I often use a Gore-Tex bivouac bag, I've stuck to regular shell fabric for my sleeping bag. This comes from a suspicion (which a call to W. L. Gore & Associates did little to dispel) that it's not a good idea to have more than a single layer of waterproof/breathable laminate. Now that Gore's iron-clad patent has expired, a number of similar proprietary fabrics have appeared, This-Tex and That-Tex.

Internal reflective barriers like Texolite, Kodalite, and Orcothane have disappeared from sleeping bags as abruptly as they burst on the scene. Durability seems to have been an issue, along with moisture transport. Kelty's Pepper Series bags have a silvery polyester inside (though I wonder if this doesn't slow sun drying), and some vapor-barrier liners (page 472), by definition nonbreathable, are reflective.

The newest trend in shells is microfibers. Also used extensively for clothing, the microfiber itself is a very fine nylon or polyester filament, a great many of which are combined to form a single thread. Thus, a 30-denier thread may incorporate 30 to 40 individual filaments. When the cloth is woven, the spaces between threads are so tight that the fabric is downproof, sheds water and wind, yet breathes. At around 1.7 oz. and 350 threads per inch, the microfiber used in sleeping-bag shells is lighter than what shows up in clothing. Pertex Microlight is a 1.3-oz. nylon microfiber (from Perserverance Mills in Padham, England) that spreads moisture over a broad area, to prevent nylon's usual wetting out. Durable water repellent (DWR) treatments are applied to ducky it up.

A full go-round with fabrics would be incomplete without at least a bow to the question of color. Conventional wisdom is to make winter bags in the hottest colors, red and orange. Following the ROYGBV spectrum, yellow and green are 3-season models, with blue and violet for summer-weights. But color preferences are so stubbornly personal that retail stores tend to lobby makers vigorously for their favorite hues. At one company, Western Mountaineering, they got so tired of this that for a while they hung their booths at trade shows with all-black sleeping bags in protest.

My observations on color are two. Light shades quickly show dirt and body grime (especially unpleasing with liners), and dark ones, particularly black and dark green, help bags to dry out faster in the sun. So whatever opalescent hue the shell may be, I prefer (vigorously, reasonably) a jet-black liner.

Hoods, collars, zippers, etc.

COLIN: *Hoods* that encapsulate your head when drawn tight form an integral part of most modern mummy-bag shells. They are important: the human animal, with two of its major evolutionary features (brain and expressive face) housed in its head, naturally serves that member with a hugely complex blood-supply system. The capillaries often travel near the surface and are therefore subject to rapid cooling (the head, like a computer, requires a more or less constant temperature—which usually means it needs cooling). The old "facts"—that at 40°F it may, if unprotected, lose up to half your heat production, at 5° up to three-quarters—have been challenged; but there can be no doubt that it is the body's prime heat-loss area. And perhaps too little attention has been paid to this problem in sleeping bags. Certainly, all hoods are not created equal, or even equal enough.

CHIP: The hood on my first down bag, an REI Skier, was a snap-on option. Like most hoods of that time, it was a flat U-shape edged with a drawstring that puckered it into a head shape. Sierra Designs (beginning with their Cloud Series) advanced the art with hoods shaped to surround the head. Warm-season bags may still have flat, U-shaped hoods or lightly contoured ones. But cold-weather bags, like the Kelty Serrano, have deeply contoured hoods with elastic brow bands or a second drawstring. Floating hoods, unconnected to the bag and thus allowing corkscrew sleepers some leeway, have faded out. The reverse-differential cut (page 464), with more liner than shell, is often used. If you're a wire-chinned chap, some nylon hood liners are so scratchy-noisy they actually keep you awake. Polyesters are quieter. Particularly silent (and warm-feeling) was the Microtherm polyester lining the hood of a Slumberjack Ranger I spent a few nights with. A new hood from Sierra Designs, called the NightCap, adjusts from a squarish fist-and-elbow-accommodating breadth to a rounded head shape with two drawcords. This combination does offer scope for eccentric sleeping styles. And it's also a further step in resolving the mummy problem. In case you hadn't noticed, most living people sleep not on their backs, faces toward heaven, but rather on their sides, with knees drawn slightly up.

COLIN: The *drawstrings* that pull the hood around your face and hold it there mostly come equipped with spring-loaded plastic toggles or other secure but quickly adjustable devices. Sometimes there are two such devices, one at each free end of the cord or tape, near the top of the zipper; but many bags now have a single toggle in the center of the hood on the opposite side from the zipper, so that you can adjust the hood with a single device instead of the two and need not loosen the drawstring if you want to open the top of the zipper (to cool off a little or to emerge briefly in the middle of the night to urinate). This arrangement means that the drawstring ends are anchored near the zipper top, one on each side, and when you tighten the hood you place strain on the zipper and may pull it open. The bag should therefore have a snap or Velcro fastener to take the strain and also keep the draft edge closed. (Velcro is easier to open and close than a snap but can, I hear, grab long hair or even beards.) One designer suggests that perhaps you really need two fasteners, each pulling at a slightly different angle.

CHIP: High on my list of unintended consequences is that sleeping-bag drawstrings and zipper pulls (often adorned with stiff, black nylon tabs) have a tendency to dangle inside the hood, poke me in the face, and summon evil dreams: for instance, kissing a porcupine's arse. I cut these tiny assassins off and replace them with soft, light-colored cloth tape. The second unintended consequence is that the Velcro tabs used to keep zippers from gapping can damage light shell fabrics by hooking into threads and jerking them out of the weave. The only solution for this is to firmly engage all hook-and-loop fasteners before stuffing the bag, and to keep a weather eye when hanging the bag up to air: a loose tab flapping in the wind can wreak minor havoc.

COLIN: *Built-in collars* that fit across the sleeper's chest and so reduce draft through the head opening are becoming more popular. They can be down-filled appendages or plain fabric. And while they may possibly reduce somewhat the bag's flexibility in wide ranges of temperatures they undoubtedly help keep you warmer in real cold. Warmer, certainly, than any makeshift measures (page 500).

CHIP: Here, the Mummy's Curse strikes again—that is, the deeply lobed yokes seen on so many synthetic bags are designed for back sleepers (or the thermocouple-equipped manikins that companies use for tests). Those of us (the majority) who rest as we did in our maternal tummies do better with a simple, tubular draft collar that lets us roll freely from side to side without fussy realignments. Serious winter bags might have draft-collar tubes both top and bottom. But unless you summer on the summit of Denali, most above-freezing bags don't need draft collars. One of my favorite hinge-season bags, the Sierra Designs Lewis, is a favorite precisely because it lacks one. My body heat tends to be low on retiring and to ramp up as the night proceeds, peaking about 3 a.m. At that point, I ventilate, which in a draft-collared bag means complicated yogic adjustments of the side zipper. And that in turn requires real thinking—sharply incompatible with renewed sleep. The draft-collarless Lewis lets me tug dreamily at the main zip and thrash my hands to open the top—back to sleep. So, despite the fact that at present this ranks with ranting against the probability of resurrection, I'd rather not have a puffy, air-blocking draft collar above 0°—Fahrenheit!*

Zippers on bags, formerly gap-toothed nylon-eating marvels, are now almost all nylon-coil type. The best coil zippers are self-healing: if the teeth pull apart, you can zip down and back up and lo! you're in business again (the first few times, anyway). For a diatribe on zippers-in-general see page 149.

Where early saber-toothed zippers could chew their way through a considerable stretch of nylon, leaving plentiful exits for down fluff, the coil type merely snags and stops—so don't force it. But ultralight fabrics can still get nastily gnawed, and thoughtful makers back the zipper with nonsnagging tape or sew a band of thicker fabric on the draft tube. Double sliders are standard, and desirable, letting you vent the foot without opening the entire flank to the elements. Also nice are swiveling pulls, with a U-shaped track on the slider to let one hangy-down serve both inside and out. Every zipper on every sleeping bag I've ever owned was made by YKK. But the WaterTight laminated polyurethane zippers

---

*The new Sierra Designs bag I'm testing, a 0°F-rated model, also lacks a draft collar. But it has stretch baffles, which hug the body and slow air circulation inside.

showing up on parkas seem like a good match for DryLoft shelled sleeping bags, if they hold up.

Zippers have migrated. The infamous army duck-down mummies had a front-and-center zip that's rarely seen these days. Early nylon bags tacked the zips along a side seam, halfway up. On bags with ground-level seams, zippers are mostly likewise, seeming always to end up underneath when you need a fast exit. Some designers now fetch the ground-level zips up toward your chin, for access reasons (but these are the worst as far as lip tickling). On at least one new bag (the Slumberjack Pumori), the zipper swoops clear across from right elbow to left shoulder—the sort of thing you either love or hate. Cascade Designs put the zip on their Quantum bags about 6 inches off the deck, where the side curves into the top. I'm a side sleeper, so this arrangement worked wonders for me, putting the zipper pull right at my fingertips though not right in my face and letting me vent freely without chilly gaps.

Current accessorizing includes upgrade hoods and insulated footsacks. On particularly bitter nights I've draped my down parka or vest over the foot of my bag, to the same effect. The new Sierra Designs bag I'm testing has four discreet loops sewn into the ground-level seams that mate up with the Pad Lock—four plastic clips and a lock on a length of light shock cord—to keep your pad where it belongs. Another clever extra is Mountain Hardwear's zip-in expander, which adds 8 inches of girth—a boon to the pregnant (down or Polarguard, 12 oz., $50). Some bags have sprouted little Velcro-flapped goodie pockets. Mountain Hardwear's Tallac bag includes a headnet that stuffs into a chest pocket, for rapid deployment. The only two items I've put in a sleeping-bag pocket are a flashlight and a handkerchief. Eyeglasses seem risky. Zip-together lovers might stash breath mints, tissues, and condoms. For the devout, the pocket could hold a compact Bible, Koran, etc. For the apprehensive, pepper spray.

Unless you hang your bag for storage, a necessary adjunct is a storage sack that protects without ruinously overcompressing the insulation, as a stuff sack does. These come with most high-quality bags, in cotton or mesh, or are easily found in shops. A king-size cotton pillowcase from a thrift store also serves.

Vapor-barrier linings (VBLs)

COLIN: VBLs have been around for years. But although embraced fanatically by a few they have not caught on. Some people, including me, still like them; others, including Chip, like hell do not.

For a brief summary of the theory behind VBLs, and some discussion of the practice, see pages 515 to 517. I have good reasons for attacking the matter there, in the Clothes Closet, rather than here; but understanding the theory so that you can practice properly is a major component of VBL usage, so I'm afraid you'll have to read most of pages 515 and 516 if you're to grasp the meat of what follows.

Both theory and practice are simpler with sleeping bags than with clothes, because in a bag you lie more or less still and your metabolic rate changes only very slowly (though the practice is complicated by your being mostly unaware of temperature changes, and the need to adjust, until cold or heat wakes you up). But even with VBL sleeping bags you must understand what you're playing with—which is something very different from a conventional breathing-shell bag.

More than three decades ago I tried a VBL bag by Warmlite, a pioneer in the field, on a five-day test up to 12,000 feet and down to a windless 16°F. In a tent, wearing little or no clothing, I found I was far too hot, soon began to sweat, and simply could not adjust the rather complicated bag to an all-around comfort level. Now, the real trouble may have been the bag's built-in foam pad. I normally lie first on one side, then on the other, moving the whole bag with me and thereby keeping any opened zipper to my front; but the built-in pad could not move with me and the opened zipper was, in one of my lying positions, bound to run close and cold to my curved back. (A reader later wrote that he'd had a similar unsatisfactory experience, and also thought the trouble was the built-in pad.) I had further minor difficulties too (though the makers assured me with heat that I had misused the bag). In the years since, I've met many people who have tried VBL bags and found them wanting. The reasons could lie in extraneous matters like that built-in pad or such personal idiosyncrasies as high metabolic rates. But I suspect that in many cases the bags were simply used in temperatures too high for the system. The maker of excellent VBLs once told me that he felt they were really not for use above 35°F. The difficulty is, of course, that many nights may begin much warmer than that but end up much colder. And one night may be much warmer, the next much colder, especially in the mountains. Bags with built-in VBLs are simply not versatile enough for such very common conditions.

The way to achieve versatility is fortunately simple: a removable VBL. I have for years carried one on all but the most guaranteed-warm trips. I'm convinced that it extends the low end of any bag's comfort level by at least 10° and probably by 20°.

The price in weight and bulk is small; in money, very reasonable. I use a simple, coated ripstop half-sac (no longer available) by Moonstone of California that weighs 4.7 oz., takes up about as much room as a pair of jockey shorts, and cost $18. True, I normally also carry a matching VB shirt (6 oz., $35—see page 517) and use it with the half-sac, but the shirt performs major daytime functions—and other warm torso clothing would often be enough in conjunction with the half-sac. By taking a bag that's a tad on the light side for a given trip (or even several tads) and regarding the VBL as a reserve for cold occasions I can save considerable weight and bulk. And if temperatures drop markedly during the night I simply slip into the VBL, which I have put ready, inside the bag. My Moonstone half-sac extends up to my upper chest and is held there by an elastic "waistband." Provided I wear polypropylene underwear (page 505) I experience little or no damp or clammy feeling—and none of the uncomfortable wrapping around legs and torso that some people report with full-length liners. I find the half-sac particularly useful with a very light bag (page 482).

Some sleeping bags have a snap or two to anchor an optional liner, and the makers tuck a VBL liner into the margins of their catalogs. Stephenson's makes VBL items from a somewhat-stretchy urethane-coated 2.2-oz. nylon knit called Fuzzy Stuff, with the soft side skinward. Feathered Friends sells a VBL liner in four sizes (about 6 oz., $35–$37). For "extreme winter camping" Western Mountaineering sells the Hot Sac, 1.1-oz. polyester with a shiny reflective lining (7 oz., $65), that can serve as an emergency bivouac bag. For a makeshift version, get an aluminized polyester "emergency bag" for $10 to $12, and try it with wicking long underwear and socks. (If the VBL aspect doesn't thrill you, you can always use it as a groundsheet.)*

But with removable liners we're beginning to move over from traditional, more-or-less-one-purpose sleeping bags into

Sleeping systems.

The idea is hardly new. One early approach was Warmlite's "solo-triple" bag that I described in *The New Complete Walker* (with two zipper-off topsides of different thicknesses that can be used alternatively or together, giving a solo sleeper three bags in one). Camp 7 for some years offered a lightweight synthetic-fill bag that could be used alone as a summer bag but would fit as an outer shell around any of Camp 7's main line

---

*CHIP: Because it seems to me that the major benefit of a VBL sleeping-bag liner is to keep moisture out of the insulation, I would now use one, if at all, for extended trips in deep cold. If you're likely to lack the benefit of a sunny dry-out before packing up and it's cold enough that progressive icing is possible, a VBL liner's survival value might outweigh its potential for serious discomfort. Besides night sweats (which are not, as some VBL devotees assert, a moral failing) another problem with VBL liners (shirts, socks, etc.) is that they create ideal conditions for bacterial growth. One of my VBL-using friends was noted, even in our scruffy crowd, for his wolverine reek. I've also heard of yeast infections, rashes, and boils being attributed to frequent VBL use. Antimicrobial powders seem advisable, and the antibacterial longjohns now available might help. So does washing occasionally.

of down bags—boosting their warmth and also protecting the down from external moisture. A removable VBL greatly increased the cellar range of either bag or of both together.

CHIP: The zipper on my ultralight down bag is on the same side as the one on my 15°F model, so despite their being from different makers I now double them up—8 inches of loft—for really cold nights. But makers of real system bags offer a calculated fit, matching zippers, etc. Mountain Hardwear has a choice of a 40° down (2 lbs. 8 oz., $165) or 45° Polarguard HV mummy bags (2 lbs. 2 oz., $105), or a 50° Polarguard HV barrel-shaped bag (2 lbs. 10 oz., $115), to fit inside their 3-season models. The upgrade hood (6 oz.) seems like a necessary component. Feathered Friends, among others, make certain bags with systemic features: their Great Auk (2 lbs. 1 oz., $288) is a roomy 20° bag with a hood and a built-in pad pocket, designed to engulf a summer or 3-season model, with a 40° boost in its comfort rating. A slick 4-season combo is the Great Auk and a Feathered Friends Rock Wren (1 lb. 15 oz., $225), a unique summer bag with zippered armholes and a drawstring foot, that doubles as a full-body camp robe. With the Rock Wren, you can get up and make coffee without leaving your sleeping bag: scary. You can also augment the Rock Wren with a down parka and booties, for hard-core bivy sacking.

Any of four Wiggy's sleeping bags, filled with a proprietary resin-bonded fiber called Lamilite, will fit into a hooded overbag that, alone, works to 35°F and adds roughly 40° to the rating of the inner bag. The Wiggy's Ultralite (3 lbs. 8 oz., $146) is rated at 20° alone or to −20° with the overbag (2 lbs. 8 oz., $144).

The inflatable Cocoon 4, by Pneugear, is probably the most elaborate sleep system going (a brochure showed up in my mailbox, but my offer to test-and-return elicited no reply). It has a contoured, 4-inch air mattress mated to an inflatable down-filled top: air pressure regulates the loft. The ensemble includes Primaloft-filled hood, zip-on stormfly and bug netting, titanium stakes, repair kit, and of course, a built-in pump (10–11 lbs., $1395).

At the spare end of the spectrum is the Fur sleep system by GoLite. Rated to 20°F, it's based on a Ray Jardine design that eliminates not only the hood (keep your hat on, says Ray) but also the underside of the sleeping bag: a 2-inch Polarguard top quilt Velcros around the edges to a tapered ⅜-inch polyethlene foam pad (6 oz.). Including the pad, the small size weighs 2 lbs. 2 oz., the medium 2 lbs. 8 oz., and the large 2 lbs. 14 oz. ($198 each). Jardine's original sleeper was a double, boosting the warmth and shaving the weight, and GoLite plans to build one, along with colder-weather models.

For the single/double option, look for a barrel-shaped bag (with a foot that unzips and perhaps a detachable hood) that mates with a *coupler,* or *doubler.* This is a single layer of fabric with straps or pockets for pads and a pillow sleeve up top. The bag zips to the undersheet for a warm-weather *paso doble.* I cherish an old Moonstone Upside-Downside because it not only incorporates this solo/duo possibility, but the bag itself has thick and thin sides. This not only lets you (solo) flop it for warm or cold nights but also gives couples a warm side and cool side. The advantages of this system, for mutual comfort and conflict avoidance, are brilliantly clear—plus it saves weight and bulk and cash. It also makes sense for those avid walkers with a partner who camps only once in a while. To go with their Flying Wide down bags, Feathered Friends makes couplers: the Toucan Ultralite in 1.1-oz. ripstop nylon (9 oz., $52), and the Toucan Deluxe in a poly/nylon blend (1 lb. 1 oz., $63). Mountain Hardwear's Duet is 12 oz. and $65.

Costs

COLIN: Any good sleeping bag is now a damnably expensive item. But the range is large—from $125 for a reasonably serviceable 2- or 3-season synthetic-filled semi-mummy to over $700 for sophisticated, superbly crafted, custom-made models for the coldest weather. Mostly—surprise!—you get what you pay for, and you must make your own decisions about what you can afford. I'm aware that backpackers who use their equipment only once or twice a year may not feel justified, in view of other responsibilities, in spending the sums now demanded for really good bags (though see page 461). The current prices may curdle your financial blood, but remember that when you take a sleeping bag out of your pack as night falls on a frigid, windswept mountain you understand without having to think about it that dollars are meaningless frivolities.

Choosing a bag that will suit your purposes

The usual criterion for gauging the efficiency of a sleeping bag is the lowest temperature at which it can be used with comfort. "This bag is excellent for use down to 25°F," the catalog may proclaim. Such generalizations have their uses. Beginners need guidelines. But there's a serious danger that people may accept the figures uncritically. Many factors other than temperature are important, and a wide variation in one or more of them can throw out the whole works. Still, the general rule is sometimes promulgated: "For summer use, with temperatures above freezing, 2 pounds of high-quality down; for temperatures down to 0°F, 3 pounds." (For most synthetics, increase weights about 35–40 percent.) For more on fills, see pages 460 to 463. For construction and other shell desiderata, see pages 463 to 469. You can check the construction of most blow-filled bags light enough for backpacking by simply holding the shell up to a strong light.

One way sometimes recommended for checking the probable efficiency of both fill and construction is to measure what's called *free loft*. Unroll the bag on a flat surface and shake its edges with a gentle fluffing action that allows air to become entrapped in the fill. Then measure the height of the bag at its midsection. The amount of loft depends on both the quality of the fill and the efficiency of the shell construction (see differential cut, page 464). Different makers apparently measure loft in different ways, but it seems reasonable to assume that, as is claimed, a relationship exists between free loft and heat-retaining efficiency. What the exact relationship is I have no idea.

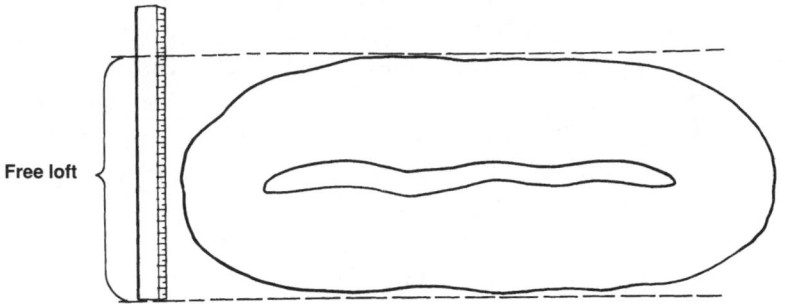

Free loft

It's important to remember that temperature-tolerance figures for sleeping bags are now generally based on the assumption that you sleep in a tent with good insulation under you. A bag that keeps you comfortably warm at 32°F on a full-length foam pad will obviously not begin to do so if you roll it out on bare ground. And the same kind of difference exists between different roofs—tent, sky, or intermediate. The temperature inside a tent may run 10° or 20° higher than outside (see table, page 387). Again, much depends on what clothes, if any, you choose to sleep in. My solution to all this is always to carry a pad (or, occasionally, an air mattress) and to take a sleeping bag, perhaps with a separate VB liner, that I judge will keep me warm under normal conditions for the time and place if I sleep without clothes or roof (except in snow), and will just about do so under the worst recorded conditions if I wear every garment in my pack and protect the bag with every form of shelter I'm carrying—whether a simple poncho or a Visklamp-and-polyethylene roof or a tent. Nowadays I seem to guess about right. I can't remember a night in the past 40 years when I've slept in a sleeping bag and been uncomfortably cold. Now, it may be that I'm a little overcautious. "When it comes to sleeping bags," a store owner once told me, "most people overbuy—and then sweat their arses off." But in a modern, full-length-zipper bag it's easy enough to stay cool. For an example of how "overcaution," at least in support items, can pay off when it really matters, see pages 569 to 574.

One major difficulty with temperature ratings for sleeping bags is that the relationship between air temperature and what the human body feels is a remarkably tenuous one.

First, weather is much more than just temperature. Above all there's wind. A bag that keeps you snugly warm in the open on a calm 10°F night may be frigidly inadequate at 32° in a 30-mile-an-hour wind. See, importantly, the windchill table on page 748—though laminated and microfiber shells may be taking the edge off the wind problem. Humidity comes into it too. Dry air is a poor conductor of heat, damp air a good one. So in wet weather the air pockets held in the fill of your sleeping bag insulate less efficiently than in dry. This is no idle theorizing. Using equipment that has proved entirely adequate in dry weather at freezing and below, you may find yourself decidedly cool in a temperature of 40° after heavy rain has saturated the atmosphere, even though your bag remains dry. It's even possible for a drop in temperature to make you feel warmer. At 34°, with the air full of water vapor, the weather may seem rawly cold. When the temperature falls a few degrees and the moisture that has been ruining the insulation freezes, you'll probably feel much cozier.

But the most variable factor of all is the individual.

Some people "sleep cold," others "hot." The theory—no more—is that the bigger you are and the more generally active, the warmer you tend to sleep. After camping under various conditions with other people using similar equipment you'll probably get a fair idea of your own rating. Or you can tap indoor experience: do bedmates regard you as iceberg or hot-water bottle? (This is a purely thermal rating, of course—nothing to do with the factor involved in that libelous dig, "Which would you rather have—an English lover or a hot-water bottle?")

Remember, too, that no individual is a neat, predictable, laboratory-conditioned guinea pig. At different times he may react very differently to similar conditions. Tiredness, emotional state, and fullness of stomach certainly come into it: someone who sleeps snugly in a given bag at zero when he's rested, secure, and well fed is unlikely to do so if he's exhausted, worried stiff about a sick companion, and hasn't eaten since morning. (Don't overlook the eating business. After a good meal your high blood sugar—available for heat production—will mean you sleep much warmer than on an empty or half-empty stomach. So if you tend to dine early consider eating a sugar-rich snack just before you go to sleep—even if you follow the Zone Diet.) Again, personal variations may be simply a matter of not being used to the cold or the heat or the elevation or whatever prime stress the situation imposes. Our bodies need time to adapt to radically changed conditions. Two or three days' acclimation may be plenty; but if the change is too abrupt those two or three days can be distressing.

The solution is to get used to a new environment gradually. One word for this process is "training." In Europe during World War II we often used to sleep in the open or in slit trenches in subfreezing weather with nothing over our distinctly temperate-country clothing except a thin antigas cape. I don't say we liked it. And I don't say we slept very well. But we slept. We were young, we were fit—and we got used to it (mainly, perhaps, because we had to). By the time I made the California walk I was a dozen years less young; but after a month of walking I was probably just as fit. Yet I remember a night in Death Valley, when I had no sleeping bag, that might make you wonder if I were the same person. That warm desert night I put on all the clothing I had—which was certainly as warm as, if not warmer than, British battle dress. Then I wrapped my poncho around me and curled up in a little gully. I had just finished a 20-mile day, and I promptly fell asleep. But before long I came half awake and tried to pull the poncho more closely around me. There was no wind; nothing that could even be called a breeze. But cool night air was moving slowly and steadily across the desert's surface. Like the tide advancing across mudflats, it penetrated every corner. It passed over me. It passed around me. It passed underneath me. Soon it seemed to be passing through me as well. Minute by minute it sucked my warmth away. No matter how closely I cuddled to the gully wall, the cold bit deeper and deeper. For shapeless hours I fought the sleep battle. Occasionally I dozed. More often I lay three-quarters awake, telling myself I was half asleep. By two o'clock the dozes had become unreal memories. And at 3:30 I got up, packed my bag and headed north into the darkness.*

Later I learned that the temperature that night never fell below 58°F. This is admittedly an official reading, taken 5 feet off the ground; but a thermometer lying beside my bed just before I left would probably have registered somewhere around the same. Now, 58° is a very mild temperature. But the reason I felt so bitterly cold is simple: I wasn't used to it. I'd been walking through deserts for more than a month, in day temperatures that had risen to a peak of 105°. Recent nights had been warm too, and the day I entered Death Valley the minimum temperature had been 80°. But what mattered most was that all this time I'd been sleeping in a highly efficient 2½-lbs.-of-goose-down mummy bag. Then, two days earlier—wanting to cut my load, and feeling I didn't need a bag

*From *The Thousand-Mile Summer,* page 86.

in night temperatures that seemed likely to fall no lower than 80°—I'd given it to two Death Valley rangers who checked my arrival at a spring at the south end of the valley. I arranged to collect the bag when I passed through a ranger station a couple of weeks later. But that same night an unexpected storm sent temperatures plunging. The next night I found myself curling up in that miserable little gully with no protection except my clothes and poncho—and, what was even more important, with my body unprepared for the shock of sleeping in what seemed reasonably warm conditions. (Note, though [pages 747 and 748], that two-thirds of maximum windchill effect occurs when the wind is blowing at only 2 miles an hour.)

Acclimation can also work the other way. One September I spent a week walking along a mountain crest that rarely fell below 12,000 feet and rose at one point to 14,000. In clear autumnal weather the panoramas and the wind were both breathtaking. On the third night my route took me down off the crest for the only time all week, and I camped in a side-canyon at 10,000 feet. At dusk my bedside thermometer read a bare degree or two below freezing. Because I was trying out a very efficient experimental mummy bag that had been designed for Alaskan mountaineering (it had 3 lbs. of down and no side zipper), I didn't bother about shelter, except to camp just below some bushes. The bushes, I felt sure, would blunt the almost inevitable down-canyon wind. To my surprise, no wind blew. Soon I was far too hot to sleep. I slipped into my wool shirt and a very thick, hooded down parka, then eased up partway out of the sleeping bag, and pulled on longjohns and pants. With the sleeping bag pulled loosely up around my midriff and a pair of big leather gauntlets to protect my hands, I immediately fell asleep.

I woke at dawn, glowingly warm, to find the thermometer registering 22°F. But what really surprised me was that during the night one glove had come off and my bare hand, lying unprotected on the grass, felt perfectly warm. The circulation in my hands had always been rather poor in cold weather, and I wouldn't have believed it possible for one of them to feel pleasantly warm at 22°—even with the rest of my body glowing and the air very dry. The point is, I think, that I'd been up in cold, windy country for two days. I very much doubt if the hand would have felt so warm under identical conditions on the night I left the car.

I hope this long discussion has not led you to believe that temperature ratings have no value as a means of expressing a sleeping bag's efficiency. I repeat: they're useful guidelines. But if uncritically accepted as absolute statements they can be dangerously misleading. Bear that danger steadily in mind when you're making your choice. And ponder ponderously. Buying a sleeping bag is a serious business. If you make a mistake you'll have many long, slow, purgatorial hours in which to repent.

. . .

These days the mountain shops tempt us with serried ranks of gorgeous, gossamer, butterfly-colored sleeping bags—gleaming, curvaceous works of art that almost demand to be stroked. Faced with such an array and the need to choose one among all those superb creations, it's often difficult to know where to begin.

In easing toward a decision you'll probably—after weighing the general and sometimes subjective elements I've outlined—move on to a relatively objective survey of shell materials, including laminates, microfibers, and VBLs. (You will, of course, buy only a bag that fits you: one so short that your feet press against its end will prove a very expensive mistake.) But in the end the elimination process may boil down, economics aside, to deciding which minor variants seem to offer some advantage. If you like a bag to turn with you as you roll over (which I do, so that a partially opened zipper stays in position along my front, where my natural curl will hold it at a distance, rather than close and cold along my back), then a slender, form-fitting mummy will probably suit you best. But if you prefer—or rather think you prefer—being able to turn over in a more or less stationary bag, then consider ampler envelopes—the barrelsome daddies or even unabashed biggies—or at least avoid those contoured to fit your feet. Next, cast a critical eye on all hoods. Then examine in the beam of your druthers such accessories as drawstrings and built-in collars. And look closely at zippers and the draft flaps or block baffles inside them. See if the base of the flap is sewn right through and might create cold spots. Check that the flap (or baffle) lies snug along the zipper line. If in any doubt on this score (and maybe even if not) take the bag into a strong light, put your head inside, and see whether, with the bag in the kind of position it will assume when full of you, any gaps show. If they do, take the bag back to a dark corner and leave it there.

In the end, though, your decision may rest on your assessment of workmanship.

Meticulous workmanship is the key to toughness and long life in any first-rate backpacking bag, stripped as it must be of every unnecessary gram. It is no assembly-line product. To ensure high quality, at least one maker has each bag "constructed by a single seamstress who is personally responsible for that bag." In the finished bag almost the only outward and visible sign of this inward and invisible pride and expertise is the stitching. Check it carefully. Check it most of all in difficult places, and those that will undergo most strain—such as around the top of the zipper. But I suspect that most backpackers are as poorly qualified to judge the quality of workmanship as I am. (Note that, in spite of earnest consultation with manufacturers, I have not—except for the words on tuck stitching [page 467]—found it possible to describe just how you should rate stitching.) In the end the safest way is probably to check reputation. Don't just shop around; check around. Pay some attention to good reports, great attention to bad ones. Finally, you may even want, if you can, to try out the model you favor by borrowing or renting one.

Makes and models

The comforting thing about the present plethora of gorgeous sleeping bags is that it has become difficult to go diabolically wrong. Fierce competition and the high costs of both materials and labor—which virtually force anyone entering the market to aim for a quality product—mean that there are few if any crummy bags around. You won't find them in reputable mountain shops or specialist catalogs—and probably not even in general sports stores.

For years now I've used only two bags for backpacking. The makers of both are out of business, but the bags' general specifications may be guidance-useful. The first, lighter one is a Bear Cub by Blue Puma (regular size, 15 oz. of 600-fill-power down, 3- to 3½-inch loft, rated to 35°F, weighs only 1 lb. 12 oz.—which is what entranced me when I bought it, almost 20 years ago). The weight is achieved by stark simplification. The bag even dispenses with baffles: it's sewn through, like a light down jacket—the way I said no self-respecting modern bag was sewn. But it works. Like hell it works. It has long been my standard mild-weather bag—often backed by a Moonstone half-sac VBL (page 473). It proved itself early by coddling me through a windless 18° night, in a tent. And down the years it has kept me warm and happy at many damp, windy, around-freezing camps.

My second bag is a mummy custom-made by Down Home—which replaced my Trailwise Slimline when that trusted old friend beat me to the punch and suffered decrepitude beyond usefulness. The transverse-baffled Down Home weighs 2 lbs. 12 oz. Its temperature rating, now befogged by time, is probably 10°F; its down fill power 700 or 800. Loft: still 8 inches. To hold the side-opening baffle closed, an internal zipper backs the two-way, almost-length-of-the-bag main one. No collar. Simple hood with toggled drawstring and opposite-side snap fastener plus Velcro strip. The bag has done me proud under all kinds of conditions; and the little Bear Cub bag fits inside it—imperfectly but usefully—to form a cold-weather rig. But I've used the combo in the field no more than two or three times: in truly bitter weather I'm now old and wise enough (or do I mean chicken enough?) to stay home.

CHIP: As choices go, deciding what to sleep in seems to rank right up there with deciding who to sleep with—so my sleeping-bag tests for this book have been selective. Rather than reeling off a list of bags I haven't slept in, for the most part I'll describe my often-lofted sweethearts. Bear in mind that our concern here is mainly backpacking, and no less, backpacking for fun—rather than expeditionary climbing, polar traverses, etc.

Below zero. Until recently my deep-winter bag was a late-Pleistocene Holubar (circa 1976), cinnamon and tan, with 3 lbs. of down, V-baffles, and a bit of age-related clumping in the hood. For that hard solstice chill (ah, distinctly I remember) I'd insert a down ultralight inside. I did nearly piss myself a few times, too sleep-muddled to solve the zipperistic puzzle I'd set up. But mostly, the bag and I got along.

A few years back, a would-be hero showed up at my house after driving hundreds of miles, having somehow forgotten his winter bag. So, with a certain amount of chin scratching (signifying severe inner stress), I loaned him mine. What afflicted me wasn't so much plain distrust as the idea that anyone hapless enough to roar off on a winter mountaineering trip without a sleeping bag probably wouldn't return. So I pulled out a stack of catalogs and picked out a new one, just in case: a Western Mountaineering Puma (0°F, 2 lbs. of down, 8 inches of loft, 3 lbs. 1 oz. total, $400). My old bag did come back—and I had my next one picked out.

But instead of taking the financial plunge, the last two winters I've taken the combo approach. Most people would consider the Sierra Designs Lewis (now replaced by the stretch-seam Night Fall long at 3 lbs. 2 oz., $240) as a 3-season bag. I think of it as my winter ultralight: a 15°F down bag that's blessedly free of a draft collar or other fashionable impediments. For bitter midnights, I line it with a Western Mountaineering Iroquois (long, 1 lb. 9 oz., $205; see next page) that closely resembles Colin's Blue Puma. And I like layering up—except for the damn zippers.

Hinge season. For me this means fall days when the jet stream dips southward and rain changes to snow. It also means the high northern spring, with long, sunstruck days and subfreezing nights, and a snowpack that alternates between boilerplate and slush. That is, it means being alert to change, and rolling with it—as much as I love downy old down, I find synthetics a blessing for hinge-y conditions.

Recently I adopted a Sierra Designs Hibernator, filled with 3 lbs. 4 oz. of Polarguard 3D and rated to 0°F (4 lbs. 15 oz., $259). What intrigued me is the Lycra baffling (known as the Flex system), the intent being to reduce the empty and potentially cold volume of air inside while allowing freedom of movement: good for those dragon battles and demon loves. The puckered seams didn't thrill me at first, but after quite a few nights the Hibernator's practical roominess (6 full inches of stretch) does.

I can roll from side to side without corkscrewing the bag and can draw up my knees without pressing the liner out into a cold spot. The broad-browed hood—called a NightCap (see page 470)—is another departure. The ground-level main zipper swerves up to the chin (I hacked the factory-installed lip-tickling zipper pulls off the first night). A second short zipper opposite the main one lets you vent or shut off the alarm watch. Four discreet loops on the ground-level seams anchor a Pad Lock—a length of light shock cord with four plastic clips to corral wandering pads. One drawback: like many warm synthetic bags, it's somewhat bulky when stuffed.

Three-season bags. This rather broad class takes in bags rated from 15°F to perhaps 40°, depending on where your three seasons are spent. I think of a 3-season bag as being mostly for cool summer nights on high. When you wake up, there's a faint mist on the lake and the grass gleams with dew. But if it freezes, you can pull on a cap and longjohns, and wake up toasty. Or on the other hand, if it's balmy, you can open things up, reaching a balance somewhere between full frontal nudity and the Heat Death of the Universe.

A 3-seasonish bag I've had for years is the Moonstone Upside-Downside, a long-discontinued semi-rectangular Polarguard bag with a doubler, already described on page 476. A couple of years ago I tested a newer Moonstone, a Minima Long of Polarguard 3D rated for a low of 25 to 40°F (2 lbs. 11 oz., $165). The liner was made of something called T-Silk, with "ZAP Electrostatic Action to move excess moisture away from the user." On one sad occasion, I had to tromp a couple of quarts of water out of the Minima and then spend a brisk spring night in it. I put on wicking underwear and socks, and crept in—a mite chilly at first. But I actually got to sleep and woke up the next morning warm, having dried out the bag (except for a patch under my butt) with body heat.

Ultralights. Being not just a warm but a geothermal sleeper, I use ultralight bags in lieu of the usual 3-season choices. My ultralight baptism was an Austrian Gold-Eck Schlafsäcke (i.e., sleeping bag) weighing 1 lb. 8 oz. that stuffed into a Quaker Oats box. God, was I smitten. Until I schlafsäcked out one 3° night (for the horror, the horror, see page 31). Summed up, it was less than Eck-static. But the gossamer sirens crooned on. So I ordered a Western Mountaineering Iroquois. The shell is a subtle blue, the liner black. The foot section has a cut like the bust on Marie Antoinette's favorite ballgown. Yet despite the legendary quality of Western Mountaineering's down and construction, I was suspicious of the sewn-through box quilting. But the anticipated cold spots didn't show up. Instead, the temperature range is magnificent—and it's now my 3-season bag. Summed up, the Iroquois (long, 1 lb. 9 oz., $205) makes me feel that money itself means very little, compared to a good sleeping bag.

Children's sleeping bags

COLIN: These bags are usually made of cheaper materials than full-size ones, are more simply constructed, and are filled with synthetics rather than down, no doubt on the reasonable assumption that if you invest in a high-quality bag you're not going to buy something your children will grow out of within a year or two. But price isn't the only reason synthetic fills are more popular than down: synthetics can be repeatedly rinsed and washed; with down you can, particularly during the diaper years, land in big trouble.

Lower-quality children's bags apparently sell very well. One possible reason is that children tend to sleep warmer than adults. In theory they should sleep colder: their smaller bodies, with a wider surface-to-volume ratio, should lose heat faster. But to balance this factor their metabolism tends to operate at a higher rate. What happens in practice is a matter of opinion, but a limited poll I conducted among friends tended to support the opinion of one mother of five children ranging from 4 to 13 years old, whose family seemed to spend half its young life camping or cabining in the mountains. "Yes," said this seasoned troop leader, "I'd say there may well be something to the sleeping-warmer business—certainly when the kids are young and covered in puppy fat. I've found our 4-year-old almost out of his bag on quite cold nights, still fast asleep. Once children start beanstalking up into their teens, though, it's rather different. It could easily be that at that stringy stage they tend to sleep somewhat colder than adults."

CHIP: In 1998, when the *Backpacker* Annual Gear Guide included a listing of children's outdoor equipment, the purveyors of kids' sleeping bags were: Eastern Mountain Sports, Feathered Friends, Ferrino, Integral Designs, Kelty, L. L. Bean, Lafuma, Molehill Mountain Equipment, Peak 1, REI, Slumberjack, Stephenson-Warmlite, Tough Traveler, and Wenzel. The bags ranged from the low-budget baby-fat types to relatively sophisticated youth models with shaped hoods, draft collars, etc. Lowest price was $21 for a Wenzel Jr. Espirit (2 lbs.). Highest was $480 for the Stephenson-Warmlite Triple (3 lbs., including pad). Median cost for synthetic bags was about $60. High-quality down bags for children were the Feathered Friends Fledgling 68-incher (1 lb. 9 oz., $195) and Fledging 72-incher (1 lb. 12 oz., $210).

For a child, a good ¾-size self-inflating pad does nicely, as do the ¾

Cascade Designs Ridge Rest (9 oz., $15) and ¾ Z-Rest (11 oz., $24). For adolescents, the Artiach midlength pads, at 63 inches (see page 448), are a good fit. Or, for that matter, an Ensolite pad can be trimmed. But don't expect your kids to nestle down happily on your old, cracked Ensolite pad while you yourself are Therm-a-Resting.

Pillows

COLIN: Some people don't mind sleeping without a pillow; others even prefer it that way. Unless I'm too tired to notice I find it disconcerting not to have one. Minor back trouble sometimes forces me to carry a specially shaped foam pillow (my "security pillow"), but mostly I still make do with older, more orthodox devices. For me, an air mattress with pillow (page 444) is ideal. With a self-inflating or foam pad I normally just roll up my long pants or down jacket or another garment and stuff it (or them) under my head. If you push the garment partway into a stuff sack you can fine-adjust pillow size to meet your need of the moment. Sometimes I bolster the clothing with a plastic canteen or the day's-ration food bag. If the night is cold enough to make me wear all the clothes I've brought, I may use a canteen alone. This arrangement helps keep the canteen unfrozen; and because I'm sure to be wearing my balaclava helmet and perhaps a hooded parka as well, it's tolerably comfortable. Or I may pad the canteen with the packbag or ration bag—making sure that soft food such as cereal is directly under my head. A convertible stuff sack from Liberty Mountain Adventure (8-by-18-inch, $12; 9-by-20-inch, $14) holds your sleeping bag and then reverses to serve as a clothing-filled pillow with a fleece panel. You can, of course, buy a separate, inflatable pillow; a synthetic-filled one; or, much more cheaply, an ordinary zip-top bag.

On sand or other loose soil the simplest and most comfortable pillow is a roughly banked-up guillotine block. No matter how much you want a soft pillow, there are precious few places left in which it is justifiable to use bough tips or moss or any natural material. Occasionally, manna falls. One reader reports that when, as a member of a large party, he was the bearer of an inflatable plastic arm splint, he found it made "a luxurious pillow."

Knee pillows

If you have any kind of back trouble (not exactly rare in *homo backpackerens*) you may find that when sitting up in your bag or lying on your back you need some kind of knee support. Anything from a down or pile jacket through food bags to the half-empty pack can be pressed into service, either inside or outside the bag. This knee pillow must be so arranged that when you turn over onto one side your knees can circum-navigate it with next to no assist from your conscious mind.

SUBSTITUTES AND SUPPLEMENTS
FOR SLEEPING BAGS

Cagoule-and-footsack bivouac

CHIP: With the rise of the 1-pound Gore-Tex bivouac bag, the former range of ingenious cagoules, footsacks, convertible down pants, and other help-me-make-it-through-the-night gear has nearly vanished. Or at least the mountaineering suppliers that used to carry such things for the most part no longer do. The divide here is between climbers and hard-core types who seek out such *déshabillé* nights and those—most of us really—for whom it represents dire emergency. The kit used by my hard-core friends is a bare-bones bivouac bag, a pack-length Ensolite pad, and an insulated cap, parka, pants, and booties. The usual down-versus-synthetic battles rage, of course. But in either wise, a knowledgeable user can spend a night or two out without serious harm—and maybe even get a few hours of sleep.

COLIN: The knee-length parka, or *cagoule* (page 547), is designed for use as a bivouac—either alone (when you draw your knees up inside it) or with a companion footsack. The idea is presumably to use the combination when nights are really warm, but there are few climates I would trust. As an emergency bivouac the rig sounds ideal. But "emergency bivouac" means sleeping out when you do not expect to—and therefore are unlikely to be carrying equipment for the job. Besides, a modern VBL shirt and pants or half-sac (page 473) do the same job better. Still, it's possible to imagine certain situations in which a cagoule-and-footsack rig might be worth packing along. Anyway, the world would be poorer without it. It's one of those intriguing items that make catalog browsing the dreamy, time-wasting, utterly delightful pursuit it is.

Note that Wiggy's still makes a classic nylon oxford cagoule with a drawcorded hood, waist, and just-above-the-knee-length skirt (in four sizes, $140). Campmor's Backpacker Rain Cagoule, in one size, costs about $40.

Packbag as emergency footsack

See page 186.

Stuff sacks

Years ago I used to stuff my sleeping bag loose into the pack or even tie it unprotected onto the outside. But eventually I became, like most people, a convert to stuff sacks. They're normally cylindrical affairs with drawcord closures, and they protect your bag—and down clothing and other items too—from unnecessary wear and tear and also from rain. If you're at all worried about the bag's getting wet, line or envelop its stuff sack with a large plastic bag filched from almost any other use.

CHIP: Most stuff sacks are made of waterproofed nylon, but some of the new fabrics seen in fly sheets, like coated polyester and ultralight silicone-impregnated nylon, are good for stuffers as well. While the fabric itself may be more or less waterproof, the usual drawstring closure is not. It can actually suck water in when the sleeping bag inside is compressed and then released, which occurs when you set an E-frame pack down in wet foliage—or wade that deeper-than-it-looks creek.

The lightest waterproof sacks are silicone-impregnated nylon parachute cloth. GoLite makes a stow sack called the Pouch, in five sizes (all in cubic inches): 125, 250, 500, 1000, and 2000. Weights range from 0.5 oz. to 2.5 oz., and prices from \$12 to \$33. The largest size will line the main compartment of a pack. The 1000-cu.-in. size works for most sleeping bags while the 1-oz.-500-cu.-incher happily swallows a lightweight. GoLite improves the usual drawstring-and-flap closure to a drawstring and collar—you stuff the sleeping bag or parka, twist the collar, and then drawstring it in place.

For ruggedness, a good waterproof fabric for stuff sacks is Hydroseal, developed by Outdoor Research (in rain-fresh Seattle). A stout 4-oz. Antron nylon is coated with a special elastomer, making it waterproof to 200 pounds per square inch (psi). Besides waterproofness, the endearing quality of Hydroseal is that the fabric is limp enough to mold itself to the contents of the sack. Hydroseal stuff sacks, sleeping-pad covers, and external pack pockets come in more sizes than I can list here. The Basic model is a drawcord/flap closure with a webbing handle at the base. The Standard adds factory-taped seams and a daisy chain for lashing down. The Advanced model drops the drawcord for a roll closure with Velcro bindings. The Advanced model also works as a compression sack—you stuff your treasure and exhaust the air, whence the limp fabric sucks together, letting you roll and tab the closure for compression as good as that in sacks with straps or laces. I used one to hold a fleece top and pants, strapping it to the front bar of a cataraft for a seven-day river run. If it failed, I figured I could always wring out the fleece and get by. But I didn't have to: many rapids (and one disgraceful flip) later, the fuzz was still dry. Outdoor Research Hydroseal stuff sacks come in eight sizes, from 300 to 2500 cu. in. The Basic runs $9.50 to $19; the Standard, $12.50 to $22.50; and the Advanced, $16.50 to $28.50. If butt compression's not enough, they now make a four-strapper bondage bag, hinged and zippered, in five sizes. Nominally, these range from 800 to 2900 cu. in., with the compression system halving that. Cost ranges from $20 to $35 (and yes, they come in black).

Most suppliers of stuff sacks have some sort of compression model, with a set of lengthwise straps, encircling straps, horizontal laces, or even a double drawstring, that lets you reduce the volume of squashables by up to half.

Another remarkable stuff sack, for quite different reasons, is the Gregory Contour, a 420-denier ripstop in three sizes (3–4 oz., $20 each), sewn in a gently rectilinear shape to fit the sleeping-bag compartments of Gregory's (and many other) packs.

Coated-nylon stuff sacks and ditty bags are simple to sew—for a pattern, look at your favorite. This makes them ideal, says Colin, "for feeling your way into the do-it-yourself field."

The small-stuff-sack fallacy

COLIN: Manufacturers tend to make stuff sacks for sleeping bags and other items as small as possible, if not smaller. Apart from saving material and a scrittage of weight, and convincing customers that the stuffed product is small and neat and probably light, the only advantage I can discern is a possible increase in waterproofness due to skintightness when packed. That may be a gain for those who carry sleeping bags outside their packs. For others it's offset with acres to spare by two weighty debits.

First, you do not, as might be imagined, save space. A tightly packed stuff sack tends to sit stalwartly and nonconformingly in its corner of a pack; unless you have soft, yielding articles to stuff around it you leave wasted space at its peripheries.

Second, and more important, there's the stuffing difficulty. A bag of such a size that you can just about cram in your sleeping bag or down jacket or whatever with no more than a minor struggle in store or living room at a windless 70°F, when you're fresh and fed, may seem beguilingly efficient. In a gale, at 20°, when you're hungry and weary and in a hurry, it transmutes into a monster.

I always try to buy a stuff sack big enough to take its load with room to spare, leaving it soft, malleable, odd-corner-fitting—and easily stuffable.

Carrying your sleeping bag: strapped outboard or stuffed inside packbag?

See pages 173 to 174.

Sleeping-bag liners (not VBLs)

CHIP: Since washing seems to break down insulation fast, especially synthetics, liners are regaining popularity, in materials that are both warmer and lighter than cotton. Fleece mummy liners with side zippers and drawstring hoods are eminently washable and add about 10°F of comfort to a compatible sleeping bag. I've also talked with ultralighters who use them in summer, with a slim bivy sack and gossamer tarp (page 394). While somewhat heavier and bulkier than an ultralight down bag, they cost half as much and aren't vulnerable to moisture. A wholesaler, Liberty Mountain Adventure, stocks Fleece Mummy Liners in midweight Polartec 200 — order through your local shop (regular: 2 lbs., $88; long: 2 lbs. 6 oz., $96). Since they're one thickness throughout, the primary kvetch seems to be cold feet.

Light cotton liners are still around but seem to be used more for dude-ranch/rental situations than backpacking. No synthetic fabric seems to have emerged as the perfect lightweight sleeping-bag liner. But an ancient one, silk, is incredibly light and compressible, fast-drying, and a comfort to the skin.

I've used a silk envelope with a Velcro-tabbed side opening and pillow sleeve called a Dreamsack (6 oz., $59), as a sleeping-bag liner. It's midnight blue—dreamy indeed, though I do get tangled up in it; a few points of attachment would help. But I find I use it more outside my sleeping bag than in. On hot-country trips my former custom was to pack an old bedsheet, fold it once lengthwise, and taco in—cheap and quite comfortable on breathless nights. But a cotton sheet weighs a pound and a half, gains water weight fast, and is slow to dry. The Dreamsack weighs next to nothing, dries in a few minutes of early sun, and stuffs into an insulated mug (or the teeny sack supplied). Westwind Trading Company imports Dreamsacks in singles, doubles, and various lengths (5–12 oz., $45–$110). For the tender-cheeked they have a silk pillowcase that stuffs to the size of a mouse, weighs less, and costs $7.

Another tiptoe in the general direction of Babylon are liners and sleeping-pad covers from Design Salt (whose ads drape them around Euro-vixens in abandoned poses). They come in sizes from child to affinity group, in silk, cotton, and blends thereof, with wild colors and patterns. A durable, washable, nonwoven nylon liner is also available.

All of which makes my old percale burrito system look like . . . sheet.

CARE OF SLEEPING BAGS

COLIN: Any sleeping bag should be aired after use. Just open the bag and leave it spread out, preferably up off the ground. With nylon-shell bags, which tend to pick up body odors, two or three days isn't too long. Outdoor airing, especially in sunshine, seems best. Purists will warn you that sunlight is nylon's archenemy. Technically, they may be right. But life is too bloody short.

It's best not to store a bag for long periods compressed in its stuff sack: if you do, the fill—especially synthetics but also resilient down— will tend to retain its cramped conformation and will therefore lose at least some of its insulating power. So lay the bag out flat, hang in a closet, or roll loosely.

Normally, cleaning should amount to no more than sponging the shell, inside and out, with a mild soap (not detergent) and tepid water. Rinse, then dry thoroughly. If a bag becomes so soiled that it demands more stringent measures, that presents no problem if it has synthetic fill: you simply wash it. (Do *not* dry-clean it.) But take care with the drying: Polarguard, for example, suffers irreversible damage at 140°F. (Note that car trunks and interiors can easily reach 140°.)

Down demands greater cleaning care. You can take the bag to reputable launderers, accustomed to down clothing, and have them wash it in soap or mild detergent and then tumble dry; but you can save a lot of money by doing the job yourself. There are now several soaps made especially for the job, including Nikwax Down Wash (10-oz. plastic bottle, $10) and Down Suds (4-oz. plastic bottle, $3; 8-oz., $5). With such soaps you can do a good job in a bathtub with tepid water. But don't use too much soap. Make sure any Velcro tabs are firmly tabbed: when open, they can damage the shell and liner fabrics. And rinse carefully. Do not man-handle the bag: soaked, wet down is so heavy that it can tear the internal baffles. Be prepared for a tedious drying job. One manufacturer recommends letting the bag drip dry for a couple of hours (in a chaise longue, say, or a hammock) or even spindrying it in the largest possible front-loading dryer at a Laundromat "for several hours (when it feels dry, give it another hour)." Set dryer to FLUFF or SYNTHETIC cycle; otherwise, you can melt nylon and fuse zippers. Don't let a bag lie in a dryer once it has stopped. Some experts recommend throwing a pair of sneakers in with the bag: "they will help pound clogged down apart, and the rubber/nylon combination generates the static electricity needed to loft the down fully." Counter-experts judge the sneakers to do more harm than good, and warn that they're especially likely to damage old bags.

A few people—even some soap makers—say that with the right soaps you can safely use tumble washers (but not top-loaders).

An alternative (for down bags, not synthetics) is dry cleaning. The experts' advice on dry-cleaning or not dry-cleaning your bag seems to change about as often as skirt lengths. So I shall stick with my first-edition advice (though there does seem to be a tendency for more and more makers to recommend dry cleaning at reputable cleaners).

Ever since one favorite old bag of mine lost a great deal of its virtue after two or three widely spaced visits to the cleaners I've tended to avoid commercial cleaning. But so that I shouldn't pass on pure hunch I made careful inquiries—only to find that "expert" opinions on acceptable dry-cleaning methods run the gamut, A through Z. As for specific trustworthy cleaners of any kind, they seem to come and go. Best bet: inquire at a good mountain shop; the staff should know which local cleaners do a restrained but effective job on sleeping bags.*

One reason it's sometimes advisable to have a bag cleaned is that in time the down begins to mat. Clumps of it coagulate, and large areas in each baffle tube are left empty. Dry cleaning certainly seems to redistribute the down effectively. But the plant manager I've quoted (and he can hardly be accused of commercial bias in this opinion) maintained that the redistribution was purely the result of mechanical tumbling in the dryer. In other words, the way to redistribute the down in your bag, especially if it has been soaked, is to put it in the tumble dryer at low heat—back home or at a Laundromat.

Warning: almost any kind of patch that's taped or glued on will come off a bag during dry cleaning, and fill will escape. So if your bag has been patched, try to avoid having it cleaned unless (or until) the patches are sewn on.

Repairing

Like it or not, small cuts and burns happen. Adhesive repair tape

---

*CHIP: Toxic solvents like perchloroethylene, the dry-cleaning industry standby, have proved to be harmful both to human health and the environment. Silicone-based wet-cleaning compounds like Rynex are being tested, but the most promising method seems to be with liquid CO_2 and a compatible detergent. Developed at North Carolina State University, this nontoxic "green cleaning" technique uses no heat and is said to strip less fiber than other methods. A new franchise called Hangers employs this CO_2 method, but the machines cost $80,000 to $100,000 each, so it might be a while taking hold.

(page 667) is the remedy. It used to be that the adhesive was enough on its own, but this no longer seems to be so. Certainly not for permanent patches. My opinion, based on many years' patching of one ancient cotton-covered bag, is apparently not purely attributable to crabbed age: I recently forced one experienced salesman to admit that, owing to the slipperiness of the new materials, the stuff really doesn't adhere the way it used to. The solution: sew permanent patches around all their edges.

CHIP: Reformulated stickum helps a lot and so does rounding the corners of the patch. I patched a crampon hole in my packcloth gaiters with Kenyon ripstop repair tape. Despite lots of step kicking and postholing, the patch still held after five years, when I gave the gaiters to a buffalo-defending youngster in West Yellowstone, Montana.

Pensioning off

COLIN: There comes a time—no matter how much cleaning or tumble drying or self-deceiving you do—when a patched and trusted old bag is no longer sure to give you a warm sleep within its temperature range. There's only one remedy. But it's always a sad moment when another old friend bites the Goodwill.

CHOOSING AND PREPARING A BEDROOM

Level bedsites

There are few simpler ways of ensuring a bad night's sleep than choosing a bed that slopes. If the slope is sideways you spend the night in a thinly conscious hassle with gravity; and you wake, tired and aching, to find yourself still pressing fiercely on the downslope with arms and knees and a battery of assistant muscles. If the slope runs from feet to head you don't go to sleep at all. No matter how gentle the incline (and it's sure to be gentle, or you would never have overlooked it) you discover the horrible truth the moment you lie down. The feeling that all the blood is going to rush to your head is so disturbing that after a few feeble attempts at telling yourself that it's all imagination, you gruntle up and switch head and feet.*

---

*CHIP: Crossing a clear-cut in the savagely logged Medicine Bow National Forest, I found a small bubble level, about the size of a pen with a pocket clip (o.6 oz.). For the rest of the trip I checked my prospective beds with it and found that my native judgment isn't as good as I thought. If you're highly sensitive to tilt, hardware stores sell both pocket-clip levels and smaller keychain-bob models (o.4 oz., $2).

If you can't possibly avoid a sloping bed you should sleep with your feet downhill. That way, if the slope isn't too severe, you spend a passably comfortable night: you may come half awake occasionally to find yourself a yard and a half downhill from pillow and groundsheet, and have to do an undignified wriggle back uphill; but you wake with nothing worse than mildly aching leg muscles.

Do everything you can, then, to organize a level bed. I routinely check by lying full length on the bare ground (or on a groundsheet if it's wet), adjusting to the most comfortable position, and then lying still long enough to make sure my head isn't too blood-collecting low. If you have to camp on generally sloping ground then try to do so on a trail or just above a tree or in some other place where there's a ready-made level platform. Or go to considerable pains to make a platform. Often you can find a place with soil loose enough to kick away with your heels. You can always do so on talus. But in heavily used country you must these days accept a bedsite that needs leveling only if the construction work will do no damage to the ground and can be completely repaired before you leave. Sand, talus, and a deep leaf carpet qualify. Grass like hell does not: leveling it means removing the roots and therefore killing it. And unless you sleep in a bureaucratically consecrated campsite where the ground is likely to be scraped or worn bare you should try to leave no sign—beyond a rectangle of crushed vegetation if you *have* to crush any—that you slept there. Leave, that is, no more trace than a bear, or even a deer.

Improving a bedsite

When I lie down to check the levelness of a bedsite I naturally discover any bumps, rocks, and other body prodders. I quickly banish the worst offenders. And if I'm sleeping on a thin, closed-cell foam pad (which nowadays is rarely) I may work with bare hands or a stick or even my toilet trowel (page 698) until the place is reasonably smooth. With a thick foam pad, a Therm-a-Rest, or an air mattress, I need take far less care.

But, provided the country and the under-bed material permit, it often makes sense to contour a bedsite to fit your form—certainly if there'll be no cushion between bag and ground; probably with a closed-cell pad; possibly even with a more voluptuous mattress. The idea is to emulate a waterbed by digging or merely boot-scratching a shallow depression for your shoulders and a rather deeper one for your butt/hips. Excavated material builds a pillow, or raises the legs a trifle. Determine your needs by trowel and error.

Choice of under-bed material

Grass is one of the poorer choices for a bedsite. Except when very long, it cushions you precious little; and even aside from the unacceptable scarring (see facing page), it is difficult to contour to fit your form. An air mattress or thick foam pad takes the sting out of loose gravel or talus, and they are far easier to contour. Bare earth is often as easy, and appreciably softer. Sand rates higher still. A deep carpet of leaves, and especially of pine needles, offers the ultimate luxury in warmth and comfort—and sometimes a monumental fire hazard. Leaves should never be chosen if you intend to light a fire. Even with a stove you must clear a hearth to bare soil—and still exercise meticulous care.*

Shelter from wind

The level-bed business is so important that when I camp at nightfall and expect to move on again first thing in the morning it's often the only campsite feature I worry about. In fair weather, that is. But when the wind rises to gale force or feels like a disembodied iceberg then shelter from wind supplants level ground as the one thing you absolutely must have.

Unless you have both a tent and confidence that you can erect it in the teeth of the gale, go to great pains to find natural shelter. I tend to do so anyway. It's much simpler, and often warmer. A clump of trees or bushes will deflect the full fury of any wind. And even in exposed places, quite minor irregularities, if themselves total windbreaks, make remarkably good refuges. I've spent comfortable nights, well sheltered from icy gales, in the troughs of shallow gullies, behind low walls, even tucked in close to a cattle trough. But the best hideout of all is an overhanging rock-ledge. (A full-fledged cave protects you better, of course; but caves tend to be both rare and unappetizing.) Even a very shallow ledge, provided it's on the lee side of a hill or rockpile, can be a snug place. The rock retains much of its daytime warmth, and after one comfortable night in such a sanctuary you understand why cold-blooded rattlesnakes like to live among rocks. The floor of the ledge is rarely as level as you'd like it to be, but there are often small rocks lying around for a rough construction job. Such construction can rarely be justified in heavily used country. Even less can the still-general practice of camping in an unprotected place and

---

*CHIP: Outdoor programs have lately been urging the practice of camping on bedrock. A wee trick—since you can't exactly level bedrock—is to roll a parka, pants, or vest, etc. and lay it along the low side under your pad. This at least keeps you from rolling downslope.

then collecting boulders and building a wall or, sometimes, an embryo cabin.*

Remember, by the way, that winds often die at dusk, then revive from a different quarter. Desert winds fairly consistently blow up canyons by day, down them (and cold) at night. The night downwind is also common on mountains in generally calm weather.

Shelter from rain

Rockledges make good shelters from rain too—and caves are even better. But beware of shallow caves in thunderstorms (page 754). Hollow tree trunks are traditional wilderness shelters but, to be honest, I've never tried one. In rain I just tend to put up whatever roof I've brought along. Naturally, I choose the most sheltered site I can find.

Shelter from snow

CHIP: An obvious refuge is under a tree—I've bivouacked often in hollows under big conifers and hung my stove from a branch, with globs of pitch making me occasionally sorry. If there's wind driving the snow, small openings in the forest are good shelter, as are brushy hollows or encircling rocks. The base of an overhanging cliff can be safe, if it overhangs enough. Otherwise, look out not just for unpredictable sloughs of snow but also for frost-wedged rocks and falling icicles.

At all events, try to avoid spots where the wind is either scouring snow away or depositing it. Scour zones have particularly strong gusts. Deposition zones, in the lee of a ridge or cliff, are calmer. But drifting snow might bury your tent as you sleep.

High winds create avalanche risk, even if it's not snowing heavily at the moment. Avoid camping under steep, treeless slopes or gullies, especially those topped with a *cornice* (the overhanging snow crest formed by the wind). If the weather's too thick for good visibility, study your topo

---

*CHIP: In the windswept Wind River Range, rock enclosures are common above treeline. Since people seem to dependably heap them up at about the same rate Forest Service wilderness rangers dismantle them, it makes sense (to me at least) to leave the most popular ones in place. I also noticed that the rocks in some of the best-built enclosures all had slow-growing lichens on their upper faces, meaning they'd been in place for a century or more. In fact, some of the structures looked very old indeed. Later, a knowledgeable Shoshone elder confirmed that his people built many stone firepits, windbreaks, shelter walls, and sweat-lodge frames at high elevations in the range. They also left convenient rings of stones on bedrock, for tent anchors. Thus, by dismantling such sites, the wilderness rangers had violated the federal Antiquities Act. Not to mention, said my Shoshone informant, courting damned bad luck.

map for hazardous terrain. As Colin advised in *Walker III*: "Before you venture out into any depth of snow in any country that's not flat or close to it, make damned sure you ascertain from a genuine avalanche authority that it's safe to do so. If not, stay at home."

There are also several good books on the subject: page 754.

For finding shelter in the snow itself, consider snow caves, *quinzhees,* and trenches—page 438.

Cold bedrooms

Meadows, especially when cradled in hollows, often collect cold, damp air. They're delightful places to camp, though, and—provided human usage is light—should not necessarily be avoided. A hillock or rockslab a few feet above the meadow itself is often enough to ward off the worst of the cold, improve the view—and spare the fragile grass.

Riverbanks also tend to be damp and therefore cold places. On a 1989 to 1990 raft journey down the Colorado, source to sea, when I had to sleep close to raft and river, I encountered in December, in desert just above the Mexican border, microclimatic riverside temperatures as low as 11°F. Still, even on nonraft backpacking trips, riverbanks can provide richly rewarding campsites. But remember that the authorities often, and with good reason, adjure you to camp not less than 30 feet from the water. And for sanitation warnings, see page 699.

Siting your bedroom to catch—or avoid—the morning sun

It can occasionally be important that your bed should catch the first rays of morning sunshine. Sometimes only the sun's warmth will make a bitter world habitable. (That's what happened, very quickly, at those frigid December-desert campsites beside the Colorado—because I took care to camp on the west bank.) Sometimes you go to sleep without a roof—because you're tired or lazy or just because you like it that way—expecting heavy dew during the night but knowing that morning sunshine will quickly dry it off and save you packing along pounds of water. Or it may be that a tent needs drying. And on days on which you're planning not to move camp, or to move late, it's always more pleasant to start the day in sunshine. At least, almost always. In deserts, in summer, you'll want to avoid the sun. And some people prefer to avoid it, especially if they want to sleep late, in all but icebergial weather.

Anyway, whatever your reason for wanting to know where the sun will rise, the solution is simple: on the first day of the trip—or before you start, if you can remember it—measure with your compass the exact bearing on which the sun rises over a flat horizon. Pencil the bearing on the back of the compass. Then, at any night camp, all you have to do is take out the compass, sight along the correct bearing, make due allowance for close or distant heightening of the horizon, and site your camp in the right place. With a little experience you can prophesy accurately enough to make use of even narrow gaps in trees.

But perhaps you know you'll forget to take a sunrise bearing before you start and are afraid there will be no sun on the first day. If you delight in dabbling with tortuous theory and have a copy of *Practical Boating: Inland and Offshore—Power and Sail* by W. S. Kals (Doubleday, 1969, now out of print) you're still in good shape: on page 121 you'll find a table showing the true bearing of the sun at sunrise, at various latitudes. Or, suggests Chip, simply take a bearing on your first morning out.

Minor factors in choosing a campsite

Your criteria for a good campsite will vary a lot with the kind of country, your expected length of stay, and your personal preferences. For the first day or two of a trip, especially in strange country, you may find yourself circling around a promising area like a dog stirred by ancestral memories. But before long you're once more recognizing a good site at a glance: not only a flat bedsite with reasonable protection from wind but also (if you want a fire) plenty of firewood and (where there's water) a bathroom.

Don't underrate the importance of a good bathroom. There's a yawning gap between a camp with running bedside water (where you can without effort scoop out drinking water, wash, wash up, and wash your feet) and a place in which you have to crash through tangled undergrowth and yards of sucking swamp to reach a tepid outpuddle of a river. By comparison, the difference between hotel rooms with and without a private bath is so much fiddle-faddle. Naturally, I'm speaking now of large lakes or rivers in genuinely remote places. In most of today's teeming wildernesses it's rarely possible to make your choices with so little consideration for fellow travelers.

You earn, by the way, an oddly satisfying bonus if you succeed in choosing a memorable camp from the map—as you can sometimes do once you grow used to a certain kind of country. If you play the percentages and hunches and get everything right—level bed, shelter from wind, firewood, water, morning sunshine, pleasing surroundings, even (and this is what makes a camp truly memorable) the stimulation or mystery or magic that can come from an isthmus of woodland or an oddly shaped hillock or a quietly gurgling backwater—if you get all these right you experience the same slightly surprised pleasure as from finding that your checkbook total tallies with the bank statement.

Dry camps

I was astonished to read in a magazine a few years back an article about the "new" practice of dry camping—that is, of carrying enough water, for a short or long distance, to enable you to choose a campsite independent of any water source. Under a wide range of conditions—from deserts to almost any place there's no regulation that you must camp in a bureaucratically consecrated campsite—I have for years carried enough canteens to give me such freedom. I may fill up at a creek and carry the necessary extra load only half a mile. Or I may lug it much farther. Sometimes this is purely a making-mileage ploy. But often it's not. And when it's not I almost always find that the extra convenience or shelter or privacy or beauty of the campsite I'm freed to select makes the effort well worthwhile. I'd guess that these days, except in well-watered high mountains, at least 50 percent of my campsites are more than half a mile from my water source.

THE BEDROOM IN ACTION

We examined most details of how the bedroom operates in our Sample Day in the Kitchen (pages 359–67 and 370–71). More appears under A Sample Day in the Rain (pages 567–74). And for modifications under various kinds of roof, see their separate subheadings in this chapter. But several points remain unmade:

KEEPING TABS ON THE FLASHLIGHT

After dark you must always know exactly where the flashlight is. Otherwise, chaos. My flashlight spends the night in an easy-to-feel position in one bedside boot. And I used to have a rule that when it was in intermittent use, such as before and during dinner, I never let go my grasp on it without putting it in the pocket designated for the night (*which* pocket depended on what I was wearing). This rule was so strict that I rarely broke it more than three or four times a night.

Nowadays the rule has been superseded: I virtually always have the flashlight tied to a large loop of nylon cord that slips over my head.

For more on flashlights, headlamps, and subgenres see pages 579 to 598. For candle lanterns and even fancier illumination, pages 599 to 606.

Fluffing up the sleeping bag

Although I'm told that many people fail to do so, it seems only common sense that before you get into bed at night you should always shake the sleeping bag by the edges and so fluff up the down or even synthetic fill and suffuse it with the air pockets that actually keep you warm. At this point in the original *Walker* I wrote: "One of these nights I must try it out." I'm happy to report that the act of writing that sentence prodded me into doing the job fairly regularly. It remains good to know, firsthand, that the book has taught somebody something.

Adjusting to suit the night

With experience (and I guess there's no other way) you can usually gauge pretty accurately how much clothing, if any, you'll need to wear in your sleeping bag. Or, in warmer weather, how tightly you need pull the hood drawstrings, and whether you should unzip the bag partway. But you'll never get so good that you always hit the nail dead center.

In general, be a pessimist: if in doubt, wear that extra layer of clothing, and pull the drawstrings tight. Sleeping too hot is uncomfortable; but sleeping cold is murder. In any case, the night will usually, though not always, get progressively colder (the coldest time typically comes either at dawn or, even more often, in the last few minutes before sunrise).

There's another and even more important reason that you do better by deliberately looking on the bleak side: boosting insulation is a major operation, reducing it a very simple one. When you wake up uncomfortably hot (and you will do so occasionally unless you consistently under-insulate, and then God help you) all you need do is slacken off the drawstrings. At least, that usually lets out enough heat, especially if you flap the bag in a bellows effect a couple of times to introduce some cold air. If you find that to establish the right balance you have to slacken the drawstrings until there's a gaping hole around your head you'll probably discover that the upper part of your body gets too cold and the lower part stays too hot. If you're wearing heavy clothes, take off one layer. (A minor disadvantage of a close-fitting bag is that putting on or taking off socks and pants "indoors" is a struggle. But it can be done. At least, taking them off can.) If you wake to find yourself too hot when you're wearing few or no clothes (which will mean that outside air temperatures are not too barbarously low), feel for the inside tab of the zipper and slide it partway or all the way down. Two-way zippers, now almost standard, allow you to open up a breathing hole at your calves as well. Once again, only experience will tell you how far to go, and also how to tuck the opening under you, or to wriggle it around on top, or away from the wind, or whatever else achieves the balance you want. If you unzip you may well have to rezip as the night grows colder, and/or to tighten the drawstrings; but you soon learn to do so without coming more than about one-eighth awake.

On really hot nights the only comfortable way to use the bag may be as a cover—fully unzipped and just spread out loosely over your body. At such times it may be most comfortable to wear a shirt to keep your shoulders warm and to tuck your feet partway into the foot of the bag. A little to my surprise, I find myself sleeping this way more and more often on windless nights when the temperature's over about 40°F. One advantage of using the bag instead of wearing a couple of layers of clothing is that as the night grows colder (which it mostly will) you can compensate, without coming even one-eighth awake, by pulling the edges of the outspread bag a little more firmly around you.

Dealing with a full bladder at night

See page 701.

Getting to sleep

An experienced outdoorsman once suggested that I include in this chapter "the ritual of getting to sleep in a bag," and as he was my editor I decided that I had better attempt the task. In an earlier edition I wrote that my technique was to lie down, close my eyes, and go to sleep. That's still true, mostly. Sleeping is one of my fields of competence. But if I experience any difficulty—as I understand some people regularly do—I now quieten myself with Selective Awareness (page 124), and soon slip down and away.

Clothes Closet

COLIN: The best dress for walking is nakedness. But our sad though fascinating world rarely generates the right mix of weather and privacy for such freedom, and even when it does the Utopia never seems to last for very long. So you always, dammit, have to worry about clothes.*

The most sensible way to set about deciding what clothing to take on a trip and what to leave behind is to consult weather statistics (page 38) and your own experience and so arrive at an estimate of the most miserable conditions of temperature, wind, exposure, humidity, and precipitation that you can reasonably expect to suffer. The worst conditions recorded in at least 20 years. Then all you have to do is judge what you need to take to keep you warm under daytime conditions when you are wearing everything and doing something or at least are only sitting down and doing nothing for short intervals. If you hit this target around about center you can feel reasonably sure that at night, with shelter and sleeping bags selected to match, you will sleep tolerably warm under the bitterest conditions possible if you wrap yourself up in every stitch of available clothing that remains dry. During the day, if you stop doing anything for any length of time and begin to feel cold, or even think that you might soon feel cold, then—provided your clothes and the weather are dry enough—you simply pupate inside the sleeping bag.

This kind of calculation involves not so much a precise balancing of conditions and clothing as an exercise in extrapolating from experience. But it works. I don't remember being seriously cold at any time in the last 40 years for more than the few minutes it took me to do something about the problem. And although I have never operated in bitter cold—never below zero, in fact—people such as Chip who do so fairly often seem to apply much the same methods of choice and the same techniques.

*The executive director of an Eastern Trail Conference once delighted me by reporting that he had walked "over 1000 miles of the Appalachian Trail wearing shoes and socks and a pack."

This general approach works irrespective of the kind of clothing you wear.

Seventy years ago mountaineers scaled formidable peaks—even challenged Everest—wearing tweed shooting jackets. Fifteen years ago most backpackers wore modified forms of their everyday informal wardrobe. (Down jackets, which transformed outdoor wear more than three decades ago, had already become part of that wardrobe. So had windbreakers.) But new synthetics, and older fibers put to new uses, have now seeded

A revolution in the clothes closet—

a continuing renovation more radical than that assailing any other sector of backpacking equipment.

The primary elements are wicking underwear, fleece or pile insulating garments, and waterproof/breathable shells. These three basic ingredients and their variations, alone or with addenda, can constitute a layered system for backpacking in all nonextreme temperatures and in almost any kind of rain you can nightmare up. For the moment, I shall speak of a simple, idealized system—though one of its advantages is that it can be modified to meet the demands of widely differing conditions as well as those of tradition, habit, and idiosyncrasy.

The proven three-layer system

offers solid advantages. Its constituent items are lighter, sometimes more durable, and generally less expensive than traditional equivalents. Properly used, they're more flexible. Above all, they work far better than traditional garments when they become wet, either from sweat or from rain that has penetrated the "waterproof" shell. Finally, each item, raw or slightly modified, can become—as the down jacket and windbreaker quickly did—a standard part of everyday town wardrobes.

The seeds of the clothing revolution, planted years ago and cultivated by succeeding generations, are now bustin' out all over; and while it's just possible that the garden will fail to flourish, I doubt it. A burgeoning band of backpackers, particularly in such aqueous places as the Pacific Northwest, became such dedicated converts to the three-layer system that they convinced the rest of us—except for a few holdouts. For an occasion on which I found it excellent, see page 567.

In addition to that system there's the older but never acutely popular vapor-barrier system—which can be used as an extension of the three-layer system. We'll examine it in due course.

Before attempting to compare traditional clothing with the slew of new systems we must take a closer look at the newcomers. But first it might be wise to review

The prime purpose of clothes.

For the moment, we'll ignore protection from rain and sun and also such ancillary matters as beautification and conventional decency (aka prudery), and will consider only warmth. And warmth only in a simple sense. For the different kinds of heat loss and heat barriers, see page 513.

Beginner backpackers sometimes overlook two basic and obvious facts. First, when you put on clothes for warmth you are not "keeping the cold out," as the old saying has it; you're conserving heat from the only available source—you. Second, you normally wear clothes not to make you as warm as possible but to maintain *thermal equilibrium*—that is, a state in which your heat production roughly balances your heat loss and you remain within your comfort range whether you're sitting still, being active enough to sweat like crazy, or, most demanding of all, sitting still after sweating.

To achieve thermal equilibrium under changing conditions your wardrobe must be versatile. Gross adjustments can sometimes be made by putting on or taking off layers in response to the weather and what you are doing. But that's often foully inconvenient or even impractical, especially in cold or wet. So you aim for as broad a range as possible over which each item or combination of items will maintain you in comfort. Generally speaking, this is best achieved by clothing that will trap dry, still air and therefore insulate you but will also, when you're being active, allow water vapor from your sweat to pass through and escape. Your sweat can then do its job of cooling you by extracting from your body the latent heat needed for water to turn to vapor. But if the clothing absorbs some of the moisture and therefore remains damp when you cease your activity and stop sweating—as old-fashioned wool does to some extent, and cotton markedly—then the absorbed water will not only reduce the clothing's ability to hold dry air and so impair its insulative value but will also continue to draw from your body the latent heat needed to turn the water into vapor. Result: you suffer from *after-exercise chill*. Experiments at the U.S. Army Research Institute of Environmental Medicine showed that "with an absorptive textile [wool-nylon] the after-exercise chill is large and persists for about two hours but with a non-absorptive type [fiber-pile] it is negligible."

This efficiency in circumventing after-exercise chill is a big reason for the ongoing popularity of the three-layer clothing system.

Some of the fabrics used in the system are now known quantities, but others have only recently achieved widespread success, at least in the backpacking field, and it seems certain that, as almost always happens during any evolutionary process, things will continue to develop. By the time this edition appears some of the current buzzword trade names may have melted away. Perhaps a fiber or two will have been superseded. So in trying to describe what is happening I shall bear in mind that we are living through the rapidly shifting arc of an ongoing continuum. Rather than simply name names, Chip or I will try to describe those properties that fit the new fibers and fabrics so snugly into the backpacker's clothes closet. With luck, you'll be able to penetrate beyond outdated trade names and understand the functions of replacement equivalents.

The strata of the present three-layer system are:

1. Next-to-the-skin layer,
2. Insulating layer,
3. Wind- and/or waterproof shell.

Next-to-the-skin layer

The breakthrough in materials came with polypropylene. Now often known as *polypro,* it's one fiber in the larger group of *polyolefins*—sometimes called just *olefins;* but for our purposes all these terms are interchangeable. The very durable fiber—derived from propylene and ethylene gases—was the lightest and least expensive of the new synthetics. It also absorbs only 1 percent of its weight in moisture. It therefore wicks moisture away from the skin very rapidly by capillary action. (Please don't ask me to explain "therefore": the molecular processes remain unclear to me and, as far as I can determine, to everyone else.) The fiber's nonabsorbency also means that polypro fabric dries out very quickly. One booster told me that "if you put a polypro undershirt in a bucket, then swing it twice over your head and put it on, within a minute it will be bone dry and you will be warm." I promptly carried out the experiment (purely for you, O buster, bustress), and I have to report that in spite of modifying the prescription to a sextupular waving and subsequently encasing myself in a pile jacket I was back at my desk five minutes later, agreeably warm but clammily short of dry. So our booster trafficked in hyperbole. It's probably true, though, that if you fall profoundly into the drink a polypro (or other synthetic) undergarment will dry out faster and more comfortably than anything else now known. But polypro was not perfect. The stuff melts at 385°F and therefore can't be ironed. If put in a dryer at high heat it would shrink, skulkingly. And some users reported that "It's hard to get the smell of sweat out of the stuff. If you've worn it for ten days you may need to wash it twice—with a lemon-scented soap." More serious was the comfort quotient: the simple, extruded, monofilament fabric, though acceptable to most people in low temperatures, tended to feel itchy as things warmed up.

CHIP: I still keep a few of those original Helly Hansen and Patagonia polypro undershirts and drawers—more for reference than for everyday use. They have a plasticky feel and a disturbing tendency to act Velcro-ish with my short and curly hairs—along with vicious butt and armpit chafing. The reason we liked them was that they didn't absorb moisture and instead wicked it away from our tender skins. So we might have been itchy and stinky, but we stayed warm. New generations of synthetic fabrics are more efficient at keeping us comfortable while feeling softer and stinking much less. For the most part, trade names change so fast that even I can't keep track. But the few that catch on seem to last, even as the makers change the fabrics themselves. Capilene (named, I'd guess, after El Capitan in Yosemite), a polyester from Patagonia (the outdoor-clothing makers in California, not the sheep-raising region in Argentina), was soft on the skin and dependably washable, though debates raged about its effectiveness. But the newest version of Capilene soothes all qualms except price. In tops and bottoms ranging from $30 to $70, it comes in four weights—silk, light, mid, and expedition—that are typical of next-to-the-skin garments in general.

Except for light briefs and bras, next-to-the-skin clothing is no longer strictly *underwear,* except in the sense it's sometimes worn under garments called *outerwear.* Some walkers add a pair of shorts, for modesty's sake or to keep from tearing holes when sitting on rocks. Whether you take this to mean that our sense of what's proper is all shot to hell or that practicality has finally triumphed is up to you. In any event, items like synthetic T-shirts and stretch fleece can be worn alone; over a thin, wicking layer; or under a shell. So, as categories go, this one's increasingly elastic.

The compounding of today's fibers and fabrics has grown so madly complex that I'll shy away from microspecifics. But some solid generalities might help. The first is that our clothing is now engineered from the molecules up. A synthetic compound such as nylon or polyester is chosen for strength, resilience, and water repellency. The resulting fiber may then be treated with a polymer, like DuPont's Teflon, to make it repel not just water but also stains and body oils. Or it can be combined with another fiber that has different properties. For instance, a nonabsorbent (*hydrophobic*) core can be surrounded with a highly absorbent (*hydrophilic*) casing to create a wicking fiber that passes moisture without absorbing, proportionally speaking, very much. Another trick is to create not just fibers but whole fabrics with two or more layers of different materials. The original Duofold underwear—cotton next to the skin and wool outside—was an early shot at this. Newer blends—for instance, Du Pont's Supplex nylon with stretchy Lycra—are widely used for outdoor-sports briefs, tights, bras, and shorts. Other successful skin snuggers from Du Pont are Cool-Max and ThermaStat (see also Socks, page 89).

New fibers combined with intricate weaving and knitting techniques now yield relatively thin fabrics with, for instance, a wicking inner face of one material, a stretchy matrix of another, and an outer layer of a third that blocks wind or repels water. To deal with the ever-present stink factor, some next-to-the-skin fibers incorporate chemicals such as zeolites that can either prevent odors from being absorbed or some, like n-halamines (stabilizers for chlorine compounds), that wipe out funk-brewing bacteria. Which leads me to speculate that someday instead of pumping water through a filter we might just strain it through our underwear.

Utterly new for regulating skin temperature are *phase-change* materials. One such material now on the market is Outlast, tiny beads of wax encapsulated in plastic. How does this stuff work? When a solid melts, the molecules break loose from their regular pattern and begin to circulate freely. The process of overcoming the bonds between molecules in a solid state requires a great deal of energy. A calorie, by definition, is the heat needed to raise 1 gram of water 1°C. But raising that gram of water the 1° from ice to liquid takes 80 calories. This energy hump is called the *heat of fusion*. When the liquid is cooled and solidifies, the heat is released. Since wax can be formulated to melt at a temperature just below that of the skin, there's no doubt that it can store body heat and release it. But the amount of heat needed is proportional to the total mass of the wax. The problem is whether a sufficient mass of wax can be placed in a fabric to make a real difference. Various phase-change materials are being tested at Colorado State University, and I've asked the researchers for some numbers rather than the high-velocity sales pitch and flashy diagrams the company hands out.*

The next big thing in your pants might be polyethylene glycol. (Automotive antifreeze/coolant is either ethylene glycol, which is toxic, or propylene glycol, which is less so.) Developed by Tyrone Vigo, of the U.S.

---

*For the few who care about such things, the equations describing changes in heat all contain "mass" as a term, e.g., for the phase-change process:

$$\text{HEAT TO MELT} = \text{MASS} \times \text{HEAT OF FUSION}$$

So the effectiveness of the wax beads depends on their weight. While I can see how enough beads could be mixed into the foam that lines a boot to do the job, it's hard to see how this could be accomplished with fibers woven into socks or underwear. But I'm ready to be surprised.

Department of Agriculture, polyethylene glycol is a polymer molecule shaped like a spring. It also acts like one, extending its coil as it absorbs heat or tightening to release it, for a temperature-moderating effect. It can be formulated to act at different temperatures. Being hydrophilic, it also draws water quickly away from the skin. Tom Lister, of the patent holder Wisconsin Global Technologies, claims that fabric bonded with polyethylene glycol not only moderates temperature but is nontoxic, antimicrobial, odor-free, anti-static, anti-wrinkle, and non-shrinking. Coming soon to a backpacking shop near you.

But good old natural hemp, which owing to antiquated laws can't be grown for fiber in the U.S., is gaining a following. It apparently can be grown with much less environmental damage than cotton and is quite rugged, though somewhat coarse in texture. Both pure and blended, it's showing up in shirts, shorts, pants, and accessories from companies like Seattle's Manastash and Portland's Deep E Company.

In the midst of synthetic miracles, wool is also making a comeback. John Gans, the head of the National Outdoor Leadership School (NOLS), tells me that the only natural fibers they stock in their retail shop are socks made of wool. SmartWool socks (page 92) are well known for their comfort and durability, and now the same company is resurrecting wool for long underwear. The top-grade merino wool is processed to remove the parts that cause shrink and scratch. After that, the fibers are coated with something or other, to replace the smelly-but-effective natural oils. The result is a soft, springy, itch-free knit. Merino signifies a breed of sheep with notably soft wool. Lamb's wool is, of course, from lambs, who are only young once. *Virgin wool* (having actually herded sheep, I'll bypass the usual joke) is the first shearing, softer than what grows out afterward—but the fineness varies markedly according to breed. Virgin merino wool is doubly soft. *New wool* is anything that hasn't been used before. *Reprocessed wool* contains mill scraps, recycled blankets, and the like, so the fibers are cut or broken, making them stiff and itchy—best for felt clogs and pac-boot liners. Despite being unable to stand regular wool against my skin (I break out in a rash) I tried a prototype pair of SmartWool longjohns. Their first outing was a winter solo on snowshoes in up-and-down country, with a full pack.

On that trip in the Snowy Range, I wore the midweight Smart-Woolies for four days straight—sans itch. It snowed 8 inches, then blew like the devil. After which, it was sunny, sweet, and clear. The lows were around 10°F, highs about 40°. Given that trip, and some shorter ones, my impression is that the SmartWool longjohns are at least as comfortable and unodiferous as the best synthetics, perhaps more so. They aren't as rugged, though. After a year, the parts that stretch—cuffs and knees—have developed holes.

But back to the problem at hand. More than getting cold, my problem is building up such thermonuclear heat on the uphills that I get sweat-soaked, and eventually chilled. What's going on? When my skin gets warm, the first thing that happens is that the capillaries open up to circulate more blood, recycling the excess heat: this is called the *aerobic stage*—the best stage to be in while exercising. If the increased circulation doesn't lower my skin temperature enough, my sweat glands kick in, to cool me down by evaporation. When liquid water changes state and becomes vapor at the surface of the skin, a tremendous amount of heat is lost: the *heat of vaporization* is 540 calories per gram, nearly seven times as much as the heat of fusion required to change ice to a liquid. It's also five times as much heat as it takes to raise water from the freezing point to the boiling point.

If the layer next to my skin sheds all this heat, I'll cool down fast, maybe too fast. The champions of SmartWool claim that it balances moisture transport and absorption in a way that quickly cools the skin, keeping it in the aerobic phase, without releasing all that heat to the outside air. Which is precisely what the synthetic phase-change materials are intended to do. The box my SmartWoolies came in shows two thermographs comparing heat loss from a layer of wool and one of polypropylene. Wool wins, of course. But there's not much unalloyed polypro around these days. And as the new generation of multicomponent and phase-change synthetics lopes onto the field, who knows?

Some fabrics, like the zeolite-impregnated ZeO_2 from Mountain Hardwear, have qualities like odor-resistance and wicking particularly suited for next-to-the-skin wear. Others in this class are Malden Polartec 100 fleece, in both regular and chamois-like microfiber versions, and Polartec Power Dry. While intended for use as a base layer, these mid- and expedition-weight garments can be worn alone, or over a lightweight base for insulation. Some, like Malden Power Stretch, of 60 percent polyester, 30 percent nylon, and 10 percent Lycra, lend themselves to a variety of uses. A lightweight pile, Power Stretch has a glossy, wind-cheating, abrasion-resistant nylon jersey side and a bum-cuddling polyester velour side. Tights made of it, for instance, can be worn with the fuzz next to the skin as a base layer, or reversed over lightweight underwear to insulate. But that takes us well into the second layer, where most convective insulation comes from

Fleece and pile.

Traditionally, *fleece* is what covers a sheep and *pile* is what that unlovable critter leaves behind. For backpackers, though, they both mean warmth in varying degrees.

COLIN: Fleece and pile garments are mostly made of polyesters: the fiber is stiff and springy (in technical jargon, "has a high modulus") and therefore holds the fabric in a lofted position that effectively traps dead air, the prime insulant.

As a backpacker's word, "pile" demands some definitions. It's often used, generically, as I have so far used it, to encompass a group of fabrics that includes "fleece" and "bunting" as well as a different end product known specifically as "pile." All three fabrics are made from the same base—a rather thin, dense knit that looks like terry cloth. First, this base passes through a "napping" machine: a series of rollers with very sharp wire wrapped around them (hooked and straight wire alternating). The wire picks out and rakes up the loops on one side of the "terry cloth." The result is a fluffier but still fairly dense fabric: "fleece." Fleece napped on both sides is called "bunting." (Polarfleece and most other backpacking fleeces are buntings.) To make "pile" you subject single-sided fleece to further processes. A "napper" machine with very sharp, straight-wire "brushes" frees and combs out the fleece's entangled surface. Next, the heated cylinders of a "polishing or ironing" machine make the fibers stand erect—and stay that way. Finally, a "shear" machine cuts off wild and uneven fiber. The resultant "pile" is a very open fabric, five times as thick as the terry-clothic base. At present all piles used in backpacking garments are single-sided and about half an inch thick.*

Piles and fleeces have been around for many years (in carpets, warm-up suits, and teddy bears, for example), but only a couple of decades ago were they introduced as backpacking clothes—by Yvon Chouinard, founder of Patagonia.

At first Chouinard and others used only pile—in the narrower sense of a one-sided, sheared fabric. It filled the bill admirably. The durable fabric makes rugged clothes with a life span still undetermined. Because of its resilience you suffer no cold patches at such pressure points as elbows or knees. The fiber's high conductivity means that when you put on a pile jacket you experience an immediate sense of warmth—"like slipping into a bed with flannel sheets," says one aficionado. (For less positive words on the quality of its warmth, see page 521.) Polyester wicks almost as efficiently as polypropylene (and various treatments and processes have

---

*Different piles may undergo variations on these processes. But that doesn't alter the basic distinctions between fleece, bunting, and pile.

I'm indebted to Malden Mills of Massachusetts for the information on fabrics, and to the 3M Company of Minnesota for basic facts about fibers.

My informant at 3M suggested that "in turning to pile as an insulant we have in a sense circled back to beginnings. Long, long ago, men wore animal furs, and furs are essentially natural piles." More accurately, of course, piles are synthetic furs. But it's a nice thought.

greatly increased its wickability), so the open-structured fabric dries out very quickly. If it gets soaking wet you can take it off and wring it out, and even while your body heat is drying it out the stiff, springy fibers retain their loft and you remain at least reasonably warm. ("You only need one experience with a wet down jacket," a certain mountaineer told me, "and you'll convert to pile.")

In other words, pile may be less efficient, weight for warmth, than new, dry down, but unlike down it's always functioning at or close to optimum. That's why it quickly caught on among boaters and especially kayakers, among fishermen (it doesn't compress to uselessness under waders), and now among backpackers—notably those who haunt soggy places. Pile also dries quickly, of course, after washing. And you can wash it easily—and repeatedly, to the point where down would simply give up—without causing harm. That makes it perfect for kids: if they wallow in dirt you just throw the jacket in the washer; and if they roll in the snow it will, I'm told, "be dry before you go brush it off."

Polyester pile (and fleece) has a rather high *fiber friction,* and you may experience some difficulty in slipping your arms down the sleeves, especially if you're wearing a chamois shirt. This is an old difficulty with other fibers: hence satin linings in formal suits. Nylon pile offers less friction than does polyester pile and retains its shape rather better (all piles stretch somewhat with use and then tend to fit better). But nylon pile is a somewhat less efficient insulator than polyester. So is acrylic pile, which once dominated the overall pile market.

Though very good indeed, those first-generation piles fell short of perfection. They compressed very little and therefore tended to take up a lot of room in your pack. Because of their open texture, most of them gave very little protection from wind. And the pile's lack of elasticity meant that jackets required ribbed cuffs and waistbands to prevent warm air from bellowing out. The trouble with this arrangement was that the polypro ribbings sucked water from the pile and dried very slowly. They were the only reason ever to put a pile garment in a dryer. And dryers—especially large commercial ones—can raise problems. At 350°F polyesters "cook": colors change, and so does the very nature of the fiber. (Some suffer damage at temperatures as low as 120°.) So if you must use a dryer, stick with the LOW or DELICATE setting. Beyond that, you really have to "blow it" to damage pile.

With a few exceptions, early pile was hardly fashion-plate stuff. And because pile garments were worn with the "roughed up" surface inside, to hold air better, the unattractive unbrushed surface was what the world saw. What's more, wear and washing tended to make the surface "pill," or generate little balls of fluff. To reduce pilling, the outsides of some piles were resinated—but that made them "boardy." All in all, no one would accuse pile of beauty. Some called it plain ugly. And that's where fleece came in.

Double-sided fleece is good-looking stuff. (Recent improvements have markedly reduced the pilling that it, too, used to suffer.) And because general-use "soft goods" now loom large in the turnover of most mountain shops, there's a tendency for makers and retailers to recommend fleece jackets as good garments for both town and backcountry. Up to a point, they're right. Fleece can indeed do both jobs. But it won't do as good a backpacking job as pile: the material is denser and therefore a less efficient insulator, ounce for ounce; and while it wards off the wind rather better (not a crucial factor, as we shall see), its density means it breathes less well and therefore has a narrower range of use. Worse still, dual-purpose garments tend to be designed with one and a half eyes on fashion and therefore to be heavier, more expensive, and less functional than they should be for the backcountry.*

CHIP: I first saw synthetic fleece for backpacking duds when I worked at Trailhead Sports in Logan, Utah. On fondling a prototype Synchilla pullover, I (loyal to my pile jacket) informed the Patagonia rep that the stuff would never catch on. Why? Because it looked too much like baby pajamas—the kind with embroidered bunnies and the feet sewn shut. He just laughed. And 20 years later, Patagonia racks up $182 million in annual sales, much of it from fuzzy, fussy fleece.

Being thus humbled in matters of prediction, I'll take a run at the current state-of-the-fleece. Patagonia's original Synchilla Snap-T is now made from recycled plastic bottles, and more fleece garments ought to be. A lot of the fleece used by Patagonia and others is made by Malden Mills of Lawrence, Massachusetts. A family-owned firm that continues—

---

*Fashion is always fighting function. And the bruises show, all the time, on all kinds of garments.

It is backpackers and climbers, presumably interested only in function, who "legitimize" the garments. They are the ones the ads feature, stalwarting on Everest. But the ads are often aimed at the general public—and the general public wants something that can be worn in town, even out to an informal dinner. Add the soft-goods orientation of today's mountain shops and it's easy to see why pile and down jackets come "styled" and hoodless, why rain jackets sprout unnecessary, percolative pockets . . . and so on down many lines.

One designer long ago told me, "Frankly, it's years since there's been a down jacket on the market that was really made for backpackers." And the current trend with fleeces is to reduce their pilling (a purely cosmetic flaw) by shifting to tighter knits with less nap—a trend that fights, head-on, the functional demand for maximum insulation.

No wonder retailers report a stream of hard-core backpackers and climbers who complain, "Why is there now so much goddamn stuff that's fashion-oriented?" But then, it always was a sad, sad world. Let's have a drink.

despite a major fire and rebuilding process—to thrive in its original location, Malden Mills is committed to "quality, to long-term relationships with customers, and to workers and the community that helped build the business." It also has a crack research-and-development team. In some cases, Malden Mills works with clothing makers like Patagonia and Lowe Alpine Sports to develop new fabrics. This is done under agreements that give the clothing maker a year or two's exclusive run with the new textile, after which Malden can place it on the general market. That's why new fabrics show up first under high-end labels in specialty shops and a few years later cover the whole map, from L. L. Bean to Wal-Mart.

Using Malden as our map—as far as fleece goes—here's a rundown of some recently availables for the insulating layer.

Lightweight fleeces like Polartec 100 are a good insulating layer for active pursuits, like carrying a pack up mountains or ski mountaineering. Generally, this type of fleece stretches in one direction, is not particularly windproof, sheds a bit more fuzz, and pills more quickly than the heavier grades. Used for pullovers, vests, and tights, it's often doubled up for collars, cuffs, elbows, knees, and other high-wear spots. Despite that, it's not fragile and is comfortable as hell.

Polartec 200 is standard-weight fleece, used for year-round pullovers, vests, and hats and for cold-weather pants. Besides the ubiquitous two-faced fuzz, some midweight fleece is now made with microfiber, to give both a fuzzy and a chamois-like face, with more wind resistance and in some cases antimicrobial properties. Bi-Polar fleece is not for people with severe mood swings. Instead, it has a pill-resistant outer side with a fluffy shearlinglike inner. This type of fleece, with the addition of a hidden barrier membrane, is called Windbloc. It didn't catch on at first, but is growing in popularity for vests, hats, and particularly for gloves. My first try with Windbloc was a pair of Lowe Alpine gloves that I sized up as good for skiing. I took them on a winter solo in the Wind Rivers to use as liners and ended up leaving my mitten shells in the pack. I've since added a Windbloc vest to my armory. (Windstopper is the Gore equivalent.) Like most midweight fleecies, these can be worn as an outer layer or under a shell.

Real fleece (i.e., from sheep) reenters the field both in 100 percent merino or lamb's wool for jerseys, vests, and pullovers, some washable. It also shows up in blends with Lycra (for tights). A company called Ibex in Woodstock, Vermont, is beating the natural-fiber drum hard enough to draw considerable notice. Schoeller has come up with a wool-nylon blend called Skifans that is light, tough, windproof, and sort of water-repellent; Ibex uses it in a range of clothing that gets raves from those in the raving business. My recent experience with the SmartWoolies suggests that we shouldn't write off sheep quite yet—as sources of fiber, that is. Schoeller also makes synthetic Dryskin Extreme, a layered fleece that wicks, insulates, and repels water. Cloudveil, a Wyoming outfit, uses it in the classy Serendipity Jacket (1 lb. 1 oz., $240) and Symmetry Pants (1 lb. 2 oz., $199). The advantage of this stuff is that you can use it as your outer layer in anything short of a downpour.

Back to Malden: Polartec 300 Series fleece is mostly used for zip jackets and vests, like Lowe Alpine's Aleutian 375 jacket and vest. With a close-cropped outer and shearling inner, Polartec 300 resembles the pile that we started with but is lighter and warmer.

At present Malden's cutting-edge fleece (forgive the mixed metaphor) is Polartec Thermal Pro, with mysterious hollow interior "pillars" that increase insulating capacity without adding weight and bulk. Still in the way-exclusive realm, it shows up in Lowe Alpine's technical Core Jacket and Core Vest, both with nice pockets and strategic panels of Power Stretch.

It's also used in Patagonia's new Regulator fleecies, which come in three weights. The reviewers at *Backpacker* like them extremely well: "Warm, soft, nonabsorbent, and virtually indestructible," says equipment editor Jonathan Dorn. "After using three Regulator jackets, I no longer equate the warmth of fleece with its thickness," says Southwest editor Annette McGivney.

"Three jackets?" says Chip Rawlins, who intends to wait for the booming and zooming to pass, and then (after the price drops) to take an unhurried look.

Outer shell material

COLIN: A shell acts as both windbreaker and rain jacket. At present it's usually made of some-waterproof-breathable-Tex or other—which we'll discuss under Rainwear (page 537).

A few further notes on the three-layer system:

As promised, we've delineated a simple, idealized system. It will often prove adequate in that form. But it's wide and pleasantly open to modification. If you like to wear a cotton T-shirt when moving in warm weather you're free to do so with no more penalty than an extra 3 or 4 ounces—dry weight, that is: soaked and wrung out, it weighs over a pound. But remember to take off the sweaty T-shirt before you bundle up in "the system"; otherwise, the wet cotton will nullify the wicking warmth of underwear and pile/fleece. If habit or tradition dictates a wool shirt or even a thin down vest, well, that's fine too. I still often take a thin wool shirt for halts, and even around camp. But once again you must guard against damp wool fouling up the wicking system. In bitterly cold weather you can, of course, add compatible layers to the system over your insulating jacket: a sleeveless pile or fleece vest (pretty damned bulky) and/or a pullover of some sort, with a deep-chested or full-length zipper for versatility (and ventilation).

I've deliberately concentrated so far on upper-body protection. Under normal backpacking conditions your prime consideration should be head and trunk: if they are warm, and reasonably dry, you'll likely be comfortable—as long as you keep moving, anyway. Old-style clothing— even shorts—will take care of your legs. But really low temperatures may demand full three-layer leg protection.

As addenda to the system or even possibly as replacement items, there lurk in the wings both old reliables like down and several "high-tech" materials. But in order to understand how the new materials work we had better pause for a look at

The fundamentals of insulation.

The ideal insulator for clothing has to meet demands different from those made on an insulator for sleeping bags (wherein the sleeper maintains a roughly constant metabolic rate). The clothing insulator must be able to cope with radical metabolic changes: when the encasee is sitting still it must, as in a sleeping bag, retain all possible heat; but when he's active it must draw the heat off, or at least allow it to escape.

The achievement of these already conflicting tasks is further befouled by the existence of four different kinds of heat loss, and therefore four kinds of heat barrier. The percentage of loss by each route, far from being constant, varies according to the channels open at the time.

Convective heat loss—the most common form—occurs when air (or, occasionally, water), after contact or near-contact with the body's surface, moves away and carries heat with it. Under normal conditions, convection accounts for the highest percentage of the body's heat loss, and most heat barriers are therefore convective: they encapsulate the body in a layer of dead air, an excellent insulator. Convective heat loss is measured by the *R factor*, familiar to anyone interested in insulating a home.

We've seen how pile, enveloped if necessary by a windproof shell, acts as a convective barrier. Down or synthetic substitutes such as Polarguard or Hollofil work the same way. Ditto Thinsulate, wool, et al.

Well-designed convective barriers are flexible: when you sit down and button up they keep most of the warmth in; as you become more active your increased body heat tends to drive warmed air out through the porous material; and before things get unpleasantly hot you begin to unbutton or unzip.

Evaporative heat loss comes from the conversion of moisture on your skin into vapor: the latent heat required to bring about this change is drawn from your body. That's why we sweat: it's the body's mechanism for shucking excess heat. See heat of vaporization, page 509. It's a very efficient method—the one we use in refrigerators and air conditioners.

But sometimes—as when we sit down after heavy exercise in sweat-soaked clothing—evaporative loss becomes undesirable and uncomfortable, even dangerous (page 509).

Fortunately, efficient modern wickers virtually prevent evaporative heat loss—by removing moisture from the skin before it vaporizes. (For the wickers' role in preventing loss from insensible sweating, see Vapor-Barrier Clothing, facing page.)

Conductive heat loss occurs when heat passes directly from the body into a stationary medium (air, water, fabric) that's in contact with it and at a lower temperature. Conductive loss is generally minor. But if you fall in a cold lake you'll lose heat almost wholly by conduction to the water surrounding you (though some will be convected away by moving water), almost none by radiant heat and absolutely none by evaporative heat. In very cold water the conductive loss may be so rapid that you soon die.

Radiant heat loss occurs without warming of the air through which the heat passes: transfer occurs only to solid objects. The sun heats the earth and other planets by radiation: sunlight doesn't warm the air directly, only by heating the soil or other solid ground objects, which in turn warm the air by convection. That's why the air is much hotter 1 inch above sunlit soil than it is 5 feet, or 5000 feet, higher.

Radiant heat loss from the human body is usually minor. But when other channels are closed, that can change, radically. If a naked man stands still in a room at the same temperature as his body, two-thirds of his heat loss may be by radiation. But in practical backpacking situations, radiant heat loss tends to occur not directly from the skin but from the fabric next to it: the body heats the fabric by other channels and then, if the next layer offers direct pathways, the fabric radiates heat outward. (Direct pathways may exist, though: hold a batt of Polarguard up to the light and you can see through its holes.)

Radiant heat loss is prevented by reflective barriers: they turn the heat back toward the body. That's fine in sleeping bags, because you want to conserve such small amounts of heat as you're generating. But it's the opposite of ideal in clothing. When you're sitting still and in the greatest need of heat conservation you're generating very little and the reflective barrier has no useful work to do; but when you're active and producing a lot of surplus heat and the problem is to dissipate it, then reflective barriers work hard, turning back toward the body heat that is not wanted there—except perhaps in the most intensely cold weather.

And that, thank God, is all we really need to know about the theory of insulation.

Vapor-barrier clothing

In outline: vapor-barrier (VB) clothing forms a system designed to conserve the heat loss due to "insensible sweat"—a constant seepage of moisture out onto the surface of the skin that we are unaware of but that occurs independently of internal or external temperatures and continues when we're at rest, including sleeping. The mechanism's apparent purpose: to keep skin moist so that it won't crack or chap.

The difficulty with VBs is "sensible sweat"—the normal, obvious moisture that sweat glands secrete when we get too hot. Its purpose: to cool the body by removing unwanted heat through evaporation (page 509). Solution to the obvious overheating and soak-wallow problem: matching armpit zippers, or "pit zips," on all garments. See page 543.

The basic system consists of polypro underwear (not always necessary) and a thin but impermeable jacket; also, for wear outside them, a pile jacket for conserving warmth when you get cool and a rain jacket for when any wind blows. *All,* remember, with matching pit zips.

I used VB clothing for years and still do occasionally under the right conditions; but although the system has—or at least had—true-believer boosters who see it as the Holy Grail, most people disliked it. And today, except for some VB clothing by Stephenson-Warmlite and VB socks for high-altitude or polar conditions (from Black Diamond, in four sizes, $19), about the only VB items sold are liners for sleeping bags.

Given this market dearth, the long VB section in the last edition no longer seems justified. Space constraints. And if the truly curious want something more than the brief summary above, we can only refer them to *Walker III,* pages 386 to 390—if you can find a copy. Not a wholly satisfactory solution, we know. But who said this was a perfect world?

Traditional versus new systems

Will the new clothing systems—strict three-layer and probable successors—make traditional backpacking wear obsolete tomorrow?

I doubt it. For one thing, we are creatures of habit. Beyond that, we rightly tend to favor things we've learned to trust. By their very nature, new systems are still used mainly by an avant-garde—and leaders usually run about five years ahead of their pack. Then there are economics: someone with a good, expensive, traditional backpacking wardrobe is unlikely to rush out and buy a radically new one just because he hears or reads that it works rather better; and many people who backpack only occasionally will no doubt continue to make do with the most suitable of their everyday informal garments (though some of the new stuff is already becoming "everyday"). I'm also willing to bet my bottom layer that many converts will still take along shirts or other old-favorite garments for use when the weather smiles.

CHIP: But since the previous edition of this book, the tables have turned: synthetics are the backpacking standard, while (with the notable exception of socks) natural fibers like loden wool and Ventile cotton are worn mostly by a privileged minority. Since I tend not to tear stuff up, I still have some "traditional" backpacking clothes that will serve for comparison and a bit of trend fuddling besides.

Weight. My old wool mountaineering sweater weighs 23 oz., while my Polarfleece zip pullover weighs 17 (6 oz. less). My original (circa 1984) Moonstone Gore-Tex parka weighs 32.5 oz., while the Lowe Lightflite (waterproof/breathable) Anorak I now use for hairballing weighs 10.5 oz. (22 oz. less). (For definitions of *parka* and *anorak,* see page 543.) My marvelous Marmot Down Sweater—really a coat without a hood—weighs 22 oz., while the GoLite Coal parka I used on recent winter trips, insulated with Polarguard 3D, weighs 15 oz. without the hood (7 oz. less)—and only 18 oz. with it. My outdoor wool pants weigh 18 oz. and my favorite Polartec tights, 10 oz. (8 oz. less). Underwear: A wool-cotton midweight top is 13.5 oz., while a Mountain Hardwear ZeO_2 polyester Zip-T is 9.5 oz. (4 oz. less). For comparable synthetics, the net saving so far is 47 oz. or nearly 3 lbs.: no contest.

Also, as Colin observes, a lot of outdoor garments are "overbuilt"—for instance, if you're layering you don't need linings, zippers, drawstrings, pockets, collars, and cuffs on every layer. And if you choose your layers to work together, according to the landscape and season, you can be shockingly comfortable with about half the weight of a haphazard selection of outdoor clothes.

Durability. The best synthetics come close to being indestructible though nothing yet made seems more indestructible than top-grade wool. Careless washing and drying, rather than normal use, seems to be the downfall of both. So it pays to be persnickety—after the trip, when you roll into town, don't let your goofy partner do your wash (or that pizza and beer might cost you a couple hundred bucks in ruined clothing).

Ease of care. Synthetics—*nolo contendere.* Though hyper-intelligent wool blends win out in some cases—particularly for socks.

Performance when wet: For the most part, synthetics triumph, particularly the newest multicomponent types. Moreover, when layered with due attention to their performance characteristics (wicking, breathability) synthetics are far less likely to get wet in the first place, and will dry out much faster when they do. To confirm this, I soaked two comparable underwear tops (both of which I like), wrung them out and whirled them around until the drips stopped coming, and then weighed them. Afterward I hung them up in the shade (37 percent relative humidity at 62°F) and weighed them at intervals. The synthetic top dripped two to three times as much water, and I was able to wring more from the lower edge.

	SmartWool midweight merino	Mountain Hardwear ZeO₂ polyester Zip-T	Difference in water weight (oz.)
Dry weight (oz.)	10.5	9.5	—
Wringing wet (oz.)	24.0	20	3.0
2 hr.	22.0	17	4.0
4 hr.	18.0	14	4.5
6 hr.	16.0	12	3.0
8 hr.	13.0	10	2.0
10 hr.	11.0	9.5	0.5
12 hr.	10.5	9.5	0

That is, while the synthetic top dried faster, both dried overnight. Despite lab tests on single synthetic fibers that show only 1 percent absorbence, when those fibers are knit into clothing they trap considerably more water. After all, steel doesn't absorb much water either, but a bucket holds quite a bit. In clothing, synthetic fibers dry considerably faster with body heat. But SmartWool socks seem (based on my chaotic and nebulous impressions) to have superior wicking qualities and comfort in boots (see page 92).

Bulk. Down triumphs, and new ultralight and microfiber shell fabrics allow the down to loft like cumulus clouds on a hot afternoon. At comparable warmth, synthetics stuff 30 to 50 percent larger. And repeated tight stuffing and washing flattens synthetics out more quickly—Polarguard seems to be farthest along at combining long life and compressibility (though I haven't personally tested Primaloft or Lamilite at length). For a given warmth, top-grade wool and synthetic fleece are just about equally compressible, while pile outbulks both. The new micropile (e.g., Power Stretch) can be jammed and crammed to some extent, without harm.

Cost varies like crazy. And since the key Gore patent expired, it's even less predictable. Since the publication of *Walker III,* there's been an overall turnaround—good natural-fiber outdoor clothing now tends to be pricier than synthetics. On the one hand you have Ibex selling a retro-chic Stornoway Parka, in 100 percent Ventile cotton for $245 (the first parka I bought, circa 1969, was Ventile cotton; soaked and frozen, as it often was, it weighed about 6 lbs.), while Red Ledge has a TH-4 synthetic waterproof/breathable seam-taped Thunderlight Parka for $50. At skin level the SmartWool 100 percent merino Zip-T runs $82, while the excellent Lowe Dryflo Zipneck top is $55. The big factors up front seem to be research and development, multiplied by labor costs. A generic fleece jacket sewn by "outsourced" Third World contract labor will cost a third or less of what a fashion-color micro-multi coat from a trendsetter does. And (sad to say) the seller of the sweatshop knockoff is probably taking more profit. The key is not to confuse price with value. I have a Patagonia shelled bunting vest that I got in, like, 1983 (bargain-binned because it was Stark Red rather than Tuscan Umber). It's still in good shape, having faded to a more tolerable hue, with the *original* zipper. Eighteen years, and I wear it *mucho:* winter, spring, summer, fall. That's value, pilgrims.*

COLIN: *Comfort range.* The breathability and nonabsorbency of synthetics mean that they can keep you "in thermal equilibrium" under a wide range of temperatures and activities. (And it's worth noting that more back-packers are now operating in early spring and again in very late fall, when the summer hordes have hibernated back into cities. Also that the new clothing works fine for skiing.) VB systems, even when constantly adjusted, seem to pose difficulties for many people in the temperate weather that houses most backpacking. Traditional wardrobes stand somewhere between these extremes.

CHIP: *Comfort against skin.* The plasticky, abrasive feel of synthetics is long gone and so is the hook-and-loop problem. New micropiles, like Malden Power Stretch, are less disconcertingly clingy than silk and older synthet-ics: you can walk for hours without having to haul them out of your bum-furrow. While the stiff, early laminates were hopeless next to or even near the skin without extensive linings, some of the new flexible shell fabrics, like Gore's Activent or Lowe Alpine's Triplepoint, can be worn over light-weight underwear for strenuous hiking with little or no moisture buildup. Being prone to frequent overheating and heavy sweating, I fully expected to get steamed—and was amazed, and happy, not to. On buggy summer eves, I even wear Lowe Alpine shell pants (in Lightflite, the pre-decessor of Triplepoint Ripstop) over bare legs without stickiness. Such material changes have led me to change my thinking on the three layers somewhat. In cold and difficult conditions, rather than putting a thin layer on my skin, piling on insulation, and then covering the whole with a shell, I now tend to reverse the two outer layers. Wicking underwear is still the basis. But the new multifiber fleeces with wind-blocking mem-branes and durable water repellency make a strikingly good outer layer, even when it's raining or snowing a bit. In practice, the body heat I pro-

---

*For those who see temptation lurking, I here state that Patagonia has neither given nor even slightly discounted a single piece of clothing to me for purposes of this book. I contacted them about a few ultra-new things to test and was roundly snubbed. And, to put it bluntly, they've long since priced themselves out of my range. Even so, I admire their work.

duce on the move keeps the wet from penetrating my outer layer (except perhaps under the yoke and pack). Without an outer shell there's far less moisture trapping going on. When I stop, and am no longer pumping out heat, on goes the shell. Despite initial worries, I seem to stay warmer and drier. After all, arctic mammals aren't covered in Gore-Tex, but in layers of fur. And I think of the shell as a portable burrow.

Another tack, in cold or blustery weather, is to wear a wicking base layer (thickness depending on how cold it is) under a thin, flexible shell. When you stop, throw on the insulated coat or vest to keep from chilling down. This puts your lofty insulating layer outside the shell—you stow it when you head out again. Given modest and shelter-seeking halts, this keeps your insulation relatively dry, since you aren't continuously steaming it up from the inside. I came up with this system on strenuous trips in the Wind Rivers, when our science loads were grindingly heavy and it was hard to keep from sweating, unless we stood absolutely still (not an option). But when we'd reach the sampling site or our base camp and dump our packs, we tended to chill hard. Not wanting to squash my dry down vest between sweaty longjohns and a steamed-up shell, I'd slip it on the outside: Bingo! The formidable Mark Twight recommends this tactic in his book *Extreme Alpinism,* which, despite his focus on high angles and altitudes, has some razor-sharp ideas for backpackers.

Given their balance of water- and wind-resistance, plus breathability, microfiber shells are perfect for this layer-swapping approach. They are, however, cacophonous in high winds. Last winter, climbing a peak on a howling day, I felt like I was being Uzi-ed by my microfiber hood. But it was simply blowing too hard to do without it. So I finally slipped a fleece headband over the bastard, and it ceased fire.

COLIN: *Quality of warmth.* Both VB and three-layer systems, though they can keep you comfortably warm and may even at times make you too hot, never seem to generate the "toastiness" that you often experience, even sitting still, when wearing a wool or cotton shirt and down jacket. Almost anyone who has tried both new and old systems will know about the difference. I recently confirmed it by ringing the changes on all three systems within a few minutes one windless evening when the thermometer registered 32°F. Yet I've never seen the difference mentioned in print, let alone described. The closest I can come is to say that "plastic warmth" rarely if ever seems to move beyond a mere absence of coldness, while "old-fashioned warmth" can and commonly does become a positive, glowing radiance—a luxurious sense of well-being, a sensual pleasure.

It's interesting, I find, that at least some textile researchers recognize the difference. But although they like hell want to understand what goes on, so that they can do something about it with improved synthetics, the causes remain unknown. Naturally, the researchers will not admit, officially, that old-fashioned warmth is necessarily "better" than plastic warmth. And I guess it could turn out that the latter is more calorie-efficient or something. Still, sensual pleasure is sensual pleasure. And you presumably go backpacking for pleasure. But pleasure can be measured in many ways, and one of them is by the lightness of your load.

So the future remains sweetly uncertain. My guess, as I've said, is that traditional clothing based on cotton and wool and on down or synthetic fills will refuse to fade away, especially in dry, temperate places. But the new systems seem likely to make heavy inroads, especially where backpackers can sometimes expect bitter cold or prolonged rain. And they'll prove irresistible to congenital equipment freaks. As for your personal choice, you will as usual have to balance the conflicting claims of old and new and then judge which works best for you, and when. To balance, that is, likelihood of getting wet against quality of warmth, to weigh the claims of versatility, and to heft your own standards of weight, cost, and perhaps bulk. I only hope you now know enough to go out and make up your own cotton- or polyester-pickin' mind.

The woman's wardrobe

CHIP: Since women are increasingly and independently active as backpackers, we consulted a qualified subcommittee. For 12 years I was married to a dauntless outdoorswoman who helped a lot with testing and comments. Also invaluable to us have been the combined wisdom and experience of the many women who've written letters in response to the previous *Walker*s (for names, see the Acknowledgments on page 825), and also those many others who kindly answered questions for this one. Rather than trying to shoehorn their contributions under this one heading, we'll continue to place them under the relevant ones. If Colin and I still get things wrong on occasions, Great Mother forgive us.

Besides word of mouth and magazine reviews, up-to-date wardrobe information can be had from catalogs such as Title Nine Sports and from Internet retailers such as *MountainWoman.com.*

COLIN: By all means consult one of the books by and for women backpackers (page 24 and Appendix IV). See also Underclothing, next page and page 530. And page 556 for keeping your loved ones warm.

An item of advice from the experienced subcommittee that I coopted for the first edition seems worth repeating. She found that by taking along one attractive garment ("something that makes me feel good") she helped sustain her beleaguered sense of femininity.

It's now time, I guess, for us to rummage through

THE CLOTHES CLOSET, GARMENT BY GARMENT.

First, a few general considerations:

For most people, choice of clothing is largely a matter of selecting each individual garment carefully for warmth in relation to weight, for toughness in wear, for versatility in use, for performance when wet, and, in rainwear, for water resistance. Also, I suspect, in response to those obscure promptings, probably aesthetic, that lurk, shadowy and often unsensed, behind most of our apparently logical choices.

On purely practical grounds, it pays to choose clothes that are dark but bright. Dark, so that they won't advertise the inevitable dirt. And bright (especially red), because you can hardly walk away from camp and leave gaudy garments lying on the ground or hanging up to dry; because if you're brave enough to go out and walk during the hunting season, a plain-as-a-pikestaff exterior may save your life; because in case of accident, worn or waved clothing may attract rescuers' attention; and because a small splash of red or orange can crystallize an otherwise amorphous color photograph.

But it has been suggested, with reason, that if backpackers chose inconspicuous clothes (and packs and shelters) it would reduce the visual impact of man on today's semicrowded wilderness. A set of outer garments in some obscurantist shade of brown or green or gray is certainly worth having for those occasions when you don't want to be seen: fishing, photographing game, keeping out of people's way, trespassing.

Whether you call it underwear, inner wear, next-to-the-skin wear, upper-mid-wear, or outer-upperwear, for simplicity we'll title the next part

Torso housings.

Underclothing. A few people still use old-style fishnet underwear. These rather unlikely looking garments are a lot of big holes tied together with string. At least, the original models were.*

---

*During World War II, I was for a time with a British unit that had been issued true fishnet vests as special mountaineering equipment. Eventually the unit was converted to cliff-assault duty and moved to a Cornish fishing village. Our string vests astonished the fishermen and their wives. For several years they had, as experienced net makers, been producing these strange devices for the war effort, in great secrecy, but they had never been able to guess what the peculiarly shaped nets were used for. No one, when sober, had seriously entertained the notion that they might be some kind of clothing.

Today fishnet underwear is hard to find. Wiggy's still stocks "string-ies"—but they're nylon (tops, $37; bottoms, $33). But whatever the fabric, the holes are the important thing: they are what keep you warm when you want to keep warm and cool when you want to keep cool. To keep warm you button up all outer clothing and close neck and wrist openings. The holes of the fishnet weave then hold air in place close to your skin, and your body heat soon warms this air.

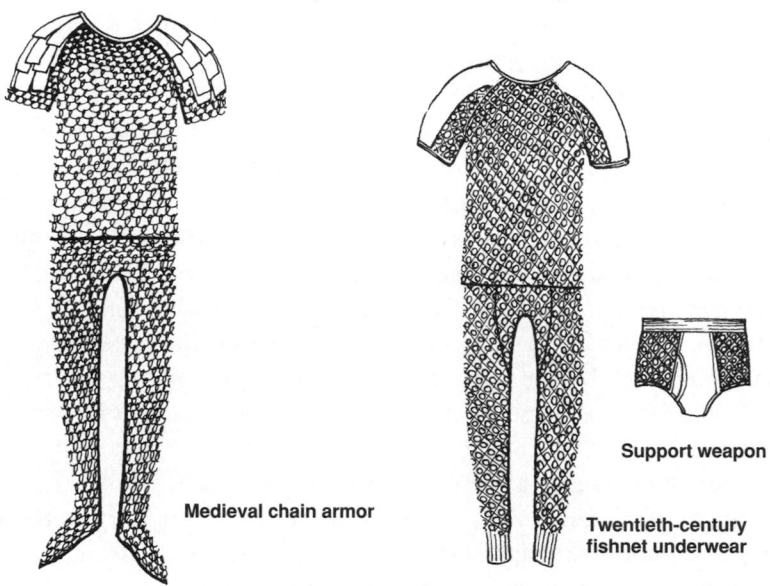

Medieval chain armor

Support weapon

Twentieth-century fishnet underwear

To cool off, you simply loosen the neck opening of your outer garments and allow warm air to escape. Loosening wrist openings speeds up the process. If you get too hot you unbutton jacket and shirt and allow all hot air to be replaced by cold. When you're unbuttoned like this, air circulates freely, and then a string vest is far cooler than conventional underwear. To get full two-way benefit, wear outer clothing that unbuttons completely down the front and carry a scarf so that you can block off the passage of air at your neck.

CHIP: My one set of net underwear chafed me badly—under the shoulder straps and back panel of my pack and in the all-important territory of my groin. Even lacking fishnet undies, women friends mention chafing around their breasts as a problem on backpacking trips, against which sports bras are the weapons of choice. Given the variations in size and shape (of both women and bras) no single type has emerged as the undoubted favorite—and preferences are fierce. Most sports bras are blends of Lycra and wicking yarns such as CoolMax. Sleeveless tops, whether extended-length sports bras or looser tank tops and camisoles, are also gaining popularity not just as a single layer for hot days but also as underwear—for warmth and to lessen the wear and tear of backpack suspensions.

Synthetic T-shirts are now a unisex staple. Nearly as dear as my own skin is my shirt-for-all-seasons, a Lowe Alpine Dryflo crewneck T (6 oz., $39). The piqué knit feels dry and light, and the dark gray-green is such a good solar absorber that I can rinse out the shirt before lunch, give it a good wring-and-swing, and drape it over a boulder in the sun. With a flip or two, it's dry by the time I finish eating. I have only one, and wear it so much—not only for backpacking but for midwinter skiing and mid-August runs down desert rivers—that it's showing fuzz where the sternum strap buckles. The rest, though, is still perfect. And of course, Lowe Alpine just discontinued it. For times when I need to change, a Patagonia silk-weight T (4.5 oz., $32) stands in. Both have proved rugged beyond their heft.

Next up in thickness and warmth are long-sleeved crewnecks: one of lightweight Capilene, one of SmartWool (page 92) in 100 percent merino. For medium-cold, these are my base layer and they're also nice shirts-in-general. On sunny days, I ruck up the sleeves (probably why the rather snug cuffs on the SmartWool top developed holes) and use a bandanna around my neck to prevent sunburn.

Then come the zip turtles, some full, some mock. If I lost everything, a zip turtleneck would be the first replacement item. My Zip-T of midweight green Capilene (9.5 oz., $43) is hanging in after lo these many years, but seams blew out at the side and cuffs and needed restitching. A new midweight, Mountain Hardwear's ZeO$_2$ Zip-T (9.5 oz., $49), is softer, wickier, pricier, and so far indestructible. When the clouds roll in, a turtle slips easily over a synthetic T-shirt. On midwinter trips, it makes a solid base layer that covers nearly up to my ears, warding off both cold and sunburn, and also unzips to vent. Linda, a longtime Capilenista, also likes both the fit and the finance of Recreational Equipment MTS (Moisture Transport System) stretchies, 92 percent polyester and 8 percent Lycra (at a reasonable $23–$32) in colors like Hyacinth and Zen Leaves. When I asked her if that would help sustain her beleaguered sense of femininity, she said, "Huh?" Dressier still is the Zuni Rose Zip-T (Wild Roses, 9 oz., $65) in Malden Power Stretch, with a pantherine cut, double side seams, and an elegantly rounded collar, in black. The distinguishing mark of new outdoor clothing by women designers is that it combines ruthless functionality with reasonably good looks.

Sloping off the stretchy knits, at times it's nice to have a woven-cloth shirt with retro features like buttons, long sleeves and cuffs, breast pockets, and a flop-over collar. For slip-on warmth, Colin likes fine wool or Viyella, a wool-cotton blend. For different reasons, I keep an eye out for 100 percent cotton twill with a sky-high thread count. Not only does cotton's aggressive chilling power work wonders for those burning afternoons but also *mosquitoes can't penetrate it.* Over the years cotton twills have spared my all-too-mortal husk many gallons of DEET and probably 7 to 10 million festering mini-welts. Columbia makes nice cotton-twill shirts. There are Supplex nylon lookalikes that last longer and dry faster, but most won't stop a skeeter beak: I watch. Patagonia cotton canvas shirts are also skeeterproof, but they weigh a ton. So on high-summer, deep-desert trips, I take a cotton-twill shirt that's ready to give up the ghost. And it does. If I was a shirt, that's how I'd choose to die.*

Pullovers. Since we're rummaging my gear closet, I might as well say that there are no longer any wool sweaters in it, though I have a couple for around town. My pullover range begins with an expedition-weight polyester zip turtle from REI (14 oz., $42) that I seldom wear these days. The successor, a Sage Creek Polartec 100 pullover (10.5 oz., $75) that I got two years ago from Wyoming Wear, now ranks as my most-worn insulation. It stuffs with room to spare in a fanny pack, so it's gone backpacking, skiing, fishing, paddling, biking, and just as often to the post office and grocery. On winter days, working on this book, I've worn it around the house. It also makes a dreamworthy pillow. Though now slightly pilled and balding in spots, it's in excellent shape considering all I've put it through. I find it adequate for all but the freezingest days. For cold-cold I switch to a Patagonia zip Synchilla pullover (17 oz.) that has a light nylon lining in front for windproofing and a zip breast pocket. The current Pata-quivalent is the Marsupial (16 oz., $80), while the newest big thing is their R1 Flash Pullover (10 oz., $98) of Regulator fleece.

Jackets. My pile jacket is a museum piece: navy-blue, with pit zips, a really high collar, deep hand-warmer pockets, and matching inner pockets for drying out gloves, etc. The shoulders are silvered by the alpine sun, and the pile is matted but still springy—or stubborn. I've donned it for cutting brush, working on cars, and even crawling under the house to solder pipes. But it won't die. And I've had it so long that if I get a new pile coat, it'll be jealous. So I'm thinking about sending it back to Sierra Designs for new zippers.

A new and somewhat hybridized category is the bi-component knit thingie with shell. I'm not sure what else to call it. The leader of the pack, as far as I'm concerned, is the Marmot DriClime Windshirt (11 oz., $125). I was a grudger at first, because it looked like a damn golf jacket (not sure why I hate golf, but I do). But the wicking liner wicks, the long tail warms, the CoolMax underarm mesh fights off swamp chafe, and the

---

*Microfiber is at least theoretically mosquito-proof. I recently got an ultralight microfiber shell (also windproof and water-resistant) that might replace the cotton-twill shirt in my kit.

shell fabric wards off meteorological slings and arrows. It has a nice collar and a zip front pocket, too. I wore it walking, skiing, snowshoeing, and paddling on windy spring creeks. In summer, it could take the place of a fleece top and shell. You can also layer it under a shell parka or insulating jacket. It does give pack waistbelts a thousand tiny legs, but so do all of the floating-shell synthetics. In all, though, it was probably the most adaptable garment I tried.

What's not in my closet? The emerging rage seems to be Malden's Polartec Thermal Pro (see page 514). This is used in Lowe Alpine's technical Core Jacket (1 lb. 6 oz., $129) with strategic panels of Power Stretch. Roughly the same fleece goes into Patagonia's new Regulator jackets, the R2 (1 lb., $120) and the R3 Radiant (1 lb. 6 oz., $134). *Backpacker* gave Regulator fleece their 2000 Editors' Choice Award. Another *BP* award winner is the Ibex Icefall (men's, 1 lb. 2 oz., $225) and Cirque (women's, 14 oz., $198) jackets, made of Schoeller Skifans, a wool-nylon blend. But I don't wear insulated jackets much, having a greater liking for

Vests. If you choose a jacket with no sleeves, the world is your pit zip. A vest keeps your breadbasket warm and your back covered while letting your arms swing free. The stark-red Patagonia shelled bunting vest (17 oz., priceless) I've worn for centuries has already been held high as an icon for value. Recently, I tried a Windbloc fleece vest from REI (10.5 oz., $45) that I've gotten attached to: it's teddy-bear brown, warm for the weight, and has that open-cockpit look. If I started feeling expeditious, I'd get something like the Lowe Alpine Core Vest (13 oz., $99), made of Malden Thermal Pro fleece and Power Stretch. But my other favorite vest is down-filled, which oozes us into

Quilted clothing (down- or synthetic-filled).

COLIN: When Western man woke up a few decades ago to the idea of taking a feather out of the birds' book and making down-filled clothing as well as sleeping bags (the Chinese apparently tumbled to the idea long ago), the result was so much more effective than anything he had used before that it revolutionized polar and high-altitude exploration. Men could operate with safety and even comfort where they once had to battle simply to exist. Even in kinder environments they quickly accepted the breakthrough with gratitude.

Then, a few years ago, synthetics began to challenge down as quilt filling—at least in part because the cost of down rocketed ruinously (page 460). As with sleeping bags, synthetic fills in clothing have steadily gained ground and will no doubt continue to do so. Although still less efficient insulants than down, warmth for weight, and less able to bounce back to full loft after many compressions, they remain markedly cheaper as well as nonallergenic—and, most important, they become far less fatally impaired when wet. For a time Polarguard led. Then it was Hollofil or Quallofil. Now Polarguard 3D and Primaloft battle for the lead. Others, capable of being sewn or blown into baffled garments even more easily, seem on the way. But for some years "quilted clothing" mostly meant "down-filled."

Down clothing is a special case of torso housing (not to mention leg and extremities housing) because it isn't really compatible with the new systems and therefore has to stand in unabashed opposition; because it has come to epitomize backwoods clothing and also old-fashioned warmth (page 521); and because a good, unimpaired down garment is still the warmest for weight by a significant margin.

Down's weakness lies in the word "unimpaired." A down jacket dampened by rain or heavy sweat loses appreciable virtue; soaked, it becomes almost useless—and is the very devil to dry. Grime can also reduce efficiency. So, eventually, can wear and tear and repeated washing. And washing a down garment is a pain in the tub (page 491). These draw-backs also apply, in varying degrees, to synthetic-filled garments. Yet, although the much cheaper pile is better on all these counts, quilted garments' advantages (including their much greater compressibility) will surely keep them around.

Unfortunately, down jackets have suffered the same Detroit syndrome as other backpacking garments: they've undergone creeping growth. Virtually all of them have for years been made for polar or mountain expeditions or for working on the Alaska pipeline or, almost as bad, for fashion-conscious urban users. So from a backpacker's point of view they've been overbuilt and overstuffed. For three-season backpacking you rarely need a bulging, Michelin Man, expedition-type jacket. And a light ripstop or taffeta shell will save almost half a pound over a more fashionable one that's designed to resist showers in town but is unnecessary for backpacking, when you'll be carrying raingear of some kind. Nor do you really need the rash of pockets beloved by town users, or heavy two-way zippers.

Four decades ago I carried on my length-of-Grand-Canyon trip a simple, hoodless jacket that weighed just 1 lb. 1 oz., and although snow fell during the first two weeks I don't remember that I was ever cold. For years such stripped-down models have been almost unobtainable—though you could sometimes find sleeveless, lightweight "vests" that weighed around ¾ pound. Fortunately, there seem to be signs, as with other garments, of a return to lighter, more genuinely serviceable down jackets.

Overengineering aside, quilted garments seem, like sleeping bags, to have attained a design plateau of excellence. Fine jackets now come from virtually all the established bag makers, and again there is generally little to choose between them. If you select from a reputable catalog or store a model that seems to meet your requirements of the moment, and examine its workmanship as for sleeping bags (page 481), you're unlikely to go far wrong. But it might pay to check certain details.

Strive for a single rather than two-way zip—and not only because of lightness and expense. In a warm store you may be able to align double sliders fairly easily, but in the field—always in a storm and often in fair weather, even in daylight and when you're not wearing gloves—the damned things generate wills of their own. And rarely if ever, except perhaps in town, do you need or even want to ventilate by unzipping from the waist. But when I tried to get a single zip put on a jacket being made for me by an experienced manufacturer he said he had none of the right length in stock because the overwhelming demand was for double zips on down jackets.

When pervestigating a new jacket don't overlook closure arrangements at wrists (Velcro or snap fasteners are fine) and waist. (Avoid models without a waist drawstring or at least a hem through which you can thread one: because you can't trap warm air inside, the jacket loses half its effectiveness.) Pockets are convenient, but they should add a minimum of weight and not reduce warmth. Above all, I would suggest—though by no means everybody would—that you buy a jacket with a hood (see heat loss from head, page 469). Snap-detachable hoods are probably the most common. But I have nightmares of mine being whisked away over a cliff in a storm, and I much prefer the safe, built-in kind. When not in use it hangs harmlessly out of the way, and if you're worried about sartorial elegance back home you simply tuck it inside. I'm told that it's no big deal to sew on a detachable hood without loss of insulation.

Prices for down jackets are now backbreaking. A simple sleeveless vest often runs from $85 to $150; a good general-duty jacket, perhaps $150 to $225; a bulbous expedition-type "parka," over $400.

CHIP: I think of this as the puff layer. For a birthday years ago, Linda gave me an unglamorous forest-green Woolrich down vest (13 oz.) that's still an essential part of my kit. Most often I use it over fleece tops and/or lightweight shells, rather than under, to ward off the chill while making camp in the blues of evening. Folded inside a fleece pullover, it makes God's Own Pillow. The other quilted stalwart is a Down Sweater (22 oz., now $189) from Marmot's last days in Colorado. The collar has vertical tubes, so it stands up rather than squashing. The down is lofty and the shell fabric light. The cuffs snug with Velcro. The pockets open upward with a zip, and the front zipper is backed with a subtle draft tube that's stiffened in front so it won't snag. The lining is black (wahoo!) and there are two big glove-drying pockets inside. All in all, it's the very soul of serviceability, while managing to look rather dashing in electric blue.

The synthetic puff-layer rivals right now are Polarguard 3D and Primaloft. The GoLite Coal parka I used last winter is filled with Polarguard 3D that's quilted to the lining at 6-inch intervals with a floating outer shell of ultralight nylon ripstop. It weighs a mere 15 oz. without the detachable hood, and 18 oz. with (and costs $195, with a silicone-impregnated stow sack). It lacks some of the features the comparably priced Marmot Down Sweater has, like a draft tube, adjustable cuffs, and interior pockets, and the loft averages 1.5 inches (to the Down Sweater's 2 inches) so it's not as warm. But the lightness and synthetic-ness make it better for hinge-season extravaganzas, when wet is the rule. I've also used it for winter camping in moderate (i.e., down to 0°F) conditions. I was wary of the light-gauge zippers, but they're holding up, and the lining is a Cremation-of-Sam-McGee yellow that warms me up just looking at it. Polarguard 3D puff-layer coats and vests can be had from Marmot, Patagonia, and others. Primaloft jackets, vests, pants, and suits, with Pertex Microfiber shells are the specialty of Canada's Integral Designs. The Integral Designers claim that Primaloft loses no insulating value whatsoever when wet, so I'll have to try it sometime. Wet.

A puff subtype consists of insulated garments made with the same materials, but without the quilting, using the floating shell we saw in ultralight synthetic sleeping bags (page 465). This boosts both the insulating capacity and compressibility while letting you slither around freely inside. My GoLite Coal parka is made this way. Patagonia's Puffball Pullover (13 oz., $145) and Vest (8 oz., $105) are likewise good examples. Like most of the above units, they have matching pants, or as Colin insists on calling them—

Leg housings.

COLIN: Nowadays I tend to walk without underwear. The practice brings you into closer conformity with the Second Law of Thermodynamic Walking: "Give your balls some air."*

---

*The first law, of course, reads, "Walk is heat and heat is walk."

A valued critic writes: "I think it would be fair to warn your readers that if they're going to go without underpants they should be careful about the pants they are wearing. I once went on a weeklong trip with no underpants. I was wearing Patagonia canvas standup shorts, and four days into the trip I had one sore tail which got a lot sorer before the week was finished. Baggies, or something smooth, would have been fine, but between the rock and your ass you don't need another hard place."

CHIP: I dispense with briefs altogether. But at times the suspended parts rub against my inner thighs, which suffer first redness, then actual loss of skin. Regular applications of talc help, but so does a pair of light synthetic sports briefs. I can't imagine wearing boxer shorts backpacking, but microfleece boxers do appear in catalogs.

Being exempt from the Second Law, women friends tend to wear briefs as a matter of course on backpacking trips. Special outdoor models, in a bouquet of synthetics, are widely sold.

Despite jokes about "Lycra Lizards," tights have long been favored by runners, bicyclists, and ski racers of both sexes, and are often seen in the wilds. There have been studies showing that the support and compression of tights assist muscles under stress. It took me a while to overcome a twofold dislike of tights—first for their clinging feel and second for what the cling revealed: they made me feel nude and spraypainted. But for skiing and hinge-season walking I now wear Insport ski racer's tights of polypro and Lycra (from which I excised the miserable stirrups) that are surprisingly weatherproof over synthetic underwear. Of a grim and uncompromising gray, they landed in a bargain bin ($12 on sale, and a mere 7 oz.). I also tried some ultralight black thermal leggings of 65 percent DuPont ThermaStat and 35 percent Lycra (now discontinued) that were unexpectedly warm under my racing grays—but damnably fragile. Those accustomed to donning pantyhose may have no problem, but after a week on the trail mine had developed so many toe holes and groin gaps that I looked like a soloist for the Royal Ballet of Hades. There are tougher tights in varying weights, from nylon/spandex lizardslicks to mammalian microfleeces and piles. For reasons I don't need to explain, you should avoid wearing tights that are even remotely flesh-colored (see page 78).

Some leg housings serve equally well as underwear or outerwear. Malden Power Stretch 50 has a glossy nylon face and a brushed polyester inner—delicious stuff, says a biologist friend who likes the familiar-but-not-grabby fit of her Sedona Rose P-tights from Wild Roses (8 oz., $65). The "P-" designation signals a discreet coil zipper that gives the wearer increased freedom to. Zippers, flaps, and similar conveniences appear on tights and pants from makers like Juno Rising, Mountain Hardwear, and Patagonia. Women experienced in their use tell me that one layer is a breeze, two requires some expertise, and with three they'd rather just drop their drawers in the time-honored fashion. In which case, wearing the P-layer next to your skin means you don't risk ultimate exposure. (There are also full drop-seats available.)

While men do have the advantage in this one respect, even as a boy I hated those awkward front overlaps that tend to make you pee on your fingers. And my now-favorite longhandles, of midweight Mountain Hardwear ZeO$_2$ (7.5 oz., \$44), have no such frontal tomfoolery.

COLIN: To most backpackers, pants still mean things that come down to your ankles. But for years now there seems to have been a sensible drift toward

Shorts. I have long been a wholeheartedly bigoted devotee—so much so that I often find myself wearing shorts until the temperature drops into the low 30s or the wind develops a really keen cutting edge. At least once I've arrived at a 14,000-foot peak in shorts. But I hasten to add that there are not too many places and days you can do such things in comfort. Some years ago I wore shorts up 5000 feet of snow, on a cloudless April day of icy winds, to the 12,000-foot rim of Fujiyama and paid for my stupidity for the rest of the week every time I tried to force red, raw legs into the steaming-hot baths that are the only form of ablution in Japanese inns, and which *noblesse* apparently obliges you to refrain from tempering with cold water. But I remain an unrepentant shorts man.*

I have for years preferred my shorts to be brown, or some other color that hides the dirt, and to have a built-in waistband, reasonably adjustable so that it can conform to a midriff that, like many people's, fluctuates in response to prolonged packing of heavy weights and to such other variables as food, love life, and tennis. I also liked my shorts to have pockets that are strong, numerous, and tailored to my fancies (preferably two hip pockets, two sidepockets, and two ticket pockets at the waistband, front—one for bookmatches and the other for fire- or stove-priming scraps of paper). In theory, I maintain these preferences; in practice, as we shall see, I seem to be retreating from them.

Shorts of any kind allow much more efficient ventilation than long pants do. And I long ago reached the point at which I feel, or imagine I feel, dragged down by the restrictiveness of long pants. Fortunately, real cold seems to override the sensation. But several times I've started out on bitter mornings in longs and have realized later, after the day had warmed up, that I was making meager progress simply because I was still wearing them. A change to shorts has usually been enough to get me moving well again.

---

*Shorts may at times even help reap you rich and unexpected rewards. Once, at a busy Tennessee trailhead, as I sat on a tree stump lacing my boots, preparing for a walk up onto the Appalachian Trail with a companion—a New Yorker born in Venezuela—I noticed a group of tourists eyeing me. I was wearing ordinary corduroy hiking shorts, chamois shirt, and beard. One of the tourists edged toward my companion and asked, in a hushed, almost awed voice, "Is he *really* a Tennessee hillbilly?"

Really pesky insects might, I guess, drive even me to give up shorts for a while.

I used to regard corduroy shorts as best: they're warm and absorbent, wash well, and wear prodigiously—provided the fabric is good quality. The quality depends on both the sturdiness of the backing and the way the cotton plush is run through it: typically, each strand of plush is attached in a simple V; but superior stuff is double-threaded in a W. Many people, I'm told, look at cords and dismiss them as "too hot"; but, provided leg openings are wide, preferably to the decency limit, I find them plenty cool. They're also tough (in the backcountry you always use unpadded chairs, often granite-rough) and wind-resistant, and provide the sort of padding I find comforting if not essential under the hipbelts of most heavily loaded packs, at least during the first few days of a trip. Still, there's no denying that they're the devil to dry out, even from sweat.

In recent years I've moved toward synthetic-fabric shorts, such as Baggies by Patagonia (about 6 oz., $35; now made from recycled materials). The great advantage of such shorts, beyond their lightness, is the speed with which they dry. Even after crossing a river you simply wade out the far side, shake your fanny, then mince on down the trail. A pair of Baggies even felt great during a weeklong snowshoe trip to 10,000 feet in deep snow but brilliant sunshine, with a 58-pound pack. And I've had no unreasonable difficulty with two areas of initial concern: wear and discomfort from sitting on the backcountry's unpadded chairs; and lack of padding against hipbelt bruising with a heavy pack (though this last may be largely due to the excellence of my Gregory hipbelt [page 139]).

CHIP: Either Colin transmits some kind of shorts virus or it's in my genes. Because I wear shorts in all but the deep-snow moons. Mostly, my layering system is a) shorts; b) gaiters with shorts; c) underwear bottoms, gaiters, and shorts; d) sleeping bag. While I carry shell pants for protection from blowing snow or tundra mosquitoes, they spend most of their time rolled up in my pack. My lifetime favorites were from Mont-Bell, of Supplex nylon, I think, with a ventilating cut, deep pockets, and that undefinably perfect feel. After countless sewings-up they reached the point of indecency, so I gave them an honorable burial last year.

I've tried to fill the aching void with others. A pair of Wyoming Wear Zephyr Shorts (6 oz., $21) in micro-ripstop are the best for hydromancy. They're way-short (4.5-inch inseam) and fast-drying. They have deep slash pockets of soft mesh and a flapped-and-zipped cache for things you can't afford to lose. I like the built-in web belt (preferable to a drawstring). And they dispense with the useless back pocket—like a balcony on a bungalow—too often found on otherwise-perfect shorts.

More commodious and highly crafted are the Mountain Hardwear Pack Shorts, with a 7-inch inseam (mine: 10 oz.; men's or women's medium: 8 oz., $75). Given the sobering price tag, I just looked them over with a laser gaze. The cloth is a two-ply Supplex nylon twill, soft yet durable, treated with the same ZeO_2 process as their funk-defying underwear. The "seamless conical" waist eliminates the bunch-up found in most shorts. Elastic draws up the casing around the built-in web belt, rather than puckering up all the layers together (smart). The belt has a low-profile cam buckle. There's a zip front fly. The pockets are unique, as pockets go: deep front scoops with mesh drains at the inside corners (smart), with the right one hiding a zip security pocket actually big enough to get your hand inside. The left pocket hides a lanyard and clip for keys, pocketknife, etc. The rear pockets transcend my dislike: rather than useless little squares, high up, they're big scoops with a hand-accommodating slant, closed with Velcro tabs. On the trail, I seldom use them except for a map, a bandanna, or a ball cap. But they're perfect for shuttling water bottles from creek to camp and keeping sundries out of the dirt. Well and good. But the hidden splendor is Micro Chamois—kitty-fuzz polyester that lines the waist and crotch—ending not only testicular chafe (and the woman's equivalent) but also the savage gnawing of a pack waistbelt under a heavy load. Mountain Hardwear does seem to have its thinking cap on. But it's embarrassing to grumble about Patagucci prices and then find myself with $75 shorts. Even if I love them.*

Cyclists started wearing their Lycra bike shorts for backpacking, and some well-seasoned walkers now swear by them. So I've been experimenting with a pair of Outdoor Research Obsidian shorts, of 160-denier Spandura (5.5 oz., $55). The support is nice, though the leg circumference of most stretch shorts (and tights) seems to be calculated for reedy thighs—initially they were squeak-tight and the bottom bands pinched like hose clamps. But they've let up a bit. They dry nearly as fast as bare skin—a decided advantage. But I miss the air circulation of baggy-type shorts—and miss the pockets severely. The problem with skintight shorts, pants, etc. is that if you put anything in the pockets (usually one skimpy little internal pouch) it rubs on you as you walk.

At the other end of the spectrum are the knee-length ultrabaggy

---

*Having pawed through bargain barrels for most of my outdoor existence, my new role in the gear judiciary does give me occasional pause—as it did when I noted the price of those excellent shorts. But I just walked out on a breezy spring day and, verily, they are a functional marvel. Meanwhile, my car, a 1978 Saab that I seldom drive, just attained 24 years of age. It runs beautifully. But the bank says it's only worth $750—the same as 10 pairs of shorts. And I spend a hell of a lot more time in shorts. So perhaps my sense of values is not disastrously out of whack.

shorts affected by pro basketballers, skateboarders, and other fashion cultists. Not properly shorts, they're more like divided skirts. It seems as if they'd be maddeningly flappy for serious walking. (If the wind comes up, tack.)

COLIN: For protecting shorts in rain, see Colin's Kilt, page 549. I have several times thought of carrying this idea a step further, following Thermodynamic writ (page 530) and Scottish precedent, and wearing a kilt of suitable material in lieu of shorts. But almost all women backpackers seem to spurn skirts, which after all amount to the same thing, so I guess hidden disadvantages lurk.

There are, of course, times when you may want to switch from shorts to longs. And catalogs occasionally feature shorts cunningly convertible to longs with zippers or studs or even Velcro strips. But I'm told they never sell.

A pair of breathing rainpants (page 547) or even rain chaps (page 549) do a good job of converting shorts instantly to viable leg housings for semicold conditions, particularly if you also put on synthetic long-johns.

Long pants are still probably more popular than shorts among back-packers. And even if you prefer shorts you almost always need a pair of longs in your pack for cold-day or -evening use.

Ordinary jeans still seem to outnumber every other kind: being cotton, they're very comfortable, breathe well, and are reasonably light—but useless when wet, and difficult to dry. In wet, wool is better, though rather too hot for general use. And now new options exist.

I presently find myself in a state of even greater evolutionary uncertainty with long pants than with shorts.

Except in low desert in high summer, I have for years almost always carried a pair of stout wool-blend whipcord longs, forest-ranger style (1 lb. 10 oz., now around $150). I rarely seem to use them, even on cool evenings, and from time to time wonder just why I carry the extra weight; but occasionally I'm thankful I do (see, for example, page 571). A functionally similar but much cheaper alternative: army-surplus pants. And there are now many other options. Chip will deal with them.

CHIP: For scorching trips, I keep a pair of well-worn cotton-twill pants around—besides coolness on sunburnt skin, they're bugproof. Filson makes great ones, but my present pair are sales-rack scoops (18 oz., about $15). Alas, they've worn so thin that the hole I just tore in the knee may prove unpatchable. Good plain-front khakis can be found in thrift shops (in locales where people wear plain-front khakis, anyhow).

Between the traditional pant-pants and waterproof/breathable shell pants lies a good bit of terrain these days. It's easy to put long legs on a good pair of shorts, so most makers do: Wyoming Wear Zephyr Pants (8 oz., $29) are of micro-ripstop with a water-repellent coating, and roll up to the size of two bagels. The superlative Mountain Hardwear shorts have their counterpart in Pack Pants (15 oz., $110).

Years ago in a bargain barrel, I found some Wild Country guide pants (15 oz.) in a heavy nylon that has prevailed against hell in various forms. Just snug enough to need ankle zips, they have deep zipper pockets that give me peace of mind when operating in steep and snowy locales. The fabric is tough as spun steel, though the seams tend to unravel every few years—they're about due for a stitch-over. Meanwhile, I'm auditioning Outdoor Research Rhyolite Tights (13 oz., $100) in 160-denier Spandura, with 3 pockets, a drawstring, and ankle zips—not as snug as the counterpart shorts, thank heavens. But they have the same tough, quick-drying fabric in an unobtrusive cut: neither arse-chafing nor loose.

If you don't mind scary colors and stripes, thrift-store jogging pants are not altogether bad, but avoid the fashionably baggy kind—unless you enjoy cracking like a banner in the gusts.

Matching the materials in jackets, insulating pants come in a boggling array: fleece, pile, Polarguard, down. For years I used Royal Robbins polypropylene sweatpants, now ragged and melted in spots from excitement with stoves. Since my work involved winter camping I got Helly Hansen bunting pants, but found I didn't use them much. On the move they were too thick, and when I hit base camp I'd usually slip into my sleeping bag. So I gave them to some suffering buffalo defenders on the borders of Yellowstone Park. As a rule-of-leg, besides your own heating capacity, consider whether you're likely to be moving very slowly or to be stopped, without the shelter of tent and sleeping bag. This is often the case on mountaineering ventures—magazine ads show puffily panted ascensionists by the dozens. But what's good at 6000 meters isn't necessarily worth a hell-damn for backpacking. Presently, I take light- and midweight base layers. Depending on conditions, I can choose either one or double them up. Lightweight shell pants top things off. For ice-boxy jaunts, I add Polartec 100 stretch tights (9.5 oz.). That is, three thin, flexible layers rather than a single fat one.

With its tight-knit face and fuzzy-skin side, Power Stretch 150 is a good single layer for cool, windy conditions, or so I hear—by the time I wear out what I've got, it'll be vastly improved. For thicker insulating layers, full-length zippers save your hopping around on one foot like a dingbat. Having seen one person, trying to get out of nonzip fleece pants while balanced on one ski, lose his balance, grab a pack strap, and topple three others, I heartily recommend full side zips.

Belt—or suspenders

COLIN: If possible, buy pants with built-in waistbands or web belts. This is not only a question of weight; any belt is uncomfortable under the waistbelt of your pack. When you go off on packless side trips and, lacking a belt bag (page 181), need something around your waist to which you can attach a poncho-wrapped lunch and a cup and camera tripod and so on, simply use a few turns of nylon cord (page 676).

Suspenders clearly overcome any pack-belt pressure problem, eliminate waist constriction, and increase midriff ventilation. But I suspect that their prime attraction may be an "in" funkiness.

Leg protectors

If you wear shorts you may find that in certain kinds of country, especially desert, you need something to stop your bare and vulnerable lower legs from being savaged by scrub, thorn brush, and cacti. The best protection I've come across is a pair of Ace bandages (that I always carry anyway; see page 681), wrapped puttee-fashion from boots to just below the knees. Or, as Chip does, use tall gaiters (page 82).

RAINWEAR

The pitch of your concern about rainwear will vary according to the places you walk. In southeast Alaska or the Pacific Northwest or, to a lesser degree, New England, the problem looms large and almost perpetually; in desert it does no more than peek occasionally. But all of us have to worry, sometime, about how to avoid getting wet when it rains. And nowadays our rainwear can and should triple as windwear and outer-warmth shell.

Even regarded only as rainwear, no single garment is "best" for all conditions. In fact, there may be no final and satisfactory response to prolonged heavy rain except getting the hell out of it. But when you're backpacking you can't always shelter. So you have to make the best of trying to reconcile apparent irreconcilables: the need to cocoon yourself against getting soaked by external wetness; and the sometimes equally pressing need to ventilate so that you don't get soaked in your own sweat. That's why rainwear has long been the least-efficient part of a backpacker's clothes closet, perhaps of all his equipment. Today it retains—along with boots, maybe—that dubious pennant. But in the last few years we've come a long way, babies.

The efficiency of any rain garment depends on:

- Its fabric;
- Its nature, design, and workmanship;
- The way you use it.

Fabrics

Backpackers and others have long sought the Holy Grail: a fabric that's waterproof but breathes. (Fabric is waterproof, says a U.S.-government ukase, when it keeps out water under a pressure of 40 pounds per square inch—though heavy wind-driven rain seems ignorant of this ruling [not to mention another that stipulates "25 pounds"]. Fabric breathes, I guess, if you can use it to cocoon yourself against rain in warm weather when walking uphill with a pack and still not get rained on by your own perspiration even if you are, like me, one of the sweaters of the half century.)

For a couple of decades most backpacking rainwear was made of woven nylon waterproofed with an inner liquid coating—usually of polyurethane (*urethane-coated*). Such fabrics are light, inexpensive, and flexible and will last several years provided they're dried after use and not overheated. Some alternative and less common coatings offer advantages but are heavier: polyvinyl chloride (PVC; *vinyl-coated*), acrylic nitrile, and neoprene. Most coated fabrics are reasonably waterproof or better, at least when new. But none breathes worth a damn.

Fine-weave cotton fabrics impregnated with various cunning concoctions tend to breathe appreciably better, but they rarely keep the rain out for very long.

All-plastic garments have always looked good to beginners—mainly because they're cheap and seem totally waterproof. But the stuff tears at the sound of a harsh word (so much so that you almost never see zippers on it, or even drawstrings). And cold weather makes it so brittle that it may crack along folds. It therefore tends to get discarded in the backcountry—and has become a hideous source of litter. Beyond all that, it breathes like a corpse.

For many years these were the only choices open to backpackers. But dreams of the Holy Grail persisted. All through the 1960s new miracle fabrics burst regularly on the scene claiming Grailhood—and consistently biting the mud because in the field, as opposed to the lab, they leaked, failed to breathe, or did both.

Then, in 1976, came Gore-Tex.

The heart of Gore-Tex is a thin, white, stretchy, microporous membrane that looks like condom material but was originally developed for surgery, to graft arteries. It's a very light, pliable form of Teflon—a petrochemical polymer called polytetrafluorethylene or PTFE. (Gore-Tex, Helly-Tech, Klimate, Sympatex, and newer versions are known collectively as PTFE laminates.) This membrane has, say its makers, 9 billion pores per square inch, each of them "20,000 times smaller than a drop of water (which makes it waterproof) but 700 times larger than a molecule of water vapor—allowing the material to 'breathe.' " This PTFE membrane or film is bonded to one or two layers of fabric to protect the membrane and make it wearable. A two-layer laminate bonds the PTFE film to an outer fabric (usually nylon). An unbonded lining is sometimes used to protect the membrane. Two-layer laminates are supple and drape well, and the lining gives the garment maker something to which he can attach accessories—storm skirts, drawstrings, and inside pockets—without external, potentially leaky seams. Three-layer laminates incorporate an inner layer of nylon tricot and are normally used without linings. In both two- and three-layer laminates the outer fabric can run from 1.1-oz. nylon taffeta to 3-oz. Taslan. The lighter fabrics save ounces and are cooler (or less warm) but abrade more easily. Heavy Taslan, though it may make the fabric stiff and "boardy," wears better and is warmer (or hotter).

PTFE laminates are windproof as well as waterproof and, as we shall see (page 550), this greatly extends their usefulness.

When it appeared, Gore-Tex was duly proclaimed the Holy Grail. But reports soon began to trickle, then flood, in of leakage through the fabric, not just seams. What had happened, it eventually emerged, was that the surface readily became contaminated in such a way that water droplets in contact with it lost their surface tension and their round, beady shape and broke down into smaller particles that could pass through the membrane's pores. The culprit might be poor laundering or spilled food or plain, earthy dirt; but the most common, almost impossible to avoid, was ordinary human body oils.

W. L. Gore, the makers, hurried back to their lab drawing board and in 1978 marketed a "second-generation" Gore-Tex that they claimed was "incapable of being contaminated" and therefore remained waterproof yet still breathed like the earlier versions.*

For a time Gore-Tex garments also suffered, as does a lot of rainwear, from seam leakage. Applying the necessary two coats of seam sealant was too labor-expensive a task to be done in the factory, and users often evaded or botched it. Then Gore came up with a machine that welds a tape onto sewn seams with hot air and pressure. The tape—itself a laminate of

---

*CHIP: The second-generation Gore-Tex membrane combined the original expanded PTFE film with a second polymer: an *oleophobic,* or oil-hating, material on the inner face that resists contamination by "body oils, cosmetics, saltwater, and insect repellents that could otherwise affect waterproofness."

Gore-Tex film between tricot knit fabric and a hot-melt adhesive—seems in its latest form to do the job. W. L. Gore leases the sealing machines to its licensees, which "allows the machines to be upgraded quickly. . . . Only Gore will match the seam tape, adhesive, and the seam-sealing machines to the fabric type and weight." Factory-sealed garments, now the rule, are certainly a marked improvement. Meanwhile, don't forget that even factory seam sealing, though good, is not perfect. The machines need good drivers. So check all tapes for wrinkles or imperfectly matched edges.

CHIP: A seismic shift in the waterproof/breathable field was the recent expiration of a key patent held by W. L. Gore. Prior to this, few alternatives existed. Fabrics had to be shipped to W. L. Gore for lamination, adding considerable cost. Further, companies using Gore-Tex had to sign a licensing agreement that ensured quality but also limited them in other respects, giving Gore-Tex a lock on the market. Despite the obstacles, competitors did manage to enter the field: Sympatex is commonly used in boots and Todd-Tex (developed by tentmaster Todd Bibler) is proven in his namesake tents, with Lowe Alpine's Triplepoint Ceramic established in the clothing end. But with the expiration of the original Gore patent, makers have announced waterproof/breathable fabrics in a bewildering array. Some of them are no doubt fully as good as Gore-Tex, while others most likely are not. It's hard to tell by looking, of course.

One cue is the series of tests specified by the International Standards Organization (ISO), a body that provides criteria for virtually everything—except perhaps virtue itself. For instance ISO 811 is a test for the waterproofness of fabric under actual use conditions—flexing, folding, and so forth. For this test, 40 pounds per square inch (psi) is a good score for a waterproof/breathable laminate. Another aspect of ISO testing is that the organization audits participating labs and makers, and awards an International Quality Registration: W. L. Gore's number is ISO-9002. Simply, this certifies that the material actually does what the maker claims.*

There are now four Gore-Tex outerwear laminates: two-layer, three-layer, three-layer LTD, and the four-layer Z-liner. Besides the original PTFE laminates, W. L. Gore has also come up with a range of outdoor products: a patented waterproof bootie, glove liners, Dryloft shell fabric for down and other insulating materials, Activent two-layer laminates for strenuous activity, Windstopper fabric and fleece, and a water-based durable water repellent called Revivex.

*The U.S. affiliate is the American National Standards Institute (ANSI). For complete information, try the Web site: *www.ansi.org.*

As far as competing "Texes," some have been around long enough to earn their spurs. Lowe Alpine's Triplepoint series of laminates is very good indeed. Linda's Lowe mountain parka of Triplepoint Ceramic has bumped the Gore-Tex parka from her starting lineup. A Lowe Alpine anorak and pants of Lightflite (predecessor of two-layer Triplepoint) have edged out my trusty-but-venerable Gore-Tex parka and bibs: the Lightflite garments neither leak nor steam up inside. There are still skirmishes along the border, but on the whole it seems that waterproof/breathable fabrics are well on the way to being a semi-invisible aspect of outdoor clothing—like zippers, which were once a revolution in themselves.

Design and workmanship in raingear

COLIN: Design features can be as important as the fabric.

Seams are the Achilles' heel of most rainwear. So the fewer seams, the better, and those that are essential should if possible (which it often isn't) avoid such vulnerable, rain-pelted places as shoulders and upper back.

Zippers also leak. Check and if necessary hand-seal all attendant seams. Full-length parka zippers should have storm flaps. Some makers maintain that they're more likely to work if the flaps are secured by Velcro tape rather than snaps. But an interesting alternative that has passed all tests to date appears in my current—but now old—Gore-Tex parka: the zipper folds around to form a flap and is protected from heavy rain when a line of snaps, with the male components 2 inches from the zipper, is closed. Seems to work.

The short neck zip on anoraks (page 543) is sometimes backed by a V-shaped piece of fabric that allows some neck ventilation but looks like a great drip catcher and I'm told is.

A two-way zip on a jacket may occasionally make ventilation easier, but I doubt that it's worth the drawbacks.

For the pros and cons of pit zips, see page 544.

CHIP: The Zipping News is a polyurethane-laminated model that's claimed to be watertight. Called the WaterTight zipper, it's used by Arc'Teryx for the pockets and pit zips on their parkas and shell pants. They left off the storm flaps altogether, so negative feedback should come in rather short order—if any. At the top of its track, the watertight slider "parks" under a molded "Zipper Garage." But the main front zipper is still a double-flapped heavy-duty type—so the watertight zips might not stand up to the heaviest use. I tried on some prototypes of the Arc'Teryx Gore-Tex jackets (Alpha, Beta, Kappa, and Theta) and was struck by the sterling quality. The cut of their hoods is unique and they fit better over a hat (or a helmet) than anything I've tried. Their stitching and flat-lock seams are brilliant, and the joints in their seam tapes are a series of mini-masterpieces. One finicky friend dug deep for an Arc'Teryx Beta LT Jacket (17.5 oz., $365) and says that it's the best thing he's ever worn.

COLIN: *Hoods.* To me, a hoodless rain garment is an idiocy. Yet some people prefer big hats and high collars. Certainly, hoods can pose problems. Because it seems impossible to make them seamless, they always have leak potential. They also tend to make ventilation difficult. So in light, warm rain without wind it may indeed be better to leave the hood down and wear a hat. But in wind-driven rain a hood is to my mind the only decent protection. As wind protector and warmth provider for the most vital part of your body (page 469), nothing compares with it. It should, of course, be big enough for you to wear at least one and maybe two balaclavas underneath. And it must be designed to pull flush around your face and so keep rain from driving in and dripping down your neck. A good system is an internal storm flap, pulled tight by the drawstring: the best allow you to pull the collar in tight under your chin, so that rain doesn't drip down your neck, or alternatively to leave it standing tall, up to your nose, as protection against wind. A small, flexible peak also helps shed rain. The more protection you get, though, the less vision you're likely to have. On balance, give me the protection. A wide field of view, though certainly pleasing, is not vital in backpacking, the way it is in cycling.

Sleeves in rainwear must be full-cut (raglan type) for free arm movement and longer than in other garments, so that they won't slide up when you extend your arms. The extra length also means that most of the time you can keep your hands protected inside them. Although you must be able to close off the wrists in cold or driving rain you must also be able to ventilate, and the best answer seems to be a simple Velcro-secured strap.

Hems, drawstrings, and storm skirts. Rainwear should always be cut fairly long, because even the best-designed models will pull up a little if you raise your arms. And whether you like it or not, a certain amount of rain will get in under the hem. A drawstring there helps, especially in keeping you warm (when that's what you want). More common, perhaps, is a drawstring at the waist, to allow more freedom of movement. A viable variation that reduces seam and wear difficulties at that crucial circumference is a storm skirt—a ring of fabric, usually nylon, elastic-hemmed, and closable with snaps. When you're not wearing a pack—the belt of which does the job, anyway—it insulates your upper body and keeps snow out yet lets the garment stand clear.

Pockets on rainwear are rarely waterproof. And they add not only weight and cost but also more seams and potential leaks. Yet although you often can't get your hands into them when you're wearing a pack, they're undeniably useful at times—and people seem to demand them. Pockets with Velcro-secured flaps are probably best. Long jackets with waist-level drawstrings or storm skirts may have low side-entry pockets without seams sewn through to the outside: such water as may possibly breach even a baffled opening will mingle more or less harmlessly (provided you don't expect to keep the contents dry) with that inevitable quotient coming up from the hem.

Kinds of rainwear

Remember in choosing any rain garment that it must be big enough to fit with something to spare over the thickest clothing you ever expect to wear with it. Restrictive rainwear is not only uncomfortable: it's likely to increase condensation.

The most obvious torso housing is some kind of *jacket.* It permits free movement yet protects you fully. And because fabric is kept to a minimum it's likely to be light. Old-style, coated-fabric jackets were a snare: you tended to soak in sweat. But Gore-Tex et al. have changed that.

There are two kinds of jacket: parkas and anoraks. *Parka* is an Aleutian word originally meaning "a fur jacket or heavy, long woolen shirt, often lined with pile or fleece, with attached hood." *Anorak* is the Greenland Eskimo name for a similar hooded garment, though it may be made of leather or cloth. But time has worked on language. Today a parka is a hooded jacket of almost any material with a full-length opening, usually zippered, down the front. An anorak is a similar garment without a front opening other than a short neck zipper. This zipper makes it possible to put an anorak on and take it off and also provides some ventilation. But although the garment's simple barrel structure makes it highly efficient as protection against both wind and rain, ventilation can be a problem. And if you've ever stood on a mountain ridge in a howling gale and tried to battle your way up into an anorak, especially one a shade small for you, or if you've taken a soaking-wet one off in order to shed a layer of clothing and then tried to reinject yourself without irrigating everything, you'll understand why parkas are more popular.

The parka's full-length front zipper, no matter how well protected against rain, is always a potential leak line—though the new laminated zippers (page 541) may change that. But a zipper certainly makes ventilation adjustment much easier. And putting on and taking off, even in rain, are relatively painless. On balance, I vote for parkas every time.

And now, with the difference between anoraks and parkas understood, we can consider both garments together, simply as jackets.

The question of whether jackets should have underarm zippers (pit zips) provides a minor backpacking battleground. "If the stuff breathes, why?" says one camp. "The wretched things always leak, too." The opposition replies: "Under certain conditions you need to vent, and the armpits are the place to do it." I agree with those who say that the "small loss of sleeve integrity" that occurs in heavy rain (I can vouch for such leakage) is worth the gain in temperature flexibility. Note that flaps, or the new laminated zippers, may help reduce the leakage. And also that, with the three-layer system, polypro underwear and pile jacket mean that rain invading down a sleeve matters very little: it's quickly wicked out and expelled. But in deciding pro or con pit zips you must strike your own balance. Make sure, though, that if you vote "yes" the pit zips extend only a short way down your torso: you'll be much happier sacrificing your arms to the rain than your ribs.

Current backpacking rainjackets, like other garments, tend to be overbuilt. But you can get lighter jackets, designed for backpackers—more sparingly constructed, often with lighter laminated fabrics. Remember, though, that lighter fabrics mean some loss in warmth and appreciable loss in abrasion resistance.

CHIP: Back to the closet. (Rummage, rummage.) For years I packed a full-featured Moonstone parka of three-layer Gore-Tex with a wicking liner (and matching bibs for Wyoming winters). Built for slithering up couloirs and ratcheting against rocks, it's overbuilt for most backpacking ventures and by current standards grievously heavy: 2 whole pounds. Since then, the vast improvement in wicking layers has made it feasible to use shells that are both light and unlined. My first (circa 1983) was a Patagonia H_2No ripstop anorak (8 oz.) that I seam-sealed and have redoused in many generations of DWR (durable water repellent) treatments (see page 565). Over a wicking layer or two, it still keeps me dry enough for comfort at one-fourth the weight of that bombproof parka. In true downpours, though, it "wets out." But Dame Progress hath proffered fresher fruits: a few years ago I got a Lowe Alpine Lightflite Anorak (10.5 oz., $99). Billed by Lowe "for the high activity mountain user who is prepared to sacrifice total waterproofness for increased breathability and lighter weight," the fabric is a nylon ripstop with a DWR-treated finish and a virtually waterproof coating—in gusty mountain thunderstorms and heavy snowfalls I have yet to get soaked from the outside. And, equally vital—despite being a sweat horse, I don't get steamed up inside. Of course, by the time I wear the Lightflite out (and assuming the survival of Western Capitalism) there'll be far, far better things. I can wait.

Still newer and gleamier are ultralight laminates. I tested a prototype Moonstone vest (6 oz.) and shell pants (8 oz.) of Gore Activent, designed for heat-producing hyperactives. Stacking the deck, I lugged a huge pack over glacial moraines during a chinook that turned the snowpack into Cream of Wheat—mile after mile, postholing on skis, expecting the worst. With no steam-up. So I retried the pants over bare skin and still couldn't achieve an annoying level of condensation. Which, being in a contrary mood that day, I was sort of hoping for.

Another sheathing for the troublesome primate is the "micro-urethane" 1.76-oz. ripstop nylon laminate in the GoLite Newt rainjacket (10 oz., $170). It, too, performs at a disgustingly high level. (Though on the prototype I tested, the internal seam tape had wrinkles and messy joints.) Still ultra-lighter is the GoLite Bark shell jacket, a slithery layer of Silmond 2.4-oz. polyester microfiber (8 oz., $95). Though it doesn't please me aesthetically (the golf-jacket issue), the Bark now teams up with the Wyoming Wear fleece pullover as my most-worn torso housing. In passing showers, water beads up on the outside and rolls off. In a continuous downpour the sky-facing parts wet out but don't really leak except under direct pressure—when I hold a sleeve under a rivulet springing off a boulder I can feel droplets pressing through. But for the most part raindrops bounce off. To work, microfiber should be kept clean and be treated after washing with a durable water repellent (see Nikwax, etc., page 565). Perhaps stretching my luck, I've been using these gossamer swaddles for winter ski trips. And have not, so far, died. Nor even suffered much. (As the 2-pound parka gathers dust.)*

For predictable drenchings and mud-wallows—rain-forest crawls in southeast Alaska—I still pack an old North Face urethane-coated rainjacket with a hood (16 oz.). It doesn't leak and though it has breathing holes (grommets, actually) under a flap, it gets steamy inside as I push through the bush. Another coated standby is the Sierra Designs Microlight hooded jacket (10 oz., $38)—if you know you'll be squeezing through sandstone slots and crashing through prickly oak, why shred a $400 Gore-Tex parka? For muddy, scratchy, thorn-studded occasions a lower-price coated nylon jacket might still be best. But the prices on waterproof/breathable laminates have dipped so sharply that they now compete: Red Ledge has a synthetic waterproof/breathable seam-taped Thunderlight Parka for $50 (I sent one to my brother Chris in Seattle for a winter workout—no leakee, says he).

---

*Given Colin's comment about overbuilding, I got out that parka and shook off the dust—to see what features I haven't used: a) Given wicking underwear, the full liner is extra weight; b) the elasticized, internal storm flap—while great for skiing Rocky Mountain powder, since it keeps snow from drafting up under your coat—is of damn little use for backpacking; c) likewise the two huge, zippered, and storm-flapped bellows pockets, which open at precisely the same height as the waistbelt of a pack; and d) while perhaps good for mixed alpine climbs, the Cordura abrasion proofing on the shoulders and forearms has been of no use for backpacking.

COLIN: *Ponchos*—once popular, now rare—offer certain advantages, especially on trips with low rain risk.

A poncho is a waterproof sheet, 4 feet by 7 feet or a little bigger, with a head hole and hood in the middle. In good backpacking ponchos the hole is placed somewhat off-center and the longer rear section covers your pack. At least, that's the theory; but if a wind is blowing don't expect too much overlap from theory into practice. Most hoods can be tightened flush around your face with a drawstring, but the rest of the sheet hangs down like a shroud and in a high wind attains a will of its own—though snap fasteners on the edges allow you to make rudimentary sleeves that may help keep the shroud from flapping too wildly. Some heavier models have a drawstring at the waist that not only cuts down the flappage but also holds in warmth—too efficiently on occasion. A length of nylon cord around your waist will do the job almost as well, though its rubbing may damage the waterproofing.

Ponchos are simple and therefore relatively light and inexpensive. They are also, except for the hood, seamless. And they are the only garments you can wear over your pack. This means you always achieve good ventilation (often, far too much) and so avoid the worst condensation problems. They're therefore still made of coated fabrics. (Note that, worn under or without a pack, ponchos can very definitely cause condensation.)

Ponchos are clearly not ultra-efficient rain-defeating devices, but they're versatile. Those snap fasteners along the edges help, and so do the grommets sometimes put in at each corner. (I always had at least one other grommet—and probably three or four—inserted along each long side; the short sides rarely have a wide enough hem to take even a small grommet.) With these simple fittings, a poncho can be much more than a waterproof garment. It can be a windbreaker—especially useful when a thin down jacket is the only warm garment you have with you. As we've seen (pages 433–36), the grommets allow you to turn it into a wild assortment of roofs and sidewalls and cocoons that will ward off snow, rain, wind, or sun. With two ponchos snapped together by their fasteners you can build a big ridge-backed shelter. Under certain conditions, you may be forced to use your poncho as a groundsheet, but in such cases don't expect it to remain waterproof for long. On packless side trips or on short walks from home or car, a bundled poncho secured around your waist with nylon cord makes a useful belt bag for lunch and oddments, especially convenient if there's a rain threat. Cunningly molded to the landscape, it can form a washbasin (page 564). Finally, it will help waterproof your pack contents during a river crossing (page 688) or make a floating bundle of your clothes and other necessaries if you're crossing without a pack (that is, will act in lieu of a white plastic sheet, page 690).

Weights run from over 2 lbs. for a rubberized surplus-type poncho down to as little as 10 oz. for a nylon or plastic one. A tough, coated-nylon poncho may cost as much as $45, though a less fancy and less durable one may run only $20; plastic horrors—eminently tearable, appallingly rich in litter potential—sell, unfortunately, for as little as $3.

Cagoules are full-cut, knee-length, sleeved capes with hoods. (The word is French and originally meant "a monk's cloak" or "penitent's cowl.") Cagoules are made primarily for mountaineers, who often have to make emergency bivouacs: you can if necessary draw your knees up inside the long "skirt" and seal yourself off by pulling tight on a drawstring that runs around the hem. If you carry a companion footsack-and-carrying-bag of the same urethane-coated nylon fabric you're in even better shape. Wiggy's makes a classic nylon Oxford cagoule with a draw-corded hood, waist, and just-  above-the-knee-length skirt in four sizes, $140. Campmor sells a 15-oz. "backpacker's" model for $40.

As day garments, cagoules are good at keeping rain out, heat and sweat in.

CHIP: For protecting your legs, *rainpants* have edged out ponchos, cagoules, batwing chaps, and similar artifacts. Logic says that rainpants should be long enough to lap over your boot tops, but if you use gaiters (I do), you might prefer a shorter, close-fitting cuff with elastic and/or a zipper. For many years coated nylon was most popular and is still a reasonable choice: Sierra Designs Microlight pants (7.5 oz., $30) are a good example, with deep sidepockets, a zip rear pocket, a drawstring waist, and shock-corded cuffs with cleverly hidden cord locks to cinch them down.

My problem with coated nylon pants (besides the incessant *sweesh-sweesh-sweesh*) was that my thighs are absolute heat pumps. To hike any distance in coated rainpants was to die, with sweat funneling down both legs and into my boot tops. So for years, I seldom put on any coated shell pants unless for some reason—rowing a raft—I had to sit unsheltered in the rain or snow.

Another rampant rainpant gremlin was that coated nylon doesn't stretch, so in order to accommodate knee flex and butt thrust, the pants had to be loose. This, in turn, not only led to flapping and sweeshing but also to condensation. But with the ongoing rush of laminates, as well as recent price dips, waterproof/breathable pants are taking over the field. A rather basic pair of Red Ledge Thunderlight TH-4 pants (7.5 oz.) with a drawstring waist and snap cuffs now costs only $35. They aren't a match in terms of features for top-notch brands, but the seams are taped, the fabric hasn't leaked (so far), and it seems to breathe as advertised.

For the last few years, both summer and winter, I've worn Lowe Alpine Lightflite Side-Zip Pants (10 oz., $85) that match my anorak (page 544). The fabric is a nylon ripstop with a DWR finish and a pretty-well-waterproof coating. They're black, and they sun-dry fast. They have full side zippers, for quick-changeability and access to the pockets in my shorts. They self-stuff into a mesh pouch and fit in the top pocket of my pack. And not least, they've kept me dry in abrupt and dramatic weather. They do lack abrasion patches, but as long as I don't do any lengthy butt glissades they should last a while.

The lightest shell pant I've tried is the GoLite Trunk (6.5 oz., $85), made of a microfiber nylon ripstop that's wind- and bugproof, water-repellent, and breathes nicely. An elasticized drawstring waist and side-pockets civilize the waist, with elastic cuffs and scuff patches below. A light desert tan, they've recently bumped the knee-holed cotton pants out of my pack for a warm-season weight savings of 11.5 oz. But since the boots or sandals must come off to slip them on, for weathery trips I prefer full zips—so does Colin.

This is a good time to poke and ponder a few more things that, as a backpacker, you don't really need. Shell pants aimed at mountaineers have stout Cordura patches on the backside, knees, and inside the ankle, to resist climbing-harness abrasion, sharp rocks, crampon points, and ski edges. Pants aimed at lift or heli skiers often have high-rise waists and built-in gaiters for ski boots. Both sorts tend to be heavier and hotter and costlier than you need for walking. Likewise—

Overalls, or *bibs,* are useful for expeditionizing in high altitudes and latitudes. But they are cumbersome, hot, and not very adaptable for walking in general—unless you plan to walk across Greenland. A one-piece sleeveless *farmer john* or *salopette* of light fleece can make life easier in the cold—and shitting harder, although some one-piece fuzzies have ventral zips, flaps, or other sanitary bomb-run arrangements. (Those fascinated should read Mark Twight's *Extreme Alpinism.*)

In that line but of more use to backpackers, the newest trend is to waterproof/breathables that stretch. These showed up first in tops (early jackets had seam tape that unfortunately didn't stretch as well as the fabric), and are just now bottoming their way into the market as pants. After being shocked speechless by the waterproofness of the stretchy SealSkinz knit sock (page 93), I no longer consider such things impossible. If the bugs can be worked out, the discussion of shell pants might, in the next edition, be short. Or missing.

Rain chaps that I found long ago in the sporting-goods section of a grocery store were a decent half measure (5 oz., $12). Tapered tubes of coated nylon with webbing tie-ons, they're good for whacking through wet or stickery brush. They were also well ventilated, by virtue of open tops, but my shorts offered nothing to tie them to. My partner brandished a rock-drill and suggested placing expansion bolts in my hipbones. But I fashioned some webbing into a backcountry garter belt.

COLIN: Chaps are definitely worth considering if your rainshell is long enough to protect your thighs and you fear prolonged rain or expect to slog for hours through sodden scrub.

You may, especially if you wear shorts, like to replace or augment rain chaps with a device that has been called

Colin's kilt—aka Everyman's Wonderful Waterproof Trash-Bag Skirt (1 or 2 oz., around $.25). To make it you take a plastic trash bag—around 30-gallon, preferably black, and as thick as you can find—and with a knife convert it to the subspecies profundissimus (i.e., bottomless). Then you step into the tube and tuck it inside your shorts top or secure it around your waist with nylon cord or what pleases you. If your rainshell is even halfway adequate the kilt will extend its protection to the bottom of your shorts. If it's not raining but you're walking through wet brush or long grass you probably won't need the shell, and the kilt is a gem: that's what I originally devised it for. You hold the kilt in place with the pack's hipbelt and raise or lower your hemline according to your warmth requirements, length of shorts, heaviness of rain, windiness of wind, and surliness of underbrush. The kilt can be invaluable when used with chaps if windblown rain threatens to breach an incipient gap between chaps and shell or poncho. For a specific occasion on which I used the kilt, see page 568.

If you carry trash bags for other uses you can, of course, create a kilt instanter and anywhere. But evolution may sweep us beyond trash bags. If some enterprising body wants to design a stronger and less tearable kilt of coated nylon or something . . . well, I've not yet patented my brainchild.

Umbrellas. You may occasionally see pictures of—or even meet—backpackers carrying umbrellas. An umbrella's huge advantage is to banish all the overheating problems. And it can, if there's not too much wind, protect your pack as well as you. But because it's almost useless, going on a menace, in high winds or middling brush or branches you more or less have to carry some more traditional rainwear as well, and that rather wipes the shine off.*

WINDWEAR

The ascendancy of waterproof/breathable rainjackets means that traditional anoraks and parkas—no more than mildly water-resistant, and primarily used as windbreakers—have become virtually obsolete. Now you need carry only one garment for both rain and wind protection—and warmth as well. But there are, I guess, certain dry conditions under which the older-type, nonwaterproof jackets might still prove useful. And in cool, breezy weather, if you expect to do some climbing or even scrambling, it might be worth considering ultralight jackets and perhaps pants that allow almost total freedom, breathe well, afford some protection against light rain, and, although not 100 percent windproof, block you off pretty well.

CHIP: This is the case for walks in predictable weather, that is, short ones. But the longer you stay out, the greater your likelihood of meeting an abrupt shift in conditions. By way of example, this last week—mid-May in Wyoming—started warm and calm with sunny 70°F mornings and breezy cloud-puffed afternoons: perfect windbreaker weather. But Wednesday dawned with a thundering downpour that swiftly accelerated to blinding hail, then bore down with a full day of wind-propelled snow. By Thursday morning we had 6 inches of sodden white on the ground. It was perfect for testing, and I dashed out repeatedly but found myself glad not to be out on some lonely plateau with ultralight and semiwaterproof gear. It's not that I'm scared of such weather. But, improperly clothed, I've spent so much time in that nether-zone of misery, halfway to hypothermia—that I know intimately the potential of such days for grinding your spirit down. So a lightweight shell-for-all-seasons that sheds water, blocks wind, and yet manages to breathe free is a kind of backpacker's Grail. And we're getting closer all the time.

A parallel development is windproof pile and fleece. This trickily involves laminating a semi-elastic membrane to a knit fabric, and not sur-

---

*CHIP: For another side of the umbrella question, see Ray Jardine's book *Beyond Backpacking* (Appendix IV). On windy days, cheapo umbrellas go inside out. But GoLite has a backpacker's umbrella, the Dome, for $23. I've carried one on a hot-season walk across a treeless expanse, for midday shade-ups. An umbrella also makes a nice cook shelter for bivy-sack trips. But a gust can surprise you: after a lengthy chase, I added a wrist loop of light webbing, which also lets me anchor the thing with a tent stake. If your arm gets tired, you can slip the shaft through the loops and tie-downs of a pack—a cool if rather silly-looking arrangement.

prisingly the leading contenders are W. L. Gore's Windstopper and Malden Mills's Windbloc (see page 513). Since blocking all air passage, as a urethane coating does, puts us back to square one, the idea is rather to blunt the force of the wind and maintain a stable boundary layer of warm air next to the skin. A permeability of 1 cubic foot per minute of air accomplishes this, holding in body heat while still being, in a practical sense, breathable. The two-layer form joins the membrane to a knit, while the three-layer version sandwiches the membrane between a face fabric and a wicking liner, both generally knit polyester.

Meanwhile, the traditional windbreaker has been resurrected in microfiber: single-layer shells whose high thread counts and tight weaves make them relatively windproof. With a durable water repellent (DWR) treatment (page 565), these can get you by where rainfall is light and/or passing.

In this vein, a new standard for sheer useful adaptability is set by the Marmot DriClime Windshirt (11 oz., $125 — *ouch* — but see page 526 for a run-up). You can use it as a windshirt, a base layer, or as a light all-in-one jacket. The shell blocks wind and will turn a drizzle, while the knit liner wicks and warms. And it has a nice zipper pocket right over the heart.

EXTREMITIES AND ANCILLARIES

Gloves

COLIN: Some hardy souls lighten their loads by going without gloves, even in spring and fall. But except in really warm weather I always take along a pair of light woolen gloves or mitts (about 2 oz., $4–$10). Mitts—in which all four fingers cohabit and only the thumb lives alone—are warmer than equivalent gloves but leave you fumble-fisted for any but the simplest tasks. A best-of-both-worlds compromise: fingerless gloves inside mitts, with a slot in the mitts, near the wrist, so that you can curl your gloved hand into a fist, slip it out through the slot, Velcro the mitt back onto your wrist, and do intricate tasks in semi-comfort. (The Manzella Convertible Glove/Mitt is 4 oz. at $15, and the Outdoor Research Magic Mitt of Gore Windstopper fleece is 3 oz. at $35.) Polypropylene gloves, though they keep your hands warm even when wet and also dry out faster than wool, are otherwise no warmer, apparently wear less well, and seem to cost more.

Standard leather or canvas/leather work gloves may be worth taking for such heavy chores as digging or wood gathering. They're also useful in mild winds and cold. I rarely carry them, but some backpackers always do—for fire lighting, cooking, and protection against sunburn and insects.

No matter what cold-weather gloves you choose you will in bitter cold probably need inners—to afford some protection when you must take off the outer gloves for a task that demands dexterity, and also to wick moisture away. Plastic bags as makeshift VB liners are said to work. And one reader strongly suggests carrying nitrile plastic gloves, used by surgeons, housepainters, et al., to go over thin liners and under insulating gloves or mitts.

CHIP: In gloves made of Malden's Windbloc and W. L. Gore's Windstopper, a stretch membrane is invisibly wed to fleece and pile. And since hands are the part of us most likely to get cold on windy days, in glove form these laminated materials prove their worth. On a trip to medium-high mountains in March, I took a pair of Lowe Alpine Polartec Windbloc gloves (2 oz., $30) in place of my usual bunting liners. In case it got nasty, I also packed shell mitts. It did get nasty enough to be interesting—two days of wind-stirred snowfall—but in fact, I wore nothing but the Windbloc gloves for the whole trip. Not only did they block/bloc the wind, but they had a greater temperature range than other synthetic gloves, made me sweat less, dried faster, and weighed a half ounce less per pair.

The layering system works for hands as well, so let's rummage the glove stash. My base layer consists of one pair of much-melted generic Thermax liners and another, likewise hammered, of Expedition-weight Capilene from Patagonia (2 oz., $24). Camp cooking is murder on synthetic gloves. So are ice axes and ski/trek poles. My insulating (or all-around) layer includes some ratty gray Patagonia (Ratty-gonia?) bunting gloves, now fetchingly melted and pilled. Still presentable are the afore-mentioned Lowe Alpine Windbloc gloves, though the palms are starting to show mileage. The new kids-in-the-box are Outdoor Research WS Grippers (3 oz., $45), of Windstopper fleece with a curved anatomical cut and rubbery goop on the palms, thumbs, and first two fingers—which should wear longer than plain fuzz.

More than one of my female advisors say that fat-fingered men's gloves don't fit. So, for women's hands, Wild Roses makes well-cut liners of Malden Power Stretch (2 oz., $20), Thermal Rose gloves of Malden Polartec 300 (3 oz., $20), Windy Rose gloves of Gore Windstopper (2 oz., $45), and mitts like the Frosty Rose of Gore DryLoft (3 oz., $35). Any of the insulating gloves can be worn under any of the shells, which come with their own Polartec 300 liners.

I still have a long-lived pet pair of Norwegian wool mittens. But the darned things need darning again. So for most trips a pair of Outdoor Research Modular Mitts has taken over—the Taslan Gore-Tex shells (5 oz., $57) have palms of rubberized Toughtek, and Velcro wrist and cuff straps that can be adjusted with your teeth. I stitched up a nose wiper (a

4-inch tube of fluffy pile) and added it to one of the wrist straps. For lightweight trips in the cold, I take the shell mitts and the Windstopper gloves. For sustained digit-freezing exposure I add Outdoor Research mitt liners, which dock inside the shells with Velcro. Of Moonlite pile, the singles (my choice) are 2.5 oz. and $14, while the double-layer mitts are 4.5 oz. and $26.

Alternately, when tinkering with buckles and bindings might lead to frostbite, a pair of Mont-Bell expedition gauntlets (9 oz.) has been invaluable, with bunting liners, a wicking midlayer, and reinforced Gore-Tex shells—so warm in fact that I use them sparingly. Since Mont-Bell hit the skids, the handsomest ultrawarm gloves I've seen are made by Granite Gear.

For fishing and hydrologizing on cold days, I use Danalco SealSkinz (3.5 oz., $28.50). A knit outer is laminated to a seamless stretch membrane, lined with wicking CoolMax and finished with a Lycra cuff. The palms have rubber grip-dots. Though their longevity is as yet undetermined, they're surprisingly waterproof and keep my hands pleasantly dry, as long as the cuffs stay above water. I formerly wore neoprene windsurfing gloves, but after a knuckle-bashing ice climb I got an infection that crept under the cuticle of my index finger and along the bone. My finger ballooned—hot soaks with lancing and draining were all I could do in camp. Back home I got antibiotics to clear up the oozing mess and now have an interesting scar. Along with a wariness of neoprene gloves.

Booties

COLIN: I have for years used down booties. Once they kept my feet totally warm—perhaps even a shade hot—in a Slimline bag, unprotected, at 11°F. On Kilimanjaro, when the temperature hardly fell below freezing but murkily miserable weather and the thin air at 16,000 feet made it seem colder, they kept my feet comfortable in a similar lightweight bag. Such booties—with light nylon shell and thick waterproof nylon sole padded with ¼-inch Ensolite—are also excellent for brief excursions from your tent out into the snow, provided the snow is cold and dry.

As far as I know, every foam-soled down bootie comes equipped with a resident little devil whose sole aim in life is to slide the foam off to one side of your foot, where it becomes comprehensively useless. Some models incorporate elastic inserts at the heels, intended to exorcise these devils. Intended.*

---

*CHIP: The Sierra Designs down booties I've used for years have the foam stitched snugly around the edges, exorcising the devils. Plain drawcord models with nonskid soles, they weigh 8 oz. a pair and cost $32. Polarguard booties weigh slightly more and cost a bit less.

Because down booties are very hard to keep dry, Polarguard-filled versions have for years threatened to replace them—without actually doing so.

Hoods and balaclavas

Never underestimate the importance of covering your head in cold weather. The head is the body's radiator (see page 469). Hence the old adage, "If you want to keep your feet warm, put your hat on."

Because time has reduced my natural head covering to a joke, I always carry at least one balaclava, for use at night.

CHIP: To get this straight, what Colin and I call a *balaclava* (after the famously chilly site of an 1854 battle in the Crimean War) is now generally known—in catalogs, not dictionaries—as a face mask. Whereas what I think of as a *face mask* seems to be widely called a balaclava. For our purposes, a mask is something that covers your face, and the best place to look for one is the Outdoor Research catalog. The various bala-face-clava-masks pictured, of Moonlite Pile and Windstopper, swaddle all but the eyes and nostrils. Some models have Velcro flaps, for ingestion, and others have mesh-covered breathing ports ($34–$37). I have seldom moved fast enough to need one. But in horrid conditions, they will keep you far warmer than you have any right to be, and will also induce nightmares in small children.

On the other hand, in *Walker*-speak a balaclava is what covers your head and neck while leaving nose, eyes, and (optionally) lips exposed.

COLIN: In any kind of cold I carry three: a silk or synthetic one for nontickling wear next to the skin; an Orlon one for general use, particularly at night; and a pile hood or balaclava by Patagonia that extends down onto the shoulders and has a drawstring for snugging around the face. You can also roll it up to make a hat. Being pile, it demands a shell, such as a hooded rainjacket, to ward off wind. But it absorbs only 2 percent of its weight in water, compared with wool's 50 percent. In action in miserable conditions, it has proved itself as a heat regulator again and again.

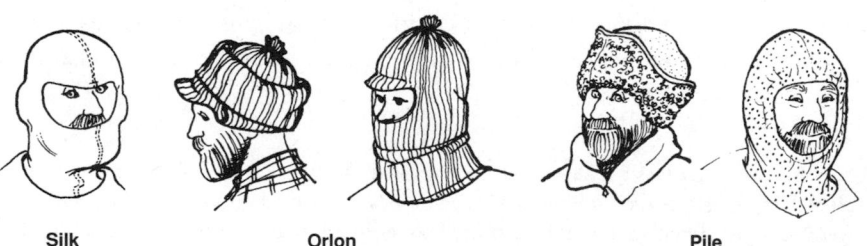

Silk   Orlon   Pile

Balaclava   **Balaclava and ball cap**   **Balaclava rolled over bill**

CHIP: I still have a silk balaclava (0.8 oz.), but when called upon to absorb the superheated steam that issues from my head with any exertion whatsoever, silk tends to get soaked, baggy, and smelly. So I got a lightweight Patagonia Capilene model (1.5 oz., $18) but found the face opening more suitable for a weasel. To shade my face, I often cover a light balaclava with a ball cap or a visor. Once I heat up, I stretch the face hole up and over the bill so my ears stay covered while my neck is free to radiate. But Patagonia's weasel-size face hole had a binding that lacked the necessary stretch, so I ripped the bottom half of the binding off and have worn it—ragged and raw—for quite a few years. Later, I found a Lowe Alpine Dryflo 170 face mask (1 oz., $19) with a stretchier opening. For rescue/loaner purposes, I often carry an extra head housing of densely knit Thermax from Wigwam (2.5 oz., $18) and at times layer it over the lightweight one, though the over-the-bill trick doesn't work with two layers. An obscure prize is the Turtle Fur something-or-other (2.5 oz., a gift) that combines an acrylic fleece "neck-gaiter" with a stretchy nylon dome. The fleecy part folds up easily over the stretchy part, making a neo-watchcap. The dome also accommodates a ball cap or other billed head appliance, and the neck-warmer can do the over-bill flip, making this (and a ball cap or visor) my secret weapon for trips where big temperature swings are likely. Given a hooded shell, I'm well covered for rain, snow, alpine sun, etc.

Other tricksy, featherweight warmers are headbands of bunting and fleece. An ounce or less, and $4 to $15, these are a boon if your ears get cold while your head is too hot, often the case for me. They can also back up an ultralight balaclava or ball cap, and restrain a maddeningly flapping hood on summit days. Curiouser still are Ear Bags. Not baggy at all, they're tidy little fleece mouse ears with spring-steel frames that (once you get the trick) flip snugly into place close to your head. At a half ounce per pair ($12), they're sleepers as far as warmth-for-weight.

Fleece hats—watchcaps, envelopes, earflaps, domes, peaks, bombers, and stockings—provide endless variations on a theme, and they all work fine—or at least, I've never had a bad one. Some even manage to look good. For smooch points, I got my honey an Ilahee Rose microfleece fez with Windbloc earflaps (2 oz., $25) from Wild Roses. Which besides being warm in a practical way is also killingly chic: proof, she tells me, that women are smarter.

Scarves

COLIN: The human neck is no doubt necessary, but it is a hell of a thing to keep warm. And it creates a weak point in almost any clothing system. Even in warm weather I always carry a small (2-oz.) wool or Orlon scarf to block off the escape of precious warm air from the main reservoir that clothing has created around my body. Unless you've tried it you'll have difficulty believing how much difference this small detail can make, especially when your clothing is on the light side. Fleece neck-gaiters (Turtle Fur acrylic, 2 oz., $7) are the present equivalent. A stray sock also works.

Keep your loved ones warm

Now offered: down cups for breasts and for genitals.*

Swimsuits

When there's a chance of a swim you may, unless you're reasonably sure of privacy, like to take along a thin nylon swimsuit. On one trip entailing repeated river crossings with my pack (page 692) in rough water and hot weather, I wore mine every time, so that in the unlikely event of being separated from the pack I would at least have some protection from the sun. If you wear Baggies or other running-type shorts they can double as swimsuit. So can underpants.

Bandannas

A large cotton bandanna or handkerchief, preferably bright-colored and therefore not easily lost, is your wardrobe's maid-of-all-work. It performs as potholder, napkin, dishcloth, washcloth, towel, emergency headgear, wet inside-the-hat cooling pad in hot weather, Lawrence-of-Arabia

---

*CHIP: Some years ago, while ski touring at −10°F, I frostbit the tip of the Rawlins Peninsula. I was wearing long underwear, but the metal zipper on my surplus wool pants conducted the chill to that tenderest part. Which I thawed in warm water—with muffled shrieks and some involuntary ballet. But no permanent damage. For just such sneaky hazards, there are now sports briefs with front panels of windproof fleece—Patagonia's Capilene Wind Briefs are 2.5 oz. and $18. Or you can mobilize the small fleece sack intended for a headlamp, candle lantern, etc. for temporary peninsular defense.

neck protector (especially cooling if damp), hand pad for snowpeg-as-trowel, snooze mask, and even fig leaf (page 567).

Traditional "cowboy kerchief" cotton bandannas or curlicue-pattern equivalents weigh about 2 oz. and come in 24-inch and 27-inch squares ($2–$3). And you can now "rub your nose in knowledge" with bandannas (same size and weight) in assorted colors and imprinted with nose-encyclopedias concerning butterflies, clouds, shells, knots, whales, animal tracks, birds of prey, and shorebirds; even various board games. But the butterflies et al. are not free: $5 to $8 each. Variations: topographic maps of popular backpacking spots, 25-by-25-inch, on microfiber.

Wash bandannas frequently. They soon dry if tied on a pack.

Hats

Hikers wear about as many different kinds of headgear as you'll see in a fully fashioned Easter parade. But the valid practical criteria are light-ness, protection afforded from heat, ventilation quotient, and ability to stand up to brutal treatment. (I pay little attention to rain resistance: I rely on parka or poncho hood. But not everyone agrees. See page 561.) Beyond such practical matters, suit your fancy—though should you be thin on top but still able to enjoy the finer things of life it's desirable that the hat be of such a nature that if it becomes dislodged during totally engrossing delights under a hot, hot desert sun it is easy, without any interruption at all, for her to reach up, if she really loves you, and replace it.

On occasion, you must be able to arrange things so that the hat will stay on your head in a half hurricane. The only way you can do so is with a chin strap. If the hat you like doesn't have one (and it probably won't) all you have to do is punch a hole in the brim on either side, close to the crown, and grommet the holes—or have a shoemaker do the job—then thread through the grommets a suitable length of braided nylon cord. (Red cord dirties less objectionably than white and also helps color pho-tography.) When not in use the chin strap goes up into the crown: you soon get used to flicking it up without thought as you put the hat on. Or, sometimes, you can tuck it into the hatband.

Some people like caps with visors—which certainly have some worth in snow. And cycling caps are light and cool, and work in fair weather (see Chip's ball-cap rhapsody below).

Down the years I have, for no clearly discernible reason, run through a mild fashion parade of hats, from felt Half Stetsons through minifacsim-iles to an ordinary U.S. Army–surplus fatigue hat. All did their job well. But they took a continuous beating: they not only got soaked and tram-pled on but spent long hours stuffed inside the pack or slung by their chin straps from the packframe or clipped onto the belt-clip-on-cord-from-top-of-packframe that was primarily there for my camera. Each lasted several years but eventually became so limp or frayed, especially around the crown, that finally I was forced to pension it off. I can never bring myself to throw such old friends away, and several of them lie on a shelf in my gear closet. Every now and again my eye lights on them and my face up.

Although I'm aware that light-colored hats reflect the heat better, I note that all mine have been brown or gray or blue—no doubt because I liked the look of them and because I knew they wouldn't show the dirt. About the only other feature they've shared is a crown high enough to leave airspace between bald pate and murderous sunshine. For more on that, see facing page.

In 1989, for my six-month raft-and-backpacking trip down the Colorado River, I bought a Tilley T3 hat (bottom row, left; now $55, mine 6 oz., complete with dirt; lightweight version now available at $62). Since then, I've used it, steadily, for backpacking.

And that's how things go in backpack hatting: it's a strictly freelance field, and you buy what and where you want—French Foreign Legion Jungle hats, Portuguese Army caps ("purchased in Mozambique . . . rather nifty . . . the neck flap offers good insect and thorn protection—such as needed when you canoe through rose bushes)." Many readers have written recommending their favorite hats with passion, eloquence, and illustrations.

Illustration by Hendrik G. Van Oss

One reader drew my attention to a hat described in *Inventions Necessity Was Not the Mother Of,* by S. V. Jones (now out of print) and invented by Harold W. Dahly of Chicago. Mr. Dahly's 1967 patent (#3,353,191) "describes a solar cell that generates current to run the motor. To regulate the speed of the fan or shut it off entirely, a cover can be swung over the cell. Air is admitted through holes in the side of the crown and is circulated for the comfort of the wearer." "It is well known," says Mr. Dahly, "that cooling the top of the head will have a cooling effect on the entire person."*

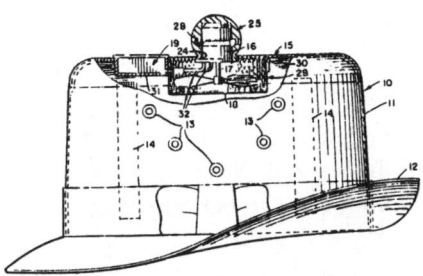

Another reader some years ago eulogized the now-popular ultimate in nonhats: the shaved head ("never overheated . . . there is something sinfully fantastic about sitting on a mountain with the air literally whistling around your ears: great, great feeling").

Shaved head or no, the way you wear the crown of your hat in hot weather can be critical. From force of city habit we tend to indent the top "stylishly." But doing so in hot weather radically reduces the vital air-insulation barrier between the top of your head and the sun's rays. The thing to do is to push the crown out to its rounded maximum.

A rounded crown hardly helps you to look intelligent, but if appearance counts enough to force you to stay with a dented crown you had better confine your walking to the financial district.

---

*CHIP: A tiny fan powered by a solar panel that clips onto a stiff-brimmed cap can be had from Real Goods for $9. I've seen similar ones installed in classic pith helmets.

Some sober and reliable people classify as pure myth the tradition that you need a hat in hot, sunny weather. But I know that if I go without a hat in any kind of hot sun I very soon feel dizzy. Or, at the least, I imagine I feel dizzy—and the two states are indistinguishable. So to me, in summer desert, a hat is no joking matter.

On my California walk, when I rested for a day at the southern end of Death Valley, the temperature was 105°F in the extremely rare shade. During the morning of that day I climbed up into some stark hills to photograph the gray trough that was the valley—the trough I would within 24 hours be walking through. All morning a strong west wind had been blowing. As I climbed, the wind increased. But the heat lost none of its intensity. By the time I reached the first summit ridge, the wind had risen to a half gale. On the ridge I stopped to take a photograph, and used my hat to shield the camera lens from the sun. Afterward, in a careless moment, I forgot to slip the chin strap back under my chin. Before I could lift a hand, the wind had snatched the hat away and sent it soaring upward.

Suddenly the sun was battering down on my head like a bludgeon.

I cannot have stood there looking at the flying hat for more than two or three seconds. But I don't think I shall ever forget my feeling of helplessness as the twirling brown shape grew smaller and smaller. I stood still, watching it twist up and away into the hard blue sky.

Then the hat dived behind one of the fantastically colored ridges that stretched back and back as far as I could see.

Its disappearance snapped the spell. I broke into a run. As I ran I remembered how, only a couple of weeks before, a wise old desert rat had shown me a magazine picture of a corpse sprawled beside a bicycle out in the Mojave Desert. "No hat—not surprised," the old-timer had said. I raced on over bare rock. A makeshift hat in Death Valley? I might go days without seeing anyone. And I knew that I could hunt for hours among those endless ridges without finding the hat. I scrambled onto a chocolate-brown crest. And there, its strap neatly looped over a spike of rock, lay the hat.

I picked it up, chin-strapped it firmly onto my head, and walked slowly back down the hill. Now the danger had passed I felt thankful that the desert had reminded me how fine a line divides safety from tragedy—and how easily a moment of carelessness can send you stumbling across it.*

Necessity being the mom of invention, you find that if you lose your hat you soon devise something as substitute. The only time I've lost mine was on a 17-day trip in Lower Grand Canyon, when temperatures ran over

*From *The Thousand-Mile Summer,* pages 82–83.

100°F just about every day. My bandanna had been acting as a wet-pad cooling system inside the hat and was lost with it. For a couple of days I used jockey shorts, then managed to lose them too. Because I was following the Colorado River and had to cross it from time to time I was carrying a life vest (page 692), and I devised a method of folding it, lightly inflated, and lashing it with nylon cord into such a conformation that, with its web belt under my chin, it would stay on top of my head. This unlikely rig, immersed every hour in the river, and with the wet swimsuit stuffed into its hollow center, turned out to be just about the coolest hat I've ever worn, even if not the most becoming. I had to hold my head fairly upright to keep it on, but that was probably good for my posture or something.

CHIP: Living in the high, brilliant light of the interior, I'm a fiend for bill caps of all kinds (see next page). For cold weather, my dry-phase pick is the South Shore by Granite Gear (3.5 oz., $33) (a), an ultralight bomber cap. Aptly, the bill, front, and sides are of Bombshell nylon, with a water-proof/breathable coating, while the floating liner and earflaps are Dyersburg ECO fleece. The top has two layers of fleece, for breathable warmth. Velcro tabs corral the earflaps, and a back strap adjusts the fit. It layers perfectly over a light balaclava or my Turtle Fur whatever-it-is.

For wet-phase cold, the Outdoor Research Hat for All Seasons (5.6 oz., $40) (b) is a favorite with high-latitude river guides, salmon trollers, and other slosh-hounds. It has a Gore-Tex shell with a bill that flips up for visibility and earflaps that flip up for—whatever. It also has a stout chin strap. The shell is lined with wicking fabric (3.9 oz.) and stands alone to keep the rain off and give moderate warmth, supplemented with an ear-snugging skullcap of Moonlite pile (1.7 oz.) that resembles a detail from a Bruegel the Elder painting. The liner can be worn under a climbing,

biking, or kayaking helmet, and also as a compact and nonitchy sleep cap that, no matter how much you thrash, won't slouch down over your eyes.

In the Hat Department of the Universe, Outdoor Research unquestionably has the biggest selection of hats that have actually been tested on human heads, out of doors. Fleece, pile, Gore-Tex, Velcro, drawstrings, sweatbands, earflaps, neck flaps, chin straps: they've got it all. Even a classic Britannic Touring Cap in Windstopper Fleece.

My own Hat Department also reveals a much-used Outdoor Research Sonora Sombrero (2.8 oz., \$31) (c), a classic flopster made of Solarplex, a nylon blend that feels cottony, its white faintly reddened by the silty rapids of Desolation Canyon, where it kept me from cooking one August. The 4-inch brim descends for shade or Velcros up at the sides while a removable chin cord keeps it from abandoning ship (or Chip). Other Outdoor Research Sombreros—Seattle, Snoqualmie, Sahale, Sitka, and Siberian—are calibrated for all known gradations of rain, snow, and sun.

After having a few suspicious sunspots excised from my brow, I've been experimenting with a portable palm tree—the Sport Hat (or Sun Half-Veil, 2 oz., \$25) (d) from an Oregon maker called Sunday Afternoons. Exceedingly light and airy, it has a 4-inch brim that tapers toward the back, where a 3.5-inch neck veil takes over. The brim arcs around the face to protect you from angled light or flips up for visibility, and is a glare-fighting green underneath. Mesh side panels increase ventilation while letting in a few droplets. A cinch headband and chin cord combine to keep your head plugged in. If you lose it, it floats. The crown could be a touch higher, but perfection's elusive. The same maker offers a Leisure—

or Adventure—Hat (2.5 oz., $33) with a 7.5-inch rear veil for increased palm-tree effect. But Wyoming winds make it unruly.

Mostly, though, I love to wear sun visors and combine them with balaclavas, headbands, mouse ears, bandannas, and such in quaintly layered compositions. Stout visors are made by Kavu and other outfits, but given a sad tendency to leave them in saloons, I now buy generic white ones in tennis shops (1.5 oz., $3). The ultimate among visors—one that I couldn't afford to leave in a pub—is one-third of the Outdoor Research Super Safari Cap, of Solarplex, with a removable crown and full-coverage neo-Bedouin neck skirt ($33)—making you feel like a pillar of wisdom.

For bug-plagued pilgrimages, a worthy adjunct is a headnet, and crummy ones are widely available in discount stores. Notably improved are the Spring Ring Headnet from Outdoor Research, an under-cap model of black no-see-um mesh with a spring-steel hoop that holds it off your face and folds up for stowing (1.5 oz., $11). Another is a nice ball cap with a headnet that drapes over the bill and stows in a pouch where brim meets crown: *La Casquette Mostiquaire* (sold as the Bug Cap by REI and others — 3.7 oz., $22) by Horizon Products of Montréal.

Ball caps come and go. Given my layering practices, I favor the old-style caps with a high crown over newer head-hugging types—the current favorite is a black one from the Seafood Producers Co-op in Sitka, Alaska. Before that came a white satin cap with NASA in gold-embroidery, fished from a tidal creek on Florida's east coast, where it was guarded by a surly pelican. I've also cherished caps of fleece and wool. But I lost them, one by one, to pubs, railway stations, ferryboats, bush planes, and thumbed rides.

And found them as well. The only light-duty bill-topper I've bought in recent memory is a Corona Cap (Outdoor Research again, 2 oz., $18). The Solarplex fabric is cool and durable, the bill is black beneath, and the light-fuzz headband sponges up sweat. And last but not least, the external Velcro cinch strap tabs neatly around a pack strap or belt loop, so I *definitely will not leave it behind.*

CARE OF CLOTHING

In the field

COLIN: In civilized temperatures I generally try to wash most of my clothes at least once a week.* This works out well because I find—and I think most people find—that about once a week you need a day's more or less complete rest from walking.

Whatever soap or detergent you choose it must, today, be bio-degradable. The stuff you use for kitchen and personal purposes (page 640) will probably do fine for most clothes. For wool articles, see Care of Socks, page 94.

The time has passed, just about everywhere in the world, for washing clothes directly in a river or lake. Suds persist, and with our numbers now over 6 billion and wanderlust epidemic, the chances are simply too great that someone a little way downstream will soon be drinking that same water. Besides, with today's heavy usage the accumulation spells undoubted pollution. (Exceptions: huge rivers, maybe; and genuinely remote country.)

The simplest solution: use your cook pot or pots. But you can also buy cheap, light buckets and basins in plastic. A collapsible plastic bucket holding 1.5 gallons (any sporting-goods store, 8.5 oz., $5–$8) will serve, and a water hauler bag (Campmor, 2.5 gallons, 3 oz., $10) will too. You can also find various breeds of folding sinks or basins for about $4 to $5. Failing bucket and basin, you can improvise a bowl from any impermeable fabric—poncho, groundsheet, fly sheet, awning—by laying it in a natural hollow, by scooping a hollow out of sand or soil that will not be damaged, or by arranging stones or wood as under-rim supports. Fill from canteens. You scoop up water in the bucket and wash clothes (and yourself) in the bowl. Dirty water can safely be ditched 50 feet back from the river or lake: it will filter clean as it seeps down through the soil.**

To dry clothes, string them out on bushes or a nylon line. I'm indebted to a New York reader who apparently carries a light nylon line for what she calls her "twist-and-shove," which she maintains is simpler than it looks and has become a one-minute-or-so part of her evening camp

---

*In really cold weather you simply don't do any washing of clothes—or of yourself, which means that when you get back to civilization that first hot shower is not only sheer heaven but highly necessary.

**CHIP: Another option is the heavy-duty zip-top bag—add water, soap, clothes, solar heat, and jiggle. Rinse likewise. A waterproof stuff sack, like the Outdoor Research Hydroseal, also works fine, and can be affixed to your pack for agitation en route. This method gets the new synthetics fairly clean with little or no detergent: just soak twice.

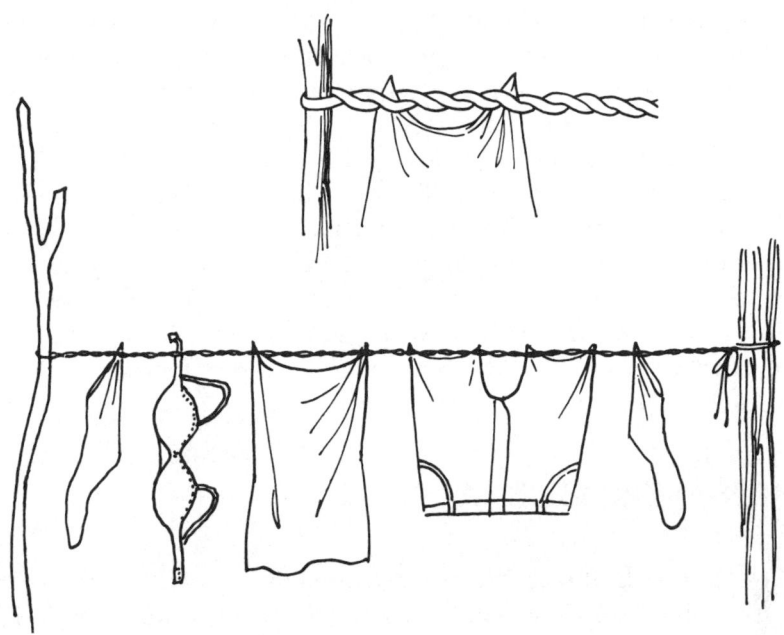

routine. You loop the line around whatever two aids you can find with the center of the line at one of them—twist tightly, then shove the clothes into two or more twist loops.*

For shirts, if you're fussy about looks, it's easy to make a clothes hanger out of a piece of stick and some nylon line. For socks, see page 94.

In wet weather the only way to dry out clothes is often a fire. But sometimes you're reduced to using the cooking stove inside your tent—if there's enough fuel. A tent with a mesh gear loft or clothesline attachment—grommeted tabs at each end of the ridge for joining with nylon cord—may allow damp clothes to dry from a combination of stove and body heat. For final drying, take clothes to bed with you.

At home

CHIP: Treat articles of outdoor clothing with due respect; i.e., read the care labels and separate accordingly for washing. But wait—according to International Standards Organization (ISO) tests, most household detergents have a disastrous effect on both waterproof/breathable laminates and durable water repellents (DWRs). For the last couple of years I've been using Nikwax washes and waterproofing treatments and have noticed a marked improvement. Tech Wash is good for synthetics in gen-

*COLIN: A reader of this paragraph in the second edition: "I used this clothesline and it was a great success. Who says book learnin' ain't scalded no hogs?"

eral and laminates in particular. For down-filled clothing, Nikwax Down Wash is the ticket (also see sleeping bags, page 491). After the article is clean, it can be resloshed in a waterproofing treatment such as Nikwax TX-Direct Wash-In (for laminates, microfibers, and synthetics in general), Nikwax Downproof (for downy-down-down), or Nikwax Cottonproof (for cotton, hemp, etc.). The fact that all these are water-based enables their use in washing machines and avoids the harm of solvent-based products. Post-wash, clothes and softgoods can be sprayed with Nikwax Tent & Gear Proof or TX Direct, both DWR finishes. Other treatments are available, such as W. L. Gore Revivex and various potions from Granger, Tectron, and others; but my impression is that Nikwax now leads the pack.*

THE WARDROBE IN ACTION

COLIN: Sartorially, hikers can be subdivided into two distinct breeds: the put-it-on-and-keep-it-on school and the keep-adjusting-your-clothing-all-day-long-so-that-you're-always-comfortable faction.

You undoubtedly save several minutes a day if you put on at the start what you judge is about right and can then stick it out hour after hour without discomfort. But I belong, unreservedly, to the fussy, thermally responsive faction. With every variation of effort and environment I button and unbutton, unzipper and rezipper, peel and restore and then peel again. I find that in any but frigid weather it takes barely a mile of walking and a side glance of sunshine to strip me down to hat, shorts, socks, and boots. That, I find, is the way to walk. With air playing freely over your skin you feel twice as fresh as you did with a shirt on. And although you may lose precious body liquids more quickly this way, experience has convinced me that you walk so much more comfortably that you more than make up for any loss. At least, I do. Besides, I enjoy myself more.

On those rare but by no means unknown occasions when you're traveling beside a river or lake in very hot, low-humidity weather, you have a cooling system ready for use. On my 17-day trip in Lower Grand Canyon, when I hiked day after day beside the Colorado River, I learned to utilize this system to the full. I found that I could keep walking comfortably,

---

*Late news: 3M Corporation recently announced it is dropping the widely used Scotchgard line of water and stain repellents because the chemicals were showing up in water, soils, and animals. While on the one hand 3M might be criticized for selling the stuff in the first place, they might also be commended for phasing it out voluntarily, without the usual lies, cover-ups, court battles, and antiregulatory bombast.

even through the heat of the day, if at the end of each halt I dived into the river wearing my drill shorts and Dacron-wool shirt. For almost the whole of the next hour the continuous evaporation from the rapidly drying clothes surrounded my body with a pleasantly cool "microclimate." For the highly efficient hat I used, purely by accident, see page 560.

Occasionally on that trip, because of a cut on one leg that I wanted to keep dry, I just soaked the clothes in the river. At other times, when the heat wasn't too ferocious, I simply draped the dripping-wet shirt around my neck and kept resoaking it with barely a check in my stride by dropping it in the river and in one easy movement pushing it under and lifting it up with the tip of my walking staff.

It's not often that you meet the right and necessary combination of weather and privacy and so can carry the keep-adjusting-your-clothing-all-day-long-so-that-you're-always-comfortable system to its logical conclusion. The first time I did so for any length of time was on my long Grand Canyon journey. Of course, I exercised due care for a few days with previously shielded sectors of my anatomy. In particular, I pressed the bandanna into service as a fig leaf. But soon I was walking almost all day long with nothing above my ankles except a hat.*

Now, nakedness is a delightful condition, and by walking naked you gain far more than coolness. You feel an unexpected sense of freedom from restraint. An uplifting and almost delirious sense of simplicity. In this new simplicity you soon find that you have become, in a new and surer sense, an integral part of the simple, complex world you're walking through. And then you are really walking.

In assembling your clothes closet for any trip you probably tend to carry, if you are wise, just a little more than common sense indicates. This overlay will, when things go wrong, leave you some margin of safety. It may take many years—and more than just unexpected cold—for events to confirm your wisdom; but you can bet your bottom layer that in due course the dice will fall appropriately. Consider

A sample day in the rain—

a Murphy-ridden day, anything but normal yet rich in precept; a day during which you do some big things wrong, thereby placing harsh and unreasonable demands on the clothes closet (and several other depart-

---

*Warning! Not everyone can take such liberties with his skin in hot sun. And most people need a lotion (page 645), at least at first.

ments) but during which you sort of make up for that by also doing a few things right; a day that might be subtitled "How to Get Yourself into a Wet Hole—and Out of It."*

You're taking a two-week trip through coastal mountains. It's November. You are, among other things, trying out several new equipment items.

You've spent most of the day walking along a 4000-foot ridge in weather that has evolved, very slowly, from calm and clear through wispy fog, mist, heavy mist, drizzle, and heavy drizzle into steady, windblown rain. Because the temperature has throughout this evolution held at an amiable 54°F, you began the day stripped to socks, boots, and a pair of corduroy shorts. (In accordance with the Second Law of Thermodynamic Walking [page 530], you wore no underpants.) As the weather deteriorated you responded only by slipping on your trash-bag kilt (page 549) and a brand-new, second-generation Gore-Tex jacket—the first you've ever tried. Initially, you wore the jacket over your bare torso. In spite of your 50-pound pack and one hour-long spell of cross-country travel across steep, rough terrain, you felt, to your surprise and pleasure, no condensation discomfort. You didn't even feel hot. Eventually, in fact, on top of an open ridge, you buffered the jacket against the rising wind with an equally untested polypropylene undervest. And after that, as long as you kept moving, you stayed just on the warm side of cool—which is how it ought to be. The only trouble has come from the pit zips. They leaked. Now, as you push on along the ridge, both your forearms are damp. But otherwise you seem to be totally dry.

"I wonder if Colin Fletcher ever has days like this?"

*I like to think of myself as a competent operator, so you can hardly expect me to admit that what follows is a drop-by-drop account of what happened to me on one damp occasion some years ago. The gear I describe is, of course, now old-hat—and old-almost-everything-else.

Around two o'clock you reach the trail that will take you eastward, down off the ridge. You're glad. The wind has risen beyond playfulness. The rain is now slanting down in deeper earnest.

Off the crest, sure enough, things are appreciably calmer.

A little before three o'clock you reach the first running water. You've been traveling since 7:30, and with only two hours of daylight left and the rain now gaining even greater momentum—though the wind is still mercifully tamed, down here at 3000 feet—you decide to camp.

You go through the routine slowly, carefully: you suspect that this may be more than an overnight camp. By the time you've chosen a flat site that won't be swamped, no matter how much rain falls, that will be partially sheltered from almost any wind, and that also looks safe from terminal compression by any of the dead trees burned in a big fire a few years ago and now crashing down in every storm, you feel a little less robustly warm. Not cold yet; not even cool. But barely warm. You eat some gorp and a couple of candies and they stoke you up a bit.

During your reconnaissance you left your pack in the lee of a tree, sheltered from the worst of the rain. Now, as deftly as possible, you slacken the flap, slip the groundsheet out from its position just under the flap, and drape it, half unfolded, over the pack. From under this protective overlay you fumble out your 4-quart canteens, fill them at the nearby creek, and stand them beside the pack, ready.

At this point you run the attributes of the chosen campsite over in your mind again, and eventually you decide that the lee of the next tree offers even greater attractions. You move the pack over to the new site and fumble out from under the groundsheet your 12-by-15-foot plastic Visqueen tarp (page 426) and its attendant plastic bag holding eight Visklamps and six lightweight pegs. By the time you've Visklamped the tarp into a defensive, battened-down configuration and have double-checked each stone-assisted peg, the rain is bloody well pouring down. Naturally, you've not yet attempted to put on any extra clothing under your Gore-Tex jacket: that would surely soggy everything. So by now, although you're still not cold, barely even cool, you're brinking. And you know that the next few minutes are the ones that count.

When the tarp was partially erected you put the pack in under it, up at the head, leaning against the tree. Now you follow it in. And just inside, up in the corner that you've predesignated the "wet or decompression chamber," you take off your dripping jacket and kilt, fold them, and stash them up in the farthest corner of the wet chamber, just clear of occasional ricochets from the lashing rain. (You've pegged the tarp so that its sides mostly reach down to ground level, but you built that corner a little higher, for access and stove lighting.) As you take off kilt and jacket you do your best to keep their insides dry, but in the gloom and damp it's difficult to tell just how successful you've been. You would like to have postponed the stripping off of outer garments, to conserve body heat, but you know that if you did so you would drip water onto everything as you unpacked. The shock of taking off the Gore-Tex jacket was substantial but bearable. As far as you can tell, your polypropylene vest is, except for the forearms, still dry.

By now the worst of the wetness has drained off both pack and covering groundsheet. But only the worst. You shake the sub-worst off the groundsheet, unfold it, and spread it out, wet side down. The "up" side seems remarkably dry. Carefully, in spite of your eagerness to get extra clothes on, you begin to unpack. You do so with some trepidation.

Among the new equipment you're testing is the pack. This is, in fact, the first time you've used an internal-frame model on a trip. You've always been careful to carry your sleeping bag inside a stout stuff sack in the very heart of your single-bloody-great-sack of a packbag, but this time you've been forced—because the configuration of the I-frame pack demands it—to stuff the sleeping bag into the bottom section of the packbag, cramming it deep into both corners so that they wrap around your hips (page 132). When you asked about the danger of the bag's getting wet in rain you were assured that it rarely happens (the "rarely" hardly comforted you), and that if a deluge threatened you should wrap the sleeping bag in one plastic trash bag and maybe line the main sack with another. You duly brought along two big black 4-mil trash bags. But that morning, because the weather was so calm and clear and because you were in a hurry to get moving, you had not thought to press them into use. Later the storm had evolved so insidiously that by the time you were sure that was indeed what you had on your hands it was too late to encapsulate the sleeping bag or line the packbag without getting everything unholy wet. Or so you had judged at the time. Now you're less sure about your decisions. And you're worrying like hell.

As soon as you begin to pull the sleeping bag out you know your worries are justified. In the failing light you can see (and also feel, though your cold and still-damp fingers are for the moment pretty poor sensors) that there are large wet patches. When you finally pull the foot of the bag free you find that part wholly wet, going on soggy. You take your flashlight from a sidepocket. Its beam confirms the diagnosis, in spades—and by chance also illuminates a patch of your bare thigh. It's goosepimpled. And all at once you realize that for the first time you are cold. Not dangerously cold. Not yet. But the objectively warm air (52°F when you checked just before pitching the tarp) is, subjectively, now a world removed from warm. You know that the objective temperature doesn't have to be very low for hypothermia to set in: exhaustion and wetness are the big deals. Though certainly not exhausted, you are by now undeniably a little tired. And it's beginning to look far from sure that you will have dry bedclothes.

Forewarned, you continue unpacking. It's neither a surprise nor a disaster to find that your undershorts and wool shirt, traveling in the pocket-on-the-flap, are only one step short of waterlogged, but the discovery adds a certain edge to the unpacking of the main sack. That edge sharpens when you find your Therm-a-Rest pad patchily damp. You unroll and inflate it, then cover it with the two dry plastic trash bags. The kingpin comes out next: your favorite down jacket—the thick, heavy one you had almost decided to leave behind this trip, in favor of a lighter model. (You have yet to buy a pile jacket.) The jacket's stuff sack is far from dry; but although the jacket itself has absorbed some moisture it seems largely unscathed, and you feel sure that, thanks to its thickness, such moisture as there is will stay clear of your inner garments and will soon be driven off by body heat. Next you pull out the cashmere sweater you rarely carry but put in at the last moment; enclosed in a plastic bag, it turns out to be bone-dry. Thankfully, you slip on over the polypropylene vest first the sweater, then the down jacket. You flip up the jacket hood, pull hood- and hem-drawstrings tight. At once you know you have stopped the worst of the heat loss. Even your forearms feel warm.

Next from the pack come your long, wool-whipcord pants. They weigh 1 lb. 10 oz. Down the years you've lugged them many a mile yet rarely used them, and lately you've seriously considered replacing them with something lighter if less protective. The pants, you discover, are essentially anhydrous. So are the new, untried polypropylene longjohns, also protected in a plastic bag.

All this time you've held your feet off to one side of the groundsheet. Now at last you take off your boots and socks—both wringing wet, in spite of gaiters—and put them near the side of the tarp. Hurriedly, you more or less dry your feet with the less soaked parts of your shirt, then slip off the damp corduroy shorts (damp, probably from sweat and general high humidity) and pull on the polypropylene longjohns and whipcord pants. The change is immediate, astonishing, delectable. Only your feet are cold now—going on icy. But two minutes after encasing them in a dry set of woolen under- and over-socks you know you have turned that corner too.

For years you've carried a small space blanket (2 oz., page 758), and although you've never used it for anything of importance you have always felt that someday it might prove its worth. You take it out of the plastic bag in which it travels, unfold it, and wrap it around the lower part of your body, clear up to your down jacket. The cocoon effect is immediate and beautiful. For the first time you feel almost sure you will spend a reasonably comfortable night. After all, you sleep like a hot-water bottle—and have grateful bedmates to vouch for it.

The discovery that your silk balaclava (page 554) is distinctly wet does little to dampen your good cheer—which is immediately fueled again, anyway, by the discovery that the thicker Orlon balaclava is wholly dry. Your scarf too. And wool gloves. You slip them all on, refit the jacket hood. Then, feeling the warmth beginning to spread outward from your core into all sectors of your body, you restoke the fires by eating a couple of candies and spirulina tablets (a first-time experiment). After that you sit for a moment and rest, recalling with pleasure how you fought off the idea that carrying two balaclavas was unnecessary, and how you chose rather heavier, long-wristed wool gloves over a lighter pair. You smile to yourself, confident that once you get a good hot meal in your gut you will positively glow.

It is while you are sitting there, beginning to plan the meal, that you remember the canteens. They're standing at the foot of the tree you originally chose as a campsite. They are standing, that is, all of 30 feet from your snug little temporary home. And outside, now, the rain is lashing down in sheets.

It doesn't take you long to reject the wrenching prospect of stripping off all those layers of wonderful, dry, heat-conserving clothes. Instead you unwrap the space blanket (which is bad enough) and pull on your coated-nylon chaps—unused to date, and still dry. Next you take off both pairs of socks (which is horrible) and slip your feet into campshoes. Then you ease up into the "wet corner" and arrange the Gore-Tex jacket over head and shoulders (finding to your joy that you apparently did a fair job of keeping the inside of the jacket dry when you took it off). You take a deep breath. Then you crawl out into the lashing rain and crouch-shamble toward the canteens. Seconds later you're crawling back in. When you strip off jacket and chaps you find that, as far as you can tell, nothing underneath has gotten wet. Within a minute or two you have your socks back on and your midriff rewrapped in space blanket, and you can feel the furnace working again. The brief spurt of exercise actually seems to have helped.

From that point on, the storm becomes a rather pleasant, restful interlude.

You cook a tasty freeze-dried Turkey Tetrazzini dinner (preheating the stove outside the tarp with fire paste [page 344]—grateful for your decision to bring the MSR stove, because it means you can, by igniting the paste "indoors" and quickly shoving the burner outside but keeping tank and controls inside, avoid both getting hands or wrists wet and also almost all danger of setting the tarp alight while the stove does its initial flaring). Sure enough, hot food stokes your fires. Soon warmth is coursing through you.

The warmth quickly dries off the worst of the dampness from the Therm-a-Rest pad. You remove the two plastic trash bags that were covering it and use one of them as a footsack. This enables you to shift the space blanket upward so that it more efficiently encases your crucial midsection. When you reinforce your socks with a backup set (that you almost decided not to bring) you find that in combination with the footsack they make you feel almost too hot. By now the upper part of the sleeping bag has begun to dry out a little, and you drape it loosely over your lower body. The trash-bag footsack and space-blanket cummerbund will protect pants and jacket from the bag's dampness, and the bag will help keep more warmth in as well as tend to dry itself out. By this time you're almost too dozy to check that the outside temperature still stands—as it will, day and night, throughout the storm—at 52°F. Before long you feel yourself drifting warmly and contentedly down into unconsciousness.

You wake in daylight, after a long, log- and toast-like sleep, to find the rain, if anything, even heavier, the wind gone steadily crazy. And you spend the entire day lying there, remarkably cozy in your small, white, double-slanting refuge. All day the wind howls and the rain cascades down. But it is Friday the 13th, so you know everything will be fine.

For a change, you brought no reading matter on this trip, yet you never, all through that day of immobility, even flirt with inaction, let alone boredom. As often happens, it is curiously difficult, looking back, to pin down just what you found to do, beyond doze occasionally. When the wind rose to gale force and the tarp began to flap rather dangerously, you certainly had to rebatten down. That meant swiveling around and crawling to the foot of the house to deal with the final two Visklamp guys; but you were able to complete even that operation without consigning anything but your hands to the perils of the storm. Several times, after things that came boomp out of the day had boomped onto the tarp (they were probably pinecones), you detected pinpricks and small slits that needed patching with ripstop tape. Soon you had a gay little galaxy of red stars pulsating overhead like a celestial Moscow parade. You also had to make ongoing checks that nothing important was getting wet—from condensation, slight galaxy leakage, or ricochets from the unfriendly outside world. In addition, there were the usual food-sorting chores. But otherwise—as far as you could remember later—you spent the time drifting into pleasant reveries, farting, and, once, exchanging world views with an orange-tinted, comfort-loving salamander that you found hunkered down among your snacks. Yet by nightfall, when you look back, that hardly seems a full day's work. The stubborn fact remains, though, that you have not even had time to finish catching up with your notes. Odd.

By that second night your body heat has dried out the sleeping bag enough for you to push your feet, still cocooned in their trash bag, inside its foot. And that not only makes you so warm that eventually you have to take off one set of socks but also helps dry the sleeping bag even further.

Next morning you awake to calm: no rain; no wind. You emerge. Above the canopy of washed and silent trees slides a hint of watery sunlight. Within half an hour you have a fire going and are beginning to dry things out. (Once again you are thankful you brought the MSR stove—and plenty of white gas: you use the stove to torch sodden wood into reluctant flame, while keeping the gas bottle a safe distance from flames and heat.)

By midafternoon you've dried everything out, sort of, and are on your way again, singing.

Back home, four days later, you learn that a weather station on the next ridge over from your cozy little refuge—less than 7 miles away—registered 11.7 inches of rain from the storm, and that even down at sea level the winds reached 71 mph.

The three-layer system in action in snow

CHIP: One good confession leads to another. October 29, the tail of the season in the Wind Rivers. It's cool, but I'm stubbornly in sandals and shorts—fortunately as it turns out. Watching a herd of mule-deer does and fawns in a riverside meadow, I ford—without proper attention—and end up chest-deep and floundering in cold, green water. On the far bank I notice my camera case is draining onto my groin (nice) and open it to find my telephoto lens has drowned. I take off pack and all clothing, spooking the deer, and wring out all that's wring-outable. Then I dig into the house on my back for a damage assessment. Dumb—I keep repeating the word—dumb. A *dumb* way to begin a trip. But surprisingly, the pack, a Dana Swiftcurrent, has kept all but a cup or so of the river out and none of my critical garments nor the all-important sleeping bag (in a truly waterproof stuff sack) are the least bit damp.

There are perhaps two hours of daylight remaining and the climb ahead is steep, so I shiver back into my wet shorts, add a fresh jersey—Lowe Dryflo polyester—and set off through thick willows, dodging around a couple of revved-up baby bull moose. (It's the end of the mating season and they, by all appearances, have not.) Leaving the level ground I punch up 3 miles of switchbacks, through silvery granite into sloping aspens, with the 13,000-foot peaks of the Divide rising into view. By the time I find a good camp, high above the river on an aspen-fringed bench set in cliffs, I'm not only dry but also warm—even sweating a bit.

In blue dusk I set up the test tent, a VauDe Galaxy Ultralight, and unfurl my vanities inside: the Skin Mat inhaling, the down sleeping bag lofting (for the gear list, see Appendix II, page 781). The shirt that I forded in hangs drying from an aspen with a few golden leaves still alight. By now I've cooled off and slide into a polyester zip T and longhandles. That feels good, so I follow it with the light fleece pullover and fleece socks. There's a downdraft breeze, but instead of matches I'm trying a sparker, and—scritch, scritch—the little cartridge stove blups into life in the lee of a lichened boulder. I start a pot of water toward boiling. Good enough.

Darkness pools in the canyon, deepening until the ridges hold the last glow, then the high rock walls far above, then the crown of fresh snow. Cold evening air ruffles the flame on the stove, a fair-weather downdraft. When the breeze dies, I can hear the river below. The first pot boils and I take the edge off with Swiss Miss and rum. There are snowpatches a few steps away, in the head of a draw, left from the last fall storm, and I dig out a potful and reboil, adding Turkish Rice Pilaf, home-dried scallions, and a dollop of margarine. Then a fresh gust from the west draws my gaze to the cloud front advancing: rain tonight, or snow, I think, and slip the fleece vest over the pullover. Out of the pot I spoon hot pilaf, hotter by virtue of home-brewed *chipotle* sauce, and then wash up in the dark, the steam curling around my bare hands in the headlamp beam.

I seek out a thick-limbed pine downwind, hang the food, and retire. Inhabiting the tent, a 5-lb. German miracle with two big vestibules, I reverse the layering process, slipping off the fleece vest and shorts, then sliding into the lightweight down bag. This being the end of hunting season, the bears are feeding on cone caches, gut piles, and hunting-camp trash, and shouldn't bother me here on this ridge; so I place the stove and pots in the vestibule. I slide out of the pullover and stuff it inside the fleece vest for a pillow, still feeling the heat of the food in my core. By headlamp I read *The Serpent and the Swan* by Boria Sax (a full pound. But it's not the sort of book you can find in a lightweight edition). As I warm up in the bag, I shuck off the underwear bottoms, then the zip top, wearing the Dryflo T as a nightshirt.

After midnight, snow sweeps in on a gust and wakes me. Over the light rasp of flakes on the fly sheet I hear hoarse breathing and hoofbeats: elk moving downcountry with the storm. Let them go. Am I happy? Warm? Yes.

And I sleep once more.

The dawn is snow-muffled blue, and the clouds course low from the west, covering the peaks of the Divide. What woke me? A congregation of ravens, raising perfect hell, north of camp. By the time I consider checking out the cause, they've stopped. The fly sheet droops with heavy snow that slides off with a flick. I unzip the side door-arch and one curve of the vestibule, loosing another mini-avalanche, and then lively up the stove. I fill the little pot, set it on, and then start the layering process—zip turtle, bottoms, socks. A pause while I dismantle the pillow. Then I don the light fleece pullover and stretch the Turtle Fur hat over my my matted locks. Last come light shell pants. I stow the sandals in favor of light-weight boots, but still warm after sleep I hold the fleece vest in reserve. The water boils and I take it off so the fly doesn't get steamed up inside.

Coffee drips through a paper filter, smelling like heaven in an insulated mug. Breakfast is oatmeal with nuts and goodies, and an ounce of Balance drink stirred in—for the strenuous day ahead. I've cleared the snow from the fly sheet and the skirts of the tent, and silently debate whether to leave it set up—shelter from the storm. The sun slips free of the Divide and lights up the tent, a wild apricot against the stainless new snow. No, I think. My plan is to first find a route down into the canyon to reach the river and then to follow it out of the mountain front. If possible. There's no trail on the map and the contour lines are mysterious. So I make haste, taking advantage of the sun's heat, shaking and hanging my camp gear for a brief dry-out before I pack up. The work heats me up as well, and once the pack is assembled I shed the pullover and stow it with the fleece hat. The brush will be snowy with drips and plops under forest trees, so I choose the light anorak. And set off in boots, stretch gaiters, lightweight bottoms, and a midweight top, under shell pants and anorak, with a gray Moonstone ball cap.

Not far from the camp several elk trails converge and drop down a series of benches into the canyon, skirting rockfaces and steep little creeks, milky with snowmelt. The sky shuts down again and starts peppering snow—little pellets called graupel, ticktocking on the hood and the bill of my cap. My hands are chilly, what with all the digestion going on, and I consider stopping to dig out fleece gloves but instead tuck my hands inside the sleeves of the anorak, making fists, tensing and letting go until they feel warm again. Going down is easy enough, though slippery: snow over foliage, mud patches, and moss-covered granite. But I make it without mishap to a long, sedgy meadow by pools of dark green. Still snowing in bursts. Needing to reach the endpoint of a previous trip, I set off upstream to explore. The river makes three log-jammed bends through rocky knuckles before the walls close up into a gorge.

The walking . . . isn't. Instead I must balance, high-step, sidle, and occasionally crawl. Having traveled so often with impatient climber types, I tend to fall into a too-rapid beat. But the canyon's rough going with a full pack, and I heat up, lowering the hood, unzipping the chest, ventilating the pants at the top—steam rising as the snow falls. With one layer for wicking and one for water shedding, I can't really take anything off. So I slow down—through ragged forest, sedge bogs, and thick snowy brush, up rockfaces and down, under deadfalls, tightroping logs bridged over tributary creeks—but never quite stop. Think of it as a stroll. Be deliberate and calm.

The sky brightens and the snow lets up, so I shed the anorak and strike up a rocky spine, overlooking the river gorge. No place to walk down there, except on a tumble of stream-polished boulders, and the water's fast and deep. So I follow the exposed heights. At last I recognize a set of cliffs above a tributary stream and find a good boulder for backrest and windbreak—and lunch. Out come the fleece pullover, the anorak, the Turtle Fur hat, and the gloves. Then, crackers and hummus and mixed dried fruit. As I eat I make notes in a K & E Mining Transit book (the hydrologist's constant companion). Done with the food, I scramble to the top of a boulder pile and take photos. Then—snow picking up again—I de-layer for the return trip, trusting my body to burn the midday fuel, keeping my precious insulation sealed away from drips, glops, and bog-downs.

So it goes. Two hours up, one hour to get back. From the point where I reached the canyon floor, a faint trail zigs through the snow-flecked woods, as the river finds ledges and cataracts, roaring by my side. Snowcovered rockslabs and multiple deadfalls make each step an exercise in judgment: observe, decide, lift, contact, stoop, and recover. My staff, with depth measurements carved in it, is a necessary third leg. The canyon drops out from under me—above, the slopes are now sheer cliffs. The river dives into slots, splits around pinnacles, froths through black logjams, and loses its smooth green composure.

The snow builds—pellets, then flakes, then pellets again—a sign that the atmosphere's roiling like the creek, moist air swirling into the cold. I'm no longer walking, but scrambling and balancing. My hands are cold now, wet from grasping wood and stone. The air lightens ahead. That might be the canyon's mouth, my goal, giving out to the broad valley. But it's not. I edge out onto a point and below there's nothing but snowy air. The river pours white through a narrow gap in bedrock and flies off into space. The snow meets hard spray. Far below is a pool, the frightening green of God's eye.

If I had a rope—. But I'm not such a fool as to rappel down an unknown waterfall, alone in a snowstorm. Unless I have to, that is. I ditch my pack and traverse right, looking for a ledge or a ramp—slippery, nothing. Wet snow on wet rock. A stack of huge boulders calls out from above, and I scramble back, grab the pack, and climb. The biggest boulder slants out toward the drop, with a lesser one cupped beneath. And it's dry.

I don't unpack the tent but instead layer up: midweights over the lights, with the shell pants rezipped. The fleece vest under the anorak, hood up. Fleece gloves. The old Norsk mittens. Turtle Fur on top. I move a few rocks to level a bed. Mate the stove to a cartridge and set it in an alcove. Reaching out from shelter, I scoop the pot full of snow, scritch a flame into life, set the water on. Swiss Miss, perhaps a ration of rum: it takes the edge off, out here on the edge. With the snow falling and the roar of the falls, this feels like the loneliest spot on earth.

Reversing my route up the canyon is easier, except for the weight of the pack. But it's strenuous—several thousand high steps. And the snow is deeper. But the night was cold enough to freeze it to the rocks, so the footing's improved. The new boots were nearly dry when I put them on, and have yet to leak. Likewise, the stretch gaiters amaze me, keeping snow out of my boots, and letting steam rise through their porous weave. Again, I'm in light bottoms, midweight top, under Lightflite shells and lunar ball cap. Taking photos (the camera and wide-angle lens are okay) and notes and detouring to the river, I work up a good blast of heat as I scramble and snap and meander up to rejoin the faint trail. From there it's a walk again—dark pines, dark firs—then it's afternoon and I climb the slippery slope back to the ridge. There are fewer bright leaves on the aspen, more lost under the snow. My first campsite is drifted in. Elk tracks punctuate the trail. As I crunch downhill, facing the wind, I need the Turtle Fur hat again, and the fleece gloves come out of the kangaroo pouch on the anorak, where they've mostly dried out.

The trail swerves down through raggedy cliffs, taking big gulps of air. I'm under the snowline now. But the wind is insistent and cold. Without stopping, hardly thinking, I know I'm too tired to make it out. Especially if I have to outmaneuver a sex-starved moose in the dark.

A rock-rimmed balcony offers itself, guarded by limber pines. Over my head, the wind hisses through their needles and draws groans from the heavy limbs, as I stack the layers on: pullover, vest, gloves, every-damn-thing I've got. The tent blossoms. The pack unburdens. Stove, pot, pad, sleeping bag—all magically find their appointed spots. Clouds race through the pinnacles, dividing, reforming. I light the stove, set the pot on, and snug back into the tent, as the last light bleeds out of the air. Time again to slip off the layers, to assemble them into a pillow, fluff the bag, ease in.

Home again.

Furniture and Appliances

No matter how grimly you pare away at the half ounces you always seem to burden your house with an astonishing clutter of furniture and appliances. At least, I do. Each item, of course, is a necessary aid to some necessary activity. For example, there's the vital matter of

SEEING.

To lighten your darkness you almost always need to carry a small, lightweight

Flashlight,

and you now have a wild and plastic selection to choose from: a flock of handheld models and a growing number of practical headlamps.

CHIP: Both hand- and head-held lights are changing fast, with leaps in the design of batteries and bulbs. Since there's determined competition for the favor of backpackers, you're ever more likely to find a light that suits you. Meanwhile, two classics survive.

The old, angular plastic Mallory still lives in many pack pockets, with the current model being sold as the Durabeam DFC Compact (empty, 1.5 oz.; with two alkaline AA batteries, 3 oz.; all told, $7). It's bright, but not waterproof, with a tapered grip that fits into some elastic and Velcro headbands, for hands-free operation. The Durabeam light costs little and will last for decades—I have a tooth-marked 1970s survivor in my glove box.

Durabeam flashlight

The other classic is the Mini Maglite (with two AA cells, 4.1 oz.,

$14.50).* Machined not of magnesium but of aluminum (Alulite just doesn't have that same ring, I guess), these are nearly indestructible. The key feature is a machined thread sealed by a rubber O-ring (water-resistant rather than -proof) that not only switches the light on but focuses the beam, from a diffused flood to a tight, brilliant spot. A semi-key feature is a selection of anodized jewel-toned cases. Linda's Mini Maglite (red) is a 1980s model and, with a couple of cleanings and one new bulb, it shines on dependably. The reason I didn't adopt one was that at low temperatures—repairing a stove, etc.—I'd get a headache from holding what amounted to a metallic cigar between my teeth. But there's now an astonishing range of accessories for the Mini Maglite:

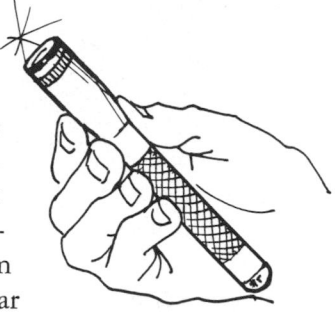

Mini Maglite with hand

headbands, holsters, wrist straps, belt clips, and, *yes,* plastic bite sockets. The Maglite Solitaire (with one AAA cell, 2 oz., $9.50) is popular for ounce paring. Extra-bright bulbs can be had ($5) if you don't mind their battery-gulping habits.

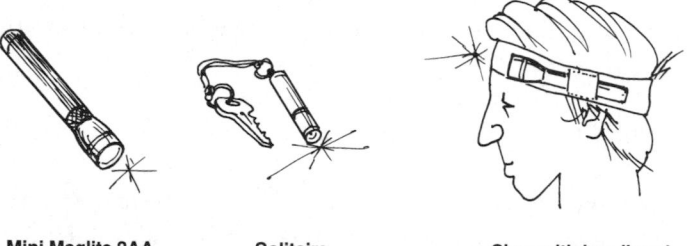

Mini Maglite 2AA　　　**Solitaire**　　　**Chap with headband**

Maglite-style switches that work by rotating the *bezel* (beh'-zel: the front part that houses the lens, reflector, and bulb) on a molded set of threads are the overwhelming choice these days. They're mechanically simple—you literally screw the bulb down into contact with the batteries. They're easy to waterproof with a rubber O-ring. But switching one on is a two-handed operation. You can accomplish it single-handedly by gripping the barrel of the light with three fingers while rotating the bezel with forefinger and thumb, though this takes practice. But—if you ease the procedure by keeping the switch/bezel near the turn-on point, the light can light up inside your pack. This happens not just from rotation

---

*Our weights for flashlights, headlamps, etc., all include the weight of the necessary batteries. For purposes of comparison, we'll choose mercury-free alkaline cells (Duracells, Energizers). But batteries vary in weight, storage capacity, and so forth—see pages 591 to 595.

but also pressure. When you take the light out the pressure is relieved and it will be off. To check, turn the bezel until the light goes off, then press down on it. Many rotary-thread models will come on for up to a half turn (180 degrees) past the apparent off-point. If your light relentlessly and mysteriously devours batteries, this might be your problem (see page 590).

Sorting the current crop of flash-lights by type—and sticking for the most part to light-weight models—let's start with some that don't have rotary-thread switches. Like the classic Mallory, the Eveready Sport Compact (with two AA cells, 4.5 oz., $6) has a rectangular reflector, but it's waterproof (and floats). The switch is a unidextrous push button clad in soft plastic; the case has molded ridges for grip; the lens is shatterproof; and there's a lanyard.

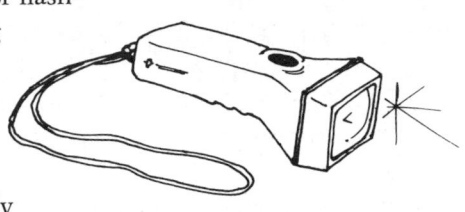

Eveready Sport light

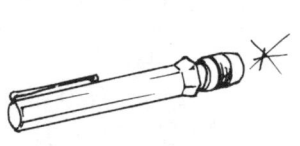

Pelican MityLite

Magnum

The following, unless noted, are all rotary-switch types that have been used for backpacking with some success. Pelican makes a series of handheld lights, flagshipped by the popular MityLite (two AAA cells, 1.7 oz., $13). Rated as waterproof to 2000 feet, it boasts a xenon seed bulb and dioptic reflector that throws a sharply focused beam. Also xenon-lamped and H_2O-proof with a longer burn time is the Pelican Magnum (two AA cells, 4 oz., $17). It has a plastic "shirt clip" that works on the bill of a cap, to free up your hands for cooking, fixing, and groping.

Princeton Tec, originally a maker of scuba divers' lights, now offers impressively waterproof and exceptionally rugged handheld models with noncorroding metal parts—the two-AA version is called the Tec 20 (3.2 oz. with batteries, $14). Princeton Tec is in New Jersey—near sea level—and when you first open the bat-tery compartments of these lights at high elevations there's a distinct

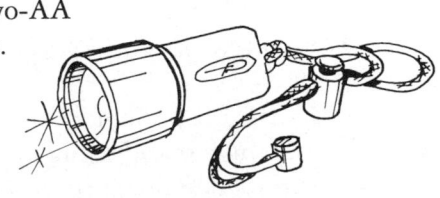

Princeton Tec 20

whoosh, which means the O-rings are good. With batteries side by side in a flat-oval cross section, the Tec 20 fits the hand nicely and also slides into most headbands, belt clips, etc.

Another compact light recommended by readers is the Streamlight Scorpion (4.4 oz.; $60 with batteries, $50 without) that runs on two 3-volt lithium cells (sold for auto-wind cameras, and hence widely available). It has a rubber-clad aluminum body and, if wallet chomping, is also bright and long-lived: a perfectionist's flashlight.

Streamlight Scorpion

A recent and well-thought-out contender is the Bison Sportslight 2AA (3.4 oz., $15), a polymer-cased handlight with a click (rather than screw-thread) rotary switch. The focusing reflector is shaped to avoid bull's-eye voids without stippling or diffusion. Two teeny bi-pin bulbs (that connect with two stiff wires) are supplied, one a high-power xenon type, with the spare nested in a semi-obscure internal cavity. The bulb change should not be done by feel in the dark, nor after encounters with John Barleycorn, Lord Ganja, or other fumble inducers. The original Bison 2C model (7 oz., $20) slings as much light as those long-barreled aluminoid cop flashers, but with better ergonomics (unless you want to club demonstrators, that is). Bison also makes a better-than-average stretch wrist-loop and belt-clip combo ($5).

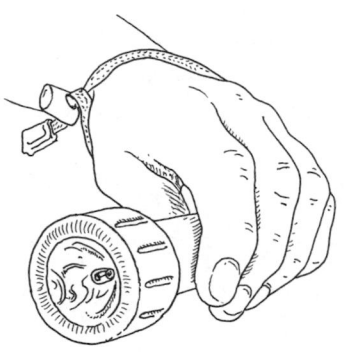

Bison 2AA

Discount-store racks have a surprising number of blister-packed two-AA flashlights with rotary-thread switches, claimed to be waterproof or -resistant, for $3 to $5 with batteries. Their weak point seems to be rapid wear on the bezel/switch/O-ring seal, causing the light to flick off without warning when jogged, or not to turn on at all. Since the mechanism resembles that of the new LED lights, see below for fixits. If you're scratching your head, "LED" is short for

Light-emitting diode,

a new and Fairy Godmotherish gift to backpackers—especially those of us who like to read at night. Unlike a bulb in which a metal filament is heated to incandescence, an LED gives off light without generating much heat. The device is made by combining a layer of semiconductor that has a small excess of electrons and a negative charge with a second layer that has electron vacancies called "holes" and a positive charge. When electron and hole meet, a photon bursts out: light. Each LED sandwich is mounted in transparent polycarbonate, which directs the light, and the resulting unit is (unlike bulbs) shock- and vibration-proof. This means extremely long life (10 or more years of continuous use) while needing only 10 to 20 percent of the power used by an incandescent bulb. The newest LED flashlights, with internal power-saving chips, can give hundreds of hours of useful light on a set of batteries. That's the revolutionary part.

Now, the liabilities: relative dimness, fuzziness, short throw, and chilly looking hues, along with some odd special effects.

Some years ago, intrigued by the possibilities, I located a single yellow LED that was soldered into a standard brass bulb-base. On rechargeable nicads it glowed a full 24 hours but was too faint for walking at a normal pace. So I used it for tenting-up and reading during storms (dim lights, thick snow, and nature's music). Recently, makers have bumped the brightness by teaming up better diodes in two-, three-, and four-LED arrays. But since the diodes themselves vary somewhat in hue, you might get a mix of bluish and yellowish haloes—a bother for reading.

Though costly (now) an LED array can save you tremendous weight and cost in batteries. A neat three-LED model in a standard 9-millimeter flange base that will drop into your favorite two- or three-cell light comes from Real Goods ($30). I tested one in a two-AA headlamp and had plenty of light for tent pitching, cooking, reading, and normal walking. After 38(!) hours the light was still bright enough for reading but too dim for confident walking. The batteries (Duracell alkaline) started fresh at 1.55 volts and ended at 1.36, so there was probably another three to four hours of useful light left. This means you can do a fairly long trip on one set of batteries. For average use—cooking and gear fiddling—you don't need much light, but for route finding and rescues, you do. So a kit of standard and extra-bright bulbs is a wise (and lightweight) backup.

LEDs arrived in a flood of Chinese-made flashlights with the diodes soldered to a flat piece of circuit board. These seem to crap out in fairly short order, first flickering when bumped, then failing to light up. A lick with a pencil eraser or fingernail file on the contact point—a blob of solder under the circuit board—might get them working again. Another caveat is that LEDs have a voltage threshold and some won't light up with even mildly depleted nicad rechargeables. In fact, many present LED configurations need three batteries (4.5 volts) to work right, so the flashlights are either long (7 inches) or wide. But not all.

The lightest useful LED backpacking light is the C. Crane Lithium Trek Light (1.6 oz. with special 3.6-volt AA cell, $40). A mere 3.5 inches

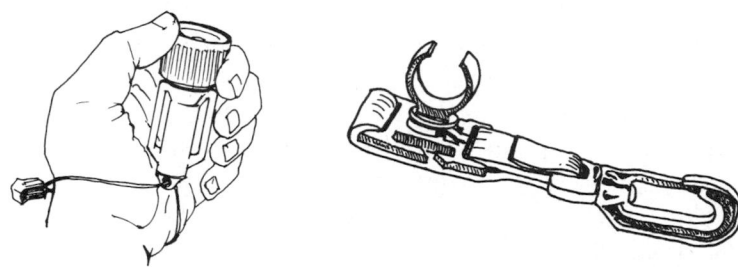

Crane Lithium Trek Light and holder

long, it has a three-LED array in a rotary-switch bezel. The 3.6-volt lithium Hawker Eternacell ($11) is rated for 50-plus hours—a very long trip or even a season—and it works in cold temperatures when alkaline cells flag and nicads are hopeless. I suggested that they include a black shield with the light as a standard item, since side glare is a problem. But as always, a wrap of duct tape works. A keen accessory is the light holder that clips to the waistband of your shorts or the lantern loop in your tent. But with careful microsawing and filing, a molded side slot on the Trek Light (ostensibly for a wrist loop) becomes a clip for a cap visor, giving you a strapless headlamp. In crash tests (I jumped out of a tree) it stayed on the cap, although the cap itself tended to fly off. The drawback with this system is that you can't adjust the angle of the beam—for walking I unclip the light and hold it low. Anyhow, at roughly the same weight as a fast-dying penlight, the Lithium Trek is a welcome surprise for determined ounce parers.

Almost as light, with the option of rechargeable batteries, is the C. Crane Mini Trek Light (3 oz. with three AAA cells, $35) in the usual black and also easy-to-find yellow. The three batteries nest in a tricky triangle, so the light's only 4 inches long, with a combination lanyard mount/bite tab and a sturdy clip for the bill of a cap—the necessary lens shield comes with it.

Brightest of the stick-type LED flashlights I tested, the Lightwave 2000 (4.5 oz. with three AA cells, $30), has a four-LED array. It also has a chip to keep the power level constant and prevent overdriving the LEDs (which accounts for the bright and dim phases of unchipped models). The chip allows three alkaline cells to yield 300 to 400 hours of illumination (I left it on for a week—168 hours—and finally got tired of checking it). The case has grip grooves, and the black bezel doesn't need a light shield. Like other lights of this sort, it's water-resistant, not -proof. The importer, LED-Lite of California, also handles a curiouser item, called the Eterna-Light.

Although lights play a role in entertainment they usually aren't the whole of it. But the EternaLight is entertaining as hell. In fact, you should be wary of lending it to impressionable tentmates, who will sit up late playing with it. Designed by Wayne Gregory, of I-frame fame, the EternaLight (4.3 oz. with three AA lithium cells, $80) has four LEDs. I tested the marine model that's watertight to 100 feet, floats (with lithium cells), and is bright enough to be useful. But the interesting part is the 18-prong internal chip, controlled by three push buttons. ON/OFF does what it says.

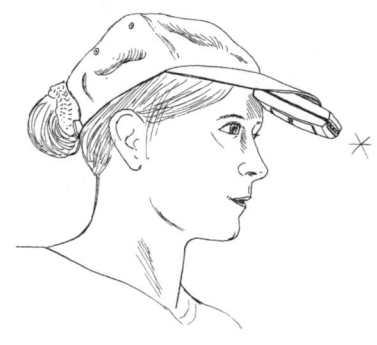

EternaLight

MODE switches seven ways, between *timer* (a 10-minute dimming to shut-off), *on/dim* (10 power levels, from 100 percent giving 50 hours to 6 percent giving 785 hours), *flasher* (all LEDs blink), *strobe* (adjustable speed), *dazzle* (LEDs wink in an attention-getting pattern), *SOS* (the Morse code signal), and *pulse* (for other signaling). The third button, RATE, controls both the power levels and the speed of the special effects. The prototype had a few glitches—foam padding that stuck to the batteries and tiny screws that fell out—and after a hearty cougar scream, I ended up stroking the rug with a magnet. When I called LED-Lite with feedback ("already changed," they said), they promised weirder and better things in the near future, including bike mounts and a headlamp. For the present, they have a nice forest-green ball cap (2 oz., $20) with Velcro loops under the bill, and a strip of hook tape for the EternaLight, making it a viable headlamp. Crash tests (jumping out of that tree again) revealed that while the light remains firmly attached to the cap, the cap—weight tripled by the light—may depart the head. In any event, I scampered out and bought an extra length of 2-inch Velcro tape for my bike helmet and am pondering other sticking points.

The business end of the Streamlight Syclone (7.6 oz., $30) pivots—fans of the old army right-angle flashlights will find it a much-improved

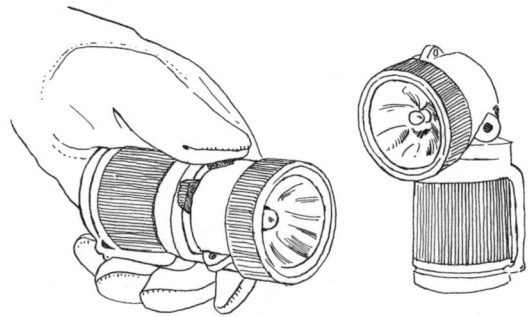

Streamlight Syclone

update. A four-AA model, the Syclone mounts a bright krypton bi-pin bulb (see page 596) and a single amber LED. On alkaline cells, the krypton bulb burns for 3.5 hours and the LED (for reading, fumbling, and careful walking) for 72. Rugged, waterproof, and only 4¾ inches long, the Syclone has a strong, rotating belt clip and a top-mounted hanger hole, so light can be directed at any angle.

Another swivel-headed model is Pelican's VersaBrite (5 oz. with two

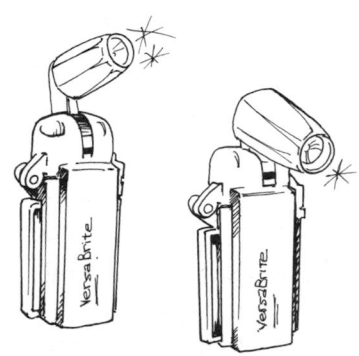

Pelican VersaBrite

AA cells, $19) that mounts a bright and focused xenon bulb. Burn time is 5 to 6 hours. With an array of clips and slots, the polycarbonate body attaches to pockets, visors, straps, and, via the Velcro tape included, to other loopy surfaces (Chesapeake Bay retrievers). There's also a magnetic mount—of limited use to backpackers, unless you have a steel plate in your head.

The Streamlight WOW (5.4 oz. with two AA cells, $14) straddles the gap between flashlight and headlamp,

with a pair of battery-holding legs that close to form a rubberized handgrip, or spread wide to encircle your brow. In like fashion, the elastic wrist lanyard becomes—voilà!— a headstrap. The lamp assembly, with a pebbled reflector and rotary switch, swivels 80 degrees up or down in either mode. The WOW light gives me mixed emotions: it

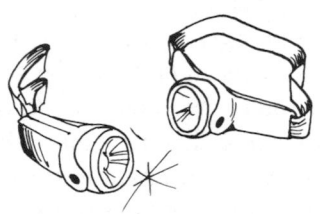

Streamlight WOW

looks like a gimcrack but turns out to be a somewhat bulky but really pretty good light (for the gadget lover, at least).

COLIN: *Dynamo lights*—which I remember as popular in the Netherlands during World War II—are interesting and economical alternatives to battery-powered flashlights: you squeeze a handle slowly and rhythmically and generate a steady light. Dropping one of these gizmos in water apparently does no damage, the handle locks away for packing, and a spare bulb sits tucked in behind the reflector. The sturdy kind of model you need (avoid flimsy lightweight versions) weighs 8 ounces; but remember you need carry no spare batteries. And although I don't dote on

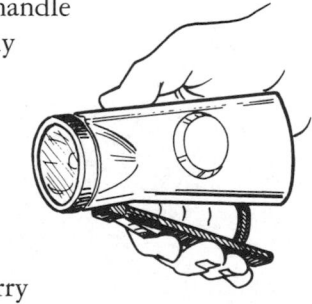

Dynamo light

the whirring noise it makes, and am underwhelmed at the thought of having to keep squeezing it for camp chores, I purr at having a surefire backup. I've used it occasionally, and with reasonable success, for following a trail at night. Real Goods still sells the kind I use (8 oz., $13), and sometimes stocks, primarily for kids, a clear plastic version ($14) that needs assembling but then—wait for it—lets you watch the wheels whir.

Many backpackers—and especially snow campers—favor

Headlamps

over hand-held models, even though they tend to be heavier. You always have both hands free—for erecting a tent, cooking, and every other chore or delight. (Along this line, a Rhode Island reader recommends, for setting up camp after dark, taping your flashlight to your knife and sticking it in a tree.)

Headlamps come in two conformations: those with the whole unit, including batteries, up on the headstrap—thereby eliminating troublesome cords but putting more weight on the head and sometimes inducing headaches, especially if you walk at night; and those with only a light bulb-and-lens unit on the headstrap and a separate battery unit, often with a built-in additional light, that can clip on clothing, travel in a pocket, or even stand alone—thereby necessitating a cord but holding headaches at bay and also keeping the batteries warm (often an important matter with all but lithium cells, as anyone who has dropped a flashlight in snow will attest).

CHIP: By the light of a flailing beam I've done things I might well have regretted: skiing out of high peaks in the December dark over snow-covered granite, with sparks spraying from the edges of my skis. For such tricks, a headlamp is mandatory (and a headache optional).

The first one I used was a Justrite Head Lantern, a steel-bezelled biggie with a lamp cord leading to a hinged steel case and four D cells (weight: a ton). Fatigued by our heroics, we forest-fire fighters often forgot to return them. In latter days, Justrite updated the beast with a polypropylene battery case and a focusing beam (1 lb. 11 oz. with four D cells, $36.50, Forestry Suppliers). About that time there were all-plastic headlamps around with basic electrical problems, odd features, and underpants-quality headstraps. Some weren't bad—Linda has a four-AA Panasonic that continues to work. I used a French Wonder Light with three brow-mounted AAs and a rotary switch, which tended to short out in rainstorms. And when I hit bumps on skis, the weight of the batteries converted it to a blindfold. So I rewired it to run off a lantern cell stowed in the top pocket of my pack. But one night when I abruptly shed my pack, the thing flew off my head and was terminally impaired by a rock.

At that point, Chouinard Equipment began selling the industrial Hartford Headlite (13.4 oz. with four AA cells, $21.50, Forestry Suppliers) of unbreakable plastic with a hole-punched rubber strap and a D-battery holder astern. With the newly available lithium D cell and matching bulb, it was the best thing going. But it was heavy and bulky, and the rear battery holder was uncomfortable for tent-bound reading. So when I saw the Petzl Micro, I pounced.

The Petzl Micro (5.2 oz. with two AA cells; $24) is a sweetly functional backpacking headlamp (though not waterproof) with a rotary bezel switch on a swiveling head, and a top strap to hold it aloft. The soft-rubber battery cover tucks a spare bulb in. It was my standby for half a decade.

Petzl Micro headlamp

Hard-core types prefer the Petzl Zoom (9 oz. with battery, $35). The flat 4.5-volt battery costs $7, for 17 hours of really bright light. An optional halogen bulb throws a 300-foot beam but cuts battery life to 6 or 7 hours. A three-AA adapter costs $5 and gives 8 to 9 hours on a krypton bulb, 3 hours on halogen—but you can also use lithium cells for longer burn time and cold conditions. C. Crane Co. sells the Petzl Zoom for $40 with a special screw-in LED array ($20 alone) that gives 35 to 40 hours of bright light and 20-plus hours of diminished output. The Crane package includes a regular krypton bulb, plus the AA adapter. Demerits: the Zoom's rear-mounted battery pack is trying if you like to read with your head propped,

Petzl Zoom headlamp
w/adapter, LED array

as I do; and for backpacking it might simply be overkill. Still more so is the NiteRider series of digitally controlled headlamps, sophisticated artifacts that start at $100-plus and rise steeply.

My current love-pet is the Princeton Tec Solo (5.5 oz. with two AA cells, $28) with the same good points as the Petzl Micro, as well as waterproof (to 2000 feet) lamp and battery cases and an easier bulb change. The Solo comes with two reflectors, a tight-beam one and a stippled one that eliminates the bull's-eye (for reading and contemplation). It

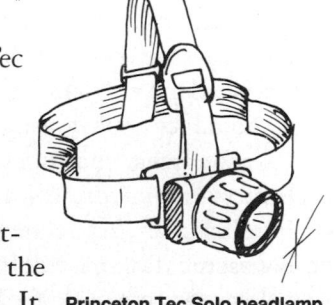

Princeton Tec Solo headlamp

also comes with two bulbs, krypton (8 hours) and halogen (2 hours), and is packed in a fleece pouch to prevent lens scratches. Now that 1.5-volt lithium AA cells (with four to five times the capacity per oz. of alkaline cells) are widely available, two-AA lamps like the Solo are nicely feasible for deep-freeze weather.

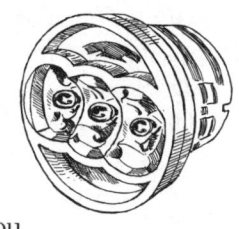

So I asked the Princeton Techies when they planned to scoop the market with an LED headlamp. Enter the Matrix (basically a Princeton Tec Solo in silver gray, 5.8 oz., $40) with a three-LED array in a plastic mount that replaces the conventional reflector/bulb assembly. It burns 40 hours on two AA alkaline cells, meaning that you can do a week's trip on a single set. The LED assembly ($30 alone) fits only Princeton Tec lights. I use it for

Princeton Tec Matrix LED array

general fumbling while keeping a spare lamp unit (a reflector/base, a spring, and a krypton bulb, included) ready to go. The changeover to tight, bright beam takes—I just timed it—18 seconds. There's a little guide groove that makes it impossible to goof up. Of course, it helps to practice the lamp change in the dark, standing up, lying down, and also to rehearse swapping batteries—in a tight situation, it's well worth the effort.

If you bash around in the dark enough to need a bright, focusing beam, another good two-AA model is the new Bison Headlamp (5.1 oz., $25). It boasts the same polymer body, battery-saving bi-pin bulb, and void-free reflector as other Bison lights. In Rimrock Purple and Aspen Yellow, it verges on fashion—without compromising function. The brightness and phenomenal throw of the beam compare favorably with much heavier lights such as the Petzl Zoom.

Bison headlamp

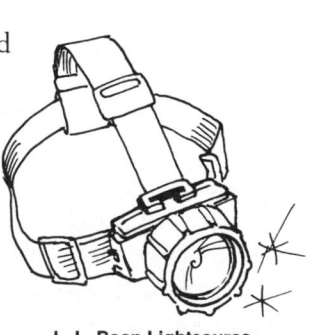

There are further dozens of perfectly good two-AA headlamps with top straps and other desirable features: the L. L. Bean Lightsource (5 oz. with two AA batteries, $29) has an optional recharging kit with two nickel-metal hydride batteries and a 110-volt charger that plugs directly into the headlamp ($20). There are also decent two-AA headlamps in the $12 to $15 range, like the Panasonic Taskmaster (8 oz., $13). Below $10, they tend to be cranky and short-lived.

L. L. Bean Lightsource headlamp

I've spent much of my adult life unplugged, with kerosene lamps and candles; for some years I even swore off flashlights, learning to negotiate the steep trail to the cabin where I lived in full, leafy dark. So I'm happy with less light than most folks. On the other hand, if you require 100-watt reading lamps and shudder between streetlights, then by all means use halogen or xenon bulbs and pack more batteries. That way you can fully illuminate your freeze-fried satay and also scan the woods for Lurking Presences.

Though, for the most part, the only Lurking Presence will be you.

Stowing the flashlight

COLIN: Naturally, you must always know exactly where your light is. During the day mine used to go into the inside pocket of the pack, where it was reasonably well protected and tolerably accessible. But my present pack has no inside pocket, and for some years the flashlight has traveled without damage in an upper outside pocket, protected by scarf or balaclava. For storage at night, see page 499.

Accidental battery drainage

CHIP: The time to put your light in order is somewhat before dark—if it doesn't work you'll have ample time to tinker. First, check the position of the switch. Slide switches and push buttons can turn on while being stuffed. Of course you can stuff the light so the switch is always pushed in the off direction. Or you can tape the switch down. The easiest way is to stick fresh tape to the body of the flashlight, with the tail extending a good 1 to 2 inches past the switch, then tab the last ¼ inch over so you'll have something to grab. New trip, new tape. For problem push buttons, keep your light on top of the load or devise some guard, like a scrap of cardboard tubing or PVC pipe. Rotary bezels can be foiled by pressure—page 580.

Putting a scrap of cardboard between a battery and contact point can prevent drainage, if the battery compartment opens easily. Reversing one cell can apparently damage batteries. Reversing all the batteries has no effect: the bulb still goes on. On new LED lights with battery-saving chips, reversing cells can ruin the chip.

Besides accidental turn-ons, another problem might be bad contact: try lightly scouring the batteries and the internal contacts with a pencil eraser or some other mild abrasive. Cleaning with alcohol (not beer) can remove scum. Moisture is another culprit. Swabbing with dry cloth or paper, or a *cautious* pass near (not directly above) a stove burner, can dry things out.

If none of that works, try the spare bulb. (If you don't have a spare, you deserve to suffer.) The chance that both bulbs will be bad is infinitesimal. For critical trips, new bulbs are not an unreasonable investment.

Batteries

Throwaway alkaline cells are now the choice of most backpackers. But the light weight, high power, cold-resistance, and long shelf life of lithium cells—newly available in the AA size—have made them semi-competitive.

The real contest now is throwaways versus rechargeables. Rechargeable nickel-cadmium cells have been around for a long time, mostly disdained by backpackers for their short life (though I use them—page 593). New rechargeable alkaline cells are gaining ground, and nickel-metal hydride (NiMH) cells also show promise.

Electricity being invisible, mostly, it's tough to sort out all the whats and wherefores. So for a table on the batteries most used by backpackers, compiled from various sources, including catalogs, manufacturers' Web sites, and consumer ratings, see page 592.*

To follow up on the table, we should brush through how each type of battery performs for backpacking. Which, for me at least, doesn't include cell phones, portable CD players, or GPS receivers. We'll look first at non-rechargeable cells.

Carbon-zinc cells have a carbon *anode* (+) surrounded by ammonium chloride paste (the electrolyte) with a zinc shell, the *cathode* (−). A chemical reaction causes electrons to flow, thus converting chemical energy directly to electrical energy. This is the magic all batteries do, in various ways. If the chemical reaction is reversible, then the battery can be recharged. But carbon-zinc cells can't be. Long the mainstay, they have now been supplanted by

Disposable alkaline cells, introduced in 1958. With a higher potential storage, they caught on, but because of their mercury content, multiplied by the sheer volume of batteries tossed out, they were soon recognized as an environmental problem. The late 1980s saw low-mercury alkaline cells, and since 1990 alkaline manganese dioxide cells (the popular Duracells, Energizers, and Rayovacs) have been mercury-free. Even so, they are discarded in such immense quantity (now 2 billion per year in the U.S.) that they still constitute toxic waste. Though the makers discourage it, it has long been known that these cells can be recharged, sort of. But they

---

*The OEM (original equipment manufacturer) sections of company Web sites often contain such things. Duracell's OEM site has a marvelous glossary of battery-related terms, but you can't print it out.

R = Rechargeable	Alkaline	Lithium Iron Disulfide	R Alkaline MNO₂ (Renewal)	R Alkaline MNO₂ (Accucell)	R Nickel-Cadmium (Pocket-Plate Type)[1]	R Nickel-Metal Hydride
Voltage	1.5	1.6	1.5	1.5	1.25	1.2
Initial charge (at purchase)	yes	yes	yes	yes	no	no
Capacity, milliamp hours (mAh)[2]						
AAA	900	n.a.	630	750	240	600
AA	2200	2900	1750	1800	750–1100	1300
C	5000	n.a.	4500	4000	2400	2200
Weight (grams)/average cost each						
AAA	9 g/$.85	n.a.	9 g/$1.75	11 g/$1.75	10 g/$1.50	9 g/$2.20
AA	24 g/$.75	14 g/$3.00	22 g/$1.75	22 g/$1.75	24 g/$2.00	25 g/$2.25
C	70 g/$1.25	n.a.	63 g/$3.25	68 g/$4.75	75 g/$4.75	75 g/$5.50
Self-discharge rate[3]	0.2%	>0.1%	0.2%	0.2%	20+%	20+%
Useful shelf life	5 years	10 years	5 years	5 years	short[4]	short[4]
Number of cycles[5]	1	1	8–25	50–500+	50–500+	50–500+
Cost per cycle	high	very high	moderate	very low	very low	very low
Memory effect	n.a.	n.a.	no	no	high	low
Solar charging[6]	no	no	no	no	yes	yes
Disposal hazard	low	low	low	very low	very high	low

[1]New high-capacity AA nicads are rated at 1000 to 1100 mAh. [2]The differing internal chemistry of the batteries listed makes mAh values hard to compare—most makers rate them for medium-drain devices like a small cassette player. [3]At 70°F/21°C. [4]Should be fully charged before use. [5]The cycle life of a rechargeable battery depends on the average depth of discharge and the rate of recharging. [6]Direct charging with a small, portable solar panel.

also might heat up and vent (i.e., blow up). If they're only partly discharged, the new microchip-controlled chargers can pump them up for a few cycles, with diminishing capacity. So, despite their popularity, they're expensive for the power you get, and given the drop-off in cold weather, far from ideal.

Lithium cells first slipped into our packs in industrial headlamps. The Chouinard-marketed Hartford Headlite, with a 3-volt bulb, used a D battery called the Eternacell, made by Power Conversion, that retailed for a stiff $20. This battery (lithium sulfur dioxide) would work in extreme cold and last for a whole expedition. But it was illegal to carry or ship it in aircraft, which put a cramp on the fun. The company, now Hawker Eternacell, has developed a lithium thionyl chloride cell that's ideal for low-drain devices like LEDs, is legal on aircraft, comes in the AA size (3.6 volts/2500 milliamp hours [mAh]), and is somewhat affordable at $9 to $11, considering that it can last a season or more. It comes with the C. Crane Lithium Trek Light (page 583) and is also available through electronic specialty houses.

Recently, Eveready Energizer has unleashed a flood of lithium-iron disulfide batteries in the 1.5-volt AA configuration. Designed for auto-wind cameras, these are now a runaway choice for camp lights. The advantages are seductive: light weight (about 60 percent of that of an alkaline cell), and a 10-year shelf life. But the word from battery specialists is that the internal chemistry of lithium cells diminishes their performance in low-drain devices such as flashlights—the exception being the use of a high-power bulb in cold weather. There seem to be few or no restrictions on shipping, air travel, and disposal. The sharpest disadvantage is cost: currently $3 each. And more significant, given that to build a small battery consumes up to 50 times the energy the battery itself can store, is the sad fact that lithium batteries can't be recharged. So while I carry lithium spares, I seldom actually use them.

Nickel-cadmium cells (nicads) combine the two metals with potassium hydroxide and water. They've been in use since the 1950s, and the best ones can deliver hundreds of cycles. But most backpackers hate them—as I did, after running head-on into their peculiarities. First, they are chemically "stiff" and need to be charged and discharged completely (unto blackout) for a few cycles to break them in. Otherwise they develop a "memory" and will take only a partial charge—a vicious, downward spiral. Not that they last a long time even when perfectly charged: a nicad stores about half as much as an alkaline cell, and yields 1.2 volts to an alkaline's 1.5. Another befoozler is that the nicad discharge curve is flat from 90 percent capacity down to 10 percent, so those little built-in voltmeters don't give you a clue as to how much power is left. The only way to get it right was to run them stone-dead, then time the charging process—

which could take 15 to 16 hours. So they also tended to get forgotten and overcharged: they heat up and are ruined. I also started out with cheap *sintered plate* nicads, which are easily damaged by overcharging—the powdered cadmium flakes off the nickel plates. And cadmium is poisonous as hell. Why bother?

Simply, if a nicad is treated right you can recharge it hundreds of times. Ten years ago, I got some quality *pocket plate* nicads (Golden Power AA, 0.8 oz., now $2.25 from Real Goods), that hold 700 mAh compared to 500 or less for sintered plate cells. I got serious about timing the charge. I also changed my battery habits, thinking of them as vessels to be filled and then emptied, like the tank of a tiny stove. I charged them before trips (they lose 1 percent per day on the shelf). And since the sun shines bright in Wyoming, I started packing a tiny solar charger to fill them up on the trail (see Solar Campsite, page 604).

Once I've conditioned a good nicad, I can count on 60 to 90 minutes from a krypton-bulbed headlamp—with the batteries kept warm by my general hotheadedness. Other AA cells I use are from Power Sonic ($2.75) and C. Crane Co. ($2). I just got some Radio Shack Hi-Capacity nicads rated at 1000 mAh ($3.50) that hold up well, and the new Panasonic P-3GPA, rated at 1100 mAh, is said to be better still, though it's hard to find (look at Costco or BJ's Wholesale for a pack with four AA cells and a charger, at $15). Though formerly a butt cramp, recharging has been made easy: new microchip-controlled home chargers analyze each battery and vary the power, with a tiny "float" charge to keep the voltage topped up. So overcharging's a thing of the past. And so is buying batteries. I haven't bought a throwaway cell in 2 or 3 years. Amazingly, after 10 years I still use those original Golden Power nicads for all but the bitterest cold. And when they do at long last go belly-up (the new chargers inform you), Real Goods will recycle them so the cadmium doesn't get loose.*

Rechargeable alkaline batteries were introduced in the U.S. in 1993 by Rayovac with a companion charger as the Renewal system. Sold elsewhere under the names Pure Energy and ALCAVA, they're properly known as rechargeable alkaline manganese dioxide zinc (RAM) cells. They have the same voltage, 1.5, as single-use alkalines and last about 85 percent as long—the first time out, at least. With each cycle, the capacity drops. Even with perfect handling, by cycle 10 it's about 60 percent. By cycle 30 it's 40 percent, and falling. (User consensus gives them 8 to 25 cycles.) So while the Renewal battery really burns out of the box, it can't match the longevity of a nicad. For longest life you should charge

---

*The Rechargeable Battery Recycling Corp., a nonprofit company funded by battery makers, has a list of stores and drop-off sites for spent nicads: 1-800-8-BATTERY; e-mail—<rbrc@rbrc.com>; Web site—*www.rbrc.com.*

Renewal cells frequently and not run them to the bitter end. The required Rayovac charger (which rejects worn-out cells) costs around $20.

A promising new RAM battery from Germany is the Accucell (Real Goods, AA, 0.8 oz., two-pack, $4; 4 pack, $7). In the AA size these pack more capacity than the Renewal, with the same constraints: frequent charging while avoiding deep discharge and heavy loads. The shelf life is the same as toss-away alkalines: 5 years or so. But Accucells are rated for hundreds of cycles—a big plus that's led me to adopt them for general use. Like the Renewal cells, they need a special charger—see below.

Nickel-metal hydride (NiMH) batteries have a capacity about halfway between that of nicads and rechargeable alkalines, and contain no toxic chemicals. Like nicads they yield 1.2 volts and can be recharged hundreds of times, but unlike nicads they have no "memory" effect. They have a short shelf life, self-discharging 1 to 4 percent of their capacity per day. Tech wizards tell me that NiMH cells work best with high-drain devices such as the Sierra Stove (page 336), and with frequent recharging. I tried some years ago and killed them off with a crude home charger. But chargers have vastly improved, and new NiMH cells are hitting the market, so I'll give them another try in my solar campsite (page 604).

Given the sheer number of batteries and bulbs now available—and my dislike for killing off batteries on the test bench—the comparison tests in the last edition are omitted from this one. For full technical details the best sources (given a healthy skepticism) are magazines such as *Consumer Reports* and the Web sites of battery makers that have OEM (original equipment manufacturer) sectors. Intended for designers and buyers, these have detailed tables, graphics, and other techno-babble, some of it in printable or downloadable forms (for fireside contemplation).

Given the considerable impact of manufacturing and dumping 2 billion batteries each year, we backpackers need to switch to rechargeable cells now. And that brings up the question of

Battery chargers.

Since the chargers sold in discount racks tend, unless carefully watched, to wreck batteries, the first step is to get one that won't. For some years, I depended on a Saitek Eco Charger (from Jade Mountain, $56). It takes AAA to D cells (no 9-volters), works with nicads and alkalines, rejects dead or damaged cells, discharges nicads to beat the memory effect, and tells you how many hours each cell will take to recharge. It runs on 6 volts, via a house-current adapter. The Eco Charger reconditioned some old nicads that were marginal, and over two years saved me about two or three times what it cost.

Last year I started using the Innovations Battery Manager Ultra

(C. Crane Co., $50) with a new pulse-charging circuit. It handles zinc chloride, alkaline, rechargeable alkaline, nicad, and nickel-metal hydride cells, AAA to D, in any combination, and rejects bad cells. Rather than telling you how long each cell will take to charge, it displays the voltage—by far the best measure once you get the feel of it—and works on a 24-hour cycle. It charges like a dream, but has a not-very-portable wedge shape. The input voltage (via adapter) is 9 volts.

I'm now trying yet another marvel, the Accucell ACL 200 (Real Goods, $99), a German-made device that mates with Accucell high-performance RAM batteries. It does all of the above tricks, with Accucell alkalines, nicads, and NiMH cells, and also charges 9-volters. It can take up to eight AA cells at once. It lacks a voltage readout, giving you a red or green light instead—the only thing I didn't like. But it charges remarkably fast, e.g., 80 minutes for a AA nicad. It's also a portable, fat-pocketbook shape and weighs 1 lb. The input is 12 volts, via the AC adapter, and it comes with an automotive plug for use in a car.

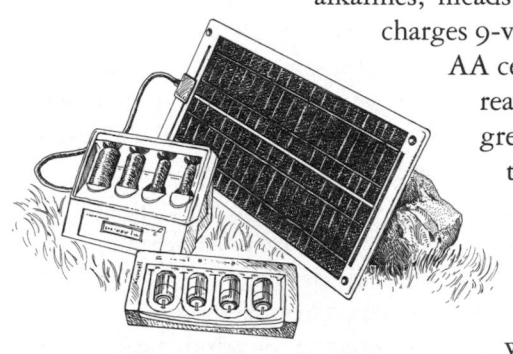

Innovations and Accucell chargers

Most people will like the Innovations charger for its charge-anything design and reasonable cost. But if you're starting from scratch and intending to spend a lot of time both outside and on the road, the Accucell charger, with a set of matching batteries, is a farsighted choice. For expeditions or groups, the Accucell charger and a 12-volt solar panel might work out. I've got a 10-watt Solarex PV210 that's 17.5 by 10.5 inches (about the same width as my shoulders, 2 lbs. 2 oz., $135) that can ride on top of a pack. New fiberglass-mounted 10-watt panels weigh only 1 lb. 2 oz. (Real Goods, $119). Solo artists will naturally want something smaller. For which, consult Solar Campsite, page 604.

Bulbs

To find the voltage of the bulb you need, multiply the number of batteries by 1.5. Thus, a light with a pair of alkaline AA, C, or D cells in series needs a 3-volt bulb. Three cells need a 4.5-volt bulb, and so on. The amps are also a factor: a light with D cells (two, three, or four) will use a 0.5-amp bulb, while two AA or two C cells need 0.25 amp or thereabouts. If you don't know what volts, amps, and watts are, for heaven's sake look it up—and in the meantime, stop babbling about *e*-this and *e*-that.

The bulb must also fit the hole. Regular incandescent bulbs with a number prefixed by "PR" are prefocused and have smooth, flanged bases; those identified by a plain number have screw bases. Another increasingly common type is the seed, or *bi-pin,* bulb of much smaller diameter, with two bendable wire connectors. These come in packs of two, possibly because you always drop the first one and lose it. To further complicate matters, all these types—flange, screw, and bi-pin—are now made in various forms, to vary both brightness and power consumption.

Krypton bulbs are the common run, filled with (Superman, look out!) krypton gas. They have a warm yellow hue, like candle flame. With long use, the vaporized tungsten of the filament gets deposited on the inside of the glass, so they dim about 25 percent before burning out. They cost $2 to $3.

Halogen bulbs have a tungsten filament in a smaller quartz-glass envelope, filled with halogen gas. They're bright, throw a long beam, focus well, and have a white light that trues up colors and details: it's a damn sight easier to field-strip a stove with a halogen bulb. The tungsten particles evaporated from the hot filament don't stick to the quartz glass—they stay with the gas and are redeposited on the filament, lengthening the life and lessening dim-out to 10 percent. (But the oils in your fingertips react with quartz glass, killing the bulb prematurely—*so install halogen bulbs with tweezers or the clean corner of a bandanna.*) Cost is $5 to $7.

Xenon bulbs are also very bright and focus well, so they're showing up in specialized lights like the Pelican Super MityLite LMX Laser Spot Xenon Watertight—a mouthful—claimed to be "600% brighter than ordinary pocket lights" (3 oz. with two AAA cells, $11). The catch: batteries get used up quickly and the xenon bulb itself lasts only 20 hours. Cost is $4 to $6.

LED arrays (nonbulbs—see page 582) are now raising their wee polycarbonate heads. They're generally dimmer than incandescents while greatly multiplying battery life. But the price is a gasp: a PR (flange-base) array of three is $30 from Real Goods, and a screw-in base array of three for Petzl lamps is $20 from C. Crane. Still, the long life and the reduced weight of spare batteries in your pack make an LED array a worthwhile investment.

A last word: pack at least one spare bulb of the type you most use. For my favorite headlamp I carry three: an LED array, a standard krypton, and a high-intensity halogen or xenon (one, of course is always in the light). Some flashlights have places for storing spares, but mine travel in a plastic film can marked "Monkey Wrenches and Dynamite."

Backup sources of light

COLIN: A chemical lightstick such as the Cyalume, Omniglow, and Snaplight (about 1 oz., $1–$2 each) is a nontoxic, nonflammable, water-proof, and windproof device that you "switch on" by just bending and shaking the plastic case and thereby mixing two chemicals. Unfortunately, you can't switch the thing off. But its surprisingly bright greenish yellow light, said to last 8 to 10 hours at around 70 to 80°F, really does so. The light is said not to attract bugs and doesn't seem to.

One stick lights a tent adequately and even lets you read smallish print—though because the all-around light, left unshielded, contracts your eye pupils it's advisable to block off the light directed toward your eyes with finger, hand, stick, shoe, or some other handy and opaque item. In some ways a lightstick outperforms a candle lantern: it cannot set a tent or anything else on fire; knocking it over won't put it out; neither will wind or rain; and you can hold it in your mouth. If, after balancing weight and cost, you decide to take lightsticks, make sure you pack out all spent ones.

Although its nonswitchoffability rules the lightstick out for general "flashlight" use, I find to my surprise that one will light your way down a faint trail that you know well, and would certainly do so on a well-defined trail. But you must use the stick properly. Tie or tape it to the end of a staff or stick and push it ahead of you like a mine detector. It's essential that, to eliminate the pupil-contracting glare, you hold staff or stick at the right, blocking angle.

CHIP: A battery-powered version, the Krill Lightstick, is a 5-inch, 3-oz. tube of "micro-encapsulated phosphors" with a 3000-hour life span. It comes in six hues, from a bright pale green to a soft red. With two AA cells, the regular model lasts 120 hours ($25) and the brighter Extreme for 50 hours ($30)—candle lanterns without candles.

Other good backups are single LED penlights (legion) and keychain lights, like the molded Photon II (1 oz., $20) with two button-type lithium cells, a single LED, and a tiny switch to keep it on without having to squeeze. A pair of obsessed chums took Photon IIs as their sole light sources on a fairly serious mountain traverse. (That it was near the summer solstice proves they're not entirely devoid of cunning.) But those Brand X ovoid keychain lights with advertising behind a wrap of clear plastic are chancy, though often free. I somehow acquired a Lumatec Flash Card, a sub-ounce battery/LED unit, 3½ by 3 by ³⁄₁₆ inches ($5), which throws enough light to walk by but isn't mouthable. Being flat, it slips in behind the signal mirror in my office-on-the-yoke (see page 180). But for those times when you're changing a headlamp bulb and the spring springs out, a mostly overlooked source of backup light is a digital watch. Mine, a Casio Alarm Chrono (0.8 oz., $14) casts a bluish phosphorescence just sufficient to get oriented and find important things, such as toilet paper and zipper pulls.

Candle lanterns

COLIN: When nights are long, and particularly if I expect to do evening reading or note taking, I sometimes carry a candle lantern. It will illuminate a decent-size tent pretty well and a small tarp shelter even better, especially if the tarp is white. You get enough light to write by, just about enough to read by if you have big print and good eyes, and more than enough to cook and housekeep by, even if you go roofless, provided you hang the lantern high so that household goods don't cast too many concealing shadows. Theoretically, candle lanterns present a fire hazard, so I take care. For roofless camping the danger is nillish, and even out in the open the best candle lanterns generate a surprisingly practical light and will withstand a certain amount of wind.

You can suspend the lantern by tying a nylon cord to its hanging bail without fear of burning the cord—and with an auxiliary sideways-pulling cord, and perhaps some such convenient handle as a staff (page 95), can adjust the sector of light so that it illuminates what you want to see while the blanked-off sector shields your eyes from bedazzlement. In good lanterns, the enclosed foot collects rather than distributes hot tallow.

You can replace a candle at night, while the wax is still hot and malleable, without too much grief—given a flashlight and reasonable familiarity with the device—though a pair of asbestos hands would help. You can replace a candle in daylight, even when the wax is cold and hard and intractable—given a stout twig to depress the candle platform, a wax-cleaning instrument such as the nail file on a small Swiss Army knife, plus a good deal of determination and patience.

CHIP: Since 1985, Northern Lights (not Lites, thank heaven) of Truckee, California, has upgraded the traditional candle lantern with innovative models such as the anodized aluminum Flip-Top (easy lighting, 7 oz. with candle, $24–$29) and the Alpine 2 (6 oz. with candle, $14.50) of thermoplastic with a glass chimney that slides, upside down, into the lantern body for transport.

Northern Lights also designed a clever oil lantern, the Ultralight (5.5 oz., $24) that either hangs or sits on a springy, stable tripod base and burns up to 17 hours per 3-fl.-oz. filling. A new variant is the Compact Oil Lantern (5.3 oz., 3 oz. fuel, $24), which resembles the Alpine candle model (above), and burns 12 hours per filling. A leakproof cap covers both

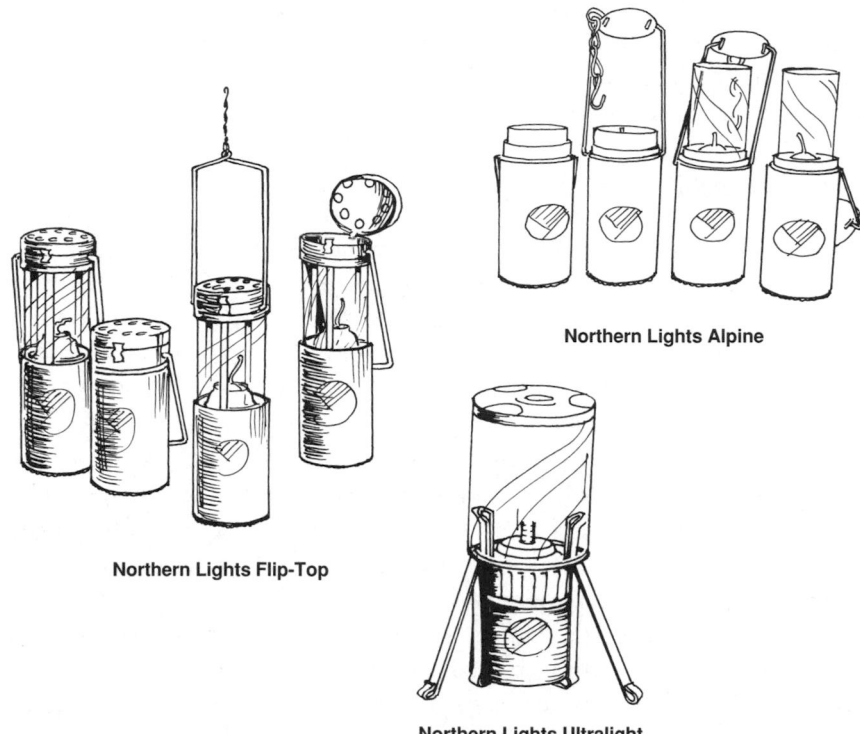

Northern Lights Alpine

Northern Lights Flip-Top

Northern Lights Ultralight

the wick and vent hole. It takes fiddling with tweezers to get the wick adjusted (barely showing above the brass tube), and the resulting flame is about half that of a candle. With the wick set for a steady, smoke-free flame, it was somewhat hard to light, so I aimed a butane lighter at the brass part for a five-count, which helped. It came with a surprisingly clunky chain, which I replaced (see lantern chains, below). Northern Lights also makes a Candoil insert ($10) of heat-resistant plastic to replace candles, with a 9-hour burn time. All these units will burn lamp oil (brightest flame — 8-oz. bottle, $2.75), deodorized kerosene ($6 per gallon) found in paint stores, or regular old stinky kerosene (cheap), available worldwide.

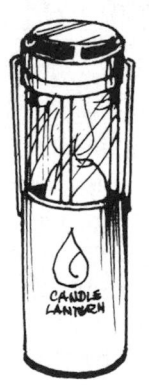

Uco Candle Lantern and mini Candle Lantern

Good candle lanterns are also made by Uco, including a slide chimney classic (7 oz., $18–$25) and a mini (3.2 oz. plus candle, $9.50) that burns tealight tub candles lasting 4 to 5 hours. The same candles fire the Olicamp Footprint Lantern, which has an unobstructed glass chimney and tripod base (3 oz. plus candle, $9.50). These newer candle and oil lanterns cast few shadows, with the metal struts thin or lacking around the glass. But if you like a one-sided light, a reflector that fits Uco and perhaps other lanterns can be had for $3.75. Lanterns with multiple candles are unwieldy for backpacking.

Lantern candles are shorter and stouter than the common household type sold in groceries, are formulated for longer burning times, and cost from $.25 to $.60 each. Since all lantern chimneys are glass, cases of neoprene or fleece reduce breakage (1 oz., $3–$5). I use candle lanterns mostly for deep-winter trips, where their warm light is a comfort and the heat helps to keep frost away.

White-gas and cartridge lanterns

COLIN: These big, heavy, fragile lanterns are hardly normal backpacking ware, but in dead of winter they lengthen an otherwise very short day and also generate a wonderful amount of heat. On short-haul, permanent-camp trips at any time of year I guess they become feasible, even desirable. They certainly have uses at roadhead camps (also known, sort of *soixante-neuf*, as trailhead camps). But remember that in backcountry a lantern screens you off from the night even more drastically than does a fire (page 288). And that although it doesn't roar the way a stove does, the damned thing hisses all the time, right there by your bloody earhole.

The most popular lantern is probably the white-gas-burning Coleman Peak 1, with a base similar to that on the most recent incarnation of the stove (page 321). It burns for three hours at 75 watts—"like a flood-light," says one backpacker I know. "It'll blast all your neighbors out of the backcountry." The current Peak 1 Dual Fuel 229 weighs 28 ounces and costs $40. Spare mantles (#20, $2 a pair) are best found where the lanterns are sold but can now be ordered from a Web site: *www.coleman. com.* Like all pressure-lantern mantles, they're very fragile for backpacking. Some years ago, reports alleged that the mantles emit dangerous radioactive material on burn-off; but Coleman assured me that, although their mantles indeed contain a small amount of thorium, users "receive at least 50,000 times more radiation due to natural radiation and about 20,000 times more radiation from radium dial watches during a normal year. The average individual dose due to *eating* a mantle is only 1% of the environmental annual dose." The company also says that independent physicists and the U.S. Nuclear Regulatory Commission have both concluded that normal use of mantles presents no radioactive hazard.

CHIP: In ever smaller and brighter designs, gas-cartridge lanterns are seeing more backcountry use, especially for group camps and snow caving. New piezoelectric ignitions make them a snap to light. And if you carry a cartridge stove, you can run a lantern on depleted cartridges that will no longer boil water (see page 301). Most use slip-on (or double-tie) mantles with a drawstring at either end that are mostly interchangeable—but those labeled by the maker of each lantern are usually better quality than discount-store brands. While safer than liquid-fuel models, cartridge lanterns still present hazards when used in a tent or other enclosed space (see page 372). And they still hiss.

Before we run down some new models, here are things to avoid. Most lanterns have a bail or chain for hanging, and if the spots where it clips are attached to the heat shield on top or in the path of the flame, then the chain will get hot enough to burn your hand or melt through a nylon loop. The now discontinued Peak 1 Micro lantern had this problem. Given the rage to miniaturize, other watchouts are that the glass chimney (or globe) fits into its cage without scratching and that the silk mantle doesn't touch the tip of the piezo lighter, which will poke a hole in it. The third deadly sin is a noisy or wavering flame.

The well-proven Primus Trekklite (8.3 oz. sans cartridge, $75) has a wire bail that hinges below the glass chimney, and a clip-in heat shield above. It has a piezo igniter and casts a steady 80 watts of shadow-free light with a medium-low noise level. A younger brother, the Primus Alpine Easy PTL, also burns at 80 watts, is lighter (7 oz.), and less of a bite ($50). Both use Primus screw-on cartridges that are widely available in outdoor shops.

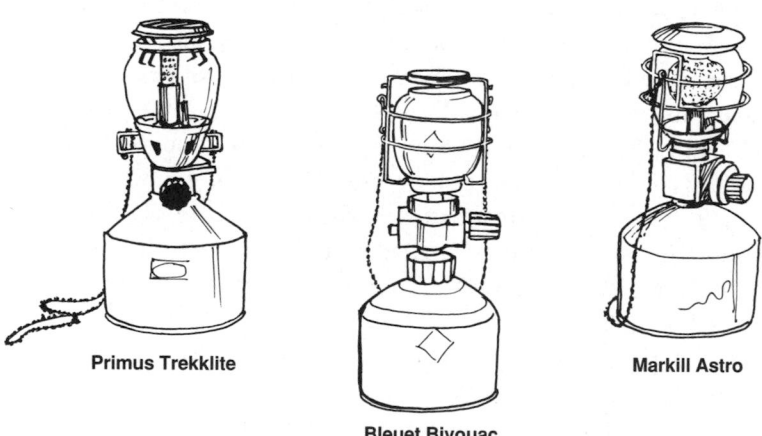

Primus Trekklite

Markill Astro

Bleuet Bivouac

Mildly updating the popular Bleuet Bivouac 270 lantern shown above, the new Campingaz Lumostar lantern is bright (80 watts) and, like its cousin the Twister 270 stove, has a blue plastic housing that locks onto the Campingaz cartridge (not compatible with other brands) and a large, cool control knob. A red button keys the piezo igniter, which works consistently. The frosted chimney casts a nice but slightly wavering light, medium noisy. While the chain doesn't get meltingly hot, I used a tent stake to handle it.

I like the well-made and affordable Markill Astro Lantern (9 oz., $30) for its steady and relatively quiet 80 to 100 watts of light. The clips are well out of the flame so the chain heats up less than others I tried. Still, I wouldn't hang it in a small backpacking tent—like lantern makers in general, Markill advises no flammable material within 4 feet above or 2 feet to the side. The reliable piezo lighter is keyed by pushing the control knob, a nice touch, though I had to trim off some scraggy wires that tore holes in mantles. But on the whole, the Astro is a good pick for road-head/trailhead/snow-cave outings.

Two smaller lanterns crossed my path. The Primus Himalayan Mesh Lantern (5 oz., $62) resembles the mini-burner unit that comes paired with a stove (page 325). It has a chimney of stainless-steel screen instead of breakable glass but includes a hang-up rig and gives a wavering 15 to 25 watts of light. A stronger step in the same direction is the Snow Peak

GigaPower Lantern GL-100, companion to their tiny and well-wrought stove (page 331). It's a spare design with a folding wire control stem and no provision for hanging; it gives a mildly wavering 80 watts of light. The brass screw-on base is compatible with Primus and Peak 1 cartridges—easier to find than Snow Peak's own. The lightest of the gaslights (4 oz., $70), it comes in a tidy plastic case 2 inches square and 4 inches high. A piezo igniter adds $17 and half an ounce. Other accessories are frosted and stainless-steel mesh globes. I took

Snow Peak GigaPower

the Snow Peak lantern on a hinge-season trip, with no tent, when I bivouacked in talus caves and under overhanging boulders. It's a good little hand warmer but so bright that it regularly blinded me when I turned my head without thinking. And, too, it made me feel conspicuous, as if the cold, blue eyes of the mountains were on me.

A wild card is the new Coleman Exponent Power-max Xcursion lantern, with a built-in tank that refills like a butane lighter. A 20-second squirt from a full Powermax cartridge (page 297 and, for the matching stove, page 330) gives 5 to 6 hours of light. It burns quiet and bright with a full tank, but after a while a ticking pulsation sets in, going from fast to slow, followed by a drop in the output. Still, looking over the prototype (the Coleman folks cautioned me that it isn't the final

Exponent Powermax Xcursion

production model) I'm struck by its cunning design. A front shell slides up to guard the glass globe and hide the ON/OFF control, preventing accidental turn-ons. The rear shell is mirrored within and can be left up or slid down to cast a full circle of light. Folded, the bail fits close for compact packing. The black base unthreads to reveal the brass filler nozzle, with room to stash a mantle or two, which you should do as a matter of course. The mantle on the lantern they sent me got pulverized in shipping, so I wouldn't count on its holding up forever in a pack. The Xcursion mantle, #9970, a small sock-type with a metal push-on fitting, is different from the #20 tie-on mantle needed for the Peak 1 Dual Fuel lantern. (Yet another type, a tube mantle with open ends, is required for the Primus, Snow Peak, and other cartridge gassers.) Given the Xcursion's innovative design, I was surprised to find that it lights via the traditional match hole—though a butane lighter with a lengthy flame does the trick. Weight, empty, is 12 oz. and the cost about $40.

Lantern chains. Some lanterns—the Markill Astro for instance—come with chains that are both light and strong, but others either have clunky chains or none. To make one, go to a hardware store and get the lightest chain they have (with twisted figure-8 links—no sharp ends poking out). You also need a small S-hook and a split ring. Crimped onto one end of the chain, the S-hook should fit through the split ring—which is rung onto the other end (total: 0.6 oz. and less than $1). The split ring can hold the bail of the lantern securely while the S-hook mates with webbing loops, etc. Or you can slip the S-hook around a tree limb and through the split ring, to swing the lantern from the hook. Length can be jockeyed by moving the split ring to another link. A lantern chain is also a useful adjunct for a hanging stove (see page 339).

If you feel like trying a radically new approach to the whole game of light and heat, you might try a

Solar campsite.

This amounts to giving up fossil fuel as your immediate source of heat and light. You sacrifice some convenience (or at least some long-standing habits). But you gain considerable freedom. With even moderate sunshine, and any sort of natural combustibles, you can extend your walking range tremendously. The equation is simple: subtract the weight of the fuel you normally consume, plus bottles or cartridges, and add the same weight of food (or an extra book).

The basic solar-camp kit is simple. First comes storage—not a fuel bottle, but AA-size rechargeable batteries, either workhorse nickel-cadmium or perhaps nickel-metal hydride, both covered a few pages back (pages 593 and 595). The light department consists of a flashlight or

Solar campsite

headlamp (pages 579–90) using the same AA cells, enhanced with an electron-stretching LED array. Heat comes from a Sierra Zzip Stove (page 336), which uses a single AA battery to blow air through a small fire in a combustion chamber, fueled with virtually anything that burns: wood chips, yak dung, or charcoal from old campfires. Finally, and the key, is a solar charger that's small and light enough to ride on top of a pack, and powerful enough to charge a pair of batteries in a day or less.

The first solar goodie I used was a Stearns Sun Shower (see page 648). They've been around forever and we all know they work. But my first inkling of a broader strategy came years ago, when poet Gary Holthaus told me of his walking several hundred miles with a Sierra Stove from Zzip Manufacturing. In crossroads stores, he said, batteries were easier to find than white gas, besides being a lighter load. After a while, he began to enjoy scrounging fuel for each meal. So I got a Sierra Stove (the new titanium version is pictured above—9.9 oz., $125) and learned how to use it—a simple process. It also didn't take long to realize that if I could recharge the stove battery en route, fuel was no longer a limiting factor.

The problem with solar energy is that you get far more than you can use—sweating up a steep snowfield and sunburning your nose—and then at sunset are plunged into an energy deficit, cold and dark. So the key is storage. I use rechargeable alkaline cells for short hops, but drawing them down shortens their life and they can't be properly charged with my small solar panel. So I settled on nicads and recently added a pair of nickel-metal hydride cells for the stove. Both types give out 1.2 volts compared to 1.5 for alkaline cells, so the fan in the Sierra Stove runs a bit slower—but not aggravatingly so. I depend on an LED headlamp with two nicads for hours of diffused-but-sufficient light for following a trail, cooking, reading, and other things I tend to do at night. For off-trail travel by dark, I switch to a halogen bulb and NiMH batteries, and keep two lithium cells handy for backup.

For long walks, with recharging en route, I now carry four high-capacity nicad AAs for my two-cell headlamp and two NiMH cells for the single-cell Sierra Stove. This means I'm doubled up on batteries, with a pair of lithium cells for emergencies (eight AA cells, total weight 6.1 oz., or less than one small gas cartridge).

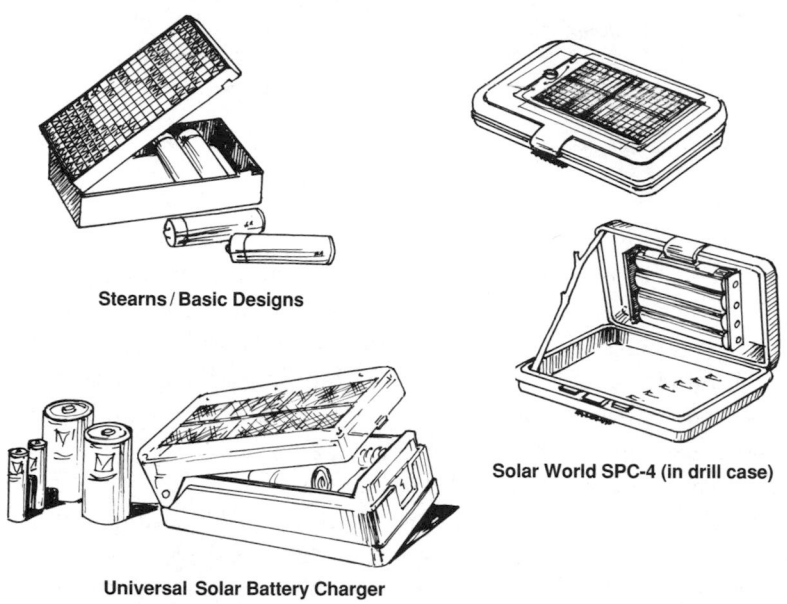

Stearns / Basic Designs

Solar World SPC-4 (in drill case)

Universal Solar Battery Charger

Portable solar chargers. If you're serious about solar camping, you need a good home charger that will handle different types of cells (see page 594). Harder to find is a portable photovoltaic (PV) charger small enough to ride on your pack and capable of pumping up a pair of batteries with 4 to 6 hours of full sun or 8 to 10 hours of partial clouds. Some small PV panels simply lack the juice. I put a meter on a Solar 4-AA Battery Charger from Stearns/Basic Designs (3.5 oz., $17) and at high noon it put out 3 volts at 48 milliamps, for 0.14 watt of power. That's not enough. A Universal Solar Battery Charger (from C. Crane Co. or Liberty Mountain Sports, 8.5 oz., $15) put out a useful 5.1 volts at 150 milliamps, for a strong 0.75 watt of power. It charges two cells at a time (AAA, AA, C, or D), but if you intend to use AA cells, the extra capacity is simply added weight. My favorite so far, the Solar World SPC-4 AA Pocket Charger (1.6 oz., $36) yielded 6.6 volts at 67 milliamps, for 0.44 watt. While the size of the solar panel provides a rule of thumb regarding output, the Stearns and the Solar World chargers have the same size panel. They're also wired differently: the Solar World puts the batteries in series and requires "jumpers" (hollow brass conductors the length of a battery, included) if you charge fewer than four cells. The Stearns/Basic Designs charger is wired in parallel, so you can charge a single cell without jumpers. (The fewer cells the more juice each one gets.)

None of these chargers will strap to a pack as is. To mount the Solar World SPC-4, I got a $.69 flexible plastic drill box from a hardware store, sliced off the internal drill holders, and cut an opening so I could silicone-seal the panel on top with the battery pack inside (see previous page, right). Then I riveted a pair of webbing loops to the bottom so it rides happily on my pack, more or less rainproof, at 3.5 oz. If the charger you find is already in a plastic case, you can stick a strip of Velcro to it and sew a corresponding patch on your pack.

The main thing is not to shade the panel with a hat, towering hair, etc. For stationary use, I now prop the drill box open with a rock (not a twig as shown), which also ensures that it won't blow over. The Solar World SPC-4 has a tiny red LED to indicate charging. A teeny built-in digital voltmeter would be great, but for now I estimate the discharge of each cell and keep track of the charging times. With power-saving tactics—an LED light and canny stove use—you can easily bridge a few cloudy days.

If you love to tinker, you might want to build your own custom charging rig. A plastic-covered mini-panel with 6-inch lead wires, rated at 6 volts and 50 milliamps, costs $18 from Solar World. You can make, or buy at stores such as Radio Shack, a "rat pack" to hold the batteries. A short length of cable with a plug lets you mount the panel on your pack and stow the batteries in the top pocket, out of the weather. But before buying anything, bone up on the electro-basics (volts × amps = watts). You need to match the solar panel to the type and number of batteries you intend to charge. Four 1.5-volt batteries = 6 volts. To charge a battery takes more voltage than the rated output, but too much juice can ruin or even explode it. I keep batteries of a single brand and type rubber-banded in pairs. Cells of different type, brand, or depth of discharge shouldn't be charged (or used) together—the weaker cell will drag the stronger one down. Since the Sierra Stove uses only one cell at a time I use one to cook dinner and the other for breakfast, to keep the discharge on a pair of batteries even.

If your home charger lacks a voltmeter, it doesn't hurt to get a simple multimeter (analog $10, digital $20) to check solar-panel output and battery voltage at home.

Not wanting to run out of juice on a long trip, I've run tabletop tests. For instance, a Power Sonic AA nicad (mid-1990s model) fresh from the home charger ran the Sierra Stove for 105 minutes. Charged with three others in the Solar World SPC-4 (8 hours in cloudy weather), it pushed the stove 55 minutes. The next day it snowed lightly. After recharging for 8 hours in low light, that same battery ran the stove for 25 minutes, a case of diminishing returns. But since the Sierra Stove can boil a quart of water in 6 to 8 minutes, I was sure that I could collect enough sunlight for my basic needs even on cloudy days.

The new Princeton Tec Matrix LED array (or equivalents, see page 588) is bright enough for confident walking and gives 18 to 20 hours on good nicads—at 3 hours per night, that's a week of Sherlock Holmes. Meanwhile, rechargeable batteries are improving so fast it's hard to keep up: a new Radio Shack Hi-Capacity nicad (1000 mAh) runs the Sierra Stove for 3 hours 30 minutes—at my usual hour-per-day of stove use, that's a bit more than three days' cooking on one AA battery. A new Rayovac NiMH cell (1300 mAh) runs the Sierra Stove for a stunning 4 hours 31 minutes—four days plus breakfast. So potentially at least, four AA rechargeables (two high-capacity nicads for the headlamp, two NiMHs for the the stove, 3.4 oz.) can power a week of walking. And the whole packet—batteries, stove, headlamp, and charger—weighs 23 oz., which strikes me as at least mildly amazing.

Of course, this monkey-tinkering is food and drink to me. And more: solar camping cuts us loose from the fossil-fuel chains that bind us to drilling rigs and unsavory politics in Third World energy colonies like Nigeria and Wyoming. (Or somewhat loose, given the petrochemistry of our beloved synthetic fibers.) But a solar-powered walkabout is several thousand long steps in the right direction.

A solo, solar-ized trip

After furious tinkering I had the Solar World charger mounted and all batteries tested and charged. At midday I drove the dirt road to a familiar trailhead. Without the usual burden of fuel bottles, my pack felt pleasantly light—full speed ahead. An hour and a steep climb from the trailhead I topped a cloud-floating pass. The trail dipped into a canyon, and I left it to pick my way upstream along a glacier-scoured bench, over a patchwork of thin turf and bedrock. The last mile or so before reaching a camp I was on the lookout for fuel and noticed a sheep bedground (i.e., where domestic sheep sleep, or have slept), so I loaded a plastic bag with dry dung before making my camp farther on.

I enjoy scouting for fuel: old, gray chips of wood, winter-range moose dung (nice, compact ovoid briquets), or charcoal from old camp- or forest fires. Resinous wood and especially conifer bark and cones will tar your pot with sticky black. If you persist, it's possible to glue the pot down (one cougar scream when you pick up the pot and the stove comes along for the ride). The best fuel is dense and nonresinous—worth stashing. It's also smart to keep some tinder and small kindling handy in your plastic bag for rainy days.

I found a good camp and unpacked: odd not to be fumbling with a fuel bottle. Firing up the Sierra Stove with dried sheep flop, like an electrified Bedouin, I cooked my pot of soup with a grin. Then I watched the sunset burn bright on 13,000-foot peaks and settled down with a book and a headlamp.

The second day I cooked breakfast and slotted the used batteries into my little pack-topping charger. The red LED glowed as I climbed up a high valley between ranks of silvery summits. I scrounged dry wood chips and some charcoal from a firepit I passed—insurance for my above-timberline camp. The trees grew stunted, then hugged the rocks, then disappeared. A bright stream dashed down a rocky fold, pooling in a chain of chill, blue lakes. At 11,000 feet, I made camp on alpine tundra, amid tussock and grit, with a great, flat, frost-spalled plinth for a table. Scouting, I found dead willow stems and also, at the base of a cliff, more sheep dung—wild bighorn, perhaps. The old black pot boiled more merrily, or did I imagine it? Replenished by hot rock-belly stew, I read for an hour by headlamp and then slept to the music of a cascade that changed pitch with the shifts of night air.

In the morning, under a light frost, I changed the battery in the stove and discovered that after boiling up for coffee, I could toast bagel halves, perfectly, on the point of my knife over the glowing coals in the Sierra Stove. It beat hell out of a gas flame. After cleaning up, I set the charger on a sunny rock, stowed my pack under talus, and set off with a dual mission: to find the highest source of the stream and to climb a peak in my sandals. The stream, a thread, tumbled out of a snowfield on a windswept col. The peak loomed above, a scary-looking blade of granite that proved to have sandal-friendly ledges and ramps all the way to the summit.

Later, as I descended, high clouds tailed in from the west, boding a change in the weather. Deciding to camp in a lower, less-exposed spot, I caught up the charger and strapped it to my pack. Taking a lower line back down the valley, and still solar-charging away, I found a troll haunt ringed by krummholz and windbreaked by a natural parapet of rock. Weathered wood, a mere double handful, with some charcoal from the plastic bag cooked my meal and brewed black tea for the evening chill.

The sun rose but the sky was occluded, clouds lowering, and the air tasted of rain. I brewed up and toasted, reloaded the batteries—still the original four—and strapped the charger to my pack to head downvalley. The clouds parted and re-formed, and I wondered whether I'd catch enough light. For the rest of the trip it stayed cloudy, raining at times with a light morning brush of snow on the highest peaks. But those same four batteries, charged by day, continued to spin the fan on my stove and light my headlamp. I never even touched the spares, let alone the emergency set, though I ate and drank heartily, and by night devoured Turgenev's *Fathers and Sons.* With the charger riding my pack I felt lighter on my feet and while scouting for fuel, goofily happy. Toasting a bagel, I beamed back at the morning sun. There's no explaining such things.

Recharge-ability can transform your notion of camping in unexpected ways. On the semifrivolous end of the spectrum, I picked up a Coghlan's 2-AA Mini-Fan (3 oz. with batteries, $3, Campmor) for a stint on a panel at a book fair. But I've ended up carrying it on summer backpacking trips, since it makes those midday, dead-air halts less deadly. A whirring minute or two dries the sweat prickles on my face and neck. Suspended with the elastic belt-clip thingie that came with a flashlight, it also makes a hot tent tenable—for the half hour or so that the batteries last (were it not for rechargeables I'd not be tempted). But with them, the Mini-Fan softens the neopuritanical aspects of solarizing with a luxurious microbreeze.

Chip and mini-fan

Direct solar heat. If you're cold, go sit in the sun—that much is obvious. But further tinkering has given mixed results. I made a snow melter for high elevations or winter camps by cutting a Maltese cross out of a discarded forest-fire shelter (reflective cloth) and duct-taping it into a tapered box-shape (18 by 9 by 5 inches, 2.5 oz.) that holds two pots. At one edge, I stuck on Velcro tabs to attach a flop-top of clear plastic (2 oz.), the stuff used for windows in tent flies, to boost the efficiency. A simpler dodge is to use a clear plastic "oven bag" that can't blow off. When it fogs up, the water's hot. To catch low winter sun, I cut a reflector (20 by 14 inches, 1.5 oz.) of the same reflective cloth, which can be stretched between sticks or pinned to a wall of packed snow. The whole thing folds flat and weighs 6 oz.—less than one gas canister. To hold the device, I carve out a recess in the snowpack, which softens surprisingly little as melting goes on. Using an MSR Blacklite Cookset (page 268), I've melted a gallon or more on sunny winter days, adding and emptying. If you pack the pots with snow and leave them alone, the yield is less but still enough to make the effort worthwhile. On a bright day, a pot packed with snow and ice at 11:00 a.m. was completely melted by 2:00 p.m. Clouds rolled in, but by 3:00 p.m. the water had heated to 95°F. (Setting a black pot on a dark rock gives similar results.) The melter is also a cooker: rice and red lentils simmered tender in 6 hours of bright sun. If you plan to occupy a base camp for several days, it can save gobs of fuel. But if you're on the move with a new camp each night, neither the solar melter nor any of the lightweight solar cookers available will do you much good—either process takes hours. Another problem is that solar cookers in the light-weight/cheap category are made of foil-coated cardboard or lightweight plastic, so the slightest gust tips them over. Carving out a recess or using stakes can help, but in any event you need to stay close by. And being tethered to a stove—even a solar one—rather defeats the purpose of being out there.

On the whole, though, solar-powered trekking is not just practical and range-extending, but actively pleasing. In regions of dependable sunshine it may in the long run prove more fail-safe than fossil-fueled stoves.

My main sources for portable solar gear (full info in Appendix III) have been C. Crane Co., Jade Mountain, Solar World, and Real Goods. In particular, Real Goods publishes a wide range of material on solar and remote living and a catalog that lists many items (LED lights, water filters, even a hiking staff with a built-in flute) of interest to backpackers. Meanwhile, I'm perennially on the lookout for new sun-driven schemes—if you have one, write. And good luck tinkering.

While you're catching bright sun on your PV charger, for your eyes' sake you should temper it with

Sunglasses and goggles.

COLIN: Dark glasses are a comfort and convenience just about anywhere, almost indispensable in deserts, totally so in snow or at high altitudes.

If you find your eyes bothered by glare in low, snow-free country, any sunglasses that are optically true should nip the trouble, even in deserts. (Notes: Blue eyes tend to be more affected than brown. And you can check the optics of sunglasses by looking at reflections of straight lines—such as fluorescent store lights—in the concave surfaces: if the lines curve near the outer edges of the lenses there is distortion.) Polaroid glasses protect eyes and also let you look through the surface glare of water—often a big advantage in fishing. Sunglasses come in various tints, and choosing between them is often a matter of personal psychological preference rather than optical efficiency: some people like the world rose- or blue-gray-tinted, others rebel.

If you wear eyeglasses all or some of the time, prescription sun-glasses will do the best job. But clip-ons or a large pair that fit over your normal glasses will do, and they certainly make good spares. (Other useful spares: the frameless, flimsy, but ultralightweight plastic affairs that oculists give you to protect your eyes after dilation; for permanence, patch with ripstop tape at the bends.) Once you've graduated to bifocals, clip-ons or big overglasses are the only practical answer if you want to read a map or indeed to see anything close up. I like clip-ons (though they're fragile and must be protected when not in use) because I can just flip them up when I walk from sunlight into shade—a surprisingly valuable bonus. You can sometimes get ordinary sunglasses big enough to wear over your prescription pair.*

At high altitude—above about 6000 feet, say—and especially in snow, your eyes, of no matter what hue, need protection from ultraviolet and infrared rays. Ultraviolets are the "tanning" rays: the skin recovers from their effects, but your retinas may not. Infrareds can also cause permanent retinal damage but, long before that, may produce fatigue and, eventually, excruciatingly painful *snow blindness*—which may not develop until hours after you've come in out of the sun. So up high, where the earth's atmosphere filters out far less of these rays than it does lower down, you need protection from both UV and IR. Glass of any kind filters out UV, but you need special darkened glasses to deal with the IR. Plastic clip-ons or overglasses that filter neither may do more harm than good: they allow your pupils to open up and admit more light to the retinas. Plastic-over-plastic guards against neither UV nor IR; plastic-over-glass at least eliminates UV.**

In snow, even low down, and especially in sun, your eyes are about as

*CHIP: Opticians are now able to supply bifocals, trifocals, and continuous-focus lenses—I have a type called Vari-focals—with full UV/IR-proof coatings in both glass and plastic. The custom lenses are in a French nylon frame labeled BREVETE SDGD that has stood so many years of daily use that it is now "retro," or so I'm told. The new domed, rainbow-hued wraparounds with polycarbonate lenses increase peripheral vison while making you look like a predatory insect. Some of these are adaptable to corrective lenses, at extra cost. Multisport goggles, while good for biking, skiing, and paddling, tend to become tiny steam chambers while back-packing—on me at least.

**CHIP: Ultraviolet radiation is now sorted into three types: UV-A, UV-B, and UV-C. Both glass and polycarbonate lenses can absorb 100 percent of all three UV frequencies. While glass can also block 100 percent of infrared (IR) as well, the best polycarbonate lenses only block about 75 percent.

much at hazard as at high altitudes. For treatment of snow blindness, see page 650 and also the first-aid references, page 652.

The standard high-altitude sunglasses were for some years those made by Vuarnet. The glass lenses are so tempered that even if broken they shatter into harmless round blobs, not lacerating shards. And the cadmium-coated lenses have green zones at top and bottom to filter glare from sky and underfoot snow, and an amber zone amidships. They work well in both sun glare and flat light. Frames are so pliable and tough that you can tie a knot in the temple and let it spring back to normal. The excellent Vuarnets became something of a fad, especially among skiers, but many viable alternatives are now cheaper or lighter or offer other advantages. The spectrum is too broad to detail here, but the names include Bollé, Bouchet, Cébé, Galibier, Julbo, Loubsol, Ray-Ban (Bausch and Lomb), and Ski Optics. Catalogs—especially REI and EMS online—teem with others. Average weight: around 2 ounces. Cost range: $35 to $150-plus. Those with polycarbonate lenses (treated to remove all or most UV as well as IR light) are lighter and less liable to fog but need greater care to prevent scratching.

Adjustable elastic restraining straps will hold glasses in place no matter what you do. The original neoprene Croakies (¼ oz., $5) are said to keep your glasses floating in water. Other styles in cotton or nylon cord (by Chums, Hotz, et al.) merely keep them on or, if slacked off, secure but resting on your chest.

Some high-altitude and snow sunglasses come with leather side-guards and noseguards for additional protection, and guards can be fitted to most glasses. Removable ones are best—to reduce misting problems in hot, humid weather. (*Note:* Sideguards are now illegal for driving in California and some other states; tickets have been issued.)

Goggles are primarily for skiers and mountain climbers, but you sometimes need them for backpacking up high or in winter. There's a wide selection from makers of sunglasses and ski-ware, ranging from $35 to hundreds of dollars for prescription-lens types. Good goggles leave room for prescription glasses inside; have breathable, hypersoft foam top and bottom; and offer amber-, rose-, or lilac-tinted lenses that both protect eyes from glare and increase contrasts in flat light.

Goggles, though highly protective, inherently tend to cause fogging as your sweat condenses on cold, poorly ventilated lenses. Various forms of ventilation combat the problem. Breathable foam padding seems the most likely to succeed in driving snow: any other system that lets in enough air also lets in snow. But some models now incorporate inner lens coatings that absorb moisture and spread it around. Others fight the fight with double lenses. A new All-Weather Vent by W. L. Gore that equalizes pressure and temperature between double lenses without letting moisture in is found on the Bollé Krait goggle ($45–$55) and perhaps others. A model with a battery-powered fan is no longer available.

Of course, you can apply anti-mist preparations to untreated goggle lenses, and you may sometimes need to do so with sunglasses, especially if they have sideguards, or even with ordinary eyeglasses. Current liquid preparations come in small plastic phials (1 oz., $3–$5), or as a wipe-on stick. A makeshift substitute: wetted soap. Apply a thin film to goggles or glasses and rub into invisibility. The effect lasts a surprisingly long time. Lacking sunglasses or goggles, you can make mild glare more penetrable by rubbing charcoal on lower eye sockets—as football players know. In an emergency, in snow, you may be able to ward off snow blindness by shielding your eyes with almost any opaque material that has cross slits or a small hole cut into it. Possibilities: cardboard from the "office" (page 661), ripstop tape (page 667), cover from a paperback book, part of a map or food wrapper.

Your seeing—of all kinds—can be greatly amplified by

Binoculars.

I am always astonished that so few hikers carry them. It's not merely that a pair of binoculars can be extremely useful—that by leapfrogging your eyes out far ahead and disclosing the curve of a creek or the impassability of a rockwall they can save you hours of wasted effort; or that they might even act as an emergency fire starter (page 354). They are the key to many unexpected and therefore doubly delightful bonuses.

They lift you up so close to a planing hawk that you feel you could reach out and straighten a misplaced wing feather. They convert a small low-flying plane from an impersonal outline into a solid construction of panels and colors and markings, even of pilot and passengers with faces and lives of their own. They transform a deer on the far rim of a sunlit meadow from a motionless silhouette into a warm, breathing individual—alert, quivering, suspicious.

You can focus most binoculars down close too—sometimes onto one of those unimportant, utterly fascinating little cameos that you're apt to stumble on when you're in the right place and the right mood, with no stupidly important things to occupy your time and attention. You can even move over into the insect world. Early one fall, on the slopes of a desert mountain, I sat idly watching with my naked eye as a clapper-rattle grasshopper made a series of noisy, stunted airborne journeys. In flight, with its wings beating furiously, it looked like a small and ungainly green butterfly. After one flight the creature landed near the edge of a gravel road 8 feet in front of me, and rested. Squatting there beside a tiny tuft of grass, it was just a small, dark smudge, barely visible. I screwed my binocular focus adjustment fully out. The grasshopper crystallized into view: huge, green-armored, and apparently wingless, its front end tapering into the kind of chinless and no-brow head that to the human mind spells vacuity. Above the head towered a gigantic forest of grass blades. After a while the grasshopper moved. It advanced, bent-stilt leg slowly following bent-stilt leg, until it came to a small blade of grass on the edge of the forest. Dreamily it reached out with one foreleg, pressed down on the blade, manipulated it, inserted the tip into its mouth, and clamped tight. Slowly it sidled around until its body and the grass blade formed a single straight line. And then, still unutterably dreamily, it proceeded to devour the grass blade as if it were a huge horizontal strand of spaghetti. It ate very slowly, moving forward from time to time with an almost imperceptible shuffle of its bent-stilt legs. All at once, when the blade of grass was about three-quarters gone, the grasshopper relinquished its grip, and the truncated blade sprang back into place on the edge of the forest. The grasshopper moved jerkily away, skirting the enormous and overhanging green forest, traversing a tract of sun-beaten sand, then lumbering out over huge boulders of gravel. Suddenly, for no apparent reason, it launched once more into clapper-rattle flight and rocketed noisily and forever out of my vivid binocular world.

If you're going to carry binoculars as a matter of habit when you go walking, be sure to get the right kind. They must be light. They must be tough enough to stand up to being banged around. And they must not tire your eyes, even when used for long periods.

In choosing a pair of glasses, people tend to consider only magnification (indicated by the first of the two numbers stamped on the casing— the 7 in an old-style average-power 7 × 35, for example). But powerful lenses magnify not only what you see but also the inevitable "jump" imparted by your hands. So, unless you can steady the glasses on something, magnification beyond a certain power—about 7 or 8 for most people—doesn't necessarily allow you to see more clearly. Generally speaking too, the greater the magnification, the narrower your field of view.

Again, if powerful glasses are not to darken what you see, they must have objective lenses (the lenses at the far, non-eye end) that are big enough to let in adequate light. The second of the two numbers on the casing—the 35 in the 7 × 35—gives the diameter of the objective lenses in millimeters, and for daylight use there's no advantage in having that second figure more than five times as big as the first: except at night, the average human eye can't use the extra light that bigger lenses let in. And big lenses mean cumbersome glasses, too heavy for ordinary use. Once the first thrill of ownership has worn off, they generally get left at home—ask anyone who has invested in a pair of those impressive looking naval-type binoculars.

New lens coatings and other technical advances mean that good-quality glasses with a magnification/objective lens ratio as low as 1:2.5—as in 8 × 20, for example—now admit enough light for perfect sunlight viewing and reasonable results in overcast or even twilight. And a 1:4 ratio can now give good definition in starlight.

On most binoculars a knurled wheel on the center post focuses both lenses, and any eye difference (except for very marked variation in long- or shortsightedness) is corrected with the right eyepiece. In other models each eyepiece focuses independently. Both systems have advantages. For quick refocusing at any range, you need center focus. Individual-focus glasses, more simply constructed, will stand up to rougher use but are now relatively rare.

Standard binoculars have cupped eyepieces that cut peripheral glare and also compel you to locate your eye pupils the right distance from the lens. But if you wear eyeglasses they force your pupils too far away and you suffer a severely restricted field of view. Models made for eyeglass wearers, distinguished by the letter *B*—as in 8 × 32B—have as eyepieces either fold-down rubber cups or push-pull sleeves that in the extended position perform the normal noneyeglass functions but can be folded down or pushed in so that with eyeglasses your pupils move in correctly close. Such devices, now a standard feature, are an advantage to anyone who ever wears sunglasses and a boon to those who often operate in snow or high altitudes and needs sunglasses or goggles for long spells.

All binoculars used to be "porro-prism": the prism system bent the light onto a new path during its passage through the glasses, so objective lenses were always wider apart than eye (or exit) lenses. But modern "roof-prism" binoculars route the light straight through and are smaller and lighter as well as more robust (though they lose some three-dimensional effect). This system led to the appearance of fully viable miniature binoculars that weigh between a quarter and half a pound and have brought joy to backpackingdom.

Within that group—and outside it—a wide selection now beckons. To decide what best suits you, balance your requirements, or priorities, in weight, magnification, field of view, toughness, waterproofness, and cost. Weight is something only you can rate. A high magnification—8 or even 10 if you have a rocklike hand—is best for route finding: you can decipher more distant details. But given a certain size (and weight) of instrument, then the larger the magnification, the narrower the field of view. *Field of view* is measured—and often marked on the binoculars—either as an angle (say 7 degrees) or as the width of view at 1000 yards (say 336 feet). And the wider the field of view, the easier it is to pick up a fleeting target such as a bird or deer. So for such tasks 7-power may be best. Backpacking demands toughness, and, generally speaking, the more you pay, the sturdier you get. "Armored" models, with impact-resistant plastic or even rubberized housings, designed for Calibans, are now both common and light—5 to 8 oz. Armored models bear the letter *A* while *C* denotes a "compact" or miniature model: a model labeled "8 × 20 BCA" has retractable eyecups, is compact, and also armored.

If moisture gets inside binoculars it may cause fogging that only the factory can remove, so unless you're always prepared to stow your binoculars away in any kind of rain, get a pair reputably described as at least "watertight." That should see you through minor drizzle, and maybe more. (Even high humidity may get moisture into cheaper models.) And if you want to operate fearlessly in downpours you should buy a pair with a reputable name that is designated "waterproof." If you pay a lot, it probably will be. Among the very best shockproof models, the Leica Trinovid 8 × 20 BCA (8 oz.) lists at $400, the 10 × 25 BCA (8.5 oz.) at $429. You can get compacts with good optics and reasonable toughness from such makers as Brunton, Bushnell, Celestron, Leica, Leupold, Minolta, Minox, Nikon, Olympus, Pentax, Steiner, Svarovski, Swift, and Zeiss at prices ranging from $50 to over $500, with quality mostly proportionate. Below $100, quality tends to fall off sharply; but if you're willing to baby your binoculars and put up with less-than-perfect optics you can still find something viable in that range, provided you shop around and outdoubt Thomas.*

Monoculars are half (or, to be more exact, rather less than half) a pair of binoculars. They therefore save ounces and dollars and are easier to carry when not in use. But they're less easy to hold steady—and demand the abnormal and therefore probably strainful business of looking through one eye. Still, some people with two eyes seem to get along fine with them. Be warned, though, that others do not. Roof-prism systems mean that monoculars can now be straight and compact and robust. Most binocular makers, up and down the scale, offer them. Good midrange models (some with a close-focus lens and microscope stand) run 3 to 5 oz.

---

*For consistency, all prices I've quoted here—and later for cameras—are "list." But list prices in this field are a chimera. Almost anywhere, anytime, you can buy "name" instruments at 30 or 40 percent below list (except that the higher-quality units tend to be more like 20 percent off). This is known as merchandising. In other fields, parallel behavior is labeled bullshit, stupidity, or deceit.

and \$100 to \$150; Minox has a 6 × 16 (3.5 oz., \$119) and Zeiss still makes an 8 × 20 (1.5 oz., \$259) and an exquisite little 5 × 10 (less than 1 oz., and only \$90). Forestry Suppliers stocks the Steiner Miniscope (3 oz., \$142)—an 8 × 22, porro-prismed unit that delivers a bright and easy-to-focus image and comes with a leather case.

Buying secondhand binoculars (or monoculars) is always a risk—unless you know exactly what you're doing. Even new ones should be bought only from reputable dealers who really understand their wares. New or old, make sure you test several pairs outside the store, in sunlight and shadow. Better still, insist on a cast-iron money-back guarantee in case you're not satisfied after, say, three days' trial: misaligned or unsuitable binoculars can cause eyestrain and will probably, like too-heavy models, soon get left at home. (Despite this good-store-only advice, I'm told that if you know precisely what you want and have a trusting nature the best buys now come from Internet sites or certain New York mail-order houses.)

Twenty years ago I grew tired of replacing good mid-price-range binoculars every couple of years (because I treated them so roughly), and invested in a pair of Leitz 8 × 20 BCA Trinovids (the company changed its name to Leica when it split from the parent firm around 1988). Like most models today, they have a broad central platform under which the barrels fold for protection and compactness, and at first that left me uneasy about retaining the all-important exactly parallel adjustment, without which the image, and your eyes, will suffer. But experience has quieted my qualms. And this little instrument is a joy to use. In theory, I should see less well in poor light and at night, but I detect little or no loss. Pundits explain that a new coating on the roof prisms "corrects the wave-optic effects of the phase shift between the two halves of the light beam split by the roof apex . . . so you can watch for longer without your eyes getting tired." Now isn't that comforting.

CHIP: As a light-and-cheap aficionado, I got by for many years with an inexpensive 8 × 21 monocular (then \$50 and always 3 oz.)—good for route finding but a trial for watching things (birds, coyotes, stars) that move.

A few years ago, Linda, an optobirdophile, doubled my wildlife horizons with some Brunton Lite-Tech 8 × 25 waterproof binoculars (11 oz.). But a recent peek through some Leica 10 × 25 BCA glasses was revelatory—I bought 'em on the spot. The clear, dry Wyoming air lets me take advantage of the 10x magnification to see across wide canyons and scout distant ridges. For an unshaky view at 10x, I rest my index finger on my brow and adjust the focus with my middle finger. Those in humid climes and vegetated landscapes might find 8x glasses a better choice.

COLIN: To get the most out of your binoculars you must learn to use them automatically, almost without thought. First, set the barrels at the widest angle that gives you a circular field of view. Note the reading on the small center dial. (Some porro-prism glasses have such a dial; some don't.) Next, focus. Do not shut one eye while you do so: you may alter the muscle positions of the open eye. Instead, keep both eyes open, cover the right front lens with one hand, and move the center-focus adjustment until a selected object is as sharp as you can make it. Shift your blocking hand to the left front lens and, still with both eyes open, move the diopter adjustment on the right eyepiece until the *same* selected object is again sharp. Then look through both eyepieces at once: the object should still be critically sharp. With center-focus binoculars, memorize the adjustment on the right eyepiece: it will be correct for your eyes at any distance. Individual-focus and rangefinder models will have further refinements; consult the directions.

Some people tend to screw their eyes up just because they're looking through an unfamiliar instrument. Naturally, their eye muscles soon tire. But if the binoculars' two barrels are properly aligned anyone can, with practice, look through them for protracted periods without strain. After all, seamen and birdwatchers do, hours at a stretch. And there is never any reason for saying, "Oh, but my eyes are too old for binoculars." Given proper eyeglasses, age need make no difference.

Some people experience difficulty at first in getting what they want into the field of view. One way is to fix your eyes on the target and simply bring the glasses into position. Another method is to draw your eyes back a few inches and align the center bar (or focusing wheel) on the target; then, without moving the instrument, shift your eyes to the eyepieces. The target should be dead center in your field of view.

Once you're so comfortable with your binoculars that you use them without a thought for technique, you'll probably find yourself taking them along whenever you go walking. And they'll always be opening up new possibilities. I still have a couple of unfulfilled wishes on my conscious waiting list. One day, for example, I'd like to look from a respectful distance straight into the eye of an ill-humored rattlesnake. For a long time I thought I also wanted to examine a nearby rainbow's end. Then, some years ago, I looked out of my bedroom window one morning soon after sunrise and saw a rainbow curving down into the foot of the hills opposite my house, barely half a mile away. I immediately turned and began hurrying for my binoculars. But halfway to the bedroom door I stopped. Faced with the impending reality, I knew that if I went ahead and looked, as I had so long thought I intended, I would find . . . nothing. So I turned and went back to the window, my dream intact. Well, almost intact.

Carrying binoculars

Back when binoculars were heavy, neck-wearying things, I used to sling mine over the projecting tubular top of one side of my E-frame, and keep them from falling too far if they bounced off by clipping them (with a belt clip, page 680) onto a length of nylon cord that was tied to a ring bolt on the frame. I even rigged a bump pad to reduce noise and damage when the binoculars bumped against the frame. But my present Trinovids are so light that even I, who fought this solution for years, almost always carry them slung around my neck, often tucked into my shirt pocket. For those who still don't like plain neck-slinging, readers have suggested various cunning devices, including an open binocular case sewn to one of the pack's shoulder straps and a metal clip, fixed to the binoculars' "camera mount," that slips into a pocket sewn to the shoulder strap. But there are now various commercially made nylon-strap-and-buckle shoulder harnesses that take most of the strain off the neck and hold binoculars (or camera) snugly against the body yet ready for instant use. For makers of such devices, and cases, see Carrying Your Camera, page 623.

For close-up seeing of such wonders as flower stamens or bug eyes it's possible to use your binoculars in reverse: you look through the objective lens and hold the eyepiece very close to the subject. But although magnification is good you get curvature distortion all around the perimeter, and I nearly always take along a ¼-oz. prospector's magnifying glass (page 287) for this job—and for others too.

RECORDING YOUR MARVEL

Nowadays most of us tend to accept that we're failing in some kind of duty if we don't record our outdoor doings on film. Chalk up another victory to advertising.

But you can fight back. And there are good, joy-filled reasons for doing so.

I've described in other books some of the less obvious and more dubious delights you can achieve with a camera.

Photography of any pretension at all eats up time at a rate that's rarely grasped by people who do no more than take snapshots of friends. And wilderness photography, even without interchangeable lenses, has its own special time-consuming idiosyncrasies. It's not just that exasperation and loving care have to fight their usual battles—first against each other, then as allies against form-balance, shadows, depth of focus, fluctuating light, parallax problems, and a wobbly tripod. You also have to cope with the irresistible beckonings of more and yet more brilliant wildflowers every time you move forward for a shot of an especially magnificent display; with the flimsy psyches of lizards; with the pathologically antisocial attitude of bighorn sheep; and with a lumpish, strapped-on pack that has to come off for almost every shot and then, by God, has to go back on again.

Now, this kind of infighting has its merits. Up to a point it can be instructive, diverting, and satisfying. Up to a point.

Not until my Grand Canyon walk did I grasp, by sheer accident, that one of the great bonuses walking has to offer is

The delight of nonphotography.

The accident that opened my eyes happened one gusty Grand Canyon afternoon when my tripod and only camera blew over and the camera gave up the ghost. At first, when I discovered that its shutter refused to function, I simmered with frustration. I knew it would be at least a week before I could get word out that I urgently needed a replacement camera—a week in which I would walk through a spectacular, rarely visited landscape that I'd almost certainly never visit again. It promised to be a bitter week. But within an hour I discovered that I had escaped from something I never quite knew existed: the tyranny of film. Photography, I suddenly understood, is not really compatible with contemplation. Its details are too insistent. They're always buzzing around your mind, clouding the fine focus of appreciation. You rarely realize this painful fact at the time, and you can't do much about it even if you do. But that day in Grand Canyon, after the camera had broken, I found myself savoring in a new way everything around me. Instead of stopping briefly to photograph and forget, I stood and stared, fixing truer images on the emulsion of memory. And the week, set free, became a carnival.

I learned my lesson. For years now I've rarely taken a camera. And if I want my walking to be, above all, carefree and therapeutic, I make sure I leave it at home—or at least carry only a roll or two of film. I find that, by and large, it works. Liberated, I have more time to stand and stare.

A Wisconsin reader suggests a less drastic antidote. "A viewfinder is restricting," he writes, "but I always take a long look at a view sans camera after I take a picture."

Now, there are certainly times when all of us, despite the delights of nonphotography, want to carry back home a thin facsimile of the marvel we have discovered; to record, that is, the highlights of a trip not to mention the lowlights and some midlights. As a writer, I often employ a camera as notebook. Occasionally I need photographs for books or articles, and then I can't use film smaller than 35 millimeter. So in practice I never do. An alternative, now: cameras taking 24-millimeter APS (Advanced

Photographic System) drop-in film. That sounds as if it meets classic backpacking criteria: equipment that's light, compact, light, simple, light, tough, and light.

Cameras and accessories

In *Walker III,* the guff on specific cameras and accessories filled eight-plus pages—and the field has grown wider and more complex. So we've decided that this time, because the subject is really peripheral to backpacking and demands pages better devoted to more central matters, we'll virtually skip it. (Besides, I've preached the joys of nonphotography and I smell near-apostasy.) If you want relevant, up-to-date advice, consult the growing flood of photography articles, pamphlets, and books.

In lieu of detailed guff we offer a compressed teach-by-example listing of what Chip and I—and one expert backpacking photographer—now find ourselves using.

If I take a camera backpacking nowadays, it's mostly my original-model Olympus XA (7.9 oz.; a shirt-pocket-size 1¼ by 2½ by 4 inches; current equivalents $120–$240). It has fewer bells and whistles than later models but, I'm told, better optics. On rare occasions—as when I may want large-animal or other telephoto shots—I take my trusty old Pentax Spotmatic (2 lbs. 6 oz. with case; 150-mm telephoto lens, 11 oz.; equivalent new single-lens-reflex models, around $450). I've tried fancy "automatic" SLRs but found them heavy and fragile—notably on a six-month raft solo down the Colorado, when I water- or sand-ruined three.

When I asked my friend John Sexton—a photographer with an international reputation—what he took backpacking when he wanted to go light and capture only nonprofessional, goofing-about images, he answered, almost apologetically: "One of the throwaway Kodak Max cameras. Often more than one." (Twenty-seven exposures of slightly cropped 35-mm film, 2.5 oz. [a roll of 35-mm film weighs 1 oz.]; little bigger than such a roll: no flash, no exposure adjustment; $13.29 at supermarkets.) John carries his in zip-top bags.

CHIP: Colin insists, so here's my current data. For serious photography and also for documenting my research on glaciers, mountains, and the like, I've used a succession of Olympus OM-1 bodies—manual with a battery-powered light meter. They're rugged, dependable in extreme cold, and as familiar as my own nose. I've got Olympus Zuiko lenses: a wide-angle 28 millimeter, a 50 millimeter "normal," and a 75 to 150 millimeter zoom. The whole mess, in a Tenba padded case that straps on my chest, weighs 3 to 4 lbs. I've tried a series of small point-and-snap cameras and after brief love affairs they've all malfunctioned, owing to cold, moisture, or electronic gremlins. So right now I either haul my antiques or use those recyclable goodies. But beware of "waterproof" cheapies in clear plastic boxes—the plastic plays nasty tricks with slanting light.

Carrying your camera

Strap-harnesses for cameras (and binoculars) now come from the well-established manufacturers Lowe Pro and Tamrac (both win consensus praise) and from Tenba and Promaster. Camera cases suitable for backpacking, too. Also allied goodies.

ROUTE FINDING

To nurture the holiday spirit on a minor trip into unfamiliar country I often go without

Maps.

Or I may take only rudimentary ones (page 625). In part, this stratagem works: it injects into each day a steady stream of that titillating element, the unexpected. But sometimes I find that traveling without a map becomes so inefficient that it diminishes my freedom rather than amplifies it. And when it's important that you get to the right place at more or less the right time, maps become indispensable. They're also a help in deciding what places you most want to see.

But maps are not merely for route finding. They can radically influence many facets of your outdoor life. They act as aids not only to keeping going and to accurate estimating (page 37) but in water logistics, foot comfort, warmth, and choice of campsites. Without a map to tell you where to find the next water—even though not always with certainty— you're liable to labor along under an unnecessary canteen load or to walk for long, half-lived hours with your awareness clogged by the gray scum of thirst. If your feet are beginning to get sore a map may help you ward off real trouble by avoiding a route that involves a long, steady, downhill, blister-inducing trek. On a day lacerated by icy winds you can with luck and a map select trails or cross-country routes that slink along in comparative coziness under the lee of a steep ridge. And with practice you can choose good campsites, hours or even days ahead—and in doing so may even collect one of walking's unexpected and delightful little bonuses (page 498).

In the United States the only maps that really convey much detailed information of the kind useful to a walker are the U.S. Geological Survey (USGS) topographical series. They're so detailed that I sometimes feel they'd be adequate to guide you on a prowl around on hands and knees. But don't be misled: although the contours rarely prove inaccurate, trails all too often do—and sometimes badly so.

By permission of Johnny Hart and Creators Syndicate, Inc.

CHIP: On 7.5-minute maps (covering about 8.5 miles north to south and 6.5 miles west to east; scale: 1:24,000; contour interval usually 40 feet; now $4.50 each) I've found occasional errors: one lake in the Wind Rivers is shown draining west instead of north. But in the late 1980s the USGS sent out a call for corrections (I submitted a batch), so new editions may have fewer boo-boos. Also useful is a series of USGS 30-by-60-minute maps (scale: 1:100,000—meaning that 1 centimeter equals 1 kilometer on the ground, and 1 inch is 1.6 miles) that cover 35 miles north to south and roughly 53 miles east to west—I say "roughly" because the distance in a minute of longitude increases, pie-slice-wise, as you approach the equator. Elevations are in meters (wake up, America) with a 50-meter contour interval (though some have a 20-meter interval), and they cost $6.50. USGS editions of both 30-by-60- and 7.5-by-7.5-minute can be had in mountain shops, some bookstores, and state geological survey offices, which stock maps for the entire state. A Bureau of Land Management (BLM) edition (for the western U.S.) of the 30-by-60-minute series has land status color-coded (yellow for BLM, green for national forest, blue for state land, and white for private land), which might be of some use in avoiding trespass.

The USGS Alaska series is 1:63,360 scale, or 1 inch to 1 mile. There is also a U.S. 1:250,000 series (almost 4 miles to 1 inch) that gives a broad overview—too broad for route finding.

The central distribution agency for all U.S. maps, including Alaska, is: USGS Information Services, P.O. Box 25286, Denver, CO 80225. You can call 888-ASK-USGS (275-8747) or check their Web site: *www. usgs.gov*. Ask for a free brochure titled *Finding Your Way with Map and*

Compass and a booklet, *Topographic Mapping,* that runs down history and techniques, including the recent digital and satellite revolution.

COLIN: Any map office or distribution center will supply you, free, with an index map of your state or area. This map enables you to find the name of the quad or quads that cover the slice of country you are interested in. It also lists places within the state from which you can buy USGS topo maps. Even if the office doesn't sell them itself, the staff will know the local retail outlets.

Topo maps for parts of the Sierra Nevada, clearly and accurately overprinted with trails (and also with an index of place-names, identifiable on the map by a grid system), are published by Wilderness Press and available in some California mountain shops. National Geographic Trails Illustrated publishes trail maps of popular backpacking areas such as national parks and monuments, with Colorado and Utah series, the Continental Divide Trail, and suchlike.

The Canadian equivalent of the USGS maps is the National Topographical Series, metric scale 1:50,000. Larger-scale maps include a 1:250,000 series. To order, contact: Federal Maps, Inc., #1, 52 Antares Drive, Nepean, Ontario, K2E 7Z1 (613-723-6366; fax—613-723-6995; e-mail—<fedmaps@fedmaps.com>). Visa, Mastercard, and Am Ex credit cards accepted for fax, e-mail, and phone orders, as well as certified checks and money orders for mail orders.

For a directory of mapping agencies and sales outlets worldwide, consult the International Map Trade Association Web site: *www.map trade.org.*

U.S. Forest Service maps generally show roads, rivers, and trails but little else. No contours. Still, it's often worth picking one up from a ranger station to check that the trail details shown on a USGS topo map are accurate and up-to-date. And I sometimes use one on a minor trip when I want to know roughly where I'm going but also want to conserve that titillating element of the unexpected.

Another way to achieve that end is to take along only an ordinary road map of the kind you can buy at any gas station. Between roads these maps are mainly blank space. At most they offer some rather speculative *hachuring*—a light shading that indicates the slope and direction of hill and valley. With such a map you can easily set yourself the vague sort of target that seems necessary to almost any kind of walk. (As someone has said, "Every journey must have a soul.") You just find a big, blank space that intrigues you, drive to the edge of it, park the car, and walk in and find out what's there. Such an expedition can take an hour, an afternoon, a weekend, or a week. With a little experience, local knowledge, and luck you may be able to burst clear not only of roads but of the last vestiges of any kind of trail.*

CHIP: For "dreaming the map," that flame-free equivalent of gazing into a campfire, some of the new digitally based, elevation-tinted relief maps deserve permanent wall space. Raven has a spectacular color map of the United States and a companion black-and-white of "Landforms and Drainage" (both 37 by 58 inches, $40). They also have large state maps in color ($25). My Wyoming neighbor Kenneth Perry worked on some Raven maps and then struck out on his own with a livelier color-set, producing a masterpiece: "The Colorado Plateau and its Drainage" (47 by 39 inches, $20), which transforms the wall above my desk. His other suit-

---

*Do not underestimate the importance of such a bursting free. There is a cardinal rule of travel, all too often overlooked, that I call The Law of Inverse Appreciation.

It states: "The less there is between you and the environment, the more you appreciate that environment."

Every walker knows, even if he hasn't thought much about it, the law's most obvious application: the bigger and more efficient your means of transportation, the more severely you become divorced from the reality through which you're traveling. A man learns a thousand times more about the sea from a kayak than from a cruise ship; euphorically more about space at the end of a cord than from inside a capsule. On land you remain in closer touch with the countryside in a slow-moving old open touring car than in an air-conditioned, tinted-glass-window, 80-miles-an-hour-and-never-notice-it behemoth. And you come in closer touch on a horse or bicycle than in any car; in closer touch on foot than on any horse or bicycle.

But the law has a second and less obvious application: your appreciation varies not only according to what you travel *in* but also according to what you travel *over*. Drive along a freeway in any kind of car and you are in almost zero contact with the country beyond the concrete. Turn off onto a minor highway and you move a notch closer. A narrow country road is better still. When you bump slowly along a jeep trail you begin at last to sense those vital details that turn mere landscape into living countryside. And a few years ago, on the East African savanna—where it was at that time not considered destructive to drive cross-country over the pale grasslands—I discovered an extending corollary to my law: "The farther you move away from any impediment to appreciation, the better it is."

These secondary discrepancies persist when you're traveling on foot. Any blacktop road holds the scrollwork of the country at arm's length: the road itself keeps stalking along on stilts or grubbing about in a trough, and your feet tread on harsh and sterile pavement. Turn off onto a dusty jeep trail and the detail moves closer. A foot trail is better still—and a barely discernible one far better than a trampled wilderness thoroughfare. But you don't really break free until you step off the trail and walk through waving grass or woodland undergrowth or across rock or smooth sand or (most perfect of all, in some ways) over virgin snow. Now you can read all the details, down to the finest print. They differ, of course, in each domain. Drifting snow crystals have barely begun to blur the four-footed signature of the marten that padded past this lodgepole pine. Or a long-legged lizard scurries for cover, kicking up little spurts of sand as it corners around a bush. Or wet, glistening granite supports an intricate mosaic of purple lichen. Or you stand in long, pale grass and watch the wave patterns of the wind until, quite suddenly, you feel seasick. And always, in snow or sand or rock or seascape grass, there is, as far as you can see in any direction, no sign of man.

That, I believe, is being in touch with the world.

able-for-dreaming maps include California and Michigan with the Upper Peninsula, and he also has CDs with screen-size state and regional maps.

USGS topographic maps have been digitized and enhanced (with brighter colors and added information) by outfits such as Maptech and DeLorme. In general, a series of maps are supplied on a CD, often with software that rotates and adds dimension for a 3-D effect (given the right computer, of course, and $30–$100). The hard-copy equivalents are plastic raised-relief topo maps in a 1:250,000 series and also for certain national parks by the Hubbard Company and others, and last but not least, bandannas and T-shirts silk-screened with topos—available in mountain shops and tourist traps.

COLIN: Occasionally, if I expect much rain or drizzle, I'll carry the map I'm currently using in a zip-top plastic bag that travels in my yoke office (page 180) and not only protects the map from moisture and dirt and general wear and tear but also seems to collect from time to time a pencil, a book of matches, camera lens tissue, and even (in heavy rain) my notebook. Simple plastic mapcases with zipper closures keep appearing in catalogs. Liberty Mountain has neat ones with an ingenious fold-and-Velcro closure in 5-by-7-, 7-by-10-, and 10-by-14-inch sizes, for $2 to $4. Cascade Designs makes good ones with a wide-track waterproof closure (8 by 12 inches, $10). There are fancier versions, too: the Silva Waterproof Map Case has a clear sleeve and various pockets for compass, fieldbook, and so on (9 oz., $21.50). Some of the fancier new yoke offices have good, protective, transparent, flip-open flaps for maps.

You used to be able to buy transparent plastic sheeting, adhesive on one side, with removable backing, that was designed to "protect maps against damage from water or wear." I tried it once, and it worked. But it seems to have vanished from stores and catalogs—probably because we now have a better maptrap. Stormproof is a liquid that impregnates and protects paper. I can confirm from field tests that, as promised, it dries quickly and is then invisible, and that it doesn't stiffen the paper, which can still be rolled or folded. Penciled notations can be easily erased; permanent ones made with waterproof ink. An advisor reports that "it held my maps together even through an 18-day canoe expedition in the Arctic, and I only brushed a coat on one side of my maps (instructions recommend impregnating both sides). It completely penetrates into the paper, giving it a bit more body and a smoother, more durable surface. The paper folds without cracking and does not shred or pull apart when the weather is damp." A half-pint of Stormproof weighs 9 oz. (so it's hardly for carrying in the pack), costs $4, and impregnates 50 square feet of paper, or about seven topo quads. Map Wrap, Map Life, and Nikwax Map Proof (4.2 oz., $8) sound like similar preparations.

Mostly, though, I just take the untreated map that I'm using, fold it rather loosely, and stuff it into my shirt pocket or the "yoke office." The practice often strikes me as dangerously slapdash, but the spring of the loosely folded map seems to hold it in place. I can remember only one occasion on which I lost a map, and that was when I needed just one small corner of a large map and had cut it down to postcard size, so that there was none of the usual fold pressure to hold it in my pocket.

I tend, especially if carrying many maps, to cut off their margins and also any areas that I know for sure I won't need, even for locating an escape route in an emergency. The actual weight saving may not amount to much, but with a really heavy load I find insupportable the knowledge that I'm carrying even one unnecessary dram.

Maps can, as I've said, furnish many bonuses that have nothing to do with efficiency. All you need to contribute is competence in using them and a certain quirky curiosity. At least, I think that is all I contribute, and I know I collect the bonuses. Map reading is one of the few arts I've been fairly competent at ever since I was a child—no doubt because I was fascinated from the start by wriggling blue rivers and amoeboid blue lakes and rhombic green woods and, above all, by the harmony and mystery of patterned red contour lines. These fascinations have never withered. I wouldn't like to say for sure that I ever walked 20 miles simply because I wanted to see the three-dimensional reality represented on my map by a dragon's-head peninsula or a perfect horseshoe river bend or an improbably vermiform labyrinth of contours. It's certainly many years since I did such a thing openly. For now that I am a man I have carefully put away such childish motives. In self-defense, I dig up more momentous reasons.

I'm aware that, for many people, a map holds neither meaning nor mystery. I can only hope, compassionately, that the rest of their existence isn't equally poverty-stricken.

Map measurer

A map measurer is a cunning little instrument with a tiny wheel that can follow any route, no matter how snaky, and which registers on its circular dial with many scales the mileage represented by the distance the wheel has rolled. Remember, though, that—except along absolutely straight roads or trails (come to think of it, who ever heard of an absolutely straight trail?)—your feet always slog a great deal farther than the wheel indicates (page 47). Still, a measurer can be a useful guide. I occasionally use mine—one of the old, round, metal kind—for planning but have never carried it in the pack.

CHIP: The lightest (2–3 oz.) and least costly ($20–$25) map measurers of reasonable quality are now plastic—from Silva, Alvin, and PECO. Impeccable metal ones such as the Minerva Curvimeter (2 oz., $138) cost more. Digital models—suitable for planning but not packing—run from $60 to $150. Forestry Suppliers has a good selection. But in the field the grid pattern on USGS maps makes it easy to eyeball distance, and I often lay a finger against the scale: at 1:100,000, the nail on my little finger is 1 kilometer long.

Trail guides

COLIN: Trail guides are now immensely popular. They line a shelf or two in every mountain shop, a column or three in most catalogs. And they continue to burgeon.

Their success is understandable. Armed with a trail guide you can plan a trip sensibly and logically, leaving very little to chance. You can strike camp each morning with a clear, numbered, and verbalized picture of what the day will unfold: its mileages, gradients, difficulties, rewards. You can rest confident that you need not miss a single important geological, botanical, or historical landmark. You will even know where to look for beauty.

My intellectual recognition of trail guides' usefulness prompted a mildly informative paragraph on them in the first edition of this book. After all, I told myself, the guides clearly met a need—or at least gave people what they thought they wanted. And some of them seemed excellent productions. But I'm sorry now that, in an attempt to be tolerant and "reasonable," I corked my true feelings. So no more pussyfooting.

I loathe trail guides, strong and sour from the bottom of my gut. They gnaw at the taproots of what I judge wilderness walking (or any kind of sane walking) to be all about. The whole idea, surely, is to cast off the coordinates of civilization. You want to "get away from it all." And, less consciously perhaps, you want to "get back to it all." To get back to old roots, that is, and renew them. So once you've sprung yourself free from roadhead, the heart of traveling ceases to be the civilized one of getting from A to B: it becomes finding out what lies between. Finding out, mark you. Not confirming mere intellectual lessons, strung out along a numbered and verbalized white line. Certainly not piling up sweaty records, mile and minute, for retail to the less stalwart. Simply finding out. Simply.

The very nature of the trail-guide beast cuts clear across this grain: the "sensible" subordination of doubt and chance; the mile-by-mile scheduling and checking; the rule of the written word. It's all inapplicable, stupid. It walls off, before you've even begun, the values you came so far to retrieve.

As I said, my aversion is a gut reaction, and I'm weightily aware that my attitude gapes with inconsistencies. After all, I recommend meticulous planning. I carry maps. And how come a writer rails against the rule of the written word? Above all, how come the writer of this how-to book—even though he has admitted misgivings (see footnote below)—inveighs against written instruction? And do we not depend, all of us, every moment we are "out," on such stiff, technological cushions as aluminum packframes and polyurethane pads and gas- or propane-burning stoves? I admit these impeachments. Yet almost all the carefulnesses I recommend impinge only on ourselves and on the little worlds we carry on our backs. They do not blight the broader world we're traveling through. And if you use the props wisely they need not curdle your appreciation of that world. Given time to break free from accustomed channels of thought, you can establish new coordinates and so move on to discovery, wonder, and illumination. But trail guides—these sensible, convenient, efficient tools—impose the old, straight-line, "civilized" coordinates, and so hold you at arm's length from the new, wilderness grid of meaning. It is, as I say, stupid. It's hardly surprising, though. One of our common stupidities is applying the criteria and then the tools of one realm to the exploration and exploitation of another.

Trail guides also do an altogether different damage. They bring people in by the goddamn horde. If I learn a once-attractive place has been trail-guided, I sadly stay away. Most horrible of all are the now-mushrooming guides to the fragile desert. The disease has even spread to ski touring. An experienced backpacker and ski tourer once said to me, "Crazy! And you know what it'll lead to? It's the old business of the cow that wandered through the bush, and the man who followed it, and then other men—and before long the engineer was following too, putting his road in." Exactly. And trail guides are engineers working on your thoughts. You know what happens when engineers lay their hands on a river and channelize it: they make it safer, easier to control, and thereby more convenient, more efficient. They also kill it.

After this little tirade—which has already made me feel a good deal better—I shall no doubt be berated as quirky, going on cranky. It will hardly be the first time. And I remain unrepentant. I'm damned if I will, this edition, recommend any guidebooks for the blind. All you've got to do if you want one, unfortunately, is browse in a catalog or mountain shop. And bad luck to you.*

---

*I actively sought criticism of and counterarguments to this section. On the whole I was pleasantly surprised. For example, the two friends who rose up in arms against my open-fires denunciation (page 290) both endorsed this one. "It rests in my gut warmly and well," wrote one of them. "At this time, when the regulatory agencies—Park Service, Forest Service, etc.— are progressing rapidly towards a requirement of designated campsites and rigid itineraries,

I never walk far without

A compass.

Yet I can remember using mine only once for its primary emergency task: showing me which way to go when I'm unable to decide on or maintain direction by any other means. On that occasion I woke up one morning in broken hill country to find that a dense fog had settled down overnight, cutting visibility to about 15 feet. I needed to get back to the

---

the philosophy you present here and in the section on maps very much needs equal time."

A request for counterarguments to a leading publisher of trail guides—before this section was written—unfortunately elicited only points that to me seem either to apply to backpacking books rather than trail guides ("guides raise the level of hikers' ecological awareness . . . help develop a reverence for the wilderness . . . help in the fight to defend the land") or to cling blindly to the straight-line, man-world coordinates ("guides help hikers enjoy the country more by acquainting them with the flora, the fauna, the geology, the history, etc. of the places they go . . . help the Park and Forest Service get their messages to users of their lands by listing rules and regulations"). Another argument was: ". . . guides spread out hikers . . . help prevent the ruination of the best-known places by all these new people."

But another author of trail guides made a cogent point. "I spent a great deal of deliberating time before writing the first guide," he wrote. "I ultimately concluded the choice lay between the North Cascades being logged, mined and otherwise resource-extracted vs. being used or, if you will, overused recreationally. . . . It seems that most of our current decisions involve choosing the lesser of two evils rather than choosing between black and white. . . . In my opinion, only enough people who are aware of an area have the political clout to keep it reasonably safeguarded."

On the other hand, Michael Parfit, writing in the *New York Times Magazine* in 1976, described guidebooks as "fine for daydreams, but destructive of mood and mystery in the manner of fluorescent tubes hung in catacombs. This way, ladies; please mind the abyss."

Readers' opinions on this section in earlier editions have varied.

One—who violently opposed my views on hunting (page 671)—supported me. He compared a dedicated trail-guide user to "the poor soul who can only look at the woods through his camera viewfinder."

A Texan admitted equivocality: he recognized that trail guides could "help keep novices out of trouble."

An Easterner protested that trail guides perform a necessary function in such places as the Appalachians, where trails mostly follow crests and water is rare and secretive. Maybe. But surely a map would do the job at least as well? And a map, though undeniably based on man-world coordinates, can be a wonderful and tickling thing.

Two friends suggested—with reason, I think—that a trail guide is a boon to a family on its first trail trip. But "perhaps Daddy could use the suggestion that he keep his burden of information under his own hat so as not to diminish the joys of exploration and discovery for the small fry."

And a stern but valued critic wrote: "It seems to me here that you fall into a particular trap: you're confusing the elements of a how-to book with your own idiosyncratic way of dealing with the world." Sure.

Chip, I'm relieved but hardly surprised to learn, votes as I do.

car that day, I had no map, and there was no general slope to the ground to show me which way to go—only a confusion of huge, rocky outcrops. And I could detect nothing that might help me hold whichever line I chose to take—not the slightest breeze, and no hint through the gray fog of where the sun lay. Fortunately I knew that only a couple of miles to the north a road ran roughly east and west. So after breakfast I struck due north by the compass. Every hundred yards or so I had to change direction as another huge, black outcrop of rock loomed up out of the fog. Under such conditions I doubt if I could have held course without the compass. But in little more than an hour I stepped onto the road.

Because of such possibilities I would feel dangerously naked without my compass. But the only purpose I use it for at all often is siting a night camp so that it will catch—or avoid—the earliest sun (page 497). It also serves, once in a while, to check my map orientation if I have not been following the detail closely enough. And I once made a pace-and-compass march out across the featureless salt flats of Death Valley to the genuinely lowest point in the Western Hemisphere. (For a pace-and-compass march you calculate from a map the magnetic bearing and the distance from starting place to invisible target. You follow this bearing either by repeatedly checking your compass or by selecting a distant point on the bearing and homing on it; and after working out how many of your paces, across that kind of terrain, will take you to the target, you count each pace taken until that number is reached. Carefully calculated and executed, it's a surprisingly accurate method, day or night.)

For years I carried a 4.5-oz., aluminum-alloy U.S. Marine Corps compass. But during a weight-paring putsch I perceived the overload and invested in a liquid-dampened Silva that weighs in at just ¾ oz. and looks like a toy but does all the things I'm likely to ask a compass to do. It will pin to your shirt; or you can carry it, as I have done, on a short, fine nylon cord that attaches, when you think you may need to check the compass frequently, to a shirt buttonhole or some other convenient point.

Compasses have radically improved in recent years, and stores and catalogs now glitter with constellations of them, basic through fancy, featherweight through ponderous. Many of those most suitable for general backpacking are plastic and at first glance look flimsy; but they turn out to be remarkably rugged.

CHIP: Silva, Suunto, and Brunton all make high-standard compasses, ranging from little jingle-bobs that hang from a zipper pull (0.5 oz., $4–$8), often co-molded with a tiny thermometer, windchill chart, whistle, or suchlike—all quite useful when (or if) you need them. The common sort of compass with a rotating bezel and clear plastic baseplate incorporating a bearing arrow, declination and measuring scales, a magnifier, etc. now costs $10 to $25. The Silva Explorer 3W (1.5 oz., $20) and Suunto A-40 Contour (1.3 oz., $17) both incorporate a map-measuring wheel. A cut higher are sighting compasses with hinged mirrors, some like the Silva Ranger (2.3 oz., $46) having automatic adjustments for declination. Global compasses, like the Suunto M3 DG (1.6 oz., $30), have needles balanced for use worldwide. And compasses like the Suunto GPS Plotter (2 oz., $30) let you spot yourself on a map using coordinates from a handheld GPS unit (about which more on page 635). For perfectionists, the Brunton Eclipse 8099 (4 oz., $60) has literally all of the above features, with a magnetic disk (1-degree accuracy) rather than a needle, three inclinometers for slope and height measurement, and a set of reference cards for compass use and survival.

COLIN: Whatever compass you choose, make sure it's tough; it may lie around in your pack for months or even years, but when a testing time comes it must be functioning perfectly. And choose a model designed to perform the fanciest function you expect to use it for.

Most people, I think, want a compass only for unfancy functions. Those functions are very simple. For the basic emergency use of holding a given line, just see where the needle or north arrow points, then walk in the direction you have decided is the one to take. Base your decision about direction on the map, knowledge of the country, intuition, guesswork, or desperation, in that order of preference; but stick with it. At night or in fog you must keep checking the compass, and hold dead on line (at night, if your compass has no printed-on luminosity, don't hold a flashlight too close: its magnetic field can deflect the needle). In good visibility a quicker and much more accurate method is to pick out a distant and distinctive point that lies on the required line, put your compass away, and head for the distant point. Provided there's no danger of your losing track of the point, you can detour as widely and as often as you like.

If you want to move in a given compass "direction" ("due north," say, or "south-southeast"), it is important to remember that *true north* and *compass north* are not the same. The difference is known as *magnetic declination.* Because the magnetic north pole presently lies among the Canadian Arctic Islands, about 1000 miles below the true north pole (it moves, slowly), the declination is different in different places. Along the West Coast of the United States, for example, it is now 15 to 20 degrees east (that is, the compass needle points well east, or right, of true north). Along the East Coast it is 15 to 20 degrees west. (The farther north you go, the greater the declination.) The declination for an area is normally given on good maps. A diagram at the foot of all USGS 7.5-minute topos shows the declination at the map's center in the year of publication, and the USGS publishes an isogenic chart showing current declinations, nationwide. For that and other geo-location topics, the best starting point is their Internet home page: *www.usgs.gov.*

For most rough-and-ready purposes, though, all you need is a round figure for magnetic declination, and the direction of error. But make sure you fix the direction of error firmly in your mind. I sometimes pencil the magnetic declination for a given area on the back of my compass before a trip, as well as the bearing of sunrise (page 497).

For fancier uses—for which you'll need to work out your individual compass error—consult one of the little paperback how-to books on the subject. For years the standard was *Be Expert with Map and Compass* by Bjorn Kjellström (IDG Books, $17) but it seems to have been nudged aside by a herd of others: see Appendix IV, Map and Compass, page 807.

Orienteering, the now-popular sport of blundering accurately around the countryside with compass and legs, has nothing to do with backpacking, of course; but if you can orienteer effectively you certainly shouldn't get lost too often while backpacking.

Alti-, baro-, and other meters

Some people regard *altimeters* as navigational aids: in theory they advise you of your elevation, and at times that could be a vast help in pin-pointing your position. The trouble is that the altimeter is also a *barometer,* and therefore a weather indicator; so when the air pressure changes, your apparent elevation will also change. Good altimeters compensate for temperature changes, and that can help dampen such errors. But good mechanical (and battery-free) altimeters are expensive. The best are by Thommen of Switzerland (TX-16, 6 oz., $280). The light-and-cheap end of the spectrum provides beguiling infuriators and dubious weather-forecasting aids. For the average backpacker, as opposed to the dyed-in-the-snowstorm mountain climber, perhaps that's all any altimeter is. But don't downplay the beguiling part (cf. thermometers, page 665).

CHIP: New on the scene are a wide, weird range of multimeasuring electronica. There are now digital compasses and altimeter/barometers by Thommen, Suunto, and others that are not only easier to read but also less costly than a corresponding array of mechanical instruments. For instance the Brunton Sherpa registers wind speed, windchill, temperature, barometric pressure, and altitude—to 30,000 feet (a mere 2 oz. with 3-volt lithium battery, $155). For the disaster-prone, there's a handheld digital Weather Monitor (4 oz., $65 from Forestry Suppliers) that logs barometric pressure, temperature (current, high, and low), and time. The display gives local forecasts in pictorial form and has built-in alarms for severe weather like thunderstorms, tornadoes, etc.

If you have an indulgent aunt and the holidays approach, mention the newest mini-whiz-bang: the Suunto Vector Wristop Computer (3 oz., $200). The same size as (and no uglier than) a fancy digital sports watch, the Vector combines watch, calendar, timer, and alarm functions with a digital altimeter, barometer, thermometer (goes down to −5 °F), and compass. There are memory/mode options for logging and comparing data, and some ranges can be field-calibrated (e.g., you can punch in a known elevation). Overall, the accuracy specs are pretty-damn-good—especially considering that the Vector's no more trouble to carry than a regular watch. Plus it's waterproof. I haven't yet actually toyed with one. But by the time this hits print, the latest models will no doubt incorporate heart monitors and broadband Internet connections.

Colin and I have made a hyperconscious decision not to cover Global Positioning System (GPS) receivers, except in passing. But before you brand us as antidigital dinosaurs, take a deep breath and consider. We both use computers to write and edit. And I've used professional GPS equipment to map glaciers—for instance, trying to find out the volume of ice in a particular one and to calculate how fast it was melting. Of course, backpacking a GPS base-station unit over a 12,000-foot pass was logistically hellish, but it saved us a full week out on the ice, exposed to crevasses and rockfall. And we got good, precise data. So I'm not dead set against GPS units—far from it. They make serious mapping and data-scrounging both easier and more accurate. But so far, I don't need a GPS unit to find my way around.

Of course, most of my backpacking life has transpired in the American West, in the central Rockies and on the Colorado Plateau, where striking features and clear sight lines make it easier to get oriented (or should I say *occidented?*). Wandering through interminable, foggy, Blair-Witch-haunted woods or on the shifting sands of the Great Erg, I might be grateful for a handheld GPS. But I've never used one.

For those who wish to quantify their location, the lightest and cutest GPS receivers at the moment are the waterproof Garmin eTrex (5.3 oz., $145) and the eTrex Summit with an altimeter/barometer (5.3 oz., $267). Major competitors are Brunton, Magellan, and several others (for addresses, consult Appendix III; for ads, open any magazine). Tech-mad friends recommend *GPS Land Navigation: A Complete Guidebook for Back-country Users of the NAVSTAR Satellite System* by Michael Ferguson (Glassford, 1997, 255 pages, $20). As of May 2000, the U.S. government improved the accuracy of signals available to the public to a standard formerly reserved for military use, with a potential error of about 60 feet.

Having used electronic devil-boxes for a great many purposes, from taking the temperatures of alpine lakes to tracking humidity in tents (page 387) it would be silly of me to rail against a whole new subdivision of human ingenuity. But since I've spent so many years peering at meters and dials, it's a grand feeling to set off utterly uninstrumented: no watch, no compass, and no thermometer, let alone all the other electro-bits. You may lose precision—the difference between saying "10.6°F" and "damn cold." What you gain is the chance to cultivate that mercurial play of nerve endings and creative memory that got our species where it is: the innate, primate sensibility that tells you much—and sometimes all—that really needs knowing.

COLIN: I suppose I should have a lot more to say about route finding. But, beyond map reading, it's mostly common sense, and I'm not very conscious of any particular techniques. Once or twice I have become aware that I was not where I thought I was because the sun hung in the wrong place or the wind blew from the wrong direction, so I suppose I must take some cognizance of such direction checks. Otherwise, route finding is largely a matter of obeying that sturdy old adage, "Never lose elevation unnecessarily," and of getting to know the idiosyncrasies of the country you are in—the pattern its ridges tend to follow, or the way its southern slopes tend to be covered with impassable scrub, or the tendency of its northern slopes to drop away in unclimbable cliffs.*

Failing your compass, you can check your bearings on a clear night by the North Star (Polaris). Pick it out by projecting the line formed by the two stars that constitute the outer lip of the Big Dipper's bowl. Project it for about five times the distance between those stars, then look a touch to the left. If you can't recognize the Big Dipper, go home. Unless, that is, you can recognize Cassiopeia. Cassiopeia is the group of five stars that sits on the opposite side of Polaris from the Big Dipper and forms an M when above it or the figure 3 or the letters W or Greek Σ (sigma) in other positions. A line drawn at right angles to the base of the M, from its right corner, points almost directly at Polaris.

For more—much more than route finding—see such books as *Stars and Planets: The Sierra Club Guide to Sky Watching and Direction Finding* by W. S. Kals (Sierra Club, 1990, $16); *The Cambridge Pocket Star Atlas* by John Cox (Cambridge University Press, 1996, $8); and—recommended by a Massachusetts reader—a children's book, *The Stars: A New Way to See Them* by H. A. Rey (Houghton Mifflin, 1976, $12). Another approach is through the Miller Planisphere: you revolve two plastic disks to match time and date and come up with a plan of the night sky for there and then,

---

*CHIP: I call this the "grain" of the country, like the pattern grown into wood. The overlapping intricacies of bedrock, drainage, landform, weather, plants, and animal life are as fascinating and variable as music, or human personality. If you can sense the grain of the country—lucky for you—you tend to avoid the traps and trials of those who can't, or won't.

with models for three latitudes (50° N for the northern tier of the U.S. and Canada, 40° N for the central tier of the U.S, and 30° N for the southern tier and northern Mexico. The 10-inch-diameter Planisphere is 2¼ oz., $10.75; the 5-inch-diameter, ⅛ oz., $5.50).

Provided you know the time, the sun's position will, of course, give you a rough, commonsense bearing.*

With experience you will in unfamiliar country come to note without much thought the landmarks and the general lay of the land that will enable you to backtrack, should that become necessary; but I occasionally stop at points that may cause confusion—such as a junction of several valleys, or a watershed with diverging drainage systems—and look back in order to memorize the way I have come. This is certainly a worthwhile precaution at any unposted trail junction.

In certain kinds of country the question of scale can become crucial to route finding. Among the repetitive rock patterns of the Grand Canyon I at first found that it was often impossible to tell from a distance, even through binoculars, whether a sheer rockface was an inconsequential 3 feet or an unclimbable 30 feet high. But eventually I realized that the agaves or century plants that grew almost everywhere were a consistent 3 or 4 feet high, and from then on I used them as gauges.

There's another helpful trick that I learned from the diaries of John Wesley Powell—who made the first known boat passage through the fast-water sections of the Green and Colorado Rivers, including the Grand Canyon.

When you look directly at a slope it's very easy to misjudge its angle—and therefore to misinterpret possible routes up it. Powell explained that all you need do is tilt your head to one side. With your head held in the normal upright position—and eyes displaced laterally—your stereoscopic vision and depth perception work well on a horizontal plane but hardly at all on the vertical. Tilt your head on one side, though—realigning your eyes vertically—and the reverse becomes true: now, almost miraculously, you can "see" the slope in a different way: can much more truly judge its general angle and can differentiate between the degrees of steepness of its various sections. That can make a vital route-finding difference.

In some kinds of country, particularly desert, game trails can be a

---

*"Yes, Aunt Josephine, the sun rises in the east. Well, kind of in the east. In summertime, if you're well north of the Equator, it'll actually rise quite a ways north of east. And in the winter, quite a ways south of east. In flat country, anyway. But at noon—standard time, not daylight saving—it's always due south. Unless, of course, it's overhead. No, that isn't very helpful, is it? And if you're in the Southern Hemisphere it'll naturally be due north at noon. . . . Yes, Auntie, unless it's overhead. . . . And yes, you're right again, it always sets in the west. Well, kind of in the west. In summertime, if you're well south of the . . ."

tremendous help. Decide by map, eye, and cogitation what seems to you the best cross-country route. Then canvass it for game trails. Look first from a distance, through binoculars. It's often easier to spot them that way than close up. If you have no luck, search carefully at constricted places such as canyon narrows, breaks in wash walls, isthmuses between lakes. In burro-traveled desert this search can be the most important thing you do all day. Once you hit a trail, latch onto it: route finding apart, it's likely to afford far easier going than cross-country. But keep firmly and continually and questioningly in mind that the animals may or may not be going the same place you are.

Wild burros are first-class trail makers. So are elk, says Chip. Wild horses are good; deer, fair; independent-minded bighorn sheep, next door to useless. The burros and horses and, to a lesser extent, the deer make excellent instructors. If you follow their trails and think, you'll soon turn from a tyro at route finding in their particular kind of country into a quick and confident expert.

Game trails tend to fade out, of course. They're especially liable to do so in wooded or scrub country at the edges of meadows or other open places—where groups break from single file and spread out to feed. Trails may also vanish unexpectedly on steep sidehills—perhaps because the animals, rather than create a human-type switchback, have taken short individual routes more or less directly up (or possibly down) the slope and then reformed in single file at a different level. So that is often where to look. (I'm indebted to an article by Sam Curtis in *Backpacker* 23 for drawing my attention to these patterns of fading game trails.)

The advent of internal-frame packs, which lack the vegetation-snagging projections of E-frames, has made game trails more feasible routes for humans who are not contortionists.*

Local human knowledge can be an invaluable aid to route finding, or at least to finding the most convenient route. But local humans are not always crystal-pure sources of information, and if you're going to travel in strange country you must command a certain proficiency in the art of sifting fact from embroidery. The only reliable informant is the person who both knows what he is talking about and is not afraid to admit he doesn't know everything. You don't meet such people every day. The surest way of

---

*CHIP: I just spent a week in an obscure and precipitous canyon where so few humans have gone that the trails are free of engineering talents—except those of moose, elk, and deer. Despite having to high-step or duck under fallen trees (back scratchers for elk) and wade soggy spots (moose trails run from bog to bog) I found passable trails going practically everywhere that I wanted to go. A general principle: animal trails blunder through endless petty irritations and undertake seemingly aimless detours in order to skirt major problems, like V-cut stream gorges and bottomless talus fields. That is, they tend to piss you off while keeping you out of real trouble.

finding out if you have just met one is to ask questions to which you know the answers.

As I approached Death Valley on my summer-long California walk I passed through Baker, at that time a very small populated road junction of the gasoline age. While I was there, one self-satisfied little man fixed me with beady eyes. "What's that?" he said. "Going through Death Valley? Huh, your feet must be stronger than your head. It'll be a hundred and ten up there by now. And climbing every day. I spent years right in the Valley, all summer too, so I know. I'm a real Desert Rat, I can tell you, a real Desert Rat."

"Oh, what sort of temperatures do they get on the floor of the Valley?" I asked—and waited.

I knew the Death Valley temperature position accurately. All-time high is a questionable 134°F, set in July 1913, that for many years held the world record. Later and more dependable readings have never risen above 127°. Most years the limit is 124° or 125°.

The Baker Rat pounced on my bait. "Summer temperatures in the Valley?" he squeaked. "Well, I can't quote exact figures, but it gets hot, believe me. Here in Baker we have summer highs of a hundred and twenty-five or thirty. And sometimes"—he turned to his wife—"sometimes we run to a hundred thirty-five, don't we?"

"Oh, not very often, dear."

"No, not too often. But it happens. And you can add a good twenty degrees for the Valley. So you'd best get ready to sweat a bit, my lad."

I didn't bother to ask the Baker Rat any of the other questions I had on my mind.*

A friend of mine who is a connoisseur of human foibles was delighted when I reported this conversation. "Now, there's a beautiful example of the dedicated weather-exaggerater at work," he said. "The real artist often uses that ploy—provoking something that seems close to dissent from one of his in-group so as to thicken the background."

It's not always so easy to winnow worthless information. Often you have to fall back on mere confirmation of details from several sources. But this technique can backfire. Many years ago, I was wandering in leisurely fashion across the Coast Range in central California, aiming broadly for the Pacific, when I emerged from forest into ranchland and almost at once met the rancher—a pleasant-faced man wearing a 10-gallon hat and a red shirt and driving a green pickup truck. We chatted cordially for some time, discussing how far it was down to the ocean and what the best routes were. An hour later, far down the hill, I came to a cattle chute. A tall, baldheaded man wearing blue overalls was inoculating a herd of

---

*If this little scene seems familiar, maybe you've read *The Thousand-Mile Summer.*

heifers. When he had finished he turned and walked toward me. Partly as an opening pleasantry, partly to confirm the figures and routes that the rancher in the green pickup had given me, I said, "Say, can you tell me how far it is down to the sea?" The man stopped and looked at me closely. Then, to my astonishment, he turned on his heel and walked back toward the chute. After a while I wandered away, wondering, through a belt of trees. Suddenly, beyond a small outbuilding, I almost walked into the green pickup. On its seat sat a familiar-looking 10-gallon hat.

Even now, all these years later, I still feel embarrassed whenever I remember that rancher.

KEEPING YOURSELF CLEAN AND COMFORTABLE

Toilet gear

forms a highly personal department that every individual will stock differently, and which he will vary to meet varying conditions.

My list expands and contracts within rather wide limits, mostly in response to how crippling the load looks like being, but also according to whether I expect to touch civilization at all. The full selection includes:

Soap. There is now a wealth of "biodegradables" around—though precious little agreement on just how rapidly biodegradable even the best of them are. The safest attitude seems to be, "It takes maybe three weeks for them to break down, so *never* wash anything directly in or into a lake or stream, especially in cold mountain waters unable to sustain the necessary bacteria. Pour the dirty water onto soil, preferably deep and sunwarmed." Among suggested brands in backpackerly sizes: Camp Soap, Camp Suds (regular, peppermint, lavender, and citronella), Pack Soap, and Dr. Bronner's Soap (Castile, Almond, Peppermint, and Eucalyptus). But everyone has his or her own favorite. I know of one man who swears by an Ivory Bar cut in half ("It's cheap, it floats, and it's 99.44 percent biodegradable").

CHIP: A compulsive skinny-dipper, I seem to stay fairly clean but still carry a few fingernail-size soap chips, in an aluminized teabag packet. Linda is fond of a teeny Nalgene jug of Dr. Bronner's, but I find the aromatic oils (peppermint and eucalyptus) too fiery on chafed parts. I've tried No Rinse Shampoo and Body Bath. If you know you'll return in a high state of reek to a waterless trailhead and must prepare for a restaurant date, then it's better than nothing—stash some in the car. But I used a whole bottle of the shampoo (you need to hugger-mugger it off with a bandanna, T-shirt, etc., so the oil and dirt end up there), and after all the fuss my hair didn't feel particularly clean.

Washcloth, towel. My washcloth *au naturel,* for that desert-varnish-like blend of sunscreen and dust that blackens my toes while hiking in sandals, is fine sand or stream grit. But for serious scrubbage, a scrap of tulle (the net used for ballet tutus) or no-see-um mesh works wonders—not only light but it dries instantaneously. For backpackpacking, cotton towels become sodden lumps (malodorous, eventually). But fast-drying viscose squares are widely sold for camp use, of which Cascade Designs PackTowls are the thickest. I got a medium one (14 by 40 inches, 3 oz., $11) and scissored it into a sweat-sopper, an eyeglass-wiper, and a bandanna-size skinny-dip towel. Viscose is madly absorbent and, unlike cotton, can be wrung nearly dry, so a small piece can dry a large body—in stages.

Tooth toiletry. Colin uses a child's toothbrush, about ¼ oz., while I still cut the tail off an adult model. They all have bristles—the main thing is a good grip. But toothpaste is a frippery, overpackaged and messy to transport. So I use tooth powder (with the same cleansing stuff, minus the water and glop—think of it as freeze-dried toothpaste). Liberty Mountain distributes a European tooth powder called EcoDent (¾ oz., $5). I use Arm and Hammer Dental Care tooth powder (4 oz., $3), which has a pleasant, neutral taste, no horrid ingredients, and is widely available. Two weeks' worth fits in a handy aluminized teabag bag. The hot ticket for dental floss, which I never fail to carry—it beats trying to tongue freeze-dried beef fibers from between my fangs—are sample micro-diskettes of W. L. Gore Glide Floss (⅒ oz.; ask your dentist) that doubles as emergency sewing thread. Another expedient is to wrap dental floss around your toothbrush handle, securing the end with a rubber band.

Deodorant, a necessity for the gringo office-mouse, can in fact ease the pheromonal stress of sharing a tent with the wilder variety of human being. Having dropped one of those mineral-salt deodorant stones (from a local natural-products emporium, $4–$6) on the bathroom tiles, I have a lifetime supply of deodorant chips: a thumbnail-size one (⅛ oz.) lasts for two weeks. Once again, I use a teabag wrapper to contain it (striving to remember that Earl Grey is *soap,* Irish Breakfast is *tooth powder,* and Lapsang souchong is *deodorant*).

COLIN: *Comb or subsititute.* A plastic Gemco "pocket hairbrush," often sold by barbers, slips over one finger and works fine (¼ oz., $1 or so). Taken if the social standards of a trip demand it. That is, damned rarely.

Toilet roll. A roll, mark you, not one of those interleaved packs that in a high wind explode like bombs. Deftly remove the deadweight cardboard liner from the roll—and learn that it's then easier to unfurl from the inside. (For using it, see Sanitation, pages 697–702.) I understand that some people, when they know that washing is going to be a problem, take along a few pads of Tucks—a medication-impregnated toilet pad. Resealable pocket packs of premoistened wipes, such as Nice 'N Clean (supermarket, 1.5 oz., $1.25), can be used for face and hands as well—but the antibacterial treatment slows down their bio-degrading, so don't strew them about.

Scissors. Now on my Swiss Army knife (page 281)—and many pocket tools. You can buy neat, folding scissors (1 oz.) that cut well (though less well than a standard pair), which you can protect in the moleskin package in the "office" (see Mirror, below).

Razors. Half a century has glided by since I used one of these barbarous instruments, but I remain aware that they still exist and that some people actually carry them in their packs.

CHIP: I do, alas, on trips lasting longer than a week, because the wiry growth at my throat, when steeped in sweat, inflames my skin. A plastic toss-away, at ⅙ oz., can lose half its handle with no loss in function, and a soap chip doubles for shaving. A fastidious woman friend, who actually shaves her legs on walking trips, claims that her biggest problem is goose bumps raised by cold water. So she carries a Solo Sunshower and warms up her bathwater on top of her pack.

COLIN: Items classifiable as "toilet gear" but discussed elsewhere:

Mirror. I used to carry one, for signaling rather than primping (see page 654). If your hand falls on the mirror a few washless days out and, by reflex action, you look into it, you may be in for a shock. It can travel conveniently in the package of moleskins, between the pads, and protect the curved points of nonfolding scissors (above).

Foot powder and rubbing alcohol. See pages 108 to 109.

Washing yourself is your business—except when it comes to polluting the water. For factors to consider—and a solution in inhabited country—see Care of Clothing, page 564. Also Soap, page 640.

Occasionally you get sensuously delightful washing surprises. I particularly like to remember finding, a couple of hundred feet below the peak of Mount Shasta, at 14,000 feet, a bubbling hot spring. The sulfurous water smelled vile. But it was very hot. And, although the sun already hung low, the air felt astonishingly warm for that elevation. So I filled both my cooking pots with snow and immersed them in the spring, which bubbles out of the ground over a fairly large area. I waited until the snow had become hot water. Then I stripped off and poured both potfuls over my head. It was a lusciously hedonistic rite.

I learned later that John Muir, the Scot who around the turn of the century did so much for the conservation of wild California, was apparently saved by this spring when caught up there in a blizzard. By lying on the hot earth and moving his body from time to time, Muir was able to keep himself comfortably warm. Well, safely warm, anyway.

There are several additional items, not strictly speaking toilet gear, that you'll often need in order to keep comfortable:

Fly dope. With luck you won't often have to use it, but once you've suffered helplessly from mosquitoes or their like you'll rarely travel without it. New and possibly better formulas appear regularly.

Muskol is perhaps the best-known current brand. It contains 100 percent active ingredients, of which 95 percent is DEET. It seems to be currently sort of accepted that DEET (N, N-diethyl-meta-toluamide)—at least in high concentrations—can do bad things to us. But it's still the most effective stuff around. It fouls up the mammal-homing mechanism of insects (which incites them to move toward greater concentrations of carbon dioxide) by kidding them that instead of finding more carbon dioxide as they move closer to skin that exudes it, they're finding less.

Repel 100 and Ben's are essentially the same as Muskol and claim to "protect for 8–10 hours" (a 1–2-oz. phial averages $5, a 1–2-oz. pump spray slightly more). This high DEET concentration is also available in lotions. But some doctors now say "avoid concentrations above 35%." Pump (as opposed to aerosol) sprays contain less DEET, and "family," "backyard," and "kids" formulations reduce the DEET to from 25 to 9 percent, which is probably the minimum for any real effect. Sawyer has DEET Plus lotions and sprays with R-326, reputed to ward off gnats, blackflies, and no-see-ums. A new "controlled-release" lotion from Sawyer with 20 percent DEET (2 oz., $5.35; 4 oz., $8) is said to remain effective for "up to 24 hours."

The severity of the insect problem varies from person to person—some seem to suffer far worse attacks than others—and also from year to year, month to month, and region to region. (Moisture and warmth are certainly relevant factors.) In the Sierra Nevada, for example, even in a bad year, summer mosquitoes are about the only serious pest. But in northern-tier states and Canada you're also likely to face, any summer, such barely carnate devils as the tiny "no-see-ums," sometimes also called "punkies" (either term appears to be generic, meaning anything that is very small and flies and bites, including gnats and sand flies and other species). There seems little doubt that for all these tormentors, in the worst locales and times, the most effective dope is that with the greatest concentration of DEET. So I play safe and go with the strong stuff. But the others are often cheaper, and you may want to use them in less pesky places and seasons.

Muskol—and no doubt the others—are said to give protection against ticks. My experience suggests that this is probably true. Some protection, anyway. Among repellent/insecticides for ticks, chiggers, and mites: Repel Permanone (6 oz. aerosol, $6.75) and Sawyer Permethrin (spray: 3 oz., $3.25; 6 oz., $7.50). They're intended for clothing, tents, etc., but *not under any circumstances skin*. For more on ticks, see page 724.

CHIP: After watching DEET dissolve plastic, I avoid the stuff nearly as much as mosquitoes do. Repellents based on natural extracts do work, though not as effectively or long-lastingly as DEET. Citronella is the main ingredient, at 10 to 15 percent. Aloe vera is often added to soothe the skin. I've used Green Ban, which also has lavender, sassafras, peppermint, myrrh, and bergamot, in regular (2.5 oz., $6.50) and double-strength (2.5 oz., $7.50). Natrapel, 10 percent citronella, which comes in a lotion (2 oz., $5.35), a dauber (2 oz., $5.75), and a pump spray (4 oz., $7), seems to work about as well. All Terrain Herbal Armor is 15 percent citronella with dashes of other botanical oils such as cedarwood, clove, lemongrass, peppermint, eucalyptus, and garlic (barely perceptible), and comes in 2- and 4-oz. pump spray ($5.75 and $8) and a 4-oz. lotion with SPF 15 sunscreen ($8). All these are labeled as safe for synthetics. Based on informal tests—it takes all my willpower to sit still and count how many mosquitoes are biting me—these compounds turn away most but not all mini-vampires. Since herbal repellents fade in an hour or so and need to be reapplied, you should pack more, compared to a DEET preparation.*

Canyon rats on the Colorado Plateau claim that Avon Skin-So-Soft is a matchless repellent for the tenacious, voracious gnats found thereabouts. I tried it and was gnawed and then tried it again and wasn't, so who knows? Basque shepherds told me that eating lots of garlic deters mosquitoes, but not flies. Once again, my field trials were inconclusive, so perhaps you need to eat garlic for an extended time. Health-food stores are often hotbeds of chatter about what vitamins or exotic herbs keep bugs away. A hush-voiced young woman from Santa Fe explained to me that "a negative aura attracts mosquitoes." Believe what you will.

A Solar Mosquito Guard from Real Goods (0.8 oz., $9) combines a tiny solar panel and rechargeable battery with a device that emits an ultrasonic whine, said to resemble that of the male mosquito. Quoth the package: "Biologists have discovered that the mosquitoes that bite humans are females. Female mosquitoes are irritated by the sound of male mosquitoes." I tried it on our local breed and they were undeterred. The package also notes: "There are more than 3000 species of mosquitoes and some may be affected by a different sound frequency." Maybe a sports broadcast, speeded up, would do the trick.

For serious bug-pro, I rely more on clothing than on chemicals. But

---

*COLIN: I just hate having to report that I've found the effect of herbal and other natural repellents on really mass mosquito attacks to be approximately nil.

I don't always think ahead. One incandescent day in August, wearing naught but shorts, I was attacked by a fog of deerflies in a desert canyon. With my back and legs running blood I cut handfuls of willow and lashed myself, *penitente*-fashion, all the way back to camp. For really vicious airborne assaults I wear long pants and a long-sleeved shirt (light cotton twill or microfiber) and use a headnet. Two favorites: the Outdoor Research Spring Ring Headnet, which goes over or under a hat, with a spring-steel hoop that keeps the mesh well off your skin and folds small (1.7 oz., $11), and *La Casquette Mostiquaire* (the Bug Cap), a Franco-Canadian nifty with no-see-um mesh tucked in a neat little roll atop the visor of a ball cap, deployable in seconds, and held off the skin by the bill of the cap and a light shock cord that goes under your arms (3.7 oz., $22). The black mesh found on both allows better vision than light colors.

COLIN: Mosquito coils are light and work well in tents or even under tarps. You can now get 10 coils and two metal stands from Coghlan's for $2.25, in a package that cautions you *not* to use them in tents or enclosed spaces.

A Pennsylvania reader reports that he always carries a fly whisk—a habit he picked up in Swaziland. "These remarkable devices, simultaneously invented in Africa, South America, Polynesia, and Australia, will ward off any nasty insect that approaches within reach, with the possible exception of wasps, which get annoyed by your whipping at them. A whisk can be used with practically no conscious thought and even less energy by simply flicking it gently and fairly

Fly whisk

constantly around your head, or wherever. It also serves as a moderately efficient broom with which to sweep out a tent—and as a conversation piece. You may get a few comments about the pleasures of little old men in certain establishments, but these can be ignored. My present whisk, which I bought in Ethiopia, is made of horsetail hairs, braided and glued into a twisted wire handle whose end will fit over your finger. It should be rather easy to make."

Sunscreen. Indispensable for those who sunburn easily, recommended for those who rather think they don't. The mountains are always full of people who did not realize how quickly skin burns at high altitudes, where there is less atmosphere to screen off the sun's ultraviolet rays. Don't underestimate the effects of such sunburn. A severely peeled nose can be painful. A raw red back or shoulders can bring the whole outfit to a screeching halt. Ditto habitually shod feet exposed too long around sun-drenched camps. And even if you have not partly or wholly stripped off but like to walk in shorts, sunburn can more or less incapacitate you (see the story of a fool on Fujiyama, page 532). If your skin happens to be going-on-black, by the way, don't imagine you're immune.

Up high, almost everyone needs some kind of skin protection. If you don't block the stronger ultraviolet rays, the result can be not only short-term painful burning but premature aging of the skin, and, in the long run, serious skin cancer.

Most good current sunscreens tell you—in fact, blare at you—their Sun Protection Factor (SPF). An SPF of 4 means that it will take four times as much sun to burn you as when unprotected, and so on up the scale. An SPF 15 rating was said to give adequate protection for most people, but lotions are now available up to SPF 50. You choose your lotion according to how high you expect to go, the degree of tanning you want, and the sensitivity of your skin. Some people get rashes from sunscreens containing para-amino-benzoic acid (PABA), but many brands are now labelled PABA-free. The best lotions are creamy but nongreasy and don't wash off easily with sweating or even swimming. But make sure you cover all exposed skin; otherwise you may end up painfully piebald. Generally speaking—surprise!—the more expensive lotions do the best job.

CHIP: Some otherwise good sunscreens have delicious fruit-and-nut scents that attract bugs, rodents, perhaps even bears. So a neutral or scent-free type is best. Another hitch: while the lotion may soak in rapidly, makers caution that it might be a half hour before the sunscreening ingredients are fully effective.

I usually get sunscreen at markets or discount stores. Ordinary Lubriderm Lotion now comes in an SPF 15 variety (a thrifty 16 oz. for $7) that's good for day trips and refilling smaller plastic bottles (I save 2- and 4-oz. sunscreen containers). Sunscreen stick (Banana Boat Sport, SPF 30, 0.55 oz., $4) slips into my yoke office (page 180), is water- and sweat-resistant, and perfect for touching up nose, feet, ear tops, and neck. Sawyer, maker of time-release bug repellent, also sells Bonding Base Sunblock, with "micro-encapsulation" claimed to provide all-day protection. Their Sun Pak with SPF 15, SPF 30, and aloe vera gel (for soothing sunburn and windburn) is handy (three 1-oz. bottles, $4.50). If you do get fried, Green Stuff is an aloe-vera-based emollient that relieves pain and speeds healing (4-oz. gel, $3.50; 8-oz. spray, $5).

Lip balm. Lips burn easily at any elevation and the cold, moistureless winds on high can make them crack and bleed. Backpacking and ski shops sell balms unavailable in supermarkets, such as Aloe Gator, Labiosan, Savex, and the formerly awful-tasting but now rather pleasant Dermatone (SPF 23, in a fat little snap-top, push-bottom tube that, washed out, also makes a dandy toothpaste carrier). Carmex and Blistex are roadside-available, with the SPF 30 Blistex Ultra in a light blue tube a particular favorite of mine.

COLIN: *Hand lotion.* For winter weather and, especially, places where the water is heavily alkaline. On the first half of the Grand Canyon trip my hands began to get raw from frequent use of Colorado water and I was thankful to be able to get a tube of lotion at the halfway mark. Ignore jibes about effeminacy. I once heard a modern-day pioneer who ranched beside an almost untouched stretch of the Colorado River, and was about as masculine a man as you'll find anywhere, say to his wife as he pulled off his boots at the end of a long day, "Better throw over the hand lotion, honey. Had my arms in that damned river half the afternoon."

Lubriderm lubes my derma (6-fl.-oz. plastic bottle, $4.29; also with SPF 15 sunscreen, 16 fl. oz., $7.50). I'm told Eucarin is good too (6-fl.-oz. bottle, $8.49; generic equivalent, 16 fl. oz., $8). You can, of course, decant from any of these into small Nalgene bottles or equivalents.

Cold protection. Certain creams (no current details available) are said to be surprisingly helpful in retaining body warmth when spread on exposed skin, hands, and feet.

CHIP: Friends (though not necessarily advisers) recommend various nostrums for cold feet, such as sprinkling cayenne in your socks or rubbing Tiger Balm (a fiercely aromatic ointment) between the toes, the object being to dilate the blood vessels near the surface of the skin. Since this also happens—uncomfortably so—in the course of irritations and inflammations, experiment close to home. Outdoor shops and catalogs sell chemical heat packs such as Shake and Warm, Warm-Packs, etc. (average prices: 9-by-13-inch sleeping-bag size $5; 4-by-5-inch jacket size, $1 each; boot size, $1.50 a pair; glove size, $1.25 a pair) that provide moderate, steady warmth for 4 to 12 hours. The contents aren't toxic: iron filings, salt, sawdust, activated carbon, vermiculite, and a catalyst—the heat comes from the accelerated rusting (oxidation) of the iron—a one-way process. For the ice-footed, there are foam footbeds with pockets for chemical heat pads (from Cabela's, $15, four pairs of refill pads, $6). Rechargeable heat pads, such as Re-Heaters (Brigade Quartermasters: 4 oz., $8; 8 oz., $10) reach 130°F and can give off diminishing heat for an hour or more. These have a nontoxic sodium acetate gel sealed in flexible plastic, with a metal catalytic disk that you flex to start the reaction: you can see cloudy crystals form. Primus sells a small round sodium-acetate heat pad (page 296) to boost their LP gas cartridges, and it slips nicely into a mitten. To regenerate the sodium acetate you have to immerse the pad in boiling water until all crystals are dissolved, a matter of 5 to 20 minutes, according to size.

From the standpoint of no-free-lunch physics, I'd rather have the same weight of chocolate.

Shower baths

The resoundingly popular Stearns Sun Shower can, as Colin puts it, be "soul-and-body-balming when you get back to roadhead and on your veranda at home too, given enough privacy or a policy of charging entertainment tax." For backcountry grime, I have a 2-liter Solo Sunshower going on 10 years old, which allows a brisk shampoo and body swish. The current Solo 3-liter size (5 oz., $10.50) gives a bit more swish and also comes in a stouter Extreme Wear roll-closure version (6 oz., $16.50). A related dodge, if you use a hydration bladder with an in-line water filter (page 251), and thus load the bladder with wild, unpurified water, is to find a suitable squirt fitting and use it as a shower. Cascade Designs makes a Pack Shower (22 oz., $30) based on a 20-liter drybag with a practically weightless shower nozzle that plugs, *squeak,* into a hydration tube. I've also used the wee nozzle with their Big Zip 4-liter bladder (6 oz., $26) and a Safewater In-line Filter (3 oz., $35) as a hydration/shower combo (for showering, unplug the filter and drinking tube to avoid contaminating it). The drawback is that heating your bathwater in the sun also promotes algae growth in your drinking reservoir. But the Big Zip has a full-width closure—easy to fill and clean. If—as a change from stringent office grooming—you're determined to get itchy and stinky, I'll not urge further unseemly luxuries on you.

MEETING EMERGENCIES

First aid

Your first-aid kit is, to some extent, your own business. But since first aid is also the duty you owe to partners, even strangers, your personal kit should contain enough to render basic assistance. How much is enough? The terrain, length of trip, your outlook, and previous experience all matter. Some people carry very little. One hard-and-fast climber-type I know has (rashly, perhaps) pared his first-aid kit to a roll of duct tape and a stash of codeine. My basic go-everywhere kit now holds:

Three feet of 1½-inch cloth adhesive tape, around a scrap of cardboard
One needle (pushed into the cardboard in the tape roll)
Two 3-by-3-inch and two 1½-by-2-inch gauze pads
Five large butterfly closures

Two knuckle bandages
One fingertip bandage
Five regular and one small strip bandages
One sheet Spenco 2nd Skin with adhesive cover fabric
Two packets Neosporin ointment (polymyxin B sulfate and bacitrin zinc,
     and neomycin—this last causes allergic reactions in some people,
     who should use Polysporin or a double antibiotic ointment instead)
One packet Benadryl (diphenhydramine hydrochloride) anti-itch cream
Two sample vials Visine (eyewash)
Tablets: four Kaopectate (antidiarrheal), eight aspirin (pain, fever), eight
     ibuprofen (pain, inflammation), eight decongestant, eight antihista-
     mine, eight hydrocodone (codeine painkiller)
Two throat lozenges with cough suppressant
Four antacid tablets
Good, sharp tweezers (brand unknown)
Pocket cards: basic first aid and artificial respiration

This collection lives in a plastic case that once held a standard first-aid kit doled out to firefighters, now held together by a rubber band and zipped in a plastic bag, in all 5 oz. The only original bits are the two pocket cards. In my pack's top pocket I also carry a 4-inch elastic wrap with closure, Ace or similar. Most of what's in the kit is there because I've needed it at one time or other: butterfly closures for a partner hit in the forehead by a chunk of falling ice (he lived), the antacid tabs for my own overindulgence in rum-and-cocoa, *ad infirmum.* But since I dig into the kit rather seldom, I have to check expiration dates.

Colin's basic kit in *Walker III* was strikingly similar, with the addition of a laxative, for that freeze-dried stopper effect, and broad-spectrum antibiotic tablets. For times when you must stay on the move despite considerable pain, where I carry straight codeine (hydrocodone) he recommended Tylenol (acetaminophen) with codeine as easier on the stomach. Tylenol works on pain and fever but has no effect on inflammation, which responds to aspirin or ibuprofen, both of which I carry instead. Because of a severe allergic reaction to a bug bite some years ago, Colin includes a small insect-sting treatment kit (page 728).

That small first-aid kit isn't the whole story, however: the average backpack contains further resources to augment your first-aid practice, including:

Scissors/tweezers/awl, etc. (on Swiss Army knife or pocket tool).
Needles, thread or dental floss for sutures (butterfly closures are less har-
     rowing).

Duct tape can close gashes and secure dressings or splints. Likewise, nylon
cord or webbing, bandanna, clean sock with toe cut off, gaiter, Velcro accessory straps.
For splints—aluminum stays, Ensolite (cut to shape) or self-inflating pad
(wrap, then inflate), beavertail panel from pack, Crazy Creek–type
folding seat (page 451), tent poles, fishing rod or case.
Irrigating wounds—purified water in squeeze bottle or hydration tube
(plus iodine and sans germy bite valve), or a clean plastic bag with a
pinhole.
Cleaning and disinfecting—moist wipes (with witch hazel or benzalko-
nium chloride), iodine water treatment, isopropyl alcohol (foot kit)
or alcoholic beverages.
Examining objects in eye, splinters, puncture wounds, insect bites, etc.—
hand lens, magnifier on compass base, signal mirror.
Taking temperatures, fever or hypothermia—plastic dial or zipper-pull
thermometer, in armpit (most register low by about 2°F).
Crutch/stretcher—trekking or ski poles, skis, snowshoes, tent, poncho,
bivy sack, space blanket.

Unlike love, your first-aid kit should alter when it alteration finds.
Terrain is a big factor. If you're headed for buggy bottomlands, antipru-
ritic ointment, swabs, or an ammonia pencil (After Bite) soothes the itch.
For deserts, where eye troubles abound, eyedrops or ointment, based on
cortisone or other steroid (also a balm for snow blindness). Knowing that
an area harbors disease-infected ticks (particularly the tiny deer ticks that
carry Lyme disease [page 724]), you should add a magnifying lens and
fine-point tweezers; and for venomous snakes, the proper antivenin kit
and/or a Sawyer Extractor (page 717). On a long trip where you might run
into a stubborn infection such as pneumonia a long way from medical
help, antibiotics can pull you through, but if you use them improperly
you might be helping germs mutate. So consult with a doctor and don't
fail to take a full course of medication, even if your symptoms disappear.
Well before such a trip, group members need to share knowledge of any
health condition, like diabetes, that might demand a quick and understanding response. All of which pivots on one fine point: how much do
you know? To do the wrong thing can be worse than to do nothing. This
is all common sense, but bears repeating.

COLIN: Because your drug requirements may be idiosyncratic, consult
your doctor before setting up your first-aid kit. If you have any particular
worries—if, for example, you are going up high for the first time—consider talking to the nearest member of the American Alpine Club medical
committee (listed in the AAC journal, which is probably available at your

local library or Sierra Club chapter HQ). Memories being what they mostly are, write down any sage advice for later reference under stress.

An experienced, first-aid-trained trip leader once echoed my uninformed gut opinion of the average prepackaged first-aid kit for backpackers: "Mostly a bunch of garbage you'll never use." But the choice is now wide enough to satisfy a hypochondriacs' union, and some are apparently good, or goodish.

CHIP: In a party, individual first-aid kits are normally supplemented, but not replaced, by a group kit. Contents will vary widely with size of party, terrain, length of trip, and philosophy of leader. Candidates include:

SAM (structural aluminum, malleable) splint material and/or air splints
CPR Microshield or Life Mask (for mouth-to-mouth breathing)
Nitrile barrier gloves (latex can cause allergic reactions)
Antivenin kit and/or Sawyer Extractor (page 717)
Oral thermometer (for fever and hypothermia; range must be 85–107°F)
Gel burn dressings (with lidocaine anesthetic)
Blunt-tipped EMT scissors
Glutose paste (with a *t*, for hypothermia, hypoglycemia, and insulin
    reaction)
Oil of cloves (for broken fillings and toothache) or dental emergency kit
Hemorrhoidal suppositories
Prescription drugs, such as antibiotics, morphine, and Dexedrine, that are
    reasonably safe when given with a competent outsider watching the
    patient's reactions

When I started wandering, "backpacker" first-aid kits were mil-spec lowest-bidder types packed in a nylon pouch rather than a steel box. But several companies now supply kits almost fiendishly calculated to who, what, where, and how many. Adventure Medical Kits has a lightweight Mountain Series with the Ouch Pouch (4 oz., $9.75), the Optimist (6 oz., $14.50), and the Trail (10 oz., $20), all suited for backpacking. They also sell kits for boating (freshwater or salt) and mountain biking, and an herbal medicine kit with a manual. The Atwater Carey series from Wisconsin Pharmacal includes the Day Hiker (4 oz., $14.50), Backpacker (4 oz., $19.50), and Walkabout (10 oz., $30), with the Pro 0.5 (9 oz., $24) a good foundation kit for fast and light trips. They come with cards and manuals. A third supplier of nicely thought-out medical kits is Outdoor Research, with the Solo (8 oz., $21) and the Hiker (8 oz., $32). When I think I might have to actually render first aid, when teaching at hydrology field school for instance, I carry the Outdoor Research Backpacker LT (14 oz., $48), a sturdy pouch with mesh pockets, one of which snaps out and is available separately (0.6 oz., $6.50) so you can prepack different sets of supplies and swap them rapidly. It also has four empty vials and a Velcro stash pocket—room to expand. But for solo excursions I revert to my self-concocted 5-ouncer.

Some kits come packed in waterproof boxes or bags. For spring trips with fast stream crossings or slot-canyon swims, I slip my first-aid kitty, elastic wrap, and sundries like matches into a waterproof pouch or box.

Since the sheer array of first-aid kits and supplies available is boggling, a chin-in-hand gaze at the charts in the catalogs will give you the excruciating details on who, what, where, and how many. First-aid-kit suppliers tend toward over-save (as opposed to over-kill). So I multiply their day/person estimates by two: a kit rated for one person and two to three days, with any luck at all, can serve me and partner on a weeklong trip. But if you're at all accident prone—and it pays to be honest with yourself—you might divide by two instead.

Most suppliers sell replacement items and also "modules" aimed at blisters, burns, cold-injuries, dental emergencies, and other subsets of outdoor distress. But my approach has been to customize and resupply from my home medicine cabinet—a practice that keeps the kit's contents fresh and wastes less—since I suffer more scrapes and gouges while fixing things around the house than while backpacking.

COLIN: An adviser suggests: "Don't take anything in your first-aid kit that you don't know how to use. If you're sitting bleeding you're in no shape to figure out how to use some unfamiliar item; you'd likely be better off using something that you do understand, fast, even if it's not quite as good. And much the same applies if someone else is hurt."

One partial solution to this knowledge dilemma is to carry some lightweight instructions. You may not look at them for years on end but in an emergency, when you find you simply don't know the correct response to the situation, they could save your life. Or somebody else's.

CHIP: Most prepacked kits now come with cards or pamphlets: the Outdoor Research Backpacker LT kit includes a very good half-ounce, 35-pager published by The Mountaineers. For more detail, there are several portable references well worth porting: *Mountaineering Medicine—and Backcountry Medical Guide* by Fred T. Darvill, Jr., M.D., an experienced outdoorsman. The book is continually updated and has sold over 150,000 copies. It gives practical advice on nearly everything from altitude sickness to ticks. Also good in the under-5-ounce class is *Wilderness and Travel Medicine* by Eric A. Weiss, M.D., with broad coverage, good illustrations, and a handy back-cover index. First-aid instructors also recommend *Back-*

country First Aid and Extended Care, by Buck Tilton; *Mountaineering First Aid: A Guide to Accident Response and First Aid Care* by Jan Carline, Martha Lentz, and Steven McDonald; *Basic Essentials: Wilderness First Aid* by William Forgey, M.D.; and *Emergency Survival Handbook* from the American Outdoor Safety League.

Tops in the pound-and-over class (for home reference or group treks) is *Medicine for the Outdoors* by Paul S. Auerbach, M.D. (1.5 lbs.). Clear, comprehensive, and well illustrated, this book covers nearly every conceivable outdoor malady. The drawback to reading it, pretrip, is that after poring over the drawings of poison spiders or the description of anisakiasis (a gruesome disorder caused by a worm found in raw or undercooked fish) you might feel more like staying home and eating popcorn.

Nevertheless, it's wise to refresh your first-aid knowledge—whether with an organized course or a lazy read under a tree. When someone actually gets hurt, I've been surprised at how my memory spits out the relevant details—if I've absorbed them, that is.

Another perennial text for group leaders and club shelves is *Medicine for Mountaineering and Other Wilderness Activities,* an emergency and health manual that goes far beyond first aid, edited by James A. Wilkerson, M.D. Others mentioned by advisers are *Wilderness First Aid: Emergency Care for Remote Locations* from the National Safety Council; *Medicine for the Backcountry* by Buck Tilton and Frank Hubbell; and *Backcountry Medical Guide* by Peter Steele, M.D.

If your health practices are greenish, there's *20 Herbs to Take Outdoors: An Herbal First-Aid Primer for the Outdoor Enthusiast* by Therese Francis. Some suppliers now sell herbal medical kits, with aloe vera gel for burns, arnica salve for soreness, and tea tree oil as antiseptic. If you want to gather your own plant remedies, seek out regional plant guides with notes on traditional uses. But just as it helps to practice first-aid drills, it makes sense to test herbal remedies close to home, watching for allergies or other reactions. On a trip some years ago, my partner carried a collection of tiny vials to practice her version of aromatherapy, which involved doing deep-breathing exercises while cocooned in her sleeping bag as odd smells wafted forth. Though for my part, not breathing exhaust fumes is the best therapy of all.

COLIN:

For hypothermia and its treatment, see page 746;

for mountain sickness, page 750;

for first aid to people struck by lightning, page 754;

for treatment of snakebite, see page 717; of tickbite, page 724; and of rashes from poison oak, ivy, and sumac, page 744.

Finally, remember that as a good backpacker you can improvise in first aid too. I once read a hiking pamphlet that recommended meat tenderizer (unseasoned), dissolved in water, as a painkiller for insect bites. I'm sure you'll value this brainstorm; after all, who ever heard of a backpacker worth his salt who did not carry, every trip, a plentiful supply of meat tenderizer (unseasoned)?

Don't forget that when there's no one around to appraise your condition objectively, from the outside, it can be difficult to judge whether you need something more drastic than first aid.

I once tackled a doctor friend on the subject.

"Would it be true to say," I asked, "that one kind of disease arises when you have many species of germs or other organisms living in or on a body in a state of mutual balance and equilibrium, and then some quite slight change occurs and one species gains the upper hand and before long becomes, by its sheer weight of numbers, a danger to the parent body?"

"Yes, I think that's a fair description of a certain kind of disease."

"Well, if you had a planetary body with many species living on it in a state of mutual balance and equilibrium, and then some slight change occurred in the head properties of one species and it gained the upper hand so that by its sheer weight of numbers it became a danger to the planet—not to mention to itself, of course—would you not call that condition a disease of a certain . . . ?"

"Oh my God, I take the Fifth Amendment."

Signaling mirror

CHIP: Anything reflective will draw attention: the sighting mirror on a compass, mirrored sunglasses, a shiny pot lid, a piece of foil, or a flopping space blanket. Colin found that the crystal of his watch did the trick, but the now-common digital watch lacks a crystal. Plastic signal mirrors about 2 by 3 inches, weighing a half ounce or so, cost from $3 up. The Starflash Signal Mirror I keep in my yoke office has a sighting hole with a star-shaped aiming point (0.7 oz., $9.25). Others have a simple range finder. Since plastic will scratch, dulling the flash, either trim the cardboard off the blister pack—but don't open it—or find a suitable protective envelope (an ink-cartridge packet, in my case). For details of use in rescues or airdrops, see pages 706 and 759.

Smoke bomb or flare

Backpacking wholesalers stock smoke bombs or flares for emergency signaling, though they're seldom seen in stores, maybe because of their vast potential for pranks. Wholesaler Liberty Mountain Sports distributes the SkyBlazer Signal Smoke that lasts 45 seconds and billows 4000 cu. ft. of orange smoke (1.5 oz., pack of two, $21.50). The SkyBlazer Aerial Flare with Launcher burns at 20,000 candlepower and shoots hundreds of feet into the air. The wilderness flare burns for 6 seconds, the marine flare for 10; both are red (no idea what they weigh; pack of three, $23). Since this last is by any definition a firework, it might be illegal on some public lands, particularly during fire closures. For use in rescues and airdrops, see page 708.

Strobe flasher

These aren't strikingly visible in daylight, nor do they show a pilot the wind direction, but they are inarguably safe and long-lasting. So they've largely replaced pyrotechnic devices, for recreational purposes at least. The long-available D-cell beacons flash 50 to 60 times a minute for 16 hours, then trail off for double that time. At $20 or so, they're water- and bombproof, and weigh 3 oz. alone—but the weight of the D cell boosts that to a hefty half pound. So lighter-weight models have flashed on the scene, like the Princeton Tec Aquastrobe (2 oz. with two AA cells, $35), lasting 8 hours and visible for 3 miles. Still lighter, and designed for hanging from a dog's collar, are the Pelican Pet Tracker (1.5 oz. with two AAA cells, $13), with half-mile visibility and an 8- to 10-hour life; and the Mini Pet Tracker, with LED and two coin-cell batteries and limited visibility but a 130-hour life (1 oz., $10). The protean EternaLight (page 584) has both strobe and code-signal settings. Of course you can simply thumb the switch on your flashlight at intervals, but the idea of a beacon is that it keeps flashing while you do other things, like eat and keep warm. When ski touring alone, I pack a Catseye LED bike taillight, a two-AAA model with both flashing and steady modes (2 oz., $10)—first removing it from my bike.

Whistle, etc.

COLIN: "A must for safety in the mountains," say some catalogs. Nowadays I always carry one (0.5 oz., about $1–$6). A possible bear warning, certainly. For whistle-thermometer-matchsafe-firestriker-compass-magnifier hybrids, and other barely imaginable artifacts, scan the catalogs.

Both plastic and metal whistles work fine—if the balls are also plastic or metal. But avoid those with cork balls. A reader whose canoe overturned says his "was never the same again." He also suggests carrying, instead of an emergency whistle, a flageolet or penny- or tin whistle: "My Generation D model ($4 in 1979) is lightweight, compact, and indestructible. It makes pretty tunes at sunset, and when I play high D they hear me in County Down." Yes, that's the trouble. It all sounds wonderfully Arcadian. But other people, well short of County Down, may be "out there" for peace and quiet, free from all works of man. Even a poorly played whistle, half a mile upwind, is less aggravating than a totebike; but if you're in the wrong mood . . .

CHIP: There are now whistles with no balls whatsoever. My Fox 40 (0.3 oz., $6.50) is the traditional shape, though plastic and pea-less, and it dangles discreetly from the inboard loop on my Possum Pocket (aka yoke office). But it doesn't sound discreet: blown near a cemetery, it will raise the dead (and they will be pissed). Other pea-less types, all a half ounce or less, are the ear-piercing Storm Safety Whistles ($5 and $7), the tooth-grinding S.O.S. Survival clip-on from Campmor ($2), and two anodized aluminum LM whistles from Liberty Mountain Sports (small shriek, $3.60; big screech, $3.90). *Caution:* If you loose a blast from any of these when you aren't in real trouble, you soon will be.

Fire starter

The patented Fire Starting Tool, Magnesium, made by Doan Machine and Equipment Co. of South Euclid, Ohio, is now nearly as ubiquitous as the safety pin. And rather simpler to operate. The magnesium bar (1 by 3 inches, 1.5 oz., $7) has a sparking insert along one edge. To use as directed, you shave off silvery curls of magnesium (a soft metal that burns at 5400°F) and collect them in a tiny heap (with tinder nested around). Then, using a knife blade, etc. you bomb the heap with sparkles. When it catches, hoo-hah! You can soak the magnesium bar in water and start a fire immediately afterward. Naturally, this is sovereign for emergencies, while the sparking insert alone handily ignites a stove (and can scorch neat little pinholes in nylon and polyester as well). I've gone entire trips without using a single match. Other more elaborate and expensive devices do the same trick. For further incendiary practices, see page 352.

Emergency fishing tackle

COLIN: The only living off the land that I normally do is fishing, and in almost any country I carry a tiny survival kit that weighs about ¼ oz. and contains:

1 spool (60 feet) 6-pound nylon line
Half-dozen hooks, assorted sizes
Half-dozen lead shot
Half-dozen trout flies

The whole kit wraps into a small, tough, polyethylene bag and travels, almost unnoticed, in the "office" (page 180).

Such a kit can augment and vary a dehydrated diet, and might even help keep you alive. In Grand Canyon I took along a 35-millimeter film can of salmon eggs. They worked well. Using my staff as rod I caught many small catfish and one carp of about 1½ lbs. Small fish of any kind demand considerable cooking effort for rather little substance, but bigger fish are rewarding. Carp need only be laid on hot embers, as their thick skin acts as aluminum foil. I often carry a little aluminum foil for less obliging species, such as trout.

For more elaborate fishing tackle, see Enjoying Extraperambulatory Activities (page 669).*

Rope

In really rough country, when there are two or more of you, a rope can be worth carrying as a safety measure. You need at least two people for a *belay* (that is, for tying yourself to rock or tree so that should your partner fall you can hold him with the rope)—or for a rescue. Alone, you'll rarely find much use for a rope, unless you expect to *rappel* down a cliff (that is, to pass the rope around your body in such a way that you can lower yourself at any desired speed by controlling with one hand the friction the rope creates on your body as you descend).**

The only time I've carried a rope was in Grand Canyon. I knew that for weeks on end I'd be walking 2000 or 3000 feet above the river, with my way down to it barred by a series of sheer cliffs. But in some places most of the cliffs had eroded nearly through, and it seemed to me that in dire emergency a rope might just allow me to rappel down an otherwise impassable barrier to the lifesaving water of the river. On short rappels I might be able to retrieve the rope for reuse by doubling it and pulling it down after me through some form of loop. (Rather than carry the ortho-

*CHIP: Inspired by the hand-carved gear of Costa Rican fishermen, the Tidelands Casting Handline (that weird object above the ice axe in the cover photo) is a pocket-size goodie in fiberglass-reinforced plastic with a rubber handgrip. After practice I could cast farther and retrieve more easily than with the short pine stick I formerly used—with the potential to land larger fish. It's made by Streamlines (see Appendix III) and comes with 140 feet of line and a practice plug (2.5 oz., $17).

**CHIP: This is tempting, when you come to one of those overhanging rims with a gorgeous canyon opening below. But before slithering down, remember that you can't rappel back up. Further, overhangs are tough to surmount even for a practiced climber with a partner to belay (or winch) you up. A great many people get badly stuck this way. For the highly relevant details of descending and ascending ropes, consult a mountaineering text. And get some hands-on-rope instruction.

dox carabiner or rappel ring for this unlikely eventuality, I decided to rely on a multiple loop of nylon cord, or perhaps a convenient tree. On long rappels I would have to use the rope single and leave it behind.) After much balancing of usefulness against weight, I took a 100-foot length of ¼-inch (6-millimeter) laid nylon rope, about 1900 pounds-test (1 lb. 14 oz.).

No dire water emergency arose. But once, reconnoitering a tricky route, I found a rather steep 10-foot rockface that I knew I could get down but didn't feel sure I could reclimb should the way ahead prove impassable. So I fastened the rope to a convenient rock pillar and hand-lined down. The route proved impassable all right, and I duly and thankfully hand-lined back up again.

I also used the rope several times to lower the pack down pitches I could manage quite confidently unladen but didn't fancy tackling with a pack. Nylon cord (page 676) will do this job, but rope is easier on the hands and waist or shoulders, which should be used for braking. Rope also gives you a better chance of pulling a pack up—though once you've tried this game with a 60-lb. external-frame pack and seen how adept the frame ends are at grabbing the rock, you'll go to some lengths to avoid a replay.

CHIP: For this sort of assisted scrambling there are now various new things that will do. Strong for the weight is 5.5-millimeter X-Cord, a blend of Kevlar and Spectra fibers that's costly ($1.13 per foot—a 25-meter length is $93) but tests at 1800 kg/3969 lbs. Standard 7-millimeter high-strength accessory cord with a nylon core and braided polyester sheath weighs half again as much, costs about $.47 a foot, and tests at 2500 pounds. The test strength has to do with impact force, since jerks or falls can subject your rope and anchor to loads many times your actual weight. Since climbing back up a skinny, stretchy cord can be problematical, when exploring slot canyons I carry a hank (35 or so feet, 8 oz.) of ½-inch tubular nylon webbing that tests at 1000 pounds and costs about $.27 per foot. For pack hauling it's easier on the hands than skinny cord, and I've also tied hand and foot loops in it for reversing short but unclamberable overhangs. It's also good for rigging tarps and a hundred what-have-yous. But it's not—nor are any of the above—fit for extended rappels or ascents. For that, get the right stuff—climbing, caving, or rescue rope—with the minimum recommended diameter about ⅜ inch, or 9.5 millimeters. Climbing ropes are *dynamic,* which means they stretch from 6 to 10 percent to absorb shock from falls. Caving and rescue ropes are *static,* with 1 to 2 percent stretch. Having the right rope doesn't automatically confer knowledge of how to use it. So get some proper instruction and enough hands-on practice that you have a sense of what can be done with a rope—and more important, what can't.

Guns

COLIN: Some years ago, a magazine printed a serious two-sided discussion on "Packing Iron" ("Should Backpackers Carry Handguns?"). The case in favor, by a writer from the National Rifle Association, quoted specious arguments and statistics to suggest that we need to protect ourselves from co-members of the species. It even called guns "good in snake-infested territory" (any informed and balanced person knows that if you really want to kill a snake the safest and surest way is with a stick). The case against gun toting, made by the National Parks and Conservation Association, advanced many of the good and obvious arguments: if someone wants to shoot you, then by the time you've got your gun out you're probably already shot; reaching for a gun is the surest way to turn threat into shooting; the terrible certainty of accidents from plain mishandling, especially by the inexperienced; the tragic danger, bordering on certainty, that some scared individual, imagining himself threatened at night by "a marauding animal," will kill a hiker. The case closed with the sensible comment that "the small benefits of carrying a gun are far outweighed by the negatives." Among the negatives it listed "increased hostility." And that, it seems to me, is the crux. The whole spirit of backpacking would be defiled. Perhaps I should add that this is no ivory-tower judgment. I once carried a handgun in Alaskan grizzly country (see page 737). During World War II I spent six years of my young life being trained to use and then using small arms for lethal purposes.

I can't help feeling that "Packing Iron" was published less because of the need for airing a genuine public controversy than because of the smell of a magazine-selling article. Unfortunately, the publicity probably increased the chances of widespread gun toting. I therefore hesitated to broach the subject here. But I guess the damage had been done. On balance, I decided, it's probably better for me to say my piece.

Happy cynics can, of course, rejoice. They'll no doubt detect another straw in the chilly wind of Industrial Devolution, another hint of impending anarchy.

IMPROVING THE MIND

Reading matter

For me, the book should be light in weight and not too leaden in content. If your natural-history knowledge is as piebald as mine, one of those little identification books on trees or reptiles or mammals or such would seem a good choice. For bird books, see page 673; for night-sky books, page 636. Generally, I find myself taking books that are relevant to some aspect of my journey but which don't deal too closely with the detail around me. On the six-month California walk I browsed slowly through a five-book paperback Mentor series on philosophy (the books were mailed ahead singly to post offices along the route). In Grand Canyon I extracted many seminal thoughts from a paperback, now apparently out of print, that dealt discursively rather than didactically with present geological knowledge. Poetry is good too: wilderness can open new windows into old lines.*

Everybody has his own reading druthers, of course, and there's huge variation. One man I know took the complete "works" of Sherlock Holmes on a monthlong trek. Another dismisses any book in the wilderness as an intrusion, almost on a par with a Walkman radio-cassette or CD player. "I'm out there to see things," he says, "not to do something I can do at home." But if you decide to take a book an apt choice might be somebody else's view of where we stand today. If you have walked properly, with your eyes open, sometimes breaking free from the confines of your own species' normal thoughtways and standing halfway outside them, then you should be in a ripe mood to consider the astonishing human bubble. Two possibilities among many are: *Earth at a Crossroads: Paths to a Sustainable Future* by Hartmut Bossel (Cambridge University Press, 1998, $21) and the latest *State of the World* annual by Lester Brown (Worldwatch Institute, $15). The chances are good that you will glean from such sources many ideas that you might when in civilization reject, out of fear—though you may discover that they are only confirmation of something you had already learned aesthetically from the green world and had accepted, utterly, with everything except your intellect. You may even find yourself sitting on a mountaintop and pondering the question: "Would it be better for the world as a whole if the human species gets itself back in hand or if it lets itself burn out?" Should you find such ruminations "pessimistic," remember that they represent no radical innovation in human thought. Even men of science have for some time been riding this road. And, at their moments, Arnold, Eliot, Picasso, Mahler, and other Travelers have long ago knocked on this same moonlit door. But never the least stir made most of us Listeners.

---

*CHIP: My reading tastes are impossible to track, let alone predict. In the Poetry Department, though, some favorite companions have been: *Cold Mountain: 100 poems by the T'ang Poet Han-Shan,* translated by Burton Watson (Columbia University, 1970, 4.5 oz.); the *Iliad* and the *Odyssey,* Homer, translated by Robert Fitzgerald (Anchor, 1974 and 1963, about 500 pages and 10 oz. each); *Narrow Road to the Interior* by Matsuo Basho, translated by Sam Hamill (Shambhala, 1991, 108 pages, 3.5 oz.); *The Essential Clare: Poems of John Clare,* selected by Carolyn Kizer (Ecco, 1992, 4 oz.); the Laurel *Emily Dickinson* (Dell, 1960, 3 oz.); and *100 Great Poems by Women,* edited by Carolyn Kizer (Ecco, 1995, 8 oz.).

Lightweight games,

which you can now buy in mountain shops and specialty stores or by mail, provide an alternative to books for tentbound times or plain relaxation. They include chess, checkers, backgammon, dominoes, Chinese checkers, and Scrabble; also foldable Frisbee-type discs, zippered football covers with grippy panels (to stuff with extra clothes), and Hacky Sack–type footbags—crochet-covered balls filled with polyethylene beads that you keep airborne, no-hands. "A great warm-up for climbing," says one happy hacker.*

My personal preferences? I've never tried any of the whole assembly. But in a public-spirited search for a game demanding only pencil and paper—and a mirror or a mirror imagination—I came up with Colinvert (patent not pending): you strive to find words with meaningful mirror images. Using suitably chaste characters, I quickly generated "mom," "wow," "oxo," "bog/pod," and "mud/bum" but soon glimpsed the awful truth: available permutations frankly fall short of those inherent in chess. Is the game worth the dandle? Of course. At the termination of your labors you can rest tolerably confident that you've done nothing to increase the risk of war, rape, taxes, or death, or to diminish the joys of walking, daydreaming, nose picking, or making love.

Notebook

If you intend to take notes of some sort on a trip but have not yet tried it, I sound a warning: time is the trouble (table, page 49). Note writing always seems to be among the activities that get consistently crowded out. I used to assume that this was a personal inefficiency, but I gather it's an occupational hazard among geologists, naturalists, and others committed to wilderness note taking. I offer no solution other than determination. Don't kid yourself, as I used to, that you will just jot down a word or two for each thought, more or less as you go, and will spend each evening—or long midday halt—expanding it. The expansion rarely happens. Certainly not if you're having to push at all hard, physically. The best I've been able to do is to jot down as much as I can in my notebook *at the time* and then attack the fuller and more discursive stuff as opportunity offers. Mostly, that means on rest days.

---

*CHIP: A compact deck of playing cards (also needed for cribbage) lightens stormed-in sojourns with solitaire or high-stakes games of poker for M&M's, lemon drops, or sips of rum. Dice also provide weight-efficient amusement (with knife fights optional). For ramblers who aren't gamblers, wholesaler A-16 carries jacks, marbles, pick-up sticks, juggling games, and such. For aggravation games such as Headlamp Tag and Scarf-the-Gorp, see *Sky's Witness: A Year in the Wind River Range.*

I generally use a plastic-covered, spiral-backed, looseleaf notebook of the kind you can buy almost anywhere. It fits conveniently into shirt pocket or yoke office (page 180), and one 60-page 3-by-5-inch book (1.5 oz., $.60) lasts at least a week. The spirals should be at the top rather than the side so that they don't catch in pocket or office. To make it easy to open the notebook at the current pages I slip rubber bands over both front and rear covers, halfway down, and slide each page under its band as I finish using it.

Waterproof pads exist that "won't wrinkle, spot, or fall apart even if soaked . . . [and will] always take a line from any pencil or pen." Rite in the Rain makes a slew of such notebooks including a 3-by-5-inch 50-sheet spiral pocket memo (2 oz., $3.15 from Forestry Suppliers—who stock many other outdoor notebooks). Chip tells me that pencil smears rather badly on waterproof paper.

Sheet paper

Waterproof sheets for field notes also exist—under such fancy names as Waterloo. See also do-it-yourself Stormproof, page 627.

I sometimes take onionskin paper for fuller notes than my notebook can absorb—and back it with a rectangle of stiff cardboard, to which I secure the paper, top and bottom, with rubber bands. The cardboard can be bent or cut in half. Paper doubles as reserve TP.*

Pens and pencils

Ballpoint pens, with refills. The press-in-to-reveal-point kind are instantly and one-handedly ready, and have no tops to be lost. But a topped, nonrefillable, half-length size (3½ inches), common in drugstores, weighs barely ¼ oz. and costs only $.50. The Fisher Space Pen, reputedly developed for the moon program, has a nitrogen-pressurized cartridge that "writes in any position and under virtually any conditions." (The compact Fisher "bullet" pen is 1 oz., $18; a Rite in the Rain "space pen" is 1 oz. and $7.25.)

I carry several pencils—two of them with pocket clips (preferably the spring-loaded kind that you open up with a fingertip as you clip or unclip the pencil to or from the yoke office). Spares go in main office. Don't sharpen pencils too fine, they'll only break. And sharp points can savage you. Both pens and pencils should be a bright, conspicuous color.

*CHIP: The margins or backside of a topographic map are a grand place for trip notes, drawings, and poems, at least for pencil scratchers like me. Transformed by art, the map becomes a topo-keepsake.

CHIP: For some reason I double-detest ballpoints, even extraterrestrial ones. Fortunately, over thousands of miles, paddle, boot, and sandal, I've managed to hold on to my grandfather's old Sheaffer mechanical pencil (bright red, 0.5 oz., priceless) with a 0.9-millimeter lead that stands up to creative frenzy—and a nice, fat eraser for afterthoughts. The original pocket clip popped off into a creek, so my Grand-pencil now sports a spring-loaded slip-on cheapster. For small notebooks, and/or small hand-writing, a finer 0.7- or 0.5-millimeter lead works better.

The office, unyoked

COLIN: I tend to use doubled zip-top bags, or sometimes a pair of such sets, to enclose the many items that need to be kept flat or otherwise pro-tected, and also small items of the kind that just ache to get lost: sheet paper for notes (often with cardboard back, as above), spare pens and pen-cils, paperback book, wilderness permit, first-aid handbook, stove-nozzle cleaner, ripstop patching material, moleskins with mirror and scissors (if carried), spare flashlight batteries, miniature can opener (page 287), rub-ber bands, maps not in use, car key, coins (for phone), spare sunglasses, and survival fishing tackle. For compact offices, yoke or belt-mounted, see page 181.

FIGURING

It would seem reasonable to suppose that you can escape from the man-world more easily if you walk out into wilderness without a

Watch.

But the stratagem may backfire. Without a watch you may find yourself operating so inefficiently (as can happen if you go without maps) that ways and means begin to obscure the things that matter. It's not sim-ply a question of knowing the time of day (provided the sun shines, you can gauge that kind of time accurately enough—though in dank or snow-clogged weather or in country so precipitous that the sun sets soon after noon, even that may prove a problem): you have lost the sharp instrument that keeps prodding you forward. That's what I find, anyway, because if time and distance are important I often mark on my map the time I stop for each halt—or at least note the time mentally. Without a watch, too, I can't work out times and distances for the way ahead. And that, for me, means a loss rather than a gain in freedom. Some people find the precise opposite. But the fact remains that after a single weeklong trip without a watch I went back to wearing one and have never rewavered.

Even without a watch, by the way, you can figure out the time at night, roughly—if you know what you're doing, which few of us do—by watching the position of the star Kochab: it circles the nearby North Star counterclockwise once every 24 hours. Or so they say.

CHIP: Unless you're one of those Rolex types, with a porter to support your wrist, or the possessor of a new multifunctional whizbang such as the Suunto Vector Wristop Computer (page 635), you probably take your everyday watch backpacking. Traditional dial types have certain advantages: they can be used as a sun compass or a signal flasher (page 654). But digital watches, in all forms, are ever more common. Colin straps on a batteryless, solar-powered, water-resistant Casio (1 oz., $27). I have a yet more basic one, the Casio Illuminator (cool name, 0.8 oz., $12) with a button-activated backlight bright enough to find a roll of TP at relatively short notice. It also has a stopwatch, a timer, and an alarm with a tortured-mouse skreek that wakes me up if I really want it to. The neo-plastique band stretches little and never stinks. I persuade myself that even H. D. Thoreau might grudgingly approve. But he'd probably write an essay decrying what I intend to replace it with: some micro-devilbox like the Suunto Vector. Still, I have to break the Illuminator first. Don't hold your breath.*

COLIN: A cruder kind of time figuring is almost always essential:

Keeping check on the days.

Even if you have no vital commitments to meet in the outside world, you should before leaving roadhead give somebody a time and a date beyond which it can be assumed that, if you have not shown up, you're in trouble (page 55). Or you may have arranged an airdrop, or a meeting with packers or other walkers. In any of these cases a mistake in the day can cost you dearly. And the mistake is remarkably easy to make.

I always prepare a table on a page near the end of my notebook (not the last page, because it may pull out). I block out the days and leave room for writing in the name, actual or fancied, of the place at which I camp each night. This detail, I find, is the one that my mind distinguishes most clearly in identifying the days. Without my calendar table I would

---

*The problem with such micro-devices is remembering all the modes and subroutines. I've been on trips with persons whose digital wonders were set for alarms at odd times, and they couldn't remember how to shut the damned things off.

often—perhaps most often—not know for sure what day it was. The table also makes it much easier to figure out, days ahead, whether I really need to hurry or can afford to amble luxuriously along.

Having a watch that reports day and date has not made me forgo the calendar-table habit. But then, I'm a cautious s.o.b.

Pedometer

Theoretically, this instrument is a valuable item. But although I own one I've never got past the finicky job of trying to calibrate it to my normal stride. Perhaps that's because I question how useful such calibration would be over any but smooth, level ground—and because I regard wilderness mileage figures as being, in most cases, singularly meaningless (page 48).

Thermometer

It's many years now since I began taking a thermometer on walks, and I still have no reasoned explanation of why it makes such a beguiling toy. I have to admit, I suppose, that it's primarily a toy. It has taught me any number of intriguing facts: the remarkably tenuous relationship that exists between air temperature and what the human body feels (page 479); the astonishingly hot surfaces your boots often have to walk on and can sometimes avoid (page 112, footnote); and the actual temperature of a river I needed to swim in (the body is a miserable judge here too, and the temperature can be critical if you have to swim far [page 690]). But the sort of information my thermometer has given me has more often been interesting than practical.

One February I took a three-day hike along Point Reyes National Seashore, just north of San Francisco. On the last day a cold, damp wind blew in from offshore fog banks. At lunchtime I sheltered from the wind in a little hollow on the edge of the sand dunes bordering the beach. Down in the hollow, the wind barely rustled the thin, tough blades of beach grass. And the sun's reflected warmth beat up genially from pale sand. After a few minutes I felt sweat beginning to trickle down my face. Idly, I checked the temperature in the shady depths of the densest grass: 64°F. Then I moved the thermometer out into the sun, on open sand. The mercury finally stopped at 112°.

For no clear or logical reason I for years checked and noted temperature readings: in shade and sun; in the air, on and below the surface; above, on, and below different neighboring surfaces; in rivers and hot springs. Once I found myself delighted by the singularly useless information that it was still 55°F in my boots half an hour after I'd taken them off, when the ground temperature had already fallen close to freezing.

I suppose I gradually gained from such readings, in an untidy and diffuse sort of way, some new and rather tangential understandings of how our fascinating world works, but I doubt that this is really why I went on with the measuring and figuring. Mostly, I think, it's just that I enjoy my thermometer. And although I play with it less nowadays I rarely go without it. It clips into my yoke office, alongside pen and pencil.

I used to carry an ordinary mercury-filled thermometer, but the glass stem regularly broke, scattering freelance blobs of mercury—now recognized as highly and persistently hazardous. One benign alternative: an Enviro-Safe model with citrus-based filler and plastic armor (1 oz., $13). But for many years I've used a nonliquid, bimetallic dial model by Taylor, with clip-equipped plastic sheath (0.5 oz.; not sure of price—they're now hard to find). In spite of the dial's being set at right angles to the stem, it's tough. Forestry Suppliers sells the similar Taylor Bi-Therm Pocket Case thermometer, −40° to 160°F (2 oz., $15). You can also get cunning little plastic thermometers, hangable "from pack or parka" (1 oz. or less, $3–$5), and thermometer/compass combinations abound at $5 to $10. For all I know, they may work.

Practical hints: Try to calibrate a new thermometer against a reliable and preferably official one. For a quick "shade" reading when there's no shade, twirl the thermometer around on the end of a length of string or nylon cord that you leave knotted to the carrying loop; but check the knot first (see knots, nylon cord, page 678). In hot weather be careful where you leave the thermometer: in the sun, surface temperatures can easily exceed 130°F; and much beyond that, if you use a glass-stemmed model, you may find yourself with an empty one. I haven't experimented to find out if a bimetallic dial goes monometallic or something.

Of course, real cognoscenti scorn thermometers. They calculate ambient temperature instantly by counting the number of times any neighboring cricket chirps in 14 seconds, then adding their age next birthday.

Windmeter

CHIP: Under certain conditions, especially in winter, knowing the wind speed might be useful as well as interesting. The Dwyer Wind Meter registers up to 66 mph (2 oz., $13.95) by means of little colored beads in a plastic tube—no batteries required. Toward the high end, the Brunton Sherpa digitally registers wind speed, windchill, temperature, barometric pressure, and altitude—to 30,000 feet (2 oz. with 3-volt lithium battery, $155). As we go to press, some makers are threatening to combine weather functions with GPS receivers, for a new generation of micro-devilboxes.

MENDING

Mending beats spending. But for laborious, blood-boiling fixes, like replacing zippers, the first step is to check the warranty. Lowe Alpine Sports and Sierra Designs have repaired fairly ancient packs and tents for me (though in one case my rezippered pack came back with a note reading "Please!!! Get a new one!!!"). Most good mountain shops will ship warranty items to companies whose gear they sell. The disadvantage is considerable downtime. Some shops also do backroom repairs or will refer you to local fix-meisters. There are also mail-order repair outfits, like Rainy Pass Repair, that specialize in hard-to-fix things like ripped Gore-Tex, and some now offer quick estimates via the Internet (see Appendix III). But you'll often want or need to do your repairs at home.

I keep swatches of fabric, repair tape, grommets-and-setting tools, plastic buckles, and other oddments in my workshop, jumbled in a cardboard box. Memory being a porous vessel, I inspect gear after—soon after—each trip, and fix things before stowing them away. This approach was not inborn but learned. Repairs made under pressure late at night before a trip can be sketchy at best, and that missing gaiter hook—how *did* I forget?—will haunt you.

My emergency repair kit, an Altoids box I call Gremlin-Smasher, weighs 3 to 4 oz., and holds:

Tape

Repair tape comes in a rainbow of colors and most outdoor-type fabrics: Cordura, ripstop, taffeta, clear, and duct. Tape in rolls and patches from Eureka, Kenyon, and W. L. Gore (black only) can be found in shops. Mostly, the stuff sticks—and will withstand a certain amount of washing but not dry cleaning. Sewing the edges makes it permanent (see page 493). If you worry about matching colors, makers sometimes include repair kits or can supply swatches, if you act while the fabric or product is in stock. New stick-ons include Scotch netting repair patches (from Moss Tents and others) for holes in no-see-um mesh. Gremlin-Smasher (my fixit kit) holds mini-rolls of regular and reflective duct tape, with light and dark ripstop tape and three mesh patches Scotch-taped under the lid. If you don't mind the fuzz, moleskin works too.

Needles and thread

Colin stores needles in his matchsafe with short lengths of strong thread threaded through three or four needles and wrapped around them like pythons. A longer reserve of thread, wrapped around a small piece of paper, goes into his "odds and ends" can.

An Alaskan reader suggests "glovers' needles," with #7 a good starter size. Glovers' needles have triangular points, and Eskimos apparently use them for skin sewing. I have a piece of cardboard scalloped at the ends, with white and black thread pythoned around it and four needles run through: two regular ones, a glover's needle for tough fabrics and leather, and a leather or canvas needle with an extra-large eye, for waxed-linen boot maker's thread (in a separate hank). For heavy sewing, the pliers on a pocket tool or a chunk of bare wood can help get the needle through.

Speedy Stitcher

For heavy repairs, the Speedy Stitcher Sewing Awl is invaluable (3-plus oz., $10). The strong wooden handle houses a replaceable bobbin of waxed thread and two interchangeable needles (straight and curved #8) 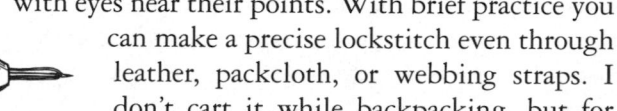 with eyes near their points. With brief practice you can make a precise lockstitch even through leather, packcloth, or webbing straps. I don't cart it while backpacking, but for large groups or remote expeditions it could save the day, particularly if pack animals are involved. And if you and the yak-wrangler hit it off, it makes a thoughtful parting gift.

Spare parts for pack, tent, snowshoes, stove, etc.

You can't carry spares for everything. But some items depend on one small piece or two whose loss or damage could screech your trip to a halt. If the maker includes a tent-pole repair sleeve or spare clevis pin, that's a strong hint. Gearheading with friends and local shop staff can provide further clues. If there are parts that need adjustment or removal en route, think about what might get dropped (God forbid!) in the snow. Plastic buckles are high on my list.

Makeshift repairs

My life is a makeshift, so my repairs tend to be pretty-damn-good. Fixing things settles my mind, and Gremlin-Smasher (my repair kit) is like a snapshot album of mishap and ill fortune, mostly resolved. It's a repository for the obvious, like safety pins, and also for all those wee trip savers that experience reveals: rivets, washers, grommets, brass tacks, teeny screws, cable ties, twist-ties, heat-shrink tubing, a precut leather patch, emery cloth (outlasts sandpaper and doesn't fall apart when wet), stainless steel, brass wire, *ad monkey-tinkerum.* Further resources such as duct tape (for everything), dental floss (for sewing), and repair compounds such as Aquaseal and Shoe Goo (for boots, sleeping pads, tent floors, etc.) are found elsewhere in my pack.

Prebagged kits are available for common horrors, like dentally impaired zippers. In fact, complete—perhaps overcomplete—repair kits are now on sale from Gear Aid and others. These tend to be well thought out, with nice surprises like a hot-melt glue stick. If you have zero, such a kit is a good start. But the drawbacks are the same as with prepacked first-aid kits. Things you already have are duplicated, at considerable expense. Quantities are overgenerous (a full-size tube of Seam Grip?). Sizes can be off, as with a generic tent-pole repair sleeve. And the total weight soon catches up with you. The Gear Aid Basic is a solid repair kit, no mistake, but it costs $25 and weighs 8 oz. And if you're overburdened with spares and repairs and quick cures, you're far more likely to need them.

Repair hints for specific items are scattered throughout this book.

ENJOYING EXTRAPERAMBULATORY ACTIVITIES

COLIN: For many people, perhaps for most, a walk is rarely a self-fulfilling operation, whether it lasts an hour or a summer. Alone, with an agreeable companion, or in a group, they walk as a means to some such specific end as hunting, fishing, photography, birdwatching, sex, or geology.

Generally speaking, I regard the equipment for such activities as outside the scope of this book. There are a few exceptions.

Fishing

An orthodox 2- or 3-piece rod is a perishing nuisance on a backpack trip. (I'm thinking primarily of trout fishing, because that's what you usually find in the wilder areas still left for backpacking. And I'm thinking above all of fly-fishing, because in most remote areas that's the way to get the most pleasure from your fishing—and sometimes to catch the most trout. But what I have to say applies to most kinds of rods.)

If you lash an orthodox rod to a pack upright—the best place for it—the risk of damage is high, though a dowel or stick rubber-banded to the uncased rod may help. If you tote along an aluminum rod case, the wretched thing tends to get in the way, especially if you use an I-frame pack. When fishing is your overriding object, the inconvenience may be worth it; but if fishing is really an excuse for escape, and even more if it's just a possible bonus, the solution lies in a portmanteau rod — 4- or even 6-piece.

The difficulty with this kind of rod is always its action: the perfect rod is a 1-piecer, and every metal ferrule marks another step down from perfection. Each ferrule also used to add critically to the weight, but new alloys have pretty well solved that problem. On this count, even some cheaper fiberglass rods now score high. And the very best dispense with metal ferrules: fiberglass fits into hollowed fiberglass. The results are featherweight wands with smooth, lively actions.

Many portmanteau rods, some of them ferruleless, now appear in outdoor catalogs. Among the best known: those by Fenwick and Daiwa. Some have reversible grips for fly-fishing or spinning.

My 4-piece, 7½-foot ferruleless fly rod, custom-made by The Winston Rod Company, formerly of San Francisco, now of Twin Bridges, Montana (2 feet, disassembled; 3 oz.; cloth cover, 2 oz.; aluminum case, 7 oz.) fits snugly down one side of the packbag, close beside the packframe. It mostly travels in the cloth cover and has never come to any harm. When using an I-frame pack I tend to carry the protective aluminum case.*

The rest of my backpack fly-fishing tackle fits into a small leather reel bag: the reel itself, six spools of nylon (2-, 3-, 4-, 6-, 8-, and 10-lb. test), a small can of flies, line lube, and fly flotant. Total: 11 oz..

Anyone with enough wit to resist the widespread fallacy that you go fishing mainly in order to catch fish will understand that spinning is a barbarous way to catch trout. But I have to admit that there are places, such as certain high mountain lakes, where fly-fishing may be useless. And there are times, of course, when you'll want to fish purely for food. For such occasions I have once or twice carried a little closed-faced abomination of a spinning reel (9 oz.) that takes most of the pleasure out of fishing but does not demand a large butt ring on the rod and can therefore be used with a fly rod. Into the abomination's little bag went some lead shot and weights, a few lures and bait hooks, and a bobber.

There are times when fly-fishing is plainly impossible. (Often, for example, when the fish are not trout.) So I have a 4-piece, 4-oz., 6-foot

---

*CHIP: Colin asked what I fish with. I've done well enough hand-lining small creeks with a piece of leader and a stick, or more recently a Streamlines casting hand-line rig (page 657, first footnote). But for serious fish-hunting I take a Sage Graphite II 4-piece fly rod, 9 feet long, that takes a 5-weight line and a Sage #106 reel (6 oz., with line), given to me as gifts. The rod and cloth case weigh 5.5 oz., and I often carry it thus, with a stout rubber band top and bottom to hold the bundle tightly together. I slip it down the side of the pack, under the compression straps and into the wand pocket, or employ the ice-axe loop and strap, aft. I've also packed it in the slim nylon bag with tent poles. All I can say is that I haven't broken it yet. The aluminum-tube case weighs 12.5 oz., and I take that only when I expect to be bushwhacking—but always use it for transport in cars.

spinning rod that breaks down to 20 inches. It was made to my specifications nearly 30 years ago from a hollow-glass blank that I selected from stock. My other spinning tackle is standard.

You can fish purely for fun—and get it—with emergency tackle (page 656) and a light switch cut from the riverbank—if cutting it seems acceptable in that place.

I'm aware that many people condemn fishing as a barbarous pursuit, lumpable with hunting. Seen from the outside, it may be—especially if the view includes close-ups of those pitiless (or, more likely, unthinking) rodmen who wrench their catch off the hook and leave it to gasp to death by inches. Even intellectually, though, I think it's possible to unlump fishing from hunting. Fish, for example, have simple nervous systems that don't seem to register pain as we mammals know it: I once hooked a small brook trout, brought it in almost to my feet before it came off the hook, and watched it swim back a few yards to its original position, then take my fly again within a minute or so. But hunters shoot birds or fellow mammals, with fellow nervous systems: a shot rabbit that just makes it back down its burrow, shattered leg gushing blood, is hardly likely to come back, like my brook trout, for another sample. Again, provided you wet your hands first and then work gently, you can, especially when fly-fishing, return without harming it almost any fish you don't want for food. (Dry hands remove protective slime and leave a fish vulnerable to disease.) But you cannot by any known means set free a doe once it is lying there with its eyeball hanging and brains spattered—even if you had thought it was a buck, or if your natural hot hunter's blood has drained away and left only chill once you stand over your twitching victim. Furthermore, I see a fly rod as a delicate wand, a gun as an instrument of war. Here we may be closing on the nub. In the end, I think the difference is aesthetic. I find fishing a gentle and artistic pastime that calms me. And I see hunting otherwise. (I speak only of hunting as a sport. I have no quarrel with hunting purely for food, as a necessity. I'd do it anytime.)

A Wisconsin reader who hunts wrote in response to the above, disagreeingly but agreeably. He asserted that hunters as a whole are "a group of dedicated, aware conservationists" but readily admits they are "severely plagued by slobs in their ranks." He also claims, with considerable reason, that we have in many cases caused overpopulation—as with deer—and that "it is therefore the responsibility of man, who threw the monkey wrench in, to correct the situation by 'removing nature's intentional excesses.'" He sounds a sincere and likable guy. And I've become increasingly aware that certain men whom I like and respect, men whose knowledge of and even veneration for wildlife is at least as great as mine, find hunting a satisfying and natural pursuit consonant with their veneration. Furthermore, I often feel more comfortable in the company of men who I know are hunters—even though I deplore what they do in that role—than I do in the company of many "ecologically aware individuals" who share my concerns but who never for one moment, by God, let you forget that they are the Chosen Defenders of the Earth. It's all very difficult—yet another instance of the not easily digested fact that you can like a man but dislike what he does. And vice versa.

Birdwatching

For the first 44 years of my life I thought of birdwatchers, when I thought of them at all, as a frustrated and ineffectual bunch of fuddy-duddies, almost certainly sex-starved, who funneled their energies into an amiable but pointless pursuit. My competence in their field was naturally close to zero. ("Naturally," because the firmest and most comfortable base from which to make sweeping judgments about any group of people is total ignorance.) But 35 years ago, on a return visit to East Africa, I bought an identification book of the astonishingly prodigal birdlife of that astonishingly prodigal land. And at once I began to understand about birdwatching. It wasn't merely that birds, really looked at, turned out to be startlingly beautiful, nor even that individual birds, like individual humans, engaged in funny, solemn, bitchy, pompous, brave, ludicrous, sexy, revolting, and tender acts; after my first real attempt to identify individuals from the book, I wrote excitedly: "Fascinating. Not just collecting species. This business makes you see." Within days I was a full-fledged convert, always eager to try out the new plumage by reaching for my birdbook.*

My conversion stuck (though it was maimed, and has never fully recovered, when someone broke into my car and stole, among other things, my American birdbook with its records of 10 years' sightings). And I long ago learned that, from a practical backpacking point of view, a convert to birdwatching will find that if he didn't take binoculars before he will certainly do so now; that he will have even more difficulty than before in not stopping and staring when he should be pounding along; and that, everywhere for a while, and in new country forever after, he will at least consider carrying a birdbook.

CHIP: Among practitioners, the preferred term is now "birding." This accords with "boating" and "biking," although watching a film is not "filming," nor is dining in a restaurant "fooding." In any event, the semi-hallowed U.S. standards for birders are two books illustrated by Roger Tory Peterson, published by Houghton Mifflin: *A Field Guide to the Birds:*

---

*Echo trouble, you say? Maybe. See *The Winds of Mara,* page 190.

A Completely New Guide to All *the Birds of Eastern and Central North America* (4th edition 1998, 384 pages, paperback, $18) and *A Field Guide to Western Birds* (reissue 1998, 431 pages, paperback, $18). The criticism one hears of these guides is that the illustrations are separated from the text, so you have to flip nimbly.

Some people prefer the *Audubon Society Field Guide to North American Birds—Eastern Region* (Alfred A. Knopf, 2nd edition 1994, 796 pages, paperback, $19). The western region guide is presently out of print. There are so many other birdbooks, each with its clamor of partisans, that we'll stick to well-trodden ground. *Birds of North America* by Chandler S. Robbins et al. (Golden Press, revised edition 1983, 360 pages, paperback, $13) is another favorite of birders. It has range maps that Colin once described in this book as "excellent" but which he was told could more accurately be designated "colorful." Another book with range maps, about which users likewise disagree, is *The National Geographic Field Guide to the Birds of North America* by Jon L. Dunn (revised and updated 3rd edition 1999, 480 pages, paperback, $21). Linda, a devout birder, prefers this last, with illustrations facing the text. She has the second edition, and the third has drawn fire for quality problems like poor color printing.

There are scads of good regional guides and also natural histories, such as the voluminously titled *Birder's Handbook: A Field Guide to the Natural History of North American Birds; Including All Species that Regularly Breed North of Mexico* by Ehrlich, Dobkin, and Wheye (Fireside, 1988, 785 pages, $20).

The Audubon Society and other birdophilic groups sell a range of belt cases, shoulder bags, book covers, tea sets, and such that is simply indescribable. Readers have suggested simple open-top bags or pockets, stitched to clothing or hanging from neck straps, possibly with extra room for protecting binoculars. One even urges the use of a "birding vest" on the order of a fly-fishing or photographer's vest, to neatly transport a full assortment of field guides plus checklists, notebook, birdcalls, sunglasses, sunscreen, lip balm, repellent, and energy bars.

COLIN: However you carry your birdbook, it may pay, if it's green like the hardback Peterson, to stick a strip of bright red ripstop tape around at least half its cover so that it will, if lost, stand out from surrounding vegetation. I learned this lesson several years ago, the hard way. At 4:00 p.m. one day I discovered that my Peterson had slipped from its makeshift, nylon-cord sling somewhere in the course of a long, rough traverse across a desert slope; at 2:00 p.m. the following day, after many sweaty retraverses, I found the book lying in the open, green and inconspicuous, in a place I had already passed at least four times. Note that I not only learned about putting red ripstop on green books but also confirmed yet again that ancient proverb: "A birdbook in the hand is worth twenty-two hours in the bush."

Boating

CHIP: Boating and backpacking were for years mutually exclusive, unless as Colin observes, you consider the canoe portage a species of backpacking.

Having used a fisherman's float tube to sample alpine lakes—with ice floating in them—I'm acutely aware not only of the weird rush of freedom I felt but also of the very real hazards. First, the cold—while float-tubing-for-science I wore a full-body drysuit that was both heavy and expensive, with a distinctly anti-recreational feel. Neoprene waders (for fishing) have the same drawbacks while offering less protection. Second, the fins you wear to propel the tube don't give you enough power to move against the wind: I had to stroke like a Viking just to stay in place. Third, you can't reasonably transport a pack. You can tow gear in a drybag, but if the wind comes up, forget it. And fourth, since your legs hang down into the water (in my case, far down) it's hard to negotiate streams of any less depth without banging, bruising, stumbling, and perhaps getting caught between rocks. A float tube is okay for a short fishing trip, on small lakes, given a sharp weather eye. But it's not reliable transportation.

In *Walker III,* Colin suggested that the inexpensive, light-enough-to-backpack inflatable kayaks then available were "essentially toys. And, in backcountry, dangerous toys. Any wind could quickly blow them just where you didn't want to go. Even given exquisite care, their durability must be suspect. And if they let you down suddenly in a mountain lake or river the cold water would give you about five minutes' survival time.

"I mention them for two reasons. People may see them and should be cautioned. And it is just possible to envision a situation in which a single, short, unhazardous water barrier, blocking off seductive terrain, might justify humping one along."

That's still the case, concerning discount-store inflatables—like floating tube-tents—that sadly end up plastered on rocks and shredded on shorelines. But there's a better way to combine backpacking and paddling in one trip. Call it

Boatpacking.

To do it right, you need a boat that's light enough to be packed, yet sturdy and stable enough to convey not only you but your chattels for some distance. I've seen those first-descent photos of hardpersons lugging hardshell kayaks down tooth-gritting trails. But any rigid kayak with the volume to stow much gear weighs at least 45 lbs. and is probably twice as long as you are: significant drawbacks. Folding kayaks are heavier still, dauntingly expensive, and likely to be destroyed on rock-studded white-water runs.

The vastly improved heavy-duty (of coated fabric rather than a single layer of polyvinyl chloride) inflatable kayaks come closer to the mark: the lightest ones now weigh about 25 lbs. and are sturdy enough to carom off several thousand rocks without expiring. Aire's Caracal I (26 lbs., $650) is a good example. It paddles nicely and you can roll it up (with the additional 6–8 lbs. of life vest, paddle, and pump) and add it to a pack with camping gear and food for several days—without red-lining, weightwise.

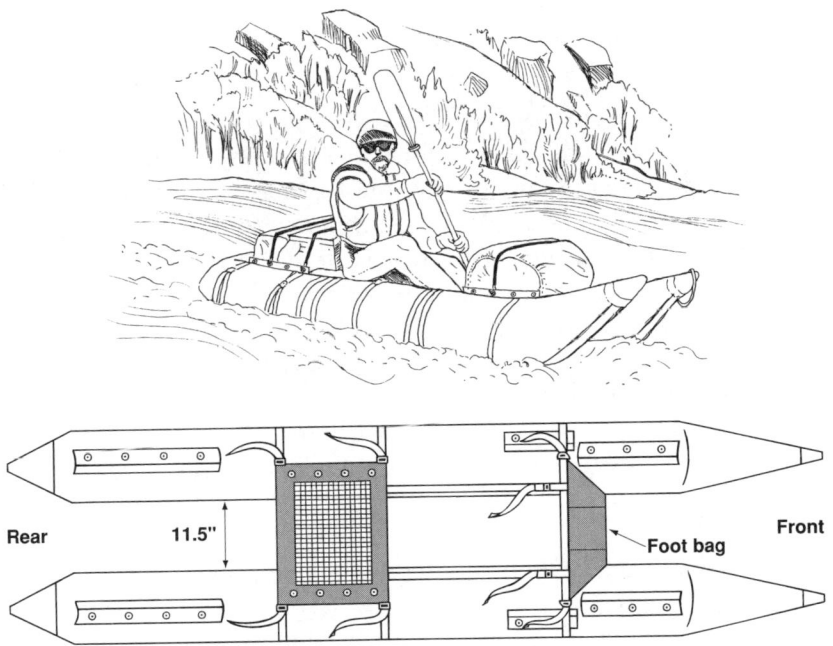

Rear   11.5"   Foot bag   Front

Even better for boatpacking is a felicitous hybrid known as the Jack's Pack Cat. Developed by Jack "Paco" Kloepfer, it's a pared-down cataraft with two 1-by-10.5-foot tubes. The two high-pressure tubes weigh 17 lbs. while the seat frame and footbar weigh 7.8 lbs., totaling 24.8 lbs. (and $935). The seat and footbar attach to the tubes with cam-buckle straps, comprising a minimalist frame. The mesh seat has an inflatable (i.e., infinitely adjustable) backrest. The footbar has a fabric guard, so you can't get trapped. You can loosen the straps and slide both seat and footbar to adjust your body position or trim the boat. While it looks odd at first gape, the Pack Cat's the most comfortable boat I've paddled—by several orders of magnitude. The two-tube design makes it strikingly stable. Add a 3-lb. kayak paddle, 2-lb. life vest, and 1.5-lb.

pump, and the package is 31 lbs. I've carried a Pack Cat up steep trails and roared down rockbound creeks that would destroy a canoe. And you can rig a week's worth of gear without seriously damping the performance.

Being four pieces rather one, the Pack Cat can be loaded and carried more handily than a one-piece inflatable. I've lugged the whole thing, plus camping gear, in a huge drybag-with-straps, and that was Sisyphean. My present tactic is to use a Coleman plastic E-frame (light, rugged, now out of production—page 176) to pack the boat and a big drybag stuffed with camp gear and food. Reaching the creek I remove the yoke and waistbelt and rig the bare packframe between the Pack-Cat tubes to support the drybag. In the event I have to hump boat-and-all back up a side-canyon to a roadhead, *presto-reverso!*

After backpacking across superheated slickrock and dusty sage flats, it's heaven to reach a stream. And then, to float off downcanyon like cottonwood fluff is heaven cubed: amphibious bliss.

With the scorch marks of Colin's fulmination on guidebooks still fresh about my ears, I'm not about to publicize my favorite boatpacking runs. You'll hear tales, no doubt, or see things written up in magazines. But don't be rash. Knowing how to paddle helps like mad. On rocky streams, so does a helmet. Besides poor technique, the major hazards are unexpected *drops* (holes and falls) and *strainers* (tree trunks or brush that catch boats and bodies, while letting the water through). So vigilant scouting and an occasional sweaty portage are necessary parts of the game. Meanwhile, the essence is to sit down with a map and figure out where you can boatpack into some remote headwater—and then float (merrily, merrily) on out again.

COLIN: The remaining furniture and appliances can best be departmentalized:

ALWAYS-COMING-IN USEFUL-AND-IN-FACT-QUITE-INDISPENSABLE DEPARTMENT

Nylon cord

The old white "parachute cord" has largely been replaced by "static accessory cord"—also with core fibers and a braided sheath—in sizes from 3 millimeters ($.19 a foot) and up. It may come in solid colors or, more often, speckled; and it's strong, low-stretch, doesn't seem to ravel too badly when carried in hanks, and has "high knotability."

I always carry four or five hanks, in 3- or 4-millimeter sizes, from about 2 to about 15 feet; and occasionally a 100-foot length (6 oz., $19).

No matter what lengths and thicknesses you choose to carry, remember that cut nylon always frays at the ends. To prevent fraying, simply fuse the ends into unravelable blobs by holding them briefly in the flame of match or stove. Hanks of all sizes can travel, easily available, in an outside pocket of your pack. Mine, for some reason, always go in the flap-top pocket.

Despite echoes from earlier pages, I think it's still worthwhile listing here—tidily bundled—some of the cord's proven multifarious uses:

- Rigging tents and allied shelters (pages 415–38)
- Clotheslines (page 564)
- Fish stringers
- Measuring lengths of fish and snakes, for later conversion to figures (mark with a knot)
- Tying socks to pack for drying
- Securing binoculars and camera—or, alternatively, hat—to pack by clip spring, so that if dislodged they cannot fall far (page 620)
- Belt for pants or for flapping poncho in high wind (page 546)
- Lowering pack down difficult places (page 657) or even pulling it up (Don't try to pull hand over hand; bend knees, pass cord belay-fashion around upper rump, straighten legs, take in slack, and repeat and repeat and repeat. . . .)
- Replacement binocular strap
- Chin band for hat (page 557)
- Lashing tent poles, fishing rod, or what-have-you to pack
- When there's no wire, hanging cooking pots over a fire, from a tree, for melting snow for water (This way you can build up a really big fire and keep warm at the same time. You do so, of course, in the uneasy knowledge that the cord may burn; but in practice, if you wet it occasionally, it doesn't seem to.)
- Wrapping around a jammed camera-case screw fitting, pulling, and so unjamming the screw for film changing
- Ditto with a jammed stove stopper (page 344)
- On packless side trips, tying poncho into lunch bundle (food, photo accessories, compass, etc.) and securing around waist (page 546)
- Makeshift loop sling for birdbook (page 673)
- On river crossings:
  (a) Lashing sleeping pad to pack
  (b) Lashing plastic sheet into virtually watertight bundle for protection of valuables, either as sanctum sanctorum of pack (page 691) or as lone floating bundle to be pushed ahead or towed on packless crossings (page 690), and

(c) Towing walking staff along behind
- Attaching flashlight to self at night with loop around neck (page 499)
- Replacing frayed gaiter underpinnings
- Spare bootlaces
- Lifting water from well in cooking pot—or from deep-cut creek (especially in snow)

Among uses I've had in mind for years but have never had occasion to try:
- Doubled or tripled or quadrupled, as "carabiner-type" loop for ensuring that doubled climbing rope used for rappeling (or roping down) can be recovered from below (page 658). Also (in extreme emergency only) as main rope for roping down low cliff: the cord might be weakened to danger point by knotting at top and by possible wear and would in any case be viciously uncomfortable even if used doubled or quadrupled.
- In river work, for pulling yourself back up against slow-to-medium river current—in case you find it necessary to float a short way past a blind headland to see if a safe land route lies ahead around dangerous rapids.

Most ordinary knots in nylon cord eventually slip. The only safe knot I know—and it's less difficult to tie and less bulky than it looks—is the fisherman's blood knot:

For permanent knots, burn-fuse all ends.*
Several readers have extolled the virtues of waxed nylon

Dental floss.

Acclaimed uses include: "most everything that nylon cord can be used for—plus fishing line"; attaching line guides to fishing rods; bind-

---

*CHIP: We once again considered a section on knots for all backpacking uses but rerejected the idea. It seems safe to say that people are either fascinated or turned off by knots. If you're fascinated, some basic books are: *The Essential Knot Book* by Colin Jarman (McGraw-Hill, 2000, $10); *Knots for the Outdoors* by Cliff Jacobson (Basic Essentials, 1999, $8); or *The Book of Camping Knots* by Peter Owen (The Lyons Press, 2000, $13).

ing around-the-neck nylon-cord loop to flashlight that lacks convenient hole; sewing thread; and toothbrush-eliminating dental care.

The only cavil: "low resistance to abrasion."

Most easily carried, primarily for teeth, in very small, ¼-oz. plastic caddy or wrapped around a card or in one of the larger tubes that it comes in—and which make good homes for needles. To prevent slippage, burn-fuse knot ends.

Rubber bands

For all-round usefulness, rubber bands rank second only to nylon cord. Their most vital function in my regimen is as weak and nonrestrictive garters for my turned-down socks, to keep stones and dirt out of the boots. Other uses: resealing opened food packages; closing food bags that are too full to be knotted at the neck; holding onionskin paper (for notes) to its rectangle of stiffening cardboard; and keeping notebook instantly openable at the current pages, front and rear (page 662).

Rubber bands have a habit of breaking and also of getting lost, and I recommend that if you use an E-frame pack and it has protruding arms, you wrap around them as many bands as you think you need ready for immediate use. Then add the same number again. Then put into a small plastic bag about 10 times as many as are on your packframe and put this reserve safely away inside the pack. Mine go into my "office" (page 663).

Plastic bags

I sometimes wonder what backpackers used as the interior walls of their houses before the days of plastic freezer bags. I use ordinary freezer, Ziploc, and OneZip bags in various sizes, including sandwich size, not only for almost every food item, but also, copiously and often double thickness, for wrapping many other things: camp moccasins, clothes (especially in wet weather), dirty socks, cooking pots, frying pan, book, rubber bands, matches, toilet gear, first-aid kit, film, camera accessories, toilet paper, spare flashlight cells, can opener, stove-nozzle cleaner, signal flare, fishing tackle, certain spare pack attachments, tarp clamps for plastic shelter, car key, and unburnable garbage. Also, sometimes, as a wallet, and even as a stove container bag. I often take along a few spare bags. Standard marine sample bags give extra-strong protection for special articles.

For details of bag sizes and uses, and hints on packing, see page 222. Ziploc and OneZip bags can double as pillows (page 486). And household trash bags can serve not only as food bags, pack liners (page 691), sleeping-bag protectors, foam-pad covers, and kilt (page 549) but also as a poncho (with arm and neck holes cut) and even bivouac bag and emergency shelter.

35-millimeter film cans/small plastic bottles

The old screw-top metal film cans made excellent containers. Current clip-on-top plastic versions look distrustable and are: I had one pop open in my pack at around 10,000 feet and spread Mautz Firepaste thin but wide. I also hear reports of squashings under pressure. And their blackness makes them eminently losable—though a red encircling tape helps. For most uses I now find the very small Nalgene bottles much safer.

Among candidate items for one or other of such small containers: salt tablets, salmon eggs for bait, and oil for lube jobs on hair and beard and even boots, not to mention for cooking. Also for odds and ends, including spare flashlight bulbs (if there's no place for them in flashlight), some strong button thread wound around a small piece of paper, and water-purifying and vitamin C tablets.

Film cans for 120 film are said to make useful makeshift matchsafes.

Belt clips/small carabiners

Swivel-mounted snap hooks on small woven nylon loops are useful for carrying certain items suspended from either your belt or the built-in waistband of your pants: a cup, in good drinking country (page 234); occasionally, your hat; the camera tripod or other light equipment, on packless side trips. Formerly brass or steel, such clips now come in high-impact plastic (Duraflex with nylon loop, ⅓ oz., $2–$3), alone or as an accessory with flashlights. But they seem to have given way to very small carabiners (about 2 inches long, 1 oz., $4).

If you use a belt clip while carrying the pack (for a cup, say), make sure you pass the hipbelt *inside* it; otherwise the belt's pressure may force the spring-loaded clip open. After a little while you find yourself flipping the cup outside automatically every time you put the pack on.

Strictly-personal-but-you'll-probably-have-your-own department

Everyone, I imagine, has little personal items that go along; they'll vary according to individual interests and frailties. Two very experienced friends of mine always carry small pliers. In addition to items I've already mentioned, such as "office" and prospector's magnifying glass, my list includes spare eyeglasses (sometimes) and (always) one or two wraparound elasticized bandages, Ace or similar. The bandages are primarily for a troublesome knee and for emergency use in case of a sprained ankle, but they've seen most use in thornbush and cactus country, wrapped puttee fashion around my bare and vulnerable lower legs (page 537).

LINKS-WITH-CIVILIZATION DEPARTMENT

Generally, the last thing you want to do out in wild country is to carry any item that helps maintain a link with civilization. But there are exceptions. For example, when it's more convenient and even cheaper to fly rather than drive to and from your chosen wilderness, you have to carry, all the way, some kind of suitable lightweight

Wallet.

The simplest and lightest is a small plastic bag. If that dissatisfies you, look in stores or catalogs for the now-popular Cordura versions. Into your choice you may want to put, according to the needs of the moment, some form of identification (driver's license is best, in case you need to drive), fishing license, and fire permit. Also some green money (although it's the most useless commodity imaginable once you're actually out in the wilderness). Consider traveler's checks too, and perhaps one or two bank checks as reserve. A credit or debit card may also be worthwhile: I once used mine to pay in advance for a short charter flight that put me down on a remote dirt road, and also for an airdrop of food that was to follow a week later.

A little cash may be worth taking along even when you'll be coming back to your car: late one fall, after a week in the mountains that ended with a fast, steep, 10,000-foot descent, I emerged with very sore feet onto a road 50 miles from my car, quickly hitched a ride in the right direction, and managed to persuade my benefactor that it was worth $5 for him to drive me several miles up a steep mountain road to where my car was parked.

Nowadays I always carry a few coins—in my "wallet" or taped to the cardboard stiffener of my "office" (page 663) or to my first-aid booklet. Few things are more frustrating than to emerge into man-country at last with a message heavy on your chest and find yourself at a remote telephone booth, coinless and therefore mute. Not all public phones can be dialed without coins and the charges assigned to a credit card or home phone number.

Car key

The obvious place to leave your car key is at the car—taped or magnet-attached to some secret corner of it, or simply hidden close by. But I once came back from a winter mountain trip and found the rear bumper of my car, with the key craftily magnet-attached inside it, buried under a 10-foot snowdrift. Fortunately, a freak of the wind had left a convenient alley along one side of the car and I was able to get at the key without too much difficulty. After that, rather to my surprise, I found that, at least on short trips, I tended to avoid vague worries about snow and torrential rain and landslides and thieves (human and other) by packing a key along with me, even though there's always one at the car, secreted away but attainable. Cached or carried, the key gets wrapped in the inevitable plastic bag.

Nowadays, burglar-alarm-and-unlocking remotes pose a mildly weightier problem. I find I normally pack mine along.

Cellular phones

CHIP: So far I've not yet seen anyone talking to their broker on a cell phone while walking a trail—but then I don't spend much time in Grand Teton National Park. When that unhappy event occurs, as I'm sure it will someday all too soon, I hope I don't react with any undue savagery. Still, as cell phones get smaller and cell-phone talkers more oblivious, one begins to wonder if it would be possible to swallow one. It could happen.

Already, rangers at Mount Rainier report a growing glut of cell-phone calls from high on the mountain itself. Along with electro-bleats for rescue, there are also a great many more asking for step-by-step route information or routine advice (e.g., *my stove won't start*). The problem, non-technologically speaking, is that many people call for assistance when they are not really in danger, placing an unfair burden on dispatchers and rescuers. And the concern, beyond burning out wilderness rangers—in general a solitude-loving group—is that such devices as GPS receivers and cell phones lend a false sense of security. The purpose of such electronica is to extend both our senses and our faculties. But the illusion of control, in turn, leads the techno-believers to stumble blindly into situations far beyond their experience and skill.

When I carried a Forest Service radio—exactly the size and weight of a brick—I found that to contact headquarters I usually had to be on a peak or ridgetop. I experimentally packed a cell phone on a recent trip into the wilderness where I'd rangered, to see if it was similarly ineffective. My route followed alpine valleys and canyon streams, and I found I could very seldom make a connection—I still had to climb to a ridge or peak, and have a line of sight to a receiving antenna. And if I can accomplish that—hell's bronze bells—*I don't need to be rescued.*

But with the dramatic calls from the doomed on Everest and a constant barrage of news items about dial-a-rescue incidents, the idea of the wireless phone as being a wilderness asset is now firmly embedded in the popular mind. Meanwhile, the towers required for wireless phone networks are desecrating high points all over the U.S., and demands are heard to place them in ever-remoter spots—even overlooking Grand Canyon. Networks using satellites rather than towers might solve the line-of-sight problem. But the emotional problem remains.

Being a pragmatical ape, I am not in any wise arguing about the utility of digitalia such as the tiny thermohygrometer I used to measure humidity in tents (page 387). Nor am I even doubting, really, the wisdom of carrying a wireless phone for that true—and fortunately very rare—backcountry emergency. In that situation, only a fool would not use one. Rather, my objection is to the inexorable (and insidious) enclosure of our senses in an ever-present electronic net.

Even in the howlingest remoteness, you can now get a precise set of directional coordinates from your GPS receiver, as you note the exact time on your digital watch. If the watch is one of those whizbang wrist computers, you can punch through a sequence of tiny buttons to find out the altitude, barometric pressure, temperature, and number of minutes since you last found out all the same things. But then what do you have?

You've got data—for the most part, numbers. Electronic gadgets are great at spewing numbers: you can, if you wish, record the air temperature at one-second intervals, with extreme precision. And by the same time the next day you have 86,400 extremely precise readings: a choking mass of data. But data, however useful, is not the same as experience.

Most of us who leave our homes to undertake long walks do so for the sake of experience. Of course, bellying down on a shag carpet in front of a television is also experience. So what we are seeking is not the mere passing of time, but something deeper. We seek the experience of walking, of course. But go to any city park and you can see your fellow citizens power walking, a sort of revved-up military march—around and around the asphalt strips that circle the close-cropped grass, and around.

So, healthful and virtuous as it may be, the physical act of walking itself is not the object.

The walk for which we go to such ends to undertake is not the dutiful circumambulation of a gym or a park, nor yet the preoccupied stroll of the window-shopper. Rather we choose a place that is passable yet only lightly marked by human works and pomps: seminatural, or perhaps comfortably wild. Our object in this is not that it passes us by like a movie, untouchably. Rather we hope that as we walk our chosen place will act on us in turn—a light wind at dawn, the scent of pine pitch, the roar of the creek.

When you're data-fying—checking a set of coordinates, a bearing, an altitude, a temperature, a barometric pressure—in physical point of fact you're hunched over staring at digits on a tiny screen.

If you step off the trail to unfold your pocket computer and uplink through your cell phone to check your e-mail for a message from your broker, your heart is a thousand miles away.

And the wilderness can have no part in you.

Housekeeping and Other Matters

ORGANIZING THE PACK

COLIN: Every backpacker eventually works out his own way of stowing gear into a pack, and it will probably be the one that best suits his equipment and techniques. But beginners may find some usable guidelines in the solutions that Chip and I have evolved. Although many of these solutions have appeared in earlier chapters it seems worthwhile to mention them here, more neatly gathered together. What we're trying to do, remember, is only to offer hints that may help beginners drift in the right direction: to provide guidelines, that is, not perpetuate idiosyncrasies.

The best way to stow your gear into your pack is to pursue, all the time, a reasonable compromise between convenience and efficient weight distribution.

For the main considerations in weight distribution and also the more precise requirements with I-frames, see page 168.

Common sense and a lick or two of experience will soon teach you the necessary refinements: after some angular item such as the stove has gouged into your back a couple of times you'll make sure, almost without thinking, that flat or soft articles pad the forward surface of the packbag's main compartment; and once you've put both the full canteens that you're carrying on the same side of the bag and found that the load then rides like a one-armed gorilla you're unlikely to repeat the mistake.

If you use a compartmented packbag your ideas on where things should go will clearly differ from those of a bloody-great-sack addict like me. But as my experience is almost entirely sackish, and because on the rare occasions I've used compartmented bags I found that the general principles held good, I'll speak purely from experience.

The most convenient way to stow gear varies from trip to trip, from day to day, from morning to evening. Obviously, the things you'll want first at the next halt should go in last. So the groundsheet will normally travel on top. In dry country, so will one canteen—though in sunny weather it should be covered with a down jacket or some other insulator. And the balance-of-the-week's-ration bag, the signal flare, reserve or empty canteens, and refills for a cartridge stove should—on the score of sheer convenience—languish down in the basement. Otherwise, the important thing is not where each item goes but that you always know where it is.

There'll be variations, of course. If rain threatens, your raingear must be on top and perhaps even sticking out, ready to be plucked into use. On cold evenings, have your heavy clothing ready to put on even before you start to make camp. If it looks as though you're going to have a long, torrid midday halt, make sure you don't have to dig down to the bottom of the packbag for plastic sheet or poncho before you can rig up an awning. But all this is just plain common sense.

I pad the forward side of my packbag with the polyethylene sit pad, or a small clothing item, or the "office," or with my camp shoes (soles facing out). In one forward corner of the main sack, fitting snugly against the packframe, go the gasoline container and usually, on top of it, the stove. If I'm carrying a second gasoline container and/or a portmanteau fishing rod, they fit into the opposite and similar corner.

There are few other firm rules for the main sack. Cooking pots and the food-for-the-day bag normally go side by side on the same level (because when I want one, I want the other), and they almost always ride high up. If space poses a problem a few small, allied, and relatively unharmable objects may travel inside the inner cooking pot, along with or in lieu of cup and spoon. Candidates include sugar and margarine containers, salt-and-pepper shaker—even my stove in its stuff sack. Otherwise, the packing arrangements depend largely on what items I expect to need next—given, of course, that I try to pack heavy articles close to the frame (see, again, page 168).

Many smaller items in my pack—particularly in the kitchen—travel in plastic bags (page 679). For stuff sacks, see pages 178 to 180 and—for The Small-Stuff-Sack Fallacy—page 489. Some people house almost everything in these light and convenient little bags; their packs become stuff-sack condominiums.

CHIP: Since, like Colin, I prefer undivided packs, the challenge is to assort the contents in some way other than a wholesale rummage. One good reason for stuff-sacking is that you can unload in rain or snow without wetting your payload. Having pitched camp several thousand times, I have a definite routine, as follows. First, I make sure of shelter. Quite often, I pack my sleeping bag, pad, bivy sac or groundsheet, and ultra-light shelter (like the Integral Designs SIL-tarp, page 394) in a single stuff sack or in the lower compartment (usually oversize for the light-weight sleeping bags I favor) of the I-frame pack. Beweathered, I can slide the shelter sack out and rezip the pack—no digging around. I keep dirt-magnet tent stakes in their own sack in an outside pocket. Then come food and drink. Pots, utensils, windscreen, and such have their own sack, with the fuel bottle in an outside pocket or plastic-bagged low and forward in the pack. The main food stash (subsacked in three or four 1-gallon zip-top bags) now occupies a Kevlar bear bag (Ursack, page 733). Spare clothes go in an Outdoor Research Cell Block, a rectangular zippered sack perfect for flat-folded duds. Puffy bits like fleece pullovers fill space at the top of the pack, rendering them accessible. Small things from snacks to water filter to toilet tissue that I need en route go in the top pocket, while raingear and other bulk items go in the rear pocket. Constant needs, like notebook, pencil, bug slather, sunscreen, and lip balm, in the Possum Pocket office-on-the-yoke.

The three levels of access are: IMMEDIATE (Possum Pocket or front pockets, tucked into yoke straps, or in the mesh water-bottle sleeves that can be reached without taking off the pack), QUICK (top and outside pockets), and SECURE (protected inside the main packbag).

Aside from conventional weight-distributive wisdom, the precise placement also depends on the pack I'm using. Panel-loading or hybrid packs, with their easy access, give more latitude to arrange gear for opti-mum weight distribution. Mountaineering packs—tall, tubular, and top-loading—should be packed with a gimlet eye to the order in which things come out. Some packs have pockets perfectly tailored for awkward stuff—the Arc'Teryx Bora 95 I use for winter struggles has a full-length rear pocket that holds (and drains, via a bottom grommet) an iced-up tent and fly. These would otherwise get snagged, if tied on the outside, or melt-moisten all else, if stuffed in the main bag. Other problem gear best stowed outboard includes tent stakes, tent poles, ice axes and crampons, and fishing rods. Since these things most often come with their own sacks, stitching on a tab with paired D-rings or Velcro can wed them to your pack.

The ideal is to evolve a seamless relationship between your pack, your gear, and the sort of trip you prefer. The corollary is that the more variation you take on in gear and trips, the more likely you'll be to have several packs. Which in turn means you'll be constantly juggling the whats and wheres. If there's a stunning disadvantage to testing many new packs, as this book demands, it's that lack of stumble-around-in-the-dark familiarity with the house on your back.

COLIN: The only radical changes in organizing the pack come at

RIVER CROSSINGS.

Crossing small creeks is mostly a simple matter, and raises no problems. You can often make it across dry-shod, on the tops of boulders that are clear of the water or slightly awash. A staff to aid balance is often a godsend. If you're wearing boots with no tread on the insteps you must make every effort to avoid the natural tendency of beginners, uncertain of their balance, to plant the instep of the boots on the curving summit of each boulder. Boots with treaded insteps make the need for such avoidance less obvious; but I still believe the ball of the foot is, in most cases, the part to plant—because it keeps you more delicately on balance.

Sometimes, of course, failing a natural log bridge or stepping-stones, you have to take off your boots and wade. At least, I do. Some people keep their boots on, but I mistrust the effect on boots and feet. Or perhaps I just mean that I abhor the idea of squelching along afterward. On easy crossings, carry your boots, with socks pushed inside. Knot the laces together and twist them around one wrist. On deeper crossings, hang the lace-linked boots on the pack. In really difficult places it's safer to stuff them inside the packbag. Sometimes you can wade in bare feet, with safety and reasonable comfort; but if your camp shoes have good-grip soles and also dry out quickly you'll often be glad to protect your feet in them.

A friend once suggested a method he uses regularly for fast and rocky rivers: take off socks, replace boots, wade river with well-protected feet, replace socks, and go on your happy and reputedly unsquelching way. Somehow, I've yet to try it out. I unfancy wet boots. If you're fishing and have waders, the problem vanishes. A possible lightweight substitute: large plastic trash bags loosely tied over each leg.

CHIP: I've tried the socks-off/boots-on method. In shallow streams, if you dash across, it works well enough—if your boots are well waterproofed and also snug enough around the tops that water doesn't funnel in. Otherwise, or in the event of repeated crossings, the insides of your boots will get wet: Blister City. A slicker approach is to carry synthetic-webbed sandals as camp shoes (page 78) and use them to wade creeks, bogs, and other water hazards. Where coarse cobbles, continuous wading, and chill water combine to peg your pain meter, a pair of neoprene or waterproof/breathable (page 93) socks will save not only your feet but in the long run your boots, which can ride high and dry in your pack.

COLIN: Provided you choose the right places you can wade surprisingly large rivers. (Fast rivers, that is, where the depth and character vary; slow, channeled rivers are normally unwadable.) It often pays to make an extensive reconnaissance along the bank in order to select a good crossing point. In extreme cases you may even need to detour for a mile or more. Generally, the safest places are the widest and, up to a point, the fastest. Most promising of all, provided the water is shallow enough and not too fierce, tend to be the fanned-out tails of wide pools. Boulders or large stones, protruding or submerged, in fairly shallow water may also indicate a good crossing place: they break the full force of racing water, and you can ease across the most dangerous places on little mounds of stone and gravel that have been deposited in the slack water behind each boulder. But always, before you start across, pick out in detail, with coldly cynical eyes, a route that looks tolerably safe—all the way. Try to choose a route with any questionable steps early, not over where you would, if turned back, have to recross most of the river. And avoid getting into any position you can't retreat from.

Experience is by far the most important aid to safe wading (I wish I had a lot more), but there are a few simple rules. Use a staff—particularly with a heavy pack. (It turns you, even more crucially than on dry land, from an insecure biped into a confident triped.) In fast current the safest route for walking, other things being equal, is one that angles down and across the current. The faster and deeper the water, the more sharply downstream you should angle. The next-best attack is up and across. Most hazardous of all—because the current can most easily sweep you off balance—is a directly-across route.

Unless you're afraid of being swept off your feet (and in that case you'd almost certainly do better to find a deep, slow section and swim across), wading doesn't call for any change in the way you pack. But before you start across you should certainly undo your waistbelt. Always. The pack (at least until it fills with water) is much more buoyant than your body and should you fall in it will, if held in place by the belt, force you under. It's easy enough to wriggle out of a shoulder yoke, particularly if it's slung over only one shoulder. At least, I have always liked to imagine so, and a reader's letter confirms my faith. She and her husband were wading a turbulent stream in Maine—waistbelts undone and hanging free—when she lost her bare footing and was swept downstream. She quickly squirmed free of the harness and within 50 feet, still hanging on to the pack, grabbed a boulder and pulled herself to safety. Afterward she realized that having her waistbelt undone had been "a great thing."

The only other precaution I sometimes take when wading, and then only at difficult crossings, is to unhitch camera and binoculars from the packframe and put them inside the pack.

But if you have to swim a river you must reorganize the pack's contents.*

The first time I tried swimming with a pack was on my Grand Canyon journey, in 1963. Because of the new Glen Canyon Dam, 100 miles upriver, the Colorado was then running at only 1200 cubic feet per second—far below its normal low-water level. Even for someone who, like me, is a poor and nervous swimmer, it seemed comparatively easy to swim across a slow, deep stretch with little danger of being swept down over the next rapids. I adopted the technique developed by the one man who had been able to help me with much information about hiking in remote parts of the Canyon. Harvey Butchart was a math professor at Arizona State College in Flagstaff. He was also, his wife said, "like a seal in the water." And he had found that by lying across his air mattress with the pack slung over one shoulder, half floating, he could, even at high water, dog-paddle across the Colorado—third-longest river in the United States and muscled accordingly. I tried his method out on several same-side detours, when sheer cliffs blocked my way, and by degrees I gained confidence in it.**

The air mattress made a good raft. Inflated not too firmly, it formed a reassuring V when I lay with my chest across it. I used it first on a pack-less reconnaissance. Remembering how during World War II we had crossed rivers by wrapping all our gear in waterproof anti-gas capes and making bundles that floated so well we could just hang on to them and kick our way forward, I wrapped the few clothes and stores I needed in a white plastic sheet (page 426) and lashed it firmly with nylon cord. It floated well. I found that by wrapping a loose end of cord around one arm I could tow it along beside me and dog-paddle fairly freely.

With the pack—an E-frame—dog-paddling turned out to be a little more restricted but still reasonably effective. The pack, slung over my left shoulder and half-floating, tended at first to keel over. But I soon found

---

*I've been taken to task for not warning you that my swimming lessons mostly apply to large desert rivers. Fast mountain rivers are generally too cold for this kind of thing. The warnings were there all right in all earlier editions, at the end of this section. But I'm now playing safe and injecting a reference to it here at the start: please read with care the last paragraph of this section, page 696.

**Harvey, after reading the first edition of this book, wrote: "I never intended to let the pack hang from one shoulder, floating in the water. This happened only by accident on two or three occasions, when I was upset. Intentionally, I have only two positions on the air mattress: crosswise—as you used your shortie—when in rough water; and lengthwise under me in calm water. If I switch positions before reaching the waves, I am reasonably sure of keeping the pack in position."

I'm glad, though, that I got it wrong. The prof specializes in two- and three-day trips, carrying relatively light packs. I found my heavy burden an impossible shoulder load when I was waterborne. But you might like to try a light pack that way.

that I could hold it steady by light pressure on the lower and upper ends of the packframe with buttocks and bald patch. It sounds awkward but worked fine.

My staff floated along behind at the end of 3 feet of nylon cord tied to the packframe. Everything else went into the pack. I had waterproofed the seams of the packbag rather hurriedly, and I found that water still seeped through. So into the bottom of the bag went bulky and buoyant articles that water couldn't damage: canteens, cooking pots, and white-gas container. Things better kept dry went in next, wrapped in the white plastic sheet. Items that just had to stay dry went on top, in what I thought of as the sanctum sanctorum: camera and accessories, flashlight and spare batteries, binoculars, watch, writing materials, and toilet paper. I tied each of these items into a plastic bag, rolled them all inside the sleeping bag, and stuffed it into the big, tough plastic bag that usually went around the cooking pots. Then I wrapped the lot in my poncho. Before strapping the packbag shut I tied the ends of the poncho outside the white plastic sheet with nylon cord. (On one trial run the pack had keeled over and water had run down inside the plastic sheet, though the sanctum had remained inviolate.) On the one complete river crossing that I had to make, nothing got even damp.

This system, or some variation of it, should prove adequate for crossing almost any river that is warm enough, provided you don't have to go through heavy rapids. I am more than half-scared of water and a very poor swimmer, and if I can succeed with it almost anyone can. The great practical advantage of this method is that you don't have to carry any special equipment. All you need is an air mattress, a poncho, and a plastic sheet or a groundsheet.

The method, by the way, turns out to be less than brand-new. A Washington State reader has shared this depiction of troops crossing a river on inflated skins—from an Assyrian relief of about 800 B.C.

Heavy rapids present a different problem. In May 1966 I took a two-week hike-and-swim trip down 70 miles of the Colorado, in Lower Grand Canyon. Although many people had run the Canyon by boat it seemed that everyone had until then had the sense to avoid attempting this very enclosed stretch on foot; but I knew from boatmen's reports that even if the route proved possible I would almost certainly have to make several river crossings. I also knew that, with the reservoir now part-filled behind Glen Canyon Dam, the river was racing down at an average of about 16,000 cubic feet per second—more than 12 times its volume on my 1963 trip. That meant I would almost certainly be carried far downstream each time I attempted a crossing. Even the calmer stretches would be swirling, whirlpooled horrors, and I'd probably be carried through at least some minor rapids. Under such conditions I wasn't willing to risk the lying-across-an-air-mattress technique, and I evolved a new method, more suitable for a timid swimmer.

Just before the trip I bought an inflatable life vest (by Stebco—no

longer available). It was made of bright yellow rubberized cotton fabric, with a valve for inflation by mouth and also a small metal cartridge that in an emergency filled the vest with carbon dioxide the instant you pulled a toggled cord. The vest yoked comfortably around the neck so that when you floated on your back your mouth was held clear of the water. When I tried it out in a side creek as soon as I reached the Colorado, I found that I could also swim very comfortably in the normal position. From the start I felt safe and confident.

I'd already decided that rather than lie across the air mattress I would this time rely solely on the life vest to keep me afloat—partly because I was afraid the vest's metal cartridge or its securing wire might puncture the mattress, but even more because I didn't fancy my chances of staying on the mattress in swirling water. (A young fellow crossing the Colorado on a trip with my math-professor friend had been swept off his mattress by a whirlpool and had drowned.) I decided that in fast water the trick would be to make the pack buoyant in its own right, and just pull or push it along with me.

The coated nylon fabric of the packbag was fully waterproof but, although I'd applied seam sealant, water still seeped in. So I decided to try to keep the pack as upright as I could in the water and stow the really vital gear, well protected, up near the top. First, for extra buoyancy high up, I put one empty plastic quart-size canteen in each of the upper sidepockets. Into the bottom of the bag as ballast went the two cooking pots and two half-gallon canteens, all filled with water. Next I lined the remaining space in the main sack with my transparent polyethylene groundsheet and left the unused portion hanging outside. Like all groundsheets, mine had developed many small holes, but I figured it would ward off the worst of any water that might seep in from the upper seams or under the flap, and that what little did get through would collect harmlessly in the bottom of the pack. The items that water couldn't damage (page 691) went in first. Next, those preferably kept dry. Then I made the sanctum sanctorum. Into the white plastic sheet (because rain was unlikely, I carried no poncho this trip) went all the things that just had to stay dry (as on page 691). Most of them were additionally protected inside an assortment of plastic bags. I lashed the white bundle firmly with nylon cord, put it on top of everything else, then folded over the unused portion of the groundsheet that was still hanging outside and carefully tucked it in between the main portion of the groundsheet and the packbag itself. I knotted down the pack flap, tight. Then I partially inflated my air mattress and lashed it securely with nylon cord to the upper half of the pack, taking care to keep it central. Finally, I took the 4-foot agave-stem walking staff that I'd cut at the start of the trip (page 101) and wedged it down into the cross-webbing of the packframe, close beside one upright.

I held the pack upright in the water for several minutes, forcing it down so that water seeped in and filled the bottom 7 or 8 inches—thereby helping, I hoped, to keep the pack upright. Then I slid down into the river beside it. With my left hand I grasped the lowest crossrung of the packframe and pulled downward. Provided I maintained a slight downward pressure (see illustration) the pack floated fairly upright, though tending to lean away from me, and I was free to swim in any position with one arm and both legs.

In addition to the inflatable vest I wore my ultralightweight nylon swimming trunks (page 556). I'd brought them because at the start, at the side creek in which I practiced, there was a possibility of meeting people. But I found that I actually wore the trunks on all crossings—to give me at least some protection from the sun if I became separated from the pack. And so that I could still light a fire in that unlikely event, I tied the waterproof matchsafe (page 285) onto the vest.

The whole rig worked magnificently. I made four crossings. The white plastic sheet hardly ever got damp, even on the outside, and the sanctum remained bone-dry, every time. So, mostly, did all other items stowed near the top of the pack. Because I could swim freely, I always got across the river reasonably fast. Each time I could have landed within half a mile of my launch site; but twice I allowed myself to be carried a little farther down to good landing places. (And as I floated down the calmer stretches on my back, with both feet resting on the packframe in front of me—my mind and body utterly relaxed, and an integral part of the huge, silent, flowing river—I found that I had discovered a new and serene and superbly included way of experiencing the Grand Canyon of the Colorado.)

I also made two same-side river detours around impassable cliffs. And one of these detours was the high point of the trip.

For the first 50 feet of the rapid I had to go through (Lower Lava Falls), the racing water battered on its left flank into a jagged rockwall. I knew that the thing I absolutely had to do was to keep an eye on this rockwall and make sure that if I swung close I fended off in time with arm or pack or legs. From the bank, the steep waves in the heart of the rapid didn't look too terrifying: not more than 3 or 4 feet high at most. But throughout the double eternity during which I swirled and wallowed through those waves—able to think of nothing except "Is it safe to grab a breath now, before I go in under that next one?"—I knew vividly and for sure that not one of them was less than $57\frac{1}{2}$ feet high. And all I saw of the rockwall was a couple of split-second glimpses—like a near-subliminal inner-thought flash from a movie.

I missed the rockwall, though—through no effort of mine—and came safely through the rapid. A belch or two in midriver cleared the soggy feeling that came from the few mouthfuls of Colorado I'd shipped; and once I got into calmer water and had time to take a look at the pack it seemed serenely shipshape. (In the rapid, frankly, I hadn't even known that I was still hanging on to it.)

The only problem now, in the fast water below the rapid, was getting back to the bank. It took me a full mile to do so.

At first I had to stay in midriver to avoid protruding rocks at the edge of another and only slightly less tumultuous rapid. Then, after I'd worked my way close to the bank, I was swept out again by tailwash from a big, barely submerged boulder. Almost at once I saw a smooth, sinister gray wave ahead, rising up out of the middle of the river. I knew at once what it was. Furiously, I swam toward the bank. A few strokes and I looked downstream once more. The wave was 5 times closer now, 10 times bigger. And I knew I could not avoid it. Just in time, I got into position with the pack held off to one side and my legs out in front of me, high in the water and slightly bent. Then I was rising up, sickeningly, onto the crest of the wave. And then I was plummeting down. As I fell, my feet brushed, very gently, over the smooth, hard surface of the hidden boulder. Then a white turmoil engulfed me. But almost instantly my head was out in the air again and I was floating along in calmer water. For a moment or two the pack looked rather waterlogged; but long before I made landfall, a couple of hundred yards downstream, it was once more floating high. When I unpacked I found the contents even drier than on some of the earlier and calmer crossings.

After those rapids and that boulder, I feel I can say that my fastwater river-crossing technique works.

That trip was something of a special case, but it taught me a useful lesson: if you have to swim a river, and have no air mattress and no inflatable vest, rig your pack somewhat after the manner I did. It will float buoyantly, and vital items will travel safely in the sanctum sanctorum. (I'm fairly sure my air mattress didn't "float" the pack, but only helped hold it upright at stressful moments.) Pull down on the bottom crossbar of the frame and swim alongside or in front or behind (in swirling water you'll do all three within seconds). A fair swimmer would have no difficulty, I imagine, in any reasonably unbroken water. And if, like me, you're a weak swimmer you could almost certainly keep yourself afloat and moving across the current by just hanging on to the pack and kicking. But if it's at all possible, try out unproven variations like this beforehand—preferably well ahead of time; or, failing that, in calm, safe water before the main attempt.

A reader suggests that for short emergency swims "a pair of tough (3 mil) plastic bags, blown up and tied or secured with rubber bands or nylon string, are very handy" for pack or person.

Don't forget that water temperature can be treacherous in river crossings. Even when you're wading, cold water can numb your feet and legs to danger point with astonishing speed. And no one can swim for long in liquid ice—can't even live in it for very long. Yet your body will work efficiently for a considerable time in 50°F water. During my 1963 Grand Canyon journey the Colorado River temperature was around 60°. On the 1966 trip it averaged about 57°, and although the water always felt perishing cold when I first got into it (which was hardly surprising, with shade temperatures rising each day to over 100°, and precious little shade anywhere) I was never once, even on the longest swim, at all conscious of being cold.

CHIP: There's an ingenious what-the-hell streak in Colin's tale that appeals to me, especially in these times of prefabricated solutions and trumped-up adventures.

In any event, nouveau gear has made deepwater crossings a lot less laborious. Available from paddling and rafting suppliers are waterproof drybags that will swallow a large pack. Cascade Designs and others make drybags with straps and hipbelts that can stand in for a regular pack (sort-of-ly anyhow—the ones I've tried are bad monkeys with any load over 35 lbs.—see page 167). And VauDe, a German firm, makes a comfortable full-suspension internal-frame backpack with waterproof roll closures (also page 167).

Along with river crossings, the application is *canyoneering,* a specialized form of backpacking through narrow canyons where pools, cascades, and even waterfalls are part of the route. Besides tumbles, flash floods are the major hazards. Several mass drownings—of Boy Scouts and guided parties—have recently made the news. Most who died resolutely ignored both weather warnings and common sense—I'd study a map of the entire watershed and err on the side of caution. I've relished some multiday walk/wade/swims on the Colorado Plateau with no mishaps, except mild tendinitis from cold spring runoff. The Fletcher pack-floating method holds true, with a drybag much more buoyant and rugged than a wrapped E-frame (most drybags float a damn sight better than they carry). If you wear a neoprene wetsuit for cold water, you can also use it to cush up your sleeping pad at night (direct contact, though, will dampen your sleeping bag).

Since people throw in a rope for stream crossings without much idea how to use it, the other observation is that it's screamingly easy to get into trouble, especially where there's a fast current and any sort of obstruction: boulders, down trees, or brush. If you lasso a tree, tie the rope around your waist, and launch straight across, you can get jerked off your feet and end up spinning like a trolling lure, unable to disengage. A short course in belay technique or whitewater rescue can hone your applied-physics grasp of what's what.

Two friends who carried a rope on a go-for-broke snowmelt traverse in the Wind Rivers ended up using it only once: to lash a log between the top fork of a cottonwood tree and a cliff, about 30 feet above a raging creek. There was just enough rope left to belay the scary balance-beam steps across. "Falling wasn't an option," said one afterward.

SANITATION

COLIN: (*Note:* Except for the paragraph on trowels, this section stands much as I wrote it 30-odd years ago. But it's now 30 times as important: our burgeoning numbers have had hideous impact. See, sadly and specifically, giardiasis, page 235. The ignorance of some newcomers about how to operate in wilderness has made a sad, self-righteous mockery of my words about the respect normally accorded the earth by those who undertake demanding journeys, but I'll let the words stand, as a goad.)

Sanitation is not a pleasant topic, but every camper must for the sake of others consider it openly, his mind unblurred by prudery.

At one extreme there's the situation in which permanent johns have been built. Always use them. If they exist, it means that the human population, at least at certain times of year, is too dense for any other healthy solution. (The National Park Service calculates that 500 people using a leach-line-system permanent john will pollute a place no more than one person leaving untreated feces, even buried.)

A big party camping in any kind of country, no matter how wild, automatically imposes a dense population on a limited area. They should always dig deep latrine holes and, if possible, carry lime or some similar disinfectant that will counteract odor, keep flies away, and hasten decomposition. And they must fill holes carefully before leaving.

A party of two or three in a remote area—and even more certainly a man on his own—must make simpler arrangements. But with proper "cat sanitation" and due care and consideration in choice of sites, no problem need arise.

"Cat sanitation" means doing what a cat does, though more efficiently: digging a hole and covering up the feces afterward. But it must be a hole, not a mere scratch. Make it at least 4 or 5 inches deep, and preferably 6 or 8. But do not dig down below topsoil into inert-looking earth where insects and decomposing bacteria will be unable to work properly. In some soils you can dig easily enough with your boots or a stick. I used to carry my sheath knife along whenever I went looking for a cat-john site, and used it if necessary for digging. Then I came across one of the plastic toilet trowels (10 inches long, 2 oz., $2) that now appear in many catalogs. At first I was merely amused. But I found that the trowel digs quickly and well and means you can cat-sanitate effectively in almost any soil. Now I always pack it along. Because these little trowels remind as well as dig, I'm tempted to suggest they be made obligatory equipment for everyone who backpacks into a national park or forest. I resist the temptation, though—not only because (human nature being what it is, thank God) any such ordinance would drive many worthy people in precisely the undesired direction but also because blanket decrees are foreign to whatever it is a man goes out into wilderness to seek, and bureaucratic decrees are worst of all because they tend to accumulate and perpetuate and harden when they're administered, as they so often are, by people who revel in enforcing petty ukases. Anyway, a rule that's impossible to enforce is a bad rule. And this one has been tried: a young reader of 89 has drawn my attention to Deuteronomy 23, verse 13 (see Appendix VI, page 816).

Your kosher plastic paddle can come in useful, by the way, when you have to melt snow for water (page 370). Conversely, a 10-inch, angled aluminum snow-peg (page 421) makes a fair toilet trowel: for digging in hard soil, pad it at the top with your ubiquitous bandanna.

In the double plastic bags that hold my roll of toilet paper lives a book of matches. I tear one match off ready beforehand and leave it protruding from the book, so that I need handle the book very little; and unless there's a severe fire hazard, when I've finished I burn all the used paper. The flames not only destroy the paper but char the feces and discourage flies. Afterward I carefully refill the hole. Unless the water situation is critical I have soap and an opened canteen waiting in camp for immediate hand-washing.

A hardy friend of mine suggests as substitutes for paper "soft grass, ferns, and broad leaves, and even the tip of firs, redwoods, etc."

In choosing a john site, remember above all that you must be able to dig. Rock is not acceptable. Rock is not acceptable. Rock is not acceptable. I am driven to reiteration by the revolting memory of a beautiful rock-girt creek in California, a long hour from roadhead but heavily fished and traveled. And that raises the only other absolute rule: always go at least 50 feet, and preferably 500, from any watercourse, even if currently dry. Soil filters; but it demands time and space. The rest is largely a matter of considering other people. Wherever possible, select tucked-away places that no one is likely to use for any purpose. But do not appropriate a place so neatly tucked away that someone may want to camp there. A little thoughtful common sense will be an adequate guide.*

All other things being equal, choose a john with a view.

*CHIP: Variations on the trusty little trowel can be had in stainless steel (U Dig It, 6 oz., $25) or with a trapdoor handle that holds a compact roll of toilet paper (Digajon, 3 oz., $10.50; paper refills, three-pack, $3.50).

When I was sampling lakes in the Wind Rivers and camping repeatedly in the same spots, I experimented a bit. My supermodified technique is to dig as above, using a stick or rock rather than a trowel—because after I shit, said stick or stone is wielded to mix soil, leaves, etc., with my deposit. Disgusting? Maybe so, but if you can mix soil in and (even better) pee on the result before covering it up, it will decompose much more quickly than if you just torch the paper and bury it. Because of my work, I was able to observe and even reuse my "experimental sites" for several years. Mixing made a big difference—even toilet tissue composted in a few weeks. But many experts now recommend packing out all tissues, wipes, and similar conveniences. A reusable plastic container (Tupperware, Rubbermaid, etc.) seems best for this. But since fecal waste isn't allowed in landfills, you either have to wait and flush what's flushable—or burn it.

Around this same time, outdoor schools began teaching pilgrims to smear their personal waste products on sunny boulders in order to hasten decomposition. Which it does. But decomposition being what it is, a group of 20 using this bravura technique had a considerable effect (you want disgusting?). A regulatory backlash developed and the practice is now disrecommended except in the remotest and rockiest spots.

In deep snow there's unfortunately nothing you can do except dig a hole, burn the paper, cover the hole, and afterward refuse to think about what will happen come hot weather. There's not much you can do, either, about having to expose your fundamentals to the elements. Actually, even in temperatures well below freezing, it turns out to be a surprisingly undistressing business for the brief interval necessary, especially if you have a tent to crawl back into. Obviously, blizzard conditions and biting cold may make the world outside your tent unlivable, even for brief intervals, but a good-size vestibule would solve this problem. For footwear when scrambling out of a tent in snow, see page 553.

It's horrifying how many people, even under conditions in which cat sanitation is easy, fail to observe the simple, basic rules. Failure to bury feces is not only barbaric; it's a danger to others. Flies are everywhere. And the barbarism is compounded by thoughtless choice of sites. I still remember the disgust I felt when, late one rainy mountain evening several years ago, I found at last what looked like an ideal campsite under a small overhanging rockface—and then saw, dead center, a cluster of filthy toilet paper and a naked human turd.

That rockledge was in a fairly remote area. The problem can be magnified when previously remote countryside is opened up to people unfit to use it. Powerboats now cruise far and wide over Powell Reservoir—officially Lake Powell—behind the Colorado's Glen Canyon Dam, and the boats' occupants are able to visit with almost no effort many ancient and fascinating Indian cliff dwellings. Before the dam was built these dwellings could be reached only by extensive foot or fastwater journeys. Now people who undertake such demanding journeys have usually (though not always) learned, through close contact with the earth, to treat it with respect—and powerboats do not bring you in close contact with the earth. I hear that most of the cliff dwellings near Powell Reservoir have now been used as toilets.*

Urination is a much less serious matter. But dense and undisciplined human populations can eventually create a smell, and although this problem normally arises only in camping areas so crowded that you might as well be on Main Street, it can also do so with locally concentrated use, especially in hot weather and when the ground is impervious to liquids. During my first Grand Canyon journey I camped on one open rockledge for four days. As the days passed, the temperature rose. On the fourth day, with the thermometer reaching 80°F in the shade—and 120° in my

---

*CHIP: Rather than cloud the reputation of the brave Major Powell, I refer to this unnatural body of water as Dominy Sump, acknowledging Floyd Dominy, former commissioner of the U.S. Bureau of Reclamation, for his part in this particular crime against nature.

unshaded camp—I several times detected whiffs of a stale odor that made me suspect I was near the lair of a large animal. I was actually hunting around for the lair when I realized that only one large animal was living on that rockledge.

But urination is usually no more than a minor inconvenience—even for those who, like me, must have been in the back row when bladders were given out. An obvious precaution is to cut down on drinking at night. No tea for me, thank you, with dinner. Yet I rarely manage to get through a night undisturbed. Fortunately, it's surprising how little you get chilled when you stand up for a few moments on quite cold nights, even naked. I go no farther than the foot of my sleeping bag, and just aim at the night (hence the "animal lair" at that rocky Grand Canyon campsite). A distaff reader wrote asking if I have any useful advice for her on this subject. Regretfully, I could offer only commiseration. But technology has now leapt into the breach (or breeches—see Chip's portion below).

And a man wrote reminding me of the Eskimo who "reaches for his urinal and without leaving the bag captures another increment for tomorrow's emptying ceremony." I duly bought a widemouth plastic bottle and have used it with total success, kneeling up, in a tent. But not, oddly enough, lying down in my bag, à la Eskimo: I find I plain fail to produce. Such a block is apparently not uncommon among the house-trained.

CHIP: The pee-jug is a winter-mountaineering institution—and so are tales about leakage, explosion-by-freezing, and the like. Meanwhile Campmor carries the Little John portable urinal for $6 and the Travel John with an "absorbent pouch that turns urine . . . into a biodegradable, odorless, self-contained Gel Bag for spill-proof disposal," also $6—reader comment invited. For womyn and grrrls, two devices in the Campmor catalog offer, if not perfect delicacy, at least some distance: the Freshette system is a form-fitting funnel that can be used with a tube for stand-up gigs or with special disposable bags in a tent (with pouch and 12 bags, $20). Similar but bagless is the Lady J, "for situations where restroom facilities are unavailable or unsanitary" ($7).

Only a minority of women readers seem to have tried these devices, and those I asked either raved (awesome!) or abominated (disgusting, never again!). The problem, one user informs me, is this: "If your rate of flow into the thing exceeds the outflow through the nozzle, you'll wet yourself—and then have to deal with both a dripping funnel and dripping pubes." My questions about aim were shrugged off.

Lady J

A related and more popular development is clothing with strategically placed zippers, such as the P-System tights and pants from Wild Roses (page 531).

A full-monty technical update (and light scatological humor) can be found in Kathleen Meyer's instant classic *How to Shit in the Woods: An Environmentally Sound Approach to a Lost Art.*

If you flinched at my (footnoted) mixmaster routine, you'll attain full shudder at this: in some heavily used areas the fecal blizzard has gotten so bad that you are now required to collect and pack out your own. A "poop tube" developed by Mark Butler of the National Park Service consists of 4-inch PVC pipe with a cap on one end and a threaded plug at the other (look in the plumbing section of your local hardware store), retained by a duct-taped piece of webbing. You poop in a paper bag and then load it into the tube (like those Civil War cannoneers in the movies). This is not as bad as it sounds, and the Germans are way ahead of us Yanks in this department. I tested one of VauDe's Wilderness Waste Systems, a 26-by-11-inch drybag with a roll closure at either end, in a 10-liter model (8 oz., $23). There's also a 15-liter size (11 oz., $30)—designed not only for terrestrial waste scenarios but also for kayakers who can't cram a river potty in. One end (IN) has a white plastic tab, the other (OUT) a black one. The instructions urge you to deploy a paper sack, dump in some sand to absorb moisture, excrete, drop in the tissues, and then file it. Unless you have pinpoint aim, the best bags are wide and short (get produce bags and trim off the tops—about 2 per oz.). Producers of polished pellets can, I suppose, deposit them on the ground and then scoop them into the sack. Since sand is both heavy and not very absorbent—and I was camping on snow—I carried sawdust in a zip-top (8 oz. lasts five days or so). Kitty litter also serves. Of course, any dry organic litter does the trick.

Most people hang the thing outside the pack using the plastic Ds on the white end. The one I used didn't seep (the horror, the horror), but if the sun is hot, the bag may inflate somewhat with methane—also known as natural gas—and you'd be wise to vent it promptly, away from fire or flame. (To suffer the explosive combustion of your toilet bag would indeed be a wretched fate—a piece of reflective space blanket or a box-wine bladder with the ends cut off will keep things cooler.) Back at the trailhead, you get a jug of water, find the nearest appropriate facility, unroll the black end—carefully, carefully—and dis-bag the contents. Then undo the white end and sluice water through to rinse and drain, resealing for transport. An eventual scrub and sanitizing is recommended.

Has it come to this?

Jawohl!

REPLENISHING SUPPLIES

COLIN: On extended trips you always face the problem of how to replenish your supplies. Generally speaking, you can't carry food for more than a week, or maybe two (page 222). Other items also need replacement: stove fuel, toilet paper, other toilet articles, perhaps powder and rubbing alcohol for your feet. You'll probably need additional film too, and new maps and replacement equipment and even special gear for certain sections of the trip.

Outposts of civilization

On my six-month California walk I was able to plan my route so that I called in every week or 10 days at remote country post offices. Before the trip I had mailed ahead to each of these post offices not only a batch of maps for the stretch of country ahead but also items of special gear, such as warm clothing for the first high mountain beyond the desert. I wrote each postmaster explaining what I was doing and asking him to hold all packages for me until at least a reasonable time after my estimated date of arrival. At each post office I mailed to the old Ski Hut, back in Berkeley, a list of the food and equipment I wanted to pick up two weeks later; and a list of film and personal requirements went to a reliable friend. So at each post-office call-in I found waiting for me everything I needed for the next leg of the journey.

These calls at outposts of civilization provided a change of diet too: there was always a store near the post office, and usually a café and a motel. I often stayed a day or two in the motel to write and mail a series of newspaper articles (and also to soak in several hot showers and cold beers). Exposed film went out in the mails, and completed notes, and sometimes equipment I no longer needed. All in all, the system worked very well. It could be adapted, with modifications to suit the needs of the moment, for many kinds of walking trips. (I used it successfully on my six-month, 1700-mile raft trip in 1989–1990. See *River: One Man's Journey Down the Colorado, Source to Sea.*)

In wild areas you have to replenish by other means. One way is to make

Caches

On the California walk I put out several water caches at critical points, and at one or two of them I also left a few cans of food. Later I realized that I should have left at least a day's nondehydrated food, for a treat—and possibly some dehydrated food for the way ahead so that I could have cut down my load.

I was able to put those caches out by car, on little-used dirt roads, but on most wilderness trips you have to pack the stuff in ahead of time. On the two-month Grand Canyon trip I put out two caches of water, food, and other supplies. From the purely logistic standpoint I should have carried these caches far down into the Canyon so that on the trip itself I wouldn't have to detour. But there is, thank God, more to walking than logistics. I'd been dreaming about the Canyon for a year, and one of the prime concerns in all my planning was to shield the dream from familiarity—that sly and deadly anesthetic. As I wrote in *The Man Who Walked Through Time,* "I knew that if I packed stores down into the Canyon I would be 'trespassing' in what I wanted to be unknown country; but I also knew that if I planted the caches outside the Rim I would in picking them up break both the real and symbolic continuity of my journey. In the end I solved the dilemma by siting each cache a few feet below the Rim."

Such delicate precautions should, I think, always be borne in mind when one of the aims of a backpacking trip, recognized or submerged, is to explore and immerse yourself in unknown country. You must avoid any kind of preview. Before my Grand Canyon trip several people said, "Why not fly over beforehand, low? That's the way to choose a safe route." But I resisted the temptation—and in the end was profoundly thankful I'd done so.

The best way to make, mark, and protect a cache will depend on local conditions. Rain and animals pose the most obvious threats. But extreme heat has to be avoided if there's film in the cache, and extreme cold if there is water. (For the protection and refinding of water caches, and the best containers, see page 258; for precautions when caching dehydrated food in damp climates, page 221.)

A cave or overhanging rockledge is probably the best protection against rain. Burying is the simplest and surest protection, especially in sandy desert, against temperature extremes and also against animals. For animals that can read, leave a note. On the California walk I put one with each cache: "If you find this cache, please leave it. I am passing through *on foot* in April or May, and am depending on it." Similar notes went on the Grand Canyon caches. But I feel fairly sure that none was ever read.

At each Grand Canyon cache all food and supplies went into a metal 5-gallon can. These cans are ideal for the job. Provided the lid is pressed firmly home, the cans are watertight, something close to airtight, and probably proof against all animals except bears and humans. I find that by packing the cans very carefully I can just squeeze in a full week's supply of everything. They're useful, too, for packing water ahead (page 259). They're also excellent for airdrops—and having them interchangeably available for caches or airdrops may help keep your plans conveniently fluid until the last possible moment. But metal cans are no longer easy to find. A good substitute for food caches: a 5-gallon plastic bucket with clip-on plastic lid of the kind now used for some foodstuffs and such construction materials as paint, adhesive, and tar (about 1.5 lbs., and anything from free to $8 for unused ones).*

Airdrops

Prearranged parachute airdrops are a highly efficient means of replenishment. But they're noisy. And I'm glad to know that in today's heavily used wilderness areas they've been banned as a normal supply method—as should all administrative, nonemergency overflights. After all, an object of going into such places—perhaps *the* object—is "to get away from it all"; and surely no one in his senses would want to inject "it" routinely in the form of low-flying aircraft. I've found, oddly enough, that the disturbance you suffer personally by having an airdrop is very small indeed; but once low-altitude flights—for any purpose at all—became anything more than very exceptional incursions they would disturb for everyone the solitude and sense of freedom from the man-world that I judge to be the essence of wilderness travel. As with sanitation, it's a matter of density.

But there are still places—especially in Alaska, Africa, and South America—in which an occasional airdrop remains a reasonable supply method as well as the only practical one. So I retain almost intact this section from earlier editions.

Although airdrops are efficient, they aren't perfect. On the ground, a practical disadvantage is that they tie you down to being at a certain place at a certain time. They're more dependable than most people imagine, but uncertainties do exist—above all, the uncertainty of weather—and I would prefer not to rely on an airdrop if there were any considerable danger that the plane might be delayed more than a day or two by storms or fog.

---

*CHIP: Plastic buckets in many sizes as well as large metal cans with FDA-approved lacquer linings (30-lb. capacity, $5.65) can be ordered from Consolidated Plastics (1-800 362-1000), and other industrial/lab suppliers. Waterproof plastic food-storage barrels (5 gallons, $13) are sold by Northwest River Supplies, 2009 S. Main St., Moscow, ID 83843; 1-800-635-5202; *www.nrsweb.com*.

Note that caches are now illegal in most designated wilderness areas in the U.S. A lawful tactic is to spot them just outside wilderness boundaries. For one winter traverse, we skied the caches in after the lakes froze and left them on small rocky islands—easy to find.

Airdrops have one important advantage over other means of supply: they act as a safety check. Once you've signaled "all's well" to the plane, everyone concerned soon knows you are safe up to that point. And if the pilot falls to locate you or sees a prearranged "in trouble—need help" signal, then rescue operations can get under immediate and well-directed way.

Airdrops are not cheap—but neither are they ruinous. Most small rural charter outfits now seem to charge around $150 to $300 for each hour of actual flying. If the base airport is within, say, 50 miles of the drop site you ought to get by on about an hour's flying time—provided the pilot has no trouble locating you. You may have to add the cost of the parachute—but see page 708.

Establishing contact is the crux of an airdrop operation.

First, make sure you've got hold of a good pilot. Unless there was no alternative I'd hesitate to depend on a man who had never done a drop before. Above all, satisfy yourself that you've got a careful and reliable man. Make local inquiries. And try to assess his qualities when you talk to him. Distrust a slapdash type whose refrain is "Just say where and when, and leave the rest to me." I admit it's a problem to know what to do if you decide, after discussing the minutest details with a pilot, that you just don't trust him. It's not easy to extricate yourself without gashing the poor fellow's feelings. The solution is probably to approach him first on a conditional basis: "Look, I find that I may need an airdrop at—." But perhaps you can dream up a better gambit.

Success in making contact depends only in part on the pilot. The recipient has a lot to do with it too. So make sure you know what the hell you're doing.

The first time I arranged an airdrop I was very conscious that I had no idea at all what the hell. The occasion was the long Grand Canyon trip. I wanted three airdrops. The pilot and I, talking over details beforehand, decided that under expected conditions the surest ground-to-air signal was mirror-flashing. I would carry a little circular mirror, about 2 inches in diameter—the kind you could then pick up for 15 cents in any variety store. The pilot, who had been an Air Force survival instructor, assured me that such a mirror was just as good as specially made mirrors with cross-slits—and, at barely an ounce, was also appreciably lighter. The trick was to practice beforehand. I soon picked up the idea. You hold the mirror as close to one eye as you can and shut the other eye. Then you extend the free hand and aim the tip of the thumb at a point (representing the plane) that's not more than about 100 yards away. You move the mirror until the sun's reflection, appearing as a bright, irregular patch of light, hits the top of your thumb. Then you tilt the mirror up a bit until only the lowest part of the patch of light remains on your thumb. The rest of it should then show up exactly on the object that represents the plane.

If it doesn't, keep practicing with fractional adjustments of mirror and thumb until you know precisely where to hold both so as to hit your target. You're now ready for the real thing. Ready, that is, to flash sunlight into the pilot's eyes.

"It's the surest way I know," said my Grand Canyon pilot. "On survival exercises I've located guys that had nothing to flash with except penknife blades or even just sunglasses. When that flash hits my eye just once, the job's done. That's all I need to know: where to look. But without something to start me off, the expanse of ground I can see, especially in broken country like the Canyon, is just too damned big."

After a few minutes' practice I had complete confidence in the mirror routine; but we also arranged that I should spread out my bright orange sleeping bag as a marker, and would have a fire and some water ready so that when the plane had located me and came over low on a trial run I could send up a plume of smoke to indicate wind direction.

Because I wasn't sure how far I could travel across very rough country in a week, and because I didn't want to be held back if I found I could move fast, we arranged primary and alternate sites for the first drop. We set zero hour at 10:00 a.m. on the eighth morning after I left an Indian village that would be my last contact with civilization. The chances were good that at ten o'clock no clouds would obscure the sun and that the day's desert winds would not yet have sprung up.

I made the alternate, farther-along site in time and, with complete confidence in the mirror-signaling technique, decided for various reasons to take the drop about 2 miles from the prearranged place, out on a flat red rock-terrace. The plane arrived dead on schedule. But it failed to see my frantic flashings and, after an hour's fruitless search around the prime site and back along the way I'd come, was heading for home and passing not too far from me when I poured water on the waiting fire and sent a column of smoke spiraling up into the clear air. Almost at once the plane banked toward me, and within minutes my supplies were sailing safely down, suspended from a big orange parachute.

Later, a park ranger in the plane told me that he'd seen the smoke the moment it rose in the air. "But we didn't see the flashing until we were almost on top of you. At a guess, I'd say you didn't shake the mirror enough. You've got to do that to set up a good flashing. Oh, and your orange sleeping bag didn't show up at all against the red rock. We could hardly see it, even on the drop run."

So my first airdrop taught me a valuable lesson: unless it's absolutely unavoidable, don't change your prearranged drop site, even by a short distance. For the two later drops on that trip we'd picked only one site, and each time I was in exactly the right place. I also had the white 8-by-9-foot plastic sheet (page 426) in my pack, and I spread it out beside the sleeping bag. Each time, the pilot saw the white patch as soon as he came within range, and although I had begun to flash with the mirror, the plane rocked its wings in recognition and I therefore stopped flashing before there was time to assess the mirror's worth. Both these later drops went off without a hitch.*

Three years later, on my 17-day hike-and-swim trip through Lower Grand Canyon, I had another airdrop. Because the route was untried I couldn't guarantee to be at the clearly defined riverside ledge that was the prime drop site, and on the scheduled morning I was still 3 miles upriver, on the most obvious and open ledge I could find—which was neither very obvious nor very open. Our plan was that if the pilot didn't see me at the prime drop site he'd fly upriver to my starting point and then return, still down in the Inner Gorge, between rockwalls more than 2000 feet high and, at their foot, barely 200 yards apart. It worked. The pilot missed me on the upriver run—because the early-morning sun was in his eyes and because I didn't have time to generate much smoke from the fire I had ready. But on the return run he saw the now healthy smoke column from far upriver, and when he turned some way below me and came back for the drop, into the blinding sun, he had no difficulty knowing where I was because of the cloud of orange smoke from a day flare that I'd carried for that specific purpose and had ignited as soon as I heard him returning downriver. The orange cloud persisted well and showed up clearly, he told me later. The parachute he used, by the way, was one he'd made by stitching together two plastic windsocks. It worked fine.

Several people have written asking what I did in the Canyon with the parachutes and other garbage. I packed the chutes and everything else into the metal 5-gallon cans that the supplies had been packed in (page 704); and I tucked the cans away out of sight. (Years later, separate people found two of them—and actually returned one to me.)

Helicopters

Useful as they may be, helicopters are—at least in wilderness—disgusting bloody machines. And I feel sure that having one land and offload supplies—and also bring you into contact with "outsiders"—would be a far more disruptive event than an airdrop. What's more, the 'copters' fiendish clatter and the way they can mosey into every corner make them even less desirable as wilderness suppliers than conventional planes. Still, I suppose there are times and places . . .

---

*Described in rather different detail in *The Man Who Walked Through Time*, pages 81–84. Note that airdrops are no longer permitted in Grand Canyon National Park. And that I now carry, for emergencies, a small dedicated signaling mirror (page 654).

Average charter rates for a *small* helicopter operating no higher than about 5000 feet start at around $250 an hour. Supercharged 'copters for mountain work may cost $500 an hour, and the newer light-turbine versions as much as $800. (Comparable rates for small conventional plane: around $150 and up.)

It's worth knowing—not so much for supply purposes but because most wilderness rescue work is now carried out by helicopters—that they can't put down just anywhere. A slope of more than about 10 degrees isn't a feasible landing place for even a small machine. In good conditions, though, on a clear surface, an expert pilot may be able to hover with one skid on a steeper slope long enough to pick up a casualty. But even for this method (known as a "toe-in") the slope can't be more than about 25 degrees.

Fixed-wing planes

In lake-rich places—notably Alaska—floatplanes are a common means of shipping backpackers into wild and largely roadless country. My only use of one worked well. See *Secret Worlds,* Chapter 5.

A couple of times, I've also chartered small wheeled planes to get quickly into remote places. Once, near Lower Grand Canyon, we achieved an interesting touchdown on a narrow dirt road.

Charter rates for small rural-based planes—for ferrying, as for parachute drops—now run around $150 to $300 for each flying hour.

Support backpackers

CHIP: A support backpacker is, in the largest sense, a pack animal. And having backpacked loads in to support friends on wilderness routes where caching was banned, I'm an honorary beast of burden. One method is portering, in which you accompany the main party in and then pull out, leaving your load. But what I've done more often is to rendezvous with someone a week or more along their route. As with airdrops, the key is having your meeting place and time absolutely riveted—and having the patience to stay put. In one sad case I watched from a rocky summit as an outdoor leadership class and their resupply train of packhorses circled my vantage point repeatedly—following, as it turned out, one another's tracks.

Auxiliary pack animals

COLIN: Indoorsmen often ask why I never use a pack animal such as a burro on any of my long walks. Blame for the thought probably lies with

Robert Louis Stevenson and his *Travels with a Donkey*—or maybe with TV prospectors who amble across parched western deserts escorted by amiable burros.

Frankly, I've never even been tempted. For one thing, I can go places a burro can't. And I blench at the prospect of looking after a burro's food and water supply. Also, although I know nothing at first hand about managing the beasts, I mistrust their dispositions. Come to think of it, I don't seem to be alone in my distrust. Precious few people use burros these days. It's perhaps significant that on one of the only two occasions I've come across this man-beast combination, the man was on one side of a small creek pulling furiously and vainly at the halter of the burro, and the burro was planted on the far bank with heels dug resolutely in.

CHIP: Climbers and some backpackers hire horse-and-mule outfitters to haul loads in, a practice known as *spot-packing.* (A *drop-camp* by contrast means that the outfitter hauls in tents, etc., and sets them up, leaving you there for a specified time.) Rates in the U.S. for a one-day spot-pack are generally a flat fee, $100 to $200, plus a charge ($50–$75) for each pack animal. If the pack animals must be trucked to the trailhead, the cost increases. If the packer stays overnight the price goes up again, steeply. And if you expect to be packed out, it costs the same again.

A recent alternative is to hire llamas or pack goats. Both can handle rougher terrain than can horses while doing less damage to trails. They might come with a handler or alone. The backpacking shop in Pinedale, Wyoming, had a rental pair of llamas and a trailer—solidly booked from June through September. For two field seasons of wilderness monitoring, I leased my own pair of llamas and found them stalwart—the larger of the two could carry 125 lbs.—and easy to handle (for more llama tales, see *Sky's Witness: A Year in the Wind River Range*). Having the snooty aloofness of their camel cousins, llamas are tractable rather than friendly. In fact, too much fussing and petting is the surest way to make them spit or kick, which they mostly do only to one another. Pack goats are incredibly agile and also friendlier, though they travel somewhat low to the ground. For more goat-lore, consult *The Pack Goat* by John Mionczynski (Pruett, 1992, $16) and, for goat-related philosophical insights, *Goatwalking* by Jim Corbett (Viking, 1991, $20).

In far-flung lands you might find reindeer, camels, or yaks for hire. Since packers can be a rough lot and large animals more so, shoving their loads into rocks and occasionally rolling over on them, things do get broken. To forestall damage, wrap your pack in a cheap Ensolite sleeping pad and/or enclose it in a duffel. Always carry cameras and such yourself.

DANGERS, REAL AND IMAGINED

COLIN: For many wilderness walkers, no single source of fear quite compares with that stirred up by

Rattlesnakes.*

Every year an almost morbid terror of the creatures ruins or at least tarnishes countless otherwise delightful hikes all over the United States and Canada. This terror is based largely on folklore and myth.

Now, rattlesnakes can be dangerous, but they're not what so many people fancy them to be: vicious and cunning brutes with a deep-seated hatred of man. In solid fact, rattlers are timid and retiring. They are highly developed reptiles but they simply don't have the brain capacity for cunning in our human sense. And although they react to man as they would to any big and threatening creature, they could hardly have built up a deep-seated hatred: the first human that one of them sees is usually the last. Finally, the risk of being bitten by a rattler is slight, and the danger that a bite will prove fatal to a healthy adult is small.**

In other words, ignorance has as usual bred deep and unreasoning fear—a fear that may even cause more harm than snakebite. Some years ago, near San Diego, California, a hunter who was spiked by barbed wire thought he'd been struck by a rattler—and very nearly died of shock.

The surest antidote to fear is knowledge. When I began my California walk I knew nothing about rattlesnakes, and the first one I met scared me purple. Killing it seemed a human duty. But by the end of the summer I no longer felt this unreasoning fear, and as a result I no longer killed rattlers—unless they lived close to places frequented by people.

Later I grew interested enough to write a magazine article about rattlesnakes, and in researching it I read the entire 1500-odd pages of the last-word bible on the subject. As I read, the fear sank even further away.

---

*Only two distinct kinds of poisonous snakes occur in the United States: the coral snakes and the pit vipers—a group that includes rattlesnakes, cottonmouths (or water moccasins) and copperheads. Coral snakes, though highly poisonous, rarely bite humans; and they're restricted to the southeast corner of the country plus one sector of Arizona.

**In the United States more people are killed and injured in their bathtubs than by snakebite. Of 270 million Americans, perhaps 1200 a year are bitten. Twelve of these (or 1 percent) may die; but this figure includes people who've been badly frightened, those with weak hearts, and small children whose bodies cannot absorb the venom. So even without treatment, the odds on survival are very, very long.

Gradually I came to accept rattlesnakes as fellow creatures with a niche in the web of life.

The book I read was *Rattlesnakes: Their Habits, Life Histories and Influence on Mankind* by Laurence M. Klauber (University of California Press, 1997; 1580 pages; $108. Abridged edition, 1982, 350 pages, $50; paperback, 1989, $17). Dr. Klauber was the world's leading authority on rattlesnakes, and in the book he sets out in detail all the known biological facts. But he does more. He examines and exposes the dense cloud of fancy and folklore that swirls around his subject. I heartily recommend this fascinating book to anyone who ever finds his peace of mind disturbed by a blind fear of rattlesnakes—and also to anyone interested in widening the fields in which he can observe and understand when he goes walking. You should find the book in any university library, and in any medium-size or large public library.

Among the many folklore fables Dr. Klauber punctures is the classic "boot story." I first heard this one down in the Colorado Desert of Southern California—and believed it. "There was this rancher," the old-timer told me, "who lived not far from here. One day he wore some kneeboots belonging to his father, who had died 10 years before. Next day the rancher's leg began to swell. It grew rapidly worse. Eventually he went to a doctor—just in time to avoid amputation from rattlesnake poisoning. Then he remembered that his father had been struck when wearing the same boots a year before he died. One of the snake's fangs had broken off and lodged in an eyehole. Eleven years later it scratched the son."

Essentially the same story was read before the Royal Society of London by a New World traveler on January 7, 1714. That version told how the boot killed three successive husbands of a Virginia woman. Today the incident may take place anywhere, coast to coast, and the boot is sometimes modernized into a struck and punctured tire that proves fatal to successive garagemen who repair it. Actually, the amount of dried venom on the point of a fang is negligible. And venom exposed to air quickly loses its potency.

Then there's the legend of the "avenging mate": kill one rattler, and its mate will vengefully seek you out. Pliny, the Roman naturalist who died in A.D. 79, told this story of European snakes, and it's still going strong over here. In 1954, after a rattlesnake had been killed in a downtown Los Angeles apartment, the occupant refused to go back because a search had failed to unearth the inevitably waiting mate.

The legend probably arose because it seems as though a male may occasionally court a freshly killed female. Some years ago a geographer friend of mine and a zoologist companion, looking for specimens for research, killed a rattler high in California's Sierra Nevada. The zoologist carried the snake 200 yards to a log and began skinning it. My friend sat facing him. Suddenly he saw another rattler crawling toward them. "It was barely four yards away," he told me later, "and heading directly for the dead snake; but it was taking its time and seemed quite unaware of our presence. We killed it before it even rattled. It was a male. The first was a female." An untrained observer might well have seen this incident as proof positive that the second snake was bent on revenge.

Toward the end of my 17-day foot trip through Lower Grand Canyon I saw with my own eyes just how another myth could have arisen. I was running very short of food, and after meeting four rattlers within four days I reluctantly decided that if I met another I'd kill and cook it. I duly met one. It was maybe 3 feet long—about as big as they grow in that country. I promptly hit it with my staff a little forward of the tail, breaking its back and immobilizing it; but before I could put it out of its pain by crushing its head, it began striking wildly about in all directions. Soon—and apparently by pure accident—it struck itself halfway down the body. It was a perfect demonstration of how the myth arose that wounded rattlers will strike themselves to commit suicide. (Quite apart from the question of whether snakes can comprehend the idea of a future death, rattlesnakes are little affected by rattlesnake venom.)

After I'd killed that snake I cut off the head, wrapped the body in a plastic bag, and put it in my pack; but I couldn't for the life of me remember what Dr. Klauber had said about eating rattlers that had struck themselves. As I walked on, thinking of the venom that was probably still circulating through the snake's blood system, I grew less and less hungry. After half an hour, feeling decidedly guilty about the unnecessary killing, I discarded the corpse. Later I found that although people are often warned against eating a rattler that has bitten itself there is in fact no danger if the meat is cooked: the poisonous quality of snake venom is destroyed by heat. It's as well to cut out the bitten part, though, just as you cut away damaged meat in an animal that's been shot. Back in the 1870s one experimenter got a big rattler to bite itself three or four times. It lived 19 hours and seemed unhurt. The man then cooked and ate it without ill effect.

According to Dr. Klauber, rattler meat has been compared with chicken, veal, frog, tortoise, quail, fish, canned tuna, and rabbit. It is, as he points out, useful as an emergency ration because it's easily hunted down and killed, even by people weakened by starvation. But there's only 1 lb. of meat on a 4-foot rattler, 2.5 lbs. on a 5-footer, and 4.5 on a 6-footer. The one small and skinny rattler I've eaten tasted of nothing in particular. And stringy.

Even straightforward information about rattlesnakes often gets hopelessly garbled in the popular imagination. For example, the only facts about rattlers that many people know for sure are that they grow an extra rattle every year, revel in blistering heat, and are fast and unfailingly deadly. Not one of these "facts" is true. Number of rattles is almost no indication of age. A rattler soon dies if the temperature around it rises much over 100°F. It crawls so slowly that the only dangerous rattler is the one you don't see. Even the strike isn't nearly as fast as was once thought. Tests prove it to be rather slower than a trained man's punching fists. If you move first—as fast as you can, and clean out of range—you may get away with it, though avoiding the strike, even if you're waiting for it, borders on the impossible.

Accurate knowledge will not only help dispel many unreasoning fears (it's nearly always the unknown that we fear the most) but can materially reduce the chances that you'll be bitten.

Take the matter of heat and cold, for example. Rattlesnakes, like all reptiles, lack an efficient mechanism such as we have for keeping body temperature constant, so they're wholly dependent on the temperature around them. In cold climates they can hibernate indefinitely at a few degrees above freezing, and have fully recovered after four hours in a deep freeze at 4°F. Yet at 45° they can hardly move, and they rarely choose to prowl in temperatures below 65°. Their "best" range is 80 to 90°. At 100° they're in danger, and at 110° they die of heat stroke. But these, remember, are *their* temperatures—that is, the temperatures their bodies attain through contact with the ground over which they're moving and with the air around them. These temperatures may differ markedly from official weather readings taken in the shade, 5 feet above ground level. When such a reading is 60°, for example, a thermometer down on sunlit sand may record 100°, and in the lowest inch of air about 80°. (See page 112.) In other words, a rattler in the right place may feel snugly comfortable in an "official" temperature of 60°. On the other hand, in a desert temperature of 80° in the shade, the sunlit sand might be over 130° and the lowest inch of air around 110°, and any rattler staying for long in such a place would die.

Once you know a few such facts you find after a little practice that your mind almost automatically tells you when to be especially watchful, and even where to avoid placing your feet. In cool early-season weather, for example, when rattlers like to bask, you'll tend to keep a sharp lookout, if the sun is shining but a cold wind is blowing, in sunlit places sheltered from the wind. And in hot desert weather you'll know that there's absolutely no danger out on open sand where there's no shade. On the other hand, the prime feeding time for rattlers in warm weather is two hours before and after sunset, when the small mammals that are their main prey tend to be on the move; so if you figure that the ground temperature during that time is liable to be around 80° to 90° you keep your eyes skinned. I don't mean that you walk in fear and trembling. But you watch your step. Given the choice, for example, you tend to bisect the space between bushes, and so reduce the chances of surprising a rattler resting unseen beneath overhanging vegetation. Once you're used to it, you do this kind of thing as a natural safe operating procedure, no more directly connected with fear than is the habit of checking the street for traffic before you step off a sidewalk.*

You'll also be able to operate more safely once you understand how rattlesnakes receive their impressions of the world around them. Their sight is poor, and they're totally deaf. But they're well equipped with other senses. Two small facial pits contain nerves so sensitive to heat that a rattler can strike accurately at warm-blooded prey in complete darkness. (Many species hunt mainly at night.) They're highly sensitive to vibration too, and have rattled at men passing out of sight 150 feet away. (Moral: in bad rattler country, at bad times, tread heavily.) Two nostrils just above a rattler's mouth furnish a sense of smell very like ours. And that's not all. A sure sign that a snake has been alerted is a flickering of its forked tongue: it is "smelling" the outside world. The tongue's moist surface picks up tiny particles floating in the air and at each flicker transfers them to two small cavities in the roof of the mouth. These cavities, called "Jacobson's organs," interpret the particles to the brain in terms of smell, much as do the moist membranes inside our noses.

In Biblical times, people wrongly associated snakes' tongues with their poison. Nothing has changed. Stand at the rattlesnake cage in any zoo and the chances are you'll soon hear somebody say, "There, did you see its stinger?" or even, "Look at it stick out its fangs!" It is true, though, that an alarmed snake will sometimes use its tongue to intimidate enemies. When it does, the forked tips quiver pugnaciously out at their limit, arching first up, then down. It's a chillingly effective display. But primarily, of course, a snake reacts to enemies with that unique rattle. Harmless in itself, it warns and intimidates, like the growl of a dog.

The rattle is a chain of hollow, interlocking segments made of the same hard and transparent keratin as human nails. The myth that each segment represents a year of the snake's age first appeared in print as early as 1615. Actually, a new segment is left each time the snake sheds its skin. Young rattlers shed frequently, and adults an average of one to three times each year. In any case, the fragile rattles rarely remain complete for very long.

In action the rattles shake so fast that they blur like the wings of a hummingbird. Small snakes merely buzz like a fly but big specimens sound off with a strident hiss that rises to a spine-chilling crescendo.

---

*CHIP: I've always been more frightened of cars than of rattlesnakes.

Someone once said that it was "like a pressure cooker with the safety valve open." Once you've heard the sound you'll never forget it.

The biggest rattlers are eastern diamondbacks: outsize specimens may weigh 30 lbs. and measure almost 8 feet. But most of the 30 different species grow to no more than 3 or 4 feet.

People often believe that rattlers will strike only when coiled, and never upward. It's true that they can strike most effectively from the alert, raised-spiral position; but they're capable of striking from any position and in any direction.

Rattlers are astonishingly tenacious of life. One old saying warns, "They're dangerous even after they're dead"—and it's true. Lab tests have shown that severed heads can bite a stick and discharge venom for up to 43 minutes. The tests even produced some support for the old notion that "rattlers never die till sundown." Decapitated bodies squirmed for as long as 7½ hours, moved when pinched for even longer. And the hearts almost always went on beating for a day, often for two days. One was still pulsating after 59 hours.

A rattlesnake's enemies include other snakes (especially king snakes and racers), birds, mammals, and even fish. In Grand Canyon I found a 3-foot rattler apparently trampled to death by wild burros. Torpid captive rattlers have been killed and partly eaten by mice put in their cages for food! Not long ago a California fisherman caught a big rainbow trout with a 9-inch rattler in its stomach. But only one species of animal makes appreciable inroads on the rattlesnake population. That species is man—to whom the warning rattle is an invitation to attack. If humans had existed in large numbers when rattlesnakes began to evolve, perhaps 6 million years ago, it's unlikely the newfangled rattlebearers would have succeeded and flourished.

In spite of stories to the contrary, a rattlesnake meeting a large animal such as man hardly ever attacks so long as the potential enemy stays outside its striking range. (Very rarely, when courting, it may just possibly attack; but so may a deer or even a rabbit.) It may move toward you, but that will be for other reasons, such as the slope of the ground. Its first reaction will most likely be to lie still and escape attention. Then it may crawl slowly for safety. Detected or alarmed, it will probably rattle and rise into its menacing defensive coil—a vibrant, open spiral quite distinct from the tightly wound pancake resting position. It may also hiss. Finally, it may strike. Usually, though by no means always, it will rattle before striking. Of course, none of these comments necessarily applies if a man treads on a snake or comes suddenly and alarmingly within its restricted little world. Then, not unnaturally, the frightened animal will often strike without warning.

But it's important to remember that rattlesnakes are as moody as men, as unpredictable as women. A man who for many years was rattlesnake-control officer of South Dakota concluded that they simply "are not to be trusted, for some will violate all rules." Certain individuals, even whole species, seem to be always "on the prod." A few habitually strike without warning. Others seem almost amiable.

Defense is not, of course, the main purpose of a rattler's venom and fangs. Primarily, they're for securing food.

The fangs, regularly replaced, are precision instruments. One slender, curving tooth on each side of the snake's upper jaw grows almost five times longer than its fellows. In large rattlers it may measure ¾ inch. A cunning pivot-and-lever bone structure ensures that when the mouth is closed these fierce barbs lie flat; but as the jaw opens wide to strike they pivot erect. Each fang is hollow. Its cavity connects with a venom sac beneath the eye, equivalent to our salivary gland. When the fangs stab into a prey the snake injects a controlled dose of venom through the cavity and out of an aperture just above the fang's point. In the small mammals that rattlers mostly feed on, the venom causes almost instant paralysis and rapid death.

A rattlesnake's venom—present from birth—is as unpredictable as its temperament. Quantity and toxicity seem to vary widely from species to species, from individual to individual. In general, though, the bigger the snake, the greater the danger: a big snake stabs deeper with its fangs and generally injects more venom. But there are other, quite unpredictable, factors in any case of snakebite. It's not just that a rattler can control, at least to some degree, the amount of venom it injects; the quantity in its sacs will vary markedly according to whether it has or has not expended venom recently in killing prey.

Treatment of snakebite

The greatest danger is probably hysteria; people bitten by harmless snakes have come close to dying from fright. What many snakebite patients need most, in fact, is rest and reassurance. But there seems little doubt that, in cases of bad bites from genuinely dangerous snakes, *quick* physical treatment, carefully applied, can prevent possibly severe illness and may even save a life—especially of a child, whose small body can absorb little venom. Remember, though, that even venomous snakes may inject little or no venom when they bite, particularly under backpacking conditions, when the snake is likely to have been surprised and to have struck defensively, perhaps almost haphazardly.

The ideal treatment is to get to a hospital as quickly as possible so that a full evaluation can be made and, if necessary, antivenin injected with the proper safeguards. "The best first aid," says one expert, "is a set of car keys."

That advice is worth bearing in mind, even for backpackers. If you're within an hour or so of roadhead and quick access to a hospital, or at least a doctor, the best response to being bitten may be to walk out "at a moderate pace, taking frequent rests, using a sling if the bite is on the hand, and abstaining from alcohol." Provided, that is, the day is not too hot and you're not too exhausted or panic-stricken. A companion who can provide physical support and also keep an eye on your condition makes walking out much more practical. And two companions can maybe rig up a makeshift stretcher. Unless roadhead is more than 36 hours away, small children weighing less than about 60 lbs. should be carried out, on shoulders or stretcher, as soon as possible. But in such cases, when other people are available, the best action may be to send out one or more fast messengers for a helicopter.

Clearly, each case is different. Judgment on the correct response demands both some knowledge of the facts and a lot of cool.

CHIP: Since the experts disagree to some extent, I boiled down pages of advice from recent or recently updated first-aid references (pages 652–53) to the treatment on which all parties agree.

The first crucial judgment is whether venom has been injected. Some strikes and bites don't penetrate the skin, so look for fang marks. Snakes have rows of sharp teeth, but fang marks are bigger and deeper. There will be from one to four of them, often at the end of a row of fainter tooth marks.

A fiery, circulating pain and swelling within 5 to 10 minutes both indicate venom. So does numbness and tingling or muscle twitches of lips, cheeks, scalp, and extremities (especially near the bite) within 30 to 90 minutes.* But immediate symptoms of this kind may owe to panicky hyperventilation rather than to venom. Other signs that appear one to two hours post-bite are a cold sweat, weakness, headache, nausea, vomiting, and fainting. The heart and breathing rate might also go up sharply. Other signs of venom in the same time span are a rusty or rubbery taste in the mouth and the appearance of bruises (i.e., hemorrhaging) around the bite.

After several hours, the spread of venom can lead to confusion, difficult breathing, large blood blisters near the bite, severe nausea, and blood in the vomit, urine, or feces. Ugly, but few people die of it (see page 711, second footnote).

---

*The bites of the Mojave rattler and the small-toothed gnawing of the coral snake cause much less immediate pain, swelling, etc. but are nonetheless serious.

Enough horrors: let's talk about what to do. If you're alone, get a grip. Even if there are definite fang marks, etc., you might not be poisoned. According to Dr. Paul S. Auerbach, author of *Medicine for the Outdoors* (Appendix IV), "Most bites, even by venomous snakes, do not result in medically significant envenomations." Got that?

So the first thing to treat for, in yourself or others, is fear itself. Don't shriek and dash off like an idiot. Sit down (not, however, on the poor snake). If you're dizzy from hyperventilating, cup your hands over your nose and mouth, breathing slowly and deeply into the little chamber thus formed (a paper bag also works). This recycles the carbon dioxide you've shed by huffing and puffing and returns the CO_2 level in your blood to normal.

If you got a good look at the snake, fine. If not, and if you're in a region where it might be any of several sorts (rattler, cottonmouth, copperhead, or coral), then try to get a peek from a safe (twice the snake's length) distance. Dr. Auerbach advises killing the snake, not for revenge but for medical reference, and carefully placing it in a fang-proof container. Dr. Weiss advises that it's not necessary to kill the snake—especially, I'd think, if it might lead to further panic, hyperventilation, or bites. (I'd probably apologize to the snake and jot down a brief description for the doctor.)

It helps me at such times to imagine my good judgment as a butterfly, floating easily and gazing with light-blue compassion on the hairy, suffering primate—me. If the hirsute beastie thrashes and squalls, the butterfly of good judgment will flutter off. So—

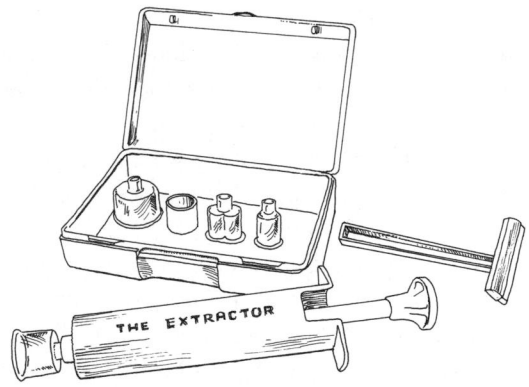

If a) there are fang marks, b) the bite is from a rattlesnake, and c) medical help is an hour or more away, then quickly rinse the bite and apply a suction device (e.g., the Sawyer Extractor, 3.5 oz., about \$12)—though a number of experts now say suction may have little value. If the area of the bite is hairy, you'll have to quickly shave it clean to maintain suction—there's a plastic safety razor in the Extractor kit—but DO NOT cut an X (nor any other letter) at the fang mark. According to Dr. Auerbach, the time-honored slash and suck method "invariably creates a nasty infection that leaves a noticeable scar; there is also the risk of blood-borne disease."

Reportedly, a suction device can remove up to one-third of the venom if it's applied soon (minutes) after the bite. If the Extractor is working, a yellowish fluid and some blood will be drawn into the Extractor cup. When it fills, empty, rinse (both bite and cup), and repeat. After 30 minutes, quit. If possible, wash the bite well with soap and water.

Meanwhile, take off watches, rings, nonstretchy clothing, etc. before swelling sets in. Ice packs evidently do no good and might cause tissue damage similar to frostbite (the last thing you want on top of snakebite).

Some first-aid texts describe another measure, called "Australian Compression," in which the bitten limb is wrapped and/or splinted. The mild pressure and immobility slow the spread of the venom. But Australia has no pit vipers, the most common poisonous snakes in the U.S., and certain other texts hold that confining rattlesnake venom with wraps, splints, or constricting bands can significantly worsen tissue damage near the bite.

One universal agreement: Drink no booze whatsoever. For the religious, prayer is the best comfort; for the irreverent, jokes.

For pain use Tylenol (acetaminophen) and/or codeine, but not aspirin, which can increase hemorrhaging. Besides the proper antivenin, an antibiotic (dicloxacillin, erythromycin, or cephalexin) can be administered by a qualified person, but possible allergic reactions to both venom and drugs are a concern.

Electrical shocks, applying the blood of the snake, and other folkloric nostrums, new and old, should be *firmly* discouraged.

COLIN: I must accent that everything we've said, except for the warning against alcohol, applies only to rattlesnakes and other pit vipers of the United States and Canada (page 711, first footnote). All have comparatively low-toxicity venom. The rare and rather docile coral snakes of Arizona are so small that they're very unlikely to be able to bite a human, and even when they do the results are short of deadly. But the larger coral snakes of Florida present more of a problem. Anyone penetrating known coral-snake country there might consider inquiring from *a reliable authority* about the possibility of carrying an antivenin. Keep in mind, though, that many experts strongly advise against such a course—for the same reason that they say it would be sheer idiocy for the layman to take antivenin in rattlesnake country: the risk from injecting it without full medical safeguards is greater than that from a rattlesnake bite. Where snakes are more deadly—as in Africa and, I understand, parts of Asia and Central and South America—the only worthwhile snakebite kit is antivenin and a syringe. But some people are very seriously allergic to the serum used in the antivenin. Before you even consider carrying a kit, check your reaction with an allergist.

I hope this rather long discourse has convinced you that rattlesnakes, although dangerous, are not the vicious and deadly brutes of legend. If you have in the past felt, as many people do, a deep and unreasoning fear of them, then I hope we've helped just a little in dispelling that fear—and have left you free to walk almost anywhere.

You may even find that your understanding of rattlesnakes passes at length beyond mere factual knowledge. I've described in *The Man Who Walked Through Time* (page 166) how I was sitting naked one afternoon on a sandbar at the edge of a willow thicket when I saw a pale pink rattlesnake come gliding over the sand, barely 6 feet away from me, clearly unaware of my presence. Sitting there watching it, I found that I felt curiosity rather than fear. Slowly, gracefully, the snake threaded its way through a forest of willow shoots. As its flank pushed past each stem I could see the individual scales tilt under the stem's pressure, then move back flush. Four feet from my left buttock the snake stopped, its head in a sun-dappled patch of sand beside a cluster of roots. Unhurriedly, it drew its body forward and curled into a flat resting coil. Then it stretched and yawned. It yawned a long and unmistakable yawn. A yawn so uninhibited that for many slow seconds I seemed to see nothing but the pale lining of its mouth and two matching arcs of small, sharp teeth. When the yawn was over at last the snake raised its head and twisted it slowly and luxuriously from side to side, as a man or a woman will do in anticipation of rest and comfort to come. Finally, with such obvious contentment that I don't think I'd have been altogether surprised to hear the creature purr, it laid its head gently on the pillow of its clean and beautifully marked body.

And all at once, for the first time in my life, I found that I'd moved "inside" a rattlesnake. Quite unexpectedly, I had shared its sleepiness and anticipation and contentment. And as I sat looking down at the sleeping snake coiled in its patch of sun-dappled shade, I found myself feeling for it something remarkably close to affection.

Frankly, the feeling has not lasted. I'm still no rattlesnake aficionado. But my fear, helped by the moment of understanding, has now contracted to vanishing point. On my 1966 trip down Lower Grand Canyon, when I met five rattlesnakes in five days, one small specimen even struck from under a stone and hit my boot (no damage done). Yet even at that moment I don't think I felt much fear: it was more a matter of interest and curiosity. But—and it may be a very big "but"—the rattlesnakes of Grand Canyon don't grow more than about 3 feet long. Whether I'd have been so consistently calm in country thick with big diamondbacks, I just don't know. I'm afraid I can guess, though.

Scorpions

A friend who does a great deal of hiking in Arizona once told me that he worried more about scorpions than about rattlesnakes. "You can see the rattlers," he said.

In Arizona there's good reason for respecting scorpions: the sting of a small, delicate, sand-colored species called the bark scorpion (*Centuroides sculpturatus*) that's found there—and in adjacent parts of New Mexico, Texas, California, and northern Mexico—is always serious and can prove fatal. Clinics in that area have antivenin, so the treatment is to chill the sting and head for the doc. But the sting of other scorpions found in North America is rarely much more serious than a bee sting. (Remember, though, that some people react violently to almost any venom. For them, even a bee sting may be fatal.)

But unless you go around turning up stones you're not very likely to see a scorpion. I've only come across two in the United States: one, rather surprisingly, was at an elevation of over 10,000 feet; the other, in my garden.

There's a well-known desert tradition that in scorpion country you always turn out your boots before putting them on in the morning. Before I went down into Grand Canyon I asked an experienced park ranger about it. "Oh, it always sounds to me like an old wives' tale," he said. Then a smile leaked slowly out over his face, and he added, "But I still do it."

In the United States the nonhuman creatures that pose the greatest real danger are, rather surprisingly, "bugs": that is, arachnids and true insects (spiders, ticks, and chiggers are arachnids). Bugs apparently cause 60 percent of total U.S. deaths from venomous animals.

Spiders

All spiders are in a sense "poisonous." That's how they make a living: they kill or incapacitate their prey by injecting small amounts of venom. But almost all spiders found in the U.S. have injecting mechanisms too delicate to penetrate human skin; and even if their venom were injected it would be close to harmless. There are three exceptions: tarantulas, black widows, and brown recluses.

Tarantulas that occur in the U.S. do not, in spite of their evil aspect and matching reputation, inflict a serious bite. No more serious, again, than a bee sting. And your chances of meeting a tarantula are small. Only in late fall, usually November, do they normally emerge from their subterranean homes and, with gleams in all eight eyes, prowl the overland world in search of mates. Even then they remain, as far as humans are concerned, unbelligerent creatures, almost passive.

But black widows are dangerous. Although they're very much smaller than tarantulas their bites are always serious and in very rare cases can prove fatal, even to adults. (Statistics are blurred, but black widows cause maybe one death a year in the U.S.) In dry parts of the West they're more common than people think. In my house we sort of cohabitate—but rarely meet.*

If you're bitten the only sensation at first may be something like a mild pinprick, though the spider may still be adhering to your skin. Two or 3 hours may pass before you suffer serious pain. But then, for 8 to 12 hours, the pain may be severe. Muscles may also cramp severely. Ice packs and Tylenol-codeine or muscle relaxers such as Valium will relieve the pain. Beyond that there seems to be no first aid of any value. Cut-and-suck treatment is useless as well as dangerous: there's simply not enough venom (which is of a neurotoxic type). So, once again, the best action, where it's possible, is hightailing (circumspectly) or being hightailed out to qualified medical treatment, which now includes an antidote for those suffering severe symptoms. If that's impractical you have, once again, to sit the thing out in a cool place—reassuring yourself with that one-death-a-year figure.

Female black widows (the males don't bite) have a shiny, rounded abdomen, from the size of an aspirin tablet up to that of a small marble. They don't have particularly noticeable legs. They're entirely black except for a red patch on the underside, shaped like an hourglass.

Brown recluse spiders were, rather surprisingly, unknown to science until the 1940s. Once only a threat in the South, they seem to be spreading—perhaps because they hole up in stored furniture and get shipped out. A brown recluse's bite is painless. The first symptom, appearing hours or even days later, may be a skin ulcer that can become gangrenous and slough off tissue several inches square. The ulceration is very slow-healing: it may last up to a year. An untreated bitee may also suffer a fever and pass dark urine. Children may even die. Beyond getting to a doctor, quick, first aid is to apply ice to the bite—and, if a blister forms and ruptures, antibiotic ointment and a sterile dressing. I've never been intro-

---

*CHIP: Apparently, some of the choicest real estate (dark, with flies) for black widows is the underside of outhouse seats. When they are disturbed by the descent of large pendulous objects (for instance, human testicles), they retaliate. Thus, an inordinate number of black widow bites are suffered on those tenderest male parts. Look well before you stoop.

duced to this fortunately rare little beauty but it's said to be a small, pale brown spider with a dark brown, violin-shaped spot on its back.

Ticks

CHIP: The inherent creepiness of ticks and my twitchy nerve endings combine to give me the best possible protection. I've picked hundreds, maybe thousands, of the little arachno-tractors off my hide and only had one drill in. But because ticks feed by inserting their mouthparts into your blood supply, they can host and transmit a number of unsavory disorders.

Lyme disease is the most common tick-borne infection in the U.S.— 5000 to 15,000 new cases a year—yet we still have much to learn. We know it's caused by a spirochete hosted by the deer tick (*Ixodes scapularis*) in the Northeast and by the black-legged tick (*I. pacificus*) in the West, and perhaps others: the dog tick, wood tick, rabbit tick, and Lone Star tick are suspect. Most cases occur in Connecticut (it was first diagnosed in the town of Lyme), New York, Pennsylvania, New Jersey, Rhode Island, Michigan, Wisconsin, Minnesota, California, and Oregon. In Europe the disease is linked to the sheep tick (*I. ricinus*) and it exists in other parts of the globe. The two known U.S. tick hosts infect not just people and whitetail deer but mice, woodrats, kangaroo rats, and other mammals— or even reptiles such as lizards.*

Ixodes ticks are pinhead size and their juvenile nymph form, which can also transmit the disease, is tinier still: the size of the period at the end of this sentence. Like most ticks, they seek heat and need a backstop to drill through your skin, so most bites occur where clothes or skin folds give them something to push against: on the trunk, upper arm, or armpit. Collars, cuffs, and shoe tops also make prime drilling sites, as do hairy locales.

Again, the best preventive measure is to keep the tick off with clothing, repellents, etc., or failing that, to get the little monster off before it drills. Since the Lyme-infected deer ticks are so small, precision tweezers, some available with a magnifier attached, are the best tool for the job (see page 726).

Some people are bitten without knowing. (Arrrgh—I keep having to stop writing in order to scratch.) Anyhow, 70 percent of those infected

---

*COLIN: Recent research at U.C. Berkeley reveals that when Lyme disease–bearing ticks attach themselves to a common Western Fence lizard—which they often do—then by the time they drop off, 85 percent of them no longer carry the disease. So I now view the Western Fence lizards that have for years patrolled my veranda as the defense league for a Limey against Lyme disease.

show a distinctive "bull's-eye" rash that clears in the center as it expands up to 6 or 7 inches across. The rash does not necessarily form around the bite—the thigh, armpit, or groin are frequent sites—and it may fade after a month or so. Hives or measleslike eruptions can also occur from 1 to 14 months after the bite. Other symptoms are flulike aches and fever, coughs, sore throat, eye irritations, and sensitivity to light. Other victims have hepatitis-like symptoms. Long-term effects include swollen joints, facial paralysis, heart and nervous-system damage, and severe arthritis, so it's vital to get treatment. (Pets can also contract Lyme disease, displaying lameness, grogginess, joint swelling, and lack of interest in food.) Various antibiotics are being tested. People who are severely infected might need some time in a hospital. So, while this might seem weird, on the whole ticks are more dangerous than rattlesnakes.

The misleadingly named *Rocky Mountain Spotted Fever* (most cases occur in southeastern states) is caused by a *Rickettsia* parasite most often hosted by the dog tick (*Dermacentor varibilis*) and the western wood tick (*D. andersoni*). To transmit RMSF a tick must remain attached to the skin for about two to six hours. If diagnosed early the disease can be quickly cured with an antibiotic (tetracycline or doxycycline) but with no treatment can prove fatal. Symptoms begin in from 2 to 14 days (average: one week) with a sudden high fever. A spotty, red rash begins on the hands and feet and spreads to the trunk, though some victims remain spotless. Flulike symptoms are also present and sometimes confuse the issue. My father was bitten by a tick while fishing, and after trying some folkloric means of removal (burnt match ends, dripping hot wax from a candle, etc.), he applied the last-ditch traditional remedy: a large dose of whisky. All of which (in those pre-antibiotical times) simply enhanced his eventual misery.

Colorado Tick Fever is caused by a virus hosted by the western wood tick (*D. andersoni*) and possibly others. A seasonal malady, it runs from late March through September, peaking in May and June. Incubation time is three to six days, with a sudden fever and flulike aches and fatigue. Other symptoms include sensitivity to light, stomach pain, nausea, and vomiting. About half of the victims have a remission after two to three days of fever—a good time to hike out since that's followed by another two to three days of misery. Long-term complications are rare. It may take a few weeks to recover full strength, but one infection seems to confer a lifelong immunity.

Other serious tick-borne diseases include *Ehrlichiosis* (a *Rickettsial* parasite spread by Lone Star ticks) and *Babesiosis* (a protozoan that invades red blood cells, spread by *I. scapularis,* the same deer tick that carries Lyme disease).

Another rare, mystifying, and potentially serious condition—neither infection nor parasite—is progressive weakness in the legs, spreading to the arms and trunk, that leads to paralysis and is potentially fatal. This is caused by a neurotoxin that builds up if a female tick is embedded for five or more days. If the tick is found—lodged behind the ear or in some other inobvious spot—and removed, recovery takes place in a matter of hours. Evidently, young people with long or thick hair are most often at risk.

COLIN: Tick time in most of the country is summer, though in drier and warmer parts of the Southwest, including California, it's winter, starting with the first rains. When conditions are right, ticks (and chiggers too) migrate to the tips of grass stems and other vegetation. If you look closely during prime time you can see battalions of the little bastards waiting for a warm-blooded host to pass. As you brush by they grasp skin or clothing (but not, I find, a cold staff). They may then spend hours crawling toward tick-Nirvanas: soft, warm sectors such as buttocks, waist, and upper back where there's pressure from clothing. This crawling phase is what gives you a break. In bad times, check frequently. The crop can sometimes be astonishing. In a heavily infested little valley I often walk through I once plucked 35 ticks off my bare legs after a passage of barely 300 yards. And by the time I was out of the valley, 30 minutes later, I'd harvested a total of 104. That morning I checked at least every hour. In any tick country you should examine yourself once or more a day. The most popular tick parking places are not all easy to examine by yourself, of course, and if you're not traveling solo, mutual search may be advisable. The only danger is that this operation, artistically conducted in the right company, may lead to such delectable results that all thought of tick removal fades.

Crawling ticks are simple to pluck off. But once they burrow in and start sucking blood it's not easy to remove them without leaving heads and pincers embedded. In disease-bearing ticks these remnants can still transmit the disease. And remnants from even the "harmless" species may cause infection. Some years ago a left-behind tick head in my groin, apparently embedded in the lymph system, sent an angry red line running up my leg, and as a registered hypochondriac I had no choice but to abort the trip and head for a doctor. Maybe wisely too.

The current gospel on removing ticks is to avoid both cigarette butts applied to tick butts (as an encouragement toward withdrawal) and also the application of oil or grease (as a suffocant). Most likely result: an embedded corpse. Instead, grasp the body with tweezers or tissue-covered fingertips and "roll" it upward, slowly but firmly, without jerk or twist. (Frankly, I've twisted counterclockwise for years, in the belief that ticks burrow in corkscrew-fashion, and have achieved considerable success.)

CHIP: The De-Ticker II ($3.50), from Macor Industries, is a sub-ounce plastic device that grips the tick while you gently unscrew it, with counterclockwiseness indicated by a convenient arrow. (Note that some tickologists vehemently discourage this unscrewing method.) The expanding dimensions of tick fear have also created a market in specialized tweezers. Some popular models are Uncle Bill's stainless-steel (1 oz., $6), Magna Point (stainless steel with a built-in 5× magnifier for deer ticks and nymphs, 1 oz., $6), and the Sawyer Tick Plier (plastic, with a 20× magnifier, 1.5 oz., $8) with scooplike jaws that slip between the skin and the tick.

The main thing is to take hold of the tick as close to the head (and your skin) as possible and to maintain a firm but gentle grip. Avoid squashing the little monster, thus injecting tick innards into your bloodstream, or jerking the body off the buried head and mouthparts. Another ploy is to apply permethrin, an insecticide used as tick repellent, to the body of the tick (but *not* your skin) using a cotton swab. This kills the tick in 10 to 15 minutes and can ease removal, though regurgitation (on the part of the dying tick) might take place.

If there are mouthparts (i.e., dark stuff) left in the skin, gently scrape them out. Some recommend using a suction extractor at this point. Then clean the area with soap and water or an antiseptic swab, and cover with a dressing. If a rash or any symptoms develop, bag the trip and see a doctor. In fact, it's wise to seek medical advice after having a tick embedded, period.

Prevention: Best of all is to scrupulously examine yourself, per Colin's advice, and if you're alone use a mirror. I also skinny-dip frequently and look myself over while drip-drying. Tuck pants into socks and wear long sleeves with tight cuffs, snug gaiters, hats with a brim, etc. Avoid thick brush and overhanging foliage, or if you can't, aim for as little contact as possible. If you find deer tracks, then ticks are there too. DEET-based repellents (page 643) help to keep ticks off, while insecticides like Sawyer permethrin or Permanone (page 644) applied to clothing—never to skin—and then air-dried before wearing can repel or kill ticks and other microdrillers for one to two weeks.*

COLIN: These tactics also work for

Chiggers.

Mostly found in the East and South, chiggers are tiny red larval

---

*COLIN: In tick country I tend to stick with my shorts. Sure, the little demons find bare skin more easily—but I can see them, almost at a glance.

forms of mites. Once beachheaded on a warm human body they head for the softest parts, such as wrists, armpits, and behind the knees. They don't actually suck blood, like ticks, but do dissolve skin cells—and set up an unholy itching. I'm told they can sometimes be removed, tediously and painfully, with extremely sticky tape. But if left alone they drop off after three or four days, and although the itching is pesky it rarely becomes serious. For severe cases, a phenol/calamine lotion or prednisone tablets, also used to treat poison oak rash, can treat the itch.

Other bugs

In the U.S., insects other than malaria-transmitting mosquitoes are mostly no worse than perishing nuisances, to be fought with tents, netting, or cheesecloth, repellents (page 643), or clothing (page 645). The pain and irritating itches left by some bites can be neutralized, I'm told, with preparations such as Sting-Eze (camphor, phenol, benzocaine, and diphenhydramine, 0.5-oz. plastic bottle, $3.50), also said to help alleviate the pain of poison-oak and -ivy rashes (page 744), or After Bite (ammonia, 0.5-oz. tube, $4.50).

But the real danger from insect bites lies in allergic reactions. In severe cases they can lead within minutes to *anaphylactic shock,* in which the patient first suffers inability to breathe properly—along with hives, vomiting, and dizziness—and occasionally, because the small air passages in his lungs close, may pass out and even die from asphyxiation. Bee stings are notoriously liable to produce life-threatening reactions in certain people. If you know or even suspect you're susceptible to reactions to any kind of bite or sting, get a doctor's prescription for an emergency insect-sting allergy kit (1½ oz., $46), containing four tablets of the antihistamine chlorpheniramine maleate and an epinephrine-loaded syringe. The syringe (and that means the whole caboodle) needs replacing every two or three years. Get the doctor to explain the kit's use. I've carried such a kit ever since suffering a mildly dramatic reaction to a bite, probably inflicted by an assassin bug that failed by a decent margin in its attempt.

Mammals

CHIP: Over the years I've had packs rifled and holes chewed in tents by—guess what? Not grizzlies. Not black bears, though one did keep me awake all night (story below). Not wolves or coyotes. Not mountain lions, jaguars, or bobcats—

Marmots. The Golden-mantled Marmot (aka Rockchuck), a large rodent, is alleged by most field guides to "feed entirely on green vegetation." But as a disgruntled eyewitness I attest that marmots have a burning yen for everything from fresh-caught trout to Swiss Miss. I've returned to camp to find a marmot inside my tent, having chewed its own ragged entrance—and exit. The next day I woke up and noticed my food-sack, suspended in bear-proof fashion, swinging violently across the rising sun with no apparent cause. As I approached, the marmot's head popped out, in a beige halo of Swiss Miss. I yelled. The marmot oozed forth, like infernal toothpaste, ascended the skinny cord to the branch, and flashed down the tree to its bouldery fortress, from whence issued a single derisory "phweeet."

Since a heavily thumped horse-packer camp was nearby, it's within a degree or two of certain that the hairy offender had not only scavenged in their bacon-strewn wake but had also likely been tossed bits of everything from cooked trout to cigar butts. So, like a junkie on the prowl, it had not only a habit but perhaps a grudge.

Field guides will also tell you that marmots are not a forest species, let alone tree climbers. Nevertheless, at least one member of the clan not only knows how but can also rappel a ¼-inch nylon cord and unpucker a stuff sack. Marmots also eat, or at least sample to the point of nonuse, the sweat-soaked headbands of caps and the shoulder straps and hipbelts on packs.

Second to marmots on my list of raiders are mice—the regular sort, plus the larger woodrats and packrats. I've opened my pack more than once to find not just a single mouse but a bright-eyed, gray-suited corporation, their built-in shredders at work. One long-ago night a packrat took a wild fancy to the key for my Svea stove and, despite the chain attaching it to the appliance proper, made off, dragging the stove several yards before I intervened. One fall night, sans tent, I was kept awake by mice dashing across my sleeping bag. Whether I was blocking some vital intermeadow route or they just liked the texture of the nylon, I'll never know. It was warm enough that I'd unzipped the sleeping bag down below and finally, despite the repeated scritch-scritch, fell asleep—only to wake up with a hairy little commuter on-ramping my leg. I shrieked and levitated. The mouse dove for safety in my crotch. The rest is a blur.

Enough. In other parts you'll hear raccoon epics or skunk legends or armadillo tales. The main point is that most of the trouble we backpack-ers have with our hairy, warm-blooded cousins is just this sort of low-level jostling. Irritating, occasionally infuriating, yes. But not a threat to life and limb.

Still, we *civilisados* are scared of other large predatory mammals quite out of proportion to any real danger. In part this may be because we see them so infrequently that most of us have no experience with them as real-life creatures. The nature-porn shown on television seems to high-light fangs, claws, blood, and gore. All of which combines to make lions and tigers and bears (Oh my!) into hobgoblins of the popular unconscious, lying in wait to bear us off for devourment.

Understand: I'm not immune—camped alone in the woods I've waked up at a noise and been seized by this same dark, unreasoning fear. This, despite my having slept more than a thousand nights out in bear country not just unharmed but unthreatened.

In Yellowstone National Park, where grizzlies coexist with intensive human use, the numbers tell the same tale: with more than 600,000 *registered* nights of backcountry use from 1980 to 1994 (not to mention even greater numbers of day hikers), there were only 21 people injured by the big bears (see page 737). That's 0.0035 percent. In short, grizzlies do their level best to avoid us and our troubles. This is not just my feeling but is well documented in the book I recommend above all: the sagacious and good-humored *Backcountry Bear Basics: The Definitive Guide to Avoiding Unpleasant Encounters* by Dave Smith (see Appendix IV), from which some of the following comes.

In fact, far more people suffer from the attacks of domestic pets and livestock than all the bears, wolves, cougars, and coyotes combined. That is, even in the wilderness, you're a lot more likely to be bitten by an out-of-control dog (or for that matter, your hiking partner) than a grizzly bear. This is not to say large predators don't attack people. A biologist friend of mine was torn up and permanently disfigured by a female grizzly. Cougars have pounced on a number of joggers. Just this year, in Great Smokies National Park, a woman was killed by a pair of black bears. But, on the other hand if you need to worry, as Colin observes, worry about bugs, not bears.

That is, concerning grizzly and brown bears, the genuine hazards are three largely controllable ones: surprise, food (and smell), and being seen as prey.*

Being surprised can make me react quite out of proportion to the cause: years ago when I was basking in the sun, a college roommate tossed a pitcher of ice water out the window and doused me. I leapt up, dashed around the building (aha!, a charge), and punched a hole through the rather stout wooden door (which he had just defensively locked). Most large animals, not just predators but also moose, bison, and such, can react in a similar way to a shock.

To lessen the element of surprise, keep your eyes open. If you walk the way most people drive—fast—with a narrow focus on the trail ahead, you can easily miss the presence of a large animal and thus blunder

---

*A single species of bear, *Ursus arctos,* is commonly called the "grizzly" in the lower 48 states and the "brown" in Canada and Alaska. The Kodiak bear (*Ursus arctos middendorffi*), found on Kodiak Island in Alaska, is now seen as a variety, not a separate species.

blindly into its personal space. Instead, slow down and scan, especially when you cross from sun to shade or top a rise or leave a meadow for the woods. Look to the side or behind occasionally. Scan the landscape ahead with binoculars. If you can see an animal, it can probably see you. But in areas with limited sight lines and sharp transitions (not to mention doting mama bears), it pays to make some noise. How much?

Some walkers in Yellowstone and Grand Teton National Parks travel in herds, festoon their packs with clappers and bells, and chatter so incessantly that *I* want to attack them. There *is* safety in numbers—bears and other large predators are less likely to approach a group—but there's no need to commit a public nuisance. The object is to alert the critter, not to annoy the hell out of every living thing within earshot. Sometimes I sing (Bob Marley, Merle Haggard, whatever), especially when walking into the wind or near a stream. Before heading into thick willows or forest understory I might clap my hands or tap my staff on a rock and say "Hey, bear. Yo, moose," in a conversational tone. (For recent findings on noise and bears, see page 741.)

Hiking at night or in a storm can sharply increase the chances of an abrupt encounter. Walking out from sampling a lake, on a moonless night, I once came upon a pair of moose that were vigorously mating—a perfectly natural act. At first glance, though, what I saw was a many-legged nightmare beast having an attack of convulsions: a heart stopper.

Big critters won't necessarily flee at the sound of your voice, particularly if they're bedded down or near a food source. So take your rest-and-gorp stops in places with good visibility on all sides. A common and bear-corrupting mistake is to ditch a goody-stuffed pack and wander off to take photos, etc. When you return, the bear is in full, toothy possession.

Food (and smell) is a complex, conjoined issue. But stated simply, a problem arises when an animal perceives you either as a) a source of food or b) as an obstacle to using a natural food source. We fuddle the issue further by permeating things like sunscreen and chewing tobacco with food-like scents. There is absolutely no survival advantage to smelling like a giant piña colada. So in bear (marmot, raccoon, hyena, coati mundi) habitat, avoid highly odiferous foods—cooking fresh meat or fish is a bio-magnet—and seek out unscented lotions and potions. Take pains to keep food and cooking smells out of your hair, clothing, sleeping bag, and tent. Since snow campers necessarily break this rule, bear gurus advise seasonal washups or using a different bag and tent for summer. Other tactics are to wash and change clothes after cooking, and/or to do your cooking and eating a bit early, then pack up and walk a half hour to make the night's camp. At a minimum, locate your sleeping area upwind and at least 100 feet from your cook site.

Smell might draw an animal's attention, but securing food, even a lick or a crumble, cements the association. Thousands of bears have been executed for going after human food, a strategy that puts the burden on the innocent. So the present push is to prevent bears from regarding humans as a food source. National parks and forests have installed bear-proof storage boxes and trash tips, with food-hanging poles and other conveniences, at popular campsites. But the first step is changing your kitchen habits: don't brush away crumbs or pour off fat, oil, cooking water, etc., in your campsite, or leave greasy paper towels smoldering like white-trash incense in the firepit. Use resealable plastic bags to hold food, cookware, and cosmetics, with another bag for trash, used tampons, spent moleskin, ucky Band-Aids, and other potential attractants. (A 1980 Yosemite Park study found that while 92 percent of campers claimed to store food properly, only 3 percent actually did.)

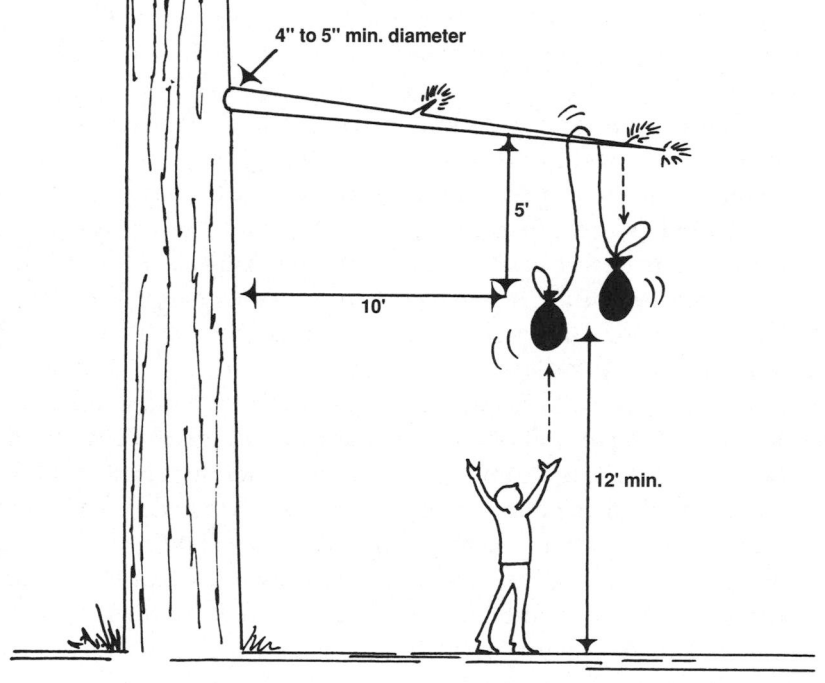

Based on a National Park Service drawing

The time-honored method is to hang a foodsack by the counterbalance method at least 10 feet above the ground on a limb too slender to support a bear (see drawing above). Gregory, among others, makes counterbalance bear bags with cords, etc. But this is only a stopgap—considering the bears' problem-solving ability with regard to knots and cords (not to mention my marmot incident above). Nevertheless, hanging nonfoods such as backpacks and trekking poles can spare them an investigative chewing.

For those of us who'd rather camp away from "developed" sites, containers that are bear- (and marmot-, raccoon-, hyena-, coati mundi–, packrat-, and mouse-) proof are a great leap forward. They're also a raging pain in the butt at first. But once you get used to them, they're better than pills to ensure a sound sleep. The proven standard is the Backpacker's Cache, a tapered canister of black plastic made by Garcia Machine in California (9 by 12 inches, 2.7 lbs., $75). The rounded contours offer little purchase for jaws and claws. A recessed trapdoor in one end has two twist-lock latches that open with a coin or a pocket tool. In the Sierra backcountry, where bear/camper disagreements had grown increasingly common, the required use of these containers has brought a sharp decrease in both scary encounters and the killing of "problem" bears. So it works.

The butt-cramp is that the rigid canister doesn't fit into most packs gracefully, especially lightweight top-loaders (which tend to look like a boa constrictor that's swallowed a beer keg). A fitted nylon carrying case with straps can be had from Garcia (3.5 oz., $18) that works fine with an E-frame but juts out awkwardly when lashed to I-frame packs. So if you're an I-framer and need serious critter-pro, choose a panel- or hybrid-loading pack.

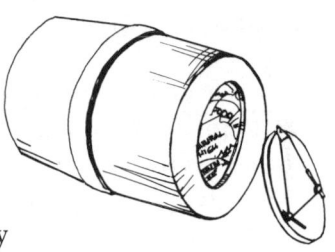

Garcia Backpacker's Cache

Other ursine calorie-deprivation setups (noted but not tested) include the aircraft-aluminum Bearcan (8 by 12 inches, 2.3 lbs., 10.5 quarts, $95) from Gio Enterprises. Both ends open with full-width covers, a plus, but the teeny screw latches are delicate, and there are four per end. After you take the food out you can set a stove on top. The Bearikade Weekender (9 by 10.4 inches, 1 lb. 10 oz., 11.3 quarts, $150) has a carbon-fiber body and aluminum ends with three latches—also somewhat delicate and hard to open. The new Purple Mountain Engineering Bear Canister is anodized aluminum (2.3 lbs., $90) available in five colors with slide-aside lid and custom engraving. Incidentally, you can put a piece of aluminum foil on a Garcia Cache and use it as a stove stand, too. One reader—the voice of experiential physics—writes to forewarn us that, "being round in cross section, most bear-proof caches will roll merrily away down slopes and into creeks, crevasses, or canyons."

A new and promising tack is a bear-defeating stuff bag called the Ursack (Minor: 8 by 13 inches, 4 oz., $40; Major: 8 by 24 inches, 6 oz., $60). Woven of pale yellow aramid fiber, of bulletproof-vest fame, the bag has a drawstring of Kevlar cord with a tensile strength of 1280 lbs. You seal your food and smellies in plastic bags, load the Ursack, tie an overhand knot above the cord lock (which is said to stand up to chomping), run the ends of the cord around a tree or other unmovable object some distance from your camp, and then rejoin them in a figure-eight knot. I did this and, lacking a bear, went after the Ursack with my fists and various garden tools, growling to get in the spirit of the thing. One zip-top bag burst inside and the granola bars went to pieces. But both fabric and cord held up. I've used the Ursack on two trips so far with no penetration by bear (marmot, raccoon, hyena, coati mundi, packrat, nor even a mouse). Some early users reported that seams unraveled, so the maker now double-stitches the seams and tapes them. The Ursack loads and packs more easily than does a rigid canister, weighs much less, and is somewhat less costly. The Ursack Minor has the same volume as the Garcia Cache (one person for four to five days). I use the Ursack Major and roll up the excess fabric. Some agencies requiring bear-proof containers might not have approved the Ursack for use, so check before embarking.

In the interests of interspecies tranquillity, you should studiously avoid getting between a large animal and its food. I say studiously because this means learning enough about the seasonal food habits of the animal whose neighborhood you're entering to avoid setting up camp in a nutritional hot spot.

For instance, from late March through April, when Yellowstone grizzlies are coming out of their dens, the green vegetation around hot springs and geysers is an important food source, as are the carcasses of winter-killed elk, deer, and bison. Hence, you should avoid camping near any of them—and also between courses, so to speak. Later in spring it's wise to avoid camping near streams where cutthroat trout are spawning.

With the fall snows, the Yellowstone bears are stripping frost-ripened berries and digging up squirrel-cached cones, particularly where whitebark pines yield fat-rich seeds. A cone cache is a heap of duff (cone scales, seed hulls, needles, and organic miscellania) under mature conifers. Little holes mean that the squirrels are burying their winter supply. Big holes mean a bear is digging the cones out to add a final coat of winter fat. Never camp on or near a cone cache that a bear is digging. It's like standing between a musk ox and his musk.*

Location is key in other ways. Bears and other large beasties tend to follow creeks or to skirt meadows using the forest edge for cover: that's

---

*One fall I was sampling the chemistry of small lakes on the west slope of the Tetons with the local trail crew foreman and two pack llamas. After climbing steep trails, we halted under a snow-threatening sky in a grove of whitebark pines. "This is where the trail crew always camps," he said. But under the trees was a massive and ancient cone cache. I looked around and saw several large digs, fresh and moist.

"There are bear digs all over," I said. "Can we pull off a ways?"

"This is where the trail crew *always* camps," said he, jaw set. That seemed to be it. After where you'll find animal trails. Developed trails often take these critter-engineered routes, so camp out in the open or well back in the woods. Forest and Park Service regulations mandate a certain distance (often 200 feet) from open water and established trails, and this is good practice for keeping out of the way of perambulating bears and moose. (Hint: they both leave big, easy-to-recognize tracks.)

On trips to griz-bear country, take a tent. Most nighttime attacks are predatory attempts, not charges, and most people injured were tent-less. If a bear cruises your tent, don't suffer in silence. Talking (not shriek-ing), unzipping the door, and flashing a light are usually enough to drive a bear away. If it returns, then yelling, rock tossing, and pepper spray are in order (see below).

Another bear attractant seems to be bright colors. David Petersen, author of *Ghost Grizzlies* (Johnson Books, 1998), tells of Yupik Eskimos warning a bear biologist "not to wear red, orange, or other bright colors." Intrigued, biologist Kellie Smith tried presenting different colored panels to brown bears, both in zoos and on the tundra. Said Smith, "A large, unbroken pattern such as a tent, even in natural colors, stands out as odd and may pique a bear's interest." Thick forest obscures such things, but in open country search-and-rescue orange is a beacon to curious bears. Smith suggests a camouflage fly—removable in case you want to attract the notice of a pilot.

Smith also built a blind on a cliff and rigged one of the widely used bear bells on the trail below and says: "In 15 trials not a single bear inves-tigated the bell or even turned to look at it." On the other hand, snapping a stick or making a loud "woof" got immediate bearish attention, ranging

---

he zipped up in his tent and commenced snoring, I slid into my bivy sac—and heard a loud, disgusted sniff from the dark. *Big nostrils,* I thought. We were close to occupied griz habitat. Maybe even in it. I flashed my light around. The two llamas swiveled like twin compass nee-dles to point at the unseen bear. The llamas turned north, east, south, west. The night wore on. Sniffs, scuffs, and grumbles kept me awake.

Occasionally I flashed my headlamp in whatever direction the llamas were pointing, but saw only grim pines, fallen trunks, and the clawed-up craters in the duff.

Just before dawn, I fell asleep. But first light revealed the circling bear to the two llamas. The larger one let out an alarm call, a rather mild expression for a sound that would peel scales off the Devil's arse. I exited the bivy sac spinning, about 5 feet in the air. The startled bear was likewise airborne and we both hit the ground at once, eye to eye.

I was fixed to the spot. But the big black bear wheeled, dashed up a 75-degree rockface, and with the rising sun glinting on its glossy, fat-shivering coat, disappeared.

Roused by the llama-klaxon, the trail crew foreman hollered, *"Jesus H. Christ!"* and promptly jammed the zipper of his tent. I yelled back that the bear had fled—just in time to keep him from slashing his way out with a Buck knife. We got the zipper unjammed. He poked his rumpled head out.

"So—the trail crew always camps here?" I said.

from a dead-stop alert to rapid flight. Given that most backpackers won't carry a bundle of sticks to snap, Smith advises handclaps and shouts.*

Do menstrual odors attract bears, let alone stimulate attacks? In 1967 in Glacier National Park two women died on the same night, August 13, from separate grizzly attacks, the first grizzly-caused deaths in the park. One was menstruating and the other carried tampons, anticipating her period. Amid a blitz of press coverage, the U.S. Park Service and several Canadian parks began issuing warnings to women to stay out of the backcountry when menstruating. While the ostensible agency concern was safety (and avoiding lawsuits), the rush to judgment raised questions in many minds. Later analysis of the fatal incidents brought the food-conditioning of both bears and the behavior of the campers to the forefront, without dissipating the cloud of doubt.

In 1980 a University of Montana student, Bruce Cushing, did a study on captive polar bears in Manitoba, using food items, human blood, and used tampons, among other things. He also did similar tests on wild bears in the field and concluded that menstrual odors did attract polar bears, though less so than fish, seal oil, chicken, and beer. (No official warning to beer drinkers was issued.) The study put park officials in a bind, since they were still issuing menstrual warnings to visitors while hiring a great many women to work as backcountry rangers. Several women who worked in Glacier National Park issued a critique of Cushing's research, and the park superintendent wrote a directive calling the study "inconclusive." But menstrual warnings continued in some parks and forests.

Further research failed to support the notion that women were significantly at risk of grizzly attacks during their periods. Dr. Stephen Herrero, researching a book on bear attacks, "did not find a correlation between attacks on women and any particular stage of their menstrual cycles."**

Another University of Montana student, Caroline Byrd, wrote a master's thesis analyzing both the Cushing study and the entire topic. Not surprisingly, she found that prevailing attitudes played at least as great a role as the sparse scientific data in associating menstruation with bear attacks. She also discovered that there was no significant correlation not just between bear attacks and menstruation, but between attacks and the sex of the victim.***

*See "The Blend-In Theory," by David Petersen, *Backpacker,* October 2000.

**Bear Attacks: Their Cause and Avoidance* by Dr. Stephen Herrero (Lyons & Burford, 1985), page 139.

***"Of Bears and Women: Investigating the Hypothesis that Menstruation Attracts Bears," by Caroline Byrd, University of Montana, 1988.

What about black bears? Biologist Lynn L. Rogers, for a 1991 paper, reviewed existing studies, did fieldwork, and questioned fellow biologists, concluding that: "Menstrual odors were essentially ignored by black bears. . . . we found no instance of black bears attacking or being attracted to menstruating women."*

In 1996 the Yellowstone Park report on 600,000 visitor-nights of backcountry use counted 21 people injured by bears—15 were men, 6 women. Most surprised a grizzly and were charged. Of the 3 people injured while camping, one was a woman, who was not menstruating at the time.**

Now that the dust has settled, the best advice seems to be to treat used tampons and underwear with the same caution as food, cosmetics, beer, and other potential attractants. Lately, a similar knee- (or higher) jerk reaction is evident in official warnings about sex being a dangerous attractant to bears. If it gets to the point where your sleeping bag crackles when you roll over and your tent acquires that monkey-house whiff, perhaps. But at this point none of us, neither scientist nor swami, let alone a gaggle of pinch-lipped prohibitory park puritans, knows for sure.

COLIN: The gospel some years ago was to walk alertly and carry a big gun. In *Walker III* I commented that "except in rare cases, this is a poor solution that could turn out to be the most dangerous of the lot." But when I made my first trip to Alaska and spent three weeks alone in a remote mountain area, a concerned Fish and Game Department biologist more or less insisted that I carry his .357 magnum revolver. Several recent and well-authenticated reports of people being killed by grizzlies overcame my reluctance. The bulky revolver, carried in a shoulder holster on my left side, proved to be no impediment and quickly became forgettable— though I remained comfortingly aware of its psychological protection.

Toward the end of my trip I "used" the gun. Two cubs and their mama ambled over a low crest in open, treeless country, directly in my path and perhaps 100 yards away. As Mama stood up to get a clear view of me (brown and indestructible, enormous, towering against the sky), I knew that the two of us were standing on the brink of that pivotal moment that always arises when a wild animal unused to humans meets one of us without clear introduction: for a brief, agonizing interval you can see the animal making up its mind whether this new creature should

---

*"Reactions of Black Bears to Human Menstrual Odors," by Lynn L. Rogers and S. S. Scott, *Journal of Wildlife Management*, 55(4), pages 632–34.

**"Bear-Inflicted Human Injuries in Yellowstone, 1980–1994," by Kerry Gunther and Hopi Hoekstra, *Yellowstone Science*, 4(1), winter 1996, pages 2–9.

be fled from, ignored, or attacked. And I understood what I had to do. I drew the revolver. Then I reached down and unclipped the Sierra Club cup that hung from my belt, moved it across my body to meet the revolver (which had miraculously shrunk to the dimensions of a peashooter), and began tapping the two metal objects together. Metal against metal is an unknown and apparently scary sound to truly wild animals. I've seen elephants veer away from it.

There on the Alaska tundra the effect was almost instantaneous. Mama came down from the sky and in the same movement turned left. On all fours she began hurrying back the way she'd come, over the crest and out of sight. The cubs followed.

Long afterward, when I had advanced beyond the crest, I glimpsed the family far downhill to the right, half a mile away, semiskulking behind a willow thicket and peering up toward me. A week later, on my first morning back in Anchorage, I woke to hear a radio report that a man had been killed and partly eaten by a grizzly less than 50 miles from where I'd been.

You can, of course, draw all kinds of conclusions from my nonadventure. Whether the metal-against-metal trick saved me, I don't know. "Ninety percent of the time," says my adviser, "nothing happens anyway, no matter what you do. It's the ten percent that's uncertain."*

CHIP: Current wisdom is that handguns are virtually worthless as grizzly bear protection—except as noisemakers. As Dave Smith writes, in *Backcountry Bear Basics:* "You're not likely to be charged by a grizzly unless you startle a bear at 60 yards or less. A grizzly can cover 60 yards in 4 to 5 seconds. It will be hurtling at you at 30 or more miles per hour. Your target area is only about 12 square inches."

Imagine having a star quarterback dash out of the brush and drill a pass right at your face—could you draw, fire, and hit the football?

A high-powered pistol is expensive and heavy. And from a statistical perspective, you're a damn sight more likely to have a stupid accident with it than to ward off a charging griz. There's also a building body of evidence that playing the *pistolero* in fact increases the chance that a bear will try to kill you—think of it from the bear's point of view.

Which brings us to pepper spray—which emerged as a self-defense tool for use against rapists and muggers, and was quickly adopted by police for use against criminals, political protesters, environmental activists, and other unruly elements. (If you've ever been on the receiving

---

*For a full account of this Alaska bear meeting, see *The Secret Worlds of Colin Fletcher,* chapter 6, page 205.

end, you know how it works.) More to the point, in the early 1980s, Charles Jonkel and other bear biologists began testing pepper spray as a means to ward off grizzly bears without permanently hurting, let alone killing, them.

The active principle is oleoresin capsicum, the oily irritant in peppers that makes Mexican, Thai, and Szechuan food a challenge. The liquid fire is extracted and mixed with a propellant, then sealed in single-use cans that resemble small chemical fire extinguishers. For bear defense, the spray should have 10 percent oleoresin capsicum (or 2 percent capsaicin), sufficient volume (7.9 oz./225 g net weight), a safety stop (some glow in the dark), and a holster or other means of keeping it in instant reach.

How well does it work? In 1995, an accounting of actual incidents showed that 20 out of 20 brown bears entering a camp were turned away. Only 2 bears made a second attempt. Out of 16 brown bear charges, pepper spray interrupted 15 (94 percent). But 6 bears that charged continued aggressive behavior, and 3 returned and attacked the sprayer.

Out of 26 black bears entering camps, 19 (73 percent) were initially deterred by spray; 14 of those left the campsite, but 6 returned. That is, out of 26 black bears sprayed only 8 (31 percent) left the area altogether. The 4 black bears pepper-sprayed after sudden encounters or predacious behavior all stopped what they were doing, but none left the area. While these are small numbers for statistical purposes, they do represent real-world encounters.*

They also point to important differences in behavior between brown or grizzly bears (*Ursus arctos*) and black bears (*Ursus americanus*). Read on for tactical tips.

Mugger/rapist sprays are useless against a bear. Designed to be used within arm's length, they come out in a diffuse fog. Bear spray issues in a denser, tighter cone, for four to nine seconds with a 15- to 35-foot range. When the canister's cold, that's halved, and wind or heavy rain sharply decrease the effective range. The orange dye lets you correct your aim. If you've never used bear spray (or a chemical fire extinguisher) it's a good idea to test-fire some—at $35 to $50 a can! So chip in with several friends and rotate squirts, but for heaven's sake watch the wind and don't get it on your hands or clothes.**

---

*"Field Use of Capsaicin Sprays as a Bear Deterrent," by Stephen Herrero and Andrew Higgins, in *Proceedings, 10th International Conference on Bear Research and Management* (Fairbanks, Alaska: IUCN Bear Specialists Group, 1995).

**A *Backpacker* magazine editor (mercifully unnamed) who kept a canister on his bedside table for burglar defense managed to let off a short burst while demonstrating to his (also naked) wife how the safety clip worked. Both ceased their behavior and immediately left the

Since pepper spray deteriorates, check by shaking the can. If it sloshes two to three times and then stops, the propellant is good. If it keeps sloshing, it's over the hill.

Other caveats: You don't want your kids firing test shots at the neighbor's dog (or each other), so keep it sequestered. If a can is triggered inside your car, you'll crash—no joke. (In sad fact this is probably more likely in statistical terms than your spraying it on a bear.) So en route, keep it double-bagged in the trunk. If you don't have a trunk, get an ammo can or other airtight container. Bush pilots now stow pepper spray outboard on a wing strut or float. Airlines forbid it entirely—you can neither carry it nor pack it in luggage, and might be fined and/or lose your ticket for trying. A different sort of fuss arises if you take U.S.-made pepper spray into Canada. The U.S. Environmental Protection Agency prohibits labeling it "for use against animals," while the Canadian government requires that it be labeled that way. In *Backcountry Bear Basics,* Dave Smith reports that Canadian customs agents will confiscate U.S. pepper spray and levy a stiff fine.

One more wrinkle: pepper spray is a *chemical weapon,* not a repellent. Spraying it on yourself will decommission your sight, breathing, smell, and most of the nerve endings in your skin for hours. Spraying it on packs, tents, etc. can actually *draw* bears, in the way that the exhaust fan of a good Mexican restaurant causes me to stop and salivate a block away. If I walked into the place and they squirted salsa in my eyes, that would be a different story. But, based on recent tests that show pepper-spray residue might actually attract bears, common sense dictates a thorough cleaning for any pepper-seasoned gear.

While I have a can of Counter Assault Bear Deterrent (11.4 oz., $47—at this date the only spray to gain EPA registration), I'm of two minds about actually carrying it. With this book in mind I've packed it on two trips and found that having it constantly at hand makes me more fearful, not less. Sleeping with it on cold nights is a downright nuisance, and the thought of rolling over and triggering a blast is sleep-banishing. No data exists on its effect on depredating marmots, and it would be sadistic to soak down a mouse. And my experience, in the country I frequent, is that unless I pull some transcendentally stupid trick like camping on a cone cache, the bears leave me alone. If I was a biologist or backcountry ranger working in griz habitat I might keep a can of the stuff in an elastic sheath on the yoke of my pack. But I'm not. Rather, I tend to

---

area. (*Backpacker,* September 2000, page 66—the article also lists and evaluates several brands of pepper spray, with a thoughtful sidebar by Jonathan Dorn on why he doesn't carry pepper spray.)

limit or avoid backcountry trips in the few places in the lower 48 where, despite a continuing loss of habitat, the big bears manage to hang on.*

While this decision might owe somewhat to inborn monkey fear, it owes more to respect for the magnificent creature that tribal people call "The Real Bear."

Anyhow, let's review tactics. Assume you've done everything right as far as food handling and storage and a bear still comes calling. What then? Some black bears can be driven off by making noise and tossing rocks (toward the bear, not at it: in Yosemite in 1996, a pack of Boy Scouts stoned a bear to death). But a bear that's snaffled food from campers might ignore the fuss. So, if possible, secure the food supply. But if the bear nails your grub, retreat. You lose (and the bear will probably get killed as a result). The following is a digest of what I've heard from people who've actually spent considerable time around bears.

If *any* bear approaches you:

- *STAND YOUR GROUND.* No matter whether you throw out your chest in defiance or are frozen with terror, stay put.
- *Don't run, try to climb a tree, or dive into a tent.* In the same way that jerking your hand back from a dog's face can cause it to bite, running away can trigger a predatory response in bears (also cougars, tigers, *et growlia*).
- *Keep your eye on the bear.* This doesn't mean staring it down. Just don't turn away. Wait for the next move. And try to decide whether it's a black bear or a grizzly. The grizzly (or brown) is both more likely to charge and more dangerous if it does.
- *Don't flop down and play dead—yet.* Unless a bear knocks you down, stay put. If it does knock you down, roll facedown, flat, and clasp the back of your neck. Hold still. The bear will most likely stop its attack, sniff, and retreat. *Stay put.* Movement can cause the bear to attack again. Steve French, codirector of the Yellowstone Grizzly Foundation and an M.D., says: "Victims who are attacked from a close-encounter situation and who immediately protect themselves and do not try to resist typically receive outpatient injuries."**

*There are six grizzly recovery areas in the U.S.: Greater Yellowstone, Northern Continental Divide (Glacier National Park), Cabinet-Yaak, Selway-Bitterroot, Selkirk, and North Cascades.

**Quoted in *Backcountry Bear Basics,* by Dave Smith, page 86.

CHIP: One consequence of playing dead when you first sight a bear is that you arouse the bear's curiosity. A friend and sometime climbing partner, one of the most accident-prone peo-

That is, don't try to fight it out with a grizzly, period. Play dead. In *very* rare cases, a black bear with cubs might charge and attack—she wants to neutralize the threat to her family as quickly as possible, then escape. Again, play dead.

But otherwise, if a black bear pursues the attack, fight like hell. Kick or use a weapon (knife, stick, rock). Punching a black bear, except squarely on the nose, has little effect and exposes your hands and forearms to serious damage.

For black bears and other predators such as cougars to ignore their instinctive caution and attempt to prey on a human being is rare indeed, but it happens. As subdivisions and vanity housing tear into their home habitat, with gourmet garbage, wandering pets, wayward children, and joggers lolloping along the trails like polychrome sausages, some predatory attacks will no doubt take place. That is, if you look like easy prey, then you might just be.

COLIN: Of course, less serious, old-style dangers remain. Backpacking in the Catskills some years ago, one reader became aware of a camp robber about four o'clock in the morning. "I moved slowly to check it out," he wrote me. "And it's just as well, because it was a rather large skunk. Right at my elbow. The disaster of a sudden move cannot be stressed too hard."

In spite of what I've written on page 671, there's still one other animal that puts the fear of God into me: *Homo sapiens nimrodamericanus,* the red-breasted, red-blooded, North American hunter. Every year, in the fall, the woods are alive with hunters, and every year a few more hunters fall dead. I know some of the massacre stories are probably apocryphal, but I play it safe: when the calendar springs the hunters loose I tend to stay at home—or at least to walk only in national parks, where hunters can't. But in the parks I must now hassle with bears. I'm sure hunters derive much sardonic amusement and also satisfaction—which may well be pragmatically sound—at the implicit ironies: we goddamned holier-than-thou backpackers must now choose between facing either marauding bears in

---

ple I've ever known, encountered a large black bear and immediately flopped down like a sick bunny. The bear, wondering what the hell was wrong with this guy, walked over and sniffed his motionless form. Then it bit down on the Snickers bar in his pants pocket, hooking its front teeth in his thigh. Whereupon he yelled and punched the bear on the nose. The bear fled. So did he. Not content with simply running away, he leapt into a nearby river and almost drowned.

After he told me this, with no hint of irony whatsoever, I quit climbing with him.

parks or the marauding hunters who probably used to keep the bears from marauding.*

Outside North America the general animal situation can be less reassuring. In Africa, for example, many rhinos and some elephants and even perhaps a rare buffalo will charge without apparent provocation. (Or does trespass on another animal's territory constitute provocation? Remember the Gulf War?) Lions, if surprised, may also attack. See page 378 too. For appropriate action on meeting unicorns, see page 96.

A possible but low-level risk in certain places and at certain times is bubonic plague, contracted from fleas from rodents, including chipmunks and squirrels. To avoid, do not feed the live animals or pick up dead bodies. Another low-level risk, almost anywhere in the world, is attack by rabid animals. I've seen only one animal that I assumed was rabid: a jackal that in broad daylight walked openly across a wheat field we were harvesting in Kenya. It seemed to be walking in a self-contained little world of its own, and it took no notice at all of either a combine or several people standing alongside. As it walked it kept twitching its head in a regular and demented fashion. It was, in other words, "acting contrary to general behavior patterns"—which is what rabid animals are described as habitually doing.

Now look, I hope you'll hold in decent perspective all these pages we've written about possible dangers of attack by wild animals. The real point, and not only with rattlesnakes and bears, is that knowledge reduces both fear and danger. Provided you behave sensibly, the risks are really very slight—probably a great deal less than those involved in getting to the wilderness, when some unprovoked animal traveling rapidly in the opposite direction may fall asleep or suffer a heart attack or burst a tire and slew across the dividing line and write an abrupt "finis" to your little game.

The only vegetable dangers you're likely to meet in the U.S. (assuming no gigantic Venus's-flytraps) are

---

*CHIP: Most grizzly deaths are still caused by hunters, who leave freshly killed game out overnight and return to find a bear contesting their possession. Since concerted efforts are being made to reduce the association of humans and food in the ursine mind, the counterproductive practice of shooting black bears over bait—horse carcasses, fish and poultry scraps, restaurant garbage, etc.—has now been banned in many states.

Further, as the western livestock industry loses its death grip on public lands, and native predators are less subject to tax-subsidized shooting, trapping, and mass poisoning, a number of species should rebound. Healthy populations of bears, wolves, cougars, lynx, and others will mean a better chance of meeting them in the wild. And it means more responsibility on the shoulders of wilderness lovers to keep the critters we esteem—and ourselves—out of trouble.

Poison oak, ivy, and sumac.

All these closely related plants cause rashes on some people—perhaps most people—if oil from leaf or stem comes in contact with the skin, directly or through transfer by clothes or other agents. The poison in all three plants is *urushiol,* an oil-soluble compound carried in canals *below* the surface of leaves and all other parts except pollen, which is nonpoisonous. So leaves or stems must be bruised in some way before you can be affected. In practice, though, almost all leaves are "bruised" by insects, weather, etc. Because urushiol's reaction with your skin begins within a minute of contact—though symptoms may take from six hours to a week to appear (commonly two days)—the sooner you start treatment after exposure the less severe the reaction is likely to be. But if you're highly susceptible and get a bad case you may spend three ghastly weeks in the hospital. (And never assume you're safe: one experienced friend of mine maintains that "the hospitals are full of people who thought they were immune." Although nobody can get a reaction on first contact, that contact—or the hundredth—may cause sensitization.) In less serious cases, affected skin reddens, swells, and develops blisters. The rash is always liable to spread, and it itches like crazy. Scratch, and you increase the irritation. Urushiol is long-lived stuff that clings to clothing, tools, pets, etc. and unless washed off can cause reactions for years.

Folklore, purveyed by hearty souls who are probably immune, goes something like this: "Can't understand what all the fuss is about. Just a good wash down with soap and hot water afterward and you'll never get any rash worth talking about. Why, I've waded thigh deep through the stuff and never had any kind of a rash at all."

Washing, especially with cold water, to close the pores, and a good soaping and rinsing indeed seem to help, if done within 30 minutes of contact—the time it takes for the resin to bond with the skin. In back-country situations, swabbing the resin off with isopropyl alcohol is more effective than haphazard washing, but bag up the swabs and any suspect clothing. Also recommended by doctors are Technu Poison Oak-N-Ivy Cleanser (alkane and alcohol) and Dr. West's Ivy Detox Cleanser (magnesium sulfate). Hot showers, later, alleviate the itching—though they may possibly prolong the symptoms. Calamine lotion, the traditional remedy, is now regarded as minor help; oral antihistamines (Benadryl, Teldrin, Claritin) may do more to reduce itching. See also Sting-Eze, page 728. A 1 percent hydrocortisone cream does a good job of suppressing symptoms if sparingly applied immediately after contact or at first blush of irritation. For severe cases, doctors sometimes prescribe prednisone tablets.

These remedies, and stronger corticosteroid prescription creams, seem to hold the reaction down, prevent spread, and almost eliminate itching. A mild rash may persist for as long as three weeks, but it never gets out of hand. At least, that has been my experience with Synalar, a cortisone-based prescription cream. In poison-oak country I always carry a small tube.

Opinion on the effectiveness of prophylactics now available, including shots, covers the whole spectrum from "useless" to "miraculous," so I guess a lot depends on the individual. Note that people who react violently to urushiol may get some reaction to prophylactics. And if over-the-counter brands containing urushiol, such as ImmunOak, ImmunIvy, and homeopathic pills, are taken during an attack they'll only make it worse. I have no firsthand experience of any prophylactic, but first-aid references recommend Ivy Block, a nonprescription lotion approved by the FDA, as well as Ivy Shield, Hollister Moisture Barrier, Hydropel, and Stokogard Outdoor Cream; people who won't be able to avoid urushiol-bearing plants can apply these products to bare skin before exposure.

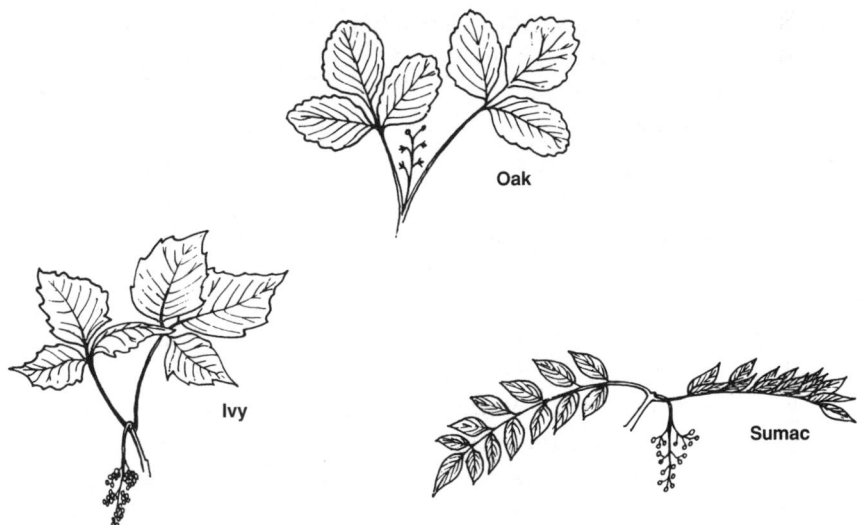

Oak

Ivy

Sumac

Many easterners now come west to backpack, and they're often confused about where to expect and how to recognize poison oak. No wonder. It's ubiquitous stuff. Although it's primarily a plant of low-altitude grasslands and forests, I've found it at nearly 7000 feet in the Sierra Nevada and, once, beside a desert creek in Southern California. And it's a botanical chameleon. Leaves are generally indented and oaklike; but they're variable. Their color is normally green, but they can be red, even in spring. Their surface is often shiny, but not always. The plant may be a single small stalk, standing on its own or lurking among others; it may climb, vinelike, far up a tree; or it may mass into dense clumps a dozen feet high and covering acres. Almost the only constant you can verbalize, in fact, is that its leaves, like those of poison ivy, *always* grow in clusters of three. Yet once you're familiar with the stuff you can recognize it readily enough; and in suspect country you soon learn to keep your eyes skinned in a barely conscious safe-operating procedure akin to that you adopt in rattler country (page 714).

I'm delighted to report that I can offer no earned enlightenment on poison ivy or sumac. But both, remember, bewitch with urushiol, and I gather that most of what I've said about the charms of poison oak apply to them.

Hypothermia

Some salient points should be understood by anyone who lives a life unwrapped in cotton and who wishes to remain among the quick.

Hypothermia (= subnormal body temperature; often called *exposure*) is not a danger restricted to high altitudes or bitter cold. Under certain conditions—wind, wetness, and a victim who is exhausted or unprepared to protect himself—deaths have occurred at sea level and at temperatures no lower than 42°F.

The progressive steps that lead to severe hypothermia can, once begun, accelerate alarmingly. A person who is exhausted—from overexertion, sickness, lack of food, or even extreme apprehension—and who becomes cold in wet, windy conditions may very quickly become colder and lose the capacity to rewarm himself. To generate heat, a cold body starts shivering—which in turn consumes a great deal of energy (page 194). Even apart from that, a cold body greatly elevates its metabolic demands (for oxygen and energy), and only a very fit person can meet them for long. In addition, hypothermia, like dehydration (page 230), quickly impairs judgment and so reduces chances of effective remedial action.

It's therefore vital that you understand the progressive symptoms of hypothermia. They're easy enough to recognize in someone else; difficult, but not impossible, to recognize in time in yourself. First, coldness and fatigue; then shivering that becomes uncontrolled; eventually—and this is the tip-off, and also the reason self-diagnosis is fiendishly difficult—increasing lethargy, until at last the patient plain gives up. In the early stages, heat loss from the central organs becomes too great for replacement by the metabolism; soon the nervous system ceases to function adequately; finally, the heart may stop.

Wet clothing is often the prime contributor. Clothing protects you by trapping body-warmed air between its layers and your skin. Water eliminates these airspaces—and conducts heat away from your body much faster than still, dry air: up to 5 times as fast in wet clothing, and 25 times as fast when you're immersed. Wool used to be by far the best material when wet, but synthetic-fiber underwear and pile garments that wick moisture away from your skin (page 510) seem to remove at least some of the danger.

Wind drastically increases chilling effect—and in theory two-thirds of the maximum increase occurs when the wind is blowing at only 2 mph. But the wind speed that counts is the one at your skin. If you're poorly dressed, that speed may approach or even equal the outside velocity. But proper windproof clothing can cut the effect to almost nil—though if the clothing is wet, wind will increase the evaporation and therefore the heat loss. The chart on the next page gives values for almost the whole human operating range. To use it, join with a ruler the wind velocity on left scale and the temperature on right scale, then read off windchill factor on diagonal—and learn that absolutely calm air at 30°F means a chill factor of 350 (cool, going on pleasant) and is the equivalent of a 2-mph wind at 58°F. Play with the chart, and think; but remember the blunting effects of good clothing.*

Aids to prevention. Try to avoid getting overfatigued: rest periodically, though not long enough to become chilled. Eat small amounts of food periodically too, to keep your metabolism fueled. Make every effort not to get wet—from rain or sweat; or wear wicking underwear and nonabsorbent insulation. Guard against anything that may cause sudden unnecessary cooling, such as ceasing to exercise and not readjusting or adding to your clothing.

Treatment. First reduce heat loss. Try to get out of the wind and put on dry clothes, or at least a windproof shell. Above all, protect the head and back of the neck (see pages 458 and 469). If stationary, insulate body from ground.

Second, produce heat. It's vital to remember that you're trying to reheat the body core, not the peripheries. One of the body's responses to cold is to reduce circulation and therefore heat flow to feet, hands, and all outlying areas, including the whole skin: as their temperature falls, so does the heat-dissipation rate. If you warm these precooled areas all you're

---

*CHIP: Maurice Bluestein, professor of engineering at Purdue University, and other thermodynamics researchers have called for an update of the windchill index, which he claims exaggerates the effect of cold on human beings by 10 to 15°F. The original research was done in the 1940s using water-filled cylinders to measure the rate of freezing, not a good model of how the human body works, said Bluestein at a meeting of the American Meteorological Society in 1998. The index also fails to take into account factors like direct solar heating. Another problem is that reported wind speeds are measured 30 feet above the ground and are faster than at a person's height. But, responds the Office of Meteorology's Mike Matthews, the National Weather Service "is going to continue using the windchill [index] in place right now until such time that the scientific community can really show and demonstrate that they have a better, improved formula."

WINDCHILL

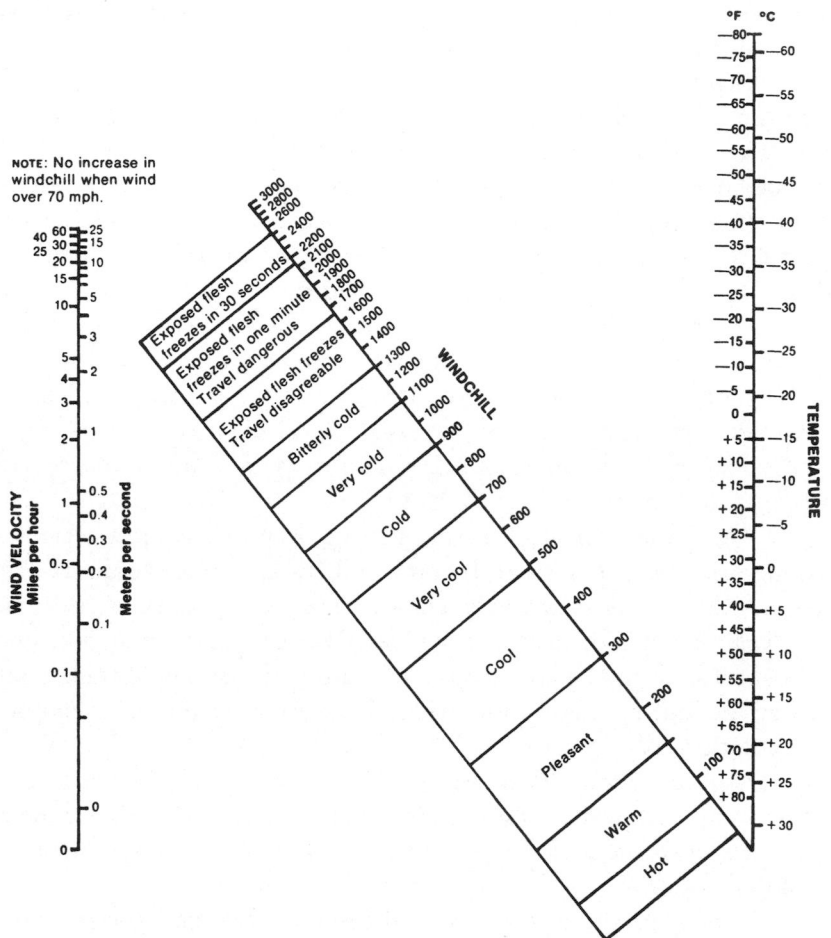

Line chart showing windchill and state of comfort under varying conditions of temperature and wind velocity. From Consolazio et al., *Metabolic Methods* (St. Louis: C. V. Mosby Company, 1951)

likely to do, at least at first, is to increase the circulation and heat flow from core to periphery—and therefore to cool the already heat-starved core, perhaps even fatally.

CHIP: By far the best-known first-aid treatment for mild hypothermia is to bundle up the victim with one or more warm companions, covered by sleeping bags. For this to work, the maximum possible skin-to-skin contact with the *torso* of the victim is crucial. Immersion in a warm bath is seldom possible in the field, but if a hot spring is handy get the person all the way in and be sure to support his head. Among possible treatments are hot, sugary drinks, if the patient is alert enough to swallow them (though *not* heavily caffeinated drinks or alcohol—Saint Bernard's kegs notwithstanding). Sips aren't enough: it takes 2 quarts of liquid at 140°F to raise the core temperature of an average-size person 1°, so keep that pot singing on the stove. Breathing warm air in a closed sleeping bag or inhaling steam over the pot are other ways to get heat to the body core. Commercial heat packs, fire-warmed rocks, and hot water in bladders or bottles should be wrapped in clothing and applied to the torso or the groin, not to the feet, hands, etc. Don't forget the option of building a fire and using a rockwall or a reflective blanket as a backdrop (page 351).

For very mild cases strenuous exercise can restore warmth, but since hypothermia is so often associated with exhaustion and dehydration, exercise in the absence of other treatment can deplete the victim's resources and make things worse. Since cold tissues and joints are subject to damage, avoid abrupt handling, or vigorous massage.

Jinglebob thermometers placed in the armpit or groin can clue you somewhat, but the only reliable indicator of core temperature is a rectal probe. If you're unprepared (or unwilling) then look for these symptoms:

Mild (core temp 95°F). The person will feel cold and shiver, remaining alert though perhaps whiny, difficult, or hostile.

Worsening (core temp below 93°—some first-aid books call this moderate). Shivering might cease, while stumbling, apathy, slurred speech, and memory loss can all take place.

Severe (core temp below 90°F). The person is unresponsive or unconscious, and other worries kick in. Chief among these is heart failure, since the heartbeat slows and becomes uneven, and fibrillation may take place. First-aid specialists agree on these principles:

- Treat the person very gently—no rough handling whatsoever; if breathing is weak (less than six breaths per minute) or absent, try rescue breathing but avoid the chest compression of CPR.
- Support the head and neck; stabilize other injuries with a splint or bandage.
- Keep the person from getting colder but get them to medical help fast.
- Since the person may be in "cold-protected state," particularly if he's fallen in cold water, rapid rewarming can bring a rush of chill, acidic blood from the extremities to the core, complicating recovery. Even people who seem to be stone cold dead have been revived. So get the poor devil to the hospital.

One of the curious and misleading things about our bodies is that we can feel bitingly cold without being in any real danger. Or on the other hand we might feel warm and happy up to and beyond the border of hypothermia. This happens because the brain gets its temperature readings from the nerves in the skin, not the core. Thus, drinking to excess makes us feel warm while actually cooling us down. Likewise, warming the hands and face can stop shivering without providing enough heat to the core to reverse hypothermia. A young man who was found dead on the west slope of the Tetons (not far from the place I was kept awake by a bear) had thrown off his clothing—a symptom of severe hypothermia known as *paradoxical undressing.* This occurs when the blood vessels in your skin abruptly dilate in response to lowering core temperature, producing an intense—but false—sensation of heat.

Mountain sickness

COLIN: An excellent little book, *Mountain Sickness: Prevention, Recognition and Treatment* by Peter H. Hackett, M.D. (American Alpine Club/The Mountaineers Books, 1980, 3 oz., 80 pages, $8.50), presents the current gospel in practical form, for laymen and physicians. It's clearly dangerous for me to attempt a summary of what turns out to be a rather complicated subject; but it might be even more dangerous—for those going up high—if I failed to make the attempt. (For suggestions on acclimation for moderately high trips, see page 44; on walking methods up high, page 121.) Dr. Hackett—Director of Medical Research for the Himalayan Rescue Association, and the fourth man (and first American) to climb to the summit of Everest alone—kindly checked this summary and the related sections. He suggested a few alterations, now incorporated.

Acute mountain sickness (AMS) is a fairly specific and potentially fatal condition with well-recognized but somewhat variable symptoms. It is, says Dr. Hackett, "not a mysterious or terribly complex entity that can only be dealt with by experienced mountain doctors. In fact, it is quite simple to recognize and easy to treat if it is recognized early enough, and requires no special medical knowledge. What it does require, however, is a high index of suspicion—which can only be based on reading about the condition or on having experienced it. Undoubtedly, the most common cause of morbidity and mortality from mountain sickness is lack of recognition because of ignorance."

AMS rarely seems to occur below 10,000 feet, though a few healthy people may begin to suffer at about 8000 and those with heart or lung problems even lower. A person's "AMS threshold" may differ appreciably on different occasions; factors that affect it certainly include rate of ascent, degree of exertion, and state of hydration.

Dr. Hackett says with obvious truth that AMS "is much better prevented than treated." Above all, he counsels careful acclimation. His measures are specifically tailored for newcomers to altitudes above 10,000 feet, but he recommends them for the experienced too: they may "mean the difference between a marginally enjoyable struggle and a comfortable, thoroughly enjoyable (and safe) trip. Why suffer?"

His main acclimating recommendations: If possible, start low and climb on foot. If you must drive or fly to above 10,000 feet, rest for 24 hours. Limit your net gain (i.e., camp to camp) to 1500 feet a day. Try to carry high (over passes, ridges) and sleep low. "It is the sleeping altitude that is critical." If continually moving higher, rest every third day.

Dr. Hackett's other recommendations: "Drink enough fluids (at least 3 quarts a day) to maintain a clear and copious urine." Do not take extra salt. Avoid overexertion. Eat a diet high in carbohydrates. And do not use medications as prophylactics: they may produce undesirable side effects and also a false sense of security. Exceptions: rescuers lifted abruptly to high elevations and people proven highly susceptible to AMS. (For them, "Diamox may be an alternative to giving up the mountains in favor of the beaches.") Another possible exception: people making a once-in-a-lifetime, limited-schedule trip up high, as to an Everest base camp, who have no time to linger and no second chance.

Headache is by far the most common AMS symptom. A mild headache that comes on after exertion and subsides after a rest or tea or coffee or maybe an aspirin, and which vanishes after a night's rest, is no more than an inconvenience. Deep breathing may help. So may massaging of the arteries at the temple. But a moderate-to-severe headache that persists after a night's rest, despite aspirin or acetaminophen and perhaps 30 milligrams of codeine, may be more serious. Stop ascending. If the headache persists after a second night's rest, descend—for at least 1000 feet.

Periodic breathing or Cheyne-Stokes syndrome (page 45) isn't serious in itself but may increase insomnia, itself a common high-altitude occurrence that tends to disappear after a week. For treatment, see page 122.

Mild gastrointestinal disorders, including loss of appetite, are not in themselves an indication of AMS but in severe form, especially as nausea, and with other symptoms, may be serious. Reduced urinary output, though difficult to distinguish from straight dehydration, should be taken as a warning sign, especially if there are other symptoms. For pulmonary symptoms, see pulmonary edema, on the next page.

The two most specific and crucial AMS symptoms are lassitude and ataxia. *Lassitude* may be distinguished from physical exhaustion, which responds to food, fluids, and a night's rest. Lassitude typically deepens over a 24- to 48-hour period. And if someone gets to the stage where he "cannot get up for meals, will not talk to anyone, and refuses to drink sufficient fluids, he soon cannot take care of himself" and may lapse into unconsciousness within 12 hours. Lassitude may be the only symptom of severe AMS. But it is usually accompanied by some degree of ataxia.

Ataxia (or loss of coordination) is another crucial sign of serious AMS—though it may occur in mild form with plain exhaustion or in hypothermia. Testing for ataxia is fortunately very simple, and every high-altitude backpacker should understand at least the heel-to-toe-walking-along-a-straight-line test often used by police to check sobriety. A normal person can "toe the line" without difficulty. Mildly ataxic people sway and show signs of difficulty in maintaining balance. In severe cases they may fall. An alternative test is the Romberg. Have the patient stand "at attention"—arms at sides, feet touching. Face him, place your arms around his upper body and tell him you won't let him fall. Then have him close his eyes. A normal person stands still. An ataxic person will start to sway within 10 to 15 seconds and may fall against your arms. The signs are obvious and impressive. Someone with ataxia can become a litter case within 6 hours and will usually do so within 24—unless sent down (never alone) for 1000 or even 3000 feet.

Peripheral edema (swelling of the face, hands, or feet) does not cause pain but can be dramatic and unsettling. It is more common in women than in men. Swelling of hands or feet is rarely serious, though rings should be removed from fingers as soon as possible. Facial edema is more likely to be a sign of AMS but normally occurs along with other symptoms.

The two extreme and dangerous conditions resulting from AMS are cerebral edema and high-altitude pulmonary edema.

Cerebral edema (CE) takes several days to develop, and is therefore of concern only if you are staying up high. Symptoms are generally severe forms of those already described, though toward the end there will probably be confusion, disorientation, sometimes hallucinations, and, ultimately, unconsciousness. "Descent is the only definitive therapy . . . as rapidly . . . and as far down as possible. . . . Taking someone down in the middle of the night instead of waiting until morning may save a life or prevent long-term brain damage."*

People developing *high-altitude pulmonary edema* (HAPE) usually exhibit at least some of the standard AMS symptoms. Specific signs include breathlessness even at rest, high breathing and pulse rates, decreased exercise capacity—and a cough. Distinguishing between a "normal" high-altitude cough due to dry air and a HAPE cough is diffi-

---

*CHIP: More recent sources also recommend giving oxygen, at 5 to 10 liters per minute and the steroid Decadron (dexamethasone). The Gamow Bag, or hyperbaric oxygen chamber, is a portable, inflatable device now used by expeditions and mountain-rescue units to treat all forms of altitude sickness.

cult. But the former will probably ease during rests and be assuaged by cough lozenges or steam inhalation. A HAPE cough persists during rests and does not respond to treatment. But it too may be "dry" at first, and only in advanced cases be accompanied by "pinkish or rusty-colored frothy sputum." These uncertainties are what make HAPE dangerous. It's difficult to diagnose. And if left untreated, death may be only hours away. Once again, the treatment is prompt and rapid descent. (A thousand feet will probably be enough, 3000 feet almost certainly.) Oxygen, if available, is very helpful.*

The basic problem of AMS seems to be "abnormal fluid shifts into the brain and lungs," so CE and HAPE often occur together. Distinguishing between them hardly matters, because treatment is the same: "When in doubt, go down!"

Treatment for milder forms of AMS includes various medications. Dr. Hackett recommends only Diamox, a prescription drug he judges useful in all forms except pulmonary edema. It need be taken only once every 8 or 12 hours, usually for only a few doses. A single tablet at bedtime will eliminate the Cheyne-Stokes periodic-breathing syndrome (page 45). Unlike some physicians, Dr. Hackett does not advocate Diamox as a prophylactic for everyone going high (for cases in which he does recommend it, see page 751). "The drug," he says, "has a number of side effects and should not be considered lightly. . . . Its effect on physical performance at altitude may also be detrimental [though] this is a subject of current controversy." Possible side effects include numbness and tingling in fingers, toes, and face; increased frequency of urination; and nausea, vomiting, and drowsiness.

In this brief summary, all I've been able to do is put out some signposts to the proper management of AMS so that no one remains totally ignorant of the basics. For full information, read Dr. Hackett's *Mountain Sickness* or one of the first-aid references on pages 652 to 653. But if you go above 10,000 feet be sure to maintain "a high index of suspicion." And remember that early diagnosis is the key and that descent, not medication, is the surest and safest cure.

Avalanches

CHIP: I guess this could be called "slopekeeping." Like any lover of the steep and deep, I've spent quite a bit of time trying to decide if a certain snow-covered slope would slip. There have been times when I argued with

---

*CHIP: Procardia (nifedipine), a drug prescribed for high blood pressure, can reportedly help treat HAPE and may prevent it in people who have a history of attacks, but it isn't yet accepted for general preventative use.

a partner about avalanche potential. In a few cases the partner tested it and down it went—with exciting though fortunately not fatal results. Given the sudden and tremendous power of avalanches, a touch of humility is only fitting. So I err on the side of caution and (knocking on whatever skis are made of these days) have never been caught.

Obviously it's not easy to study avalanches firsthand, so a short course with a book is a necessary prelude to traveling the mountain snowpack. I have an ancient copy of *The Avalanche Handbook* (USDA Handbook #489, U.S. Government Printing Office, Washington, DC 20402). There's also a private-sector *Avalanche Handbook* by David McClung and Peter Schaerer (The Mountaineers, 256 pages, $20). Another time-tested compact reference is *The ABC of Avalanche Safety* by Edward R. La Chapelle (The Mountaineers, 2nd edition 1985, $7). Also portable and inexpensive is *Basic Essentials of Avalanche Safety* (ICS Books, 1992, 72 pages, $6) by Buck Tilton.

Other books recommended by friends are *Avalanche Safety for Skiers and Climbers* by Tony Daffern (The Mountaineers, 2nd edition 1999, 192 pages, $17); *Avalanche Aware: Safe Travel in Avalanche Country* by John Moynier (Falcon, 1998, 128 pages, $7); and *Snow Sense: A Guide to Evaluating Snow Avalanche Hazard* by Jill Fredston and Doug Fesler (see Appendix IV). A more general guide is the *AMC Guide to Winter Camping: Wilderness Travel and Adventure in the Cold-weather Months* by Stephen Gorman (see Appendix IV).

Given a choice, I'd rather look at avalanches than books. Watching big gleaming spring slabs peel off and roar down with a thump and a thunder—from a comfortable distance—is worth any 10 good movies.

Another brief-but-beautiful phenomenon you need to treat with caution is

Lightning.

COLIN: Lightning is a low-risk danger worth learning something about: knowledge can reduce the hazard to vanishing point.

For walkers, mountains are the dangerous places. American Alpine Club statistics show that in a fairly recent 22-year span there were 14 lightning accidents on U.S. mountains. Twenty-eight people were involved. Seven died. But mountains are by no means the most dangerous places. And even in other wild areas the risk remains low. (In the metal-rich man-world, though, it's surprisingly high: lightning kills about 150 Americans a year—more than tornadoes or hurricanes—and injures about 250, predominantly east of the Mississippi.)

If you're caught up high in a storm the first thing to remember is the old mountaineering maxim: "In a storm, get off peaks and ridges." Avoid steep inclines (where the current flows fastest) and seek out flat ledges or gentle slopes. If possible get near a pinnacle that will act as a lightning rod. Stay a little way out from its base but not farther away than its height. Crouch low, touching the ground only with your feet, or sit on some insulator such as a coiled climbing rope. Keep clear of metal, such as your packframe or an aluminum staff. A cave, though the obvious shelter, is probably the most dangerous place of all unless it's very deep and high-roofed. Stay resolutely clear of shallow, low-roofed caves that are really no more than overhanging ledges. On August 4, 1948, a party of four California climbers was surprised by a storm near the summit of Bugaboo Spire in British Columbia and took shelter in just such a "cave." Almost at once a bolt of lightning struck outside the entrance. Two of the party died; the other two, dazed and burned, barely managed to make their way down safely.

No matter how careful you are, of course, the element of luck remains. On Bugaboo Spire it was the chance positioning of the four members of that party at the moment of the strike that determined who would live and who would die. Remember, though, that near-strikes such as the Bugaboo party suffered are not always serious. That day three other parties of the same expedition were all "hit," out in the open, with no ill effects. And mountains are by no means the only dangerous places. On the same day as the Bugaboo accident two children were killed by lightning in an open field in Oklahoma.

Useful facts: To estimate the distance in miles to a thunderstorm (and gain some idea of how much time you have to get the hell out of there) count the number of seconds between lightning and thunder and divide by 5.

At roadhead, the inside of your car is almost certainly the safest place around.

First aid. Persons struck by lightning receive a severe electrical shock and may be burned, but they carry no electrical charge and can be handled safely. A person "killed" by lightning can often be revived by prompt rescue breathing and CPR. In a group struck by lightning, the apparently dead should be treated first; those who show vital signs will probably recover spontaneously, although burns and other injuries may require treatment. Recovery from lightning strikes is usually complete except for possible impairment or loss of sight or hearing.*

---

*Source: "Death from Lightning and the Possibility of Living Again," by H. B. Taussig, *Annals of Internal Medicine,* Vol. 68, No. 6, June 1968. For further details, consult *All About Lightning* by Martin Uman (Dover, 1986, $8).

Many experienced outdoorsmen—and all reasonable hiking organizations—contend that one of the greatest dangers in wilderness travel is a practice that permeates this book:

Walking alone.

They may have something too. But once you've discovered solitude—the gigantic, enveloping, including, renewing solitude of wild and silent places—and have learned to put it to creative use, you're likely to accept without a second thought such small additional dangers as the solitude imposes. Naturally, you're careful. You make darned sure that someone always knows where you are, and when you'll be "out." You leave broad margins of safety in everything you do: hurrying (or not hurrying) over rough country to make up time; crossing (or not crossing) the creek on that narrow log; inching past (or not inching past) that perilously perched boulder. And when it comes to the all-important matter of luck you keep firmly in mind the Persian proverb I've already quoted: "Fortune is infatuated with the efficient."

But if you judge safety to be the paramount consideration in life you should never, under any circumstances, go on long hikes alone. Don't take short hikes alone either—or, for that matter, go anywhere alone. And avoid at all costs such foolhardy activities as driving, falling in love, or inhaling air that is almost certainly riddled with deadly germs. Wear wool next to the skin. Insure every good and chattel you possess against every conceivable contingency the future might bring, even if the premiums half-cripple the present. Never cross an intersection against a red light, even when you can see that all roads are clear for miles. And never, of course, explore the guts of an idea that seems as if it might threaten one of your more cherished beliefs. In your wisdom you will probably live to a ripe old age. But you may discover, just before you die, that you have been dead for a long, long time.

A book like this should obviously have something to say about

SURVIVAL.

But I find to my surprise that I can rake up precious little—and that I've never really given the matter the thought it seems to deserve.

Hoping to fill this awkward and humiliating gap in my knowledge, I asked a friend of mine—an experienced hiker, a cross-country skier of repute, and an expert climber who has been on Alaskan and Himalayan expeditions—for suggestions about books to read. "Oh, I dunno," he said. "I never read them. And I guess I never give the matter much thought."

Somewhat relieved but still uneasy, I turned for counsel to a practical outdoorsman who is in heavy demand as an instructor of survival and associated crafts. We talked for some time, but with each subject he brought up—water sources, signal flares, first-aid and snakebite kits, loosening waistbelt when wading rivers, and so on—I found myself saying, "Oh, but I've discussed that in the book as part of normal operating procedure."

After four or five such answers my counselor paused. "Yes," he said slowly. "Come to think of it, I guess you could say, really, that if you know how to operate properly in wilderness, then you know most of what there is to know about survival.

"What it generally amounts to, anyway, with inexperienced people, is simply not giving in to terror. That's what usually happens: ignorance—then panic. If your partner breaks a leg, for instance, you're in bad shape if you start thinking, 'Is it safe to leave him here, with all these wild animals around?' Of course it's safe—provided he's warm and comfortable. But if you don't know that, and feel suddenly overwhelmed and alone, you're liable to give way to panic. Naturally, you must be able to find your way out to civilization or the nearest help, and then guide rescuers back unerringly to the right place . . . but here we're back with plain competence in operating. And this is the kind of survival problem that's most likely to arise with walkers in the United States. Almost anywhere, outside of Alaska, you can get out to civilization—if you can walk—within two days at most. The old idea of survival as the problem of having to look after yourself for six months, completely cut off, when you're in good physical shape just doesn't apply here any more. And the rest amounts in most cases to medical knowledge and common sense."

In other words, this kind of "survival" mostly amounts to "experience." But "experience" isn't easy to assess. When I left the Mexican border at the start of my summer-long walk up California in 1958, at the age of 35, I had never spent a night on my own, away from the man-world, dependent *entirely* on what I carried on my back. (It was only some years later, I think, that I registered this fact—with considerable surprise.) I'm more than a little leery, now, of admitting my "inexperience" at that time: I might encourage tyros to attempt stupid and dangerous things. But even on the day I walked north from the Mexican border I was no tyro. Not really. I had considerable experience, in war and peace, of walking with loads and also of being alone in the bush for days on end—in cabins, for example, and canoeing around a remote Canadian lake. Also, in addition to being drum-tight with determination, I knew the limitations of my experience. I knew I had a lot to learn as I went along. That was important. People often get into trouble because they unwittingly—often unthinkingly—bite off more than they know how to chew. And sometimes, then, they don't survive.

"Survival" in the sense of living off the land (pages 30 and 188) poses a different problem. It's a real one all right, but most answers are specifically local. Knowing what to eat and what not to eat in the Sierra Nevada will get you nowhere in the Adirondacks, and even less place in the Mojave Desert. In each kind of country you have to learn it all again—from local and regional sources, experienced people, and even that immemorial standby, trial and error.

If you want reassurance on the broader questions of survival, and if you're a reader of books on such matters (and I guess you are if you've come 758 pages with us), there's plenty of material. The list waxes and wanes, so consult your local library or search the Internet. There are many and various sets of pocket-size survival cards available—you could fill a whole pack with them.

But perhaps, like me, you're lazy or a touch skeptical about such reading. If so, just remember, comfortably, that survival is 80 percent competence, 20 percent local knowledge, and 100 percent keeping your cool.

"The best single survival item you can carry," an experienced backpacker once said to me, " is a

Space blanket.

Now mostly called *emergency blankets,* these ultralightweight, aluminized Mylar sheets (56 by 84 inches, 2 oz., \$1–\$4 depending on quality) certainly have a lot going for them. Wrapped around as makeshift blanket, "they reflect up to 90% of a person's body heat back to him." They are wind- and waterproof. The original, high-quality versions remain flexible at 60°F below and, unlike some counterfeits, are very difficult to tear. They fold down to the size of a deck of survival cards. Proclaimed uses include: emergency blanket; lean-to protection against wind, rain, or snow; sun awning; short-term groundsheet (though they'll soon puncture); litter for carrying an injured person; heat reflector behind your back at campfire; reflector for ovens; fill-in reflector for photography; and a signal to aircraft or ground (sun reflection with the silver side, or color contrast with the orange side). For an occasion on which I was thankful I had gone back to carrying one—after a stretch when I didn't—see page 571. The blanket is almost always worth taking, I now feel, even if only as insurance on away-from-the-pack side trips. And I testify that as a pocket-stuffable item for covering your legs in frigid ballparks, nothing I know of can hold a candlestick to it.

Emergency signals

These days, almost any search operation for people believed lost in wild country is carried out, at least at first, from the air. So it pays to carry something that'll enable you to signal to a search plane even if you're injured and can move very little or not at all. A mirror, a smoke flare, and a strobe flasher are obvious candidates. But if you're able to build a fire and have water available, natural smoke may be the best bet. For details of flares and flashers, see page 654. For use and usefulness of mirror, flares, and smoke, see page 706; for a makeshift mirror substitute use anything shiny or reflective: knifeblade, watch crystal, mirrored sunglasses, Mylar space blanket, etc.

The same signals can, of course, be used for establishing contact with search parties on the ground. So can a whistle (page 655).

For places a helicopter can and cannot land, see page 709.

Keeping an eye on the weather

is an ongoing and all-pervasive part of "survival." Yet it's surprisingly difficult to formulate satisfactory guidelines. In fact, I find it hard to focus anything really worth saying, beyond "In any but the safest places and seasons—and perhaps even then—don't forget to keep a corner of your mind ready to detect any hint of a change." Above all, watch the wind. It can tip you off to what the general high-low atmospheric patterns are doing at that moment in your corner of the planet, and they, more than anything else, control and convey the storms that are what we mostly mean when we say "weather" in this context. But the nature of the clouds, which are often what you use to detect the wind, can be highly significant too. A book by Walter F. Dabberdt, *Weather for Outdoorsmen* (out of print), has cloud-formation photographs as endpapers and some useful information in between. But a lot of the most vital weather lore is a local matter. In the Sierra Nevada, for example, any persistent wind with some south in it should be regarded as a warning signal, and at certain times of year, under certain conditions, as an almost explicit warning to run for lower ground. But that gem won't apply in many other places, of course.

Local weather books are rare, but *Weathering the Wilderness: The Sierra Club Guide to Practical Meteorology* by William F. Reifsnyder (out of print) devotes less than half its 275 pages to weather in general, the rest to eight regional climates: Northern and Southern Appalachians, Great Lakes Basin, Northern and Southern Rockies, Cascades, Olympics, and Sierra Nevada. The book is, according to a harsh critic of my acquaintance, "a brave attempt at an impossible task." A new regional book: *Northwest*

Mountain Weather: Understanding and Forecasting for the Backcountry User by Jeff Renner (The Mountaineers, 96 pages, $11). But the best teachers are probably an alert awareness and years of experience. For weather radios and other devices, see catalogs (and pages 40 and 634).

No matter how you get your knowledge, though, use it constantly. Watch the clouds, wind, temperature. Mark any changes. And remember that a bad storm can convert a smiling playground into a potential morgue. Avoiding that potential is, of course, survival.

PRESERVING THE WILDERNESS

I've decided not to update this section, beyond a word here and there. It still reflects my views. And by leaving it essentially as it appeared in *Walker III* I hope to demonstrate that it's not flighty-by-night stuff. After all, it has already hung around for 17 years. Most of it, in three editions, for 30 years. Keeping things as they were, and saying I've done so, may also make it harder for new readers to brush off the darker elements as mere GOMP (Grumpy Old Man Perspective).

In the first two editions of this book I wrote, "Once you become a walker, you become a conservationist: no one can walk for days on end through wild and unspoiled country and then stumble on some man-perpetrated horror without having his blood start to boil." I'm now far less sure in my assertion than I used to be, but the principle stands.

Please don't misread me. On balance, I'm in favor of man. At times, though, my vote might just go the other way—and such moments mostly come when I've stumbled on the atrocities of the feeble-minded. I still remember vividly, from 40 years ago, walking across a secluded forest glade and all at once finding myself standing stock-still beside an old campsite that was a carnage of beer cans and cardboard boxes and torn plastic sheeting and dirty aluminum-foil plates and crumpled, soggy newspapers. Once, deep in a sidecanyon that led to the Inner Gorge of the Grand Canyon of the Colorado, I passed half a dozen pale pink boulders that the ages had worn into smooth and sensuous sculpture but which had recently been overprinted with crude black drawings and the timeless legend "Batman." Such droppings of bat-witted individuals are bad enough; but it angers me far more when a whole segment of society goes in for large-scale desecration. Many years ago, for two long and satisfying summers, I walked the virgin forests of western Vancouver Island, British Columbia, prospecting and staking claims for a mining company (and hoping, with some confidence, that the claims would never be developed). At intervals during those two summers I would emerge without warning

from the coolness and cloistered calm of huge trees and green undergrowth into the glare and heat and desolation of gouged earth and splin-
tered wood. I have never recovered from those moments: clear-cut logging
is still the one provocation that I acknowledge might drive me to murder.

Logging at least has some solid justifications: it generates both
needed wood products and also a satisfying life for some people. The same
cannot be said for an exploding, flippant, quintessentially modern
scourge, only somewhat less destructive, that I see as man at his blind
worst. Off-Road Vehicles (ORVs) undoubtedly give users a lot of pleasure.
We mustn't forget that. In fact, we should try to empathize. But freedom
to enjoy yourself is contingent on not harming your neighbors—your
human and other neighbors. It's rather like freedom of speech, which does
not include shouting "Fire!" in a crowded theater. For example, doing
motorcycle slaloms around Arlington National Cemetery would no doubt
be fun; but few people would condone such desecration. Yet many places
beloved by ORV users and being desecrated by them—such as the California deserts—are just as beautiful and fragile as Arlington. For those
with tuned-in eyes they carry at least as much significance. If left intact
they'll last a great deal longer. And we have no damned right to butcher
them for brief bursts of fun. Now, ORVs are expensive toys. Makers have
a huge stake in protecting their use, and the ORV lobby is therefore well
organized and carries heavy political clout. Since 1968, when the original
Walker appeared, the number of ORVs in the U.S. alone has zoomed from
a handful to multimillions. So their users' political influence has also
zoomed. The butchery too.

Make no mistake about the butchery. Accumulated results can be
appalling. A single motorcycle or all-terrain vehicle crossing fragile desert
or certain kinds of grassland leaves a compacted track. Scars can last for
years, decades, even centuries. And where one wheel passes, others almost
always follow. The increasingly popular cross-desert motorcycle races are
only a part of the problem. On some grassy hills near Gorman, 50 miles
north of Los Angeles, the ORV trail network could, even 15 years ago, be
seen from a plane flying at 30,000 feet.

The physical butchery—butchery of precious places that were until
recently free from the vehicular yoke that lies so heavy across most of our
land—is the obvious and brutal part. But those of us who walk for pleasure and beyond know that the ORVs' stark, straight-line, engineering
tracks—visible and invisible—crucify two of the essences of wilderness:
silence; and nature's soft and subtle curves and rhythms. In other words,
this relatively new scourge is, at root, yet another arm of a menace I have
railed against before: the deadly tentacles of the engineering mind.

More and more, it seems, the engineers are gathering up the reins of
power. And they are little men, most of them, with no concept at all of

what their projects are doing to the face of the earth. They will, if it serves any half-baked economic purpose, slash a freeway through irreplaceable redwood groves. Driven by a perfectly understandable professional challenge and an equally understandable desire to have plenty of work in the years ahead (and also driven, even less consciously, by the built-in self-aggrandizement mechanism that rots into the structure of almost all our human institutions), they will concoct plans for gigantic, unnecessary dams. That particular urge now seems to have ebbed. But other, more recent tides have come and gone: such propositions as the MX missile racecourse madness and oil rigs spattered through protected wildernesses. And as we look around the world today, it seems difficult to avoid the conclusion that many of our current problems stem from the application of engineering overlays to biological systems.*

Of course, the engineers don't always have their way. In recent decades we've protected many new wilderness areas from "progress." But

*A Missouri engineer has written complaining of an attack, similar to the above, that I made against engineers in the second edition. He wrote civilly and cogently. He pointed out that we need technology—"a necessary evil"—to maintain any kind of progress, even to ward off starvation. He said he was a Sierra Club member and worked actively to protect and increase wilderness areas. He said a lot more, with eloquence and sincerity. "So you see," he concluded, "just because I am an engineer, I'm not necessarily a mad despoiler. I hope you will think twice before you again condemn an entire group of people in print."

He's dead right, of course. I do not back down an inch from my inveighings against the dangers of the mass engineering mind, but I should not have appeared to pour scorn on all engineers. And I apologize.

I'm grateful to the man from Missouri for drawing my attention to this error and also for underlining something else, at least as important, that I tried to say in the second edition: my engineering outburst, left unqualified as it was, bordered on or even blundered into arrogant self-righteousness. And self-righteousness is an occupational hazard for all of us who call ourselves conservationists or preservationists or environmentalists—or, if you must, "ecologists."

Now, it doesn't matter much that self-righteousness begets crashing bores—the sort of people you're always slipping away from at parties. What does matter is that as soon as we raise our self-righteous banners we lose our effectiveness. The Sierra Club, of which I was once a member, though hardly an active one, remains an effective U.S. conservationist voice. But, like cooperative societies and organized religious bodies, it tends to be a holier-than-thou organization. The maggot is built in. As a result, the words "Sierra Club" are liable to raise, even in neutral circles, a chorus of groans—not to mention such pungent bumper stickers as "Sierra Club, kiss my axe." You can see the same effect on a small scale when we who are rabid antilitter fiends forget that we are human and start throwing our holy weights around: the result may well be a hostile group strewing their every last can and food wrapper about the landscape, deliberately and gleefully.

So we must always be on guard against our self-righteousness. It's difficult, I know. I, too, am pretty damned sure that we are holier than the litterlouts and the blinder engineers. But we must try to suppress the conviction—not just because it may possibly be unfounded, or even because it's bad for our souls or something, but because it reduces the chances that we'll achieve what we desperately want and need to achieve.

we mustn't take for granted these precious, last unmammonized oases—
or much that marches alongside them. We must continue to respond, vig-
ilantly, to the old shibboleth "You can't stop progress" by saying, "Sure,
but you can redefine it." And we must remember that, in the end, the
politicians are not necessarily the guilty ones. The enemy, as usual, is us—
the whole damned clutch of *Homo insapiens.* We all tend to get trapped in
the human corner. We repeatedly forget—or, encouraged by most of our
current religious systems, have never truly grasped—that there's more to
the world than us. We become hopelessly homocentric, perceptually
myopic. We say, for example, that the U.S. (or maybe the Western world)
is in economic trouble, and that therefore we must make major fiscal and
social adjustments. To me, it seems much truer and pragmatically more
fruitful to say that humanity is in trouble because it has moved out of harmony with the rest of the world, and that the only response that makes
any sense is striving to restore that harmony. "Hardheaded realists" tend
to label those who voice such thoughts as "impractical dreamers." But
Robert McNamara was once an archetypical hardheaded realist, and he
did a full one-eighty. There are plenty of clear early-warning signs, anyway: acid rain, toxic spills, vanishing rain forests, ozone holes, carbon-
dioxide buildup—and, still, the shadow of nuclear war.

Yet even when we correct our myopia and shrug off the omens for a
moment, the very signposts to the way ahead remain far from clear. Julian
Huxley defined man as "nothing else than evolution become conscious
of itself." Others consider us the brain of the planetary organism. It certainly seems not unreasonable to see ourselves as the current spearhead of
evolution. And once you start trying to discern the spear's trajectory you
eventually ask, "What are people for?" Huxley responded—rather surprisingly for a biologist—"The answer has something to do with their
quality." But that thought, warm and socially seminal though it may be,
is less relevant for our present purposes than Lewis Thomas's insight—
equally surprising from a physician—that what we seem to do best, or at
least better than any other organism, is communicate, and that perhaps
we should therefore consider communication our "biological function."
As a writer, I naturally tend to buy that. But I find myself unwilling even
to rent one of Thomas's follow-up suggestions, made in the early 1970s:
"There may be some laws about [our] kind of communication, mandating
a critical density and mass before it can function with efficiency. Only in
this century have we been brought close enough to each other, in great
numbers, to begin the fusion around the earth, and from now on the
process may move very rapidly. . . . What we need is more crowding,
more unrestrained and obsessive communication." This scenario meshes
with my acceptance of the view that evolution seems to move in the direction of increasing complexity. But it runs head-on into two opposing con-

victions. First, that there are already far too many of our species on the planet for its overall and necessary harmony, not to mention for our own health and safety, and that our most urgent need is, for starters, to cut our numbers, radically. We're unlikely to do this job ourselves other than by nuclear war, which seems certain to impose gross, totally inharmonious, and "unacceptable" side effects on the rest of the planet. (It's essential, of course, that we protect other gene pools with potential for alternative lines of progress should our spearhead shatter.) Yet if we are not culled in some relatively benign way, and soon—perhaps by some deadly, wide-spread, and human-specific disease, such as Very Easily Acquired Immune Deficiency Syndrome—the human bubble seems in imminent danger of bursting. My second opposing conviction, strong and gut, and entwined with the first, is that we need more wide and protected reaches of the planet, still rich and complicated and harmonious, where we do not dominate everything so stunningly.

I have for some time struggled with these opposing and apparently contradictory views—the need for greater density and the needs for culling and for wild places—and at last I have, with a little help from my friends, come up with a possible reconciliation. What we may need is more crowding together in certain restricted but fluidly interconnected localities, so that we generate even tenser communications—but also, at the same time, an overall retrenchment that will allow us to protect those precious wild places where we can stand back and contemplate and gain at least a whiff of perspective. Frank Herbert's *Dune* dwellers understood: they knew that "polish comes from the cities, wisdom from the desert."

Perhaps you're complaining by now that these reflections are neither profound nor even very satisfactory. But I shall let them stand, even though I might do better tomorrow. I am still seeking—even if it's for solutions to insoluble problems. And perhaps that's the point. It could be that what I'm really trying to say is: "Note that reflections like this are what seem to emerge in the end whenever you push hard at your worries about how to continue preserving the green world that opens up so richly once you've become a reasonably complete walker."

LEARN OF THE GREEN WORLD

Learn of the green world what can be thy place.

Ezra Pound

Learn of the Green World

The wilderness has a mysterious tongue,
which teaches awful doubt.

Quoted by Charles Darwin
in *The Voyage of the* Beagle

COLIN: When I began this book it was my intention to examine, here at the end, the delights of walking in different kinds of country. For I was afraid that in the course of several hundred fundamentally how-to pages we might have forgotten the feel-how—afraid that the ways and means might have masked the joys and insights that can come, in the end, from the simple act of walking. I'm still afraid that such an eclipse may have occurred. But I see now that the delights of different places are not what I must write about. They too are only means to an end.

Now, I'm the last person to deny that each kind of country—and also each season of the year and each hour of the day—has its own very special enchantments.

Mountains offer the slow unfolding of panoramas and the exhilaration of high places. Their summits, even the humble ones, are nearly always pinnacles of experience. And afterward you come back down. You ease back, step by step, from stark rock and snow into the world of observable life: first, a single tuft of vegetation in a windswept saddle; then the tracks of a small mammal; two hours later, the first tree; then the first tree that can stand upright against the wind; then the tracks of a large two-footed animal that was wearing lug-sole boots; then undeniable soil; soon trees that would be trees in any company; finally, thick undergrowth beneath the trees—and you pat your pocket to make sure the snakebite kit is still there.

In the desert you rediscover, every time you go back, the cleanness that exists in spite of the dust, the complexity that underlies the apparent openness, and the intricate web of life that stretches over the apparent barrenness; but above all you rediscover the echoing silence that you had thought you would never forget. Then there is untrodden snow country, silent with its own kind of silence. And the surging seashore. And other dominions too, each with its own signature: estuaries, the river worlds, marshland, farmlands, moors, and the open plain.

But in the course of time the memories meld. For they come, all of them, from the green world.

When I open my own mind and let the memories spill out, I find a many-hued mosaic. I remember the odd excitement and the restricted yet infinitely open world I have moved through several times when I have clambered up—very late at night, and following the little pool from my flashlight beam—to the flat, grassy summit of the hill on which I wrote at last the opening chapter of this book. I remember a three-day walk along an unspoiled beach with the wind always barreling in from the Pacific and the sand dunes always humping up on my left; and I remember the ceaseless surging and drawing back of the sea, with its final, curving excursions into smooth sand—excursions that sometimes left stranded, high and almost dry, little fragments of transparent protoplasm (which set me thinking, "This is the stuff we came from") and sometimes cast up a bottle that I could peer at (laughing at myself for being so childlike) in the hope that it might contain a message. I remember standing on snowshoes outside my half-buried tent after a four-day storm, in a newly gleaming white world, and watching the guilty, cloud-bearing southwest wind trying to reassert itself; I remember feeling a northeast breeze spring up, and almost hearing it take a deep breath and say, "They shall not pass," and then begin to blow in earnest; and I remember watching, thankfully, as the line of dark clouds was held along a front, horizon to horizon, and then was driven back, slowly but inexorably, until at last it retreated behind the peaks and the sky was left to the triumphant northeast wind and the warm and welcome sun. I remember trying to clamber up a steep woodland bank after dark, somewhere in the deep South (I think it was in Alabama), and finding myself in an enchanted world of fireflies and twisted tree roots and fireflies and clumps of grass and fireflies and wildflowers and fireflies and fireflies and fireflies—a world suddenly filled with a magic that I had not glimpsed since I was ten, and had almost come to disbelieve in. I remember striding down a desert road as dusk fell, with the wind catching my pack and billowing out the poncho like a sail and carrying me almost effortlessly along before it; and I remember how, when the rain came, it stung my bare legs, refreshing without hurting. I remember, in a different, sagebrush desert, coming to the edge of a village and passing a wooden building with three cars and a truck parked outside, and a battered sign that said PENTECOSTAL CHURCH OF GOD, EVERYONE WELCOME; I remember that the church door stood open to the warm evening, and that I could hear a piano and the congregation following along, with only a hint of exasperation, a half-beat behind a contralto whom nature had endowed with the volume, tempo, rigidity, and determination of a brass band. In another desert village—a long-dead ghost town, this one—I remember a clump of wild blue irises growing inside the worn wooden threshold of a once busy home. I remember red, red sunsets in a small desert valley when I was not alone. I remember, further back, a dead native cow in a clearing in the dry African bush; and, in the blood-softened soil beside its torn-out entrails, a single huge paw mark. I remember the small, round, furry heads of the hyraxes that would solemnly examine us from the boulders just behind our 13,000-foot camp up near Lewis Glacier on Mount Kenya. Further back still, I remember three otters cavorting across a moonlit Devonshire meadow; and a stag on a Scottish moor, silhouetted, elemental; and a shoal of small fish swimming slowly over a sloping bed of brown gravel that I can still see, stone fitting into stone, down a seventy-year tunnel. And now, vaulting back into yesterday, I find I'm remembering an elk that stands regally among redwood trees and the last tendrils of morning mist, and a surprised beaver that crouches almost at my feet and eyes me for clues, and a solitary evening primrose that has prospered in a desolation of desert talus, and a rainbow that arches over a dark mountain tarn, and the huge and solemn silence that encompasses, always, the buttes and mesas and cliffs and hanging terraces of the Grand Canyon of the Colorado.

Everyone who walks has his own floodlit memories—his own fluttering windwheel of scenes and sounds and scents. (It's often the scents that linger longest, though you don't know it until they come again.) But no matter what the hue of the individual memories, they all come from the green world. And in the end, when you have learned to connect—only to connect—you understand that it is simply the green world that you seek.

I suppose you could say that going out into this older world is rather like going to church. I know that it is in my case, anyway. For me, praying is no good: my god, if I have one, is a kind of space-age Pan, and It is not interested in what happens to me personally. But by walking out alone into wilderness I can elude the pressures of the pounding modern world, and in the sanctity of silence and solitude—the solitude seems to be a vital part of it—I can after a while begin to see and to hear and to think and in the end to feel with a new and exciting accuracy. And that, it seems to me, is just the kind of vision you should be hoping to find when you go to church.

Now, I don't want to suggest that out in the wilderness my mind—or, I suspect, anyone else's mind—is always soaring. Most of the time it operates on a mundanely down-to-earth level. In the course of a four-day hike taken primarily so that I could sort out ideas and directions for the first edition of this book, I tried to write down before they had faded away the thoughts that had run through my head while I was climbing one afternoon up a long and fairly steep hill. What I scribbled down was, in part: "Wonder how far now, over top and down to next creek. Maybe should have half-filled canteen from that last spring. . . . Oh hell, left heel again! Hope it's not a blister. Moleskin? No, not yet. Oh, look at that squirrel! Sun caught it beautifully, coming in from behind at an angle. Hm, horse tracks. Wonder how old. . . . Phew! Pretty damned hot for January. Better take off shirt at next halt. Almost time for rest anyway. Only five minutes. That should just get me to top of hill. . . . Hey, what's that on my leg? Oh, just water dripping off wet socks, on pack. . . . Oh my God, look! It'll be at least ten or fifteen minutes to top of bloody hill. Maybe more. . . . Say, your thoughts really do run on, don't they? Normally, don't notice it much, but . . . wait a minute, better jot down what I've been thinking, as accurately and as far back as I can. Might just be worth using in the walking book. Yes, out notebook right now. . . ."

Twice more on that four-day trip I jotted down odd islets of thought that jutted up from what was no doubt a continuous stream. Once, on a slightly less mundane but still distinctly unsoaring level, I found that as I walked I had concocted a mnemonic sentence ("King Philip, come out, for God's sake!") for a sequence that often leaves me groping: the hierarchy of categories into which biologists divide the living world (kingdom, phylum, class, order, family, genus, species). And one evening I was warming myself by a campfire and looking up at the dark pine trees silhouetted against a quarter-moon and beginning to think of beauty and life and death (or so my notes assure me) when I realized with some surprise that I was at the same time singing quietly to myself the soulful and almost immortal refrain from a song that was implanted in my mind somewhere deep in half-forgotten childhood: "And the captain sat in the captain's chair, and he played his ukulele as the ship went down."

But in trying to preclude a false impression I must not overcompensate. There are, of course, times when your mind soars or floats or hangs free and impartial—or dives into the depths.

For even in wilderness you may, very occasionally, plunge into despair—into the blackness that exists, I suppose, deep down in all our lives, waiting to blot out the underpinnings and so keep us honest. I remember a desert canyon in which, as I lay quiet beneath the stars, man was a pointless imposter on the bleak and ancient surface of the earth, and I knew I would never hope again. And I remember a night on a mountain when all that existed out in the blackness beyond my campfire was a small hemlock, and even the hemlock only flickered into and out of existence at the mercy of the fickle firelight; a night on which, for an endless, empty span, that little tree with its dark, stark needles was more lasting and more real than I was, and so claimed a crushing victory; a night on which, above all, the blackness beyond the tree was tragically and incontestably more real than the fragile tree, and therefore claimed the final, aching, desolate triumph. Such interludes—in which the keepers of the void ensnare you and all, all is vanity—are rare in wilderness. But they happen. And, although I would like to deny it, they are worse than in the city. While they last, the blackness is blacker, more hopeless, more desolately victorious. This time you cannot appeal to a more profound reality.

Far more often than despair, though, you taste elation. A squirrel leaps across a gap in the trees, a hundred feet above your head, and your mind, caught by the beauty, leaps too—across the gap between the dragging everyday world and the universals. Two swallows, bound head to tail in tight and perfect formation, bank up and away from a cliff face in a joyous arc of freedom. A quartet of beavers browses by the margin of a backwater, silent and serene, a tableau from a calmer age. Or you sit, triumphant, on a rocky peak and look and look at the whole world spread out below; and for a while, though still human, you are no longer merely human.

At such moments you do not "commune with nature" (a trite phrase that seems to classify nature as something outside and separate from us humans). At such moments you know, deep down in your fabric, with a certainty far more secure than intellect can offer, that you are a part of the web of life, and that the web of life is a part of the rock and air and water of pre-life. You know the wholeness of the universe, the great unity. And if you keep walking long enough—for several weeks or for several months—you may with care and good fortune experience whole days or even series of days during which you exist in this happy, included state.

They do not last, of course, these rich cadenzas. But their echoes linger. When you first return to the world of man there is a period of readjustment, just as there was when you left it and went out into the wilderness. After that first glorious hot shower (which is always—and always to your new surprise—a great experience in itself) you may find that for a day, or perhaps three days, or even a week, you live an unreal, cut-off-by-a-screen-of-gauze sort of existence. But once you've readjusted to hot showers and radios and orthodox beds and automobiles and parking meters and sidewalks and elevators and other people and other people's points of view, you begin to find that you have regained thrust and direction and hope and wonder and other such vital intangibles whose presence or absence color so indelibly the tenor of our lives, but which are very difficult to discuss without sententiousness. You find yourself refreshed, that is, for the eternal struggle of trying to see things as you more or less know they are, not merely as other people tell you they are. Above all, you find that you have recomprehended—totally, so that it's there behind every thought—the knowledge that we have arisen from everything that has gone before. You know, steadily, that we are more than just a fascinating and deadly and richly promising species that has begun to take over the face of the earth. You know again, fully, that this species you belong to is the current spearhead of life—and that your personal meaning is that you are a part of the spearhead. And so you find that you can take up once more the struggle we all have to make in our own several and quirky ways if we are to succeed in living lives that are truly human—the struggle to discern some glimmering of sense in the extraordinary phenomenon that is man.

And that, I guess, is quite a lot to get out of such a simple thing as walking.

Basic Checklist of Equipment

Note: For the most part, the cover photo is keyed to this list, starting at bottom with staff, boots, and other Foundations, and circling counterclockwise through Walls, Kitchen, Bedroom, and Clothes Closet to finish up with Furniture & Appliances and Housekeeping on (and below) the blue Therm-a-Rest pad. The obscure little black pouch (below the Atlas snowshoe, center right) is a rain cover for the Mountainsmith pack. The blue and black hieroglyph above the ice axe (bottom left center) is a Tidelands Casting Handline. Other mysteries have been solved by your reading of the book, or so we hope.

CHIP: In time, you're sure to evolve your own list—or lists, since your needs will change according to season and terrain. I try to anticipate the country and weather, and then imagine myself passing through: an enjoyable process that gives me ideas about what to take.

But any scatter-gun list of gear—one that tries to cover every exigency—will be too long and the resulting pack too heavy. So your next step is to make a trip-specific list that leaves out quite a lot. This leaving-out will make further demands on your imagination, as you consider ditching the tent (6.5 lbs.) in favor of a tarp (2 lbs.) and think of ways to cope should the weather shift dramatically.

The third step, and the charm, is the final paring-down. Just remember Colin's dictum: "Look after the ounces and the pounds will take care of themselves." But however you go about it, your end result will be somehow more than a list.

This basic list is weightless. For any given item the weights are so various that an average is meaningless. Sample lists *with weights* for some of my recent trips follow in Appendix II.

COLIN: *Suggestion:* Photocopy the following basic list, rule columns in both margins, and before a trip check off each item as you put it ready (on an old groundsheet or whatever), perhaps again as you transfer each item to the pack—and possibly even once more, at trailhead, before you finally strike out and away from civilization.

Remember, your final selection for any trip will always fall far short of the complete list. (Italics are in the hope of warding off the occasional misreaders' letters that bleat, "Surely you don't take *all* that stuff along with you?")

Foundations

Walls

Kitchen

Bedroom

Clothes Closet

525	Long-sleeved shirt	613	Goggles
529	Down vest	614	Anti-mist preparation
528	Down jacket	614	Binoculars
530	Next-to-skin bottom(s)	622	Camera, film, etc.
531	Briefs	623	Maps
532	Shorts	627	Mapcase
531	Tights	631	Compass/navigating device
535	Long pants	640	Soap or detergent
536	Fleece or pile pants	641	Pack towel
537	Belt or suspenders	641	Toothbrush
543	Rainjacket	641	Dentifrice
543	Parka or anorak	641	Comb
546	Poncho	641	Toilet paper
547	Cagoule	642	Scissors
547	Rainpants	643	Insect repellent
549	Rain chaps	645	Sunscreen
549	Colin's kilt	646	Lip balm
550	Wind jacket	647	Hand lotion
550	Windpants	647	Heat pads
551	Mittens (shells and/or liners)	648	First-aid kit
551	Gloves	654	Signal mirror
552	Liner gloves	654	Smoke bomb/Flare/Flasher
553	Booties	655	Whistle
554	Balaclava(s)	656	Fire starter
556	Scarf	656	Emergency fishing tackle
556	Swimsuit	657	Rope
556	Bandanna	659	Book(s)
557	Hat	661	Notebook
563	Head net	661	Paper for notes
564	Bucket and basin set	662	Pencils, pens, refills
686	Stuff sack(s) or zipper bags	663	Office
		663	Watch
		665	Pedometer

Furniture and Appliances

		665	Thermometer
		667	Repair tape (ripstop, duct, etc.)
579	Flashlight	667	Needles and thread
587	Headlamp	668	Spare clevis pins, plastic buckles, etc.
591	Spare batteries		
596	Spare bulb(s)	669	Fishing tackle
606	Solar-battery charger	672	Field guide (plants, birds)
599	Candle lantern/oil lamp	676	Nylon cord
600	Candles/lamp oil	658	Webbing
601	Gas lantern	678	Dental floss
598	Lightstick	679	Rubber bands
611	Sunglasses	679	Spare plastic bags

Housekeeping

Load Details for Various Trips by Length and Season

CHIP: These are lists for some of my recent solo trips, each chosen as an example of a particular approach:

- A) an ultralight solar-powered trip to the high desert in late spring;
- B) a fanny-pack overnighter during the hinge season in the mountains;
- C) an average-weight working trip to the mountains in stormy fall weather;
- D) a lightweight winter excursion on snowshoes.

One striking change from previous *Walkers* is how few individual items weigh more than 1 pound—I've gone from paring ounces to paring tenths of an ounce, so I list weights accordingly: in pounds, ounces, and tenths. The lists are arranged by the way I loaded my packs—where a stuff sack or pouch is listed, the items it held follow with an indent. Since there's a two-page ounce- and calorie-counting food table on pages 224 to 225—and because I was itching to *go*—for these trips I weighed the food bag as a unit. The lists don't include water weight: 1 liter = 2.2 lbs. and 1 quart = 2.1 lbs. Note that weights given below for some items might differ slightly from those in the text, owing to second-guess-weighing, wear and tear, duct-tape patches, or an occasional wash.

For more on the FSO (From the Skin Out) concept, see page 32.

A) SOLAR CAMPSITE, 7 DAYS, LATE SPRING, COLORADO PLATEAU
5000–7000 feet; 70–85°F days, 45–55° nights; passing rain

PACK, CONTENTS, AND ATTACHMENTS

	lb.	oz.
pack: GoLite Breeze		12.4
tarp/fly: Integral Designs SIL Shelter		
(not including sand)		15.0

	lb.	*oz.*
stakes (for sand and hardpan):		
Hilleberg, soft ground, 6 @ 0.6 oz.		3.6
and Black Diamond T, 9 in., 2 @ 2.2 oz.		4.4
3 mm static cord, 35 ft.		1.6
½-in. high-strength nylon webbing, 40 ft.		8.5
sleeping-bag stow sack: GoLite Pouch, medium		1.0
sleeping bag: Western Mountaineering Iroquois,		
down, long	1	11.0
Mylar reflective blanket (groundsheet)		1.7
book: *M'Asal Beag Dubh and Other Stories*		
by Padraic O Conaire		4.5

Solar campsite (page 604)

	lb.	*oz.*
battery charger: Solar World SPC-4, built into plastic box		3.8
headlamp: Princeton Tec Matrix LED (without batteries)		4.2
lamp batteries: AA high-capacity nicad, 2 @ 0.8 oz.		1.6
stove batteries: AA NiMH, 2 @ 0.9 oz.		1.8
emergency batteries: AA lithium Energizer, 2 @ 0.5 oz.		1.0
large zip-top plastic bag (for gathering fuel)		0.4
stove/pot bag (including soot)		1.2
stove: Sierra Zzip Titanium		9.9
pot with lid (serves as plate): Olicamp titanium		3.8
insulated mug, less handle: Aladdin, 12 fl. oz.		4.8
spoon: Snow Peak titanium		0.6
refillable butane lighter		0.6
stainless tea ball		0.5
viscose pack towel (partial)		0.3
scrubber		0.1
food bag (Ursack Major) and contents	13	4.8

Storage/water filtering (page 252)

	lb.	*oz.*
inlet screen, float and tube: Sweetwater		1.4
"bulk shampoo" pump		2.0
in-line cartridge filter: Safewater		3.0
bladder with hose and bite valve: Platypus Big Zip, 4-liter		4.5
zip bag: Outdoor Research Cell Block #5		2.5
lightweight balaclava: Patagonia Capilene		1.2
headnet: Outdoor Research Spring Ring		1.1
zip turtleneck: Mountain Hardwear ZeO_2 XL		9.4
pullover: Wyoming Wear Polartec 100		10.3
shell jacket: GoLite Bark microfiber L		8.2
lightweight bottoms: Patagonia Capilene XL		6.2
socks: Wyoming Wear Fleece Feet		3.0
liner socks: Bridgedale CoolMax		1.2

	lb.	*oz.*
mesh ditty bag		0.5
flashlight: C. Crane Lithium Trek		1.6
dial thermometer		0.6
digital alarm watch		0.6
regular eyeglasses		1.6
hardshell eyeglass case		1.4
cotton pocket handkerchief		1.0
toilet tissue and moist wipes in plastic bag		3.0
toothbrush, toothpowder, floss, soap (in harmonica box)		1.4
First-aid kit, plastic box (bandages, moleskin, aspirin, etc.)		5.0
foot cream: Neutrogena		3.0
lotion with sunscreen		3.5
elastic bandage		1.7
duct tape		0.3
yoke office: Outdoor Research Possum Pocket		3.0
maps		4.0
mechanical pencil		0.5
spiral notebook, 5″ × 3″		1.5
lip balm with sunscreen		0.2
pocket tool: Coast Micro-plier		1.7
whistle: Fox 40 Classic		0.4
signal mirror (Starflash plastic) in ink-cartridge bag		0.8
firestarting tool: Doan's magnesium		1.5
sweat wiper, viscose (cut from pack towel)		0.2
Pack and contents	**26 lbs.**	**4.1 oz.**

Worn or carried at the start of the trip

ball cap: Outdoor Research Corona		2.0
sunglasses		1.8
cotton pocket handkerchief		1.0
T-shirt: Lowe Alpine Dryflo		6.0
long-sleeved shirt: Columbia, cotton twill XL		10.5
shorts: Mountain Hardwear Pack XL		10.0
sandals: Chaco Elan, men's 12	1	13.0
staff: Cascade Designs Tracks Superlite 3		9.5
Total weight FSO	**30 lbs.**	**9.9 oz.**

B) TWO DAYS, ONE NIGHT, FALL, CENTRAL ROCKIES
8500–10,000 feet; 50°F days, 25° nights; light snowfall

FANNY PACK, CONTENTS, AND ATTACHMENTS

	lb.	*oz.*
fanny pack: Mountainsmith Day with strapettes	1	13.0

	lb.	oz.
sleeping bag: Western Mountaineering Iroquois long, in stuff sack	1	12.0
bivouac bag: Outdoor Research Deluxe	1	8.6
sleeping pad: Therm-a-Rest, ¾ Ultralite		15.0
book: *Grendel* by John Gardner		3.0
stove: Esbit tablet		3.0
fuel tablets @ 0.75 oz. × 8		6.0
refillable butane lighter		0.6
kettle with lid-plate, Olicamp Space Saver titanium		3.6
utensils: Snow Peak titanium, in sheath		2.0
insulated mug: Aladdin, 12 fl. oz. (less handle)		4.8
large zip-top plastic bag		0.4
water bladder: Platypus, 1-liter		1.0
water filter: Katadyn Mini Ceramic, in mesh bag		9.0
Recycled plastic water bottle: Schweppes Tonic		1.5
toilet tissue in plastic bag		1.0
toothbrush, toothpowder, floss, soap (in harmonica box)		1.4
First-aid kit, plastic box (bandages, moleskin, aspirin, etc.)		4.4
elastic bandage		1.7
headlamp: Princeton Tec Solo 2 AA		5.8
spare bulb, fleece sack		1.0
digital alarm watch		0.6
eyeglasses		1.8
hard-shell eyeglass case		1.4
rechargeable AA Accucell, 2 @ 0.75 oz.		1.5
plastic matchcase: Coghlan's, wood matches		1.0
duct tape		0.3
shock cord, ⅛ in.		0.2
yoke office: Outdoor Research Possum Pocket		3.0
mechanical pencil		0.5
map		2.0
spiral notebook, 5 × 3 in. (for gear notes)		1.5
lip balm with sunscreen		0.2
lotion with sunscreen		1.0
knife: Victorinox Tinker		3.1
whistle: Fox 40 Classic		0.4
signal mirror (Starflash plastic) in blister pack		0.7
firestarting tool: Doan's, magnesium		1.5
balaclava: Turtle Fur		2.9
red bandanna		1.4
midweight zip turtleneck: Mountain Hardwear L		7.5
anorak: Lowe Lightflite L		10.4
full-zip pants: Lowe Lightflite L		10.3
midweight bottoms: Mountain Hardwear XL		7.5
fleece gloves: Lowe Windbloc		2.3

	lb.	*oz.*
socks: Wyoming Wear Fleece Feet		3.0
neoprene socks: Gator XL		5.8
liner socks: Wigwam Ultimax		1.6
food canister (formerly held single-malt scotch)		4.0
food (packaged weight—not enough, see page 32)	1	7.6
Pack and contents	**15 lbs.**	**7.8 oz.**

Worn or carried at the start of the trip:

	lb.	*oz.*
cotton ball cap: Moonstone		2.3
sunglasses		1.8
leather side shields		0.2
eyeglass retainer: Croakies		0.4
T-shirt: Lowe Dryflo		6.5
fleece pullover: Wyoming Wear Sage Creek, XL		10.3
shorts: Wyoming Wear Zephyr, XL		6.5
sandals: Chaco Elan, men's 12	1	13.0
blue bandanna		1.4
staff (lodgepole marked with feet and tenths)		15.0
Total weight FSO	**20 lbs.**	**1.2 oz.**

Science gear (not used by the average backpacker)

	lb.	*oz.*
35 mm SLR Olympus camera, lenses, film, chest case	3	8.0
100 ft. tape (for stream-channel measurement)	1	7.6
aluminum stakes (to anchor tape)		2.6
K + E mining transit book (for stream data)		9.3
FSO with science gear	**25 lbs.**	**12.7 oz.**

C) FIVE DAYS, FOUR NIGHTS, LATE FALL, CENTRAL ROCKIES

7000–9500 feet; 35–50°F days, 20–30° nights; wind, rain, and 4 inches of snow

PACK, CONTENTS, AND ATTACHMENTS

	lb.	*oz.*
pack: Dana Design Swiftcurrent L	6	4.0
tent: VauDe Galaxy Ultralight (with stuff sack)	5	13.0
stuff sack: Outdoor Research #4 Hydroseal		4.8
sleeping bag: Sierra Designs Lewis, down, long	2	8.2
sleeping pad: Artiach Skin Mat, 72 in.	1	14.4
stove: Snow Peak GigaPower (3 oz.) + case (1 oz.)		4.0
gas cartridges: 1 Primus 2202 (15.9 oz. net)	1	5.3
1 Primus 2207 (7.6 oz. net)		11.7

	lb.	oz.
cookset: Snow Peak Mini Solo aluminum, in mesh bag		8.3
utensils: Snow Peak titanium, in sheath		2.0
insulated mug: Aladdin, 12 fl. oz. less handle		4.8
water bladder: Platypus, 1-liter		1.0
water filter: Coghlan's, with bag		6.5
viscose pack towel (partial)		1.0
toilet tissue in plastic bag		2.0
toothbrush, toothpowder, floss, soap (in harmonica box)		1.4
First-aid kit, plastic box (bandages, moleskin, aspirin, etc.)		4.4
elastic bandage		1.7
ditty bag: basic black nylon		4.0
headlamp, Princeton Tec Solo 2 AA		5.8
spare reflector, bulbs, fleece sack		1.2
digital alarm watch		0.6
eyeglasses		1.8
hard-shell eyeglass case		1.4
rechargeable AA Accucells, 2 @ 0.75 oz.		1.5
emergency lithium AA cells, Energizer, 2 @ 0.5 oz.		1.0
plastic matchcase: Coghlan's, wood matches		1.0
duct tape		0.3
shock cord, ⅛ in.		0.2
digital thermohygrometer (to measure temperature and relative humidity in and around tent)		1.8
yoke office: Outdoor Research Possum Pocket		3.0
mechanical pencil		0.7
spiral notebook, 5 × 3 in. (for gear notes)		1.5
lip balm with sunscreen		0.2
lotion with sunscreen		1.7
knife: Victorinox Tinker		3.1
whistle: Fox 40 Classic		0.4
signal mirror (Starflash plastic) in blister pack		0.7
firestarting tool: Doan's, magnesium		1.5
sandals: Chaco Elan, men's 12	1	13.0
neoprene socks: Gator XL		5.8
socks: Dahlgren, lightweight hiker		2.4
liner socks: Wigwam Ultimax		1.6
low-stretch gaiters: La Sportiva Gasket		2.6
stuff sack: Outdoor Research #4 Hydroseal		4.8
balaclava: Turtle Fur		2.9
red bandanna		1.4
midweight zip turtleneck: Mountain Hardwear ZeO$_2$ L		7.5
anorak: Lowe Lightflite L		10.4
fleece vest: REI Windbloc M		14.2
full-zip pants: Lowe Lightflite L		10.3
lightweight bottoms: Patagonia Capilene L		6.2

	lb.	*oz.*
midweight bottoms: Mountain Hardwear ZeO$_2$ XL		7.5
liner gloves: Wigwam polypropylene (partly melted)		2.0
fleece gloves: Lowe Windbloc		2.3
mittens: Norwegian wool (heavily darned)		3.0
large zip-top plastic bag		0.4
K + E mining transit book (for stream data)		9.3
book: *The Serpent and the Swan* by Boria Sax	1	0.0
map		2.0
bearproof canister: Garcia Backpacker's Cache	2	8.0
Food (packaged weight)	7	11
Pack and contents	**42 lbs.**	**4.5 oz.**

Worn or carried at the start of the trip

	lb.	*oz.*
ball cap: Moonstone, cotton		2.3
sunglasses with side shields		2.0
eyeglass retainer: Croakies		0.4
blue bandanna		1.4
T-shirt: Lowe Dryflo piqué		6.5
fleece pullover: Wyoming Wear Sage Creek XL		10.3
shorts: Wyoming Wear Zephyr XL		6.5
Boots: La Sportiva Storm GTX, men's 12	3	6.0
Socks: Bridgedale lightweight hiker		2.5
35 mm SLR Olympus camera, lenses, film, chest case	3	8.0
Total weight FSO	**51 lbs.**	**2.4 oz.**

D) THREE DAYS, TWO NIGHTS, EARLY WINTER, CENTRAL ROCKIES

7500–9500 feet; 25°F days, 15° nights; 1 foot of snow on ground, windy with 4–6 inches of snow

PACK, CONTENTS, AND ATTACHMENTS

	lb.	*oz.*
pack: Mountainsmith MountainLight 3500 L	3	10.0
solo tent: Hilleberg Akto with footprint, in stuff sack	3	3.2
stakes (for hard ground and snow), with extra guy lines, sack		12.0
sleeping bag: Sierra Designs Lewis, down, L, in stuff sack	2	13.0
sleeping pad: Therm-a-Rest ¾ Ultralite		15.0
groundsheet: Reflectix insulation, 76 in.		11.0
book: *The Lion, the Witch, and the Wardrobe* by C. S. Lewis		5.5
stove: Peak 1 Xtreme, in homemade hanging rig		15.0
fuel cartridges: Powermax, 1 @ 13.9 oz., 1 @ 7.8 oz.	1	5.7
lantern/stove chain		0.6

	lb.	*oz.*
butane lighter		0.6
matchsafe: Coghlan's, wood matches		1.0
pots with lid and lifter: MSR Blacklite	1	0.3
insulated mug: Aladdin, 12 fl. oz. less handle		4.8
coffee sling: Sierra Designs		1.0
spoon: GSI Tekk Lexan		0.3
viscose pack towel (partial)		0.3
recycled plastic water bottle, foil-taped		2.2
food bag (Ursack Major) and contents	4	8.5
mesh ditty bag		0.5
headlamp: Princeton Tec Solo with 2 AA Accucells		5.8
spare bulb, fleece sack		1.0
emergency batteries: AA lithium Energizer, 2 @ 0.5 oz.		1.0
dial thermometer		0.6
digital alarm watch		0.6
regular eyeglasses		1.6
hard-shell eyeglass case		1.4
cotton pocket handkerchief		1.0
toilet tissue in plastic bag		1.5
toothbrush, toothpowder, floss, soap (in harmonica box)		1.4
First-aid kit, plastic box (bandages, moleskin, aspirin, etc.)		4.4
elastic bandage		1.7
duct tape		0.3
yoke office: Outdoor Research Possum Pocket		3.0
mechanical pencil		0.5
spiral notebook, 5 × 3 in. (for gear notes)		1.5
lip balm with sunscreen		0.2
lotion with sunscreen		1.5
pocket tool: Coast Micro-plier		1.7
whistle: Fox 40 Classic		0.4
signal mirror (Starflash plastic) in ink-cartridge sack		0.8
firestarting tool: Doan's, magnesium		1.5
viscose eyeglass wiper (cut from pack towel)		0.2
zip bag: Outdoor Research Cell Block #8		3.0
bomber hat: Granite Gear South Shore		3.5
shell jacket: GoLite Bark microfiber L		8.2
shell pants: GoLite Trunk L		6.4
down vest: Woolrich L and stuff sack		14.0
shell mitts: Outdoor Research Gore-Tex		4.7
lightweight bottoms: Patagonia Capilene L		6.0
socks: Wigwam Ultimax		3.7
liner socks: Wigwam Ultimax		1.6
down booties: Sierra Designs		8.8
Pack and contents	**26 lb.**	**12.0 oz.**

Worn or carried at the start of the trip

	lb.	oz.
tennis visor, discount store		1.8
lightweight balaclava: Patagonia Capilene		1.2
sunglasses and side shields		2.0
Zip turtleneck: Mountain Hardwear ZeO$_2$, L		9.4
fleece pullover: Wyoming Wear Polartec 100		10.3
fleece gloves: Outdoor Research W. S. Gripper		3.4
leggings: Ridgeview Thermal Thinskins		3.5
tights: Outdoor Research Rhyolite XL		13.0
socks: Bridgedale GTX Trekker		3.2
low gaiters: Outdoor Research Flex-Tex		3.0
boots: Alico Ultrex, men's 12	3	9.6
staff: Cascade Designs Tracks Superlite 3 (with snow basket)		10.6
snowshoes: Little Bear Saguache Lexan	4	1.6
Total weight FSO	**38 lbs.**	**4.6 oz.**

Sources of Equipment, Food, and Services

The next best thing to knowing something
is knowing where to find it.

Samuel Johnson

CHIP: The following list is arranged in the same way as the book. Within each chapter or heading, the alphabet rules. One exception: rather than list catchall suppliers such as REI or Campmor repeatedly, there's an all-around category up front. *Note:* Since most e-mail addresses are also Web addresses (and e-mail can be sent through Web sites), I listed an e-mail address only in cases where no Web site was available.

All-around

Adventure 16, 4620 Alvarado Canyon Rd., San Diego, CA 92120, 619-283-6314, *www.adventure16.com*

ALPS Mountaineering, 1 White Pine, New Haven, MO 63068, 573-459-2577, *www.alpsmountaineering.com*

Black Diamond Equipment, 2084 E. 3900 S, Salt Lake City, UT 84124, 801-278-5533, *www.bdel.com*

Brigade Quartermasters, 1025 Cobb International Blvd., Kennesaw, GA 30152, 800-338-4327, *www.actiongear.com*

Cabela's, 1 Cabela Dr., Sidney, NE 69160, 800-234-4444, *www.cabelas.com*

Campmor, P.O. Box 700-A, Saddle River, NJ 07458, 800-226-7667, *www.campmor.com*

Climb High, 135 Northside Dr., Shelburne, VT 05482, 802-985-5056, *www.climbhigh.com*

Coghlan's, Ltd., 121 Irene St., Winnipeg, MB R3T 4C7, Canada 204-284-9550, <coghlans@coghlansinfo.ca>

Coleman Exponent (Peak 1), 3600 N. Hydraulic, Wichita, KS 67219, 800-835-3278, *www.coleman.com*

Dana Design, 19215 Vashon Hwy. SW, Vashon, WA 98070, 888-357-3262, *www.danadesign.com*

Eastern Mountain Sports, 1 Vose Farm Rd., Peterborough, NH 03458, 603-924-9571, *www.emsonline.com*

Eureka, 1326 Willow Rd., Sturtevant, WI 53177, 800-345-7622, *www.eurekatent.com*

Forestry Suppliers, P.O. Box 8397, Jackson, MS 39284-8397, 800-647-5368, *www.forestry-suppliers.com*

GoLite, 5785 Arapahoe, Ste. D, Boulder, CO 80303, 888-546-5483, *www.golite.com*

Integral Designs, 5516 Third St. SE, Calgary, AB, Canada T2H 1J9, 403-640-1445, *www.integraldesigns.com*

Kelty, 6235 G Lookout Rd., Boulder, CO 80301, 800-423-2320, *www.kelty.com*

Lafuma America, 6662 Gunpark Dr., Ste. 101, Boulder, CO 80301, 303-527-1460, *www.lafuma.com*

Liberty Mountain Adventure, 4375 W. 1980 S, Salt Lake City, UT 84104, 801-954-0741, *www.libertymountain.com*

Light is Right, 419 Vilas Ave., Guthrie, OK 73044, 800-955-3080, *www.lightisright.com*

L. L. Bean, Casco St., Freeport, ME 04033, 800-809-7057, *www.llbean.com*

Lowe Alpine, 2325 Midway Blvd., Broomfield, CO 80020, 303-465-3706, *www.lowealpine.com*

Marmot Mountain Ltd., 2321 Circadian Way, Santa Rosa, CA 95407, 707-544-4590, *www.marmot.com*

Mountain Equipment Co-op, 130 W. Broadway, Vancouver, BC, Canada V5Y 4A6, 800-663-2667, *www.mec.ca*

Mountain Gear, 730 N. Hamilton, Spokane, WA 99202, 800-829-2009, *www.mgear.com*

Mountain Hardwear, 4911 Central Ave., Richmond, CA 94804, 800-953-8375, *www.mountainhardwear.com*

Mountain Safety Research, 3800 First Ave., Seattle, WA 98134, 800-877-9677, *www.msrcorp.com*

Mountain Tools, P.O. Box 22788, Carmel, CA 93922, 831-620-0911, *www.mtntools.com*

Northwest River Supplies, 2009 S. Main St., Moscow, ID 83843, 800-243-1677, *www.nrsweb.com*

Outbound Products, 8585 Fraser St., Vancouver, BC, Canada V5X 3Y1, 604-321-5464, *www.outbound.ca*

Outdoor Research, 2203 First Ave. S, Seattle, WA 98134, 888-467-4327, *www.orgear.com*

Peak 1 — see Coleman Exponent

Quest, P.O. Box 1500, Williston, VT 05495, 800-222-3088, *www.peregrineoutfitters.com*

Recreational Equipment, Inc., 6750 S. 228th St., Kent, WA 98032, 800-426-4840, *www.rei.com*

Sierra Designs, 1255 Powell St., Emeryville, CA 94608, 800-635-0461, *www.sierradesigns.com*

Sierra Trading Post, 5025 Campstool Rd., Cheyenne, WY 82007, 800-713-4534, *www.sierratradingpost.com*

VauDe Sports, P.O. Box 3413, Mammoth Lakes, CA 93546, 800-447-1539, *www.vaude.com*

Wild Country/Climb High, 135 Northside Dr., Shelburne, VT 05482, 802-985-5056, *www.climbhigh.com*

GROUND PLAN

Trade and Watchdog Groups

National Labor Committee, 212-242-3002, *www.nlcnet.org*

Outdoor Recreation Coalition of America, P.O. Box 1319, Boulder, CO 80306, 1-888-854-6722, *www.orca.org*

FOUNDATIONS

Boots, Shoes, and Sandals

Alico Sport, 324 Bluff Rd., Newton VT 05855, 514-871-0774, *www.alicosport.com*

Asolo USA, 190 Hanover St., Lebanon, NH 03766, 603-448-8827, *www.asolo.com*

Chaco Sandals, P.O. Box 388, Paonia, CO 81428, 970-527-4990, *www.chacosan.com*

Danner, 12722 Airport Way, Portland, OR 97230, 1-800-345-0430, *www.danner.com*

FitSystem (for boots) by Phil Oren, HC 30 Box 911, Prescott, AZ 86301, 520-445-0031

Garmont USA, 170 Boyer Circle, Ste. 20, Williston, VT 05495, 802-658-8322, *www.garmontusa.com*

Hi-Tec Sports, 4801 Stoddard Rd., Modesto, CA 95356, 209-545-1111, *www.hi-tec.com*

La Sportiva/Lizard Sandals, 3280 Pearl St., Boulder, CO 80403, 303-443-8710, *www.sportiva.com*

Limmer Boots, HC 68, Box 248C, Center Conway, NH 03813, 603-694-2668, *www.limmerboot.com*

Lowa Boots, P.O. Box 407, Old Greenwich, CT 06870, 203-353-0116, *www.lowaboots.com*

Merrell Performance Footwear, 9431 Courtland Dr., Rockford, MI 49351, 888-637-7001, *www.merrellboot.com*

Minnetonka Moccasin Co., 1113 E. Hennepin Ave., Minneapolis, MN 55414, 612-331-3721

Montrail, 1003 Sixth Ave. S, Seattle, WA 98134, 1-800-647-0224, *www.montrail.com*

NEOS, P.O. Box 540, Charlotte, VT 05445, 802-425-4848, *www.overshoe.com*

Raichle Outdoor, P.O. Box 2913, Jackson, WY 83001, 307-733-2266, *www.raichleoutdoor.com*

Salomon North America, 9401 Nimbus Ave., Beaverton, OR 97076, 877-272-5666, *www.salomonsports.com*

Schnee's Boots & Shoes, 121 W. Main St., Bozeman, MT 59715, 406-587-0981, *www.schnees.com*

Tecnica USA, 19 Technology Dr., West Lebanon, NH 03784, 603-298-8032, *www.tecnicausa.com*

Teva Sandals, P.O. Box 968, Flagstaff, AZ 86002, 800-367-8382, *www.teva.com*

Vasque, 314 Main St., Red Wing, MN 55066, 800-224-4453, *www.vasque.com*

Boot Repairs and Resoles

Carter Boot Repair, 11 East Main St., Bozeman, MT 59715, 406-585-8607, <lacarter98@yahoo.com>

Cobbler and Cordwainer, 73 Crescent Ave., New Rochelle, NY 10801, 914-632-8312, *www.cobcord.com*

Dave Page, Cobbler, 3509 Evanston Ave. N, Seattle, WA 98103, 800-252-1229, *www.davepagecobbler.com*

Down East Service Center, 50 Spring St., New York, NY 10012, 212-925-2632, <cphilip938@aol.com>

Komito Boots, 235 W. Riverside, P.O. Box 2106, Estes Park, CO 80517, 800-422-2668

Mekan Boot, 116 E 3645 S, Salt Lake City, UT 84124, 800-657-2884, *www.mekan.citysearch.com*

Mountain Soles, P.O. Box 28, Trout Lake, WA 98650, 503-236-0785, *www.mtnsoles.com*

Progressive Outdoor Footwear Repair, 4760 Unit D, Mission Gorge Pl., San Diego, CA 92021, 800-783-7764

Rocky Mountain Resole, 211 Oak St., Salida, CO 81201, 800-228-2668, *www.rmresole.com*

Wyoming Foot Comfort, Buffalo, WY 82834, 307-684-8718, <mitch dashoe@rocketmail.com>

Footbeds and Insoles

Arch Crafters/Amfit, 2850 Bowers Ave., Santa Clara, CA 95051, 408-986-1232, *www.amfit.com*

Heat Factory, 6054 Corte del Cedro, Carlsbad, CA 92009, 800-993-4328, *www.heatfactory.com*

Orthofeet, 152A Veterans Dr., Northvale, NJ 07647, 201-767-6224, <orthofeet@aol.com>

Sof Sole, 9221 Globe Center Dr., Morrisville, NC 27560, 919-544-7900, *www.sofsole.com*

Spenco Medical, P.O. Box 2501, Waco, TX 76702, 800-877-3626, *www.spenco.com*

Spirakut/Footfix, P.O. Box 3430, Hailey, ID 83333, 208-726-2205, *www.footfix.com*

Superfeet, 1419 Whitehorn St., Ferndale, WA 98248, 800-634-6618, *www.superfeet.com*

Wyoming Foot Comfort, Buffalo, WY 82834, 307-684-8718, <mitch dashoe@rocketmail.com>

Waterproofing/Washing/Repair Compounds

Aquaseal/Seam Grip, McNett, 1405 Fraser St., Bellingham, WA 98226, 360-671-2227, <office@mcnett.com>

Granger's/MPI Outdoors, 10 Industrial Dr., Windham, NH 03087, 603-890-0455, *www.mpioutdoor.com*

Nikwax USA, P.O. Box 1572, Everett, WA 98026, 425-339-5393, *www.nikwax-usa.com*

Tectron/Blue Magic, 4445 E. Fremont St., Stockton, CA 95215, 800-289-2583, *www.bluemagic.com*

Socks

Ballston/Brown Wooten Mills, P.O. Box 1440, Burlington, NC 27216, 336-227-1291, *www.brownwooten.com*

Bridgedale, P.O. Box 12278, Everett, WA 98206, 425-339-5393, *www.bridgedale.co.uk*

Dahlgren Footwear, P.O. Box 660614, Arcadia, CA 91066, 626-334-7119, <dahlgren@ix.netcom.com>

Fox River/Wick-Dry, P.O. Box 298, Osage, IA 50461, 515-732-3798, *www.foxrivermills.com*

Gator Sports, 3789 S. 300 W., Salt Lake City, UT 84115, 801-261-3729, <gatorsports@juno.com>

Outlast Technologies, 6235 Lookout Rd., Boulder, CO 80301, 303-581-0801, *www.outlast.com*

Patagonia, 239 W. Santa Clara St., Ventura, CA 93001, 800-638-6464, *www.patagonia.com*

Ridgeview/Seneca, 2101 N. Main Ave., Newton, NC 28658, 828-464-2972

Rohner Socks, 102 Kimball Ave., Ste. 12, S. Burlington, VT 05403, 802-862-3347, *www.sportdinacocorp.com*

SealSkinz/Danalco, 1020 Hamilton, Duarte, CA 91010, 626-303-4019, *www.sealskinz.com*

SmartWool/Duke Designs, 14 Prestwick Pl., Durham, NC 27705, 919-383-6644, *www.smartwool.com*

Thorlo, 2210 Newton Dr., Statesville, NC 28677, 704-872-6522, *www.thorlo.com*

Wigwam Mills, 3402 Crocker Ave., Sheboygan, WI 53081, 414-457-5551

Wyoming Wear, P.O. Box 3127, Jackson, WY 83001, 307-733-2889, *www.wyomingwear.com*

Snowshoes

Atlas Snow-Shoe Co., 1830 Harrison St., San Francisco, CA 94103, 800-645-7463, *www.atlassnowshoe.com*

G & V, P.O. Box 87, Loretteville, Quebec, Canada G2B 3W6, 418-842-2003, *www.gvsnowshoes.ca*

Little Bear, 2477 I Rd., Grand Junction, CO 81505, 800-655-8984, *www.springbrook.com*

Mountain Safety Research, P.O. Box 24547, Seattle, WA 98124, 800-877-9677, *www.msrcorp.com*

Northern Lites, 1300 Cleveland, Wausau, WI 54401, 800-360-5483, *www.northernlites.com*

Redfeather, 4955-D Peoria St., Denver CO 80239, 303-375-0410, *www.redfeather.com*

Sherpa Snowshoes, P.O. Box 607, Milwaukee, WI 53201, 800-621-2277, *www.sherpasnowshoes.com*

Tubbs Snowshoe Co., 52 River Rd., Stowe, VT 05672, 800-882-2748, *www.tubbssnowshoes.com*

Ursus Outdoor Equipment, 2019 E. 7th Ave., Vancouver, BC, Canada V5N 1S5, 604-254-4517

Staffs and Trekking Poles

Alico Sport, 324 Bluff Rd., Newton VT 05855, 514-871-0774, *www.alicosport.com*

Alpina Sports, P.O. Box 23, Hanover, NH 03755, 603-448-1586, *www.alpinasports.com*

Cascade Designs/Tracks, 4000 First Ave. S, Seattle, WA 98134, 800-531-9531, *www.cascadedesigns.com*

Komperdell, St. Lorenz 300, Mondsee, Austria 5310, 001143-6232-42010, *www.komperdell.com*

Leki USA, 356 Sonwil Dr., Buffalo, NY 14225, 800-255-9982, *www.leki.com*

Life-Link, P.O. Box 2913, Jackson, WY 83001, 800-443-8620, *www.life-link.com*

Mountain Properties, P.O. Box 159, Sumas, WA 98295, 800-919-9699, *www.mtnprop.com*

Stoney Point, P.O. Box 234, New Ulm, MN 56073, 507-354-3360, *www.stoneypoint.com*

WALLS

Packs

Arc'Teryx, 4250 Manor St., Burnaby, BC, Canada V5G 1B2, 800-985-6681, *www.arcteryx.com*

Camp Trails, 625 Conklin Rd., Binghamton, NY 13903, 800-345-7622, *www.camptrails.com*

Cascade Designs/Platypus, 4000 First Ave. S, Seattle, WA 98134, 800-531-9531, *www.cascadedesigns.com*

Cirqueworks, 1017 SE 34th Ave., Portland, OR 97214, 503-238-8798, *www.cirqueworks.com*

Dana Design, 19215 Vashon Hwy. SW, Vashon, WA 98070, 888-357-3262, *www.danadesign.com*

Eagle Creek Travel Gear, 3055 Enterprise Ct., Vista, CA 92008, 800-874-9925, *www.eaglecreek.com*

Ferrino USA, P.O. Box 4383, Charlottesville, VA 22905, 888-219-8641, *www.ferrino-usa.com*

GoLite, 5785 Arapahoe, Ste. D, Boulder, CO 80303, 888-546-5483, *www.golite.com*

Granite Gear, 2312 10th St., Two Harbors, MN 55616, 218-834-6157, *www.granitegear.com*

Gregory Mountain Products, P.O. Box 9015, Temecula, CA 92589, 800-477-3420, *www.gregorypacks.com*

JanSport, N850 County Hwy. CB, Appleton, WI 54914, 920-831-2288, *www.jansport.com*

Kelty, 6235 G Lookout Rd., Boulder, CO 80301, 800-423-2320, *www.kelty.com*

Lowe Alpine, 2325 Midway Blvd., Broomfield, CO 80020, 303-465-3706, *www.lowealpine.com*

Madden Mountaineering, 2400 Central Ave., Ste. F, Boulder, CO 80301, 303-442-5828, *www.maddenusa.com*

Mark Pack Works, 230 Madison St., Oakland, CA 94607, 510-452-0243

McHale & Co., 6431 Seaview Ave. NW, Seattle, WA 98107, 206-783-3996, *www.mchalepacks.com*

Mountainsmith, 18301 W. Colfax Blvd., Bldg. P, Golden, CO 80401, 303-279-5930, *www.mountainsmith.com*

Mountain Tools, P.O. Box 22788, Carmel, CA 93922, 831-620-0911, *www. mtntools.com*

Osprey Packs 115 W. Progress Circle, Cortez, CO 81321, 970-564-5900, *www.ospreypacks.com*

The North Face, 2013 Farallon Dr., San Leandro, CA 94577, 800-535-3331, *www.thenorthface.com*

Tough Traveler, 1012 State St., Schenectady, NY 12307, 518-377-8526, *www.toughtraveler.com*

VauDe Sports, P.O. Box 3413, Mammoth Lakes, CA 93546, 800-447-1539, *www.vaude.com*

Vortex, 1414 S. 700 W., Salt Lake City, UT 84104, 801-978-2207, *www. vortexbackpacks.com*

Dog Stuff

Power Bone, 5800 McLeod Rd., Suite G, Albuquerque, NM 87109, 505-830-0322, *www.powerbone.com*

Ruff Wear, P.O. Box 1363, Bend, OR 97709, 541-388-1821, *www. ruffwear.com*

Walkies Outdoor Dog Gear, 2838 Zamora Ln., Davis, CA 95616, 530-297-7529, <kear@calweb.com>

Wolf Packs, 1940 Soda Mtn. Rd., Ashland, OR 97520, 541-482-7669, *www.wolfpacks.com*

KITCHEN

Food and Drink

Adventure Foods, 481 Banjo Ln., Whittier, NC 28789, 828-497-4113, *www.adventurefoods.com*

AlpineAire Foods, 4031 Alvis Ct., Rocklin, CA 95677, 800-322-6325, *www.alpineairefoods.com*

Backpacker's Pantry, 6350 Gunpark Dr., Boulder, CO 80301, 303-581-0518, *www.backpackerspantry.com*

Balance Bar Co., 1015 Mark Ave., Carpenteria, CA 93013, 805-566-0234, *www.balance.com*

Bear Valley/Intermountain Trading, P.O. Box 6157, Albany, CA 94706, 800-323-0042

BTU Stoker, P.O. Box 408, San Anselmo, CA 94979, 415-257-2210

Clif Bars, 1610 Fifth St., Berkeley, CA 94710, 510-558-7855, *www. clifbar.com*

Gookinaid ERG, 8525 Arjons Dr., Ste. L., San Diego, CA 92126, 619-689-1959, <gookinaid@aol.com>

Grabber Performance Group, 4600 Danvers SE, Grand Rapids, MI 49512, 616-940-1914, *www.grabberman.com*

GU, 1221 Eighth St., Berkeley, CA 94710, 510-527-4664, *www.gusports.com*

Harvest Foodworks, RR 1, Toronto, ON, Canada K0E 1Y0, 800-268-4268, *www.harvest.on.ca*

Mountain House, P.O. Box 1048, Albany, OR 97321, 541-926-6001, *www.mountainhouse.com*

Odwalla, 120 Stone Pine Rd., Half Moon Bay, CA 94109, 800-639-2552, *www.odwalla.com*

Paradise Farm Organics, 1000 Wild Iris Ln., Moscow, ID 83843, 800-758-2418, *www.backcountryfood.com*

Peak Bar/Way Cool Inc., 220 W. Del Norte, Colorado Springs, CO 80907, 888-922-9285, *www.peakbar.com*

Power Bar, 2150 Shattuck Ave., Berkeley, CA 94704, 510-843-1330, *www.powerbar.com*

Richmoor Corp., P.O. Box 8092, Van Nuys, CA 91409, 818-787-2510, *www.richmoor.com*

Trail Gourmet, P.O. Box 167, Amherst, OH 44001, 877-888-9355, *www.TrailGourmet.com*

Zone Diet, information: *www.drsears.com*

ZonePerfect (food, energy bars), 100 Cummings Ctr., Beverly, MA 01915, 800-666-6830, *www.zoneperfect.com*

Cookware, Food Storage, Etc.

Duromatic/Kuhn Rikon, P.O. Box 1184, Enfield, CT 06083, 800-662-5882

EverNew America, 2408 Via Rafael, Palos Verdes Estates, CA 90274, 310-375-2648

Evolution Cookwear, Outback Oven—see Backpacker's Pantry under Food and Drink

GSI Outdoors, 1023 S. Pines Rd., Spokane, WA 99206, 800-704-4474, *www.gsioutdoors.com*

Olicamp/Liberty Mountain Adventure, 4375 W. 1980 S., Salt Lake City, UT 84104, 801-954-0741, *www.libertymountain.com*

Sigg, Distributed by A-16, 4620 Alvarado Canyon Rd., San Diego, CA 92120, 619-283-6314, *www.adventure16.com*

Strike 2 Industries, Spokane, WA 99207, 509-484-3701

Knives and Pocket Tools

Coast Cutlery, 2045 SE Ankeny St., Portland, OR 97214, 800-426-5858, <info@coastcutlery.com>

Gerber Legendary Blades, 14200 SW 72nd Ave., Portland, OR 97281, 503-639-6161, *www.gerberblades.com*

Imperial Schrade, 7 Schrade Ct., Ellenville, NY 12428, 914-647-7601, *www.schradeknives.com*

Kershaw Knives, 25300 SW Pkwy., Wilsonville, OR 97070, 503-682-7168, *www.kershawknives.com*

Leatherman Tool Group, P.O. Box 20595, Portland, OR 97294, 503-253-7826, *www.leatherman.com*

SOG Specialty Knives & Tools, 6521 212th St. SW, Lynnwood, WA 98036, 425-771-6230, *www.sogknives.com*

Swiss-Tech/LKL, 8613 East Ave., Mentor, OH 44060, 440-974-7655, *www.swisstechtools.com*

Victorinox/Swiss Army Brands, P.O. Box 874, Shelton, CT 06484, 800-442-2706, *www.swissarmy.com*

Wenger North America, 15 Corporate Dr., Orangeburg, NY 10962, 914-365-3500, *www.wengerna.com*

Water Bottles, Filters, and Purification

AquaMira/McNett Outdoor, P.O. Box 996, Bellingham, WA 98227, 360-671-2227, *www.mcnett.com*

Bota of Boulder, P.O. Box 3374, Boulder, CO 80307, 303-494-8489, *www.botaofboulder.com*

CamelBak, P.O. Box 1029, Weatherford, TX 76086, 817-594-1000, *www.camelbak.com*

Coghlan's, Ltd., 121 Irene St., Winnipeg, MB, Canada R3T 4C7, 204-284-9550, <coghlans@coghlansinfo.ca>

Exstream Water Technologies, 1035 Bruce St., Milwaukee, WI 53204, 800-563-6968, *www.exstreamwater.com*

First Need/General Ecology, 151 Sheree Blvd., Exton, PA 19341, 800-441-8166, *www.generalecology.com*

Katadyn/Suunto USA, 2151 Las Palmas Dr., Ste. F, Carlsbad, CA 92009, 800-441-8166, *www.suuntousa.com*

Mountain Safety Research, 3800 First Ave., Seattle, WA 98134, 800-877-9677, *www.msrcorp.com*

Nalgene, 75 Panorama Ck. Dr., Rochester, NY 14602, 877-523-0635, *www.nalgene-outdoor.com*

Platypus/Cascade Designs, 4000 1st Ave. S, Seattle, WA, 98134, 800-531-9531, *www.sweetwaterfilters.com*

Potable Aqua/WPC Brands, P.O. Box 198, Jackson, WI 53037, 800-558-6614, *www.wpcbrands.com*

PUR, 9300 N. 75th Ave., Minneapolis, MN 55428, 800-787-5463, *www.purwater.com*

Safewater Anywhere, 208 Oak St., Ste. 106, Ashland, OR 97520, 800-675-4401, *www.safewateranywhere.com*

Sweetwater/Cascade Designs, 4000 1st Ave. S, Seattle, WA, 98134, 800-531-9531, *www.sweetwaterfilters.com*

TFO Inc., 953 W. 700 N., Suite 107, Logan, UT 84321, 888-463-5394, *www.tfoinc.com*

Timberline Filters, 1880 S. Flatiron Ct. H-2, Boulder, CO 80301, 303-440-8779, <aew@t-line.com>

Ultimate Direction, 1488 N. Salem Rd., Rexburg, ID 83440, 208-356-0385, *www.ultdir.com*

Stoves, Fuel Bottles, and Gas Cartridges

Campingaz/Coleman, 3600 N. Hydraulic, Wichita, KS 67219, 800-835-3278, *www.coleman.com*

Coleman Exponent (Peak 1), 3600 N. Hydraulic, Wichita, KS 67219, 800-835-3278, *www.coleman.com*

Markill/VauDe Sports, P.O. Box 3413, Mammoth Lakes, CA 93546, 800-447-1539, *www.vaude.com*

Mountain Safety Research, 3800 First Ave., Seattle, WA 98134, 800-877-9677, *www.msrcorp.com*

Optimus, 620 E. Monroe Ave., Riverton, WY 82501, 307-856-6559, *www.optimususa.com*

Primus/Suunto USA, 2151 Las Palmas Dr., Ste. F, Carlsbad, CA 92009, 760-931-6788, *www.suuntousa.com*

Sierra Stove/ZZ Mfg., 1520A Industrial Park St., Covina, CA 91722, 800-594-9046, *www.gorp.com/zzstove*

Sigg, Distributed by A-16, 4620 Alvarado Canyon Rd., San Diego, CA 92120, 619-283-6314, *www.adventure16.com*

Snow Peak USA, 4754 Avery Ln., Lake Oswego, OR 97035, 503-697-3330, *www.snowpeak.com*

Trangia—see Mountain Safety Research

BEDROOM

Tents, Tarps, Wings, and Bivy Sacks

Asage, P.O. Box 286, Girdwood, AK 99587, 907-566-2580, *www.asage.com*

Bibler Tents, 2084 E. 3900 S., Salt Lake City, UT 84124, 801-278-5533, *www.biblertents.com*

Dana Design, 19215 Vashon Hwy. SW, Vashon, WA 98070, 1-888-357-3262, *www.danadesign.com*

Eureka, 1326 Willow Rd., Sturtevant, WI 53177, 800-345-7622, *www.eurekatent.com*

Ferrino USA, P.O. Box 4383, Charlottesville, VA 22905, 888-219-8641, *www.ferrino-usa.com*

Hilleberg USA, 15387 NE 90th, Redmond, WA 98052, 425-883-0101, *www.hilleberg.com*

Integral Designs, 5516 3rd St., Calgary, AB, Canada, T2H 1J9, 403-640-1445, *www.integraldesigns.com*

Kelty, 6235 G Lookout Rd., Boulder, CO 80301, 1-800-423-2320, *www.kelty.com*

Marmot Mountain Ltd., 2321 Circadian Way, Santa Rosa, CA 95407, 707-544-4590, *www.marmot.com*

Moss Tents, 3800 First Ave., Seattle, WA 98134, 800-877-9677, *www.mosstents.com*

Mountain Hardwear, 4911 Central Ave., Richmond, CA 94804, 800-953-8375, *www.mountainhardwear.com*

Noall Tents, 59530 Devils Ladder Rd. #26 GV, Mountain Center, CA 92561, 909-659-4219

Outdoor Research, 2203 First Ave. S, Seattle, WA 98134, 888-467-4327, *www.orgear.com*

Sierra Designs, 1255 Powell St., Emeryville, CA 94608, 800-635-0461, *www.sierradesigns.com*

SMC, 12880 NE 21st Pl., Bellevue, WA 98005, 800-426-6251, <smc@accessone.ocm>

Stephenson-Warmlite, 22 Hook Rd., Gilford, NH 03246, 603-293-7016, *www.warmlite.com*

The North Face, 407 Merrill Ave., Carbondale, CO 81623, 888-251-9464, *www.thenorthface.com*

VauDe Sports, P.O. Box 3413, Mammoth Lakes, CA 93546, 800-447-1539, *www.vaude.com*

Walrus, 3800 First Ave., Seattle, WA 98134, 800-877-9677, *www.walrusgear.com*

Sleeping Bags and Liners

Design Salt, P.O. Box 1220, Redway, CA 95560, 800-254-7258, *www.designsalt.com*

Dreamsacks, 271 Morton St., Ashland, OR 97520, 800-670-7661, *www.dreamsack.com*

Feathered Friends, 119 Yale Ave. N, Seattle, WA 98109, 206-292-6292, *www.featheredfriends.com*

GoLite, 5785 Arapahoe, Ste. D, Boulder, CO 80303, 888-546-5483, *www.golite.com*

Integral Designs, 5516 Third St. SE, Calgary, AB, Canada T2H 1J9, 403-640-1445, *www.integraldesigns.com*

Kelty, 6235 G Lookout Rd., Boulder, CO 80301, 800-423-2320, *www.kelty.com*

Kluane Mountaineering, 10324-82 Ave., Edmonton, AB, Canada, T6E 1Z8, 780-433-9986, *www.kluane.ab.ca*

Marmot Mountain Ltd., 2321 Circadian Way, Santa Rosa, CA 95407, 707-544-4590, *www.marmot.com*

Moonstone Mountain Equipment, 2955 80th Ave. SE, Mercer Island, WA 98040, 800-390-3312, *www.moonstone.com*

Mountain Hardwear, 4911 Central Ave., Richmond, CA 94804, 800-953-8375, *www.mountainhardwear.com*

Sierra Designs, 1255 Powell St., Emeryville, CA 94608, 800-635-0461, *www.sierradesigns.com*

Slumberjack, 1224 Fern Ridge Pkwy., St. Louis, MO 63141, 800-233-6538, *www.slumberjack.com*

Stearns, Inc., P.O. Box 1498, St. Cloud, MN 56302, 320-252-1642, *www.stearnsinc.com*

Stephenson-Warmlite, 22 Hook Rd., Gilford, NH 03246, 603-293-7016, *www.warmlite.com*

The North Face, 2013 Farallon Dr., San Leandro, CA 94577, 800-535-3331, *www.thenorthface.com*

Wenzel, 1224 Fern Ridge Pkwy., St. Louis, MO 63141, 800-325-4121, *www.wenzelco.com*

Western Mountaineering, 1025 S. Fifth St., San Jose, CA 95112, 408-287-8944, *www.westernmountaineering.com*

Wiggy's, P.O. Box 2124, Grand Junction, CO 81502, 800-748-1827, *www.wiggys.com*

Woods Canada, Ltd., 1430 Birchmount Rd., Toronto, ON, Canada M1P 2E8, 416-465-2403, *www.woodscanada.com*

Sleeping Pads and Soft Chairs

Artiach/Appalachian Mountain Supply, 731 Highland Ave., Ste. C, Atlanta, GA 30312, 800-569-4110, *www.amsgear.com*

Crazy Creek, Inc., P.O. Box 1050, Red Lodge, MT 59068, 800-331-0304, *www.crazycreek.com*

Mountain Hardwear, 4911 Central Ave., Richmond, CA 94804, 800-953-8375, *www.mountainhardwear.com*

Nada Chair, 2448 Larpenteur Ave. W., St. Paul, MN 55113, 800-223-9348, *www.nadachair.com*

Stephenson-Warmlite, 22 Hook Rd., Gilford, NH 03246, 603-293-7016, *www.warmlite.com*

Therm-a-Rest/Cascade Designs, 4000 1st Ave. S, Seattle, WA, 98134, 800-531-9531, *www.cascadedesigns.com*

Hammocks and Hanging Shelters

DrYad/Terrelogic, Inc., 590 King St. W., Ste. 403, Toronto, ON, Canada M5V 1M4, 888-693-7923, *www.terrelogic.com*

Hangouts, 1328 Pearl St. Mall, Boulder, CO 80301, 800-426-4688, *www.hangouts.com*

Jungle Hammock/Clark Outdoor, 4637 S. 300 W., Salt Lake City, UT 84107, 800-468-4635, *www.junglehammock.com*

Lawson Hammocks, P.O. Box 12602, Raleigh, NC 27605, 919-829-7076, *www.lawsonhammockco.com*

New Tribe, Inc., 5517 Riverbanks Rd., Grants Pass, OR 97527, 541-476-9492, <newtribe@cds.net>

CLOTHES CLOSET

Torso and Leg Housings

Arc'Teryx, 4250 Manor St., Burnaby, BC, Canada V5G 1B2, 800-985-6681, *www.arcteryx.com*

Cloudveil, P.O. Box 11810, Jackson, WY 83002, 888-763-5969, *www.cloudveil.com*

Columbia Sportswear, P.O. Box 83289, Portland, OR 97283, 800-622-2693, *www.columbia.com*

Deep E. Co., 404 NW 10th Ave., Ste. 201, Portland, OR 97209, 503-299-6647, *www.deep-eco.com*

Duofold, 1 Liberty St., Tamaqua, PA 18252, 570-668-6615, *www.duofold.com*

Filson, P.O. Box 34020, Seattle, WA 98124, 206-624-4437, *www.filson.com*

GoLite, 5785 Arapahoe, Ste. D, Boulder, CO 80303, 888-546-5483, *www.golite.com*

Helly Hansen, 17275 NE 67th Ct., Redmond, WA 98052, 425-883-8823, *www.hellyhansen.com*

Ibex Outdoor Clothing, P.O. Box 297, Woodstock, VT 05091, 800-773-9647, *www.ibexwear.com*

Integral Designs, 5516 Third St. SE, Calgary, AB, Canada T2H 1J9, 403-640-1445, *www.integraldesigns.com*

Juno, 130 Prim St., Ste. 309, Colchester, VT 05446, 802-862-3351, *www.junorising.com*

Lowe Alpine, 2325 Midway Blvd., Broomfield, CO 80020, 303-465-3706, *www.lowealpine.com*

Malden Mills, 550 Broadway, Lawrence, MA 01842, *www.polartec.com*

Manastash, 600 First Ave., Ste. 106, Seattle, WA 98104, 206-903-1351, *www.manastash.com*

Manzella Productions, 80 Sonwil St., Buffalo, NY 14225, 716-681-8880, *www.manzella.com*

Marmot Mountain Ltd., 2321 Circadian Way, Santa Rosa, CA 95407, 707-544-4590, *www.marmot.com*

Moonstone Mountain Equipment, 2955 80th Ave. SE, Mercer Island, WA 98040, 800-390-3312, *www.moonstone.com*

Mountain Hardwear, 4911 Central Ave., Richmond, CA 94804, 800-953-8375, *www.mountainhardwear.com*

Outdoor Research, 2203 First Ave. S, Seattle, WA 98134, 888-467-4327, *www.orgear.com*

Patagonia, 239 W. Santa Clara St., Ventura, CA 93001, 800-638-6464, *www.patagonia.com*

Red Ledge, 685 Rte. 10 E, Randolph, NJ 07869, 973-328-8678, *www.redledge.com*

Royal Robbins Co., 1314 Coldwell Ave., Modesto, CA 95350, 209-529-6913, *www.royalrobbins.com*

SealSkinz/Danalco, 1020 Hamilton, Duarte, CA 91010, 626-303-4019, *www.sealskinz.com*

Sierra Designs, 1255 Powell St., Emeryville, CA 94608, 800-635-0461, *www.sierradesigns.com*

SmartWool/Duke Designs, 14 Prestwick Pl., Durham, NC 27705, 919-383-6644, *www.smartwool.com*

Title Nine Sports, 5743 Landregan St., Emeryville, CA 94608, 800-609-0092, *www.title9sports.com*

Wiggy's, P.O. Box 2124, Grand Junction, CO 81502, 800-748-1827, *www.wiggys.com*

Wild Roses, 2203 First Ave. S, Seattle, WA 98134, 877-953-7673, *www.wrgear.com*

W. L. Gore & Assoc., 105 Vieve's Way, Elkton, MD 21921, 800-431-4673, *www.gore-tex.com*

Woolrich, 1 Mill St., Woolrich, PA 17779, 717-769-6471, *www.woolrich.com*

Wyoming Wear, P.O. Box 3127, Jackson, WY 83001, 307-733-2889, *www.wyomingwear.com*

Head and Ears

Bug Cap/Horizon Products, Montréal, Quebec, Canada H3N 2C7, 888-284-1227

Ear Bagz of Sweden, 475 Park Ave. S., New York, NY 10016, 888-327-2241

Granite Gear, 2312 10th St., Two Harbors, MN 55616, 218-834-6157, *www.granitegear.com*

Outdoor Research, 2203 First Ave. S, Seattle, WA 98134, 888-467-4327, *www.orgear.com*

Real Goods, 200 Clara Ave., Ukiah, CA 95482, 800-762-7325, *www.realgoods.com*

Sunday Afternoons, 173 Hummingbird Ln., Talent, OR 97540, 888-874-2642, *www.sundayafternoons.com*

Tilley Endurables, 300 Langner Rd., West Seneca, NY 14224, 716-822-3052, *www.tilley.com*

Turtle Fur, P.O. Box 1010, Morrisville, VT 05661, 802-888-6400, *www.turtlefur.com*

FURNITURE AND APPLIANCES

Lights and Batteries, Solar Chargers

Accucell-USA, 1683 Brandywine Dr., Bloomfield, MI 48304, *www.accucell usa.com*

Bison Sportslights, 15350 Hinsdale Dr. Unit A, Englewood, CO 80112, 303-680-0304, *www.bisonsportslights.com*

C. Crane Co., 1001 Main St., Fortuna, CA 95540-2008, 800-522-8863, *www.ccrane.com*

Duracell, Berkshire Corporate Park, Bethel, CT 06801, *www.duracell.com*

Energizer/Eveready Battery Co., 8800 N. Allen Rd., Peoria, IL 61615

EternaLight/Technology Assoc., 959 W. 5th St., Reno, NV 89503, 775-322-6875, *www.techass.com*

Hawker Eternacell, 495 Boulevard, Elmwood Park, NJ 07407, 201-796-4800, *www.eternacell.com*

Jade Mountain, P.O. Box 4616, Boulder, CO 80306, 800-442-1972, *www.jademountain.com*

LED-Lite, 925 Hale Pl., Ste. B-10, Chula Vista, CA 91914, 877-309-0530

Mag Instrument, 1635 S. Sacramento Ave., Ontario, CA 91761, 800-289-6241, *www.maglite.com*

Pelican Products, 23215 Early Ave., Torrance, CA 90505, 800-473-5422, *www.pelican.com*

Petzl America, P.O. Box 160447, Clearfield, UT 84016, 801-327-3805, *www.petzl.com*

Princeton Tec Sport Lights, P.O. Box 8057, Trenton, NJ 08650, 800-390-7793, *www.princetontec.com*

Rayovac, 601 Rayovac Dr., Madison, WI 53711, 800-237-7000, *www.rayovac.com*

Real Goods, 200 Clara Ave., Ukiah, CA 95482, 800-762-7325, *www.realgoods.com*

Solar World, 2807 N. Prospect, Colorado Springs, CO 80907, 719-635-5125, *www.solar-world.com*

Streamlight, 1030 W. Germantown Pike, Norristown, PA 19403, 800-523-7488, *www.streamlight.com*

Candle Lanterns and Oil Lamps

Northern Lights, P.O. Box 2692, Truckee, CA 96160, 530-550-0738, *www.candle-lanterns.com*

UCO Corp., 9225 151st Ave. NE, Redmond, WA 98052, 425-883-6600, *www.ucocorp.com*

Gas Lanterns (see Kitchen/Stoves)

Compasses and Navigation-in-General

Brunton Co., 620 E. Monroe St., Riverton, WY 82501, 307-856-6559, *www.brunton.com*

Garmin International, 1200 E. 151st St., Olathe, KS 66062, 913-397-8200, *www.garmin.com*

Magellan Systems, 960 Overland Ct., San Dimas, CA 91773, 800-767-9034, *www.magellangps.com*

Silva/Johnson Worldwide Assoc., 1326 Willow Rd., Sturtevant, WI 53177, 414-884-1500, *www.jwa.com*

Suunto USA, 2151 Las Palmas Dr., Ste. F, Carlsbad, CA 92009, 760-931-6788, *www.suuntousa.com*

Maps, Hard and Soft

DeLorme, 2 DeLorme Dr., Yarmouth, ME 04096, 800-452-5931, *www.delorme.com*

Kenneth Perry/Chalk Butte, Inc., 137 Steele Lane, Boulder, WY 82923, 307-537-5283

Maptech, 655 Portsmouth Ave., Greenland, NH 03840, 800-627-7236, *www.maptech.com*

National Geographic Maps/Trails Illustrated, P.O. Box 4357, Evergreen, CO 80437, 800-962-1643, *www.colorado.com/trails*

Raven Maps & Images, P.O. Box 850, Medford, OR 97501, 800-237-0798, *www.ravenmaps.com*

U.S. Geological Survey, 800-872-6277, *www.usgs.gov*

Lotions and Potions (Sunscreen, Bug Repellent, Etc.)

All-Terrain, 315 3275 Corporate View Dr., Vista, CA 92083, 800-246-7328, *www.allterrainco.com*

Aloe Gator Suncare, 2104 Regency Dr., Irving TX 75062, 800-531-5731, <aloegatr@flash.net>

Dermatone Laboratories, 80 King Spring St., Windsor Locks, CT 06096, 800-999-0475, *www.dermatone.com*

Labiosan USA, P.O. Box 5454, Denver, CO 80217, 303-337-3227

No-Rinse, N/R Laboratories, 900 E. Franklin St., Centerville, OH 45459, 800-223-9348

Sawyer Products, P.O. Box 188, Safety Harbor, FL 34695, 800-940-4464, *www.sawyerproducts.com*

Tender Corp., P.O. Box 290, Littleton, NH 03561, 800-258-4696, *www.tendercorp.com*

Wisconsin Pharmacal, P.O. Box 198, Jackson, WI 53037, 800-558-9006, *www.destinationoutdoors.com*

First-Aid Kits and Supplies

Adventure Medical Kits, P.O. Box 43309, Oakland, CA 94624, 800-324-3517, *www.adventuremedicalkits.com*

Atwater Carey/Wisconsin Pharmacal, P.O. Box 198, Jackson, WI 53037, 800-558-9006, *www.destinationoutdoors.com*

Outdoor Research, 2203 First Ave. S, Seattle, WA 98134, 888-467-4327, *www.orgear.com*

Miscellania

Fox 40/Ascent Inc., 856 Glenwood Ave., Burlington ON, Canada L7T 2J9, 800-361-0473

Gear Aid, P.O. Box 7622, Edmond, OK 73083, 888-750-4327, *www.gearaid.com*

Pack Cat/Jack's Plastic Welding, 115 S. Main, Aztec, NM 87410, 505-334-8748, *www.jpwinc.com*

Rainy Pass Repair, 5307 Roosevelt Way NE, Seattle, WA 98105, 800-733-4340, *www.rainypass.com*

Streamlines, P.O. Box 2214, Paso Robles, CA 93447, 805-237-2313, *www.streamlines.com*

HOUSEKEEPING

Sanitation

Freshette/Sani-fem, P.O. Box 4117, Downey, CA 90241, 800-542-5580, *www.freshette.com*

Bears, Snakes, Ticks, Etc.

Bear Can/Gio Enterprises, P.O. Box 4507, Oceanside, CA 92052, 760-945-9034, *www.bearcan.com*

Bearikade/Wild Ideas, P.O. Box 60813, Santa Barbara, CA 93160, 805-693-0550, *www.wild-ideas.net*

Counter Assault, 120 Industry Ct., Kalispell, MT 59901, 800-695-3394, *www.counterassault.com*

De-Ticker II/Macor Industries, P.O. Box 2108, Cary, NC 27512, 800-859-7691

Garcia Machine, 14097 Ave. 272, Visalia, CA 93292, 559-732-3875

Purple Mountain Engineering, 813 W. Ave L-8, Ste. D, Lancaster, CA 93534, 661-726-1021, *www.purplemountainengineer.com*

Sawyer Products, P.O. Box 188, Safety Harbor, FL 34695, 800-940-4464, *www.sawyerproducts.com*

Tender Corp., P.O. Box 290, Littleton, NH 03561, 800-258-4696, *www.tendercorp.com*

Ursack, P.O. Box 5002, Mill Valley, CA 94942, 415-786-8772, *www.ursack.com*

Magazines, Books, and Other Publications

CHIP: In the text and footnotes, we've mentioned a great many books, so treat this as a supplement rather than an all-encompassing list. To conserve ink, once again I rounded all prices ending in .95 to the nearest dollar. The best way to get current titles is to visit your local shop or search on-line. Most often I use *www.booksense.com*, which has a search function and fewer annoying ads than some other on-line booksellers. For some small presses, I've listed the address so you can order direct.

MAGAZINES

AMC Outdoors (Appalachian Mountain Club), 5 Joy St., Boston, MA 02108, 617-523-0722 (membership, 12x yr., $40)

Backpacker editorial: 33 E. Minor St., Emmaus, PA 18098, 610-967-8296; to subscribe, 800-666-3434; *www.backpacker.com*

Canadian Geographic, The Royal Canadian Geographic Society, 39 McArthur Ave., Ottawa, ON, Canada K1L 8L7, *www.canadiangeographic.ca* ($30 yr.)

Orion and Orion Afield, 195 Main, Great Barrington, MA 01230, 413-528-4422, *www.orionsociety.org* (membership includes both magazines, 4x yr., $30)

Outside, editorial: 400 Market St., Santa Fe, NM 87501, 505-989-7100; to subscribe, 800-678-1131, *www.outsidemag.com*

Mountainfreak, 122½ N. Oak St., Telluride, CO 81535, 970-728-9821, *www.mountainfreak.com* (6x yr., $20)

Mountain Gazette, 5355 Montezuma Rd., Montezuma, CO 80435, 970-513-9865, *www.mountaingazette.com*

Resurgence, Rocksea Farmhouse, St. Mabin, Bodmin, Cornwall, PL30 3BR, UK; Doormouse Distribution, 9 Davies Ave., Suite 202, Toronto, ON, Canada, M4M 2A6; or P.O. Box 404, Freeland, WA, USA 98249, 360-321-5424, *www.resurgence.org* (6x yr. plus airmail to USA, $62)

Snowshoer, P.O. Box 458, Washburn, WI 54891, 715-373-5556 (5x yr., $12)

Wilderness Way, P.O. Box 203, Lufkin, TX 75902, 409-632-8746, *www.powerpc.com/wildernessway* (4x yr., $16)

Wilds Woman, P.O. Box 11311, Truckee, CA 96162 (single $3; 4x yr., $10)

BOOKS AND PUBLISHERS (LISTED BY AUTHOR)

Backpacking-Affairs-in-General

Berger, Karen. *Advanced Backpacking.* W. W. Norton, 1998, $18.

Berger, Karen. *Everyday Wisdom: 1001 Expert Tips for Hikers.* The Mountaineers Books (Backpacker Magazine Series), 1997, $17.

Berger, Karen. *Hiking and Backpacking: A Complete Guide.* W. W. Norton, 1995, $15.

Bossel, Hartmut. *Earth at a Crossroads.* Cambridge University Press, 1998, $25.

Curtis, Rick. *The Backpacker's Field Manual: A Comprehensive Guide to Mastering Backcountry Skills.* Three Rivers Press, 1998, $15.

Hampton, Bruce, and David Cole. *Soft Paths: How to Enjoy the Wilderness Without Harming It.* National Outdoor Leadership School, 1995, $15.

Hart, John. *Walking Softly in the Wilderness: The Sierra Club Guide to Backpacking.* Sierra Club Books, 1998, $12.

Howe, Steve, ed. *Making Camp: The Complete Guide for Hikers, Mountain Bikers, Paddlers, and Skiers.* The Mountaineers Books (Backpacker Magazine Series), 1997, $17.

Logue, Victoria. *Backpacking in the 90s: Tips, Techniques, and Secrets.* Menasha Ridge Press, 1995, $15.

Logue, Frank, and Victoria Logue. *The Appalachian Trail Backpacker: Trail-Proven Advice for Hikes of Any Length.* Menasha Ridge Press, 1994, $15.

McGivney, Annette. *Leave No Trace: A Practical Guide to the New Wilderness Ethic.* The Mountaineers Books (Backpacker Magazine Series), 1998, $11.

McManners, Hugh. *The Complete Wilderness Training Book.* Dorling Kindersley, 1994, $14.

Mouland, Michael. *The Complete Idiot's Guide to Camping and Hiking.* Alpha/Macmillan, 2000, $17.

Mueser, Roland. *Long-Distance Hiking: Lessons from the Appalachian Trail.* McGraw-Hill, 1998, $17.

Mullally, Linda B. *Hiking with Dogs: Becoming a Wilderness-wise Dog Owner.* Falcon Press, 1999, $7.

Niemi, Judith. *Women in the Outdoors.* Globe Pequot, 1999, $8.

Randall, Glenn. *The Modern Backpacker's Handbook.* The Lyons Press, 1994, $15.

Roberts, Harry. *Backpacking.* Globe Pequot, 1989, $8.

Ross, Cindy, and Todd Gladfelter. *A Hiker's Companion: 12,000 Miles of Trail-Tested Wisdom.* The Mountaineers Books, 1993, $13.

Smith, Dave. *Backcountry Bear Basics.* The Mountaineers Books, 1997, $11.

Townsend, Chris. *The Backpacker's Handbook.* McGraw-Hill, 2nd edition 1996, $15.

Wiseman, John. *The SAS Survival Handbook.* HarperCollins, 1986, $24.

Ultralight Gear and Technique

Jardine, Ray. *Beyond Backpacking—Ray Jardine's Guide to Lightweight Hiking.* AdventureLore Press, P.O. Box 804, LaPine, OR 97739, 800-247-6553, *www.AdventureLore.com,* 1996, $20 postpaid.

Twight, Mark, and James Martin. *Extreme Alpinism: Climbing Light, Fast, and High.* The Mountaineers Books, 1999, $28.

Food and Cookery

Brunell, Valerie. *Wilderness Ranger Cookbook.* Falcon, 1991, $7.

Harrington, H. D. *Edible Native Plants of the Rocky Mountains.* University of New Mexico Press, 1977, $19.

Kesselheim, Alan. *Trail Food: Drying and Cooking Food for Backpackers and Paddlers.* McGraw-Hill, 1998, $9.

McHugh, Gretchen. *The Hungry Hiker's Book of Good Cooking.* Knopf, 1982, $20.

McTaggart, Bonnie, Jill Bryant, and Chum McLeod. *The Wilderness Cookbook: A Guide to Good Food on the Trail.* Second Story Press, 1999, $13.

Miller, Dorcas S. *Backcountry Cooking: From Pack to Plate in 10 Minutes.* The Mountaineers Books (Backpacker Magazine Series), 1998, $17.

Netzer, Corinne T. *The Complete Book of Food Counts.* Dell, 5th edition 2000, $7.50.

Yaffe, Linda. *High Trail Cookery.* Chicago Review Press, 1997, $13.

Map and Compass

Burns, Bob, Mike Burns, and Paul Hughes. *Wilderness Navigation: Finding Your Way Using Map, Compass, Altimeter, and GPS.* The Mountaineers Books, 1999, $10.

Boga, Steven. *Orienteering.* Stackpole Books, 1997, $18.

Fleming, June. *Staying Found: The Complete Map and Compass Guidebook.* The Mountaineers Books, 1994, $13.

Hodgson, Michael. *Compass and Map Navigator. The Complete Guide to Staying Found.* Globe Pequot, 2000, $15.

Jacobson, Cliff. *Basic Essentials: Map and Compass.* ICS Books, 1997, $7.

Kals, William S. *Land Navigation Handbook: The Sierra Club Guide to Map and Compass.* Sierra Club Books, 1983, $15.

Kjellstrom, Bjorn. *Be Expert with Map and Compass: The Complete Orienteeering Handbook.* IDG Books Worldwide, 1994, $17.

Randall, Glenn. *The Outward Bound Map and Compass Handbook.* Lyons & Burford, 1989, $9.

First Aid, Health, and Sanitation

Auerbach, Paul S. *Medicine for the Outdoors: The Essential Guide to Emergency Medical Procedures and First Aid.* The Lyons Press, 1999, $22.50.

Carline, Jan, Martha Lentz, and Steven McDonald. *Mountaineering First Aid: A Guide to Accident Response and First Aid Care.* The Mountaineers Books, 4th edition 1996, $11.

Colombo, Luann. *How to Have Sex in the Woods.* Three Rivers Press, 1999, $10.

Cooney, David O. *Purification of Wilderness Waters: A Practical Guide.* Balsam Books, 1070 Inca Dr., Laramie, WY 82072, 1998, $13.

Darvill, Fred T., Jr., M.D. *Mountaineering Medicine and Backcountry Medical Guide.* Wilderness Press, 14th edition 1998, $8.

Emergency Survival Handbook. American Outdoor Safety League. The Mountaineers Books, 1989, $3.50.

Forgey, William, M.D. *Basic Essentials: Wilderness First Aid.* Globe Pequot, 2nd edition 1999, $8.

Francis, Therese. *20 Herbs to Take Outdoors: An Herbal First-Aid Primer for the Outdoor Enthusiast.* Crossquarter Breeze, 1998, $7.

Meyer, Kathleen. *How to Shit in the Woods: An Environmentally Sound Approach to a Lost Art.* Ten Speed Press, 1994, $6.

Steele, Peter, M.D. *Backcountry Medical Guide.* The Mountaineers Books, 2nd edition 1999, $15.

Tilton, Buck. *Backcountry First Aid and Extended Care.* Globe Pequot, 3rd edition 1998, $5.

Tilton, Buck, and Frank Hubbell. *Medicine for the Backcountry.* Globe Pequot, 1999, $14.

Weiss, Eric A., M.D. *Wilderness and Travel Medicine.* Adventure Medical Kits, 2nd edition 1997, $7.

Weiss, Eric A., M.D. *Wilderness 911: A Step-by-Step Guide for Medical Emergency and Improvised Care in the Backcountry.* The Mountaineers Books/Backpacker Magazine, $17.

Wilkerson, James A., M.D., ed. *Medicine for Mountaineering and Other Wilderness Activities.* The Mountaineers Books, 4th edition 1993, $18.

Snow Travel and Camping

Conover, Garrett, and Alexandra Conover. *A Snow Walker's Companion: Winter Trail Skills from the Far North.* McGraw-Hill, 1994, $20.

Cook, Charles. *The Essential Guide to Cross-Country Skiing and Snowshoeing in the United States.* Holt, 1997, $18.

Fredston, Jill, and Doug Fesler. *Snow Sense: A Guide to Evaluating Snow Avalanche Hazard.* Alaska Mountain Safety Center, 9140 Brewsters Dr., Anchorage, AK 99516, 907-345-3566, $9.

Gorman, Stephen. *AMC Guide to Winter Camping: Wilderness Travel and*

Adventure in the Cold-Weather Months. Appalachian Mountain Club, 1991, $13.

Halfpenny, James, and Ray Ozanne. *Winter: An Ecological Handbook.* Johnson Books, 1989, $17.

Olmsted, Larry. *Snowshoeing: A Trailside Guide.* W. W. Norton, 1998, $18.

Zwosta, Marianne. *The Essential Snowshoer: A Step By Step Guide.* McGraw-Hill, 1997, $16.

Organizations That Promote Walking or Sound Outdoor Practices

CHIP: As Colin lamented in *Walker III,* "Any list like this is sure to be incomplete, and it begins to die before it is born." So, after amassing a sheaf of addresses that would choke a hungry hippo—I concluded that there are now far too many state and local groups to list them all here. Instead, I'm listing various national and regional groups, some mentioned in the text, some not.

Boinking around the Internet is by far the most efficient way to get up-to-date information. Some groups (notably the American Hiking Society) maintain Web sites with links to state and local groups. Large nonprofit conservation groups, such as the Audubon Society, National Wildlife Federation, and Sierra Club, sponsor walking trips both nationally and at the local level. In Wyoming, for example, state groups such as the Wyoming Outdoor Council, and local ones such as Friends of the Bow, organize regular outings: join up and you'll be in touch. Colleges usually support free or low-cost outings programs, as do groups such as the YMCA, YMHA, and religious congregations.

When writing local groups for information, put a first-class stamp on a regular business envelope, address it to yourself, fold it three times, and enclose it with your request. That way you'll avoid straining shoestring budgets—and get a quick reply.

NOTE: <@> indicates an electronic-mail address; *www.* indicates an Internet Web site.

United States, National

Access Fund, P.O. Box 17010, Boulder, CO 80308, 303-545-6772, *www.accessfund.org*

American Alpine Club, 710 Tenth St., Ste. 100, Golden, CO 80401, 303-384-0110, *www.americanalpineclub.org*

American Hiking Society, P.O. Box 20160, Washington, DC 20041, 888-766-4453, *www.americanhiking.org*

Big City Mountaineers, 210 Beaver Brook Cyn. Rd., Ste. 200, Evergreen, CO 80439, 800-644-2122, *www.bigcitymt.org*

EMS Trail Fund, 1 Vose Farm Rd., Peterborough, NH 03458, *www. emsonline.com*

Leave No Trace, P.O. Box 997, Boulder, CO 80306, 800-442-8222, *www. lnt.org*

National Audubon Society, 700 Broadway, New York, NY 10003, 212-979-3000, *www.audubon.org*

National Outdoor Leadership School, 288 Main, Lander, WY 82520-3140, 307-332-5300, *www.nols.edu*

National Trails Day, 1-888-766-4453, *www.ahs.simplenet.com*

National Wildlife Federation, 1400 Sixteenth St. NW, Washington, DC 20036, 800-822-9919, *www.nwf.org*

Outward Bound—for the many state, regional, and worldwide programs, try a Web search under *"outward."*

Sierra Club, 85 Second St., 2nd floor, San Francisco, CA 94105, <national outings@sierraclub.org>, *www.sierraclub.org*

Student Conservation Association, 1265 S. Main St., #201, Seattle, WA 98144, *www.sca-inc.org*

Wilderness Inquiry, 1313 Fifth St. SE, Box 84, Minneapolis, MN 55414-1546, 800-728-0719, *www.wildernessinquiry.org*

The Wilderness Society, 900 Seventeenth St. NW, Washington, DC 20006, 202-833-2300, *www.tws.org*

U.S., Regional

American Discovery Trail Society, P.O. Box 3672, Frederick, MD 21705, 301-668-2202, *www.discoverytrail.org*

American Long Distance Hikers Association—West, P.O. Box 651, Vancouver, WA 98666, *www.aldha.org/aldawest*

Appalachian Long Distance Hikers Association, 10 Benning St., PMB 224, West Lebanon, NH 03784, *www.aldha.org*

Appalachian Mountain Club, 5 Joy St., Boston, MA 02108, 617-523-0722, *www.outdoors.org*

Appalachian Trail Conference, P.O. Box 807, Harpers Ferry, WV 25425, 304-535-6331, *www.atconf.org*

Continental Divide Trail Alliance, P.O. Box 628, Pine, CO 80470, 303-838-3760, *www.cdtrail.org*

East Coast Greenway Alliance, 135 Main St., Wakefield, RI 02879, 401-789-4625, *www.greenway.org*

Mountaineers, 300 Third Ave. W, Seattle, WA 98119, 206-284-6310, *www.mountaineers.org*

North Country Trail Association, 49 Monroe Center NW, Ste. 2006, Grand Rapids, MI 49503, 616-454-5506, *www.northcountrytrail.org*

Ozark Society, 1509 Old Forge, Little Rock, AR 72227, 501-666-2989, *www.ozarksociety.net*

Pacific Crest Trail Association, 5325 Elkhorn Blvd,. PMB #256, Sacramento, CA 95842, 888-728-7245, *www.pcta.org*

Canada

Alberta Trail Net, 548-11 St. NE, Medicine Hat, AB, Canada T1A 1T3, 403-527-2052, *www.health-in-action.org*

Alpine Club of Canada, P.O. Box 8040, Canmore, AB, Canada T1W 2T8, 403-678-3200, *www.alpineclubofcanada.ca*

Canadian Hostelling Association, 400-205 Catherine St., Ottawa, ON, Canada K2P 1C3, 800-663-5777, *www.iyhf.org*

The Audubon Society, Sierra Club, and other groups have chapters in Canada: Web links via U.S. listings.

UK and Ireland

For a complete list of walking and camping groups, with copious links: Lancaster University Hiking Club, *www.comp.lancs.ac.uk/rec-and-travel/ users/uns026/links/clubs.html*

England

The Ramblers' Association, 1/5 Wandsworth Rd., London SW8 2XX, 0171-339-8500, *www.ramblers.org.uk*

Scotland

The Ramblers' Association, Kingfisher House, Auld Business Mart Park, Milnathort, Kinross, KY13 9DA, <enquiries@scotland.ramblers.org.uk>

Wales

The Ramblers' Association, Ty'r Cerddwyr, High St., Gresford, Wrexham, Clwyd LL12 8PT, 01978-855148, <cerddwyr@wales.ramblers.org.uk>

Everywhere

For a worldwide list of hiking and mountaineering clubs, maintained by the Chamois Mountaineering Club: *www.chamois.org.uk/world/shtml*

Pleasant Quotes
for Contemplative Walkers

I nauseate walking.
WILLIAM CONGREVE

When you have worn out your shoes, the strength of the shoe leather has passed into the fiber of your body. . . . He is the richest man who pays the largest debt to his shoemaker.
EMERSON

The longing to be primitive is a disease of culture.
GEORGE SANTAYANA

There is something about the idea of an encounter with nature that has a powerful hold on the American imagination—an idea of independence, of self-reliance, self-sufficiency and autonomy. These are ideas that lie very close to the heart of the cultural values we prize most, and that seem to be most threatened by the style of modern, urban, industrial society.
JOSEPH L. SAX

If you pick 'em up, O Lord, I'll put 'em down
ANONYMOUS
"The Prayer of the Tired Walker"

Our mental make-up is suited to a life of very severe physical labor. I used, when I was younger, to take my holidays walking. I would cover 25 miles a day, and when the evening came I had no need of anything to keep me from boredom, since the delight of sitting amply sufficed. . . .

When crowds assemble . . . to cheer to the echo an announcement that the government has decided to have them killed, they would not do so if they had all walked 25 miles that day.

BERTRAND RUSSELL

I drew my bride, beneath the moon,
Across my threshold; happy hour!
But, ah, the walk that afternoon
We saw the water-flags in flower!

COVENTRY PATMORE

I want a divorce.

BARBARA BAILEY MARCUS
(Response suggested for Mrs. Coventry Patmore)

If you are ready to leave father and mother, and brother and sister, and wife and child and friends, and never see them again—if you have paid your debts, and made your will, and settled all your affairs, and are a free man, then you are ready for a walk.

THOREAU

Huh, your feet must be stronger than your head!

STRANGER
To Colin Fletcher,
during thousand-mile walk

The civilized man has built a coach, but he has lost the use of his feet.

EMERSON

In properly developed countries, the inhabitants regard walkers with grave suspicion and have taught their dogs to do the same.

ALAN BOOTH

If I couldn't walk fast and far, I should explode and perish.

CHARLES DICKENS

The swiftest traveler is he that goes afoot.
> THOREAU

There is more to life than increasing its speed.
> GANDHI

"I'm sure nobody walks much faster than I do."

"He can't do that," said the King, "or else he'd have been here first."
> LEWIS CARROLL
> *Through the Looking-Glass*

The man who goes alone can start today; but he who travels with another must wait till that other is ready, and it may be a long time before they get off.
> THOREAU

Now, to be properly enjoyed, a walking tour should be gone upon alone. . . . because freedom is of the essence.
> ROBERT LOUIS STEVENSON

Never did I think so much, exist so vividly, and experience so much, never have I been so much myself—if I may use that expression—as in the journeys I have taken alone and on foot.
> JEAN-JACQUES ROUSSEAU

Take this simple test to see if you qualify for solo camping. Shine a flashlight in one ear. If the beam shines out the other ear, do not go into the woods alone.
> BRUCE COCHRAN
> *Everything You Never Wanted to Know*
> *About Camping*

In solitude
What happiness? Who can enjoy alone,
Or all enjoying, what contentment find?
> MILTON
> *Paradise Lost*

Solitude is as needful to the imagination as society is wholesome for the character.

> JAMES RUSSELL LOWELL

That inward eye which is the bliss of solitude.

> WORDSWORTH

> O Solitude! where are the charms
> That sages have seen in thy face?
>> WILLIAM COWPER
>> "Verses Supposed to Be Written
>> by Alexander Selkirk"

Bear bells provide an element of safety for hikers in grizzly country. The tricky part is getting them on the bears.

> BRUCE COCHRAN
> *Everything You Never Wanted to Know*
> *About Camping*

> The true male never yet walked
> Who liked to listen when his mate talked.
>> ANNA WICKHAM
>> (Mrs. Patrick Hepburn)

Thou shalt have a place also without the camp, whither thou shalt go forth abroad: and thou shalt have a paddle upon thy weapon; and it shall be, when thou wilt ease thyself abroad, thou shalt dig therewith, and shalt turn back and cover that which cometh from thee.

> DEUTERONOMY XXIII: 13

He went back through the Wet Wild Woods, waving his wild tail, and walking by his wild lone. But he never told anybody.

> RUDYARD KIPLING
> "The Cat That Walked by Himself"

> O why do you walk through the fields in gloves,
> Missing so much and so much?
>> FRANCES CORNFORD
>> "To a Fat Lady Seen from the Train"

Oh, he's a genuine backpacker, all right. He's got a filed-down toothbrush.

OVERHEARD BY COLIN FLETCHER

Who walks with beauty has no need of fear;
The sun and moon and stars keep pace with him;
Invisible hands restore the ruined year,
And time, itself, grows beautifully dim.

DAVID MORTON

There's night and day, brother, both sweet things; sun, moon, and stars, brother, all sweet things; there's likewise a wind on the heath. Life is very sweet, brother; who would wish to die?

GEORGE BORROW
Lavengro

You ask me:
        Why do I live
        on this green mountain?
This is
        another sky
No likeness
        to that human world below.

LI PO

Range after range of mountains
Year after year after year
I am still in love.

GARY SNYDER

What men call gallantry, and gods adult'ry,
Is much more common where the climate's sultry.

BYRON
Don Juan

Three things there are that ease the heart—water, green grass, and the beauty of woman.

FRANK HERBERT
Dune

"Would you tell me, please, which way I ought to go from here?"

"That depends a good deal on where you want to go to," said the Cat.

"I don't much care where—" said Alice.

"Then it doesn't matter which way you go," said the Cat.

"—so long as I get *somewhere*," Alice added as an explanation.

"Oh, you're sure to do that," said the Cat, "if you only walk long enough."

LEWIS CARROLL
Alice in Wonderland

The Promised Land always lies on the other side of a wilderness.

HAVELOCK ELLIS

The walking stick serves the purpose of an advertisement that the bearer's hands are employed otherwise than in useful effort, and it therefore has utility as an evidence of leisure.

THORSTEIN VEBLEN
The Theory of the Leisure Class

Dear Uncle Colin: I'm haveing fun at camp My counselors he Read one of your Books anb he said it gave him sore Feet.

POSTCARD FROM HONORARY NEPHEW

Hi-Rise Campsites, Inc., has announced plans to construct a 20-story campground in downtown New Orleans. . . . Plans for the $4 million project call for 8 lower floors of parking and 12 upper stories with 240 individual sites equipped with utility hookups for campers . . . and campsites carpeted with artificial turf, and a rooftop pool.

"This will be unique—the first of its kind anywhere," said Wesley Hurley of Hi-Rise. "It is designed for today's different kind of camping. People don't want the woodsy bit now; they want to camp in comfort near the city."

ASSOCIATED PRESS REPORT
[Sub-historical footnote: The facility was never built.]

I find that the three truly great times for thinking thoughts are when I am standing in the shower, sitting on the john, or walking. And the greatest of these, by far, is walking.

COLIN FLETCHER

It is interesting that in both Japanese Zen and Plains Indian ani-
mism, there are walking and sitting forms of contemplation.
ROB SCHULTHEIS
The Hidden West

Man is a thinking reed but his great works are done when he is
not calculating and thinking.
DAISETZ T. SUZUKI

In my room, the world is beyond my understanding,
But when I walk I see that it consists of three or four hills and a
cloud.
WALLACE STEVENS

He likes the country, but in truth must own,
Most likes it when he studies it in town.
WILLIAM COWPER

Thou canst not stir a flower
Without troubling of a star.
FRANCIS THOMPSON

To a person uninstructed in natural history, his country or seaside
stroll is a walk through a gallery filled with wonderful works of
art, nine-tenths of which have their faces turned to the wall.
THOMAS HUXLEY

The last word in ignorance is the man who says of a plant or animal, "What good is it?" If the land mechanism as a whole is good,
then every part of it is good, whether we understand it or not.
ALDO LEOPOLD

Solvency is entirely a matter of temperament and not of income.
LOGAN PEARSALL SMITH

There is no cure for birth and death save to enjoy the interval.
GEORGE SANTAYANA

To understand life, man must learn to shudder.
> QUOTED BY LOREN EISLEY

Comedy is tragedy plus time.
> ATTRIBUTED TO CAROL BURNETT'S
> MOTHER

Humor and knowledge are the two great hopes of civilization.
> KONRAD LORENZ

I went to the woods because I wished to live deliberately, to front only the essential facts of life, and see if I could not learn what it had to teach, and not, when I came to die, discover that I had not lived.
> THOREAU

To enjoy the full flavor of life, take big bites. Moderation is for monks.
> ROBERT HEINLEIN
> *Time Enough for Love*

Early and provident fear is the mother of safety.
> EDMUND BURKE

The beginning of wisdom is a salutary shock.
> ARNOLD TOYNBEE

All paths lead nowhere, so it is important to choose a path that has heart.
> CARLOS CASTANEDA

Improvement makes straight roads; but the crooked roads without improvement are roads of genius.
> WILLIAM BLAKE

Man . . . walks up the stairs of his concepts, [and] emerges ahead of his accomplishments.
> JOHN STEINBECK

Man discovers that he is nothing else than evolution become conscious of itself.

JULIAN HUXLEY

. . . man, in his paranoid arrogance, has perpetrated the greatest blasphemy of all time by stating in the Bible, "So God created Man in his own image." . . . There is a God all around us which man has refused to accept but he abuses and exploits her forgetting that she of all deities is our own true God. . . . Man's greatest enemy is his own kind and upon an understanding of this fact depends his chances of survival in the future.

PHILIP E. GLOVER
Tsavo Research Project, Kenya

The human race is bound to defile, I've often noticed it,
Whatever they can reach or name, they'd shit on the morning star
If they could reach. . . .
A day will come when the earth will scratch herself and smile and
    rub off humanity.

ROBINSON JEFFERS

It is in the long run essential to the growth of any new and high civilization that small groups of people can escape from their neighbors and from their governments, to go and live as they please in the wilderness.

FREEMAN DYSON
Disturbing the Universe

Men and their works have been a disease on the surface of their planets before now. . . . Nature tends to compensate for diseases, to remove or encapsulate them, to incorporate them into the system in her own way.

FRANK HERBERT
Dune (set in the far future)

The . . . scientists were wrong . . . the most persistent principles of the universe were accident and error.

FRANK HERBERT
Dune

Let a man once overcome his selfish terror at his own finitude, and his finitude is, in one sense, overcome.

GEORGE SANTAYANA

The concept of progress acts as a protective mechanism to shield us from the terrors of the future.

FRANK HERBERT
Dune

Change is inevitable, progress possible.

JULIAN HUXLEY

If one advances confidently in the direction of his dreams, and endeavors to live the life which he has imagined, he will meet with a success unexpected in common hours.

THOREAU

Grow up as soon as you can. It pays. The only time you really live fully is from thirty to sixty. . . . The young are slaves to dreams; the old, servants of regrets. Only the middle-aged have all their five senses in the keeping of their wits.

HERVEY ALLEN

There are three terrible ages of childhood: 1 to 10, 10 to 20, and 20 to 30.

CLEVELAND AMORY

Walk while ye have the light, lest darkness come upon you.

ST. JOHN XII:35

I speak truth, not so much as I would, but as much as I dare; and I dare a little the more, as I grow older.

MONTAIGNE

Growing old isn't so bad—when you consider the alternative.

MAURICE CHEVALIER

We will go no more to the woods, the laurel-trees are cut.
THÉODORE DE BANVILLE

And as I turn me home,
My shadow walks before.
ROBERT BRIDGES

Metric Conversions

LENGTH

1 inch = 2.54 centimeters or 25.4 millimeters
1 foot = 30.48 centimeters or 0.3048 meters
1 yard = 91.44 centimeters or 0.9144 meters
1 mile = 1.6094 kilometers

MASS

1 ounce (avoir.) = 28.4 grams
1 ounce (troy) = 37.3 grams
1 U.S. fluid ounce = 29.573 milliliters
1 pound = 453.6 grams or 0.4536 kilograms

VOLUME

1 cubic inch = 16.4 cubic centimeters
1 pint = 0.568 liter
1 quart = 1.136 liters
1 gallon = 4.546 liters

TEMPERATURE

To convert from °Fahrenheit to °Centigrade, subtract 32,
   multiply by 5 and divide by 9.
Example: *50°F* minus 32 is 18, times 5 is 90, divided by 9 yields *10°C*
From °Centigrade to °Fahrenheit, multiply by 9, divide by 5, and add 32.
Example: *10°C* times 9 is 90, divided by 5 is 18, plus 32 yields *50°F*
Or see the scale at right.

PRESSURE

1 pound per square inch = 51.7 millimeters of Hg or 70.33 grams per square
   centimeter

Acknowledgments

COLIN: Injustice lurks in every list of acknowledgments: there's no really practical way to distinguish between major donors of time or expertise and those who kindly dotted a few "i"s. But before we move to the main list, Chip and I must single out those who contributed mightily and steadily throughout the three years we worked on this edition.

Carl D. Brandt, as usual and from the earliest drafts, acted not only as our literary agent but also as a literary and backpacking critic. And . . .

CHIP: Along with her patience and good grace, Linda Baker tested gear and lent us her seasoned outdoor perspective. Fellow writer Mark Jenkins served as a guide to the jungles of commerce and also provided a sharp and friendly ear. Florence Shepard offered safe haven in Salt Lake City during the outdoor trade shows. Kitty Graham answered more than her share of questions and welcomed me to Seattle's vibrant outdoor community. And Deb Donahue, environmental law scholar and wildlife biologist, has partnered me on both off-trail scrambles and daily walks—and in other ways as well: we were married July 15, 2000.

A further supporting cast (along with those named in the text) includes people who over the years advised in specific fields, readers who contributed ideas, owners and representatives of companies that make outdoor gear, and those who produced this book.

The list is long (as I know all too well, having rummaged my files to compile it under a looming deadline). But that simply reflects how much human effort and thought has gone into this book. If we missed someone, we're sorry. We really appreciate the help.

ADVICE AND HELP IN SPECIFIC FIELDS: John Sexton (photography and other wisdoms); Dan Innamorato (a rich assortment of criticisms and suggestions and even samples); Janice Herald of the Community Hospital of the Monterey Peninsula, CA (nutrition); Donald B. Kunkel, M.D.

(snakebite); John Davis (spiders); David P. Graber, Barrie Gilbert, David Petersen, and Douglas Peacock (bear behavior); Harvey Neuber (pack mathematics); Douglas Hittle, Colorado State University (phase-change materials); Nalini Nadkarni, Evergreen State College, WA (arboreal pursuits); and Jack and Lauri Kloepfer (boatpacking).

READERS WHO OFFERED VALID IDEAS, SUGGESTIONS, OR COMMENTS: *Alabama:* Jim Hipp; *Arizona:* John W. Burns, Mark Hunt; *Arkansas:* John Matthews; *California:* William DeFrance, David Donohoe, Marlene Furtado, Tom Galloway, W. D. Grissom, Fred Hottenroth, Elaine Kane, M. Imajo, Larry Nelson, Steve Olsen, Steve Perez, Vince Pettit, Doug Robinson, Robert Stephens, Frank Tehan, Sherrill K. Walker, Michael White, Ruth Wise; *Colorado:* Henry Cavalier, Michael Galvin, Ken Koerwitz, Bert Newman; *Connecticut:* Nori Hoffman; *Florida:* William A. Raventos; *Hawaii:* Jahan Byrne, Boyd Hill; *Idaho:* Steve Schelly; *Illinois:* Jeffrey Benner; *Indiana:* Jacob Schor; *Louisiana:* Russ Panecki; *Massachusetts:* Mark Howard, Maria Louisa Michele; *Michigan:* Wes Boyd, Ellsworth Littler, Russell M. Reid; *Minnesota:* Chauncey L. Greene; *Missouri:* Teri Smillie, Paul Stamler; *Nebraska:* Sharon Johnson Alford; *Nevada:* Hendrik G. Van Oss; *New Hampshire:* John Foley, Pete Tandy; *New Jersey:* Karl Brand, Dave Teich; *New York:* Charle Cook, Ralph Lia, Fred A. Meyer, Morris Pejsach, Jay Peters, Gilbert Plantinga, Jay Wopperer; *North Carolina:* Neri G. Terry; *Ohio:* Brian Rohal, Luke Seubert; *Oregon:* Maria Faber, Dan Karwoski, Chuck Kennedy, Bob Walker; *Pennsylvania:* Leonard X. Finegold, Clarke A. Green, Jim and Jan Hamilton; *Utah:* Larry D. Hall, Christopher McKellar; *Washington:* Jon R. Charno, Joseph L. Drew, Mark Oberle; *Wisconsin:* Michael Bergum, Tom Haberski; *Wyoming:* Maureen Ryan; *Canada:* John LaBella, Renald-Nelson Dunn, Maria Schoenefeld; *England:* W. G. Conyers; *Scotland:* J. Haldane Tait; *Denmark:* Torbjörn Johansson.

INDIVIDUALS, FIRMS, OR AGENCIES: *Hometown store folks:* Larry and Jane Arthur of Mountain Tools (Carmel, CA); Jeff Alford of Keeble & Shucat (Palo Alto, CA); Steve Myrick of Myrick Photographic (Monterey, CA); Scott von Coops of Wolf Camera (Carmel, CA); Scott and Jessie Datwyler of Trailhead Sports (Logan, UT); Rex and Linda Poulson of the Great Outdoor Shop (Pinedale, WY), and Ken Cramer of Cross Country Connection (Laramie, WY).

Nationwide: Michael Wayne and Jenny Case of Adventure-16; Chris Gubera of Adventure Medical Kits; Reid Cooper of Alico Sport; Russell Sonneborn of AlpineAire Foods; Brian Schmid of Appalachian Mountain Supply; Michael Blenkarn and Tom Duguid of Arc'Teryx; Joe Ifi of Asolo/Benetton; Oliver Olin of Atlas Snow-Shoe Co.; Rodney Smith and Greg Tantum of Backpacker's Pantry; Charlotte Norrie of Balance Bar Co.; Marilyn Perkey of

Ballston/Brown Wooten Mills; Stephen Halasz of Bison Sportslights; Lindsay Cousley of Bridgedale; Kitty Graham, Tom Myers, and Jim Marson of Cascade Designs; Elaine Kane of C. Crane Co.; Mark Paigen of Chaco Sandals; Collin Whitehead of CirqueWorks; Jane Hagen of Clif Bar; Wendy Fahs of Bota of Boulder; David Grissom of Cloud Peak Equipment; David Brands of Coast Cutlery; Wayne Tegeler of Coghlan's; Anne Walden of Coleman/Peak 1/Exponent; Kristy Dahlgren of Dahlgren Footwear; Gayle Mauer of Dana Design; Krista Clark of Robley Marketing/Danner; Bob Farentinos of Deep E; and Nancy Morgan of Dreamsacks.

Sarah Marcikonis and Le Do of EMS (Ft. Collins, CO); Peter Hickner of Feathered Friends; Kurt Heisler of Eureka/JWA; Jennifer Dow of Fox River/Wick-Dry; Caroline Fleischer and Tony Fleming of Freebairn, Inc. (Eureka, Camp Trails, Leica, and Silva); Richard Garcia of Garcia Machine; John Coleman of Gear Aid; General Ecology, Inc.; Demetri Coupounas and Coral Darby of GoLite; John Cron of Granite Gear; Paul Gagner and Wayne Gregory of Gregory Mountain Products; Marty Heister of GSI Outdoors; Petra Hilleberg of Hilleberg the Tentmaker; Shari Arakelian of Hi-Tec; Jerry Parker of JanSport; Laura Orlowski of Kelty; Charly Oliver of La Sportiva; Amy Mentuck and Scott Reid of Leave No Trace; Christa Fiehler of LED-Lite; Leki USA; John Pedersen and Matt Hader of Liberty Mountain Adventure/Advance Base Camp; Heidi Kessler of Lowe Alpine; Carole Godfrey of Macor Industries; Diana Tepe of Madden Mountaineering; John Cooley and Neil Munro of Marmot Mountain Ltd.; Amy Torgeson and Linda Wenzelberger of Moonstone Mountain Equipment; Cindy Hazard of Montrail; Ted Dishner and Terry Breaux of Moss Tents; Paige Boucher of Mountain Hardwear; Mike Harrelson and Kristine Carey of Mountainsmith; and Jennifer Gombas and Jim Trombly of Mountain Safety Research.

Victor Toso of Nada Chair; John Gans of the National Outdoor Leadership School; Michael O'Farrell of NEOS; Sophia Sparks of New Tribe; Mark Samuelson of Nikwax; Joanne Holden of the Nutrient Data Laboratory (Beltsville, MD); Erik Hamerschlag and Erik Wegner of Osprey Packs; Brian Hewitt and Jim Meyers of Outdoor Research; Mary Jane Butters of Paradise Farm Organics; Brian Scott Fritz of Peak Bar; Lisa Winston of Peak Exposure (Lowe Alpine and Safewater Anywhere); Michael Fattori of Princeton Tec; Philippe de Serres of Produits Horizon; Rick Appelsies of PUR; Lisa McClain of Real Goods; Kristen Wappler of Recreational Equipment; Thorn Luth of Redfeather Snowshoes; Red Ledge/Tahsin Industrial Corp. USA; Ander Horne of Ridgeview; Tristin Thomas Ferguson of Safewater Anywhere; Cheryl Iachini of Sawyer Products; Phil Hofstee of SealSkinz/Danalco; Jan McCallum of Sherpa Snowshoes; Fred Dieter, Sharon Leicham, and Ted Ganio of Sierra Designs; Joel Anderson of Slumberjack; Gardner Flanigan of SmartWool/Duke Designs; Tomo Sekiguchi of Snow Peak USA; Ryan Eittreim of Spirakut; Jack Stephenson of Stephenson-Warmlite; Mary Snyder of Stearns; Tom Peterson of Stoney Point; Mary Ellen Gianiulio of Streamlight; Angeline Lacey of Sunday Afternoons; Evan Wert of Superfeet; Lauren Zimmerman of Suunto USA; Susan Killoran of Tecnica; Naomi Girouard of Tender Corp.; Michael de Jong of Terrelogic; David Hennel of Trail Gourmet; Kathleen Murphy of Tubbs Snowshoe Co.; Susan Marsh and Lynn Pisano-Pedigo of the U.S. Forest Service; Steve Reiter of the U.S. Geological Survey; Gordon Lehmann of Vasque; Sam Roney of VauDe Sports; Tom Cohen of Ursack; Bill Crawley of Vortex Backpacks; Todd Bloxham of Walrus Tents; John Francis Maggio and Gary Schaezlin of Western Mountaineering; Jay Kroll and Donna Fischer of Wigwam/Ultimax; Kristin Wolfe of Wilderness Press; Frannie Huff and Heidi Niehues of Wyoming Wear; and Duane Spoelstra of ZZ Manufacturing.

THOSE WHO PRODUCED THE BOOK: Thanks to everybody at Alfred A. Knopf, who teamed up with the two of us (plus illustrators Vanna Prince and Hannah Hinchman) to ensure the best of all possible works. In particular we thank Ashbel Green, senior editor, who oversaw these semiorderly proceedings with patience and good humor. Jonathan Fasman, his assistant, braved blizzards of detail. Virginia Tan, art director, sorted out complex matters of illustration. Kathleen Fridella, production editor, worked out the hitches in usage between Britannic Fletcher and Americat Rawlins. Finally, we bow to Ruth Elwell, whose index adds the tail to this particular shaggy dog.

Index

COLIN FLETCHER was born in Wales and educated in England. After six years' World War II service in the Royal Marines, he went to East Africa in 1947, farmed for four years in Kenya, and later surveyed and built a road over a virgin mountain in southern Rhodesia (now Zimbabwe). In the 1950s he crossed the Atlantic and prospected—among other pursuits—in northern and western Canada. In 1956 he moved south to California. Soon afterward he spent a summer walking from Mexico to Oregon across California's deserts and mountains. Later he became the first man known to have walked the length of Grand Canyon National Park within the Canyon's rim. Each of these feats generated a book: *The Thousand-Mile Summer* and *The Man Who Walked Through Time.* Mr. Fletcher continues to walk, and to write books: *The Complete Walker* (here revised for the third time), *The Winds of Mara,* and *The Man from the Cave, The Secret Worlds of Colin Fletcher,* and *River.*

CHIP RAWLINS has lived outdoors, working as a guide and outdoor teacher, a forest ranger and firefighter, and a wilderness hydrologist before becoming a full-time writer in 1992. His books (as C. L. Rawlins) include *A Ceremony on Bare Ground* (1985), *Sky's Witness* (1993), *Broken Country* (1996), and *In Gravity National Park* (1998). Along with bachelor's and master's degrees from Utah State University, a Stegner Fellowship at Stanford, and various literary prizes, he has received the U.S. Forest Service Primitive Skills Award for monitoring air pollution in Wyoming's Wind River Range. Rawlins has served as a volunteer and board member with the Greater Yellowstone Coalition, the Wyoming Outdoor Council, and the Wyoming Coalition for the Homeless. He lives near Laramie, Wyoming, and is now spending a year in New Zealand while his spouse, scholar Deb Donahue, studies conservation and biodiversity law.

A NOTE ON THE TYPE

THE TEXT of this book was set in Garamond No. 3. It is not a true copy of any of the designs of Claude Garamond (ca. 1480–1561), but an adaptation of his types, which set the European standard for two centuries. It probably owes as much to the designs of Jean Jannon, a Protestant printer working in Sedan in the early seventeenth century, who had worked with Garamond's romans earlier in Paris but who was denied their use because of Catholic censorship. Jannon's matrices came into the possession of the Imprimerie nationale, where they were thought to be by Garamond himself, and were so described when the Imprimerie revived the type in 1900. This particular version is based on an adaptation by Morris Fuller Benton.

Composed by North Market Street Graphics, Lancaster, Pennsylvania
Printed and bound by Quebecor World, Fairfield, Pennsylvania